A
People
and a
Nation

A
People
and a
Nation

A History of the United States

FIFTH EDITION

Mary Beth Norton
Cornell University

David M. Katzman
University of Kansas

Paul D. Escott
Wake Forest University

Howard P. Chudacoff
Brown University

Thomas G. Paterson
University of Connecticut

William M. Tuttle, Jr.
University of Kansas

Houghton Mifflin Company   Boston   New York

Senior sponsoring editor: Patricia A. Coryell
Senior associate editor: Jeffrey Greene
Basic book editor: Ann West
Senior project editor: Carol Newman
Senior production/design coordinator: Carol Merrigan
Manufacturing manager: Florence Cadran

Cover design: Henry Rachlin
Cover image: *Harry Howard, Chief Engineer of the New York Volunteer Fire Department*, by unidentified artist, American, c. 1857, painted wood, purchase Ellie Nadelman. Photo by Glen Castellano; from the collection of the New-York Historical Society.

About the Buttons

The icons used for the chapter title pages and headings within each chapter are photographs of buttons dating from the late nineteenth century. The button used in Volume I is a brass cutout of wheat over a wood background. The button for Volume II, known by collectors as "Brooklyn Bridge," is stamped brass. It may have been produced to commemorate the opening of the bridge in 1883. Picture buttons were popular in the late nineteenth century for women's clothing, often to celebrate major events, plays, and operas. Both buttons, despite their different appearance, were likely constructed from the same manufacturing technique—using a die to strike metal and then assembled into buttons with a wire shank at the back.

Printed in the U.S.A.

Library of Congress Catalog Card Number: 97-72526

ISBN: 0-395-78882-X

123456789-VH-01 00 99 98 97

Brief Contents

Contents

Charts

Maps

Preface

Some twenty years ago, when we first embarked on this textbook-writing adventure, most survey texts adequately covered American politics and diplomacy, important historical events, and the famous people at the top of the hierarchy of power, but something was missing: the stories of ordinary Americans. Our experience as teachers told us that, although a rich scholarship in social history had emerged, it was not yet being incorporated into survey texts. We set out to weave this significant dimension of American history into the traditional fabric of party politics, congressional legislation, wars, economic patterns, and local and state government. The response to our approach proved exceptionally gratifying.

As we wrote subsequent editions, always challenged by enriching scholarship, the task changed from "inserting" social history to integrating it fully into the historical narrative and treating social history not only as the study of the private lives of Americans but also as power relationships among competing groups that looked to the public sphere of politics and government to mediate their differences. In this new edition we especially worked to accomplish this new task. After all, like other teachers and students, we are always re-creating our past, restructuring our memory, rediscovering the personalities and events that have shaped us, inspired us, and bedeviled us. This book represents our rediscovery of America's history—its diverse people and the nation they created and have sustained. As this book demonstrates, there are many different Americans and many different memories. We have sought to present all of them, in both triumph and tragedy, in both division and unity.

After meeting in frank and searching planning sessions, critiquing one another's work, and reading numerous evaluations of the fourth edition of *A People and a Nation*, we developed a plan for this edition. Guided by up-to-date scholarship, we decided to place new emphasis on several themes and subjects that we had discussed in previous editions but believed needed more attention: the interaction of the private sphere of everyday life with the public sphere of politics

New Thematic Emphases

and government; grassroots movements; religion; the emerging cultural globalism of American foreign relations; the development of the American West; and the relationship of people to the land, including conflict over access to natural resources. By reexamining every sentence, editing every paragraph, and condensing, reconfiguring, and reconceptualizing chapters (see below), we accomplished a thorough revision (reducing the book by one chapter) while including a considerable amount of fresh material for new emphases, examples, and interpretations.

As before, we challenge students to think about the meaning of American history, not just to memorize facts. Through a readable narrative about all of the American people, we invite students to take themselves back in time to experience what it was like to live in—and to make life's choices in—a different era. Chapter-opening vignettes that dramatically recount stories of people contending with their times help define the key questions of a chapter (two-thirds of the vignettes are new to this edition). Succinct, focused introductions and conclusions frame each chapter. Illustrations, graphs, tables, and maps tied closely to text encourage visual and statistical explorations. We do not detail historiographical debates, but we acknowledge interpretations different from our own, and in the "Suggestions for Further Reading" sections at the end of each chapter we cite works with varying points of view to demonstrate that the writing of history is very much infused with debate.

Especially successful in the fourth edition, and strengthened here, is the "How Do Historians Know?" feature, which explains how historians go about using evidence to arrive at conclusions. In this highlighted section, our discussion—coupled with illustrations—explores how historians can draw conclusions from a variety of sources: crafts, political cartoons, maps, medical records, diaries, tape recordings, postcards, census data, telegrams, popular art, photographs, and more. This feature also helps students to understand how scholars can claim knowledge about historical events and trends. More than half of these discussions are new to this edition.

"How Do Historians Know?"

A People and a Nation is comprehensive in its treatment of the many ways in which Americans have defined themselves—by gender, race, class, region, ethnicity, religion, sexual orientation—and of the many subjects that have reflected Americans' multidimensional experiences: social, political, economic, diplomatic, military, environmental, intellectual, cultural, and more. We highlight the remarkably diverse everyday life of the American people—in cities and on farms and ranches, in factories and in corporate headquarters, in neighborhood meetings and in powerful political chambers, in love relationships and in hate groups, in recreation and in the workplace, in the classroom and in military uniform, in secret national security conferences and in public foreign relations debates, in church and in prison, in polluted environments and in conservation areas. We pay particular attention to lifestyles, diet and dress, family life and structure, labor conditions, gender roles, and childbearing and child rearing. By discussing music, sports, theater, print media, film, radio, television, graphic arts, and literature—in both "high" culture and "low" culture—we explore how Americans have entertained and informed themselves.

The private sphere of everyday life always interacts with the public sphere of politics and government. To understand how Americans have sought to protect their different ways of life and to work out solutions to thorny problems, we emphasize their expectations of government at the local, state, and federal levels; government's role in providing answers; the lobbying of interest groups; the campaigns and outcomes of elections; and the hierarchy of power in any period. Because the United States has long been a major participant in world affairs, we explore America's descent into wars, interventions in other nations, empire building, immigration patterns, images of foreign peoples, cross-national cultural ties, and international economic trends.

Mary Beth Norton, who had primary responsibility for Chapters 1 through 8, further developed her comparative focus in Chapters 1 and 2, explaining the growth of contrasting American, African, and European societies in the colonial world, giving new attention to the Spanish borderlands. Chapter 3 includes new discussion of the introduction of slavery into English mainland colonies and comparisons with New France and the Spanish borderlands. Chapter 4 has been recast with new emphasis on intercultural interactions among Indians and Europeans and comparisons of families in New France, the Spanish borderlands, and the English colonies (including Indian and mixed-race families). Chapter 7 includes new material on economic/fiscal issues in the Confederation period.

David M. Katzman, who had primary responsibility for Chapters 9, 10, 12, and 13, rewrote to emphasize the role of the federal government and debates over centralized political authority. New emphases are found in his discussion of the conquering of the West (including a new vignette featuring Lewis and Clark in Chapter 9) and the growth of a Mexican-American culture in the Southwest (Chapter 12). He also widened his presentation of ethnic diversity, mental health reform, family and marriage (including divorce laws and women's property legislation), and manifest destiny.

Paul D. Escott, who had primary responsibility for Chapters 11, 14, 15, and 16, introduced new material on the westward movement of slaveholders and slaves and attitudes toward centralized government, African-American soldiers during the Civil War, and Confederate relations with Indians in the West. A new chart details the unprecedented losses of the Civil War, and several new and rarely seen photographs capture the drama of the Civil War period on many levels.

Howard P. Chudacoff, who had primary responsibility for Chapters 17 through 21 and 24, added new material on and gave new thematic emphasis to land (and water) control, conflict over access to natural resources, and environmental management in a newly titled Chapter 17, "The Development of the West and South, 1877–1892." Multiracial composition and racial tensions in the West are highlighted in Chapters 17 and 19, and new material is also presented on home life—indoor and family amusements and the impact of engineers and technology on household life—in Chapter 19. Chudacoff also reworked the section on agrarian protest and Populism, especially in the Rockies and Far West, and reconceptualized Gilded Age politics, adding the religio-cultural dimension (Chapter 20). To his discussion of Progressive reform (Chapter 21), he added coverage of women's clubs, the National Consumer's League, and federal policy on resource conservation. In his new account of the 1920s (Chapter 24), he emphasized the clash between "tried-and-

How We Study the Past

Major Changes in This Edition

true" and "modern" values and added new references to lobbying as a major influence in political decision making.

Thomas G. Paterson, who had primary responsibility for Chapters 22, 23, 26, 29, and 30, gave added emphasis to the theme of cultural relations and the conditioning of the foreign relations decision-making environment by ideology and images of foreign peoples. For Chapter 22, he included new material on relations with Africa, Canada, China, Chile, and Hawaii and on international environmental agreements. In Chapter 23, on the First World War, the role of women in the peace movement, African-American attitudes toward the war, the economic impact of the war, and treatment of the war dead also received added attention. In Chapter 26, newly titled "Peaceseekers and Warmakers: United States Foreign Relations, 1920–1941," Paterson integrated new material on the role of nongovernmental organizations such as the Rockefeller Foundation and the Americanization of Europe. As part of the restructuring of the post-1945 chapters in the text, Chapters 29 and 30 carry the foreign relations story to the present. These chapters, well cross-referenced, especially reflect the post–Cold War declassification of documents from foreign sources (Russian, Chinese, and German, for example). Here the reader will discover new examinations of the origins of the Korean War, the Cuban missile crisis, Japan's "economic miracle," covert activities of the Central Intelligence Agency, human rights, United States Information Agency propaganda, the Middle East peace process, Haiti, and the debate over foreign aid. In lengthy coverage of the Vietnam War, Paterson included new material on Ho Chi Minh's relationship with Americans in 1945, the Tonkin Gulf crisis, and the My Lai massacre.

William M. Tuttle, Jr., had primary responsibility for Chapters 25 and 27, and the post-1945 Chapters 28 and 31 through 33. In Chapter 25, he added new material on Social Security and the end of the New Deal. In Chapter 27 on the Second World War, readers will find new discussions of race and ethnic relations, women and children, and the decision to drop the atomic bomb. Tuttle substantially rewrote and reorganized the material on post-1945 domestic history, reducing the number of chapters covering this period by one. In a new Chapter 28 he interweaves the political, economic, social, and cultural history from 1945 to 1961, adding fresh material on Cold War politics, civil rights, and the baby boom. Chapter 31 takes the story from 1961 to 1974, shedding new light on the Equal Rights Amendment, women in the civil rights movement, *Roe v. Wade*, and Richard Nixon and the Watergate tapes. The next chapter incorporates recent studies on economic woes, the new immigration from Latin America and Asia, social polarization, and the rise of political and cultural conservatism in the 1970s and 1980s. Chapter 33, which concludes the book, is a new history of the 1990s, focusing on Americans' political disaffection and on their hopes and fears as they approach the twenty-first century.

The multidimensional Appendix, prepared by Thomas G. Paterson, includes a new, extensive table on the "Fifty States, the District of Columbia, and Puerto Rico." Here students will discover essential information on dates of admission with rank, capital cities, population with rank, racial/ethnic distribution, per capita personal income with rank, and total area in square miles. Once again, the Appendix begins with a guide to reference works on key subjects in American history. Students may wish to use this updated and enlarged list of encyclopedias, atlases, chronologies, and other books when they start to explore topics for research papers, when they seek precise definitions or dates, when they need biographical profiles, or when they chart territorial or demographic changes. The table of statistics on key features of the American people and nation also have been updated and expanded, as have the tables on presidential elections, the cabinet members of all administrations, party strength in Congress, and the justices of the Supreme Court.

Many instructors and students who have used this book in their courses have found its many learning and teaching aids very useful. The most exciting addition to our ancillary lineup is *@history: an interactive American history source*. This multimedia teaching/learning package combines a variety of material—primary sources (text and graphic), videos, audio, and links to Web sites—with activities that can be used to analyze, interpret, and discuss primary sources; to enhance collaborative learning; and to create multimedia presentations. *@history* provides instructors with an interactive multimedia tool that can improve the analytical skills of students and introduce them to historical sources.

Study and Teaching Aids

The *Study Guide*, prepared by George Warren and Cynthia Ricketson of Central Piedmont Community College, includes an introductory chapter on studying history that focuses on interpreting historical facts, test-taking hints, and critical analysis. The guide also includes learning objectives, a thematic guide, lists of terms, multiple-choice and essay questions for each chapter, as well as map exercises and sections on organizing information for some chapters. An answer key alerts students to the correct response and also explains why the other choices are wrong.

A *Computerized Study Guide* is also available for students. It provides approximately 15 multiple-choice questions for each chapter and functions as a tutorial that gives students information on incorrect as well as correct answers. The computerized guide is available in Macintosh, IBM, and IBM-compatible formats.

"A new *Instructor's Resource Manual*, prepared by Donald Frazier, Marvin Schultz, and Bruce Winders of Texas Christian University and Robert Pace of Longwood College, contains ten chronological resource units in addition to teaching ideas for each chapter of the textbook. Each chronological resource unit includes sections on geography, technology, physical and material culture (artifacts), historical sites, documentary films, popular films, and music. The manual also includes for each textbook chapter a content overview, a brief list of learning objectives, a comprehensive chapter outline, ideas for classroom activities, discussion questions, and ideas for paper topics.

A *Test Items* file, also prepared by George Warren, provides approximately 1,700 new multiple-choice questions, more than 1,000 identification terms, and approximately 500 essay questions.

A *Computerized Test Items File* for IBM and Macintosh computers is available to adopters. This computerized version of the printed *Test Items* file allows professors to create customized tests by editing and adding questions.

A set of full-color map transparencies is also available to instructors on adoption. A variety of videos—documentaries and docudramas by major film producers—is available for use with *A People and a Nation*.

At each stage of this project, historians read drafts of our chapters. Their suggestions, corrections, and pleas helped guide us through our revisions. We could not include all of their recommendations, but the book is better for our having heeded most of their advice.

Acknowledgments

We heartily thank

Diane Allen, *Columbia Gorge Community College*
David E. Conrad, *Southern Illinois University*
Paige Cubbison, *Miami Dade Community College, Kendall*
Joseph A. Devine, Jr., *Stephen F. Austin State University*
Shirley M. Eoff, *Angelo State University*
Maurine Greenwald, *University of Pittsburgh*
Melanie Gustafson, *University of Vermont*
D. Harland Hagler, *University of North Texas*
Craig Hendricks, *Long Beach City College*
Robert Kenzer, *University of Richmond*
Timothy Koerner, *Oakland Community College*
Lisa M. Lane, *Miracosta College*
Larry MacLestch, *Mendocino College*
Jeff Ostler, *University of Oregon*
William Robbins, *Oregon State University*
Athan Theoharis, *Marquette University*
Lynn Weiner, *Roosevelt University*
Marianne S. Wokeck, *Indiana University–Purdue University of Indianapolis*
Gerald Wolff, *University of South Dakota*

Once again we thank the extraordinary Houghton Mifflin team who designed, edited, produced, and nourished this book. Their high standards and careful attention to both general structure and fine detail are unmatched in publishing. Many thanks to Jean Woy, editor-in-chief; Pat Coryell, senior sponsoring editor; Ann West, basic book editor; Jeffrey Greene, senior associate editor, Keith Mahoney, assistant editor; Carol Newman, senior project editor; Carol Merrigan, senior production/design coordinator; Charlotte Miller, art editor; and Florence Cadran, manufacturing manager.

For helping us in many essential ways, we also extend our thanks to Michael Donoghue, Jan D. Emerson, Steven Jacobson, Andrea Katzman, Eric Katzman, Sharyn Brooks Katzman, Walter D. Kamphoefner, G. Stanley Lemons, Pam Levitt, Shane J. Maddock, Jill Norgren, Aaron M. Paterson, Norman G. Radford, Zil-e-Rehman, Paul L. Silver, Peter Solonysznyi, Julee Stephens, Luci Tapahonso, Kathryn Nemeth Tuttle, Samuel Watkins Tuttle, and Daniel H. Usner, Jr. Some of these individuals sent us suggestions for improving *A People and a Nation*, and we took their recommendations seriously. We welcome comments from professors and students about this new edition, too.

For the authors, THOMAS G. PATERSON

The Authors

Mary Beth Norton

Born in Ann Arbor, Michigan, Mary Beth Norton received her B.A. from the University of Michigan (1964) and her Ph.D. from Harvard University (1969). She is now Mary Donlon Alger Professor of American History at Cornell University. Her dissertation won the Allan Nevins Prize. She has written *The British-Americans* (1972), *Liberty's Daughters* (1980), and *Founding Mothers and Fathers* (1996), which was one of three finalists for the Pulitzer Prize in 1997. She has coedited *To Toil the Livelong Day* (1987), *Women of America* (1979), and *Major Problems in American Women's History* (1995). Her articles have appeared in such journals as the *William and Mary Quarterly, Signs*, and the *American Historical Review*. Mary Beth has served on the National Council on the Humanities, as president of the Berkshire Conference of Women Historians, as vice president for research of the American Historical Association, and as general editor of the *AHA Guide to Historical Literature* (3rd edition, 1995). She has advised colleges on curriculum development in gender studies. The National Endowment for the Humanities, Guggenheim Foundation, and Rockefeller Foundation have assisted her scholarship.

David M. Katzman

Born in New York City and a graduate of Queens College (B.A., 1963) and the University of Michigan (Ph.D., 1969), David M. Katzman is professor of history and chair of American studies at the University of Kansas. He has written *Before the Ghetto* (1973) and *Seven Days a Week* (1978), which won the Philip Taft Labor History Prize. He has coedited *Plain Folk* (1982) and *Technical Knowledge in American Culture* (1996). He has also coauthored *Three Generations in Twentieth-Century America* (1982). David has been a visiting professor at University College, Dublin, Ireland, and at the University of Birmingham, England. He has also directed National Endowment for the Humanities Summer Seminars for College Teachers. He has sat on the Board of Directors of the National Commission on Social Studies and is coeditor of *American Studies*. At the University of Kansas, he is a former director of the College Honors Program. The Guggenheim Foundation, National Endowment for the Humanities, Ford Foundation, and Rockefeller Foundation have supported his research.

Paul D. Escott

Born and raised in the Midwest (St. Louis, Missouri), Paul D. Escott studied in New England (Harvard College, B.A., 1969) and the South (Duke University, Ph.D., 1974). He is Reynolds Professor of History and Dean of the College at Wake Forest University. He has written *After Secession* (1978), *Slavery Remembered* (1979), *Many Excellent People* (1985), and *A History of African Americans in North Carolina* (with Jeffrey J. Crow and Flora J. Hatley, 1992). Paul is the editor of *W. J. Cash and the Minds of the South* (1992) and coeditor of *Major Problems in the History of the American South* (with David R. Goldfield, 1990). His most recent publication is *North Carolina Yeoman* (1996). Paul's articles have appeared in *Civil War History, The Journal of Southern History*, and *The North Carolina Historical Review*. He was a member of the editorial board and a contributor to *The Encyclopedia of the Confederacy* (1993). The American Council of Learned Societies, Whitney M. Young, Jr., Foundation, and Rockefeller Foundation have assisted his research.

Howard P. Chudacoff

A professor of history at Brown University, Howard P. Chudacoff was born in Omaha, Nebraska. He earned his A.B. (1965) and Ph.D. (1969) degrees from the University of Chicago. He has written three books: *Mobile Americans* (1972), *The Evolution of American Urban Society* (with Judith Smith, 4th edition, 1993), and *How Old Are You?* (1989). He has also edited *Major Problems in American Urban History* (1993). His articles have appeared in such journals as the *Journal of Family History, Reviews in American History*, and *Journal of American History*. At Brown University, Howard has cochaired the American Civilization Program, chaired the department of history, and since 1990 has been faculty adviser to the women's basketball team. He has also served on the board of directors of the Urban History Association. The National Endowment for the Humanities, Ford Foundation, and Rockefeller Foundation have given him awards to advance his scholarship.

Thomas G. Paterson

Born in Oregon City, Oregon, and graduated from the University of New Hampshire (B.A., 1963) and the University of California, Berkeley (Ph.D., 1968), Thomas G. Paterson is professor of history at the University of Connecticut. He has written *Soviet-American Confrontation* (1973), *Meeting the Communist Threat* (1988), *On Every Front* (1992), *Contesting Castro* (1994), *American Foreign Relations* (with J. Garry Clifford and Kenneth J. Hagan, 1994), and *America Ascendant* (with Clifford, 1995). Tom has also edited *Kennedy's Quest for Victory* (1989), *Explaining the History of American Foreign Relations* (with Michael J. Hogan, 1991), and *Major Problems in American Foreign Relations* (with Dennis Merrill, 1994). With Bruce Jentleson he was senior editor for the four-volume *Encyclopedia of U.S. Foreign Relations* (1997). He has served on the editorial boards of the *Journal of American History* and *Diplomatic History*. He has been president of the Society for Historians of American Foreign Relations and has directed National Endowment for the Humanities Summer Seminars for College Teachers. His most recent award was a fellowship from the Guggenheim Foundation.

William M. Tuttle, Jr.

A native of Detroit, Michigan, William M. Tuttle, Jr., received his B.A. from Denison University (1959) and his Ph.D. from the University of Wisconsin (1967). A professor of history and American studies at the University of Kansas, Bill has written *Race Riot* (2nd edition, 1996) and *"Daddy's Gone to War"* (1993). He has also edited *W.E.B. DuBois* (1973) and coedited *Plain Folk* (1982). His articles have appeared in such journals as the *Journal of American History*, *American Studies*, and *Child Welfare*. He has been a research associate at the Institute of Human Development at the University of California, Berkeley. As a historical consultant, Bill has helped prepare several public television documentaries and docudramas, including *The Killing Floor*, which appeared on PBS's "American Playhouse." Bill's scholarly work has been assisted by the American Council of Learned Societies, Institute of Southern History at Johns Hopkins University, Charles Warren Center, Guggenheim Foundation, Stanford Humanities Center, Radcliffe College, and National Endowment for the Humanities. In 1995, Bill was awarded the Denison University Alumni Citation.

A
People
and a
Nation

CHAPTER

1

Three Old Worlds
Create a New
1492–1600

A t birth, she was called Malinalli. The Spaniards christened her Doña Marina. History knows her as Malinche, a name formed by adding the Aztec suffix *che*, a term of respect, to her original name. She has been celebrated as the symbolic mother of the modern Mexican people and maligned as a traitor to Mexico's ancient residents.

Born near the Gulf Coast of Mexico sometime between 1502 and 1505, Malinalli was the daughter of a cacique, or village chief, within the Aztec Empire. Her father died while she was young, and her mother soon remarried. To protect the inheritance of the son born to that second marriage, the mother sold her daughter into slavery. Eventually, Malinalli came to live with Mayan-speaking people in the province of Tabasco.

Along with nineteen other enslaved women, she was presented as a gift to the Spanish conquistador Hernán Cortés when he marched through Tabasco in 1519. Cortés, who first arrived in the Spanish West Indies in 1504, embarked for the mainland in search of wealthy cities rumored to exist there. Little did he know that the young woman whom the Spaniards baptized as a Christian and renamed Doña Marina would be one of the keys to his conquest of Mexico.

Doña Marina, who spoke both Nahuatl (the language of her birth and of the Aztecs) and Mayan (the language of her masters), and who soon learned Spanish, became Cortés's translator and mistress. She bore him a son, Martín—one of the first *mestizos*, or mixed-blood children. Accompanying Cortés on his travels in Mexico, she did more than simply interpret words for him: she explained the meanings that lay behind the language, opening the Aztec world to the Spaniards.

An illustration in the *Codex Florentino*, one of the few surviving works produced by Aztec scribes, shows Malinche, dressed in traditional garb, translating for the Spaniards and the Aztecs. Pictographs representing words come from her mouth, linking the two groups. In the background stands an Aztec building.
Biblioteca Medicia Laurenziana, Florence.
Photo: Alberto Scardigli

Bernal Diaz del Castillo, one of Cortés's lieutenants, greatly admired Doña Marina. In his *History of the Conquest of New Spain*, he observed that she was "a valuable instrument to us. . . . without her we never should have understood the Mexican language, and, upon the whole, have been unable to surmount many difficulties." The Aztecs even called Cortés "El Malinche," or "the captain of Marina," Bernal Diaz explained, because she "was always in his company, especially when ambassadors arrived and during talks with chiefs." The Aztecs and subsequent Mexican historians have blamed Malinche for betraying her own people. But who were her people? The Aztecs, in whose empire she had been born and who had sold her as a slave? The Mayas, among whom she was raised? Or the Europeans, who relied on her translations?

Malinche's life history, and her dual image as betrayer of ancient Mexico and symbolic mother of the modern mixed-race nation, encapsulate many of the ambiguities of the first encounter between Europeans and Americans. Sold into slavery by her Aztec-connected family, she owed that people little loyalty. The Spaniards gave her respect, yet she did not become Spanish: Cortés never married her, although she was the mother of his son. She did eventually marry one of Cortés's subordinates, but it is unclear whether she had any choice in the matter. Malinche may simply have been passed from one conquistador to another, much as her family sold her to slave traders or the Tabascans gave her to the Europeans.

Until she died around 1540, Malinche was caught between two worlds, part of both and of neither, alternately praised and blamed for her actions. Many people from both sides of the Atlantic were to meet the same fate as they attempted to cope with the rapidly changing world of the fifteenth and sixteenth centuries.

For thousands of years before 1492, human societies in the Americas had developed in isolation from the rest of the world. The era that began in the Christian fifteenth century brought that longstanding isolation to an end. As European explorers and colonizers sought to exploit the resources of the rest of the globe, peoples from different races and cultural traditions came into regular contact for the first time. All were profoundly changed by the resulting interaction. By the time Cortés and his troops invaded Mexico in 1519, the age of European expansion and colonization was already well under way. Over the next 350 years, Europeans would spread their influence across the globe. The history

of the tiny colonies in North America that became the first components of the United States must be seen in this broad context of European exploration and exploitation.

The continents that European sailors reached in the late fifteenth century had their own history, one the invaders largely ignored. The residents of the Americas were the world's most skillful plant breeders; they had developed vegetable crops more nutritious and productive than those grown in Europe, Asia, or Africa. They had invented systems of writing and mathematics and had created calendars fully as accurate as those used on the other side of the Atlantic. In the Americas, as in Europe, states rose and fell as leaders succeeded or failed at the goal of expanding their political and economic power. The Europeans' arrival in their world immeasurably altered the Americans' struggles with each other.

After 1400, European nations tried to improve their positions relative to neighboring countries not only by waging wars on their own continent but also by acquiring valuable colonies and trading posts elsewhere in the world. In response, nations in Asia, Africa, and the Americas attempted to use the alien intruders to their own advantage or, failing that, to adapt successfully to the Europeans' presence in their midst. All the participants in the resulting interaction of divergent cultures were indelibly affected by the process. The contest among Europeans for control of the Americas and Africa changed the course of history on four continents. Strategies selected by American and African leaders influenced the outcome of the Europeans' competition and determined the fates of their own societies. Although in the end Europeans emerged politically dominant, they did not control many aspects of the interactions among the divergent cultures of the Americas and Africa.

 American Societies

Human beings probably originated on the continent of Africa, where humanlike remains about 3 million years old have been found in what is now Ethiopia. Over many millennia, the growing human population slowly dispersed to the other continents. Because the climate was then far colder than it is now, much of the earth's water was concentrated in huge rivers of ice called glaciers. Sea levels were accordingly lower, and land masses covered a larger proportion of the earth's surface than they do today. About 30,000 years ago, a land bridge that scholars

• *Important Events* •

30,000–10,000 B.C.E.	Paleo-Indians began migrating from Asia to North American across the Beringia land bridge	**1494**	Treaty of Tordesillas divides land claims between Spain and Portugal in Africa, India, and South America
7000 B.C.E.	Cultivation of food crops begins in America	**1496**	Last of the Canary Islands falls to Spanish attack
c. 1000 B.C.E.	Olmec civilization appears	**1497**	John Cabot reaches North American coast
c. 300–600 C.E.	Height of influence of Teotihuacán	**1513**	Ponce de León explores Florida
c. 600–900 C.E.	Classic Mayan civilization	**1518–30**	Smallpox epidemic devastates Indian population of West Indies and Central and South America
1000 C.E.	Anasazi settlements in modern states of Arizona and New Mexico flourish as trading centers	**1519**	Hernán Cortés invades Mexico
1001	Norse establish settlement in "Vineland" (Newfoundland)	**1521**	Tenochtitlán surrenders to Cortés; Aztec Empire falls to Spaniards
1050–1250	Height of influence of Cahokia; prevalence of Mississippian culture in midwestern and southeastern United States	**1534–35**	Jacques Cartier explores St. Lawrence River
14th century	Aztec rise to power	**1539–42**	Hernando de Soto explores southeastern United States
1450s–80s	Portuguese explore and colonize islands in the Mediterranean Atlantic and São Tomé in Gulf of Guinea	**1540–42**	Francisco Vásquez de Coronado explores southwestern United States
1477	Publication of Marco Polo's *Travels*, describing China	**1587–90**	Sir Walter Raleigh's Roanoke colony vanishes
1492	Christopher Columbus reaches Bahama Islands	**1588**	Thomas Harriot publishes *A Briefe and True Report of the New Found Land of Virginia*

have called Beringia linked the Asian and North American continents at the site of the Bering Strait. Some of the peoples participating in the vast worldwide migration crossed this land bridge. When the climate warmed, the glaciers receded, and the sea levels rose about 10,000 years ago, those migrants were irrevocably separated from their fellow human beings who had remained on the connected continents of Asia, Africa, and Europe.

Those forerunners of the American population are known as Paleo-Indians. The earliest confirmed evidence of their presence in the Americas dates

Paleo-Indians

to approximately 28,000 years ago. The Paleo-Indians were nomadic hunters of game and gatherers of wild plants. Spreading throughout North and South America, they probably moved as extended families, or *bands*. By about 11,500 years ago the Paleo-Indians were mak-

ing fine stone projectile points, which they attached to wooden spears and used to kill and butcher bison (buffalo), woolly mammoths, and other large mammals then living in the Americas. But as the Ice Age ended and the human population increased, all the large American mammals except the bison disappeared. Scholars cannot agree whether overhunting or the change in climate caused their demise. In either case, deprived of their primary source of meat, the Paleo-Indians had to find new ways of survival.

Consequently, by approximately 9,000 years ago, the residents of what is now central Mexico began to cultivate food crops, especially maize (corn),

Importance of Agriculture

squash, beans, and peppers. In the Andes Mountains of South America, people started to grow potatoes. As knowledge of agricultural techniques improved and spread through the Americas, vegetables and maize proved a more reliable source of food than hunting and gathering. Except for those living in the harshest climates, most Americans started to adopt a more sedentary style of life so they could tend fields regularly. Some established permanent settlements; others moved several times a year among fixed sites. They became adept at clearing forests through the use of controlled burning. All the American cultures emphasized producing sufficient food to support themselves. Although they traded goods, no society ever became dependent on another group for items vital to its survival.

Wherever agriculture dominated the economy, complex civilizations flourished. Such societies, assured of steady supplies of grains and vegetables, no longer had to devote all their energies to subsistence. Instead, they were able to accumulate wealth, produce ornamental objects, and create elaborate rituals and ceremonies. In North America, the successful cultivation of nutritious crops such as maize, beans, and squash seems to have led to the growth and development of all the major civilizations: first the large city-states of Mesoamerica (modern Mexico and Guatemala), then the urban clusters known collectively as the Mississippian culture and located in the present-day United States. Each of these societies, many historians and archaeologists now believe, reached its height of population and influence only after achieving success in agriculture. Each later declined and collapsed after reaching the limits of its food supply, with dire political and military consequences. Even the powerful Aztec Empire that the Spaniards encountered in 1519 is thought to have been approaching the point at which it could no longer sustain its population.

The Aztecs were the heirs of a series of Mesoamerican civilizations, the history of which stretched back to the Olmecs, who about 3,000 years

Mesoamerican Civilizations

ago lived near the Gulf of Mexico in large cities dominated by temple pyramids. More than 1,000 years later, the Mayan civilization developed on the Yucatán Peninsula. The Mayas built large urban centers containing tall pyramids and temples with brightly painted stuccoed and carved façades. They studied astronomy, created the first writing system in the Americas, and developed a richly symbolic religious life in which rituals of bloodletting played a major role. By the fifth century C.E. (Common Era), or about 1,500 years ago, the kings of the Mayan city-states started to war with each other, attempting

conquest on a grand scale. But no king or city could win total victory. Eventually, the constant fighting combined with overpopulation and resulting environmental stress to cause the collapse of the most powerful cities, ending the classic era of Mayan civilization by 900 C.E. By the time the Spaniards arrived, only a few remnants of the once-mighty society remained intact.

The largest Mesoamerican metropolis was contemporary with, and a major trading partner of, the Mayas. Teotihuacán, founded about 300 B.C.E. (Before the Common Era)—some 2,300 years ago—in the Valley of Mexico, was one of the largest cities in the world in the fifth century C.E., with a population of over 100,000. (By contrast, Paris had only about 10,000 residents at that time.) The rulers of Teotihuacán gained their position chiefly through commerce; their trading network extended hundreds of miles in all directions. Thousands of craftspeople lived in the city, many of whom were especially skilled in working the green glass called obsidian, which was valued throughout the region as a source of fine knives and mirrors. Teotihuacán also served as a religious center; pilgrims must have come long distances to visit the impressive Pyramid of the Sun, Pyramid of the Moon, and the great temple of Quetzalcoatl—the feathered serpent, the primary god of central Mexico.

Teotihuacán's influence was felt so widely in Mesoamerica before its decline in the eighth century C.E. that some scholars have argued that this

Moundbuilders, Anasazi, and Mississippians

Mexican city-state also influenced societies farther north, in what is now the United States. The Moundbuilders of the Ohio River region, who flourished about two thousand years ago, just as Teotihuacán rose to prominence, constructed earthen mounds. But the Ohioan mounds were used as burial sites, not as bases for temple pyramids. Also, the Moundbuilders' economy, which was based on hunting and gathering, bore little resemblance to that of Mesoamerica. Trade goods from as far away as the Great Lakes and the Gulf of Mexico have been found in the mounds, but direct evidence of contact with Teotihuacán is lacking.

The same is true for sites inhabited by the Anasazi peoples in the modern states of Arizona and New Mexico. Pueblo Bonito in Chaco Canyon, a city that by 1000 C.E. consisted of many large adobe buildings constructed along the sides of the canyon, sat at the juncture of over 400 miles of roads and

Pueblo Bonito in Chaco Canyon in what is now the state of New Mexico. More than six hundred buildings were present on the well-defended site. The circular structures were kivas, used for food storage and for religious rituals.   David Muench photography.

served as a major regional trading center. The Anasazi cultivated maize and other Mesoamerican crops, but they did not construct temple pyramids, nor did their towns resemble those built by their contemporaries in what is now Mexico. Accordingly, scholars have concluded that their contact with Mesoamerica was slight.

More likely, Teotihuacán and later Mesoamerican empires like that of the Aztecs had an impact on the development of the Mississippian culture, which flourished around 1000 C.E. in what is now the midwestern and southeastern United States. (Indeed, the historian Francis Jennings has recently argued that some of the Mississippians were "colonists" dispatched from Teotihuacán.) This civilization, like those to the south, was based on the cultivation of maize, beans, and squash. Not until about 700 to 900 C.E. were these crops grown successfully in the present-day United States; soon after their introduction, large cities with plazas and earthen pyramids first appeared in the region. The largest of the cities was Cahokia, near modern St. Louis. At its peak (in the twelfth century), Cahokia covered more than 5 square miles and had a population of at least 15,000—small by Mesoamerican standards but larger than any other northern community. Like

Teotihuacán, Cahokia was a religious and trading center. Its main pyramid, today called the Monk's Mound, was in 1492 the third largest structure in the Western Hemisphere. Although Cahokia's power declined after about 1250 C.E., Spanish explorers encountered Mississippian peoples in present-day South Carolina, Alabama, and Georgia in the midsixteenth century. The Natchez, a society characterized by temple mounds and autocratic priestly rulers, survived in the lower Mississippi River valley until the 1720s.

The Aztecs' histories tell of the long migration of their people (who called themselves Mexica) into the Valley of Mexico during the twelfth century.

Aztecs

The uninhabited ruins of Teotihuacán, which by then had been deserted for at least two hundred years, awed and mystified the migrants. The Aztecs' primary god, Huitzilopochtli, was a god of war represented by an eagle. Aztec chronicles record that Huitzilopochtli directed the Aztecs to establish their capital at the spot on an island where they saw an eagle eating a serpent (thus symbolizing Huitzilopochtli's triumph over the traditional deity, Quetzalcoatl). That island city became Tenochtitlán, the center of a rigidly

How do historians know that the ruins of Teotihuacán "awed and mystified" the Aztecs (see page 7) when they arrived in the Valley of Mexico at least two hundred years after that city had been abandoned by its inhabitants? One striking indication of the Aztecs' attitude toward the earlier civilization is this beautiful greenstone mask with polished obsidian eyes, which was created at Teotihuacán. Archaeologists found it not there but rather in the ruins of the Aztecs' Templo Mayor, constructed in Tenochtitlán (the site of modern Mexico City) about a thousand years after the mask was sculpted. The temple had two sides, one dedicated to the war god Huitzilopochtli, the other to the rain

god Tlaloc. The place where the two sides met was at the heart of the Aztecs' most sacred site. There they buried this mask, which they must have found at Teotihuacán, about 20 miles from Tenochtitlán. Although we cannot know for certain what the Aztecs intended to accomplish by this gesture, it seems reasonable to conclude that they hoped to draw on the mysterious powers that the mask (and the civilization it represented) symbolized for them. Had they not been awed by it, they never would have buried the mask where they did.   Michel Zabe-Thiriat.

stratified society composed of hereditary classes of warriors, merchants, priests, common folk, and slaves.

The Aztecs conquered their neighbors and forced them to pay tribute in luxury items, raw materials, and human beings who could be sacrificed to Huitzilopochtli. They also engaged in ritual combat, known as "flowery wars," to obtain further sacrificial victims. The war god's taste for blood was not easily quenched. In the Aztec year Ten Rabbit (1502) at the coronation of Motecuhzoma II (the Spaniards could not pronounce his name correctly, so they called him Montezuma), five thousand people are thought to have been sacrificed by having their still-beating hearts torn from their bodies.

The Aztecs believed that they lived in the age of the Fifth Sun. Four times previously, they wrote, the earth and all the people who lived on it had been destroyed. They predicted that their own world would end in earthquakes and hunger. In the Aztec year Thirteen Flint, volcanoes erupted, sickness and hunger spread, wild beasts attacked the Aztecs' children, and an eclipse of the sun darkened the sky. Did some priest wonder whether the Fifth Sun was approaching its end? Eventually, the Aztecs learned that their year Thirteen Flint was called 1492 by the Europeans.

 ## North America in 1492

Over the centuries, the Americans who lived north of Mexico had adapted their once-similar ways of life to very different geographical settings, thus creating the diverse cultures that the Europeans encountered when they first arrived (see map, page 9). Bands that lived in environments not well suited to agriculture—because of inadequate rainfall or poor soil, for example—followed a nomadic lifestyle similar to that of the Paleo-Indians. Within the area of the present-day United States, these groups included the Paiutes and Shoshones, who inhabited the Great Basin (now Nevada and Utah). Because of the difficulty of finding sufficient food for more than a few people, such hunter-gatherer bands were small. They usually were composed of one or more related families, with men hunting small animals and women gathering seeds and berries. Where large game was more plentiful and food supplies therefore more certain, as in present-day Canada and the Great Plains, bands of hunters were somewhat larger.

In more favorable environments, larger groups combined agriculture with gathering, hunting, and fishing. Those who lived near the seacoasts, like the Chinooks of present-day Washington and Oregon,

Primary mode of subsistence:

- Agriculture
- Hunting
- Hunting-gathering
- Fishing

Native Cultures of North America *The natives of the North American continent effectively used the resources of the regions in which they lived. As this map shows, coastal groups relied on fishing, residents of fertile areas engaged in agriculture, and other peoples employed hunting (often combined with gathering) as a primary mode of subsistence.*

consumed fish and shellfish in addition to growing crops and gathering seeds and berries. Residents of the interior (for example, the Arikaras of the Missouri River valley) hunted large animals while also cultivating maize, squash, and beans. The Algonkian-speaking peoples of what is now eastern Canada and the northeastern United States also combined hunting and agriculture. Every few years they set fire to forests and underbrush to clear new fields, create open grasslands that would attract deer, and enrich the soil (the ashes made excellent fertilizer).

Societies that relied primarily on hunting large animals like deer and buffalo assigned that task to men and allotted food processing, clothing production, and child rearing to women. Before such nomadic bands

Sexual Division of Labor in North America

acquired horses from the Spaniards, women—occasionally assisted by dogs—also carried the family's belongings whenever the band relocated. Such a sexual division of labor was universal among hunting peoples, regardless of their location. Agricultural societies, by contrast, differed in their assignments of work to the sexes. In what is now the southwestern United States, the Pueblo peoples, who lived in sixty or seventy autonomous villages and spoke five different languages, defined agricultural labor as men's work. In the East, Algonkian, Iroquoian, and Muskogean peoples allocated most agricultural chores to women, although men cleared the land. In all the farming societies, women gathered wild foods, prepared food for consumption or storage, and cared for children, while men were responsible for hunting.

The southwestern and eastern agricultural peoples had similar social organizations. They lived in villages, sometimes sizable ones with a thousand or more inhabitants. The Pueblos, descendants of the Anasazi, lived in large, multistory buildings constructed on terraces along the sides of cliffs or other easily defended sites. Northern Iroquois villages (in modern New York State) were composed of large, rectangular, bark-covered structures, or long houses; the name Haudenosaunee (which the Iroquois called themselves) means "People of the Long House." In the present-day southeastern United States, Muskogeans and southern Algonkians lived in large houses made of thatch. Most of the eastern villages were surrounded by wood palisades and ditches to aid in fending off attackers. The defensive design of such villages and of the western pueblos discloses the sig-

nificance of warfare in pre-Columbian America. Long before the Europeans arrived, the residents of North America fought with each other for control of the best hunting and fishing territories, the most fertile agricultural lands, or the sources of essential items like salt (for preserving meat) and flint (for making knives and arrowheads).

In all these agricultural societies, each dwelling housed an extended family defined *matrilineally* (through a female line of descent). Mothers, their married daughters, and their daughters' husbands and children all lived together. Matrilineal descent did not imply *matriarchy*, or the wielding of power by women, but rather served as a means of reckoning kinship. Extended families were linked into *clans*, also defined by matrilineal ties. The nomadic bands of the Great Plains, by contrast, were most often related *patrilineally* (through the male line). They lacked settled villages and defended themselves from attack primarily through their ability to move to safer locations when necessary.

American leaders governed largely through consensus, but political structures in the various groups differed considerably. Among Pueblo and Muskogean peoples, the village council, composed of ten to thirty men,

Native American Politics and Religion

was the highest political authority; no government structure connected the villages. Nomadic hunters also lacked formal links among separate bands. The Iroquois, by contrast, had an elaborate political hierarchy incorporating villages into nations and nations into a widespread confederation. In all the North American cultures, political power was divided between civil and war leaders, who wielded authority only so long as they retained the confidence of the people. Autocratic rule of the sort common in Europe (see page 15) was foreign to these political systems.

The political position of women varied. Women were more likely to assume leadership roles among agricultural peoples, especially those in which females were the primary cultivators, than among nomadic hunters. Squaw sachems (female rulers) led Algonkian villages in what is now Massachusetts, but women were never chosen as heads of hunting bands of the Great Plains. Iroquois women did not become chiefs, yet clan matrons exercised political power (see page 77). Probably the most powerful female chiefs were found in what is now the southeastern United States. In the mid-sixteenth century a female

Jacques Le Moyne, an artist accompanying the French settlement in Florida in the 1560s (see page 35), produced some of the first European images of North American peoples. His depiction of native agricultural practices shows the sexual division of labor: men breaking up the ground with fish-bone hoes before women drop seeds into the holes. But Le Moyne's version of the scene cannot be accepted uncritically: unable to abandon a European view of proper farming methods, he erroneously drew plowed furrows in the soil. John Carter Brown Library at Brown University.

ruler known as the Lady of Cofitachequi governed a large group of villages in present-day western South Carolina.

Americans' religious beliefs varied even more than did their political systems, but all the peoples were *polytheistic*, worshiping a multitude of gods. One common thread was their integration with nature. Thus each group's most important beliefs and rituals were closely tied to its economy. The major deities of agricultural peoples like the Pueblos and Muskogeans were associated with cultivation, and their chief festivals centered on planting and harvest. The most important gods of hunters (such as those living on the Great Plains) were associated with animals, and their major festivals were related to hunting. A band's economy and women's role in it helped to determine women's potential as religious leaders. Women held the most prominent positions in those agricultural societies (like the Iroquois) in which they were also the chief food producers, whereas in hunting societies men took the lead in religious as well as political affairs.

A wide variety of cultures, comprising more than 5 million people, thus inhabited mainland North America when Europeans arrived. The hierarchical kingdoms of Mesoamerica bore little resemblance to the nomadic hunting societies of the Great Plains or to the agricultural societies that dominated a significant share of the continent. The diverse inhabitants of North America spoke well over one thousand different languages. For obvious reasons, they did not consider themselves one people, nor did they—for the most part—think of uniting to repel the European invaders. Instead, each village or band continued to try to better its circumstances relative to its neighbors, regardless of whether those neighbors were of American or European origin.

 ## African Societies

Fifteenth-century Africa, like fifteenth-century America, housed a variety of cultures adapted to different geographical settings (see map). Many of these cultures were of great antiquity. In the north, along the Mediterranean Sea, lived the Berbers, a Muslim people. (Muslims are adherents of Islam, founded by the prophet Mohammed in the seventh century C.E.) On the east coast of Africa, Muslim city-states engaged in extensive trade with India, the Moluccas (part of modern Indonesia), and China. In these ports, sustained contact and intermarriage among Arabs and Africans created the Swahili language and culture. Through the East African city-states passed a considerable share of the trade between the eastern Mediterranean and the Far East; the rest followed the long land route across Central Asia known as the Silk Road.

In the African interior, south of the Mediterranean coast, lie the great Sahara and Libyan deserts, vast expanses of nearly waterless terrain that served as a barrier to some types of travel yet also acted as a highway for transmitting religious and cultural ideas throughout the region. Below the deserts, much of the continent is divided between tropical rain forests (along the coasts) and grassy plains (in the interior). People speaking a variety of languages and pursuing different economic strategies lived in a wide belt south of the deserts. South of the Gulf of Guinea (see map, page 13), the grassy landscape came to be dominated by Bantu-speaking peoples, who left their homeland in modern Nigeria about two thousand years ago and slowly migrated south and east across the continent.

Most of the enslaved people carried to North America came from West Africa, which the Europeans called Guinea, a land of tropical forests, fishing, and agriculture that had been inhabited for at least ten thousand years before Europeans set foot there in the fifteenth century. The northern region of West Africa, or Upper Guinea, was heavily influenced by the Islamic culture of the Mediterranean. As early as the eleventh century C.E., many

West Africa (Guinea)

of the region's inhabitants had become Muslims. Trade between Upper Guinea and the Muslim Mediterranean was sub-Saharan Africa's major connection to Europe and the Middle East. In return for salt, dates, silk, and cotton cloth, Africans exchanged ivory, gold, and slaves with northern merchants.

Upper Guinea runs roughly north-south from Cape Verde to Cape Palmas. The people of its northernmost region, the so-called Rice Coast (present-day Gambia, Sénégal, and Guinea), fished and cultivated rice in coastal swamplands. The Grain Coast, the next region to the south, was thinly populated and not readily accessible from the sea because it had only one good harbor (modern Freetown, Sierra Leone). Its people concentrated on farming and raising livestock. Both the Rice and the Grain Coasts—especially the former—supplied slaves destined for sale in the Americas, but even more enslaved people came from Lower Guinea, to the east of Cape Palmas.

In the fifteenth century, most Africans in Lower Guinea practiced traditional religions, not the precepts of Islam. As in the religions of the agricultural peoples of the Americas, their beliefs revolved around rituals intended to ensure good harvests. Throughout the region, individual villages composed of groups of kin were linked into small, hierarchical kingdoms. At the time of initial contact with the Europeans, the region was characterized by decentralized political and social authority.

West African law did not permit individual ownership of land; instead, land belonged temporarily to anyone who cultivated it. Africans held in slavery on their own continent—primarily criminals, debtors, or wartime captives, and their descendants—were therefore essential components of the economy, because only the ownership of people allowed the accumulation of wealth. An African who possessed slaves also had a right to the products of their labor. Accordingly, an internal traffic in slaves thrived long before Europeans' ships arrived off the West African coast. The first slave voyages merely diverted some of that trade to Europe or the Americas.

Slavery in West Africa

Many of the first slaves destined for sale across the Atlantic came from the Gold Coast, composed of thirty little kingdoms known as the Akan States. By the eighteenth century, though, it was the area farther east, the modern nations of Togo and Benin, that supplied most of the slaves sold in the English

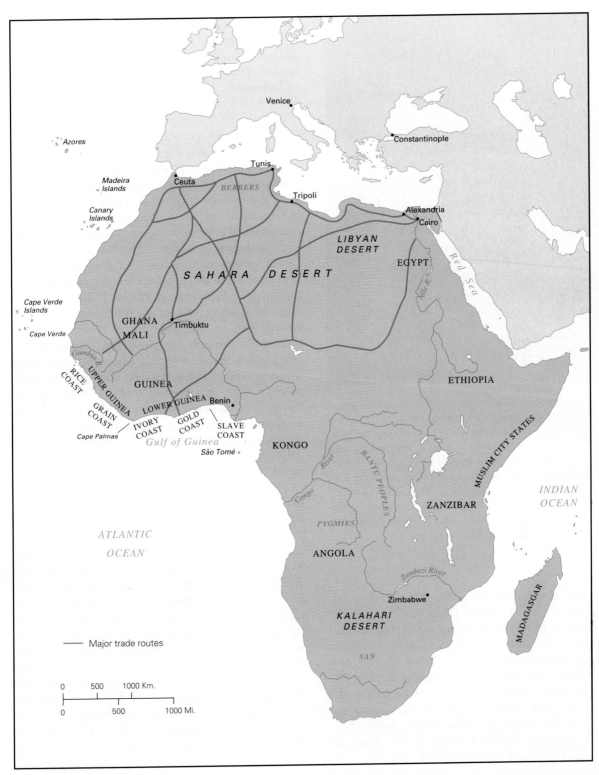

Africa and Its Peoples, c. 1400 *On the African continent resided many different peoples in a variety of eco-logical settings and political units. Even before Europeans began to explore Africa's coastlines, its northern regions were linked to the Mediterranean (and thus to Europe) by a network of trade routes.*

This decorative brass weight, created by the Asante peoples of Lower Guinea, was used for measuring gold dust. It depicts a family pounding fu-fu, a food made by mashing together plantains (a kind of banana), yams, and cassava. The paste was then shaped into balls to be eaten with soup. This weight, probably used in trading with Europeans, shows a scene combining foods of African origin (plantains and yams) with an import from the Americas (cassava), thus bringing the three continents together in ways both symbolic and real. Trustees of the British Museum. Photo by Michael Holford.

colonies. The Adja kings of the region, which became known as the Slave Coast, encouraged the founding of slave-trading posts and served as middlemen in the trade. Access to valuable European trade goods enhanced their positions in their own societies and improved their kingdoms' standing relative to their neighbors. Initially, those sent to the Americas came from the ranks of the already enslaved. By the early eighteenth century, however, after the demand for bondspeople in the American colonies had increased dramatically (see page 70), African rulers appear to have warred on other groups primarily to obtain slaves for sale.

The societies of West Africa, like those of the Americas, assigned different tasks to men and women. In general, the sexes shared agricultural duties. Men also hunted, managed livestock, and did most of the fishing. Women were responsible for childcare, food preparation, and cloth manufacture. Everywhere in West Africa women were the primary local traders. They managed the extensive local and regional networks through which goods were exchanged among the various families, villages, and small kingdoms.

Sexual Division of Labor in West Africa

Despite their different economies and the rivalries among states, the peoples of Lower Guinea had similar social systems organized on the basis of what anthropologists have called the *dual-sex principle*. In Lower Guinea, each sex handled its own affairs: just as male political and religious leaders governed men, so females ruled women. In the Dahomean kingdom, for example, every male official had his female counterpart; in the Akan States, chiefs inherited their status through the female line, and each male chief had a female assistant who supervised other women. Many West African societies practiced *polygyny* (one man having several wives, each of whom lived separately with her children). Thus few adults lived permanently in marital households, but the dual-sex system ensured that their actions were subject to scrutiny by members of their own sex, if not by a spouse.

Throughout Lower Guinea religious beliefs likewise stressed complementary male and female roles. Both women and men served as heads of the cults and secret societies that directed the spiritual life of the villages. Young women were initiated into the Sandé cult, young men into Poro. Neither cult was allowed to reveal its secrets to the opposite sex. Although West African women (unlike some of their Native American contemporaries) rarely held formal power over men, female religious leaders did govern other members of their sex within the Sandé cult, enforcing conformity to accepted norms of behavior and overseeing their spiritual well-being.

West African Religion

The West Africans brought to the Americas, then, were agricultural peoples, skilled at tending livestock, hunting, fishing, and manufacturing cloth from plant fibers and animal skins. Both men and women were accustomed to working communally, alongside other members of their own sex. They were also accustomed to a relatively egalitarian relationship between the sexes, especially within the context of religion. In the Americas, they entered societies that used their labor but had little respect for their cultural traditions.

 ## European Societies

In the fifteenth century, Europeans, too, were agricultural peoples. The daily lives of Europe's rural people had changed little for several hundred years. Split into numerous small, warring countries, Europe was divided linguistically, politically, and economically, yet in social terms Europeans' lives were more similar than different. European societies were hierarchical: a few families wielded arbitrary power over the majority of the people. English society in particular was organized as a series of interlocking hierarchies; each person (except those at the very top or bottom) was superior to some, inferior to others. Europe's kingdoms accordingly resembled those of Africa or Mesoamerica but differed greatly from the more egalitarian, consensus-based societies then established in America north of Mexico.

Most Europeans, like most Africans and Americans, lived in small villages. Only a few cities dotted the landscape, most of them political capitals.

Sexual Division of Labor in Europe European farmers, who were called *peasants*, owned or leased separate landholdings, but they worked the fields communally. Because fields had to lie fallow (unplanted) every second or third year to regain fertility, a family could not have ensured itself a regular food supply had not the work and the crop been shared annually by all the villagers. Men did most of the fieldwork; women helped out chiefly at planting and harvest. In some areas men concentrated on herding livestock. Women's duties consisted primarily of childcare and household tasks, including preserving food, milking cows, and caring for poultry. If a woman's husband was an artisan or a storekeeper in a city, she might assist him in business. Since Europeans kept domesticated animals (pigs, goats, sheep, and cattle) for meat, hunting had little economic importance in their cultures. Instead, hunting was primarily a sport for male aristocrats.

Unlike African and American societies, in which women often played prominent roles in politics and religion, men dominated all areas of life in Europe.

A few women—notably Queen Elizabeth I of England—achieved status or power, but the vast majority were excluded from positions of political authority. In the Roman Catholic Church and later in the new Protestant denominations, leadership roles were reserved for men. Husbands and fathers likewise expected to control their families. In short, European women generally held inferior social, economic, and political positions, yet within their own families they wielded power over children and servants.

Black Death When the fifteenth century began, European nations were slowly beginning to recover from the devastating epidemic of plague known as the Black Death, which first struck them in 1346. Bubonic plague, spread by rats and fleas as well as by human contact, arrived in Europe from China, traveling with long-distance traders along the Silk Road. The disease then recurred with particular severity in the 1360s and 1370s. Although no precise figures are available and the impact of the Black Death varied from region to region, the best estimate is that fully one-third of Europe's people died during those terrible years. That led to a precipitous economic decline—in some regions more than half of the workers were lost—and to severe social, political, and religious disruption because of the deaths of clergymen and other leading figures.

Political, Economic, and Technological Change As plague ravaged the population, England and France waged the Hundred Years War (1337–1453), initiated because the English monarchy claimed the French throne. The war interrupted overland trade routes through France that connected northern Europe to the Italian city-states and thence to Central Asia. Merchants in the eastern Mediterranean thus had to find new ways of reaching their northern markets. They solved that dilemma by forging a regular maritime link with the north to replace the overland route. The use of a triangular, or lateen, sail (rather than the then-standard square rigging) improved the maneuverability of ships, enabling them to sail out of the Mediterranean and into the North Sea. Also of key importance was the perfection of navigational instruments like the astrolabe and the quadrant, which allowed oceangoing sailors to estimate their position (latitude) by measuring the relationship of sun, moon, or stars to the horizon.

In the aftermath of the Hundred Years War, European monarchs relied on nationalistic feelings fostered by the conflict to consolidate their previously diffuse political power and to raise new revenues through increased taxation of an already hard-pressed peasantry. The long military struggle led to new pride in national identity (regional loyalties had previously held sway) and to heightened hostility toward foreigners. In England, Henry VII in 1485 founded the Tudor dynasty and began uniting a previously divided land. In France, the successors of Charles VII unified the kingdom and levied new taxes. Most successful of all were Ferdinand of Aragón and Isabella of Castile. In 1469 they married and combined their kingdoms, thereby creating the foundation of a strongly Catholic Spain. In 1492, they defeated the Muslims, who had lived in Spain and Portugal for centuries, thereafter expelling all Jews and Muslims from their domain.

The fifteenth century also brought technological change to Europe. Movable type and the printing press, invented in Germany in the 1450s, made information more accessible than ever before. Printing stimulated the Europeans' curiosity about fabled lands across the seas, lands they could now read about in books. The most important such work was Marco Polo's *Travels*, which recounted a Venetian merchant's adventures in thirteenth-century China and described that nation as bordered on the east by an ocean. Polo's account circulated widely among Europe's educated elites after it was printed in 1477. The book led many Europeans to believe that they could trade directly with China in oceangoing vessels instead of relying on the Silk Road or the trade route through East Africa. The transoceanic route, if it existed, would allow them to circumvent the Muslim and Mediterranean merchants who hitherto had controlled their access to Asian goods.

The European explorations of the fifteenth and sixteenth centuries were made possible by technological advances and by the growing strength of newly powerful national rulers. The primary motivation for exploratory voyages was each country's craving for easy access to desirable African and Asian goods—spices like pepper, cloves, cinnamon, and nutmeg (to season the bland European diet), silk, dyes, perfumes, jewels, and gold. Avoiding middlemen and acquiring such valuable products directly would improve a nation's income and its standing relative to other countries.

Motives for Exploration

That economic motive was supported by a secondary concern about spreading Christianity around the world. The linking of materialist and spiritual goals might seem contradictory today, but fifteenth-century Europeans saw no necessary conflict between the two. Explorers and colonizers could honestly want to convert "heathen" peoples to Christianity. At the same time they could hope to increase their nation's wealth by establishing direct trade with Africa, China, India, and the Moluccas (also known as the Spice Islands).

Early European Explorations and the Columbus Voyages

Before European mariners could discover new lands, they had to discover the oceans. To reach Asia, seafarers needed not just the maneuverable vessels and navigational aids increasingly used in the fourteenth century, but also knowledge of the sea, its currents, and especially its winds. Wind would power their ships. But how did the winds run? Where would Atlantic breezes carry their square-rigged ships, which, even with the addition of a triangular sail, needed to run before the wind (that is, to have the wind directly behind the vessel)?

Europeans learned the answers to these questions in the region that has been called the Mediterranean Atlantic, the expanse of the Atlantic that is south and west of Spain and is bounded by the island groups of the Azores (on the west) and the Canaries (on the south), with the Madeiras in their midst (see map, page 18). Europeans reached all three sets of islands during the fourteenth century. The Canaries proved a popular destination for mariners from Iberia (the peninsula that includes Spain and Portugal). Sailing to the Canaries from Europe was easy, because strong winds known as the Northeast Trades blow southward along the Iberian and African coastlines. The voyage took about a week, and the volcanic peaks on the islands made them difficult to miss even with navigational instruments that were less than precise.

Sailing in the Mediterranean Atlantic

The problem was getting back. The Iberian sailor attempting to return home faced a major obstacle: the very winds that had brought him so quickly to the Canaries now blew directly at him. Early travelers to the islands sometimes used galleys powered by oarsmen as well as by sails, but even oarsmen had a difficult time fighting the contrary winds and currents. Another alternative was similarly tedious: tacking back and forth to the east and west, attempting each time to make more headway north. The problem seemed intractable, and in earlier eras European sailors had been unable to solve it. When confronted with contrary winds, they simply waited for the wind to change. But for the most part, the Northeast Trades did not change. They blew steadily, never reversing course, though shifting slightly with the seasons.

What could be done? Some unknown seafarer figured out the answer: sailing "around the wind." If a mariner could not sail against the trade winds, he had to sail as close as possible to the direction from which the wind was coming without being forced to tack. In the Mediterranean Atlantic, that meant pointing his vessel northwest into the open ocean, away from land, until—weeks later—he reached the winds that would carry him home, the so-called Westerlies. Those winds blow (we now know, though the mariners at first did not) northward along the coast of North America before heading east toward Europe.

This solution must at first have seemed to defy common sense, but it proved to be the key to successful exploration of both the Atlantic and the Pacific Oceans. Once a sailor understood the winds and their allied currents, he no longer feared leaving Europe without being able to return. Faced with a contrary wind, all he had to do was sail around it until he found a wind to carry him in the proper direction. This strategy might seem to take him hundreds of miles out of the way, but in the long run it was safer and surer than attempting the monumental task of tacking against the wind.

During the fifteenth century, armed with knowledge of the winds and currents of the Mediterranean Atlantic, Iberian seamen regularly visited its islands, all of which they could reach in two weeks or less. The uninhabited Azores were soon settled by Portuguese migrants who raised wheat for sale in Europe and sold livestock to passing sailors. Madeira also had no native peoples, and by the 1450s Portuguese colonists were employing slaves (probably Jews and Muslims brought from Iberia) to grow large quantities of sugar for export to the mainland. Madeira thus developed by the 1470s into the world's first colonial plantation economy.

Islands of the Mediterranean Atlantic

One of the few surviving contemporary illustrations of a fifteenth-century European vessel, the caravel, is this engraving by the Flemish artist Peter Breughel. Notice the combination of square-rigged and lateen sails, the former for moving as efficiently as possible with a following breeze, the latter for maneuvering in unfavorable winds.   Private Collection.

The first islands the Europeans found—arriving as early as the 1330s—were the Canaries, inhabited by the Guanche people, who began trading animal skins and dyes with their European visitors. In 1402 the French attacked one of the islands; thereafter, Portuguese and Spanish expeditions continued the sporadic assaults. The Guanches resisted vigorously, but one by one the seven islands came under European control. The Guanches were then carried off as slaves to the Madeiras or the Iberian Peninsula. The last island fell to the Spanish in 1496, and the last known Guanche died in the middle of the next century. The Spanish conquerors then devoted the land of the Canary Islands to sugar cultivation. Collectively, the Canaries and Madeira became known as the Wine Islands because much of their sugar production was employed to make sweet wines.

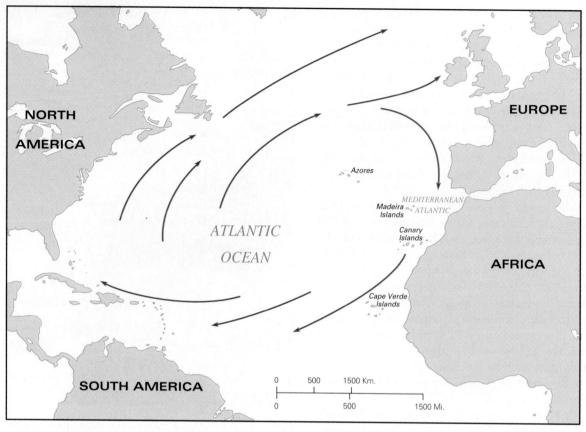

Atlantic Winds and Islands   *European mariners had to explore the oceans before they could find new lands. The first realm they discovered was that of Atlantic winds and islands.*

While some Europeans concentrated on exploiting the islands of the Mediterranean Atlantic, others used them as steppingstones to Africa. In 1415, Portugal seized control of Ceuta, a Muslim city in North Africa (see map, page 13). Prince Henry the Navigator, son of King John I of Portugal, knew that vast wealth awaited the first European nation to tap the riches of Africa and Asia directly. Each year he dispatched ships southward along the African coast, attempting to discover an oceanic route to Asia. But not until after Prince Henry's death did Bartholomew Dias round the southern tip of Africa (1488) and Vasco da Gama finally reach India (1498).

Portuguese Trading Posts in Africa

Long before that, though, Portugal reaped the benefits of its seafarers' voyages. Although West African states successfully resisted European penetration of the interior, they allowed the Portuguese to establish trading posts along their coasts. Charging the traders rent and levying duties on the goods they imported, the African kingdoms set the terms of exchange and benefited considerably from their new, easier access to European manufactures. The Portuguese gained too, for they no longer had to rely on the long trans-Saharan trade route. They earned immense profits by swiftly transporting African gold to Europe. Another valuable cargo for the Portuguese traders was slaves. When they carried previously enslaved Africans back to the Iberian Peninsula, the Portuguese introduced black slavery into Europe.

An island off the African coast, previously uninhabited, proved critical to Portuguese success. São Tomé, located in the Gulf of Guinea (see map, page 13) was colonized in the 1480s. By that time Madeira had already reached the limit of its capacity to produce sugar. The soil of São Tomé proved ideal for raising that valuable crop, and plantation agriculture there expanded rapidly. Large numbers of slaves were imported from the mainland to work in the cane fields, thus creating the first economy based primarily on the bondage of black Africans.

By the 1490s, even before Christopher Columbus set sail to the west, Europeans had learned three key lessons of colonization from their experiences in

Lessons of Early Colonization

the islands of the Mediterranean Atlantic and the African coast. First, they knew that they could transplant their crops and livestock successfully to exotic locations. Second, they learned that the native peoples of unknown lands could be either conquered (the Guanches) or exploited (the Africans) to European advantage. Third, they successfully developed a model of plantation slavery—an exploitative economy based on the labor of large numbers of people held in perpetual bondage—and a system for supplying nearly unlimited quantities of such workers. The stage was set for a critical moment in world history, and the man of the hour was a sailor named Christopher Columbus.

Columbus was well schooled in the lessons of the Mediterranean Atlantic. Born in 1451 in the Italian city-state of Genoa, Columbus, the largely

Christopher Columbus

self-educated son of a wool merchant, was by the 1490s an experienced sailor and mapmaker. Like many mariners of the day, he was drawn to Portugal and its islands, especially Madeira, where he commanded a merchant vessel. At least once he voyaged to the Portuguese outpost on the Gold Coast. There he acquired an obsession with gold, and there he came to understand the economic potential of the slave trade.

Like all accomplished seafarers, Columbus knew the world was round. (So, indeed, did most educated people: the idea that his contemporaries believed the world to be flat is a myth dating from the nineteenth century.) But he differed from other cartographers in his estimate of the earth's size: he thought that Japan lay only 3,000 miles from the southern European coast. Thus, he argued, it would be easier to reach Asia by sailing west than by making a difficult voyage around the southern tip of Africa. Experts scoffed at this crackpot notion, accurately predicting that the two continents lay 12,000 miles apart. When Columbus in 1484 asked the Portuguese authorities to back his plan to sail west to Asia, they rejected the proposal. After all, why should they adopt

such a crazy scheme just as their efforts to round the Cape of Good Hope promised success?

Ferdinand and Isabella of Spain, ruling a newly united kingdom and jealous of Portugal's successes in Africa, were more receptive to Columbus's ideas. Urged on by some Spanish noblemen and a group of Italian merchants residing in Castile, the monarchs agreed to finance the risky voyage, in part because they hoped the profits would pay for an expedition to conquer Muslim-held Jerusalem. And so, on August 3, 1492, in command of three ships—the *Pinta*, the *Niña*, and the *Santa Maria*—Columbus set sail from the southern Spanish port of Palos.

The first part of the journey must have been very familiar, for the ships steered down the Northeast Trades to the Canary Islands. There Columbus refitted his square-rigged ships, adding triangular sails to make them more maneuverable. On September 6, the ships weighed anchor and headed out into the unknown ocean.

Just over a month later, pushed by the favorable trade winds, the vessels found land approximately where Columbus had predicted (see map, page 18). On October 12, he and his men landed on an island in the Bahamas, which its inhabitants called Guanahaní but which he renamed San Salvador. (Because Columbus's sketchy description of his landfall can be variously interpreted, two different places—Watling Island and Samana Cay—are today proposed as possible contenders for Columbus's landing site.) Later he went on to explore the islands now known as Cuba and Hispaniola, which their residents, the Taíno people, called Colba and Bohío. Because he thought he had reached the Indies, Columbus referred to the inhabitants of the region as *Indians*.

Three themes predominate in Columbus's log, the major source of information on this first encounter. First, he insistently asked the Taínos where

Columbus's Observations

he could find gold, pearls, and valuable spices. Each time, his informants replied (largely via signs) that such products could be obtained on other islands, on the mainland, or in cities in the interior. Eventually he came to mistrust such answers, noting, "I am beginning to believe . . . they will tell me anything I want to hear."

Second, Columbus wrote repeatedly of the strange and beautiful plants and animals. "Here the fishes are so unlike ours that it is amazing. . . . The colors are so bright that anyone would marvel," he noted, and again, "The song of the little birds

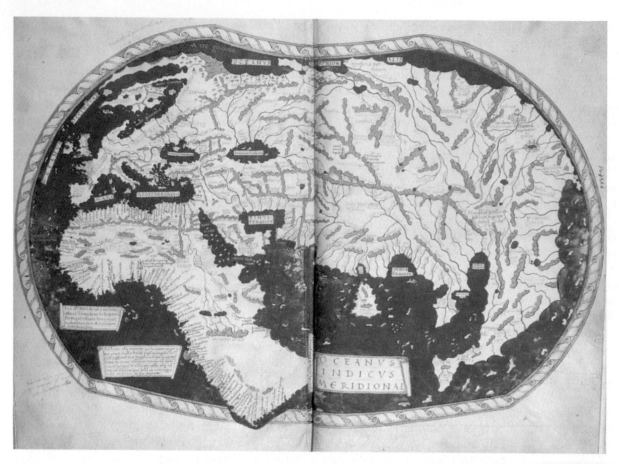

This map, produced in 1489 by Henricus Marcellus, represents the world as Christopher Columbus knew it, for it incorporates information obtained after Bartholomew Dias, a Portuguese sailor, rounded the Cape of Good Hope at the southern tip of Africa in 1488. Marcellus did not try to estimate the extent of the ocean separating the west coast of Europe from the east coast of Asia. Trustees of the British Library.

might make a man wish never to leave here. I never tire from looking at such luxurious vegetation." Yet Columbus's interest was not only aesthetic. "I believe that there are many plants and trees here that could be worth a lot in Spain for use as dyes, spices, and medicines," he observed, adding that he was carrying home to Europe "a sample of everything I can," so that experts could examine them.

Third, Columbus also described the islands' human residents, and he seized some to take back to Spain. The Taínos were, he said, very handsome, gentle, and friendly, though they told him of fierce people who raided their villages and lived on other nearby islands. The Caniba (today called Caribs), from whose name the word *cannibal* is derived, were reported to eat their captives (today

The Taíno People

scholars disagree about whether the tales were true). Columbus believed the Taínos to be likely converts to Catholicism, remarking that "if devout religious persons knew the Indian language well, all these people would soon become Christians." But he had more in mind than conversion. The islanders "ought to make good and skilled servants," Columbus declared. It would be easy, he asserted, to "subject everyone and make them do what you wished."

Thus the very first encounter between Europeans and America and its residents revealed a theme that would be of enormous significance for centuries to come: the Europeans' desire to extract profits from North and South America by exploiting their natural resources, including plants, animals, and peoples alike.

Christopher Columbus made three more voyages to the west, exploring most of the major

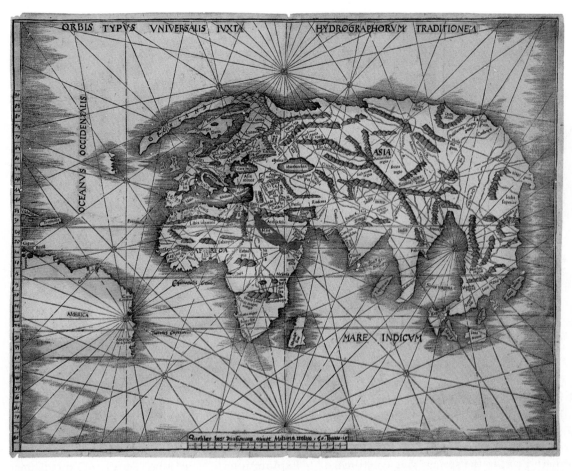

In 1507 Martin Waldseemüller, a German mapmaker, was the first person to designate the newly discovered southern continent as "America." He named the continent after Amerigo Vespucci, the Italian explorer who realized that he had reached a "new world" rather than islands off the coast of Asia. John Carter Brown Library at Brown University.

Caribbean islands and sailing along the coasts of Central and South America. Until the day he died in 1506 at the age of fifty-five, Columbus believed that he had reached Asia. Even before his death, others knew better. Because the Florentine Amerigo Vespucci, who explored the South American coast in 1499, was the first to publish the idea that a new continent had been discovered, Martin Waldseemüller in 1507 labeled the land "America," as is evident in his map (reproduced above). By then, Spain, Portugal, and Pope Alexander VI had signed the Treaty of Tordesillas (1494), confirming Portugal's dominance in Africa and Brazil in exchange for Spanish preeminence in the rest of the New World.

Naming of America

The first mariners to explore the region of North America that was to become the United States and Canada followed a very different route. Some historians argue that European sailors may have found the rich Newfoundland fishing grounds in the 1480s, even before Columbus's first voyage, but kept their discoveries a secret so that they alone could exploit the sea's bounty. Whether or not fishermen had crossed the entire width of the Atlantic, they had thoroughly explored its northern reaches. In the same way the Portuguese traveled regularly in the Mediterranean Atlantic, fifteenth-century English seafarers and others voyaged among the European continent, England, Ireland, and Iceland.

Northern Voyages

The winds these seafarers confronted posed problems on their outbound rather than homeward journeys. The same Westerlies that carried Colum-

Columbus received gold and this elaborate belt from a Taíno leader. In exchange, his log reveals, he presented the Taíno man with red shoes and an amber necklace. Museum Für Völkerkunde, Vienna.

bus and other southern voyagers back to Europe blew in the faces of northerners looking west. But sailors soon learned that the strongest winds shifted southward during the winter and that, by departing from northern ports in the spring, they could make adequate headway if they steered northward to catch sporadic easterly breezes. Thus, whereas the first landfall of most sailors to the south was somewhere in the Caribbean, those taking the northern route usually reached America along the coast of what is now Maine or the Canadian maritime provinces.

Five hundred years before Columbus, in the year 1001, the Norseman Leif Ericsson and other explorers from Greenland briefly established a settlement at a western site they named Vineland. (In the 1960s, archaeologists determined that this encampment was located at what is now L'anse aux Meadows, Newfoundland.) Attacks by local residents forced them to depart hurriedly, the tale of their exploits subsequently being preserved in oral-history sagas. Therefore, the European generally credited with "discovering" North America is John Cabot. More precisely, it might be said that Cabot brought to Europe the first formal knowledge of the northern coastline of the continent.

Like Columbus, Cabot was a master mariner from the Italian city-state of Genoa. He is known to

John Cabot's Explorations

have been in Spain when Columbus returned from his first trip to America. Calculating that England—which traded with Asia only through a long series of middlemen stretching from Belgium to Venice to the Muslim world—would be eager to sponsor exploratory voyages, Cabot sought and won the support of King Henry VII. He set sail from Bristol in late May 1497 in the *Mathew*, reaching his destination on June 24. Scholars disagree about the location of his landfall (some say it was Cape Breton Island, others Newfoundland), but all recognize the importance of his month-long exploration of the coast. Having achieved his goal, Cabot rode the Westerlies back to England, arriving just fifteen days after he left North America.

The voyages of Columbus, Cabot, and their successors finally brought the Eastern and Western Hemispheres together. The Portuguese explorer Pedro Alvares Cabral reached Brazil in 1500; John Cabot's son Sebastian followed his father to North America in 1507; France financed Giovanni da Verrazzano in 1524 and Jacques Cartier in 1534; and in 1609 and 1610 Henry Hudson explored the North American coast for the Dutch West India Company (see map). All these men were primarily

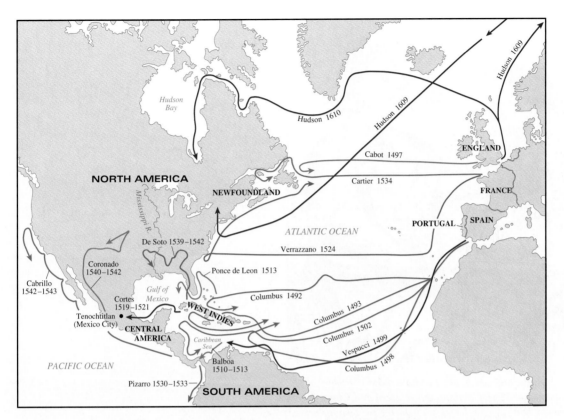

European Explorations in America   *In the century following Columbus's voyages, European adventurers explored the coasts and parts of the interior of North and South America.*

searching for the legendary, nonexistent "Northwest Passage" through the Americas, hoping to find an easy route to the riches of Asia. Although they did not attempt to plant colonies in the Western Hemisphere, their discoveries interested European nations in exploring North and South America.

Spanish Colonization and the Exchange of Diseases, Plants, and Animals

The Europeans' greatest impact on the Americas was unintended. Diseases carried from Europe and Africa by the alien invaders killed millions of Indians, who had no immunity to germs that had infested the other continents for centuries. The statistics are staggering. When Columbus landed on Hispaniola in 1492, more than 1 million people

Smallpox and Other Diseases

probably resided there. Fifty years later, only 500 were still alive. Within thirty years of the first landfall at Guanahaní, not one Taíno survived in the Bahamas. The lethal combination of diseases and slave-raiding parties had wiped them out.

Although measles, influenza, and other illnesses severely afflicted the Native Americans, the greatest killer was smallpox, which was spread by direct human contact. A Spanish priest recorded the words of an old Aztec man who survived the first smallpox epidemic in Tenochtitlán, the Aztec capital. That epidemic began in Hispaniola in 1518 and was carried to the mainland by Cortés and his army of invaders. The epidemic peaked in 1520, during the Aztec month of Tepeilhuitl, and it fatally weakened Tenochtitlán's defenders. "It spread over the people as great destruction," the elderly Aztec remembered. "Some it quite covered [with pustules] on all parts—their faces, their heads, their breasts. . . . There was great havoc. Very many died of it. . . . Great was its destruction." In the Aztec year Three House, on the

The Codex Florentino, *which has the fullest Aztec account of the Spaniards' conquest of Mexico, contains this image of an Indian afflicted with the smallpox that ravaged Tenochtitlán during the Spanish siege of the city.* Biblioteca Medicea Laurenziana, Florence.

day One Serpent (August 1521), Tenochtitlán surrendered. On the site of the Aztec capital, the Spaniards built what is now Mexico City.

Far to the north, where smaller American populations encountered only a few European explorers, missionaries, traders, and fishermen, disease also ravaged the countryside. A great epidemic, most likely chickenpox, swept through the villages along the coast north of Cape Cod from 1616 to 1618. The mortality rate may have been as high as 90 percent. An English traveler several years later commented that the people had "died on heaps, as they lay in their houses," and that bones and skulls covered the ruins of villages. Because of this dramatic depopulation of the area, just a few years later English colonists were able to establish settlements virtually unopposed.

The Americans, though, took a revenge of sorts. They gave the Europeans syphilis, a virulent venereal disease. The first recorded case of the new disease in Europe occurred in Barcelona, Spain, in 1493, shortly after Columbus's return from the Caribbean. Although less likely than smallpox to cause immediate death, syphilis was extremely dangerous and debilitating. Carried by soldiers, sailors, and prostitutes, it spread quickly through Europe and Asia, reaching as far as China by 1505.

The exchange of diseases was only part of a broader mutual transfer of plants and animals that resulted directly from European voyages. The two hemispheres had evolved separately for millions of years, developing widely different forms of life. Many large mammals like cattle and horses were native to the connected continents of Europe, Asia, and Africa, but the Americas contained no domesticated beasts larger than dogs and llamas. However, the vegetable crops of the Americas—particularly corn, beans, squash, cassava, and potatoes—were more nutritious and produced higher yields than those of the Old, like wheat and rye. In time, the Native Americans learned to raise and consume European livestock, and the Europeans and Africans became accustomed to planting and eating American crops. As a result, the diets of

Exchange of Plants and Animals

A European artist recorded this scene of a Carib war dance. The leaders in the middle of the circle blow tobacco smoke on the dancers to give them courage in the coming battles. MAPes MONDe Ltd.

all three peoples were vastly enriched. One consequence was the doubling of the world's population over the next three hundred years.

The exchange of two other commodities significantly influenced European and American civilizations. In America, Europeans encountered tobacco, which was at first believed to have beneficial medicinal effects. Smoking and chewing the "Indian weed" became a fad in the Old World after it was planted in Turkey in the sixteenth century. Despite the efforts of such skeptics as King James I of England, who in 1604 pronounced smoking "loathsome to the eye, hatefull to the Nose, harmfull to the brain, [and] dangerous to the Lungs," tobacco's popularity climbed. Its contribution to another disease, lung cancer, was discovered only in the twentieth century.

Also important was the impact of the horse on some Indian cultures. Horses brought to America by the Spaniards inevitably fell into the hands of Native Americans. Traded northward, they eventually became essential to the life of the nomadic buffalo hunters of the Great Plains. Sioux, Comanches, and Blackfeet, among others, used horses for transportation and hunting, calculated their wealth in the number of horses owned, and waged wars primarily from horseback. Women no longer had to carry the bands' belongings on their backs. Some groups that previously had cultivated crops abandoned agriculture altogether. Through the acquisition of horses, then, a mode of subsistence that had been based on hunting several different animals, in combination with gathering and agriculture, became one focused almost wholly on hunting buffalo.

The European and African invasion of the Americas therefore had a significant biological component, for the invaders carried plants and animals with them. Some creatures, such as livestock, they brought deliberately. Others, including rats (which infested their ships), weeds, and diseases, arrived unexpectedly. And the same process occurred in reverse. When the Europeans returned home, they deliberately took back such crops as corn, potatoes, and tobacco, along with that unanticipated hitchhiker, syphilis.

Only in the areas that Spain explored and claimed did formal colonization begin immediately. On his second voyage in 1493, Columbus brought to Hispaniola seventeen ships loaded with twelve hundred

Spanish Colonization

men, seeds, plants, livestock, chickens, and dogs—along with microbes and weeds. The settlement named Isabela (in the modern Dominican Republic) and its successors became the staging area for the Spanish invasion of America. On the islands of Cuba and Hispaniola the Europeans learned to adapt to the new environment, as did the horses, cattle, and hogs they imported. When the Spaniards explored the mainland, they rode island-bred horses and ate island-bred cattle and hogs. Everywhere the Spaniards went they carried with them what the historian Alfred Crosby has termed their "invasion team": European diseases and hooved animals. Those microorganisms and livestock ensured the Spaniards' success.

At first, Spanish explorers fanned out around the Caribbean basin. In 1513, Juan Ponce de León reached Florida and Vasco Núñez de Balboa crossed the Isthmus of Panama to the Pacific Ocean. Eight years later, the Spaniards' dreams of wealth were realized when Cortés conquered the Aztec Empire, seizing a fabulous treasure of gold and silver. Venturing northward, conquistadors like Juan Rodriguez Cabrillo (who sailed along the California coast), Hernando de Soto (who journeyed to the Mississippi River), and Francisco Vásquez de Coronado (who explored the southwestern portion of what is now the United States) found few of the products the Spanish coveted. By contrast, Francisco Pizarro, who explored the western coast of South America, acquired the richest silver mines in the world by conquering and enslaving the Incas in 1535. Pizarro was able to defeat the Incas in part because many of their leaders had been wiped out by a smallpox epidemic shortly before his arrival. Just a half-century after Columbus's first voyage, the Spanish monarchs—who treated the American territories as their personal possessions—controlled the richest, most extensive empire Europe had known since ancient Rome.

Spain established the model of colonization that other countries later attempted to imitate, a model with three major elements. First, the Crown maintained tight control over the colonies, establishing a hierarchical government that allowed little autonomy to New World jurisdictions. That control included, for example, limiting the number of people permitted to emigrate to America and insisting that the colonies import all their manufactured goods from Spain. Roman Catholic priests were dispatched to ensure the colonists' conformity with orthodox religious views. Second, most of the colonists sent from Spain were male. They married Indian—and later African—women, thereby creating the racially mixed population that characterizes much of Latin America to the present day.

Third, the colonies' wealth was based on the exploitation of both the native population and slaves imported from Africa. The Mesoamerican peoples, many of whom lived in urban areas, were accustomed to autocratic rule. Spaniards simply took over roles once assumed by native leaders, who had also exacted labor and tribute from their subjects. The *encomienda* system, which granted tribute from Indian villages to individual conquistadors as a reward for their services to the Crown, in effect legalized Indian slavery. Yet in 1542 a new code of laws reformed the system, forbidding Spaniards from enslaving Indians while still allowing them to collect money and goods from their tributary villages. In response, the conquerors, familiar with slavery in Spain, began to import Africans in order to increase the labor force under their direct control. Indian and African workers were primarily employed on huge ranches, which raised horses, cattle, and sheep; in gold and silver mines; and on sugar plantations. Yet African slavery failed to be adopted on a large scale everywhere in New Spain: it was far more common in the Greater Antilles (the major Caribbean islands) than on the Mexican mainland.

In this early view of a Spanish gold mine in South America, enslaved Africans process gold—mining, washing, and drying the nuggets before giving them to a Spanish overseer.   Pierpont Morgan Library/Art Resource, NY.

The New World's gold and silver, initially a boon, ultimately brought about the decline of Spain as a major power. The influx of unprecedented wealth led to rapid inflation, which (among other adverse effects) caused Spanish products to be overpriced in international markets and imported goods to become cheaper in Spain. The once-profitable Spanish textile-manufacturing industry collapsed, as did scores of other businesses. The seemingly endless income from American colonies emboldened successive Spanish monarchs

Spain's Economy Crumbles

to spend lavishly on wars against the Dutch and the English. Several times in the late sixteenth and early seventeenth centuries the monarchs repudiated the state debt, thus wreaking havoc on the nation's finances. When the South American gold and silver mines started to give out in the mid-seventeenth century, Spain's economy crumbled and the nation lost its international importance.

Spanish wealth derived from American suffering. The Spaniards deliberately leveled American cities, building cathedrals and monasteries on sites once occupied by Aztec, Incan, and Mayan temples. Some conquistadors sought to erase all vestiges of the great Indian cultures by burning the written records they found. With traditional ways of life in disarray, devastated by disease, and compelled to labor for their conquerors, many demoralized residents of Mesoamerica accepted the Christian religion brought to New Spain by friars of the Franciscan and Dominican orders.

The friars devoted their energies to persuading Mesoamerican people to move into new towns and to build Roman Catholic churches. In such towns, they were exposed to European customs and to religious rituals newly elaborated in an attempt to assimilate Christianity and pagan beliefs. For example, the friars deliberately juxtaposed the cult of the Virgin Mary with that of the corn goddess. These conversion efforts met with remarkable success. Thousands of Indians residing in Spanish territory embraced Catholicism, at least partly because it was the religion of their new rulers and they were accustomed to obedience.

Christianity in New Spain

European Traders, Fishermen, and Early Settlements

Other European nations did not start at once to colonize the coasts their sailors had explored. The Portuguese finally turned their attention away from Africa and India to Brazil, founding a small colony there in 1532. Not until after the middle of the century, however, did Brazil begin to develop a booming economy based on large-scale sugar production for the European market. By 1600, Portuguese ships were annually carrying thousands of enslaved Africans from Lower Guinea to labor on Brazilian sugar plantations.

Northern Europeans, denied access to the wealth of Mesoamerica by the Spanish and beaten to South America by the Portuguese, were initially more interested in exploiting North America's abundant natural resources than in the difficult task of establishing colonies on the mainland. John Cabot reported that fish were so plentiful along the North American coastline that they could be caught merely by lowering baskets over the side of a vessel. Europeans rushed to take advantage of the abundance of fish, a product in great demand in their homelands as an inexpensive source of nourishment. By the

1570s, more than 350 ships were exploiting the bounty of the Newfoundland Banks each year.

European fishermen soon learned that they could supplement their profits by exchanging cloth and metal goods like pots and knives for the Native Americans' beaver pelts, which Europeans used to make fashionable hats. At first the Europeans conducted their trading from ships sailing along the coast, but later they established permanent outposts on the mainland to centralize and control the traffic in furs (see pages 36–37). All were inhabited primarily by male adventurers, whose chief aim was to send as many pelts as possible home to Europe.

Northern Traders

The Europeans' insatiable demand for furs, especially beaver, was matched by the Native Americans' desire for European goods that could make their lives easier and establish their superiority over their neighbors. Some bands began to concentrate so completely on trapping for the European market that they abandoned their traditional economies. The Abenakis of Maine, for example, became partially dependent on food supplied by their neighbors to the south, the Massachusett tribe, because they devoted most of their energies to catching beaver to sell to French traders. The Massachusetts, in turn, intensified their production of foodstuffs, which they traded to the Abenakis in exchange for the European metal tools they preferred to their own handmade stone implements. The intensive trade in pelts also had serious ecological consequences. In some regions, beavers were completely wiped out. The disappearance of their dams led to soil erosion, especially when combined with the extensive clearing of forests by later European settlers.

Although their nation reaped handsome profits from fishing, English merchants and political leaders watched enviously as Spain's American possessions enriched Spain immeasurably. In the mid-sixteenth century, English "sea dogs" like John Hawkins and Sir Francis Drake began to raid Spanish treasure fleets sailing home from the West Indies. Their actions caused friction between the two countries and helped to foment a war that in 1588 culminated in the defeat of a huge invasion force—the Spanish Armada—off the English coast. As a part of the contest with Spain, English leaders started to think about planting colonies in the Western Hemisphere, thereby gaining better access to valuable trade goods and simultaneously preventing their enemy from dominating the Americas.

The first English colonial planners took Spain's possessions as both a model and a challenge. They hoped to reproduce Spanish successes by dispatching to America men who would sim-

Sir Walter Raleigh's Roanoke Colony

ilarly exploit the native peoples for their own and their nation's benefit. In the 1580s, a group that included Sir Humphrey Gilbert and his younger half-brother Sir Walter Raleigh promoted a scheme to establish outposts that could trade with the Indians and provide bases for attacks on New Spain. Approving the idea, Queen Elizabeth I authorized Raleigh and Gilbert to colonize North America.

Gilbert failed to plant a colony in Newfoundland, dying in the attempt, and Raleigh was only briefly more successful. After two preliminary expeditions, in 1587 he sent 117 colonists to the territory he named Virginia, after Elizabeth, the "Virgin Queen." They established a settlement on Roanoke Island, in what is now North Carolina, but in 1590 a resupply ship—delayed in leaving England because of the Spanish Armada—could not find them. The colonists had vanished, leaving only the word *Croatoan* (the name of a nearby island) carved on a tree.

Thus England's first attempt to plant a permanent settlement on the North American coast failed, as had earlier efforts by Portugal on Cape Breton Island (early 1520s) and France in northern Florida (mid-1560s). All three enterprises collapsed for the same reasons: inability to be self-sustaining with respect to food, and hostile neighbors, both American and European. Spanish soldiers wiped out the French colony in 1565 (see pages 34–35), and neither the Portuguese nor the English were able to maintain friendly relations with local Indians for very long.

The explanation for such failings becomes clear in Thomas Harriot's *A Briefe and True Report of the New Found Land of Virginia*, published in 1588 to publicize Raleigh's colony. Har-

Thomas Harriot's *Briefe and True Report*

riot, a noted scientist who sailed with the second of the preliminary voyages to Roanoke, was charged with describing the animals, plants, and people of the region for an English readership. His account revealed that although the explorers were almost wholly dependent on nearby villagers for food, they needlessly antagonized their neighbors by killing some of them for what Harriot himself admitted were unjustifiable reasons.

John White, an artist with Raleigh's 1585 expedition (and later the governor of the ill-fated 1587 colony), illustrated three different fishing techniques used by Carolina Indians: to the left, the construction of weirs and traps; in the background, spearfishing in shallow water; in the foreground, fishing from dugout canoes. The fish are accurately drawn and can be identified today.   Trustees of the British Museum.

The scientist concluded by advising later colonizers to deal with the native peoples of America more humanely than his comrades had done. But the content of his book suggested why that advice would rarely be followed. *A Briefe and True Report* examined the possibilities for economic development in America. Harriot stressed three points: the availability of commodities familiar to Europeans, like grapes, iron, copper, and fur-bearing animals; the potential profitability of exotic American products such as maize, cassava, and tobacco; and the relative ease of manipulating the native population to the Europeans' advantage. Should the Americans attempt to resist the English by force, Harriot asserted, the latter's advantages of disciplined soldiers and superior weaponry would quickly deliver victory.

Harriot's *Briefe and True Report* thus depicted for his English readers a bountiful land full of opportunities for a quick profit. The people already residing there would, he thought, "in a short time be brought to civilitie" through conversion to Christianity, admiration for European superiority, or conquest—if they did not die from disease, the ravages of which he witnessed. Thomas Harriot understood the key elements of the story, but his prediction was far off the mark. European dominance of North America was to be difficult to achieve. Indeed, some historians today argue that it never was fully achieved, in the sense Harriot and his compatriots intended, and that the societies that subsequently developed in North America owed as much to their native origins as to their immigrant ones.

 ## Conclusion

The process of initial contact between Europeans and Americans that ended with Thomas Harriot near the close of the sixteenth century had begun approximately 250 years earlier when Portuguese sailors first set out to explore the Mediterranean Atlantic and to settle on its islands. That region of the Atlantic so close to European and African shores nurtured the mariners who, like Christopher Columbus, ventured into previously unknown waters—those who sailed to India and Brazil as well as to the Caribbean and the North American coast. When Columbus first reached the Americas, he thought he had found Asia, his intended destination. Later explorers knew better but, except for the Spanish, regarded the Americas primarily as a barrier that prevented them from reaching their long-sought goal of an oceanic route to the riches of China and the Moluccas. Ordinary European fishermen were the first to realize that the northern coasts had valuable products to offer: fish and furs, both much in demand in their homelands.

The wealth of the north could not compare to that of Mesoamerica. The Aztec Empire, heir to the trading networks of Teotihuacán as well as to the intellectual sophistication of the Mayas, dazzled the conquistadors with the magnificence of its buildings and its seemingly unlimited wealth. As an old man, Bernal Diaz del Castillo recalled his first sight of Tenochtitlán, situated in the midst of Lake Texcoco: "We were amazed and said that it was like the enchantments . . . on account of the great towers and cues [temples] and buildings rising from the water, and all built of masonry." Some soldiers asked, he remembered, "whether the things that we saw were not a dream."

The Aztecs had predicted that their Fifth Sun would end in earthquakes and hunger. Hunger they surely experienced after Cortés's invasion; and, if there were no earthquakes, the great temples tumbled to the ground nevertheless, as the Spaniards used their stones (and Indian laborers) to construct cathedrals honoring their God and his son Jesus rather than Huitzilopochtli. The conquerors employed first American and later enslaved African workers to till the fields, mine the precious metals, and herd the livestock that earned immense profits for themselves and their mother country.

The initial impact of Europeans on the Americas proved devastating. Flourishing civilizations were, if not entirely destroyed, markedly altered in just a few short decades. The Europeans' invasion team of diseases and livestock, along with a wide range of other imported plants and animals, irrevocably changed the American environment, affecting the lives of the Western Hemisphere's inhabitants. By the end of the sixteenth century, many fewer people resided in North America than had lived there before Columbus's arrival, even taking into account the arrival of many Europeans and Africans. And the people who did live there—Indian, African, and European—resided in a world that was literally new—a world engaged in the unprecedented process of combining foods, religions, economies, styles of life, and political systems that had developed separately for millennia. Understandably, conflict and dissension permeated that process.

Suggestions for Further Reading

General

Alfred W. Crosby, *The Columbian Exchange: Biological and Cultural Consequences of 1492* (1972); Alfred W. Crosby, *Ecological Imperialism: The Biological Expansion of Europe, 800–1900* (1986); Bernard Lewis, *Cultures in Conflict: Christians, Muslims, and Jews in the Age of Discovery* (1995); William H. McNeill, *Plagues and Peoples* (1976); D. W. Meinig, *Atlantic America, 1492–1800* (1986); Herman Viola and Carolyn Margolis, eds., *Seeds of Change: Five Hundred Years Since Columbus* (1991); Eric Wolf, *Europe and the People Without History* (1982).

Mesoamerican Civilizations

Inga Clendinnen, *Aztecs: An Interpretation* (1991); Michael Coe, *Mexico*, 3d. ed. (1984); Brian Fagan, *Kingdoms of Gold, Kingdoms of Jade: The Americas Before Columbus* (1991); Eduardo Matos Moctezuma and David Carrasco, *Moctezuma's Mexico: Visions of the Aztec World* (1992); Linda Schele and David Friedel, *A Forest of Kings* [on the Mayas] (1990); Smithsonian Institution, *Handbook of Middle American Indians*, 16 vols. (1964–1976).

North American Indians

Brian Fagan, *Ancient North America: The Archaeology of a Continent* (1991); Brian Fagan, *The Great Journey: The Peopling of Ancient America* (1987); Francis Jennings, *The Founders of America: From the Earliest Migrations to the Present* (1993); Alvin Josephy, Jr., ed., *America in 1492* (1992); Alice B. Kehoe, *North American Indians* (1981); Mark Mehrer, *Cahokia's Countryside: Household Archaeology, Settlement Patterns, and Social Power* (1995); Lynda N. Shaffer, *Native Americans Before 1492: The Moundbuilding Centers of the Eastern Woodlands* (1992); Smithsonian Institution, *Handbook of North American Indians*, 8 vols. (1978–1990); Colin F. Taylor, ed., *The Native Americans: The Indigenous People of North America* (1992); Bruce Trigger and Wilcomb Washburn, eds., *The Cambridge History of the Native Peoples of the Americas*, Vol. 1: *North America* (1996).

Africa

Jacob Ade Ajayi and Michael Crowder, *History of West Africa* (1985); Paul Bohannon and Philip Curtin, *Africa and Africans* (1988); John Iliffe, *Africans: The History of a Continent* (1996); Robert July, *A History of the African People* (1992); Roland Oliver, ed., *The Cambridge History of Africa, vol. 3: c. 1050–c. 1600* (1977); Roland Oliver and J. D. Fage, *A Short History of Africa* (1988); John Thornton, *Africa and Africans in the Making of the Atlantic World, 1400–1680* (1992).

Exploration and Discovery

Emerson Baker et al., eds., *American Beginnings: Exploration, Culture, and Cartography in the Land of Norumbega* (1994); Fredi Chiappelli et al., eds., *First Images of America: The Impact of the New World on the Old*, 2 vols. (1976); Felipe Fernández-Armesto, *Before Columbus: Exploration and Colonization from the Mediterranean to the Atlantic, 1229–1492* (1987); Felipe Fernández-Armesto, *Columbus* (1991); Jerald T. Milanich, *Florida Indians and the Invasion from Europe* (1995); Jerald T. Milanich and Susan Milbrath, eds., *First Encounters: Spanish Explorations in the Caribbean and the United States, 1492–1570* (1989); Samuel Eliot Morison, *The European Discovery of America: The Northern Voyages, A.D. 1500–1600* (1971); Samuel Eliot Morison, *The European Discovery of America: The Southern Voyages, A.D. 1492–1616* (1974); J. H. Parry, *The Age of Reconnaissance* (1963); J. H. Parry, *The Discovery of the Sea* (1974); William and Carla Phillips, *The Worlds of Christopher Columbus* (1992); David B. Quinn, *North America from Earliest Discovery to First Settlements* (1977); Irving Rouse, *The Tainos: Rise and Decline of the People Who Greeted Columbus* (1992); Kirsten Seaver, *The Frozen Echo: Greenland and the Exploration of North America, ca. A.D. 1000–1500* (1995); Roger C. Smith, *Vanguard of Empire: Ships of Exploration in the Age of Columbus* (1993); Paolo Emilio Taviani, *Columbus: The Great Adventure* (1991).

The Conquest of Mexico

Sandra Cypess, *La Malinche in Mexican Literature* (1991); Ross Hassig, *Mexico and the Spanish Conquest* (1994); Miguel León-Portilla, ed., *The Broken Spears: The Aztec Account of the Conquest of Mexico* (1992); James Lockhart, ed. and trans., *We People Here: Nahuatl Accounts of the Conquest of Mexico* (1993); Lord Thomas, *Conquest: Montezuma, Cortés, and the Fall of Old Mexico* (1993).

Early European Settlements

Kenneth Andrews, *Trade, Plunder and Settlement: Maritime Enterprise and the Genesis of the British Empire, 1480–1630* (1984); Nancy Farriss, *Maya Society Under Colonial Rule* (1984); Charles Gibson, *Spain in America* (1966); Karen O. Kupperman, *Roanoke, the Abandoned Colony* (1984); James Lockhart, *The Nahuas After the Conquest: A Social and Cultural History of the Indians of Central Mexico, Sixteenth Through Eighteenth Centuries* (1992); A. J. R. Russell-Wood, *A World on the Move: The Portuguese in Africa, Asia, and America, 1415–1808* (1993); David J. Weber, *The Spanish Frontier in North America* (1992).

CHAPTER

2

Europeans Colonize North America

1600–1640

I n August 1630, Fray Alonso de Benavides brought thrilling news to Madrid. Franciscan friars in the remote territory called New Mexico had successfully converted to Roman Catholicism at least eighty thousand heathens. In village after village and even among the nomadic Apaches and Navajos, Indians had eagerly embraced baptism in the new faith, had built beautiful churches and schools with their own hands, and had demonstrated their willing adherence to the true religion of Jesus Christ. Moreover, the friars' missionary activities had repeatedly benefited from God's "wonders and miracles." For example, when an old woman from the Taos pueblo tried to convince four others to renounce their Christian marriages, "a bolt of lightning flashed from a clear untroubled sky, killing that infernal agent of the demon."

Fray Alonso, who was born in the Azores in the 1570s, supervised the New Mexico missions from 1626 to 1629. His account of the Franciscans' miraculous successes, like Theodor de Bry's depiction of America as in the illustration opposite, created a sensation in Europe. Alonso's *Memorial* not only was immediately published in Spanish but also was quickly translated into Latin, French, Dutch, and German. Fray Alonso undertook the arduous journey to Spain to convince the king to increase his financial and administrative support of the Franciscan missions. He achieved that goal: King Phillip IV agreed to send additional friars to New Mexico at his own personal expense, and he ordered the colonial governor to assist the missionaries' efforts actively.

Yet even Fray Alonso de Benavides's enthusiastic and optimistic report contained a troubling undercurrent. The colonial capital at Santa Fe, he noted, was inhabited by only about 250 Spaniards (along with

33

another 750 Pueblos and mestizos). The soldiers were "few and poorly equipped," and the church had been "a miserable hut" before Fray Alonso ordered the construction of a new one. Furthermore, not all the local Indians had been receptive to the friars' message. The residents of Picurís pueblo, for one, were "treacherous" and "on various occasions" had tried to murder the priests stationed there. Many of the miracles Fray Alonso described (such as the one recounted above) had been necessitated by the Indians' resistance to Christianity. For example, the skepticism of some Hopis about Christian teachings had led one friar to cause a boy blind from birth to see for the first time, and a Franciscan attempting to convert a group of Apaches had been saved from death only because at the last minute his attackers miraculously "did not dare shoot" the arrows they were aiming at him.

So, while praising the Spaniards' stunning successes in New Mexico, Fray Alonso revealed their equally striking weaknesses: more than a few Native Americans staunchly combated their missionizing; both priests and soldiers lacked adequate financial resources; and the one tiny, impoverished European settlement was surrounded by tens of thousands of potentially troublesome Pueblos, Apaches, and Navajos. Fray Alonso furthermore failed to identify an additional problem: royal governors often clashed with the Franciscans in a struggle for primacy in the region. A half-century later, such weaknesses helped to lead to a successful Pueblo revolt.

By the time Fray Alonso arrived in Madrid in 1630, England, France, and the Netherlands had also founded permanent colonies in North America. No longer were the Spaniards the only Europeans on that vast continent. Just as Franciscans played a major role in the Spanish settlements, so too Jesuit priests were active in New France. The French and Dutch colonies, like the Spanish outposts, were peopled largely by European men. Like the conquistadors, French and Dutch merchants (on the mainland) and planters (in the Caribbean islands) hoped to make a quick profit and then perhaps return to their homelands. The English, as Thomas Harriot made clear in the 1580s, were just as interested in profiting from North America. But they pursued those profits in a different way.

In contrast to other Europeans, most of the English settlers came to America intending to stay. Especially along the northeast Atlantic coast of the continent, in the area that came to be known as New

England, they arrived in family groups, sometimes along with friends and relatives from neighboring villages back home. They recreated European society and family life to an extent not possible in the other colonies, where migrant men had to find their sexual partners within the Native American or African populations. Among the English colonies, those in the Chesapeake region and on the Caribbean islands most closely resembled colonies founded by other nations. Their economies, like those of Hispaniola or Brazil, soon came to be based on large-scale production for the international market by a labor force composed of bonded servants and slaves.

Wherever they settled, the English, like other Europeans, did not prosper until they learned to adapt to the alien environment. The first permanent English colonies survived only because nearby Indians assisted the newcomers. The settlers had to learn to grow unfamiliar American crops such as maize (corn) and tobacco. They also had to develop extensive trading relationships with Native Americans and with colonies established by other European countries. In need of laborers for their fields, they first used English indentured servants, then later began to import African slaves, copying the example of the Spanish in the Atlantic and Caribbean islands, and the Portuguese in São Tomé and Brazil. Thus the early history of the region that became the United States and the English Caribbean can best be understood as a series of complex interactions among a variety of European, African, and American peoples and environments rather than as a simple story of English colonization.

New Spain, New France, New Netherland, and the Caribbean

Spaniards were the first Europeans to establish a permanent settlement within the boundaries of the modern United States, but they were not the first to attempt that feat. Twice in the 1560s groups of French Protestants (Huguenots) sought to escape from persecution in their homeland by planting colonies on the south Atlantic coast. The first colony, in present-day South Carolina, collapsed when its starving inhabitants had to

Florida

be rescued by a passing ship. The second, near modern Jacksonville, Florida, was destroyed in 1565 by a Spanish expedition under the command of Pedro Menéndez de Avilés. To ensure Spanish domination of the strategically important region (located near sea lanes used by Spanish treasure ships bound for Europe), Menéndez set up a small fortified outpost, which he named St. Augustine—now the oldest continuously inhabited European settlement in the United States. Franciscan missionaries soon followed, but nearby Indians fiercely resisted the friars' efforts to Christianize them. Only after the native peoples were forcibly moved to mission towns did many assent to baptism. Even so, by the end of the sixteenth century a chain of Franciscan missions stretched across northern Florida.

More than thirty years passed after the founding of St. Augustine before conquistadors ventured anew into the present-day United States. In 1598,

New Mexico

drawn northward by rumors of rich cities, Juan de Oñate, a Mexican-born adventurer, led a group of about five hundred soldiers and settlers to New Mexico. At first, the Pueblos greeted the interlopers cordially. When the Spaniards began to use torture, murder, and rape to extort food and clothing from the villagers, however, the residents of Acoma pueblo killed several soldiers. The invaders responded ferociously, killing more than eight hundred people and capturing the remainder. All the captives above the age of twelve were ordered enslaved for twenty years, and men older than twenty-five had one foot amputated. Not surprisingly, the other Pueblo villages surrendered.

Yet Oñate's bloody victory proved illusory, for New Mexico held little wealth. It also was too far

*The women of Acoma pueblo have long been accomplished pot-
ters. Before the arrival of Europeans with iron utensils, residents of the pueblo stored food and water in pots like this. The
unusual shape derived from its function: the low center of gravity allowed a woman to balance the pot easily on her head as she
carried water from a cistern to the top of the mesa.*   The Field
Museum #A109998c.

from the Pacific coast to assist in protecting Spanish
sea lanes, which had been one of Oñate's aims (he,
like others, initially believed the continent to be
much narrower than it actually is). Many of the
Spaniards returned to Mexico, and officials considered abandoning the isolated colony, which lay 800
miles north of the nearest Spanish settlement. Instead, in 1609, the authorities decided to maintain a
small military outpost and a few Christian missions
in the area, with the capital at Santa Fe (founded in
1610). This was the constricted world in which Fray
Alonso de Benavides arrived in 1626 and on which
he made his mark.

After Spain's destruction of France's Florida settlement in 1565, the French turned their attention
northward, to the area that Jacques Cartier had

New France

explored in the 1530s. Several
times in the late sixteenth century they tried futilely to establish permanent bases along the
coast of what is now Canada. Finally, in 1608 Samuel
de Champlain founded a trading post at an interior
site the local Iroquois had called Stadacona when
Cartier spent the winter there seventy-five years earlier. Champlain renamed it Quebec. He had chosen
well: Quebec was the most easily defended spot in

the entire St. Lawrence River valley, a stronghold
that controlled access to the heartland of the continent. In 1642, the French established a second post,
Montréal, at the falls of the St. Lawrence (and thus
at the end of navigation by oceangoing vessels), a
place the Indians called Hochelaga.

Before the founding of Quebec and Montréal,
French fishermen served as the major conduits
through which North American beaver pelts
reached France, but the two new posts quickly took
over control of the lucrative trade in furs. The settlements had only a few European residents, most of
them men, some of whom married Native American
women. The colony's leaders offered land grants
along the river to prospective settlers, including
wealthy seigneurs (nobles) who were expected to import tenants to work their farms. A small number of
Frenchmen brought their wives and took up agriculture; even so, more than twenty-five years after
Quebec's founding, it had just sixty-four resident
families, along with traders and soldiers. With respect to territory occupied and farmed, northern
New France never grew much beyond the confines
of the river valley between Quebec and Montréal.

One other important group was part of the population of New France: missionaries of the Society
of Jesus (Jesuits), a Roman Catholic order dedicated
to converting nonbelievers to
Christianity. First arriving in
the colony in 1625, the Jesuits,
whom the Native Americans
called Black Robes, initially
tried to persuade indigenous peoples to live near
French settlements and to adopt European agricultural methods as well as the Europeans' religion.
When that effort failed, the Jesuits concluded that
they could introduce Roman Catholicism to their
new charges without insisting that they fundamentally alter their traditional ways of life. Accordingly,
the Black Robes learned Native American languages
and traveled to remote regions of the interior, where
they lived in twos and threes among hundreds of potential converts.

Using a variety of strategies, Jesuits sought to
undermine the authority of village shamans (the traditional religious leaders) and to gain the confidence
of leaders who could influence others. Trained in
rhetoric, they won admirers by their eloquence. Immune to smallpox (for all had survived the disease already), they explained epidemics among the Indians
as God's punishment for sin, their arguments aided
by the ineffectiveness of the shamans' traditional

**Jesuit Missions
in New France**

The Founding of Permanent European Colonies in North America, 1565–1640

Colony	Founder(s)	Date	Basis of Economy
Florida	Pedro Menéndez de Avilés	1565	Farming
New Mexico	Juan de Oñate	1598	Livestock
Virginia	Virginia Company	1607	Tobacco
New France	France	1608	Fur trading
New Netherland	Dutch West India Company	1614	Fur trading
Plymouth	Pilgrims	1620	Farming, fishing
Maine	Sir Ferdinando Gorges	1622	Fishing
St. Kitts, Barbados, et al.	European migrants	1624	Sugar
Massachusetts Bay	Massachusetts Bay Company	1630	Farming, fishing, fur trading
Maryland	Cecilius Calvert	1634	Tobacco
Rhode Island	Roger Williams	1635	Farming
Connecticut	Thomas Hooker	1636	Farming, fur trading
New Haven	Massachusetts migrants	1638	Farming
New Hampshire	Massachusetts migrants	1638	Farming, fishing

remedies against the new pestilence. Drawing on European science, Jesuits predicted solar and lunar eclipses. Perhaps most important, they amazed the villagers by communicating with each other over long distances and periods of time by employing marks on paper. The Native Americans' desire to learn how to harness the extraordinary power of literacy was one of the most critical factors in making them receptive to the missionaries' message.

Although the process took many years, the Jesuits slowly gained thousands of converts, some of whom moved to reserves set aside for Christian Indians. In those communities they followed Catholic teachings with fervor and piety. The converts replaced their own culture's traditional equal treatment of men and women with notions more congenial to the Europeans' insistence on male dominance and female subordination. Further, they altered their practice of allowing premarital sexual relationships and easy divorce because Catholic doctrine prohibited both customs.

Jesuit missionaries faced little competition from other Europeans for Native Americans' souls, but French fur traders had to confront a direct challenge. In 1614, only five years after Henry Hudson sailed up the river that now bears his name, his spon-sor, the Dutch West India Company, established an outpost (Fort Orange) on that river at the site of present-day Albany, New York. Like the French, the Dutch sought beaver pelts, and their presence so close to Quebec posed a threat to French domination of the region. The Netherlands, at the time the world's dominant commercial power, was interested primarily in trade rather than colonization. Thus New Netherland, like New France, remained small, also focused on a river valley that offered easy access to its settlements. The colony's southern anchor was New Amsterdam, a town founded in 1624 on Manhattan Island, at the mouth of the Hudson River.

As the Dutch West India Company's colony in North America, New Netherland was a relatively unimportant part of a vast commercial empire that

New Netherland

included posts in Africa, Brazil, the West Indies, and modern-day Indonesia. Autocratic directors-general ruled the colony for the company; with no elected assembly, settlers felt little loyalty to their nominal leaders. Migration was sparse. Even a company policy of 1629 that offered a large land grant, or patroonship, to anyone who would bring fifty settlers to the province failed to attract takers. (Only one such tract—Rensselaerswyck, near Albany—was ever fully developed.) As late as the mid-1660s, New Netherland had only about five thousand inhabitants. Some of those were Swedes, who resided in the former colony of New Sweden (founded in 1638 on the Delaware River; (see map, page 40) which was taken over by the Dutch in 1655.

Despite their geographical proximity and their trading rivalry, New France and New Netherland did not come into armed conflict with each other. Yet their Native American allies did. In the 1640s, the Iroquois, who traded chiefly with the Dutch and lived in modern upstate New York, went to war against their northern neighbors the Hurons, who traded primarily with the French and lived in present-day Ontario. The Iroquois wanted to become the major supplier of pelts to Europeans and to ensure the security of their hunting territories. They achieved both goals by using guns supplied by the Dutch to largely exterminate the Hurons, whose population had already been decimated by an epidemic. The Iroquois thus established themselves as a major force in the region, one that Europeans could ignore only at their peril.

It was in the Caribbean, though, that France, the Netherlands, and England—the third entrant into the contest for North America—clashed most openly in the first half of the seventeenth century. The Spanish concentrated their colonization efforts on the Greater Antilles— Cuba, Hispaniola, Jamaica, and Puerto Rico. They left many smaller islands alone, partly because of resistance by their Carib inhabitants, partly because the mainland offered greater wealth for less effort. But to other European powers, the tiny islands were attractive targets: they could provide bases from which to attack Spanish vessels loaded with American gold and silver, and they could serve as sources of valuable tropical products such as spices, dyes, and fruits.

The Caribbean

England was the first northern European nation to establish a permanent foothold in the smaller West Indian islands (the Lesser Antilles). English people settled on St. Christopher (St. Kitts) in 1624, then later on other islands such as Barbados (1627). France was able to colonize Guadeloupe and Martinique only after overcoming fierce resistance by native Caribs, whereas the Dutch more easily gained control of St. Eustatius (strategically located near St. Kitts). In addition to native inhabitants, the European interlopers had to worry about conflicts with Spaniards and with each other. Most of the islands

were attacked at least once during the course of the century, and some changed hands. For example, the English drove the Spanish out of Jamaica in 1655, and the French soon thereafter took over half of Hispaniola, creating the colony of St. Domingue (modern Haiti).

Why did other Europeans devote so much energy to gaining control of these tiny bits of land neglected by Spain? The primary answer to that question was

Satisfying Europe's Sweet Tooth

sugar. Early in the 1640s, English residents of Barbados discovered that the island's soil and climate were ideally suited for cultivating sugar cane, then the major source of sweetness in the human diet. Europeans at the time grew that expensive, desirable luxury food in only a few widely scattered locations: Madeira, the Canaries, São Tomé, and Brazil.

Sugar was one of the most important components of the post-Columbian exchange of plants and animals. First domesticated in the East Indies, it was being grown in North Africa and southern Spain by 1000 C.E. But neither those regions nor the Atlantic islands settled in the fifteenth century could supply the demands of Europe's insatiable sweet tooth. Canary Island sugar canes were among the plants Columbus carried to Hispaniola on his 1493 voyage; by the 1520s, plantations (probably worked by African slaves) in the Greater Antilles were regularly shipping cargoes of sugar to Spain. Because of its focus on the mainland, though, the Spanish government did not encourage Caribbean sugar cultivation. At the end of the sixteenth century, most American sugar was being produced in Brazil.

The Dutch provided the key to the introduction of sugar cane to the newly colonized Lesser Antilles. In 1630 they seized control of northeastern Brazil from the Portuguese, holding the region until 1654. There the Dutch learned how to grow the canes and to process them into molasses and refined brown and white sugars. When they taught those skills to Barbadians, they were not being altruistic. The Dutch expected to sell African slaves to West Indian planters and to carry to Europe barrels of molasses and rum, which was distilled from sugar. The results must have exceeded their wildest dreams. The Barbados sugar boom in the 1640s was both explosive and lucrative. Planters, slave traders, and Dutch shipping interests alike earned immense profits.

Of course, as other Caribbean planters adopted sugar-cane cultivation, Barbadians' profits fell. Even so, sugar remained the most valuable American

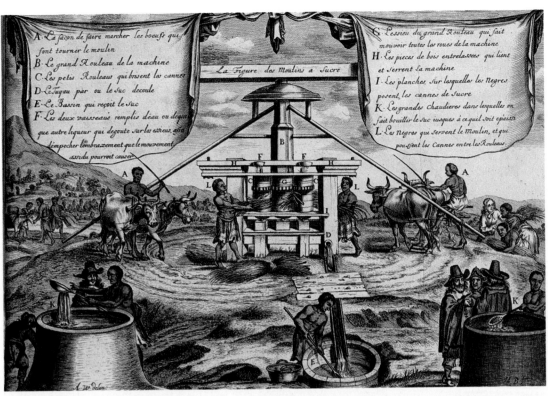

In the 1660s, a French book illustrated the various phases of sugar processing for curious European readers. Teams of oxen (A) turned the mill, the rollers of which crushed the canes (C), producing the sap (D), which was collected in a vat (E), then boiled down into molasses (K). African slaves, with minimal supervision by a few Europeans (foreground), managed all phases of the process. Library Company of Philadelphia.

commodity for more than one hundred years. In the eighteenth century, sugar grown by slaves in British Jamaica and French St. Domingue dominated the world market. Yet, in the long run, the future economic importance of the Europeans' American colonies lay on the mainland rather than in the Caribbean.

 ## England Colonizes Mainland North America

The failure of Raleigh's attempt to colonize Virginia ended English efforts to settle in North America for nearly two decades. When the English decided in 1606 to try once more, they again planned colonies that imitated the Spanish model. Success came only when they abandoned that model and founded settlements very different from those of other European powers. Unlike Spain, France, or the Netherlands, England eventually sent large numbers of men and women to set up agriculturally based

colonies on the mainland. Two major developments prompted approximately 200,000 ordinary English men and women to move to North America in the seventeenth century and led their government to encourage that migration.

The first major development that led English folk to move to North America was the onset of dramatic social and economic change caused by the doubling of the English population in the 150-year period after 1530, largely as a result of the introduction of nutritious American crops into Europe. All those additional people needed food, clothing, and other goods. The competition for goods led to high inflation, coupled with a fall in real wages as the number of workers increased. In these new economic and demographic circumstances, some English people—especially those with sizable landholdings that could produce food and clothing fibers for the growing population—substantially improved their lot. Others, particularly landless laborers and those with very

Social Change in England

European Settlements and Indian Tribes in Eastern North America, 1650 *The few European settlements established in the east before 1650 were widely scattered, hugging the shores of the Atlantic Ocean and the banks of its major rivers. By contrast, America's native inhabitants controlled the vast interior expanse of the continent and Spaniards had begun to move into the West.*

small amounts of land, fell into unremitting poverty. When landowners raised rents or decided to enclose and combine small holdings into large units, they forced tenant farmers off the land. As a result, geographical as well as social mobility increased, and the population of the cities swelled. London, for example, more than tripled in size between 1550 and 1650. By the latter year 375,000 residents were living on its crowded streets.

Well-to-do English people reacted with alarm to what they saw as the disappearance of traditional ways of life. Steady streams of the landless and homeless filled the streets and highways. Obsessed with the problem of maintaining order, officials came to believe that England was overcrowded. They concluded that colonies established in North America could siphon off England's "surplus population," thus easing social strains at home. For similar reasons, many English people decided that they could improve their circumstances by migrating from a small, land-scarce, apparently overpopulated island to a large, land-rich continent. Such economic considerations were rendered even more significant in light of the second development, a major change in English religious practice.

The sixteenth century witnessed a religious transformation that eventually led large numbers of English dissenters to leave their homeland. In 1533,

English Reformation

Henry VIII, wanting a male heir and infatuated with Anne Boleyn, sought to annul his marriage to his Spanish-born queen, Catherine of Aragon, despite nearly twenty years of marriage and the birth of a daughter. When the pope refused to approve the annulment, Henry left the Roman Catholic Church. He founded the Church of England and—with Parliament's concurrence—proclaimed himself its head. The English people welcomed the schism. Many had little respect for the English Catholic Church, which at the time was filled with corrupt bishops and ignorant priests. At first the reformed Church of England differed little from Catholicism in its practices, but under Henry's daughter Elizabeth I (child of his marriage to Anne Boleyn), new currents of religious belief that had originated on the European continent early in the sixteenth century dramatically affected the English church.

The leaders of the continental Protestant Reformation were Martin Luther, a German monk, and John Calvin, a French cleric and lawyer. Combating the Catholic doctrine that priests must serve as in-

Tudor and Stuart Monarchs of England, 1509–1649

Monarch	Reign	Relation to Predecessor
Henry VIII	1509–1547	Son
Edward VI	1547–1553	Son
Mary I	1553–1558	Half-sister
Elizabeth I	1558–1603	Half-sister
James I	1603–1625	Cousin
Charles I	1625–1649	Son

termediaries between laypeople and God, Luther and Calvin insisted that each person could interpret the Bible for himself or herself. One result of that notion was the spread of literacy: to understand and interpret the Bible, people had to learn how to read. Both Luther and Calvin rejected Catholic rituals and denied the need for an elaborate church hierarchy. They also asserted that salvation came through faith alone, rather than—as Catholic teaching had it— through a combination of faith and good works. Calvin, though, went further than Luther in stressing God's absolute omnipotence and emphasizing the need for people to submit totally to God's will.

Elizabeth I tolerated religious diversity among her subjects as long as they generally acknowledged her authority as head of the Church of England.

Puritans

Accordingly, during her long reign (1558–1603) Calvin's ideas gained influence within the English church. By the late sixteenth century, many English Calvinists—those who came to be called Puritans because they wanted to purify the Church of England—believed that the English Reformation had not gone far enough. Henry had simplified the church hierarchy; they wanted to abolish it altogether. Henry had subordinated the church to the interests of the state; they wanted a church free from political interference. And the Church of England, like the Roman Catholic church, continued to include all English people in its membership. The Puritans preferred a more restricted definition; they wanted to confine church membership to persons they believed to be "saved."

Elizabeth I's Stuart successors, her cousin James I (1603–1625) and his son Charles I (1625–1649), were

London in 1616, with London Bridge at center right. Overcrowding in the city led many observers to conclude that American colonization could remove "excess" population and provide new employment for poverty-stricken persons. The rapidly growing community of London merchants also sought to develop new sources of overseas profits.

less tolerant of Puritans than she. As Scots, they also had little respect for the traditions of representative government that had developed in England under the Tudors and their predecessors. The wealthy landowners who sat in Parliament had grown accustomed to having considerable influence on government policies, especially taxation. But James I, taking a position later endorsed by his son, publicly declared his adherence to the theory of the *divine right of kings.* The Stuarts insisted that a monarch's power came directly from God and that his subjects had a duty to obey him. A king's authority was absolute, they argued, just like the authority of a father over his children.

Both James I and Charles I believed that their authority included the power to enforce religious conformity among their subjects. Because Puritans were challenging many of the most important precepts of the English church, the monarchs authorized the removal of Puritan clergymen from their pulpits. In the 1620s and 1630s a number of English Puritans accordingly decided to move to America, where they hoped to put their religious beliefs into practice unmolested by the Stuarts or the church hierarchy.

However, the initial impetus for the establishment of what was to become England's first permanent colony in the Western Hemisphere came not from the Puritans but from a group of merchants and wealthy gentry. In 1606, envisioning the possibility of earning great profits by finding precious metals and opening new trade routes, the men established a joint-stock venture, the Virginia Company, to plant colonies in America.

The First Stuart Monarchs

Joint-stock companies had been developed in England during the sixteenth century as a mechanism for pooling the resources of many small investors. These forerunners of modern corporations were funded through the sale of stock. Until the founding of the Virginia Company, they had been used primarily to finance trading voyages. For that purpose they worked well: no one risked too much money, and investors usually received quick returns. Joint-stock companies turned out to be a poor way to finance colonies, because the early settlements required enormous amounts of capital and, with rare exceptions, failed to return much immediate profit. Colonies founded by joint-stock companies consequently suffered from a chronic lack of capital and from constant tension between stockholders and colonists, who claimed they were not being adequately supported by the investors.

Joint-Stock Companies

The Virginia Company was no exception to this rule. Chartered by James I in 1606, the company tried but failed to start a colony in Maine and barely succeeded in planting one in Virginia. In 1607 it dispatched to North America an expedition consisting exclusively of men and boys. In May, 104 Englishmen landed in a region called Tsenacomoco by the native inhabitants. There they established the settlement called Jamestown on a swampy peninsula in a river they also named for their monarch. The colonists were ill equipped for survival in the unfamiliar environment, and the settlement was afflicted by dissension and disease.

Founding of Virginia

By January 1608, only thirty-eight of the original colonists were still alive. Many of the first migrants were gentlemen unaccustomed to working with their hands and artisans with irrelevant skills like glassmaking. Having come to Virginia expecting to make easy fortunes, most could not adjust to the conditions they encountered. They resisted living "like savages," retaining English dress and casual work habits despite their desperate circumstances. Such attitudes, combined with the effects of chronic malnutrition and epidemic disease, took a terrible toll. Only when Captain John Smith, one of the colony's founders, imposed military discipline on the colonists in 1608 was Jamestown saved from collapse. But after Smith's departure the settlement experienced a severe "starving time" (the winter of 1609–1610), during which at least one colonist re-

Theodor de Bry's America *depicted crucial events in the continents' history. This illustration is de Bry's version of the kidnapping of Pocahontas, Powhatan's daughter, in 1612. In the foreground, two other Native Americans are enticing Pocahontas to join the English; at right center, she is being led onto a ship; in the background, English raiders are burning the villages of Powhatan's people.* Library of Congress.

sorted to cannibalism. Although more settlers (including a few women and children) arrived in 1608 and 1609 and living conditions slowly improved, as late as 1624 only 1,300 of approximately 8,000 English migrants to Virginia remained alive.

That Jamestown survived was a tribute not to the English but rather to the Native Americans within whose territories they settled, a group of six Algonkian tribes known as the Powhatan Confederacy (see map, page 40). A shrewd and powerful leader, Powhatan was aggressively consolidating his authority over some twenty-five other small bands when the Europeans arrived. Fortunately for the colonists, Powhatan at first viewed them as potential allies. He found the English colony a reliable source of items such as steel knives and guns, which gave him a technological advantage over his Indian neighbors. In return, Powhatan's people traded their excess corn and other foodstuffs to the starving settlers. The initially cordial relationship soon deteriorated, however. The English colonists kidnapped Powhatan's daughter, Pocahontas, holding her as a hostage in retaliation for Powhatan's seizure of several settlers. In captivity, she agreed in 1614 to

Powhatan Confederacy

marry a colonist, John Rolfe; she sailed with him to England, where she died in 1616.

The relationship between the Jamestown colony and the coastal Indians was uneasy. English and Algonkian peoples had much in common: deep religious beliefs, a lifestyle oriented around agriculture, clear political and social hierarchies, and sharply defined gender roles. Yet the English and the Powhatans themselves usually focused on their cultural differences, not their similarities. English men thought that Indian men were lazy because they did not work in the fields and spent much of their time hunting (which was a sport to the English). Indian men thought English men effeminate because they did "women's work" of cultivation. In the same vein, the English believed that Algonkian women were oppressed because they did heavy field labor.

Other differences between the two cultures caused serious misunderstandings. Although both societies were hierarchical, the nature of the hierarchies differed considerably. Among the East Coast Algonkians, people were not born to positions of leadership, nor were political power and social status necessarily inherited through the male line. Members of the English gentry inherited their position from their fathers, and English political and military leaders tended to rule autocratically. By contrast, the authority of Algonkian leaders rested on consensus. Accustomed to the European concept of powerful kings, the English sought such figures in native villages. Often (for example, when negotiating treaties) they willfully overestimated the ability of chiefs to make independent decisions for their people.

Algonkian and English Cultural Differences

Furthermore, the Algonkians and the English had very different notions of property ownership. In most Algonkian villages, land was held communally by the entire group. It could not be bought or sold absolutely, although certain rights to use the land (for example, for hunting or fishing) could be transferred. English people, in contrast, were accustomed to individual farms and to buying and selling land. In addition, the English refused to accept the validity of Indians' claims to traditional hunting territories, insisting that only land intensively cultivated could be regarded as owned or occupied. As one colonist put it, the English believed that "salvadge peoples" who "rambled" over a region without farming it could claim no "title or propertye" in the land.

Above all, the English settlers believed unwaveringly in the superiority of their civilization. Although in the early years of colonization they often anticipated living peacefully alongside Native Americans, they always assumed that they would dictate the terms of such coexistence. Like Thomas Harriot at Roanoke, they expected Native Americans to adopt English customs and to convert to Christianity. They showed little respect for traditional Indian ways of life, especially when they believed their own interests were at stake. That attitude was clearly revealed in the Virginia colony's treatment of the Powhatan Confederacy in subsequent years.

The spread of tobacco cultivation upset the balance of power in early Virginia. In tobacco—the American crop previously introduced to Europe by the Spanish—the settlers and the Virginia Company found the salable commodity for which they had been searching. John Rolfe planted the first crop in 1611. In 1620 Virginians exported 40,000 pounds of cured leaves, and by the end of that decade shipments had jumped dramatically to 1.5 million pounds. The great tobacco boom had begun, fueled by high prices and substantial profits for planters. The price later fell almost as sharply as it had risen, and it fluctuated wildly from year to year in response to increasing supply and international competition. Nevertheless, tobacco became the foundation of Virginia's economic prosperity, and the colony developed from a small outpost peopled exclusively by males into an agricultural settlement inhabited by both men and women.

Tobacco: The Basis of Virginia's Success

Successful tobacco cultivation required abundant land, since the crop quickly drained soil of nutrients. Planters soon learned that a field could produce only about three satisfactory crops before it had to lie fallow for several years to regain its fertility. Thus the once-small English settlements began to expand rapidly: eager planters applied to the Virginia Company for large land grants on both sides of the James River and its tributary streams. Lulled into a false sense of security by years of peace, the planters established farms at some distance from one another along the river banks—a settlement pattern convenient for tobacco cultivation but poorly designed for defense.

Opechancanough, Powhatan's brother and successor, watched the English colonists steadily encroaching on the confederacy's lands and attempting to convert its members to Christianity. Recognizing the danger his brother had overlooked, the war leader launched coordinated attacks all along the river on March 22, 1622. By the end of the day, 347 colonists (about one-quarter of the total) lay dead, and only a timely warning from two Christian converts saved Jamestown itself from destruction.

Indian Uprising

Virginia reeled from the blow but did not collapse. Reinforced by new shipments of men and arms from England, the settlers attacked Opechancanough's villages. For some years an uneasy peace prevailed, but then in April 1644 Opechancanough tried one last time to repel the invaders. He failed, losing his life in the war that ensued. In 1646, survivors of the Powhatan Confederacy accepted a treaty formally subordinating them to English authority. Although they continued to live in the region, their alliance crumbled and their efforts to resist the spread of European settlement ended.

Life in the Chesapeake: Virginia and Maryland

The 1622 Powhatan uprising that failed to destroy the colony did succeed in killing its parent. The Virginia Company never made any profits from the enterprise, for all its earnings were offset by the heavy cost of supporting the settlers and by internal corruption. In 1624 James I revoked the charter, transforming Virginia into a *royal colony*—a colony ruled by the king through appointed officials. Yet he nevertheless continued the company policy (adopted in 1617) of attracting settlers through a "headright" system. Every new arrival paying his or her own way was promised a land grant of 50 acres; those who financed the passage of others received similar headrights for each person. To ordinary English farmers, many of whom owned little or no land, the headright system offered a powerful incentive to migrate to Virginia. To wealthy gentry, it promised even more: the possibility of establishing vast agricultural enterprises worked by large numbers of laborers.

Headrights

In 1619, the company had introduced a second policy that James was more reluctant to retain: it

had authorized the landowning men of the major Virginia settlements to elect representatives to an assembly called the House of Burgesses. Although England was a monarchy, English landholders had long been accustomed to electing members of Parliament and controlling their own local governments. In accordance with his belief in the absolute power of the monarchy and his distrust of legislative bodies, James at first abolished the assembly. But Virginians protested so vigorously that by 1629 the House of Burgesses was functioning once again. Only two decades after the first permanent English settlement was planted in North America, the colonists successfully insisted on governing themselves at the local level. Thus the political structure of England's American possessions came to differ from that of New Spain, New France, and New Netherland, all of which were ruled autocratically.

The House of Burgesses

By the 1630s, tobacco was firmly established in Virginia as the staple crop and chief source of revenue. It quickly became just as important in the second English colony planted on Chesapeake Bay: Maryland, settled in 1634 and given by Charles I to the Calvert family as a personal possession, a *proprietorship*. (Because Virginia and Maryland both border Chesapeake Bay—see map, page 40—they are often referred to collectively as "the Chesapeake.") The Calverts intended the colony to serve as a haven for their fellow Roman Catholics, who were being persecuted in England. Cecilius Calvert, second Lord Baltimore, became the first colonizer to offer freedom of religion to all Christian settlers; he understood that protecting the Protestant majority was the only way to ensure Catholics' rights.

Founding of Maryland

In everything but religion the two Chesapeake colonies resembled each other. In Maryland as in Virginia, tobacco planters spread out along the river banks, establishing isolated farms instead of towns. The region's deep, wide rivers offered dependable water transportation in an age of few and inadequate roads. Each farm or group of farms had its own wharf, where oceangoing vessels could take on or discharge cargo. As a result, Virginia and Maryland had few towns, for their residents did not need commercial centers in order to buy and sell goods.

The planting, cultivation, and harvesting of tobacco had to be done by hand; these tasks did not

How do historians know what seventeenth-century settlements looked like? Recent excavations at St. Mary's City, Maryland, founded as the capital and sole town of Calvert's colony in 1634, demonstrate the importance of cooperation between historians and archaeologists. St. Mary's City is one of only two major seventeenth-century English settlements in America not now buried under modern cities. (The other, Jamestown, was located in 1996, although for many years historians believed that it had been eroded into the James River.) The site of St. Mary's City was abandoned in 1696 when the colonial capital was moved to Annapolis; later the area was incorporated into a tobacco plantation. Working from written documents like deeds and wills, historians created

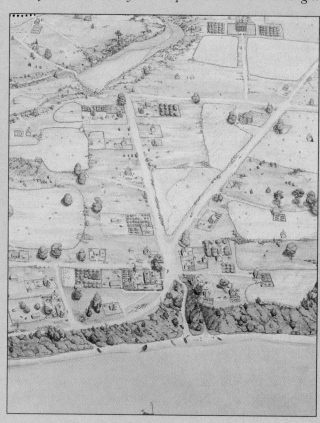

hypotheses about the layout of the town. But when archaeologists began digging into the soil, they discovered what the documents had not revealed: the town plan was based on triangles intersecting at the town's central square. A modern artist's reconstruction of the town as it might have looked in 1685 shows portions of those triangles. At far right, top, is the Jesuit chapel, the first Catholic church in Anglo-America. At center is the square, with the large Country's House, the building once used as the capitol, on the left. (The new state house constructed in 1676 is off this map to the far left, at the point of a triangle at the same distance from the square as the chapel.) The artist needed both archival and archaeological data to produce this drawing. Historic St. Mary's City Commission.

take much skill, but they were repetitious, time-consuming, and labor-intensive. Clearing land for new fields, a necessary process every few years, was also a slow, labor-intensive task. Above all else, then, successful Chesapeake tobacco plantations required laborers. But where and how could they be obtained? Nearby Indians, their numbers reduced by war and disease, could not supply the needed workers. Dutch traders carried a few Africans to the Chesapeake beginning in 1619, but such merchants could more easily and profitably sell slaves in the West Indies, their first American landfall. In the first half of the seventeenth century, therefore, only a few

Need for Laborers

Africans, some of them free, arrived in the Chesapeake. By 1650, about three hundred blacks lived in Virginia—a tiny fraction of the population.

Chesapeake tobacco planters thus looked primarily to England to supply their labor needs. Because of the headright system (which Maryland also adopted in 1640), a prospective tobacco planter anywhere in the Chesapeake could simultaneously obtain both land and labor by importing workers from England. Good management could make the process self-perpetuating: a planter could use his profits to pay for the passage of more workers and thereby gain title to more land.

Since men did the agricultural work in European societies, planters and workers alike assumed that field laborers should be men. Such male laborers, along with a few women, migrated to America as *indentured servants*—that is, in return for their passage they contracted to work for planters for periods ranging from four to seven years. Indentured servants accounted for 75 to 85 percent of the approximately 130,000 English migrants to Virginia and Maryland during the seventeenth century; the rest were mostly young couples with one or two children.

English Migrants

Roughly three-quarters of the servant migrants were males between the ages of fifteen and twenty-four; only one in five or six was female. Most of the men had been farmers and laborers, and many came from parts of England experiencing severe social disruption. Some had already moved several times within England before migrating to America; they came from the middling ranks of society—what their contemporaries called the "common sort." Their youth indicated that most of them probably had not yet established themselves in their homeland.

For such people the Chesapeake appeared to offer good prospects. After fulfilling the terms of their indentures, servants were promised "freedom dues" consisting of clothes, tools, livestock, casks of corn and tobacco, and sometimes even land. From a distance at least, America seemed to hold out chances for advancement unavailable in England. Yet the migrants' lives were difficult. Servants typically worked six days a

Conditions of Servitude

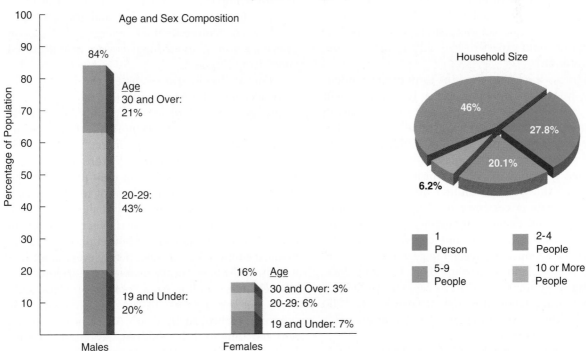

The Population of Virginia, 1625

Population of Virginia, 1625 The only detailed census taken in the English mainland North American colonies during the seventeenth century was prepared in Virginia in 1625. It listed a total of 1,218 people, comprising 309 "households" and living in 278 dwellings—so some houses contained more than one family. The chart shows, on the left, the proportionate age and gender distribution of the 765 individuals for whom full information was recorded, and, on the right, the percentage variation in the sizes of the 309 households. The approximately 42 percent of the residents of the colony who were servants were concentrated in 30 percent of the households. Nearly 70 percent of the households had no servants at all. Source of data: Robert V. Wells, *The Population of the British Colonies in America Before 1776: A Survey of Census Data* (Princeton: Princeton University Press, 1975), tables V-5 and V-6 and pp. 165–166.

week, ten to fourteen hours a day, in a climate much warmer than they were accustomed to. Their masters could discipline or sell them, and they faced severe penalties for running away. Even so, the laws did offer them some protection. For example, their masters were supposed to supply them with sufficient food, clothing, and shelter, and they were not to be beaten excessively. Servants who were especially cruelly treated turned to the courts for assistance, sometimes winning verdicts directing that they be sold to more humane masters or freed from their indentures.

Servants and planters alike had to contend with epidemic disease but not with the same illnesses that continued to kill Native Americans in large numbers. Migrants first had to survive the process the colonists called "seasoning"—a bout with disease (probably malaria) that usually occurred during their first Chesapeake summer. They then had to endure recurrences of malaria, along with dysentery, typhoid fever, and other diseases. As a result, approximately 40 percent of male servants did not survive long enough to become freedmen. Even young men of twenty-two who had successfully weathered their seasoning could expect to live only another twenty years at best.

For those who survived the term of their indentures, however, the opportunities for advancement were real. Until the last decades of the seventeenth century, former servants were usually able to become independent planters ("freeholders") and to live a modest but comfortable existence. Some even assumed positions of political prominence such as justice of the peace or militia officer. But in the 1670s tobacco prices entered a fifty-year period of stagnation and decline. Simultaneously, good land grew increasingly scarce and expensive. In 1681 Maryland dropped its legal requirement that servants receive land as part of their freedom dues, forcing large numbers of freed servants to live for years as wage laborers or tenant farmers. By 1700 the Chesapeake was no longer the land of opportunity it once had been.

Life in the early Chesapeake was hard for everyone, regardless of sex or status. Farmers (and sometimes their wives) toiled in the fields alongside

Standard of Living

servants, laboriously clearing land, then planting and harvesting tobacco and corn. Because hogs could forage for themselves in the forests and needed little tending, Chesapeake households subsisted mainly on pork and corn, which were filling but did not supply sufficient nutrients. Planter families supplemented this monotonous fare by eating fish, shellfish, and wildfowl, in addition to vegetables such as lettuce and peas, which they grew in small gardens. The health problems caused by epidemic disease were magnified by the near impossibility of preserving food for safe winter consumption. Salting, drying, and smoking, the only methods the colonists knew, did not always prevent spoilage.

Few households had many material possessions other than farm implements, bedding, and basic cooking and eating utensils. Chairs, tables, candles, and knives and forks were luxury items. Most people rose and went to bed with the sun, sat on crude benches or storage chests, and held plates or bowls in their hands while eating meat and vegetable stews with spoons. The tiny houses were ramshackle dwellings with just one or two rooms. Planters devoted their income to improving their farms, buying livestock, and purchasing more laborers rather than to improving their standard of living. Instead of making items such as clothing and tools, planter families concentrated their energies chiefly on growing tobacco, importing necessary manufactured goods from England.

The predominance of males, the incidence of servitude, and the high mortality rates combined to produce unusual patterns of family life. Female

Chesapeake Families

servants normally were not allowed to marry during their terms of indenture because masters did not want pregnancies to deprive them of workers. Many male ex-servants could not marry at all because there were relatively few women; such men lived alone, in pairs, or as third members of households containing married couples. In contrast, nearly every adult free woman in the Chesapeake married, and widows usually remarried within a few months of a husband's death. Yet because their marriages were delayed by servitude or broken by death, Chesapeake women bore only one to three children, in contrast to English women, who normally had at least five.

Thus Chesapeake families were few, small, and short-lived. The migrants could not reproduce the English system of family governance, for they came to America as individuals free of paternal control and tended to die while their own children were still quite young. In one Virginia county, for example, more than three-quarters of the children had lost at least one parent by the time they either married or reached age twenty-one.

As a result of the demographic patterns that led to a low rate of natural increase, migrants made up a majority of the Chesapeake population throughout the seventeenth century. That

Chesapeake Politics

fact had important implications for politics in Maryland and Virginia. Since migrants dominated the population, they also composed the vast majority of the membership of Virginia's House of Burgesses and Maryland's House of Delegates (established in 1635). So, too, in each colony they dominated the governor's council, which was simultaneously the colony's highest court, part of the legislature, and executive adviser to the governor.

English-born colonists naturally tended to look to England for solutions to their problems, and migrants frequently relied on English allies to advance their cause. Because of the low birth rates and high mortality, no cohesive native-born ruling elite emerged until the early eighteenth century. Before that, the Chesapeake colonies' immigrant leaders engaged in bitter and prolonged struggles for power and personal economic advantage. The incessant quarreling and convoluted political tangles thwarted the ability of the Virginia and Maryland governments to function effectively.

Representative institutions based on the consent of the governed are usually seen as a major source of political stability. In the seventeenth-century Chesapeake, most property-owning white males could vote, and such freeholders chose as their legislators the local elites who seemed to be the natural leaders of their respective areas. But because most such men were migrants without strong ties to each other or to the colonies, the assemblies' existence did not lead to political stability. Unusual demographic patterns thus produced the region's especially contentious politics.

The Founding of New England

The economic motives that prompted English people to move to the Chesapeake colonies also drew men and women to New England (see map). But because Puritans organized the New England colonies, and also because of environmental differences between the two regions, the northern settlements turned out very differently from those in the South. The northern climate was too cold and the soil too infertile to raise tobacco on a large scale or to raise

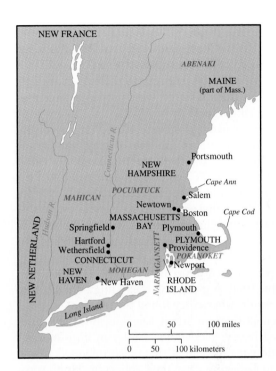

New England Colonies, 1650 *The most densely settled region of the mainland was New England, where English settlements and Indian villages existed side by side.*

sugar cane at all. Accordingly, diversified small farms dominated the landscape. Except for the Catholics who moved to Maryland, migrants to the Chesapeake seem to have been little affected by religious motives. Yet religion was a primary motivating factor in the minds of many, though certainly not all, of the people who colonized New England. The Puritan church quickly became one of the most important institutions in colonial New England; neither the Church of England nor Roman Catholicism had much impact on the settlers or the development of the Chesapeake colonies.

Religion was a constant presence in the lives of pious Puritans. As followers of John Calvin, they believed that an omnipotent God predestined souls to

Puritan Beliefs

heaven or hell before birth and that Christians could do nothing to change their ultimate fate. One of their primary duties as Christians, though, was to assess the state of their own souls. They devoted themselves to self-examination and Bible study, and families prayed together each day under the guidance of the husband and father. Yet even the most pious could never be absolutely certain that they were numbered among the saved (or elect). Consequently, devout Puritans were filled with anxiety about their spiritual state. That anxiety lent a special intensity to their religious beliefs and to their concern with proper behavior— their own and others'.

Some Puritans (called Congregationalists) wanted to reform the Church of England rather than abandon it. Another group, known as Separatists, believed the Church of England to be so corrupt that it could not be salvaged. The only way to purify it, they believed, was to start anew, establishing their own religious bodies, with membership restricted to the saved, as nearly as they could be identified.

Separatists were the first to move to New England. In 1609 a group of them migrated to the Netherlands, where they found the freedom of worship denied them in Stuart England. But they were troubled by the Netherlands' tolerant atmosphere: the nation that tolerated them also tolerated religions and behaviors that they abhorred. Hoping to isolate themselves and their children from the corrupting influence of worldly temptations, these people, who were to become known as Pilgrims, received permission from the Virginia Company to colonize the northern part of its territory.

In September 1620, more than one hundred people, only thirty of them Separatists, set sail from England on the old and crowded *Mayflower.* Two months later they landed in America, but farther north than they had intended. Still, given the lateness of the season, they decided to stay where they were. They established their colony on a fine harbor previously visited by the French explorer Champlain, whose drawing of it appears on page 51. The English named their settlement Plymouth, locating it on the site of an Indian village whose inhabitants had died in the chickenpox epidemic of 1616–1618.

**Founding
of Plymouth**

Even before they landed, the Pilgrims had to surmount their first challenge—from the "strangers," or non-Puritans, who had sailed with them to America. Because they landed outside the jurisdiction of the Virginia Company, some of the strangers questioned the authority of the colony's leaders. In response, the Mayflower Compact, signed in November 1620 while everyone was still on board the *Mayflower,* established a "Civil Body Politic" and a rudimentary legal authority for the colony. The settlers elected a governor and

at first made all decisions for the colony at town meetings. Later, after more towns had been founded and the population had increased, Plymouth, like Virginia and Maryland, created an assembly to which the landowning male settlers elected representatives.

A second challenge facing the Pilgrims was simple survival. Like the Jamestown settlers before them, they were poorly prepared to subsist in the new environment. Their difficulties were compounded by the season of their arrival, for winter quickly descended on them. Only half of the *Mayflower*'s passengers were still alive by spring. But, again like the Virginians, the Pilgrims benefited from the political circumstances of their Native American neighbors.

The Pokanokets (a branch of the Wampanoags) controlled the area in which the Pilgrims had settled. Their villages had suffered terrible losses in the recent chickenpox epidemic, so to protect themselves from the powerful Narragansetts of the southern New England coast (who had been spared the ravages of the disease), the Pokanokets decided to ally themselves with the newcomers. In the spring of 1621, their leader, Massasoit, signed a treaty with the Pilgrims, and during the colony's first difficult years the Pokanokets supplied the English with essential foodstuffs. The settlers were also assisted by Squanto, a Pokanaket, who, like Malinche (see Chapter 1), served as a conduit between the Native Americans and the Europeans. Captured by fishermen in the early 1610s and taken to England, Squanto learned to speak English. When he returned to North America, he discovered that his village had been wiped out by the epidemic. Squanto became the Pilgrims' interpreter and a major source of information about the unfamiliar environment.

Pokanokets

Before the 1620s ended, another group of Puritans—this time Congregationalists—launched the colonial enterprise that would come to dominate New England and would absorb Plymouth in 1691. The event that stimulated their interest in North America was Charles I's accession to the throne in 1625. Charles was more hostile to Puritan beliefs than his father had been, and for eleven years after 1629 he refused to call Parliament into session because it was dominated by Puritans. In 1633 he named William Laud, a prominent persecutor of Puritans, as archbishop of Canterbury, the most important post in the Church of England. Some non-Separatists

**Massachusetts
Bay Company**

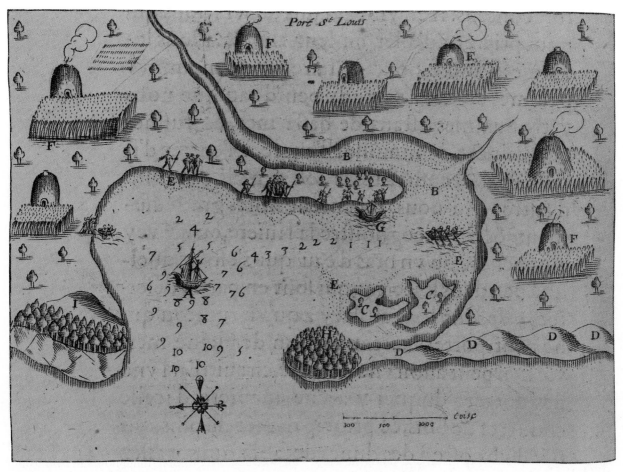

When Samuel de Champlain mapped the New England coast while on the exploratory voyage for France that led him to the St. Lawrence River, he drew the harbor on which the Pilgrims settled about a decade and a half later. Most of the people of the village he depicted, probably the home of Squanto before he was kidnapped and carried to England around 1611, died in the chicken pox epidemic of 1616–1618.   John Carter Brown Library at Brown University.

therefore began to think about settling in America. A group of Congregationalist merchants sent out a body of colonists to Cape Ann, north of Cape Cod, in 1628. The following year the merchants obtained a royal charter, constituting themselves as the Massachusetts Bay Company.

The new joint-stock company quickly attracted the attention of Puritans of the "middling sort" who were becoming increasingly convinced that they no longer would be able to practice their religion freely in England. They remained committed to the goal of reforming the Church of England but concluded that they should pursue that aim in America rather than at home. In a dramatic move, the Congregationalist merchants boldly decided to transfer the Massachusetts Bay Company's headquarters to New England. The settlers would then be answerable to no one in the mother country and would be able to handle their affairs, secular and religious, as they pleased.

The most important recruit to the new venture was John Winthrop, a member of the lesser English gentry. In October 1629, the Massachusetts Bay Company elected Winthrop as its governor. (Until his death twenty years later, he served the colony continuously in one leadership post or another.) It fell to Winthrop to organize the initial segment of the great Puritan migration to America. In 1630 more than one thousand English men and women moved to Massachusetts—most of them to Boston,

Governor John Winthrop

which soon became the largest town in English North America. By 1643 nearly twenty thousand compatriots had followed them.

On board the *Arbella*, en route to New England in 1630, John Winthrop preached a sermon, "A Modell of Christian Charity," laying out his expectations for the new colony. Above all, he stressed the communal nature of the endeavor on which he and his fellow settlers had embarked. God, he explained, "hath so disposed of the condition of mankind as in all times some must be rich, some poor, some high and eminent in power and dignity, others mean and in subjection." But differences in status did not imply differences in worth. On the contrary: God had planned the world so that "every man might have need of other, and from hence they might be all knit more nearly together in the bond of brotherly affection." In America, Winthrop asserted, "we shall be as a city upon a hill, the eyes of all people are upon us." If the Puritans failed to carry out their "special commission" from God, "the Lord will surely break out in wrath against us."

Winthrop's was a transcendent vision. The society he foresaw in Puritan America was a true *commonwealth*, a community in which each person put the good of the whole ahead of his or her private concerns. Although, like seventeenth-century England, that society was to be characterized by social inequality and clear hierarchies of status and power, it was also to be a society whose members all lived according to the precepts of Christian love. Of course, such an ideal was beyond human reach. Early New England had its share of bitter quarrels and unchristian behavior. What is remarkable is how long the ideal prevailed as a goal to be sought, though seldom attained.

The Puritans expressed their communal ideal chiefly in the doctrine of the covenant. They believed God had made a covenant—that is, an agreement or contract—with them when they were chosen for the special mission to America. In turn they covenanted with each other, promising to work together toward their goals. The founders of churches and towns in the new land often drafted formal documents setting forth the principles on which such institutions would be based. The same was true of the colonial governments of New England. The Pilgrims' Mayflower Compact was a covenant; so too was the Fundamental Orders of Connecticut (1639), which laid down the basic law for the settlements established

Ideal of the Covenant

along the Connecticut River valley in 1636 and thereafter.

The leaders of Massachusetts Bay likewise transformed their original joint-stock company charter into the basis for a covenanted community based on mutual consent. Under pressure from landowning male settlers, they gradually changed the General Court—officially the company's small governing body—into a colonial legislature. They also granted the status of freeman, or voting member of the company, to all property-owning adult male church members residing in Massachusetts. Less than two decades after the first large group of Puritans had arrived in Massachusetts Bay, the colony had a functioning system of self-government composed of a governor and a two-house legislature. The General Court also established a judicial system modeled on England's.

The colony's method of distributing land helped to further the communal ideal. Unlike Virginia and Maryland, where individual applicants sought headrights for themselves and their servants, in Massachusetts groups of families—often from the same region of England—applied together to the General Court for grants of land on which to establish towns. The men who received the original town grant had the sole authority to determine how the land would be distributed.

New England Towns

Understandably, they copied the villages from which they had come. First they laid out town lots for houses and a church. Then they gave each family parcels of land scattered around the town center: pasture here, a woodlot there, an arable field elsewhere. They reserved the best and largest plots for the most distinguished among them (including the minister). People who had been low on the social scale in England were given much smaller and less desirable allotments. Still, every man received land, thus sharply differentiating these villages from their English counterparts.

When migrants began to move beyond the territorial limits of the Massachusetts Bay colony into Connecticut (1636), New Haven (1638), and New Hampshire (1638), the same pattern of town land grants was maintained. Only Maine, with coastal regions thinly populated by fishermen and their families, deviated from the standard practice.

Thus New England settlements initially tended to be more compact than those of the Chesapeake.

Town centers grew up quickly, developing in three distinctly different ways. Some, chiefly isolated agricultural settlements in the interior, tried to sustain Winthrop's vision of harmonious community life based on diversified family farms. A second group, the coastal towns like Boston and Salem, became bustling seaports, serving as places of entry for thousands of new migrants and as focal points for trade. The third category, commercialized agricultural towns, grew up in the Connecticut River valley, where easy water transportation made it possible for farmers to sell surplus goods readily. In Springfield, Massachusetts, for example, the merchant-entrepreneur William Pynchon and his son John began as fur traders and ended as large landowners with thousands of acres on which tenant farmers produced grain for export. Even in Puritan New England the acquisitive, individualistic spirit characteristic of the Chesapeake found some room for expression.

The migration to the Connecticut valley ended the Puritans' relative freedom from clashes with their Native American neighbors. The first English settlers in the valley moved there from Newtown (Cambridge, Massachusetts), under the direction of their minister, Thomas Hooker. Connecticut was fertile, though remote from the other English towns, and the wide river promised ready access to the ocean. The site had just one problem: it fell within the territory controlled by the powerful Pequots.

The Pequots' dominance was based on their role as primary middlemen in the trade between New England Indians and the Dutch in New Netherland.

Pequot War

The arrival of English settlers signaled the end of the Pequots' power over the regional trading networks, for their tributary bands could now trade directly with Europeans. Clashes between Pequots and English colonists began even before the Connecticut valley settlements were established, but their founding tipped the balance toward war. The Pequots tried without success to enlist other Indians in resisting English expansion. After two English traders were killed (probably not by Pequots), the English raided a Pequot village. In return, the Pequots attacked the new town of Wethersfield in April 1637, killing nine and capturing two of the colonists. To retaliate, a Massachusetts Bay expedition the following month attacked and burned the main Pequot town on the Mystic River. The Englishmen and their Narragansett allies

An English beaver felt hat, made by combining American beaver fur with wool and other fibers. Men and women in England and on the European continent wore such fashionable items, thus creating the insatiable demand for pelts that fueled the fur trade for many years. The Pilgrim Society, Plymouth, Massachusetts.

slaughtered at least four hundred Pequots, mostly women and children, and captured the few survivors.

For the next thirty years, the New England Indians tried to accommodate themselves to the spread of European settlement. They traded with the newcomers and sometimes worked for them, but for the most part they resisted acculturation or incorporation into English society. The Native Americans clung to their traditional farming methods, which did not employ plows or fences, and women rather than men continued to be the chief cultivators. When men whose hunting territories had become English farms did learn "European" trades in order to survive, they chose those that—like broom making, basket weaving, and shingle splitting—most nearly accorded with their customary occupations and simultaneously ensured both independence and income. The one European practice they adopted was keeping livestock, for in the absence of game, domesticated animals provided excellent alternative sources of meat.

Although the official seal of the Massachusetts Bay colony showed an Indian crying "Come over and

Among John Eliot's principal converts to Christianity was a young Native American named Daniel Takawampbartis. Ordained as a minister, he served at the head of the Indian congregation at Natick, Massachusetts, a "Praying Town," until his death in 1716. Members of his congregation made this desk for him in about 1677, incorporating elements of English design (brass pulls), Native American motifs (incised lines), and uniquely American hooved feet. The top, a hinged box, is intended to hold a Bible.   The Morse Institute, Natick, Massachusetts. Photo by Mark Sexton of the Peabody and Essex Museum, Salem.

he established, and just 10 percent of those town residents had been formally baptized.

The Jesuits' successful missions in New France contrasted sharply with the Puritans' failure to win many converts and the Franciscans' mixed results in New Mexico. Initially, Catholicism had several advantages over Puritanism (advantages more fully exploited by Jesuits than by Franciscans). The Catholic Church employed attractive rituals, instructed converts that through good works they could help to earn their own salvation, and offered Indian women an inspiring role model— the Virgin Mary. In Montréal and Quebec but not in New Mexico, communities of nuns taught Indian women and children and ministered to their needs. Furthermore, the few French colonists on the St. Lawrence did not alienate potential converts by encroaching steadily on their lands (as did New Englanders) or by demanding labor tribute (as did New Mexicans). Perhaps most important, the Jesuits understood that Christian beliefs were to some extent compatible with Native American culture. Unlike Puritans and Franciscans, Jesuits were willing to accept converts who did not wholly adopt European styles of life.

Puritan, Franciscan, and Jesuit Missions Compared

What attracted Native Americans to these religious ideas? Conversion often alienated the new Christians (both Catholic and Puritan) from their relatives and traditions—a likely outcome that must have caused many potential converts to think twice about making such a commitment. But surely one primary motive was a desire to use the Europeans' religion as a means of coping with the dramatic changes the intruders had wrought. The combination of disease, alcohol, new trading patterns, and loss of territory disrupted customary ways of life to an unprecedented extent. Shamans had little success in restoring traditional ways. Many Native Americans must have concluded that the Europeans' own ideas could provide the key to survival in the new circumstances.

John Winthrop's description of a smallpox epidemic that swept through southern New England in the early 1630s reveals the relationship among smallpox, conversion to Christianity, and English land claims. "A great mortality among the Indians," he noted in his diary in 1633. "Divers of them, in their sickness, confessed that the Englishmen's God was a good God; and that if they recovered, they

help us," most colonists showed little interest in converting the New England Algonkians to Christianity. Only a few Massachusetts clerics, most notably John Eliot, seriously undertook missionary activities. Eliot insisted that converts reside in towns, farm the land in English fashion, assume English names, wear European-style clothing and shoes, cut their hair, and stop observing a wide range of their own customs. Since Eliot was demanding a total cultural transformation from his adherents—on the theory that Indians could not be properly Christianized unless they were also "civilized"—he understandably met with little success. At the peak of Eliot's efforts, only eleven hundred Native Americans lived in the fourteen "Praying Towns"

John Eliot and the Praying Towns

Father Claude Chauchetière, a Jesuit in New France, sketched scenes of life in the colony's missions. His drawing of Indian women worshiping at a shrine of the Virgin Mary includes (at the rear) a view of one woman cutting her hair to conform more closely to European fashion. The other female converts show no evidence of having adopted European dress or hairstyles. Archives Departmentales de la Gironde, France.

would serve him." But most did not recover: in January 1634 an English scout reported that smallpox had spread "as far as any Indian plantation was known to the west." By July, Winthrop observed that most of the Indians within a 300-mile radius of Boston had died of the disease. Therefore, he declared with satisfaction, "the Lord hathe cleared our title to what we possess."

 ## Life in New England

New England's colonizers adopted lifestyles that differed considerably from those of both their Indian neighbors and their European counterparts in the Chesapeake. Algonkian bands usually moved four or five times each year to take full advantage of their environment. In spring, women planted the fields, but once crops were established they did not need regular attention for several months. Villages then divided into small groups, women gathering wild foods and men hunting and fishing. The villagers returned to their fields for harvest, then separated again for fall hunting. Finally, the people wintered together in a sheltered spot before returning to the fields to start the cycle anew the following spring.

Unlike the mobile Algonkians, English people lived year-round in the same location. And unlike residents of the Chesapeake, New Englanders constructed sturdy dwellings intended to last. (Indeed, some survive to this day.) They used the same fields again and again, believing it was less arduous to employ manure as fertilizer than to clear new fields every few years. Furthermore, they had to fence their croplands to prevent them from being overrun by the cattle, sheep, and hogs that were their chief sources of meat. When New Englanders began to spread out over the countryside, the reason was not so much human crowding as it was animal crowding. All that livestock constantly needed more pasturage.

New England Families

Because Puritans commonly moved to America in family groups, the age range in early New England was wide; and because many more women went to New England than to the tobacco colonies, the population could immediately begin to reproduce itself. Moreover, New England was much healthier than the Chesapeake. Once Puritan settlements had survived the difficult first two or three years and established self-sufficiency in foodstuffs, New England proved to be even healthier than the mother country. Adult male migrants to the Chesapeake lost about ten years from their English life expectancy of fifty to fifty-five years; their Massachusetts counterparts gained five or more years.

Consequently, while Chesapeake population patterns gave rise to families that were few in number, small in size, and transitory, the demographic characteristics of New England made families there numerous, large, and long-lived. In New England most men were able to marry; migrant women married young (at age twenty, on the average); and marriages lasted longer and produced more children, who were more likely to live to maturity. If seventeenth-century Chesapeake women could expect to rear one to three healthy children, New England women could anticipate raising five to seven.

Both children and older people flourished in the healthy climate of colonial New England. More infants survived their first year of life than in other contemporary societies, and more people lived longer. Thus settlers with numerous children needed high-chairs, like this one made in seventeenth-century Massachusetts for the use of the Mather family. American Antiquarian Society. Gift of Hannah Mather Crocker, 1819.

The nature of the population had other major implications for family life. New England in effect created grandparents, since in England people rarely lived long enough to know their children's children. And whereas early southern parents commonly died before their children married, northern parents exercised a good deal of control over their adult children. Young men could not marry without acreage to cultivate, and because of the communal land-grant system they were dependent on their fathers to supply them with that land. Daughters, too, needed the dowry of household goods that their parents would give them when they married. Yet parents needed their children's labor and often were reluctant to see them marry and start their own households. These needs at times led to considerable conflict between the generations. On the whole, though, children seem to have obeyed their parents' wishes, for they had few alternatives.

Another important difference lay in the influence of religion on New Englanders' lives. Puritans controlled the governments of Massachusetts Bay, Plymouth, Connecticut, and all the other early northern colonies.

Impact of Religion

Congregationalism was the only officially recognized religion; except in Rhode Island, which was founded by dissenters from Massachusetts, members of other sects had no freedom of worship. Some non-Puritans voted in town meetings, but in Massachusetts Bay and New Haven, church membership was a prerequisite for voting in colony elections. All households were taxed to build meetinghouses and pay ministers' salaries. Massachusetts's first legal codes (1641 and 1648) incorporated regulations drawn from Old Testament scriptures into the laws of the colony; those codes were later copied by New Haven, Plymouth, New Hampshire, and Connecticut. All colonists were required to attend religious services, whether or not they were church members, and anyone who expressed contempt for ministers or their preaching was punished with fines or whippings.

In addition, the Puritan colonies attempted to enforce strict codes of moral conduct. Colonists there were frequently tried for drunkenness, card-playing, even idleness. Couples who had sex during their engagement—as revealed by the birth of a baby less than nine months after their wedding—were fined and publicly humiliated. (Maryland, by contrast, did not penalize premarital pregnancy, only bastardy.) More harshly treated in both regions were men—and a handful of women—who engaged in behaviors that today would be called homosexual. (The term did not then exist, nor were some people thought to be more likely than others to perform such acts.) Several men who had consenting same-sex relationships were hanged, as were other men suspected of bestiality (sex with animals). One unfortunate resident of New Haven was executed because the colonists believed he had fathered a piglet, now known to be a biological impossibility.

In New England, church and state were thus intertwined, for Puritans believed they were following Old Testament rules in assigning such penalties to moral miscreants. Puritans objected to secular interference in religious affairs but at the same time expected the church to influence the conduct of politics and the affairs of society. They also believed that the state had an obligation to support and protect the one true church—theirs. As a result, though they came to America seeking freedom to worship as they wished, they saw no contradiction in their refusal to grant that freedom to others. Indeed, the two most significant divisions in early Massachusetts were caused by religious disputes and by Massachusetts Bay's unwillingness to tolerate dissent.

Roger Williams, a Separatist, migrated to Massachusetts Bay in 1631. He soon began to express some eccentric ideas: that the king of England had

Roger Williams

no right to give away land already occupied by Native Americans, that church and state should be kept entirely separate, and that Puritans should not impose their religious beliefs on others. Banished from Massachusetts in late 1635, Williams founded the town of Providence on Narragansett Bay a few months later. Because of Williams's beliefs, Providence and other towns in what became the colony of Rhode Island adopted a policy of tolerating all religions, including Judaism.

The other dissenter, and an even greater challenge to Massachusetts Bay orthodoxy, was Mistress Anne Marbury Hutchinson. A skilled medical

Anne Hutchinson

practitioner popular with the women of Boston, she was a follower of John Cotton, a minister who stressed the *covenant of grace*, or God's free gift of salvation to unworthy human beings. By contrast, most Massachusetts clerics emphasized the need for Puritans to engage in good works, study, and reflection in preparation for receiving God's grace. (In its most extreme form, such a doctrine could verge on the *covenant of works*, or the idea that people could earn their own salvation.) After spreading her ideas for months in the context of childbed discussions (when no men were present), Mistress Hutchinson began holding women's meetings in her home to discuss Cotton's sermons. She emphasized the covenant of grace more than did Cotton himself, and she even adopted the belief that the elect could be assured of salvation and communicate directly with God. Such ideas had an immense appeal for Puritans. Anne Hutchinson offered them certainty of salvation instead of a state of constant anxiety. Her approach also lessened the importance of the institutional church and its ministers.

Mistress Hutchinson's ideas were a dangerous threat to Puritan orthodoxy. So in November 1637, the leaders of the General Court charged her with

Many New England men and women lived to become grandparents. Few, however, equaled the life span of Mary Mirick Davie, who died at the age of 117 in 1752. Massachusetts Historical Society.

having maligned the colony's ministers by accusing them of preaching the covenant of works. For two days she defended herself cleverly against her accusers, matching scriptural references and wits with John Winthrop himself. But then Mistress Hutchinson triumphantly and boldly declared that God had spoken to her "by an immediate revelation," telling her that he would curse the Puritans' descendants for generations if they harmed her. That assertion assured her banishment. After she had also been excommunicated from the church, she and her family, along with some faithful followers, were exiled to Rhode Island. Several years later, after she moved to New Netherland, she and most of her children were killed by Indians.

The authorities in Massachusetts Bay perceived Anne Hutchinson as doubly dangerous to the existing order: she threatened not only religious orthodoxy but also traditional gender roles. Puritans believed in the equality before God of all souls, including those of women, but they considered actual women (as distinct from their spiritual selves) inferior to men. Christians had long followed Saint Paul's dictum that women should keep silent in church and be submissive to their husbands. Mistress Hutchinson did neither. The magistrates' comments during her trial reveal that they were almost as outraged by her "masculine" behavior as by her religious beliefs. Winthrop charged her with having set wife against husband, since so many of her followers were women. A minister at her church trial told her bluntly: "You have stept out of your place, you have rather bine a Husband than a Wife and a preacher than a Hearer; and a Magistrate than a Subject."

The New England authorities' reaction to Anne Hutchinson reveals the depth of their adherence to European gender-role concepts. To them, an orderly society required the submission of wives to husbands as well as the obedience of subjects to rulers. English people intended to change many aspects of their lives by colonizing North America, but not the sexual division of labor or the assumption of male superiority.

 ## Conclusion

By the middle of the seventeenth century, Europeans had unquestionably come to North America to stay, a fact that signaled major changes for the peoples of both hemispheres. Europeans had indelibly altered not only their own lives but also those of the Native Americans. Europeans killed Indians with their weapons and diseases and had but limited success in converting them to European religions. Contacts with the Native Americans taught Europeans to eat new foods, speak new languages, and recognize—however reluctantly—the persistence of other cultural patterns. The prosperity and even survival of many of the European colonies depended heavily on the cultivation of American crops (maize and tobacco) and an Asian crop (sugar), thus attesting to the importance of post-Columbian ecological change.

European political rivalries, once confined to Europe, now spread around the globe, as England, Spain, Portugal, France, and the Netherlands vied for control of the peoples and resources of Asia, Africa, and the Americas. In America, Spaniards reaped the benefits of their South and Central American gold and silver mines, while French people earned their primary profits from Indian trade (in Canada) and cultivating sugar cane (in the Caribbean). Sugar also enriched the Portuguese.

The Dutch, by contrast, concentrated on commerce—trading in furs and sugar as well as carrying human cargoes of enslaved Africans to South America and the Caribbean.

Of these nations, only France and Spain went beyond the economic relationships they established with native peoples to attempt to Christianize them. In missions scattered in remote locations such as northern Florida, the St. Lawrence valley, and New Mexico, Catholic priests like Fray Alonso de Benavides worked with dedication to convert the Indians and to persuade them of the truth of Europeans' religious beliefs.

Although the English colonies, too, at first sought to rely on trade, they quickly took another form altogether when so many English people of the "middling sort" decided to migrate to North America. To a greater extent than their European counterparts, the English transferred the society and politics of their homeland to a new environment. Their sheer numbers, coupled with their need for vast quantities of land on which to grow their crops and raise their livestock, inevitably brought them into conflict with their Native American neighbors. New England and the Chesapeake differed in the sex ratio and age range of their migrant populations, in the nature of their developing economies, in their settlement patterns, and in the impact of religious beliefs on their settlers' lives. Yet both were English in origin, and in the years to come both regions would be drawn into the increasingly fierce rivalries besetting the European powers. Those rivalries would continue to affect Americans of all races until after France and England fought the greatest war yet known in the mid-eighteenth century and the Anglo-American colonies had won their independence.

Suggestions for Further Reading

General

Charles M. Andrews, *The Colonial Period of American History: The Settlements*, 3 vols. (1934–1937); David Hackett Fischer, *Albion's Seed: Four British Folkways in America* (1989); Karen O. Kupperman, ed., *America in European Consciousness, 1493–1750* (1995); D. W. Meinig, *Atlantic America, 1492–1800* (1986); Gary B. Nash, *Red, White, and Black: The Peoples of Early America*, 2d ed. (1982); Mary Beth Norton, *Founding Mothers & Fathers: Gendered Power and the Forming of American Society* (1996); John E. Pomfret, *Founding the American Colonies, 1583–1660* (1970); Paula Treckel, *To Comfort the Heart: Women in Seventeenth-Century America* (1996); Alden T. Vaughan, *Roots of American Racism* (1994).

New Spain, New Netherland, New France, and the Caribbean

Karen Anderson, *Chain Her by One Foot: The Subjugation of Native Women in Seventeenth-Century New France* (1991); Charles R. Boxer, *The Dutch Seaborne Empire, 1600–1800* (1965); Denys Delâge, *Bitter Feast: Amerindians and Europeans in Northeastern North America, 1600–64* (1993); Richard S. Dunn, *Sugar and Slaves: The Rise of the Planter Class in the English West Indies, 1624–1713* (1972); William J. Eccles, *France in America*, rev. ed. (1990); Carol Hoffecker et al., eds., *New Sweden in America* (1995); Jonathan Israel, *Dutch Primacy in World Trade, 1585–1740* (1989); Donna Merwick, *Possessing Albany, 1630–1710* (1990); Sidney Mintz, *Sweetness and Power: The Place of Sugar in Modern History* (1985); Marc Simmons, *The Last Conquistador: Juan de Oñate and the Settling of the Far Southwest* (1991); David J. Weber, *The Spanish Frontier in North America* (1992).

England

Susan Dwyer Amussen, *An Ordered Society: Gender and Class in Early Modern England* (1988); Carl Bridenbaugh, *Vexed and Troubled Englishmen, 1590–1642*, rev. ed. (1976); Peter Laslett, *The World We Have Lost*, 3d ed. (1984); Wallace Notestein, *The English People on the Eve of Colonization, 1603–1630* (1954); Michael Walzer, *The Revolution of the Saints* (1965); Keith Wrightson, *English Society, 1580–1680* (1982).

Early Contact Between Europeans and Indians

James Axtell, *The Invasion Within: The Contest of Cultures in Colonial North America* (1985); Philip Barbour, *Pocahontas and Her World* (1970); William Cronon, *Changes in the Land: Indians, Colonists, and the Ecology of New England* (1983); Francis Jennings, *The Invasion of America: Indians, Colonialism, and the Cant of Conquest* (1975); Karen O. Kupperman, *Settling with the Indians: The Meeting of English and Indian Cultures in America, 1580–1640* (1980); Patrick Malone, *The Skulking Way of War: Technology and Tactics Among the Indians of New England (1991)*; Kenneth Morrison, *The Embattled Northeast: The Elusive Ideal of Alliance in Abnaki-Euroamerican Relations* (1984); Helen C. Rountree, *Pocahontas's People: The Powhatan Indians of Virginia Through Four Centuries* (1990); Neal Salisbury, *Manitou and Providence: Indians, Europeans, and the Making of New England, 1500–1643* (1982); Bernard Sheehan, *Savagism and Civility: Indians and Englishmen in Colonial Virginia* (1980); Timothy Silver, *A New Face on the Countryside: Indians, Colonists, and Slaves in South Atlantic Forests, 1500–1800* (1990); Alden T. Vaughan, *The New England Frontier: Puritans and Indians, 1620–1675*, rev. ed. (1979); Peter Wood et al., eds., *Powhatan's Mantle: Indians in the Colonial Southeast* (1989).

Chesapeake Society and Politics

Lois Green Carr et al., *Robert Cole's World: Agriculture and Society in Early Maryland* (1991); David Galenson, *White Servitude in Colonial America: An Economic Analysis* (1981); James Horn, *Adapting to a New World: English Society in the Seventeenth-Century Chesapeake* (1994); Ivor Noël Hume, *The Virginia Adventure: Roanoke to James Towne* (1994); A. J. Leo Lemay, *The American Dream of Captain John Smith* (1991); Gloria L. Main, *Tobacco Colony: Life in Early Maryland, 1650–1720* (1983); Edmund S. Morgan, *American Slavery, American Freedom: The Ordeal of Colonial Virginia* (1975); James Perry, *The Formation of a Society on Virginia's Eastern Shore, 1615–1655* (1990); Darrett Rutman and Anita Rutman, *A Place in Time: Middlesex County, Virginia, 1650–1750* (1984); Alden T. Vaughan, *American Genesis: Captain John Smith and the Founding of Virginia* (1975).

New England Communities, Politics, and Religion

David Grayson Allen, *In English Ways: The Movement of Societies and the Transferral of English Law and Custom to Massachusetts Bay in the 17th Century* (1981); Virginia DeJohn Anderson, *New England's Generation: The Great Migration and the Formation of Society and Culture in the 17th Century* (1991); Charles Cohen, *God's Caress: The Psychology of Puritan Religious Experience* (1986); David D. Hall, *Worlds of Wonder, Days of Judgment: Popular Religious Belief in Early New England* (1989); Stephen Innes, *Creating the Commonwealth: The Economic Culture of Puritan New England* (1995); Stephen Innes, *Labor in a New Land: Economy and Society in 17th-Century Springfield* (1983); Sydney V. James, *Colonial Rhode Island* (1975); George Langdon, *Pilgrim Colony: A History of New Plymouth, 1620–1691* (1966); Kenneth A. Lockridge, *A New England Town: The First Hundred Years (Dedham, Massachusetts, 1636–1736)* (1970); John Frederick Martin, *Profits in the Wilderness: Entrepreneurship and the Founding of New England Towns in the 17th Century* (1991); Edmund S. Morgan, *The Puritan Dilemma: The Story of John Winthrop* (1958); Darrett Rutman, *Winthrop's Boston* (1965).

New England Women and Family Life

David Cressy, *Coming Over: Migration and Communication Between England and New England in the Seventeenth Century* (1987); John Demos, *A Little Commonwealth: Family Life in Plymouth Colony* (1970); Philip J. Greven, Jr., *Four Generations: Population, Land, and Family in Colonial Andover, Massachusetts* (1970); Lyle Koehler, *A Search for Power: The "Weaker Sex" in Seventeenth-Century New England* (1980); Edmund S. Morgan, *The Puritan Family*, rev. ed. (1966); Roger Thompson, *Sex in Middlesex: Popular Mores in a Massachusetts County, 1649–1699* (1986).

Why, why should the world be minding
Here a world of Evill Finding Thy Farres
Then Farrell Ioies thy Wiles Thy Warrs
Trifly thy Ioies thy Wiles Thy Warrs
Thy Ioues Retreat: I am not sorye
The Eternall Drawes to him my heart
By Faith (which can my Force Subvert)
Crowne me (after Grace) with Glory.

CHAPTER

3

American Society Takes Shape
1640–1720

Standing on a ladder with the condemned man, the hangman tightened the noose around his neck and shoved him off the ladder. The rope broke, and the notorious pirate Captain William Kidd lay on the ground, dazed. The hangman repeated the procedure with a new rope. This time it held, and Kidd died violently, as he had lived. It was May 23, 1701; the site was Wapping, near the London docks. As a warning to others, Kidd's body was left dangling from a gibbet on the bank of the Thames.

William Kidd, born in Scotland, had made his home in New York, the port once known as New Amsterdam. Merchants there were none too choosy about how they earned their profits, and at the end of the seventeenth century the vast expansion of worldwide trading networks opened practically unlimited opportunities for buccaneers who preyed on ships carrying valuable commodities long distances by sea. The merchants of Manhattan eagerly provisioned pirates' ships and purchased their loot. In the 1690s, the economy of the town depended on this illegal trade. For years Kidd and other pirates could count on the complicity of New York's governors, who ignored their activities in exchange for shares of the bounty.

Why was Captain Kidd condemned to die? His fatal buccaneering voyage began in London in early 1696, when he gained financial backing from several powerful and prominent English investors. After recruiting a crew in New York, Kidd sailed for Madagascar, the main pirate haven in the Indian Ocean. He captured all the likely vessels he encountered—a ship from Bombay flying the English flag, a Dutch merchantman, a Portuguese vessel. His most valuable prize, the *Quedah Merchant*, carried a large cargo of cloth, sugar, opium, and iron.

After more than a year of buccaneering, Kidd returned to New York by way of the Caribbean, hoping to avoid prosecution for piracy by paying off his investors in full and by bribing colonial officials. Unfortunately for Kidd, one of his financial backers, the earl of Bellomont, had become governor of New York. Bellomont was waging a vigorous campaign against piracy and could not afford to protect Kidd. In addition, as governor he could claim for his personal use one-third of any confiscated illegal cargo, whereas as a backer he was entitled to less than one-fifth of the partnership's proceeds. Kidd's fate was sealed when Bellomont ordered his arrest and shipped him back to England for trial.

The saga of William Kidd illustrates above all the involvement of the English mainland colonies in a growing network of trade and international contacts, not all of them legal. North America, like England itself, was becoming increasingly embedded in a worldwide matrix of exchange and warfare. The web woven by oceangoing vessels—once composed of only a few strands spun by Christopher Columbus, John Cabot, and their successors—now crisscrossed the globe, carrying West Indian sugar to Europe, Africans to America, cloth and spices from the East Indies to Africa, and New England fish and wood products to the Caribbean. Formerly tiny outposts, the North American colonies expanded their territorial claims and embarked on a deliberate course of economic development. In response, the English government for the first time began to adopt policies to systematize colonial administration, passing laws that regulated trade and reshaped the American governments.

Three developments shaped life in the mainland English colonies between 1640 and 1720: the introduction of a system of chattel slavery, especially in the south Atlantic coastal regions; changes in the colonies' relationship with their mother country; and increasing conflicts with their North American neighbors, both European and Native American. All these developments were intimately connected with the historical processes that produced Captain Kidd and others like him.

The explosive growth of the slave trade was of critical significance in the Anglo-American economy. Carrying human cargoes paid off handsomely, as many slave traders learned; planters who could afford to buy slaves also reaped huge profits. The arrival of large numbers of West African peoples dramatically reshaped colonial society and fueled the

international trading system. The burgeoning North American economy, invigorated by the arrival of so many laborers, attracted new attention from colonial administrators. Especially after the Stuarts had been restored to the throne (having lost it for a time as a result of the English Civil War in the 1640s), rulers and bureaucrats in London attempted to supervise the American settlements more effectively and to ensure that the mother country benefited from their economic growth.

Neither English colonists nor London administrators could ignore other peoples living on the North American continent. As the English settlements expanded, they came into violent conflict not only with the powerful Indians of the interior but also with the Dutch, the Spanish, and especially the French. By 1720, war—between Europeans and Indians, among Europeans, and among Indians allied with different colonial powers—had become an all-too-frequent feature of American life. No longer isolated from each other or from Europe, the people and products of the North American colonies were now integral to the world trading system and inextricably enmeshed in its conflicts.

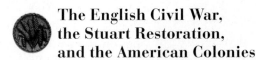

The English Civil War, the Stuart Restoration, and the American Colonies

In 1642, England erupted into civil war. Disputes over taxation, religion, and other issues led to armed conflict between supporters of the Puritan-dominated Parliament and King Charles I. After four

Stuart Monarchs of England, 1660–1714

Monarch	Reign	Relation to Predecessor
Charles II	1660–1685	Son
James II	1685–1688	Brother
Mary	1688–1694	Daughter
William	1688–1702	Son-in-law
Anne	1702–1714	Sister, sister-in-law

• *Important Events* •

1642–46	English Civil War; end of first New England economic system based on furs and migrants	**1681**	Pennsylvania chartered
1649	Charles I executed	**1685**	James II becomes king
1651	First Navigation Act passed to regulate colonial trade	**1686–89**	Dominion of New England established, superseding all charters of colonies from Maine to New Jersey
1660	Stuarts restored to throne; Charles II becomes king	**1688–89**	James II deposed in Glorious Revolution; William and Mary ascend throne
1662	Halfway Covenant drafted in New England, creating category of partial membership in Congregational churches	**1689–97**	King William's War fought on northern New England frontier
1663	Carolina chartered	**1692**	Witchcraft outbreak in Salem Village; nineteen executions result
1664	English conquer New Netherland; New York founded; New Jersey established	**1696**	Board of Trade and Plantations established to coordinate English colonial administration
1670s	Jacques Marquette, Louis Jolliet, and Robert Cavelier de La Salle explore the Great Lakes and Mississippi valley for France	**1701**	Iroquois adopt neutrality policy toward France and England
1675–76	King Philip's (Metacom's) War devastates New England	**1702–13**	Queen Anne's War fought by French and English
1676	Bacon's Rebellion disrupts Virginia government; Jamestown destroyed	**1711–13**	Tuscarora War (North Carolina) leads to capture or migration of most Tuscaroras
1680–92	Pueblo revolt temporarily drives Spaniards from New Mexico	**1715**	Yamasee War nearly destroys South Carolina
		1718	New Orleans founded in French Louisiana
		1732	Georgia chartered

years of warfare, Parliament triumphed. Charles I was executed in 1649, and the parliamentary army's leader, Oliver Cromwell, assumed control of the government. Yet after Cromwell's death in 1658 Parliament decided to restore the monarchy if Charles I's son and heir would agree to restrictions on his authority. In 1660, Charles II ascended the throne, having promised to support the Church of England and to seek Parliament's consent for any new taxes. Thus ended the tumultuous chapter in English history known as the Interregnum (Latin for "between reigns") or Commonwealth period.

The Civil War, the Interregnum, and the reign of Charles II (1660–1685) had far-reaching significance for the Anglo-American colonies. During the Civil War and the Commonwealth period, Puritans controlled the English government. Thus the migration to New England largely ceased, and some

colonists packed up to return home. During the subsequent reign of Charles II, six of the thirteen colonies that eventually would form the American nation were either founded or came under English rule: New York, New Jersey, Pennsylvania (including Delaware), and North and South Carolina (see map, page 64). All were proprietorships; like Maryland they were granted in their entirety to one man or to a group of men who held title to the soil and controlled the government. Charles II gave these vast American holdings as rewards to men who had supported him during the Civil War. Several of his favorites even shared in more than one grant. Collectively, these became known as the Restoration colonies, because they were created by the restored Stuart monarchy.

One of the first to benefit was Charles's younger brother James, the duke of York. In 1664, acting as

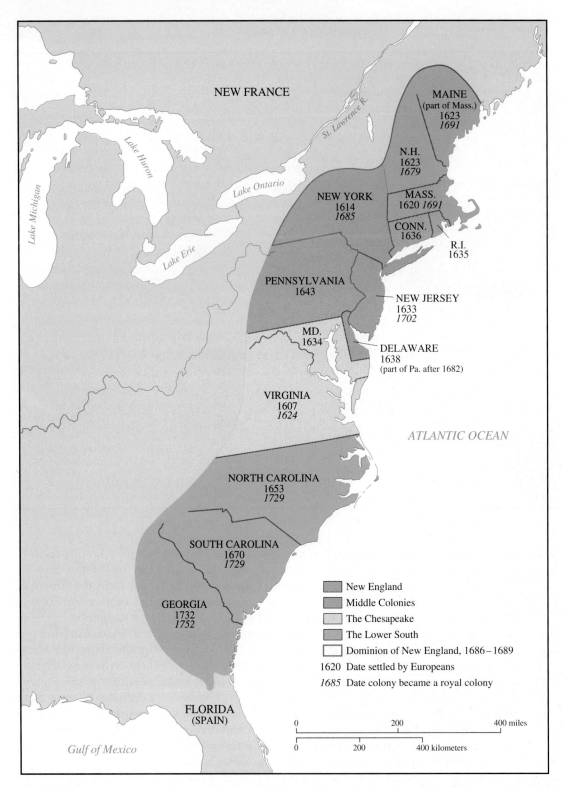

The Anglo-American Colonies in the Early Eighteenth Century *By the early eighteenth century, the English colonies nominally dominated the Atlantic coastline of North America. But the colonies' formal boundary lines are deceiving, because the western reaches of each colony were still largely unfamiliar to Europeans and because much of the land was still inhabited by Native Americans.*

The Founding of English Colonies in North America, 1664–1732

Colony	Founder(s)	Date	Basis of Economy
New York (formerly New Netherland)	James, duke of York	1664	Farming, fur trading
New Jersey	Sir George Carteret, John Lord Berkeley	1664	Farming
North Carolina	Carolina proprietors	1665	Tobacco, forest products
South Carolina	Carolina proprietors	1670	Rice, indigo
Pennsylvania	William Penn	1681	Farming
Georgia	James Oglethorpe	1732	Rice, forest products

though the Dutch colony of New Netherland did not exist, Charles II gave James the region between the Connecticut and Delaware Rivers, including the Hudson valley and Long Island. James immediately organized an invasion fleet. In late August the vessels anchored off Manhattan Island and demanded New Netherland's surrender. The colony complied without resistance. Although the Netherlands briefly regained control of the colony in 1672, the Dutch permanently ceded the province in 1674.

New Netherland Becomes New York

Thus England acquired a tiny but heterogeneous possession. In 1664, an appreciable minority of English people (mostly Puritan New Englanders who had moved to Long Island) already lived in the colony. New York, as it was now called, also included sizable numbers of Native Americans, Germans, French-speaking Walloons (from the southern part of modern Belgium), Scandinavians, and Africans, as well as a smattering of other European peoples. The Dutch West India Company, the world's greatest slave-trading power at midcentury (see page 70), had actively imported slaves into the colony, intending some of them for resale in the Chesapeake. Many, though, remained in New Netherland as laborers; at the time of the English conquest, almost one-fifth of Manhattan's approximately fifteen hundred inhabitants were of African descent. In fact, slaves constituted a higher proportion of New York's urban population than of the Chesapeake's at the same time.

Recognizing the population's diversity, the duke of York's representatives moved cautiously in their efforts to establish English authority. The Duke's Laws, a legal code proclaimed in 1665, at first applied solely to the English settlements on Long Island, only later being extended to the rest of the colony. Dutch forms of local government were maintained, Dutch land titles confirmed, and Dutch residents allowed to maintain customary legal practices. Religious toleration was guaranteed through a multiple establishment: each town was permitted to decide which church to support with its tax revenues. Much to the dismay of English residents of the colony, the Duke's Laws made no provision for a representative assembly. Like other Stuarts, James was suspicious of legislative bodies, and not until 1683 did he agree to the colonists' requests for an elected legislature. Before then, New York was ruled by an autocratic governor as it had been under the Dutch.

The English takeover thus had little immediate effect on the colony. Its population grew slowly, barely reaching eighteen thousand by the time of the first English census in 1698. Until the second decade of the eighteenth century, New York City remained a commercial backwater within the orbit of Boston.

One of the chief reasons why the English conquest brought so little change to New York was that the duke of York in 1664 regranted the land between the Hudson and Delaware Rivers—East and West Jersey—to his friends Sir George Carteret and John Lord Berkeley. That grant left his own colony confined between Connecticut to the east and the Jerseys to the west and south, depriving it of much fertile land and hindering its economic growth. He also failed to

Founding of New Jersey

In 1679 a traveler drew this picture of the Stadt Huys (State House) on Manhattan Island, in the colony of New York. The government building and its adjoining houses, built under Dutch rule while the settlement was still called New Amsterdam, make the scene look more like the Netherlands than like England.   Brooklyn Historical Society.

promote migration. Meanwhile, the Jersey proprietors acted rapidly to attract settlers, promising generous land grants, limited freedom of religion, and—without authorization from the Crown—a representative assembly. In response, large numbers of Puritan New Englanders migrated southward to the Jerseys, along with some Dutch New Yorkers and a contingent of families from Barbados. New Jersey grew quickly; in 1726, at the time of its first census as a united colony, it had 32,500 inhabitants, only 8,000 fewer than New York.

Within twenty years, Berkeley and Carteret sold their interests in the Jerseys to separate groups of investors. The purchasers of all of Carteret's share (West Jersey) and portions of Berkeley's (East Jersey)

were members of the Society of Friends, seeking a refuge from persecution in England. The Society of Friends, also called Quakers, denied the need for intermediaries between individuals and God. They believed that anyone could receive the "inner light" and be saved and that all were equal in God's sight. They had no formally trained clergy; any Quaker, male or female, could become a "public Friend" and travel from meeting to meeting to discuss God's word. Moreover, any member could speak in meetings if he or she desired. The Quaker message of radical egalitarianism was not welcome in the hierarchical society of seventeenth-century England or, for that matter, in Puritan New England. For example, Mary Dyer—who had followed Anne Hutchinson into exile—became a Quaker, returned to Boston as a missionary, and was hanged (along with several men) for preaching Quaker doctrines.

The Quakers obtained their own colony in 1681, when Charles II granted the region between Maryland and New York to his close, personal friend William Penn, a prominent member of the sect. Penn was then thirty-seven years old; he held the colony as a personal proprietorship, one that earned profits for his descendants until the American Revolution. Even so, Penn, like the Roman Catholic Calverts of Maryland before him, saw his province not merely as a source of revenue but also as a haven for his persecuted coreligionists. Penn offered land to all comers on liberal terms, promised toleration of all religions (though only Christians were given the vote), guaranteed English liberties such as the right to bail and trial by jury, and pledged to establish a representative assembly.

Pennsylvania: A Quaker Haven

He also publicized the ready availability of land in Pennsylvania through promotional tracts printed in German, French, and Dutch and distributed widely throughout Europe.

Penn's activities and the attraction of his lands for Quakers gave rise to a migration whose magnitude was equaled only by the Puritan exodus to New England in the 1630s. By mid-1683, over three thousand people—among them Welsh, Irish, Dutch, and Germans—had already moved to Pennsylvania, and within five years the population reached twelve thousand. (By contrast, it took Virginia more than thirty years to achieve a comparable population.) Philadelphia, carefully planned to be the major city in the province, drew merchants and artisans from throughout the English-speaking world. From mainland and West Indian colonies alike came Quakers seeking religious freedom; they brought with them years of experience on American soil and well-established trading connections. Pennsylvania's lands were both plentiful and fertile, and the colony

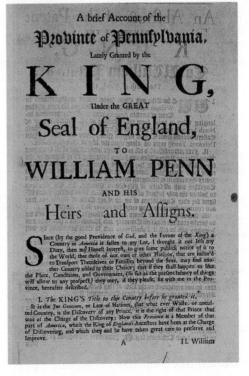

William Penn, later the proprietor of Pennsylvania, as he looked during his youth in Ireland. In such pamphlets as the one shown here, Penn spread the word about his new colony to thousands of readers in England and its other colonial possessions.   Portrait and Pamphlet: Historical Society of Pennsylvania.

soon began exporting flour and other foodstuffs to the West Indies. Practically overnight Philadelphia acquired more than two thousand citizens and began to challenge Boston's commercial dominance.

A pacifist with egalitarian principles, Penn attempted to treat Native Americans fairly. He learned to speak the language of the Delawares (or Lenapes),

William Penn's Indian Policy

from whom he purchased tracts of land to sell to European settlers. Penn also established strict regulations for trade and forbade the sale of alcohol to Indians.

His policies attracted Indians who moved to Pennsylvania near the end of the seventeenth century to escape repeated clashes with English colonists in Maryland, Virginia, and North Carolina. Most important were the Tuscaroras, whose experiences are described later in this chapter. Likewise, Shawnees and Miamis chose to move eastward from the Ohio valley. By a supreme irony, however, the same toleration that attracted Native Americans also brought non-Quaker Europeans who showed little respect for Indian claims to the soil. In effect, Penn's policy was so successful that it caused its own downfall. The Scots-Irish, Palatine Germans, and Swiss who settled in Pennsylvania in the first half of the eighteenth century clashed repeatedly over land with groups of Indians who had also recently migrated to the colony.

The other proprietary colony, granted by Charles II in 1663, encompassed a huge tract of land stretching from the southern boundary of Virginia to Spanish Florida. The area

Founding of Carolina

had great strategic importance; a successful English settlement there would prevent Spaniards from pushing farther north. The semitropical land was also extremely fertile, holding forth the promise of producing exotic and valuable commodities such as figs, olives, wines, and silk. The proprietors named their new province Carolina in honor of Charles, whose Latin name was *Carolus*. The "Fundamental Constitutions of Carolina," which they asked the political philosopher John Locke to draft for them, set forth an elaborate plan for a colony governed by a hierarchy of landholding aristocrats and characterized by a carefully structured distribution of political and economic power. But Carolina failed to follow the course the proprietors laid out. Instead, it quickly developed two distinct population centers, which in 1729 permanently split into two separate colonies.

The Albemarle region that became North Carolina was settled by Virginia planters. They established a society much like their own, with an economy based on tobacco cultivation and the export of such forest products as pitch, tar, and timber. Because North Carolina lacked a satisfactory harbor, its planters continued to rely on Virginia's ports and merchants to conduct their trade, and the two colonies remained tightly linked. Although North Carolina planters held some slaves, they never became as dependent on slave labor as did the other population center in Carolina.

Charleston, South Carolina, was founded in 1670 by a group of settlers from the island of Barbados, which was already overcrowded less than fifty years after English people first moved there. The English migrants from Barbados brought with them the slaves who had worked on their sugar plantations and the legal codes that had governed those laborers, thereby shaping the future of South Carolina and the subsequent history of the United States.

The North American Slave Trade and the Enslavement of Africans

Since England had no tradition of slavery, why did English settlers in North America and the Caribbean islands begin to enslave Africans around the middle of the seventeenth century? The answer to that question lies in a combination of the settlers' need for labor and the experience of other Europeans.

Although the English had not previously practiced slavery, other Europeans had. As noted in Chapter 1, the Spanish and Portuguese imported enslaved Africans as laborers into the islands of the Mediterranean Atlantic during the fifteenth century. They then extended that practice to their American possessions, New Spain and Brazil. No free people of any description were willing to toil for wages in the difficult and dangerous conditions of South American mines or Caribbean sugar plantations. To produce the profitable goods they had come to America to seek, Europeans needed bound laborers—people who, by law or contract, could be forced to work at jobs that no person would do voluntarily. Dutch, French, and English Caribbean planters eagerly purchased slaves from the 1640s on. Then, twenty years later, the supply of English indentured servants in the Chesapeake started to dry up. Because population pressures had eased in England,

and because the founding of the new Restoration colonies meant that prospective migrants could choose other American destinations, Chesapeake planters were deprived of an ample number of English laborers. Consequently, they too turned to Africans.

In the early mainland English settlements, the few residents of African descent varied in status: some were free, some indentured, some enslaved. All came from a population that the historian Ira Berlin recently termed "Atlantic creoles"—people who participated in the new international system of trade and piracy that encompassed Captain Kidd. Often of mixed race, they were already familiar with Europeans and fitted easily into established niches in the many-faceted hierarchical social structures of the early colonies. Slave status was not clearly defined in law, and individuals moved back and forth across boundaries of freedom, indenture, and enslavement.

Atlantic Creoles

Before the 1660s, none of the English mainland colonies systematically categorized Africans as slaves.

Systematic Enslavement of Africans

But after Chesapeake planters began to import already enslaved Africans from Caribbean sugar islands and then to purchase slaves directly from Africa, that situation changed decisively. As increasing numbers of slaves arrived each year beginning in the 1670s, the enslaved population changed from acculturated creole to newly imported African, and the laws governing enslaved people were more comprehensively and tightly drawn. Most of the English colonies, even those without many bondspeople, adopted codes to govern slaves' behavior. By the end of the century, African slavery was firmly established as the basis of the economy in the Chesapeake as well as in the Caribbean.

One of the most remarkable aspects of the adoption of the slave system was English enslavers' evident lack of moral qualms. No one at the time seems to have questioned—or even felt the need to justify with racist rationalizations—the decision to hold Africans and their descendants in perpetual bondage. That fact suggests the importance both of

At forts along the African coast, Europeans purchased slaves from local rulers. This contemporary illustration of such a transaction is taken from a book published in 1729.   Library of Congress.

prior Spanish and Portuguese practice and of economic motives in leading to this momentous development. Certainly economics, not racism, was the theme of one New Englander's argument for acquiring slaves in 1645. The problem with indentured servants, he pointed out, was that they would become free "and not stay but for verie great wages." Further, "wee shall maynteyne 20 Moores [Africans] cheaper then one Englishe servant." He concluded, "I doe not see how wee can thrive untill we gett into a stock of slaves suffitient to doe all our buisnes." Nowhere did he consider the morality of the course he advocated, nor did he contend that Africans were inferior to other peoples. Accepting their already enslaved status, he simply wanted to employ them to his advantage.

Between 1492 and 1770 more Africans than Europeans came to the Americas. The vast majority of them went to Brazil or the Caribbean: of at least 10 million enslaved people brought to the Americas during the existence of slavery, only about 120,000 by 1740, or 260,000 by 1775, were imported into the region that later became the United States. The magnitude of the slave trade raises three related questions. What was its impact on West Africa and Europe? How was the trade organized and conducted? What was its effect on the people it carried and on the region to which they were taken?

West Africa was one of the most fertile and densely inhabited regions of the continent, so the trade in human beings did not seriously depopulate the area. That was true even

West Africa and the Slave Trade

after the demand for slaves grew so great that the sale of previously enslaved prisoners could not meet it and African raiding parties began regularly setting out to capture the unwary. Even so, because American planters preferred to purchase male slaves, the trade significantly affected the sex ratio of the remaining population. The relative lack of men increased the work demands on women and simultaneously encouraged polygyny.

In Guinea, the primary consequences of the trade were political and economic. Coastal rulers—like the one pictured on page 69—served as middlemen, allowing the establishment of permanent slave-trading posts in their territories and supplying resident Europeans with slaves to fill ships that stopped regularly at the coastal forts. Such rulers controlled European traders' access to slaves and at the same time controlled inland peoples' access

to desirable European goods like cloth, alcohol, tobacco, firearms, and iron bars that could be made into useful tools. The centralizing tendencies of the slave trade helped to create such powerful eighteenth-century kingdoms as Dahomey and Asante (formed from the Akan States; see page 12). Smaller polities were destroyed and traditional economic patterns disrupted, as trade once sent north toward the Mediterranean was redirected to the coast, and as local manufactures declined in the face of European competition.

Europeans were the chief beneficiaries of this traffic in slaves, despite its importance to some African kings. The expanding network of trade between

Europe and the Slave Trade

Europe and its colonies in the seventeenth and eighteenth centuries was fueled by the sale and transportation of slaves, the exchange of commodities produced by slave labor, and the need to feed and clothe so many bound laborers. The sugar planters of the Caribbean and Brazil, along with the tobacco and rice planters of North America, eagerly purchased slaves from Africa, dispatched shiploads of valuable staple crops to Europe, and bought large quantities of cheap food, much of it from elsewhere in the Americas. By the 1720s, more than 80 percent of English cotton textile exports was traded to Africa or slaveholding American colonies.

The European economy, previously oriented toward the Mediterranean and Asia, shifted its emphasis to the Atlantic Ocean. Whereas European merchants' profits had once come primarily from trade with North Africa, the eastern Mediterranean, and China, by the late seventeenth century commerce in slaves and the products of slave labor constituted the basis of the European economic system. The irony of Columbus's discoveries was thus complete: seeking the wealth of Asia, Columbus found instead the lands that ultimately replaced Asia as the source of European prosperity.

European nations fought bitterly to control the slave trade. The Portuguese, who at first dominated the trade, were supplanted by the Dutch in the 1630s. The Dutch in turn lost out to the English, who controlled the trade through the Royal African Company, a joint-stock company chartered by Charles II in 1672. Holding a monopoly on all English trade with sub-Saharan Africa, the company built and maintained eight forts, dispatched to West Africa hundreds of ships carrying English manufactured goods, and transported more than 120,000

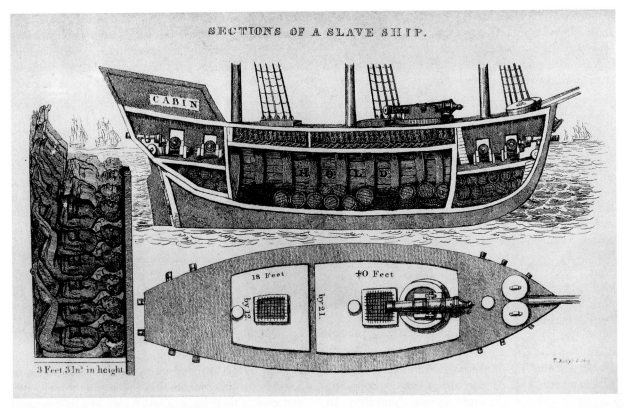

Slave traders tightly packed their human cargoes, attempting to carry as many people as possible on each voyage. This cutaway view of a typical vessel gives the ship's dimensions and shows the way slaves were transported in cramped quarters, with only small openings providing light and air.   British Library.

slaves to England's colonies in the Caribbean and on the mainland. Yet even before the company's monopoly expired in 1712, many individual English traders had illegally entered the market for slaves. By the early eighteenth century, such independent traders were carrying most of the Africans imported into the colonies, earning huge profits from successful voyages.

The experience of the Middle Passage (thus named because it was the middle section of the so-called triangular trade among England, Africa, and the Americas; see pages 81–82) was always traumatic and sometimes fatal for the Africans who made up a ship's cargo. An average of 10 to 20 percent of slaves died en route. On voyages that were unusually long or plagued by epidemic diseases, mortality rates were much higher. In addition, some slaves died either before the ships left Africa or shortly after their arrival in the Americas. Their European captors also died at high rates, chiefly through exposure to dis-

The Middle Passage

eases endemic to Africa. Just 10 percent of the men sent to run the Royal African Company's forts in Lower Guinea lived to return home to England, and one in every four or five European sailors died on the Middle Passage. Once again, the exchange of diseases caused unanticipated death and destruction.

One of the most vivid accounts of the Middle Passage was written by Olaudah Equiano, who was eleven years old in 1756 when African raiders kidnapped him from his Ibo village in what is now Nigeria. Terrified by the light complexions, long hair, and strange language of the sailors, he was afraid that "I had gotten into a world of bad spirits and that they were going to kill me." Equiano was placed below decks, where "with the loathsomeness of the stench and crying together, I became so sick and low that I was not able to eat, nor had I the least desire to taste anything." The slavers flogged him to make him eat. Equiano thought about killing himself by jumping overboard but was too closely watched. At last some other Ibos told him that they were being taken to their captors' country to work.

"I then was a little revived," Equiano remembered, "and thought if it were no worse than working, my situation was not so desperate."

After a long voyage during which many of the Africans died of disease brought on by the cramped, unsanitary conditions and poor food, the ship arrived at Barbados. Equiano and his shipmates feared that "these ugly men" were cannibals, but experienced slaves came on board to assure them that they would not be eaten and that many Africans like themselves lived on the island. "This report eased us much," Equiano recalled, "and sure enough soon after we landed there came to us Africans of all languages." Equiano was not purchased in the West Indies, instead being carried to Virginia, where he was soon sold and put to work on a tobacco plantation before being resold to a visiting ship captain.

The voyage Equiano described was typical, for most slave ships followed the Northeast Trades to the Caribbean before heading north to Virginia. So many Africans were imported so rapidly that as early as 1690 the Chesapeake colonies had more African slaves than English indentured servants, and by 1710 one-fifth of the region's population was of African descent. Slaves usually cost about two-and-a-half times as much as servants, but they repaid the greater investment with a lifetime of service.

Slavery in the Chesapeake

Yet many planters could not afford to purchase such expensive workers. Accordingly, the transition from indentured to enslaved labor increased the social and economic distance between richer and poorer planters. Those with enough money could acquire slaves and accumulate greater wealth, whereas the less affluent could not even buy indentured servants, whose price was driven up by scarcity. As time passed, Anglo-American society in the Chesapeake became more and more stratified—that is, the gap between rich and poor steadily widened. The introduction of large numbers of Africans into the Chesapeake thus had a significant impact on Anglo-American society, in addition to reshaping the population as a whole.

That impact involved cultural values as well as demographic and economic change. Without realizing it, Anglo-Americans in the Chesapeake adopted African modes of thought about the use of time and the nature of work. Africans were more accustomed than European migrants to life in a hot climate. Anglo-Americans soon learned the benefits of African patterns of time usage—working early and late, taking a long rest in the midday heat. They also assimilated African attitudes toward work, which were far more casual than those of New England. There, Puritans emphasized the necessity of "improving" every moment and scorned all leisure-time activities. In the Chesapeake, Anglo- and African-Americans alike came to recognize the importance of recreation and to understand that work could be performed at a leisurely pace on most occasions.

Since Africans were included among the first colonists to come to South Carolina from Barbados in 1670, they composed one-quarter to one-third of the early population. The Barbadian slaveowners quickly discovered that Africans had a variety of skills well suited to the semitropical environment of South Carolina. African-style dugout canoes became the chief means of transportation in the colony, which was crisscrossed by rivers. Fishing nets copied from African models proved more efficient than those of English origin. Baskets that enslaved laborers wove and gourds that they hollowed out came into general use as containers for food and drink. Africans' skill at killing crocodiles equipped them to handle alligators. And, finally, Africans adapted their traditional techniques of cattle herding for use in America. Since meat and hides—not the exotic products originally envisioned—were the colony's chief exports in its earliest years, Africans contributed significantly to South Carolina's prosperity.

African-Americans in South Carolina

The similarity of South Carolina's environment to West Africa's, coupled with the large proportion of Africans in the population, ensured that more aspects of West African culture survived in that colony than elsewhere on the North American mainland. Only in South Carolina did enslaved parents continue to give their children African names; only there did a dialect develop that combined English words with African terms. (Known as Gullah, it has survived to the present day in isolated areas.) African skills remained useful, so techniques that in other regions were lost when the migrant generation died were instead passed down to the migrants' children. And in South Carolina, as in Guinea, African women were the primary traders, dominating the markets of Charleston as they did those of Guinea.

Significantly, the importation of large numbers of Africans near the end of the seventeenth century

How do historians know that enslaved Africans were able to preserve at least some aspects of their cultural heritage in colonial North America? Although most enslaved people were illiterate and thus did not leave written records describing their cultural beliefs or practices, African-Americans did create objects that showed their connections to their homeland even more vividly than words on a page could have done. Many such objects have been found in the United States. The drum on the left was constructed on the Gold Coast of Africa in the nineteenth century, the one on the right in Virginia sometime before the middle of the eighteenth century. The similarities of style and decoration suggest strong cultural affinities between the two drum builders even though they were separated by 3,000 miles of ocean and at least one hundred years. Photo: Trustees of The British Museum; Smithsonian Institution, Washington, D.C.

coincided with the successful introduction of rice as a staple crop in South Carolina. English people knew little about the techniques of growing and processing rice, and their first attempts to raise the crop were not successful. But people from Africa's Rice Coast (see Chapter 1, page 12) had spent their lives working with the crop. Although the evidence is circumstantial, it seems likely that the Africans' expertise enabled their English masters to cultivate the crop profitably. After rice had become South Carolina's major export, 43 percent of the Africans imported into the colony came from rice-producing regions, and enslaved Africans' central position in the economy was unchallenged.

Rice and Indigo

South Carolina later developed a second staple crop, and it too made use of slaves' special skills. The crop was indigo, much prized in Europe as a source of blue dye for clothing. In the early 1740s, Eliza Lucas, a young woman who was managing her father's plantations, began to experiment with indigo cultivation. Drawing on the knowledge of slaves and overseers from the West Indies, she developed the planting and processing techniques later adopted throughout the colony. Indigo was grown on high ground, and rice was planted in low-lying swampy areas; rice and indigo also had different growing seasons. Thus the two crops complemented each other perfectly. Although South Carolina indigo never matched the quality of that raised in the West Indies, the indigo industry flourished because Parliament offered Carolinians a bounty on every pound they exported to Great Britain.

After 1700, therefore, southern planters, large and small alike, were irrevocably committed to slavery as their chief source of labor. The same was not true of northerners. Only a

Slavery in the North

small proportion of the Africans brought to the English colonies in America went to the northern mainland provinces, and most of those worked as enslaved domestic servants. Lacking large-scale agricultural enterprises, the rural North did not demand many bound laborers. In northern urban areas, though, European domestic servants were hard to find and harder to keep because other jobs in the labor-scarce economy earned higher wages. Thus enslaved Africans there filled an identifiable need. In some northern colonial cities (notably Newport, Rhode Island, and New York City), slaves accounted for more than 10 percent of the population.

The introduction of large-scale slavery in the South, coupled with its near absence in the rural North, accentuated regional differences that already had begun to develop in England's American colonies. To the distinction between diversified agriculture and staple-crop production was now added a difference in the status of most laborers. That difference was one of degree, for slavery was legal everywhere in the colonies, but it was nonetheless crucial. For the next 150 years the continent's society and politics were to be indelibly shaped by decisions made in the late seventeenth century.

Relations Between Europeans and Indians

Everywhere in North America, European colonizers depended heavily on the labor of native peoples, but their reliance took varying forms in different parts of the continent. In the Northeast, France, England, and the Netherlands competed for the pelts supplied by Indian trappers. In the Southeast, England, Spain, and later France each tried to control a thriving trade with the Native Americans in deerskins and Indian slaves. In the Southwest, meanwhile, Spain attempted to exploit the agricultural and artisan skills of the Pueblo peoples (see map).

After Fray Alonzo de Benavides departed for Madrid in 1629 (see Chapter 2), Franciscan friars continued their conversion efforts, with mixed success.

Popé and the Pueblo Revolt

The Pueblo peoples were willing to add Christianity to their own religious beliefs but not to give up their indigenous rituals. Friars and secular colonists who held *encomiendas* also placed heavy demands on the Indians. As the decades passed, Franciscans adopted brutal and violent tactics in an attempt to wipe out all traces of the native religion. Finally, in 1680 the Pueblos revolted under the leadership of Popé, a respected shaman, and successfully drove the Spaniards out of New Mexico. Although Spanish authority was restored in 1692, Spain had learned its lesson. From that time on, Spanish governors stressed cooperation with the Pueblos, rather than confrontation, and no longer attempted to reduce them to bondage or to violate their cultural integrity. The Pueblo revolt was the most successful and longest-sustained Indian resistance movement in colonial North America.

When the Spanish expanded their territorial claims to the east and north, they followed the same strategy they had used in New Mexico, establishing

Spain's North American Possessions

their presence through military outposts and Franciscan missions. The army's role was to maintain order among the subject Indians—to protect them from attack and ensure the availability of their labor—and to guard the boundaries of the Spanish Empire from possible incursions, especially by the French. The friars concentrated on conversions. By the late eighteenth century, Spain claimed a vast territory that stretched from California (first colonized in 1769 to prevent Russian sea-otter trappers from taking over the region) through Texas (settled after 1700) to the Gulf Coast. Throughout that region, the Spanish presence consisted of a mixture of missions and forts dotting the countryside, sometimes at considerable distances from each other.

Europeans along the eastern seaboard valued Indians as hunters rather than as agricultural workers, but they were no less dependent on Indian labor than were Spaniards in the Southwest. To obtain pelts and deerskins from indigenous peoples, Europeans—French, Spanish, and English alike—had to supply trade goods the Indians wanted. Such commodities included ammunition, clothing, and alcohol (usually rum distilled from West Indian molasses). Although in the seventeenth century Indians

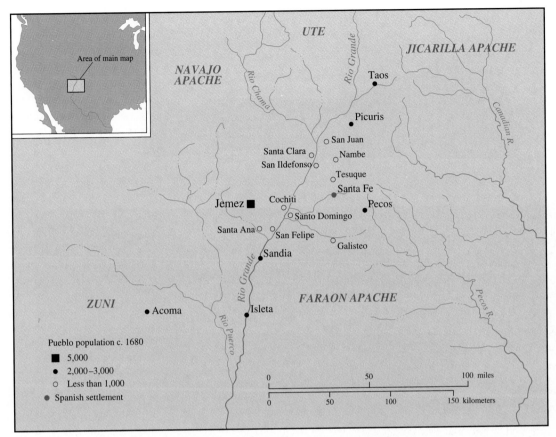

New Mexico, c. 1680 *In 1680, the lone Spanish settlement at Santa Fe was surrounded and vastly outnumbered by the many Pueblo villages nearby.*   Source: Adapted from *Apache, Navaho, and Spaniard*, by Jack D. Forbes. Copyright © 1960 by the University of Oklahoma Press. Used by permission.

primarily obtained rum at settlers' taverns or in gift exchanges accompanying trade or treaty negotiations, by 1720 European and Indian traders were carrying casks of rum far into the American interior. Indians' demand for alcohol (a commodity to which they were introduced by the traders) made rum a key component of colonial commerce, and alcohol abuse hastened the deterioration of villages already devastated by disease and dislocation.

Also destructive of tribal communities was traffic in Indian slaves. Carolina Indians, especially the Creeks, profited from selling their captive enemies to the English, who either kept them as slaves or exported them to other mainland settlements or to the West Indies. There are no reliable statistics on the extent of the trade in Indian slaves, but in 1708 they composed 14 percent of the South

Indian Slave Trade in the Southeast

Carolina population. Many were Catholics converted by the Spanish missions in northern Florida, then captured by Englishmen or their Native American allies.

Bitter conflicts between the Carolina settlers and indigenous peoples produced not only slaves but also mass migrations. In 1711 the Tuscaroras, an Iroquoian people, attacked a Swiss-German settlement at New Bern, which had expropriated their lands without payment. The Tuscaroras had been avid slavers and had sold to the Europeans many captives seized from their Algonkian neighbors. Those Indians took the opportunity to settle old scores, joining with the English colonists to defeat their enemy in a bloody two-year war. In the end, more than a thousand Tuscaroras were themselves sold into slavery, and the remnants of the group

Tuscarora and Yamasee Wars

Trade between Europeans and Indians provided both societies with essential items. The Europeans manufactured tomahawks specifically for the Native American market. Likewise, the Indians of Long Island increased their production of wampum (made from clam shells) when English and Dutch colonists adopted the purple and white beads as a medium of exchange. Wampum served as a substitute for European coins, which were scarce in the remote colonial outposts.   Tomahawk: Peabody and Essex Museum. Belt: Peabody and Essex Museum

drifted northward, where they joined the Five Nations Iroquois in New York.

The slave trade's abuses led to yet another Indian war in Carolina. Colonial traders regularly engaged in corrupt, brutal, and fraudulent practices. They were notorious for cheating Native Americans, physically abusing them (including raping women), and selling friendly peoples into slavery when no enemy captives came readily to hand. In the spring and summer of 1715, the Yamasees, aided by Creeks and others, retaliated by attacking English settlements. Refugees by the hundreds streamed into Charleston; the Creek-Yamasee offensive came close to driving the intruders from the mainland altogether. But colonial reinforcements arrived from the north, and Cherokees joined English settlers to fight the Creeks, their ancient enemies.

The war pointed up both the difficulty of achieving unity among the Indians and their critical dependence on European weapons. When the Creeks and Yamasees depleted their stores of ammunition and could not repair their broken guns, their cause was lost. The Yamasees moved south to Florida, and the Creeks retreated to villages in the west. South Carolina did not fully recover from the effects of the Yamasee War for many years, but the existence of the colony was never again seriously threatened.

That the Yamasees could escape by migrating southward exposed the one remaining gap in the line

Founding of Georgia

of English coastal settlements, the area between South Carolina's southern border and Spanish Florida (see map, page 64). The gap was plugged in 1732 with the chartering of Georgia, the last of the colonies that would become part of the United States. Intended as a haven for English debtors by its founder James Oglethorpe, Georgia was specifically designed as a garrison province. Since all its landholders were expected to serve as militiamen to defend English settlements, the charter prohibited women from inheriting or purchasing land in the colony. The charter also prohibited slavery and the use of alcoholic beverages. Such provisions reveal the founders' intention that Georgia should be peopled by sturdy, sober yeoman farmers who could take up their weapons at a moment's notice against Native Americans or Spaniards. None of the original conditions of the charter were enforced, however, and all of them had been abandoned by 1752, when Georgia became a royal colony.

Iroquois Confederacy

In the Northeast, relationships were complicated by the number of European and Indian nations involved in the fur trade. The key players were the Iroquois, not one tribe but five—the Mohawks, Oneidas, Onondagas, Cayugas, and Senecas. (In 1722, the Tuscaroras became the sixth.) Under the terms of a defensive alliance forged early in the sixteenth century, decisions of war and peace for the entire Iroquois Confederacy were made by a council composed of tribal representatives. Each nation retained some autonomy and could not be forced to comply with a council directive against its will.

The Iroquois were unique among Native Americans, not only because of the strength and persistence of their alliance but also because of the role played by their clan matrons. The older women of each village chose its chief and could either start wars (by calling for the capture of prisoners to replace dead relatives) or stop them (by refusing to supply warriors with necessary foodstuffs).

Philip Georg Friedrich von Reck, an artist who visited Georgia in the early years of English settlement there, recorded a festival celebrated by the local Yuchi Indians in 1736. European guns hang from the rafters of the open shelter, showing that extensive trade connections already existed between the two peoples.   Royal Library, Copenhagen.

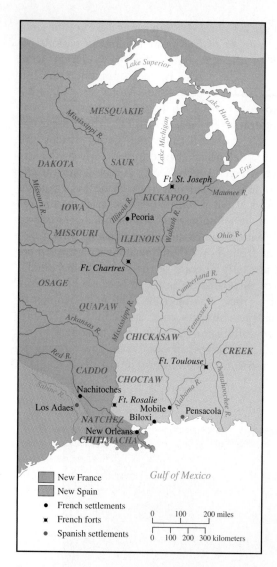

Louisiana, c. 1720 *By 1720, French forts and settlements dotted the Mississippi River and its tributaries in the interior of North America. Two isolated Spanish outposts were situated near the Gulf of Mexico.* Source: Adapted from *France in America*, by William J. Eccles. Copyright © 1972 by William J. Eccles. Reprinted by permission of Harper & Row, Publishers, Inc.

Before the arrival of Europeans, the Iroquois waged wars primarily to acquire captives to replenish their population. Contact with foreign traders brought ravaging disease as early as 1633 and thus intensified the need for captives. Simultaneously, the Europeans' coming created an economic motive for warfare: the desire to control the fur trade and gain unimpeded access to European goods. The war with the Hurons in the 1640s (see page 38) was but the

first of a series of conflicts with other tribes known as the Beaver Wars, in which the Iroquois fought desperately to maintain a dominant position in the trade.

In the mid-1670s, just when they were achieving their goal, the French stepped in; an Iroquois triumph would have destroyed France's plans to trade directly with the Indians of the Great Lakes and Mississippi valley. Over the next twenty years the French launched repeated attacks on Iroquois villages. The English offered little assistance other than weapons to their trading partners and nominal allies. Their people and resources depleted by constant warfare, the Iroquois in 1701 negotiated neutrality treaties with France, England, and their Indian neighbors. For the next half-century they maintained their power through trade and skillful diplomacy rather than warfare.

The wars against the Iroquois Confederacy were crucial components of French Canada's plan to penetrate the heartland of North America. In the 1670s, Louis de Buade de Frontenac, the governor-general of Canada, encouraged the explorations of Father Jacques Marquette, Louis Jolliet, and Robert Cavelier de La Salle in the Great Lakes and Mississippi valley regions. Officials in France approved the expeditions because they wanted to find a trade route to Mexico. La Salle and Frontenac, by contrast, hoped to profit personally, monopolizing the fur trade by establishing trading posts along the Mississippi River.

French Expansion

Unlike Spaniards, French adventurers did not attempt to subjugate the Native Americans they encountered. Nor, at first, did they even claim the territory formally for France. Still, when France decided to strengthen its presence near the Gulf of Mexico by founding New Orleans in 1718—to counter both the westward thrust of the English colonies and the eastward moves of the Spanish— the Mississippi posts became the glue of empire. *Coureurs de bois* (literally, "forest runners") used the rivers and lakes of the American interior to travel regularly between Quebec and Louisiana, carrying French goods to outposts such as Michilimackinac (at the junction of Lakes Michigan and Huron), Cahokia and Kaskaskia (in present-day Illinois), and Fort Rosalie (Natchez), on the lower Mississippi River (see map).

Most of the posts consisted of a small military garrison and a priest, surrounded by powerful nations such as the Choctaws, Chickasaws, Osages, and

Illinois. The Indians permitted French soldiers and traders to remain among them because they wanted easy access to valuable European goods. The French, for their part, sought political as well as economic ends, attempting to prevent the English from encroaching too far into the interior. Their goals were limited; they did not engage in systematic efforts to convert nearby Native American peoples to Christianity.

Along the Mississippi just south of modern St. Louis and north of Fort Chartres (see map, page 78), migrants from Quebec and Montréal established six small villages (known collectively as *le pays de Illinois*, the Illinois country) that produced wheat for export to New Orleans. But a shortage of manpower—the population never rose much above three thousand—meant that the French could not significantly expand the amount of land under cultivation. And the lack of French women led to interracial unions between French men and Native American women and to the creation of mixed-race people known as *metís*.

Matters were very different in the English colonies, where white colonists had an avid interest in acquiring more land. In Virginia, the conflict was especially acute because of the colonists' insatiable hunger for tobacco acreage.

By the early 1670s, some Virginians were eagerly eyeing rich lands north of the York River that early treaties had reserved for Native Americans.

Bacon's Rebellion

Using as a pretext the July 1675 killing of an English servant by some Doeg Indians, they attacked not only the Doegs but also the Susquehannocks, a powerful tribe that had recently occupied the area. In retaliation, Susquehannock bands raided frontier plantations in the winter of 1676. The land-hungry Anglo-Americans rallied behind the leadership of Nathaniel Bacon, a recently arrived planter, who, like many of his followers, had immigrated too late to acquire fertile lands in the already settled tidewater region. Bacon and his followers wanted, in his words, "to ruine and extirpate all Indians in general." Governor William Berkeley, however, hoped to avoid setting off a major war, which might devastate the colony.

Berkeley and Bacon soon clashed. After Bacon forced the House of Burgesses to authorize him to attack the Indians, Berkeley declared Bacon and his men to be in rebellion. As the chaotic summer of 1676 wore on, Bacon alternately pursued Indians and battled with the governor's supporters. In Sep-

tember Bacon marched on Jamestown itself and burned the capital to the ground. But when Bacon died of dysentery the following month, the rebellion collapsed. Even so, a new treaty signed in 1677 opened much of the disputed territory to English settlement.

More than coincidentally, New England—also colonized more than fifty years earlier—was wracked by conflict with Native Americans at precisely the same time. In both areas, the colonists' original accommodation with the Indians, reached after the defeat of the Pequots in the North and the Powhatan Confederacy in the South, no longer satisfied both parties. In New England, though, it was the indigenous peoples, rather than the colonists, who felt aggrieved.

In the half-century since the founding of New England, colonial settlement had spread far into the interior of Massachusetts and Connecticut. In

King Philip's War

the process, the colonists had completely surrounded the ancestral lands of the Pokanokets (Wampanoags) on Narragansett Bay. Their chief, Metacom (known to the English as King Philip), was the son of Massasoit, who had signed the treaty with the Pilgrims in 1621. Troubled by encroachments on Pokanoket lands and equally concerned about the impact European culture and Christianity were having on his people, Metacom led his warriors in attacks on nearby communities in June 1675.

The Nipmucks and the Narragansetts soon joined Metacom's forces. In the fall, the three Indian nations jointly attacked settlements in the northern Connecticut River valley. In early 1676, they devastated well-established villages and even attacked Plymouth and Providence. Altogether, the alliance totally destroyed twelve of the ninety Puritan towns and attacked forty others. One-tenth of the able-bodied adult male colonists in Massachusetts were captured or killed. Proportional to population, it was the most costly war in American history. New England's very survival seemed at stake.

But the tide turned in the summer of 1676. The Indian coalition ran short of food and ammunition, and colonists began to use Christian Indians as guides and scouts. After Metacom was killed in an ambush in August, the alliance crumbled. Many surviving Pokanokets, Nipmucks, and Narragansetts, including Metacom's wife and son, were captured and sold into slavery in the West Indies. The power of New England's coastal tribes was broken. There-after they lived in small clusters, subordinated to the colonists and often working as servants or sailors. Only on the isolated island of Martha's Vineyard were some surviving Wampanoags able to preserve their cultural identity intact.

 ## New England and the Web of Imperial Trade

From the early years of colonization to the close of the seventeenth century, New England changed in three major ways. The population grew dramati-cally; the residents' relationship to Puritanism al-tered; and the economy developed in unanticipated ways.

Population expansion resulted not from contin-ued migration from England (for that largely ceased after the outbreak of the English Civil War in 1642) but rather from natural increase.

Population Pressures

The original settlers' many chil-dren also produced many chil-dren, and subsequent genera-tions followed suit. By 1700, New England's population had quadrupled to reach approximately 100,000. Such an increase placed great pressure on available land, and many members of the third and fourth generations of New Eng-landers had to migrate—north to New Hampshire or Maine, south to New York, west beyond the Con-necticut River—to find sufficient farmland for themselves and their children. Others abandoned agriculture and learned skills like blacksmithing or carpentry so they could support themselves in the growing number of towns dotting the countryside.

The passage of time also brought changes in Pu-ritanism, for two of the Puritans' fundamental be-liefs came inevitably into conflict. Puritans practiced infant baptism, yet at the same time they insisted that only the saved could be members of their churches. No one foresaw the problem that con-fronted congregations in the 1660s: young people baptized as children married and had babies before undergoing the searching examination of their faith required to join a church. Could the offspring of such couples be baptized? The need to answer that question led to the convening of a synod of clergy-men in 1662 and to the adoption of the so-called Halfway Covenant, which established a category of "halfway" membership in Puritan congregations. If previously baptized adults acknowledged the

church's authority over them, the ministers declared, they could have their children baptized.

By the 1660s, women were far more likely than men to become either full or halfway members of Pu-ritan congregations. Searching for the cause of this

Women, Men, and Puritan Churches

phenomenon, Cotton Mather, the most prominent member of a family of distinguished ministers, speculated that the fear of dying in childbirth made women espe-cially sensitive to their spiritual state. By contrast, modern historians have argued that women were attracted to religion because the church offered them spiritual equality to offset their secular inferiority.

Whatever the explanation, the increasingly fe-male composition of his audiences prompted Mather to deliver sermons outlining women's proper role in church and society—the first formal examination of that theme in American history. Mather was the first of many men to publish sermons urging American women to be submissive to their husbands, watchful of their children, and attentive to religious duty.

If Mather thought to ask the parallel question—why had New England's men become more reluctant to acknowledge the church's authority over them?—he did not propose an answer, though scholars have done so. One historian hypothesizes that the con-nection between church membership and political obligation was critical. Believing with good reason that unchurched men were unlikely to be elected to office, male New Englanders may well have failed to join congregations because they wanted to avoid having to serve as constables or militia officers. Such time-consuming and onerous jobs not only took them away from their farms and families but also could cause dissension in their neighborhoods.

Another hypothesis focuses on the male resi-dents of seaport towns such as Boston and Salem. Men in these urban areas, some historians argue, be-came more worldly and less interested in religion as the economy of the New England colonies changed after the outbreak of the English Civil War.

Initially, New England's economy rested on two foundations: the fur trade and the constant flow of mi-grants. Together, those had allowed New Englanders

New England's First Economy

to acquire the manufactured goods they needed. The fur trade gave them valuable pelts to sell in England, and the migrants were always willing to exchange cloth-ing and other items for the earlier settlers' surplus

The harbor of Christiansted, St. Croix, in the Danish West Indies. Although this view was painted over one hundred years after the events discussed in this chapter, the town had not changed much in the interim. Scenes like this would have been very familiar to Captain William Kidd and his contemporaries, for such tiny ports existed all over the Caribbean. Anchored merchant vessels await the hogsheads of molasses being prepared for shipment at the wharf.   MAPes MONDe Ltd.

seed, grains, and livestock. But New England's supply of furs was quickly exhausted by excessive trapping, and the migrants stopped coming after the English Civil War began. Thus in the early 1640s that first economic system collapsed.

The Puritans then began a search for new markets and salable crops. They found such crops in the waters off the coast—fish—and on their own land—grain and wood products. By 1643 they had also found the necessary markets: first the Wine Islands and then the English colonies in the Caribbean. All these islands lacked precisely the goods that New England could produce in abundance: cheap food (corn and salted fish) to feed to slaves and wood for barrels to hold wine and molasses (the form in which sugar was shipped).

Thus developed the series of transactions that has become known, inaccurately, as the triangular trade. The northern colonists sold their goods in the West Indies and elsewhere to earn the money with which to purchase English imports.

Atlantic Trading System

There soon grew up in New England's ports a cadre of merchants who acquired—usually through barter—cargoes of timber and foodstuffs, which they then dispatched to the West Indies for sale. In the Caribbean, the ships sailed from island to island, exchanging fish, barrel staves, and grains for molasses, fruit, spices, and slaves. Once they had a full load, the ships returned to Boston, Newport, or New Haven to dispose of their cargoes. New Englanders traded the items they did not use to other colonies or to England.

Most important, northerners distilled West Indian molasses into rum, a key component of the only

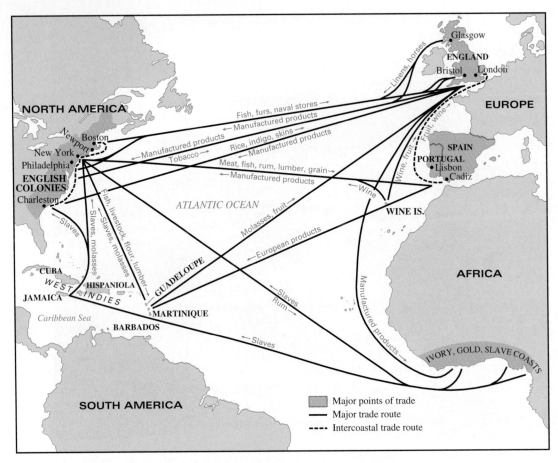

Atlantic Trade Routes *By the late seventeenth century, an elaborate trade network linked the countries and colonies bordering the Atlantic Ocean. The most valuable commodities exchanged were enslaved people and the products of slave labor.*

part of the trade that could be termed triangular. Rhode Islanders took rum to Africa and traded it for slaves, whom they carried to the West Indies to exchange for more molasses to produce still more rum. With that exception, the trading pattern was not a triangle but a shifting set of two-way voyages (see map). Its sole constant was uncertainty, due to the weather, rapid shifts in supply and demand in the small island markets, and the delicate system of credit on which the entire structure depended.

The New Englanders who ventured into commerce were soon differentiated from their rural counterparts by their ties to a wider transatlantic world and their preoccupation with material endeavors. As time passed, increasing numbers of Puritans became involved in trade. Small investors who

owned shares of voyages soon dominated the field numerically if not monetarily.

The gulf between commercial and farming interests widened after 1660, when, with Stuart Restoration, merchants who were members of the Church of England (Anglicans) began to migrate to New England to participate directly in the booming trade in slaves and staple crops produced by enslaved laborers. Such men had little stake in the survival of Massachusetts Bay and Connecticut in their original forms, and some were openly antagonistic to Puritan traditions. As non-Congregationalists they were denied the vote, but they were still taxed to support the church. Further, Anglicans were forbidden to practice their own religion freely. They resented their exclusion from the governing elite, believing that their wealth and social status entitled them to political power. Congregationalist clergymen returned their hostility, preaching sermons lamenting New England's new commercial orientation. The Reverend Increase Mather (Cotton Mather's father) reminded his congregation in 1676 that "Religion and not the World was that which our Fathers came hither for."

But Mather spoke for the past, not for the future or even for many of his own contemporaries. By the 1670s, New England and the other American colonies were deeply enmeshed in an intricate international trading network. The early colonies may have been even more dependent on overseas markets and on imported goods than eighteenth-century America would be. During the 1600s the colonies lacked sufficient population to support manufacturing. For example, all attempts to establish ironworks or glass factories in the first decades of settlement failed because there simply were not enough colonial consumers. Furthermore, the colonies' economic fortunes depended on the sale of their exports in foreign markets: furs, deerskins, sugar, tobacco, rice, fish, and timber products together formed the basis for Anglo-America's prosperity.

English officials seeking a new source of revenue after the disruptions of the Civil War realized that the colonies could make important contributions to England's economic well-being. Chesapeake tobacco and West Indian sugar had obvious value, but other colonial products also had profitable potential. Additional tax revenues could put England back on a sound financial footing, and English merchants wanted to ensure that they—not their Dutch rivals—reaped the benefits of trading with the English colonies. Parliament and the restored Stuart monarchs accordingly began to draft laws designed to confine the profits of colonial trade primarily to the mother country.

Mercantilism

Like other European nations, England based its commercial policy on a series of assumptions about the operations of the world's economic system. Collectively, these assumptions are usually called *mercantilism*, though neither the term itself nor a unified mercantilist theory was formulated until a century later. The economic world was seen as a collection of national states, whose governments actively competed for shares of a finite amount of wealth. What one nation gained was automatically another nation's loss. Each nation's goal was to become as economically self-sufficient as possible while maintaining a favorable balance of trade with other countries by exporting more than it imported. Colonies had an important role to play in such a scheme. They could supply the mother country with valuable raw materials to be consumed at home or sent abroad, and they could serve as a market for the mother country's manufactured goods.

Parliament applied mercantilist thinking to the American colonies in laws known as the Navigation Acts. The major acts—passed between 1651 and 1673—established three main principles. First, only English or colonial merchants and ships could engage in trade in the colonies. Second, certain valuable American products could be sold only in the mother country or in other English colonies. At first, these "enumerated" goods were wool, sugar, tobacco, indigo, ginger, and dyes; later acts added rice, naval stores (masts, spars, pitch, tar, and turpentine), copper, and furs to the list. Third, all foreign goods destined for sale in the colonies had to be shipped by way of England and were subject to English import duties. Some years later, a new series of laws established a fourth principle: the colonies could not export items (such as wool clothing, hats, or iron) that competed with English products.

Navigation Acts

The intention of the Navigation Acts was clear: American trade was to center on England. The mother country was to benefit from colonial imports and exports both. England had first claim on the most valuable colonial exports, and all foreign imports into the colonies had to pass through England first, enriching its customs revenues in the process. Some colonies, like those in the West Indies and the Chesapeake, were adversely affected by the laws because they could not seek new markets for their staple crops. In others, the impact was less severe. Builders and owners of ships benefited from the monopoly on American trade given to English and colonial merchants. And the northern and middle colonies in particular produced many goods that were not enumerated—for example, fish, flour, and barrel staves. These products could be traded directly to foreign purchasers as long as they were carried in English or American ships.

The English authorities soon learned that it was easier to write mercantilist legislation than to enforce it. The many harbors of the American coast provided ready havens for smugglers, and colonial officials often looked the other way when illegally imported goods were offered for sale. In ports such as St. Eustatius in the Dutch West Indies, American merchants could easily dispose of enumerated goods and purchase foreign items on which duty had not been paid. Consequently, Parliament in 1696 enacted another Navigation Act. This law established in America a number of vice-admiralty courts, which operated without juries. In England such courts dealt only with cases involving piracy, vessels taken as wartime prizes, and the like. But since American juries had already demonstrated a tendency to favor local smugglers over customs officers (a colonial customs service was instituted in 1671), Parliament decided to remove Navigation Act cases from the regular colonial courts.

England took another major step in colonial administration in 1696 by creating the fifteen-member Board of Trade and Plantations, which thereafter served as the chief organ of government concerned with the

Board of Trade and Plantations

American colonies. (Previously, no single body had that responsibility.) It gathered information, reviewed Crown appointments in America, scrutinized legislation passed by colonial assemblies, supervised trade policies, and advised successive ministries on colonial issues. Still, the Board of Trade did not have any direct powers of enforcement. It also shared jurisdiction over American affairs not only with the customs service and the navy but also with the secretary of state for the southern department, the member of the ministry responsible for the colonies. In short, although the Stuart monarchs' reforms considerably improved the quality of colonial administration, supervision of the American provinces remained decentralized and haphazard.

 ## Colonial Political Development and Imperial Reorganization

English officials in the 1670s and 1680s confronted not only resistance to the Navigation Acts but also a bewildering array of colonial governments. Massachusetts Bay and Plymouth functioned under their original charters. Neighboring Connecticut (including the formerly independent New Haven) and Rhode Island had been granted charters by Charles II in 1662 and 1663, respectively. Virginia was a royal colony, and New York also became one when

its proprietor ascended the throne in 1685 as James II. All the other mainland settlements were proprietorships, whose royal charters gave the proprietors a great deal of leeway in how they governed their possessions.

Still, in political structure the colonies shared certain characteristics. Most were ruled by a governor and a two-house legislature. In New England, the governors were elected by property-holding men or by the

Colonial Political Structures

legislature; in the Chesapeake and the middle colonies, they were appointed by the king or the proprietor. A council, either elected or appointed, advised the governor on matters of policy and sometimes served as the colony's highest court. The councils also served as upper houses of colonial legislatures. At first, councilors and elected representatives met jointly to debate and adopt laws affecting the colony. But as time passed, the fundamental differences between the two legislative groups' purposes and constituencies led them to separate (the first such division occurred in Massachusetts in 1644). Thus developed the two-house legislature still used in almost all of the states.

Meanwhile, local political institutions were taking shape. In New England, elected selectmen initially governed the towns, but by the end of the century town meetings—held at least annually and attended by most free adult male residents—handled matters of local concern. In the Chesapeake colonies and both of the Carolinas, appointed justices of the peace ran local governments. At first the same was true in Pennsylvania, but by the early eighteenth century elected county officials began to take over some government functions. And in New York, local elections were the rule even before the establishment of the colonial assembly in 1683.

By late in the seventeenth century, therefore, Anglo-American colonists were everywhere accustomed to exercising a considerable degree of local political autonomy. The tradition of consent was especially firmly established in New England. Massachusetts, Plymouth, Connecticut, and Rhode Island were, in effect, independent entities, subject neither to the direct authority of the king nor to a proprietor. Everywhere in the English colonies, free adult men who owned more than a stated minimum amount of property (which varied from province to province) expected to have an influential voice in how they were governed—and especially in how they were taxed.

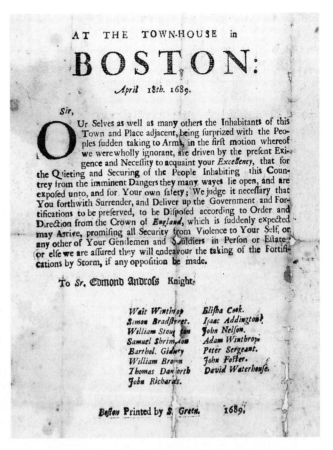

Sir Edmund Andros (1637–1714), the much-detested autocratic governor of the Dominion of New England, and a broadside issued at the height of the crisis caused by the Glorious Revolution, calling on Andros to surrender control of the government. The signers were the foremost leaders of the Massachusetts Bay colony, among them a son and grandson of John Winthrop.   Portrait: Massachusetts State Archives. Broadside: Massachusetts Historical Society.

After James II became king, these expectations clashed with those of the monarch. The new king and his successors sought to bring order to the apparently chaotic state of colonial administration by tightening the reins of government and reducing the colonies' political autonomy. (Simultaneously, they used the Navigation Acts to reduce the colonies' economic autonomy.) They began to chip away at the privileges granted in colonial charters and to reclaim proprietorships for the Crown. New Hampshire (1679), its parent colony Massachusetts (1691), New Jersey (1702), and the Carolinas (1729) all became royal colonies. The charters of Rhode Island, Connecticut, Maryland, and Pennsylvania were temporarily suspended but ultimately were restored to their original status.

The most drastic reordering of colonial administration targeted Puritan New England. Reports from America convinced English officials that New

Dominion of New England

England was a hotbed of smuggling. Moreover, Puritans refused to allow freedom of religion to non-Congregationalists and insisted on maintaining laws that ran counter to English practice. New England thus seemed an appropriate place to exert English authority with greater vigor. The charters of all the colonies from New Jersey to Maine (then part of Massachusetts) were revoked, and a Dominion of New England was established in 1686. (For the boundaries of the Dominion, see the map on page 64.) Sir Edmund Andros, the governor, was given immense power: all the assemblies were dissolved, and he needed only the consent of an appointed council to make laws and levy taxes.

New Englanders endured Andros's autocratic rule for more than two years. Then came the dramatic news that James II had been overthrown in a bloodless coup known as the Glorious Revolution and had been replaced on the throne by his daughter Mary and her husband, the Dutch prince William of Orange. James II, like his father Charles I, had levied taxes without parliamentary approval. He also had announced his conversion to Roman Catholicism. When Parliament offered the throne to the Protestants William and Mary, the Glorious Revolution affirmed the supremacy of both Parliament and Protestantism.

Seizing the opportunity to rid themselves of the hated Dominion, New Englanders jailed Andros and his associates, proclaimed their loyalty to William and Mary, and wrote to England for instructions about the form of government they should adopt. Most of Massachusetts Bay's political leaders hoped that the new monarchs would renew their original charter, revoked in 1684 prior to establishment of the Dominion.

Glorious Revolution in America

In other American colonies, too, the Glorious Revolution was a signal for revolt. In Maryland the Protestant Association overturned the government of the Catholic proprietor, and in New York a militia officer of German origin, Jacob Leisler, assumed control of the government. Like the New Englanders, the Maryland and New York rebels allied themselves with the supporters of William and Mary. They saw themselves as carrying out the colonial phase of the English revolt against Stuart absolutism.

William and Mary, however, like James II, believed that England should exercise tighter control over its unruly American possessions. Consequently, the only American rebellion that received royal sanction was that in Maryland, primarily because of its anti-Catholic thrust. In New York, Jacob Leisler was hanged for treason, and Massachusetts (including the formerly independent jurisdiction of Plymouth) became a royal colony with an appointed governor. The province was allowed to retain its town meeting system of local government and to elect its council, but the new charter issued in 1691 eliminated the traditional religious test for voting and officeholding. An Anglican parish was set up in the heart of Boston. The "city upon a hill" as John Winthrop had envisioned it was no more.

Compounding New England's difficulties in a time of political upheaval and economic uncertainty was a war with the French and their Native Ameri-

can allies. King Louis XIV of France allied himself with the deposed James II, and England declared war on France in 1689. The conflict, which lasted until 1697, was known in Europe as the War of the League of Augsburg, but the colonists called it King William's War. The American war was fought chiefly on the northern frontiers of New England and New York; among the English settlements devastated by enemy attacks in 1690 were Schenectady, New York, and Casco (now Falmouth), Maine. Expeditions organized by the colonies against Montréal and Quebec that same year both failed miserably, and throughout the rest of the war New England found itself on the defensive.

In this period of extreme stress occurred an outbreak of witchcraft accusations in Salem Village (now Danvers), Massachusetts. Like their contemporaries elsewhere, seventeenth-century New Englanders believed in the existence of witches, whose evil powers came from the Devil. If people could not find other explanations for their troubles, they tended to suspect they were bewitched. Before 1689, 103 New Englanders, most of them middle-aged women, had been charged with practicing witchcraft, chiefly by neighbors who attributed their misfortunes to the suspected witch. Only a few of the accused were convicted, and fewer still were executed. Most such incidents were isolated; nothing else in New England's history came close to matching the Salem Village cataclysm.

Witchcraft in Salem Village

The crisis began in early 1692 when a group of girls and young women accused some older female neighbors of having bewitched them. Before the hysteria spent itself ten months later, nineteen people (including several men, most of them related to convicted female witches) were hanged, one was pressed to death with heavy stones, and more than one hundred persons were jailed. Historians have proposed various explanations for this puzzling episode, but to be understood it must be seen in the context of political and legal disorder, Indian war, and religious and economic crises. Puritan New Englanders must have felt as though their entire world was collapsing. At the very least they could have had no sense of security about their future.

Nowhere was that more true than in Salem Village, a farming town torn between old and new styles of life because of its position on the edge of the bustling port of Salem. And no residents of the village had more reason to feel insecure than those who issued the first accusations. Many of them had been orphaned in the recent Indian attacks on Maine; they were living in Salem Village as domestic servants. Their involvement with witchcraft began as an experiment with fortunetelling as a means of foreseeing their futures, in particular the identities of their eventual husbands. As the most powerless people in a town apparently powerless to direct its fate, they offered their fellow New Englanders a compelling explanation for the seemingly endless chain of troubles afflicting them: their province was under direct attack from the Devil and his legion of witches. Accordingly, it is not so much the number of witchcraft prosecutions that seems surprising but rather their abrupt cessation in the fall of 1692.

There were three reasons for the rapid end to the crisis. First, the accusers grew too bold. When they began to charge some of the colony's most distinguished and respected residents with being in league with the Devil, members of the ruling elite began to doubt their veracity. Second, the colony's ministers, led by Increase Mather, formally expressed strong reservations about the validity of the spectral evidence used against most of the accused. Third, the implementation of the new royal charter ended the worst period of political uncertainty, eliminating a major source of stress. King William's War continued, but, although the Puritans were not entirely pleased with the new charter, at least order had formally been restored.

Over the course of the next three decades, Massachusetts and the rest of the English colonies in America accommodated themselves to the new imperial order. Most colonists resented alien officials who arrived in America determined to implement the policies of king and Parliament, but they adjusted to their demands and to the trade restrictions imposed by the Navigation Acts. They fought another imperial war—the War of the Spanish Succession, or Queen Anne's War—from 1702 to 1713, without enduring the stresses of the first, despite the heavy economic burdens the conflict imposed. Colonists who allied themselves with royal government received patronage in the form of offices and land grants and composed "court parties" that supported English officials. Others, who were either less fortunate in their friends or more principled in defense of colonial autonomy, made up the opposition, or "country" interest. By the end of the first quarter of the eighteenth century, most men in both

No seventeenth-century New Englander ever drew a picture of a witchcraft trial or execution, but an artist did record the hanging of several witches in England around 1650. The multiple executions of Salem witches in the summer of 1692 probably resembled this gallows scene.   Folger Shakespeare Library.

groups had been born in America and were members of elite families whose wealth derived from staple-crop production in the South and commerce in the North.

 ## Conclusion

The eighty years from 1640 to 1720 established the basic economic and political patterns that were to structure all subsequent changes in mainland colonial society. In 1640 there were just two isolated centers of English population, New England and the Chesapeake. In 1720, nearly the entire east coast of North America was in English hands, and Indian power east of the Appalachian Mountains had been broken. What had been a migrant population was now mostly American-born; economies originally based on the fur trade had become far more complex and more closely linked with the mother country; and a wide variety of political structures had been reshaped into a more uniform pattern. Yet at the same time the introduction of large-scale slavery into the Chesapeake and the Carolinas irrevocably differentiated their societies from those of the colonies to the north. Staple-crop production for the market was not the key distinguishing feature of the southern regional economies; rather, their uniqueness lay in their reliance on a system of perpetual servitude.

Meanwhile, from a small outpost in Santa Fe, New Mexico, and missions in Florida, the Spanish had expanded their influence throughout the Gulf Coast region and, by just after midcentury, as far north as California. The French had moved from a few settlements along the St. Lawrence to dominate the length of the Mississippi River and the entire Great Lakes region. Both groups of colonists lived near Indian nations and were dependent on the indigenous people's labor and goodwill. The French and Spanish could not fully control their Native American allies—and the French did not even try. The extensive Spanish and French presence to the south and west of the English settlements meant that future conflicts among the European powers in North America were nearly inevitable.

By 1720, the essential elements of the imperial administrative structure that would govern the English colonies until 1775 were firmly in place. The regional economic systems originating in the late seventeenth and early eighteenth centuries also continued to dominate North American life for another century—until after independence had been won. And Anglo-Americans had developed the commitment to autonomous local government that later would lead them into conflict with Parliament and the king.

Suggestions for Further Reading

General

Wesley Frank Craven, *The Colonies in Transition, 1660–1713* (1968); W. J. Eccles, *France in America*, rev. ed. (1990); Jack P. Greene and J. R. Pole, eds., *Colonial British America* (1984); John J. McCusker and Russell R. Menard, *The Economy of British America, 1607–1789* (1985).

New Netherland and the Restoration Colonies

Edwin Bronner, *William Penn's "Holy Experiment": The Founding of Pennsylvania, 1681–1701* (1962); Wesley Frank Craven, *New Jersey and the English Colonization of North America* (1964); Joyce Goodfriend, *Before the Melting Pot: Society and Culture in Colonial New York City, 1664–1730* (1992); Oliver Rink, *Holland on the Hudson: An Economic and Social History of Dutch New York* (1986); Robert C. Ritchie, *The Duke's Province: A Study of Politics and Society in Colonial New York, 1660–1691* (1977); Robert M. Weir, *Colonial South Carolina: A History* (1983).

Africa and the Slave Trade

Jay Coughtry, *The Notorious Triangle: Rhode Island and the African Slave Trade, 1700–1807* (1981); Philip D. Curtin, *The Atlantic Slave Trade: A Census* (1969); David Brion Davis, *The Problem of Slavery in Western Culture* (1966); Joseph Inikori and Stanley Engerman, eds., *The Atlantic Slave Trade* (1992); Herbert Klein, *The Middle Passage* (1978); Robin Law, *The Slave Coast of West*

Africa, 1550–1750: The Impact of the Atlantic Slave Trade on an African Society (1991); Daniel C. Littlefield, *Rice and Slaves: Ethnicity and the Slave Trade in Colonial South Carolina* (1981); James Rawley, *The Transatlantic Slave Trade: A History* (1981); Barbara Solow, ed., *Slavery and the Rise of the Atlantic System* (1991).

Africans in Anglo-America

T. H. Breen and Stephen Innes, *"Myne Owne Ground": Race and Freedom on Virginia's Eastern Shore, 1640–1676* (1980); Douglas Deal, *Race and Class in Colonial Virginia: Indians, Englishmen, and Africans on the Eastern Shore During the Seventeenth Century* (1993); Allan Kulikoff, *Tobacco and Slaves: The Development of Southern Cultures in the Chesapeake, 1680–1800* (1986); Edgar J. McManus, *Black Bondage in the North* (1973); Edmund S. Morgan, *American Slavery, American Freedom: The Ordeal of Colonial Virginia* (1975); Peter H. Wood, *Black Majority: Negroes in Colonial South Carolina from 1670 Through the Stono Rebellion* (1974).

European–Native American Relations in the North

Russell Bourne, *The Red King's Rebellion: Racial Politics in New England, 1675–1678* (1991); John Demos, *The Unredeemed Captive: A Family Story from Early America* (1994); Matthew Dennis, *Cultivating a Landscape of Peace: Iroquois-European Encounter in Seventeenth-Century America* (1993); Francis Jennings, *The Ambiguous Iroquois Empire* (1984); Peter Mancall, *Deadly Medicine: Indians and Alcohol in Early America* (1995); Michael Puglisi, *Puritans Beseiged: The Legacies of King Philip's War in the Massachusetts Bay Colony* (1991); Daniel Richter, *The Ordeal of the Longhouse: The Peoples of the Iroquois League in the Era of European Colonization* (1992); Daniel Richter and James Merrell, eds., *Beyond the Covenant Chain: The Iroquois and Their Neighbors in Indian America, 1600–1800* (1987); Dean Snow, *The Iroquois* (1992); Richard White, *The Middle Ground: Indians, Empires, and Republics in the Great Lakes Region, 1650–1815* (1991).

European–Native American Relations in the South and West

David H. Corkran, *The Creek Frontier, 1540–1783* (1967); Verner W. Crane, *The Southern Frontier, 1660–1732* (1929); Ramón Gutiérrez, *When Jesus Came, the Corn Mothers Went Away: Marriage, Sexuality, and Power in New Mexico, 1500–1846* (1991); Elizabeth A. H. John, *Storms Brewed in Other Men's Worlds: The Confrontation of Indians, Spanish, and French in the Southwest, 1540–1795* (1975); Andrew Knaut, *The Pueblo Revolt of 1680* (1995); James Merrell, *The Indians' New World: Catawbas and Their Neighbors from European Contact through the Era of Removal* (1989); Daniel H. Usner, Jr., *Indians, Settlers, and Slaves in a Frontier Exchange Economy: The Lower Mississippi Valley before 1783* (1992).

New England

Bernard Bailyn, *The New England Merchants in the Seventeenth Century* (1955); Richard Bushman, *From Puritan to Yankee: Character and the Social Order in Connecticut, 1690–1765* (1967); Christine Heyrman, *Commerce and Culture: The Maritime Communities of Colonial Massachusetts, 1690–1750* (1984); Richard Melvoin, *New England Outpost: War and Society in Colonial Deerfield* (1990); Robert Pope, *The Half-Way Covenant* (1969); Amanda Porterfield, *Female Piety in Puritan New England* (1991);

Laurel Thatcher Ulrich, *Good Wives: Image and Reality in the Lives of Women in Northern New England, 1650–1750* (1982).

New England Witchcraft

Paul Boyer and Stephen Nissenbaum, *Salem Possessed: The Social Origins of Witchcraft* (1974); Elaine Breslaw, *Tituba, Reluctant Witch of Salem: Devilish Indians and Puritan Fantasies* (1996); John Demos, *Entertaining Satan: Witchcraft and the Culture of Early New England* (1982); Richard Godbeer, *The Devil's Dominion: Magic and Religion in Early New England* (1992); Peter Hoffer, *The Devil's Disciples: Makers of the Salem Witchcraft Trials* (1996); Carol Karlsen, *The Devil in the Shape of a Woman: Witchcraft in Early New England* (1987); Bernard Rosenthal, *Salem Story: Reading the Witch Trials of 1692* (1993); Richard Weisman, *Witchcraft, Magic, and Religion in 17th-Century Massachusetts* (1984).

Colonial Politics

Lois Green Carr and David W. Jordan, *Maryland's Revolution of Government, 1689–1692* (1974); Richard P. Johnson, *Adjustment to Empire: The New England Colonies, 1675–1715* (1981); David S.

Lovejoy, *The Glorious Revolution in America* (1972); Jack M. Sosin, *English America and Imperial Inconstancy: The Rise of Provincial Autonomy, 1696–1715* (1985); Jack M. Sosin, *English America and the Restoration Monarchy of Charles II* (1980); Jack M. Sosin, *English America and the Revolution of 1688* (1982).

Imperial Trade and Administration

Robert M. Bliss, *Revolution and Empire: English Politics and the American Colonies in the Seventeenth Century* (1991); Lawrence W. Harper, *The English Navigation Laws: A Seventeenth-Century Experiment in Social Engineering* (1939); Marcus Rediker, *Between the Devil and the Deep Blue Sea: Merchant Seamen, Pirates, and the Anglo-American Maritime World, 1700–1750* (1987); Robert C. Ritchie, *Captain Kidd and the War Against the Pirates* (1986); I. K. Steele, *Politics of Colonial Policy: The Board of Trade in Colonial Administration* (1968); Stephen Saunders Webb, *Lord Churchill's Coup: The Anglo-American Empire and the Glorious Revolution Reconsidered* (1995); Stephen Saunders Webb, *1676: The End of American Independence* (1984); Stephen Saunders Webb, *The Governors-General: The English Army and the Definition of the Empire, 1569–1681* (1979).

4

Growth and Diversity
1720–1770

Maturina, a free black resident of New Orleans, awoke with a start at 3 A.M. on June 2 to the shouts of her neighbor, a slave woman named Louisa. "Maturina, someone has stolen your hens!" Louisa yelled. Leaping from her bed, Maturina ran to investigate, accompanied by her son and her brother Nicolas. They quickly located three of the hens, which had escaped from the robber's grasp, but could search no more until daylight.

Maturina knew where to look for missing chickens. At dawn, she and her relatives went to the city market on the levee (river bank), where they soon encountered a man carrying three fowls they recognized as hers. By threatening him with prosecution, they extracted the information that he had purchased the hens from a French grocer named La Rochelle. So the three confronted La Rochelle at his hut, where they found yet another of the birds. Under their questioning, the grocer reluctantly admitted that "it was a negro who had brought them to him to sell," informing Maturina and Nicolas "that he must be on the levee, or in some of the huts."

Suspicious, Maturina searched La Rochelle's own hut, rousting out the thief, who was hiding within. He tried to escape, but Nicolas pursued and captured him. Brought before the authorities, the thief proved to be Juan, a runaway slave from the countryside. The official investigation revealed that several times in the previous month Juan had successfully sold other stolen poultry at the levee market.

That much of the action in the story of Maturina, Nicolas, and Juan took place on the Mississippi River levee is not surprising. In the mid-eighteenth century, the crude market centered there was as much a focal point of New Orleans as were its formal government buildings. (The theft occurred in 1782, when New Orleans was ruled by Spain [see page 125], but the same events could have happened at any time in

More than fifty years after Maturina found her missing chickens at the New Orleans market (see vignette), Benjamin Henry Latrobe sketched these "Market Folks" buying and selling goods on the levee. Maturina would have recognized this scene, even though it occurred in 1819. African-Americans, European-Americans, and Native Americans all actively participated in market exchanges in both eras. *Maryland Historical Society, Baltimore.*

the preceding three decades.) To the levee came Indian traders, French and German farmers, free and enslaved Africans—all intent on buying and selling. One contemporary observed in 1761 that the Germans' Saturday morning market on the levee supplied the city with "cabbages, salads, fruits, greens . . . as well as vast quantities of wildfowl, salt pork, and many excellent sorts of fish." About 2,000 people, or one-fourth of the population of Louisiana, lived in New Orleans in 1763, and they regularly mingled at the levee market.

The lively markets in New Orleans and Anglo-American cities such as Boston and Philadelphia illuminate several key themes of colonial development in the mid-eighteenth century: population growth, ethnic diversity, the increasing importance of colonial urban centers, the creation of an urban elite that purchased food and clothing from other colonists, rising levels of consumption for all social ranks, and the new significance of internal markets. In the French and English mainland colonies, exports continued to dominate the economy. Settlers along the Atlantic and Gulf of Mexico coasts were tied to an international commercial system that fluctuated wildly for reasons having little to do with the colonies but inescapable in their effects. Yet expanding local populations demanded greater quantities and types of goods, and Europe could not supply all those needs. Therefore, in English and French America, as well as in the northern portions of New Spain known as the Borderlands (where exports were never an important element of the economy), colonists came increasingly to depend on exploiting and consuming their own resources.

Ethnic diversity was especially pronounced in the small colonial cities, but even the countryside attracted settlers from a wide range of nations. For example, an Englishman traveling in the vicinity of New Orleans in 1770 encountered not merely the French, Indian, and African residents one might expect, but also Germans, Acadians (see page 124), Irish, Scots, a native of the Spanish island of Minorca, a Slav, and several Anglo-Americans. The Spanish Borderlands and rural New England were the only exceptions; they attracted few new migrants of any description, their population growth stemming entirely from natural increase. The middle and southern Anglo-American colonies attracted by far the largest number of newcomers, both free and enslaved. Their arrival not only swelled the total population but also altered political balances and affected the religious climate by introducing new sects.

The ruling elites in the colonies paid little heed to the newcomers. In New France and New Spain, ordinary settlers were already denied any voice in their government, but even in English America elected and appointed leaders often refused to allow recent migrants from Europe adequate representation and government services. A series of violent clashes ensued after midcentury. By that time, native-born elites dominated the English colonies and contended with governors and other officials born in the mother country for control of the government machinery.

Intermarried webs of wealthy families developed in each of Europe's American possessions by the 1760s. Such well-off, educated colonists participated in transatlantic intellectual communities, whereas many colonists of the "lesser sort" could neither read nor write. The elites lived in comfortable houses and enjoyed leisure-time activities. Most colonists, whether free or enslaved, struggled just to survive, working daily from dawn to dark. Such divisions were most pronounced in British America, the largest and most prosperous settlements on the continent. By the last half of the century, the social and economic distance among different ranks of Anglo-Americans had widened noticeably.

Wealthy Anglo-Americans in particular were heavily influenced by the Enlightenment, the prevailing European intellectual movement of the day. The Enlightenment stressed reason and empirical knowledge, deliberately discarding superstition and instinct as guides to human behavior. Enlightened thinkers saw God as a distant presence who had ordered the world, setting forth natural laws that humans could discover through careful investigation and logical thought. From this perspective grew a distaste for emotion of any sort. Thus the religious revival known as the Great Awakening, which erupted in the English colonies in the 1740s, aroused much opposition from elites, because that revival drew primarily on the Calvinistic concept of a God that people could never fully comprehend. To a believer in the primacy of reason, the passions of the newly "awakened" were incomprehensible.

In 1720, much of the North American continent still fell under Indian control. By 1770, in sharp contrast, settlements of Europeans and Africans ruled by Great Britain filled almost all of the region between the Appalachian Mountains and the Atlantic Ocean; and the British, thanks to their victory over France in the Seven Years War (see pages 124–125), dominated the extensive system of rivers and lakes

• *Important Events* •

1690	Locke's *Essay Concerning Human Understanding* published, a key example of Enlightenment thought		**1741**	New York City "conspiracy" reflects whites' continuing fears of slave revolts
1720–40	Black population of Chesapeake begins to grow by natural increase, contributing to rise of large plantations		**1760s**	Baptist congregations take root in Virginia
			1760–75	Peak of eighteenth-century European and African migration to English colonies
1739	Stono Rebellion (South Carolina) leads to increased white fears of slave revolts		**1765–66**	Hudson River land riots pit tenants and squatters against large landlords
	George Whitefield arrives in America; Great Awakening broadens		**1767–69**	Regulator movement (South Carolina) tries to establish order in back country
1739–48	King George's War disrupts American economy		**1771**	North Carolina Regulators defeated by eastern militia at Battle of Alamance

running through the heart of the continent. Spanish missions extended in a great arc from present-day northern California to the Gulf Coast. Such geographic, economic, and social changes transformed the character of Europe's North American possessions.

Population Growth and Ethnic Diversity

One of the most striking characteristics of the English mainland colonies in the eighteenth century was their rapid population growth. Only about 250,000 European- and African-Americans resided in the colonies in 1700. Thirty years later, that number had more than doubled, and by 1775 it had become 2.5 million. Such rapid expansion appears even more remarkable when compared to the modest changes that occurred in Louisiana, New Mexico, California, and Texas. By the last quarter of the eighteenth century, Texas had only about 2,500 Spanish residents and California even fewer; the largest Spanish colony, New Mexico, included just 20,000 or so. The total European population of New France expanded from approximately 15,000 in 1700 to about 70,000 in the 1760s, but only along the St. Lawrence River between Quebec and Montréal and in New Orleans were there significant concentrations of French settlers.

Although migration accounted for a considerable share of the growth in English America, most of the growth resulted from natural increase. Once the difficult early decades of settlement had passed, the American population doubled approximately every twenty-five years. Such a rate of growth was unparalleled in human history until very recent times. It had a variety of causes, chief among them women's youthful age at the onset of childbearing (early twenties for Europeans, late teens for Africans). Since married women became pregnant every two or three years, women normally bore five to ten children. Because the colonies were healthful places to live (especially north of Virginia), a large proportion of children who survived infancy reached maturity and began families of their own. As a result, about half of the American population was under sixteen years old in 1775. (By contrast, only about one-third of the American population was under sixteen in 1990.)

Africans (about 278,000) constituted the largest racial or ethnic group that came to the mainland English colonies during the eighteenth century.

Newcomers from Africa and Europe In the slaveholding societies of South America and the Caribbean, a surplus of males over females and appallingly high mortality rates meant that only a large, continuing flow of enslaved Africans could maintain the captive work force at constant levels. South Carolina, where rice cultivation was difficult and unhealthy (chiefly because malaria-carrying mosquitoes bred in the rice swamps), and where planters preferred to purchase men, bore some resemblance to such colonies because it too required an inflow of Africans to sustain as well as expand its labor force. But in the Chesapeake the number of black residents grew especially

"Rachel Weeping" by Charles Willson Peale conveys as few other colonial portraits can the affection of eighteenth-century parents for their children and the grief they felt when those children died (as was so often the case) at an early age. Peale movingly revealed his wife's sorrow at the death of their daughter; thus his painting helps to refute the interpretation—advanced by some historians—that high levels of infant mortality led colonists to avoid becoming too attached to their young children. Philadelphia Museum of Art, the Barra Foundation.

rapidly, because the new African workers were added to a population that began to sustain itself through natural increase after 1740.

The offspring of slaves were also slaves, whereas the children of servants were free. The consequences of this important difference between enslaved and indentured labor were not clear until after 1720. It then became evident that a planter who owned adult female slaves could watch the size of his labor force increase steadily—through the births of their children—without making additional major investments in workers. Not coincidentally, the first truly large Chesapeake plantations appeared in the 1740s. Some years later, the slaveholder Thomas Jefferson indicated that he fully understood the connections when he declared, "I consider a woman who brings a child every two years more profitable than the best man of the farm. What she produces is an addition to the capital, while his labors disappear in mere consumption."

In addition to the new group of Africans, about 585,000 Europeans moved to North America during the eighteenth century, most of them after 1730 (see maps, page 95). Because some of these migrants (for example, convicts sentenced to exile by English courts) and all the slaves did not freely choose to come to the colonies, approximately one-third of the newcomers moved to America against their will. That contrasts sharply with later voluntary migrations from Europe, Asia, and the Americas in the nineteenth and twentieth centuries.

One of the largest groups of immigrants—nearly 150,000—came from Ireland or Scotland. About 66,000 were Scots-Irish, descended from Presbyterian Scots who had settled in the north of Ireland during the seventeenth century.

Scots-Irish, Germans, and Scots

Some 35,000 people came directly to America from Scotland. Another 43,000, both Protestants and Catholics, migrated from southern Ireland. Fleeing economic distress and (in Ireland) religious discrimination, they were also lured by hopes of obtaining land. Scots, Irish, and Scots-Irish immigrants usually landed in Philadelphia. They moved west and south, settling chiefly in Pennsylvania, Maryland, Virginia, and the Carolinas. Frequently unable to afford any acreage, they squatted on land belonging to Indians, land speculators, or colonial governments.

Migrants from Germany numbered about 85,000. Most emigrated from the Rhineland between 1730 and 1755, also usually arriving in Philadelphia. They became known locally as Pennsylvania Dutch (a corruption of *Deutsch*, as the Germans called themselves); late in the century they and their descendants accounted for one-third of Pennsylvania's residents. But many other Germans moved west and then south along the eastern slope of the Appalachian Mountains, eventually finding homes in western Maryland and Virginia. Others sailed first to Charleston or Savannah and settled in the interior of South Carolina or Georgia, often initially living under very difficult conditions, as is evident in the drawing on page 96. The Germans belonged to a wide variety of Protestant sects—primarily Lutheran, German Reformed, and Moravian—and therefore added to the already substantial religious diversity of the middle colonies.

The most concentrated period of immigration to the colonies fell between 1760 and 1775. Tough times in Germany and the British Isles led many to

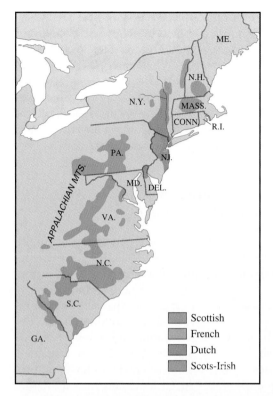
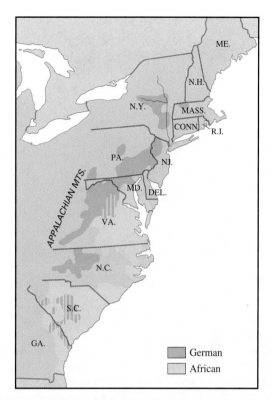

Non-English Ethnic Groups in the British Colonies, c. 1775 *Non-African immigrants arriving in the years after 1720 were pushed to the peripheries of settlement, as is shown by these maps. Scottish, Scots-Irish, French, and German newcomers had to move to the frontiers. The Dutch remained where they had originally settled in the seventeenth century. Africans were concentrated in coastal plantation regions.*

decide to seek a better life in America; simultaneously, the slave trade burgeoned. In those fifteen years alone arrived more than 220,000 persons—or nearly 10 percent of the entire population of British North America in 1775. Late-arriving free immigrants had little choice but to remain in the cities or move to the edges of settlement; land elsewhere was fully occupied. In the peripheries they became the tenants of, or bought property from, land speculators who had purchased giant tracts in the (usually vain) hope of making a fortune.

Because of these migration patterns and the concentration of slaveholding in the South, half of the colonial population south of New England was of non-English origin by 1775. Whether the migrants assimilated readily into Anglo-American culture depended on patterns of settlement, the size of the group, and the strength of the migrants' ties to their common culture. For example, the Huguenots—French Protestants who fled religious persecution in their homeland after

Effects of Ethnic Diversity

1685—settled in tiny enclaves in American cities like Charleston and New York. They were unable to sustain either their language or their religious practices, and within two generations they were almost wholly absorbed into Anglo-American culture. By contrast, the equally small group of colonial Jews maintained a distinct identity. Most Jews in early America were Sephardic—that is, they were descended from the group of Jews who had escaped persecution in Spain and Portugal by migrating to the Netherlands and later to Dutch colonies in the New World. In a few cities—notably New York and Newport, Rhode Island—they established synagogues and worked actively to preserve their culture (for example, by opposing intermarriage with Christians).

Members of the larger groups of migrants (Germans, Irish, and Scots) found it easier to sustain Old World ways. Countless localities were settled almost exclusively by one group or another. Near Frederick, Maryland, a visitor would have heard more German than English; in Anson and Cumberland Counties, North Carolina, the same visitor might have

The first German immigrants in Georgia lived in crude shelters they erected in the wilderness at the settlement they named New Ebenezer. Notice the similarity to the structures inhabited by the Indians of the region, illustrated in a painting by the same artist, Philip Georg Friedrich von Reck, on page 77.   The Royal Library, Copenhagen.

thought she was in Scotland. Where migrants from different countries settled in the same region, ethnic antagonisms often surfaced. One German clergyman, for example, explained his efforts to prevent German youths from marrying people of different ethnic origins by asserting that the Scots-Irish were "lazy, dissipated and poor" and that "it is very seldom that German and English blood is happily united in wedlock."

Recognizing the benefits of keeping other racial and ethnic groups divided, the English elites on occasion deliberately fostered such antagonisms. When the targets of their policies were European migrants, the goal was the maintenance of political and economic power. When the targets were Indians and Africans, as they were in South Carolina, the stakes were considerably higher. In 1758 one official reported, "It has been allways the policy of this government to create an aversion in them [Indians] to Negroes." South Carolinians of English origin, a minority of the population, wanted to prevent Indians and Africans from making common cause against them. To keep slaves from running away to join the Indians, Anglo-Americans hired Indians as slave catchers. To keep Indians from trusting Africans, slaves were employed as soldiers in Indian wars.

The elites probably would have preferred to ignore the English colonies' growing racial and ethnic diversity, but they could not do so for long and still maintain their power. When such men decided to lead a revolution in the 1770s, they recognized that they needed the support of non-English Americans. Quite deliberately, they then began to speak of "the rights of man," rather than "English liberties," when they sought recruits for their cause.

Economic Growth and Development

The dramatic increase in the population of Anglo-America served as a source of stability for the colonial economy and provided a firm basis for further growth. Again, a comparison to French and Spanish America reveals significant differences. The population and economy of New Spain's Borderlands stagnated. The isolated settlements produced few items for export (notably, hides and skins, most obtained through trade with Indians); residents were more likely to exchange goods illegally with their French and English neighbors than with the distant centers of Spanish Mexico or the Caribbean. French Canada exported large quantities of furs and fish, but monopolistic trade practices ensured that most of the profits ended up in the home country. The Louisiana colony required substantial government subsidies to survive, despite its active internal trade and some agricultural exports such as tobacco and rice. Of France's American possessions, only the Caribbean islands flourished economically.

British, French, and Spanish Colonies Compared

In British North America, by contrast, each year the rising population generated ever-greater demands for goods and services, which led to the development of small-scale colonial manufacturing and a complex network of internal trade. As the area of settlement expanded, roads, bridges, mills, and stores were built to serve the new communities. A lively coastal trade developed; by the late 1760s, 54 percent of the vessels leaving Boston harbor were sailing to other mainland colonies rather than to foreign ports. Such ships not only collected goods for export and distributed imports but also sold items made in America. The colonies thus began to move away from their earlier pattern of near total dependence on Europe for manufactured goods. For the

Who Moved to America from England and Scotland in the Early 1770s, and Why?

	English Emigrants	Scottish Emigrants	Free American Population
Destination			
13 British colonies	81.1%	92.7%	—
Canada	12.1%	4.2%	—
West Indies	6.8%	3.1%	—
Age Distribution			
Under 21	26.8%	45.3%	56.8%
21–25	37.1%	19.9%	9.7%
26–44	33.3%	29.5%	20.4%
45 and over	2.7%	5.3%	13.1%
Sex Distribution			
Male	83.8%	59.9%	—
Female	16.2%	40.1%	—
Unknown	4.2%	13.5%	—
Traveling Alone or with Families			
In families	20.0%	48.0%	—
Alone	80.0%	52.0%	—
Known Occupation or Status			
Gentry	2.5%	1.2%	—
Merchandising	5.2%	5.2%	—
Agriculture	17.8%	24.0%	—
Artisanry	54.2%	37.7%	—
Laborer	20.3%	31.9%	—
Why They Left			
Positive reasons (e.g., desire to better one's position)	90.0%	36.0%	—
Negative reasons (e.g., poverty, unemployment)	10.0%	64.0%	—

Source of data: Bernard Bailyn, *Voyagers to the West* (New York: Knopf, 1986), Tables 4.1, 5.2, 5.4, 5.7, 5.23, and 6.1.

Note: Between December 1773 and March 1776, the British government questioned individuals and families leaving ports in Scotland and England for the American colonies to learn who they were, where they were going, and why they were leaving. This table summarizes just a few of the findings of the official inquiries, which revealed a number of significant differences between the Scottish and English emigrants.

How do historians know that the residents of colonial North America began to purchase luxury items in the eighteenth century and that those goods came from wide-ranging trade networks? Probate inventories—written records of what people possessed at the time of their deaths—are a useful documentary source. But perhaps even more revealing are the results of archaeological excavations at the sites of colonial settlements. The shards shown below were found at one of the first French outposts in Louisiana—Old Mobile, established in 1702 on Mobile Bay, in what is now Alabama. The pots, of which only these small pieces remain (see the complete example), represent the final stage in a long trade route originating in China. The Chinese sold ceramics to traders in the Philippines, which Spain controlled, in exchange for Mexican silver. Spanish ships then carried the porcelain across the Pacific to Mexico, where it was purchased at annual fairs in Acapulco, carried by mule train across Mexico to Vera Cruz, then shipped to Caribbean ports and to Spain itself. The three hundred or so residents of Old Mobile bought such items from the Spanish settlement at Pensacola in nearby Florida. A brief description in an inventory could not convey so much information nearly as vividly as do these small bits of pottery.   Fragments: The Magazine Antiques. Pot: The Metropolitan Museum of Art.

first time, the American population was generating sufficient demand to encourage manufacturing enterprises. The largest indigenous industry was iron making; by 1775, 82 American furnaces and 175 forges were producing more iron than was England itself. Almost all of that iron was for domestic consumption.

The major energizing, yet destabilizing, influence on the colonial economy nevertheless remained foreign trade. Colonial prosperity still depended heavily on overseas demand for American products like tobacco, rice, indigo, fish, and barrel staves; the sale of such items earned the colonists the credit they needed to purchase English and European imports. If demand for American exports slowed, the colonists' income dropped and so did their ability to buy imported goods. Merchants were particularly vulnerable to economic downswings, and bankruptcies were common.

Despite fluctuations, the economy grew slowly during the eighteenth century. That growth, which resulted in part from Americans' higher earnings

Growth of Consumption

from their exports, in turn produced better standards of living for all property-owning Americans. In the first two decades of the century, as the price of British manufactures fell in relation to Americans' incomes, households began to acquire amenities such as chairs and earthenware dishes. Diet also improved as trading networks brought access to more varied foodstuffs. After 1750, luxury items like silver plate could be found in the homes of the wealthy, and the "middling sort" started to purchase imported English ceramics and teapots. Even the poorest property owners had more and better household possessions. Thus the colonists became *consumers*, in the sense that for the first time they could make choices among a wide variety of products and also could afford to buy items not absolutely essential for survival and subsistence.

Yet the benefits of economic growth were not evenly distributed: wealthy Americans improved their position relative to other colonists. The native-born elite families who dominated American political, economic, and social life by 1750 were those who had begun the century with sufficient capital to take advantage of the changes caused by population growth. They were the urban merchants who exported raw materials and imported luxury goods, the large landowners who rented small farms to immigrant tenants, the slave traders who supplied equally wealthy planters with their bondspeople, and the owners of rum distilleries. The rise of this group of moneyed families helped to make the social and economic structure of mid-eighteenth-century America more stratified than before.

New arrivals did not have the opportunities for advancement that had greeted their predecessors. Even so, there seems to have been relatively little severe poverty among free settlers in rural areas, where 90 percent of the colonists lived. But in the cities, the story was different. Families of urban laborers lived on the edge of desti-

Urban Poverty

tution. In Philadelphia, for instance, a male laborer's average annual earnings fell short of the amount needed to supply his family with the bare necessities. Even in a good year, his wife or children had to do wage work; in a bad year, the family could be reduced to beggary. By the 1760s public urban poor-relief systems were overwhelmed with applicants for assistance, and some cities began to build workhouses or almshouses to shelter the growing number of poor people. Among them were recent immigrants, the elderly and infirm, and widows, especially those with small children.

Within this overall picture, it is important to distinguish among the various regions: New England, the middle colonies, the Chesapeake, and the Lower South (the Carolinas and Georgia). Each region of the colonies had its own economic rhythm derived from the nature of its export trade.

In New England, three elements combined to influence economic development: the nature of the landscape, New England's leadership in colonial

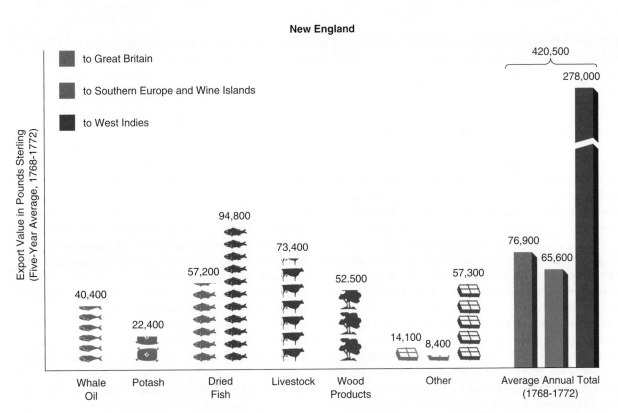

Regional Trading Patterns: New England *New England's major exports—dried fish, livestock, and wood products—were sold primarily in the West Indies.* Source: James F. Shepherd and Gary M. Walton, *Shipping, Maritime Trade, and the Economic Development of Colonial North America* (Cambridge: Cambridge University Press, 1972). Copyright 1972. Used by permission of Cambridge University Press.

Middle Colonies

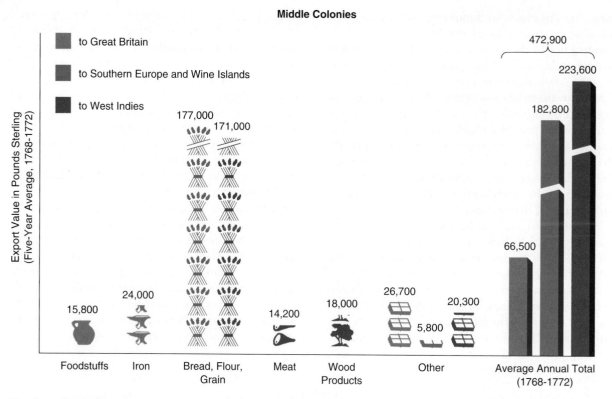

Regional Trading Patterns: Middle Colonies   The middle colonies' major trading partners were the West Indies, the Wine Islands, and southern Europe. Bread, flour, and grains were the region's most valuable exports.   Source: James F. Shepherd and Gary M. Walton, *Shipping, Maritime Trade, and the Economic Development of Colonial North America* (Cambridge: Cambridge University Press, 1972). Copyright 1972. Used by permission of Cambridge University Press.

New England and King George's War

shipping, and the impact of imperial wars. New England's poor soil did not produce salable surpluses other than livestock, so wood products constituted a major cash crop. Farms were worked primarily by family members; the region had relatively few hired laborers. It also had the lowest average wealth per freeholder in the colonies. But New England had many wealthy men: merchants and professionals whose income was drawn from trade with the West Indies in items such as dried fish, livestock, and molasses.

Boston, by the 1730s a major shipbuilding center, soon felt the effects when warfare resumed in 1739. British vessels clashed with Spanish ships in the Caribbean, setting off a conflict that became known in America as King George's War. Nominally the war was fought to determine who would sit on the Austrian throne (in Europe it was called the War of the Austrian Succession), but one of its causes was

European commercial rivalries in the Americas, as nations jockeyed for position in the lucrative West Indian trade. The war's first impact on Boston's economy was positive. Ships—and sailors—were in great demand to serve as privateers (privately owned vessels authorized by the British to capture the enemy's commercial shipping). Wealthy merchants became even wealthier by profiting from contracts to supply military expeditions.

But Boston suffered heavy losses of manpower in Caribbean battles and in forays against the French in Canada. The most successful expedition was also the most costly. In 1745 a Massachusetts force captured the French fortress of Louisbourg (in modern Nova Scotia), which guarded the sea lanes leading to New France. Afterward, though, Massachusetts had to levy heavy taxes on its residents to pay for the expensive effort. For decades Boston's economy felt the continuing effects of King George's War. The city was left with unprecedented numbers of widows and children on its relief rolls. The boom in shipbuilding ended when the war did, and taxes remained high. As a final blow to the colony, Britain gave Louisbourg back to France in the Treaty of Aix-la-Chapelle (1748).

The middle colonies were more positively affected by King George's War and its aftermath because of the greater fertility of the soil in New York and Pennsylvania, where commercial farming was the norm.

Prosperity of the Middle Colonies

An average Pennsylvania farm family consumed only 40 percent of what it produced, selling the rest. New York and New Jersey both had many tenant farmers, who rented acreage from large landowners and often paid their rental fees by sharing crops with their landlords. Prosperous landlords and farmers were thus in an ideal position to profit from the wartime demand for grain and meat, especially in the West Indies. After the war a series of poor grain harvests in Europe

caused flour prices to rise rapidly. Philadelphia and New York, which could draw on large fertile grain- and livestock-producing areas, took the lead in the foodstuffs trade. Meanwhile, Boston, which had no such fertile hinterland, found its economy stagnating.

Increased European demand for grain had a significant impact on the Chesapeake as well. After 1745, when the price of grain began rising faster than that of tobacco, some Chesapeake planters began to convert tobacco fields to wheat and corn. By diversifying their crops, they could avoid dependency on one product for their income. Tobacco still ruled the region and remained the largest single export from the mainland colonies. (The value of tobacco exports was nearly double that of grain products, the next contender.) Yet the conversion to grain cultivation brought about the first significant

Change in the Chesapeake

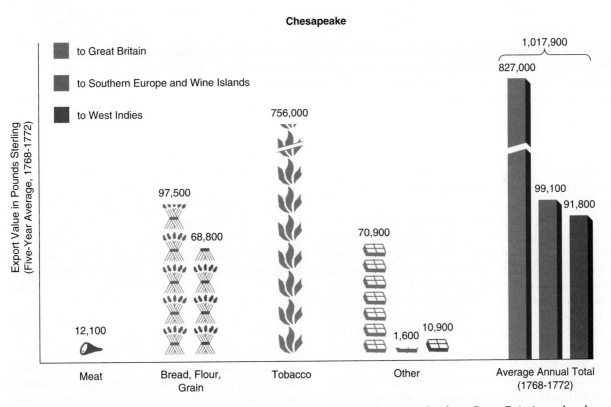

Regional Trading Patterns: The Chesapeake *Tobacco—legally exported only to Great Britain under the terms of the Navigation Acts—was the Chesapeake's dominant product. Grain made up an increasing proportion of the crops this region sold to other destinations.* Source: James F. Shepherd and Gary M. Walton, *Shipping, Maritime Trade, and the Economic Development of Colonial North America* (Cambridge: Cambridge University Press, 1972). Copyright 1972. Used by permission of Cambridge University Press.

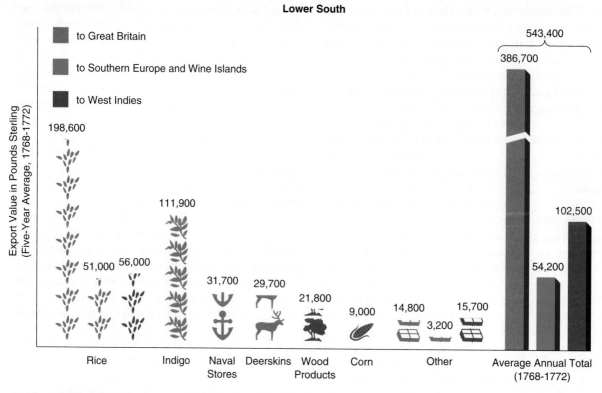

Regional Trading Patterns: The Lower South *Rice and indigo, sold primarily in the mother country, dominated the exports of the Lower South.* Source: James F. Shepherd and Gary M. Walton, *Shipping, Maritime Trade, and the Economic Development of Colonial North America* (Cambridge: Cambridge University Press, 1972). Copyright 1972. Used by permission of Cambridge University Press.

change in Chesapeake settlement patterns by encouraging the development of port towns (like Baltimore) to house the merchants who marketed the new products.

Like the Chesapeake, the Lower South depended on staple crops and an enslaved labor force, but its pattern of economic growth was distinctive.

Trade and the Lower South

In contrast to tobacco prices, which rose slowly through the middle decades of the century, rice prices climbed steeply, doubling by the late 1730s. The sharp rise was caused primarily by heavy demand for rice in southern Europe. Because Parliament removed rice from the list of enumerated products (see page 83) in 1730, South Carolinians were able to do what colonial tobacco planters never could: trade directly with continental Europe. But dependence on European sales had its drawbacks, as rice growers discovered at the outbreak of King George's War in 1739. Trade with the European continent was dis-

rupted, rice prices plummeted, and South Carolina entered a depression from which it did not emerge for a decade. Still, prosperity returned by the 1760s because of rapidly rising European demand for South Carolina's exports; indeed, the Lower South experienced more rapid economic growth in that period than did the other regions of the colonies. Partly as a result, it had the highest average wealth per freeholder in Anglo-America by the time of the American Revolution.

Although King George's War at first helped New England and hurt the Lower South, in the long run those effects were reversed. In the Chesapeake and the middle colonies, the war ushered in a long period of prosperity. These variations in economic experience point up a crucial fact about the English mainland colonies: they did not compose a unified whole. They were linked economically into regions, but they had few political or social ties beyond or even within those regions. Despite the growing coastal trade, the individual colonies' economic fortunes depended not on their neighbors in America but rather on the shifting markets of Europe and the West Indies. Had it not been for an unprecedented crisis in the British imperial system (discussed in Chapter 5), it is hard to see how they could have been persuaded to join in a common endeavor. Even with that impetus, they found unity difficult to maintain.

Colonial Cultures

Genteel Culture

A seventeenth-century resident of England's American possessions miraculously transported to 1750 would have been surprised not only by the denser and more diverse population but also by what the historian Richard Bushman has termed "the refinement of America." Those colonists who acquired wealth through trade, agriculture, or manufacturing spent their money ostentatiously, dressing at the height of fashion, traveling in horse-drawn carriages driven by uniformed servants, and entertaining each other at lavish parties. Most notably, they built large houses containing rooms specifically designed for such forms of socializing as dancing, cardplaying, or drinking tea. Sufficiently well-off to enjoy "leisure" time (a first for North America), they attended concerts and the theater, gambled at horse races, and played billiards and other games. They also cultivated polite manners, adopting stylized forms of address and paying attention to "proper" ways of behaving. Although the effects of accumulated wealth were most pronounced in Anglo-America, elite families in New Mexico, Louisiana, and Quebec as well, set themselves off from the "lesser sort." Together these wealthy families deliberately constructed a genteel culture quite different from that of the seventeenth-century colonies or of ordinary colonists in their own day.

Men from such families prided themselves not only on their possessions and on their positions in the colonial political, social, and economic hierarchy,

Education and the Enlightenment

but also on their level of education and their intellectual connections to Europe. Many had been tutored by private teachers hired by their families; some even attended college in Europe or America. (Harvard, the first colonial college, founded in 1636, was joined by William and Mary in 1693, Yale in 1701, and later by several others—for example, Princeton, established in 1747.) In the seventeenth century, only aspiring clergymen attended college, and their studies focused heavily on ancient languages and theology. But by the mid-eighteenth century, colleges broadened their curricula to include courses on mathematics, the natural sciences, law, and medicine. Accordingly, young men from elite

The profits earned by tobacco planters with large holdings of land and slaves enabled them to buy luxurious items unimaginable to earlier colonists. This handpainted ivory fan and elaborate gold and enamel watch belonged to female members of the Byrd family of Virginia in the mid-eighteenth century. Watch: Virginia Historical Society. Fan: Virginia Historical Society.

Nabby Martin, an eighteenth-century girl living in Providence, depicted in her needlework sampler buildings representing higher education (University Hall at Brown University) and politics (the Rhode Island State House). Ironically, she was excluded from participating in both on account of her sex. Museum of Art, Rhode Island School of Design, Providence, R.I.

or upwardly mobile families enrolled in college to study for careers other than the ministry. American women, though, were uniformly excluded from advanced education. The only exceptions were some of the young women who joined convents in Canada or Louisiana; a few were able to engage in sustained study within the convent walls.

The learned clergymen who headed colonial colleges in the eighteenth century were deeply affected by the intellectual current known as the Enlightenment. About the middle of the previous century, some European thinkers began to analyze nature in an effort to determine the laws that govern the universe. They employed experimentation and abstract reasoning to discover general principles behind phenomena such as the motions of planets and

stars, the behavior of falling objects, and the characteristics of light and sound. Above all, Enlightenment philosophers emphasized acquiring knowledge through reason, taking particular delight in challenging previously unquestioned assumptions. John Locke's *Essay Concerning Human Understanding* (1690), for example, disputed the notion that human beings are born already imprinted with innate ideas. All knowledge, Locke asserted, derives from one's observations of the external world.

The Enlightenment had an enormous impact on educated, well-to-do people in Europe and America. It supplied them with a common vocabulary and a unified view of the world, one that insisted that the enlightened eighteenth century was better than all previous ages. It joined them in a common endeavor, the effort to make sense of God's orderly creation. Thus American naturalists like John and William Bartram supplied European scientists with information about New World plants and animals so that they could be included in newly formulated universal classification systems. So, too, Americans interested in astronomy took part in an international effort to learn about the solar system by studying a rare occurrence, the transit of Venus across the face of the sun in 1769.

Enlightenment rationalism affected politics as well as science. Locke's *Two Treatises of Government* (1691) and other works by French and Scottish philosophers challenged previous concepts of a divinely sanctioned political order. Governments, declared Locke, were created by men and so could be altered by them. If a ruler broke his contract with the people and did not protect their rights, he could legitimately be ousted from power by peaceful—or even violent—means. The aim of government was the good of the people, Enlightenment theorists proclaimed. A proper political order could prevent the rise of tyrants; even the power of monarchs was subject to God's natural laws.

Yet the world in which such ideas were discussed was that of the few, not the many. Most residents of North America did not know how to read or write.

Oral Cultures   Even those with basic literacy skills—a small proportion in French or Spanish America, about half of the people in British America—were familiar only with the rudiments. Books were scarce and expensive (the one book households tended to own was the Bible), and ordinary folk rarely had occasion to write a letter. Public schools supported by tax levies were few and far between, even in such colonies as Massachusetts, which nominally required towns to provide schooling for local children. European youngsters who learned to read usually did so in their own homes, taught by their parents or older siblings. A few months at a private "dame school" run by a literate local widow might complete their education by teaching them the basics of writing and simple arithmetic. Enslaved African-American children were denied even that level of learning; teaching slaves to read and write was forbidden as too subversive of the social order. And only the most zealous Indian converts were taught Europeans' literacy skills.

Thus the cultures of colonial North America were primarily oral, communal, and—at least through the first half of the eighteenth century—intensely local. In the absence of literacy, the major means of communication was face-to-face conversation. Information tended to travel slowly and within relatively confined regions. Different locales developed divergent cultural traditions, and racial and ethnic variations heightened those differences. Public rituals served as the chief means through which the colonists forged their cultural identities.

Attendance at church was perhaps the most important such ritual. In Congregational (Puritan) churches, seating was assigned by church leaders to reflect standing in the community. In early New England, men

Religious Rituals

and women sat on opposite sides of a central aisle, arranged in ranks according to age, wealth, and church membership. By the mid-eighteenth century, wealthy men and their wives sat in privately owned pews; their children, servants, and the less fortunate were still seated in sex-segregated fashion at the rear or sides of the church. In eighteenth-century Virginia, seating in Anglican parishes also conformed to the local status hierarchy. Planter families purchased their own pews, and in some parishes landed gentlemen customarily strode into church as a group just before the service, deliberately drawing attention to their exalted position. In the city of Quebec, Catholic feast days were celebrated by formal processions of men into the parish church; each participant's rank determined his placement in the procession. By contrast, Quaker meetinghouses in Pennsylvania and elsewhere used an egalitarian but sex-segregated seating system. The rituals surrounding people's entrance into and seating in colonial churches, in other words, symbolized their place in society and the values of the local community.

Communal culture centered on the civic sphere as well. In New England, colonial governments proclaimed official days of thanksgiving (for good harvests, victories in war, and so forth) and days of fasting and prayer (when the colony was experiencing difficulties such as droughts or epidemics). Everyone was expected to participate in the public rituals held in churches on such occasions. Monthly militia musters (known as training days) also brought the community together, since all able-bodied men between the ages of sixteen and sixty were members of the militia.

Civic Rituals

In the Chesapeake, important cultural rituals occurred on court and election days. When the county court was in session, men would come from miles around to file suits, appear as witnesses, serve as jurors, or simply observe the goings-on. Attendance at court functioned as a method of civic education; from watching the proceedings men learned what behavior their neighbors expected of them. Elections served the same purpose, for freeholders voted in public. An election official, often flanked by the candidates for the office in question, would call each man forward to declare his preference. The voter would then be thanked politely by the gentleman for whom he had cast his oral ballot. Traditionally, the candidates treated their supporters to rum at nearby taverns.

Everywhere in colonial North America, the public punishment of criminals served not just to humiliate the offender but also to remind the community of proper standards of behavior. Public hangings and whippings expressed the community's outrage about crimes and restored harmony to its ranks. Judges often assigned penalties that shamed miscreants in especially appropriate ways. In San Antonio, Texas, for example, one cattle thief was sentenced to be led through the town's streets "with the entrails hanging from his neck"; and when a New Mexico man assaulted his father-in-law, he was directed not merely to pay medical expenses but also to kneel before him and to beg his forgiveness publicly, in front of the entire community. New Englanders who were convicted of capital offenses but not hanged did not thereby escape public humiliation: frequently they were ordered to wear nooses around their necks for years as a constant reminder to themselves, their families, and their neighbors of their heinous violation of community norms.

The wide availability of consumer goods after the early years of the eighteenth century fostered

Convicted criminals were publicly punished and shamed in front of their friends, relatives, and neighbors. A man might be put in the stocks for offenses such as contempt of authority, drunken and disorderly conduct, or theft. The intent was not simply to deter him from future misbehavior but to let his fate serve as a warning to all who saw his humiliating posture.   Library of Congress.

Rituals of Consumption

new rituals centered on consumption, establishing novel links among the various residents of North America and creating what historians have termed "an empire of goods." The rituals began with the acquisition of desirable items. In the seventeenth century, settlers acquired necessities by bartering with neighbors or by ordering products from a home-country merchant. By the middle of the eighteenth century, specialized shops selling nonessentials had proliferated in cities such as New York, Philadelphia, and New Orleans. In 1770, Boston alone had more than five hundred stores, which offered consumers a vast selection of millinery, sewing supplies, tobacco, gloves, tableware, and the like. Even small and medium-size towns had one or two retail establishments by then. A colonist with money to spend would set aside time to "go shopping," a novel and pleasurable activity. A shopkeeper would display his (or occasionally her) wares to the customer, who was treated with respect and offered choices undreamed of by previous generations of colonists. The subsequent purchase of a desired object—for example, a ceramic bowl, a mirror, or a length of beautiful fabric—marked only the beginning of consumption rituals.

Consumers would then deploy their purchases in an appropriate manner: hanging the mirror prominently on a wall of the house, displaying the bowl on a table or sideboard, turning the fabric into a piece of clothing that could be worn on special occasions. Individual colonists clearly took personal pleasure in owning lovely objects, but they also could take pride in displaying their acquisitions (and thus their wealth and good taste) publicly to kin and neighbors. A particularly rich man might even hire a portraitist to paint his family using the objects and wearing the clothing, thereby creating a pictorial record that also would be displayed to others.

Tea drinking played an especially important role in Anglo-American consumption rituals. From early in the eighteenth century, households with aspirations to genteel status sought to acquire the items necessary for the proper consumption of tea: not just pots and cups but also strainers, sugar tongs, bowls, and even special tables. Tea provided a focal point for socializing and, because of its cost, served as a crucial marker of status. A hot drink that was mildly stimulating, it was seen as healthful as well. Thus poor households also consumed tea, although they could not afford the fancy equipment used by their better-off neighbors. Even some Mohawk Indians adopted the custom, much to the surprise of a traveler from Sweden, who observed them drinking tea in the late 1740s.

Just as civic, religious, and consumption rituals helped to bring certain communities together, so too they allowed the disparate cultures of colonial North America to interact with one another. Particularly important were the rituals that developed on what the historian Richard White has termed "the middle ground"—that is, the psychological and geographical space in which Indians and Europeans encountered each other. Most of those cultural encounters occurred in the context of trade or warfare.

Intercultural Rituals

When Europeans sought to trade with Indians, they came into contact with an indigenous system of exchange that stressed gift giving rather than formalized buying and selling. Although French and English traders complained constantly about the need to present Indians with gifts prior to negotiating with them for furs and skins, such a step was essential to successful bargaining. Over time, an appropriate ritual developed. A European trader arriving at a village would give gifts (cloth, rum, gunpowder, and other items) to Indian hunters. Eventually, those gifts would be reciprocated, and further exchanges would then take place. To the detriment of Indian societies, rum became a crucial component of these intercultural trading rituals. With some reason, traders came to believe that drunken Indians would sell their furs more cheaply; and some Indians refused to hunt or trade unless they were first supplied with alcohol.

Rituals surrounding murders were also critical points of cultural interaction. Indians and Europeans both believed that murders required a compensatory act, but the two groups had different notions of what that act should be. Europeans sought primarily to identify the murderer and to punish, perhaps to kill, that person. Such "eye for an eye" re-

This trade card (advertisement) issued by a Philadelphia tobacco dealer in 1770 shows a convivial group of wealthy men at a tavern. Both the leisurely activity depicted here and the advertisement itself were signs of the new rituals of consumption. Merchants began to advertise only when their customers could choose among different ways of spending money. Library Company of Philadelphia.

venge was for Indians only one of a number of possible responses to murder. Compensation could also be accomplished by capturing someone who could take the dead person's place or—most important for maintaining peace on the frontiers—by "covering the dead," or providing the family of the deceased with goods that could compensate for the loss. Eventually, the French and the Algonkians in particular evolved an elaborate ritual for handling frontier murders—a ritual that encompassed elements of both societies' traditions: murders were investigated and murderers identified, but by mutual agreement deaths were usually "covered" by trade goods rather than by blood revenge.

Throughout colonial North America, therefore, a variety of rituals both cemented ties and established rank within communities and allowed those communities to interact peacefully with one another. Such rituals were economic, political, and religious in nature, and all residents of the continent participated in them to some extent.

 ## Colonial Families

As Europeans consolidated their hold on the North American continent during the first three quarters of the eighteenth century, Native Americans were

Indian and Mixed-Race Families

forced to adapt to novel circumstances. As noted in Chapter 1, Spanish horses dramatically changed the lives of Plains Indians, and diseases ravaged even those groups that had little direct contact with Europeans. Bands reduced in numbers by disease and warfare recombined into new units; for example, the group later known as the Catawbas emerged in the 1730s in the western Carolinas from the fragmentary remains of several earlier Indian nations, including the Yamasees. Likewise, Indian family forms were reshaped under pressure from European secular and religious authorities. Whereas many Indian societies had permitted easy divorce, English, French, and Spanish missionaries frowned on such practices; and those societies that had allowed polygynous marriages (including New England Algonkians) redefined such relationships, designating one wife as "legitimate" and others as "concubines."

Continued high mortality rates created Indian societies in which extended kin took on new importance, for when parents died, aunts, uncles, and other relatives—even occasionally nonkin—assumed child-rearing responsibilities. Furthermore, once European dominance was established in any region, Indians there were commonly unable to pursue traditional modes of subsistence. That led to unusual family forms as well as to a variety of economic strategies. In New England, for instance, Algonkian husbands and wives often could not live together, for adults sought to support themselves by working separately for Anglo-Americans (perhaps wives as domestic servants, husbands as sailors). And in New Mexico, detribalized Navajos, Pueblos, and Apaches employed as servants by Spanish settlers clustered in the small towns of the Borderlands. Known collectively as *genizaros*, they lost contact with Indian cultures and instead lived on the fringes of Hispanic society.

Wherever there were relatively few European women in the population, sexual liaisons (both inside and outside marriage) occurred among European men and Indian women. The resulting mixed-race population of mestizos and métis worked as a familial "middle ground" to ease other cultural interactions. In New France and the Anglo-American backcountry, such families frequently resided in Indian villages and were enmeshed in trading networks; often, children of these unions became prominent leaders of Native American societies. (For example, Peter Chartier, the son of a Shawnee mother and a French father, led a pro-French Shawnee band in western Pennsylvania in the 1740s.) By contrast, in the Spanish Borderlands the offspring of Europeans and genizaros were treated as degraded individuals. Largely denied the privilege of legal marriage, they bore generations of "illegitimate" children of various racial mixtures, giving rise in Hispanic society to a wide range of labels describing degrees of skin color with a precision unknown in English or French America.

Family life among the many European migrants to North America was far more stable than that among Indian and mestizo peoples. Families (rather than individuals) constituted the basic units of colonial society.

European-American Families

Headed by European men or their widows, households were the chief mechanisms of production and consumption. Their members—bound by ties of blood or servitude—worked together to produce goods for consumption or sale. The head of the household represented it to the outside world, managing the finances and hold-

Farmer Abraham's Almanac, published in Philadelphia in 1759, contained this crude woodcut showing women engaged in chores associated with dairying: at right, milking a cow; at left, churning butter.   American Antiquarian Society.

ing legal authority over the rest of the family—his wife, his children, and his servants or slaves. (Eighteenth-century Americans used the word *family* for people who occupied one house, whether or not they were blood kin.) Such households were considerably larger than American families today; in 1790, the average home in the United States housed 5.7 whites. Most of those large families were nuclear—that is, unlike Indian families they did not include extended kin like aunts, uncles, or grandparents.

In English, French, and Spanish America alike, the vast majority of European families supported themselves through agriculture by cultivating crops and raising livestock. The scale and nature of the work varied: the production of indigo in Louisiana or tobacco in the Chesapeake required different sorts of labor from subsistence farming in New England or cattle ranching in New Mexico and Texas. Still, just as in the European, African, and Native American societies discussed in Chapter 1, household tasks were allocated by sex. The master, his sons, and his male servants or slaves performed one

set of chores; the mistress, her daughters, and her female servants or slaves, an entirely different set.

The mistress was responsible for what Anglo-Americans called "indoor affairs." She and her female helpers prepared food, cleaned the house, did laundry, and often made clothing. These basic chores were complex and time-consuming. Preparing food, for instance, involved planting and cultivating a garden, harvesting and preserving vegetables, salting and smoking meat, drying apples and pressing cider, milking cows and making butter and cheese, not to mention cooking and baking. The head of the household and his male helpers, responsible for "outdoor affairs," also had heavy workloads. They had to plant and cultivate the fields, build fences, chop wood for the fireplace, harvest and market crops, care for livestock, and butcher cattle and hogs to provide the household with meat. So extensive was the work involved in maintaining a farm household that a married couple could not do it alone. They had to have help. If they had no children, they then turned to servants or slaves.

The larger population in colonial towns and cities offered women opportunities for employment unknown in the countryside. One such Bostonian was Ann Arnold, a wet nurse known as Jersey Nanny (probably a native of the English Isle of Jersey), who was portrayed in 1748 by John Greenwood.   Museum of Fine Arts, Boston. Gift of Henry Lee Shattuck.

African-American Families

A European-American man's household could include African-American families as well as his own kin. More than 95 percent of colonial African-Americans were held in perpetual bondage. Although many African-Americans lived on farms with only one or two other slaves, the majority had the experience of living and working in a largely black setting. In South Carolina and Louisiana, a majority of the population was of African origin; in Georgia, about half; and in the Chesapeake, 40 percent. Indeed, portions of the Carolina low country were nearly 90 percent African-American by 1790.

Large plantations allowed for the specialization of labor. Each had its own enslaved male blacksmiths, carpenters, and shoemakers, along with slave women who worked as seamstresses, cooks, dairymaids, and midwives. These skilled slaves—between 10 and 20 percent of the African-American population—were essential to the smooth functioning of the plantation. But most slaves, male or female, worked in the fields. Since West African women were accustomed to agricultural labor, that task must have coincided with their own cultural expectations. To European-Americans, however, black women's work in the fields connoted inferior status.

Because all the colonies legally permitted slavery, African-Americans had few potential refuges from bondage. Some recently arrived Africans stole boats to try to return home or ran off in groups to frontier regions to join the Indians. Some slaves from South Carolina and Georgia managed to reach Spanish Florida, where they were allowed to establish a free community, Gracia Real de Santa Teresa de Mose, on the outskirts of St. Augustine. Violent resistance had even less to recommend it than running away. European-American colonists may have been in the minority in some areas, but they controlled the guns and ammunition. Even if a revolt succeeded for a time, masters could easily muster the armed force necessary to put it down. Only in unusual circumstances, then, did colonial slaves rebel collectively.

Yet the lack of rebellion did not imply an absence of resistance to enslavement. Family ties often provided a key means for such resistance. Even though slaves were not allowed to marry legally, they established strong family structures in which youngsters usually carried their parents' and grandparents' names. Extended-kin groups protested excessive punishment of relatives and asked to live in the same quarters. The links that developed among African-American families who had lived on the same plantation for several generations served as insurance against the uncertainties of existence under slavery. If a nuclear family was broken up by sale, other relatives could help with child rearing and similar tasks. Among African-Americans, just as among Indians, the extended family served a more important function than it did among European-Americans.

Most slave families managed to carve out a small measure of autonomy, especially in their working and spiritual lives. Enslaved Muslims often clung to their Islamic faith, a pattern especially evident in Louisiana. Many other Africans, though, converted to Christianity, finding comfort in the assurances of their new religion that all people would be free and equal in heaven. On many plantations, slaves were allowed or required to plant their own gardens, hunt, or fish in order to supplement the minimal diet their masters supplied. In some regions, most notably South Carolina and Louisiana, enslaved people were allowed to accumulate personal property by working for themselves once they had finished their assigned tasks. Late in the century, some Chesapeake planters with a surplus of laborers began to hire out slaves to others, often allowing the workers to keep a small part of their earnings. Such accumulated property could buy desired goods or serve as a legacy for children.

Just as African- and European-Americans lived together on plantations, so too both groups were found in cities. Yet the few colonial cities were nothing but large towns by today's standards. In 1750 the largest, Boston and Philadelphia, had just seventeen thousand and thirteen thousand inhabitants respectively. Life in the cities differed considerably from that on northern farms, southern plantations, or southwestern ranches. City dwellers everywhere, not just those in New Orleans who went to the levee, purchased foodstuffs and wood at markets and cloth in shops, instead of laboriously producing such items themselves. City people also had much more contact with the world beyond their own homes than did their rural counterparts.

Life in the Cities

By the 1750s, most major cities had at least one weekly newspaper, and some had two or three. Anglo-American newspapers printed the latest "advices from London" (usually two to three months old) and news from other English colonies, as well as local reports. Newspapers were available at taverns and inns, so people who could not afford to buy them could catch up on the news. Even illiterates could do so, since literate customers often read the papers aloud. Contact with the outside world, however, had drawbacks. Sailors sometimes brought exotic and deadly diseases into port. Boston, New York, Philadelphia, and New Orleans endured terrible epidemics of smallpox and yellow fever, which Europeans and Africans in the countryside largely escaped.

 ## Politics and Religion: Stability and Crisis in British America

In the first decades of the eighteenth century, Anglo-American political life exhibited a new stability. Despite substantial migration from overseas, most residents of the mainland had been born in America. Men from genteel families dominated the political structures in each province, for voters (free male property holders) tended to defer to their well-educated "betters" on election days.

Throughout the Anglo-American colonies, political leaders sought to increase the powers of elected assemblies relative to the powers of the governors and other appointed officials. Assemblies began to claim privileges associated with the British House of Commons, such as the rights to initiate all tax legislation and to control the militia. The assemblies also developed effective ways of influencing British appointees, especially by threatening to withhold their salaries. In some colonies (Virginia and South Carolina, for example), elite members of the assemblies usually presented a united front to royal officials, but in others (like New York), they fought with each other long and bitterly. New York took the first steps on the road to modern American democracy. In an attempt to win hotly contested elections, the province's genteel leaders began to appeal to "the people," competing openly for the votes of ordinary freeholders. Yet in 1733 that same New York government imprisoned a newspaper editor, John Peter Zenger, who had too vigorously criticized its actions. Defending Zenger against the charge of "seditious libel," his lawyer argued that the truth could not be defamatory, thus helping to establish a free-press principle now found in American law.

Rise of the Assemblies

Eighteenth-century assemblies bore little resemblance to twentieth-century state legislatures. Much of their business would today be termed administrative; only on rare occasions did they formulate new policies or pass laws of real importance. Members of the assemblies also saw their roles differently than do modern legislators. Instead of believing that they should act positively to improve the lives of their constituents, eighteenth-century assemblymen saw themselves as acting defensively to prevent encroachments on the people's rights. In their minds, their primary function was, for example, to stop the governors or councils from enacting oppressive taxes, rather than to pass laws that would actively benefit their constituents.

By midcentury, politically aware colonists commonly drew analogies between their own governments and Great Britain's balance of king, lords, and

In 1713, the colony of Massachusetts constructed its impressive State House in Boston. Here met the assembly and the council. The solidity and imposing nature of the building must have symbolized for its users the increasing consolidation of power in the hands of the Massachusetts legislature.   The Bostonian Society.

commons—a combination that had been thought to produce a stable polity since the days of ancient Greece and Rome. Although the analogy was not exact, political leaders equated their governors with the monarch, their councils with the aristocracy, and their assemblies with the House of Commons. All three were thought essential to good government, but Americans did not regard them with the same degree of approval. They viewed governors and appointed councils as posing potential threats to colonial freedoms and customary ways of life. As representatives of England rather than America, the governors and councils were to be feared rather than trusted. Colonists saw the assemblies, however, as the people's protectors. And in turn the assemblies regarded themselves as representatives of the people.

Again, though, such beliefs should not be equated with modern practice. The assemblies, firmly controlled by dominant families whose members were reelected year after year, rarely responded to the concerns of their poorer constituents. Although settlement continually spread westward, assemblies failed to reapportion themselves to provide adequate representation for newer communities—a lack of action that led to serious grievances among frontier dwellers, especially those from non-English ethnic groups. Thus it is important to distinguish between the colonial ideal, which placed the assembly at the forefront in the protection of people's liberties, and the reality, which was that most of those who were protected tended to be the wealthy and the assembly members themselves.

At midcentury, the political structures that had stabilized in a period of relative calm were confronted with a series of crises. None affected all the mainland provinces, but no colony escaped wholly untouched by at least one. The crises were of various sorts—ethnic, racial, economic, religious. They exposed the internal tensions building in the pluralistic American society, foreshadowing the greater disorder of the revolutionary era. Most important, they demonstrated that the political accommodations arrived at in the aftermath of the Glorious Revolution were no longer adequate to govern Britain's American empire. Once again, changes appeared necessary.

One of the first and greatest crises occurred in South Carolina. Early one morning in September 1739, about twenty South Carolina slaves gathered near the Stono River south of Charleston. Seizing guns and ammunition from a store, they killed the storekeepers and some nearby planter families. Then, joined by other local slaves, they headed south toward Florida in hopes of finding refuge at Gracia Real de Santa Teresa de Mose. By midday, however, the alarm had been sounded among slaveowners in the district. That afternoon a troop of militia attacked the fugitives, who then numbered about a hundred, killing some and dispersing the rest. More than a week later, most of the remaining conspirators were captured. Those not killed on the spot were later executed, but for over two years renegades were rumored to be at large.

Stono Rebellion

The Stono Rebellion shocked slaveholding South Carolinians and residents of other colonies as well. Throughout British America, laws governing the behavior of African-Americans were stiffened. But the most immediate response came in New York City, which had suffered a slave revolt in 1712. There the news from the South, coupled with fears of Spain generated by the outbreak of King George's War, set off a reign of terror in the summer of 1741. Hysterical whites interpreted a biracial gang of thieves and arsonists as malevolent conspirators who wanted to foment a slave uprising under the guidance of a supposed priest in the pay of Spain. By summer's end, thirty-one blacks and four whites had been executed for participating in the supposed plot. The Stono Rebellion and the New York conspiracy not only exposed and confirmed Anglo-Americans' deepest fears about the dangers of slaveholding but

also revealed the assemblies' inability to prevent serious internal disorder. Events of the next two decades confirmed that pattern.

By midcentury, most of the fertile land east of the Appalachians had been purchased or occupied. As a result, conflicts over land titles and conditions of landholding grew in number and frequency as colonists competed for control of land good for farming. In 1746, for example, some New Jersey farmers clashed violently with agents of the East Jersey proprietors. The proprietors claimed the farmers' land as theirs and demanded annual payments, called quitrents, for the use of the property. Similar violence occurred in the 1760s in the region that later became Vermont. There, farmers holding land grants issued by New Hampshire battled with speculators claiming title to the area through grants from New York authorities.

Land Riots in New Jersey and New York

The most serious land riots of the period took place along the Hudson River in 1765 and 1766. Late in the seventeenth century, Governor Benjamin Fletcher of New York had granted several huge tracts in the lower Hudson valley to prominent colonial families. The proprietors in turn divided these estates into small farms, which they rented chiefly to poor Dutch and German migrants who regarded tenancy as a step on the road to independent freeholder status. By the 1750s some proprietors were earning large sums annually from quitrents and other fees.

After 1740, though, increasing migration from New England brought conflict to the great New York estates. The New Englanders did not want to become tenants. Many squatted on vacant portions of the manors and resisted all attempts at eviction. In the mid-1760s the Philipse family brought suit against the New Englanders, some of whom had lived on Philipse land for twenty or thirty years. New York courts upheld the Philipse claim and ordered squatters to make way for tenants with valid leases. Instead of complying, the farmers organized a rebellion against the proprietors. For nearly a year insurgent farmers controlled much of the Hudson valley. They terrorized proprietors and loyal tenants, freed their friends from jail, and on one occasion battled a county sheriff and his posse. The rebellion was put down only after British troops dispatched from New York City captured the rebellion's leaders.

Built in the late eighteenth century and still standing in Fairfax County, Virginia, the Frying Pan Meetinghouse was one of the Baptist churches with a racially integrated congregation from its earliest years. The existence of such egalitarian religious bodies directly challenged the colony's hierarchical society. Virginia Department of Historic Resources, VA.

bined to create these disturbances, which ultimately arose from frontier people's dissatisfaction with the Carolina governments.

The most widespread crisis, however, was religious. From the late 1730s through the 1760s, waves of religious revivalism—today known collectively as the Great Awakening—swept over various parts of the

First Great Awakening

colonies, primarily New England (1735–1745) and Virginia (1750s and 1760s). Orthodox Calvinists were eager to combat Enlightenment rationalism, which denied innate human depravity. Simultaneously, the economic and political uncertainty accompanying King George's War made colonists receptive to the spiritual certainty offered by evangelical religion. In addition, many recent immigrants and residents of the backcountry had no prior religious affiliation, thus presenting evangelists with a potential source of converts.

The first signs of what was to become the Great Awakening appeared in western Massachusetts, in the Northampton Congregational Church led by the Reverend Jonathan Edwards, a noted preacher and theologian. During 1734 and 1735, Edwards noticed a remarkable response among the youthful members of his flock to a message based squarely on Calvinist principles. Individuals could attain salvation, Edwards contended, only through recognition of their own depraved natures and the need to surrender completely to God's will. Such surrender brought to members of his congregation an intensely emotional release from sin and came to be seen as a single identifiable moment of conversion.

The effects of such conversions remained isolated until 1739, when George Whitefield, an English Anglican cleric, arrived in America. For fifteen

George Whitefield

months he toured the British colonies, preaching to large audiences from Georgia to New England and concentrating his efforts in the major cities: Boston, New York, Philadelphia, Charleston, and Savannah. A gripping orator, Whitefield was the chief generating force behind the Great Awakening. The historian Harry Stout has termed him "the first modern celebrity," because he was skilled at self-promotion and cleverly manipulated both his listeners and the newspapers. Everywhere he traveled, his fame preceded him. Thousands turned out to listen—and to experience conversion. Whitefield's journey, the first such ever undertaken, created

Violent conflicts of a different sort erupted just a few years later in the Carolinas. The Regulator movements of the late 1760s (South Carolina) and early 1770s (North Caro-

Regulators in the Carolinas

lina) pitted backcountry farmers against wealthy eastern planters who controlled the provincial governments. Frontier dwellers, most of whom were Scots-Irish, protested their lack of an adequate voice in colonial political affairs. South Carolinians for months policed the countryside in vigilante bands, contending that law enforcement in the region was too lax and biased against them. North Carolinians, whose primary grievance was heavy taxation, fought and lost a battle with eastern militiamen at Alamance in 1771. Regional, ethnic, and economic tensions thus com-

new interconnections among the previously distinct colonies.

Regular clerics initially welcomed Whitefield and the American-born itinerant evangelist preachers who sprang up to imitate him. Soon, however, many clergymen began to realize that although "revived" religion filled their churches, it ran counter to their own approach to doctrine and matters of faith. They disliked the emotional style of the revivalists, whose itinerancy also disrupted normal patterns of church attendance because it took churchgoers away from the services they usually attended.

Opposition to the Awakening heightened rapidly, causing large numbers of congregations to splinter. "Old Lights"—traditional clerics and their followers—engaged in bitter disputes with the "New Light" evangelicals. Already characterized by numerous sects, American Protestantism became further divided as the major denominations split into Old Light and New Light factions and as new evangelical sects—Methodists and Baptists—gained adherents. Paradoxically, the angry fights and the rapid rise in the number of distinct denominations eventually led to an American willingness to tolerate religious diversity. No single sect could make an unequivocal claim to orthodoxy, so they had to coexist if they were to exist at all.

The most important effect of the Awakening was its impact on American modes of thought. The revivalists' message directly challenged the colonial

Impact of the Awakening

tradition of deference. Itinerant preachers, only a few of whom were ordained clergymen, claimed they understood the will of God better than did orthodox clerics. The Awakening's emphasis on emotion rather than learning undermined the validity of received wisdom, and New Lights questioned not only religious but also social and political orthodoxy. For example, New Lights began to defend the rights of groups and individuals to dissent from a community consensus, thereby challenging one of the most fundamental tenets of colonial political life.

Nowhere was this trend more evident than in Virginia, where the plantation gentry and their ostentatious lifestyle dominated society. By the 1760s

Virginia Baptists

Baptists had gained a secure foothold in Virginia; their beliefs and behavior were openly at odds with the way most genteel families lived. They rejected as sinful the horseracing, gambling, and dancing that occupied much of the gentry's leisure time. Like Quakers before them, they dressed plainly, in contrast to the gentry's fashionable opulence. They addressed each other as "brother" and "sister" regardless of social status, and they elected the leaders of their congregations—more than ninety of them by 1776. Their monthly "great meetings," which attracted hundreds of people, introduced new public rituals that rivaled the weekly Anglican services.

Strikingly, almost all the Virginia Baptist congregations included both black and white members. When the Dan River Baptist Church was founded in 1760, for example, eleven of its original seventy-four members were African-Americans, and other congregations had African-American majorities. Church rules applied equally to all members; interracial sexual relationships, divorce, and adultery were forbidden to everyone. In addition, masters were directed not to break up slave marriages through sale. Biracial committees investigated complaints about church members' misbehavior. Churches excommunicated slaves for stealing from their masters, but they also excommunicated masters for physically abusing their slaves. One such slaveowner excommunicated in 1772 experienced a true conversion. Penalized for "burning" one of his slaves, Charles Cook apologized to the congregation and became a preacher in a largely African-American church. Other Baptists decided that owning slaves was "unrighteous" and freed their bondspeople; Robert Carter manumitted more than nine hundred slaves.

 ## Conclusion

The Great Awakening thus injected an egalitarian strain into Anglo-American life at midcentury and further disrupted traditional structures of existence. Although primarily a religious movement, the Awakening also had important social and political consequences, calling into question habitual modes of behavior in the secular as well as the religious realm. In short, the Great Awakening helped to break Anglo-Americans' ties to their limited seventeenth-century origins. So, too, did the newcomers from Germany, Scotland, Ireland, and Africa, who brought their languages, customs, and religions to British North America. The European immigrants settled throughout the English colonies but were concentrated in the growing cities and in the backcountry. By contrast, enslaved migrants from Africa lived and worked primarily within 100 miles of the Atlantic coast. In many areas of the colonial South, 50 to 90 percent of the population was of African origin.

The economic life of all Europe's North American colonies proceeded simultaneously on two levels. On the farms, plantations, and ranches on which most colonists resided, the daily, weekly, monthly, and yearly rounds of chores for men, women, and children alike dominated people's lives while providing the goods consumed by households and sold in the marketplace. At the same time, the British, French, and Spanish colonies were enmeshed in an international network of trade that affected their local economic circumstances. The bitter wars fought by European nations during the eighteenth century inevitably involved the colonists by creating new opportunities for overseas sales or by disrupting their traditional markets. Above all, the colonial economy was volatile, fluctuating for reasons beyond Americans' control. Those fortunate few who—through skill, control of essential resources, or luck—reaped the profits of international trade made up the wealthy class of merchants and landowners who dominated colonial political and social life.

A century and a half after European peoples first settled in North America, the colonies mixed diverse European, American, and African traditions into a novel cultural blend that owed much to Europe but just as much, if not more, to North America itself. Europeans who interacted regularly with peoples of African and American origin—and with Europeans who came from nations other than their own—had to develop new methods of accommodating intercultural differences in addition to creating ties within their own potentially fragmenting communities. Yet at the same time the dominant colonists continued to identify themselves as French, Spanish, or British rather than as Americans. That did not change in Canada, Louisiana, or the Spanish Borderlands, but in the 1760s some Anglo-Americans began to realize that their interests were not necessarily identical to those of Great Britain or its monarch. For the first time, they offered a direct challenge to British authority.

Suggestions for Further Reading

General

Jack P. Greene, *Pursuits of Happiness: The Social Development of the Early Modern British Colonies and the Formation of American Culture*

(1988); Richard Hofstadter, *America at 1750: A Social Portrait* (1971); Peter C. Mancall, *Deadly Medicine: Indians and Alcohol in Early America* (1995); D. W. Meinig, *Atlantic America, 1492–1800* (1986); Stephanie G. Wolf, *As Various as Their Land: The Everyday Lives of 18th Century Americans* (1992).

New France and New Spain

Ramón Gutiérrez, *When Jesus Came, the Corn Mothers Went Away: Marriage, Sexuality, and Power in New Mexico, 1500–1846* (1991); Gwendolyn Midlo Hall, *Africans in Colonial Louisiana: The Development of Afro-Creole Culture in the Eighteenth Century* (1992); Dale Miquelon, *New France, 1701–1744* (1987); G. F. G. Stanley, *New France, 1744–1760* (1968); Daniel H. Usner, Jr., *Indians, Settlers, and Slaves in a Frontier Exchange Economy: The Lower Mississippi Valley Before 1783* (1992); David J. Weber, *The Spanish Frontier in North America* (1992); Richard White, *The Middle Ground: Indians, Empires, and Republics in the Great Lakes Region, 1650–1815* (1991).

Anglo-American Society

T. H. Breen, *Tobacco Culture* (1985); Carl Bridenbaugh, *Cities in Revolt: Urban Life in America, 1743–1776* (1955); Lois Green Carr et al., eds., *Colonial Chesapeake Society* (1988); David Conroy, *In Public Houses: Drink and the Revolution of Authority in Colonial Massachusetts* (1995); Rhys Isaac, *The Transformation of Virginia, 1740–1790* (1982); Christopher Jedrey, *The World of John Cleaveland: Family and Community in Eighteenth-Century New England* (1979); Sung Bok Kim, *Landlord and Tenant in Colonial New York: Manorial Society, 1664–1775* (1978); Peter C. Mancall, *Valley of Opportunity: Economic Culture Along the Upper Susquehanna, 1700–1800* (1991); Gary B. Nash, *The Urban Crucible: Social Change, Political Consciousness, and the Origins of the American Revolution* (1979); Michael Zuckerman, *Peaceable Kingdoms: New England Towns in the Eighteenth Century* (1970).

Anglo-American Economic Development

Richard Bushman, *The Refinement of America: Persons, Houses, Cities* (1992); Cary Carson et al., eds., *Of Consuming Interests: The Style of Life in the Eighteenth Century* (1994); Stephen Innes, ed., *Work and Labor in Early America* (1988); Alice Hanson Jones, *Wealth of a Nation to Be: The American Colonies on the Eve of the Revolution* (1980); John J. McCusker and Russell R. Menard, *The Economy of British America, 1607–1789* (1985); Edwin J. Perkins, *The Economy of Colonial America* (1980); Gary M. Walton and James F. Shepherd, *The Economic Rise of Early America* (1979).

Anglo-American Politics

Bernard Bailyn, *The Origins of American Politics* (1968); Patricia U. Bonomi, *A Factious People: Politics and Society in Colonial New York* (1971); Richard Bushman, *King and People in Provincial Massachusetts* (1985); Edward M. Cook, Jr., *The Fathers of the Towns: Leadership and Community Structure in Eighteenth-Century New England* (1976); Jack P. Greene, *The Quest for Power: The Lower Houses of Assembly in the Southern Royal Colonies, 1689–1776* (1963).

Immigration to British America

Bernard Bailyn, *The Peopling of British North America* (1986); Bernard Bailyn, *Voyagers to the West* (1986); Bernard Bailyn and

Philip Morgan, eds., *Strangers Within the Realm* (1991); Jon Butler, *The Huguenots in America* (1983); R. J. Dickson, *Ulster Immigration to Colonial America, 1718–1775* (1966); David Dobson, *Scottish Immigration to Colonial America, 1607–1785* (1994); A. Roger Ekirch, *Bound for America: The Transportation of British Convicts to the Colonies, 1718–1775* (1987); Ned Landsman, *Scotland and Its First American Colony* (1985); A. G. Roeber, *Palatines, Liberty, and Property: German Lutherans in Colonial British America* (1993).

African-Americans

Ira Berlin and Philip Morgan, eds., *Cultivation and Culture: Labor and the Shaping of Slave Life in the Americas* (1993); Thomas J. Davis, *A Rumor of Revolt: The "Great Negro Plot" in Colonial New York* (1985); Marvin L. Michael Kay and Lorin Lee Cary, *Slavery in North Carolina, 1748–1775* (1995); Allan Kulikoff, *Tobacco and Slaves: The Development of Southern Cultures in the Chesapeake, 1680–1800* (1986); Gerald [Michael] Mullin, *Flight and Rebellion: Slave Resistance in Eighteenth-Century Virginia* (1972); Michael Mullin, *Africa in America: Slave Acculturation and Resistance in the American South and the British Caribbean, 1736–1834* (1992); William Pierson, *Black Yankees: The Development of an Afro-American Subculture in Eighteenth-Century New England* (1988); Mechal Sobel, *The World They Made Together: Black and White Values in Eighteenth-Century Virginia* (1987); Betty Wood, *Women's Work, Men's Work: The Informal Slave Economies of Low Country Georgia* (1995); Anne Yentsch, *A Chesapeake Family and Their Slaves* (1994).

Anglo-American Women and Families

Kathleen M. Brown, *Good Wives, Nasty Wenches, and Anxious Patriarchs: Gender, Race, and Power in Colonial Virginia* (1996); Cornelia Hughes Dayton, *Women Before the Bar: Gender, Law, and Society in Connecticut, 1639–1789* (1995); Philip J. Greven, *The Protestant Temperament: Patterns of Child-Rearing, Religious Experience, and the Self in Early America* (1977); Joan Gundersen, *To Be Useful to the World: Women in Eighteenth-Century America* (1996); Barry J. Levy, *Quakers and the American Family* (1988); June Namias, *White Captives: Gender and Ethnicity on the American Frontier* (1993); Marylynn Salmon, *Women and the Law of Property in Early America* (1986); Daniel Blake Smith, *Inside the Great House: Planter Family Life in Eighteenth-Century Chesapeake Society* (1980); Merril D. Smith, *Breaking the Bonds: Marital Discord in Pennsylvania, 1730–1830* (1992).

Anglo-American Education, Science, and the Enlightenment

Patricia Cline Cohen, *A Calculating People: The Spread of Numeracy in Early America* (1982); Lawrence A. Cremin, *American Education: The Colonial Experience, 1607–1783* (1970); Richard Beale Davis, *Intellectual Life in the Colonial South, 1585–1763* (1978); Brooke Hindle, *The Pursuit of Science in Revolutionary America* (1956); Kenneth Lockridge, *Literacy in Colonial New England* (1974); Henry F. May, *The Enlightenment in America* (1976); Thomas P. Slaughter, *The Natures of John and William Bartram* (1996); William Sloan and Julie Williams, *The Early American Press, 1690–1783* (1994); Raymond P. Stearns, *Science in the British Colonies of America* (1970).

Religion and the Great Awakening

Patricia U. Bonomi, *Under the Cope of Heaven: Religion, Society, and Politics in Colonial America* (1986); J. M. Bumstead and John E. Van de Wetering, *What Must I Do to Be Saved? The Great Awakening in Colonial America* (1976); Jon Butler, *Awash in a Sea of Faith: Christianizing the American People* (1990); Michael Crawford, *Seasons of Grace: Colonial New England's Revival Tradition in Its British Context* (1991); Alan E. Heimert, *Religion and the American Mind: From the Great Awakening to the Revolution* (1966); David S. Lovejoy, *Religious Enthusiasm in the New World* (1985); Harry S. Stout, *The Divine Dramatist: George Whitefield and the Rise of Modern Evangelicalism* (1991); Patricia Tracy, *Jonathan Edwards, Pastor* (1980).

5

Severing the Bonds
of Empire
1754 – 1774

T he two men must have found the occasion remarkable. The artist customarily painted portraits of the wealthy and high born, not of artisans, even well-connected, affluent ones. The subject himself was an artist—a maker of beautiful silver and gold objects, an engraver of cartoons and townscapes. The political sympathies of the painter, John Singleton Copley, lay primarily with Boston's conservatives, whereas the sitter, Paul Revere, was a noted leader of resistance to British policies. Yet some time in 1768 Revere commissioned Copley to paint his portrait, and the result (opposite page) is one the greatest works of American art.

Copley was thirty, Revere thirty-four. Each man had learned his trade from a parent. Revere's father Apollos, who arrived in Boston as a teenage Huguenot refugee early in the century, was an accomplished gold- and silversmith; Paul served as his father's apprentice and took over the family business when Apollos died in 1754. Copley, whose Irish parents had immigrated to Boston in the 1730s, was taught to paint by his stepfather, Peter Pelham, an English artist. The two young tradesmen had undoubtedly known each other for years. In 1763 and thereafter Copley hired Revere to make silver and gold frames for the miniature portraits that were among his earliest works.

But their finest collaboration was the painting reproduced here. Copley portrayed Revere surrounded by the tools of his trade and contemplating a teapot he was crafting. The silversmith wears a loose-fitting linen shirt and an open vest rather than the formal dress usually worn by colonial artists' subjects. Even so, Revere is not actually at work: his clothes are too clean, the table too polished to be a work surface. The

John Singleton Copley's portrait of Paul Revere is generally regarded as one of his masterpieces. Copley captured Revere's character as a hard-working, respectable artisan—a man unafraid of displaying his humble origins to the world.
Museum of Fine Arts, Boston. Gift of Joseph W., William B., and Edward H. R. Revere.

119

silversmith's pose and apparel convey an impression of thoughtfulness, virtuous labor, and solidity. The teapot too carries a message, especially in the year 1768. Simultaneously a reflection of a craftsman's skills and a prominent emblem of the new "empire of goods" in British America, it resonated with symbolism because, as shall be seen later in this chapter, tea boycotts were an important component of colonial resistance to Great Britain. Both artist and subject, indeed, were to be active participants (though in very different ways) in the 1773 event known to history as the Boston Tea Party.

In retrospect, John Adams identified the years between 1760 and 1775 as the era of the true American Revolution. The Revolution, Adams declared, was completed before the fighting started, for it was "in the Minds of the people," involving not the actual winning of independence but a fundamental shift of allegiance from Britain to America. Today, not all historians would agree with Adams's assertion that that shift constituted the Revolution. But none would deny the importance of the events of those crucial years, which divided the American population along political lines and set the colonies on the road to independence.

The story of the 1760s and early 1770s describes an ever-widening split between Great Britain and Anglo-America and among their respective supporters in the colonies. In the long history of British settlement in the Western Hemisphere, considerable tension at times had marred the relationship between individual provinces and the mother country. Still, that tension rarely had been sustained for long, nor had it been widespread, except during the crisis following the Glorious Revolution in 1689. The primary divisions affecting the colonies had been internal rather than external. In the 1750s, however, a series of events began to draw the colonists' attention from domestic matters to their relations with Great Britain. It all started with the Seven Years War.

Britain's overwhelming victory in that war, confirmed by treaty in 1763, forever altered the balance of power in North America. France was ousted from the continent and Spain from Florida, events with major consequences for both the indigenous peoples of the interior and the residents of the British colonies. Indians could no longer play off European powers against one another and so lost one of their major diplomatic tools. Anglo-Americans, for their part, no longer had to fear the French threat on their northern and western borders or the Spanish in the Southeast. The British colonies along the coast would never have dared to break with their mother country, some historians contend, if France and its Indian allies had continued to control the interior of the continent.

The British victory in 1763, then, constituted a major turning point in American history because of

The Colonial Wars, 1689–1763

American Name	European Name	Dates	Participants	American Sites	Dispute
King William's War	War of the League of Augsburg	1689–97	England, Holland versus France, Spain	New England, New York, Canada	French power
Queen Anne's War	War of Spanish Succession	1702–13	England, Holland, Austria versus France, Spain	Florida, New England	Throne of Spain
King George's War	War of Austrian Succession	1739–48	England, Holland, Austria versus France, Spain, Prussia	West Indies, New England, Canada	Throne of Austria
French and Indian War	Seven Years War	1756–63	England versus France, Spain	Ohio country, Canada	Possession of Ohio country

• *Important Events* •

1754	Albany Congress meets to try to forge colonial unity Fighting breaks out with Washington's defeat at Fort Necessity
1756	Britain declares war on France; Seven Years War officially begins
1759	British forces take Quebec
1760	American phase of war ends with fall of Montréal to British troops George III becomes king
1763	Treaty of Paris ends Seven Years War Pontiac's allies attack British forts in West Proclamation of 1763 attempts to close land west of Appalachians to English settlement
1764	Sugar Act lays new duties on molasses, tightens customs regulations Currency Act outlaws paper money issued by the colonies
1765	Stamp Act requires stamps on all printed materials in colonies Sons of Liberty formed
1766	Stamp Act repealed Declaratory Act insists that Parliament can tax the colonies
1767	Townshend Acts lay duties on trade within the empire, send new officials and judges to America
1768–70	Resistance to Townshend duties takes form of boycotts and public demonstrations but divides merchants and urban artisans
1770	Lord North becomes prime minister Townshend duties repealed, except for tea tax Boston Massacre kills five colonial rioters
1772	Boston Committee of Correspondence formed
1773	Tea Act aids East India Company Boston Tea Party protests the Tea Act
1774	Coercive Acts punish Boston and Massachusetts as a whole Quebec Act reforms government of Quebec

its direct effect on all the residents of North America. It also had a significant impact on Great Britain, one that soon affected the colonies as well. To win the war, Britain went heavily into debt. To reduce the debt, Parliament for the first time imposed revenue-raising taxes on the colonies in addition to the customs duties that had long regulated trade. That decision exposed differences in the political thinking of Americans and Britons—differences that until then had been obscured by a shared political vocabulary.

During the 1760s and early 1770s a broad coalition of the residents of Anglo-America, men and women alike, resisted new tax levies and attempts by British officials to tighten controls over provincial governments. The colonies' elected leaders became ever more suspicious of Britain's motives as the years passed. They laid aside old antagonisms to coordinate their response to the new measures, and they slowly began to reorient their political thinking. As late as the summer of 1774, though, most were still seeking a solution within the framework of the empire; few harbored thoughts of independence.

 ## Renewed Warfare Among Europeans and Indians

The English colonies along the Atlantic seaboard were surrounded by hostile, or potentially hostile, neighbors: Indians everywhere, the Spanish in Florida and along the coast of the Gulf of Mexico, the French along the great inland system of rivers and lakes that stretched from the St. Lawrence to the Mississippi. The Spanish outposts posed little direct threat, for Spain's days as a major power had passed. The French were another matter. Their long chain of forts and settlements dominated the North American interior, facilitating trading partnerships and alliances with the Indians. In none of the three wars fought between 1689 and 1748 was England able to shake France's hold on the American frontier. Under the Peace of Utrecht, which ended Queen Anne's War in 1713, the English won control of such peripheral northern areas as Newfoundland, Hudson's Bay, and Nova Scotia (Acadia). But Britain made no territorial gains in King George's War (see map, page 126).

An eighteenth-century Iroquois warrior as depicted by a European artist. Such men of the Six Nations confederacy dominated the North American interior before the Seven Years War. Lines drawn on maps by colonizing powers and the incursions of traders made little impact on their power. Library of Congress, Rare Book and Special Collections Division.

During both Queen Anne's War and King George's War, the Iroquois Confederacy maintained the policy of neutrality it first developed in 1701.

Iroquois Neutrality

While British and French forces fought for nominal control of the North American continent, the confederacy—which actually dominated a large portion of that continent—skillfully played the Europeans off against each other, refusing to commit its warriors fully to either side despite being showered with gifts by both. Instead, the Iroquois fought only their traditional southern enemies, the Catawbas. Since France repeatedly urged them to attack the Catawbas, who were allied with Britain, the Iroquois achieved desirable goals. They kept the French happy and simultaneously consolidated their control over the entire interior region north of Virginia. The campaign against a common enemy also enabled the confederacy to cement its alliance with its weaker tributaries, the Shawnees and Delawares, and to ensure the continued subordination of those groups.

But even careful Iroquois diplomats could not prevent the region inhabited by the Shawnees and Delawares (now western Pennsylvania and eastern Ohio) from providing the spark that set off a major war. That conflict spread from America to Europe (a significant reversal of previous patterns), proving decisive in the contest for North America. Trouble began in 1752 when Anglo-American fur traders ventured into the area known as the Ohio country (see map, page 123). The French could not permit their rivals to gain a foothold in the region, for it contained the source of the Ohio River, which offered direct access by water to French posts on the Mississippi. A permanent British presence in the Ohio country could challenge France's control of the western fur trade and even threaten its prominence in the Mississippi valley. Accordingly, in 1753 the French pushed southward from Lake Erie, building fortified outposts at strategic points.

In response to the French threat to their western frontiers, delegates from seven northern and middle colonies gathered in Albany, New York, in June 1754. With the backing of administrators in London, they sought two goals: to persuade the Iroquois to abandon their traditional neutrality and to coordinate the defenses of the colonies. They succeeded in neither. The Iroquois listened politely to the colonists' arguments but saw no reason to change a policy that had served them well for half a century. And although the Albany Congress delegates adopted a Plan of Union (which would have established an elected intercolonial legislature with the power to tax), their provincial governments uniformly rejected the plan—primarily because those governments feared a loss of autonomy.

Albany Congress

While the Albany Congress delegates deliberated, the war they sought to prepare for was already beginning. Governor Robert Dinwiddie of Virginia had sent a small militia force westward to counter the French moves. Virginia claimed ownership of the Ohio country, and Dinwiddie was eager to prevent the French from establishing a permanent post there. But the Virginia militiamen arrived too late.

European Settlements and Native American Tribes, 1750 *By 1750, Europeans had expanded the limits of the English colonies to the eastern slopes of the Appalachian Mountains. Few independent Indian nations still existed in the East, but beyond the mountains they controlled the countryside. Only a few widely scattered English and French forts maintained the Europeans' presence there.*

A colonial soldier in 1758 etched onto his powder horn images of Indians and English troops fighting in the Seven Years War.   New York Historical Society.

The French had already taken possession of the strategic point—now Pittsburgh—where the Allegheny and Monongahela Rivers meet to form the Ohio, and they were busily engaged in constructing Fort Duquesne. The inexperienced young officer who commanded the Virginians attacked a French detachment and then allowed himself to be trapped in his crudely built Fort Necessity at Great Meadows, Pennsylvania. After a day-long battle (on July 3, 1754), during which more than one-third of his men were killed or wounded, twenty-two-year-old George Washington surrendered. He and his men were allowed to return to Virginia.

Washington had blundered grievously, setting off a war that eventually would encompass nearly the entire world. He also en-

Seven Years War

sured that the Ohio valley Indians, many of whom had moved west to escape Iroquois domination and to trade with the French, would for the most part support France in the conflict. The Indians took Washington's mistakes as an indication of Britain's inability to win the war, and nothing that occurred in the next four years made them change their minds. In July 1755, a few miles south of Fort Duquesne, a combined force of French and Indians ambushed British and colonial troops readying for a renewed assault on the fort. General Edward Braddock was killed, and his men were demoralized by a devastating defeat. After news of the debacle reached London, Britain declared war on France in 1756, thus formally beginning the conflict known as the Seven Years War.

For three more years one disaster followed another for Great Britain. The war went so badly that Britain began to fear that France would attempt to retake Newfoundland and Nova Scotia. Attempting to solidify their hold on that area, the British administrators of Nova Scotia forced its French residents to leave the homes they had occupied for generations—the first modern deportation of an entire people. After years of wandering, many of these Acadian exiles made their way to Louisiana, where they became known as Cajuns.

At last, under the leadership of William Pitt, who was named secretary of state in 1757, Britain mounted the effort that won the war in North America. Pitt encouraged cooperation between the colonists and Great Britain, agreeing to reimburse the colonies for their military expenditures and placing troop recruitment wholly in local hands. He thereby gained wholehearted American support for the war effort. Earlier in the war—in the years of England's many defeats—British officers had instead tried to coerce the colonies into supplying men and materiel to the army.

In July 1758, British forces recaptured the fortress at Louisbourg, winning control of the entrance to the St. Lawrence River and breaking the major French supply route. Then, in a surprise night attack in September 1759, General James Wolfe's soldiers defeated the French on the Plains of Abraham and took Quebec. Sensing a British victory, the Iroquois abandoned their policy of neutrality and allied themselves with Britain, hoping to gain some diplomatic leverage. A year later the British captured

Montréal, the last French stronghold on the continent, and the American phase of the war ended.

In the Treaty of Paris (1763), France ceded its major North American holdings to Britain. Spain, an ally of France toward the end of the war, gave Florida to the victors. Britain, fearing the presence of France on its western borders, forced the French to cede Louisiana to Spain. The British thus gained control of the fur trade of the entire continent. And no longer would the English seacoast colonies have to worry about the threat to their existence posed by France's extensive North American territories (see maps, page 126).

Because most of the fighting had occurred in the Northeast, the war had especially pronounced effects on New Englanders. As many as one-third of all Massachusetts men between the ages of sixteen and twenty-nine served for a time in the provincial army. Wartime service left a lasting impression on these

American Soldiers

soldiers. For the first time, ordinary Americans came into extended contact with Britons—and they did not like what they saw. The provincials regarded the British troops (called "redcoats" because of the color of their uniforms) as haughty, profane Sabbath-breakers who arbitrarily imposed overly harsh punishments on anyone who broke the rules. Nearly sixty years later a veteran still vividly recalled an incident in 1762 when a British soldier inflicted hundreds of lashes on three men for "some trifling offense. . . . I felt at the time as though I could have taken summary vengeance on those who were the authors of it," he wrote in his memoirs.

The New England soldiers also learned that British troops did not share their adherence to principles of contract and consensus—the values that had governed their lives at home. Colonial regiments mutinied or rebelled en masse if they believed they were being treated unfairly, as happened, for example, when they were not allowed to leave at the end of their formal enlistments. One private in these

On the night of September 13, 1759, British forces under General James Wolfe scaled the heights of Quebec and defeated the French army led by General Louis Joseph Montcalm. Both generals died on the battlefield.   Library of Congress.

European Claims in North America *The dramatic results of the British victory in the Seven Years (French and Indian) War are vividly demonstrated in these maps, which depict the abandonment of French claims to the mainland after the Treaty of Paris in 1763.*

circumstances grumbled in his journal in 1759, "Although we be Englishmen born, we are debarred Englishmen's liberty. . . . [The British soldiers] are but little better than slaves to their officers. And when I get out of their [power] I shall take care how I get in again." Such men would later recall their personal experience of British "tyranny" when they decided to support the Revolution.

The overwhelming British triumph stimulated some Americans to think expansively about the colonies' future. People like the Philadelphia printer Benjamin Franklin, who had long touted the colonies' wealth and potential, predicted a glorious new future for British North America—a future that included not just geographical expansion but also economic development and population growth. Such men were to lead the resistance to British measures in the years after 1763. They uniformly opposed any laws that would retard America's growth and persistently supported steps to increase Americans' control over their own destiny.

 ## 1763: A Turning Point

The great victory over France had an irreversible impact on North America, felt first by the indigenous peoples of the interior. With France excluded from the continent altogether and Spanish territory now confined to the area west of the Mississippi, the diplomatic strategy that had served the Indians well for so long could no longer be employed. The consequences were immediate and devastating.

Even before the Treaty of Paris, southern Indians had to adjust to the new circumstances. After Britain gained the upper hand in the American war in 1758, Creeks and Cherokees lost their ability to force concessions by threatening to turn instead to France or Spain. In desperation, and in retaliation for British atrocities, Cherokees attacked the Carolina and Virginia frontiers in 1760. Though initially victorious, the Indians were defeated the following year by a force of British regulars and colonial militia. Late in 1761 the two sides concluded a treaty under which the Cherokees allowed the construction of British forts in their territories and opened a large tract of land to European settlement.

The fate of the Cherokees in the South was a portent of things to come in the Ohio country. There, the Ottawas, Chippewas, and Potawatomis reacted angrily when Great Britain, no longer facing French competition, raised the price of trade goods and ended traditional gift-giving practices. Britain also allowed settlers to move into the Monongahela and Susquehanna valleys, onto Delaware and Iroquois lands. A shaman named Neolin (also known as the Delaware Prophet) warned his people of impending doom and urged them to resist British encroachments.

Pontiac, the war chief of an Ottawa village near Detroit, understood the implications of British policies. Only unity among the western tribes, he realized, could prevent total dependence on and subordination to the victorious British. Using his considerable powers of persuasion, in the spring of 1763 he

Pontiac's Uprising

forged an unprecedented alliance among Hurons, Chippewas, Potawatomis, Delawares, Shawnees, and even some Mingoes (Pennsylvania Iroquois). Pontiac then laid siege to Fort Detroit while war parties attacked other British outposts in the Great Lakes region. Detroit withstood the siege, but by late June all the other forts west of Niagara and north of Fort Pitt (old Fort Duquesne) had fallen to the Indian alliance.

That was the high point of the uprising. Indians raided the Virginia and Pennsylvania frontiers at will throughout the summer, killing at least two thousand settlers. But they could not take the strongholds of Niagara, Fort Pitt, or Detroit. In early August, colonial militiamen soundly defeated a combined force of Delawares, Shawnees, Hurons, and Mingoes at Bushy Run, Pennsylvania. Conflict ceased when Pontiac broke off the siege of Detroit in late October. A treaty ending the war was finally negotiated three years later.

Pontiac's uprising showed Great Britain that the huge territory it had just acquired from France would not be easy to govern. The central administration in London had no prior experience managing such a vast tract of land, particularly one inhabited by such restive peoples—the remaining French settlers along the St. Lawrence and the many different Indian

Proclamation of 1763

Benjamin West, the first well-known American artist, engraved this picture of a prisoner exchange at the end of Pontiac's Uprising, with Colonel Henry Bouquet supervising the return of settlers abducted during the war. In the foreground, a child resists leaving the Indian parents he had grown to love. Many colonists were fascinated by the phenomenon West depicted—the reluctance of captives to abandon their adoptive Indian families. Ohio Historical Society.

groups. In October, in a futile attempt to assert control over the interior, the British ministry issued the Proclamation of 1763, which declared the headwaters of rivers flowing into the Atlantic from the Appalachian Mountains to be the temporary western boundary for colonial settlement (see map, page 123). The proclamation was intended to prevent clashes between Indians and colonists by forbidding whites to move onto Indian lands until tribes had given up their land by treaty. But many whites had already established farms or purchased property west of the proclamation line, and from the outset the unenforceable policy was doomed to failure.

Other decisions made in London in 1763 and thereafter had a wider impact in British North

America. The hard-won victory created both problems and opportunities for the British government. The most pressing problem, Britain's immense war debt, had to be solved by King George III and his new prime minister, George Grenville.

George III succeeded his grandfather, George II, on the British throne in 1760. The twenty-two-year-old king, a man of mediocre intellect and even more mediocre education, was unfortunately also an erratic judge of character. During the crucial years between 1763 and 1770, when the rift with the colonies was growing ever wider, he replaced ministries with bewildering rapidity. Though determined to assert the power of the monarchy, the king was immature and unsure of himself. He often substituted stubbornness for intelligence, and he regarded adherence to the status quo as the hallmark of patriotism.

George III

The man he selected as prime minister in 1763, George Grenville, believed that the American colonies should be more tightly administered than in the past. Grenville confronted a financial crisis: England's burden of indebtedness had nearly doubled since 1754, from £73 million to £137 million. Annual expenditures before the war had amounted to no more than £8 million; now the yearly interest on the debt alone came to £5 million. Grenville's ministry had to find new sources of funds, and the British people themselves were already heavily taxed. Since the colonists had benefited greatly from the wartime expenditures, Grenville concluded that Anglo-Americans should be asked to pay a greater share of the cost of running the empire.

Grenville did not question Great Britain's right to levy taxes on the colonies. Like all his countrymen, he believed that the government's legitimacy derived ultimately from the consent of the people, but he defined consent far more loosely than did the colonists. Americans had come to believe that they could be represented only by men for whom they or their property-holding neighbors actually voted; otherwise, they could not count on legislators to represent their interests properly. Grenville and his English contemporaries, however, believed that Parliament—king, lords, and commons acting together—by definition represented all British subjects, wherever they resided (even overseas) and whether or not they could vote.

Theories of Representation

Parliament saw itself as collectively representing the entire nation; the particular constituency that chose a member of the House of Commons had no special claim on that member's vote. According to this theory of government, called *virtual representation*, the colonists were seen as virtually, if not actually, represented in Parliament. Thus their consent to acts of Parliament could be presumed. By contrast, in the colonies members of the lower houses of the assemblies were viewed as specifically representing the regions that had elected them. Before Grenville proposed to tax the colonists, the two notions coexisted without apparent contradiction. But the events of the 1760s pointed up the difference between the two definitions of representation.

The same events threw into sharp relief Americans' attitudes toward political power. The colonists had become accustomed to a central government that wielded only limited authority over them and affected their daily lives very little. In consequence, they believed that a good government was one that largely left them alone, a view in keeping with the theories of a group of British writers known as the Real Whigs. Drawing on a tradition of dissenting thought that reached back to John Locke and even to the Civil War, the Real Whigs stressed the dangers inherent in a powerful government, particularly one headed by a monarch. Some of them even favored republicanism, which proposed to eliminate monarchs altogether and rest political power more directly on the will of the people. Real Whigs warned the people to guard constantly against government's attempts to encroach on their liberty and seize their property. Political power was always to be feared, wrote John Trenchard and Thomas Gordon in their essay series *Cato's Letters* (originally published in London in 1720–1723 and reprinted many times thereafter in the colonies). Rulers would try to corrupt and oppress the people. Only the perpetual vigilance of people and their elected representatives could preserve their fragile yet precious liberty, which was closely linked to their right to hold private property.

Real Whigs

Britain's attempts to tighten the reins of government and raise revenues from the colonies in the 1760s and early 1770s convinced many Americans that the Real Whigs' reasoning applied to their circumstances, especially because of the link between liberty and property rights. Excessive and unjust taxation, they believed, could destroy their freedoms.

They began to interpret British measures in light of the Real Whigs' warnings and to see oppressive designs behind the actions of Grenville and his successors. Historians disagree over the extent to which those perceptions were correct, but by 1775 a large number of colonists believed they were. In the mid-1760s, however, colonial leaders did not immediately accuse Grenville of an intent to oppress them. They at first simply questioned the wisdom of the laws he proposed.

Parliament passed the first such measures, the Sugar and Currency Acts, in 1764. The Sugar Act (also known as the Revenue Act) revised existing customs regulations and laid new duties on some foreign imports into the colonies. It also estab-

Sugar and Currency Acts

lished a vice-admiralty court at Halifax, Nova Scotia, and included provisions aimed at stopping the widespread smuggling of molasses, one of the chief commodities in American trade. Although the Sugar Act appeared to resemble the Navigation Acts, which the colonies had long accepted as legitimate, it broke with tradition because it was explicitly designed to raise revenue, not to channel American trade through Britain. The Currency Act effectively outlawed colonial issues of paper money. (British merchants had complained that Americans were paying their debts in inflated local currencies.) Americans could accumulate little sterling, since they imported more than they exported; thus the act seemed to the colonists to deprive them of a useful medium of exchange.

The Sugar and Currency Acts were imposed on an economy already in the midst of depression. A business boom accompanied the Seven Years War, but the brief spell of prosperity ended abruptly in 1760 when the war shifted overseas. Urban merchants could not sell all their imported goods to colonial customers alone, and without the military's demand for foodstuffs, American farmers found fewer buyers for their products. The bottom dropped out of the European tobacco market, threatening the livelihood of Chesapeake planters. Sailors were thrown out of work, and artisans found few customers. In such circumstances, the prospect of increased import duties and inadequate supplies of currency aroused merchants' hostility.

Individual American essayists and colonial governments protested the new policies. But, lacking any precedent for a united campaign against acts of Parliament, Americans in 1764 took only hesitant and uncoordinated steps. Eight colonial legislatures sent separate petitions to Parliament requesting the Sugar Act's repeal. They argued that its commercial restrictions would hurt Britain as well as the colonies and that they had not consented to its passage. The protests had no effect. The law remained in force, and Grenville proceeded with another revenue plan.

 ## The Stamp Act Crisis

The Stamp Act (1765), Grenville's most important proposal, was modeled on a law that had been in effect in Great Britain for almost a century. It touched nearly every colonist by requiring tax stamps on most printed materials, but it placed the heaviest burden on merchants and other members of the colonial elite, who used printed matter more frequently than did ordinary folk. Anyone who purchased a newspaper or pamphlet, made a will, transferred land, bought dice or playing cards, needed a liquor license, accepted a government appointment, or borrowed money would have to pay the tax. Never before had a revenue measure of such scope been proposed for the colonies. The act also required that tax stamps be paid for with sterling, which was scarce, and that violators be tried in vice-admiralty courts, which operated without juries. (Previously, such courts had heard only cases involving violations of maritime law.) Americans feared the loss of their right to trial by a jury of their peers. Finally, such a law would break decisively with the colonial tradition of self-imposed taxation.

The most important colonial pamphlet protesting the Sugar Act and the proposed Stamp Act was *The Rights of the British Colonies Asserted and Proved,*

James Otis's *Rights of the British Colonies*

by James Otis, Jr., a brilliant young Massachusetts attorney. Otis starkly exposed the ideological dilemma that was to confound the colonists for the next decade. How could they justify their opposition to certain acts of Parliament without questioning Parliament's authority over them? On the one hand, Otis asserted, Americans were "entitled to all the natural, essential, inherent, and inseparable rights" of Britons, including the right not to be taxed without their consent. "No man or body of men, not excepting the parliament . . . can

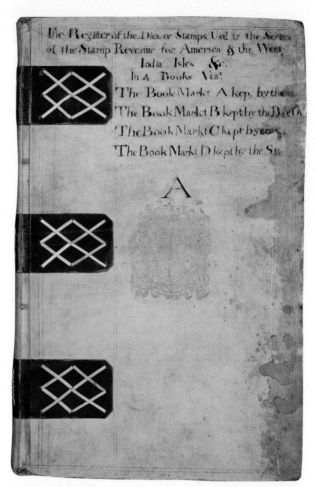

The Register of the Dies or Stamps Used in the Service of the Stamp Revenue for America & the West India Isles &c.
In 4 Books Viz!
The Book Markt A kep. by the
The Book Markt B kept by the Rec
The Book Markt C kept by
The Book Markt D kept by the S

A

In 1765 a clerk in the offices of British tax officials prepared this register to contain examples of the tax stamps intended for use in the American colonies. But because the law was never enforced and soon repealed, the register is largely empty, and the other volumes the clerk anticipated were never readied at all.   The British Library Philatelic Section, Inland Revenue Archives.

ment: that Parliament was the sole, supreme authority in the empire. Even unconstitutional laws enacted by Parliament had to be obeyed until Parliament decided to repeal them.

According to orthodox British political theory, there could be no middle ground between absolute submission to Parliament and a frontal challenge to its authority. Otis tried to find such a middle ground by proposing colonial representation in Parliament, but his idea was never taken seriously on either side of the Atlantic. The British believed that colonists were already virtually represented in Parliament, and Anglo-Americans quickly realized that a handful of colonial delegates to London would simply be outvoted.

Otis published his pamphlet before the Stamp Act was passed. When Americans first learned of the act's adoption in the spring of 1765, they were uncertain how to react. Few colonists—even appointed government officials—publicly favored the law. But colonial petitions had already failed to prevent its adoption, and further lobbying appeared futile. Perhaps Otis was right that the only course open to Americans was to pay the stamp tax, reluctantly but loyally. Acting on that assumption, colonial agents in London sought the appointment of their American friends as stamp distributors so that the law would at least be enforced equitably.

Not all the colonists were resigned to paying the new tax. Among them was a twenty-nine-year-old lawyer serving his first term in the Virginia House of Burgesses. Patrick Henry later recalled that he was "young, inexperienced, unacquainted with the forms of the house and the members that composed it"—and appalled by his fellow legislators' unwillingness to oppose the Stamp Act. Henry decided to act. "Alone, unadvised, and unassisted, on a blank leaf of an old law book," he wrote the Virginia Stamp Act Resolves.

Patrick Henry and the Virginia Stamp Act Resolves

Little in Henry's earlier life foreshadowed his success in the political arena he entered so dramatically. The son of a prosperous Scottish immigrant to western Virginia, Henry had little formal education. After marrying at eighteen, he failed at both farming and storekeeping before turning to the law as a means of supporting his wife and their six children. Henry lacked legal training, but his oratorical skills made him an effective advocate, first for his clients and later for his political beliefs. A prominent Virginia lawyer

take [those rights] away," he declared. On the other hand, Otis was forced to admit, under the British system established after the Glorious Revolution, "the power of parliament is uncontrollable but by themselves, and we must obey. . . . Let the parliament lay what burthens they please on us, we must, it is our duty to submit and patiently bear them, till they will be pleased to relieve us."

Otis's first contention, drawing on colonial notions of representation, implied that Parliament could not constitutionally tax the colonies because Americans were not represented in its ranks. Yet his second point both acknowledged political reality and accepted the prevailing theory of British govern-

observed, "He is by far the most powerful speaker I ever heard. Every word he says not only engages, but commands the attention; and your passions are no longer your own when he addresses them."

Patrick Henry introduced his seven proposals near the end of the legislative session, when many burgesses had already departed for home. Henry's fiery speech led the Speaker of the House to accuse him of treason. (Henry denied the charge, contrary to the nineteenth-century myth that he exclaimed, "If this be treason, make the most of it!") The few burgesses remaining in Williamsburg adopted five of Henry's resolutions by a bare majority. Although they repealed the most radical of the five the next day, their action had far-reaching effects. Some colonial newspapers printed Henry's seven original resolutions as if they had been uniformly passed by the House, even though one had been rescinded and two others were never debated or voted on at all.

The four propositions adopted by the burgesses repeated Otis's arguments, asserting that the colonists had never forfeited the rights of British subjects, among which was consent to taxation. The other three resolutions went much further. The one that was repealed claimed for the burgesses "the only exclusive right" to tax Virginians, and the final two (those never considered) asserted that residents of Virginia need not obey tax laws passed by other legislative bodies (namely Parliament), terming any opponent of that opinion "an Enemy to this his Majesty's Colony."

The burgesses' decision to accept only the first four of Henry's resolutions anticipated the position most Americans would adopt throughout the following decade. Though willing to contend for their rights, the colonists did not seek independence. They rather wanted some measure of self-government. Accordingly, they backed away from the assertions that they owed Parliament no obedience and that only their own assemblies could tax them. Indeed, declared the Maryland lawyer Daniel Dulany, whose *Considerations on the Propriety of Imposing Taxes on the British Colonies* was the most widely read pamphlet of 1765, "The colonies are dependent upon Great Britain, and the supreme authority vested in the king, lords, and commons, may justly be exercised to secure, or preserve their dependence." But, warned Dulany, a superior did not have the right "to seize the property of his inferior when he pleases"; there was a

Continuing Loyalty to Britain

crucial distinction between a condition of "dependence and *inferiority*" and one of "absolute *vassalage* and slavery."

Over the next ten years, America's political leaders searched for a formula that would enable them to control their internal affairs, especially taxation, but remain under British rule. The chief difficulty lay in British officials' inability to compromise on the issue of parliamentary power. The notion that Parliament could exercise absolute authority over all colonial possessions was basic to the British theory of government. Even the harshest British critics of the ministries of the 1760s and 1770s questioned only the wisdom of specific policies, not the principles on which they were based. In effect, the Americans wanted British leaders to revise their fundamental understanding of the workings of their government. But that was simply too much to expect.

The ultimate effectiveness of Americans' opposition to the Stamp Act rested on more than ideological arguments over parliamentary power. What

In 1795 the artist Lawrence Sully painted the only known life portrait of Patrick Henry. The old man's fierce gaze reflects the same intensity that marked his actions thirty years earlier, when he introduced the Virginia Stamp Act Resolves in the House of Burgesses. Mead Art Museum, Amherst College. Bequest of Herbert L. Pratt, Class of 1985.

gave the resistance its primary force were the decisive and inventive actions of some colonists during the late summer and fall of 1765.

In August the Loyal Nine, a Boston social club of printers, distillers, and other artisans, organized a demonstration against the Stamp Act. Hoping to show that people of all ranks opposed the act, they approached the leaders of the city's rival laborers' associations, based in Boston's North End and South End neighborhoods. The two gangs, composed of unskilled workers and poor tradesmen, often battled each other, but the Loyal Nine convinced them to lay aside their differences to participate in the demonstration. All colonists, not just affluent ones, would have to pay the stamp taxes.

Loyal Nine

Early on August 14, the demonstrators hung an effigy of Andrew Oliver, the province's stamp distributor, from a tree on Boston Common. That night a large crowd led by a group of about fifty well-dressed tradesmen paraded the effigy around the city. The crowd tore down a small building they thought was intended as the stamp office and built a bonfire near Oliver's house with wood from the destroyed building. They then beheaded the effigy and added it to the flames. Demonstrators broke most of Oliver's windows and threw stones at officials who tried to disperse them. In the midst of the melée, the North End and South End leaders drank a toast to their successful union. The Loyal Nine achieved success when Oliver publicly promised not to fulfill the duties of his office. One Bostonian jubilantly wrote to a relative, "I believe people never was more Universally pleased not so much one could I hear say he was sorry, but a smile sat on almost every ones countinance."

But another crowd action twelve days later, aimed this time at Oliver's brother-in-law, Lieutenant Governor Thomas Hutchinson, drew no praise from Boston's respectable citizens. On the night of August 26, a mob reportedly led by the South End leader Ebenezer MacIntosh attacked the homes of several customs officers. The crowd then completely destroyed Hutchinson's elaborately furnished townhouse in one of Boston's most fashionable districts. The lieutenant governor reported that by the next morning "one of the best finished houses in the Province had nothing remaining but the bare walls and floors." His trees and garden were ruined, his valuable library was lost, and the mob "emptied the house of every thing whatsoever except a part of the kitchen furniture." But Hutchinson took some comfort in the fact that "the encouragers of the first mob never intended matters should go this length and the people in general express the utmost detestation of this unparalleled outrage." (A portrait of Hutchinson is on page 141.)

The differences between the two Boston mobs of August 1765 exposed divisions that would continue to characterize subsequent colonial protests.

Americans' Divergent Interests

Few residents of the colonies sided with Great Britain during the 1760s, but various colonial groups had divergent goals. The skilled craftsmen who composed the Loyal Nine, and merchants, lawyers, and other members of the educated elite preferred orderly demonstrations confined to political issues. For the city's laborers, by contrast, economic grievances may have been paramount. Certainly, their "hellish Fury" as they wrecked Hutchinson's house suggests a resentment against his ostentatious display of wealth.

Colonists, like Britons, had a long tradition of crowd action in which disfranchised people took to the streets to redress deeply felt local grievances. But the Stamp Act controversy drew ordinary urban folk into the vortex of transatlantic politics for the first time. Matters that previously had been of concern only to the gentry or to members of colonial legislatures were now discussed on every street corner. Benjamin Franklin's daughter observed as much when she informed her father, then serving as a colonial agent in London, that "nothing else is talked of, the Dutch [Germans] talk of the stompt act the Negroes of the tamp, in short every body has something to say."

The entry of unskilled workers, slaves, and women into the realm of imperial politics both threatened and afforded an opportunity to the elite men who wanted to mount effective opposition to British measures. On the one hand, crowd action could have a stunning impact. Anti–Stamp Act demonstrations occurred in cities and towns stretching from Halifax, Nova Scotia, in the north, to the Caribbean island of Antigua in the south (see maps, page 133). They were so successful that by November 1, when the law was scheduled to take effect, not one stamp distributor was willing to carry out his official duties. Thus the act could not be enforced. But on the other hand, wealthy men recognized that mobs composed of the formerly

Sites of Major Demonstrations Against the Stamp Act *Every place named on these maps was the site of a demonstration against the Stamp Act of 1765; British colonies outside the eventual United States joined in the nearly universal opposition to the hated measure.* Source: From Lester J. Cappon et al., eds., *Atlas of Early American History: The Revolutionary Era, 1760–1790.* Copyright © 1976 by Princeton University Press. Reprinted by permission of Princeton University Press.

powerless—whose goals were not always identical to theirs (as the Boston experience showed)—could endanger their own dominance of the society. What would happen, they wondered, if the "hellish Fury" of the crowd were turned against them?

They therefore attempted to channel resistance into acceptable forms by creating an intercolonial association, the Sons of Liberty. The first such group was created in New York in early November, and branches

Sons of Liberty

spread rapidly through the coastal cities. Composed of merchants, lawyers, prosperous tradesmen like Paul Revere, and others, the Sons of Liberty by early 1766 linked protest leaders from Charleston, South Carolina, to Portsmouth, New Hampshire.

The Sons of Liberty could influence events but not control them. In Charleston in October 1765, an informally organized crowd shouting "Liberty Liberty and stamp'd paper" forced the resignation of

the South Carolina stamp distributor. The victory celebration a few days later—the largest demonstration the city had ever known—featured a British flag with the word "Liberty" emblazoned on it. But the new Charleston chapter of the Sons of Liberty was horrified when in January 1766 local slaves paraded through the streets similarly crying "Liberty." That was not the sort of liberty elite slaveowners had in mind.

In Philadelphia, resistance leaders were dismayed when an angry mob threatened to attack Benjamin Franklin's house. The city's laborers believed Franklin to be partly responsible for the Stamp Act, since he had obtained the post of stamp distributor for a close friend. But Philadelphia's artisans—the backbone of the opposition movement there and elsewhere—were fiercely loyal to Franklin, one of their own who had made good. They gathered to protect his home and family from the crowd. The house was saved, but the resulting split between the

British Ministries and Their American Policies

Head of Ministry	Major Acts
George Grenville	Sugar Act (1764) Currency Act (1764) Stamp Act (1765)
Lord Rockingham	Stamp Act repealed (1766) Declaratory Act (1766)
William Pitt/Charles Townshend	Townshend Acts (1767)
Lord North	Townshend duties (except for the tea tax) repealed (1770) Coercive Acts (1774) Quebec Act (1774)

better-off tradesmen and the common laborers prevented the establishment of a successful workingmen's alliance like that of Boston.

During the fall and winter of 1765–1766, opposition to the Stamp Act proceeded on three separate fronts. Colonial legislatures petitioned Parliament to repeal the hated law and in October sent delegates to an intercolonial congress, the first since 1754. The Stamp Act Congress met in New York to draft a unified but conservative statement of protest. At the same time, the Sons of Liberty held mass meetings, attempting to rally public support for the resistance movement. Finally, American merchants organized nonimportation associations to pressure British exporters. By the 1760s, one-quarter of all British exports were being sent to the colonies, and American merchants reasoned that London merchants whose sales suffered severely would lobby for repeal. Since times were bad and American merchants were finding few customers for imported goods anyway, a general moratorium on future purchases would also help to reduce their bloated inventories.

In March 1766, Parliament repealed the Stamp Act. The nonimportation agreements had had the anticipated effect, creating allies for the colonies among wealthy London merchants. But boycotts, formal protests, and crowd actions were less important in winning repeal than was the appointment of a new prime minister, chosen by George III for reasons unrelated to colonial politics. Lord Rockingham, who replaced Grenville in the summer of 1765, had opposed the Stamp Act, not because he believed

**Repeal of
the Stamp Act**

Parliament lacked power to tax the colonies but because he thought the law unwise and divisive. Thus although Rockingham proposed repeal, he linked it to passage of the Declaratory Act, which asserted Parliament's ability to tax and legislate for Britain's American possessions "in all cases whatsoever."

News of the repeal arrived in Newport, Rhode Island, in May, and the Sons of Liberty quickly dispatched messengers to carry the welcome tidings throughout the colonies. They organized celebrations commemorating the glorious event, which all stressed the Americans' unwavering loyalty to Great Britain. Their goal achieved, the Sons of Liberty dissolved. Few colonists saw the ominous implications of the Declaratory Act.

 Resistance to the Townshend Acts

The colonists had accomplished their immediate aim, but the long-term prospects were unclear. In the summer of 1766, another change in the ministry in London revealed how fragile their victory had been. The new prime minister was William Pitt, who as Britain's secretary of state had fostered cooperation between the colonies and Great Britain during the Seven Years War (see page 124). Now, however, Pitt was ill much of the time, and another minister, Charles Townshend, became the dominant force in the ministry. An ally of Grenville and a supporter of colonial taxation, Townshend decided to renew the attempt to obtain additional funds from Britain's American possessions.

The taxes Townshend proposed in 1767 were to be levied on trade goods like paper, glass, and tea, and thus seemed to be nothing more than extensions of the existing Navigation Acts. But the Townshend duties differed from previous customs duties in two ways. First, they were levied on items imported into the colonies from Britain, not from foreign countries. Thus they were at odds with mercantilist theory (see page 83). Second, they were designed to raise money to pay the salaries of some royal officials in the colonies. That posed a direct challenge to the colonial assemblies, which derived considerable power from threatening to withhold officials' salaries. In addition, Townshend's scheme provided for the creation of an American Board of Customs Commissioners and of vice-admiralty courts at Boston, Philadelphia, and Charleston. Both moves angered merchants, whose profits would be threatened by more vigorous enforcement of the Navigation Acts.

In 1765, months had passed before the colonists began to protest the Stamp Act. The passage of the Townshend Acts, however, drew a quick response. One series of essays in particular, *Letters from a Farmer in Pennsylvania* by the prominent lawyer John Dickinson, expressed a broad consensus. Eventually all but four colonial newspapers printed Dickinson's essays; in pamphlet form they went through seven American editions. Dickinson contended that Parliament could regulate colonial trade but could not exercise that power to raise revenue. By drawing a distinction between trade regulation and unacceptable commercial taxation, Dickinson avoided the sticky issue of consent and how it affected colonial subordination to Parliament. But his argument created a different, and equally knotty, problem. In effect it obligated the colonies to assess Parliament's motives in passing any law pertaining to trade before deciding whether to obey it. That was in the long run an unworkable position.

John Dickinson's Farmer's Letters

The Massachusetts assembly responded to the Townshend Acts by drafting a letter to be circulated among the other colonial legislatures, calling for unity and suggesting a joint petition of protest. Not the letter itself but the ministry's reaction to it united the colonies. When Lord Hillsborough, recently named to the new post of secretary of state for America, learned of the circular letter, he ordered Governor Francis Bernard of Massachusetts to insist that the assembly recall it. He also directed other governors to prevent their assemblies from discussing the letter. Hillsborough's order gave colonial assemblies the incentive they needed to join forces to oppose this new threat to their prerogatives. In late 1768 the Massachusetts legislature met, debated, and resoundingly rejected recall by a vote of 92 to 17. Bernard immediately dissolved the assembly, and other governors followed suit when their legislatures debated the circular letter.

Massachusetts Assembly Dissolved

The number of votes cast against recalling the circular letter—92—assumed ritual significance for the supporters of resistance. The figure 45 already had symbolic meaning because John Wilkes, a radical Londoner sympathetic to the American cause, had been jailed for libel in Britain for publishing an essay entitled *The North Briton No. 45*. In Boston, Paul Revere made a punchbowl weighing 45 ounces that held 45 gills (half-cups) and was engraved with the names of the 92 legislators; James Otis, John Adams, and others publicly drank 45 toasts from it. In Charleston, the city's tradesmen decorated a tree with 45 lights and set off 45 rockets. Carrying 45 candles, they adjourned to a tavern, where 45 tables were set with 45 bowls of wine, 45 bowls of punch, and 92 glasses.

Rituals of Resistance

Such public rituals served important educational functions. Just as the pamphlets by Otis, Dulany, Dickinson, and others acquainted literate colonists with the issues raised by British actions, so public rituals taught illiterate Americans about the reasons for resistance and familiarized them with the terms of the argument. When Boston's revived Sons of Liberty invited hundreds of city residents to dine with them each August 14 to commemorate the first Stamp Act uprising, and the Charleston Sons of Liberty held their meetings in public, crowds gathered to watch and listen. Likewise, the public singing of songs supporting the American cause helped to spread the word. The participants in such events were openly expressing their commitment to the cause of resistance and encouraging others to join them.

During the campaign against the Townshend duties, the Sons of Liberty and other American leaders made a deliberate effort to involve ordinary folk in the resistance movement. Most important, they urged colonists of all ranks and both sexes to sign agreements not to purchase or consume British

A Society of Patriotic Ladies (1775), attributed to Philip Dawes, an English printmaker. This grotesque caricature of female patriots shows the women emptying their tea into a chamber pot (at left) and flirting with their male counterparts (at center), while a neglected child sits below the table. The cartoon bears no resemblance to the actual event, the signing of an anti-British petition by female residents of Edenton, North Carolina.   Library of Congress.

walking through town in a solemn procession. Women throughout the colonies exchanged recipes for tea substitutes or drank coffee instead. The best known of the protests (because it was satirized in a British cartoon reproduced here), the so-called Edenton Ladies Tea Party, actually had little to do with tea. It was a meeting of prominent North Carolina women who pledged formally to work for the public good and to support resistance to British measures.

Women also encouraged home manufacturing. In many towns, young women calling themselves Daughters of Liberty met to spin in public in an effort to persuade other women to make homespun and thus end the colonies' dependence on British cloth. These symbolic displays of patriotism—publicized by newspapers and broadsides—served the same purpose as the male rituals involving the numbers 45 and 92. When young ladies from well-to-do families sat publicly at spinning wheels all day, eating only American food and drinking local herbal tea, and later listening to patriotic sermons, they were serving as political instructors. Many women took great satisfaction in their new-found role. When a New England satirist hinted that women discussed only "such triffling subjects as Dress, Scandal and Detraction" during their spinning bees, three Boston women replied angrily: "Inferior in abusive sarcasm, in personal invective, in low wit, we glory to be, but inferior in veracity, sincerity, love of virtue, of liberty and of our country, we would not willingly be to any."

But the colonists were by no means united in support of nonimportation and nonconsumption. If the Stamp Act protests had occasionally (as in Boston and Philadelphia) revealed a division between artisans and merchants on the one side and common laborers on the other, resistance to the Townshend Acts exposed new splits in American ranks. The most significant divided urban artisans and merchants, allies in 1765 and 1766, and it arose from a change in economic circumstances.

Divided Opinion over Boycotts

The Stamp Act boycotts had helped to revive a depressed economy by creating a demand for local products and reducing merchants' inventories. But in 1768 and 1769, merchants were enjoying boom times and had no financial incentive to support a boycott. As a result, merchants signed the agreements only reluctantly, sometimes violating them se-

products. The new consumerism that previously had linked colonists economically now linked them politically as well, supplying them with a ready method of displaying their allegiance. As "A Tradesman" wrote in a Philadelphia paper in 1770, it was essential "for the Good of the Whole, to strengthen the Hands of the Patriotic Majority, by agreeing not to purchase British Goods."

As the primary purchasers of textiles and household goods, women played a central role in the nonconsumption movement. In Boston more than three hundred matrons publicly promised not to buy or drink tea, "Sickness excepted." The women of Wilmington, North Carolina, burned their tea after

Daughters of Liberty

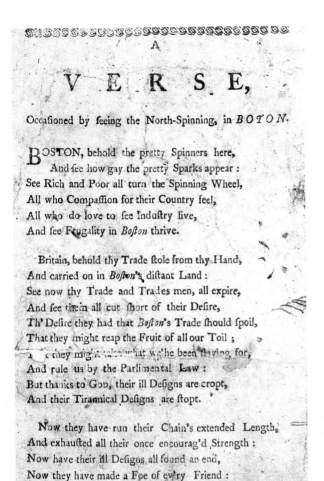

A VERSE,

Occasioned by feeing the North-Spinning, in *BOSTON.*

BOSTON, behold the pretty Spinners here,
    And fee how gay the pretty Sparks appear :
See Rich and Poor all turn the Spinning Wheel,
All who Compaffion for their Country feel,
All who do love to fee Induftry live,
And fee Frugality in *Bofton* thrive.

    Britain, behold thy Trade ftole from thy Hand,
And carried on in *Bofton's* diftant Land :
See now thy Trade and Tradesmen, all expire,
And fee them all cut fhort of their Defire,
Th' Defire they had that *Bofton's* Trade fhould fpoil,
That they might reap the Fruit of all our Toil ;
. . they might . . what we'he been ſlaving for,
And rule us by the Parlimental Law :
But thanks to GOD, their ill Defigns are cropt,
And their Tirannical Defigns are ftopt.

    Now they have run their Chain's extended Length,
And exhaufted all their once encourag'd Strength :
Now have their ill Defigns, all found an end,
Now they have made a Foe of every Friend :
Now let them ftarve and die the Death of thofe,
Who do the Intereft of their King oppofe.

    BOSTON: Printed and Sold 1769.

A 1769 Boston broadside commended the spinners, "Rich and Poor," who had "Compassion for their Country" and promoted "Frugality" during the Townshend Act crisis. The poet put into verse precisely the message the spinners intended to convey. Massachusetts Historical Society.

cretly. In contrast, artisans supported nonimportation enthusiastically, recognizing that the absence of British goods would create a ready market for their own manufactures. Thus tradesmen formed the core of the crowds that coerced both importers and their customers by picketing stores, publicizing offenders' names, and sometimes destroying property.

Such tactics were effective: colonial imports from England dropped dramatically in 1769, especially in New York, New England, and Pennsylvania.

But they also aroused heated opposition, creating a second major division among the colonists. Some Americans who supported resistance to British measures began to question the use of violence to force others to join the boycott. In addition, wealthier and more conservative colonists were frightened by the threat to private property inherent in the campaign. Political activism by ordinary colonists challenged the ruling elite's domination, just as its members had feared in 1765.

Disclosures that leading merchants were violating the nonimportation agreement caused dissension in the ranks of the boycotters, so Americans were relieved when news arrived in April 1770 that the Townshend duties had been repealed, with the exception of the tea tax. A new prime minister, Lord North, had persuaded Parliament that duties on trade within the empire were bad policy. Although some colonial leaders argued that nonimportation should continue until the tea tax was repealed, merchants quickly resumed importing. The rest of the Townshend Acts remained in force, but repeal of the taxes made the other laws appear less objectionable.

Repeal of the Townshend Duties

Growing Rifts

At first the new ministry in London did nothing to antagonize the colonists. Yet on the very day Lord North proposed repeal of the Townshend duties, a clash between civilians and soldiers in Boston led to the death of five Americans. The origins of the event that patriots called the Boston Massacre lay in repeated clashes between customs officers and the people of Massachusetts. The decision to base the American Board of Customs Commissioners in Boston was the source of the problem.

From the day of their arrival in November 1767, the customs commissioners were frequent targets of mob action. In June 1768 their seizure of patriot leader John Hancock's sloop *Liberty* on suspicion of smuggling caused a riot in which prominent customs officers' property was destroyed. The riot in turn helped to convince the ministry in London that troops were needed to maintain order in the unruly port. The assignment of two regiments of regulars to their city confirmed Bostonians' worst fears; the redcoats were a constant reminder of the oppressive potential of British power.

Bostonians found themselves hemmed in at every turn. Guards on Boston Neck, the entrance to the city, checked all travelers and their goods. Redcoat patrols roamed the city day and night, questioning and sometimes harassing passersby. Military parades were held on Boston Common, accompanied by martial music and often the public whipping of deserters and other violators of army rules. Parents began to fear for the safety of their daughters, who were subjected to soldiers' coarse sexual insults. But the greatest potential for violence lay in the uneasy relationship between the soldiers and Boston laborers. Many redcoats sought employment in their off-duty hours, competing for unskilled jobs with the city's ordinary workingmen. Members of the two groups brawled repeatedly in taverns and on the streets.

Early on the evening of March 5, 1770, a crowd of laborers began throwing hard-packed snowballs at soldiers guarding the Customs House. Goaded

Boston Massacre

beyond endurance, the sentries acted against express orders to the contrary and fired on the crowd, killing four and wounding eight, one of whom died a few days later. Resistance leaders idealized the dead rioters as martyrs for the cause of liberty, holding a solemn funeral and later commemorating March 5 annually with patriotic orations. Paul Revere's engraving of the massacre (based on a drawing by John Singleton Copley's half brother Henry Pelham and reproduced on page 139) was part of the propaganda campaign.

Leading patriots wanted to ensure that the soldiers did not become martyrs as well. Despite the political benefits the patriots derived from the massacre, it is unlikely that they approved of the crowd action that provoked it. Ever since the destruction of Hutchinson's house in August 1765, men allied with the Sons of Liberty had supported orderly demonstrations and expressed distaste for uncontrolled riots, of which the Boston Massacre was a prime example. Thus when the soldiers were tried for the killings in November, they were defended by John Adams and Josiah Quincy, Jr., both unwavering patriots. All but two of the accused men were acquitted, and those convicted were released after being branded on the thumb. Undoubtedly the favorable outcome of the trials prevented London officials from taking further steps against the city.

For more than two years after the Boston Massacre and the repeal of the Townshend duties, a superficial calm descended on the colonies. The most

A British Plot?

outspoken colonial newspapers, such as the *Boston Gazette*, the *Pennsylvania Journal*, and the *South Carolina Gazette*, published essays drawing on Real Whig ideology and accusing Great Britain of a deliberate plan to oppress the colonies. After the Stamp Act's repeal, the patriots had praised Parliament; following repeal of the Townshend duties, they warned of impending tyranny. What had seemed to be an isolated mistake, a single ill-chosen stamp tax, now appeared to be part of a plot against American liberties. Essayists pointed to Parliament's persecution of the British radical John Wilkes, the stationing of troops in Boston, and the growing number of vice-admiralty courts as evidence of plans to enslave the colonists. Indeed, patriot writers played repeatedly on the word *enslavement*. Most white colonists had direct knowledge of slavery (either as slaveholders themselves or as neighbors of slaveowners), and the threat of enslavement by Britain must have hit them with peculiar force.

Still, no one yet advocated complete independence from the mother country. Though the patriots were becoming increasingly convinced that they should seek freedom from parliamentary authority, they continued to acknowledge their British identity and their allegiance to George III. They began, therefore, to envision a system that would enable them to be ruled by their own elected legislatures while remaining loyal to the king. But any such scheme was alien to Britons' conception of the nature of their government, which was that Parliament held sole undivided sovereignty over the empire. Furthermore, in the British mind, Parliament encompassed the king as well as lords and commons, so separating the monarch from the legislature was impossible.

Then, in the fall of 1772, the North ministry began to implement the Townshend Act that provided for governors and judges to be paid from customs revenues. In early November, voters at a Boston town meeting established a Committee of Correspondence to publicize the decision by exchanging letters with other Massachusetts towns. Heading the committee was the man who had proposed its formation, Samuel Adams.

Samuel Adams was fifty-one in 1772, thirteen years older than his distant cousin John and by a

How do historians know whether ordinary people were familiar with the ideas propounded by the leaders of the American Revolution? This is a difficult question to answer, because most of the evidence about the patriots' ideology comes from pamphlets and newspapers aimed at the well educated. People who could read at only a basic level might not have been able to understand the sophisticated criticisms of British policies advanced in such writings. But because an engraver made his point visually rather than verbally, anyone, even illiterate folk, could interpret an image like Paul Revere's masterful portrayal of the Boston Massacre. The label "Butcher's Hall" on the Customs House merely reinforces the patriot view of the incident on March 5, 1770. The British soldiers are shown firing on an unresisting crowd (not the aggressive, angry mob described at the soldiers' trial), and a gun with smoke drifting up from its barrel emerges from a window above the redcoats, suggesting the complicity of civilian officials in what the patriots interpreted as an outrageous act.   Photo: Library of Congress.

decade the senior of most other leaders of American resistance. He had been a Boston tax collector, a member and clerk of the Massachusetts assembly, an ally of the Loyal Nine, and a member of the Sons of Liberty. His primary forum

Samuel Adams

was the Boston town meeting. Unswerving in his devotion to the American cause, Adams drew a sharp contrast between a corrupt, vice-ridden Britain and the colonies, peopled by simple, liberty-loving folk. An experienced political organizer, Adams continually stressed the necessity of prudent collective action. His Committee of Correspondence thus undertook the task of creating an informed consensus among all the residents of Massachusetts.

Such committees, which were eventually established throughout the colonies, represented the next logical step in the organization of American resistance. Until 1772, the protest movement was largely confined to the seacoast and primarily to major cities and towns (see maps, page 133). Adams realized that the time had come to widen the movement's geographic scope, to attempt to involve the residents of the interior in the struggle. Accordingly, the Boston town meeting directed the Committee of Correspondence "to state the Rights of the Colonists and of this Province in particular," to list "the Infringements and Violations thereof that have been, or from time to time may be made," and to send copies to the other towns in the province. In return, Boston requested "a free communication of their Sentiments on this Subject."

Boston Committee of Correspondence

The statement of colonial rights prepared by the Bostonians declared that Americans had absolute rights to life, liberty, and property. The idea that "a British house of commons, should have a right, at pleasure, to give and grant the property of the colonists" was "irreconcileable" with "the first principles of natural law and Justice . . . and of the British Constitution in particular." The list of grievances complained of taxation without representation, the presence of unnecessary troops and customs officers on American soil, the use of imperial revenues to pay colonial officials, the expanded jurisdiction of vice-admiralty courts, and even the nature of the instructions given to American governors by their superiors in London.

The entire document, which was printed as a pamphlet for distribution to the towns, exhibited none of the hesitation that had characterized colonial claims against Parliament in the 1760s. No longer were patriots—at least in Boston—preoccupied with defining the precise limits of parliamentary authority. No longer did they mention the necessity of obedience to Parliament. They were committed to a course that placed American rights first, loyalty to Great Britain a distant second.

The response of the Massachusetts towns to the committee's pamphlet must have caused Samuel Adams to rejoice. Some towns disagreed with Boston's assessment of the state of affairs, but most

aligned themselves with the city. From Braintree came the assertion that "all civil officers are or ought to be Servants to the people and dependent upon them for their official Support, and every instance to the Contrary from the Governor downwards tends to crush and destroy civil liberty." The town of Holden declared that "the People of New England have never given the People of Britain any Right of Jurisdiction over us." The citizens of Petersham commented that resistance to tyranny was "the first and highest social Duty of this people." And Pownallborough warned, "Allegiance is a relative Term and like Kingdoms and commonwealths is local and has its bounds." Beliefs like these made the next crisis in Anglo-American affairs the final one.

 ## The Boston Tea Party

The only one of the Townshend duties still in effect by 1773 was the tax on tea. In the years after 1770 some Americans continued to boycott English tea, while others resumed drinking it either openly or in secret. As explained in Chapter 4, tea was important in the colonists' diet and in their social lives, so observing the boycott required them not only to forgo a favorite beverage but also to alter habitual forms of socializing. Tea thus retained an explosively symbolic character even though the boycott was less than fully effective after 1770.

In May 1773, Parliament passed an act designed to save the East India Company from bankruptcy. The company, which held a legal monopoly on British trade with the East Indies, was of critical importance to the British economy (and to the financial well-being of many prominent British politicians who had invested in its stock). According to the Tea Act, certain duties paid on tea were to be returned to the company, and tea was to be sold only by designated agents, a method of distribution that would enable the East India Company to avoid colonial middlemen and undersell any competitors, even smugglers.

Tea Act

The net result of bypassing the middlemen would be cheaper tea for American consumers. Resistance leaders, however, interpreted the new measure as a pernicious device to make them admit Parliament's right to tax them, for the less-expensive tea would still be taxed under the Townshend law. Others saw the Tea Act as the first step in the establishment of an East India Company monopoly of all colonial trade. Residents of the four cities designated to receive the first shipments of tea accordingly prepared to respond to what they perceived as a new threat to their freedom.

In New York City, the tea ships failed to arrive on schedule. In Philadelphia, the governor of Pennsylvania persuaded the captain to turn around and sail back to Britain. In Charleston, the tea was unloaded, stored under the direction of local tradesmen, and later destroyed. The only confrontation occurred in Boston, where both sides—the town meeting, joined by participants from nearby towns, and Governor Thomas Hutchinson, two of whose sons were tea agents—rejected compromise.

The first of three tea ships, the *Dartmouth*, entered Boston harbor on November 28. The customs laws required cargo to be landed and the appropriate duty paid by its owners within twenty days of a ship's arrival; otherwise, the cargo had to be seized by customs officers and sold at auction. After a series of mass meetings, Bostonians voted to post guards on the wharf to prevent the tea from being unloaded. Hutchinson, for his part, refused to permit the vessels to leave the harbor. John Singleton Copley, whose father-in-law was a tea agent, tried to mediate the dispute.

On December 16, one day before the cargo would have been confiscated, more than five thousand people (nearly a third of the city's population) crowded into Old South Church. The meeting, chaired by Samuel Adams, made a final attempt to persuade Hutchinson to send the tea back to England. But the governor remained adamant. In the early evening Adams reportedly announced "that he could think of nothing further to be done—that they had now done all they could for the Salvation of their Country." Cries then rang out from the back of the crowd: "Boston harbor a tea-pot tonight! The Mohawks are come!" Small groups pushed their way out of the meeting. Within a few minutes, about sixty men crudely disguised as Indians assembled at the wharf, boarded the three ships, and dumped the cargo into the harbor. By 9 P.M. their work was done: 342 chests of tea worth approximately £10,000 floated in splinters on the water.

Among the "Indians" were many representatives of Boston's artisans, including Paul Revere. Five masons, eleven carpenters and builders, three leatherworkers, a blacksmith, two barbers, a coachmaker, and twelve apprentices have been identified as par-

Thomas Hutchinson, the governor of Massachusetts, helped to incite the Boston Tea Party by refusing to allow the tea ships to leave the harbor. This portrait conveys the governor's haughty demeanor.   Massachusetts Historical Society.

ticipants. That their ranks also included four farmers from outside Boston, ten merchants, two doctors, a teacher, and a bookseller illustrated the widespread support for the resistance movement. The next day John Adams exulted in his diary that the Tea Party was "so bold, so daring, so firm, intrepid and inflexible" that "I can't but consider it as an epocha in history."

The North administration reacted with considerably less enthusiasm when it learned of the Tea Party. In March 1774, Parliament adopted the first of four laws that became known as the Coercive, or Intolerable, Acts. It ordered the port of Boston closed until the tea was paid for, prohibiting all but coastal trade in food and firewood. Later in the spring, Parliament passed three other punitive measures. The Massachusetts Government Act altered

Coercive and Quebec Acts

the province's charter, substituting an appointed council for the elected one, increasing the governor's powers, and forbidding most town meetings. The Justice Act provided that a person accused of committing murder in the course of suppressing a riot or enforcing the laws could be tried outside the colony where the incident had occurred. Finally, the Quartering Act gave broad authority to military commanders seeking to house their troops in private dwellings. Thus the Coercive Acts punished not only Boston but also Massachusetts as a whole, alerting other colonies to the possibility that their residents, too, could be subject to retaliation if they opposed British authority.

After passing the last of the Coercive Acts, Parliament turned its attention to much-needed reforms in the government of Quebec. The Quebec Act thereby became linked with the Coercive Acts in the minds of the patriots. Intended to ease strains that had arisen since the British conquest of the formerly French colony, the Quebec Act granted greater religious freedom to Catholics—alarming Protestant colonists, who equated Roman Catholicism with religious and political despotism. It also reinstated French civil law, which had been replaced by British procedures in 1763, and it established an appointed council (rather than an elected legislature) as the governing body of the colony. Finally, in an attempt to provide northern Indians with some protection against Anglo-American settlement, the act annexed to Quebec the area east of the Mississippi River and north of the Ohio River. That region, parts of which were claimed by individual seacoast colonies, was thus removed from their jurisdiction.

Members of Parliament who voted for the punitive legislation believed that the acts would be obeyed and that at long last they had solved the

Implications of the Coercive Acts
problem posed by the troublesome Americans. But the patriots showed little inclination to bow to the wishes of Parliament. In their eyes, the Coercive Acts and the Quebec Act proved what they had feared since 1768: that Great Britain had embarked on a deliberate plan to oppress them. If the port of Boston could be closed, why not the ports of Philadelphia or New York? If the royal charter of Massachusetts could be changed, why not the charter of South Carolina? If certain people could be removed from their home colonies for trial, why not

all violators of all laws? If troops could be forcibly quartered in private houses, did not that action pave the way for the occupation of all of America? If the Roman Catholic Church could receive favored status in Quebec, why not everywhere? It seemed as though the full dimensions of the plot against American rights and liberties had at last been revealed.

The Boston Committee of Correspondence urged all the colonies to join in an immediate renewed boycott of British goods. But the other provinces were not yet ready to take such a drastic step. They suggested that another intercolonial congress be convened to consider an appropriate response. Few people wanted to take hasty action; even the most ardent patriots remained loyal to Britain and hoped for reconciliation with its leaders. Despite their objections to British policy, they continued to see themselves as part of the empire. Americans were approaching the brink of confrontation, but they had not committed themselves to an irrevocable break. So the colonies agreed to send delegates to Philadelphia in September to attend a Continental Congress.

 Conclusion

During the preceding decade, momentous changes had occurred in the ways colonists thought about themselves and their allegiance. The number of colonists who defined themselves as political actors had increased substantially. Once linked unquestioningly to Great Britain, they had begun to develop a sense of their own identity as Americans, including a recognition of the cultural and social gulf that separated them from Britons. They had started to realize that their concept of the political process differed from that held by people in the mother country. They also had come to understand that their economic interests did not necessarily coincide with those of Great Britain. Colonial political leaders reached such conclusions only after a long train of events, some of them violent, had altered their understanding of their relationship with the mother country. Parliamentary acts such as the Stamp Act and the Townshend Acts had elicited colonial responses—both ideological and practical—that produced further responses from Britain. Tensions escalated until they climaxed in the Tea Party. From that point on, there was to be no turning back.

In the late summer of 1774, the Americans were committed to resistance but not to independence.

Even so, they had started to sever the bonds of empire. During the next decade, they would forge the bonds of a new American nationality to replace those rejected Anglo-American ties.

Suggestions for Further Reading

General

Ian R. Christie and Benjamin W. Labaree, *Empire or Independence, 1760–1776: A British-American Dialogue on the Coming of the American Revolution* (1976); Edward Countryman, *The American Revolution* (1985); Marc Egnal, *A Mighty Empire: The Origins of the American Revolution* (1988); Ronald Hoffman and Peter Albert, eds., *The Transforming Hand of Revolution: Reconsidering the American Revolution as a Social Movement* (1995); Merrill Jensen, *The Founding of a Nation: A History of the American Revolution, 1763–1776* (1968); John Phillip Reid, *The Constitutional History of the American Revolution* (1995); Robert W. Tucker and David C. Hendrickson, *The Fall of the First British Empire: Origins of the War of American Independence* (1982).

Colonial Warfare and the British Empire

Fred Anderson, *A People's Army: Massachusetts Soldiers and Society in the Seven Years' War* (1984); Lawrence Henry Gipson, *The British Empire Before the American Revolution* (1936–1970); Douglas Leach, *Roots of Conflict: British Armed Forces and Colonial Americans, 1677–1763* (1986); Robert C. Newbold, *The Albany Congress and Plan of Union of 1754* (1955); William Pencak, *War, Politics, and Revolution in Provincial Massachusetts* (1981); Alan Rogers, *Empire and Liberty: American Resistance to British Authority, 1755–1763* (1974); John Shy, *Toward Lexington: The Role of the British Army in the Coming of the American Revolution* (1965); James Titus, *The Old Dominion at War: Society, Politics, and Warfare in Late Colonial Virginia* (1991).

British Politics and Policy

Colin Bonwick, *English Radicals and the American Revolution* (1977); James E. Bradley, *Popular Politics and the American Revolution in England* (1986); John Brewer, *Party Ideology and Popular Politics at the Accession of George III* (1976); John Brooke, *King George III* (1972); John L. Bullion, *A Great and Necessary Measure: George Grenville and the Genesis of the Stamp Act, 1763–1765* (1981); Michael Kammen, *A Rope of Sand: The Colonial Agents, British Politics, and the American Revolution* (1968); Nancy F. Koehn, *The Power of Commerce: Economy and Governance in the First British Empire* (1994); P. D. G. Thomas, *Tea Party to Independence* (1991); P. D. G. Thomas, *The Townshend Duties Crisis* (1987); P. D. G. Thomas, *British Politics and the Stamp Act Crisis* (1975).

Native Americans and the West

Richard Aquila, *The Iroquois Restoration: Iroquois Diplomacy on the Colonial Frontier, 1701–1754* (1983); David H. Corkran, *The Cherokee Frontier: Conflict and Survival, 1740–1762* (1962); Gregory Dowd, *A Spirited Resistance: The North American Indian Struggle for Unity, 1745–1815* (1992); Francis Jennings, *Empire of Fortune: Crowns, Colonies and Tribes in the Seven Years' War in America* (1988); Howard H. Peckham, *Pontiac and the Indian Uprising* (1947); Jack M. Sosin, *Whitehall and the Wilderness: The Middle West in British Colonial Policy, 1760–1775* (1961); Richard White, *The Middle Ground: Indians, Empires and Republics in the Great Lakes Region, 1650–1815* (1991).

Political and Economic Thought

Bernard Bailyn, *The Ideological Origins of the American Revolution* (1967); J. C. D. Clark, *The Language of Liberty, 1660–1832: Political Discourse and Social Dynamics in the Anglo-American World* (1994); J. E. Crowley, *This Sheba, Self: The Conceptualization of Economic Life in Eighteenth-Century America* (1974); Jay Fliegelman, *Prodigals and Pilgrims: The American Revolution Against Patriarchal Authority, 1750–1800* (1982).

American Resistance

David Ammerman, *In the Common Cause: American Response to the Coercive Acts of 1774* (1974); T. H. Breen, *Tobacco Culture: The Mentality of the Great Tidewater Planters on the Eve of the Revolution* (1985); Richard D. Brown, *Revolutionary Politics in Massachusetts: The Boston Committee of Correspondence and the Towns, 1772–1774* (1970); Joseph Albert Ernst, *Money and Politics in America, 1755–1775: A Study in the Currency Act of 1764 and the Political Economy of Revolution* (1973); Paul Gilje, *The Road to Mobocracy: Popular Disorder in New York City, 1763–1834* (1987); Dirk Hoerder, *Crowd Action in Revolutionary Massachusetts, 1765–1780* (1977); Benjamin W. Labaree, *The Boston Tea Party* (1964); Pauline R. Maier, *The Old Revolutionaries: Political Lives in the Age of Samuel Adams* (1980); Pauline R. Maier, *From Resistance to Revolution: Colonial Radicals and the Development of American Opposition to Britain, 1765–1776* (1972); Edmund S. Morgan and Helen M. Morgan, *The Stamp Act Crisis: Prologue to Revolution* (1953); Gary B. Nash, *The Urban Crucible: Social Change, Political Consciousness, and the Origins of the American Revolution* (1979); Bruce A. Ragsdale, *A Planters' Republic: The Search for Economic Independence in Revolutionary Virginia* (1996); Richard Ryerson, *The Revolution Has Now Begun: The Radical Committees of Philadelphia, 1765–1776* (1978); Peter Shaw, *American Patriots and the Rituals of Revolution* (1981); John W. Tyler, *Smugglers and Patriots: Boston Merchants and the Advent of the American Revolution* (1986); Richard Walsh, *Charleston's Sons of Liberty: A Study of the Artisans, 1763–1789* (1959); Hiller B. Zobel, *The Boston Massacre* (1970).

CHAPTER

6

A Revolution, Indeed
1774–1783

W hen John Provey and Richard Weaver appeared before the loyalist claims commissioners in London at the end of the Revolution, the commissioners were not impressed with their descriptions of losses and loyal service to the king. Such men had "no right to ask or expect any thing from Government," the commissioners declared. Their applications "hardly deserve[d] a serious Investigation or a serious Answer." So Provey and Weaver, along with most of the forty-five other men in the same circumstances, were denied any assistance from the funds allocated by Parliament to compensate loyalists for the damages they had incurred by opposing the Revolution. Why were Weaver and Provey treated thus? They were African-Americans.

John Provey, a North Carolinian, had been the slave of a lawyer; Richard Weaver, a Philadelphian, was freeborn. Provey served in a black corps of the British army during the war; Weaver left Philadelphia with the British troops when they evacuated that city in 1778 and made his way to London the following year. Both had wives and children at the time they requested government assistance. Because they were denied the help they sought, they and their families, along with hundreds of other African-Americans, became dependent on charity disbursed by a group of civic-minded London merchants, the Committee to Aid the Black Poor, which was formed in 1786.

Seeing no future for themselves in London, they both agreed to emigrate to West Africa, to the new colony of Sierra Leone, which was sponsored by the Black Poor Committee. John Provey died on shipboard before the vessels even left London. But Richard Weaver went to Sierra Leone and was elected the first governor of the tiny colony, composed largely of exiled African-American loyalists. Conflicts with a nearby ruler and with slavers who established a post near the settlement almost

In 1787, John Trumbull painted Washington and his officers participating in "The Surrender of Lord Cornwallis at Yorktown" six years earlier. Trumbull devoted his career to painting large, patriotic canvases that illustrated important moments in the nation's history. Although he was not present at the events he portrayed, he sketched his subjects from life and relied on their descriptions when he composed his works, which always depicted the nation's leaders in heroic fashion.

Yale University Art Gallery (a detail) Trumbull Collection

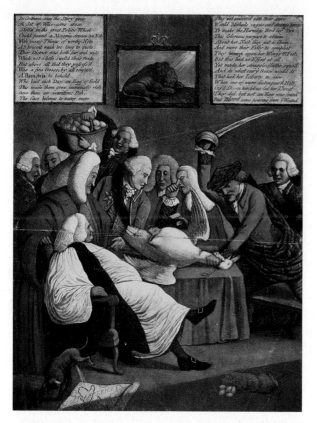

"The Wise Men of Gotham and Their Goose," published in 1776, was a British satirist's look at his nation's American policy. The cartoonist showed British politicians in the process of killing the colonial goose that laid the golden eggs (displayed in a basket in the background) while the British lion slumbers overhead and the king watches unemotionally. As in the cartoon of the "Patriotic Ladies" on page 136, a urinating dog symbolizes the artist's disgust with the proceedings. John Carter Brown Library at Brown University.

destroyed it. But in 1792 the future of the colony was assured when an additional twelve hundred African-American refugees arrived from Nova Scotia, where they had fled immediately after the war.

The little-known tale of the black loyalists who returned to the homeland of their ancestors is but one dramatic example of the disruptive effects of the American Revolution. The Revolution was more than just a series of clashes between British and patriot armies with the victors emerging nobly, as the illustration on page 144 might imply. The Revolution uprooted thousands of families, disrupted the economy, reshaped society by forcing many colonists into permanent exile, led Americans to develop new conceptions of politics, and created a na-

tion from thirteen separate colonies. Thus it marked a significant turning point in Americans' collective history.

The struggle for independence required revolutionary leaders to accomplish three separate but closely related tasks. The first was political and ideological: transforming a consensus favoring loyal resistance into a coalition supporting independence. They accordingly adopted a variety of measures (ranging from persuasion to coercion) to enlist all European-Americans in the patriot cause. Fearing with some reason that Indians and blacks would side with Britain, the colonies' elected leaders hoped at least to ensure those groups' neutrality in the impending conflict.

The second task involved foreign relations. To win independence, patriot leaders knew they needed international recognition and aid, particularly from France. Thus they dispatched to Paris the most experienced American diplomat, Benjamin Franklin, who had served for years as a colonial agent in London. Franklin skillfully negotiated the Franco-American alliance of 1778, which was to prove crucial to winning independence.

Only the third task directly involved the British. George Washington, commander-in-chief of the American army, soon recognized that his primary goal should be not to win battles but to avoid losing them decisively. The outcome of any one battle was less important than ensuring that his army survived to fight another day. Consequently, the story of the Revolutionary War reveals British action and American reaction, British attacks and American defenses. The American war effort was aided by the failure of British military planners to analyze accurately the problem confronting them. Until it was too late, they treated the war against the colonists as they treated wars against other Europeans: they concentrated on winning battles and did not consider the difficulties of achieving their main goal, retaining the colonies' allegiance. In the end, the Americans' triumph owed more to their own endurance and to Britain's mistakes than to their military prowess.

 ## Government by Congress and Committee

When the fifty-five delegates to the First Continental Congress convened in Philadelphia in September 1774, they knew that any measures they adopted were likely to enjoy support among many of their

• *Important Events* •

1774	First Continental Congress meets in Philadelphia, adopts Declaration of Rights and Grievances
	Continental Association implements economic boycott of Britain; committees of observation established to oversee boycott
1774–75	Provincial conventions replace collapsing colonial governments
1775	Battles of Lexington and Concord; first shots of war fired
	Second Continental Congress begins
	Lord Dunmore's proclamation offers freedom to patriots' slaves if they join British forces
1776	Thomas Paine publishes *Common Sense*, advocating independence
	British evacuate Boston
	Declaration of Independence adopted
	New York City falls to British
1777	British take Philadelphia
	Burgoyne surrenders at Saratoga
1778	French alliance brings vital assistance to the United States
	British evacuate Philadelphia
1779	Sullivan expedition destroys Iroquois villages
1780	British take Charleston
1781	Cornwallis surrenders at Yorktown
1782	Peace negotiations begin
1783	Treaty of Paris signed, granting independence to the United States

fellow countrymen and countrywomen. That summer, open meetings held throughout the colonies had endorsed the idea of another nonimportation pact. Participants in such meetings promised (in the words of the freeholders of Johnston County, North Carolina) to "strictly adhere to, and abide by, such Regulations and Restrictions as the Members of the said General Congress shall agree to and judge most convenient." Committees of correspondence publicized these meetings so effectively that Americans everywhere knew about them. Most of the congressional delegates were selected by extralegal provincial conventions whose members were chosen at such local gatherings, since governors had forbidden regular assemblies to conduct formal elections. Thus the very act of designating delegates to attend the Congress involved Americans in open defiance of British authority.

The colonies' leading political figures—most of them lawyers, merchants, and planters—attended the Philadelphia Congress. The Massachusetts delegation included both Samuel

First Continental Congress

Adams, the experienced organizer of Boston resistance, and his younger cousin John, an ambitious lawyer. Among others, New York sent John Jay, a talented young attorney. From Pennsylvania came the

conservative Joseph Galloway and his long-time rival, John Dickinson. Virginia elected Richard Henry Lee and Patrick Henry, both noted for their patriotic zeal, as well as George Washington. Most of these men had never met, but in the weeks, months, and years that followed they became the chief architects of the new nation.

The congressmen faced three tasks when they convened at Carpenters Hall on September 5, 1774. The first two were explicit: defining American grievances and developing a plan for resistance. The third—outlining a theory of their constitutional relationship with Great Britain—was less clear-cut and proved troublesome. The most radical congressmen, like Lee of Virginia, argued that colonists owed allegiance only to George III and that Parliament was nothing more than a local legislature for Great Britain with no authority over the colonies. The conservatives—Joseph Galloway and his allies—proposed a formal plan of union that would have required Parliament and a new American legislature to consent jointly to all laws pertaining to the colonies. After heated debate, delegates narrowly rejected Galloway's proposal, but they were not prepared to accept the radicals' position either.

Finally, they accepted a compromise position worked out by John Adams. The crucial clause that Adams drafted in the Congress's Declaration of

Declaration of Rights and Grievances

Rights and Grievances read in part: "From the necessity of the case, and a regard to the mutual interest of both countries, we cheerfully consent to the operation of such acts of the British parliament, as are bona fide, restrained to the regulation of our external commerce." Notice the key phrases. "From the necessity of the case" declared that Americans would obey Parliament only because they thought that doing so was in the best interest of both countries. "Bona fide, restrained to the regulation of our external commerce" made it clear to Lord North that they would continue to resist taxes in disguise, like the Townshend duties. Most striking of all was that such language—which only a few years before would have been regarded as irredeemably radical—could be presented and accepted as a compromise in the fall of 1774. The Americans had come a long way since their first hesitant protests against the Sugar Act ten years earlier.

With the constitutional issue resolved, the delegates readily agreed on the laws they wanted repealed (notably the Coercive Acts) and decided to implement an economic boycott while petitioning the king for relief. They adopted the Continental Association, which called for nonimportation of British goods (effective December 1, 1774), nonconsumption of British products (effective March 1, 1775), and nonexportation of American goods to Britain and the British West Indies (effective September 10, 1775, so that southern planters could market their 1774 tobacco crop, which had to be dried and cured before sale).

To enforce the Continental Association, Congress recommended the election of committees of observation and inspection in every American locality. By specifying that committee members be chosen by all persons qualified to vote for members of the lower house of the colonial legislatures, Congress guaranteed the committees a broad popular base. In some places the committeemen were former local officeholders; in other towns they were men who had never before held office. Everywhere, these committeemen—perhaps seven to eight thousand of them in the colonies as a whole—became the local leaders of American resistance.

Such committees were officially charged only with overseeing implementation of the boycott, but

Committees of Observation

over the next six months they became de facto governments. They examined merchants' records and published the names of those who continued to import British goods. They also promoted home manufactures, encouraging Americans to adopt simple modes of dress and behavior to symbolize their commitment to liberty and virtuous behavior. Since expensive leisure-time activities were believed to reflect vice and corruption, Congress urged Americans to forgo dancing, gambling, horseracing, cockfighting, and other forms of "extravagance and dissipation." Some committees accordingly forbade dancing, extracted apologies from people caught gambling or racing, prohibited the slaughter of lambs (because of the need for wool), and offered prizes for the best locally made cloth.

Thus the committees gradually extended their authority over many aspects of American life. They attempted to identify opponents of American resistance, developing elaborate spy networks, circulating copies of the Continental Association for signatures, and investigating reports of dissident remarks and activities. Suspected dissenters were first urged to support the colonial cause; if they failed to do so, the committees had them watched, restricted their movements, or tried to force them to leave the area. People engaging in casual political exchanges with friends one day could find themselves charged with "treasonable conversation" the next. One Massachusetts man, for example, was called before his local committee for maligning the Congress as "a Pack or Parcell of Fools" that was "as tyrannical as Lord North and ought to be opposed & resisted." When he refused to recant, the committee ordered him watched.

Those who dissented more openly received harsher treatment, as the experiences of the Reverend John Agnew of Virginia demonstrate. Agnew, an Anglican, insisted on warning his congregation of "the danger and sin of rebellion." He rejected the committee's summons and was thereafter ostracized by its order. Millers would not grind his corn, and doctors would not treat his sick wife and children. The committee tried to intimidate him by sending armed men to his church to beat drums and drill during services. When that failed, patriots nailed shut the church's doors and windows. Finally Agnew and his oldest son fled, but the persecution of his wife and younger children continued. She was, she later recalled, "daily insulted and robbed . . . [and] searched under various pretense."

While the committees of observation were expanding their power during the winter and early spring of 1775, the regular colonial governments were collapsing. Only in Connecticut, Rhode Island, Delaware, and Pennsylvania did legislatures continue to meet without encountering patriot challenges to their authority. In every other colony, popularly elected provincial conventions took over the task of running the government, sometimes entirely replacing the legislatures and at other times holding concurrent sessions. In late 1774 and early 1775, these conventions approved the Continental Association, elected delegates to the Second Continental Congress (scheduled for May), organized militia units, and gathered arms and ammunition. Unable to stem the tide of resistance, the British-appointed governors and councils watched helplessly as their authority crumbled.

Provincial Conventions

The frustrating experience of Governor Josiah Martin of North Carolina is a case in point. After a provincial convention was called to meet at New Bern on April 4, 1775—the same day the legislature was to convene—Martin asked all citizens to "renounce disclaim and discourage all such meetings cabals and illegal proceedings . . . which can only tend to introduce disorder and anarchy." When the convention met at New Bern, its membership proved to be virtually identical to that of the colonial legislature. The delegates proceeded to act alternately in both capacities and even passed some joint resolves. Continuing the farce, the exasperated Martin delivered a speech to the assembly denouncing the convention. Three days later, Martin wrote to officials in London, admitting that his government was "absolutely prostrate, impotent, and that nothing but the shadow of it is left."

Royal officials in other colonies suffered similar humiliations. Courts were prevented from holding sessions; taxes were paid to the conventions' agents rather than to provincial tax collectors; sheriffs' powers were challenged; and militiamen would muster only when committees ordered. In short, during the six months preceding the battles at Lexington and Concord, independence was being won at the local level, but without formal acknowledgment and for the most part without bloodshed. Not many Americans fully realized what was happening. The vast majority still proclaimed their loyalty to Great Britain and denied that they sought to leave the empire. Among the few who most clearly recognized the trend toward independence were those who opposed it.

Choosing Sides: Loyalists, African-Americans, and Indians

The first protests against British measures, in the mid-1760s, had won the support of most colonists. Only in the late 1760s and early 1770s did a significant number of Americans begin to question both aims and tactics of the resistance movement. By 1774 and 1775 such people found themselves in a difficult position. Like their more radical counterparts, most of them objected to parliamentary policies, favoring some kind of constitutional reform. Joseph Galloway, for instance, was a conservative by American standards, but his plan for restructuring the empire was too novel for Britain to accept. Nevertheless, if forced to a choice, these colonists sympathized with Great Britain rather than with an independent America. The events of the crucial year between the passage of the Coercive Acts and the outbreak of fighting in Massachusetts crystallized their thinking. Their objections to violent protest, their desire to uphold the legally constituted colonial governments, and their fears of anarchy combined to make them especially sensitive to the dangers of resistance.

Some conservatives began in 1774 and 1775 to publish essays and pamphlets critical of the Congress and its allied committees. In New York City, a group of Anglican clergymen jointly wrote pamphlets and essays arguing the importance of maintaining a cordial connection between Britain and America. In Pennsylvania, Joseph Galloway published *A Candid Examination of the Mutual Claims of Great Britain and the Colonies*, attacking the Continental Congress for rejecting his plan of union. In Massachusetts, the young attorney Daniel Leonard, writing under the pseudonym Massachusettensis, engaged in a prolonged newspaper debate with Novanglus (John Adams). Leonard and others realized that what had begun as a dispute over the nature of American subordination to Parliament was now raising the question of whether the colonies would remain linked to Great Britain at all. "Rouse up at last from your slumber!" the Reverend Thomas Bradbury Chandler of New Jersey cried out to Americans. "There is a set of people

John Singleton Copley married into a loyalist family. His father-in-law, Richard Clarke, was one of the Boston tea agents in 1773. Copley was in Italy studying art when the war began but joined his exiled wife and father-in-law in London in 1776. His sentimental portrait of the family (with himself in the background) commemorated their reunion. The only person in the painting who ever returned to America was his daughter Elizabeth (center), who grew up to marry a Bostonian. Andrew W. Mellon Fund © National Gallery of Art, Washington, D.C.

among us . . . who have formed a scheme for establishing an independent government or empire in America."

Some colonists heeded the conservative pamphleteers' warnings. About one-fifth of the Anglo-American population remained loyal to Great Britain, actively opposing independence and remaining true to a self-conception that patriots proved willing to abandon. That there were so few active loyalists is surprising, since joining the patriot cause required a far more significant change of allegiance than did loyalism.

Loyalists, Patriots, and Neutrals

With notable exceptions, most people of the following descriptions remained loyal to the Crown: British-appointed government officials; merchants whose trade depended on imperial connections; Anglican clergy everywhere and lay Anglicans in the North, where their denomination was in the minority (the king was the head of their church as well as head of state); former officers and enlisted men from the British army, many of whom had settled in America after 1763; non-English ethnic minorities, especially Scots; tenant farmers, particularly those whose landlords sided with the patriots; members of persecuted religious sects; and many of the back-country southerners who had rebelled against eastern rule in the 1760s and early 1770s. All these people had one thing in common: patriot leaders were their long-standing opponents, though for varying reasons. Ethnic minorities in particular had long felt excluded from the colonial political process. Local and provincial disputes thus helped to determine which side people chose in the imperial conflict.

Active patriots, who accounted for about two-fifths of the population, came chiefly from the groups that had dominated colonial society, either numerically or politically. Among them were yeoman farmers, members of dominant Protestant sects (both Old and New Lights), Chesapeake gentry, merchants dealing mainly in American commodities, city artisans, elected officeholders, and people of English descent. Wives usually but not always adopted their husbands' political beliefs. Although all these patriots supported the Revolution, they pursued divergent goals within the broader coalition, as they had in the 1760s. Some sought limited political reform, others extensive political change, and still others social and economic reforms. (The ways in which their concerns interacted are discussed in Chapter 7.)

There remained in the middle perhaps two-fifths of the white population. Some of those who tried to avoid taking sides were sincere pacifists, such as Quakers. Others opportunistically shifted their allegiance to whatever side happened to be winning at the time. Still others simply wanted to be left alone; they cared little about politics and usually obeyed whoever was in power. But such colonists also resisted British and Americans alike when the demands on them seemed too heavy—when taxes became too high, for example, or when calls for militia service came too often. Their attitude might best be summed up in the phrase "a plague on both your houses." Such persons made up an especially large proportion of the population in the southern backcountry, where Scots-Irish settlers had little love for either the patriot gentry or the English authorities.

To American patriots, apathy or neutrality was a crime as heinous as loyalism. In their minds, those who were not for them were against them. By the winter of 1775–1776, the Second Continental Congress was recommending that all "disaffected" persons be disarmed and arrested. State legislatures passed laws prescribing severe penalties for suspected loyalists. Many began to require all voters (or, in some cases, all free adult men) to take oaths of allegiance; the penalty for refusal was usually banishment or extra taxes. After 1777, many states confiscated the property of banished loyalists and used the proceeds for the war effort.

During the war, loyalists congregated in cities held by the British army. When those posts were evacuated at war's end, loyalists scattered to different parts of the British Empire—Britain, the West Indies, and especially Canada. In the provinces of Nova Scotia, New Brunswick, and Ontario they recreated their lives as colonists, laying the foundations of British Canada. All told, perhaps as many as 100,000 Americans preferred to leave their homeland rather than live in a nation independent of British rule. That preference attests to the depth of their loyalty to the monarchy and their Anglo-American identity.

The patriots' policies helped to ensure that the scattered and persecuted loyalists could not band together to threaten the revolutionary cause. But loyalists were not the patriots' only worry. They feared that Indians and slaves might join the forces arrayed against them. Early in the war, free blacks from New England enlisted in local patriot militias, but the revolutionaries could not assume that enslaved African-Americans would also support the struggle for independence.

Bondspeople faced a dilemma at the beginning of the Revolution: how could they best pursue their goal of escaping slavery? Should they fight with or against their masters? With no correct choice immediately apparent, African-Americans made different decisions. Some indeed joined the revolutionaries, but to most an alliance with Great Britain appeared more promising. Thus news of slave conspiracies surfaced in different parts of the colonies in late 1774 and early 1775. All shared a common element: a plan to assist the British in return for freedom. One group of slaves futilely petitioned General Thomas Gage, the commander-in-chief of the British army in Boston, promising to fight for the redcoats if he would liberate them. The most serious incident occurred in 1775 in Charleston, where Thomas Jeremiah, a free black harbor pilot, was brutally executed after being convicted of attempting to foment a slave revolt.

African-Americans' Dilemma

Fear of such acts made sugar planters in the British West Indian colonies more cautious in their opposition to parliamentary policies than were their counterparts on the mainland. On most of the Caribbean islands, slaves outnumbered their masters by six or seven to one. With the ever-present threat of slave revolt or foreign attack hanging over their heads, planters could not afford to risk opposing Britain, their chief protector. The Jamaica assembly agreed with the mainland colonial legislatures that citizens should not be bound by laws to which they had not consented. Nevertheless, its members assured the king in 1774 that "it cannot be supposed, that we now intend, or ever could have intended Resistance to Great Britain." They cited as reasons Jamaica's "weak and feeble" condition, "its very small number of white inhabitants, and . . . the incumbrance of more than Two hundred thousand Slaves."

Slavery affected politics in the continental colonies as well. In the North, with few resident slaves, revolutionary fervor was at its height. In

Slavery and Patriotic Fervor

Virginia and Maryland, where free people also constituted a safe majority, there was occasional alarm over potential slave revolts but no disabling fear. But South Carolina and Georgia, where slaves composed more than half of the population, were noticeably less enthusiastic about resistance. Georgia sent no delegates to the First Continental Congress and reminded its representatives at the second one to consider its circumstances, "with our blacks and tories [loyalists] within us," when voting on the question of independence.

The slaveowners' worst fears were realized in November 1775, when Lord Dunmore, the governor of Virginia, offered to free any slaves and indentured servants who would leave their patriot masters to join the British forces. Dunmore hoped to use African-Americans in his fight against the revolutionaries and to disrupt the economy by depriving planters of their labor force. But at most only two thousand African-Americans rallied to the British standard, and many of them perished in a smallpox epidemic. Even so, Dunmore's proclamation led Congress in January 1776 to modify an earlier policy that had prohibited the enlistment of African-Americans in the regular American army.

Although slaves did not pose a serious threat to the revolutionary cause in its early years, the patriots turned rumors of slave uprisings to their own advantage. In South Carolina, resistance leaders argued that unity under the Continental Association would protect masters from their slaves at a time when royal government was unable to muster adequate defense forces. Undoubtedly many wavering Carolinians were drawn into the revolutionary camp by fear

that an overt division among the colony's free people would encourage a slave revolt.

Similarly, the threat of Indian attacks helped persuade some reluctant westerners to support the struggle against Great Britain. In the years since the Proclamation of 1763, British officials had won the trust of the interior tribes by attempting to protect them from land-hungry European-Americans. British-appointed superintendents of Indian affairs, John Stuart in the South and Sir William Johnson in the North, lived among and understood the Indians. In 1768, Stuart and Johnson negotiated separate agreements modifying the proclamation line and attempting to draw realistic, defensible boundaries between tribal holdings and European-American settlements. The treaties supposedly established permanent western borders for the colonies. But just a few years later, in 1770 and 1773, the British pushed the southern boundary even farther west to accommodate the demands of settlers in western Georgia and Kentucky.

By 1775, many Indian groups were impatient with European-Americans' aggressive pressure on their lands. Relationships on the frontier were filled

Indians' Grievances

with bitterness, misunderstanding, and occasional bloody encounters. In combination with the tribes' confidence in Stuart and Johnson, such grievances predisposed most Indians toward an alliance with Great Britain. Even so, the latter hesitated to make full and immediate use of these potential allies. The superintendents were aware that neither the Indians' style of fighting nor tribal war aims were necessarily compatible with those of the British. Accordingly, Stuart and Guy Johnson (who became northern superintendent following his uncle's death) sought from the tribes only a promise of neutrality. The superintendents even helped to avert a general Indian uprising in the summer of 1774 by preventing the Shawnees from recruiting allies for attacks on frontier villages in Kentucky. Lord Dunmore's War, between the Shawnees and the Virginia militia, thus ended with Kentucky being opened to European-American settlement but with hunting and fishing rights still reserved to the Shawnees.

Recognizing that their standing with native peoples was poor, the patriots also sought the Indians' neutrality. In 1775 the Second Continental Congress sent a general message to Indian nations describing the war as "a family quarrel between us and Old England" and requesting that they "not join on either side" since "you Indians are not concerned in it." A group of Cherokees led by Chief Dragging Canoe nevertheless decided that the "family quarrel" would allow them to settle some old scores. They attacked settlements along the western borders of the Carolinas and Virginia in the summer of 1776. But a militia campaign destroyed many of their towns, along with crops and large quantities of supplies. Dragging Canoe and his diehard followers fled to the west, establishing new outposts; the rest of the Cherokees agreed to a treaty that ceded still more of their land.

The fate of the Shawnees and Cherokees foreshadowed the history of Indian involvement in the Revolution. The British victory over France in

Native Americans' Diverse Interests

1763 had removed the Indians' strongest weapon: their ability to play the European powers off against one another. Successful strategies were difficult to envision under these new circumstances, and even if the interests of several neighboring tribes coincided, old enmities kept them from forming alliances. Consequently, during the Revolution many Indian nations pursued a course that aligned them with neither side and (as the American leaders wanted) avoided active involvement in the war.

Thus although patriots could never completely ignore the threats posed by loyalists, neutrals, slaves, and Indians, only rarely did fear of these groups seriously hamper the revolutionary movement. Occasionally frontier militiamen refused to turn out for duty on the seacoast because they feared Indians would attack in their absence. Sometimes southern troops refused to serve in the North because they (and their political leaders) were unwilling to leave their regions unprotected against a slave insurrection. But the practical impossibility of a large-scale slave revolt, coupled with tribal feuds and the patriots' successful campaign to disarm and neutralize loyalists, ensured that the revolutionaries would remain firmly in control as they fought for independence.

 ## War Begins

On January 27, 1775, Lord Dartmouth, secretary of state for America, addressed a fateful letter to General Thomas Gage in Boston. Expressing his belief

In 1776 Benjamin West painted this portrait of Colonel Guy Johnson, the superintendent for Indian affairs in the northern district of America, while Johnson was in London for consultations with British officials. In the background is a man thought to be the Mohawk chief Joseph Brant (see page 163). Andrew Mellon Fund © National Gallery of Art, Washington, D.C.

that American resistance was nothing more than the response of a "rude rabble without plan," Dartmouth urged Gage to take a decisive step. Opposition could not be "very formidable," Dartmouth wrote, and even if it were, "it will surely be better that the Conflict should be brought on, upon such ground, than in a riper state of Rebellion."

Dartmouth's letter did not reach Gage until April 14. He responded by sending an expedition to confiscate provincial military supplies stockpiled at

Battles of Lexington and Concord

Concord. Bostonians dispatched two messengers, William Dawes and Paul Revere (later joined by Dr. Samuel Prescott), to rouse the countryside. So when the British vanguard of several hundred

In 1775, an unknown artist painted the redcoats entering Concord. The fighting at North Bridge, which occurred just a few hours after this triumphal entry, signaled the start of open warfare between Britain and the colonies.   Photography Courtesy of Concord Museum, Concord, MA.

men approached Lexington at dawn on April 19, they found a ragtag group of seventy militiamen— about half of the adult male population of the town—drawn up before them on the common. The Americans' commander ordered his men to withdraw, realizing they could not halt the redcoats' advance. But as they began to disperse, a shot rang out; the British soldiers then fired several volleys. When they stopped, eight Americans lay dead and another ten had been wounded. The British moved on to Concord, 5 miles away.

There the contingents of militia were larger, Concord residents having been joined by groups of men from nearby towns. An exchange of gunfire at the North Bridge spilled the first British blood of the Revolution: three men were killed and nine wounded. Thousands of militiamen then fired from houses and from behind trees and bushes at the

British forces as they retreated to Boston. By the end of the day, the redcoats had suffered 272 casualties, including 70 deaths. Only the arrival of reinforcements and the American militia's lack of coordination prevented much heavier British losses. The patriots suffered just 93 casualties.

By the evening of April 20, perhaps as many as twenty thousand American militiamen had gathered around Boston, summoned by local committees that spread the alarm across the countryside. Many did not stay long, since they were needed at home for spring planting, but those who remained dug in along siege lines encircling the city. For nearly a year the two armies sat and stared at each other across those lines. The redcoats attacked their besiegers only once, on June 17, when they drove the Americans from

First Year of War

trenches atop Breed's Hill in Charlestown. In that misnamed Battle of Bunker Hill, the British incurred their greatest losses of the entire war: over 800 wounded and 228 killed. The Americans, though forced to abandon their position, lost less than half that number.

During the same eleven-month period, patriots captured Fort Ticonderoga, a British fort on Lake Champlain, acquiring much-needed cannon. Trying to bring Canada into the war on the American side, they also mounted an uncoordinated northern campaign that ended in disaster at Quebec in early 1776. But the chief significance of the war's first year lay in the long lull in fighting between the main armies at Boston. The delay gave both sides a chance to regroup, organize, and plan their strategies.

Lord North and his new American secretary, Lord George Germain, made three central assumptions about the war they faced. First, they concluded

British Strategy

that patriot forces could not withstand the assaults of trained British regulars. They and their generals were convinced that the 1776 campaign would be the first and last of the war. Accordingly, they dispatched to America the largest force Great Britain had ever assembled anywhere: 370 transport ships carrying 32,000 troops and tons of supplies, accompanied by 73 naval vessels and 13,000 sailors. Such an extraordinary effort, they thought, would ensure a quick victory. Among the troops were thousands of Hessian mercenaries (from the German state of Hesse); eighteenth-century armies were often composed of such professional soldiers who hired out to the highest bidder.

Second, British officials and army officers treated this war as comparable to wars they had fought successfully in Europe. They adopted a conventional strategy of capturing major American cities and defeating the rebel army decisively without suffering serious casualties themselves. Third, they assumed that a clear-cut military victory would automatically bring about their goal of retaining the colonies' allegiance.

All these assumptions proved false. North and Germain, like Lord Dartmouth before them, vastly underestimated Americans' commitment to armed resistance. Battlefield defeats did not lead patriots to abandon their political aims and sue for peace. The ministers in London also failed to recognize the significance of the American population's dispersal over an area 1,500 miles long and more than 100 miles

wide. Although Great Britain would control each of the most important American ports at one time or another during the war, less than 5 percent of the population lived in those cities. Furthermore, the coast offered so many excellent harbors that essential commerce was easily rerouted. In other words, the loss of cities did little to damage the American cause, whereas the aim of capturing such ports repeatedly led redcoat generals astray.

Most of all, British officials did not at first understand that military triumph would not necessarily lead to political victory. Securing the colonies permanently would require hundreds of thousands of Americans to return to their original allegiance. The conquest of America was thus a far more complicated task than the defeat of France twelve years earlier. Great Britain needed not only to overpower the patriots but also to convert them. After 1778, the ministry adopted a strategy designed to achieve that goal through the expanded use of loyalist forces and the restoration of civilian authority in occupied areas. But the new policy came too late. Britain's leaders never fully realized that they were fighting not a conventional European war but rather an entirely new kind of conflict: the first modern war of national liberation.

Great Britain at least had a bureaucracy ready to supervise the war effort. The Americans had only the Second Continental Congress, originally

Second Continental Congress

planned as a brief gathering to consider the ministry's response to the Continental Association. Instead, the delegates who convened in Philadelphia on May 10, 1775, found that they had to assume the mantle of intercolonial government. "Such a vast Multitude of objects, civil, political, commercial and military, press and crowd upon us so fast, that we know not what to do first," John Adams wrote a close friend early in the session. Yet as the summer passed, Congress slowly organized the colonies for war. It authorized the printing of money with which to purchase necessary goods, established a committee to supervise relations with foreign countries, and took steps to strengthen the militia. Most important, it created the Continental Army and appointed its generals.

Until Congress met, the Massachusetts provincial congress had taken responsibility for organizing the militiamen encamped at Boston. But that army, composed of men from all the New England states,

The plight of the redcoat soldiers besieged in Boston during the fall and winter of 1775–1776 attracted the sympathies of a British cartoonist. For "Six-Pence a Day," he noted, soldiers were exposed to "Yankees, Fire and Water, Sword and Famine," while their wives and children begged for assistance at home. The artist hoped to persuade men not to enlist in the British army. The British Museum, Department of Prints and Drawings, Satires.

constituted a heavy drain on limited local resources. Consequently, Massachusetts asked the Continental Congress to assume the task of directing the army. As a first step, Congress had to choose a commander-in-chief. Since the war had thus far been a wholly northern affair, many delegates recognized the importance of naming someone who was not a New Englander. There seemed only one obvious candidate: they unanimously selected their fellow delegate, the Virginian George Washington.

Washington was no fiery radical, nor was he a reflective political thinker. He had not played a prominent role in the prerevolutionary agitation, but his devotion to the American cause was unquestioned. He was dignified, conservative, and respectable—a man of unimpeachable integrity. The younger son of a Virginia planter, Washington did not expect to inherit substantial property and planned to make his living as a surveyor. But the early death of his older brother and his marriage to the wealthy widow Martha Custis made George Washington a rich man. Though unmistakably an aristocrat, he was unswervingly committed to representative government. He had other desirable traits as well. His stamina was remarkable: in more than eight years of war, Washington never had a serious illness and took only one brief leave of absence. Moreover, he both looked and acted like a leader. More than six feet tall in an era when most men were five inches shorter, he displayed a stately and commanding presence. Other patriots praised his judgment, steadiness, and discretion, and even a loyalist admitted that Washington could "atone for many demerits by the extraordinary coolness and caution which distinguish his character."

Washington needed all the coolness and caution he could muster when he took command of the army

George Washington: A Portrait of Leadership

outside Boston in July 1775. It took him months to impose hierarchy and discipline on the unruly troops and to bring order to the supply system. But by March 1776, when the arrival of cannon from Ticonderoga finally enabled him to

British Evacuate Boston

put direct pressure on the redcoats in the city, the army was prepared to act. As it happened, an assault on Boston proved unnecessary. Sir William Howe, who had replaced Gage, had for some time been considering an evacuation; he wanted to transfer his troops to New York City. The patriots' new cannon decided the matter. On March 17, the British and more than a thousand of their loyalist allies abandoned Boston forever.

That spring of 1776, as the British fleet left Boston for the temporary haven of Halifax, Nova Scotia, the colonies were moving inexorably toward the act the Massachusetts loyalists on board the British ships feared most: a declaration of independence. Even months after fighting began, American leaders still denied seeking a break with Great Britain. But in January 1776 there appeared a pamphlet by a man who both thought and advocated the unthinkable.

Thomas Paine's *Common Sense* exploded on the American scene like a bombshell. Within three months of publication, it sold 120,000 copies. The author, a radical English printer who had lived in America

Thomas Paine's *Common Sense*

only since 1774, called stridently and stirringly for independence. More than that: Paine challenged many common American assumptions about government and the colonies' relationship to Britain. Rejecting the notion that a balance of monarchy, aristocracy, and democracy was necessary to preserve freedom, he advocated the establishment of a *republic*, a government by the people with no king or nobility. Instead of acknowledging the benefits of links to the mother country, Paine insisted that Britain had exploited the colonies unmercifully. In place of the frequently heard assertion that an independent America would be weak and divided, he substituted an unlimited confidence in America's strength when freed from European control.

These striking statements were expressed in equally striking prose. Scorning the rational style of most other pamphleteers, Paine adopted a furious, enraged tone. The king, he declared, was a "royal brute," a "wretch" who only pretended concern for the colonists' welfare. The pamphlet indeed reflected the oral culture of ordinary folk. Couched in everyday language, it relied heavily on the Bible— the only book familiar to most Americans—as a primary source of authority. No wonder the pamphlet had a wider distribution than any other political publication of its day.

There is no way of knowing how many people were converted to the cause of independence by reading *Common Sense*. But by late spring in 1776 independence had become inevitable. On May 10, the Second Continental Congress formally recommended that individual colonies "adopt such governments as shall, in the opinion of the representatives of the people, best conduce to the happiness and safety of their constituents in particular, and America in general." From that source stemmed the first state constitutions. Perceiving the trend of events, the few loyalists still connected with Congress severed their ties to that body.

Thomas Paine, the English radical who wrote Common Sense. *James Watson prepared this 1783 engraving from a portrait by Charles Willson Peale, who depicted his subject accompanied by the tools of the writer's trade—several sheets of paper and a quill pen.* National Portrait Gallery, Smithsonian Institution, Washington, D.C.

Then on June 7 came confirmation of the movement toward independence. Richard Henry Lee of Virginia, seconded by John Adams of Massachusetts, introduced the crucial resolution: "that these United Colonies are, and of right ought to be, free and independent States, that they are absolved of all allegiance to the British Crown, and that all political connection between them and the State of Great Britain is, and ought to be, totally dissolved." Congress debated but did not immediately adopt Lee's resolution. Instead, it postponed a vote until early July, to allow time for consultation and public reaction. In the meantime, a five-man committee—including Thomas Jefferson, John Adams, and Benjamin Franklin—was directed to draft a declaration of independence.

The committee assigned primary responsibility for writing the declaration to Jefferson, who was well known for his apt and eloquent style. Years later John Adams recalled that Jefferson had modestly protested his selection, suggesting that Adams prepare the initial draft. The Massachusetts revolutionary recorded his frank response: "You can write ten times better than I can."

Thomas Jefferson was at the time thirty-four years old, a Virginia lawyer educated at the College of William and Mary and in the law offices of a prominent attorney. A member

Thomas Jefferson and the Declaration of Independence

of the House of Burgesses, he had read widely in history and political theory. His broad knowledge was evident not only in the declaration but also in his draft of the Virginia state constitution, completed just a few days before his appointment to the committee. Jefferson, an intensely private man, loved his home and family deeply. This early stage of his political career was marked by his beloved wife Martha's repeated difficulties in childbearing. While he wrote and debated in Philadelphia, she suffered a miscarriage at their home, Monticello. Not until after her death in 1782, from complications following the birth of their sixth (but only third surviving) child in ten years of marriage, did Jefferson fully commit himself to public service.

The draft of the declaration was laid before Congress on June 28, 1776. The delegates officially voted for independence four days later, then debated the wording of the declaration for two more days, adopting it with some changes on July 4. Since

Americans had long ago ceased to see themselves as legitimate subjects of Parliament, the Declaration of Independence concentrated on George III (see the Appendix). That focus also provided an identifiable villain. The document accused the king of attempting to destroy representative government in the colonies and of oppressing Americans through the unjustified use of excessive force.

The declaration's chief long-term importance, however, did not lie in its lengthy catalogue of grievances against George III (including, in a section omitted by Congress, Jefferson's charge that the British monarchy had introduced slavery into America). It lay instead in the ringing statements of principle that have served ever since as the ideal to which Americans aspire: "We hold these truths to be self-evident: That all men are created equal; that they are endowed by their Creator with certain unalienable rights; that among these are life, liberty and the pursuit of happiness; that, to secure these rights, governments are instituted among men, deriving their just powers from the consent of the governed; that whenever any form of government becomes destructive of these ends, it is the right of the people to alter or to abolish it, and to institute new government." These phrases have echoed down through American history like no others.

The delegates in Philadelphia who voted to accept the Declaration of Independence did not have the advantage of our two centuries of hindsight. When they adopted the declaration, they risked their necks: they were committing treason. Thus when they concluded the declaration with the assertion that they "mutually pledge[d] to each other our lives, our fortunes, and our sacred honor," they spoke no less than the truth. The real struggle still lay before them, and few had Thomas Paine's boundless confidence in success.

 ## The Long Struggle in the North

In late June 1776, the first ships carrying Sir William Howe's troops from Halifax appeared off the coast of New York (see map, page 159). On July 2, the day

Loss of New York City

Congress voted for independence, redcoats landed on Staten Island. Howe, though, waited until mid-August, after the arrival of more troops from England, to begin his attack on the city. The delay gave Washington sufficient time to march his army of seventeen thousand south from Boston to meet the threat. But both he and his men, still inexperienced in fighting and maneuvering, made major mistakes, losing battles at Brooklyn Heights and on Manhattan Island. The city fell to the British, who captured nearly three thousand American soldiers. Those men spent most of the rest of the war imprisoned on British vessels anchored in New York harbor, where many died of disease.

During the autumn months, Washington retreated across New Jersey, with Howe in leisurely pursuit. The British took control of most of the state, and hundreds of New Jerseyites and Pennsylvanians (among them Joseph Galloway) accepted pardons for their "treasonous" activities. Occupying troops met little opposition, and the revolutionary cause appeared to be in disarray. "These are the times that try men's souls," wrote Thomas Paine in his pamphlet *The Crisis*. "The summer soldier and the sunshine patriot will, in this crisis, shrink from the service of his country; . . . yet we have this consolation with us, that the harder the conflict, the more glorious the triumph."

Campaign in New Jersey

The British let their advantage slip away as redcoats stationed in New Jersey went on a rampage of rape and plunder. Because loyalists and patriots were indistinguishable to British and Hessian troops, families on both sides suffered nearly equally. Livestock, crops, and firewood were seized for use by the British army. Houses were looted and burned, churches and public buildings desecrated. Yet nothing was better calculated to rally doubtful Americans to the cause than the murder of innocent civilians and the rape of women.

The soldiers' marauding alienated potentially loyal New Jerseyites and Pennsylvanians whose allegiance the British could ill afford to lose. It also spurred Washington's determination to strike back. Moving quickly, he attacked a Hessian encampment at Trenton early in the morning of December 26, while the redcoats were still reeling from their Christmas celebration. The patriots captured more than nine hundred Hessians and killed another thirty; only three Americans were wounded. A few days later, Washington attacked again at Princeton. Having gained command of the field and buoyed American spirits with the two swift victories, Wash-

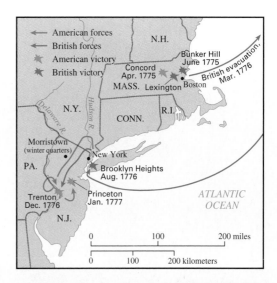

The War in the North, 1775–1777 *The early phase of the Revolutionary War was dominated by British troop movements in the Boston area, the redcoats' evacuation to Nova Scotia in the spring of 1776, and the subsequent British invasion of New York and New Jersey.*

ington set up winter quarters at Morristown, New Jersey.

The 1776 campaign established patterns that persisted throughout much of the war, despite changes in British leadership and strategy. The British forces were usually more numerous and often better led than the Americans. But their ponderous style of maneuvering, lack of familiarity with the terrain, and inability to live off the land without antagonizing the populace partially offset those advantages. Furthermore, although Washington always seemed to lack regular troops—the Continental Army never numbered more than 18,500 men—he could usually count on the militia to join him at crucial times. American militiamen did not like to sign up for long terms of service or to fight far from home; but when their homes were threatened, they rallied to the cause. Washington and his officers complained about the militiamen's habit of disappearing during planting or harvesting. But time and again their presence, however brief, enabled the Americans to launch an attack or counter an important British thrust.

As the war dragged on, the Continental Army and the militia took on decidedly different characters. State governments, responsible for filling

At the Battle of Princeton in early 1777, American forces under George Washington cemented the victory they had won a few days earlier at Trenton. This view was painted in 1787 by James Peale, who fought in the battle.   Princeton University Library.

The American Army

military quotas, discovered that most men willing to enlist for long periods in the regular army were young, single, and footloose. Farmers with families tended to prefer short-term militia duty. As the supply of men willing to sign up with the Continentals dwindled, recruiters in northern states turned increasingly to African-Americans, both slave and free. Perhaps as many as five thousand blacks eventually served in the army, and most of them won their freedom as a result. They commonly served in racially integrated units but were assigned tasks that others shunned, such as cooking, foraging for food, and driving wagons. Also attached to the American forces were a number of women, the wives and widows of poor soldiers. Such camp followers worked as cooks, nurses, and launderers in return for rations and low wages. The presence of women, as well as militiamen who floated in and out of the American camp at irregular intervals, made for an unwieldy army that officers found difficult to manage. Yet the army's shapelessness also reflected its greatest strength: an almost unlimited reservoir of manpower and womanpower.

The officers of the Continental Army—those who enlisted for long periods or for the war's duration—developed an intense sense of pride and commitment to the revolutionary cause. The hardships they endured, the battles they fought, the difficulties they overcame all helped to forge an esprit de corps that outlasted the war. The realities of warfare were often dirty, messy, and corrupt, but the officers drew strength from a developing image of themselves as professionals who sacrificed personal gain for the good of the entire nation. When Benedict Arnold—an officer who fought heroically for the patriot cause early in the war—violated that virtuous self-image by defecting to the British, they made his name a metaphor for villainy. "How black, how despised, loved by none, and hated by all," wrote one patriot.

In 1777, the chief British effort was planned by the flashy "Gentleman Johnny" Burgoyne, a playboy general as much at home at the gaming tables of London as on the battlefield. A subordinate of Howe, Burgoyne spent the winter of 1776–1777 in London, where he gained the ear of Lord George Germain. Burgoyne convinced Germain that he could lead an invading force of redcoats and Indians down the Hudson River from Canada, cutting off New England from the rest of the states. He proposed to rendezvous near Albany with a similar force that would move east along the Mohawk River valley. The combined forces would then presumably link up with Sir William Howe's troops in New York City.

Planning the 1777 Campaign

That Burgoyne's scheme would give "Gentleman Johnny" all the glory and relegate Howe to a supporting role did not escape Sir William's notice. While Burgoyne was plotting in London, Howe was laying his own plans in New York. Joseph Galloway and other Pennsylvania loyalists persuaded Howe that Philadelphia could be taken easily and that many loyal residents would welcome his troops. Just as Burgoyne left Howe out of his plans, Howe left Burgoyne out of his. Thus the two major British armies in America would operate independently in 1777, and the result would be a disaster (see map).

Howe captured Philadelphia, but he did so in inexplicable fashion, delaying for months before beginning the campaign, then taking six weeks to transport his troops by sea instead of marching them overland. That maneuver cost him at least a month, debilitated his men, and depleted his supplies. Incredibly, at the end of the lengthy voyage, he was only 40 miles closer to Philadelphia than when he started. By the time Howe was ready to move on Philadelphia, Washington had had time to prepare its defenses. Twice, at Brandywine Creek and again at Germantown, the two armies clashed near the patriot capital. Although the British won both engagements, the Americans handled themselves well. The redcoats took Philadelphia in late September, but to little effect; the campaign season was nearly over; the revolutionary army had gained confidence in itself and its leaders; few welcoming loyalists had ma-

Howe Takes Philadelphia

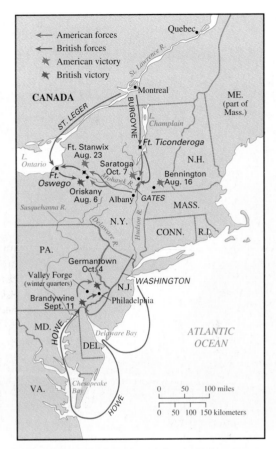

Campaign of 1777 *The crucial campaign of 1777 was fought on two fronts: along the upper Hudson and Mohawk river valleys, and in the vicinity of Philadelphia. The rebels won in the north; the British triumphed—at least nominally—in the south. The capture of Philadelphia, however, did the redcoats little good, and they abandoned the city the following year.*

terialized; and, far to the north, Burgoyne was going down to defeat.

Burgoyne and his men set out from Montréal in mid-June 1777, floating down Lake Champlain into New York in canoes and flat-bottom boats. They easily took Fort Ticonderoga from its outnumbered and outgunned patriot defenders. Trouble began, however, when Burgoyne began an overland march. His clumsy artillery carriages and baggage wagons foundered in the heavy forests and ravines. Patriot militia felled giant trees across

Burgoyne's Campaign in New York

This kettledrum belonged to the band of the Royal Norfolk Regiment, a British infantry unit that surrendered to the Americans at Saratoga. The drum was sent to West Point, where it has remained ever since, a symbol of the new nation's first great victory of the Revolution.   The West Point Museum Collection, U.S. Military Academy, West Point, NY. Photo by Paul Warchal.

his path to slow his progress. Consequently, Burgoyne's troops took twenty-four days to travel 23 miles. In August, the campaign suffered two sharp blows—first, when the redcoats and Indians marching east along the Mohawk River turned back after a battle at Oriskany, New York; second, when in a clash near Bennington, Vermont, American militiamen nearly wiped out eight hundred of Burgoyne's German mercenaries. Yet the general continued to dawdle, giving the Americans more than enough time to prepare for his coming. After several skirmishes with an American army commanded by General Horatio Gates, Burgoyne was surrounded near Saratoga, New York. On October 17, 1777, he surrendered his entire force of more than six thousand men.

The August 1777 battle at Oriskany was also important because it revealed a division in the Iroquois Confederacy (see pages 77–78). In 1776 the Six

Split of the Iroquois Confederacy

Nations had formally pledged to remain neutral in the Anglo-American struggle. But two influential Mohawk leaders, Joseph and Mary Brant, worked tirelessly to persuade their fellow Iroquois to join the British. Mary Brant, a powerful tribal matron, was also the widow of the Indian superintendent Sir William Johnson. Her younger brother Joseph, a renowned warrior, was convinced that the Six Nations should ally themselves with the British in order to prevent American encroachment on their lands. The Brants won over to the British the Senecas, Cayugas, and Mohawks, all of whom contributed warriors to the 1777 expedition. But the Oneidas—who had been converted to Christianity by Protestant missionaries—preferred the American side and brought the Tuscaroras with them. The Onondagas split into three factions, one on each side and one supporting neutrality. At Oriskany, some Oneidas and Tuscaroras joined patriot militiamen in fighting their Iroquois brethren; thus a league of friendship that had survived over three hundred years was torn apart.

The collapse of Iroquois unity and the confederacy's abandonment of neutrality had significant consequences. In 1778, Iroquois warriors allied with the British raided frontier villages in Pennsylvania and New York. To retaliate, the Americans dispatched an expedition under General John Sullivan the following summer to burn Iroquois crops, orchards, and settlements. The destruction was so thorough that many bands had to leave their ancestral homeland to seek food and shelter north of the Great Lakes during the winter of 1779–1780. A large number of Iroquois people never returned to New York but settled permanently in British Canada.

Burgoyne's surrender at Saratoga brought joy to patriots, discouragement to loyalists and Britons. In exile in London, Thomas Hutchinson wrote of "universal dejection" among loyalists there. "Everybody in a gloom," he commented; "most of us expect to lay our bones here." The disaster prompted Lord North to authorize a peace commission to offer the Americans what they had requested in 1774—in effect, a return to the imperial system of 1763. It was, of course, far too late for that: the patriots rejected the overture, and the peace commission sailed back to England empty-handed in mid-1778.

Most important of all, the American victory at Saratoga drew France formally into the conflict. Ever since 1763, the French had sought to avenge their defeat in the Seven Years War, and the American Revolution gave them that opportunity. Even before Benjamin Franklin arrived in Paris in late 1776, France was covertly supplying the revolutionaries with military necessities. Indeed, 90 percent of the gunpowder used by the Americans during the war's first two years came from France.

Benjamin Franklin worked tirelessly to strengthen ties between the two nations. He deliberately assumed a plain style of dress that made him stand out amid the luxury of the court of King Louis XVI. Presenting himself as a representative of American simplicity, he played on the French image of Americans as virtuous yeomen. Franklin's efforts culminated in 1778 when the countries signed two treaties. In the Treaty of Amity and Commerce, France recognized

Franco-American Alliance of 1778

Joseph Brant, the Iroquois leader who helped to persuade the Mohawks, Senecas, and Cayugas to support the British in the latter stages of the Revolution, as painted by Charles Willson Peale in 1797. Independence National Historic Park Collection.

American independence and established trade ties with the new nation. In the Treaty of Alliance, France and the United States promised—assuming that France would go to war with Britain, which it soon did—that neither would negotiate peace with the enemy without consulting the other. France also abandoned all its claims to Canada and to North American territory east of the Mississippi River. The most visible symbol of Franco-American cooperation in the years that followed was the Marquis de Lafayette, a young nobleman who volunteered for service with George Washington in 1777 and fought with American forces until the conflict ended.

The French alliance had two major benefits for the patriot cause. First, France began to aid the Americans openly, sending troops and naval vessels in addition to arms, ammunition, clothing, and blankets. Second, Great Britain could no longer focus solely on the American mainland, for it had to fight France in the Caribbean and elsewhere. Spain's entry into the war in 1779 as an ally of France (but not of the United States) further magnified Britain's problems, for the Revolution then became a global

James Armistead Lafayette, a Virginia slave, was first a spy and later a courier for General Lafayette during the Revolution. After the war, he adopted Lafayette's surname as his own and was freed by a special act of the state legislature. Valentine Museum, Gift of Mr. Louis E. Franck, Jr.

war. French assistance was important to Americans throughout the conflict, but in its last years the aid was particularly vital.

 The Long Struggle in the South

In the aftermath of the Saratoga disaster, Lord George Germain and British military officials reassessed their strategy. Maneuvering in the North had done them little good; perhaps shifting the field of battle southward would bring success. Many loyalist exiles in London encouraged this line of thinking. They argued that loyal southerners would welcome the redcoat army as liberators and that the region could serve as a base for attacking the North, once it had been pacified and returned to civilian control.

In early 1778 Sir William Howe was replaced by Sir Henry Clinton, who oversaw the regrouping of British forces in America. He ordered the evacuation of Philadelphia in June 1778 and dispatched a small expedition to Georgia at the end of the year. When Savannah and then Augusta fell easily into British hands, Clinton became convinced that a southern strategy would succeed. In late 1779 he sailed down the coast from New York to attack Charleston, the most important city in the South (see map, page 166).

The Americans worked hard to bolster Charleston's defenses, but the city fell to the British on May 12, 1780. General Benjamin Lincoln surrendered the entire southern army—5,500 men—to the invaders. In the weeks that followed, the redcoats spread through South Carolina, establishing garrisons at key points in the interior. Hundreds of South Carolinians renounced allegiance to the United States and proclaimed their loyalty to the Crown. Clinton organized loyalist regiments, and the process of pacification began.

Fall of Charleston

Yet the British triumph was less complete than it appeared. The success of the southern campaign depended on British control of the seas, for the British armies were so widely dispersed and travel by land so difficult that only through British naval vessels could the armies coordinate their efforts. For the moment, the Royal Navy safely dominated the American coastline, but French naval power posed a threat to the entire southern enterprise. Moreover, the redcoats never managed to establish full control of the areas they seized. Patriot bands operated freely throughout the state, and loyalists could not be guaranteed protection against their enemies. Last but not least, the fall of Charleston did not dishearten the patriots; instead, it spurred them to greater exertions. As one Marylander declared confidently, "The Fate of America is not to be decided by the Loss of a Town or Two." Patriot women in four states formed the Ladies Association, which collected money to purchase shirts for needy soldiers. Recruiting efforts were stepped up.

Nevertheless, the war in South Carolina went badly for the patriots throughout most of 1780. In August, a reorganized southern army under Horatio Gates was crushingly defeated at Camden by the forces of Lord Cornwallis, the new British commander in the South. The redcoats were joined wherever they went by hundreds, even thousands, of enslaved African-Americans seeking freedom on the basis of Lord Dunmore's proclamation. They ran away from their patriot masters individually and as families in such numbers that they seriously disrupted planting and harvesting in 1780 and 1781. More than fifty-five thousand slaves were lost to their owners as a result of the war. Not all of them joined the British or won their freedom if they did, but their flight had exactly the effect Dunmore wanted. Many served the British well as scouts, guides, and laborers.

A British cartoon published in 1780. Even after Spain and the Netherlands had joined France in supporting the Americans' quest for independence, this artist had confidence in Britain's ability to outweigh the alliance in "The Ballance of Power." Miriam and Ira D. Wallach Division of Art, Prints and Photographs, The New York Public Library.

After the defeat at Camden, Washington (who had to remain in the North to oppose the British army occupying New York) appointed General Nathanael Greene of Rhode Island to command the southern campaign. Greene was appalled by what he found in South Carolina. "The word difficulty when applied to the state of things here . . . is almost without meaning, it falls so far short" of reality, he wrote to a friend. His troops needed clothing, blankets, and food, but "a great part of this country is already laid waste and in the utmost danger of becoming a desert." Incessant guerrilla warfare had, he commented, "so corrupted the principles of the people that they think of nothing but plundering one another."

In such circumstances, Greene had to move cautiously. He adopted a conciliatory policy toward loy-

Greene Rallies South Carolina

alists and neutrals, persuading the governor of South Carolina to offer pardons to those who had fought for the British if they would join the patriot militia. He also ordered his troops to treat captives fairly and not to loot loyalist property. Greene recognized that the patriots could win only by convincing the populace that they could bring stability to the region. He thus helped the shattered provincial congresses of Georgia and South Carolina to begin reestablishing civilian authority in the interior—a goal the British were never able to accomplish, even along the coast.

Greene also took a conciliatory approach to the southern Indians. With his desperate need for soldiers, he could not afford to have frontier militia companies occupied in defending their homes against Indian attacks. Since he had so few regulars (only sixteen hundred when he took command), Greene had to rely on western volunteers. Although

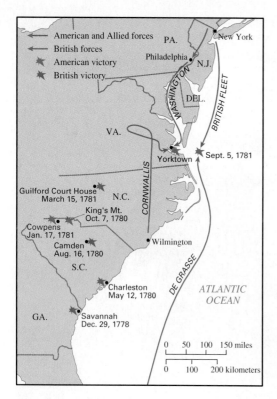

The War in the South *The southern war— after the British invasion of Georgia in late 1778—was characterized by a series of British thrusts into the interior, leading to battles with American defenders in both North and South Carolina. Finally, after promising beginnings, Cornwallis's foray into Virginia ended with disaster at Yorktown in October 1781.*

royal officials cooperating with the redcoat invaders initially won some Indian allies, Greene's careful diplomacy eventually proved successful. By war's end, only the Creeks remained allied with Great Britain.

Even before Greene took command of the southern army in December 1780, the tide had begun to turn. In October, at King's Mountain, a force from the settlements west of the Appalachians defeated a large party of redcoats and loyalists. Then in January 1781 Greene's trusted aide Brigadier General Daniel Morgan brilliantly defeated the crack British regiment Tarleton's Legion at Cowpens. Greene himself confronted the main body of British troops under Lord Cornwallis at Guilford Court House, North Carolina, in March. Although Cornwallis controlled the field at the end of the day, most of his army had been destroyed. He had to retreat to

Wilmington, on the coast, to receive supplies and fresh troops from New York by sea. Meanwhile, Greene returned to South Carolina, where, in a series of swift strikes, he forced the redcoats to abandon their interior posts and retire to Charleston.

Cornwallis had already ignored explicit orders not to leave South Carolina unless the state was safely in British hands. He headed north into Virginia, where he joined forces with a detachment of redcoats commanded by the American traitor Benedict Arnold. Instead of acting decisively with his new army of 7,200 men, Cornwallis withdrew to the peninsula between the York and James Rivers, where he fortified Yorktown and waited for supplies and reinforcements. Seizing the opportunity, Washington quickly moved more than 7,000 troops south from New York City. When a French fleet under the Comte de Grasse arrived from the Caribbean in time to defeat the Royal Navy vessels sent to relieve Cornwallis, the British general was trapped (see map). On October 19, 1781, Cornwallis surrendered to the combined American and French forces.

Surrender at Yorktown

When news of the surrender reached London, Lord North's ministry fell. Parliament voted to cease offensive operations in America and authorized peace negotiations. But guerrilla warfare between patriots and loyalists continued to ravage the Carolinas and Georgia for more than a year, and in the North vicious raids by both sides kept the frontier aflame. The persistence of conflict among guerrillas, frontiersmen, and Indians after the Battle of Yorktown, too often overlooked in accounts of the Revolution, serves to underscore the significance of the internal conflict that accompanied the more famous battles between the British and American armies.

Often overlooked also are the heavy costs of winning independence. More than twenty-five thousand American men died in the war, only about one-quarter of them from wounds suffered in battle. The rest were declared missing in action or died of disease or as prisoners of war. In the South, years of guerrilla warfare and the loss of thousands of runaway slaves shattered the economy. Indebtedness soared, and local governments were crippled for lack of funds, since few people could afford to pay their taxes. In the 1780s in Charles County, Maryland, for example, men commonly refused to serve in elective or appointive office because their personal estates would become liable for any taxes or fines they were unable to collect. Many of the county's formerly

How do historians know that Americans had only incomplete knowledge of the boundaries of their new nation? They know from consulting written documents and from looking at early maps like this one, "A New and Correct Map of the United States of North America," produced in 1784. New it certainly was, but correct it was not. A comparison with a standard map of the United States and Canada today shows many errors of scale, proportion, and placement of natural features. To point out just a few: the Ohio River is shown much too far south; the northern part of the Mississippi River is misplaced to the west; Lake Superior is too small, and its islands are too large; and the Nova Scotia peninsula is misshapen. What links all these features is that they were on the periphery of the new nation and thus on the margins of Americans' knowledge. But even so well known a waterway as Chesapeake Bay is inaccurately drawn, suggesting that residents of the United States still had much to learn about the geography of their country. Photo: New Jersey Historical Society.

Measles, typhus, diphtheria, dysentery, and other diseases ravaged military encampments, so medicine chests like the one shown here were essential equipment for the army. Doctors used crude remedies that often did more harm than good, for little was known about the causes of such afflictions. Smallpox was one of the few epidemics that eighteenth-century doctors could combat: inoculation was known to be an effective preventive measure as early as the 1720s.   The West Point Museum Collection, U.S. Military Academy, West Point, NY. Photo by Josh Nefsky.

wealthy planters descended into insolvency as a result of the war, and in the 1790s a traveler observed that "the country . . . wears a most dreary aspect," remarking on the "old dilapidated mansions" that had once housed well-to-do slaveowners.

Yet Charles County residents and Americans in general "all rejoiced" when they learned of the signing of a preliminary peace treaty at Paris in November 1782. The American diplomats—Benjamin Franklin, John Jay, and John Adams—ignored their instructions from Congress to be guided by France and instead negotiated directly with Great Britain. Their instincts were sound: the French government was more an enemy to Britain than a friend to the United States. In fact, French ministers worked secretly behind the scenes to try to prevent the establishment of a strong and unified government in America. Spain's desire to lay claim to the region between the Appalachian Mountains and the Mississippi River further complicated the negotiations. But the American delegates proved adept at power politics and achieved their main goal: independence as a united nation. The new British ministry, headed by Lord Shelburne (formerly an outspoken critic of Lord North's American poli-

Treaty of Paris

cies), was weary of war and made numerous concessions—so many, in fact, that Parliament ousted the ministry shortly after peace terms were approved.

The treaty, signed formally on September 3, 1783, granted the Americans unconditional independence. The boundaries of the new nation were generous: to the north, approximately the present-day boundary with Canada; to the south, the 31st parallel (about the modern northern border of Florida); to the west, the Mississippi River. Florida, which Britain had acquired in 1763, was returned to Spain. The Americans also gained unlimited fishing rights off Newfoundland. In ceding so much land to the United States, Great Britain ignored the territorial rights of its Indian allies, sacrificing their interests to the demands of European politics. Loyalists and British merchants were also poorly served by British diplomats. The treaty's ambiguously worded clauses pertaining to the payment of prewar debts and the postwar treatment of loyalists caused trouble for years to come and proved impossible to enforce.

 Conclusion

The long war was finally over, and the victorious Americans could look back on their achievement with satisfaction and awe. In 1775, with an inexperienced ragtag army, they had taken on the greatest military power in the world—and eight years later they had won. They accomplished their goal more through persistence and commitment than through brilliance on the battlefield. Actual victories were few, but their army always survived defeats and standoffs to fight again. Ultimately, the Americans simply wore their enemy down.

In winning the war, the Americans reshaped the physical and mental landscapes in which they lived. They abandoned the British identity that once was so important to them, excluding from their new nation all those unwilling to make a break with the mother country. In the Continental Army in particular they began the process of creating loyalty to an entity that had no prior existence—a nation they named "the United States of America." They also established a claim to most of the territory east of the Mississippi River and south of the Great Lakes, thereby greatly expanding the land potentially open to their settlements.

In achieving independence, Americans surmounted formidable challenges. But in the future they faced perhaps even greater ones: establishing stable republican governments at the state and national levels to replace the monarchy they had rejected, and ensuring their government's continued existence in a world of bitter rivalries among the major powers— Britain, France, and Spain. Those European rivalries worked to the Americans' advantage during the war, but in the decades to come they would pose significant threats to the survival of the new nation.

Suggestions for Further Reading

General

Colin Bonwick, *The American Revolution* (1991); Edward Countryman, *The American Revolution* (1985); Theodore Draper, *A Struggle for Power: The American Revolution* (1996); Stephen G. Kurtz and James H. Hutson, eds., *Essays on the American Revolution* (1973); Robert Middlekauff, *The Glorious Cause: The American Revolution, 1763–1783* (1982); Harry M. Ward, *The American Revolution: Nationhood Achieved, 1763–1788* (1995); Alfred F. Young, ed., *Beyond the American Revolution* (1993); Alfred F. Young, ed., *The American Revolution: Explorations in the History of American Radicalism* (1976).

Military Affairs

Jeremy Black, *War for America: The Fight for Independence, 1775–1783* (1991); E. Wayne Carp, *To Starve the Army at Pleasure: Continental Army Administration and American Political Culture, 1775–1783* (1984); Stephen Conway, *The War of American Independence, 1775–1783* (1995); John C. Dann, ed., *The Revolution Remembered: Eyewitness Accounts of the War for Independence* (1980); Don Higginbotham, *The War of American Independence: Military Attitudes, Policies, and Practice, 1763–1789* (1971); Ronald Hoffman and Peter Albert, eds., *Arms and Independence: The Military Character of the American Revolution* (1984); Piers Mackesy, *The War for America, 1775–1783* (1964); James K. Martin, *Benedict Arnold, Revolutionary Hero* (1997); Charles P. Niemeyer, *America Goes to War: A Social History of the Continental Army* (1997); Charles Royster, *A Revolutionary People at War: The Continental Army and American Character, 1775–1783* (1980); John Shy, *A People Numerous and Armed: Reflections on the Military Struggle for American Independence*, rev. ed. (1990).

Local and Regional Studies

Richard Buel, *Dear Liberty: Connecticut's Mobilization for the Revolutionary War* (1980); Edward Countryman, *A People in Revolution: The American Revolution and Political Society in New York, 1760–1790* (1981); Jeffrey Crow and Larry Tise, eds., *The Southern Experience in the American Revolution* (1978); Thomas Doerflinger, *A Vigorous Spirit of Enterprise: Merchants and Economic Development in Revolutionary Philadelphia* (1986); David Hackett Fischer, *Paul Revere's Ride* (1994); Robert A. Gross, *The Minutemen and Their World* (1976); Ronald Hoffman, *A Spirit of Dissension: Economics, Politics, and the Revolution in Maryland* (1973); Ronald Hoffman, Thad W. Tate, and Peter Albert, eds., *An Uncivil War: The Southern Backcountry During the American Revolution* (1985); Jean B. Lee, *The Price of Nationhood: The American Revolution in Charles County* (1994); Bruce A. Ragsdale,

A Planters' Republic: The Search for Economic Independence in Revolutionary Virginia (1996); Stephen Rosswurm, *Arms, Country, and Class: The Philadelphia Militia and the "Lower Sort" During the American Revolution* (1988); John Selby, *The Revolution in Virginia, 1775–1783* (1988).

Indians and African-Americans

Colin Calloway, *The American Revolution in Indian Country: Crisis and Diversity in Native American Communities* (1995); Sylvia Frey, *Water from the Rock: Black Resistance in a Revolutionary Age* (1991); Barbara Graymont, *The Iroquois in the American Revolution* (1972); Isabel T. Kelsey, *Joseph Brant, 1743–1807: Man of Two Worlds* (1984); James H. O'Donnell III, *Southern Indians in the American Revolution* (1973); Anthony F. C. Wallace, *The Death and Rebirth of the Seneca* (1969).

Loyalists

Bernard Bailyn, *The Ordeal of Thomas Hutchinson* (1974); Robert McCluer Calhoon, *The Loyalists in Revolutionary America, 1760–1781* (1973); Mary Beth Norton, *The British-Americans: The Loyalist Exiles in England, 1774–1789* (1972); Janice Potter, *The Liberty We Seek: Loyalist Ideology in Colonial New York and Massachusetts* (1983); Paul H. Smith, *Loyalists and Redcoats: A Study in British Revolutionary Policy* (1964); James W. St. G. Walker, *The Black Loyalists: The Search for a Promised Land in Nova Scotia and Sierra Leone, 1783–1870* (1976).

Women

Richard Buel and Joy Buel, *The Way of Duty: A Woman and Her Family in Revolutionary America* (1984); Ronald Hoffman and Peter Albert, eds., *Women in the Age of the American Revolution* (1989); Linda K. Kerber, *Women of the Republic: Intellect and Ideology in Revolutionary America* (1980); Mary Beth Norton, *Liberty's Daughters: The Revolutionary Experience of American Women, 1750–1800* (1980).

Foreign Policy

Jonathan Dull, *A Diplomatic History of the American Revolution* (1985); Ronald Hoffman and Peter Albert, eds., *Peace and the Peacemakers: The Treaty of 1783* (1986); Ronald Hoffman and Peter Albert, eds., *Diplomacy and Revolution: The Franco-American Alliance of 1778* (1981); Lawrence Kaplan, ed., *The American Revolution and a "Candid World"* (1977); Jan Willem Schulte Nordholt, *The Dutch Republic and American Independence* (1982); Richard W. Van Alstyne, *Empire and Independence: The International History of the American Revolution* (1965).

Patriot Leaders

Fawn M. Brodie, *Thomas Jefferson: An Intimate History* (1974); Richard Brookhiser, *Founding Father: Rediscovering George Washington* (1996); Joseph Ellis, *American Sphinx: The Character of Thomas Jefferson* (1997); John E. Ferling, *The First of Men: A Life of George Washington* (1988); Eric Foner, *Tom Paine and Revolutionary America* (1976); Norman Risjord, *Thomas Jefferson* (1994); Charles Royster, *Light-Horse Harry Lee and the Legacy of the American Revolution* (1981); Peter Shaw, *The Character of John Adams* (1976); Sheila Skemp, *Benjamin and William Franklin: Father and Son, Patriot and Loyalist* (1994); Esmond Wright, *Franklin of Philadelphia* (1986).

7

Forging a National Republic
1776–1789

On January 25, 1787, an army of fifteen hundred farmers from the hills and valleys of western Massachusetts advanced on the Springfield federal armory, which housed 450 tons of military supplies, including seven thousand muskets and thirteen hundred barrels of gunpowder. Inside the arsenal, General William Shepard prepared his group of one thousand militiamen to resist the assault. First, though, he dispatched two aides to warn the farmers that they would soon "inevitably" draw the fire of men who had been their officers during the Revolutionary War. "That is all we want, by God!" replied one of the rebels. The farmers moved toward the armory, urged on by the commands of Daniel Shays, one of their leaders. "March, God Damn you, March!" he shouted. Shepard fired two cannon over the heads of the farmers, and then—when that did not frighten them—ordered his men to shoot directly at the straggling ranks. Four men died, twenty were wounded, and the rebels withdrew.

What caused this violent clash between former comrades in arms, so soon after the war? Massachusetts farmers were angered by high taxes and the scarcity of money. Since the preceding summer, they had organized committees and crowd actions—the tactics used so successfully in the 1760s and early 1770s—to halt state efforts to seize property for nonpayment of taxes. Many of the insurgents were respected war veterans, described as "gentlemen" in contemporary accounts of the riots. Daniel Shays, their nominal leader (he disclaimed the title), had been a captain in the Continental Army. Clearly the episode could not be dismissed as the work of an unruly rabble. What did the uprising mean for the republic's future? Was it a sign of impending anarchy?

The protesters explained their position in an address to the Massachusetts government. They proclaimed their loyalty to the nation but

A woodcut of Daniel Shays and one of his chief officers, Job Shattuck, in 1787.   National Portrait Gallery, Smithsonian Institution, Washington, D.C.

objected to the state's fiscal policies, which, they said, prevented them from providing adequately for their families. Referring to their experience as revolutionary soldiers, they asserted that they "esteem[ed] one moment of Liberty to be worth an eternity of Bondage." One rebel sympathizer explained, "Whenever any encroachments are made either upon the liberties or properties of the people, if redress cannot be had without, it is virtue in them to disturb government." The Massachusetts government was "tyrannical," Shays asserted, and, like that of Great Britain, deserved to be overthrown.

To the state's elected leaders, the most ominous aspect of the uprising was the farmers' attempt to link their rebellion with the earlier struggle for independence. The state legislature insisted that "in a republican government the majority must govern. If the minor part governs it becomes aristocracy; if every one opposed at his pleasure, it is no government, it is anarchy and confusion." In short, the crowd actions that once had been a justifiable response to British tyranny were no longer legitimate.

In a republic, reform had to come through the ballot box rather than by force. If the nation's citizens refused to submit to legitimate authority, the result would be chaos and political collapse.

The confrontation at the Springfield armory symbolized for many Americans the trials facing the new nation. That the rebels were dispersed easily, that their leaders (including Shays) had to flee to neighboring states for asylum, that two of the insurgents were hanged, and that a newly elected legislature adopted conciliatory measures—none of these outcomes altered American political leaders' interpretation of the events in western Massachusetts. In Shays's Rebellion they thought they discerned the first signs of disintegration of the republic they had worked so hard to establish.

Republicanism—the idea that governments should be based wholly on the consent of the people—originated with political theorists in ancient Greece and Rome. Republics, such writers declared, were desirable yet fragile forms of government. Unless their citizens were especially virtuous—that is,

• *Important Events* •

1776	Second Continental Congress directs states to draft constitutions	**1788**	Hamilton, Jay, and Madison write *The Federalist* to urge ratification of the Constitution by New York Constitution ratified
1777	Articles of Confederation sent to states for ratification	**1794**	Defeat of Miami Confederacy at Fallen Timbers
1781	Articles of Confederation ratified	**1795**	Treaty of Greenville opens Ohio to white settlement
1786	Annapolis Convention meets, discusses reforming government	**1800**	Mason Locke Weems publishes his *Life of Washington*
1786–87	Shays's Rebellion in western Massachusetts raises questions about future of the republic		
1787	Northwest Ordinance organizes territory north of Ohio River and east of Mississippi River Constitutional Convention drafts new form of government		

sober, moral, and industrious—and largely in agreement on key issues, republics were doomed to failure. When Americans left the British Empire, they abandoned the idea that the best system of government balanced monarchy, aristocracy, and democracy—or, to put it another way, that a stable polity required participation by a king, the nobility, and the people. They substituted a belief in the superiority of republicanism, in which the people, not Parliament, were sovereign. Now Americans had to deal with the potentially unwelcome consequences of that decision. How could they best ensure political stability? How could they foster consensus among the populace? How could they create and sustain a virtuous republic?

America's political and intellectual leaders worked hard to inculcate virtue in their fellow countrymen and countrywomen. After 1776, American literature, theater, art, architecture, and education all pursued explicitly moral goals. The education of women was considered particularly important, for as the mothers of the republic's children, they were primarily responsible for ensuring the nation's future. On such matters Americans could agree, but they disagreed on many other critical issues. Almost all white men concurred that women, Indians, and African-Americans should be excluded from formal participation in politics, but they found it difficult to reach a

consensus on how many of their own number should be included, how often elections should be held, or how their new governments should be structured.

Republican citizens had to make many other decisions as well. Should a republic conduct its dealings with Indian nations and foreign countries any differently than other types of governments did? Were republics, in other words, obliged to negotiate fairly and honestly at all times? And then there were Thomas Jefferson's words in the Declaration of Independence: "all men are created equal." Given that bold statement of principle, how could white republicans justify holding African-Americans in perpetual bondage? Some answered that question by freeing their slaves or by voting for state laws that abolished slavery. Others responded by denying that blacks were "men" in the same sense as whites.

The most important task facing Americans in these years was the construction of a genuinely national government. Before 1765, the British mainland colonies had rarely cooperated on common endeavors. Many circumstances separated them: their diverse economies, varying religious traditions and ethnic compositions, competing land claims (especially in the West), and different political systems. But fighting the Revolutionary War brought them together and created a new nationalistic spirit, especially among those who served in the Continental

Army or the diplomatic corps. Wartime experiences broke down at least some of the boundaries that previously had divided Americans, replacing loyalties to state and region with loyalties to the nation.

Still, forging a national republic (as opposed to a set of loosely connected state republics) was neither easy nor simple. America's first such government, under the Articles of Confederation, proved to be inadequate. But some of the nation's political leaders learned from their experiences and tried another approach when they drafted the Constitution in 1787. Some historians have argued that the Articles of Confederation and the Constitution reflect opposing political philosophies, the Constitution representing an "aristocratic" counterrevolution against the "democratic" Articles. The two documents are more accurately viewed as successive attempts to solve the same problems. Both applied theories of republicanism to practical problems of governance; neither was entirely successful in resolving those difficulties.

 ## Creating a Virtuous Republic

When the colonies declared their independence from Great Britain, John Dickinson recalled many years later, "there was no question concerning forms of Government, no enquiry whether a Republic or a limited Monarchy was best. . . . We knew that the people of this country must unite themselves under some form of Government and that this could be no other than the republican form." But how should that goal be implemented?

Three different definitions of *republicanism* emerged in the new United States. The first, held chiefly by members of the educated elite (such as the

Varieties of Republicanism

Adamses of Massachusetts), was based directly on ancient history and political theory. The histories of popular governments in Greece and Rome seemed to prove that republics could succeed only if they were small in size and homogeneous in population. Unless a republic's citizens were willing to sacrifice their own private interests for the good of the whole, the government would collapse. A truly virtuous man, classical republican theory insisted, had to forgo personal profit and work solely for the best interests of the nation. In return for sacrifices, though, a republic offered its citizens equality of opportunity. Under such a government, rank would be based

on merit rather than on inherited wealth and status. Society would be governed by members of a "natural aristocracy," men whose talent had elevated them from what might have been humble beginnings to positions of power and privilege. Rank would not be abolished but instead would be founded on merit.

A second definition, advanced by other members of the elite but also by some skilled craftsmen, drew more on economic theory than on political thought. Instead of perceiving the nation as an organic whole composed of people nobly sacrificing for the common good, this version of republicanism followed the Scottish theorist Adam Smith in emphasizing individuals' pursuit of rational self-interest. The applicability of this approach was underscored by the huge profits some men reaped from patriotism by selling supplies to the army. The nation could only benefit from aggressive economic expansion, argued men such as Alexander Hamilton. When republican men sought to improve their own economic and social circumstances, the entire nation would benefit. Republican virtue would be achieved through the pursuit of private interests, rather than through subordination to some communal ideal.

The third notion of republicanism was more egalitarian than the other two, which both contained considerable potential for inequality. This view was less influential because many of its proponents were illiterate or barely literate and thus wrote little to promote their beliefs. Men who advanced the third version of republicanism, the most prominent of whom was Thomas Paine, called for widening men's participation in the political process. They also wanted government to respond directly to the needs of ordinary folk, rejecting any notion that the "lesser sort" should automatically defer to their "betters." They were, indeed, democrats in more or less the modern sense. For them, republican virtue was embodied in the untutored wisdom of the people as a whole, rather than in the special insights of a natural aristocracy or the pronouncements of wealthy individuals.

Despite the differences, the three strands of republicanism shared many of the same assumptions. For example, all three contrasted a virtuous, industrious America to the corruption of Britain and Europe. In the first version, that virtue manifested itself in frugality and self-sacrifice; in the second, it would prevent self-interest from becoming vice; in the third, it was the justification for including even propertyless free men in the ranks of voters. "Virtue,

Virtue alone . . . is the basis of a republic," asserted Dr. Benjamin Rush of Philadelphia, an ardent patriot, in 1778. His fellow Americans concurred, even if they defined virtue in divergent ways. Most agreed that a virtuous country would be composed of hard-working citizens who would dress simply and live plainly, elect wise leaders to public office, and forgo the conspicuous consumption of luxury goods.

As citizens of the United States set out to construct their republic, they believed they were embarking on an unprecedented enterprise. With great pride in their new nation, they expected to replace the vices of monarchical Europe—immorality, selfishness, and lack of public-spiritedness—with the sober virtues of republican America. They wanted to embody republican principles not only in their governments but also in their society and culture. They looked to painting, literature, drama, and architecture to convey messages of nationalism and virtue to the public.

Virtue and the Arts

Americans faced a crucial contradiction at the very outset of their efforts. To some republicans, the fine arts themselves were manifestations of vice. Their existence in a virtuous society, many contended, signaled the arrival of luxury and corruption. What need did a frugal yeoman have for a painting—or, worse yet, a novel? Why should anyone spend hard-earned wages to see a play in a lavishly decorated theater? The first American artists, playwrights, and authors thus confronted an impossible dilemma. They wanted to produce works embodying virtue, but those very works, regardless of their content, were viewed by many as corrupting.

Still, they tried. William Hill Brown's *The Power of Sympathy* (1789), the first novel written in the United States, was a lurid tale of seduction intended as a warning to young women, who made up a large proportion of America's fiction readers. In Royall Tyler's *The Contrast* (1787), the first successful American play, the virtuous conduct of Colonel Manly was contrasted (hence the title) with the reprehensible behavior of the fop Billy Dimple. The most popular book of the era, Mason Locke Weems's *Life of Washington*, published in 1800 shortly after George Washington's death, was intended by its author to "hold up his great Virtues . . . to the imitation of Our Youth." Weems could hardly be accused of subtlety. The famous tale he invented—six-year-old George bravely admitting cutting down his father's favorite cherry tree—ended with George's father exclaiming, "Run to my arms, you dearest boy. . . . Such an act of heroism in my son, is worth more than a thousand trees, though blossomed with silver, and their fruit of purest gold."

Painting and architecture, too, were expected to embody high moral standards. Two of the most prominent artists of the period, Gilbert Stuart and Charles Willson Peale, painted innumerable portraits of upstanding republican citizens. John Trumbull's vast canvases depicted milestones of American history such as the Battle of Bunker Hill, Burgoyne's surrender at Saratoga, and Cornwallis's capitulation at Yorktown. Such portraits and historical scenes were intended to instill patriotic sentiments in their viewers. Architects likewise hoped to convey in their buildings a sense of the young republic's ideals. When the Virginia government asked Thomas Jefferson, then minister to France, for advice on the design of the state capitol in Richmond, Jefferson unhesitatingly recommended copying a Roman building, the Maison Carrée at Nîmes. "It is very simple," he explained, "but it is noble beyond expression." Jefferson set forth ideals that would guide American architecture for a generation to come: simplicity of line, harmonious proportions, a feeling of grandeur. Nowhere were these rational goals of republican art manifested more clearly than in Benjamin H. Latrobe's plans for the majestic domed United States Capitol in Washington, D.C., built shortly after the turn of the century.

Despite the artists' efforts (or, some would have said, because of them), some Americans were beginning to detect signs of luxury and corruption by the mid-1780s. The resumption of European trade after the war brought a return to fashionable clothing for both men and women and abandonment of the simpler homespun garments patriots had once worn with pride. Elite families again attended balls and concerts. Parties no longer seemed complete without gambling and cardplaying. Social clubs for young people multiplied; Samuel Adams worried in print about the opportunities for corruption lurking behind plans for tea drinking and genteel conversation among Boston youths. Especially alarming to fervent republicans was the establishment in 1783 of the Society of the Cincinnati, a hereditary organization of Revolutionary War officers and their descendants. Many feared that the group would become the nucleus of a native-born aristocracy. All these developments directly challenged the United States's self-image as a virtuous republic.

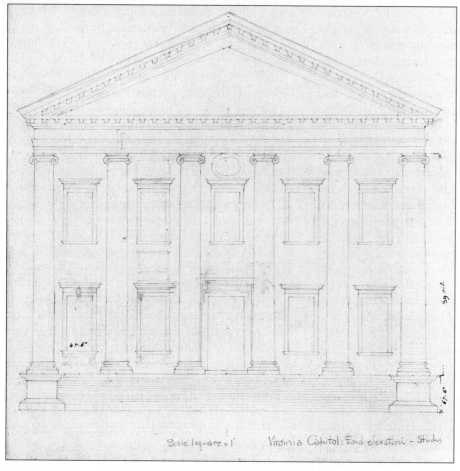

Thomas Jefferson's design for the front of the Virginia state capitol (c. 1785) epitomized the architectural ideals of the republic.   Massachusetts Historical Society.

Americans' deep-seated concern for the future of the infant republic focused their attention on their children, the "rising generation." Throughout the history of the colonies, education had been seen chiefly as a private means to personal advancement, of concern only to individual families. Now, though, education would serve a public purpose. If young people were to resist the temptations of vice, they would have to learn the lessons of virtue at home and at school. In fact, the very survival of the nation depended on it. The early republican period was thus a time of major educational reform.

Educational Reform

The 1780s and 1790s brought two significant changes in American educational practice. First, in contrast to the colonies, where nearly all education had been privately financed, some northern states began to use tax money to support public elementary schools. In 1789, Massachusetts became one of the first states to require towns to offer their citizens free public elementary education.

Second, schooling for girls was improved. Americans' recognition of the importance of the rising generation led to the realization that mothers would have to be properly educated if they were to instruct their children adequately. Therefore Massachusetts insisted in its 1789 law that town elementary schools be open to girls as well as boys. Throughout the United States, private academies were founded to give teenage girls from well-to-do families an opportunity for advanced schooling. No one yet proposed opening colleges to women, but a few fortunate girls could study history, geography, rhetoric, and mathematics. The academies also trained female students in fancy needlework—the only artistic endeavor considered appropriate for genteel women.

The chief theorist of women's education in the early republic was Judith Sargent Murray of Gloucester, Massachusetts. In a series of essays published in the 1780s and 1790s, Murray argued that women and men had equal intellectual capacities, though women's inadequate education might make them seem less intelligent. "We can only reason from what we know," she declared, "and if an opportunity of acquiring knowledge hath been denied us, the inferiority of our sex cannot fairly be deduced from thence." Therefore, concluded Murray, boys and girls should be offered equivalent scholastic training. She further contended that girls should be taught to support themselves by their own efforts: "Independence should be placed within their grasp."

Judith Sargent Murray and Women's Education

Murray's direct challenge to the traditional colonial belief that, as one man put it, girls "knew quite enough if they could make a shirt and a pudding" was part of a general rethinking of women's position that occurred as a result of the Revolution. Male patriots who enlisted in the army or served in Congress were away from home for long periods of time. In their absence their wives, who previously had handled only the "indoor affairs" of the household, shouldered the responsibility for "outdoor affairs" as well. As the wife of a Connecticut militiaman later recalled, her husband "was out more or less during the remainder of the war [after 1777], so much so as to be unable to do anything on our farm. What was done, was done by myself." Similarly, John and Abigail Adams took great pride in Abigail's developing skills as a "farmeress." Like her female contemporaries, Abigail Adams stopped calling the farm "yours" in letters to her husband and began referring to it as "ours"—a revealing change of pronoun. Both men and women realized that female patriots had made vital and important contributions to winning the war through their work at home and that their notions of proper gender roles had to be rethought. Americans began to develop new ideas about the role women should play in a republican society.

The best-known example of those new ideas is a letter Abigail Adams addressed to her husband

Judith Sargent (1751–1820), later Mrs. John Murray, painted by John Singleton Copley when she was in her late teens. Although her steady gaze suggests clear-headed intelligence, there is little in the stylized portrait—typical of Copley's work at the time—to suggest her later emergence as the first notable American feminist theorist. Frick Art Reference Library.

in March 1776. "In the new Code of Laws which I suppose it will be necessary for you to make I desire you would Remember the Ladies," she wrote. "Remember all Men would be tyrants if they could. . . . If perticuliar care and attention is not paid to the Laidies we are determined to foment a Rebelion, and will not hold ourselves bound by any Laws in which we have no voice, or Representation." With these words, Abigail Adams took a step that was soon to be duplicated by other disfranchised Americans. She deliberately applied the ideology developed to combat parliamentary supremacy to purposes revolutionary leaders had never intended. Since men were

Abigail Adams: "Remember the Ladies"

"Naturally Tyrannical," she argued, the United States should reform colonial marriage laws, which made wives subordinate to their husbands.

Abigail Adams did not ask that women be allowed to vote, but others claimed that right. The men who drafted the New Jersey state constitution in 1776 defined voters carelessly as "all free inhabitants" who met certain property qualifications. They thereby unintentionally gave the vote to property-holding white spinsters and widows, as well as to free blacks. Qualified women and African-Americans regularly voted in New Jersey's local and congressional elections until 1807, when they were disfranchised by the state legislature, which falsely alleged that they had engaged in widespread vote fraud. Yet the fact that women voted at all was evidence of their altered perception of their place in the political life of the country.

Such dramatic episodes were unusual. After the war, European-Americans still viewed women in traditional terms, continuing to believe that women's primary function was to be good wives, mothers, and mistresses of households. They perceived significant differences between male and female characters. That distinction eventually enabled Americans to resolve the conflict between the two most influential strands of republican thought and led to new roles for some women. Because wives could not own property or participate directly in economic life, women in general came to be seen as the embodiment of self-sacrificing, disinterested republicanism. Through new female-run charitable associations founded after the war, better-off women assumed public responsibilities, in particular through caring for poor widows and orphaned children. Thus men were freed from the naggings of conscience as they pursued their economic self-interest (that other republican virtue), secure in the knowledge that their wives and daughters were fulfilling the family's obligation to the common good. The ideal republican man, therefore, was an individualist, seeking advancement for himself and his family. The ideal republican woman, by contrast, always put the well-being of others ahead of her own.

Women's Role in the Republic

Together white men and women established the context for the creation of a virtuous republic. But nearly 20 percent of the American population was black. How did approximately 700,000 African-Americans fit into the developing national plan?

Emancipation and the Growth of Racism

Revolutionary ideology exposed one of the primary contradictions in American society. Both blacks and whites saw the irony in slaveholding Americans' claims that one of their aims in taking up arms was to prevent Britain from "enslaving" them. Many revolutionary leaders voiced the theme. In 1773 Dr. Benjamin Rush called slavery "a vice which degrades human nature," warning ominously that "the plant of liberty is of so tender a nature that it cannot thrive long in the neighborhood of slavery." Common folk also saw the contradiction. When Josiah Atkins, a Connecticut soldier marching south, saw Washington's plantation, he observed in his journal: "Alas! That persons who pretend to stand for the rights of mankind for the liberties of society, can delight in oppression, & that even of the worst kind!"

African-Americans did not need revolutionary ideology to tell them that slavery was wrong, but they quickly took advantage of that ideology. In 1779 a group of slaves from Portsmouth, New Hampshire, asked the state legislature "from what authority [our masters] assume to dispose of our lives, freedom and property," pleading "that the name of slave may not more be heard in a land gloriously contending for the sweets of freedom." The same year several bondspeople in Fairfield, Connecticut, petitioned the legislature for their freedom, characterizing slavery as a "dreadful Evil" and "flagrant Injustice." How could men who were "nobly contending in the Cause of Liberty," they asked, continue "this detestable Practice"?

Both legislatures responded negatively, but the postwar years did witness the gradual abolition of slavery in the North. Vermont abolished slavery in its 1777 constitution. Massachusetts courts decided in the 1780s that a clause in the state constitution prohibited slavery. Pennsylvania passed an abolition law in 1780; four years later Rhode Island and Connecticut provided for gradual emancipation, followed by New York (1799) and New Jersey (1804). Although New Hampshire did not formally abolish slavery, only eight slaves were reported on the 1800 census, and none remained a decade later.

Gradual Emancipation

No southern state adopted similar general emancipation laws, but the legislatures of Virginia (1782), Delaware (1787), and Maryland (1790 and

1796) altered laws that previously had restricted slaveowners' ability to free their bondspeople. South Carolina and Georgia never considered adopting such acts, and North Carolina insisted that all manumissions (emancipations of individual slaves) be approved by county courts.

Revolutionary ideology thus had limited impact on the well-entrenched economic interests of large slaveholders. Only in the North, where slaves were relatively rare and where little money was invested in human capital, could state legislatures easily vote to abolish slavery. Even there, legislators' concern for property rights—the Revolution, after all, was fought for property as well as life and liberty—led them to favor gradual emancipation over immediate abolition. Most states provided only for the freeing of children born after passage of the law, not for the emancipation of adults. And even those children were to remain slaves until reaching adulthood. Still, by 1840 in only one northern state—New Jersey—were African-Americans legally held in bondage.

Despite the slow progress of abolition, the number of free people of African descent in the United States grew dramatically in the first years after the Revolution. Before the war there had been few free blacks in America. According to a 1755 Maryland census, for example, only 4 percent of the African-Americans in the colony were free. Most blacks emancipated before the war were *mulattos*, born of unions between enslaved women and their masters, who then manumitted the children. But wartime disruptions radically changed the size and composition of the freed population. Slaves who had escaped from plantations during the war, others who had served in the American army, and still others who had been emancipated by their owners or by state laws were now free. By 1790 there were nearly 60,000 free people of color in the United States; ten years later they numbered more than 108,000, nearly 11 percent of the total African-American population.

Growth of Free Black Population

The effects of postwar manumissions were felt most sharply in the Chesapeake, where they were fostered by economic changes such as declining soil fertility and the shift from tobacco to grain production. Since grain cultivation was less labor-intensive than tobacco growing, planters began to complain about "excess" slaves. They occasionally solved that problem by freeing some of their less productive or

Robert Carter was one of the largest slaveholders in Virginia. After the state altered its manumission laws and he had become a Baptist, he decided to free all his bondspeople. He worked out a plan of gradual emancipation, freeing some slaves each year for several years. Hannah, one of his weavers, wrote to him in April 1792, requesting that she be allowed to buy her loom when she was emancipated the following January. This is one of only a handful of documents known to be written by literate slave women during the eighteenth century. Chicago Historical Society, Robert Carter Papers.

more favored bondspeople. The free black population of Virginia more than doubled between 1790 and 1810, and by the latter year nearly one-quarter of Maryland's African-American population was no longer in legal bondage.

In the 1780s and thereafter, freed people often made their way to northern port cities. Boston and Philadelphia, where slavery was abolished sooner than in New York City, were popular destinations. Women outnumbered men among the migrants by a margin of three to two. Black women found more opportunities for employment, particularly as domestic servants, in the cities than in the countryside. Some freedmen also worked in domestic service, but larger numbers were employed as unskilled laborers and seamen. A few of the women

Migration to Northern Cities

How do historians know that the 1780s and 1790s marked a key turning point in the history of slavery and racism in the United States? The emancipation and manumission laws adopted by state legislatures, coupled with debates in pamphlets and newspapers, are important indications of a shift in Americans' thinking. But a painting such as the one reproduced here, Liberty Displaying the Arts and Sciences, offers a unique visual perspective on the same developments. In 1792, the Library Company of Philadelphia, a private lending library founded in the mid-eighteenth century, commissioned the artist Samuel Jennings to produce a depiction of slavery and abolitionism showing the "figure of Liberty (with her Cap and proper Insignia) displaying the arts." The library's directors reportedly were well pleased with the results. The painting, probably the first to celebrate emancipation, shows the blonde goddess presenting books (symbolizing knowledge and freedom) to several suppliant and grateful blacks, while in the background a group of former slaves dances joyfully around a liberty pole. Although the theme is abolition and the African-Americans in the foreground have realistic features, the portrayal of blacks in passive roles and diminutive sizes portends future stereotypical images. Thus the picture simultaneously linked emancipation and the growth of racism.   The Library Company of Philadelphia.

and a sizable proportion of men (nearly one-third of those in Philadelphia in 1795) were skilled workers or retailers. These people chose new names for themselves, exchanging the surnames of former masters for names like Newman or Brown, and as soon as possible they established independent two-parent nuclear families instead of continuing to live in their employers' households. They also began to occupy distinct neighborhoods, probably as the combined result of discrimination and a desire for racial solidarity.

Emancipation did not bring equality. Even whites who recognized African-Americans' right to freedom were unwilling to accept them as equals. Laws discriminated against emancipated blacks as they had against slaves. South Carolina, for example, did not permit free blacks to testify against whites in court. Public schools often refused to educate their children. Freedmen found it difficult to purchase property and find good jobs. And though in many areas African-Americans were accepted as members—even ministers—of evangelical churches, whites rarely allowed them an equal voice in church affairs.

Gradually, freed people developed their own institutions, often based in their own neighborhoods. In Charleston, mulattos formed the Brown Fellowship

Freed People's Churches and Associations

Society, which provided insurance coverage for its members, financed a school, and helped to support orphans. In 1794, blacks in Philadelphia and Baltimore founded societies that eventually became the African Methodist Episcopal (AME) denomination. AME churches later sponsored schools in a number of cities and, along with African Baptist, African Episcopal, and African Presbyterian churches, became cultural centers of the free black community. Freed people quickly learned that, to survive and prosper, they had to rely on their own collective efforts rather than on the benevolence or goodwill of their white compatriots.

Their endeavors were all the more necessary because the postrevolutionary years witnessed the development of a coherent racist theory in the United States. Whites had long regarded

Development of Racist Theory

their slaves as inferior, but the most influential writers on race attributed that inferiority to environmental factors. They argued that blacks' seemingly debased character derived from their enslavement,

rather than enslavement being the consequence of inherited inferiority. In the Revolution's aftermath, though, white southerners needed to defend their enslavement of other human beings against the notion that "all men are created equal." Consequently, they began to argue that blacks were less than fully human and that the principles of republican equality applied only to whites. In other words, to avoid having to confront the contradiction between their practice and the egalitarian implications of revolutionary theory, they redefined the theory so that it would not apply to African-Americans.

This racism had several intertwined elements. First was the asssertion that, as Thomas Jefferson suggested in 1781, blacks were "inferior to the whites in the endowments both of body and mind." Then came the belief that blacks were congenitally lazy, dishonest, and uncivilized (or uncivilizable). Third, and of crucial importance, was the notion that all blacks were sexually promiscuous and that black men lusted after white women. The specter of interracial sexual intercourse involving black men and white women haunted early American racist thought. Significantly, the more common reverse circumstance—the sexual exploitation of enslaved women by their white masters—aroused little comment.

African-Americans did not allow these developing racist notions to go unchallenged. Benjamin Banneker, a free black surveyor, astronomer, and mathematical genius, directly disputed Thomas Jefferson's belief in blacks' intellectual inferiority. In 1791 Banneker sent Jefferson a copy of his latest almanac (which included his astronomical calculations) as an example of blacks' mental powers. Jefferson's response admitted Banneker's capability but indicated that he regarded Banneker as exceptional; Jefferson insisted that he needed more evidence before he would change his mind.

At its birth, then, the republic was defined by its leaders as an exclusively white enterprise. Indeed, some historians have argued that the subjugation of

A Republic for Whites Only

blacks was a necessary precondition for equality among whites. They have pointed out that identifying a common racial antagonist helped to create white solidarity and to lessen the threat to gentry power posed by the enfranchisement of poorer whites. Some have asserted that it was less dangerous to allow whites with little property to participate formally in politics than to open the possibility that they might join with former slaves to question the rule of the "better sort." That was perhaps one reason why after the Revolution the division of American society between slave and free was transformed into a division between blacks—some of whom were free—and whites. The wielders of power ensured their continued dominance in part by substituting race for enslavement as the primary determinant of African-Americans' status.

 ## Designing Republican Governments

In May 1776, even before adoption of the Declaration of Independence, the Second Continental Congress directed states to devise new republican governments to replace the provincial congresses and committees that had met since 1774. Thus Americans initially concentrated on drafting state constitutions and devoted little attention to their national government—an oversight they later were forced to remedy.

At the state level, they immediately faced the problem of defining just what a constitution was. The British Constitution could not serve as a model

Drafting of State Constitutions

because it was a mixture of law and custom; Americans wanted tangible documents specifying the fundamental structures of government. Several years passed before states concluded that their constitutions, unlike ordinary laws, could not be drafted by regular legislative bodies. Following the lead established by Vermont in 1777 and Massachusetts in 1780, they began to call conventions for the sole purpose of drafting constitutions. Thus states sought direct authorization from the people—the theoretical sovereigns in a republic—before establishing new governments. After preparing new constitutions, delegates submitted them to voters for ratification.

The framers of state constitutions concerned themselves primarily with outlining the distribution of and limitations on government power. Both issues were crucial to the survival of republics. If authority was improperly distributed among the branches of government, or not confined within reasonable limits, the states might become tyrannical, as Britain had. Americans' experience with British rule permeated every provision of their new constitutions. States experimented with different solutions to the

problems the framers perceived, and the early constitutions varied considerably in specifics while remaining broadly comparable in outline.

Under their colonial charters, Americans had learned to fear the power of the governor—usually, the appointed agent of king or proprietor—and to see the legislature as their defender. Accordingly, the first state constitutions typically provided for the governor to be elected annually (commonly by the legislature), limited the number of terms he could serve, and gave him little independent authority. Simultaneously, the constitutions expanded the legislature's powers. Every state except Pennsylvania and Vermont retained a two-house structure, with members of the upper house having longer terms and being required to meet higher property-holding standards than members of the lower house. But they also redrew electoral districts to reflect population patterns more accurately, and they increased the number of members in both houses. Finally, most states lowered property qualifications for voting. As a result the legislatures came to include some members who before the war would not have been eligible to vote. Thus the revolutionary era witnessed the first deliberate attempt to broaden the base of American government, a process that has continued into our own day.

But the state constitutions' authors knew that governments designed to be responsive to the people would not necessarily provide sufficient protection if tyrants were elected to office.

Limits on State Governments

They consequently included explicit limitations on government authority in the documents they composed. Seven of the constitutions contained formal bills of rights, and the others had similar clauses. Most guaranteed citizens freedom of the press and of religion, the right to a fair trial, the right of consent to taxation, and protection against general search warrants. An independent judiciary was charged with upholding such rights.

In sum, the constitution makers put far greater emphasis on preventing state governments from becoming tyrannical than on making them effective wielders of political authority. Their approach to shaping governments was understandable, given the American experience with Great Britain. But establishing such weak political units, especially in wartime, practically ensured that the constitutions soon would need revision. As early as the 1780s some states began to rewrite constitutions they had drafted in 1776 and 1777.

Invariably, the revised versions increased the powers of the governor and reduced the scope of the legislature's authority. Only then, a decade after the Declaration of Independence, did Americans start to develop a formal theory of checks and balances as the primary means of controlling government power. Once they realized that legislative supremacy did not in itself guarantee good government, Americans attempted to achieve that goal by balancing the powers of the legislative, executive, and judicial branches against one another. The national constitution they drafted in 1787 embodied that principle.

The constitutional theories that Americans applied at the state level did not at first influence their conception of national government. Since American political leaders had little time to devote to legitimizing their de facto government while organizing the military struggle against Britain, the powers and structure of the Continental Congress evolved by default early in the war. Not until late 1777 did Congress send the Articles of Confederation to the states for ratification.

The Articles largely wrote into law the unplanned arrangements of the Continental Congress. The chief organ of national government was a unicameral (one-house) legislature in which each state had **Articles of** one vote. Its powers included **Confederation** conducting foreign relations, settling disputes between states, controlling maritime affairs, regulating Indian trade, and valuing state and national coinage. The Articles did not give the national government the ability to raise revenue effectively or to enforce a uniform commercial policy. The United States of America was described as "a firm league of friendship" in which each state "retains its sovereignty, freedom and independence, and every Power, Jurisdiction and right, which is not by this confederation expressly delegated to the United States, in Congress assembled." (See the Appendix for the text of the Articles.)

The Articles required the unanimous consent of the state legislatures for ratification or amendment, and a clause concerning western lands proved troublesome. The draft accepted by Congress allowed states to retain all land claims derived from their original colonial charters. But states with definite western boundaries spelled out in their charters (like Maryland and New Jersey) wanted other states to cede to the national government their landholdings west of the Appalachian Mountains. Otherwise, they

feared, states with large claims could expand and overpower their smaller neighbors. Maryland refused to accept the Articles until 1781, when Virginia finally promised to surrender its western holdings to national jurisdiction (see map, page 184). Other states followed suit, establishing the principle that unorganized lands would be held by the nation as a whole.

The capacity of a single state to delay ratification for three years was a portent of the fate of American government under the Articles of Confederation. The unicameral legislature, whether it was called the Second Continental Congress (until 1781) or the Confederation Congress (thereafter), was too inefficient and unwieldy to govern effectively. The Articles' authors had not given adequate thought to the distribution of power within the national government or to the relationship between the Confederation and the states. The Congress they created was simultaneously a legislative body and a collective executive, but it had no independent income and no authority to compel the states to accept its rulings. What is surprising is not how poorly the Confederation functioned but rather how much the government was able to accomplish.

 ## Trials of the Confederation

The most persistent problem faced by the American governments, state and national, was finance. Because legislators at all levels were reluctant to levy taxes, both Congress and the **Financial** states tried to finance the war by **Problems** printing currency. Even though the money was backed by nothing but good faith, it circulated freely and without excessive depreciation during 1775 and most of 1776. Demand for military supplies and civilian goods was high, stimulating trade (especially with France) and local production. Indeed, the amount of money issued in those years was probably no more than what a healthy economy required as a medium of exchange.

But in late 1776, as the American army suffered reverses in New York and New Jersey, prices began to rise and inflation set in. The currency's value rested on Americans' faith in their government, a faith that was sorely tested in the years that followed, especially during the dark days of early British triumphs in the South (1779 and 1780). State governments fought inflation by controlling wages and

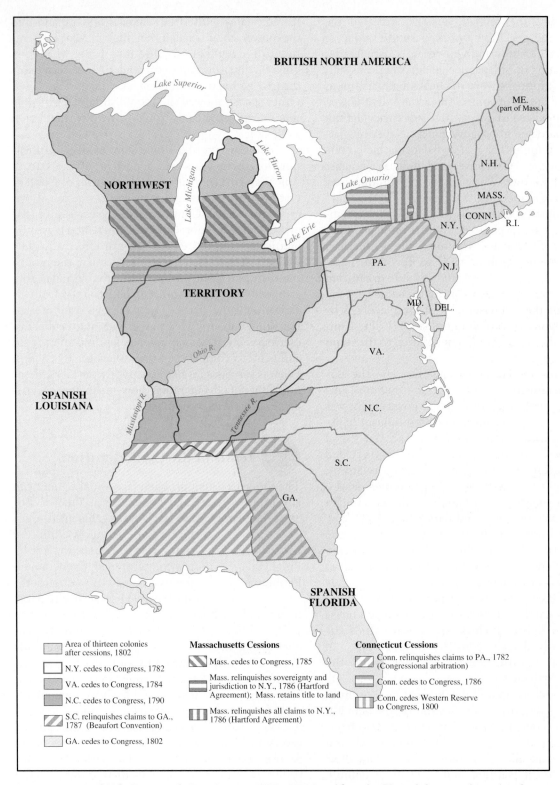

Western Land Claims and Cessions, 1782–1802 *After the United States achieved independence, states competed with each other for control of valuable lands to which they had possible claims under
their original charters. That competition led to a series of compromises among the states or between individual states and the new nation, which are indicated on this map.*

prices and requiring acceptance of paper currency on an equal footing with hard money. States also borrowed funds, established lotteries, and even levied taxes. Their efforts were futile. So too was Congress's attempt to stop printing currency altogether and to rely solely on money contributed by the states. By early 1780 it took forty paper dollars to purchase one silver dollar. Soon, Continental currency was worthless.

In 1781, faced with total collapse of the monetary system, the congressmen undertook ambitious reforms. After establishing a department of finance under the wealthy Philadelphia merchant Robert Morris, they asked the states to amend the Articles of Confederation to allow Congress to levy a duty of 5 percent on imported goods. Morris put national finances on a solid footing, but the customs duty was never adopted. First Rhode Island and then New York refused to agree to the tax. The states' resistance reflected fear of a too-powerful central government. As one worried citizen wrote in 1783, "If permanent Funds are given to Congress, the aristocratical Influence, which predominates in more than a major part of the United States, will fully establish an arbitrary Government." But states too needed revenue; when they enacted new, heavy taxes after the war, farmers resisted *their* authority. Shays's Rebellion was the most dramatic result of that resistance.

Congress also faced major diplomatic problems at the close of the war. Chief among them were issues involving the peace treaty itself. Article 4,

Weakness in Foreign Affairs and Commerce

which promised the repayment of prewar debts (most of them owed by Americans to British merchants), and Article 5, which recommended that states allow loyalists to recover their confiscated property, aroused considerable opposition. States passed laws denying British subjects the right to sue for recovery of debts or property in American courts, and town meetings decried the loyalists' return. As residents of Norwalk, Connecticut, put it, few Americans wanted to permit the "Tory Villains" to return "while filial Tears are fresh upon our Cheeks and our Murdered Brethren scarcely cold in their Graves." State governments also had reason to oppose enforcement of the treaty. Sales of loyalists' land, houses, and other possessions had helped to finance the war. Since most of the purchasers were prominent patriots, states had no desire to raise questions about the legitimacy of their property titles.

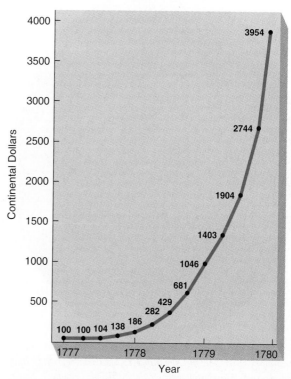

Depreciation of Continental Currency, 1777–1780

* Currency abandoned in April 1780

Depreciation of Continental Currency, 1777–1780 *The depreciation of Continental currency accelerated in 1778, as is shown in this graph measuring its value against one hundred silver dollars. Thereafter, its value dropped almost daily.*   Source: Data from John J. McCusker, "How Much Is That in Real Money? A Historical Price Index for Use as a Deflator of Money Values in the Economy of the United States," *Proceedings of the American Antiquarian Society,* Vol. 101, Pt. 2 (1991), Table C-1.

The refusal of state and local governments to comply with Articles 4 and 5 gave Britain an excuse to maintain military posts on the Great Lakes long after its troops were supposed to have withdrawn. Furthermore, Congress's inability to convince states to implement the treaty pointed up its lack of power, even in an area—foreign affairs—in which it had authority under the Articles of Confederation. Concerned nationalists argued publicly that enforcement of the treaty, however unpopular, was a crucial test for the republic. "Will foreign nations be willing to undertake anything with us or for us," asked Alexander Hamilton, "when they find that the nature of our

Because of their citizens' resistance to taxation, the early state governments found it hard to raise sufficient revenues. Some, like Massachusetts, turned to state-run lotteries to make up the shortfall. Here a New Englander proudly poses with a lottery ticket, demonstrating his support for the state.   Milwaukee Art Museum Purchase, Layton Art Collection.

governments will allow no dependence to be placed on our engagements?"

Congress's weakness was especially evident in the realm of trade because the Articles of Confederation denied it the power to establish a national commercial policy. Immediately after the war, Britain, France, and Spain all restricted American trade with their colonies. Americans, who had hoped independence would bring about trade with all nations, were outraged but could do little to change matters. Members of Congress watched helplessly as British manufactured goods flooded the United States while American produce could no longer be sold in the British West Indies, once its prime market. Although Americans reopened commerce with other European countries and started a profitable trade with China in 1784, neither substituted for access to closer and larger markets.

Congress also had difficulty dealing with the threat posed by Spain's presence on the nation's southern and western borders. Determined to prevent the

Failed Negotiations with Spain

republic's expansion, Spain in 1784 closed the Mississippi River to American navigation. It thus deprived the growing settlements west of the Appalachians of their major access route to the rest of the nation and the world. Congress opened negotiations with Spain in 1785, but even John Jay, one of the nation's most experienced diplomats, could not win the necessary concessions on navigation. The talks collapsed the following year after Congress divided sharply on the question of whether agreement should be sought on other issues. Southerners, voting as a bloc, insisted on navigation rights on the Mississippi; northerners were willing to abandon that claim in order to win commercial concessions. The impasse raised doubts about the possibility of a national consensus on foreign affairs.

Diplomatic problems of another sort confronted congressmen when they considered the status of land beyond the Appalachians. Although tribal claims were not discussed by British and American diplomats, the United States assumed that the Treaty of Paris (1783) cleared its title to all land east of the Mississippi except the area still held by Spain. But recognizing that some sort of land cession should be obtained from the most powerful tribes, Congress initiated negotiations with both northern and southern Indians (see map, page 187). At Fort Stanwix, New York, in 1784, and at Hopewell, South Carolina, in late 1785 and early 1786, American diplomats signed separate treaties with chiefs purporting to represent the Iroquois and with emissaries from the Choctaw, Chickasaw, and Cherokee nations. Later, both groups of Indians denied that the men who agreed to the treaties had been authorized to speak for them. But the United States still took the treaties as confirmation of its sovereignty over the territories in question and authorized settlers to move onto the land. European-Americans soon poured over the southern Appalachians, provoking the Creeks—who had not agreed to the Hopewell treaties—to defend their territory by declaring war. Only in 1790 did they come to terms with the United States.

In the North, meanwhile, the Iroquois Confederacy was in disarray. Members of the Six Nations who had not fled to Canada in 1779 found that they had little bargaining power left. In 1786 they repudiated the Fort Stanwix treaty and threatened new

Encroachment on Indian Lands

attacks on frontier settlements, but everyone knew the threat was empty. The flawed treaty stood by default. At intervals until the end of the decade New York State purchased large tracts of land from individual Iroquois nations. By 1790 the once-dominant confederacy was confined to a few scattered reservations.

Led by a remarkable prophet, Handsome Lake, the Iroquois sought to adapt to their new circumstances by embracing the traditional values of their culture and renouncing drinking alcohol, gambling, and other destructive European customs. Yet simultaneously, with Handsome Lake's approval, Quaker missionaries taught the Iroquois Anglo-American styles of agricultural subsistence. Men were now to be cultivators rather than hunters—since their hunting territories were lost—and women to be housekeepers rather than cultivators. Paradoxically, only by adopting a sexual division of labor that had originated in Europe could the Iroquois maintain a semblance of their culture.

Handsome Lake's Reforms

Western nations such as the Shawnees, Chippewas, Ottawas, and Potawatomis previously had allowed the Iroquois to speak for them. After the collapse of Iroquois power, they formed their own confederacy and demanded direct negotiations with the United States. Their aim was to present a united front so as to avoid the piecemeal surrender of land by individual hands and villages.

At first the national government ignored the western confederacy. Shortly after state land cessions were completed, Congress began to organize the Northwest Territory, bounded by the Mississippi River, the Great Lakes, and the Ohio River (see map). Ordinances passed in 1784, 1785, and 1787 outlined the process through which the land could be sold to settlers and formal governments could be organized.

Northwest Ordinances

To ensure orderly development, Congress in 1785 directed that the land be surveyed into townships 6 miles square, each divided into thirty-six sections of 640 acres (1 square mile). Revenue from the sale of the sixteenth section of each township was to be reserved for the support of public schools—the first instance of federal aid to education in American history. The minimum price per acre was set at one dollar, and the minimum sale was one section. Congress was not especially concerned about helping the

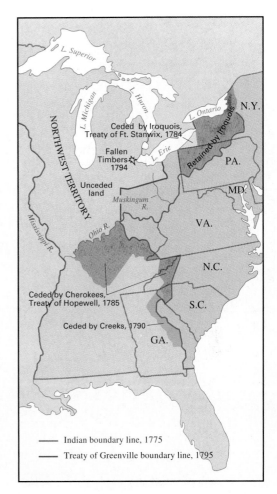

Cession of Tribal Lands to the United States, 1775–1790 *The land claims of the United States meant little as long as Indian nations still controlled vast territories within the new country's formal boundaries. A series of treaties in the 1780s and 1790s opened some lands to white settlement.* Source: From Lester J. Cappon et al., eds., *Atlas of Early American History: The Revolutionary Era, 1760–1790.* Copyright © 1976 by Princeton University Press. Reprinted by permission of Princeton University Press.

small farmer: the resulting minimum outlay of $640 was beyond the reach of ordinary Americans (except those veterans who received part of their army pay in land warrants). Proceeds from land sales were the first independent revenues available to the national government.

The most important ordinance was the third, passed in 1787. The Northwest Ordinance contained a bill of rights guaranteeing settlers freedom

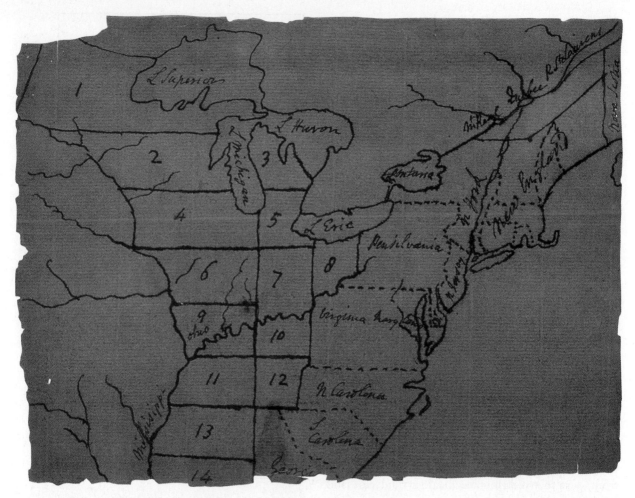

In 1784, Thomas Jefferson proposed a scheme for organizing the new nation's western lands. His plan would have divided the region on a grid pattern, yielding fourteen new states (with names such as "Metropotamia" and "Pelisipia") composed of 10-mile-square "hundreds." After a year of debate, Jefferson's plan was replaced by the one adopted in the Land Ordinance of 1785, which is described in the text. Notice that Jefferson's outline map contains some of the same errors evident in "A New and Correct Map" on page 167. Clements Library, University of Michigan.

of religion and the right to a jury trial, forbidding cruel and unusual punishments, and nominally prohibiting slavery. Eventually, that prohibition was to become an important symbol for antislavery northerners, but at the time it had little effect. Some residents of the territory already held slaves, and Congress did not intend to deprive them of their property. Moreover, the ordinance also contained a provision allowing slaveowners to "lawfully reclaim" runaway bondspeople who took refuge in the territory—the first national fugitive slave law. The ordinance prevented slavery from taking deep root by discouraging slaveholders from moving into the territory with their human chattel, but not until 1848

was enslavement abolished throughout the region, now known as the Old Northwest.

The ordinance also specified the process by which residents of the territory could organize state governments and seek admission to the Union "on an equal footing with the original States." Early in the nation's history, therefore, Congress laid down a policy of admitting new states on the same basis as the old and assuring residents of the territories the same rights held by citizens of the original states. Having suffered under the rule of a colonial power, congressmen understood the importance of preparing the new nation's first "colony" for eventual self-government. Nineteenth- and twentieth-century

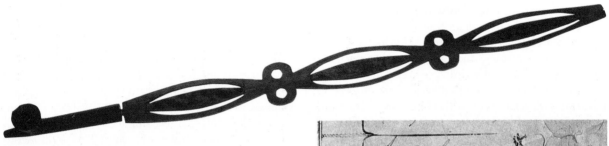

Americans were to be less generous in their attitudes toward residents of later territories, many of whom were non-European or non-Protestant. But the nation never fully lost sight of the egalitarian principles of the Northwest Ordinance.

In a sense, though, the ordinance was purely theoretical at the time it was passed. The Miamis, Shawnees, and Delawares refused to acknowledge American sovereignty. They opposed settlement violently, attacking unwary pioneers who ventured too far north of the Ohio River. In 1788 the Ohio Company, to which Congress had sold a large tract of land at reduced rates, established the town of Marietta at the juncture of the Ohio and Muskingum Rivers. But Indians prevented the company from extending settlement very far into the interior. After General Arthur St. Clair, the Northwest Territory's first governor, failed to negotiate a meaningful treaty with the Indians in early 1789, it was apparent that the United States could not avoid a clash with a western confederacy composed of eight nations and led by the Miamis.

Little Turtle, the able war chief of the Miami Confederacy, defeated first General Josiah Harmar (1790) and then St. Clair himself (1791) in major battles near the present border between Indiana and Ohio. More than six hundred of St. Clair's men were killed and scores more wounded; it was the whites' worst defeat in the entire history of the American frontier. In 1793 the Miami Confederacy declared that peace could be achieved only if the United States recognized the Ohio River as its northwestern boundary. But the national government refused to relinquish its claim in the region. A new army under the command of General Anthony Wayne, a Revolutionary War hero, attacked and defeated the confederacy in August 1794 at the Battle of Fallen Timbers (near present-day Toledo, Ohio; see map, page 187). Peace negotiations began after the victory.

**War in the
Old Northwest**

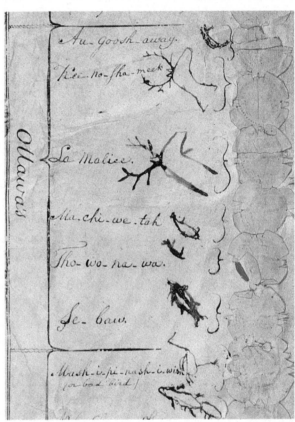

In the summer of 1795, the United States and the Miami Confederacy signed the Treaty of Greenville, bringing an end to open conflict after several years of warfare. All the participants smoked the calumet (peace pipe) pictured here, symbolizing their acceptance of the treaty. Because there were so many signatories, the ceremony took a long time. Pipe: Ohio Historical Society, Treaty: National Archives.

By the summer of 1795, Wayne reached agreement with the Miami Confederacy. The Treaty of Greenville gave each side a portion of what it wanted. The United States gained the right to settle much of what was to become Ohio, the indigenous peoples retaining only the northwest corner of the region. Indians, though, received the acknowledgment they had long sought: American recognition of their rights to the soil. At Greenville, the United

States formally accepted the principle of Indian sovereignty, by virtue of residence, over all lands the native peoples had not ceded. Never again would the United States government claim that it had acquired Indian territory solely through negotiation with a European or North American country.

The problems the United States encountered in ensuring safe settlement of the Northwest Territory pointed up the basic weakness of the Confederation government. Not until after the Articles of Confederation were replaced with a new constitution could the United States muster sufficient force to implement the Northwest Ordinance. Thus, although the ordinance is often viewed as one of the few lasting accomplishments of the Confederation Congress, it must be seen within a context of political impotence.

 ## From Crisis to the Constitution

The Americans most deeply concerned about the inadequacies of the Articles of Confederation were those involved in finance, overseas trade, and foreign affairs. In those areas the Articles were obviously deficient: Congress could not levy taxes, nor could it impose its will on the states to establish a uniform commercial policy or to ensure the enforcement of treaties.

The problems involving trade were particularly serious. Less than a year after the war's end, the American economy slid into a depression. Exporters of staple crops (especially tobacco and rice) and importers of manufactured goods were harmed by the postwar restrictions European powers imposed on American commerce. Although some of the restrictions were eased and recovery began by 1786, the war's effects proved impossible to erase entirely, particularly in the Lower South. Some estimates suggest that between 1775 and 1790 America's per capita gross national product declined by nearly 50 percent.

The war, indeed, had wrought permanent change in the American economy. The near total cessation of foreign commerce in nonmilitary items during the war years stimulated domestic manufacturing. Con-

Economic Change

sequently, despite the influx of European goods after 1783, the postwar period witnessed the stirrings of American industrial development. For ex-

ample, the first American textile mill began production in Pawtucket, Rhode Island, in 1793. Because of continuing population growth, the domestic market assumed greater relative importance in the overall economy. Moreover, foreign trade patterns shifted from Europe and toward the West Indies, continuing a trend that had begun before the war. Foodstuffs shipped to the French and Dutch Caribbean islands became America's largest single export, replacing tobacco (and thus accelerating the Chesapeake's conversion from tobacco to grain production).

Recognizing the Confederation Congress's inability to deal with commercial matters, Virginia invited the other states to a convention at Annapolis,

Annapolis Convention

Maryland, to discuss trade policy. Although eight states named representatives to the meeting in September 1786, only five delegations attended. Those present realized that they were too few in number to have any real impact on the political system. They issued a call for another convention, to be held in Philadelphia nine months later, "to devise such further provisions as shall . . . appear necessary to render the constitution of the federal government adequate to the exigencies of the Union."

The other states did not respond immediately. But then Shays's Rebellion convinced many political leaders that the nation's problems extended far beyond trade policy. The reaction to the rebellion hastened the movement toward comprehensive revision of the Articles. After most of the states had already appointed delegates, the Confederation Congress belatedly endorsed the convention. In mid-May 1787, fifty-five men, representing all the states but Rhode Island, assembled in Philadelphia to begin their deliberations.

The vast majority of delegates to the Constitutional Convention were men of property and substance. They all favored reform; otherwise, they would not have come to Philadel-

Constitutional Convention in Philadelphia

phia. Most wanted to invigorate the national government and to give it new authority over taxation and foreign commerce. Many had been members of state legislatures, and some had helped to draft state constitutions. All were influenced in their Philadelphia deliberations by their understanding of the success or failure of those constitutions' provisions. Among their number were merchants, planters, physicians,

The Constitutional Convention met in the state capitol of Pennsylvania, now known as Independence Hall. This view dates from 1778. Independence National Historic Park.

generals, governors, and especially lawyers—twenty-three had studied the law. Most had been born in America, and many came from families that had arrived in the seventeenth century. In an era when only a tiny proportion of the population had any advanced education, more than half of the delegates had attended college. A few had been educated in Britain, but most were graduates of American institutions: Princeton, with ten, had the most alumni participants. The youngest delegate was twenty-six, the oldest—Benjamin Franklin—eighty-one. Like George Washington, whom they elected their presiding officer, most were in their vigorous middle years. A dozen men did the bulk of the convention's work. Of these, James Madison of Virginia was by far the most important; he truly deserves the title "Father of the Constitution."

The frail, shy James Madison was thirty-six years old in 1787. Raised in western Virginia, he attended

James Madison: Father of the Constitution

Princeton, served on the local Committee of Safety, and was elected successively to the provincial convention, the state's lower and upper houses, and the Continental Congress (1780–1783). Although Madison returned to Virginia to serve in the state legislature in 1784, he remained in touch with national politics, partly through his continuing correspondence with his close friend Thomas Jefferson. A promoter of the Annapolis Convention, he strongly supported its call for further reform.

Madison was unique among the delegates in his systematic preparation for the Philadelphia meeting. Through Jefferson in Paris he bought more than two hundred books on history and government, carefully analyzing their accounts of past confederacies and republics. A month before the Constitutional Convention began, he summed up the results

James Madison (1751–1836), the youthful scholar and skilled politician who earned the title "Father of the Constitution." Library of Congress.

of his research in a lengthy paper entitled "Vices of the Political System of the United States." After listing the flaws he perceived in the current structure of the government (among them "encroachments by the states on the federal authority" and lack of unity "in matters where common interest requires it"), Madison revealed the conclusion that would guide his actions over the next few months. What the government most needed, he declared, was "such a modification of the sovereignty as will render it sufficiently neutral between the different interests and factions, to controul one part of the society from invading the rights of another, and at the same time sufficiently controuled itself, from setting up an interest adverse to that of the whole Society."

Thus Madison set forth the principle of checks and balances. The government, he believed, had to be constructed in such a way that it could not become tyrannical or fall wholly under the influence of a particular interest group. He regarded the large

size of a potential national republic as an advantage in that respect. Rejecting the common assertion that republics had to be small to survive, Madison argued that a large, diverse republic should be preferred. Because the nation would include many different interest groups, no one of them would be able to control the government. Political stability would result from compromises among the contending parties.

Madison's conception of national government was embodied in the so-called Virginia Plan, introduced on May 29 by his fellow Virginian Edmund Randolph. The plan provided for a two-house legislature, the lower house elected directly by the people and the upper house selected by the lower; proportional representation in both houses; an executive elected by Congress; a national judiciary; and congressional veto over state laws. The Virginia Plan gave Congress the broad power to legislate "in all cases to which the separate states are incompetent." Had it been adopted intact, it would have created a government in which national authority reigned unchallenged and state power was greatly diminished. Proportional representation in both houses would also have given large states a dominant voice in the national government.

Virginia and New Jersey Plans

The convention included many delegates who recognized the need for change but believed the Virginians had gone too far in the direction of national consolidation. After two weeks of debate on Randolph's proposal, the disaffected delegates united under the leadership of William Paterson of New Jersey. On June 15 Paterson presented an alternative scheme, the New Jersey Plan, calling for modifying the Articles rather than completely overhauling the government. Paterson proposed retaining a unicameral congress but giving it new powers of taxation and trade regulation. Paterson earlier had made his position clear in debate. Asserting that the Articles were "the proper basis of all the proceedings of the convention," he contended that the delegates' proper task was "to mark the orbits of the states with due precision and provide for the use of coercion" by the national government. Although the convention initially rejected Paterson's position, he and his allies won a number of victories in the months that followed.

The delegates began their work by discussing the structure and functions of Congress. They readily agreed that the new national government should

The Debates: Houses of Congress

have a two-house (bicameral) legislature. But they then discovered that they differed widely in their answers to three key questions: Should representation in both houses of Congress be proportional to population? How was representation in either or both houses to be apportioned among the states? And, finally, how were the members of the two houses to be elected?

The last issue was the easiest to resolve. To quote John Dickinson, the delegates thought it "essential" that members of the lower branch of Congress be elected directly by the people and "expedient" that members of the upper house be chosen by state legislatures. Since legislatures had selected delegates to the Confederation Congress, they would expect a similar privilege in the new government. If the convention had not agreed to allow state legislatures to elect senators, the Constitution would have aroused significant opposition among state political leaders.

Considerably more difficult was the matter of proportional representation in the Senate. The delegates accepted without much debate the principle of proportional representation in the lower house. But small states, through their spokesman Luther Martin of Maryland, argued for equal representation in the Senate, while large states supported a proportional plan for the upper house. For weeks the convention deadlocked on the issue, neither side able to obtain a majority. A committee appointed to work out a compromise recommended equal representation in the Senate, coupled with a proviso that all appropriation bills originate in the lower house. But not until the convention accepted a suggestion that a state's two senators vote as individuals rather than as a unit was a breakdown averted.

The remaining critical question divided the nation along sectional lines rather than by size of state: how was representation in the lower house to be apportioned among states? Delegates from states with large numbers of slaves wanted African and European inhabitants to be counted equally; delegates from states with few slaves wanted only free people to be counted. So slavery became inextricably linked to the foundation of the new government. Delegates resolved the dispute by using a formula developed by the Confederation Congress in

The Debates: Slavery and Representation

1783 to allocate financial assessments among states: three-fifths of slaves would be included in population totals. (The formula reflected delegates' judgment that slaves were less efficient producers of wealth than free people, not that they were 60 percent human and 40 percent property.) The three-fifths compromise on representation won unanimous approval. Only two delegates, Gouverneur Morris of New York and George Mason of Virginia, later spoke out against the institution of slavery.

Although the words *slave* and *slavery* do not appear in the Constitution (the framers used euphemisms such as *other persons*), direct and indirect protections for slavery were deeply embedded in the document. The three-fifths clause, for example, assured white southern voters not only congressional representation out of proportion to their numbers but also a disproportionate influence on the selection of the president, since the number of each state's electoral votes was determined by the size of its congressional delegation. Congress was prevented from outlawing the slave trade for at least twenty years, and the fugitive slave clause required all states to return runaways to their masters. By guaranteeing that the national government would aid any states threatened with "domestic violence," the Constitution promised aid in putting down future slave revolts, as well as incidents like Shays's Rebellion.

Constitutional Protections for Slavery

Once agreement was reached on the knotty, conjoined problems of slavery and representation, the delegates readily achieved consensus on the other issues confronting them. All agreed that the national government needed the authority to tax and to regulate commerce. But instead of giving Congress the nearly unlimited scope proposed in the Virginia Plan, delegates enumerated congressional powers and then provided for flexibility by granting all authority "necessary and proper" to carry out those powers. Discarding the legislative veto contained in the Virginia Plan, the convention implied a judicial veto instead. The Constitution plus national laws and treaties would constitute "the supreme law of the land; and the judges in every state shall be bound thereby." As another means of circumscribing state powers, delegates drafted a long list of actions forbidden to states.

The convention placed primary responsibility for conducting foreign affairs in the hands of the president, who was also designated commander-in-chief of the armed forces. That

The Presidency

decision raised the question, left unspecified in the Constitution's text, of whether the president (or Congress, for that matter) acquired special powers in times of war. With the consent of the Senate, the president could appoint judges and other federal officers. To select the president, delegates established an elaborate mechanism, the electoral college, whose members would be chosen in each state by legislatures or qualified voters. This system, they hoped, would ensure that the executive would be independent of the national legislature—and of the people. They also agreed that the chief executive should serve a four-year term but be eligible for re-election.

The final document still showed signs of its origins in the Virginia Plan, but compromises created a system of government less powerful at the national level than Madison and Randolph had envisioned. The key

Separation of Powers

to the Constitution was the distribution of political authority—separation of powers among executive, legislative, and judicial branches of the national government, and division of powers between states and nation. Concurrence of two-thirds of Congress and three-fourths of the states, for example, was required for amendments. The branches were balanced against one another, their powers deliberately entwined to prevent them from acting independently. The president was given a veto over congressional legislation, but his treaties and major appointments required the Senate's consent. Congress could impeach the president and federal judges, but courts appeared to have the final say on interpreting the Constitution. These checks and balances would make it difficult for the government to become tyrannical. At the same time, though, the elaborate system would sometimes prevent the government from acting quickly and decisively. Furthermore, the line between state and national powers was so ambiguously and vaguely drawn that the United States had to fight a civil war in the next century before the issue was fully resolved.

The convention held its last session on September 17, 1787. Of the forty-two delegates present, only three refused to sign the Constitution. (Two of the three declined in part because of the lack of a bill of rights.) Benjamin Franklin had written a speech calling for unity; because his voice was too weak to

be heard, another delegate read it for him. "I confess that there are several parts of this constitution which I do not at present approve," Franklin admitted. Yet he urged its acceptance "because I expect no better, and because I am not sure, that it is not the best." Only then was the Constitution made public. The convention's proceedings had been entirely secret—and remained so until the delegates' private notes were published in the nineteenth century. (See the Appendix for the full text of the Constitution.)

 Opposition and Ratification

Later the same month, the Confederation Congress submitted the Constitution to the states but did not formally recommend approval. The ratification clause provided for the new system to take effect once it was approved by special conventions in at least nine states, with delegates being elected by qualified voters. Thus the national Constitution, unlike the Articles of Confederation, would rest directly on popular authority (and the presumably hostile state legislatures would be circumvented).

As states began to elect delegates to the special conventions, discussion of the proposed government grew more heated. Federalists (supporters of the Constitution) and Antifederalists (its opponents) published newspaper essays and pamphlets vigorously defending or attacking the convention's decisions. The extent of the debate was unprecedented. Every newspaper in the country printed the full text of the Constitution, and most newspapers supported its adoption. Even so, it quickly became apparent that the disputes within the Constitutional Convention had been mild compared with divisions of opinion within the populace as a whole. Although most politically aware citizens concurred that the national government should have more power over taxation and foreign commerce, some believed that the proposed government held the potential for tyranny.

Federalists built on the notions of classical republicanism, holding forth a vision of a virtuous, self-sacrificing republic vigorously led by an aristocracy of talent. They claimed that the

Federalists

nation did not need to fear centralized authority when good men were in charge and that the carefully structured government would preclude the possibility of tyranny. A republic could be large, they declared, if the government was designed to prevent any one group from controlling it. The separation of powers among legislative, executive, and judicial branches, and the division of powers between states and nation, would accomplish that goal. Thus people did not need to be protected from the powers of the new government in a formal way.

Antifederalists feared a too-powerful central government, although they recognized the need for a national source of revenue. They saw the states as

Antifederalists

the chief protectors of individual rights; consequently, their weakening could bring the onset of arbitrary power. Antifederalist arguments against the Constitution often consisted of lists of potential abuses of government authority.

Heirs of the Real Whig ideology of the late 1760s and early 1770s, Antifederalists stressed the need for constant popular vigilance to avert oppression. Indeed, some of the Antifederalists were the very men who originally promulgated those ideas—Samuel Adams, Patrick Henry, and Richard Henry Lee were leaders of the opposition to the Constitution. The Antifederalist ranks were heavily peopled by such older Americans, whose political opinions had been shaped prior to the centralizing, nationalistic Revolution. Joining them were small farmers, who were preoccupied with guarding their property against excessive taxation, and ambitious, upwardly mobile men who would gain more from an economic and political system less tightly controlled than the one the Constitution promised to establish.

As public debate continued, Antifederalists focused on the Constitution's lack of a bill of rights. Even if states were weakened by the new sys-

Importance of a Bill of Rights

tem, they believed, people could still be protected from tyranny if their rights were specifically guaranteed. The Constitution did contain some prohibitions on congressional power. For example, the writ of habeas corpus, which prevented arbitrary imprisonment, could not be suspended except in dire emergencies. But Antifederalists found such constitutional provisions inadequate. Nor were they reassured by Federalist assertions that, since the new government was one of limited powers, it could not violate people's rights.

Letters of a Federal Farmer, perhaps the most widely read Antifederalist pamphlet, listed the rights that should be protected: freedom of the press and of religion, the right to trial by jury, and guarantees against unreasonable search warrants. From Paris, Thomas Jefferson added his voice to the chorus. Re-

The Federal Almanack *for 1789 trumpeted the virtues of the new Constitution. Not all Americans were so certain that the national government, here symbolized as an edifice supported by thirteen pillars, was as "solid, strong as time" as the printer proclaimed.* American Antiquarian Society.

plying to Madison's letter conveying a copy of the Constitution, Jefferson declared, "I like much the general idea" but not "the omission of a bill of rights. . . . A bill of rights is what the people are entitled to against every government on earth, general or particular, and what no just government should refuse, or rest on inference."

As state conventions met to consider ratification, the lack of a bill of rights loomed ever larger as a flaw in the proposed government. Four of the first

**Ratification
of the
Constitution**

five states to ratify did so unanimously, but serious disagreements then surfaced. Massachusetts, in which Antifederalist forces had been bolstered by a backlash against the state government's heavy-handed treatment of the Shays rebels, ratified by a majority of only 19 votes out of 355 cast. In June 1788, when New Hampshire ratified, the requirement of nine states was satisfied. But New York and Virginia had not yet voted, and everyone realized the new Constitution could not succeed unless those key states accepted it.

Despite a valiant effort by the Antifederalist Patrick Henry, pro-Constitution forces won by 10 votes in the Virginia convention. In New York, James Madison, John Jay, and Alexander Hamilton campaigned for ratification by publishing *The Federalist*, a political tract that explained the theory behind the Constitution and masterfully answered its critics. Their reasoned arguments, coupled with Federalists' promise to add a bill of rights to the Constitution, helped win the battle. On July 26, 1788, New York ratified the Constitution by the slim margin of 3 votes. Although the last state (Rhode Island) did not formally join the Union until 1790, the new government was a reality.

 Conclusion

During the 1770s and 1780s the nation took shape as a political union. It began to develop an economy independent of the British Empire, and it designed a foreign policy that attempted to chart its own course in the world in order to protect the national interest, defend the country's borders, and promote beneficial trade. Some Americans prescribed rules for the cultural and intellectual life they thought appropriate for a republic, outlining artistic and educational goals for a properly virtuous people. An integral part of the formation of the Union was the systematic formulation of American racist thought. Emphasizing race (rather than status as slave or free) as a determinant of African-Americans' standing in the nation allowed white men to define republicanism to exclude all people but themselves and to ensure that they would dominate the country for the foreseeable future.

The experience of fighting a war and of struggling for survival as an independent nation altered

the political context of American life in the 1780s. At the outset of the war, most politically aware Americans believed that "that government which governs best governs least," but by the late 1780s many had changed their minds. These were the drafters and supporters of the Constitution, who concluded from the republic's vicissitudes under the Articles of Confederation that the United States needed a more powerful central government. They contended during ratification debates that their proposed solution to the nation's problems was just as "republican" in conception (if not more so) as the Articles.

Both sides concurred in a general adherence to republican principles, but they emphasized different views of republicanism. Federalists advanced a position based on the principles of classical republicanism. Antifederalists, fearing that elected leaders would not subordinate personal gain to the good of the whole, wanted a weak central government, formal protection of individual rights, and a loosely regulated economy.

The Federalists won their point when the Constitution was adopted, however narrowly. The process of consolidating the states into a national whole was thereby formalized. The 1790s, the first decade of government under the Constitution, would witness hesitant steps toward the creation of a true nation, the *United* States of America.

Suggestions for Further Reading

General

Richard Beeman et al., eds., *Beyond Confederation: Origins of the Constitution and American National Identity* (1987); John E. Crowley, *The Privileges of Independence: Neomercantilism and the American Revolution* (1993); Ronald Hoffman et al., eds., *The Economy of Early America: The Revolutionary Period, 1763–1790* (1988); Cathy Matson and Peter S. Onuf, *A Union of Interests: Political and Economic Thought in Revolutionary America* (1990); Forrest McDonald, *Novus Ordo Seclorum: The Intellectual Origins of the Constitution* (1985); Edmund S. Morgan, *Inventing the People: The Rise of Popular Sovereignty in England and America* (1988); Gordon S. Wood, *The Radicalism of the American Revolution* (1992); Gordon S. Wood, *The Creation of the American Republic, 1776–1787* (1969); Alfred F. Young et al, eds., *We the People: Voices and Images of the New Nation* (1993); Rosemarie Zagarri, *The Politics of Size: Representation in the United States, 1776–1850* (1988).

Continental Congress and Articles of Confederation

E. James Ferguson, *The Power of the Purse: A History of American Public Finance, 1776–1790* (1961); H. James Henderson, *Party Politics in the Continental Congress* (1974); Merrill Jensen, *The New Nation: A History of the United States During the Confederation,*

1781–1789 (1950); Jerrilyn G. Marston, *King and Congress: The Transfer of Political Legitimacy, 1774–1776* (1987); Richard B. Morris, *The Forging of the Union, 1781–1789* (1987); Peter S. Onuf, *Statehood and Union: A History of the Northwest Ordinance* (1987); Jack N. Rakove, *The Beginnings of National Politics: An Interpretive History of the Continental Congress* (1979); Ann Withington, *Toward a More Perfect Union: Virtue and the Formation of American Republics* (1992).

State Politics

Willi Paul Adams, *The First American Constitutions: Republican Ideology and the Making of the State Constitutions in the Revolutionary Era* (1980); Robert Gross, ed., *In Debt to Shays* (1992); Ronald Hoffman and Peter Albert, eds., *Sovereign States in an Age of Uncertainty* (1981); Donald Lutz, *Popular Consent and Popular Control: Whig Political Theory in the Early State Constitutions* (1980); Jackson Turner Main, *Political Parties Before the Constitution* (1973); Jackson Turner Main, *The Sovereign States, 1775–1783* (1973); David P. Szatmary, *Shays' Rebellion: The Making of an Agrarian Insurrection* (1980).

The Constitution

Thornton Anderson, *Creating the Constitution: The Convention of 1787 and the First Congress* (1993); Lance Banning, *The Sacred Fire of Liberty: James Madison and the Founding of the Federal Republic* (1995); Roger H. Brown, *Redeeming the Republic: Federalists, Taxation, and the Origins of the Constitution* (1993); Christopher Duncan, *The Anti-Federalists and Early American Political Thought* (1995); Jackson Turner Main, *The Anti-Federalists: Critics of the Constitution, 1781–1788* (1961); Frederick W. Marks III, *Independence on Trial: Foreign Affairs and the Making of the Constitution* (1973); Jack N. Rakove, *Original Meanings: Politics and Ideas in the Making of the Constitution* (1996); Robert A. Rutland, *The Ordeal of the Constitution: The Antifederalists and the Ratification Struggle of 1787–88* (1966); Abraham Sofaer, *War, Foreign Affairs, and Constitutional Power*, vol. 1, *The Origins* (1976).

Education and Culture

Cathy N. Davidson, *Revolution and the Word: The Rise of the Novel in America* (1987); Joseph M. Ellis, *After the Revolution: Profiles of Early American Culture* (1979); Carl F. Kaestle, *Pillars of the Republic: Common Schools and American Society, 1780–1860* (1983); Russel B. Nye, *The Cultural Life of the New Nation, 1776–1803*

(1960); Kenneth Silverman, *A Cultural History of the American Revolution* (1976).

Women

Edith Gelles, *Portia: The World of Abigail Adams* (1992); Ronald Hoffman and Peter Albert, eds., *Women in the Age of the American Revolution* (1989); Susan Juster, *Disorderly Women: Sexual Politics and Evangelicalism in Revolutionary New England* (1994); Linda K. Kerber, *Women of the Republic: Intellect and Ideology in Revolutionary America* (1980); Mary Beth Norton, *Liberty's Daughters: The Revolutionary Experience of American Women, 1750–1800* (1980); Rosemarie Zagarri, *A Woman's Dilemma: Mercy Otis Warren and the American Revolution* (1995).

African-Americans and Slavery

Ira Berlin and Ronald Hoffman, eds., *Slavery and Freedom in the Age of the American Revolution* (1983); David Brion Davis, *The Problem of Slavery in the Age of Revolution, 1770–1823* (1975); Paul Finkelman, *Slavery and the Founders: Race and Liberty in the Age of Jefferson* (1996); Carol V. R. George, *Segregated Sabbaths: Richard Allen and the Emergence of Independent Black Churches, 1760–1840* (1973); Winthrop Jordan, *White over Black: American Attitudes Toward the Negro, 1550–1812* (1968); Duncan J. Macleod, *Slavery, Race, and the American Revolution* (1974); Gary Nash, *Forging Freedom: The Formation of Philadelphia's Black Community, 1720–1840* (1988); Donald L. Robinson, *Slavery in the Structure of American Politics, 1765–1820* (1971); Shane White, *Somewhat More Independent: The End of Slavery in New York City, 1770–1810* (1991); Arthur Zilversmit, *The First Emancipation: The Abolition of Slavery in the North* (1967).

Indians

Harvey L. Carter, *The Life and Times of Little Turtle* (1987); Gregory E. Dowd, *A Spirited Resistance: The North American Indian Struggle for Unity, 1745–1815* (1992); Dorothy Jones, *License for Empire: Colonialism by Treaty in Early America* (1982); Francis Paul Prucha, *American Indian Policy in the Formative Years: The Indian Trade and Intercourse Acts, 1790–1834* (1962); Wiley Sword, *President Washington's Indian War: The Struggle for the Old Northwest, 1790–1795* (1985); Anthony F. C. Wallace, *The Death and Rebirth of the Seneca* (1969); Richard White, *The Middle Ground: Indians, Empires, and Republics in the Great Lakes Region, 1650–1815* (1991).

CHAPTER

8

Politics and Society in the Early Republic
1789–1800

"S hall I commence my journal, my dear Elizabeth, with a description of the pain I felt at taking leave of all my friends, or shall I leave you to imagine?" wrote Margaret Dwight as she began a chronicle of her arduous journey from New Haven, Connecticut, to Warren, Ohio. An orphan at age twenty, Margaret was traveling west to live with relatives who had already migrated to the region known as New Connecticut. Her diary, kept at a cousin's request, described not only the difficult trip but also the reactions of a genteely bred young woman to the rough life of the early American frontier.

Margaret filled her pages with comments on poor roads, dangerous river crossings, dirty taverns, profane wagoneers, troublesome fellow travelers, and brawling "dutchmen" (Germans), whose failure to observe the Sabbath disgusted her. "We have concluded the reason so few are willing to return from the Western country," she remarked, "is not that the country is so good, but because the journey is so bad." Disconcerted by her inability to understand the Germans' "Jabbering," Margaret also noticed differences in English usage: "The people here talk curiously, they all reckon instead of expect—Youns is a word I have heard used several times, but what it means I don't know."

Many people she encountered assumed that Margaret was moving west to find a husband. One innkeeper's wife predicted that she "would certainly be married in a little while"; a man "at once concluded" that she and a traveling companion "were going to the Hio . . . to get husbands." But Margaret resisted, writing that she was "determin'd not to oblige myself to spend my days there, by marrying should I even have an opport[unit]y." She was "encouraged" by meeting a young *unmarried*

The "American Stage Waggon" is depicted in 1807 leaving a tavern on the road between Lancaster and Pittsburgh, Pennsylvania—the route traveled by Margaret Dwight on her move from Connecticut to Ohio. Perhaps she stopped for the night or a meal at this very place. Travelers better off than Margaret and her companions might choose such stages; Margaret had to travel in a crude farm wagon. *American Antiquarian Society.*

woman traveling from Ohio back to the East, "a thing I never before heard of, & had begun to think impossible." Yet at the end of her trip Margaret found Warren "pleasanter than I expected." About a year later, she married William Bell, a local merchant who soon relocated to Pittsburgh, the western Pennsylvania town that had grown up around Fort Pitt. Eventually, she gave birth to eight children in the West she had disdained.

Margaret Dwight was just one of the many thousand people who moved west in the decades following the Revolution. Their mobility signaled the beginnings of a new age, as large numbers of European-Americans and African-Americans poured through the Appalachian Mountains for the first time. North of the Ohio River (Margaret's destination), the strength of the Miami Confederacy blocked westward expansion until after the Treaty of Greenville in 1795. South of the river, western settlements appeared as early as the 1770s, but they were isolated from the Atlantic coast by the long chain of mountains. Not until the first years of the nineteenth century did those settlements become more fully integrated into American life through the vehicle of the Second Great Awakening, a religious revival that swept both the East and the West.

The dispersal of the population was accompanied by political fragmentation and economic difficulties. The United States economy still depended on the export trade. When warfare between England and France resumed in 1793, Americans found their commerce disrupted yet again, with consequent fluctuations in their income and profits. And the fight over the Constitution presaged an even wider division over the major political, economic, and diplomatic questions confronting the young republic. To make matters worse, Americans did not anticipate the political disagreements that characterized the 1790s. Believing that the Constitution would resolve the problems that had arisen during the Confederation period, they expected the new government to rule largely by consensus.

Accordingly, many Americans found it difficult to understand the partisan tensions that accompanied disputes over fundamental issues such as the extent to which authority (especially fiscal authority) should be centralized in the national government, the formulation of foreign policy in an era of continual warfare in Europe, and the limits of dissent. They could not understand or fully accept the division of America's political leaders into two fac-

tions—not yet political parties—known as Federalists and Republicans, because factions were believed to be legitimate only in monarchies. In republics, it was thought, the rise of factions was a sign of decay and corruption. As the decade closed with the first fully partisan presidential election, Americans still had not come to terms with the implications of partisan politics.

 ## Building a Workable Government

Americans in many cities celebrated the ratification of the Constitution with a series of parades on July 4, 1788. The processions were carefully planned to symbolize the unity of the new nation and to recall its history to the minds of the watching throngs. Like prerevolutionary protest meetings, the parades served as political lessons for literate and illiterate Americans alike. Men and women who could not read were thereby educated about the significance of the new Constitution for the nation. They also were instructed about political leaders' hopes for industry and frugality on the part of a virtuous American public.

Celebrating Ratification

The Philadelphia parade, planned by the artist Charles Willson Peale, was filled with symbols that expressed those goals. About five thousand people took part in the procession, which stretched for a mile and a half and lasted three hours. The parade featured floats portraying themes such as "The Grand Federal Edifice." Marchers representing the first pioneers and revolutionary war troops were joined by groups of farmers and artisans dramatizing their work. More than forty groups of tradesmen, including barbers, hatters, printers, cloth manufacturers, and clockmakers, sponsored floats. The artisans were followed by lawyers, doctors, clergymen of all denominations, and congressmen. Bringing up the rear was a symbol of the nation's future, students from the University of Pennsylvania and other city schools, bearing a flag labeled "The Rising Generation." After the parade, the marchers imbibed beer and cider, the "Federal liquors" celebrated in a broadside circulated at the time.

The nationalistic spirit expressed in the ratification processions carried over to the first session of Congress. Only a few Antifederalists ran for office in

• *Important Events* •

1789	George Washington inaugurated as first president
	Judiciary Act of 1789 organizes federal court system
	French Revolution begins
1790	Alexander Hamilton's *Report on Public Credit* proposes assumption of state debts
1791	First ten amendments (Bill of Rights) ratified
1793	France declares war on Britain, Spain, and Holland
	Washington's neutrality proclamation keeps the United States out of the war
	Democratic-Republican societies founded, the first grassroots political organizations
1794	Whiskey Rebellion in western Pennsylvania protests taxation
1795	Jay Treaty with England
1796	First contested presidential election: John Adams elected president, Thomas Jefferson vice president
1798	XYZ affair arouses American opinion against France
	Alien and Sedition Acts punish political dissenters
	Virginia and Kentucky resolutions protest suppression of dissent
1798–99	Quasi-War with France
1800	Franco-American Convention ends the Quasi-War
	Jefferson elected president, Aaron Burr vice president
	Gabriel's Rebellion threatens Virginia whites
1801	Second Great Awakening sweeps through Kentucky

Nationalism in the First Congress

the congressional elections held late in 1788, and even fewer were elected. Thus the First Congress consisted chiefly of men who supported a strong national government. The drafters of the Constitution had deliberately left many key issues undecided, so the nationalists' domination of Congress meant that their views on those points quickly prevailed.

Congress faced four immediate tasks when it convened in April 1789: raising revenue to support the new government, responding to state ratification conventions' call for a bill of rights, setting up executive departments, and organizing the federal judiciary. The last task was especially important. The Constitution established a Supreme Court but left it to Congress to decide whether to have other federal courts as well.

James Madison, who had been elected to the House of Representatives, soon became as influential in Congress as he had been at the Constitutional Convention. A few months into the first session, he persuaded Congress to adopt the Revenue Act of 1789, imposing a 5 percent tariff on certain imports. Thus the First Congress quickly achieved what the

IN HONOUR OF AMERICAN
BEER and CYDER,

It is hereby recorded, for the information of strangers and posterity, that 17 000 people assembled on this green, on the 4th of July, 1788, to celebrate the establishment of the constitution of the United States, and that they separated at an early hour, without intoxication, or a single quarrel.----They drank nothing but Beer and Cyder. Learn, reader, to prize those invaluable FEDERAL liquors, and to consider them as the companions of those virtues that can alone render our country free and respectable.

Learn likewise to despise

SPIRITOUS LIQUORS, as

Anti-federal, and to consider them as the companions of all those vices, that are calculated to dishonour and enslave our country.

Drinking beer and cider (instead of imported spirits like brandy) took on patriotic meaning in the celebrations of the Constitution's ratification. Other forms of alcohol, this broadside proclaimed, were "Anti-federal" and thus inappropriate for the nation's citizens. Rare Book and Manuscript Division, New York Public Library, Astor, Lenox, and Tilden Foundations.

The first census in 1790, demonstrating that the United States had nearly 4 million residents, was a source of pride to the young republic. A jug of Liverpool ware commemorated the count by reproducing the figures surrounded by symbols of the nation's prosperity—agricultural produce, buildings, a ship, and other items. Division of Political History, Smithsonian Institution, Washington, D.C.

Confederation Congress never had: an effective national tax law. The new government would have problems in its first years, but lack of revenue was not one of them.

Madison also took the lead on the issue of constitutional amendments. At the convention and thereafter, he had consistently opposed additional limitations on the national government. He believed it unnecessary to guarantee people's rights explicitly when the government was one of delegated powers. But Madison recognized that public opinion, as expressed in state ratifying conventions, was against him. Accordingly, he placed nineteen proposed amendments before the House. Eventually, the states ratified ten, which officially became part of the Constitution on December 15, 1791 (see the Appendix for the Constitution and all amendments). Their adoption defused Antifederalist opposition and rallied support for the new government.

Bill of Rights

The First Amendment specifically prohibited Congress from passing any law restricting the right to freedom of religion, speech, press, peaceable assembly, or petition. The next two amendments arose directly from the former colonists' fear of standing armies as a threat to freedom. The Second Amendment guaranteed people's right "to keep and bear arms" because of the need for a "well-regulated Militia." Thus the constitutional right to bear arms was based on the expectation that most able-bodied men would serve the nation as citizen soldiers and there would be little need for a standing army. The Third Amendment defined the circumstances in which troops could be quartered in private homes. The next five pertained to judicial procedures. The Fourth Amendment prohibited "unreasonable searches and seizures"; the Fifth and Sixth established the rights of accused persons; the Seventh specified the conditions for jury trials in civil (as opposed to criminal) cases; and the Eighth forbade "cruel and unusual punishments." The Ninth and Tenth Amendments reserved to the people and the states other unspecified rights and powers. In short, the amendments' authors made clear that, in listing some rights, they did not mean to preclude the exercise of others.

While debating proposed amendments, Congress also considered the organization of the executive branch. It readily agreed to continue the three administrative departments established under the Articles of Confederation: War, Foreign Affairs (renamed State), and Treasury. Congress instituted two lesser posts: the attorney general—the nation's official lawyer—and the postmaster general. Controversy arose over whether the president alone could dismiss officials whom he originally had appointed with the Senate's consent. After some debate, the House and Senate agreed that he had such authority. Thus was established the important principle that the heads of executive departments are responsible to the president.

Executive Branch

Aside from constitutional amendments, the most far-reaching piece of legislation enacted by the First Congress was the Judiciary Act of 1789, which defined the jurisdiction of the federal judiciary and established a six-member Supreme Court, thirteen district courts, and three circuit courts of appeal. Its most important provision, Section 25, al-

Judiciary Act of 1789

lowed appeals from state courts to federal courts when cases raised certain types of constitutional issues. Section 25 thus implemented Article VI of the Constitution, which stated that federal laws and treaties were to be considered "the supreme Law of the Land." For Article VI to be enforced uniformly, the national judiciary had to be able to overturn state court decisions in cases involving the Constitution, federal laws, or treaties. Yet nowhere did the Constitution explicitly permit such action by federal courts. The Judiciary Act of 1789 presumed that the wording of Article VI implied the right of appeal from state to federal courts. In the nineteenth century, however, judges and legislators committed to states' rights challenged that interpretation.

During its first decade, the Supreme Court handled few cases of any importance, and there was considerable turnover in its membership. (John Jay, the first chief justice, served only

The Early Supreme Court

six years.) But in a significant 1796 decision, *Ware* v. *Hylton*, the Court for the first time declared a state law unconstitutional. That same year it also reviewed the constitutionality of an act of Congress, upholding its validity in the case of *Hylton* v. *U.S.* The most important case of the decade, *Chisholm* v. *Georgia* (1793), established that states could be sued in federal courts by citizens of other states. This decision, unpopular with state governments, was overruled five years later by the Eleventh Amendment to the Constitution.

Domestic Policy Under Washington and Hamilton

George Washington did not seek the presidency. In 1783 he returned to Mount Vernon, his plantation on the Potomac River, eager for the peaceful life of a Virginia planter. But his

Election of the First President

fellow countrymen never regarded Washington as just another private citizen. He was unanimously elected the presiding officer of the Constitutional Convention. As such, he did not participate in debates, but he consistently voted for a strong national government and served as a steadying influence. Once the proposed structure of the government was presented to the public, Americans concurred that only George Washington had sufficient stature to serve as the re-

public's first president. The unanimous vote of the electoral college was just a formality.

Washington was reluctant to return to public life but knew he could not ignore his country's call. Awaiting the summons to New York City, the nation's capital, he wrote to an old friend, "My movements to the chair of Government will be accompanied by feelings not unlike those of a culprit who is going to the place of his execution. . . . I am sensible, that I am embarking the voice of my Countrymen and a good name of my own, on this voyage, but what returns will be made for them, Heaven alone can foretell."

Washington acted cautiously during his first months in office, knowing that whatever he did would set precedents for the future. When the title by which he should be addressed aroused controversy (Vice President John Adams favored "His Highness, the President of the United States of America, and

Washington's First Steps

Protector of their Liberties"), Washington said nothing. The accepted title soon became a plain "Mr. President." By using the heads of the executive departments collectively as his chief advisers, he created the cabinet. As the Constitution required, he sent Congress an annual State of the Union message. Washington also concluded that he should exercise his veto power over congressional legislation very sparingly—only, indeed, if he was convinced a bill was unconstitutional.

Washington's first major task as president was to choose the heads of the executive departments. For the War Department he selected an old comrade-in-arms, Henry Knox, who had been his reliable general of artillery during much of the Revolution. His choice for the State Department was his fellow Virginian Thomas Jefferson, who had just returned to the United States from his post as minister to France. And for the crucial position of secretary of the treasury, the president chose the brilliant, intensely ambitious Alexander Hamilton.

The illegitimate son of a Scottish aristocrat and a woman whose husband had divorced her for adultery and desertion, Hamilton was born in the British West Indies in 1757. His early years were spent in poverty; after

Alexander Hamilton

his mother's death when he was eleven, he worked as a clerk for a mercantile firm. In 1773 Hamilton enrolled in King's College (later Columbia University) in New York City; only eighteen months

John Trumbull, known primarily for his larger-than-life portraits of patriot leaders, painted this miniature of George Washington, who posed for it during his presidency (c. 1792–1794).   Division of Political History, Smithsonian Institution, Washington, D.C.

later, the precocious seventeen-year-old contributed a pamphlet to the prerevolutionary publication wars of late 1774. Devoted to the patriot cause, Hamilton volunteered for service in the American army, where he came to the attention of George Washington. In 1777 Washington appointed the young man as one of his aides, and the two developed great affection for one another. Indeed, in some respects Hamilton became the son Washington never had.

The general's patronage helped the poor youth of dubious background to marry well. At twenty-three he took as his wife Elizabeth Schuyler, daughter of a wealthy New York family. After the war, Hamilton practiced law in New York City and served as a delegate first to the Annapolis Convention and then to the Constitutional Convention. Though he exerted little influence at either gather-

ing, his contributions to *The Federalist* in 1788 revealed him to be one of the chief political thinkers in the republic.

In his dual role as secretary of the treasury and one of Washington's major advisers, two traits distinguished Hamilton from most of his contemporaries. First, he displayed an undivided loyalty to the nation as a whole. As a West Indian who had lived on the mainland only briefly before the war, Hamilton had no ties to a particular state. He showed little sympathy for, or understanding of, demands for local autonomy. Thus the aim of his fiscal policies was always to consolidate power at the national level. Further, he never feared the exercise of centralized executive authority, as did older counterparts who had clashed repeatedly with colonial governors, nor was he afraid of maintaining close political and economic ties with Britain.

Second, he regarded his fellow human beings with unvarnished cynicism. Perhaps because of his difficult early life and his own overriding ambition, Hamilton believed people to be motivated primarily, if not entirely, by self-interest—particularly economic self-interest. He placed no reliance on people's capacity for virtuous and self-sacrificing behavior. This outlook set him apart from those Americans who foresaw a rosy future in which public-spirited citizens would pursue the common good rather than their own private advantage. Although other Americans (like Madison) also stressed the role of private interests in a republic, Hamilton went beyond them in his emphasis on self-interest as the major motivator of human behavior. And his beliefs significantly influenced the way in which he tackled the monumental task before him: straightening out the new nation's tangled finances.

In 1789, Congress ordered the new secretary of the treasury to assess the public debt and to submit recommendations for supporting the government's credit. Hamilton found that the country's remaining war debts fell into three categories: those owed by the nation to foreign governments and investors, mostly to France (about $11 million); those owed by the national government to merchants, former soldiers, holders of revolutionary bonds, and the like (about $27 million); and, finally, similar debts owed by state governments (roughly $25 million). With respect to the national debt, there was little disagreement: politically aware Americans recognized that if their new

National and State Debts

government was to succeed it would have to repay at full face value those financial obligations incurred by the nation while winning independence.

The state debts were another matter. Some states—notably Virginia, Maryland, North Carolina, and Georgia—already had paid off most of their war debts. They would oppose the national government's assumption of responsibility for other states' debts, because their citizens would be taxed to pay such obligations. Massachusetts, Connecticut, and South Carolina, by contrast, still had sizable unpaid debts and would welcome a system of national assumption. The possible assumption of state debts also had political implications. Consolidating the debt in the hands of the national government would help to concentrate economic and political power at the national level. A contrary policy would reserve greater independence of action for the states.

Hamilton's first *Report on Public Credit*, sent to Congress in January 1790, reflected both his national loyalty and his cynicism. He proposed that Congress assume outstanding state debts, combine them with national obligations, and issue new securities covering both the principal and the accumulated unpaid interest. Current holders of state or national debt certificates would have the option of taking a portion of their payment in western lands. Hamilton's aims were clear: he wanted to expand the financial reach of the United States government, simultaneously reducing the states' economic power. He also wanted to ensure that holders of public securities—many of them wealthy merchants and speculators—would have a significant financial stake in the survival of the national government.

Hamilton's Financial Plan

Hamilton's plan stimulated lively debate in Congress. The opposition coalesced around his former ally James Madison, who opposed the assumption of state debts because his own state of Virginia had already paid off most of its obligations. As a congressman tied to agrarian rather than moneyed interests, Madison also criticized the proposal to compensate only the current holders of public securities. Well aware that speculators had purchased large quantities of debt certificates at a small fraction of their face value, Madison proposed that the original holders of the debt also be compensated by the government. Madison's plan, though fairer than Hamilton's, would have been difficult, if not impossible, to administer. The House of Representatives rejected it.

Alexander Hamilton (1757–1804) sat for this miniature by Charles Willson Peale in 1780. The determination and purposefulness of the future secretary of the treasury are reflected even in this early portrait.   Columbiana Collection, Columbia University.

At first, the House also rejected the assumption of state debts. The Senate, however, adopted Hamilton's plan largely intact, and a series of compromises followed. Hamilton agreed to changes in the assumption plan that would benefit Virginia in particular. The assumption bill also became linked in a complex way to the other controversial issue of that congressional session: the location of the permanent national capital. Both northerners and southerners wanted the capital in their region. The legend that Hamilton and Madison agreed over Jefferson's dinner table to exchange assumption of state debts for a southern site is not supported by the surviving evidence, but a political deal was undoubtedly struck. The Potomac River was designated as the site for the capital, and the first part of Hamilton's financial program became law in August 1790.

Four months later Hamilton submitted to Congress a second report on public credit, recommending the chartering of a national bank. This proposal too aroused considerable opposition, though primarily after Congress had already passed the bill to establish the bank.

First Bank of the United States

Hamilton modeled his bank on the Bank of England. The Bank of the United States was to be capitalized at $10 million, of which only $2 million would come from public funds. Private investors would supply the rest. The bank's charter would run for twenty years, and the government would name one-fifth of the directors. The bank's notes would circulate as the nation's currency. The bank would also act as collecting and disbursing agent for the Treasury and would lend money to the government. Most political leaders recognized that such an institution would be beneficial, especially because it would solve the problem of America's perpetual shortage of an acceptable medium of exchange. But another issue loomed large: did the Constitution give Congress the power to establish such a bank?

James Madison answered that question with a resounding no. He pointed out that Constitutional Convention delegates had specifically rejected a clause authorizing Congress to issue corporate charters. Consequently, he argued, that power could not be inferred from other parts of the Constitution.

Madison's contention disturbed President Washington, who decided to request other opinions before signing the bill into law. Edmund Randolph, the attorney general, and Thomas Jefferson, the secretary of state, agreed with Madison that the bank was unconstitutional. Jefferson referred to Article I, Section 8, of the Constitution, which gave Congress the power "to make all Laws which shall be necessary and proper for carrying into Execution the foregoing Powers." The key word, Jefferson argued, was *necessary*: Congress could do what was needed but could not do (without specific constitutional authorization) what was merely desirable. Thus Jefferson formulated the strict-constructionist interpretation of the Constitution.

Strict and Broad Constructions of the Constitution

Washington asked Hamilton to reply to the negative assessments of his proposal. Hamilton's *Defense of the Constitutionality of the Bank*, presented to the president in February 1791, was a brilliant exposition of what has become known as the broad-

Although Congress did not react positively to the arguments in Hamilton's Report on Manufactures, *the owners of America's burgeoning industries recognized the importance of the policy Hamilton advocated. Ebenezer Clough, a Boston maker of wallpaper, incorporated into his letterhead the exhortation "Americans, Encourage the Manufactories of your Country, if you wish for its prosperity."* American Antiquarian Society.

constructionist view of the Constitution. Hamilton argued forcefully that Congress could choose any means not specifically prohibited by the Constitution to achieve a constitutional end. If the end was constitutional and the means was not unconstitutional, then the means also was constitutional.

Washington was convinced. The bill became law; the bank proved successful. So did the scheme for funding the national debt and assuming the states' debts. The new nation's securities became desirable investments for its own citizens and for wealthy foreigners, especially those in the Netherlands, who rushed to purchase American debt certificates. The influx of new capital, coupled with the high prices American produce now commanded in European markets, eased farmers' debt burdens and contributed to a new prosperity. But two other aspects of Alexander Hamilton's wide-ranging financial scheme did not fare so well.

In December 1791, Hamilton presented to Congress his *Report on Manufactures*, the third and last of his prescriptions for the American economy. In it he outlined an ambitious plan for encouraging and protecting the United States's infant industries, like shoemaking and textile manufacturing. Hamilton argued that the nation could never be truly independent as long as it relied heavily on Europe for manufactured goods. He thus urged Congress to promote the immigration of technicians and laborers and to support industrial development through a limited use of protective tariffs. Many of Hamilton's ideas were implemented in later decades, but few congressmen in 1791 could see much merit in his proposals. They firmly believed that America's future lay in agriculture and the carrying trade and that the mainstay of the republic was the virtuous yeoman farmer. Therefore, Congress rejected the report.

That same year Congress accepted another feature of Hamilton's financial program, an excise tax on whiskey. Although proceeds from the Revenue Act of 1789 were sufficient to pay interest on the national debt alone, the decision to fund state debts meant that the national government required additional income. An excise tax on whiskey was attractive because it affected relatively few farmers—those in the West who sold their grain in the form of distilled spirits as a means of avoiding the high cost of transportation—and because it might reduce consump-

Whiskey Rebellion

tion of whiskey. (Eighteenth-century Americans were notorious for their heavy drinking; annual per capita consumption of alcohol was about double today's rate.) Moreover, Hamilton knew that those western farmers were Jefferson's supporters, and he saw the benefits of taxing them rather than the merchants who supported his own policies.

News of the excise law set off protests in frontier areas of Pennsylvania, where residents were already dissatisfied with the army's as yet unsuccessful attempts to defeat the Miami Confederacy (see pages 188–189). To their minds, the same government that was protecting them inadequately was now proposing to tax them disproportionately. Unrest continued for two years on the frontiers of Pennsylvania, Maryland, and Virginia. Crowds of men drafted petitions protesting the excise, raised liberty poles (deliberately imitating actions taken in the 1760s), and occasionally harassed tax collectors.

President Washington responded with restraint until violence erupted in July 1794, when western Pennsylvania farmers resisted a federal marshal and a tax collector trying to enforce the law. Three rioters were killed and several militiamen wounded. About seven thousand rebels convened on August 1 to plot the destruction of Pittsburgh but decided not to face the heavy guns of the fort guarding the town. Washington then took decisive action to prevent a crisis reminiscent of Shays's Rebellion. On August 7, he called on the insurgents to disperse and summoned nearly thirteen thousand militia from Pennsylvania and neighboring states. By the time federal forces marched westward in October and November (led at times by Washington himself), the disturbances had ended. The troops met little resistance and arrested only twenty suspects. Two, neither of them prominent leaders of the rioters, were convicted of treason, but—continuing his policy of restraint—Washington pardoned both. The leaderless and unorganized rebellion ended almost without bloodshed.

The chief importance of the Whiskey Rebellion was not military victory over the rebels—for there was none—but the forceful message it conveyed to the American public. The national government, Washington had demonstrated, would not tyrannize its citizens, but it also would not allow violent resistance to its laws. In the republic, change would be effected peacefully, by legal means. People dissatisfied with the law should try to amend or repeal it, not take extralegal action.

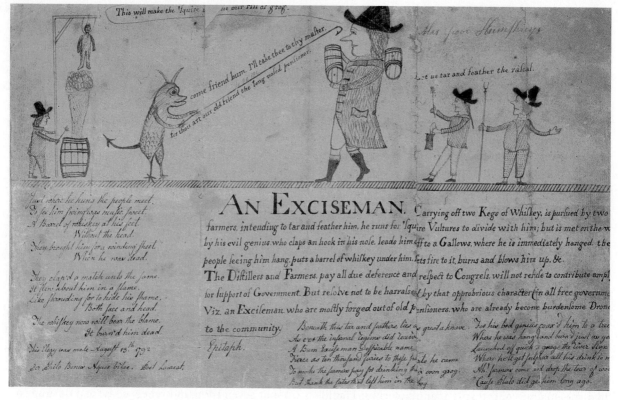

A cartoon from the mid-1790s showed the fate of an exciseman who confiscated two kegs of whiskey: pursued by two farmers, he allies himself with a devil and is hanged from a gallows. Atwater Kent Museum.

By 1794, a group of Americans were already beginning to seek change systematically through electoral politics, even though traditional political theory regarded organized opposition—especially in a republic—as illegitimate. In a monarchy, opposition groups were to be expected, even encouraged. In a government of the people, by contrast, serious and sustained disagreement was taken as a sign of corruption and subversion. Yet the opposition leaders Thomas Jefferson and James Madison became convinced as early as 1792 that Hamilton's policies of favoring wealthy commercial interests at the expense of agriculture aimed at imposing a corrupt, aristocratic government on the United States. They contended that they were the true heirs of the Revolution and that Hamilton was plotting to subvert republican principles. To dramatize their point, Jefferson, Madison, and their

Republicans and Federalists

followers in Congress began calling themselves *Republicans.*

Hamilton in turn accused Jefferson and Madison of the same crime: attempting to destroy the republic. Hamilton and his supporters began calling themselves *Federalists,* to legitimize their claims and link themselves with the Constitution. In short, each group accused the other of being an illicit faction working to destroy the republican principles of the Revolution. (In the traditional sense of the term, a *faction* was by definition dangerous and opposed to the public good.)

At first, President Washington tried to remain aloof from the political dispute that divided Hamilton and Jefferson, his chief advisers. Even so, the controversy helped persuade him to seek a second term of office in 1792 in hopes of promoting political unity. But in 1793 and thereafter, developments in foreign affairs magnified the disagreements.

Partisan Politics and Foreign Policy

The initial years under the Constitution were blessed by international peace. Soon, however, the French Revolution, which began in 1789, brought about the resumption of hostilities between France, America's wartime ally, and Great Britain, America's most important trading partner.

At first Americans welcomed the news that France was turning toward republicanism. The French people's success in limiting, then overthrowing, an oppressive monarchy seemed to vindicate America's own revolution. Americans saw themselves as the vanguard of an inevitable historical trend that would reshape the world for the better. But by the early 1790s the reports from France were disquieting. Outbreaks of violence continued; ministries succeeded each other with bewildering rapidity; executions were commonplace. The king himself was beheaded in early 1793. Although many Americans, including Jefferson and Madison, retained their sympathy for the revolutionaries, others began to view France as a prime example of the perversion of republicanism. As might be expected, Alexander Hamilton fell into the latter group.

The French Revolution

When France declared war on Britain, Spain, and Holland in 1793, the Americans faced a dilemma. The 1778 Treaty of Alliance with France bound them to that nation "forever," and a mutual commitment to republicanism created ideological bonds. Yet the United States was connected to Great Britain as well. Aside from their shared history and language, America and Britain were economic partners. Americans still purchased most of their manufactured goods from Great Britain. Indeed, since the financial system of the United States depended heavily on import tariffs as a source of revenue, the nation's economic health in effect required uninterrupted trade with the former mother country.

The political and diplomatic climate was further complicated in April 1793, when Citizen Edmond Genêt, a representative of the French government, landed in Charleston. As Genêt made his way northward to New York City, he recruited Americans for expeditions against British and Spanish colonies in the Western Hemisphere, and he distributed privateering commissions with a

Citizen Genêt

generous hand. Genêt's arrival raised a series of troubling questions for President Washington. Should he receive Genêt, thus officially recognizing the French revolutionary government? Should he acknowledge an obligation to aid France under the terms of the 1778 Treaty of Alliance? Or should he proclaim American neutrality?

For once, Hamilton and Jefferson saw eye to eye. Both told Washington that the United States could not afford to ally itself with either side. Washington agreed. He received Genêt but also issued a proclamation informing the world that the United States would adopt "a conduct friendly and impartial toward the belligerent powers." In deference to Jefferson's continued support for France, the word *neutrality* did not appear in the declaration, but its meaning was clear.

Genêt himself was removed from politics when his faction fell from power in Paris; he subsequently sought political asylum in the United States. But his disappearance from the diplomatic scene did not lessen the impact of the French Revolution in America. The domestic divisions Genêt helped to widen were perpetuated by clubs called Democratic-Republican societies, formed by Americans sympathetic to the French Revolution and worried about the policies of the Washington administration. Such societies expressed a growing grassroots concern about the same developments that troubled Jefferson and Madison.

More than forty Democratic-Republican societies were organized between 1793 and 1800. Their members saw themselves as heirs of the Sons of Liberty, seeking the same goal as their predecessors: protection of people's liberties against encroachments by corrupt and self-serving rulers. To that end, they publicly protested government fiscal and foreign policy and repeatedly proclaimed their belief in "the equal rights of man," particularly the rights to free speech, free press, and assembly. Like the Sons of Liberty, the Democratic-Republican societies were composed chiefly of artisans and craftsmen, although professionals, farmers, and merchants also joined.

Democratic-Republican Societies

The rapid growth of such groups, outspoken in their criticism of the Washington administration for its failure to come to the aid of France and for its domestic economic policies, deeply disturbed Hamilton and eventually Washington himself. Some news-

Citizen Edmond Genêt's visit caused the first major diplomatic crisis in the new nation. His attempts to enlist Americans in support of the French Revolution raised troubling questions about the international role of the United States.   Collection of the Albany Institute of History and Art. Bequest of George Genêt.

papers charged that the societies were subversive agents of a foreign power. Their "real design," one asserted, was "to involve the country in war, to assume the reins of government and tyrannize over the people." The climax of the counterattack came in the fall of 1794, when Washington accused the societies of having fomented the Whiskey Rebellion.

In retrospect, Washington and Hamilton's reaction to the Democratic-Republican societies seems disproportionately hostile. But it must be recalled that factional disputes were believed to endanger the survival of republics. As the first organized political dissenters in the United States, the Democratic-Republican societies alarmed elected officials, who had not yet accepted the idea that one component of a free government was an organized loyal opposition.

Also in 1794 George Washington dispatched Chief Justice John Jay to London to negotiate four unresolved questions affecting Anglo-American af-

fairs. The first point at issue was recent British seizures of American merchant ships trading in the French West Indies. The United States wanted to establish the principle of freedom of the seas and to assert its right, as a neutral nation, to trade freely with both combatants. Second, in violation of the 1783 peace treaty, Great Britain had not yet evacuated its posts in the American Northwest. Settlers there believed that the British were responsible for the renewed warfare in the region (see pages 183–189), and they wanted that threat removed. The Americans also hoped for a commercial treaty and sought compensation for the slaves who had left with the British army at the end of the war.

Jay Treaty

The negotiations in London proved difficult, since Jay had little to offer in exchange for the concessions he sought. Britain did agree to evacuate the western forts and ease restrictions on American trade to England and the West Indies. (Some limitations were retained, however, violating the Americans' stated commitment to open commerce.) No compensation for slaves was agreed to, but the treaty established two arbitration commissions—one to deal with prewar debts Americans owed to British creditors and the other to hear claims for captured American merchant ships. Under the circumstances, Jay did remarkably well: the treaty averted war with England at a time when the United States, which lacked an effective navy, could not have hoped to win such a conflict. Nevertheless, most Americans, including the president, were dissatisfied with at least some parts of the treaty.

At first, potential opposition was blunted because the Senate debated and ratified the treaty in secret. Not until after it was approved by a vote of 20 to 10 in June 1795 was the public informed of its provisions. The Democratic-Republican societies led protests against the treaty, which were especially intense in the South. Planters criticized the commission on prewar debts and the failure to obtain compensation for runaway slaves. Once President Washington had signed the treaty, though, there seemed to be little the Republicans could do to prevent it from taking effect. Just one opportunity remained: Congress had to appropriate funds to carry out the treaty provisions and, according to the Constitution, appropriation bills had to originate in the House of Representatives.

When the House debated the issue in March 1796, members opposing the treaty tried to prevent approval of the appropriations. To that end, they asked Washington to submit to the House all documents pertinent to the negotiations. In successfully resisting the House's request, Washington established the doctrine of *executive privilege*—the power of the president to withhold information from Congress if he believes circumstances warrant doing so.

The treaty's opponents initially appeared to be in the majority, but pressure for approval built as time passed. Frontier residents were eager to have the British posts evacuated, fearing a new outbreak of Indian war despite the signing of the Treaty of Greenville. Merchants wanted to reap benefits from expanded trade. Furthermore, Thomas Pinckney of South Carolina had negotiated a treaty with Spain giving the United States navigation privileges on the Mississippi, which would be an economic boost to the West and South. The popularity of Pinckney's Treaty (the Senate ratified it unanimously) helped to overcome opposition to the Jay Treaty. For all these reasons, the House voted the necessary funds by the narrow margin of 51 to 48.

Analysis of the vote reveals both the regional nature of the division and the growing cohesion of the Republican and Federalist factions in Congress.

Partisan Divisions in Congress

Voting for the appropriations were 44 Federalists and 7 Republicans; voting against were 45 Republicans and 3 Federalists. The final tally was also split by region. The vast majority of votes against the bill were cast by southerners (including three Virginia Federalists). The bill's supporters were from New England and the middle states, with the exception of two South Carolina Federalists. The seven Republicans who voted for the appropriations were from commercial areas in New York, Pennsylvania, and Maryland.

The small number of defectors on both sides reveals a new force at work in American politics: partisanship. Voting statistics from the first four Congresses show the ever-increasing tendency of members of the House of Representatives to vote as cohesive groups, rather than as individuals. If factional loyalty is defined as voting together at least two-thirds of the time on national issues, the percentage of nonaligned congressmen dropped from 42 percent in 1790 to just 7 percent in 1796. Significantly, this trend toward party cohesion occurred even though Congress experienced heavy turnover. Most congressmen served only one or two terms in office, and fewer than 10 percent were reelected more than three times. During the 1790s the majority slowly shifted from Federalist to Republican. Federalists controlled the first three Congresses, through the spring of 1795. Republicans gained ascendancy in the Fourth Congress. Federalists returned to power with slight majorities in the Fifth and Sixth Congresses, but the Republicans took over—more or less for good—in the Seventh Congress in 1801.

To describe these shifts is easier than to explain them. The growing division cannot be accurately explained in the terms used by Jefferson and Madison (aristocrats versus the people) or by Hamilton and Washington (true patriots versus subversive rabble). Simple economic differences between agrarian and commercial interests do not provide the answer either, since more than 90 percent of Americans in the 1790s lived in rural areas. Moreover, Jefferson's vision of a prosperous agrarian America was based on commercial farming, not rural self-sufficiency. Nor did the Federalist-Republican division simply repeat the Federalist-Antifederalist debate of 1787–1788. Even though most Antifederalists became Republicans, the party's leaders, Madison and Jefferson, had supported the Constitution.

Bases of Partisanship

Yet certain distinctions can be made. Republicans, who were especially prominent in the southern and middle states, tended to be self-assured, confident, and optimistic about both politics and the economy. Southern planters, firmly in control of their region and of a class of enslaved laborers, did not fear instability, at least among the European-American population. They foresaw a prosperous future based partly on continued westward expansion, which they expected to dominate. Republicans employed democratic rhetoric to win the allegiance of small farmers south of New England. Members of non-English ethnic groups—especially Irish, Scots, and Germans—found Republicans' words attractive. Also included in the Republican coalition were artisans, who saw themselves as the urban equivalent of yeoman farmers and valued their independence from domineering bosses. Republicans of all descriptions emphasized developing America's own resources and were less concerned than the Federalists about the nation's position in the world. Republicans also remained sympathetic to France in international affairs.

By contrast, Federalists, concentrated in New England, came mostly from English stock. They

How do historians know that *Americans were intensely patriotic in the early years of the republic? One piece of evidence is supplied by the many items incorporating patriotic motifs that decorated the homes of American citizens. The artisans of the new nation (and of England as well) quickly recognized that "patriotism sold," so they created a wide variety of objects to satisfy Americans' demand for furniture, wallpaper, curtains, and pottery goods displaying such themes. (See, for example, the jug made in Eng-land and reproduced on page 202.) Only middling and well-to-do Americans could afford to buy such items, but a less-well-off American woman could produce some of these goods for herself. We do not know who made this eagle hooked rug, but a poor woman with just a few moments to spare each day could well have labored for months to display her allegiance to the new nation in this fashion.*   New York State Historical Association, Cooperstown.

drew considerable support from commercial interests and were insecure, uncertain of the future. They stressed the need for order, authority, and regularity in the political world. Federalists had no grassroots political organization and put little emphasis on involving ordinary people in government. Not all Federalists were wealthy merchants; many were farmers who, prevented from expanding agricultural production because of New England's poor soil, gravitated toward the more conservative party. Federalists, like Republicans, assumed that southern interests would dominate the land west of the mountains, so they had little incentive to work actively to develop that potentially rich territory. In Federalist eyes, the nation was perpetually threatened by potential enemies, both internal and external, and was best protected by a continuing alliance with Great Britain. Their vision of international affairs may have been more accurate than that of the Republicans, given the warfare in Europe, but it was also narrow and unattractive. Since the Federalist view held out little hope of a better future to the voters of any region, it is not surprising that Republicans eventually prevailed.

The presence of the two organized groups—not yet parties in the modern sense but active contenders for office nonetheless—made the presidential election of 1796 the first that was seriously contested. Tired of the criticism to which he had been subjected, George Washington decided to retire from office. (Presidents had not yet been limited to two terms by constitutional amendment.) In September Washington published his Farewell Address, most of which had been written by Hamilton. In it Washington out-

Washington's Farewell Address

lined two principles that guided American foreign policy at least until the late 1940s: to maintain commercial but not political ties to other nations and to enter no permanent alliances. He also drew sharp distinctions between the United States and Europe, stressing America's uniqueness and the need for unilateralism (independent action in foreign affairs).

Domestically, Washington lamented the existence of factional divisions among his countrymen. Historians have often interpreted his call for an end to partisan strife as the statement of a man who could see beyond political affiliations to the good of the whole. But it is more accurately read in the context of its day as an attack on the legitimacy of the Republican opposition. What Washington wanted was unity behind the Federalist banner, which he saw as the only proper political stance. The Federalists (like the Republicans) continued to see themselves as the sole guardians of the truth and the only true heirs of the Revolution; they perceived their opponents as misguided, unpatriotic troublemakers who were undermining the revolutionary ideals.

To succeed Washington, the Federalists in Congress put forward Vice President John Adams, with the diplomat Thomas Pinckney as his running mate.

Election of 1796

Congressional Republicans caucused and chose Thomas Jefferson as their presidential candidate; the lawyer, Revolutionary War veteran, and active Republican politician Aaron Burr of New York agreed to run for vice president.

That the election was contested did not mean that its outcome was decided by the people. Voters could cast their ballots only for electors, not for the candidates themselves, and not all electors publicly declared their preferences. More than 40 percent of the members of the electoral college were chosen by state legislatures rather than by popular vote, and some were picked even before the presidential candidates had been named by congressional caucuses. Moreover, the method of voting in the electoral college did not take into account the possibility of party slates. The Constitution's drafters had not foreseen the development of competing national political organizations, so the Constitution provided no way to express support for one person for president and another for vice president. The electors simply voted for two people. The man with the highest total became president; the second highest, vice president.

This procedure proved to be the Federalists' undoing. Adams won the presidency with 71 votes, but a number of Federalist electors (especially those from New England) did not cast ballots for Pinckney. Thomas Jefferson won 68 votes, 9 more than Pinckney, and became vice president. The incoming administration was thus politically divided. The next four years were to see the new president and vice president, once allies and close friends, become bitter enemies.

 ## John Adams and Political Dissent

John Adams took over the presidency peculiarly blind to the partisan developments of the previous four years. As president he never abandoned an outdated notion discarded by George Washington as early as 1794: that the president should be above politics, an independent and dignified figure who did not seek petty factional advantage. Thus Adams kept Washington's cabinet intact, despite its key members' allegiance to his chief rival, Alexander Hamilton. Adams often adopted a passive posture, letting others (usually Hamilton) take the lead when he should have acted decisively. As a result, his administration gained a reputation for inconsistency. When Adams's term ended, the Federalists were severely divided, and the Republicans had won the presidency. But Adams's detachment from Hamilton's maneuverings did enable him to weather the greatest international crisis the republic had yet faced: the so-called Quasi-War with France.

The Jay Treaty improved America's relationship with Great Britain, but it provoked retaliation by France. Angry that the United States had reached agreement with its enemy, the French government ordered its vessels to seize American ships carrying British goods. In response, Adams appointed three commissioners to try to reach a settlement with France. Simultaneously, Congress increased military spending, authorizing the building of ships and the stockpiling of weapons and ammunition.

For months, the American commissioners sought negotiations with Talleyrand, the French foreign minister, but Talleyrand's agents demanded a bribe of $250,000 before talks could begin. The Americans retorted, "No, no; not a sixpence," and reported the incident in dispatches that President Adams received in early March 1798. Adams informed Congress of the impasse and recommended increased appropriations for defense.

XYZ Affair

This cartoon drawn during the XYZ affair depicts the United States as a maiden being victimized by the five leaders of the French government's directorate. In the background, John Bull (England) watches from on high, while other European nations discuss the situation. The Lilly Library, Indiana University, Bloomington, Indiana.

Convinced that Adams had deliberately sabotaged the negotiations, congressional Republicans insisted that the dispatches be turned over to Congress. Adams complied, aware that releasing the reports would work to his advantage. He withheld only the names of the French agents, referring to them as *X, Y,* and *Z.* The revelation that the Americans had been treated with contempt stimulated a wave of anti-French sentiment in the United States. A journalist's version of the commissioners' reply, "Millions for defense, but not a cent for tribute," became the national slogan. Cries for war filled the air. Congress formally abrogated the Treaty of Alliance and authorized American ships to seize French vessels.

Thus began an undeclared war with France. The so-called Quasi-War was fought in the West Indies, between warships of the United States Navy and French privateers seeking to capture American merchant vessels. Although initial American losses of merchant shipping were heavy, by early 1799 the United

Quasi-War with France

States Navy had established its superiority in Caribbean waters. Its ships captured eight French privateers and naval vessels, easing the threat to America's vital West Indian trade.

The Republicans, who opposed war and continued to sympathize with France, could do little to stem the tide of anti-French feelings. Since Agent Y had boasted of the existence of a "French party in America," Federalists flatly accused Republicans of traitorous designs. A New York newspaper declared that anyone who remained "lukewarm" after reading the XYZ dispatches was a "criminal—and the man who does not warmly reprobate the conduct of the French must have a soul black enough to be *fit* for *treason Strategems* and *spoils.*" John Adams wavered between calling the Republicans traitors and acknowledging their right to oppose administration measures. His wife was less tolerant. "Those whom the French boast of as their Partizans," Abigail Adams declared, should be "adjudged traitors to their country." If Jefferson had been president, she added, "we should all have been sold to the French."

Federalists saw this climate of opinion as an opportunity to deal a death blow to their Republican opponents. Now that the country seemed to see the truth of what they had been saying ever since the Whiskey Rebellion in 1794—that Republicans were subversive foreign agents—Federalists sought to codify that belief into law. In 1798, the Federalist-controlled Congress adopted a set of four laws known as the Alien and Sedition Acts, intended to suppress dissent and to prevent further growth of the Republican party.

Alien and Sedition Acts

Three of the acts were aimed at immigrants, whom Federalists accurately suspected of being Republican in their sympathies. The Naturalization Act lengthened the residency period required for citizenship and ordered all resident aliens to register with the federal government. The two Alien Acts provided for the detention of enemy aliens in time of war and gave the president authority to deport any alien he deemed dangerous to the nation's security. Neither act was implemented during the Adams administration, however.

The fourth act, the Sedition Act, sought to control both citizens and aliens. It outlawed conspiracies to prevent the enforcement of federal laws and set the maximum punishment for such offenses at five years in prison and a $5,000 fine. The act also tried to control speech. Writing, printing, or uttering "false, scandalous and malicious" statements against the government or the president "with intent to defame . . . or to bring them or either of them, into contempt or disrepute" became a crime punishable by as much as two years' imprisonment and a fine of $2,000. Today any such law punishing speech alone would be considered unconstitutional. But in the eighteenth century, when organized political opposition was regarded with suspicion, the restrictions that the Sedition Act placed on speech were acceptable to many.

The Sedition Act led to fifteen indictments and ten convictions. Most of the accused were outspoken Republican newspaper editors who failed to mute their criticism of the administration in response to the law. But the first victim—whose story may serve as an example of the rest—was a hot-tempered Republican congressman from Vermont, Matthew Lyon. The Irish-born Lyon, a former indentured servant who had purchased his freedom and fought in the Revolution, was indicted for declaring in print that John Adams had displayed "a continual grasp for power" and "an unbounded thirst for ridiculous pomp, foolish adulation, and selfish avarice." Though convicted, fined $1,000, and sent to prison for four months, Lyon was not silenced. He conducted his reelection campaign from jail, winning an overwhelming majority. The fine was ceremoniously paid for him by contributions from leading Republicans around the country.

Faced with prosecutions of their supporters, Jefferson and Madison sought an effective means of combating the acts. Petitioning the Federalist-controlled Congress to repeal the laws would clearly do no good. Furthermore, Federalist judges refused to allow accused individuals to question the Sedition Act's constitutionality. Accordingly, the Republican leaders turned to the only other forum available for protest: state legislatures. Carefully concealing their own role—it would not have been desirable for the vice president to be indicted for sedition—Jefferson and Madison each drafted a set of resolutions. Introduced into the Kentucky and Virginia legislatures, respectively, in the fall of 1798, the resolutions differed somewhat but had the same import. Since the Constitution was created by a compact among the states, they contended, people speaking through their states had a legitimate right to judge the constitutionality of actions taken by the federal government. Both sets of resolutions pronounced the Alien and Sedition Acts null and void and asked other states to join in the protest.

Virginia and Kentucky Resolutions

Although no other state endorsed them, the Virginia and Kentucky resolutions were nevertheless influential. First, they were superb political propaganda, rallying Republican opinion throughout the country. They placed the opposition party squarely in the revolutionary tradition of resistance to tyrannical authority. Second, the theory of union that they proposed inspired southern states' rights advocates in the 1830s and thereafter. Jefferson and Madison had identified a key constitutional issue: how far could states go in opposing the national government? How could a conflict between the two be resolved? These questions were not to be definitively answered until the Civil War.

Ironically, just as the Sedition Act was being implemented and northern state legislatures were rejecting the Virginia and Kentucky resolutions,

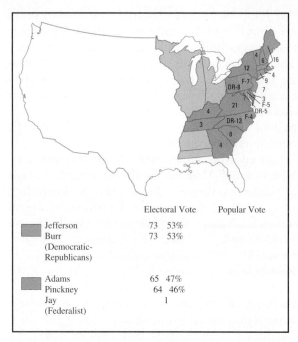

	Electoral Vote	Popular Vote
Jefferson	73	53%
Burr	73	53%
(Democratic-Republicans)		
Adams	65	47%
Pinckney	64	46%
Jay	1	
(Federalist)		

Presidential Election, 1800   The Democratic-Republicans, with their candidates Thomas Jefferson and Aaron Burr, won the electoral votes of the southern states, while the Federalists, the party of John Adams and Charles Cotesworth Pinckney, received votes primarily in New England. The parties split the votes of the middle states, but the Democratic-Republicans dominated the electoral-vote count there and won the election.

Convention of 1800

Federalists split over the course of action the United States should take toward France. Hamilton and his supporters still called for a declaration legitimizing the undeclared naval war. But Adams received a number of private signals that the French government regretted its treatment of the American commissioners. Acting on these assurances, he dispatched the envoy William Vans Murray to Paris. The United States asked for two things: compensation for ships the French had seized since 1793 and abrogation of the treaty of 1778. The Convention of 1800, which ended the Quasi-War, provided for the latter but not the former. Still, it freed the United States from its only permanent alliance, thus allowing it to follow the independent diplomatic course George Washington outlined in his Farewell Address.

The results of the negotiations were not known in the United States until after the presidential election of 1800. Even so, since Hamilton and many of his followers wanted to widen the Quasi-War, Adams's decision to seek a peaceful settlement probably cost him reelection because of the divisions it caused in Federalist ranks.

The Republicans entered the 1800 presidential race firmly united behind Jefferson and Burr. Although they won the election, their lack of foresight almost cost them dearly. The problem was the system of voting in the electoral college, which Federalists understood better than Republicans.

Election of 1800

The Federalists arranged in advance for one of their electors to fail to vote for Charles Cotesworth Pinckney, their vice-presidential candidate. John Adams thus received the higher number of Federalist votes (65 to Pinckney's 64). The Republicans failed to make the same distinction between their candidates, and all 73 of their electors cast ballots for both Jefferson and Burr (see map). Because neither Republican had a plurality, the Constitution required that the contest be decided in the House of Representatives, with each state's congressmen voting as a unit. Since the new House, dominated by Republicans, would not take office for some months, Federalist congressmen decided the election. It took them thirty-five ballots to decide that Jefferson would be a lesser evil than Burr. In response to the tangle, the Twelfth Amendment to the Constitution (1804) changed the method of voting in the electoral college to allow for a party ticket.

 **Westward Expansion, Social Change, and Religious Ferment**

The United States experienced a dramatic increase in internal migration in the postrevolutionary years. As much as 5 to 10 percent of the population moved each year, approximately half relocating to another state. Young European-American men were the most mobile segment of the populace, but all groups moved with similar frequency. The major population shifts were from east to west (see map, page 218): from New England to upstate New York and Ohio, from New Jersey to western Pennsylvania, from the Chesapeake to the new states of Kentucky

In 1805, an unidentified artist painted Benjamin Hawkins, a trader and United States agent to the Indians of the Southeast, at the Creek agency near Macon, Georgia. Hawkins introduced European-style agriculture to the Creeks, who are shown here with vegetables from their fields. Throughout the eastern United States, Indian nations had to make similar adaptations of their traditional lifestyles in order to maintain their group identity.   Collection of the Greenville County Art Museum, South Carolina.

and Tennessee, which entered the Union in 1792 and 1796 respectively. Very few people moved north or south, but some southerners (perhaps yeoman farmers escaping the expansion of slavery) did seek new homes farther north.

Some of these migrants moved west of the Appalachian Mountains. The first permanent white settlements beyond the mountains were established in western North Carolina in 1771. But not until after the defeat of the Shawnees in 1774 and the Cherokees in 1776 (see pages 152–153) was the way cleared for a more general migration. Small groups of families filtered through the Cumberland Gap into Kentucky, following the Wilderness Road carved out in 1775. At war's end, Americans streamed over the

Settlement in the West

mountains in considerably larger numbers. In 1783, only about 12,000 whites and blacks lived west of the mountains and south of the Ohio River; less than a decade later, the 1790 census counted more than 100,000 residents of the future states of Kentucky and Tennessee.

Settlements grew more slowly north of the Ohio River because of the strength of the Miami Confederacy. But once the Treaty of Greenville was signed in 1795, the Ohio country also grew rapidly. Many easterners traveled by land to Pittsburgh, then floated down the Ohio River on flatboats and rafts to Marietta. Others, like Margaret Dwight, moved to land that Connecticut had claimed under its colonial charter—the so-called Western Reserve (see map, page 184). All these settlers repeated the process of transforming the environment that their fore-

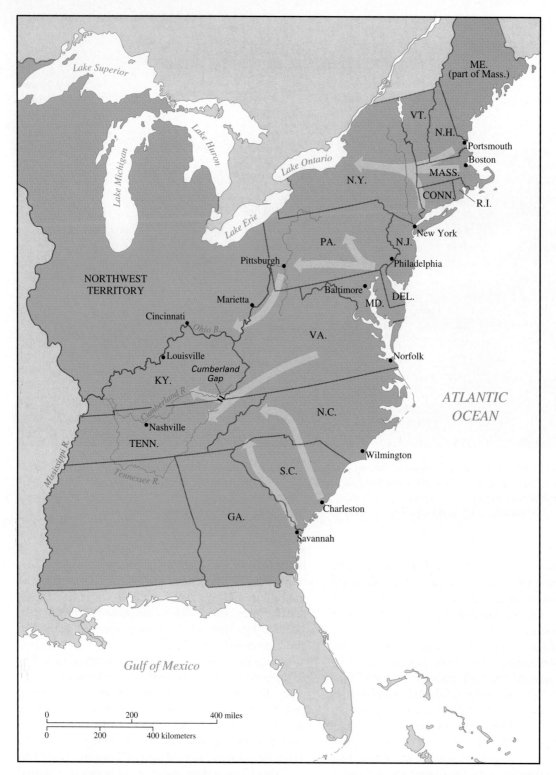

Western Expansion, 1785–1805 *After the Revolutionary War, large numbers of white and black Americans ventured west of the Appalachian Mountains for the first time. Following certain distinct routes, they moved along rivers like the Mohawk (in New York) and the Ohio or through passes like the Cumberland Gap.*

bears had undertaken: cutting down forests, clearing fields, building fences, and, in general, imposing patterns of land usage derived from European practice on a landscape previously managed quite differently by Indians.

The transplanted New Englanders in particular did their best to re-create the societies they had left behind, laying out farms and towns in neat checkerboard patterns and founding libraries and Congregational churches. Early arrivals' enthusiastic letters describing Ohio's rich soil and potential for growth recruited others to join them, setting off a phenomenon known in New England as "Ohio Fever." The New Englanders, proud of their literate, orderly culture, viewed their neighbors with disdain. Ohioans, said one, were "intelligent, industrious, and thriving," whereas the Virginians who had settled across the river in Kentucky were "ignorant, lazy, and poor." He continued the contrast: "Here the buildings are neat, . . . there the habitations are miserable cabins. Here the grounds are laid out in a regular manner . . . ; there the fields are surrounded by a rough zigzag log fence."

The westward migration of slaveholders, first to Kentucky and Tennessee and then later into the rich lands of western Georgia and eventually the Gulf Coast, had an adverse impact on African-Americans. The web of family connections built up over several generations of residence in the Chesapeake was torn apart by the population movement. Even those few large planters who moved their entire slave force west rarely owned all the members of every family on their plantations. Most commonly the migrants were either younger sons of eastern slaveholders, whose inheritance included only a portion of the family's slaves, or small farmers with just one or two bondspeople. In the early years of American settlement in the West, the population was widely dispersed; accordingly, African-Americans raised among large numbers of kin in the Chesapeake had to adapt to lonely lives on isolated farms, far from their parents, siblings, or even spouses and children. The approximately 100,000 African-Americans forcibly moved west by 1810 had to begin to build new families there to replace those unwillingly left behind in the East. They succeeded well, as Chapter 11 shows.

The mobility of the population created a volatile mix in southern frontier areas. Everyone was new to the region, and few had relatives nearby. Since most

African-Americans in the West

of the migrants were young, single men just starting to lead independent lives, western society was at first unstable. Like the seventeenth-century Chesapeake, the late-eighteenth-century American West was a society in which single women like Margaret Dwight married quickly. The other side of the same coin was that the few women among the migrants lamented their lack of congenial female friends. Isolated, far from familiar surroundings, women and men strove to create new communities to replace those left behind. Perhaps the most meaningful of the new communities was the affiliation supplied by evangelical religion.

Second Great Awakening

Among the migrants to Kentucky and Tennessee were clergymen and committed lay members of the evangelical sects that had arisen in America after the Great Awakening of the 1730s through the 1760s—Baptists, Presbyterians, and Methodists. That First Awakening had flourished in the southern backcountry well into the 1760s, and the Second Great Awakening, which began around 1800 in the West and continued into the 1840s (see pages 348–349), was an extension of the earlier revival. Laymen and clerics alike spread the doctrine of evangelical Christianity through the countryside, carrying the message of salvation to the rootless and mostly uneducated frontier folk.

At camp meetings, sometimes attended by thousands of people and usually lasting from three days to a week, clergymen exhorted their audiences to repent their sins and become genuine Christians. Many declared that salvation was open to all, rejecting the Calvinistic doctrine of predestination. Stressing the emotional nature of the conversion experience and downplaying the need for Bible study, such preachers brought the message of religion to the people in more ways than one. They were in effect democratizing American religion, making it available to all rather than to a preselected and educated elite.

The most famous camp meeting took place in August 1801 at Cane Ridge, in central Kentucky. At a time when the largest settlement in the state had no more than two thousand inhabitants, about ten thousand people came to Cane Ridge, attracted to a scheduled Presbyterian communion service after a summer filled with smaller revivals. Twenty Presbyterian and Methodist clergymen preached to the throngs; they were joined by an estimated three hundred lay exhorters, who began speaking to the crowd

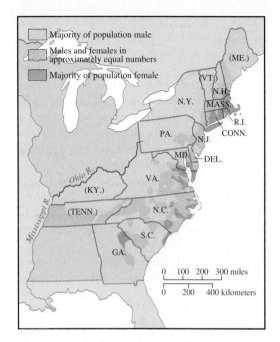

Sex Ratio of White Population, 1790
The first census revealed that the sex ratio varied dramatically in different parts of the country. In many older, coastal areas, women predominated; on the frontier, men were in the majority. The variations had important implications for life in those regions, as the text points out.   Source: From Lester J. Cappon et al., eds., *Atlas of Early American History: The Revolutionary Era, 1760–1790.* Copyright © 1976 by Princeton University Press. Reprinted by permission of Princeton University Press.

spontaneously. One witness saw "sinners dropping down on every hand, shrieking, groaning, crying for mercy, . . . some singing, some shouting, clapping their hands, hugging and even kissing, laughing." Such scenes were to be repeated many times in the decades that followed. Revivals swept across different regions of the country until nearly the middle of the century, leaving an indelible legacy of evangelism to many American Protestant churches.

The established churches of the colonial era—supported, like the Congregationalists in Massachusetts or the Anglicans in Virginia, by tax revenues—

Attacks on Established Churches

came under vigorous attack from dissenters who used revolutionary ideology to great advantage. Isaac Backus, a New England Baptist, pointed out forcefully that "many, who are filling the

nation with the cry of liberty and against *oppressors* are at the same time themselves violating that dearest of all rights, liberty of conscience." Legislators found it impossible to resist the logic of such arguments. Many states dissolved their ties to churches during or immediately after the war, and others vastly reduced state support for established denominations.

These changes meant that congregations could no longer rely on public funds and that all churches were placed on the same footing with respect to government. Church membership became voluntary, as did monetary contributions from members. If congregations were to survive, they had to generate new sources of support. Revivals, which were genuine outpourings of religious sentiment, also proved a convenient means of increasing church membership.

An analysis of secular society can help to explain the conversion patterns of the Second Awakening. Unlike the First Great Awakening, when converts were evenly divided by sex, more women than men—particularly

Women and the Second Awakening

young women—answered the call of Christianity during the Second Awakening. The increase in female converts seems to have been directly related to fundamental changes in women's circumstances in the late eighteenth century. In some areas of the country, especially New England (where the revival movement flourished), women outnumbered men after 1790, for many young men had migrated westward (see map). Thus eastern girls could no longer count on finding marital partners. The uncertainty of their social and familial position seems to have led them to seek spiritual certainty in the church.

Young women's domestic roles changed dramatically at the same time, for cloth production was beginning to move from the household to the factory (see page 349). Deprived of their chief household role as spinners and weavers, New England daughters found in the church a realm where they could continue to make useful contributions to society. Church missionary societies and charitable associations provided an acceptable outlet for their talents. One of the most striking developments of the early nineteenth century was the creation of hundreds of female associations to aid widows and orphans, collect money for foreign missions, and improve the quality of maternal care. Thus American women collectively assumed the role of keepers of the nation's conscience, taking the lead in charitable enterprises and freeing their husbands from concern for such moral issues.

The religious ferment in frontier regions of the Upper South contributed to racial ferment as well, for people of both races attended the camp meetings to hear black and white preachers. When revivals spread eastward into more heavily slaveholding areas, planters became fearful of the egalitarianism implied in the evangelical message of universal salvation and harmony. Their fear was heightened by events in the West Indies. In 1793, in the French colony of Saint Domingue (Haiti), mulattos and blacks under the leadership of Toussaint L'Ouverture overthrew European rule in a bloody revolt characterized by numerous atrocities on both sides. News of the successful rebellion traveled rapidly among slaves and slaveowners in the South, which at that time was experiencing rapid demographic change.

Unrest Among African-Americans

The expansion of cotton production after the invention of the cotton gin in 1793 and the beginnings of large-scale westward migration increased the demand for slaves. Planters rushed to purchase new enslaved laborers, both to take advantage of the new technology and to replace the bondspeople lost during the Revolution. The postwar decades therefore witnessed the single most massive inflow of Africans into North America since the beginnings of the slave trade. Before the legal trade was halted in 1808, more than ninety thousand new Africans had been imported into the United States (see map). Their mere presence increased slaveholders' anxieties about the possibilities for revolt, while simultaneously the postwar increase in the number of free blacks severely challenged the slave system. Like their white compatriots, African-Americans (both slave and free) had become familiar with notions of liberty and equality. They also had witnessed the benefits of fighting collectively for freedom, rather than resisting individually or running away. The circumstances were ripe for an explosion.

Gabriel's Rebellion

At this juncture in Virginia, Gabriel, an enslaved Richmond blacksmith who argued that African-Americans should fight for their freedom, planned a large-scale revolt. Identifying his targets not as all whites but rather as those "merchants" who oppressed artisans of both races, Gabriel first recruited to his cause other skilled African-Americans who like himself lived in semifreedom under minimal supervision. Next he enlisted rural slaves. The conspirators planned to attack Richmond on the night of August 30, 1800, setting fire to the city, seizing the state capitol, and capturing the governor. At that point, Gabriel believed, other slaves and sympathetic poor whites would join in.

The plan showed considerable political sophistication, but heavy rain forced a postponement. Several planters then learned of the plan from their slaves and spread the alarm. Gabriel avoided capture for some weeks, but most of the other leaders of the rebellion were quickly arrested and interrogated.

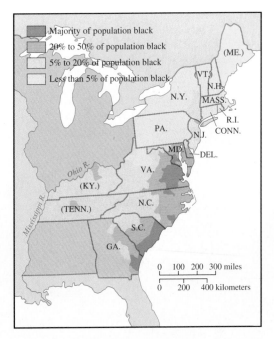

African-American Population, 1790: Proportion of Total Population *The first census clearly indicated that the African-American population was heavily concentrated in just a few areas of the United States, most notably in coastal regions of South Carolina, Georgia, and Virginia. Although there were growing numbers of blacks in the backcountry—presumably taken there by migrating slaveowners—most parts of the North and East, with the exception of the immediate vicinity of New York City, had few African-American residents.* Source: From Lester J. Cappon et al., eds., *Atlas of Early American History: The Revolutionary Era, 1760–1790.* Copyright © 1976 by Princeton University Press. Reprinted by permission of Princeton University Press.

Richmond, Virginia, at the time of Gabriel's Rebellion. This was the city as Gabriel knew it. The state capitol, the rebels' intended target, dominates the city's skyline as it dominated Gabriel's thinking.   Virginia Historical Society.

Twenty-six conspirators, including Gabriel himself, were hanged, but that outcome did not put an end to unrest among Virginia's slaves.

In 1802, a waterman named Sancho—a peripheral participant in Gabriel's plot—revived the plans for a revolt. This time word spread along Virginia and North Carolina rivers, carried by slaves who, like Sancho, worked on the boats that plied the two states' interconnected waterways. The plans were still incomplete when the plots were revealed. Again, trials and executions followed, and twenty-five more African-Americans lost their lives on the gallows.

At his trial two years earlier, one of Gabriel's followers had made explicit the links that so frightened Chesapeake slaveholders. He told his judges that, like George Washington, "I have adventured my life in endeavouring to obtain the liberty of my countrymen, and am a willing sacrifice in their cause." Southern state legislatures responded to such claims by increasing the severity of the laws regulating slav-ery. Before long, all talk of emancipation (gradual or otherwise) ceased, and slavery became even more firmly entrenched as an economic institution and way of life.

 Conclusion

As the nineteenth century began, inhabitants of the United States were moving toward an accommodation to their changed lives in the new republic. Native American peoples east of the Mississippi found that they had to give up some parts of their traditional culture to preserve others. African-Americans and European-Americans tried to create new lives for themselves in the West and to adjust to changed economic circumstances in the East. Building on successful negotiations with both Britain (the Jay Treaty) and France (the Convention of 1800), the United States developed its diplomatic independence, striving to avoid entanglement with the European powers. The 1790s spawned vigorous debates over foreign and domestic policy and saw the beginnings of a system of political parties. Dissent was discouraged but not successfully suppressed. Religious revivals swept portions of the countryside and contributed to social unrest, as they had done in the eighteenth century.

At the end of the 1790s, after years of struggle, the Jeffersonian interpretation of republicanism finally prevailed over Hamilton's approach. As a result, in the years to come the country would be characterized by a decentralized economy, minimal government (especially at the national level), and maximum freedom of action and mobility for individual white men. Jeffersonian Republicans, like other white men before them, failed to extend to white women, Indian peoples, and African-Americans the freedom and individuality they recognized as essential for themselves.

Suggestions for Further Reading

National Government and Administration

Kenneth Bowling, *The Creation of Washington, D.C.* (1991); Ralph Adams Brown, *The Presidency of John Adams* (1975); William R. Casto, *The Supreme Court in the Early Republic: The Chief Justiceships of John Jay and Oliver Ellsworth* (1995); Stanley Elkins and Eric McKitrick, *The Age of Federalism, 1788–1800* (1993); Morton Frisch, *Alexander Hamilton and the Political Order* (1991); Richard H. Kohn, *Eagle and Sword: The Federalists and the Creation of the Military Establishment in America, 1783–1802* (1975); Tadahisa Kuroda, *The Origins of the Twelfth Amendment: The Electoral College in the Early Republic, 1787–1804* (1994); Forrest McDonald, *Alexander Hamilton* (1979); Forrest McDonald, *The Presidency of George Washington* (1974); John R. Nelson, Jr., *Liberty and Property: Political Economy and Policymaking in the New Nation, 1789–1812* (1987); James R. Sharp, *American Politics in the Early Republic: The New Nation in Crisis* (1993); Garry Wills, *Cincinnatus: George Washington and the Enlightenment* (1984).

Partisan Politics

Joyce Appleby, *Capitalism and a New Social Order: The Republican Vision of the 1790s* (1984); Lance Banning, *The Jeffersonian Persuasion: Evolution of a Party Ideology* (1978); Richard Buel, *Securing the Revolution: Ideology in American Politics, 1789–1815* (1972); Joseph Charles, *The Origins of the American Party System* (1956); Noble E. Cunningham, *The Jeffersonian Republicans: The Formation of Party Organization, 1789–1801* (1957); Manning J. Dauer, *The Adams Federalists* (1953); Richard Hofstadter, *The Idea of a Party System: The Rise of Legitimate Opposition in the United States, 1780–1840* (1970); John Zvesper, *Political Philosophy and Rhetoric: A Study of the Origins of American Party Politics* (1977).

Foreign Policy

Harry Ammon, *The Genêt Mission* (1973); Samuel F. Bemis, *Jay's Treaty*, 2d ed. (1962); Samuel F. Bemis, *Pinckney's Treaty*, 2d ed. (1960); Jerald A. Combs, *The Jay Treaty* (1970); Alexander DeConde, *The Quasi-War: Politics and Diplomacy of the Undeclared War with France, 1797–1801* (1966); Alexander DeConde, *Entangling Alliance: Politics and Diplomacy Under George Washington* (1958); Felix Gilbert, *To the Farewell Address: Ideas of Early American Foreign Policy* (1961); Reginald Horsman, *The Diplomacy of the New Republic, 1776–1815* (1985); Lawrence Kaplan, "Entangling Alliances with None": American Foreign Policy in the Age of Jefferson* (1987); Bradford Perkins, *The First Rapprochement: England and the United States, 1795–1805* (1967); William Stinchcombe, *The XYZ Affair* (1981).

Civil Liberties

Leonard W. Levy, *Emergence of a Free Press* (1985); Leonard W. Levy, *Origins of the Fifth Amendment* (1968); Robert A. Rutland, *The Birth of the Bill of Rights, 1776–1791*, rev. ed. (1983); James Morton Smith, *Freedom's Fetters: The Alien and Sedition Laws and American Civil Liberties* (1956).

Social Change and Westward Expansion

Andrew Cayton, *The Frontier Republic: Ideology and Politics in the Ohio Country, 1789–1812* (1986); Nancy F. Cott, *The Bonds of Womanhood: "Woman's Sphere" in New England, 1780–1835* (1977); Douglas Egerton, *Gabriel's Rebellion: The Virginia Slave Conspiracies of 1800 and 1802* (1993); John Mack Faragher, *Daniel Boone: The Life and Legend of an American Pioneer* (1992); Reginald Horsman, *The Frontier in the Formative Years, 1783–1815* (1970); Allen Kulikoff, *The Agrarian Origins of American Capitalism* (1992); Malcolm Rohrbough, *The Trans-Appalachian Frontier: Peoples, Societies, and Institutions, 1775–1850* (1979); Thomas Slaughter, *The Whiskey Rebellion* (1986).

Religion

Catharine Albanese, *Sons of the Fathers: The Civil Religion of the American Revolution* (1976); Ruth Bloch, *Visionary Republic: Millennial Themes in American Thought* (1985); Jon Butler, *Awash in a Sea of Faith: Christianizing the American People* (1990); Paul Conkin, *Cane Ridge: America's Pentecost* (1990); Nathan O. Hatch, *The Democratization of American Christianity* (1990); Ronald Hoffman and Peter J. Albert, eds., *Religion in a Revolutionary Age* (1994); Fred J. Hood, *Reformed America, 1783–1837* (1980); William McLoughlin, *Revivals, Awakenings, and Reform* (1978).

O.C.SELTZER.

9

The Empire of Liberty
1801 – 1824

Nez Perce villagers on the western slope of the Rockies were stunned on September 20, 1805, when a ragtag group of white men descended on them. Some boys playing in a field first spotted the intruders, a scouting group headed by William Clark. Terrified, the boys fled. Clark, leaving his gun and horse behind him, chased the boys and found them hiding. The boys returned to their village with gifts of ribbon.

An old man soon came to greet the bearded strangers. Using signs to communicate, he invited them to his village. As elderly men and women of all ages looked on with fear, the Indian leader told Clark that the village head, Broken Arm, and the men were away on a raid. They fed Clark and his group with pieces of buffalo, dried salmon, and camas bread.

In the next village, the Nez Perce greeted the Clark party in much the same way. They welcomed the strangers and watched them gather food. A Nez Perce chief mapped out the terrain for them, indicating that in another camp was an important leader, Twisted Hair. Clark then sent a message to his partner Meriwether Lewis and the majority of the exploring group, saying he and his companions would meet them at Twisted Hair's settlement. The villagers watched on September 22 as the two separate groups joined.

According to the Nez Perce's oral tradition, their cautious but friendly welcome of Lewis and Clark was due in part to the efforts of an elderly woman whose experience with white people had been positive. Watkuweis, whose name meant "returned from a far country," had once been a slave of a white trader. When Clark arrived at her village, she said: "These are the people who helped me. Do them no hurt." The Nez Perce also welcomed Lewis and Clark because they wanted guns and ammunition, which the expedition was carrying. In the spring of 1805 men from Broken Arm's band had traded with other Indians for six guns and had heard about the Lewis and Clark expedition. Lewis and Clark gave the chiefs the usual gifts—tobacco, clothing, flags, and medals—but Nez Perce self-interest, not trading goods, was responsible for the good relations.

The Nez Perce crossed the rugged mountains regularly and safely, but the Lewis and Clark expedition found the terrain perilous. Early in September 1805 as the explorers had moved through the Rockies in present-day Montana and Idaho, they crossed what expedition member Sergeant Patrick Gass in his diary described as "the most terrible mountains I ever beheld." Shoshone Indians had warned them that the trail was treacherous, and that little game was to be had. But they also told Lewis and Clark that the Nez Perce traversed it frequently, and the American explorers believed that if the Indians could make the climb, so could they.

The trip had proved as difficult as predicted. The Americans lost their way a number of times and tumbled down steep mountain trails. They slept in the snow, bone cold. Short of food, they killed a horse for meat. Finally, the thirty survivors of the fifty-man group reached level land and the Nez Perce villages. From there they went on to the Pacific Ocean and then spent another year on the return journey.

President Thomas Jefferson had commissioned Lewis and Clark in 1803 to explore the newly purchased Lousiana Territory. The twenty-nine-year-old Lewis had been a regular army officer in the 1790s and was Jefferson's private secretary. The thirty-three-year-old Clark was an explorer and former soldier who had fought and negotiated with Native Americans. Aware of the risks as well as the scientific and political importance of their mission, both itched to explore the West. They gathered information on the natural history of the areas they passed through, but they had political goals as well: to counter British advances to the Indians and to map the territory so that it could be opened to settlement and exploitation.

The Lewis and Clark expedition (1804–1806) proved successful. The explorers reached the Pacific, and their good relations with the Indians and the fame of their travels led to the opening of the territory to settlement and prevented British advances. Their collection of information about natural specimens and artifacts from the area was thorough. Along the way they had been aided by trappers and

Native Americans, including Sacagawea, a young Shoshone woman companion to a French-Canadian trader, who joined the expedition. Sacagawea helped negotiate safe passage in the Far West, and she interpreted the terrain and the languages of the West for the explorers.

The Lewis and Clark expedition was part of American expansion. Like the purchase of the Louisiana Territory from France in 1803 it extended, in Jefferson's phrase, the American "empire of liberty." Through buckskin diplomacy, Lewis and Clark made friends beyond the limits of United States settlement. They were harbingers of the future, of the expansion and settlement of the United States.

Americans passed a political test at home when President Jefferson succeeded President Adams peacefully in 1800, despite the bitterness of the election and political intrigue. Presidential succession by ballot rather than arms helped secure constitutional government.

The transfer of power to the Republicans from the Federalists intensified political conflict. In the tradition of the Revolution, Republican presidents would seek to restrain the national government, believing that limited government would foster republican virtue. The Federalists would advocate a strong national government with centralized authority to promote economic development. As both factions competed for popular support, they laid the basis for the evolution of democratic politics. But factionalism, personal animosities, and partisanship within each group prevented the development of cohesive political parties, and the Federalists, unable to build a strong base of popular support, slowly faded away.

Events abroad and in the West encouraged and threatened Americans. Seizing one opportunity, the United States purchased the Louisiana Territory, pushing its border to the Pacific Ocean. But then from the high seas came war. Caught between the warring British and French, the United States found its ships seized and its sailors impressed, in violation of its rights as a neutral and independent nation. When the humiliation and threat to United States interests became too great, Americans took up arms in the War of 1812 both to defend their rights as a nation and to expand farther to the west and north. Though unprepared for combat, the United States fought Great Britain to a standstill. The Americans also routed Indian resistance and shattered Native American unity. A peace treaty restored the prewar

• *Important Events* •

1801	John Marshall becomes Chief Justice of the United States Thomas Jefferson inaugurated as first Republican president
1801–05	United States defeats Barbary pirates in Tripoli War
1803	*Marbury* v. *Madison* establishes judicial review United States purchases Louisiana Territory from France
1804	Burr kills Hamilton in a duel Jefferson reelected
1804–06	Lewis and Clark explore Louisiana Territory
1805	Prophet emerges as Shawnee leader
1807	*Chesapeake* affair almost leads to war with Great Britain Embargo Act halts foreign trade
1808	Congress bans importation of slaves to the United States James Madison elected president
1808–13	Prophet and Tecumseh organize Native American tribal resistance
1812–15	United States and Great Britain fight the War of 1812
1813	Death of Tecumseh ends effective pan-Indian resistance
1814	Andrew Jackson's defeat of Creeks at Battle of Horseshoe Bend begins Indian removal from the South Treaty of Ghent ends the War of 1812
1814–15	Hartford Convention undermines Federalists
1815	Battle of New Orleans makes Jackson a national hero
1816	Second Bank of the United States chartered James Monroe elected president
1817	Rush-Bagot Treaty limits British and American naval forces on Lake Champlain and the Great Lakes
1819	*McCulloch* v. *Maryland* establishes supremacy of federal over state law Adams-Onís Treaty with Spain gives Florida to United States and defines Louisiana territorial border
1819–23	Financial panic and depression: hard times for Americans
1820	Missouri Compromise creates a formula for admitting slave and free states Monroe reelected
1823	Monroe Doctrine closes Western Hemisphere to European intervention

status quo, but the war and the treaty reaffirmed American independence and strengthened American determination to steer clear of European conflicts.

The War of 1812 unleashed a wave of nationalism and self-confidence. War needs promoted domestic manufacturing and internal improvements. With peace, the federal government championed business and the construction of roads and canals. The new spirit encouraged economic growth and western expansion at home, trade abroad, and assertiveness throughout the Western Hemisphere. By the 1820s, the United States was no longer an experiment; a new nation had emerged. Free of its colonial past, the country began energetically shaping its own identity.

Economic growth and territorial expansion, however, generated new problems. In 1819 a finan-cial panic brought hardship and conflict that sowed the seeds for the Jacksonian movement in the 1820s and 1830s. More ominously, sectional differences and the presence of slavery created divisions that would widen in the wake of further westward expansion during the 1840s and 1850s.

 Jefferson in Power

Thomas Jefferson viewed the election of 1800 as a revolution that restored government to its limited role. He stressed republican virtues of independence, self-reliance, and equality. He believed in a limited and frugal government. In contrast to the formality of the Federalist presidents Washington and Adams, Jefferson and his fellow Republicans

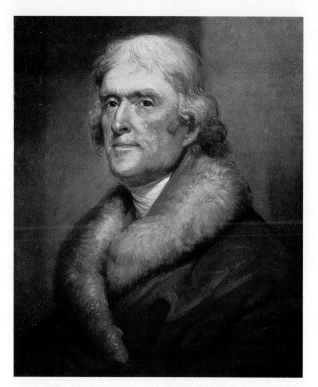

This portrait of President Thomas Jefferson was painted by Rembrandt Peale in 1805. Charles Willson Peale (Rembrandt's father) and his five sons helped establish the reputation of American art in the new nation. Rembrandt Peale was most famous for his presidential portraits; here he captured Jefferson in a noble pose without the usual symbols of office or power, befitting the Republican age.   New-York Historical Society.

preferred simplicity, wearing ordinary clothes instead of the aristocratic wigs and breeches (knee-length trousers) the first two presidents had favored.

Jefferson considered the United States "the world's best hope" and set the United States on a course to live up to that assessment. Although as president he cut federal operations, he and his Republican successors (James Madison and James Monroe) invigorated the federal government over the next two decades. He did not hesitate to use federal power, even when questionable, as in the purchase of Louisiana. Although he stressed the importance of domestic issues, during his term of office foreign crises, in particular, strengthened federal institutions.

The election campaign of 1800 had been so bitter that Jefferson in his inaugural address sought unity by declaring, "We are all Republicans, we are all Federalists." Still, the Federalists and Republi-

cans continued to distrust each other. John Adams, the outgoing president, and Jefferson had once been close friends but now disliked each other intensely. Both were thin-skinned and not only quick to take offense but also quick to give it. On inaugural day Adams had left Washington before dawn to avoid the Republican takeover. Republicans considered Federalists antidemocratic. Federalists accused Republicans of favoring egalitarianism, which they believed had recently led to anarchy in France. By doing away with Federalist social pomp and excessive government, Jefferson intended to restore the simplicity and civic virtue that had fueled the American Revolution.

Jefferson aggressively extended the Republicans' grasp on the national government. Virtually all of the six hundred or so officials appointed during the administrations of Washington and Adams were loyal Federalists; only six were known Republicans. To bring into his administration men who shared his vision of an agrarian republic and individual liberty, Jefferson refused to recognize appointments that Adams had made in the last days of his presidency, and he dismissed Federalist customs collectors from New England ports and awarded vacant treasury and judicial offices to Republicans. By July 1803 Federalists still held only 130 of 316 presidentially controlled offices. Jefferson adroitly used patronage to build a party organization, compete with the Federalists, and restore political balance in government.

Republican Appointments

The Republican Congress proceeded to affirm its belief in limited government. Albert Gallatin, secretary of the treasury, and John Randolph of Virginia, Jefferson's ally in the House of Representatives, translated ideology into policy, putting the federal government on a diet. Congress repealed all internal taxes, including the whiskey tax. Gallatin cut the army budget in half and reduced the 1802 navy budget by two-thirds. Gallatin moved to reduce the national debt—which Alexander Hamilton viewed as the engine of economic growth—from $83 million to $57 million, as part of a plan to retire it altogether by 1817. Jefferson even closed two of the nation's five diplomatic missions abroad—at The Hague and Berlin—to save money.

More than frugality, however, distinguished Republicans from Federalists. Before Jefferson's election, opposition to the Alien and Sedition Acts of 1798 had helped unite Republicans (see page

215). Jefferson now declined to use the acts against his opponents (as President Adams had done in suppressing Republican editors) and pardoned those who had been convicted under the acts. Congress let expire the Sedition Act in 1801 and the Alien Act in 1802. Congress also repealed the Naturalization Act of 1798, which had required fourteen years of residency for citizenship. The 1802 act that replaced it required only five years of residency, loyalty to the Constitution, and the forsaking of foreign allegiance and titles. It also, however, continued provisions for the registration of aliens. The new act, which made it easier to become a citizen, would remain the basis of naturalized American citizenship into the twentieth century.

The Republicans turned next to the judiciary, the last stronghold of Federalist power. During the 1790s not a single Republican had occupied the federal bench. The Judiciary Act of 1801, passed in the final days of the Adams administration, created fifteen new judgeships, which Adams filled by signing midnight appointments until his term was just hours away from expiring. The act also reduced by attrition the number of justices on the Supreme Court from six to five. Since that reduction would have denied Jefferson a Supreme Court appointment until two vacancies had occurred, the new Republican-dominated Congress repealed the 1801 act.

The Republicans also targeted opposition judges for removal. Federalist judges had refused to review the Sedition Act under which Federalists had prosecuted critics of the Adams administration. At Jefferson's prompting, the House impeached (indicted) Federal District Judge John Pickering of New Hampshire, an emotionally disturbed alcoholic, and in 1804 the Senate removed him from office. The Republicans were moving against the partisan Federalist judiciary.

Attacks on the Judiciary

The day Pickering was convicted, the House impeached Supreme Court Justice Samuel Chase for judicial misconduct. A staunch Federalist, Chase had led in pressing for convictions under the Sedition Act and repeatedly had denounced Jefferson's administration from the bench. The Republicans, however, failed to muster the two-thirds majority of senators necessary to convict him. Their failure to remove Chase preserved the Court's independence and established the precedent that criminal actions, not political disagreements, were the only proper grounds for impeachment. Time soon cured the Re-

publicans' grievances; in his tenure as president, Jefferson appointed three new Supreme Court justices. Nonetheless, the Court remained a Federalist stronghold under Chief Justice of the United States John Marshall.

Marshall, a Virginia Federalist, was an astute lawyer with keen political sense. He had served as minister to France and then secretary of state under Adams before being named to the Supreme Court. Though an autocrat by nature, Marshall possessed a grace and openness of manner that complemented the new Republican political style. Charles de Saint-Memin's portrait of Marshall in 1801 captured both his autocratic bearing and his direct manner. Under Marshall's domination, however, the Supreme Court retained a Federalist outlook even after Republican justices achieved a majority in 1811. Throughout his tenure (from

John Marshall

John Marshall (1755–1835) was Chief Justice of the United States from 1801 to 1835. He posed for this portrait by the French artist Charles Balthazar Julien Fevret de Saint-Memin in 1801, the year he joined the Court. The artist captured the power and strength with which Marshall would dominate the Court. Duke University Archives.

1801 until 1835), the Court consistently upheld federal supremacy over the states and protected the interests of commerce and capital.

Marshall made the Court an equal branch of government in practice as well as theory. Service on the Court became a coveted honor for ambitious and talented men. Marshall unified the Court, influencing the justices to issue joint majority opinions rather than a host of individual concurring judgments. Marshall himself became the voice of the majority: from 1801 through 1805 he wrote twenty-four of the Court's twenty-six decisions; through 1810 he wrote 85 percent of the Court's opinions, including every important decision.

Marshall also increased the Court's power, notably in the landmark case *Marbury* v. *Madison* (1803). William Marbury, one of Adams's midnight appointees, had been named a justice of the peace in the District of Columbia. James Madison, Jefferson's new secretary of state, declined to certify Marbury's appointment so that the president could appoint a Republican. Marbury sued, requesting a writ of mandamus (a court order forcing the president to appoint him). The case presented a political dilemma. If the Supreme Court ruled in favor of Marbury and issued a writ of mandamus, the president probably would not comply with it, and the Supreme Court had no way to force him to do so. But if the Federalist-dominated Court refused to issue the writ, it would be handing the Republicans a victory.

**Marbury
v. Madison**

Marshall avoided both pitfalls. Speaking for the Court, he ruled that Marbury had a right to his appointment but that the Court could not compel Madison to honor the appointment because the Constitution did not grant the Court power to issue a writ of mandamus. In the absence of any specific mention in the Constitution, Marshall ruled, the section of the Judiciary Act of 1789 that authorized the Court to issue such writs was unconstitutional. In *Marbury* v. *Madison*, the Supreme Court denied itself the power to issue writs of mandamus but established its great power to judge the constitutionality of laws passed by Congress.

In succeeding years Marshall fashioned the theory of *judicial review*, the power of the Court to decide the constitutionality of legislation. Since the Constitution was the supreme law, he reasoned, any federal or state act contrary to the Constitution must be null and void. The Supreme Court, whose duty it was to uphold the law, would decide whether or not a legislative act contradicted the Constitution. The power of judicial review established with *Marbury* v. *Madison* permanently enhanced the independence of the judiciary.

While Marshall was enlarging the power of the Court, President Jefferson had his eye on enlarging the borders of the nation. Jefferson shared with other Americans the belief that the United States was destined to expand its "empire of liberty." But there were four obstacles: the French in New Orleans and in the Louisiana Territory; the Spanish in Florida and Mexico; the British in Canada; and Native Americans throughout the continent. The obstacle posed by the French in New Orleans and Louisiana was the first to be overcome.

Since American independence, Louisiana had held a special place in the young nation's expansionist dreams. Louisiana defined the western border of the United States along the Mississippi from the Gulf of Mexico to present-day Minnesota. Spain had acquired the Louisiana Territory from France in 1763, at the end of the Seven Years War (see page 125). By 1800 hundreds of thousands of Americans in search of land had settled in the rich Mississippi and Ohio valleys, intruding on tribal lands. These settlers floated their farm goods down the Mississippi and Ohio Rivers to New Orleans for export. Whoever controlled the port of New Orleans thus had a hand on the throat of the American economy. Americans preferred Spanish control of Louisiana to control by France, a much stronger power.

**Louisiana
Purchase**

Rumors of the transfer of Louisiana back to France proved true in 1802. France had acquired the territory in secret pacts with Spain in 1800 and 1801, but the United States learned of the transfer only in 1802, when Napoleon threatened to rebuild a French empire in the New World. "Every eye in the United States is now focused on the affairs of Louisiana," Jefferson wrote to Robert R. Livingston, the American minister in Paris. American concerns intensified in October 1802 when Spanish officials, on the eve of ceding control to the French, violated Pinckney's Treaty (see page 211) by denying Americans the privilege of storing their products at New Orleans prior to transshipment to foreign markets. "The Mississippi," Secretary of State James Madison wrote, "is to them everything. It is the Hudson, the

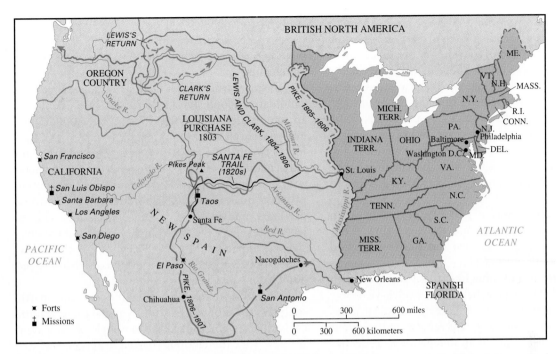

Louisiana Purchase   *The Louisiana Purchase (1803) doubled the area of the United States and opened the trans-Mississippi West for American settlement.*

Delaware, the Potomac and all navigable rivers of the Atlantic States formed into one stream." Western farmers and eastern merchants thought a devious Napoleon had closed the port; they grumbled and talked war.

To relieve the pressure for war and to win western farm support, Jefferson prepared for war while sending James Monroe to join Robert Livingston in France to try to buy the port of New Orleans. Meanwhile, Congress authorized the call-up of eighty thousand militiamen in case war became necessary. Arriving in Paris in April, Monroe was astonished to learn that France already had offered to sell all 827,000 square miles of Louisiana to the United States for a mere $15 million. On April 30 Monroe and Livingston signed the Louisiana treaty to purchase the vast territory, whose borders were undefined and whose land was uncharted (see map).

At one stroke of a pen, the Louisiana Purchase doubled the size of the nation and opened the way for continental expansion. It was also the most popular achievement of Jefferson's presidency. But for Jefferson, the purchase presented a dilemma. It promised fulfillment of his dream of a continental nation reaching to the Pacific, "with room enough for our descendants to the hundredth and thousandth generation." It provided a means to resolve Indian-settler conflict in the West by making available land to which eastern tribes could be forcibly removed. But was it legal?

The Constitution did not authorize the president to acquire new territory and incorporate it into the nation. Jefferson considered proposing a constitutional amendment to allow the purchase but decided not to. His justification for authorizing the purchase was that he was exercising the president's implied powers to protect the nation. The people signaled their approval of Jefferson's decision on election day in 1804.

Americans eager to expand the nation sought information and routes westward. Lieutenant Zebulon Pike followed Lewis and Clark in 1805 and 1806 in

Exploration of the West

search of the source of the Mississippi and a navigable water route to the Far West. The vast lands were not uninhabited, as Lewis and Clark had demonstrated. When Pike and his men wandered into

Spanish territory to the south, the Spanish held them captive for several months in Mexico. After his release, Pike wrote an account of his experiences that set commercial minds spinning. He described a potential commercial market in southwestern Spanish cities as well as bountiful furs and precious minerals. Over the next few decades, as Americans avidly read accounts of western exploration, expansion seized their imagination. The vision of a road to the Southwest became a reality with the opening of the Santa Fe Trail in the 1820s, and settlement followed the trail.

Tejas—Texas—was a buffer province between Spain's Mexican colonies and the Louisiana Territory. Texas officials welcomed Americans interested in the land south of Louisiana. American immigrants began to drift in, and some fought as volunteers with Indians and Mexican rebels in a twelve-year war with Spain that ended in 1821 with Mexican independence. The establishment of an independent Mexico stirred dreams of an independent Texas nation. Many Americans, however, were suspicious of all Mexicans. They did not want to include Mexicans—a mix of European, Indian, and African peoples—in the "empire of liberty."

Republicans Versus Federalists

Prior to the Republican victory in 1800, most Federalists had disdained popular campaigning. They believed in government by the "best" people—those whose education, wealth, and experience qualified them to be leaders. For candidates to debate their own merits in front of their inferiors—the voters— was believed to be demeaning. The direct appeals of the Republicans struck the Federalists as a subversion of the natural political order.

After the resounding Federalist defeat in 1800, however, a younger generation of Federalists began to imitate the Republicans. Led by men like Josiah Quincy, a Massachusetts congressman, the Younger Federalists campaigned for popular support. Quincy cleverly presented the Federalists as the people's party, attacking Republicans as autocratic planters. "Jeffersonian Democracy," Quincy gibed in 1804, was "an Indian word, signifying '*a great tobacco planter who had herds of black slaves.*'" In attacking frugal government, the Younger Federalists played on fears of a weakened army and navy. Eastern

Political Campaigning

merchants depended on a strong navy to protect ocean trade; westerners looked to the army for support as they encroached on the territory of Native Americans.

In states where both factions organized and ran candidates, people became more involved in politics. In some states about 90 percent of the eligible voters—nearly all of whom were white males—cast ballots between 1804 and 1816. As popular interest and participation in elections increased, states expanded suffrage. But the popular base remained restricted: property qualifications for voting and holding office persisted, and in six states the legislatures still selected presidential electors in 1804. Fearing the divisiveness of partisanship, even Republicans restrained their organizational efforts, and most leaders shied away from cohesive political movements.

Yet political competition and a vigorous, partisan press prompted grassroots campaigning. Political barbecues symbolized the new style of campaign. In New York the factions roasted oxen; on the New England coast they baked clams; in Maryland they served oysters. Guests washed down their meals with beer and punch and sometimes competed in corn shuckings or horse pulls. Voters displayed their allegiance by attending these events and displaying images of their party leaders, such as the portrait of Jefferson on a snuff box. Oratory was a popular form of entertainment, and candidates delivered lengthy and uninhibited speeches at barbecues. They often made wild accusations, which—given the slow speed of communications—might go unanswered until after the election.

Both factions held political barbecues, but the Federalists never fully mastered the art of wooing voters. Older Federalists still opposed blatant campaigning. And though strong in Connecticut, Delaware, and a few other states, the Federalists never offered the Republicans sustained competition. Divisions among Federalists often undermined their success, and the extremism of some Older Federalists discredited them all. A case in point was Timothy Pickering, a Massachusetts congressman and former secretary of state. Pickering opposed the Louisiana Purchase, feared Jefferson's reelection, and urged the secession of New England in 1803 and 1804. He won some support, but most Federalists opposed his plan for secession. Ever the opportunist, Vice President Aaron Burr flirted with Pickering, fantasizing about leading New York into secession, with other states following. But when Burr lost his bid to become governor of New York in 1804, his

How do historians know that popular interest in elections was increasing early in the nineteenth century? Election data are not available, but paintings like John Lewis Krimmel's Election Day in Philadelphia *(1815) convey that interest. Only white males could vote at the time, and the crowd is composed mostly of white men, although at least one African-American and some women and children are present. The artist depicts a festive occasion. Citizens riding on a float in the background carry their own flag; they have created a parade. A holiday spirit seems to prevail as men cluster in groups talking, arguing, sharing jokes, and generally appearing to have a good time. Perhaps there is a hint of overindulgence as well. The man sitting in front of an overturned chair (left foreground), with his hat on the ground behind him,* seems to have fallen, perhaps from too much drink—a common affliction in the party atmosphere of election day. Among the spectators are two women (center foreground), one of whom is holding the hand of a little girl. They suggest a restraining force on the raucous scene. The woman dressed in white and her friend offer a common female image of the time: the woman as an emblem of republican virtue. The space between the female and male figures suggests that the women stand apart not only as nonvoters but also as symbols of virtue and seriousness absent in the male world. Overall, the painting depicts a popular event, mixing a party atmosphere with civic duty. From a sober exercise of democratic responsibility, voting had become a popular, festive occasion.   Photo: Winterthur Museum.

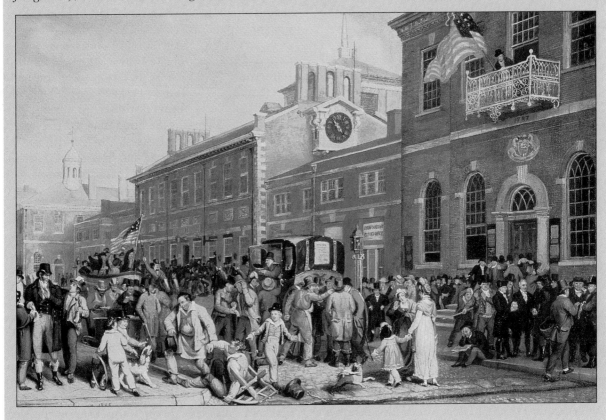

and Pickering's dream of a northern confederacy evaporated.

The controversies surrounding Burr highlight some of the shortcomings of the emerging political system. Personal animosities were as strong a force as ideology, and temporary factions flourished. Moreover, although politicians courted voters and participation in politics broadened, the electoral base remained narrow. The election of 1804 showed the Federalists could offer only weak competition at

Voters expressed their party loyalty by displaying portraits of party leaders, as in this Thomas Jefferson commemorative pitcher. It also shows the extent of grass-roots involvement in presidential politics.   Collection of David J. and Janet L. Frent.

the national level. And where Federalists were too weak to pose a threat, Republicans fought among themselves.

Both Republicans and Federalists suffered from divisiveness and personal animosities. The charismatic and ambitious Aaron Burr and Alexander Hamilton, for instance, had long despised each other. Hamilton always seemed to block Burr's path. He thwarted Burr's attempt to steal the election of 1800 from Jefferson, and in the 1804 New York gubernatorial race Burr lost to a rival Republican faction backed by the Federalist Hamilton. Burr turned his resentment on Hamilton, who had charged that he was too dangerous and unfit to hold office, and challenged Hamilton to a duel. His honor at stake, Hamilton accepted Burr's challenge, though he found dueling repugnant. Because New York had outlawed dueling, the two men met across the Hudson River at Weehawken, New Jersey. Hamilton did not fire and paid for that decision with his life. But in killing Hamilton, Burr only added to his dishonor in the public's

Hamilton-Burr Duel

eyes. He was indicted for murder in New York and New Jersey and faced immediate arrest if he returned to either state.

His political career in ruins, Burr plotted to create in the Southwest a new empire carved out of the Louisiana Territory. With the collusion of General James Wilkinson, the United States commander in the Mississippi valley, Burr planned to raise a private army to grab land from the United States or from Spain (his exact plans remain uncertain). Wilkinson switched sides and informed President Jefferson of Burr's intention. Jefferson personally assisted the prosecution in Burr's 1807 trial for treason, over which Chief Justice Marshall presided. The jury acquitted Burr, who fled to Europe to avoid further prosecution.

Campaigning for reelection in 1804, Jefferson claimed credit for western expansion and the restoration of republican values. He considered the acquisition of Louisiana among his greatest presidential accomplishments. Jefferson and the Republicans bragged of ending the Federalist threat to liberty by repealing the Alien and Sedition and Judiciary Acts. They also had reduced the size of government by cutting spending. Despite his opponents' charges, Jefferson had demonstrated that Republicans supported commerce and promoted free trade. American trade with Europe was flourishing. Unwisely, Federalists who earlier had criticized Jefferson for not seizing Louisiana now attacked the president for paying too much for it and for exceeding his powers in buying it.

Jefferson's Reelection

Jefferson's opponent was Charles Cotesworth Pinckney, a wealthy South Carolina lawyer and former Revolutionary War aide to George Washington. As Adams's vice-presidential running mate in 1800, Pinckney had inherited the Federalist leadership. Jefferson dumped the disloyal and unreliable Aaron Burr from the 1804 ticket, and he and his running mate, George Clinton of New York, swamped Pinckney and New Yorker Rufus King in the electoral college by 162 votes to 14, carrying fifteen of the seventeen states.

Jefferson's reelection was both a personal and an organizational triumph. The political dissenters of the 1790s had fashioned the Democratic-Republican societies into successful political organizations. More than anything else, opposition to the Federalists had given them cohesion. Indeed, in areas where the Federalists were strongest—in commercial New York and Pennsylvania in the 1790s and in New England in the 1800s—the Republicans had organized most effectively.

Although this period is commonly called the era of the first party system, parties as such were not fully developed. Competition at the polls encouraged rudimentary party organization, but personal ambition, personality clashes, and local, state, and regional loyalties undermined it. Increasingly, too, external events overpowered party ties.

 ## Preserving American Neutrality in a World at War

"Peace, commerce, and honest friendship with all nations, entangling alliance with none," President Jefferson had proclaimed in his first inaugural address. Jefferson's efforts to stand aloof from European conflict were successful until 1805. Thereafter, the pursuit of peace and undisturbed commerce occupied nearly his entire second administration, but they proved elusive goals.

After the Senate ratified Jay's Treaty in 1795 (see page 210), the United States and Great Britain appeared to reconcile their differences. Britain withdrew from its western forts and interfered less in American trade with France. Increased trade helped: the United States became Britain's best customer, and the British Empire in turn bought the bulk of American exports.

But in May 1803, two weeks after Napoleon sold Louisiana to the United States, renewal of the Napoleonic wars between France and Britain (and Britain's continental allies, Prussia, Austria, and Russia) again trapped the United States between Britain and France on the high seas. For two years American commerce benefited from the conflict. As the world's largest neutral carrier, the United States became the chief supplier of food to Europe. American merchants also gained control of most of the West Indian trade.

Meanwhile, United States victory in the Tripoli War on the north coast of Africa (against the Barbary states) provided Jefferson with his one clear success in protecting American trading rights. In 1801 the sultan of Tripoli had demanded payment not to prey on American vessels and sailors in the Mediterranean. Jefferson refused to pay and instead sent a naval squadron to protect American merchant ships from the Barbary pirates. In 1803–1804, under Lieutenant Stephen Decatur, the navy blockaded Tripoli

harbor while marines marched overland from Egypt to seize the port of Derna. The United States ransomed its hostages and signed a peace treaty with Tripoli in 1805 but continued to pay tribute to other Barbary states until 1815. That year the navy, again under Decatur, forced Algiers and Tunis to renounce attacks against Americans. The Tripoli War and its aftermath made clear that the United States would protect its commerce anywhere, and it helped make the Mediterranean safe for commerce again.

American merchants grew increasingly concerned about Anglo-French interference with trade. In October 1805 Britain tightened its control of the high seas by defeating the French and Spanish fleets at the Battle of Trafalgar. Two months later Napoleon defeated the Russian and Austrian armies at Austerlitz. Stalemated, France and Britain launched a commercial war, blockading each other's trade. As a trading partner of both countries, the United States paid a high price.

Britain, whose navy was the world's largest, was suffering a severe shortage of sailors. Few men were enlisting, and those in service frequently deserted, demoralized by poor shipboard conditions. Some British subjects found work on United States merchant ships, where conditions were better. The Royal Navy resorted to stopping American ships and seizing British deserters, British-born naturalized American seamen, and other unlucky sailors suspected of being British. Perhaps six to eight thousand Americans were impressed (forcibly drafted) in this way between 1803 and 1812. Americans saw impressment as a direct assault on the independence of their new republic. The principle of "once a British subject, always a British subject" ignored United States citizenship and sovereignty. The alleged deserters—many of them American citizens—faced British court-martial.

Impressment of American Sailors

In February 1806 the Senate denounced British impressment as aggression and a violation of America's neutral rights. In protest, Congress passed the Non-Importation Act, prohibiting importation from Great Britain of cloth and metal articles. In November Jefferson suspended the act temporarily while William Pinckney, a Baltimore lawyer, joined James Monroe in London to negotiate a settlement. But the treaty Monroe and Pinckney carried home violated their instructions—it did not mention impressment—and Jefferson never submitted it to the Senate for ratification.

The United States merchant marine facilitated economic growth in the early republic. But protection of neutral shipping rights and impressment of American seamen by the British navy stirred conflict between the United States and Britain and helped bring about the War of 1812. Here George Ropes, Jr., depicts the launching of the merchant ship Fame *in 1802 at Salem, Massachusetts.*   Peabody Essex Museum.

Less than a year later, the *Chesapeake* affair exposed American military weakness and intensified the emotional impact of impressment on the public.

Chesapeake Affair

In June 1807 the forty-gun frigate U.S.S. *Chesapeake* left Norfolk, Virginia, on a mission to protect American ships in the Mediterranean. About 10 miles out, still inside American territorial waters, it met the fifty-gun British frigate *Leopard*. When the *Chesapeake* refused to be searched for deserters, the *Leopard* repeatedly fired its guns broadside into the American ship. Three Americans were killed and eighteen wounded, including the ship's captain. The British seized four deserters from the Royal Navy—three of them American citizens; one of them, Jenkin Ratford, was hanged. Damaged and humiliated, the *Chesapeake* returned to port.

Had the United States been better prepared militarily, the ensuing howl of public indignation might have brought about a declaration of war. But the United States was ill equipped to defend its neutral rights with force; it was no match for the British navy. With Congress in recess, Jefferson was able to avoid hostilities. In July, the president closed American waters to British warships to prevent similar incidents, and soon thereafter he increased military and naval expenditures. In December Jefferson again put economic pressure on Great Britain by invoking the Non-Importation Act, followed eight days later by a new restriction, the Embargo Act.

The Embargo Act was intended to avoid war. Jefferson thought of it as a short-term measure to prevent confrontation between American merchant vessels and British and French warships and to put pressure on France and England by denying them American products. The embargo forbade virtually all exports from the United States to any country. Foreign ships deliver-

Embargo Act

ing goods left American ports with empty holds. Smuggling blossomed overnight.

Few American policies were as well intentioned or as unpopular and unsuccessful as Jefferson's embargo. Although "peaceable coercion" was an enlightened concept in international affairs, some Republicans felt uneasy about interfering with trade. Federalists opposed the embargo vociferously. Some feared its impact abroad. "If England [were to] sink," Federalist vice-presidential candidate Rufus King said in 1808, "her fall will prove the grave of our liberties." Mercantile New England, the heart of Federalist opposition to Jefferson, felt the brunt of the resulting economic depression. Shipping collapsed as exports fell by 80 percent between 1807 and 1808. In the winter of 1808–1809, talk of secession spread through New England port cities.

Although general unemployment soared, some individuals benefited from the embargo. Merchants with ships abroad (thus not idled by the embargo) and merchants willing to risk the lax enforcement to trade illegally could garner enormous profits. United States manufacturers—the early textile mills, for instance—received a boost, since the domestic market became theirs exclusively.

Great Britain, meanwhile, was only mildly affected by the embargo. The British most severely hurt—West Indians and factory workers—had no voice in policy. English merchants actually gained because they took over the Atlantic carrying trade from the stalled American ships. And because of a successful British blockade of Europe, the embargo had little practical effect on the French. Indeed, it gave France an excuse to set privateers against American ships that had escaped the embargo. The French cynically claimed that such ships were British ships in disguise, because the embargo prevented American vessels from sailing.

In the election of 1808, the Republicans faced not only the Federalists but also dissatisfaction with the embargo and factional dissent. Although nine

Election of 1808

state legislatures passed resolutions urging Jefferson to run again, the president followed Washington's lead in renouncing a third term. He supported James Madison, his secretary of state, as the Republican standard-bearer. For the first time, however, the Republican nomination was contested. Madison won the endorsement of the Republican congressional caucus, but Virginia Republicans put forth James Monroe (who later withdrew), and some east-

ern Republicans supported Vice President George Clinton.

Charles Cotesworth Pinckney and Rufus King again headed the Federalist ticket, but with new vigor. The Younger Federalists, led by Harrison Gray Otis and other Bostonians, made the most of the widespread disaffection with Republican policy, especially the embargo. Although Pinckney received only 47 electoral votes to Madison's 122, the Federalists offered genuine competition. Pinckney carried all of New England except Vermont, and he won Delaware and some electoral votes in two other states. Federalists also gained seats in Congress and captured the New York state legislature. The Federalist future looked promising.

Under the pressure of domestic opposition, the embargo eventually collapsed. Jefferson felt the weight of his failure: "never did a prisoner, released from his chains," he wrote on leaving office, "feel such relief as I in shaking off the shackles of power." In his last days in office Jefferson had tried to lighten the burden through the Non-Intercourse Act of 1809. This act reopened trade with all nations except Britain and France, and it authorized the president to resume trade with Britain or France if either of them ceased to violate neutral rights.

Non-Intercourse Act

The new act solved only the problems created by the embargo; it did not prevent further British and French interference with American commerce. For one brief moment it appeared to work. In June 1809 President Madison reopened trade with England after the British minister to the United States assured him that Britain would repeal restrictions on American commerce. His Majesty's government in London, however, repudiated the minister's assurances, and Madison reverted to nonintercourse.

When the Non-Intercourse Act expired in 1810, Congress substituted a variant, Macon's Bill Number 2, that exchanged the proverbial stick for a carrot. The bill reopened trade with both Great Britain and France but provided that when either nation stopped violating American commercial rights, the president could suspend American commerce with the other. Madison, eager to avoid war, was tricked at his own game. When Napoleon accepted the offer, Madison declared nonintercourse with Great Britain in 1811. Napoleon, however, did not keep his word. The French continued to seize American ships, and nonintercourse failed a second time. But because the Royal Navy dominated the seas, Britain,

The Shawnee chiefs Prophet (left) and Tecumseh (right). The two brothers led a revival of traditional Shawnee culture and preached Native American federation against white encroachment. In the War of 1812 they allied themselves with the British, but Tecumseh's death at the Battle of the Thames (1813) and British indifference thereafter caused Native Americans' resistance and unity to collapse. Prophet: National Museum of American Art, Smithsonian Institution; Tecumseh: Field Museum of Natural History, FMNH Neg. #A93851.

not France, became the main target of American hostility.

Angry American leaders tended to blame even Indian resistance in the West on British agitation, ignoring the Native Americans' legitimate protests against treaty violations. In the early 1800s two Shawnee brothers, Prophet and Tecumseh, attempted to build a pan-Indian federation, taking advantage of Anglo-American friction. Prophet's early experiences typified the experiences of the Indians of the Old Northwest. Born in 1775, a few months after his father's death in battle, Prophet, called Lalawethika ("Noisemaker") as a young man, was expelled to Ohio along with other Shawnees under the 1795 Treaty of Greenville (see page 189), and he later moved to Indiana. Within the shrunken territory granted the Shawnees, game soon became scarce. Encroachment by whites and the periodic ravages of disease brought further misery, and, like many other

Shawnee Resistance

Native Americans, Lalawethika turned to whiskey. He also turned to traditional folk knowledge and remedies and in 1804 became a tribal medicine man. His medicine, however, could not stop the white man's diseases from ravaging his village.

Lalawethika emerged from his own battle with illness in 1805 as a new man, called Tenskwatawa ("the Open Door"), or "the Prophet." Claiming to have died and been resurrected, he traveled widely in the Ohio River valley as a religious leader, attacking the decline of moral values among Native Americans, warning of damnation for those who drank whiskey, condemning intertribal battles, and stressing harmony and respect for elders. He urged Indians to return to the old ways and abandon white customs: to hunt with bows and arrows, not guns; to stop wearing hats; and to refrain from eating bread and instead to cultivate corn and beans.

Prophet's message reassured the Shawnees, Potawatomis, and other western Indians who felt unsettled and threatened by non-Indians. Prophet won converts by performing miracles—he seemed to darken the sun by timing his invocations to coincide with a solar eclipse—and he used opposition to federal Indian policy to draw others into his camp. His message spread to southern tribes as well, and the federal government and white settlers became alarmed.

By 1808, Prophet and his older brother Tecumseh were talking less about spiritual renewal and more about resisting American aggression. Their refusal to leave lands claimed by the government was encouraged by the British, who looked to alliances with Native Americans after renewed Anglo-American hostilities followed the *Chesapeake* affair of 1807. In repudiating land cessions to the government under the Treaty of Fort Wayne (1809), Tecumseh told Indiana's governor William Henry Harrison at Vincennes in 1810 that "the only way to check and stop this evil is, for all the red men to unite in claiming a common and equal right in the land, as it was at first, and should be yet; for it . . . belongs to all, for the use of each. . . . No part has a right to sell, even to each other, much less to strangers."

The Prophet and Tecumseh

Tecumseh, a towering six-foot warrior and charismatic orator, soon overshadowed his brother as Shawnee leader; his message found greater reception among younger Indians. Warriors found Tecumseh's political visions more relevant than Prophet's spirituality in protecting themselves against the United States. Convinced that only an Indian federation could stop the advance of white settlement, Tecumseh sought to unify northern and southern Indians. He traveled widely, preaching Indian resistance. And he warned Harrison that Indians would resist white occupation of the 2.5 million acres on the Wabash River that they had ceded in the Treaty of Fort Wayne.

 ## The War of 1812

Conflict over Native American loyalties in the West and over impressment on the seas strained relations between Britain and the United States. Having exhausted all efforts to alter British policy, the United States in 1811 and early 1812 drifted toward war with Great Britain until Republican "War Hawks" elected to Congress in 1810 led the charge to war. Meanwhile, in June 1812, Britain reopened the seas to American shipping. Hard times had hit the British Isles: the Anglo-French conflict had blocked much of British commerce with the European continent, and exports to the United States had fallen 80 percent. But two days after the change in British policy, before word of it had crossed the Atlantic, Congress declared war.

The War of 1812, the nation's first general war, was the logical outcome of United States policy after the renewal of warfare in Europe in 1803.

The Vote for War

The grievances President Madison enumerated in his message to Congress on June 1, 1812, were old ones: impressment, interference with neutral commerce, and British alliances with the western tribes. What brought the United States to this point, however, were Republicans' resolve to defend American independence and honor and American expansionists' thirst for British Canada.

The war Congress was a partisan one. Much of the war fever came from the so-called War Hawks, land-hungry southerners and westerners, all Republicans, led by John C. Calhoun of South Carolina and first-term congressman and House Speaker Henry Clay of Kentucky. Westerners had increased their numbers in Congress following reapportionment after the 1810 census, and the enlarged delegation was concerned equally with national honor and expansion. Most representatives from the coastal states opposed war, because armed conflict with the great naval power would interrupt American shipping. On June 4, the House voted 79 to 49 for war; two weeks later the Senate voted 19 to 13 in favor. Republicans favored war by a vote of 98 to 23; Federalists opposed it 39 to 0. On June 19, President Madison signed the declaration of war.

Though unprepared for war in 1812, the United States could not avoid it. The United States had tried economic pressure but had failed to protect American ships and sailors. The United States Army and Navy and the state militias were not fully prepared to wage war against the British.

The war turned out to be mostly a series of scuffles and skirmishes. The military campaigns were poorly executed; full-scale battles were rare (see map, page 240). The Americans had the advantage of fighting close to home. The war's outcome affirmed the freedom won in the Revolutionary War and dealt a serious blow to Indian resistance to American expansion. It also stimulated American nationalism and self-confidence.

After six months of preparation, American forces were still not ready for war. The United

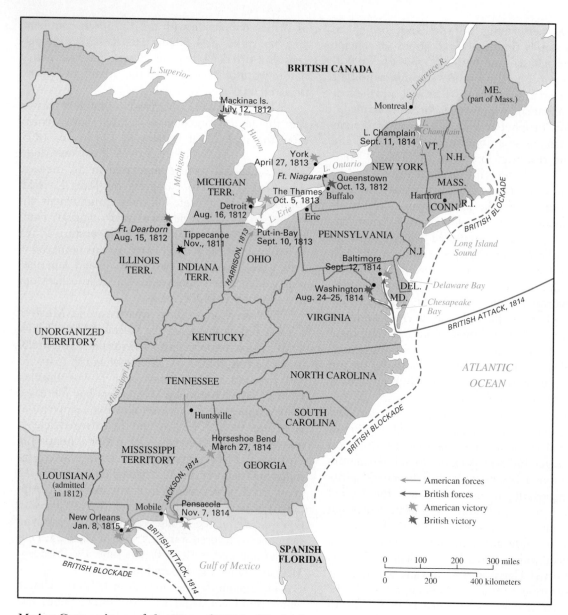

Major Campaigns of the War of 1812 *The land war centered on the American-Canadian border, the Chesapeake Bay, and the Louisiana and Mississippi Territories.*

States Navy had a corps of experienced officers who had proved their mettle in protecting American merchant ships from the Barbary pirates. But in comparison with the Royal Navy, the ruler of the seas, the American navy was minuscule. Jefferson's warning that "our constitution is a peace establishment—it is not calculated for war" proved true. The United States Army had neither an able staff nor an adequate force of enlisted men. By 1812 the United

Recruiting an Army

States Military Academy at West Point, founded in 1802, had produced only eighty-nine regular officers. The American army thus turned to political leaders and the state militias to recruit volunteers, and not all states cooperated. Much of the war effort, including planning, was decentralized. The government offered enlistees a sign-up bonus of $16, monthly pay of $5, a full set of clothes, and a promise of three months' pay and 160 acres of western land upon discharge. Forty-two percent of the enlistees were illiterate.

At first, recruitment in the West went well. Civic spirit, desire for land, and strong anti-Indian sentiment stimulated thousands of enlistments from the Old Northwest, Kentucky, Tennessee, and the southern frontier. The army made itself more acceptable to new recruits by abolishing flogging in 1812. Within a year, however, frontier enlistments were declining. Word spread that the War Department was often slow in meeting its payroll and supplying clothing.

In New England, raising an army proved even more difficult. Many viewed the conflict as a Republican war—"Mr. Madison's War"—and Federalists discouraged enlistments. Even some New England Republicans declined to raise volunteer companies. Those who accepted promised their men that they would serve only a defensive role, as in Maine where they guarded the coastline. Indeed, the inability of the United States to mount a successful invasion of Canada was due in part to the army's failure to assemble an effective force. State militias in New England and New York often declined to fight outside the borders of their own state.

Canada offered the United States the only readily available battlefront on which to confront Great Britain and conquer land. The mighty Royal Navy

Invasion of Canada

could not reach the Great Lakes separating the United States and Canada, because there was no river access to them from the Atlantic (see map, page 240). Canada, thousands of miles from British supply sources, was vulnerable to American attack.

Begun with high hopes, the invasion of Canada ended in disaster. The American strategy concentrated on the West, aiming to split Canadian forces and isolate the Indians who were supporting the British. Tecumseh joined the British when the war began in return for the promise of an Indian nation in the Great Lakes region. United States General William Hull, governor of the Michigan Territory, marched his troops into Upper Canada, near Detroit. More experienced as a politician than as a soldier, Hull had surrounded himself with newly minted colonels who were as politically astute and militarily ignorant as he was. Although his forces in the area were twice as large as those of the British and their Indian allies, Hull waged a timid campaign, retreating more than he attacked. His abandonment of Mackinac Island and Fort Dearborn in Chicago and his surrender of Fort Detroit left the entire Midwest exposed to the enemy. The only

bright spot was the September 1812 defense of Fort Harrison in Indiana Territory by Captain Zachary Taylor, who provided the Americans with their first land victory. By the winter of 1812–1813, the British controlled about half of the Old Northwest.

The United States had no greater success on the Niagara front, where New York borders Canada. At the Battle of Queenstown, in Canada north of Niagara, the United States Army met defeat because the New York militia refused to leave New York. This scenario was repeated near Lake Champlain, where American plans to attack Montréal were foiled when the New York militia again declined to cross the border into Canada. The American offensives in the North were probably doomed to fail anyway; the United States lacked the means to hold any part of Canada permanently.

The navy provided the only bright ray in the first year of the war: the U.S.S. *Constitution*, the U.S.S. *Wasp*, and the U.S.S. *United States* all bested British warships on the Atlantic. The *Constitution*'s rout of H.M.S. *Guerrière* in the Atlantic emboldened the United States Navy and earned the American ship the nickname "Old Ironsides." In victory, the Americans lost 20 percent of their ships. In defeat, however, the British lost just 1 percent of their naval strength. The British admiralty simply shifted its fleet away from the American ships, and by 1813 the Royal Navy again commanded the seas.

The Royal Navy blockaded the Chesapeake and Delaware Bays in December 1812, and by 1814 the blockade covered nearly all American ports along the Atlantic and Gulf coasts. Since 1811, American trade overseas had declined nearly 90 percent, and the decline in revenues from customs duties threatened to bankrupt the federal government.

The contest for control of the Great Lakes, the key to the war in the Northwest, was largely a shipbuilding race. Under Master Commandant Oliver

Great Lakes Campaign

Hazard Perry and shipbuilder Noah Brown, the United States outbuilt the British on Lake Erie and defeated them at the bloody Battle of Put-in-Bay on September 10, 1813. With this costly victory, the Americans gained control of Lake Erie.

General William Henry Harrison then began the march that proved to be among the United States's most successful moments in the war. The volunteers who constituted the majority of Harrison's command were a ragged group. Volunteers in the Kentucky militia, they had been drafted into the

In the first year of the War of 1812, only the United States Navy proved equal to British forces. In August 1812, the U.S.S. Constitution *defeated and sank* H.M.S. Guerrière *in the Atlantic 750 miles east of Boston. The* Guerrière *had long plagued American ships, and the victory was widely cheered in the states. Thomas Birch's painting* Constitution and the Guerrière *re-creates the fury of the encounter.*   United States Naval Academy Museum.

regular army and sent to fight in Upper Canada; they marched 20 to 30 miles a day to join Harrison's forces in Ohio, receiving no training and armed only with swords and knives.

Harrison's force of forty-five hundred men attacked and took Detroit and then entered Canada. They pursued the British, Shawnee, and Chippewa forces, defeating them on October 5 at the Battle of the Thames. This victory permitted the United States to retain control of the Old Northwest. Tecumseh died in the battle, and with his death expired Native American unity. After the Battle of the Thames, the Americans razed York (now Toronto), the Canadian capital. They looted and burned the Parliament building before withdrawing; they did not have enough troops to hold the city.

After defeating Napoleon in April 1814, the British stepped up the land campaign against the United States, concentrating on the Chesapeake Bay region. In retaliation for the burning of York—and

to divert American troops from Lake Champlain, where the British planned a new offensive—royal troops occupied Washington, D.C., in August and set it ablaze, leaving the presidential mansion scarred by fire. The attack on the capital, however, was only a diversion. The major battle occurred at Baltimore, where the Americans held firm. Francis Scott Key, witnessing the British fleet's bombardment of Fort McHenry in Baltimore harbor, was inspired to write the verses of "The Star-Spangled Banner" (which became the national anthem in 1931). Although the British inflicted heavy damage both materially and psychologically, they achieved little militarily. Equally unsuccessful was their offensive at Lake Champlain, where an American fleet turned back a British flotilla at Plattsburgh. The offensive was discontinued, and the war was essentially a stalemate.

The last campaigns of the war were waged in the South, along the Gulf of Mexico against the Creeks and against the British around New Orleans (see map, page 240). The Creeks—also known as the Red Sticks—had responded to Tecumseh and Prophet's calls to resist United States expansion. Some had died in Indiana Territory, at Prophetstown on Tippecanoe Creek, when General Harrison's troops routed Shawnee forces there in 1811. In December 1812 General Andrew Jackson raised his Tennessee militia to fight the Creeks. By late 1813 his anti-Creek campaign was stalled by lack of supplies, and his men, who had signed up for a year, were talking about going home. Jackson refused to discharge them; they could not, he said, leave their posts on enemy ground. Officers repeatedly threatened to shoot any man who left. In March 1814 Jackson executed John Woods, a militiaman, for disobedience and mutiny. This act broke the opposition within the ranks, and Jackson's men defeated the Creek nation at the Battle of Horseshoe Bend in Mississippi Territory in March 1814.

**Campaign
Against
the Creeks**

Andrew Jackson's defeat of the Creek nation began his rise to political prominence. In the August 1814 Treaty of Fort Jackson, the Creeks ceded two-thirds of their land and withdrew to the southern and western part of Mississippi Territory, in what is now Alabama; the removal of Indians from the South had begun. Jackson became a major general in the regular army and continued south toward the Gulf of Mexico. To forestall a British invasion at Pensacola Bay, which guarded an overland route to New Orleans, Jackson seized Pensacola—in Spanish Florida—in November 1814. Then, after securing Mobile, he marched on to New Orleans to defend it against the British.

The Battle of New Orleans was the last campaign of the war. Early in December the British fleet landed fifteen hundred men east of the city, hoping to control the Mississippi River and thus strangle the lifeline of the American West. They faced American regulars, Tennessee and Kentucky volunteers, and two

---
**Battle of
New Orleans**

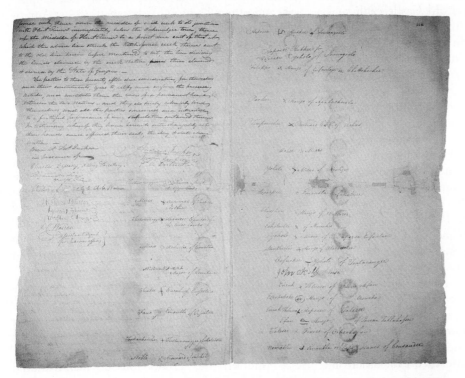

Andrew Jackson imposed the Treaty of Fort Jackson on the Creek nation, ending the campaign against the Red Sticks. The treaty required the Creeks to pay the costs of the war, which Jackson estimated at the equivalent of 20 million acres. In forcing the Creeks out of what is now central Alabama, Jackson initiated the Indians' forced removal from the South. Ironically, of the thirty-five chiefs who made their mark on the treaty, part of which is shown here, only one was a member of the Creek nation.   National Archives.

companies of free African-American volunteers from New Orleans. For three weeks the British under Sir Edward Pakenham and the Americans led by Jackson played cat-and-mouse. Finally, on January 8, 1815, the two forces met head-on. In fortified positions, Jackson's poorly trained army held its ground against two frontal assaults from a British contingent of six thousand. At day's end, more than two thousand British soldiers lay dead or wounded; the Americans suffered only twenty-one casualties. Andrew Jackson emerged a national hero, and the battle was memorialized in song and paintings. The Battle of New Orleans actually was fought two weeks after the end of the war. Unknown to the participants, a treaty had been signed in Ghent, Belgium, on December 24, 1814.

The United States government had gone to war reluctantly and throughout the conflict probed for a diplomatic end to hostilities. In 1813, President Madison eagerly accepted a Russian offer to mediate, but Great Britain balked. Three months later, British foreign minister Lord Castlereagh suggested opening peace talks. It took over ten months to arrange meetings, but in August 1814 a team of American negotiators, including John Quincy Adams and Henry Clay, began talks with the British in Ghent.

Treaty of Ghent

The Ghent treaty made no mention of the issues that had led to war. The United States received no satisfaction on impressment, blockades, or other maritime rights for neutrals. British demands for an independent Indian nation in the Northwest and territorial cessions from Maine to Minnesota were not satisfied. Essentially, the Treaty of Ghent restored the prewar status quo. It provided for an end to hostilities with the British and with Native Americans, release of prisoners, restoration of conquered territory, and arbitration of boundary disputes.

Why did the negotiators settle for so little? Events in Europe had made peace and the status quo acceptable at the end of 1814, as they had not been in 1812. Napoleon's fall from power allowed the United States to abandon its demands, since peace in Europe made impressment and interference with American commerce moot questions. Similarly, war-weary Britain—its treasury nearly depleted—stopped pressing for a military victory.

The War of 1812 affirmed the independence of the American republic. Nearly three hundred thousand troops had taken up arms to maintain

Consequences of the War of 1812

independence; almost two thousand died and four thousand were wounded. Although conflict with Great Britain continued, it never again led to war. The experience strengthened America's resolve to steer clear of European politics, for it had been the British-French conflict that had drawn the United States into war. For the rest of the century the United States would shun involvement in European political issues and wars.

The war had disastrous results for most Native Americans. Although they were not a party to the Treaty of Ghent, the ninth article of the treaty pledged the United States to end hostilities and to restore "all the possessions, rights, and privileges" that Indians had enjoyed before the war. More than a dozen treaties were signed with midwestern Indian leaders in 1815, but they had little meaning. With the death of Tecumseh, the Indians had lost their most powerful political and military leader; with the withdrawal of the British, they had lost their strongest ally. The Shawnees, Potawatomis, Chippewas, and others had lost the means to resist American expansion.

Domestically, the war exposed weaknesses in defense and transportation. American generals had found American roads inadequate to move troops and supplies. In the Northwest, General Harrison's troops had depended on homemade cartridges and gifts of clothing from Ohio residents; in Maine, troops had melted down spoons to make bullets. Improved transportation and a well-equipped army became national priorities; both were vital for westward expansion. In 1815, President Madison responded by centralizing control of the military and by building a line of forts for coastal defense, and Congress voted a standing army of ten thousand men—one-third of the army's wartime strength but three times the size of the army during Jefferson's administration. After the war, improved transportation would facilitate western settlement.

Perhaps most important of all, the war stimulated economic growth. The embargo, the Non-Importation and Non-Intercourse Acts, and the war itself spurred the production of manufactured goods: New England capitalists began to invest in home manufactures. The effects of these changes were to be far-reaching (see Chapter 10).

Finally, the war sealed the fate of the Federalists. Realizing that they could not win a presidential election in wartime, the Federalists joined renegade Republicans in supporting DeWitt Clinton of New York in 1812. This was the high point of Federalist organization at the state level, and the Younger Federalists campaigned hard. Clinton nevertheless lost to President Madison by 128 to 89 electoral votes; areas that favored the war (the South and West) remained solidly Republican. The Federalists gained some congressional seats and carried many local elections, but once again extremism undermined the Federalists.

During the war Federalists had revived talk of secession. With the war stalemated, delegates from New England states met in Hartford, Connecticut,

Hartford Convention

for three weeks in the winter of 1814–1815 to discuss revising the national compact or pulling out of the republic. Moderates prevented a resolution of secession, but convention members condemned the war and the embargo and endorsed radical changes in the Constitution. They wanted to restrict the presidency to one term and require a two-thirds congressional vote to admit new states to the Union. They proposed forbidding naturalized citizens from holding office. The proceedings were a fruitless attempt to preserve New England Federalist political power as electoral strength shifted to the South and West and immigrants became politically active.

The timing of the Hartford Convention proved lethal. The victory at New Orleans and news of the peace treaty made the convention, with its talk of secession and constitutional amendments, look ridiculous if not treasonous. Rather than harassing a beleaguered wartime administration, the Federalists found themselves in retreat before a rising tide of nationalism. Though Federalism survived in a handful of states until the 1820s, the Federalist faction began to dissolve. The War of 1812, at first a source of revival as opponents of war flocked to the Federalist banner, helped bring its demise.

Postwar Nationalism and Diplomacy

With peace came a new surge of American nationalism. Self-confident, the nation asserted itself at home and abroad as Republicans borrowed a page from Federalists' agenda and encouraged commerce and economic development. In his message to Congress in December 1815, President Madison embraced Federalist doctrine by recommending military expansion and a program of economic growth. Wartime experiences, he said, had demonstrated the need for a national bank (the charter of the first Bank of the United States had expired in 1811) and for better transportation. To raise government revenues and perpetuate the wartime growth of manufacturing, Madison called for a protective tariff—a tax on imported goods designed to protect American manufactures. Though he strayed from Jeffersonian Republicanism, Madison did so within limits. Only a constitutional amendment, he argued, could give the federal government the authority to build roads and canals that were less than national in scope.

The congressional leadership pushed Madison's nationalist program energetically in the belief that it would unify the country. Republican Congressman John C. Calhoun of South Car-

Nationalist Program

olina and Speaker of the House Henry Clay of Kentucky believed the tariff would stimulate industry. The agricultural South and West would sell cotton to the new mills and sell food to the millworkers. New roads would make possible the flow of produce and goods, and tariff revenues would provide the money to build them. A national bank would facilitate all these transactions.

The Republican Congress enacted much of the nationalist program. They chartered the Second Bank of the United States just five years after they had let the charter of the first Bank of the United States run out. The Republicans recognized that they needed a national bank to assist the government and to issue currency. The bank opened its doors in Philadelphia in 1817. The government provided $7 million of the initial $35 million in capital and appointed one-fifth of the directors.

Congress did not share Madison's scruples about the constitutionality of using federal funds to build local roads. "Let us, then, bind the republic together," Calhoun declared, "with a perfect system of roads and canals." Madison, however, vetoed Calhoun's internal-improvements bill, which would have funded mostly local roads, declaring it unconstitutional. Internal improvements, Madison insisted, were the province of the states and of private enterprise. He did, however, approve funds for the extension of the National Road, which began in western Maryland, to Ohio, on the grounds that the road was a military necessity.

To aid American industry, Congress passed the first substantial protective tariffs. The embargo and the war had stimulated domestic industry—especially the manufacture of cloth and iron—but resumption of overseas trade after the war revived competition from abroad. The Tariff of 1816 levied taxes on imported woolens and cottons and on iron, leather, hats, paper, and sugar, in effect raising their prices in the United States. Some New England congressmen viewed the tariff as interference in free trade, and southern congressmen (except Calhoun and a few others) opposed it because it would increase the prices that southern families paid for imported goods. But with support in the western and Middle Atlantic states, the tariff passed.

James Monroe, elected president in 1816, continued Madison's domestic program, supporting tariffs and vetoing internal improvements on constitutional grounds. Monroe was the third Virginian elected president between 1801 and 1825. A former senator, twice governor of Virginia, and an experienced diplomat, he had served under Madison as secretary of state and secretary of war. Monroe fulfilled his ambition to be president largely through perseverance and close association with Jefferson and Madison.

Even Madison's admirers admitted that, among the nation's founders, he was an ordinary and colorless man who rarely had an original idea. He rode into office on Republican coattails, easily defeating the last Federalist nominee, Rufus King, and sweeping all the states except the Federalist strongholds of Massachusetts, Connecticut, and Delaware. "Discord does not belong to our system," Monroe optimistically declared, calling the American people "one great family with a common interest." A Boston newspaper dubbed the one-party period the "Era of Good Feelings."

Led by Federalist chief justice John Marshall, the Supreme Court became the bulwark of a nationalist point of view. In *McCulloch* v. *Maryland* (1819),

McCulloch v. Maryland

the Court struck down a Maryland law taxing a branch of the federally chartered Second Bank of the United States. Maryland had imposed the tax in an effort to destroy the bank's Baltimore branch. The issue was thus one of state versus federal jurisdiction. Speaking for a unanimous Court, Marshall asserted the supremacy of the federal government over the states. "The Constitution and the laws thereof are supreme," he declared. "They control the constitution and laws of the respective states and cannot be controlled by them."

The Court went on to consider whether Congress could issue a bank charter. The Constitution did not spell out such power, but Marshall noted that Congress had the authority to pass "all laws which shall be necessary and proper for carrying into execution" the enumerated powers of the government. Echoing Alexander Hamilton's notion of implied powers, Marshall ruled that Congress could legally exercise "those great powers on which the welfare of the nation essentially depends." If the ends were legitimate and the means were not prohibited, Marshall ruled, a law was constitutional. The Constitution was, in Marshall's words, "intended to endure for ages to come, and consequently, to be adapted to the various causes of human affairs." The bank charter was declared legal.

McCulloch v. *Maryland* thus joined Federalist nationalism and Federalist economic views. By asserting federal supremacy, Marshall was protecting the commercial and industrial interests that favored a national bank; this was federalism in the tradition of Alexander Hamilton. The decision was only one in a series. In *Fletcher* v. *Peck* (1810), the Court had voided a Georgia law that violated individuals' rights to make contracts. In *Dartmouth College* v. *Woodward* (1819), the Court nullified a New Hampshire act altering the charter of Dartmouth College. Marshall ruled that the charter was a contract, and in protecting such contracts he thwarted state interference in commerce and business. *Gibbons* v. *Ogden* (1824) confirmed federal supremacy in interstate commerce.

Monroe's secretary of state, John Quincy Adams, matched the self-confident Marshall Court in assertiveness and nationalism. A small, austere

John Quincy Adams as Secretary of State

man once described by a British official as a "bulldog among spaniels," Adams, the son of John and Abigail Adams, was a superb diplomat who spoke six languages. From 1817 to 1825 he brilliantly managed the nation's foreign policy, stubbornly pushing for expansion, fishing rights for Americans in Atlantic waters, political distance from the Old World, and peace. An ardent expansionist, he nonetheless placed conditions on expansion, believing that it must come about through negotiations, not war, and that newly acquired territories must bar slavery. He urged restraint. The United States, Adams said in an 1821 Fourth of July speech, "goes not abroad, in search of monsters to destroy. She is the well-wisher to the freedom and independence of all."

An Anglophobe, Adams nonetheless worked to strengthen the peace with Great Britain. In 1817 the two nations agreed in the Rush-Bagot Treaty to limit their naval forces to one ship each on Lake Champlain and Lake Ontario and to two ships each on the four other Great lakes. This first disarmament treaty of modern times led to the demilitarization of the border between the United States and Canada.

Adams then pushed for the Convention of 1818, which fixed the United States–Canadian border from Lake of the Woods in Minnesota westward to the Rockies along the 49th parallel (see map, page 250). When agreement could not be reached on the territory west of the Rockies, Britain and the United States settled on joint occupation of Oregon for ten years (renewed indefinitely in 1827). Adams wanted to fix the border along the 49th parallel all the way to the Pacific Ocean, thereby gaining the important inland waterways of Juan de Fuca Strait and Puget Sound, and he hoped for a better negotiating position when the treaty lapsed.

Adams's next moved to settle long-term disputes with Spain. Although the 1803 Louisiana Purchase had omitted reference to Spanish-ruled West Florida, the United States claimed the territory as far east as the Perdido River (the present-day Florida-Alabama border) but occupied only a small finger of the area. During the War of 1812 the United States had seized Mobile and the remainder of West Florida. After the war Adams took advantage of Spain's preoccupation with domestic and colonial troubles to negotiate for the purchase of East Florida. During the talks, which took place in 1818, General Andrew Jackson took it on himself to occupy much of present-day Florida on the pretext of suppressing Seminole raids against American settlements across the border. Adams was furious with Jackson but defended his brazen act.

The following year, Don Luís de Onís, the Spanish minister to the United States, agreed to cede Florida to the United States without payment.

Adams-Onís Treaty

The Adams-Onís, or Transcontinental, Treaty also defined the southwestern boundary of the Louisiana Purchase, a jagged line across the West from Texas to the Pacific Ocean (see map, page 231). (Spain retained present-day Texas, New Mexico, and California.) In return, the United States government assumed $5 million worth of claims by American citizens against Spain and gave up its dubious claim

John Quincy Adams (1767–1848), architect of the Monroe Doctrine, was secretary of state from 1817 to 1825. Thomas Sully's portrait, painted in 1825, captured Adams's determination and stubbornness.   New York State, Office of Parks, Recreation, and Historic Preservation, Philipse Manor Hall State Historic Site.

to northern Mexico (Texas). Expansion was thus achieved at little cost and without war.

When the Spanish flag was last raised over St. Augustine on July 10, 1821, and at Pensacola on July 17, the residents of Florida differed in the welcome they gave to the United States and the American colonial governor, General Andrew Jackson. Some planter-slaveholders and traders were pleased to be living under the American flag, but Creeks and Seminoles, free blacks, runaway slaves who had escaped to Florida, smugglers who worked the coast, and Spanish-speaking town dwellers, were not pleased. General Jackson had led raids against the Seminoles in Florida in 1814 and 1818 and was feared by many. The last colonial Spanish governor, José María Coppinger, encouraged residents to resettle in Mexico, Cuba, or Texas. The Spanish urged the Seminoles to move to the Texas–United States border to discourage American penetration into

Texas. Most Florida residents stayed put but were wary of the United States.

Conflict between the United States and European nations was temporarily resolved by the Rush-Bagot Treaty, the Convention of 1818, and the Adams-Onís Treaty, but events to the south still threatened American interests. John Quincy Adams's desire to insulate the United States and the Western Hemisphere from European conflict brought about his greatest achievement: the Monroe Doctrine.

The immediate issue was the recognition of new governments in Latin America. Between 1808 and 1822, the United Provinces of the Río de la Plata (present-day northern Argentina, Paraguay, and Uruguay), Chile, Peru, Colombia, and Mexico all broke free from Spain. Mindful of the United States's own revolutionary tradition, many Americans favored recognizing their independence, but Monroe and Adams moved cautiously. They sought to avoid conflict with Spain and to be assured of the stability of the new regimes. Then in 1822, shortly after the Adams-Onís Treaty was signed and ratified, the United States became the first nation outside Latin America to recognize the new states, including Mexico.

Soon events in Europe again threatened the stability of the New World. Spain suffered a domestic revolt, and France, in an attempt to bolster the weak Spanish monarchy against the rebels, occupied Spain. The United States feared that France would return the new Latin American states to colonial rule. Great Britain, similarly distrustful of France, proposed a joint United States–British declaration against European intervention in the Western Hemisphere and a joint disavowal of territorial ambitions in the region. Adams rejected the British overture. In accordance with George Washington's admonition to avoid foreign entanglements, he insisted that the United States act independently.

Determined to avoid joint action with Great Britain, Adams would not budge. Those who favored joint action believed the United States needed British naval power to prevent French or Russian expansion in the New World. But Adams won. "It would be more candid, as well as more dignified," he argued, "to avow our principles explicitly to Russia and France, than to come in as a cockboat in the wake of the British man-of-war." Adams interpreted the British proposal to disavow territorial ambitions as a deliberate attempt by London to prevent further American expansion.

President Monroe presented the American position—the Monroe Doctrine—to Congress in December 1823. His message called for *noncolonization* of the Western Hemisphere by European nations, a principle that addressed American anxiety not only about Latin America but also about Russian expansion on the West Coast. (Russia held Alaska and had built settlements and forts as far south as California.) He also demanded *nonintervention* by Europe in the affairs of independent New World nations, and he pledged *noninterference* by the United States in European affairs, including those of Europe's existing New World colonies.

Monroe Doctrine

The Monroe Doctrine proved popular at home as an anti-British, anti-European assertion of American nationalism, and it eventually became the foundation of American policy in the Western Hemisphere. Monroe's words, however, carried no force. Indeed, the policy could not have succeeded without the support of the British, who already were committed to keeping other European nations out of the hemisphere to protect their dominance in the Atlantic trade. Europeans ignored the Monroe Doctrine; it was the Royal Navy they respected, not American policy.

The Panic of 1819 and Renewed Sectionalism

Monroe's domestic record did not match the diplomatic successes of his administration. In 1819, financial panic subverted postwar confidence and revived sectional loyalties. Neither panic nor the resurgence of sectionalism hurt Monroe politically; without a rival political party to rally opposition, he won a second term in 1820 unopposed.

But hard economic times spread. The postwar expansion has been built on easy credit; state banks had printed notes too freely, fueling speculative buying of western land. Speculators had bought acreage to sell at a profit rather than to farm. When manufacturing fell in 1818, prices spiraled downward. The Second Bank of the United States cut back on loans, thus further contracting the economy. Distressed urban workers became politically involved by demonstrating for easy credit and internal improvements. Farmers

Hard Times

clamored for lower tariffs on imported manufactured goods. Hurt by a sharp decline in the price of cotton, southern planters railed at the protective Tariff of 1816, which had raised prices on all imported goods. The Virginia Agricultural Society of Fredericksburg, for example, protested that the tariff violated the principles on which the nation had been founded. In a memorial to Congress in 1820, the society called the tariff an unequal tax that awarded exclusive privileges to manufacturers—"oppressive monopolies, which are ultimately to grind both us and our children after us 'into dust and ashes.'" Manufacturers, by contrast, demanded greater tariff protection and eventually got it in the Tariff of 1824.

Western farmers suffered, too. Those who had purchased public land on credit could not repay their loans. To avoid mass bankruptcy, Congress delayed the deadlines for repayment, and western state legislatures passed "stay laws" restricting mortgage foreclosures. Many westerners blamed the panic on the Second Bank of the United States for tightening the money supply. As state banks folded, westerners bitterly accused the Second Bank of saving itself while the nation went to ruin. Although the economy recovered in the mid-1820s, resentment of the bank contributed to the rise of the Jacksonian movement (see pages 358–361).

Far more divisive was the question of slavery. Ever since the drafting of the Constitution, political leaders had tried to avoid the issue. The one exception was an act ending the foreign slave trade after January 1, 1808, which passed without much opposition. The act followed the expiration of the constitutional ban (Article I, Section 9) on ending the slave trade before 1808. In 1819, however, slavery crept onto the political agenda when Missouri residents petitioned Congress for admission to the Union as a slave state. For the next two-and-a-half years the issue dominated all congressional action. "This momentous question," wrote Thomas Jefferson, fearful for the life of the Union, "like a fire bell in the night, awakened and filled me with terror."

The debate transcended slavery in Missouri. At stake were the compromises that had kept the issue under wraps since the Constitutional Convention. Five new states had joined the Union since 1812: Louisiana (1812), Indiana (1816), Mississippi (1817), Illinois (1818), and Alabama (1819). Of these, Louisiana, Mississippi, and Alabama permitted slav-

"Fire Bell in the Night"

ery. Because Missouri was on the same latitude as free Illinois, Indiana, and Ohio (a state since 1803), its admission as a slave state would thrust slavery farther northward. It would also tilt the uneasy political balance in the Senate toward the slave states. In 1819 the Union consisted of eleven slave and eleven free states. If Missouri joined, slave states would have a one-vote edge in the Senate.

The moral issues made slavery an explosive question. The settlers of Missouri were mostly Kentuckians and Tennesseeans who had grown up with slavery. But in the North slavery was slowly dying out, and many northerners had concluded that it was evil. When Representative James Tallmadge, Jr., of New York proposed gradual emancipation in Missouri, a passionate and sometimes violent debate ensued. Southerners accused the North of threatening to destroy the Union. "If you persist, the Union will be dissolved," Thomas W. Cobb of Georgia shouted at Tallmadge. "Seas of blood can only extinguish" the fire Tallmadge was starting, Cobb warned. "Let it come," retorted Tallmadge. The House, which had a northern majority, passed the Tallmadge amendment, but the Senate rejected it. The two sides were deadlocked.

A compromise emerged in 1820 under pressure from House Speaker Henry Clay: the admission of free Maine, carved out of Massachusetts, was linked with the admission of slave Missouri. In the rest of the Louisiana Territory north of latitude 36°30' (Missouri's southern boundary), slavery was prohibited forever (see map, page 250). The compromise carried, but the agreement almost came apart in November when Missouri submitted a constitution that barred free blacks from entering the state. Opponents contended that the proposed state constitution violated the federal Constitution's provision that "the citizens of each State shall be entitled to all privileges and immunities of citizens in the several States." Advocates argued that restrictions on free blacks were common in both North and South. In 1821, Clay produced a second compromise: Missouri guaranteed that none of its laws would discriminate against citizens of other states. (Once admitted to the Union, however, Missouri twice adopted laws banning free blacks.)

Missouri Compromise

Although political leaders succeeded in removing slavery from the congressional agenda, sectional issues undermined Republican unity and ended the

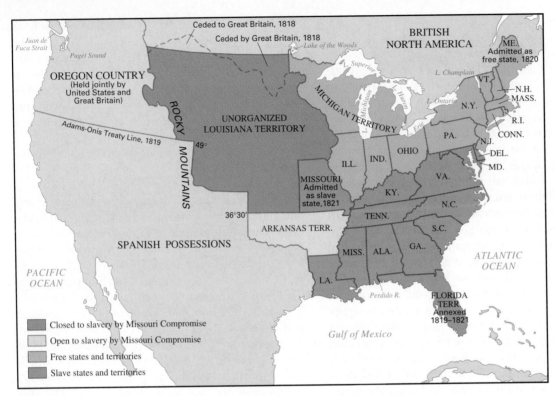

Missouri Compromise and the State of the Union, 1820 *The compromise worked out by House Speaker Henry Clay established a formula that avoided debate over whether new states would allow or prohibit slavery. In the process, it divided the United States into northern and southern regions.*

reign of the Virginia presidential dynasty. The Republican party came apart in 1824 as presidential candidates from different sections of the country scrambled for support. Sectionalism and the question of slavery ultimately would threaten the Union itself.

 **Conclusion**

The first decades of the nineteenth century were a time of self-definition and growth for the young republic. Political parties broadened white male involvement in politics and quieted factional divisions. A tradition of peaceful transition of power through presidential elections was established. And the United States expanded continuously, from the acquisition of Louisiana to the purchase of Florida.

The Revolution still cast a shadow over the new nation. Federalists harked back to British precedents. Republicans sought to maintain the ideals and virtues associated with the Revolution and the founding of a republic in which citizens would place

civic virtue above individual gain. A second war with Britain—the War of 1812—reaffirmed American independence and thwarted Indian opposition to United States expansion; thereafter the nation was able to settle most foreign disputes at the bargaining table.

The War of 1812 and diplomatic assertiveness brought a sense of national identity and self-confidence. Americans claimed victory, and after the war, all branches of the government, responding to the popular mood, pursued a vigorous national policy. The Supreme Court promoted national unity by extending federal power over the states and encouraging commerce and economic growth. In spite of Jefferson's vision of an agrarian society, the country was gradually shifting to a market economy in which people produced goods to sell to others (see Chapter 10). Embargo and war had promoted the manufacturing of goods in the United States, lessening dependence on imports from Europe. Developments in transportation further stimulated the economy and expansion. Under the guidance of John Quincy Adams, the United States pursued its interests through diplomacy, not direct intervention. The Monroe Doctrine was among his finest achievements.

Sectionalism accompanied nationalism and geographic expansion. War, tariffs, economic hard times, and slavery brought out sectional discord. While manufacturers and merchants in the North and agricultural producers in the West became linked through transportation and trade, the South was developing its own economy and culture based on cotton, export markets, a plantation system, and slavery (see Chapter 11). Politicians kept the question of slavery off the national agenda as long as possible and worked out the Missouri Compromise as a stopgap measure. But territorial acquisitions and further westward expansion in the 1840s and 1850s would collide with a rising tide of reform to make the question of slavery unavoidable (see Chapters 13 and 14).

Over the next two decades, the way Americans lived and worked changed at a quickening pace. The colonial and revolutionary generations were fading away. The deaths of John Adams and Thomas Jefferson within a few hours of each other on July 4, 1826—the fiftieth anniversary of the signing of the Declaration of Independence—symbolized that passing. As citizens mourned those political giants, they recognized that their future would be very different from the world of the founders. Economic development, rising population, the spread of settlement, and the growth of cities were transforming people, their lives, and their communities.

Suggestions for Further Reading

General

Henry Adams, *History of the United States of America During the Administration of Thomas Jefferson and of James Madison*, 9 vols. (1889–1891); Noble E. Cunningham, Jr., *The United States in 1800: Henry Adams Revisited* (1988); George Dangerfield, *The Awakening of American Nationalism, 1815–1828* (1965); George Dangerfield, *The Era of Good Feelings* (1952); Jean V. Matthews, *Toward a New Society: American Thought and Culture, 1800–1830* (1991); John Mayfield, *The New Nation, 1800–1845* (1981); Marshall Smelser, *The Democratic Republic, 1801–1815* (1968).

Party Politics

James M. Banner, *To the Hartford Convention: The Federalists and the Origins of Party Politics in the Early Republic, 1789–1815* (1967); Noble E. Cunningham, Jr., *The Jeffersonian Republicans in Power: Party Operations, 1801–1809* (1963); David Hackett Fischer, *The Revolution of American Conservatism: The Federalist Party in the Era*

of Jeffersonian Democracy (1965); Linda K. Kerber, *Federalists in Dissent* (1970); Shaw Livermore, *Twilight of Federalism: The Disintegration of the Federalist Party, 1815–1830* (1962); Milton Lomask, *Aaron Burr*, 2 vols. (1979, 1983); Richard P. McCormick, *The Presidential Game: The Origins of American Presidential Politics* (1982); Drew McCoy, *The Elusive Republic* (1980); Robert V. Remini, *Henry Clay: Statesman for the Union* (1991); James Sterling Young, *The Washington Community, 1800–1828* (1966).

The Virginia Presidents

Harry Ammon, *James Monroe: The Quest for National Identity* (1971); Noble E. Cunningham, Jr., *In Pursuit of Reason: The Life of Thomas Jefferson* (1987); Noble E. Cunningham, Jr., *The Process of Government Under Jefferson* (1978); Ralph Ketcham, *Presidents Above Party: The First American Presidency, 1789–1829* (1984); Drew R. McCoy, *The Last of the Fathers: James Madison and the Republican Legacy* (1989); Merrill D. Peterson, *Thomas Jefferson and the New Nation* (1970); Norman K. Risjord, *Thomas Jefferson* (1994); Robert Allen Rutland, *The Presidency of James Madison* (1990); Robert W. Tucker and David C. Hendrickson, *Empire of Liberty: The Statecraft of Thomas Jefferson* (1990).

The Supreme Court and the Law

Leonard Baker, *John Marshall: A Life in Law* (1974); Robert Lowry Clinton, *Marbury v. Madison and Judicial Review* (1989); Richard E. Ellis, *The Jeffersonian Crisis: Courts and Politics in the Young Republic* (1971); Morton J. Horowitz, *The Transformation of American Law, 1780–1860* (1977); R. Kent Newmyer, *The Supreme Court Under Marshall and Taney* (1968); Thomas C. Shevory, *John Marshall's Law: Interpretation, Ideology, and Interest* (1994); Francis N. Stites, *John Marshall: Defender of the Constitution* (1981).

Expansionism, the War of 1812, and Diplomacy

Roger H. Brown, *The Republic in Peril* (1964); Alexander De Conde, *This Affair of Louisiana* (1976); R. David Edmunds, *Tecumseh and the Quest for Indian Leadership* (1984); R. David Edmunds, *The Shawnee Prophet* (1983); Clifford L. Egan, *Neither Peace nor War: Franco-American Relations, 1803–1812* (1983); Kenneth J. Hagan, *This People's Navy* (1991); Donald R. Hickey, *The War of 1812* (1989); Bradford Perkins, *The Creation of a Republican Empire, 1776–1865* (1993); Julius W. Pratt, *Expansionists of 1812* (1925); James P. Ronda, *Lewis and Clark Among the Indians* (1984); Greg Russell, *John Quincy Adams and the Public Virtues of Diplomacy* (1995); J. C. A. Stagg, *Mr. Madison's War: Politics, Diplomacy, and Warfare in the Early Republic, 1783–1830* (1983); Anders Stephanson, *Manifest Destiny: American Expansionism and the Empire of Right* (1995); Steve Watts, *The Republic Reborn: War and the Making of a Liberal America, 1790–1820* (1987); David J. Weber, *The Spanish Frontier in North America* (1992).

The Monroe Doctrine

Samuel F. Bemis, *John Quincy Adams and the Foundations of American Foreign Policy* (1949); Walter LaFeber, ed., *John Quincy Adams and American Continental Empire* (1965); Ernest R. May, *The Making of the Monroe Doctrine* (1976); Dexter Perkins, *Hands Off: A History of the Monroe Doctrine* (1941).

THE OLD GRANITE STATE,

Judson.   Abby.   John.   Asa

A SONG,

Price 50 Ce

COMPOSED, ARRANGED AND SUNG, BY

THE HUTCHINSON FAMIL

CHAPTER

10

Rails, Markets, and Mills: The North and West 1800–1860

The Hutchinson family, also known as the Tribe of Jesse, was the most popular singing group in nineteenth-century America. Abby, Asa, Jesse, John, and Judson Hutchinson—five members of a family of sixteen children from rural New Hampshire—performed throughout the United States and across the Atlantic, singing the patriotic, religious, and sentimental songs that had dominated popular music since the Revolution. Twentieth-century commentators have compared them to Woody Guthrie, Chuck Berry, Bruce Springsteen, and even the Beatles for initiating new musical styles, for their popularity and energy as performers, and for writing their own socially aware lyrics.

The family members were accomplished entertainers. Unlike most groups that just sang, the Tribe of Jesse presented well-rehearsed and elaborately produced performances. They used traditional airs that the audiences knew and found comforting, but they wrote new lyrics exploring controversial social problems and reform, abolitionism, and temperance. For example, "'Get Off the Track!' represented the railroad with all its terrible enginery and speed and danger," according to a contemporary editor. When first performed in 1844, the song was too inflammatory for any publisher to print. The Hutchinsons sang it on stage, and the abolitionist press carried its lyrics until a publisher finally printed songsheets.

The Hutchinson Family celebrated their native rural New Hampshire in "The Old Granite State," their most popular song. They made a business of performing, and hawkers sold their sheet music at concerts. *Lynn Historical Society.*

Ho! the Car Emancipation
Rides majestic thro' our nation
Bearing on its Train, the story.
LIBERTY! a Nation's Glory.
  Roll it along, thro' the Nation
  Freedom's Car, Emancipation.

The song became one of the Hutchinsons' trademarks, rousing antislavery audiences.

The Hutchinson Family was part of a new phenomenon: singers, songwriters, musicians, publishers, and managers who made a business of music and entertainment. Drawing their largest audiences in the growing cities, they entered the commercial world and made a living from writing and performing music. The Hutchinson Family's fee for a single night in the 1840s reached $1,000. Each performance was planned and choreographed, and the group had an entourage of managers, agents, publishers, and concert-hall representatives. Hawkers sold sheet music, portraits, and songbooks at the Hutchinsons' concerts. A traditional rural pastime had become a big business.

The Hutchinsons' own lives, too, bridged the old and the new. Their roots were in the farm country of New Hampshire, the "Old Granite State" celebrated in their most popular song. But they left the farm to sing to millworkers, laborers, homemakers, and reformers in the industrial North.

Besides their musical talent, the Hutchinson Family seemed to offer their audiences reassurance in a time of rapid and thoroughgoing change. By setting their lyrics to traditional hymns, they connected change and reform with time-tested values. And by describing a bucolic future, they reassured their audiences that the present, with all its turmoil and change, would turn out well.

The Hutchinsons were able to tour the nation in concert because of advances in transportation and communications that linked the growing national economy between 1800 and 1860. The canal boat, steamboat, locomotive, and telegraph made possible a Hutchinson Family concert tour. But more enduringly, these technological advances opened up the frontier and helped expand farm production for markets at home and abroad. Ready-made men's garments manufactured in New York and Cincinnati could be purchased across the nation. Increasingly, farmers grew more crops for the internal market, and urban producers worked for wages. Improved transportation was the most tangible change, but equally significant was increased specialization in agriculture, manufacturing, and finance, which fostered a nationwide, capitalist, market-oriented economy.

This dramatic transformation began early in the century and spread nearly everywhere. In 1800 most of the 5.3 million Americans earned their living working the land or serving those who did. Settlements clustered on the East Coast, along the Ohio and Mississippi river valleys, along the Gulf Coast, across present-day Texas, and on the West Coast. By 1860, 31.4 million Americans had spread across the continent: some midwestern farms were 1,500 miles from the Atlantic, and settlement on the Pacific Slope was booming. A continental nation had been forged. Meanwhile, the economy, though still primarily agricultural, was being transformed by enormous commercial and manufacturing expansion.

Promotion of economic growth became the hallmark of the federal government, especially during the period of fervent nationalism after the War of 1812. The government encouraged individual enterprise by promoting an environment in which farming and industry could flourish. New financial institutions amassed the capital for large-scale enterprises like factories and railroads. Mechanization took hold; factories and precision-made machinery competed successfully with home workshops and handmade goods, and reapers and sowers revolutionized farming.

New tensions accompanied economic expansion, and not everyone profited in wealth and opportunity as the Hutchinson Family did. The experience of a journeyman tailor displaced by retailers and cheaper labor was far different than that of the new merchant princes. New England farm daughters who became wage workers found their world changing no less radically. Farmers everywhere experienced tensions between their traditional way of life and the opportunities and demands of market-oriented production. Moreover, boom-and-bust cycles became part of the fabric of ordinary life. And canals, railroads, and urban and industrial growth brought with them destruction of the environment. But whatever its benefits and drawbacks, economic development was irreversible.

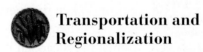

Transportation and Regionalization

The North, South, and West followed distinct economic paths between 1800 and 1860. Everywhere, agriculture remained the foundation of the American economy. Nevertheless, the North increasingly invested its resources in industry, commerce, and finance; the South in plantations and subsistence farms; and the West in commercialized family farms, agricultural processing, and implement manufactur-

• *Important Events* •

1790	First American textile mill, using water-powered spinning machines, opens in Pawtucket, Rhode Island	**1825**	Erie Canal completed
1807	Robert Fulton's steamboat, *Clermont*, makes its debut	**1830**	Baltimore and Ohio Railroad begins operation
		1831	McCormick invents the reaper
1812–15	War of 1812 stimulates domestic manufactures War of 1812 fought	**1834**	Women workers strike at Lowell textile mills
		1836	Second Bank of the United States closes
1813	New England capitalists found the Boston Manufacturing Company and build the first large-scale American factory	**1837**	*Charles River Bridge* v. *Warren Bridge* encourages new enterprises
		1839–43	Hard times strike again
1816	Tariff of 1816 introduces first substantial protective tariff Congress charters the Second Bank of the United States	**1844**	A government grant develops telegraph line between Baltimore and Washington
		1848	Regularly scheduled steamship passage begins between Liverpool and New York City
1818	National Road reaches Wheeling, Virginia, opening the West	**1849**	California gold rush transforms the West Coast
1819	*Dartmouth College* v. *Woodward* protects the sanctity of contracts	**1853**	British study of American system of manufacturing
1819–23	Hard times bring unemployment and business bankruptcies	**1854**	Railroad reaches the Mississippi River
1820s	New England textile mills expand	**1857**	Hard times mark end of third boom-or-bust cycle
1824	*Gibbons* v. *Ogden* affirms federal over state authority in interstate commerce		

ing. This tendency toward regional specialization made the various sections of the country at once less alike and more interdependent. All looked to transportation to link the various sections' economic activities.

The revolution in transportation and communications was probably the single overriding cause of these changes. Heavy investment in canals and railroads made the North the center of American commerce; its growing seaboard cities distributed western produce and New England textiles. New York financial and commercial houses linked the southern cotton-exporting economy to the North and Europe. The South, with most of its capital invested in slave labor, built fewer canals, railroads, and factories and remained mostly rural and undeveloped (see Chapter 11).

Before the 1820s and 1830s, it was by no means certain that New England and the Middle Atlantic states would dominate American finance and commerce. Indeed, the natural orientation of the 1800 frontier—Tennessee, Kentucky, and Ohio—was toward the South. The southward-flowing Ohio and Mississippi Rivers were the lifelines of early western settlement. Flatboats transported western grain and hogs southward for consumption or transfer to oceangoing vessels at New Orleans. Southern products—first tobacco, then lumber and cotton—flowed directly to Europe. Steamboats, successfully introduced in 1807 when Robert Fulton's *Clermont* paddled up the Hudson River from New York City, began in 1815 to carry cargo upstream on the Mississippi and Ohio Rivers, further reinforcing ties between the South and the West.

Change in Trade Routes

But this pattern changed in the 1820s when new arteries opened up east-west travel. The National

The town of Lockport, New York, owed its existence to the Erie Canal, and serving boats, freight, and passengers was its major industry. This view of the town was rendered in 1836, eleven years after the canal was opened.   Library of Congress, hand-colored by Sandi Rygiel, Picture Research Consultants, Inc.

Road—a stone-based, gravel-topped highway originating in Cumberland, Maryland—reached Wheeling, Virginia (now West Virginia), in 1818 and Columbus, Ohio, in 1833. (Today, highways U.S. 40 and I-70 follow the same route.) More important, the Erie Canal, completed in 1825, linked the Great Lakes with New York City and the Atlantic Ocean. The canal carried easterners and then immigrants to settle the Old Northwest and the frontier beyond; in the opposite direction, it transported western grain to the large and growing eastern markets. Railroads and later the telegraph would solidify these east-west links. By contrast, at only one place—Bowling Green, Kentucky—did northern and southern railroads connect with one another. Although trade still moved southward along the Ohio and Mississippi, the bulk of western trade flowed eastward by 1850. Thus by the eve of the Civil War, the northern and Middle Atlantic states were closely linked to the former frontier of the Old Northwest.

Construction of the 363-mile-long Erie Canal was a visionary enterprise. When the state of New York authorized it in 1817, the longest American canal was only 28 miles long.

Canals

Vigorously promoted by Governor DeWitt Clinton, the Erie cost $7 million, much of it in loans from British investors. The canal shortened the journey between Buffalo and New York City from twenty to six days and reduced freight charges from $100 to $5 a ton. By 1835, traffic was so heavy that the canal had to be widened from forty to seventy feet and deepened from four to seven feet. Skeptics who had called the canal "Clinton's big ditch" had long since fallen silent. The expanding midwestern population would lay the basis for Chicago to dominate the central region.

The success of the Erie Canal triggered an explosion of canal building. Sensing the advantage New York had gained, other states and cities rushed to follow suit. By 1840, canals crisscrossed the Northeast and Midwest, and total canal mileage reached 3,300—an increase of more than 2,000 miles in a single decade (see map, page 257). Unfortunately for investors, none of these canals enjoyed the financial success achieved by the Erie. As the high cost of construction combined with an economic contraction, investment in canals began to slump in the 1830s. By 1850 more miles were being abandoned than built, and the canal era had unmistakably ended.

Meanwhile, railroad construction boomed. The railroad era in the United States began in 1830 when Peter Cooper's locomotive Tom Thumb first steamed along 13 miles of track constructed by the Baltimore and Ohio Railroad. In 1833 the nation's second railroad ran 136 miles from Charleston to Hamburg in South Carolina. By 1850 the United States had nearly 9,000 miles of railroad; by 1860, roughly 31,000 (see map below and figure on page 258). Canal fever stimulated this early railroad construction. Promoters of the Baltimore and Ohio believed that railroads

Railroads

would compete successfully with canals. Similarly, the line between Boston and Worcester in Massachusetts was intended as the first link in a rail line to Albany, at the eastern end of the Erie Canal. In Providence, Rhode Island, and other port cities, the railroads extended to the water's edge.

The earliest railroads connected nearby cities; not until the 1850s did railroads offer long-distance service at reasonable rates. The early lines had technical problems to overcome. Locomotives heavy enough to climb steep grades and pull long trains required strong rails and resilient trackbeds. Engineers met those needs by replacing wooden tracks with iron rails and by supporting the rails with ties embedded in gravel. A new wheel alignment—the swivel truck—permitted heavy engines to hold the track on sharp curves. Other problems persisted: the use of hand brakes severely restricted speed, and

Major Railroads, Canals, and Roads in 1860 *Transportation networks linked port cities to the interior. These links were most dense in the populous Northeast and the Old Northwest.*

Railroad Mileage, 1830–1860

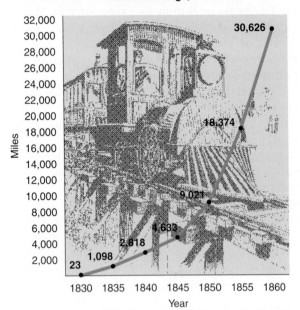

Railroad Mileage, 1830–1860 *In the 1850s, railroads developed a national rail network east of the Mississippi River.* Source: U.S. Bureau of the Census, *Historical Statistics of the United States, Colonial Times to 1970,* 2 parts (Washington, D.C., 1975), Part 2, p. 731.

the lack of a standard gauge for the width of track thwarted development of a national system. Pennsylvania and Ohio railroads, for instance, had no fewer than seven different track widths. A journey from Philadelphia to Charleston, South Carolina, involved eight different gauges, which meant that passengers had to change trains seven times.

In the 1850s technological improvements, competition, economic recovery, and a desire for national unity prompted development of regional and, eventually, national rail networks. By 1853 rail lines linked Chicago to eastern cities, and a year later track reached the Mississippi River. By 1860 rails stretched as far west as St. Joseph, Missouri. Short lines merged to create two unified systems, the New York Central and the Pennsylvania Railroad. Most lines, however, were still independently run. Differences in gauge, scheduling, car design, and a commitment to serve their hometowns first and foremost prevented cooperation and mergers.

Railroads were the most popular symbol of technological change. The Hutchinson Family capitalized on that image in "Get Off the Track!"; they dressed emancipation in railroad symbolism: all-out speed, unstoppable power, and energetic change.

Railroads did not completely replace water transportation. The federal government assisted water transportation by improving ports and clearing rivers for navigation. Shipping routes linked newer areas, like Texas and California, to the rest of the United States. At mid-century, steamships still carried bulk cargo more cheaply than railroads except during freezing weather. The sealike Great Lakes accommodated giant ships with propellers in place of paddlewheels; these leviathans carried heavy bulk cargoes like lumber, grain, and ore. On the high seas, steamships gradually replaced sailing vessels, which were dependent on prevailing winds and thus usually could not meet regular schedules. The biggest breakthrough occurred in 1848, when Samuel Cunard introduced regularly scheduled steamships between Liverpool and New York, reducing travel time across the Atlantic from twenty-five days eastbound and forty-nine days westbound to between ten and fourteen days each way. Sailing ships quickly lost first-class passengers and light cargo to steamships, although they continued to carry immigrants and bulk cargo. By 1860, only the freight trade remained to them.

Steamboats

By far the fastest-spreading technological advance of the era was the magnetic telegraph. Invented by artist Samuel F. B. Morse, the telegraph made it possible for distant messages to travel faster than any messenger could; instantaneous communication became possible even over long distances. By 1853, only nine years after construction of the first experimental telegraph line, 23,000 miles of telegraph wire had spread across the United States; by 1860, 50,000 miles were in use. In 1861 the telegraph bridged the continent, connecting the East, Gulf, and West Coasts, literally joining the nation together and ending the isolation of Texans and Californians. Rarely has an innovation had so great an impact so quickly: it revolutionized newsgathering, provided advance information for railroads, and altered patterns of business and finance.

Telegraph

Time was key to the revolutionary changes in transportation and communications that took place from 1800 to 1860. In 1800 it took four days to travel by coach from New York City to Baltimore and nearly four weeks to reach Detroit. By 1830 Baltimore was only a day-and-a-half away, and Detroit was only a two-week journey by way of the Erie Canal. By 1857 Detroit was an overnight train ride

In Providence, Rhode Island, locomotives replaced horses in transporting freight and people. In Atlantic ports and cities on navigable rivers, the rail lines extended to the water's edge to meet the steamers and sailing ships.   Museum of Art, Rhode Island School of Design.

from New York City, and in a week a traveler could reach Texas or western Missouri by rail. Reduced travel time not only saved money and facilitated commerce but also brought frontier areas under the control of Chicago and eastern businesses. During the first two decades of the century, wagon transportation cost 30 to 70 cents per ton per mile. By 1860, railroads in New York State carried freight at an average charge of 2.2 cents per ton-mile, and wheat moved from Chicago to New York for 1.2 cents per ton-mile. In sum, the transportation revolution transformed the economy.

 ## The Market Economy

Before the transportation revolution, most farmers had geared production to family needs and to local and foreign markets. They lived in interdependent communities and kept detailed accounts of labor and goods exchanged with their neighbors. Farm families produced much of what they needed—food, clothing, candles, soap, and the like—and traded for or purchased items they could not produce, such as cooking pots, horseshoes, coffee, tea, and sugar.

By the Civil War the United States was industrializing, and most Americans were involved in the market economy. More men and women worked for wages, and most people outside the South—farmers and workers alike—purchased increasing amounts of store-bought goods produced in workshops and factories.

In the market economy, men and women grew crops and produced goods for sale at home or abroad. The money that individuals received from market transactions—from the sale of goods or from the sale of a person's labor—purchased items produced by other people. Such a system encouraged specialization. Farmers began to grow only one or two crops or raise only cows, pigs, or sheep for market. Farm women gave up spinning and weaving and purchased fabric produced by wage-earning farm girls in Massachusetts textile mills.

Definition of a Market Economy

Improvements in transportation and technology, the division of labor, and new methods of financing all fueled the expansion of the economy. Goods and services multiplied. This growth, in turn, prompted new improvements and greater opportunities for wage labor. The effect was cumulative; by the 1840s the economy was growing at a faster rate than in the previous four decades. While per capita

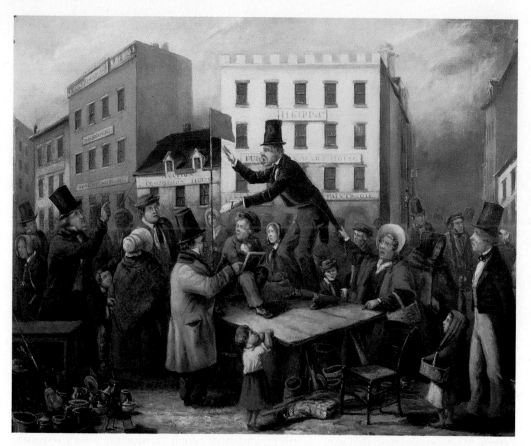

E. Didier painted Auction in Chatham Street *in 1834. Auction houses in New York and other cities boomed during hard times.*   Museum of the City of New York.

income doubled between 1800 and 1860, the price of manufactured goods and food fell.

The pace of economic growth, however, was uneven. Prosperity reigned during two long periods, from 1823 to 1835 and from 1843 to 1857. But there were long stretches of economic contraction as well. The interruption in trade between Jefferson's 1807 embargo and the end of the War of 1812 had contributed to a negative growth rate—that is, fewer goods and services were produced. Contraction and deflation (decline in the general price level) occurred again during the hard times of 1819–1823, 1839–1843, and 1857. During these periods banks collapsed, businesses went under, wages and prices declined, and jobs were hard to find or to keep.

Boom-and-Bust Cycles

As a Baltimore physician noted in 1819, working people felt hard times "a thousand fold more than the merchants." Wage earners could not build up sufficient financial reserves in good times to get them through the next bout of hard times; often they could not even make it through the winter without drawing on charity for food, clothing, and firewood. In the 1820s and 1830s, free laborers in Baltimore typically found steady work from March through October, then unemployment and hunger from November through February.

If even good times were hard on workers and their families, hard times devastated them. In 1839 in Baltimore, when hundreds of small manufacturers for the local market closed their doors, tailors, shoemakers, milliners, and shipyard and construction workers lost their jobs. Ninety miles to the north, Philadelphia took on an eerie aura. "The streets seemed deserted," Sidney George Fisher observed in 1842. "The largest [merchant] houses are shut up and to rent, there is no business . . . no money, no confidence." Only auctions boomed, as sheriffs sold off seized property at a quarter of predepression prices, as the artist E. Didier portrayed in *Auction in Chatham Street* in nearby New York. In Philadelphia and other cities, soup societies fed the hungry. In New York, bread lines and beggars crowded the sidewalks. In smaller cities like Lynn, Massachusetts, the poor became scavengers, digging for clams and harvesting dandelions.

Hard times struck again in 1857. The Mercantile Agency—the forerunner of Dun and Bradstreet—recorded 5,123 bankruptcies in 1857, nearly double the number of the previous year. The bankrupt firms owed $300 million, only half of which would be paid off. Contemporary reports estimated twenty to thirty thousand unemployed people in Philadelphia, and thirty to forty thousand in New York City. Female benevolent societies expanded their soup kitchens and distributed free firewood to the needy. In Chicago, charities reorganized to meet the needs of the poor; in New York, the city hired the unemployed to repair streets and develop Central Park. And in Fall River, Massachusetts, a citizens' committee disbursed public funds on a weekly basis to nine hundred families. The soup kitchen, the bread line, and public aid had become fixtures in urban America.

What caused the boom-and-bust cycles that brought about such suffering? Generally speaking, they were a direct result of the market economy.

Cause of Boom-and-Bust Cycles

Prosperity stimulated demand for staples and for finished goods such as clothing and furniture. Increased demand in turn led not only to higher prices and still higher production but also, because of business confidence and expectation of higher prices, to speculation in land and to the flow of foreign currency into the country. Eventually production surpassed demand, causing prices and wages to fall; in response, inflated land and stock values collapsed. The inflow of foreign money led first to easy credit and then to collapse when unhappy investors withdrew their funds.

Some contemporary economists considered this process beneficial—a self-adjusting cycle in which unprofitable economic ventures were eliminated. In theory, people concentrated on the activities they did best, and the economy as a whole became more efficient. Advocates of the system also argued that it enhanced individual freedom, since theoretically each seller, whether of goods or labor, was free to determine the conditions of the sale. But in fact the system tied workers to a perpetual roller coaster; they became dependent on wages—and on the availability of jobs—for their very existence. The cycles that governed the market economy dominated every corner of the country as even small localities became tied to regional and national markets.

People experienced the market economy in a variety of ways. In the course of the nineteenth century, traditional farm women who had contributed to the family as unpaid labor—producing cloth, clothing, and dairy products for family use—found their lives altered. They increasingly contributed cash, first from the sale of eggs, butter, cheese, and poultry, and then, in New England and the Middle Atlantic states, from industrial work at home, weaving cloth and sewing shoes for contractors who paid them by the piece. By midcentury many women's earnings sustained their families.

The market economy also ushered in another type of boom-and-bust cycle: harvest and destruction. Canals and railroads stimulated demand for distant resources, then accelerated the destruction of forests, natural waterways, and any landscape features that represented obstacles. Railroads made possible large-scale lumbering of pinewood forests in northern Michigan, Wisconsin, and Minnesota. During the 1850s, 40 million acres were cleared of lumber, leaving most of that land unfit even for agriculture. Similarly, the extension of railroads to Kansas and Nebraska brought hunters who slaughtered the great herds of bison for sport. The process of harvest and destruction eventually would change the ecology of the United States.

Government Promotes Economic Growth

The eighteenth-century political ideas that had captured the imagination of the Revolutionary War generation and found expression in the ideal of republican virtue had economic counterparts in the writings of Adam Smith, a Scottish political economist. Smith's *The Wealth of Nations* first appeared in 1776, the year of the Declaration of Independence. Both works emphasized individual liberty, and both were reactions against active government: Thomas Jefferson denounced monarchy and distant government; Smith rejected mercantilism, or government regulation of the economy to benefit the state (see page 83). Both declared that virtue resided in individual freedom and that the community would benefit most from individuals' pursuit of their own self-interest.

Jefferson, influenced by the economic and egalitarian ideas of republicanism (see pages 172–174), believed that freedom thrived where individuals had scope for independence, creativity, and choice—individuals fettered by government, monopoly, or economic dependence could not be free. Limited government was not an end, according to Jefferson, but a means to greater freedom. Committed to the idea that republican democracy would flourish best in a nation of independent farmers and artisans and in an atmosphere of widespread political participation, Jefferson recognized that government was needed to promote individual freedom. Beginning with the purchase of Louisiana in 1803, Republican policy, no less than that of the Federalists, endorsed using the federal government to promote economic growth. The result was faith in a market economy in which government played an active role.

After acquiring Louisiana, the federal government facilitated economic growth and geographic expansion by encouraging westward exploration and settlement, by promoting agriculture, and by developing transportation. The Lewis and Clark expedition (see page 231) began ongoing federal interest in geographic and geologic surveying and opened western lands to exploitation and settlement.

New steps followed quickly. In 1817–1818 Henry Rowe Schoolcraft explored the Missouri and Arkansas region, reporting on its geology and mineral resources. In 1819–1820 Major Stephen Long explored the Great Plains, mapping the area between the Platte and Canadian Rivers. Between 1827 and 1840 the government surveyed about fifty potential railroad routes. The final door to western settlement was opened in 1843–1844 by John C. Frémont's expedition, which followed the Oregon Trail to the Pacific, turned south to California, and then returned east by way of the Great Salt Lake. Frémont, later a California senator and in 1856 the first Republican presidential candidate, gained fame as a soldier-surveyor of the West. His report of his journey dispelled a long-standing myth that the middle of the continent was a desert.

To encourage settlement and cultivation of western lands, the federal government evicted Indians from their traditional lands and offered the land at reasonable prices (see pages 281–282). And because transportation was crucial to the development of the frontier, the government first financed roads and canals and later subsidized railroad construction by means of land grants. Even the State Department aided agriculture: its consular offices overseas collected horticultural information, seeds, and cuttings,

and it published technical reports in an effort to improve American farming.

The federal government also played an active role in technological and industrial growth. Federal arsenals pioneered new manufacturing techniques and helped to develop the machine-tool industry. The United States Post Office provided a communications link that stimulated interregional trade and briefly played a crucial role in the development of the telegraph. The federal government financed the first telegraph line, from Washington to Baltimore, in 1844; it was briefly managed by the Post Office. To create an atmosphere conducive to economic growth and individual creativity, the government protected inventions and domestic industries. Patent laws gave inventors a seventeen-year monopoly on their inventions, and tariffs protected American industry from foreign competition.

The federal judiciary validated government promotion of the economy and encouraged business enterprise. In *Gibbons* v. *Ogden* (1824), the Supreme Court overturned the New York State law that had given Robert Fulton and Robert Livingston a monopoly on the New York–New Jersey steamboat trade. Aaron Ogden, their successor, lost the monopoly when Chief Justice of the United States John Marshall ruled that the congressional prerogative of licensing new enterprises took precedence over New York's grant of monopoly rights to Fulton and Livingston. Marshall declared that Congress's power under the commerce clause of the Constitution extended to "every species of commercial intercourse," including transportation systems. Within a year, forty-three steamboats were plying Ogden's route.

Legal Foundations of Commerce

In defining interstate commerce broadly, the Marshall Court expanded federal powers over the economy while restricting the ability of states to control economic activity within their borders. Its action was consistent with the Court's earlier decision in *Dartmouth College* v. *Woodward* (1819), which protected the sanctity of contracts against interference by the states (see page 246). "If business is to prosper," Marshall wrote, "men must have assurance that contracts will be enforced."

Federal and state courts, in conjunction with state legislatures, also encouraged the proliferation of corporations—organizations entitled to hold property and transact business as if they were a per-

The Marshall Court encouraged business competition by ending state-licensed monopolies on inland waterways. Gibbons v. Ogden *(1824) opened up the New York–New Jersey trade to new lines, and within a short time dozens of steamboats were ferrying passengers and freight across the Hudson River.*   New-York Historical Society.

son. Corporation owners, called shareholders, were granted *limited liability*, or freedom from responsibility for the company's debts. An attractive feature to potential investors, limited liability encouraged people to back new business ventures. In 1800 the United States had about three hundred incorporated firms; in 1817 there were about two thousand. By 1830 the New England states alone had issued nineteen hundred charters, one-third to manufacturing and mining firms. At first each firm needed a special legislative act to incorporate, but after the 1830s applications became so numerous that states established routine procedures allowing firms to incorporate.

Though legislative action created corporations, the courts played a crucial role in defining their status, extending their powers, and protecting them. A particular encouragement to corporate development and free enterprise was the Supreme Court's ruling in *Charles River Bridge* v. *Warren Bridge* (1837) that new enterprises could not be restrained by implied privileges under old charters. The case involved issues of great importance: should a new interest be allowed to compete against existing enterprises,

and should the state protect existing privilege or encourage innovation and the growth of commerce through competition?

The Massachusetts legislature had chartered the Charles River Bridge Company in 1785 and six years later extended its charter for seventy years. In return for assuming the risk of building a bridge between Charlestown and Boston, the owners were granted the privilege of collecting tolls. In 1828 the legislature chartered another company to build the Warren Bridge across the Charles nearby; the owner would have the right to collect tolls for six years, after which the bridge would be turned over to the state and be free of tolls. The Charles River Bridge Company sued in 1829, claiming that the new bridge breached the earlier charter and contradicted the principles in *Dartmouth College* v. *Woodward*.

Speaking for the Court majority, Marshall's successor Roger Taney declared that the original charter did not confer the privilege of monopoly and that exclusivity could not therefore be implied. Focusing on the question of corporate privilege rather than the law of contracts, Taney ruled that charter grants should be interpreted narrowly and that ambiguities would be decided in favor of the public interest. New enterprises should not be restricted by old charters, and economic growth would best be served by narrowing the application of the *Dartmouth College* decision. Thus the judiciary supported economic expansion and individual economic opportunity.

In promoting the economy, state governments far surpassed the federal government. From 1815 through 1860, for example, 73 percent of the $135 million invested in canals was government money, most of it from the states. In the 1830s the states started to invest in rail construction. Though the federal government played a larger role in constructing railroads than in building canals, state and local governments provided more than half of the capital for southern rail lines. State governments also invested in corporate and bank stocks, providing corporations and banks with much-needed capital. In fact, states actually equaled or surpassed private enterprise in their investments.

State Promotion of the Economy

Pennsylvania, probably the most active state in promoting its economy, invested a total of $100 million in canals, railroads, banks, and manufacturing firms; its appointees sat on more than 150 corporate boards of directors. Pennsylvania was the largest state in area, extending west from the Delaware River to beyond the mountains, and thus developed the most extensive program of internal improvements to stimulate settlement and economic growth. But Pennsylvania and other states did more than invest in industry. Through special acts and incorporation laws, they regulated the nature and activities of corporations and banks. They also used their licensing capacity to regulate industry. Georgia, for example, regulated the grading and marketing of tobacco.

Largely as a result of these government efforts, the United States experienced uneven but sustained economic growth from the end of the War of 1812 until 1860. Political controversy raged over questions of state versus federal activity—especially with regard to internal improvements and banking—but all parties agreed on the general goal of economic expansion. Indeed, during these years the major restraint on government action was not philosophical but financial: the public purse was small. As the private sector grew more vigorous, entrepreneurs looked less to government for financial support, and the states played less of a role in investment.

 ## The Rise of Manufacturing and Commerce

The London *Times* ridiculed the McCormick reaper, invented by Virginia farmer Cyrus McCormick in 1831, as "a cross between a flying machine, a wheelbarrow, and an Astly chariot." In one continuous motion, a revolving drum on the horse-drawn reaper positioned grain stalks in front of a blade; the cut grain fell onto a platform. Put to a competitive test through rain-soaked wheat, only the Chicago-made reaper passed, to the cheers of the skeptical English spectators.

The reaper and hundreds of other American products made their international debut at the 1851 London Crystal Palace Exhibition, the first modern world's fair. There the design and quality of American machines and wares—from familiar farm tools to exotic devices such as the reaper and an ice-cream freezer—astonished observers. American manufacturers returned home with dozens of medals, including all three prizes for piano making. Most impressive to the Europeans were three simple machines: Alfred C. Hobb's unpickable padlocks, Samuel Colt's revolvers, and Robbins and Lawrence's rifles with completely interchangeable parts. All were machine-tooled rather than handmade, products of what the British called the American system of manufacturing.

So impressed were the British—whose nation was the leading industrial power of the time—that in 1853 they sent a parliamentary commission to study the American system. A year later a second committee returned to examine the firearms industry in detail. The committee's report described an astonishing experiment performed at the federal armory in Springfield, Massachusetts. To test the interchangeability of machine-made musket parts, the committee selected rifles made in each of the previous ten years. While the committee watched, the guns were dismantled "and the parts placed in a row of boxes, mixed up together." The Englishmen "then requested the workman, whose duty it is to 'assemble' the arms, to put them together, which he did—the Committee handing him the parts, taken at hazard—with the use of a turnscrew only, and as quickly as though they had been English muskets, whose parts had carefully been kept separate." Britain's Enfield arsenal subsequently converted to American equipment. Other nations quickly followed Great Britain's lead, sending delegations across the Atlantic to bring back American machines.

The American system of manufacturing used precision machinery to produce interchangeable parts that did not require individual adjustment to fit. Eli Whitney, a Yale graduate and inventor, had promoted the idea of interchangeable parts in 1798 when he contracted with the federal government to make ten thousand rifles in twenty-eight months. By the 1820s the United States Ordnance Department had contracted with private firms to introduce machine-made interchangeable parts for firearms. The American system quickly spread beyond the arsenals, giving birth to the machine-tool industry—the manufacture of machines for the purposes of mass production. One outcome was an explosion in consumer goods. Because the time and skill involved in manufacturing were greatly reduced, the new system permitted mass production at low cost: Waltham watches, Yale locks, and other goods became household items, inexpensive yet of uniformly high quality.

American System of Manufacturing

Interchangeable parts and the machine-tool industry were uniquely American contributions to the industrial revolution. Both paved the way for the swift industrialization that the nation experienced after the Civil War. In 1800, however, manufacturing was a relatively unimportant component of the American economy. Most took place in small workshops and homes, where master craftsmen supervised journeymen and taught apprentices and women worked alone spinning thread and weaving cloth. Tailors, shoemakers, and blacksmiths made articles by hand, to order for specific customers.

The rise of textile mills illustrates the changes in manufacturing wrought by the market economy. Some farm families continued to make their own cloth, but mill-produced cloth increasingly became the source of clothing. The nineteenth-century machine-tool industry made textile and clothing production a function of mills and factories rather than kitchens and home workshops. Cotton-textile mills in New England processed cotton grown in the slave South. Fed by the population boom, the expanding market economy created a demand for manufactured cotton goods. The first American textile mill—Almy and Brown's 1790 Pawtucket, Rhode Island, factory—used water-powered spinning machines constructed from British models by the

Production of Cloth

English immigrant Samuel Slater. Slater employed women and children as cheap labor and sold the thread they manufactured from Maine to Maryland. Soon other mills sprang up, stimulated by the embargo on British imports from 1807 through 1815. From 1809 through 1813 alone, 151 cotton and woolen companies incorporated.

These early mills, dependent on waterpower, were located in rural areas. By erecting dams and watercourses, mill owners diverted water from farmers and destroyed fishing, an important source of income and protein in rural and village America. To protect their customary rights, fishermen and farmers fought the manufacturers in New England state legislatures, but petitions from hopeful job seekers in the mill environs supported the manufacturers. The ensuing compromises promoted mill development.

Construction of the first American power loom and the chartering of the Boston Manufacturing Company in 1813 radically transformed textile manufacturing. The corporation was capitalized at $400,000—ten times the amount behind the Rhode Island mills—by Francis Cabot Lowell and other Boston merchants. Its goal was to eliminate the problems of coordination, quality control, and shipping inherent in the subcontracting of work in the putting-out system. The owners erected their factories in Waltham, Massachusetts, bringing all the manufacturing processes to a single location. They employed a resident manager to run the mill, thus separating ownership from management. Workers were paid by the piece or by the hour, and the cloth was sold throughout the United States.

Waltham (Lowell) System

The company's cloth was so inexpensive that many women began to purchase it rather than make their own. Nonetheless, spinning and especially weaving remained women's work in many rural homes. Women who traditonally had spun their own yarn and woven it into cloth now received yarn from the mills and returned finished cloth. The change was subtle but significant: although the work itself was familiar, women were operating their looms for piece-rate wages, not primarily to make cloth for their families.

When managers could not find enough hands in rural Waltham to staff the mill, they recruited New England farm daughters, accepting responsibility for their living conditions. As inducements, they offered

In the 1830s an unknown artist painted Middlesex Company Woolen Mills, *portraying the hulking mass of the mill buildings. The company organized all the manufacturing processes at a single location, in Lowell, Massachusetts, on the Merrimack River.* Museum of American Textile History.

cash wages, company-run boarding houses, and cultural events such as evening lectures—none of which was available on the farm. This paternalistic approach, called the Waltham (or Lowell) system, was adopted in other mills erected alongside New England rivers.

By 1860 a cotton mill resembled a modern factory. The work force consisted mainly of immigrant Irish women who lived at home, not in mill-subsidized housing. New England farm women continued to live in the few remaining boarding houses. Technological improvements in the looms and other machinery had made the work less skilled and more routine. The mills could thus pay lower wages, drawing from a reservoir of unskilled labor.

Textile Mills

Textile manufacturing changed New England and had its greatest impact on Lowell, Massachusetts. Among the Lowell mills was the Middlesex Company. The population of Lowell, the "city of spindles" and the prototype of early American industrialization, grew from twenty-five hundred to thirty-three thousand between 1826 and 1850. It was the largest of the cotton-mill towns before the Civil War and had the biggest work force, the greatest output, and the most capital invested. It also led in technological change.

Textiles became the most important industry in the nation before the Civil War, employing 115,000 workers in 1860, more than half of them women and immigrants. The key to the success of the textile industry was that the machines, not the women, spun the yarn and wove the cloth. Workers watched the machines and intervened to maintain smooth operation. When a thread broke, the machine stopped automatically; a worker found the break, pieced the ends together, and restarted the machine. New England textile mills used increasingly specialized machines, relying heavily on advances in the machine-tool industry. Their application of the American system of manufacturing enabled American firms to compete successfully with British cotton mills (see figure, page 267).

Outside New England—for example, in Pennsylvania's Delaware valley—the textile industry grew more slowly, combining traditional ways with technology. A decade after the Waltham mills first appeared, entrepreneurs in Rockdale, Pennsylvania, converted paper mills to cotton manufacturing. Organized as partnerships rather than corporations, these businesses could not raise the large sums available to the Lowell mills. Unlike their counterparts in Waltham and Lowell, the owners lived and worked in the mill villages. Small factories employed entire families, and unmarried workers boarded in other workers' homes. Many Pennsylvania textile workers sought to save money to buy western land, and a number of them were successful. Growth and change occurred at a modest pace; not until the 1850s would a major manufacturing center arise in once-rural southeastern Pennsylvania.

The appearance of ready-made clothing was the other great change in the textile industry. Before the 1820s, most clothing was sewn at home by women, and some people purchased used clothing. Tailors and seamstresses made wealthy men's and women's clothing to order. By the 1820s and 1830s, ready-made clothing became common. Manufacturers used two methods, either separately or in combination, to produce it. One was production within a factory. The other was, again, the putting-out system: this time, typically, a journeyman tailor cut the fabric panels in the factory, and the sewing was put out at piece rates to unskilled or semiskilled labor, often women working in their own homes.

Ready-made Clothing

In 1832, Boston manufacturers employed three hundred journeyman tailors at $2 per day and thirteen hundred women and one hundred boys at 50 cents a day. Apprentices, if used at all, were no longer learning a trade; they were a permanent source of cheap labor. Women learned their sewing skills at home; they were passed down from mother to daughter. By the late 1850s, as many as seventeen different pairs of hands were involved in making a single pair of pants under the putting-out system.

Most of the first mass-produced clothes, crudely made and limited to a few loose-fitting sizes, were produced for men, and they were purchased by men who lived in city boarding houses and rooming houses, far from the female kin who previously would have made their clothes. Most women made their own clothes, but those who could afford to do so employed seamstresses. Improvements in fit and changes in men's fashion eventually made ready-to-wear apparel more acceptable to white-collar and

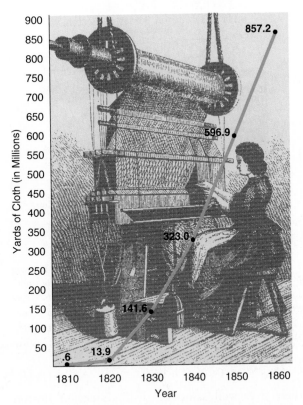

New England Cotton Industry Cloth Production, 1810–1860

New England Cotton-Industry Cloth Production, 1810–1860 Textiles was the most important manufacturing industry in the United States in the 1830s, 1840s, and 1850s. The production of cloth increased six-fold during that time. Source: James F. Willis and Martin L. Primack, *An Economic History of the United States*, 2d ed. (Englewood Cliffs, N.J.: Prentice-Hall, 1989), p. 171.

professional men. By the 1850s the short sack coat, which did not taper at the waist, had replaced the embroidered waistcoat. This forerunner of the modern suit jacket fit loosely and needed little custom tailoring. Now even upper-class men were willing to consider ready-made apparel. In 1818 Henry Sands Brooks (later Brooks Brothers), offered tailoring services and ready-made apparel to the carriage trade.

Retail clothing stores well stocked with ready-made clothes appeared in the 1820s. T. S. Whitmarsh of Boston advertised in 1827 that "he keeps constantly for Sale, from 5 to 10,000 Fashionable ready-made Garments." In 1830, J. T. Jacobs of New York boasted that "Gentlemen can rely upon being as well fitted from the shelves as if their measures were taken—their stock being very extensive and

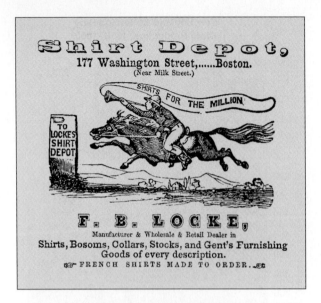

F. B. Locke adapted to the new market for ready-made clothing by becoming a manufacturer, wholesaler, and retailer of men's shirts. Although he continued to make shirts to order, the staple of his Shirt Depot was mass-produced shirts, as this advertisement from the Boston Directory *for 1848–1849 indicates.* Warshaw Collection of Business Americana, Smithsonian Institution, Washington, D.C.

their sizes well assorted." F. B. Locke of Boston made and sold "shirts for the million."

Such merchants often bought goods wholesale, though many manufactured garments in their own factories. Lewis and Hanford of New York City boasted of cutting more than one hundred thousand garments in the winter of 1848–1849. The New York firm sold most of its clothing in the South and owned its own retail outlet in New Orleans. Paul Tulane, a New Orleans competitor, owned a New York factory that made goods for his Louisiana store. In the West, Cincinnati became the center of the new men's clothing industry. By midcentury, Cincinnati's ready-to-wear apparel industry employed fifteen hundred men and ten thousand women. As in Boston, most of the women did outwork.

Though cotton-textile mills and factories were in the vanguard, large-scale manufacturing also transformed woolen textiles, farm implements, machine tools, iron, steel, glass, and finished consumer goods. "White coal"—waterpower—was widely used to run the machines. By 1860, manufacturing accounted for one-third of the nation's total production, an increase of 200 percent in twenty years.

To a striking extent, large-scale manufacturing in this period was an outcome rather than an agent of change in American life. Ever since Alexander Hamilton's *Report on Manufactures* (see page 207), national pride had spurred the development of American industry. Contrary to Hamilton's hopes, however, more capital flowed into the merchant marine than into industry between 1789 and 1808. In the early republic, greater profits could be made by transporting British products to the United States than by producing the same items at home. But the embargo and the War of 1812 reversed this situation, and merchants began to shift their capital from shipping to manufacturing (see pages 239–245). It was in this new economic environment that the Waltham system took root.

Stimulants to Industry

Other factors also stimulated industry. Population growth, especially in urban areas and the Old Northwest, created a large domestic market for finished goods (see maps, page 269). As the rise of commercial agriculture drew farmers more into the market economy, they purchased more manufactured goods. Specialty merchants and new modes of transportation hastened the development of these new markets. To sell more, merchants had to find ways to produce more goods with less skilled labor. Government policy assisted manufacturing expansion. Beginning with the Tariff of 1816 and culminating in the Tariff of Abominations of 1828, Congress imposed tariffs more to protect the market for domestic manufactures than to increase government revenue.

Commerce expanded hand in hand with manufacturing. Cotton, for instance, had once been traded by plantation agents, who sold the raw cotton and bought manufactured goods that they then sold to plantation owners, extending them credit when necessary. As cotton became a great staple export after the invention of the cotton gin in 1793, cotton exports rose from half a million pounds in that year to 83 million pounds in 1815. Gradually, some agents came to specialize in finance alone: they were cotton brokers, who for a commission brought together buyers and sellers. Similarly, wheat and hog brokers sprang up in the West—in Cincinnati, Louisville, and St. Louis. The distribution of finished goods also became more specialized as wholesalers bought large quantities of particular items from manufacturers, and jobbers broke down the wholesale lots for retail stores and country merchants.

Specialization of Commerce

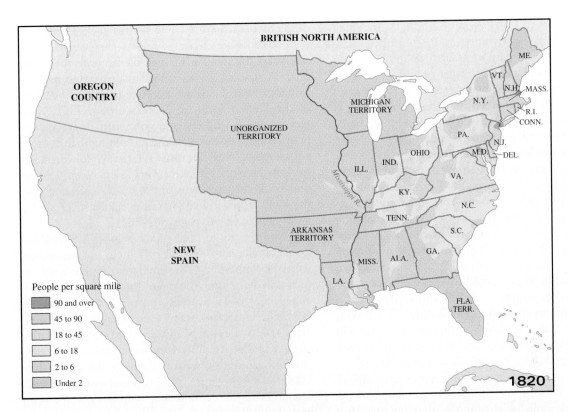

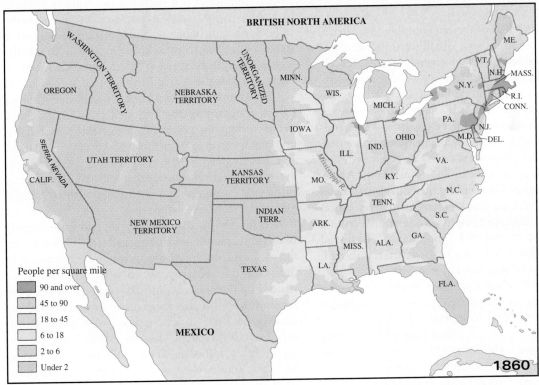

United States Population, 1820 and 1860 *Between 1820 and 1860, the population of the United States grew from 9.6 million to 31.4 million, and the density increased significantly in the North, the Old Northwest, and California. Settlement, too, spread farther away from the eastern seaboard.*

General merchants persisted longer in small towns than in cities. Such merchants continued to exchange some goods with local farm women—trading flour or pots and pans for eggs or other produce. They left the sale of finished goods, such as shoes and clothing, to local craftsmen. In some rural areas and on the frontier, peddlers acted as general merchants. But as transportation improved and towns grew, even small-town merchants began to specialize.

Commercial specialization transformed some traders in big cities, especially New York, into virtual merchant princes. New York had emerged as the dominant port in the late 1790s, outstripping Philadelphia and Boston. After the Erie Canal opened, New York City became a standard stop on every major trade route from Europe, the southern ports, and the West. New York traders were the middlemen for southern cotton and western grain trading. Merchants in other cities played a similar role within their own regions. Newly rich traders in turn invested their profits in processing enterprises and then in manufacturing, further stimulating the growth of northern cities. Some cities specialized: Rochester became a milling center, and Cincinnati—"Porkopolis"—became the first meatpacking center.

Merchants who engaged in complex commercial transactions required large office staffs. Most of the all-male office staff worked on high stools, laboriously copying business forms and correspondence. At the bottom of the office hierarchy were messenger boys, often preteens, who delivered documents. Above them were the ordinary copyists, who hand-copied documents in ink as many times as needed. Clerks handled assignments such as customs-house clearances, shipping papers, and translations. Above them were the bookkeeper and the confidential chief clerk. Those seeking employment in such an office, called a countinghouse, often took a course from a writing master to acquire a "good hand." All hoped to rise someday to the status of partner, although their chances of doing so were dim.

Banks and other financial institutions, which played a significant role in the expansion of commerce and manufacturing, also became a leading industry themselves. Financial institutions (banks, insurance companies, and corporations) linked savers—those who deposited money in banks—with producers and speculators who wished to borrow money. The expiration

Banking and Credit Systems

of the first Bank of the United States in 1811 acted as a stimulus to state-chartered banks, and over the next five years the number of such banks more than doubled. When state banks proved inadequate to spur national growth, Congress chartered the Second Bank of the United States in 1816 (see page 245). Many farmers, local bankers, and politicians, however, denounced the bank as a monster, claiming that it served national, not local, interests. Western landowners, like Andrew Jackson, suffered severe losses when the Second Bank reduced loans in the western states during the Panic of 1819. In 1836 critics finally succeeded in killing the bank (see pages 362–363).

The closing of the Second Bank in 1836 caused a nationwide credit shortage, which, in conjunction with the Panic of 1837, stimulated fundamental reforms in banking. Michigan and New York introduced charter laws promoting what was called *free banking*. Many other states soon followed suit. Previously, every new bank needed a special legislative charter before it could open for business; thus each bank incorporation was in effect a political decision. Under the new laws, any proposed bank that met certain minimum conditions—amount of capital invested, number of notes issued, and types of loans to be made—would receive a state charter automatically. Banks in Michigan, New York, and soon, other states were thus freer to incorporate, although the legislatures placed some restrictions on their operation to reduce the risk of bank failure.

Free banking proved to be a significant stimulus to the economy in the late 1840s and 1850s. New banks sprang up everywhere, providing merchants and manufacturers with the credit they needed. The free-banking laws also served as a precedent for general incorporation statutes that allowed manufacturing firms to receive state charters without special acts of the state legislature.

In the 1850s, with both credit and capital easily obtainable, manufacturing spread. In the North, industry began to rival agriculture and commerce in dollar volume. Meanwhile, commercial farming, financed by the credit boom, was integrating the early frontier into the northern economy. By 1860 six northern states—Massachusetts, New York, Pennsylvania, Connecticut, Rhode Island, and Ohio—were highly industrialized. Their clothing, textile, and shoe industries employed more than one hundred thousand workers each; lumber, seventy-five thousand; iron, sixty-five thousand; and woolens and leather, fifty thousand. Although agriculture still predominated even in these states, industrial employment would soon surpass it.

Workers and the Workplace

Oh, sing me the song of the Factory Girl!
So merry and glad and free!
The bloom in her cheeks, of health how it speaks,
Oh! a happy creature is she!
She tends the loom, she watches the spindle,
And cheerfully toileth away,
Amid the din of wheels, how her bright eyes kindle,
And her bosom is ever gay.

This idyllic portrait of factory work appeared in the Chicopee, Massachusetts, *Telegraph* in 1850. It was a fitting anthem for the teenage single women who first left the villages and farms of New England to work in the mills. New England mill owners, convinced that the degradation of English factory workers arose from their living conditions and not from the work itself, designed boarding-house communities offering airy courtyards and river views, prepared meals, and cultural activities. Housekeepers enforced strict curfews, banned alcohol, and reported to the corporations on workers' behavior and church attendance.

The promise of steady work, good pay, and kinship ties at first lured eager rural young women to the mills. Many pairs of sisters and cousins worked in the same mill and lived in the same boarding house. They helped each other adjust, and their letters home drew other kin to the mills. Young women then had few opportunities for work outside their own homes, and the commercial production of yarn and cloth had reduced their workload in New England farm households. Averaging sixteen and one-half years of age when they entered the mills, the girls usually stayed only about five years—few intended to stay longer. Their earnings brought them independence and the freedom of deciding whether to spend or save their earnings. That satisfaction was not sufficient, however, to change their ambitions to be wives and mothers. Most left the mills to marry and were replaced by other women interested in earning a wage.

Between 1837 and 1842, most mills ran only part-time because of a decline in demand for cloth. Subsequently managers applied still greater pressures on workers by means of the speed-up, the stretch-out, and the premium system. The speed-up

This young mill girl at Waltham or Lowell, probably in the late 1840s, posed for an early daguerreotype. Her swollen and rough hands contrast with her youth, neat dress, and carefully tied, beribboned hair. Her hands suggest that she worked, as did most twelve- and thirteen-year-olds, as a warper, straightening the strands of cotton or wool as they entered the looms. Courtesy of Jack Naylor.

increased the speed of the machines; the stretch-out increased the number of machines each worker had to operate; and premiums paid to the overseers whose departments produced the most cloth encouraged them to pressure workers for greater output. The result in Lowell was that the number of spindles and looms increased 150 and 140 percent respectively between 1836 and 1850, while the number of workers increased by only 50 percent. The corporation's goal of building an industrial empire and maximizing profits took precedence over its paternalistic concern for workers' living conditions. In the race for profits, owners lengthened hours, cut wages, and tightened discipline. Some millworkers began to think of themselves as slaves. The boarding houses became more crowded.

New England millworkers responded to their deteriorating working conditions by organizing and striking. In 1834, in reaction to a 25 percent wage cut, they unsuccessfully "turned out" (struck) against the Lowell mills. Two years later, when boarding-house rates increased, they turned out again.

Protests by Mill Women

As conditions continued to worsen, workers adopted new methods of resistance. In the 1840s, strikes gave way to a concerted effort to shorten the workday. Massachusetts mill women joined forces with other workers to press for state legislation mandating a ten-hour day. Eliza R. Hemingway, a three-year veteran of two different Lowell mills, told a Massachusetts House of Representatives committee in 1845 that workers' hours were too long, "her time for meals too limited. In the summer season, the work is commenced at 5 o'clock, A.M., and continued 'til 7 o'clock, P.M., with half an hour for breakfast and three quarters of an hour for dinner."

They aired their complaints in worker-run newspapers: in 1842, the *Factory Girl* appeared in New Hampshire, the *Wampanoag and Operatives' Journal* in Massachusetts. Two years later the *Factory Girl's Garland* and the *Voice of Industry*, nicknamed "the factory girl's voice," were founded. Even the *Lowell Offering*, the owner-sponsored paper that was the pride of millworkers and managers alike, became embroiled in controversy when workers charged that articles critical of working conditions had been suppressed.

The millworkers' rebellion against paternalism and exploitation took many forms. Their newspapers exposed worsening work conditions, their strikes provoked confrontations, and their songs expressed their resolve and unity, as in "The Factory Girl's Come-All-Ye" (about 1850):

No more I'll take my bobbins out,
No more I'll put them in,
No more the overseer will say
"You're weaving your cloth too thin!"

No more will I eat cold pudding,
No more will I eat hard bread,
No more will I eat those half-baked beans,
For I vow! They're killing me dead!

I'm going back to Boston town
And live on Tremont Street;
And I want all you fact'ry girls
To come to my house and eat!

The women's labor organizations were weakened by the short tenure of most workers. Few of the militant native-born millworkers stayed on to fight the managers and owners, and gradually there were fewer New England daughters to enter the mills. By the end of the 1850s the women who constituted the majority of millworkers were mostly Irish immigrants, driven to the mills by the need to support their families and unable to afford to complain about their working conditions.

A growing gender division in the workplace, especially in the textile, clothing, and shoemaking industries, was one important outcome of large-scale manufacturing. Although women and men in traditional agricultural and artisan households tended to perform different tasks, they worked as a family unit. As wage work spread, however, men's and women's work cultures became increasingly separate. The women and girls who left home to work in textile mills worked and lived in a mostly female world. In the clothing and shoemaking industries, whose male artisans had once worked at home assisted by unpaid family labor, men began working outside the home while women continued to work at home through the putting-out system. Tasks and wages, too, became rigidly differentiated: women sewed, whereas men shaped materials and finished products, receiving higher wages in shops employing men only. These new work patterns contributed to social and economic differences between men and women (see pages 327–328).

Gender Divisions in Work

The market system, wage labor, and the specialization of labor had an impact on unpaid household labor as well. As home and workplace became separate and labor came to be defined in terms of wages (what could be sold in the marketplace) rather than production, the unpaid labor of women was devalued. In a money-based economy in which families increasingly recorded their incomes and expenditures in account books, there was no category in which to enter women's unpaid labor and services. Yet those labors were extensive; indeed, the family depended on women's work within the household. And as the family became more dependent on wage labor, more family members sought outside employment and had less time to do their share of household labor. Thus gender defined household labor and placed a low value on it.

The new textile mills, shoe factories, iron mills, wholesale stores, and railroads were the antithesis of traditional workshop and household production.

**Changes in
the Workplace**

Factories created a workplace in which authority was hierarchically organized. Factory workers lost their sense of autonomy as impersonal market forces seemed to dominate their lives. Competition among mills in the growing textile industry of the 1820s and 1830s led to layoffs and the replacement of operatives with cheaper, less-skilled workers or children. The formal rules of the factory contrasted sharply with the more relaxed pace and atmosphere of artisan shops and farm households. Supervisors represented owners whom workers never saw. The division of labor and the use of machines narrowed the skills required of workers. And the flow of work was governed by the bell, the steam whistle, or the clock. In 1844 the *Factory Girl's Garland* published a poem describing how the ringing of the factory bell controlled when the workers awoke, ate, began and ended work, and went to sleep. The central problem, of course, was the quickening pace of the work between the bells. Since owners and managers no longer shared the workers' tasks, they did not consider the plight of the worker when they imposed a speed-up.

Many workers welcomed the new manufacturing methods at first; new jobs and higher wages seemed adequate compensation. But wage reductions, speed-ups, and stretch-outs later changed their minds. Other conditions were trying, too. Millworkers had to tolerate the roar of the looms, and all workers on power machines risked accidents that could kill or maim. Perhaps most demoralizing, opportunities for advancement in the new system were virtually nil.

Changes in the workplace in turn transformed the workers. Initially, mill women drew on kinship, village, and gender ties to build supportive networks in factories. In the 1840s and after, as recently arrived Irish immigrant women came to predominate, more workers were strangers to each other before they entered the mills. Once employed, their only bases for friendship and mutual support were their work experiences. As a sense of distance from their employers took hold, so did deep-seated differences among workers.

Nationality, religion, education, and future prospects separated Irish and Yankee millworkers. Many New England women resented the immigrants, and management set one group against the other through selective hiring and promotions. Mill work was not a stage in the life of most Irish women; it was permanent employment. Unlike their Yankee sisters, they could not risk striking and losing their jobs; they and their families were dependent on their earnings. With legions of unskilled immigrants looking for work, Irish millworkers considered themselves fortunate to hold on to their jobs, even though the mills cut wages three times in the 1850s and continued the speed-ups and stretch-outs. The Irish workers assisted one another as much as possible but rarely engaged in formal protest.

As wage work became common and workers sensed a loss of independence, they experienced an erosion of the republican virtues that an earlier generation of artisans had shared with the Revolutionary War generation. Thomas Jefferson had hoped to preserve these values with the purchase of the Louisiana Territory and the encouragement of a market economy, but factory work and boom-and-bust cycles did not enhance individual freedom. Those who stayed in the master-journeyman-apprentice system or remained on farms after the 1830s saw themselves as distinct from the new wage workers. So, too, did many of the first generation of Yankee millworkers, for whom factory work was a stage in the life cycle before marriage.

While female textile workers and shoemakers organized and protested, male workers responded to changes in the nature of work by participating actively in reform politics. Labor parties arose in Pennsylvania, New York, and Massachusetts in the 1820s and eventually spread to a dozen states. These parties advocated free public education, abolition of imprisonment for debt, and opposition to banks and monopolies. The interests of workers' reform parties often coincided with those of middle-class benevolent movements. The two groups shared a concern not only for public education but also for public morals: temperance, observance of the Sabbath, and suppression of vice (see Chapter 13). Ironically, however, reform politics tended to divide workers. Many of the reforms—moral education, temperance, Sabbath closings—served the interests of merchants and industrialists seeking a more disciplined work force. Temperance and Sabbath closings also pitted the native-born against immigrant workers, many of whom were Catholic. Anti-immigrant and anti-Catholic movements further divided workers.

Journeymen recognized that the new system of manufacturing threatened them. When master

How do historians know what working conditions New England millworkers experienced? This 1853 timetable from the Lowell Mills is among the rich sources historians consult to reconstruct workers' experiences in the mills. Textile factories were the first corporations to impose rigid work rules. The size of the labor force, the management structure, and the organization of the work made it necessary to publish work rules. Exact times were established for beginning and ending work and for meals. Few workers carried their own timepieces, so a system of bells regulated the lives of the factory community. From March 20 to September 19, when work began at 6:30 A.M., bells alerted the workers at 4:30 and 5:50 A.M. and again at 6:20 A.M., ten minutes before they had to be at the factory. For their main meal at midday, they had forty-five minutes away from work; the 12:35 P.M. bell warned that they had ten minutes to return. For young mill women from the New England countryside, and later for Irish women, such regimentation must have seemed a world apart from the rhythms of rural life. Photo: Museum of American Textile History.

TIME TABLE OF THE LOWELL MILLS,

Arranged to make the working time throughout the year average 11 hours per day

TO TAKE EFFECT SEPTEMBER 21st., 1853.

The Standard time being that of the meridian of Lowell, as shown by the Regulato Clock of AMOS SANBORN, Post Office Corner, Central Street.

From March 20th to September 19th, inclusive.

COMMENCE WORK, at 6.30 A.M. LEAVE OFF WORK, at 6.30 P.M., except on Saturday Evenings
BREAKFAST at 6 A.M. DINNER, at 12 M. Commence Work, after dinner, 12.45 P.M.

From September 20th to March 19th, inclusive.

COMMENCE WORK at 7.00 A.M. LEAVE OFF WORK, at 7.00 P.M., except on Saturday Evening
BREAKFAST at 6.30 A.M. DINNER, at 12.30 P.M. Commence Work, after dinner, 1.15 P.M.

BELLS.

From March 20th to September 19th, inclusive.

Morning Bells.	Dinner Bells.	Evening Bells.
First bell,............4.30 A.M.	Ring out,..............12.00 M.	Ring out,...........6.30 P.M
Second, 5.30 A.M.; Third, 6.20.	Ring in,............12.35 P.M.	Except on Saturday Evenings.

From September 20th to March 19th, inclusive.

Morning Bells.	Dinner Bells.	Evening Bells.
First bell,............5.00 A.M.	Ring out,..............12.30 P.M.	Ring out at...........7.00 P.M
Second, 6.00 A.M.; Third, 6.50.	Ring in,............1.05 P.M.	Except on Saturday Evenings.

SATURDAY EVENING BELLS.

During APRIL, MAY, JUNE, JULY, and AUGUST, Ring Out, at 6.00 P.M.
The remaining Saturday Evenings in the year, ring out as follows :

SEPTEMBER.	NOVEMBER.	JANUARY.
First Saturday, ring out 6.00 P.M.	Third Saturday ring out 4.00 P.M.	Third Saturday, ring out 4.25 P.M
Second " " 5.45 "	Fourth " " 3.55 "	Fourth " " 4.35 "
Third " " 5.30 "		
Fourth " " 5.20 "	DECEMBER.	FEBRUARY.
	First Saturday, ring out 3.50 P.M.	First Saturday, ring out 4.45 P.M.
OCTOBER.	Second " " 3.55 "	Second " " 4.55 "
First Saturday, ring out 5.05 P.M.	Third " " 3.55 "	Third " " 5.00 "
Second " " 4.55 "	Fourth " " 4.00 "	Fourth " " 5.10 "
Third " " 4.45 "	Fifth " " 4.00 "	
Fourth " " 4.35 "		MARCH.
Fifth " " 4.25 "	JANUARY.	First Saturday, ring out 5.25 P.M
NOVEMBER.	First Saturday, ring out 4.10 P.M.	Second " " 5.30 "
First Saturday, ring out 4.15 P.M.	Second " " 4.15 "	Third " " 5.35 "
Second " " 4.05 "		Fourth " " 5.45 "

YARD GATES will be opened at the first stroke of the bells for entering or leaving the Mills.

∴   SPEED GATES commence hoisting three minutes before commencing work.

craftsmen in shoemaking, textiles, and apparel manufacturing attempted to keep up with change by turning their workshops into small factories with themselves as managers, the gap between master and journeymen threatened to become insurmountable. The market economy seemed to free masters and to make journeymen more dependent. Masters stressed individuals' freedom to contract for their labor; journeymen sought out the mutual protection of their fellow workers.

Organized labor's greatest achievement during this period was to gain relief from the threat of conspiracy laws. When journeyman shoemakers organized during the first decade

Emergence of a Labor Movement

of the century, their employers turned to the courts, charging criminal conspiracy. The cordwainers' (shoemakers') cases, which resulted in six trials between 1806 and 1815, left labor organizations in a tenuous position. Although the journeymen's right to organize was acknowledged, the courts ruled unlawful any coercive action by them that would harm other businesses or the public. In other words, strikes were ruled illegal. Eventually a Massachusetts case, *Commonwealth* v. *Hunt* (1842), effectively reversed this decision when Chief Justice Lemuel Shaw ruled that Boston journeyman bootmakers could strike "in such manner as best to subserve their own interests." Conspiracy laws no longer thwarted unionization.

Yet permanent labor organizations were difficult to maintain. Most workers outside the crafts were unskilled or semiskilled at best. Moreover, religion, race, ethnicity, and gender divided workers. The first unions arose among urban journeymen in printing, woodworking, shoemaking, and tailoring. These early labor unions tended to be local; the strongest resembled medieval guilds in that members sought to protect themselves against the competition of inferior workmen by regulating apprenticeship and establishing minimum wages. They also excluded women and African-Americans. (Massachusetts mill women organized their own unions.)

Umbrella organizations composed of individual craft unions, like the National Trades Union (1834), arose in several cities in the 1820s and 1830s. But the movement fell apart amid wage reductions and unemployment in the hard times of 1839–1843. In the 1850s the deterioration of working conditions strengthened the labor movement again, and affiliated craft unions began to organize into national unions. Workers won a reduction in hours, and the ten-hour day became standard. Though the Panic of 1857 wiped out the umbrella organizations, some of the new national unions in specific trades—notably printers, hat finishers, and stonecutters—survived. By 1860 national unions had also been organized by the painters, cordwainers, cotton spinners, iron molders, and machinists.

Economic and technological change inevitably affected individual workers more heavily than it affected their organizations. As a group, workers' share of the national wealth declined after the 1830s.

Individual producers—craftsmen, factory workers, and farmers—had less economic power than they had had a generation or two earlier. And workers were increasingly losing control over their own work.

 ## Commercial Farming

Although manufacturing increased steadily, agriculture remained the backbone of the economy. In 1800 New England and Middle Atlantic farmers worked as their fathers and mothers had. Life centered around a household economy in which the needs of the family and the labor at its disposal determined what was produced and in what amounts. Most implements—wooden plows, rakes, shovels, and yokes—were homemade, with iron parts obtained from the local blacksmith.

When canals and railroads began transporting grain, especially wheat, eastward from the fertile Old Northwest, northeastern agriculture could not compete. Eastern farmers had already

Northeastern Agriculture

cultivated all the land available to them; expansion was impossible. Moreover, small New England farms with their uneven terrain did not lend themselves to the new labor-saving farm implements introduced in the 1830s—mechanical sowers, reapers, threshers, and balers. In response to these problems and to competition from the West, many northern farmers either moved west or gave up farming for jobs in the merchant houses and factories.

Many eastern farm sons and daughters moved to western New York. After the Erie Canal was completed, these Yankees and New Yorkers settled on more fertile and cheaper land in Ohio and Indiana and then in Michigan, Illinois, and Wisconsin. Farm daughters who did not go west flocked to the early textile mills. Still other New Englanders—urban, better educated, and often experienced in trade—flocked to the countinghouses in New York, Boston, and Philadelphia. Between 1820 and 1860 the percentage of the population of the North living on farms declined from 71 to 40 percent.

But neither the countinghouse nor the factory depleted New England agriculture. The farmers who remained proved as adaptable on the farm as were their children working at copy desks and water-powered looms. By the 1850s many New England and Middle Atlantic farm families had abandoned the commercial production of wheat and corn and

Many women made butter for market in the early nineteenth century. Women's production and sale of butter, cheese, and other goods were an essential part of farm families' adaptation to the market economy.   The Sinclair Hamilton Collection of American Illustrated Books, Princeton University Library.

stopped tilling poor land. Instead, they were improving their livestock, especially cattle, and specializing in vegetable and fruit production and dairy farming, financing these initiatives through land sales and borrowing. In fact, their greatest potential profit was from increasing land values, not from farming itself.

Farm families everywhere gradually adjusted to market conditions. In 1820 about one-third of all food produced was intended for market. By 1860 the amount had increased to about two-thirds. Middlemen specializing in the grain and food trades replaced the country storekeepers who had handled all transactions for local farmers, acting both as retailers and as marketing and purchasing agents.

Women's earning power from wages or market sales was an important factor in the market economy. With increasing commercialization and dependency on cash, women's earnings became essential to the survival of the family farm. The put-out work that women did in New England had its parallel in the

Women's Paid Labor

Middle Atlantic states and in Ohio—especially near towns and cities—in women's dairy production, which was crucial to family income. Butter and cheese making for local and regional markets replaced spinning and weaving as farm women's major activity, now that cloth could be purchased so cheaply. The work was physically demanding and did not replace regular home and farm chores but was added to them. Yet women took pride in their work; it gave many a sense of independence. Esther Lewis, a widow who sent from seventy-five to one hundred pounds of butter monthly to Philadelphia in the 1830s, even hired other women to increase production of milk products.

Women's success at butter and cheese making led some farms to specialize in dairy products and some entrepreneurs to seize the opportunity to profit by expanding production. Beginning in 1847 in Ohio, entrepreneurs built cheese factories in rural towns and contracted to buy curd from local dairy farmers. One such factory in Gustavus, Ohio, produced 5,000 pounds of cheese a day from the milk of 2,500 cows in 1852. The cheese was shipped by canal and railroad to cities and eastern ports, where merchants sold to consumers as far away as California, England, and China. By 1860 Ohio dairies were producing 21.6 million pounds of cheese a year for market.

Most farm families seemed to welcome the opportunities offered by the market economy. While continuing to take pride in self-sufficiency and to value rural culture, they shifted toward specialization and market-oriented production. The rewards for such flexibility were great. Produce sold at market financed land and equipment purchases and made credit arrangements possible. Many farm families flourished.

Meanwhile, the economic distance widened between farm owners on the one hand and tenants and hired hands on the other. The rising cost of land and of farming meant that opportunities for hired hands to acquire their own farms were shrinking. By the 1850s it took from ten to twenty years for a rural laborer to save enough money to farm for himself. Thus the number of tenant farmers increased. Previously farmers had relied on the labor of unpaid family members or enslaved workers; now paid farm labor became commonplace. In the North in 1860 there was one hired hand for every 2.3 farms.

Individually and collectively, Americans still valued agrarian life. State governments energetically promoted commercial agriculture to spur economic growth and sustain the values of an agrarian-based republic. Massachusetts in 1817 and New York in 1819 subsidized agricultural prizes and county fairs. New York required contestants to submit written descriptions of how they grew their prize crops; the state then published the best essays to encourage the use of new methods and promote specialization. Farm journals also helped familiarize farmers with developments in agriculture. By 1860 nearly sixty journals had a combined circulation of from 250,000 to 300,000.

Even so, the Old Northwest gradually and inevitably replaced the northeastern states as the center of American family agriculture. Farms in the Old Northwest were much larger and better suited to the new mechanized farming implements than were their northeastern counterparts. The farmers of the region bought machines such as the McCormick reaper on credit and paid for them with the profits from their high yields. By 1847 Cyrus McCormick was selling a thousand reapers a year. By introducing

Mechanization of Agriculture

interchangeable parts, he expanded production to five thousand a year, but demand still outstripped supply. Similarly, John Deere's steel plow, invented in 1837, replaced the inadequate iron plow; steel blades kept the soil from sticking and were tough enough to break the roots of prairie grass. By 1856, Deere's sixty-five employees were making 13,500 plows a year.

Mechanized farming was the basis of expanded production. In the 1850s alone wheat production surged 70 percent. By that time the area that had been the western wilderness in 1800 had become one of the world's leading agricultural regions. Midwestern farm families fed an entire nation, including a generation of immigrants—and still had enough food to export.

Settling and Conquering the West

Integral to the development of the market economy was the steady expansion of the United States. In 1800 the edge of settlement within the United States extended in an arc from western New York State through the new states of Kentucky and Tennessee and south to Georgia. By 1820, with the acquisition of the Louisiana Territory and Florida, it had shifted westward to Ohio, Indiana, and Illinois in the North, and Louisiana, Alabama, and Mississippi in the South. By 1860, Texas and California were states, and settlement had reached its twentieth-century continental limits. Unsettled and sporadically settled land remained—mostly the plains and mountain territory between the Mississippi River and the Sierra Nevada—but elsewhere the land and its Native American inhabitants had given way to white settlement (see pages 334–339).

The legal boundaries of the country were also changing rapidly during this period. Between 1803 and 1853 the United States pushed its original boundaries to their present continental limits (except for Alaska). The Louisiana Purchase roughly doubled the nation's size, and the acquisition of Florida from Spain in 1819 secured the Southeast. In the 1840s the United States annexed the Republic of Texas, defined its northern border with Canada, and acquired California, Nevada, Utah, and most of Arizona through war with Mexico (see pages 376–378). Finally, in 1853 the Gadsden Purchase added southern Arizona and New Mexico.

Most Americans saw western settlers as civilizers; a minority, including Indians, viewed them

The fur trade was part of a market system that extended from the Far West through St. Louis, Montréal, and New York to the hat merchants of Europe. These Ottawa fur traders, painted at Fort Michilimackinac in Upper Michigan, most likely traded with fur merchants based in Montréal.   National Archives of Canada.

as conquerors. In myth, literature, and song Americans glorified the explorers, fur trappers and scouts, and pioneers. James Fenimore Cooper's Leatherstocking tales, a series of novels that began appearing in 1823, introduced Hawkeye (Natty Bumppo), America's first popular fictional hero. At heart a romantic, Hawkeye preferred the freedom of the virgin forest to domesticated society. Yet whatever noble Eden the wilderness offered, it inevitably gave way, as Cooper described in *The Last of the Mohicans* (1826), to civilization. Like the Hutchinson Family's emancipation railroad, progress was unstoppable. The public snapped up tales of pioneers civilizing the wilderness.

The Hutchinson Family expressed doubt about the price of American expansion. In "The Indian's

Conquerors and Civilizers

Lament" (1846) they took an Indian voice and imagined Indian culture dying out:

> And I, and I stand alone as the last of my race,
> Upon this earth I feel I no more have a place,
> Since my home, friends, and kindred are driven away,
> For the steel of the white man, has swept them away.

What awaits the Indian is death, but it would bring release, in "the bright blissful shores, and the fair forest shade. / Where the steel of the white man, will never invade."

"The steel of the white man" referred to an iron will as well as to the military might that conquered the West. The frontier represented not only the peaceful settlement of the West and the extension of farming and republican virtue but also the conquering of the native inhabitants and the environment.

The history of the West was often violent and intolerant. The Mormons who sought a new Jerusalem near the Great Salt Lake were fleeing the gehenna (hell) imposed on them by frontier folk farther east (see page 317). Those who sought to farm the land, dig the gold, trap the furs, and cut the lumber destroyed the natural landscape and ecological balance in the name of progress and development.

The market economy provided a great impetus for expansion. Early on, the fur trapper system brought the Far West—way beyond settlement—into a market system that extended through St. Louis, Montréal, and New York to the hat merchants of Europe. Then, in the late 1840s, settlement jumped over the trapping areas to the West Coast of the American continent, when the promise of instant wealth in the form of gold sparked a gold rush.

Gold stimulated a mass migration to the West Coast. The United States had acquired Alta California in the Treaty of Guadalupe Hidalgo (see page 378) from Mexico, and the province was inhabited mostly by native peoples, some Mexicans living on large estates, and a chain of small settlements around military forts (presidios) and missions. That changed almost overnight after James Marshall, a

California Gold Rush

carpenter, spotted gold particles in the millrace at Sutter's Mill (now Coloma, California, northwest of Sacramento) in January 1848. Word of the discovery spread, and other Californians rushed to scrabble for instant fortunes. When John C. Frémont reached San Francisco five months later, he found that "all, or nearly all, its male inhabitants had gone to the mines." The town, "which a few months before was so busy and thriving, was then almost deserted."

By 1849 the news had spread around the world, and hundreds of thousands of fortune seekers, mostly young men, streamed in from Mexico, England, Germany, France, Ireland, and all over the United States. The newcomers came for one reason: instant wealth. In search of gold and silver, they mined the lodes and washed away the surface soil with hydraulic mining, leaving the land unsuitable for anything after they abandoned it.

Success in the market economy required capital, hard labor, and time; by contrast, gold mining seemed to promise instant riches. Most "forty-niners," however, never found enough gold to pay their expenses. "The stories you hear frequently in the States," one gold seeker wrote home, "are the most extravagant lies imaginable—the mines are a humbug. . . . The almost universal feeling is to get

Frank Marryat, a young English artist and writer, painted this scene of San Francisco around 1849. Gateway to the gold fields, San Francisco grew from one thousand residents in 1848 to thirty-five thousand two years later. Ships bringing people and supplies are anchored in the harbor.   Print collection of Miriam and Ira D. Wallach, Division of Arts, Prints, and Photographs. The New York Public Library. Astor, Lenox and Tilden Foundations.

Women who traveled west with their husbands found their domestic skills in great demand. In this watercolor entitled Laying Out of Karns' City, Minnesota *(1856), E. Whitefield shows a woman preparing a meal out of her lean-to kitchen for her husband and their guests.*   Chicago Historical Society.

home." But many stayed, either unable to afford the passage home or tempted by the growing labor shortage in California's cities and agricultural districts.

San Francisco, the former presido and mission of Yerba Buena, the gateway from the West Coast to the interior, became an instant city, ballooning to thirty-five thousand people in 1850. In 1848 it had been a small settlement of about a thousand Mexicans, Anglos, soldiers, friars, and Indians. Ships bringing people and supplies continuously jammed the harbor, a scene that artist Frank Marryat captured in an 1849 painting. A French visitor in that year wrote, "At San Francisco, where fifteen months ago one found only a half dozen large cabins, one finds today a stock exchange, a theater, churches of all Christian cults, and a large number of quite beautiful homes."

The forty-niners had their eyes on gold nuggets, but they had to be fed. Thus began the great Cali-

fornia agricultural boom. Wheat was the preferred staple; it required minimal investment, was easily planted, and offered a quick return at the end of a relatively short growing season. California farmers eagerly imported machinery, since labor was scarce (and thus expensive) and the flat, treeless valleys were well suited to horse-drawn machines. By the mid-1850s, California was exporting wheat. Meanwhile, enterprising merchants rushed to supply, feed, and clothe the new settlers. One such merchant was Levi Strauss, a German Jewish immigrant, whose tough mining pants found an enduring and eventually worldwide market as blue jeans.

In the Midwest, family farms were the basic unit of production. In California, by contrast, mining, grazing, and large-scale wheat farming were overwhelmingly male occupations. The experiences of women, who

Women Settlers constituted about one-seventh of the travelers on the overland trails, differed from those of men moving westward. Most men came alone, drawn by a sense of adventure and personal opportunity. Women who accompanied their husbands found their lives uprooted. Moving was a traumatic experience for many; they left behind networks of friends and kin to journey, often with children, along an unknown path to a strange environment. Yet in the West their domestic skills were in great demand. They received high fees for cooking, laundering, and sewing, and they ran boarding houses and hotels (men shunned domestic work).

Not all women, however, were entrepreneurs. Some wives, at their spouses' behest, cooked for and served their husbands' friends, enabling their husbands to build reputations as hosts. Abigail Scott Duniway, a leading western crusader for women's suffrage and a veteran of the Overland Trail to Oregon, wrote in 1859 that she lived in a "neighborhood composed chiefly of bachelors, who found comfort in mobilizing at meal time at the homes of the few married men of the township, and seemed especially fond of congregating at the hospitable cabin home of my good husband, who was never quite so much in his glory as when entertaining men at this fireside, while I, if not washing, scrubbing, churning, or nursing the baby, was preparing their meals in our lean-to kitchen."

Gold altered the pattern of settlement along the entire Pacific coast. Before 1848 most overland traffic flowed north over the Oregon Trail; few pioneers turned south to California. By 1849 a pioneer observed that the Oregon Trail "bore no evidence of having been much traveled this year." Traffic was flowing south instead, and California was becoming the new population center of the Pacific Slope. One measure of this shift was the overland mail routes. In the 1840s the Oregon Trail had been the main communications link between the Midwest and the Pacific. But the post office officials who organized mail routes in the 1850s terminated them in California, not Oregon; there was no route north of Sacramento.

By 1860 farmers in California, as in the Great Plains and prairies farther east, had become firmly linked to the market economy. They cleared the land of trees or prairie grass, hoed corn and wheat, fenced in animals, and constructed cabins of logs or sod. Success often depended on their access to water, and they sought to divert the streams and rivers of

Western Farming

the West to irrigate their land. As settled areas expanded, farmers built roads to carry their stock and produce to market and bring back supplies they could not produce for themselves. Growth brought specialization; as western farmers shifted from self-sufficiency to commercial farming, they too tended to concentrate on one crop. As land prices rose, families seeking new land had to go farther west to find land they could afford.

Though often thought of as outposts of rugged individualism, many early agricultural settlements depended heavily on family and kinship networks and communal cooperation. Sugar Creek on the Sangamon River in central Illinois exemplified this cooperative spirit. The white settlers who arrived in 1817 named the settlement for its sugar maples, tapped first by the Kickapoos and then by the American settlers. Although the settlement was based on private land ownership, most newcomers over the next decade were members of kin networks who assisted each other in clearing land and turning temporary dwellings into permanent cabins. Whether raising hogs or children, Sugar Creek families depended on kin and friends for support. In crises, too, they rose to the occasion. When someone "would be sick with chills or jaundice, or something else," Sugar Creek farmer James Megredy recalled, "his neighbors would meet and take care of his harvest, get up wood, or repair his cabin, or plant his corn." Neighbors set up a "borrowing system" whereby scarce tools and labor constantly circulated through the neighborhood. Settlers who came without previous ties, if they stayed, did not long remain strangers.

What made possible settlements such as Sugar Creek was the availability of land and credit. Some public lands were granted as a reward for military service: veterans of the War of 1812 received 160 acres; veterans of the Mexican War (see Chapter 14) could purchase land at reduced prices. And until 1820, civilians could buy government land at $2 an acre (a relatively high price) on a liberal four-year payment plan. From 1800 to 1817 the government successively reduced the minimum purchase from 640 to 80 acres, bringing the land within the reach of more Americans. But when the availability of land prompted the flurry of land speculation that ended in the Panic of 1819 (see page 248), the government discontinued credit sales. Instead, it reduced the price further, to $1.25 an acre.

Land Grants and Sales

Some eager pioneers settled land before it had been surveyed and offered for sale. Such illegal settlers, or squatters, then had to buy the land at auction and faced the risk of being unable to purchase it. Often neighbors protected squatters; in Sugar Creek, Illinois, they even helped them buy land. In 1841, to facilitate settlement and end property disputes, Congress passed the Pre-emption Act, which legalized settlement prior to surveying.

Since most settlers needed to borrow money, private credit systems arose: banks, private investors, country storekeepers, and speculators all extended credit to farmers. Railroads also sold land on credit—land they had received from the government as construction subsidies. (The Illinois Central, for example, received 2.6 million acres in 1850.) Indeed, nearly all economic activity in the West involved credit, from land sales to the shipping of produce to railroad construction. In 1816, 1836, and 1855, easy credit helped boost land prices. When land prices increased beyond farmers' abilities to pay interest or repay their loans, or when farm prices or weather conditions reduced farmers' income, farmland values collapsed, ending the speculative bubble. Mortgage bankers and speculators then purchased much land cheaply. As a consequence, many farmers became renters instead of owners of land; tenancy became more common in the West than it had been in New England.

From the start, the agricultural West was dependent on its links with towns and cities. Cities along the Ohio River—Louisville and Cincinnati—and the old French settlements—Detroit on the Great Lakes, St. Louis on the Mississippi River—predated and promoted the earliest settlement of much of the West.

Frontier Cities

New population centers, however, bypassed such old French towns as Vincennes and Kaskaskia. Chicago spearheaded settlement farther west. Steamboats connected the river cities with eastern markets and ports, carrying grain east and returning with finished goods. As the center of a rail network, Chicago exercised sway over the settling and development of most of the middle United States. Like cities in the Northeast, these western cities eventually developed into manufacturing centers as merchants shifted their investments from commerce to industry. Chicago became a center for the manufacture of farm implements, Louisville, of textiles. Smaller cities specialized in flour mills, and all produced consumer goods for the hinterlands.

Urban growth in the West was so spectacular that by 1860 Cincinnati, St. Louis, and Chicago each had populations exceeding one hundred thousand, and Buffalo, Louisville, San Francisco, Pittsburgh, Detroit, and Milwaukee had surpassed forty thousand. Thus commerce, urban growth, and industrialization overtook the farmers' frontier, wedding the West to the Northeast.

 ## Conclusion

For the North and the West the period from 1800 through 1860 was one of explosive growth. Population increased sixfold. The United States now extended from sea to sea, incorporating new peoples—Indians, Mexicans, Californians—sending out settlers to plow the land and inhabit the cities, and recruiting immigrants from around the world. Agriculture, which had completely dominated the nation at the turn of the century, was by midcentury being challenged by a booming manufacturing sector. And agriculture itself was becoming market-oriented and mechanized.

Economic development changed the way people lived. Canals, railroads, steamboats, and telegraph lines linked economic activities hundreds and even thousands of miles apart. The market economy brought sustained growth; it also ushered in cycles of boom and bust. Hard times and unemployment became frequent occurrences. The growing economy also meant larger-scale destruction of the environment: mills exploited New England waterways as a source of power, Michigan was denuded of its pine forests, and the gold rush destroyed land in California.

Large-scale manufacturing also altered traditional patterns of production and consumption. Farmers began to purchase goods formerly made by their wives and daughters, and farm families geared production to faraway markets. Farm women increasingly contributed income from market sales to the family farm. In New England many young women left the family farm to become the first factory workers in the new textile industry. As workshops and factories replaced household production, and the master-journeyman-apprentice system faded away, workplace relations became more impersonal and working conditions harsher, and men's and women's work became increasingly dissimilar. Industrial jobs began to attract large numbers of immigrants, and some workers organized labor unions.

The American people, too, were changing. Immigration and western expansion were making the population more diverse. Urbanization, commerce, and industry were creating significant divisions among Americans, reaching deeply into the home as well as the workshop. The South was not totally insulated from these changes, but its dependence on slave rather than free labor set it apart. Above all else, slavery defined the South.

Suggestions for Further Reading

General

Stuart Bruchey, *The Roots of American Economic Growth, 1607–1861: An Essay in Social Causation* (1965); David Klingaman and Richard Vedder, eds., *Essays in Nineteenth-Century History* (1975); Jack Larkin, *The Reshaping of Everyday Life, 1790–1840* (1988); Otto Mayr and Robert C. Post, eds., *Yankee Enterprise: The Rise of the American System of Manufactures* (1981); D. W. Meinig, *The Shaping of America: A Geographical Perspective on 500 Years of History*, vol. 2, *Continental America, 1800–1867* (1993); Douglass C. North, *Economic Growth of the United States, 1790–1860* (1966); Nathan Rosenberg, *Technology and American Economic Growth* (1972); Melvyn Stokes and Stephen Conway (eds.), *The Market Revolution in America: Social, Political, and Religious Expressions, 1800–1860* (1996).

Transportation

Robert G. Albion, *The Rise of New York Port, 1815–1860* (1939); Albert Fishlow, *American Railroads and the Transformation of the Ante-Bellum Economy* (1965); Carter Goodrich, *Government Promotion of American Canals and Railroads, 1800–1890* (1960); Louis C. Hunter, *Steamboats on the Western Rivers* (1949); Harry N. Scheiber, *Ohio Canal Era: A Case Study of Government and the Economy, 1820–1861* (1969); Ronald E. Shaw, *Canals for a Nation: The Canal Era in the United States, 1790–1860* (1990); George R. Taylor, *The Transportation Revolution, 1815–1860* (1951); James A. Ward, *Railroads and the Character of America, 1820–1887* (1986).

Commerce and Manufacturing

Alfred D. Chandler, Jr., *The Visible Hand: Managerial Revolution in American Business* (1977); Thomas C. Cochran, *Frontiers of Change: Early Industrialization in America* (1981); Robert F. Dalzell, Jr., *Enterprising Elite: The Boston Associates and the World They Made* (1987); Louis Hartz, *Economic Policy and Democratic Thought: Pennsylvania, 1776–1860* (1954); David A. Hounshell, *From the American System to Mass Production, 1800–1932: The Development of Manufacturing Technology in the United States* (1984); David J. Jeremy, *Transatlantic Industrial Revolution: The Diffusion of Textile Technologies Between Britain and America, 1790s–1830s* (1981); Stanley I. Kutler, *Privilege and Creative Destruction: The Charles River Bridge Case* (1971); Walter Licht, *Industrializing America: The Nineteenth Century* (1995); Merritt

Roe Smith, *Harpers Ferry Armory and the New Technology* (1977); Theodore Steinberg, *Nature Incorporated: Industrialization and the Waters of New England* (1991); Barbara M. Tucker, *Samuel Slater and the Origins of the American Textile Industry, 1790–1860* (1984); Anthony F. C. Wallace, *Rockdale: The Growth of an American Village in the Early Industrial Revolution* (1978).

Agriculture

"American Agriculture, 1790–1840, A Symposium," *Agricultural History* 46 (January 1972); Jeremy Atack and Fred Bateman, *To Their Own Soil: Agriculture in the Antebellum North* (1987); Allen G. Bogue, *From Prairie to Corn Belt: Farming on the Illinois and Iowa Prairies in the Nineteenth Century* (1963); Christopher Clark, *The Roots of Rural Capitalism: Western Massachusetts, 1780–1860* (1990); Clarence Danhof, *Change in Agriculture: The Northern United States, 1820–1870* (1969); John Mack Faragher, *Sugar Creek: Life on the Illinois Prairie* (1986); Paul W. Gates, *The Farmer's Age: Agriculture, 1815–1860* (1962); Benjamin H. Hibbard, *A History of Public Land Policies* (1939); Joan M. Jensen, *Loosening the Bonds: Mid-Atlantic Farm Women, 1750–1850* (1986); Robert Leslie Jones, *History of Agriculture in Ohio to 1880* (1983); Sally McMurry, *Transforming Rural Life: Dairying Families and Agricultural Change, 1820–1885* (1995).

Conquerors and Civilizers

William Cronon, *Nature's Metropolis: Chicago and the Great West* (1991); John Mack Faragher, *Women and Men on the Overland Trail* (1979); William H. Goetzmann, *Exploration and Empire: The Explorer and the Scientist in the Winning of the American West* (1966); Julie Roy Jeffrey, *Frontier Women: The Trans-Mississippi West, 1840–1880* (1979); Theodore J. Karamanski, *Fur Trade and Exploration: Opening the Far Northwest, 1821–1852* (1983); Lillian Schlissel, *Women's Diaries of the Westward Journey* (1982); Duane A. Smith, *Mining America: The Industry and the Environment, 1800–1980* (1987); John D. Unruh, Jr., *The Overland Emigrants and the Trans-Mississippi West, 1840–1860* (1979); David J. Weber, *The Spanish Frontier in North America* (1992).

Workers

Mary H. Blewett, *Men, Women, and Work: Class, Gender, and Protest in the New England Shoe Industry, 1780–1910* (1988); Jeanne Boydston, *Home and Work: Housework, Wages, and the Ideology of Labor in the Early Republic* (1990); Alan Dawley, *Class and Community: The Industrial Revolution in Lynn* (1977); Thomas Dublin, *Transforming Women's Work: New England Lives in the Industrial Revolution* (1994); Thomas Dublin, *Women at Work: The Transformation of Work and Community in Lowell, Massachusetts, 1826–1860* (1979); Bruce Laurie, *Artisans into Workers: Labor in Nineteenth-Century America* (1989); Jonathan Prude, *The Coming of Industrial Order: Town and Factory Life in Rural Massachusetts, 1810–1860* (1983); Howard B. Rock, Paul A. Gilje, and Robert Asher, eds., *American Artisans: Crafting Social Identity, 1750–1850* (1995); Norman Ware, *The Industrial Worker, 1840–1860* (1924); Sean Wilentz, *Chants Democratic: New York City and the Rise of the American Working Class, 1788–1850* (1984); David A. Zonderman, *Aspirations and Anxieties: New England Workers and the Mechanized Factory System, 1815–1850* (1992).

CHAPTER

11

Slavery and the Growth of the South

1800–1860

S he looked out of place in the dirty yard of the slave trader's establishment. Dressed in silk and adorned in jewelry, Eliza seemed bewildered as she clung to the hands of her children, a little boy and a girl. That morning in 1841 Eliza had been told that she was going into Washington, D.C., to receive her long-promised freedom. Now she found herself in "a slave pen within the very shadow of the Capitol."

Eliza had been the concubine of her owner, Elisha Berry, but a division of his property placed her under the control of his resentful daughter, who promptly decided to remove all evidence of her father's illicit relationship. As the reality of her situation sank in, Eliza began to fear most that she would be separated from her children.

Within a few days the slave trader moved her and the children to Richmond, Virginia, and then by ship to New Orleans, where planters in the booming Gulf region needed many more slaves. At the New Orleans slave market a man offered to purchase her son. Eliza pleaded with him to buy the family group and promised "to be the most faithful slave that ever lived." When he answered that he could not afford it, Eliza "burst into a paroxysm of grief, weeping plaintively." Later, when her daughter was sold away, Eliza had to be physically torn apart from the last person she loved.

Sent to work in the fields of a plantation on Bayou Boeuf, Eliza grew "feeble and emaciated" though she was still a young woman. Within two years she was dead. Eliza's fate was one of many human tragedies accompanying the vast expansion of plantation slavery that took place between 1800 and 1860. Tens of thousands of African-Americans suffered as slavery spread westward; across the Mississippi River and into Texas.

Louisiana sugar planters were among the richest of the southern slaveholders. Those who had enjoyed their wealth for a few decades often laid out spacious plantations and built large mansions, many of which survive today. *Louisiana State University Museum of Art, Baton Rouge.*

285

Many northerners remained undisturbed in this period by the progress of human bondage, but a growing number came to see it as shocking and backward. In the years after the Revolution, northerners—possessing few slaves and influenced by the revolutionary concept of natural rights—had adopted gradual emancipation laws (see page 178). At the same time they developed a dynamic market economy and embarked on an industrial revolution. These changes rendered forced labor obsolete. An industrializing, free-labor society saw no use for slavery (see Chapter 10).

Meanwhile, the South witnessed a different kind of growth and prosperity. New lands were settled and new states peopled, but as the North grew and changed, economically the South merely grew. And growth there only reinforced existing economic patterns. Steadily the South emerged as the world's most extensive and vigorous slave economy. Slavery had a far-reaching influence on the whole society. Southerners were slaves, slaveholders, and nonslaveholders rather than farmers, merchants, mechanics, mill girls, and manufacturers. Southern wealth came from export crops rather than from commerce, manufacturing, and crops sold at home. The southern population was almost wholly rural rather than both rural and urban.

These facts meant that the economic and social lives of southerners were unavoidably distinct from those of northerners. Nonslaveholders operated their family farms in a society dominated by slaveholding planters. A handful of planters developed an aristocratic lifestyle, while slaves—one-third of the South's people—lived without freedom, struggling to develop a culture that sustained hope. The influence of slavery spread throughout the social system, affecting not just southern economics but southern values, customs, and laws.

Migration, Growth, and the Cotton Boom

Between 1800 and 1860, small farmers and slaveowning planters migrated westward and brought new territory under cultivation. As human labor, both voluntary and coerced, built a vastly larger slaveholding society, farms and plantations spread across the landscape. The attraction of rich new lands drew thousands of southerners across the Appalachian Mountains. Early settlers told people back east about "dark, heavy forests, . . . wide, thick canebrakes, [and] clear running river[s], full of fish." These accounts created in many men an irresistible urge to move. Small farmers and ambitious slaveowners poured across the mountains, pushing the Indians off their lands in the Gulf region (see pages 334–339). The floodtide of westward migration reached Alabama and Mississippi in the 1830s, then spilled into Texas in the 1850s.

The earliest settlers in the swelling stream of migration were often yeomen—small farmers, most of whom owned no slaves. Yeomen pioneered the southern wilderness, moving into undeveloped regions and building log cabins. After the War of 1812 they moved in successive waves down the southern Appalachians into new Gulf lands, first as herders of livestock and then as farmers.

Yeoman Farmers

Migration became almost a way of life for some yeoman families. Lured by stories of good land beyond the horizon, many men uprooted their wives and children repeatedly. Each new land seemed "like a paradise" to many eager settlers. The Alabama Territory, wrote one new arrival, had "the greatest prospect of corn and cotton I ever saw." Writing to friends in older parts of the South, he asked, "Why will you stay . . . and work them poor stony ridges when one half of the labor and one third of the ground heare will bring you more?" So many shared the excitement over new lands that one North Carolinian wrote in alarm, "The *Alabama Fever* rages here with great violence. . . . I am apprehensive if it continues to spread as it has done, it will almost depopulate the country."

On the southern frontier men worked hard to clear fields and establish a farm, while their wives labored in the household economy and patiently re-created the social ties—to relatives, neighbors, fellow churchgoers—that enriched everyone's experience. Women seldom shared the men's excitement about moving. They dreaded the isolation and loneliness of the frontier, but few had a voice in the decision. "We have been [moving] all our lives," lamented one woman. "As soon as ever we git comfortably settled, it is time to be off to something new." Maria Lides's father took the family from South Carolina to Alabama, but "his having such a good crop" there, Maria wrote to a relative, "seems to make him more anxious to move." She almost wished that another restless relative, her brother, would decide on California, because "he would be obliged to stop then for he could go no farther."

• *Important Events* •

1793	Eli Whitney invents the cotton gin Production of short-staple cotton begins to expand		**1832**	Virginia holds last serious debate in South about the future of slavery
1800	Gabriel's conspiracy is discovered in Virginia		**1832 and after**	Legislators in several states increase restrictions on slaves
1808	Congress bans further importation of slaves		**1830s**	Class tensions lead to electoral reforms in much of the South
1810–20	137,000 slaves are forced to move from North Carolina and the Chesapeake to Alabama, Mississippi, and other western regions		**1836**	Arkansas gains admission to the Union
			1839	Mississippi's Married Women's Property Act gives married women some property rights
1812	Louisiana gains admission to the Union		**1845**	Florida and Texas gain admission to the Union
1817	Mississippi gains admission to the Union			
1819	Alabama gains admission to the Union		**1857**	North Carolina slaveholder Hinton R. Helper denounces the slave system in *The Impending Crisis*
1822	Denmark Vesey's plot is discovered in South Carolina			
1831	Nat Turner leads a violent rebellion in Virginia			

Some yeomen acquired large tracts of level land, purchased slaves, and became wealthy. Others clung to the beautiful mountainous areas they loved or kept moving as independent subsistence farmers because, as one frontiersman put it, he disliked "seeing the nose of my neighbor sticking out between the trees." Those who moved tended to stick to the climate and soils they knew best. Yeomen could not afford the richest bottomlands, which were swampy and required expensive draining, but they acquired land almost everywhere else.

For slaveholding southerners another powerful motive impelled westward movement: the chance to profit from a spectacular cotton boom. Southern planters were not sentimental-

Rise of the Cotton South

ists, holding onto slavery while northerners grew rich from commerce and the industrial revolution. Like other Americans, slaveholding southerners were profit oriented, and the cotton boom caused nonmechanized, slave-based agriculture to remain highly profitable in the South, sustaining the plantation economy.

This outcome had not always seemed likely. At the time of the Revolution, slave-based agriculture was not very profitable in the Upper South, where most southerners then lived. Persistent debt plagued Virginia's extravagant and aristocratic tobacco growers. Farther south, along the coast of the Carolinas and Georgia, slaves grew rice and some indigo. Cotton was a profitable crop only for the Sea Island planters of South Carolina and Georgia, who grew the luxurious long-staple variety. Short-staple cotton, which grew readily in the interior, was unmarketable because its sticky seeds lay tangled in the fibers. Yet, in spite of the limited usefulness of slavery, much wealth was tied up in it. Ingrained social forces and fear of slave revolts prevented its abolition.

Then, late in the eighteenth century, England's burgeoning textile industry demanded more and more cotton. Sea Island cotton became so profitable between 1785 and 1795 that thousands of farmers in the interior tried growing the short-staple variety; by the early 1790s southern farmers were growing 2 to 3 million pounds of it each year, despite their inability to remove the seeds. Some of this cotton was meant for domestic use, but most was grown in the hope that some innovation would make the crop salable to the English. In such circumstances the invention of a cotton gin was almost inevitable, and Eli Whitney, an inventor from Connecticut, responded

New Orleans, the South's largest city and a major port, was a wealthy hub of the cotton trade. This view from 1860 shows hundreds of cotton bales and dozens of steamboats waiting to receive them.   Chicago Historical Society.

in 1793 with a simple machine that removed the seeds from the fibers. By 1800 cotton was spreading rapidly westward from the seaboard states.

The voracious appetite of English mills caused a meteoric rise in cotton production (see maps, page 289). From 1800 until the Civil War, British demand for cotton multiplied rapidly, and southern planters rushed to increase their acreage. Despite occasional periods of low prices, the demand for cotton surged ahead every decade. Southerners with capital bought more land and more slaves and planted ever more cotton. Cotton growers boosted production so successfully that by 1825 the South was the world's dominant supplier of cotton; by the 1850s the South was the source of over 70 percent of all the cotton that Britain imported.

Thus the antebellum South—the Old South before the Civil War—became primarily a cotton South. Large amounts of tobacco and hemp continued to be grown in the Upper South, and rice and sugar were important crops in certain coastal areas, especially in South Carolina, Georgia, and Louisiana. Thousands of southerners grew only food crops, but cotton was the largest and most widespread cash crop, and the wealth it generated shaped the society and fueled the South's hunger for new territory.

Small slaveowners and wealthier planters (those who owned twenty or more slaves) sought out alluvial bottomland and other fertile soils, eager to grasp the opportunity for wealth the cotton boom offered. A Virginian who visited Vicksburg, Mississippi, in 1836 marveled at the atmosphere: "They do business in a kind of frenzy," he wrote. That frenzy produced many brand-new aristocrats. Some old Virginia and South Carolina families were represented among the proud new "cotton snobs," but most of the wealthy were newly rich.

The desire to plant more cotton and buy more slaves often caused men with new wealth to postpone the enjoyment of luxuries. Many first-generation planters lived for decades in their original log cabins, improved only by clapboards or a frame addition. "If you wish to see people worth millions living as [if] they were not worth hundreds," a Mississippi gentleman remarked, "come down here." Yet the planters' wealth put ease and refinement within their grasp, and riches and high social status arrived quickly for some.

A case in point is the family of Jefferson Davis, who later became president of the Confederacy. Like Abraham Lincoln, Davis was born in Kentucky amid humble circumstances. His father was one of the thousands of American farmers on the western frontier who moved frequently, seeking but never finding his fortune. Luckily for Jefferson Davis, his older brother migrated to Mississippi and made good. Settling on rich bottom-

One-Generation Aristocrats

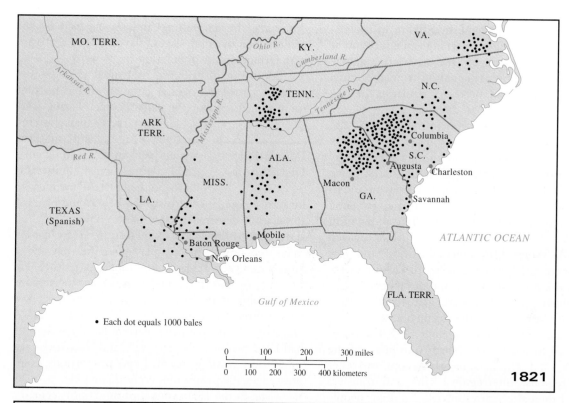

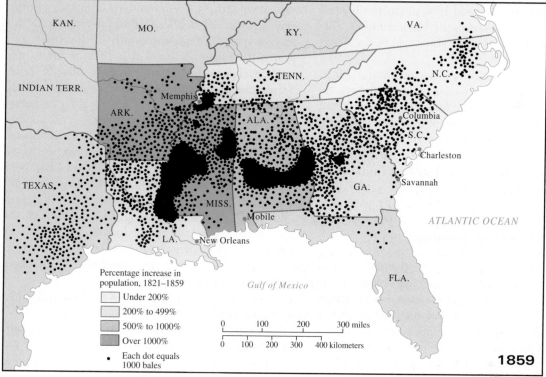

Cotton Production in the South   *These two maps reveal the rapid westward expansion of cotton production and its importance to the antebellum South.*

lands next to the Mississippi River, Joseph Davis expanded his holdings of land and slaves and grew rich. Soon he was an established figure in society, and he used his influence to arrange an education at West Point for his younger brother. A large plantation awaited Jefferson's resignation from the army. The Davis family had become aristocrats in one generation.

The rise of new aristocrats in the Gulf and the migration of thousands of aspiring slaveholders across the Appalachians meant another kind of migration—involuntary—for black southerners. Since Congress had closed the international slave trade in 1808, slaves for new cotton regions had to come from the Upper South, where the slave population was growing through natural increase while tobacco prices fell. Worried by soil exhaustion and low prices, planters in Virginia and North Carolina were shifting toward wheat and corn, crops that were less labor-intensive, and they were glad to sell excess slaves to fertile regions in the cotton South.

Between 1810 and 1820 alone, 137,000 slaves were forced to move from North Carolina and the Chesapeake states to Alabama, Mississippi, and other western regions. Interregional sales and transfers continued thereafter: an estimated 2 million people were sold between 1820 and 1860 to satisfy the need for slave labor. Thousands of black families, like Eliza's, were disrupted every year to serve the needs of the cotton economy.

To white southerners the period from 1800 to 1860 was a time of great change and progress, no less than in the North. The South was growing and expanding, driven by excitement over new lands and energies related to the cotton boom. But the South's growth was different from the North's: its distinguishing features were those of an agricultural and a slave society.

An Agrarian Society

The South did exhibit some of the diversity of the bustling, urbanizing, commercial North. There were merchants, artisans, and craftsmen in the larger cities, as well as men of commerce who promoted railways and transportation improvements. Immigrants from Ireland and other parts of Europe arrived in Savannah, New Orleans, and other southern ports in dramatically increasing numbers during the 1840s and 1850s. But these developments were only faint shadows of their northern counterparts and had relatively little impact. Southern development was dominated by agriculture and slavery and by the prominence of rural slaves, slaveholders, and yeoman farmers in the population.

Population distribution remained thin. Cotton growers spread out over as large an area as possible to maximize production and income. Farms were set far apart, rather than clustered around villages, and southern society remained predominantly rural. Because most immigrants to the United States sought urban locations, population growth fell behind the North's. Population density was low in the older plantation states and extremely low in the frontier areas. In 1860 there were only 2.3 people per square mile in vast and largely unsettled Texas, 15.6 in Louisiana, and 18.0 in Georgia. By contrast, population density in the non-slaveholding states east of the Mississippi River was almost three times higher. The Northeast had an average of 65.4 people per square mile. Massachusetts had 153.1 people per square mile, and New York City, where overcrowding reached epic proportions, compressed 86,400 people into each square mile.

Population Distribution

Even in the 1850s, much of the South seemed a virtual wilderness. Frederick Law Olmsted, a northerner later renowned as a landscape architect, made several trips through the South in the 1850s as a journalist. Olmsted found that the few trains and stagecoaches available to travelers offered crude accommodations and kept their schedules poorly. Indeed, he had to do most of his traveling on horseback along primitive trails. Between Columbus, Georgia, and Montgomery, Alabama, Olmsted found "a hilly wilderness, with a few dreary villages, and many isolated cotton farms." Alabama had been frontier as recently as 1800, but Olmsted encountered similar conditions in parts of eastern Virginia: "For hours and hours one has to ride through the unlimited, continual, all-shadowing, all-embracing forest. . . . [F]or days and days he may sometimes travel and see never two dwellings of mankind within sight of each other."

Society in such rural areas was characterized by relatively weak institutions outside the family, for it takes a concentration of people to create and support organized activity. Where people were scarce, it was difficult to finance and operate schools, churches, libraries, or even inns, restaurants, and other amenities. Southerners were strongly committed to their

This painting of the Alabama River at Selma (c. 1853–1855), attributed to William Frye, suggests the South's rural nature and the small size of its urban centers.   Selma-Dallas County Library and Birmingham Museum of Art.

churches, and some believed in the importance of universities, but all such institutions were far less fully developed than those in the North.

The South's cities were likewise smaller and less developed. Confined to the region's perimeter, the largest urban areas functioned as ports rather than centers of a vigorous internal commerce. They exported mainly staple crops, such as cotton or tobacco, and imported only a few necessary manufactured goods and luxuries. Factories—stimulus to urban growth in the North—were rare because planters invested most of their capital in slaves. A few southerners did invest in iron or textiles on a small scale. But the largest southern "industry" was lumbering, and the largest factories used slave labor to make cigars.

More decisively, the South was slower than the North to develop a unified market economy and a regional transportation network. Because planters

Weak Urban Sector

were eager to invest in land and slaves and often could use waterways for transportation, far less money was spent on canals, turnpikes, or railroads. The South had only 26 percent of the nation's railroad mileage in 1850 and, despite concerted efforts, only 35 percent in 1860. As a result, urban growth after 1820 was far less vigorous than in the North, and metropolitan centers were almost nonexistent. In 1860 only 49,000 out of 704,000 South Carolinians lived in towns with 2,500 or more residents, and less than 3 percent of Mississippi's population lived in places of comparable size. In the same year, the population of Charleston, South Carolina, was only 41,000, that of Richmond, Virginia, 38,000. New Orleans, Louisiana, by far the largest southern city, had only 169,000 residents and was being left behind because it was not linked to the national railroad network, even though it was a major port.

Thus although the South sold huge amounts of cotton on the international market, its economy at home was semideveloped relative to other sections of the country. Its white people were prospering, but not as rapidly as most residents of the North. There, changes in commerce and industry brought unprecedented advances in productivity, raising the average person's standard of living and widening the range of affordable goods and services (see Chapter 12). In the South, change was quantitative rather than qualitative. Using the same farming techniques, southern planters and farmers sought to grow more, but their region remained rural and its internal market undeveloped.

Free Southerners: Farmers, Planters, and Free Blacks

A large majority of white southern families (three-quarters in 1860) owned no slaves. Some lived in towns and ran stores or businesses, but most were yeoman farmers who owned their own land and grew their own food. They were the typical whites, but the social distance between different groups of whites was great. Still greater was the distance between whites and blacks.

The yeomen were independent, individualistic, and given to hard work and self-reliance. They could be independent thinkers as well, but their status as a numerical majority did not mean that they set the direction of the slave society. Absorbed in the work of their farms, they normally occupied a relatively autonomous position within the slavery-based staple-crop economy expanding around them. By slowly improving their acreage or settling new and better land, yeoman families improved their lot and made steady progress.

But the lives of most southern yeomen, unlike the lives of their northern counterparts, had not been transformed by improvements in transportation. Because few railroads penetrated the southern interior, yeomen generally had little contact with the market or the type of progress it could introduce. Families might raise a small surplus to sell for cash or to trade for needed items, but they were remote from large market networks and therefore not particularly concerned about increasing their cash income. Instead, they valued their self-reliance and freedom from others' control. Living an isolated, demanding rural life, yeomen constituted an important, though often silent, part of southern society. If their rights were threatened, however, they could react strongly.

The yeomen enjoyed a folk culture based on family, church, and neighborhood. They spoke with a drawl, and their inflections were reminiscent of their Scottish and Irish backgrounds. Once a year they flocked to religious revivals called protracted meetings or camp meetings, and in between they enjoyed house-raisings, logrollings, quilting bees, and corn-shuckings. Such occasions combined work with fun, offered food in abundance, and usually included liquor. They also provided fellowship that was especially welcome to isolated rural dwellers.

Folk Culture of the Yeomen

Social conventions imposed uniform roles on yeoman women. A demanding round of work and family responsibilities shaped their lives in the home. At harvest yeoman women frequently helped in the fields, and throughout the year the drying, preserving, and preparing of food consumed much of their time. Household tasks continued during frequent pregnancies and the care of small children. Primary nursing and medical care also fell to the mother, who might have a book of remedies to aid her but often relied on family and folk wisdom. In some evangelical churches women played respected roles on certain committees, but overwhelmingly the busy life of the yeoman woman was tied to the home.

Among the men there were many who aspired to wealth, eager to join the race for slaves, land, and profits from cotton. Such an individual was a North Carolinian named John F. Flintoff, whose diary reveals that the road to wealth was not always easy. At age eighteen in 1841, Flintoff went to Mississippi to seek his fortune. Like other aspiring yeomen, he worked as an overseer of slaves but often found it impossible to please his employers. At one point he gave up and returned to North Carolina, where he married and lived for a while in his parents' house. But Flintoff was "impatient to get along in the world," so he tried Louisiana next and then Mississippi again.

For Flintoff, the fertile Gulf region had its disadvantages. "My health has been very bad here," he wrote. "Chills and fever occasionally has hold of me." Routinely, "first rate employment" alternated with "very low wages." Moreover, as a young man working on isolated plantations, Flintoff often felt lonely. Even a revival meeting in 1844 proved "an extremely cold time" with "little warm feeling." His uncle and other employers found fault with his

How do historians know about the values and ways of life of nonslaveholders in the South? Letters, diaries, and family papers of these people, who generally were not rich or famous, have not been preserved as frequently as the records of the slaveholding elite. Thus historians have turned to various other sources—including travelers' accounts, folklore, and United States census records—to learn more about them. This page from the manuscript "Population Schedules" of the census of 1860 supplies information on family structure and a variety of personal characteristics. The "Census of Agriculture" contains much additional information about the size of each family's farm and the crops grown there.   Photo: North Carolina Division of Archives and History.

Most white southerners were not wealthy slaveowners but yeoman farmers. Artist John Bunyan Bristol called this painting of a farmer's home in northern Florida On the St. Johns River.   Collection of Samuel H. and Roberta Vickers/The Florida Collection.

work, and in 1846 Flintoff concluded in despair that "managing negroes and large farms is soul destroying."

A desire to succeed kept him going. At twenty-six, even before he owned any land, Flintoff bought his first slave, "a negro boy 7 years old." Soon he had purchased two more children, the cheapest slaves available. Conscious of his status as a slaveowner, Flintoff resented the low wages he was paid and complained that his uncle offered him *"hand pay,"* wages suitable for a day laborer rather than a slaveowner and manager. In 1853, with nine young slaves and a growing family, Flintoff faced "the most unhappy time of my life." Fired by his uncle, he returned to North Carolina, sold some of his slaves, and purchased 124 acres with help from his in-laws. Flintoff grew corn, wheat, and tobacco and earned extra cash hauling wood in his wagon. By 1860 he owned three horses, twenty-six hogs, ten head of cattle, and several slaves and was paying off his debts. As the Civil War approached, he looked forward to acquiring more land and slaves, freeing his wife from much of the labor of yeoman women, and possibly sending his sons to college. Although

Flintoff eventually achieved success, his path had not been easy, and he never became the cotton planter he had aspired to be.

Probably more typical of the southern yeoman was Ferdinand L. Steel, who as a young man moved from North Carolina to Tennessee to work as a hatter and river boatman but eventually took up farming in Mississippi. Steel rose every day at five and worked until sundown. With the help of his family he raised corn, wheat, pork, and vegetables for the family table. Cotton was his cash crop: he sold five or six bales (about 2,000 pounds) a year to obtain money for sugar, coffee, salt, calico, gunpowder, and a few other store-bought goods.

Steel picked his cotton himself (never exceeding 120 pounds per day, less than many slaves averaged) and complained that cotton cultivation was arduous and time-consuming. The market fluctuated, and if cotton prices fell, a small grower like Steel could be driven into debt and lose his farm. In fact, he wanted to grow less cotton. "We are too weak handed" to manage it, he noted in his diary. "We had better . . . raise corn and keep out of debt and we will have no necessity of raising cotton."

Steel's life in Mississippi in the 1840s retained much of the flavor of the frontier. He made all the family's shoes; his wife and sister sewed dresses, shirts, and "pantiloons." The Steel women also rendered their own soap and spun and wove cotton into cloth; the men hunted game. House-raisings and corn-shuckings provided entertainment, and Steel doctored his illnesses with boneset tea and other herbs.

The focus of Steel's life was family and religion. Family members prayed together every morning and night, and he prayed and studied Scripture for an hour after lunch. Steel joined a temperance society and looked forward to church and camp meetings. "My Faith increases, & I enjoy much of that peace which the world cannot give," he wrote in 1841. Seeking to improve himself and be ready for Judgment Day, Steel borrowed histories, Latin and Greek grammars, and religious books from his church. Eventually he became a traveling Methodist minister. "My life is one of toil," he reflected, "but blessed be God that it is as well with me as it is."

Toil with even less security was the lot of two other groups of free southerners: landless whites and free blacks. A sizable minority of white southern workers—from 25 to 40 percent, depending on the state—were unskilled laborers who owned no land and worked for others in the countryside and towns. Their property consisted of a few household items and some animals—usually pigs—that could feed themselves on the open range. The landless included some immigrants, especially Irish, who did heavy and dangerous work such as building railroads and digging ditches. By 1860 immigrants were becoming numerous in Savannah, New Orleans, and a few other port cities.

Landless Whites

In the countryside, white farm laborers struggled to become yeomen in the face of low wages or, if they rented, unpredictable market prices for their crops. The shortage of well-paying jobs and competition from speculators made it difficult for them to buy land. Some fell into debt and were frequently sued. By scrimping and saving and finding odd jobs, others managed to climb into the ranks of yeomen. When James and Nancy Bennitt of North Carolina succeeded in their ten-year struggle to buy land, they decided to avoid the unstable market in cotton; thereafter they raised extra corn and wheat as sources of cash. People like the Bennitts viewed pigs and livestock as a major economic asset; good steady

employment was uncertain in a region whose large producers relied on slave labor.

For the nearly quarter-million free blacks in the South in 1860, conditions were generally worse than the yeoman's and often little better than the slave's. The free blacks of the Upper South were usually descendants of men and women emancipated by their owners in the 1780s and 1790s. Some made substantial progress in towns or cities, but most lived in rural areas and had few material advantages. They usually did not own land and had to labor in someone else's fields, often beside slaves. By law free blacks could not own a gun, buy liquor, violate curfew, assemble except in church, testify in court, or (throughout the South after 1835) vote. Despite these obstacles, a minority bought land, and others found jobs as artisans, draymen, boatmen, and fishermen. A few prospered and bought slave laborers, but most who owned slaves had purchased their own wives and children (whom they could not free, since laws required newly emancipated blacks to leave their state).

Free Blacks

Farther south, in the cotton and Gulf regions, a large proportion of free blacks were mulattos, the privileged offspring of wealthy planters. Not all planters freed their mixed-race offspring, but those who did often recognized a moral obligation and gave their children good educations and financial backing. In a few cities like New Orleans and Mobile, extensive interracial sex had produced a mulatto population that was recognized as a distinct class. These people formed a society of their own and sought a status above slaves and other freedmen, if not equal to that of planters. But outside New Orleans, Mobile, and Charleston, such groups were rare, and most mulattos experienced more disadvantages than benefits from their light skin. (For a more detailed discussion of free blacks during this period, see Chapter 12.)

At the opposite end of the social spectrum from free blacks were slaveholders. As a group they lived well, on incomes that enabled them to enjoy superior housing, food, clothing, and luxuries. But most lived in comfortable farmhouses, not on the opulent scale that legend suggests. A few statistics tell the story: 50 percent of southern slaveholders had fewer than five slaves; 72 percent had fewer than ten; 88 percent had fewer than twenty. Thus the average slaveholder was not a wealthy aristocrat but an aspiring farmer, usually a person of

Planters

Most slaveowners lived in comfortable country homes rather than in stately mansions. This rare daguerreo-type, dating from about 1853, shows a family in front of their home. Notice the presence of a male slave in the left background.   The J. Paul Getty Museum, Los Angeles, California.

humble origins, with little formal education and many rough edges to his manner. In fact, he probably had little to distinguish him from a nonslaveholder beyond a degree of wealth and greater ambition.

Consider the Louisiana cotton planter Bennet Barrow, who was neither polished nor unusually coarse. His considerable wealth was new, and he was preoccupied with moneymaking: he worried constantly over his cotton crop, filling his diary with tedious weather reports and gloomy predictions of his yields. Yet Barrow also strove to appear above such worries, and in boom times he grandly cosigned loans for men who later defaulted and left him saddled with debt.

Barrow hunted frequently and had a passion for racing horses and raising hounds. He could report the loss of a slave without feeling, but emotion broke through his laconic manner when illness afflicted his sporting animals. "Never was a person more unlucky than I am," he mourned. "My favorite pup never lives." His strongest feelings surfaced when his horse

Jos Bell—equal to "the best Horse in the South"—"broke down running a mile . . . ruined for Ever." The same day the distraught Barrow gave his field hands a "general Whipping." Barrow was rich but not a cultured or gentle man.

The richest planters used their wealth to model genteel sophistication. Rather than eating abundant country food in a spacious, comfortable farmhouse, they served to guests in their mansions a choice of gourmet foods: "gumbo, ducks and olives, *supreme de volaille*, chickens in jelly, oysters, lettuce salad, chocolate cream, jelly cake, claret cup, etc." A traveler in Mississippi saw gentlemen on county court day dressed in "black cloth coats, black cravats and satin or embroidered silk waistcoats; all, too, sleek as if just from a barber's hands, and redolent of perfumes." Extended visits, parties, and balls to which women wore the latest fashions provided opportunities for friendship, courtship, and display.

Slaveholding men dominated society and, especially among the wealthiest and oldest families, justified their dominance through a paternalistic ideology.

Southern Paternalism

Instead of stressing the profitable aspects of commercial agriculture, they focused on noblesse oblige, seeing themselves as custodians of the welfare of society as a whole and of the black families who depended on them in particular. The paternalistic planter viewed himself not as an oppressor but as the benevolent guardian of an inferior race. He developed affectionate feelings toward his slaves (as long as they knew their place) and was genuinely shocked at criticism of his behavior.

The letters of Paul Carrington Cameron, North Carolina's largest slaveholder, illustrate this mentality. After a period of sickness among his one thousand North Carolina slaves (he had hundreds more in Alabama and Mississippi), Cameron wrote, "I fear the Negroes have suffered much from the want of proper attention and kindness under this late distemper . . . no love of lucre shall ever induce me to be cruel, or even to make or permit to be made any great exposure of their persons at inclement seasons." On another occasion he described to his sister the sense of responsibility he felt: "Do you remember a cold & frosty morning, during [our mother's] illness, when she said to me 'Paul my son the people ought to be shod' this is ever in my ears, whenever I see any ones shoes in bad order; and in my ears it will be, so long as I am master."

It was comforting to the richest southern planters to see themselves in this way, and slaves—accommodating to the realities of power—encouraged their masters to think their benevolence was appreciated. Paternalism also served as a defense against abolitionist criticism. Still, paternalism affected the manner and not the substance of most planters' behavior. Its softness and warmth were a matter of style, covering harsher assumptions: blacks were inferior, and planters should make money. As talk of paternalistic duties increased, theories about the complete and permanent inferiority of blacks also multiplied.

Even Paul Cameron's benevolence vanished with changed circumstances. After the Civil War, he bristled at African-Americans' efforts to be free and made sweeping economic decisions without regard to their welfare. Writing on Christmas Day 1865, Cameron showed little Christian charity (but a healthy profit motive) when he declared, "I am convinced that the people who gets rid of the free negro first will be the first to advance in improved agriculture. Have made no effort to retain any of mine [and] will not attempt a crop beyond the capacity of 30 hands." With that he turned off his land nearly a thousand black agriculturalists, rented his fields to several white farmers, and invested in industry, which he considered more promising economically.

Relations between men and women in the planter class were similarly paternalistic. The life of an upper-class southern woman was bound by the household, and she was raised and educated to be a wife,

Elite Women's Role

mother, and subordinate companion to men. South Carolina's Mary Boykin Chesnut wrote of her husband, "He is master of the house. To hear is to obey. . . . All the comfort of my life depends upon his being in a good humor." In a social system based on the coercion of an entire race, women were not allowed to challenge society's rules on sexual or racial relations. If a woman defied or questioned the status quo, she risked universal condemnation.

After spending her early years within the family circle, a planter's daughter usually attended one of the South's rapidly multiplying academies or boarding schools. There she formed friendships with other girls and received an education that emphasized grammar, composition, penmanship, geography, literature, and languages, but little science and mathematics. Typically the young woman maintained dutiful and affectionate ties with her parents and entertained suitors whom they approved. But very soon she had to choose a husband and commit herself for life to a man whom she generally had known for only a brief time.

Upon marriage, she ceded to her husband most of her legal rights, became part of his family, and was expected to get along with numerous in-laws during extended visits. Most of the year she was isolated on a large plantation, where she had to oversee the cooking and preserving of food, manage the house, supervise care of the children, and attend sick slaves. She was forbidden to travel unless accompanied by a man. All these realities were more rigid and confining on the frontier, where isolation was greater and opportunities for social interaction were fewer.

It is not surprising that an intelligent and perceptive young woman sometimes approached marriage with anxiety, for her future depended on the man she chose. Lucy Breckinridge, a wealthy Virginia girl of twenty, sensed how much autonomy she would have to surrender on her wedding day. In her diary she recorded this unvarnished observation on

Miss Mattie G. Shorter, the daughter of a governor of Alabama, was among the southern women who enjoyed greater opportunities for education. She is shown here with her diploma from Union Female College.   Shorter Mansion and Birmingham Museum of Art.

marriage: "If [husbands] care for their wives at all it is only as a sort of servant, a being made to attend to their comforts and to keep the children out of the way. . . . A woman's life after she is married, unless there is an immense amount of love, is nothing but suffering and hard work."

Lucy loved young children but knew that childbearing often involved grief, poor health, and death. In 1840 the birth rate for white southern women in their childbearing years was almost 30 percent higher than the national average. The average southern white woman could expect to bear eight children in 1800; by 1860 the figure had decreased only to six, with one or more miscarriages likely. For those women who wanted to plan their families, methods of contraception were uncertain, and doctors had few remedies for infection or irritation of the reproductive tract. Complications of childbirth were a major cause of death, occurring twice as often in the hot, moist South as in the Northeast. Moreover, a mother had to endure the loss of many of the infants she bore. Infant mortality in the first year of life exceeded 10 percent and remained high during early childhood. In the South in 1860 almost five out of ten

children died before age five, and in South Carolina more than six in ten failed to reach age twenty.

Slavery was another source of problems that white women had to endure but were not supposed to notice. "Violations of the moral law . . . made mulattoes as common as blackberries," protested a woman in Georgia, but wives had to play "the ostrich game." "A magnate who runs a hideous black harem," wrote Mrs. Chesnut, ". . . poses as the model of all human virtues to these poor women whom God and the laws have given him. From the height of his awful majesty, he scolds and thunders at them, as if he never did wrong in his life."

In the early 1800s, some southern women, especially Quakers, had spoken out against slavery. Although most white women did not criticize the "peculiar institution," they often viewed it less as a system and more as a series of relationships among individuals. Perhaps sensing this, southern men tolerated no discussion by women of the slavery issue. In the 1840s and 1850s, as northern and international criticism of slavery increased, southern men published a barrage of articles stressing that women should restrict their concerns to the home. A writer in the *Southern Literary Messenger* bemoaned "these days of Women's Rights," and the *Southern Quarterly Review* declared, "The proper place for a woman is at home. One of her highest privileges, to be politically merged in the existence of her husband."

But some southern women were beginning to seek a larger role. A study of women in Petersburg, Virginia, a large tobacco-manufacturing town, has revealed behavior that valued financial autonomy. Over several decades before 1860, the proportion of women who never married, or did not remarry after the death of a spouse, grew to exceed 33 percent. Likewise the number of women who worked for wages, controlled their own property, and ran millinery or dressmaking businesses increased. In managing property, these and other women benefited from legal changes—beginning with Mississippi's Married Women's Property Act of 1839—that had not been intended to increase female independence. To protect families from the husband's indebtedness during business panics and recessions, legal reforms gave married women some property rights.

For a large category of southern men and women, rights were nil, freedom was wholly denied, and education in any form was not allowed. Male and female, slaves were expected to accept bondage and ignorance as their condition.

 ## Slaves and Their Status in Bondage

For African-Americans, slavery was a curse that brought no blessings other than the strengths they developed to survive it. Slaves knew a life of poverty, coercion, toil, heartbreak, and resentment. They had few hopes that were not denied; often they had to bear separation from their loved ones; and they were despised as an inferior race. That they endured and found loyalty and strength among themselves is a tribute to their courage, but it could not make up for a life without freedom, dignity, or opportunity.

Southern slaves enjoyed few material comforts beyond the bare necessities. Although they generally had enough to eat, their diet was plain and monotonous. The basic ration was cornmeal, fat pork, molasses, and occasionally coffee. Many masters allowed slaves to tend gardens, which provided the variety and extra nutrition of greens and

Slaves' Diet, Clothing, and Housing

sweet potatoes, and some could fish and hunt. "It was nothin' fine," recalled one woman, "but it was good plain eatin' what filled you up."* Most slave-owners did not starve their slaves, but there is considerable evidence that slaves often suffered the effects of beriberi, pellagra, and other dietary-deficiency diseases.

Clothing too was plain, coarse, and inexpensive. Few slaves received more than one or two changes of clothing for hot and cold seasons and one blanket each winter. Children of both sexes ran naked in hot weather and wore long cotton shirts in winter. When big enough to go to the fields, boys received a work shirt and a pair of breeches, and girls a simple dress. On many plantations slave women made their own clothing of osnaburg, a coarse cotton fabric that whites called "nigger cloth." The minority who were allowed to earn a little money by doing extra work often bought additional clothing. Many slaves had to go without shoes until December, even as far north as Virginia. The shoes they received were frequent objects of complaint—uncomfortable brass-toed brogans or stiff wraparounds made from leather tanned on the plantation.

Summer and winter, slaves typically lived in small one-room cabins, possibly with a window opening but no glass. Some of the richer plantations provided more substantial houses, some of which survive today, but the average slave lived in crude accommodations. Logs chinked with mud formed the walls; dirt was the only floor; and a wattle-and-daub or stone chimney vented the fireplace, which provided both heat and light. Bedding consisted of heaps of straw, straw mattresses, or wooden bedframes lashed to the walls with rope. A few crude pieces of furniture and cooking utensils completed the furnishings. The gravest drawback of slave cabins, however, was not lack of comfort but their unhealthfulness. Each small cabin housed one or two entire families. Crowding and lack of sanitation fostered the spread of infection and contagious diseases. Many slaves (and whites) carried worms and intestinal parasites picked up from feces or soil. Lice were widespread in both races, and flies and other

---

*Accounts by ex-slaves are quoted from *The American Slave: A Composite Autobiography*, edited by George P. Rawick (Westport, Conn.: Greenwood Press, First Reprint Edition 1972, Second Reprint Edition 1974), from materials gathered by the Federal Writers' Project and originally published in 1941. The spelling in these accounts has been standardized.

George Fuller, an itinerant painter from Massachusetts, worked from 1856 to 1858 in Alabama, where he made this sketch in ink and pencil of a slave and her mistress at work on washday.   Pocumtuck Valley Memorial Association.

insects spread virulent diseases such as typhoid fever, malaria, and dysentery.

Hard work was the central fact of slaves' existence. The long hours and large work gangs that characterized Gulf Coast cotton districts seemed like factories in the field compared to the small clusters of slaves who had worked in the eighteenth-century Chesapeake.

Slaves' Work Routines

Overseers rang the morning bell before dawn—so early that some slaves remembered being "afraid to start work for fear that they would cover the cotton plants with dirt because they couldn't see clearly." And, as one woman recalled when interviewed by workers in the Federal Writers' Project of the 1930s, "it was way after sundown 'fore they could stop that field work. Then they had to hustle to finish their night work [such as watering livestock or cleaning cotton] in time for supper, or go to bed without it."

Except in urban settings and on some rice plantations, where slaves were assigned daily tasks to complete at their own pace, working "from sun to sun" became universal in the South. Long hours and hard work were at the heart of the advantage that slave labor gave slaveowners. As one planter put it, slaves were the best labor because "you could command them and *make* them do what was right." White workers, by contrast, could not be driven: "they wouldn't stand it." Slaves who cultivated tobacco in the Upper South worked long hours picking the sticky, sometimes noxious, tobacco leaves under harsh discipline. The slaves had to "sucker" the plants—pinch off secondary shoots to increase the size of the leaves—and remove tobacco worms by hand. According to many former slaves, workers who overlooked worms were forced to eat them. No free laborers in the South endured such treatment.

Profit also took precedence over paternalistic "protection" of women: slave women did heavy fieldwork, often as much as the men and even during pregnancy. Old people—of whom there were few—were kept busy caring for young children, doing light chores, or carding, ginning, and spinning cotton. Children had to gather kindling, carry water to the fields, or sweep the yard.

Slaves had a variety of ways to keep from being worked to death. It was impossible to supervise every slave every minute, and slaves slacked off when they were not being watched. Thus travelers saw slaves "go through the motions of labor without putting strength into them," and owners complained that slaves "never would lay out their strength freely. . . . It was impossible to make them do it." Stubborn misunderstanding and literal-mindedness were another defense. One exasperated Virginia planter voiced his irritation (and the racism nurtured by slavery) when he said, "You can make a nigger work, *but you cannot make him think.*"

Slaves could not slow their pace too much, of course, because the owner enjoyed a monopoly on force and violence. Whites throughout the South believed that slaves "can't be governed except with the whip." One South Carolinian frankly explained to a northern journalist that he had whipped his slaves occasionally, "say once a fortnight; . . . the fear of the lash kept them in good order." Evidence suggests that whippings were less frequent on small farms than on large plantations, but even most small farmers plied the lash. These beatings symbolized authority to the master and tyranny to the slaves, who made them a benchmark for evaluating a master. In the words of former slaves, a good owner was one who did not "whip too much," whereas a bad owner "whipped till he's bloodied you and blistered you."

Physical and Mental Abuse of Slaves

As these reports suggest, terrible abuses could and did occur. The master wielded virtually absolute authority on his plantation, and courts did not recognize the word of chattel. Pregnant women were whipped, and there were burnings, mutilations, tortures, and murders. Yet physical cruelty may have been less prevalent in the United States than in other slaveholding parts of the New World. In sugar-growing and mining regions of the Western Hemisphere in the 1800s, slaves were regarded as an expendable resource to be replaced after seven years. Treatment was so poor that death rates were high and the heavily male slave population rapidly shrank in size. In the United States, by contrast, the slave population experienced a steady natural increase as births exceeded deaths and each generation grew larger.

The worst evil of American slavery was not its physical cruelty but the nature of slavery itself: coercion, lack of freedom, belonging to another person, virtually no hope for change. Recalling their days in bondage, some former slaves emphasized the physical abuse—those were "bullwhip days" to one woman. Another woman complained that the black slave "got [his] back cut in slavery time, didn't he?" But their comments focused on the tyranny of whipping as much as the pain. A woman named Delia Garlic made the essential point when she said, "It's bad to belong to folks that own you soul an' body. I could tell you 'bout it all day, but even then you couldn't guess the awfulness of it." A man named Thomas Lewis put it this way: "There was no such thing as being good to slaves. Many people were better than others, but a slave belonged to his master and there was no way to get out of it."

As these comments reveal, the great majority of American slaves retained their mental independence and self-respect despite their bondage. They hated their oppression and, contrary to whites' stereotype of slaves as docile Sambos, were not grateful to their oppressors. They had to be subservient and speak honeyed words to their masters, but they talked quite differently among themselves. The evidence of their resistant attitudes comes from their actions and their own life stories.

Former slaves reported some warm feelings between masters and slaves, but the prevailing picture was one of antagonism and resistance. Slaves mistrusted kindness from whites and saw the self-interest in it. One woman called her mistress "a mighty good somebody to belong to" but explained that the woman was kind "'cause she was raisin' us to work for her." A man recalled that his owners took good care of their slaves, "and Grandma Maria say, 'Why shouldn't they—it was their money.'" Christmas presents of clothing from the master did not mean anything, observed another, "'cause he was going to [buy] that anyhow."

Slaves' Attitudes Toward Whites

Slaves also saw their owners as people who used human beings as beasts of burden. One man observed that his master "fed us reg'lar on good, 'stantial food, just like you'd tend to your horse, if you had a real good one." Another recalled his master eyeing the slave children and saying, "'That one will be worth a thousand dollars.' . . . You see, it was just like raisin' young mules."

Slaves were alert to the thousand daily signs of their degraded status. One man recalled the general rule that slaves ate cornbread and owners ate biscuits. If blacks did get biscuits, "the flour that we made the biscuits out of was the third-grade shorts." A former slave recalled, "Us catch lots of 'possums," but "the white folks ate 'em. Our mouths would water for some of that 'possum, but it wasn't often they let us have none." If the owner took his slaves' garden produce to town and sold it for them, the slaves suspected him of pocketing part of the profits.

Suspicion and resentment often grew into hatred. According to a former slave from Virginia, white people treated blacks "so mean that all the slaves prayed God to punish their cruel masters." When a yellow-fever epidemic struck in 1852, many slaves saw it as God's retribution. As late as the 1930s an elderly ex-slave named Minnie Fulkes cherished the conviction that God was going to punish white people for their cruelty to blacks. She described the whippings that her mother had had to endure, and then she exclaimed, "Lord, Lord, I hate white people and the flood waters goin' to drown some more."

On the plantation, of course, slaves had to keep such thoughts to themselves. Often they expressed one feeling to whites, another within their own race and culture.

 ## Slave Culture and Everyday Life

The resource that enabled slaves to maintain such defiance was their culture: a body of beliefs and values born of their past and their present and of fellowship in their own community. It was not possible for slaves to change their world, but by drawing strength from their culture they could resist their condition and struggle on against it.

Slave culture changed significantly after the turn of the century. For a few years South Carolina reopened the international slave trade. After 1808, however, when Congress banned further importations, the proportion of native-born blacks rose steadily, reaching 96 percent in 1840 and almost 100 percent in 1860 (see figure, page 303). (For this reason many blacks can trace their American ancestry back farther than many white Americans can.) Meanwhile, more and more slaves adopted Christianity as African culture gave way to a maturing African-American culture.

African influences remained strong, for African practices and beliefs reminded slaves that they were and ought to be different from their oppressors. The most visible features of African culture were slaves' appearance and forms of recreation. Some slave men plaited their hair into rows and fancy designs; slave

Influence of African Culture

women often wore their hair "in string"—tied in small bunches secured by a string or piece of cloth. A few men and many women wrapped their heads in kerchiefs of the styles and colors of West Africa.

For entertainment slaves made musical instruments with carved motifs that resembled African stringed instruments. Their drumming and dancing clearly followed African patterns; whites marveled at them. One visitor to Georgia in the 1860s described a ritual dance of African origin: "A ring of singers is formed. . . . They then utter a kind of melodious chant, which gradually increases in strength, and in noise, until it fairly shakes the house, and it can be heard for a long distance." This observer also noted the agility of the dancers and the African call-and-response pattern in their chanting.

Many slaves continued to see and believe in spirits. Whites, too, believed in ghosts, but the slaves' belief resembled the African concept of the living dead—the idea that deceased relatives visit the earth for many years until the process of dying is complete. Slaves also practiced conjuration, voodoo, and quasi-magical root medicine. By 1860 the most notable conjurers and root doctors were reputed to live in South Carolina, Georgia, Louisiana, and other isolated coastal areas of heavy slave importation.

These cultural survivals provided slaves with a sense of their separate past. Black achievement in music and dance was so exceptional that some whites became aware that the slave community was a different world and that they did not "know" their slaves. Conjuration and folklore also directly fed resistance; slaves could cast a spell or direct the power of a hand (a bag of articles belonging to the person to be conjured) against the master. Not all masters felt confident enough to dismiss such a threat.

Slaves fashioned Christianity into an instrument of support and resistance. Theirs was a religion of justice, quite unlike the religious propaganda their masters pushed at them. "You ought to have heard that preachin'," said one man. "'Obey your master and mistress, don't steal chickens and eggs and meat,' but nary a word about havin' a soul to save." Slaves believed that Jesus cared about their souls and their plight. They rejected the idea that in heaven whites would have "the colored folks . . . there to wait on 'em." Instead, slaveholders would be "broilin' in hell for their sin" when God's justice came.

Slaves' Religion

For slaves, Christianity was a religion of personal and group salvation. Devout men and women worshiped and prayed every day, "in the field or by the side of the road," or in special "prayer grounds" such as a "twisted thick-rooted muscadine bush" that afforded privacy. Beyond seeking personal guidance, slaves prayed for deliverance. Some held fervent secret prayer meetings that lasted far into the night. Many slaves nurtured an unshakable belief that God would end their bondage. "It was the plans of God to free us," one man asserted. This faith—and the joy and emotional release that accompanied worship—sustained blacks.

Enslaved African-Americans also developed a sense of racial identity. Their experience taught them that whites despised their race. As one ex-slave put it, white people "have been and are now and always will be against the Negro." Even "the best white woman that ever broke bread wasn't much," said another, "'cause they all hated [us]." Blacks naturally drew together, helping each other in danger, need, and resistance. "We never told on each other," one woman declared. Although some slaves did betray others, former slaves were virtually unanimous in denouncing those who were disloyal to the group or sought personal gain through allegiance to whites.

Of course, different jobs, talents, and circumstances created variations in status among slaves. But most slaves did not encounter a class system within the black community. Only one-quarter of all slaves lived on plantations of fifty or more blacks, so few sensed a wide chasm separating house servants and lowly field hands. Many slaves did both housework and fieldwork, depending on their age and the season, and this arrangement helped create unity rather than division.

The main source of support for individuals was the family. Slave families faced severe dangers. At any moment the master could sell a husband or wife, give a slave child away as a wedding present, or die in debt, forcing a division of his property. Many families were broken up in such ways. Others were separated in the trans-Appalachian expansion of the South, which caused the forced migration and sale of Eliza and her children and hundreds of thousands of other slaves. When the Union Army registered thousands of black marriages in Mississippi and Louisiana in 1864 and 1865, fully 25 percent of the men over forty reported that they had been forcibly separated from a previous wife. A similar proportion of former slaves later recalled that slavery had destroyed one of their marriages.

Slaves' Family Life

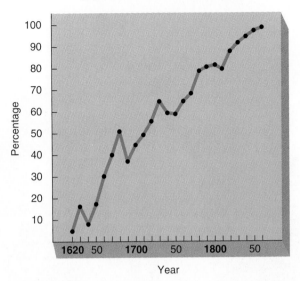

Percentage of African-Americans Born in the Colonies or the United States

Percentage of African-Americans Born in the Colonies or the United States The North American slave population increased through natural reproduction. That fact, plus Congress's closing of the international slave trade in 1808, ensured that by 1860 virtually all African-Americans had been born in the United States.

But this did not mean that slave families could not exist. American slaves clung tenaciously to the personal relationships that gave meaning to life. Although American law did not protect slave families, masters permitted them; in fact, slaveowners expected slaves to form families and have children. As a result, even along the rapidly expanding edge of the cotton kingdom, where the effects of the slave trade would have been most visible, there was a normal ratio of men to women, young to old.

Following African kinship taboos, African-Americans avoided marriage between cousins (commonplace among aristocratic slaveowners). Adapting the West African custom of polygyny to American circumstances, they did not condemn unwed mothers but did expect a young woman to enter a monogamous relationship after one pregnancy, if not before. By naming their children after relatives of past generations, African-Americans emphasized their family histories. If they chose to bear the surname of a slaveowner, it was often the name not of their current master but of the owner under whom their family had begun in America.

Slaves hated interference in their family lives. Some of their strongest protests sought to prevent

This photograph of five generations of a slave family, taken in Beaufort, South Carolina, in 1862, is silent but powerful testimony to the importance that enslaved African-Americans placed on their ever-threatened family ties.   Library of Congress.

the breakup of a family. Indeed, some individuals refused to accept such separations and struggled for years to maintain or reestablish contact. Rape was a horror for both men and women. Some husbands faced death rather than permit their wives to be sexually abused, and the women sometimes fought back. In other cases slaves seethed with anger at the injustice but could do nothing except soothe each other and condemn the guilty party.

Slave men and women followed gender roles familiar to whites and similar to West African customs. After work in the fields was done, men's

**Gender
Roles
in Slavery**

activities focused on "outdoor" tasks and women did "indoor" work. Men hunted and fished for the family stewpot, made furniture, and repaired implements; women cooked, mended, and cleaned house. Slave families resembled white families in that African-American men held a respected

place in their homes. Since slave marriages were not legal, husbands did not have legal power over their wives and did not dominate them in a manner similar to that of free husbands. It would be misleading, however, to say that slave women enjoyed equality in gender roles and family life. Under the pressures of bondage men and women had to share parental and household responsibilities. At any time, each might have to stand in for the other and assume extra duties. Similarly, uncles, aunts, and grandparents sometimes raised the children of those who had been sold away.

Work routines frequently promoted among slave women close associations that heightened their sense of sisterhood. On plantations young girls worked together as house servants. Nursing mothers got together to feed and care for their children, and adults worked together at tasks like soap making and stitching quilts like the one shown on page 305, prepared for the annual visit of a Texas bishop. Old women gathered to spin thread or supervise a nursery. Female slaves thus spent significant portions of their lives as participants in a group of women, an experience that strengthened their ties to each other.

Slave marriage ceremonies were usually brief, often involving jumping over a broomstick in the master's presence. But partners "stuck lots closer then," in one woman's words. "[When] they marries they stay married," said another. When husbands and wives lived on neighboring plantations, visits on Wednesday and Saturday nights included big dinners of welcome and celebration. Christmas was a similarly joyous time "'cause husbands is coming home and families is getting united again."

Slaves brought to their efforts at resistance the same common sense, determination, and practicality that characterized their family lives. American

Resistance to Slavery

slavery produced some fearless and implacable revolutionaries. Gabriel's conspiracy apparently was known to more than a thousand slaves when it was discovered in 1800, just before it was put into action (see pages 221–222). A similar conspiracy in Charleston in 1822, led by a free black named Denmark Vesey, involved many of the prominent whites' most trusted slaves. And the most famous rebel of all, Nat Turner, rose in violence in Southampton County, Virginia, in 1831.

The son of an African woman who passionately hated her enslavement, Nat Turner was a precocious child who learned to read when he was very young.

Nat Turner Rebellion

Encouraged by his first owner to study the Bible, he enjoyed certain privileges but also endured hard work and changes of masters. His father, who successfully escaped to freedom, inspired him as an example of defiance. Eventually young Nat became a preacher with a reputation for eloquence among whites as well as blacks. He also developed a tendency toward mysticism and became increasingly withdrawn. After nurturing his plan for several years, Turner led a band of rebels from farm to farm in the predawn

In addition to the heavy labor required on southern plantations, slaves also performed work of fine craftsmanship in furniture making, needlework, and other areas. This dining-room corner cupboard is walnut veneer on pine and cedar and was built around 1840. The quilt, emblazoned with chalice cups to celebrate the annual visit of an Anglican bishop, was made around 1860. Both are from Texas. Cupboard: Courtesy of the Witte Museum and the San Antonio Museum Association, San Antonio, Texas. Quilt: The American Museum in Britain, photo courtesy of The Museum of the Confederacy.

darkness of August 22, 1831. The group severed limbs and crushed skulls with axes or killed their victims with guns. Before alarmed planters stopped them, Nat Turner and his followers had slaughtered sixty whites of both sexes and all ages. The rebellion was soon put down, and in retaliation, whites killed slaves at random all over the country. Turner was eventually caught and then hanged. As many as two hundred African-Americans, including innocent victims of marauding whites, lost their lives as a result of the rebellion.

Most slave resistance, however, was not violent, for the odds against revolution were especially poor in North America, compared to South America and the Caribbean islands, where some successful revolts did occur. Among slaveholding societies, the South had the highest ratio of whites to blacks in the hemisphere and, because most plantations were small, whites could thoroughly supervise the slaves' activities. There was thus literal truth to one slave's remark that "the white man was the slave's jail." In addition, the South lacked the geographic and demographic features of South America and the Caribbean that made revolt more possible. The South offered no jungles and few mountain fastnesses to which rebels could flee. Furthermore, compared with slave importations in South America, southern slave importations were neither large nor prolonged. The South therefore lacked a preponderance of young male slaves who might be more likely and able to rebel. Nor were its military forces weak and overtaxed like those of many Latin American nations and colonies. In the South, slave patrols and militias were always ready to suppress rebellion, and federal troops were also available under the Constitution.

The scales weighed heavily against revolution, and the slaves knew it. Consequently they directed their energies toward creating the means of survival and resistance within slavery. Many individual slaves attempted to run away to the North, and some received assistance from a loose network of sympathetic citizens, known collectively as the Underground Railroad. But it was more common for slaves to run off temporarily to hide in the woods. There they were close to friends and allies who could help them escape capture in an area they knew well. Every day that a slave "lay out" in this way, the master lost a day's labor. Most owners chose not to mount an exhaustive search and instead sent word that the slave's grievances would be redressed. The

runaway would then return to bargain with the master, who often was glad to have his property back.

Other modes of resistance had the same object: to resist but survive under bondage. Appropriating food (stealing, in the master's eyes) was so common that even whites sang humorous songs about it. Blacks also learned to ingratiate themselves and play off one white person against another. Field hands frequently tested a new overseer to intimidate him or win more favorable working conditions. Some blacks fought with patrollers, and others argued with overseers and even resorted to physical violence to deter or resist beatings.

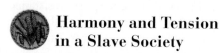

Harmony and Tension in a Slave Society

As the 1800s advanced, slavery impinged on laws and customs, individual values, and—increasingly—every aspect of southern politics. Legal restrictions on slaves, in effect since the seventeenth century, steadily increased. In all things, from their workaday movements to Sunday worship, slaves fell under the supervision of whites. State courts held that a slave "has no civil right" and could not even hold property "except at the will and pleasure of his master." In response to revolts, legislators tightened the legal straitjacket: after the Nat Turner insurrection of 1831, for example, they prohibited owners from teaching their slaves to read. As political conflicts between North and South deepened, fears of slave revolt grew, and restrictions on slaves increased accordingly.

State and federal laws aided the capture of fugitive slaves and required nonslaveholders to support the slave system. All white male citizens had a legal duty to ride in patrols to discourage slave movements at night. Ship captains, harbor masters, and other whites in strategic positions were required to scrutinize the papers of African-Americans who might be attempting to escape bondage. Urban residents who did not supervise their domestic slaves as closely as planters did were subject to criticism for endangering the community. And the South's few manufacturers, instead of receiving encouragement to expand their enterprises, often felt pressure to substitute slave for free labor.

Slavery had a deep effect on southern values precisely because it was the main determinant of wealth in the South. Ownership of slaves guaranteed

Slavery as the Basis of Wealth and Social Standing

the labor to produce cotton and other crops on a large scale—labor otherwise unavailable in rural society. Slaves were therefore vital to the acquisition of a fortune. Beyond that, they were a commodity and an investment, much like gold; people bought them on speculation, hoping for a steady rise in their value. In fact, throughout southern society, slaveholding indicated overall wealth with remarkable precision. Variations in wealth from county to county corresponded very closely to variations in slaveholding; important economic enterprises not based on slavery were too rare to have an effect on the pattern.

Wealth in slaves also translated into political power: a solid majority of political officeholders were slaveholders, and the most powerful were usually large-scale slaveholders. Lawyers and newspaper editors were sometimes influential, but they did not hold independent positions in the economy or society. Dependent on planters for business and support, they served planters' interests and reflected their outlook.

Slavery's influence spread throughout the social system until even the values and mores of nonslaveholders bore its imprint. The availability of slave labor tended to devalue free labor: where strenuous work under another's supervision was reserved for an enslaved race, few free people relished working like a slave. Nonslaveholders preferred to work for themselves, and those who had to sell their labor tended to resent or reject tasks that seemed degrading. This kind of thinking engendered an aristocratic value system ill suited to a newly established democracy.

The values of the aristocrat—lineage, privilege, pride, and refinement of person and manner—gained considerable respect among the masses. Many of those qualities were in short supply, however, in the recently settled portions of the cotton kingdom, where frontier values of courage and self-reliance modified the aristocratic ideal.

Aristocratic Values and Frontier Individualism

Thus independence and defense of one's honor became highly valued traits for planter and frontier farmer alike.

Fights and even duels over personal slights were not uncommon in southern communities. Instead of gradually disappearing as it did in the North,

A bill of sale documents that this slave woman, Louisa, was owned by the young child whom she holds on her lap. In the future Louisa's life would be subject to his wishes and decisions. Missouri Historical Society.

the *code duello*, which required men to defend their honor through violence, hung on in the South and gained acceptance throughout the society. In North Carolina in 1851 a wealthy planter named Samuel Fleming responded to a series of disputes with the lawyer William Waightstill Avery by "cowhiding" (whipping) him on a public street. According to the code, Avery had two choices: to redeem his honor violently or to brand himself a coward through inaction. Three weeks later Avery shot Fleming dead at point-blank range during a session of Burke County Superior Court, with Judge William Battle and numerous spectators looking on. A jury later took only ten minutes to find Avery not guilty, and the spectators gave him a standing ovation. Though some, including Judge Battle, were troubled by this outcome, most white males seemed satisfied.

Other aristocratic values of the planter class were less acceptable to the average voter. Planters believed they were better than other people. In their pride, they expected not only to wield power but to receive special treatment. By the 1850s, some planters openly rejected the democratic creed, vilifying Thomas Jefferson for his statement that all men were equal.

Such beliefs were never acceptable to the individualistic members of the yeoman class. Independent and proud, yeomen resisted any infringement of their rights. They believed they were as good as anyone, and many belonged to evangelical faiths that exalted values of simplicity and otherworldliness that were alien to the planters' love of wealth. They were conscious, too, that they lived in a nation in which democratic ideals were gaining strength. Thus occasional conflicts erupted between aristocratic pretensions and democratic zeal. Mary Boykin Chesnut described a South Carolina aristocrat who refused to make the necessary gestures of respect toward the average voter—mingling with the crowd, exchanging jokes and compliments. Such haughtiness doomed this man's hopes for political leadership. The voters would not accept him.

Class tensions emerged in the western parts of the seaboard states during the 1820s and 1830s. There yeoman farmers and other citizens resented

Movements for Electoral Reform

their underrepresentation in state legislatures, the corruption in government, and the undemocratic control over local government. After vigorous debate, the reformers won most of their battles. Voters in more recently settled areas—Alabama, Mississippi, Tennessee, Arkansas, and Texas—adopted white manhood suffrage and other electoral reforms, including popular election of governors, legislative apportionment based on white population only, and locally chosen county government. Kentucky enacted all these measures except for elected county governments. Georgia, Florida, and Louisiana were not far behind, and reformers won significant concessions in Maryland and made some headway in North Carolina. Only South Carolina and Virginia effectively defended property qualifications for office, legislative malapportionment, ap-

pointment of county officials, and selection of the governor by lawmakers. The formal structure of government thus became more democratic than many planters wished.

Slaveowners knew that a more open government structure could permit troubling issues to arise. In Virginia, nonslaveholding westerners raised a basic challenge to the slave system in 1832, a year after the Nat Turner Rebellion. Advocates of gradual abolition forced a two-week legislative debate on slavery, arguing that it was injurious to the state and inherently dangerous. When the House of Delegates finally voted, the motion favoring abolition lost by just 73 to 58. This was the last public debate on slavery in the antebellum South.

Given such tensions, it was perhaps remarkable that slaveholders and nonslaveholders did not experience more overt conflict. Why were class

Relations Between the Classes

confrontations among whites so infrequent? Historians have given several answers. One of the most important factors was race. The South's racial ideology stressed the superiority of all whites to blacks. Thus slavery became the basis of equality among whites, and racism inflated the status of poor whites and gave them a common interest with the rich. Moreover, family ties linked some nonslaveholders to wealthy planters. The experience of frontier living, in which all were starting out together, also created a relatively informal, egalitarian atmosphere.

The cotton boom itself relieved tension by bringing opportunity to thousands of whites. The "Old South" was a new and mobile society in which many people rose in status by acquiring land or slaves and far more moved about geographically. Even in cotton-rich Alabama in the 1850s, fewer than half of the richest families in a typical county belonged to its elite ten years later. Most did not die or lose their wealth; they merely moved on to some new state. This constant mobility meant that southern society did not settle into a rigid, unchanging pattern.

Most importantly, in their daily lives yeomen and slaveholders were seldom in conflict. Before the Civil War most yeomen were able to pursue unhindered their independent lifestyle. Marginally involved in the market economy, they worked their farms, avoided debt, and marked progress for their families that was unrelated to slaveholding. Moreover, yeomen lived in a rural and uncrowded region: travel was difficult, and daily life usually took place within the family unit. Consequently, they lived their lives with little reference to, or interference from, slaveholders. As long as they could follow their values and aspirations, yeomen had no grievance.

Likewise, slaveholders pursued their goals quite independently of yeomen. Planters farmed for the market but also for themselves. The complementary growing patterns of corn and cotton allowed them to raise food for their animals and laborers without reducing cotton production: from spring to December slaves could work first in the cotton fields, then move to fields of corn, and cultivate both. Thus the planter did not depend on the nonslaveholder as a producer of food crops. In politics, too, national economic issues, such as the tariff, that affected planters rarely had much meaning to yeomen because they were not enmeshed in the market economy.

Suppression of dissent also played a significant and increasing role. After 1830 white southerners who criticized the slave system out of moral conviction or class resentment were intimidated, attacked, or legally prosecuted. (Some, like James Birney, went north and joined the antislavery movement. Two sisters from Charleston, Angelina and Sarah Grimké, became leading advocates of both abolition and women's rights—see page 357.) Southern cities impounded abolitionist literature and sought to bar antislavery influences. Intellectuals developed elaborate justifications for slavery as newspapers railed at northern antislavery agitation. By the 1850s the defense of slavery's interests dominated public discussion, and politicians vied with each other in an aggressive defense of the South's peculiar institution. The slavery issue exerted an ever-more-powerful influence on southern politics and society.

Still, there were signs that the relative lack of conflict between slaveholders and nonslaveholders was coming to an end. As cotton lands filled up, nonslaveholders saw their opportunities beginning to narrow; meanwhile, wealthy planters enjoyed expanding profits. The risks of entering cotton production were becoming too great and the cost of slaves too high for many yeomen to rise in society. From 1830 to 1860 the percentage of white southern families holding slaves declined steadily from 36 to 25 percent. At the same time, the monetary gap between the classes was widening. Although nonslaveholders were becoming more prosperous, slaveowners' wealth was increasing much faster. And although slaveowners accounted for a smaller portion of the population in 1860 than in 1830, their share of the South's agricultural wealth remained at between 90 and 95 percent. In fact, the average slaveholder was almost fourteen times as rich as the average nonslaveholder.

Hardening of Class Lines

Urban artisans and mechanics felt the pinch acutely. Their numbers were few, their place in society was hardly recognized, and in bad times they were often the first to lose work. Moreover, they faced stiff competition from urban slaves, whose masters wanted to hire them out to practice trades. White workers in Charleston, Wilmington, and elsewhere staged protests demanding that economic competition from slaves be forbidden, but they were ignored. The powerful slaveowners would not tolerate interference with their property and their income. The angry protests of white workers, however, resulted in harsh restrictions on *free* African-American workers and craftsmen, who had no powerful allies to defend their interests. On the eve of the Civil War, many successful free blacks actually felt compelled to leave Charleston for fear of being reenslaved.

Pre–Civil War politics reflected these tensions. Anticipating the prospect of a war to defend slavery, slaveowners expressed growing fear about the loyalty of nonslaveholders. Schemes to widen the ownership of slaves were discussed, including reopening the African slave trade. In North Carolina, a prolonged and increasingly bitter controversy over the combination of high taxes on land and low taxes on slaves erupted, and a class-conscious nonslaveholder named Hinton R. Helper denounced the slave system. Convinced that slavery had impoverished many whites and retarded the whole region, Helper attacked the institution in *The Impending Crisis*, published in New York in 1857. Discerning planters knew that such fiery controversies could easily erupt in every southern state.

But for the moment slaveowners stood secure. They occupied from 50 to 85 percent of the seats in state legislatures and a similarly high percentage of the South's congressional seats. In addition to their near monopoly on political office, they had established their point of view in all the other major social institutions. Professors who criticized slavery had been dismissed from colleges and universities;

schoolbooks that contained "unsound" ideas had been replaced. And almost all the Methodist and Baptist clergy, some of whom had criticized slavery in the 1790s, had given up preaching against it. In fact, except for a few obscure persons of conscience, southern clergy had become slavery's most vocal defenders.

 Conclusion

The South of the early to mid-1800s was a diverse society that embraced a variety of elements and differing viewpoints, but the coercive influence of slavery was increasingly pressing the region into a single mold. The reality of the South's rapid growth and mobility contrasted with its increasing ideological emphasis on conservatism and stability. The values of democratic yeomen and aristocratic planters clashed, despite the rhetoric of white supremacy. Simmering resentments generated by slavery's oppression gave the lie to the benevolent image of bondage put forth in paternalist ideology. Yet leading southerners ignored evidence of diversity, preferring to submerge these contradictions in visions of a stable, slaveholding social order.

Slavery's extent and influence in the South grew markedly after 1800. Powerful groups dependent on slavery worked tirelessly to promote unity and eradicate dissent. The potential for conflict persisted, but few southerners saw it. As the influence of the peculiar institution spread through the region, the evolving South took on the aspect of a conservative and traditional society wedded to slavery. The social order as southerners knew it seemed to be stable, with threats to the status quo under control.

Outside the South, however, society was anything but stable. Market forces and the rise of industry were producing an increasingly diverse population in the North. Social and economic changes were transforming the North, and the currents of change eventually would affect the South as well.

Suggestions for Further Reading

Southern Society

Edward L. Ayers, *Vengeance and Justice* (1984); Bradley G. Bond, *Political Culture in the Nineteenth-Century South* (1995); William J. Cooper, *The South and the Politics of Slavery, 1828–1856* (1978); Clement Eaton, *The Growth of Southern Civilization, 1790–1860* (1961); Clement Eaton, *Freedom of Thought in the Old South*

(1940); William W. Freehling, *Prelude to Civil War* (1965); Eugene D. Genovese, *The Political Economy of Slavery* (1965); Peter Kolchin, *Unfree Labor: American Slavery and Russian Serfdom* (1987); Donald G. Mathews, *Religion in the Old South* (1977); Robert McColley, *Slavery and Jeffersonian Virginia* (1964); James Hebron Moore, *The Emergence of the Cotton Kingdom in the Old Southwest: Mississippi, 1770–1860* (1987); Frederick Law Olmsted, *The Slave States*, ed. Harvey Wish (1959); Charles S. Sydnor, *The Development of Southern Sectionalism, 1819–1848* (1948); Larry E. Tise, *Proslavery* (1987); Ralph A. Wooster, *Politicians, Planters, and Plain Folk* (1975); Ralph A. Wooster, *The People in Power* (1969); Gavin Wright, *The Political Economy of the Cotton South* (1978); Bertram Wyatt-Brown, *Southern Honor* (1982).

Slaveholders and Nonslaveholders

Edward L. Ayers and John C. Willis, eds., *The Edge of the South* (1991); Bennet H. Barrow, *Plantation Life in the Florida Parishes of Louisiana, as Reflected in the Diary of Bennet H. Barrow*, ed. Edwin Adams Davis (1943); Ira Berlin, *Slaves Without Masters* (1974); Joan E. Cashin, *A Family Venture* (1991); Bill Cecil-Fronsman, *The Common Whites* (1992); Charles B. Dew, *Bond of Iron* (1995); Everett Dick, *The Dixie Frontier* (1948); Clement Eaton, *The Mind of the Old South* (1967); Paul D. Escott, ed., *North Carolina Yeoman* (1996); Drew Faust, *James Henry Hammond and the Old South* (1982); Drew Faust, *A Sacred Circle: The Dilemma of the Intellectual in the Old South* (1977); John Hope Franklin, *The Militant South, 1800–1861* (1956); John Inscoe, *Mountain Masters* (1989); Michael P. Johnson and James L. Roark, *Black Masters* (1984); Robert E. May, *John A. Quitman* (1985); Stephanie McCurry, *Masters of Small Worlds* (1995); Robert Manson Myers, ed., *The Children of Pride* (1972); James Oakes, *The Ruling Race* (1982); Frank L. Owsley, *Plain Folk of the Old South* (1949); Loren Schweninger, *Black Property Owners in the South, 1790–1915* (1990); J. Mills Thornton III, *Politics and Power in a Slave Society: Alabama, 1800–1860* (1978).

Southern Women

Carol Bleser, *In Joy and in Sorrow* (1990); Carol Bleser, ed., *Tokens of Affection* (1995); Victoria Bynum, *Unruly Women* (1992); Jane Turner Censer, *North Carolina Planters and Their Children, 1800–1860* (1984); Catherine Clinton, *The Plantation Mistress* (1982); Elizabeth Fox-Genovese, *Within the Plantation Household* (1988); Jean E. Friedman, *The Enclosed Garden* (1985); Harriet Jacobs, *Incidents in the Life of a Slave Girl*, ed. Jean Fagan Yellin (1987); Jacqueline Jones, *Labor of Love, Labor of Sorrow* (1985); Frances Anne Kemble, *Journal of a Residence on a Georgia Plantation in 1838–1839* (1863); Suzanne Lebsock, *Free Women of Petersburg* (1984); Sally McMillen, *Motherhood in the Old South* (1990); Patricia Morton, ed., *Discovering the Women in Slavery* (1995); Elisabeth Muhlenfeld, *Mary Boykin Chesnut* (1981); Mary D. Robertson, ed., *Lucy Breckinridge of Grove Hill* (1979); Ann Firor Scott, *The Southern Lady* (1970); Deborah G. White, *Ar'n't I a Woman?* (1985); Virginia Ingraham Burr, ed., *The Secret Eye* (1990).

Conditions of Slavery

Kenneth F. Kiple and Virginia H. Kiple, "Black Tongue and Black Men," *Journal of Southern History* 43 (August 1977): 411–428; Peter Kolcin, *American Slavery, 1619–1877* (1993); Ronald L.

Lewis, *Coal, Iron, and Slaves* (1979); Richard G. Lowe and Randolph B. Campbell, "The Slave Breeding Hypothesis," *Journal of Southern History* 42 (August 1976): 400–412; Willie Lee Rose, ed., *A Documentary History of Slavery in North America* (1976); Todd L. Savitt, *Medicine and Slavery* (1978); Kenneth M. Stampp, *The Peculiar Institution* (1956); Robert S. Starobin, *Industrial Slavery in the Old South* (1970); Michael Tadman, *Speculators and Slaves* (1989).

Slave Culture and Resistance

Herbert Aptheker, *American Negro Slave Revolts* (1943); John W. Blassingame, *The Slave Community* (1979); Judith Wragg Chase, *Afro-American Art and Craft* (1971); Douglas Egerton, *Gabriel's Rebellion* (1993); Dena J. Epstein, *Sinful Tunes and Spirituals* (1977); Paul D. Escott, *Slavery Remembered: A Record of Twentieth-Century Slave Narratives* (1979); Eric Foner, ed., *Nat Turner* (1971); Eugene D. Genovese, *From Rebellion to Revolution* (1979); Eugene D. Genovese, *Roll, Jordan, Roll* (1974); Herbert G. Gutman, *The Black Family in Slavery and Freedom, 1750–1925* (1976); Vincent Harding, *There Is a River* (1981); Charles Joyner, *Down by the Riverside* (1984); Lawrence W. Levine, *Black Culture and Black Consciousness* (1977); Stephen B. Oates, *The Fires of Jubilee* (1975); Albert J. Raboteau, *Slave Religion* (1978); Robert S. Starobin, *Denmark Vesey* (1970); Sterling Stuckey, *Slave Culture* (1987).

CHAPTER

12

The American Social Landscape
1800–1860

I hope that things will get better," Anna Maria Klinger wrote from New York to her family in Württemberg, Germany, in March 1849. "For it's always like that, no one really likes it at first, and especially if you are so lonely and forlorn in a foreign land like I am, no friends or relatives around." Twenty-eight-year-old Anna Maria had crossed the Atlantic among strangers. Her religious faith kept her going. "The dear Lord is my shield and refuge," she wrote home.

It had taken 105 days to reach America, including seven weeks docked in Plymouth, England, while the ship was fitted. Three other young women migrants to America proved unsuitable as traveling companions. They "started behaving so badly" with young men, Anna Maria wrote her parents, that "I got annoyed because I couldn't stand such loose behavior."

Her luck improved in New York. She quickly found a job at $4 a month as a domestic servant with a German family. New York was so large, she wrote her parents, that she could not walk around it in one day. She counted nearly two hundred churches and reported that there were "about 4,000 German residents alone." There were actually fifty-six thousand Germans in the city at the time.

Anna Maria Klinger had left Germany during the political and economic crises of 1848. She was the first in her immediate family to emigrate, though two cousins had come to America some years before. Soon after arriving in New York, she met her future husband, Franz Schano, a deserter from the Bavarian army. Over the next decade she and Schano brought five of her siblings to New York: Babett, Gottlieb, Katharina, Daniel, and finally in 1858 the youngest, Rosina.

Moving Day in Philadelphia (c. 1850) commonly was May Day. On that day, literally, the life of the city was in the streets. The density, competition, and even violence of urban life was becoming common to Americans. *Courtesy of Mr. and Mrs. Screvan Lorillard.*

313

Finding work could be difficult—Franz, a stone-cutter, was unemployed for a time—but teenagers like Babett and Katharina could always get jobs as servants. Babett, who now called herself Barbara, came in 1852 and adjusted quickly. "Here you don't go out of the house without a hat or a bonnet," she wrote her parents, "you don't go out on the *Striet* [street] with your head bare, they all look at you and you'd be laughed at. If I were to run into you, none of you would recognize me with my hat on." Barbara was a servant, first for an English family then for a French family, and quickly repaid her sister for her fare to America.

Within a year of Barbara's arrival, Franz wrote home that she had taken up with a young man whom "we could see from the start would not be to her advantage." They "tried everything to dissuade her, but to no use." She soon gave birth to a baby son, "for whom she has a father all right but no husband, and when we noticed that she was expecting, we urged him to marry her but then he said he had never promised to marry her and he wouldn't ever marry her." He did provide a cash settlement of $80 to Barbara.

Anna Maria, assisted by Franz, guided the family, keeping them together by sheer force of will. But the siblings' lives eventually diverged. In 1855 Anna Maria and Franz moved to Albany, New York, where Franz opened his own business and they bought a house for $1,000.

When the Schanos moved to Albany, Barbara went west, leaving her son with Anna Maria and Franz. Within a year she wrote that she was in Indiana, married and living in a log cabin on forty acres of land. She wanted her son at first but said that the distance between Albany and Indiana prevented her from fetching him. She complained that living in rural Indiana was boring. In 1861 she finally got her son from Anna Maria. In the 1860s, a widow, she remarried and raised seven "Christian children" on her Indiana farm.

In 1860 Franz Schano died of consumption. Thirteen months later Anna Maria married Adam Plantz, a Prussian-born blacksmith; he too died of consumption, only five weeks after the wedding. Anna Maria now had a son, a nephew, and a stepson to support. She feared losing her home, but she had been left enough money to prosper. As Anna Maria became more preoccupied with providing for her son and stepson, her brother Gottlieb took over the role of head of the family.

Through Gottlieb, the Klinger siblings stayed in touch for most of their lives. Gottlieb and his brother, Daniel, settled in Albany near Anna Maria and rode the roller coaster of the economy, prospering in good times, unemployed in hard times. Gottlieb ran a saloon, lost it, then worked in a piano factory and later as a wood carver. Daniel worked as a teamster. Eventually, they lost touch with two of their sisters. After Katharina, a widow, married a prosperous New York grocer, they no longer heard from her. They also lost contact with Rosina, who had moved to Canada. Years later they heard she was living again in New York and had "a whole brood of children" with her tinsmith husband.

Despite jealousies and conflicts, the Klingers remained close, helped each other, and regularly sent money to their parents. They represented both the old values of traditional culture and the new values of the market system. Anna Maria worked hard, saved money, and found success in Albany even though widowhood twice threatened her security. Barbara lived a hard-scrabble life and was an unwed mother. She reestablished her life 700 miles from New York, eventually finding peace in a German-American rural community. Katharina worked hard but spent most of her income on herself, saving very little; her siblings complained of her selfishness. Even after years in the United States, the Klinger siblings were only partially Americanized. They always lived in German neighborhoods, and they socialized almost exclusively with family and fellow immigrants from Württemberg.

The Klinger family's experiences were similar to those of millions of other Americans. From the 1830s through the 1850s, millions of immigrants arrived on America's shores, and hundreds of thousands of native-born Americans moved from farm to town and from town to city. The American population grew so much—largely through natural increase in the first two decades of the century, then through immigration—that most Americans were newcomers in their neighborhoods and on the job. The populations of the largest cities numbered in the hundreds of thousands and were highly diverse ethnically, religiously, and racially. Within large cities and in the countryside, whole districts became enclaves of ethnic groups.

What it meant to be an American changed. The Revolution and early nation building diminished as sources of American identity. European immigrants, slaves, free people of color, and Native Americans

• *Important Events* •

1810	New York City surpasses Philadelphia in population	**1835**	Arkansas passes first women's property law
1821	Horse racing legalized in New York State	**1835–42**	Seminoles resist removal in Second Seminole War
1823	Catharine and Mary Beecher establish Hartford Female Seminary	**1837**	Boston employs paid policemen Ralph Waldo Emerson's *Nature* appears
1824	President Monroe proposes removal of Indians west of the Mississippi	**1837–48**	Horace Mann heads the Massachusetts Board of Education
1827	*Freedom's Journal*, first African-American newspaper, appears	**1841–47**	Brook Farm combines spirituality, work, and play in a utopian rural community
1830	Joseph Smith founds Mormon Church Congress passes Indian Removal Act	**1842**	Knickerbocker baseball club formed
1830s–50s	Urban riots commonplace	**1844**	Nativist riots peak in Philadelphia
1831	Cherokees turn to courts to defend treaty rights in *Cherokee Nation v. Georgia*	**1845**	Start of the Irish potato famine
1831–32	Alexis de Tocqueville travels across America: his observations form the basis for *Democracy in America*	**1846–47**	Mormon trek to the Great Salt Lake
		1847–57	Peak period of immigration before the Civil War
1831–38	Indian tribes resettled in the West	**1848**	Abortive revolutions in German states
1832	Chief Justice Marshall declares the Cherokee nation to be a distinct political community in *Worcester v. Georgia*, but the ruling is never enforced		

had cultural traditions different than those of the American colonial past. New cultural patterns flourished. Economic opportunity, the market economy, and expansionism energized Americans. In the nation's cities, opulent mansions rose within sight of notorious slums, and both wealth and poverty reached extremes unknown in agrarian America. As in the past, Americans sought community in their neighborhoods, not in the nation, but ethnic, racial, and religious differences were greater than ever before. Farm families attempted to maintain cohesive, rural villages while utopians and groups like the Mormons sought to create self-governing communal havens.

Family life was changing too. With the growth of commerce and industry, the home began to lose its function as a workplace and center of leisure. Cities took over some of the traditional family's educational role, and consumer items and leisure became commodities to be purchased. Families shrank in size, and more people lived outside family units.

Free people of color and Native Americans were at a particular disadvantage in a society that considered their very presence disturbing. Native Americans struggled to maintain their traditional lands but were forced to resettle beyond the Mississippi River. Free people of color fought against their second-class status. They founded the institutions and communities that would be the basis of modern African-American life.

Many Americans were uncomfortable with the new direction of American life. Antipathy toward immigrants was common among native-born Americans, who feared competition for jobs. Riots and violence became commonplace in cities. In a society growing ever more diverse and complex, conflict became common.

The United States remained a predominantly agricultural country, but economic and social traditions were yielding to the influence of the market economy, urban growth, and immigration. Although this change intensified in the final three decades of the century, an industrializing, urbanizing, and pluralist society was emerging before the Civil War.

 ## Country Life

Rural life changed significantly in the first half of the nineteenth century. Within a generation many western settlements became sources rather than destinations of migrants. The villages of western New York State had lured the sons and daughters of New England in the first two decades of the century; after the mid-1820s when the Erie Canal opened, New York sent its young people to new lands in the Midwest. Later, Ohio and Michigan towns and farms would watch their young people move farther west. Their counterparts in the Upper South went to Illinois and Ohio, and those farther south settled the Gulf states.

For all the romance of moving westward, many longed for a sense of community. In *Domestic Manners of the Americans* (1832) Frances Trollope, an English writer, described her visit to a farm family near Cincinnati. The family produced all their necessities except coffee, tea, and whiskey, which they acquired by sending butter and chickens to market. But until other settlers moved near them, they lacked the human contact that a community provides. For their inexpensive land and self-sufficiency they paid the price of isolation and loneliness. "'Tis strange to us to see company," observed the mother. "I expect the sun may rise and set a hundred times before I shall see another human that does not belong to the family."

Government policy fostered farm life. Farming was associated with virtue, productivity, and independence—essential values in the new republic. The acquisition of Louisiana in 1803 and later annexations of Florida, Texas, and Oregon all increased available agricultural land. The internal improvements—harbors, roads, canals, and railroads—following the War of 1812 were a boost to agriculture. Indian removal opened additional land for farmers, and the inexpensive sale of public lands facilitated new farm settlements. State governments promoted agricultural education through schools and county and state fairs.

The farm village, with its churches, post office, general store, and tavern, was the center of rural life—the farmers' link with religion, politics, and the

Farm Communities

outside world. But rural social life was not limited to trips to the village; families gathered on one another's farms to accomplish as a community what they could not manage individually. Barn-raisings regularly brought people together. A farmer and an itinerant carpenter prepared the site before the neighbors arrived by buggy and wagon to help on the appointed day. After the walls were put together and raised into position, they attached a roof. Then everyone celebrated with a communal meal and sang, danced, and played games. They might compete in foot races, wrestling, or marksmanship, and on occasion they raced horses. Similar gatherings took place at harvest time and on special occasions.

Men and women had active, social lives. Men met frequently at general stores, weekly markets, and taverns, and they hunted and fished together. Some women also attended market, especially those engaged in dairy farming. More typically they met at after-church dinners, prayer and Bible-study groups, sewing and corn-husking bees, and quilting parties. These were occasions to exchange experiences, thoughts, and spiritual support, and to swap letters, books, and news.

Irene Hardy, who grew up in rural southwestern Ohio in the 1840s, left a memoir of the gatherings she had attended as a girl. Fifty years later she recalled apple bees at which neighbors gathered to make apple butter or preserves. Typical of rural society, bees combined leisure and work activities. A dinner feast followed, Hardy recalled. After cleaning up, "the old folks went home to send their young ones for their share of work and fun." The elders gossiped; the youngsters joked and teased each other and flirted. "Then came supper, apple and pumpkin pies, cider, doughnuts, cakes, cold chicken and turkey," Hardy wrote, "after which games, 'Forfeits,' 'Building a Bridge,' 'Snatchability,' even 'Blind Man's Bluff' and 'Pussy Wants a Corner.'"

Traditional country bees had their town counterparts. Fredrika Bremer, a Swedish visitor to the United States, described a sewing bee in Cambridge, Massachusetts, in 1849, at which neighborhood women made clothes for "a family who had lost all their clothing by fire." Yet town bees were not the all-day family affairs of the countryside, and when the Hardy family moved to the town of Eaton, Ohio, Irene missed the country gatherings. Life was changing: the families of Eaton seldom held bees, and they purchased most of their goods at the store. They were wage earners and consumers, and the market economy shaped their daily lives. Many felt a loss of autonomy.

Americans were increasingly conscious of such changes. Some turned to rural utopian experiments in an effort to find an antidote to the market economy and the untamed growth of large urban communities and an opportunity to restore tradition and social cohesion. In the religious ferment of the Second Great Awakening (see pages 219–220), many people reacted favorably to new religious communities, whatever their philosophy. Utopian experiments offered to restore order and regularity to daily life and to provide a cooperative rather than competitive environment. Virtually all of the utopian experiments offered communal living and nontraditional work, family, and gender roles.

The Shakers, named for the way they danced at worship services, undertook one of the earliest utopian experiments. Founder Ann Lee imported

Shakers

this offshoot of the Quakers to America in 1774. While living in England, she had experienced a vision foretelling Jesus's second coming in America and urging her to go there. The Shakers believed that the end of the world was near and that sin entered the world through sexual intercourse. They considered existing churches too worldly and viewed the Shaker community as the instrument of salvation.

After the death of Mother Ann Lee in 1784, the Shakers turned to communal living to fulfill their mission. In 1787 they "gathered in" at New Lebanon, New York, to live and work communally. At its peak, between 1820 and 1860, the sect had recruited about six thousand members in twenty settlements in eight states; it was the largest and most permanent of the utopian experiments. Shaker communities emphasized agriculture and handcrafts; most managed to become self-sufficient and profitable enterprises. Shaker furniture became famous for its simplicity, excellent construction, and beauty of design.

Though economically conservative, the Shakers were social radicals. They abolished individual families; each colony was one large family. They also gave women new prospects for spiritual leadership. During its period of greatest growth, the Shaker ministry was headed by a woman, Lucy Wright. The sect's practice of celibacy, however, led inevitably to its demise. Because Shakers have been unable to perpetuate themselves naturally, only one Shaker colony remains in the late twentieth century.

The most successful communitarian group was the Church of Jesus Christ of Latter-day Saints, known as the Mormons. Joseph Smith, a young

Mormon Community of Saints

farmer in western New York, reported in 1827—a time of religious ferment in the Northeast—that he had been visited by the angel Moroni, who gave him a set of gold plates engraved with divine revelation. Smith published his revelations as the *Book of Mormon* and organized a church in western New York in 1830. Violence stalked the Mormons; angry mobs drove them from Ohio, Illinois, and Missouri. People objected most to the Mormon belief in continuous revelation and the practice of allowing men to have several wives at once. Finally in 1846 and 1847 the Mormons found a home in the Great Salt Lake valley. There, under Brigham Young, head of the Twelve Apostles (the Mormons' governing body), they established a patriarchal community of Saints based on communal republicanism. They achieved not only religious freedom but also political self-government.

Religious conviction fortified the Latter-day Saints to withstand persecution and economic hardship. The Mormon Church offered success and community in this world and salvation in the next to anyone who would join. Indeed, many recruits were poor and uneducated. The Mormons also held out a hand of fellowship to those who rejected existing churches. Mormonism offered religious certainty within a tight-knit society.

In Utah the Mormons distributed agricultural land according to family size. An extensive irrigation system, constructed by men who contributed their labor in proportion to the quantity of land they received and the amount of water they expected to use, transformed the arid valley into a rich oasis. As the colony developed, the church elders gained control of water, trade, industry, and even the territorial government of Utah.

Not all utopian communities were founded by religious sects. In 1825 Robert Owen, a wealthy Scottish industrialist, attempted to establish a socialist utopia in New Harmony, Indiana. According to his plan, its nine hundred members were to exchange their labor for goods at a communal store. Handicrafts (hat and boot making) flourished at New Harmony, but a textile mill—which was to have been the economic base of the community—failed after Owen gave it to the community to run. The turnover in membership at New Harmony was so great that the community never developed cohesion, and by 1827 Owen's experiment had ended.

The impact of the Brook Farm cooperative in West Roxbury, Massachusetts, was longer lasting, although its achievements were more artistic than economic. Inspired by transcendentalism—the belief that the

Brook Farm

physical world is secondary to the spiritual realm, which human beings can know by ignoring custom and experience and relying instead on intuition—Brook Farm's members rejected materialism in favor of rural communalism, combining spirituality, manual labor, intellectual life, and play. Founded in 1841 by the Unitarian minister George Ripley, a literary critic and friend of transcendentalist lecturer and essayist Ralph Waldo Emerson, Brook Farm attracted farmers, craftsmen, and writers, among them the novelist Nathaniel Hawthorne. Indeed, the fame of Brook Farm rested on the intellectual achievements of its members. Its school drew students from outside the community, and its residents contributed regularly to the *Dial*, the leading transcendentalist journal. In 1845 Brook Farm's hundred members organized themselves into model phalanxes (working-living units) in keeping with the philosophy of the French utopian Charles Fourier. Rigid regimentation replaced individualism, and membership dropped. After a disastrous fire in 1846, the experiment collapsed in 1847.

Though short-lived, Brook Farm played a significant role in the flowering of a national literature. During these years Hawthorne, Emerson, and Margaret Fuller, the *Dial*'s editor, joined Henry David Thoreau, James Fenimore Cooper, Herman Melville, and others in creating what is known today as the American Renaissance. In its philosophical intensity and moral idealism, their work was both distinctively American and an outgrowth of the European romantic movement. Their themes were universal, their settings and character American. Cooper, for instance, used the frontier as a backdrop, and Melville wrote of great spiritual quests as seafaring adventures.

The essayist Ralph Waldo Emerson was the prime mover of the American Renaissance and a pillar of the transcendental movement. Emerson had followed his father and grandfather into the ministry but quit his Boston Unitarian pulpit in 1831. After a two-year sojourn in Europe, he returned to lecture and write, preaching individualism and self-reliance. "We live in succession, in division, in parts, in particles," Emerson wrote. "We see the world piece by piece, as the sun, the moon, the animal, the tree; but the whole, of which these are the shining parts, is the soul." Intuitive experience of God is attainable, insisted Emerson, because "the Highest dwells" within every individual in the form of the "Over-soul." What gave Emerson's writings force was his simple, direct prose. In his first book, *Nature* (1836), and in "The American Scholar" (1837), a Phi Beta Kappa address at Harvard, Emerson explored human nature and American culture. Widely admired, he influenced Thoreau, Fuller, Hawthorne, and other members of Brook Farm.

Utopian communities can be seen as attempts to recapture the cohesiveness of traditional agricultural and artisan life in reaction to the competitive pressures of the market economy and urbanization. Utopians resembled Puritan perfectionists; like the Separatists of seventeenth-century New England (see page 50), they sought to begin anew in their own colonies.

 ## City Life

The transportation revolution and the expansion of commerce and manufacturing enabled the urban population to grow geometrically between 1800 and 1860, especially in the North. The nation's population increased during this period from 5 million to 31 million. Meanwhile, settlement spread westward, and small rural settlements became towns. In 1800 the nation had only 33 towns with 2,500 or more people and only 3 with more than 25,000. By 1860, 392 towns exceeded 2,500 residents, 35 had more than 25,000, and 9 exceeded 100,000 (see maps, page 319). In the Northeast, the percentage of people living in urban areas grew from 9 to 35 percent between 1800 and 1860.

Some cities became great metropolitan centers. By 1810, New York City passed Philadelphia as the nation's most populous city and major commercial center. By 1860, Baltimore and New Orleans dominated the South, and San Francisco was the leading West Coast city. In the Midwest, the new lake cities (Chicago, Detroit, and Cleveland) began to overtake the frontier river cities (Cincinnati, Louisville, and Pittsburgh) founded a generation earlier. The largest cities of the North belonged to a nationwide

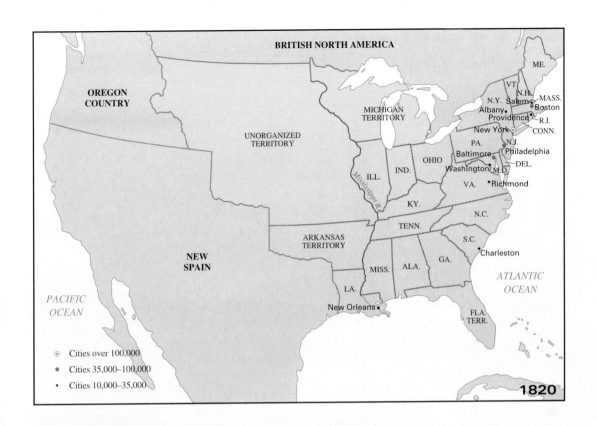

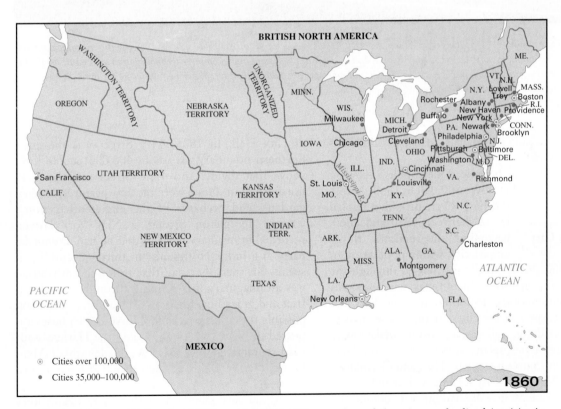

Major American Cities in 1820 and 1860 *The number of Americans who lived in cities increased rapidly between 1820 and 1860, and the number of large cities grew as well. In 1820, only New York had a population exceeding one hundred thousand; forty years later, eight more cities had surpassed that level.*

The Lackawanna Valley (1855) by George Inness. Hired by the Lackawanna Railroad to paint a picture showing the company's new roundhouse at Scranton, in northeastern Pennsylvania, Inness combined landscape and locomotive technology into an organic whole. Industrialism, Inness seemed to say, belonged to the American landscape; it would neither overpower nor obliterate the land. Gift of Mrs. Huttleston Rogers, © National Gallery of Art, Washington, D.C.

urban network linked by canals, roads, and railroads (see Chapter 10).

New York City became a metropolis, growing from 60,500 in 1800 to over 800,000 in 1860. Across the East River, Brooklyn tripled in size between 1850 and 1860, becoming the nation's third-largest city, with a population of over 260,000. Many people just passed through the two cities; the majority did not stay ten years. Although contemporary depictions of New York appear almost pastoral, the city's energy and aromas of sweat, horse dung, and garbage would make twentieth-century cities seem sanitized in comparison. An immigrant port city, mostly Irish and German by the 1850s, New York City teemed with people.

New York City

New York City literally had burst its boundaries in the 1820s. Up to that time New Yorkers regarded the city of 150,000 as a village because they could walk from one end to the other in an hour. Until the 1820s nearly all New Yorkers lived within two miles of City Hall. In 1825, 14th Street was the city's northern boundary. By 1860, 400,000 people lived above that divide, and 42nd Street was the city's northern limit. Gone were the cow pastures, kitchen gardens, and orchards of the eighteenth century. George Templeton Strong, a New York lawyer, recorded in his diary in 1856 that he had attended a party at a Judge Hoffman's "in thirty-seventh!!!—it seems but the other day that thirty-seventh Street was an imaginary line running through a rural district and grazed over by cows." Mass transit made it possible for cities to expand. Horse-drawn buses appeared in New York in 1827, and the Harlem Railroad, completed in 1832, ran the length of Manhattan. By the 1850s all big cities had horse-drawn streetcars.

By modern standards early-nineteenth-century cities were disorderly, unsafe, and unhealthy. Expansion occurred so rapidly that few cities could handle the problems it brought. For example, migrants from rural areas were accustomed to relieving themselves outside and throwing refuse in any vacant area. In the city, such waste smelled, spread disease, and polluted water. New York City partially solved the problem in the 1840s by abandoning wells in favor of reservoir water piped into buildings and outdoor fountains. In some districts, scavengers and refuse collectors carted away garbage and human waste, but in much of the city it just rotted on the ground. Only one-quarter of New York City's streets had sewers by 1857.

New York and other cities lacked adequate taxing power to provide services for all. The best the city could do was to assess the adjoining property for the cost of sewers, street paving, and water mains. Thus the spread of new services and basic sanitation depended on residents' ability to pay. As a result, those most in need of services typically got them last. Another solution was to charter private companies to sell basic services. This plan worked well with gas service. Baltimore first chartered a private gas company in 1816; New York did so in 1842. By mid-century every major city was lit by a private gas supplier. The private sector, however, failed to supply the water the cities needed. Private firms lacked the capital to build adequate systems, and they laid pipe only in commercial and well-to-do residential areas, ignoring the poor. As population grew, city governments had to take over.

A singular urban innovation was the creation of public education. In 1800 there were no public schools outside New England; by 1860 every state offered some public education.

Horace Mann and Public Schools

Massachusetts, which had taken the lead in education since Puritan times, again led in expansion of schooling under Horace Mann, secretary of the state board of education from 1837 to 1848. Massachusetts established a minimum school term of six months, formalized the training of teachers, and emphasized secular subjects and applied skills rather than religious training. In the process, schoolteaching became a woman's profession. "Females govern with less resort to physical force," Mann asserted, "and exert a more kindly, humanizing and refining influence upon the dispositions and manners of their pupils."

Horace Mann was an evangelist for public education and school reform; his preaching on behalf of free, state-sponsored education changed schooling throughout the nation. "If we do not prepare children to become good citizens," Mann argued, "if we do not develop their capacities, . . . imbue their hearts with the love of truth and duty, and a reverence for all things sacred and holy, then our republic must go down to destruction." The abolition of ignorance, according to Mann, would end misery, crime, and suffering. He advocated educating all children. Mann and others were responding to the changes wrought by the market economy, urbanization, and immigration. The typical city dweller was a newcomer, whether from abroad or from the country. Public schools would take the children of strangers and give them shared values.

Free public schools altered the scope of education. Schooling previously had focused on literacy, religious training, and discipline. Under Mann's leadership, the school curriculum became more secular and appropriate for the future clerks, farmers, and workers of America. Students studied geography, American history, arithmetic, and science. Moral education was retained, but direct religious indoctrination was dropped. However, the basic texts—*McGuffey's Eclectic Readers*—used Protestant Scripture to teach children to accept their position in society. A good child, McGuffey taught, does not envy the rich: "It is God who makes some poor and others rich." McGuffey further preached that "the rich have troubles which we know nothing of; and . . . the poor, if they are good, may be very happy."

Catholics, immigrants, blacks, and working-class people sought to have local control over their own schools, but the state legislatures established secular statewide standards under Protestant educators. Catholics in New York responded by building their own educational system over the next half-century. When Los Angeles became a city in 1850, it attempted to establish bilingual Spanish-English instruction. Trained bilingual teachers could not be found, however, and when the schools opened, only English was permitted.

Urban population concentration, growth in commerce, and shifts in work altered patterns of leisure. In rural society, as Irene Hardy recalled, both leisure activities and work often took place at home. But

Leisure

in cities, new dedicated spaces— streets, theaters, sports fields— constituted a social sphere where people could come together away from home. Through the sale of admission tickets or membership in various types of associations, leisure became a commodity to be purchased. As the population became more diverse, leisure associations reflected ethnic, racial, and class divisions.

Traditional colonial leisure pursuits continued in the city. Men frequented taverns and spent spare time drinking and playing tavern games of skill and strength—arm wrestling, ninepins, and pitching coins. Though city dwellers had less opportunity than their rural counterparts to ride and hunt, fishing remained popular among both men and women. Churches continued to remain centers for leisure, especially for women interested in religious activities and in clubs that combined socializing with good works.

Americans read more. Thanks to the expansion of public education, the vast majority of native-born white Americans were literate by the 1850s. Power printing presses and better transportation made possible wide distribution of books and periodicals. The religious press—of both traditional sects and dissenters—produced pamphlets, hymnbooks, Bibles, and religious newspapers. Americans also read secular publications. Newspapers and magazines—political organs, literary journals, and the voices of specialized groups like millworkers—abounded in the 1830s and after. In Brookfield, Massachusetts, in 1798, the mails brought one weekly newspaper; fifty years later, in 1848, fifty different newspapers and another fifty-five monthly magazines arrived on subscribers' doorsteps every week.

Fiction and autobiographies competed with religious tracts as popular literature. Newspapers and magazines printed fiction, and bookstores and stationers in large cities sold book-length novels and autobiographies. Susanna Rowson's 1794 novel *Charlotte Temple*, which offered a critique of women's dependence on men, and the powerful attack on slavery in the *Narrative of the Life of Frederick Douglass, an American Slave, Written by Himself* (1845) were widely read. Many popular novels, written by women, often for women, were set in the home and upheld Christian values. They reflected growing gender differences in American society in their exploration of the divisions between home and work, between emotion and authority, and between sentimentality and power. Yet in their support of traditional female moral roles, they also can be read as a challenge to prevailing values. Rowson's *Charlotte Temple*, for instance, never depicts the heroine performing domestic chores. And, although Susan Warners' *The Wide, Wide, Wide World* (1850), Nathaniel Hawthorne's *The House of the Seven Gables* (1851), and Fanny Fern's *Ruth Hall* (1855) did not challenge women's traditional domestic roles, they gave women a special moral bearing. In describing in positive terms community and republican virtue, they implicitly criticized the growing market economy.

Theater was a central institution in American life and provided a social sphere in which both men and women could gather. A theater was often the second public building constructed in a town—after a church. Large cities boasted two or more theaters catering to different classes. In New York City the Park Theater enjoyed the patronage of the carriage trade, the Bowery drew the middle class, and the Chatham attracted workers. Some plays cut across class lines. Shakespeare was performed so often and appreciated so widely that even illiterate theatergoers knew passages of his blank verse well. In the 1840s, musical and dramatic presentations took on a more professional tone; like the Hutchinson Family (see pages 253–254), newly popular minstrel shows and traveling circuses offered carefully rehearsed routines. Dancing and music remained popular.

Sports, like theater, increasingly involved city dwellers as spectators. Horseracing, boxing, walking races, and, in the 1850s, baseball began to attract large urban male crowds. More and more people purchased leisure by buying a ticket.

After New York State legalized horseracing in 1821, a track opened in Queens County across the East River from New York City. Two years later a single race drew fifty thousand people, and the newspapers reported a massive traffic jam of carriages from the ferry to the racecourse. Many spectators found betting as compelling as the sport. From 1831, enthusiasts could follow sports in a sports newspaper, *Spirit of the Times*. By 1849 boxing was so popular that a round-by-round account of a Maryland boxing match was telegraphed throughout the East.

Sports

Increasingly, urban sports and recreation became more formal and a commodity to be purchased. They had become less spontaneous and relied increasingly on formal rules. A group of Wall Street office workers formed the Knickerbocker Club in 1842, and in 1845 they drew up rules for the game of baseball. Their rules were widely adopted and continue to serve as the basis for the game. Entertainment became a commodity: one had to buy a ticket to go to the theater, the circus, P. T. Barnum's American Museum in New York City, the racetrack, or the ballpark.

Ironically, public leisure soon developed a private dimension. Exclusive private associations arose to provide space and occasions for leisure. Some

Nicholino Calyo's watercolor Soap-Locks, or Bowery Boys *(c. 1847) captured the bold body language and showy dress of the youths who controlled the sidewalks of the Bowery.*   New-York Historical Society.

represented class divisions as the growing middle and upper classes distanced themselves from the crowds and rowdiness of public events. In 1829 a group of Ohio merchants organized the Cincinnati Angling Club, which had a formal constitution and bylaws and limited membership to twenty-five. Ethnic, racial, religious groups seeking to socialize and share and preserve similar traditions formed clubs and societies. The Irish formed the Hibernian Society and the Sons of Erin; Germans brought Turnvereine physical-cultural clubs from across the Atlantic; Jews founded B'nai B'rith as a men's club; and African-Americans had chapters of the Prince Hall Masons in nearly every community. Women too organized their own associations, ranging from social organizations to benevolent societies.

As cities grew, their populations seemed increasingly fragmented. Finding people similar to one-self required more of a conscious effort. The new associations served as a bulwark against the cultures of other groups—immigrants, migrants, blacks, and artisans. Middle- and upper-class New Yorkers who felt alienated in the city of their birth founded exclusive clubs. Some joined the Masonic order, which offered everything

City Culture

the bustling city did not: an elaborate hierarchy, an orderly code of deference between ranks, harmony, and shared values. Members knew each other. The Masonic order played a political role as well: Masons recruited officeholders and marched in the parades that were a regular feature of the city's political life. Americans of all sorts—native- and foreign-born, black and white—also formed churches and church-associated clubs. Associations brought together like people, but they also formalized divisions between different groups.

Divisions seemed to occur naturally on city streets. A youth culture developed on the Bowery in the 1840s. In the evenings the broad street—lined with theaters, dance halls, ice-cream shops, and cafés—became an urban midway. Older New Yorkers feared the "Bowery boys and gals," whose ostentatious dress and behavior seemed threatening to them. Around 1847, artist Nicholino Calyo depicted three Bowery boys in a watercolor painting. A Bowery boy had long hair, often greased into a roll. He wore a broad-brimmed black hat, an open shirt collar, a black frock coat that reached below the knee, and as much jewelry as he could afford. His swaggering gait, especially when he had a girlfriend on his arm, frightened many in the middle class. Equally disturbing to old New Yorkers were the young working women who promenaded on the Bowery. They came in groups to enjoy each other's company and to meet Bowery boys. Unlike more genteel ladies who wore modest veils or bonnets, Bowery "gals" drew attention to themselves with bright, outlandish clothes and ornate hats.

Cities offered diversity and anonymity. People interested in same-sex liaisons, though often publicly ostracized, could find each other in the city and live together in urban boarding houses.

Most working people spent much of their lives outdoors; they worked in the streets as laborers, shopped in open markets, and paraded on special occasions. Young people courted, neighbors argued, and ethnic groups defended their turf on the streets. Increasingly, urban streets served as a political arena as crowds formed to listen to speakers, to parade, and sometimes to form mobs.

Economic, political, social, and ethnic conflict erupted on city streets. In the 1830s riots became commonplace as professionals and merchants, craftsmen, and laborers vented their rage against political and economic rivals. "Gentlemen of property and standing," unnerved by antislavery proponents, sacked abolitionist and antislavery organizations, even murdering newspaper editor Elijah Lovejoy in Alton, Illinois, in 1837. In the 1840s, "respectable" citizens drove the Mormons out of Illinois and Missouri. In Philadelphia native-born workers attacked Irish weavers in 1828, and whites and blacks fought on the docks in 1834 and 1835. Residents of North Philadelphia took to the streets continuously from 1840 to 1842 until the construction of a railroad through their neighborhood was abandoned. These disturbances came to a head in the Philadelphia riots of 1844, in which mostly Protestant skilled workers attacked Irish Catholics. Smaller cities, too, became battlegrounds as nativist riots peaked in the 1850s; Louisville, for instance, witnessed an anti-German riot in 1855. By 1840 more than 125 people had died in urban riots, and by 1860 fatalities exceeded 1,000.

Urban Riots

As public disorder spread, Boston hired uniformed policemen in 1837 to supplement its part-time watchmen and constables, and New York in 1845 established an entirely uniformed force. Nonetheless, middle-class men and women did not venture out alone at night, and even during the day they avoided certain districts. The police tried to control and suppress street activity, as did local ordinances that licensed and regulated street vendors and banned bells and horns. Local laws against vagrancy and disturbing the peace often were used against free blacks and immigrants. The continuing inflow of immigrants to the cities worsened social tensions by pitting people of dissimilar backgrounds against each other in the contest for jobs and housing. In the midst of so much noise, crime, and conflict, the lavish residences of the very rich rose like a deliberate affront to those struggling to survive.

 ## Extremes of Wealth

The French nobleman Alexis de Tocqueville and other observers characterized the United States before the Civil War as primarily a place of equality and opportunity. Tocqueville and his companion Gustave de Beaumont traveled 4,000 miles and visited all twenty-four states over a nine-month period in 1831 and 1832. Tocqueville opened *Democracy in America*, his classic analysis of the American people and nation, with this statement: "No novelty in the United States struck me more vividly during my stay there than the equality of conditions."

Tocqueville attributed American equality—the relative fluidity of the social order—to Americans' mobility and restlessness. Geographic mobility offered people a chance to start anew regardless of where they came from or who they were. Wealth and family mattered little; a person could be known by deeds alone. Indeed, Americans seemed driven by restlessness and ambition. "An American will build a house in which to pass his old age," Tocqueville wrote, "and sell it before the roof is on; he will plant a garden and rent it just as the trees are coming into bearing; he will clear a field and leave others to reap the harvest; he will take up a profession and leave it, settle in one place and soon go off elsewhere with his changing desires."

Most Americans believed that hard work reaped rewards. This belief was supported by traditional religious values and a deeply rooted work ethic. According to the conventional wisdom, anyone could advance by working hard and saving money. A local legend from Newburyport, Massachusetts, illustrated this theme. Tristram Dalton, a Federalist lawyer, wanted his carriage repaired. Moses Brown, an ambitious mechanic, refused to wait for Dalton's servants to tow the carriage to his shop; he sought out the vehicle and fixed it on the spot. After Dalton's death his heirs squandered the family fortune, but Brown's industriousness paid off. Through hard work the humble carriage craftsman became one of Massachusetts's richest men, eventually buying the Dalton homestead and living out his life there. The moral was clear: "Men succeed or fail . . . not from accident or external surroundings," as the *Newburyport Herald* put it in 1856, but from "possessing or wanting the elements of success in themselves."

Others disagreed with this egalitarian view of American life. Among those who traced the rise of a new aristocracy based on wealth and power was *New York Sun* publisher Moses Yale Beach. Author of twelve editions of *Wealth and Biography of the Wealthy Citizens of New York City*, Beach listed 750 New Yorkers

"If Not an Aristocracy"

with assets of $100,000 or more in 1845. John Jacob Astor led the list of nineteen millionaires with a fortune of $25 million. Ten years later, Beach reported more than a thousand New Yorkers worth $100,000, among them twenty-eight millionaires. Combining gossip-column items with wild guesses at people's wealth, Beach's publications suggest the enormous wealth of New York's upper class. Tocqueville himself, sensitive to conflicting trends in American life, had described the new industrial wealth. The rich and well educated "come forward to exploit industries," Tocqueville wrote, and become "more and more like the administrators of a huge empire. . . . What is this if not an aristocracy?"

Wealth throughout the United States was becoming concentrated in the hands of a relatively small number of people. In New York City between 1828 and 1845, the richest 4 percent of the city's population increased their holdings from an estimated 63 percent to 80 percent of all individual wealth. Meanwhile, the holdings of many ordinary people virtually disappeared. In Brooklyn between 1810 and 1841, the share of wealth held by the bottom two-thirds of families decreased from 10 percent to almost nothing. By 1860 the top 5 percent of American families owned more than half of the nation's wealth, and the top 10 percent owned more than 70 percent.

Meanwhile, a cloud of uncertainty hovered over working men and women. Many feared hard times and resented the competition of immigrant and slave labor. They dreaded the insecurities and indignities of poverty, chronic illness, disability, old age, widowhood, and desertion. Women feared having to raise a family without a spouse. And they had good reason: few women could find a job that paid sufficient money to support a family. Fear of poverty prompted the Klinger sisters, for instance, to marry again and again.

Urban Poverty

Poverty dogged the urban working class. Newly arrived immigrants, indigent free blacks, the working poor, and thieves, beggars, and prostitutes eked out a living in urban slums. New York City's Five Points, a few blocks from City Hall, was notorious for its squalor. Dominated by the Old Brewery, which had been converted to housing for hundreds of adults and children in 1837, the neighborhood was predominantly Irish and black. Lacking running water and sewers, Five Points exemplified the worst of urban life. Contemporaries estimated that more than a thousand people lived in its rooms, cellars, and subcellars. Throughout the city, workers' housing was at a premium. Houses built for two families often held four; tenements built for six families held twelve. Many families took in lodgers to help pay the rent.

New York and other large cities harbored "street rats," boys without families, who earned their living on the streets by petty thievery. They slept on boats, in haylofts, or in warehouses. Charles Loring Brace, a founder of the Children's Aid Society (1853), described them in *Dangerous Classes of New York* (1872): "Like the rats, they were too quick and cunning to be often caught in their petty plunderings, so they gnawed away at the foundations of society undisturbed." Brace and others considered such rootlessness a threat to American society more serious than Shays's Rebellion or Burr's conspiracies. "They will vote—they will have the same rights as we ourselves," warned the first report of the Children's Aid Society in 1854, "though they have grown up ignorant of moral principle, as any savage or Indian. . . . They will perhaps be embittered at the wealth and luxuries they never share. Then let society beware, when the vicious, reckless multitude of New York boys, swarming now in every foul alley and low street, come to know their power and use it!"

A world apart from Five Points and the people of the streets, though only a short walk away, lived the upper-class elite society of Philip Hone, one-time mayor of New York. Hone's diary, meticulously kept from 1826 until his death in 1851, records the activities of an American aristocrat. On February 28, 1840, for instance, Hone attended a masked ball at the Fifth Avenue mansion of Henry Breevoort, Jr.,

The Urban Elite

This view of the Five Points section of New York City's Sixth Ward, around 1829, depicts life in what was probably the worst slum in pre–Civil War America. Immodestly dressed prostitutes cruise the streets, attracting the attention of well-dressed men in top hats while a pig runs loose in their midst.   Courtesy of Mr. and Mrs. Screven Lorillard.

and Laura Carson Breevoort. The ball began at the fashionable hour of 10 P.M., and the five hundred ladies and gentlemen who filled the mansion wore costumes adorned with ermine and gold. For more than a week, Hone believed, the affair "occupied the minds of people of all stations, ranks, and employments." At one time or another similar parties were held in Boston, Philadelphia, Baltimore, and Charleston.

Hone regularly attended elegant dinner parties graced by fine cuisine and imported wines. The New York elite who filled the pages of Hone's diary—the 1 percent of the population who owned 50 percent of the city's wealth—lived in mansions attended by a corps of servants. In the summer, country estates, ocean resorts, mineral spas, and grand tours of Europe offered relief from the strenuous winter and spring social seasons and escape from the heat and smell of the city.

Much of this new wealth was inherited. For every John Jacob Astor who made millions in the western fur trade or George Law who left a farm to become a millionaire contractor and investor, ten

others used money they had inherited or married as a steppingstone to additional wealth. Andrew H. Mickle, a poor Irish immigrant who became a millionaire and mayor of New York City, derived his fortune from marrying the daughter of his employer. Many of the wealthiest New Yorkers bore the names of the colonial commercial elite: Beekman, Breevoort, Roosevelt, Van Rensselaer, and Whitney. These rich New Yorkers were not idle; they worked at increasing their fortunes and power. Urban capitalists like Philip Hone and the fashionable elite profited enormously from the transportation, commercial, and manufacturing revolutions. Wealth begat wealth, and marriage cemented family ties.

Meanwhile, a distinct middle class became part of the urban scene, and the growth and specialization of trade rapidly increased its numbers. The men were businessmen or professionals, the women homemakers and volunteers. Middle-class families enjoyed the new consumer items: wool carpeting, fine wallpaper, and rooms full of furniture replaced

The Middle Class

the bare floors, whitewashed walls, and relative sparseness of eighteenth-century homes. Houses were large, often having from four to six rooms. Middle-class children slept one to a bed, and by the 1840s and 1850s middle-class families used indoor toilets. When Philadelphia publishing agent Joseph Engles died in 1861, an inventory of his estate indicated that his parlor contained two sofas, thirteen chairs, three card tables, a fancy table, a piano, a mirror, and a fine carpet. Other rooms were similarly furnished.

Middle-class families formed the backbone of the rich associational life that Tocqueville had observed in America. They filled the family pews in church on Sundays; their children pursued whatever educational opportunities were available. They were as distant from Philip Hone's world as they were from the working class and the poor. Increasingly they looked to the family and home as the core of middle-class life.

 ## Women, Families, and the Domestic Ideal

Distinctions among families grew in the nineteenth century. Once primarily an economic unit, nonfarm families lost their role as producers (see Chapter 10). And as manufacturing left the home, so did wage workers. One result was specialization of roles by gender and by life stage.

The family was dominated by the husband and father. English common law gave husbands control over the family. The men owned their wives' personal property; they were legal guardians of the children; and they owned whatever family members produced or earned. A father still had the legal authority to oppose his daughter's choice of husband. Nonetheless, most American women, with their parents' blessing, were choosing their own marriage partners.

Marriage and family life were the central adult experiences of most women. Although married women still had limited legal rights and standing, they made modest gains in property and spousal rights from the 1830s on. Arkansas in 1835 passed the first women's property law, and by 1860 sixteen more states had followed suit. In those states, women, including wives, could own and convey property: when a wife inherited, earned, or acquired property, it was hers, not her husband's; and she could write a will. In the 1830s states began to liberalize divorce,

The homes of middle-class citizens were a world apart from the slums of New York City. This 1828 oil painting (by an unknown artist) shows the luxurious domestic furnishings, tailored clothing, and African-American servant of a family in York, Pennsylvania. The Saint Louis Art Museum, Bequest of Edgar William and Bernice Chrysler Garbisch.

adding cruelty and desertion as grounds for divorce. Women who had the financial means could leave unhappy marriages.

As the urban workplace and home became separate, men worked for wages outside the home. Rural sons worked on their family farms, worked for hire on other people's farms, or sought wage work in towns. New England daughters left farms to work in textile mills. In the 1840s the new urban department stores hired young women as clerks and cash runners. Many women worked for a time as teachers, usually for two to five years. Paid employment typically represented a brief stage in women's lives before they left their parental households and entered their marital households.

Supporting Families

Rebecca Lukens pioneered in an unusual role for a woman in early-nineteenth-century America: she ran the Lukens Steel Company in eastern Pennsylvania from 1825 until she died in 1854. The deaths of her father in 1823 and of her husband in 1825 left her with the mill and large debts. She revived the steel company and soon was shipping iron plates as far away as Europe. Lukens Steel Company.

Working-class women—the poor, widows, and free blacks—worked to support themselves and their families. Leaving their parental homes as early as age twelve, they earned wages most of their lives, with only short respites for bearing and rearing children. But unlike men and New England farm daughters, most of these women did not work in the new shops and factories. Instead, they sold their domestic skills for wages outside their own households. Unmarried girls and women worked as domestic servants in other women's homes; married and widowed women worked as laundresses, seamstresses, and cooks. Some hawked food and wares on city streets; others did piecework sewing; and some became prostitutes. Few of these occupations enabled them to support themselves or a family at a respectable level.

Most women's work continued to be unpaid labor in the home. As the urban family lost its role in the production of goods, household upkeep and child rearing claimed women's full-time attention. Religion, morality, domestic arts, and music and literature filled the void left by the decline in the economic functions of the family; these realms came to be known as woman's sphere. A woman who achieved mastery in these areas lived up to the middle-class ideal of the cult of domesticity.

Middle-class Americans idealized the family as a moral institution characterized by selflessness and cooperation. Many viewed the family as a utopian retreat. Women were idealized in turn as the embodiment of self-sacrificing republicanism. The role of the mother was to strengthen the nation by rearing her children in a spiritual and virtuous environment unlike the world outside the home. The world of work—the market economy—was seen as an arena of conflict increasingly identified with men and dominated by base self-interest. In a rapidly changing world, the family represented stability and traditional values. But the family, no less than other American institutions, was also in flux.

The domestic ideal restricted the range of paying jobs available to middle-class women. Most paid work was viewed with disapproval, but one occupation was considered consonant with the genteel female role: teaching. In 1823 the Beecher sisters, Catharine and Mary, established the Hartford Female Seminary and offered history and science in addition to the traditional women's curriculum of domestic arts and religion. A decade later Catharine Beecher successfully campaigned for teacher-training schools for women. By the 1850s teaching was regarded as a woman's vocation, and most urban teachers were women, nearly all unmarried. Men teachers, few in number, were often paid twice as much as women teachers. For society, the services of talented, educated women were a bargain.

Meanwhile, family size was shrinking. In 1800 American women bore an average of six to seven children. By 1860 the figure had dropped to five, by 1900 to four. This decline occurred even though many immigrants with large-family traditions were settling in the United States; thus the birth rate among native-born women declined even more steeply. Although rural families remained larger than their urban counterparts, birth rates among both groups declined comparably.

Decline in Family Size

A number of factors reduced family size. Small families were viewed as increasingly desirable in an economy in which the family was a unit of consumption rather than production. Children in smaller families would have greater opportunities: parents could give them more attention, better education, and more financial help. Also, contemporary marriage manuals stressed that too many births had a harmful effect on a woman's health, weakening her physically and overworking her as a mother. Thus, evidence suggests, many wives and husbands made deliberate decisions to limit the size of families. In places where farmland was relatively expensive, for instance, family size was smaller than in cheaper agricultural districts. In urban areas, children tended to become an economic burden rather than an asset as the family lost its role as a producer of goods.

How did men and women limit their families in the early nineteenth century? Average age at marriage rose, thus shortening the period of potential childbearing. Women also bore

Limiting Families

their last child at a younger age, dropping from around forty in the mid-eighteenth century to around thirty-five in the mid-nineteenth. This change suggests that family planning was becoming more common. Many couples used traditional forms of birth control, such as coitus interruptus (withdrawal of the male before completion of the sexual act) and breast-feeding, which makes some women temporarily infertile. Medical devices, however, were beginning to compete with these ancient and imperfect practices. Although animal-skin condoms imported from France were too expensive for popular use, cheap rubber condoms became available in the 1850s. Some couples used the rhythm method—attempting to confine intercourse to a woman's infertile periods. Awareness of the "safe period," however, was uncertain, even among physicians.

If all else failed, abortion was available, especially after 1830. Ineffective folk methods of self-induced abortion had been around for centuries, but in the 1830s abortionists, mostly women, advertised surgical services in large cities. To protect women from unqualified abortionists, and in response to reformers opposed to abortion, states began to regulate abortions. Between 1821 and 1841, ten states and one territory either restricted late-term abortions or prohibited abortion altogether; by 1860, twenty states had adopted such restrictions. Only three of those twenty states punished the women who chose to end a pregnancy; the abortionists were considered to be the criminals. Such laws, however, were rarely enforced.

Significantly, the birth-control methods that women themselves controlled—the rhythm method, abstinence, and abortion—became increasingly common. The new emphasis on domesticity encouraged women's autonomy in the home and by extension gave them greater control over their own bodies. Women ruled the household, including the bedroom, with refinement and purity. As one woman put it, "woman's duty was to subdue male passions, not to kindle them."

Smaller families and fewer births changed women's lives. At one time birth and infant care had occupied virtually the entire span of women's adult lives, and few mothers had lived to see their youngest child reach maturity. After the 1830s many women found time for other activities. Smaller families also allowed women to devote more time to their older children, and childhood gradually came to be perceived as a distinct period in the life span. The expansion of public education in the 1830s and the policy of grouping schoolchildren by age reinforced this trend.

Urban life always offered a place for men outside families. Rooming and boarding houses provided them with places to live. The expansion of cities and the market economy offered independence for women outside

Single Men and Women

families as well. Single women departed from the centuries-old pattern in which a woman moved from her father's household to the household of her husband. Louisa May Alcott (1832–1888), the author of *Little Women* (1868), sought independence and financial security for herself. Her father, the philosopher Bronson Alcott, never adequately supported his family. Not even the family's participation in a utopian cooperative put enough food on the table. Alcott worked as a seamstress, governess, teacher, and housemaid before her writing brought her success. "I think I shall come out right, and prove that though an *Alcott*, I *can* support myself," she wrote her father in 1856. "I like the independent feeling; and though not an easy life, it is a free one, and I enjoy it. I can't do much with my hands; so I will make a battering-ram of my head and make a way through this rough-and-tumble world."

Louisa May Alcott foreswore marriage. She and other unmarried women pursued careers and lives defined by female relationships. Given the difficulty women had finding work that would allow them to be self-supporting, they undertook independence at great risk. Nonetheless, the proportion of single women in the population increased significantly in the first three quarters of the nineteenth century. In Massachusetts in 1850, 17 percent of native-born women never married—a far larger percentage than in colonial days. Independent white women, in sum, were taking advantage of new opportunities offered by the market economy and urban expansion.

 ## Immigrant Lives in America

The United States continued to be a nation of newcomers; the 5 million immigrants who came to the United States between 1820 and 1860 outnumbered the entire population of the country recorded in the first census in 1790. They came from every continent, though the vast majority were European (see figure, page 331). During the peak period of pre–Civil War immigration, from 1847 through 1857, 3.3 million immigrants entered the United States; 1.3 million were from Ireland and 1.1 million from the German states. By 1860, 15 percent of the white population was foreign-born.

This massive migration had been set in motion decades earlier. At the turn of the nineteenth century, the Napoleonic wars had given rise to one of the greatest population shifts in history; it was ultimately to last more than a century. War, revolution, famine, religious persecution, and the lure of industrialization led many Europeans to leave home. Most Asian immigrants came from southern China to work in heavy construction. The United States beckoned, offering economic opportunity and religious freedom.

Both private firms and governments recruited European immigrants. Midwestern and western states lured potential settlers to promote economic growth. Two transplanted New Yorkers, Augustus and Joe Kirby Allen, for instance, in 1836 set themselves up in what became Houston, Texas, and advertised in newspapers for settlers. In the 1850s, Wisconsin appointed a commissioner of emigration, who advertised the state's advantages in European newspapers. Wisconsin also opened an office in New York and hired European agents to compete with other

Promotion of Immigration

states and with firms like the Illinois Central Railroad in recruiting immigrants.

Large construction projects and mines needed strong young laborers. Textile mills and cities attracted young women workers. Europeans' awareness of the United States grew as employers, states, and shipping companies advertised opportunities across the Atlantic. Often the message was stark: work and prosper in America or starve in Europe. The price of a ticket on the regularly scheduled sailing ships crossing the ocean after 1848 was within easy reach of millions of Europeans.

Success in America stimulated further emigration. "I wish, and do often say that we wish you were all in this happy land," wrote shoemaker John West of Germantown, Pennsylvania, to his kin in Corsley, England, in 1831, adding: "A man nor woman need not stay out of employment one hour here." John Down, a weaver from Frome, England, who emigrated to New York without his family, wrote to his wife in 1830 to describe the bountiful meal he had shared with a farmer's family: "They had on the table puddings, pyes, and fruit of all kind that was in season, and preserves, pickles, vegetables, meats, and everything that a person would wish, and the servants [farm hands] set down at the same table with their masters." Though Down sorely missed his family, he wrote, "I do not repent of coming, for you know that there was nothing but poverty before me, and to see you and the dear children want was what I could not bear. *I would rather cross the Atlantic ten times than hear my children cry for victuals once.*" Such testimonials to the success of pauper immigrants in America were widely circulated in Europe.

So they came, enduring the hardships of travel and of living in a strange land. The average trans-Atlantic crossing took six weeks; in bad weather it could take three months. Joseph Gear made sketches during his crowded, unpleasant journey to the United States aboard the *Acasta* in 1824. Disease spread unchecked among people packed together like cattle in steerage. More than seventeen thousand immigrants, mostly Irish, died from "ship fever" in 1847. On arrival, immigrants became fair game for the con artists and swindlers who worked the docks. Boarding-house and employment agents tried to lure them from their chosen destinations. In response, New York State established Castle Garden as an immigrant center in 1855. There, at the tip of Manhattan Island, the major port for European entry, immigrants were somewhat sheltered from fraud. Authorized transportation companies main-

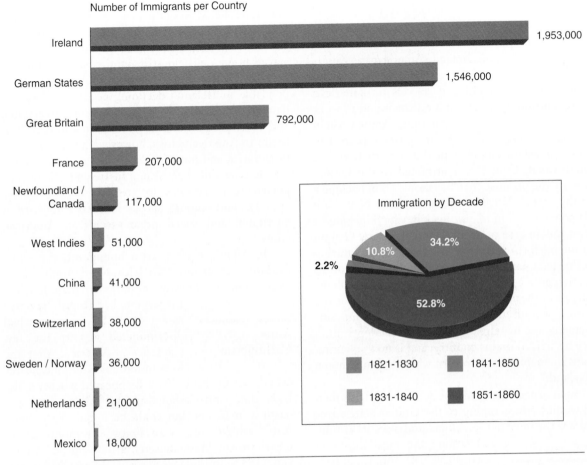

Major Sources of Immigration to the United States, 1821–1860

Number of Immigrants per Country

Country	Number
Ireland	1,953,000
German States	1,546,000
Great Britain	792,000
France	207,000
Newfoundland / Canada	117,000
West Indies	51,000
China	41,000
Switzerland	38,000
Sweden / Norway	36,000
Netherlands	21,000
Mexico	18,000

Immigration by Decade

34.2% · 10.8% · 2.2% · 52.8%

1821-1830 · 1841-1850 · 1831-1840 · 1851-1860

Major Sources of Immigration to the United States, 1821–1860   *Most immigrants came from two areas: Great Britain, of which Ireland was a part, and the German states. These two areas sent more immigrants between 1820 and 1860 than the inhabitants of the United States enumerated at the first census in 1790. By 1860, 15 percent of the white population was of foreign birth.*   Source: U.S. Bureau of the Census, *Historical Statistics of the United States, Colonial Times to 1970*, 2 parts (Washington, D.C., 1975), Part 1, pp. 206, 208.

tained offices in the large rotunda and assisted new arrivals with their travel plans.

Most immigrants gravitated toward cities, since only a minority had farming experience or the means to purchase land and equipment. Many stayed in New York City itself. By 1855 52 percent of its 623,000 inhabitants were immigrants, 28 percent from Ireland and 16 percent from the German states. Boston, another major entry port for the Irish, took on a European tone; throughout the 1850s the city was about 35 percent foreign-born, of whom more than two-thirds were Irish. Southern cities also had sizable immigrant populations. In 1860 New Orleans was 44

percent foreign-born, Savannah 33 percent, and the western city of St. Louis 61 percent. On the West Coast, San Francisco had a foreign-born majority.

Some immigrants settled in rural areas. German, Dutch, and Scandinavian farmers, in particular, gravitated toward the Midwest. Greater percentages of Scandinavians and Netherlanders took up farming than did other nationalities; both groups came mostly as religious dissenters and migrated in family units. The Dutch who founded colonies in Michigan and Wisconsin, for instance, had seceded from the official Reformed Church of the Netherlands, fleeing persecution in their native land to establish new and more pious communities such as Holland and Zeeland in Michigan.

Not all immigrants found success in the United States; hundreds of thousands returned to their homelands disappointed. Before the potato blight hit Ireland, American recruiters had lured many Irish to swing picks and shovels on American canals and railroads and to work in construction. Among them was Michael Gaugin, who for thirteen years had been an assistant engineer in the construction of a Dublin canal. Gaugin was attracted to the United States by the promise that "he should soon become a wealthy man." The Dublin agent for a New York firm convinced him to quit his job, which included a house and an acre of ground, and emigrate. Gaugin had the misfortune to land in New York City during the financial panic of 1837, and within two months of arriving he was a pauper. Gaugin told an Irish investigation that he was "now without means for the support of himself and his family, and has no employment, and has already suffered great deprivation since he arrived in this country; and is now soliciting means to enable him to return with his family home to Ireland."

Immigrant Disenchantment

Such experiences did not deter other Irish men and women from coming to the United States. Ireland was the most densely populated place in Europe and among the most impoverished. From 1815 on, small harvests prompted a steady stream of Irish to emigrate to America. Then in 1845 and 1846 potatoes—Ireland's staple food—rotted in the fields. From 1845 to 1849, death from starvation, malnutrition, and typhus spread. In all, 1 million died and about 1.5 million fled, two-thirds of them to the United States. Ireland's major export was its people. At the peak of Irish immigration, from 1847 to 1854, 1.2 million Irish men and women entered the United States. Each year between 1820 and 1854, with only two exceptions, the Irish constituted the largest group of immigrants. By the end of the nineteenth century there would be more Irish in the United States than in Ireland.

Irish Immigrants

The new Irish immigrants differed greatly from those who had left Ireland to settle in the American colonies. The Protestant Scots-Irish who predominated in the eighteenth century (see page 94) had journeyed from one part of the British Empire to another. The nineteenth-century Irish immigrants to America, however, were mostly Roman Catholic, and they moved from a British colony to an independent republic. Most of the new immigrants from Ireland were young, female, and from rural counties. Eldest sons, who expected to inherit family farms, stayed home, and eldest daughters stayed home to care for their parents. Younger children were expendable in Ireland's declining economy. Farmers' daughters could find work only as domestic servants, and poverty-stricken Ireland could not absorb all of them. In American cities, however, they found work in factories and households. If they wed, they married late, as did their sisters in Ireland. They supported their families in Ireland, built Catholic churches and schools, and established a network of charitable and social organizations in American cities.

In American cities Irish immigrants met anti-Catholic sentiment. "No Irish Need Apply" signs were common. During the colonial period, white Protestants had feared "popery" as a system of tyranny and had discriminated against the few Catholics in America. After the Revolution anti-Catholicism receded, but in the 1830s it reappeared wherever the Irish did. Anti-Catholicism was most overt and nastiest in Boston but could be found everywhere. Anti-Catholic riots were almost commonplace. In Charlestown, Massachusetts, a mob burned a convent (1834); in Philadelphia a crowd attacked priests and nuns and vandalized churches (1844); and in Lawrence, Massachusetts, a mob leveled the Irish neighborhood (1854).

Anti-Catholicism

The native-born who embraced anti-Catholicism were motivated largely by anxiety. They feared the Roman Catholic Church, unskilled Irish workers, and the urban slums inhabited by the Irish (among others). They blamed every social problem—from immorality and alcoholism to poverty and economic upheaval—on immigrant Irish Catholics. Impoverished native-born workers complained to the Massachusetts legislature in 1845 that the Irish displaced "the honest and respectable laborers of the State . . . and from their manner of living . . . work for much less per day . . . being satisfied with food to support the animal existence alone." American workers, they claimed, "not only labor for the body but for the mind, the soul, and the State." The new public schools, with their Protestant bias, represented another form of attack on Irish Catholics. Friction increased as Irish-American men fought back by entering politics.

In 1854, Germans replaced the Irish as the largest group of new arrivals. The Klinger family was part of this migration. Potato blight also had prompted emigration from the German states in the 1840s; other hardships added to the steady stream. Many people came from regions where small landholdings made it hard to eke out a living. Others were craftsmen displaced by the industrial revolution. These refugees were joined by middle-class Germans—a whole generation of liberals and freethinkers, some of whom were socialists, communists, and anarchists—who emigrated to the United States after the abortive revolutions of 1848.

German Immigrants

It is not easy to characterize German-Americans. There was not a single German culture. Though New York had a sizable German population, making it the world's third great German-speaking city—after Vienna and Berlin—Germans settled everywhere in the United States. In the South they were peddlers and merchants; in the North and West they worked as farmers, urban laborers, and businessmen. Their tendency to migrate as families and groups helped them maintain German culture and institutions. Many settled in small towns and rural areas where they could preserve their local and regional identities. In larger cities immigrants from the same German states tended to cluster together. Their presence transformed the tone and culture of cities like Cincinnati and Milwaukee.

Native-born Americans accepted German immigrants more readily than they accepted the Irish, stereotyping Germans as hard working, self-reliant, and intelligent. Many believed that Germans would "harmonize" better with American culture. Nevertheless, Germans, too, encountered hostility. A significant number of German immigrants were Jewish, and they experienced anti-Semitism. Many German immigrants were Catholic, and their Sabbath traditions differed from those of Protestants. On Sundays urban German families customarily gathered at beer gardens to eat and drink beer, to dance, sing, and listen to band music, and sometimes to play cards. Protestants were outraged by this behavior, which they believed to be a violation of the Lord's day. The Germans' persistent use of their native language also set them apart. Even German Protestants, mostly Lutherans, founded their own churches and German-language schools.

Some Hispanic groups became "immigrants" to the United States without actually moving. Mexican

This painting (c. 1840) of Saint Isadore of Madrid, patron saint of farmers, is attributed to Rafael Aragon. Hispanic farmers in the Southwest sought the aid of Saint Isadore as they struggled to raise crops and preserve their culture.   Courtesy of Dr. and Mrs. Ward Alan Minge.

inhabitants of northern Mexico—present-day New Mexico and California—were unhappy because under the Mexican constitution of 1824 they lived in Mexican territory, not states. Similarly Texas was part of the Mexican state of Coahuila. Lack of political autonomy made Mexicans in these areas unhappy, and many welcomed the events that brought them into the United States: the independence and later annexation of Texas, the Mexican War, and the Gadsden Purchase (see pages 369, 376).

Hispanics

In Texas, Anglos and European immigrants seized economic and political power. Tejanos retained their language, Roman Catholic religion, and community affiliations by means of newspapers, mutual-aid societies, schools, and the church, but they lost power and status to Anglos. In Nueces County, Texas, at the time of the Texas Revolution (1836), Mexicans held all the land; twenty years later, they had lost it all. Commerce eclipsed their agricultural and ranching economy; rancheros and vaqueros—cowboys—became obsolete. Although many Tejanos had fought for Texas's independence, arriving Anglo settlers tended to treat them as inferiors. They became second-class citizens on land where they had lived for generations.

Nonetheless, Tejanos retained their culture. They held fast to Roman Catholic and Hispanic traditions. San Antonio, Mexican from 1821 to 1836 and thereafter a Texas city, illustrates the persistence of Hispanic culture. The church, free public schools (established in 1827), life-cycle events from baptism to marriage to funerals, and public holidays and celebrations all supported Hispanic Roman Catholic traditions. Thus during the period of Texas independence, from 1836 to 1845, and after Texas statehood in 1845, Hispanic identity continued even in the face of a loss of political power.

In California—unlike Texas, New Mexico, and Arizona—Hispanic culture as well as political power quickly gave way to American and European culture. Californios, the Mexican population, numbered 10,000 in 1848, or two-thirds of the non-Indian population. By the end of the century the Hispanic population was 15,000 out of 1.5 million, and Hispanic culture was only a remnant, though it would be reestablished by Mexican immigrants in the twentieth century.

For immigrants, becoming part of American society involved conflict, but once in the United States they claimed their right to a fair economic and political share. Native Americans, however, like the Hispanics in the Southwest, had to defend what they regarded as prior rights. Their lands, their religions, and their ways of life came under constant attack because Americans viewed them as obstacles to expansion and economic growth.

Native American Resistance and Removal

The Constitution gave the United States government responsibility for dealing with Native Americans. For better or worse, there had to be a federal Indian policy. From the Indians' point of view, it usually was for the worse. United States territorial expansion took place at the Indians' expense. The result was removal of the great Native American nations to lands west of the Mississippi. While the population of other groups was increasing by leaps and bounds, the Indian population was shrinking.

Alexis de Tocqueville noticed the contrast. "Not only have these wild tribes receded, but they are destroyed," Tocqueville concluded, after personally observing the tragedy of forced removal, "and as they give way or perish, an immense and increasing people fill their place. There is no instance upon record of so prodigious a growth or so rapid a destruction." War, forced removal, disease—especially smallpox—and malnutrition reduced many Indian nations by half. More than half of the Pawnees, Omahas, Otoes, Missouris, and Kansas died in the 1830s alone.

Like the colonial powers in North America, the United States government treated Native American groups as sovereign nations, until Congress ended the practice in 1871. In its relations with Indian leaders, the government followed international protocol. Indian delegations to Washington were received with the appropriate pomp and ceremony. Native American and United States leaders exchanged presents as tokens of friendship, and commemorative flags and silver medals with presidents' likenesses became prized possessions among Indian chiefs. Agreements between a given Indian nation and the United States were signed, sealed, and ratified like any other international pact.

In practice, however, Native American sovereignty was a fiction. Protocol appeared to signify mutual respect and independence, but treaty negotiations exposed the sham. Treaty making was essentially a tactic that the American government used to acquire Indian land. Instead of bargains struck by two equal nations, treaties often were agreements imposed by the victor on the vanquished. Old treaties gave way to new ones requiring Native Americans to cede their traditional holdings in exchange for other land in the West. Beginning with President Jefferson, the federal government withheld payments for land cessions to pressure Native Americans to sign new treaties.

The War of 1812 snuffed out whatever realistic hopes eastern Indian leaders had of resisting American expansion by warfare. After the war, armed resistance by the Indians persisted, and blood was shed on both sides, as in the Seminole Wars (see pages 247, 338). But it only delayed the inevitable. The Shawnee chiefs Prophet and Tecumseh led the most significant movement against the United States (see pages 238–239), but Prophet failed to sustain the movement after Tecumseh's death.

The experiences of Prophet and other Shawnees were typical of the wanderings of an uprooted people. Until the 1870s only the Delawares and Kickapoos moved more. After

Shawnees

giving up 17 million acres in Ohio in the 1795 Treaty of Greenville (see pages 189–190), the Shawnees scattered to Indiana and eastern Missouri. After the War of 1812, Prophet's Indiana group withdrew to Canada under British protection. In 1822 other Shawnees sought Mexican protection and moved from Missouri to present-day eastern Texas. As the United States government began promoting removal to Kansas, Prophet returned from Canada to lead a group to the new Shawnee lands in eastern Kansas in 1825. When Missouri achieved statehood in 1821, Shawnees living there were also forced to move to Kansas, where they were joined in the 1830s by Shawnees removed from Ohio and others expelled from Texas. By 1854 Kansas was open to white settlement, and the Shawnees had to cede back seven-eighths of their land there—1.4 million acres.

Removal had a profound impact on all Shawnees. The men had to give up their traditional role as providers; their methods of hunting and their knowledge of woodland animals were useless on the prairies of Kansas. As grain became the tribe's dietary staple, Shawnee women played a greater role as providers, supplemented by government aid under treaty provisions. (Typically, treaties required annual distributions of grain, blankets, and cash payments.) Remarkably, the Shawnees preserved their language and culture in the face of these drastic changes. Although resistance proved incapable of protecting their lands, it did help maintain their culture.

In the 1820s Native Americans in Ohio, southern Indiana and Illinois, southwestern Michigan, most of Missouri, central Alabama, and southern

Federal Indian Policy

Mississippi were pressured to cede their lands. They gave up nearly 200 million acres for pennies an acre. The appetite of the United States for land was insatiable. The federal Indian agency system, which monopolized trade with Native Americans and paid out the rations, supplies, and annuities they received in exchange for abandoning their land, made Indians dependent on government payments. Dependency made them pliant in treaty negotiations and furthered assimilation by bringing them into the market system.

Ever since the early days of European colonization, the assimilation of Native Americans through education and Christianity had been an explicit goal of whites (see page 54). It took on renewed urgency as the United States expanded westward. "Put into the hand of [Indian] children the primer and the hoe," the House Committee on Indian Affairs recommended in 1818, "and they will naturally, in time, take hold of the plough; and, as their minds become enlightened and expand, the Bible will be their book, and they will grow up in habits of morality and industry . . . and become useful members of society." In 1819, in response to missionary lobbying, Congress appropriated $10,000 annually for "civilization of the tribes adjoining the frontier settlements." Protestant missionaries administered the "civilizing fund" and established mission schools.

Within five years thirty-two such schools were in operation. These new boarding schools substituted English for Native American languages and taught agriculture alongside the Christian Gospel. The emphasis on agriculture was intended to demonstrate the value of private property and hard work and to lay the basis for stable Christian communities. But to settlers eyeing Native American land, assimilation through education seemed too slow a process. At any given time there were never more than fifteen hundred students in all the schools; at that rate it would take centuries to assimilate all the Indians. Thus wherever Native Americans lived, illegal settlers disrupted their lives. Though obligated to protect the integrity of treaty lands, the federal government did so only halfheartedly. With government supporting westward expansion, legitimate Indian claims had to give way to the advance of white civilization.

In the 1820s it became apparent that neither economic dependency, education, nor Christianity could persuade Native Americans to cede enough land to satisfy the expansionists. Attention focused on southeastern tribes—Cherokees, Creeks, Choctaws, Chickasaws, and Seminoles—because much of their land remained intact after the War of 1812 and because they aggressively resisted white encroachment. Possessing some formal political institutions, they were better organized than the northern tribes to resist.

In his last annual message to Congress in late 1824, President James Monroe suggested that all Indians be moved beyond the Mississippi River. Three

Indian Removal to the West

days later he sent a special message to Congress proposing removal. Monroe described his proposal as an "honorable" one that would protect Indians from invasion and provide them with independence for "improvement and civilization." Force would be unnecessary, he believed; the promise of a home free from white encroachment would be sufficient to win Indian acceptance.

The proposal was aimed at the Cherokees, Creeks, Choctaws, and Chickasaws, and they unanimously rejected it. Between 1789 and 1825 they had negotiated thirty treaties with the United States. They had reached the limits of their tolerance. They wished to remain on what was left of their ancestral land.

Pressure from Georgia had prompted Monroe's policy. Cherokees and Creeks lived in northwestern Georgia, and in the 1820s the state accused the federal government of not fulfilling its 1802 promise to remove the Indians in return for the state's renunciation of its claim to western lands. Georgia was satisfied neither by Monroe's removal messages nor by further cessions by the Creeks. In 1826, under federal pressure, the Creek nation ceded all but a small strip of its Georgia acreage. But Georgia still was not satisfied. Only the removal of the Georgia Creeks to the West could resolve the conflict between Georgia and the federal government.

For the Creeks the outcome was a devastating blow. In an ultimately unsuccessful attempt to hold fast to the remainder of their traditional lands, which were in Alabama, they radically altered their political structure. In 1829, at the expense of traditional village autonomy, they centralized tribal authority and forbade any chief from ceding land. So in the end, they lost not only their land but their traditional forms of social and political organization.

If civilizing Indians was the American goal, no tribe met that test better than the Cherokees. Between 1819 and 1829 the tribe became economically self-sufficient and politically self-governing: during this Cherokee renaissance the twelve to fifteen thousand adult

Cherokees

Cherokees came to think of themselves as a nation, not a collection of villages. In 1821 and 1822 Sequoyah, a self-educated Cherokee, devised an eighty-six-character phonetic alphabet that made possible a Cherokee-language Bible and a bilingual tribal newspaper, *Cherokee Phoenix* (1828). Between 1820 and 1823 the Cherokees created a formal government with a bicameral legislature, a court system, and a salaried bureaucracy. In 1827 they adopted a written constitution, modeled after that of the United States. Cherokee land laws, however, differed from United States law. The tribe as a whole owned all Cherokee land, and complex provisions covered land sales (forbidden to outsiders) and the proximity of farms (minimum distance apart was one-quarter mile). Nonetheless, the Cherokees assimilated American cultural patterns. By 1833 they held fifteen hundred black slaves whose legal status was the same as that of slaves held by southern whites. Moreover, missionaries had been so successful that the Cherokees could be considered a Christian community.

Although the Cherokees developed a political system similar to that of an American state, they failed to win respect or acceptance from southerners. Georgia pressed them to sell the 7,200 square miles of land they held in the state. Congress appropriated $30,000 in 1822 to buy the Cherokee land in Georgia, but the Cherokees preferred to stay where they were. Impatient with their refusals to negotiate cession, Georgia annulled the Cherokee's constitution, extended the state's sovereignty over them, and ordered their lands seized.

Backed by sympathetic whites but not by the new president, Andrew Jackson, the Cherokees under Chief John Ross turned to the federal courts to defend their treaty with the United States and prevent Georgia's seizure of their land. Their legal strategy reflected their growing political sophistication. In *Cherokee Nation* v. *Georgia* (1831), Chief Justice John Marshall ruled that under the federal Constitution an Indian tribe was neither a foreign nation nor a state and therefore had no standing in federal courts. Nonetheless, said Marshall, the Indians had an unquestionable right to their lands; they could lose title only by voluntarily giving it up. A year later, in *Worcester* v. *Georgia*, Marshall defined the Cherokee position more clearly. The Indian nation was, he declared, a distinct political community in which "the laws of Georgia can have no force" and into which Georgians could not enter without permission or treaty privilege. Georgia refused to comply.

Cherokee Nation v. Georgia

President Andrew Jackson, whose reputation had been built as an Indian fighter, refused to interfere because the case involved a state action. It was widely reported that Jackson had said, "John Marshall has made his decision: now let him enforce it." Keen to open up new lands for settlement, Jackson was determined to remove the Cherokees. In the Removal Act of 1830 Congress provided Jackson with the funds he needed to negotiate new treaties

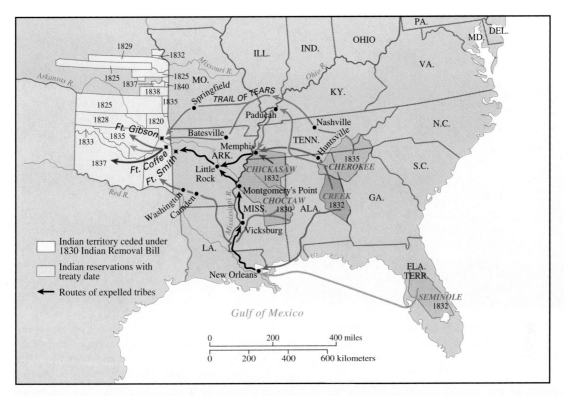

Removal of Native Americans from the South, 1820–1840   *Over a twenty-year period, the federal government and southern states forced Native Americans to exchange their traditional homes for western land. Some tribal groups remained in the South, but most settled in the alien western environment.*   Source: Acknowledgment is due to Martin Gilbert and George Weidenfeld and Nicholson Limited for permission to reproduce this map taken from *American History Atlas.*

and resettle the resistant tribes west of the Mississippi (see map).

The Choctaws were the first to go; they made the forced journey from Mississippi and Alabama to the West in the winter of 1831 and 1832. Alexis de Tocqueville was visiting Memphis when they arrived there: "The wounded, the sick, new-born babies, and the old men on the point of death. . . . I saw them embark to cross the great river," he wrote, "and the sight will never fade from my memory. Neither sob nor complaint rose from that silent assembly. Their afflictions were of long standing, and they felt them to be irremediable." Other tribes soon joined the forced march. The Creeks in Alabama resisted removal until 1836, when the army pushed them westward. A year later the Chickasaws followed.

Trail of Tears

Having fought removal in the courts, the Cherokees were divided. Some believed that further resistance was hopeless and accepted removal as the only

chance to preserve their civilization. The leaders of this minority agreed in 1835 to exchange their southern home for western land in the Treaty of New Echota. John Ross, with petitions signed by fifteen thousand Cherokees, lobbied Congress against ratification. They lost. But when the time for evacuation came in 1838, most Cherokees refused to move. President Martin Van Buren sent federal troops to round them up. About twenty thousand Cherokees were evicted, held in detention camps, and marched to Indian Territory in present-day Oklahoma under military escort. Nearly one-quarter of them died of disease and exhaustion on what came to be known as the Trail of Tears.

When the forced march to the West ended, the Indians had traded about 100 million acres east of the Mississippi for 32 million acres west of the river plus $68 million. Only a few scattered remnants, among them the Seminoles in Florida and the Cherokees in the southern Appalachian Mountains, remained in the East and South.

The Trail of Tears *by contemporary Cherokee artist Brummet Echohawk. About twenty thousand Cherokees were evicted in 1838–1839, and about one quarter of them died on the forced march to present-day Oklahoma.* Thomas Gilcrease Institute of American History and Art.

The impact of the forced removal on Native American life was disastrous. In the West they encountered an alien environment, and, lacking traditional ties with the new land, few felt at peace with it. The animals and plants they found were unfamiliar. No longer able to live off the land, many Native Americans became dependent on government payments for survival. Removal also brought new internal conflicts. The Cherokees in particular struggled over their tribal government. In 1839 followers of John Ross assassinated the leaders of the protreaty faction. Violence continued sporadically until a new treaty in 1846 imposed a temporary truce. In 1861 the American Civil War renewed the factionalism, forever shattering Cherokee unity.

Conflicts also arose among migrating Native American groups from the South and East and Indians already living in the West, as they were forced to share land and scarce resources. Nearly one hundred thousand newcomers settled west of the Mississippi, and the existing game could not support them all. The Osages and Pawnees fought the newcomers who were invading their land and homes. The story was repeated among the Apaches and Comanches in the Southwest, as the pressure of white settlement led to treaties, cession, and removal and then to new treaties, further cession, and removal.

In the Southeast a small band of Seminoles successfully resisted removal and remained in Florida.

They had resisted Andrew Jackson's 1818 campaign against the Seminoles in Florida.

Second Seminole War

Some Seminole leaders agreed in the 1832 Treaty of Payne's Landing to relocate to the West within three years. Others opposed the treaty, and some probably did not know it existed. A minority under Osceola, a charismatic leader, refused to vacate their homes and fought the protreaty group. When federal troops were sent to impose removal in 1835, Osceola waged a fierce guerrilla war against them.

The Florida Indians were a varied group that included many Creeks and mixed Indian–African Americans (ex-slaves or descendants of runaway slaves). The American army, however, considered them all Seminoles, subject to removal. General Thomas Jesup believed that the runaway-slave population was the key to the war. "This, you may be assured, is a Negro, not an Indian war," he wrote a friend in 1836, "and if it be not speedily put down, the South will feel the effects of it on their slave population before the end of the next season."

Osceola was captured under a white flag of truce and died in an army prison in 1838, but the Seminoles fought on under Chief Coacoochee (Wild Cat) and other leaders. In 1842 the United States abandoned the removal effort. Most of Osceola's followers agreed to move west to Indian Territory in 1858, but many Seminoles remained in the Florida Everglades, proud of having resisted conquest.

Native Americans in the West found themselves pressured to cede land. To facilitate white settlement, Commissioner of Indian Affairs William Medill in 1848 proposed gathering the western Indians onto two great reservations, one northern and one southern, separated by a wide corridor for white settlers to use on their way westward. In 1853 and 1854, however, the federal government took back most of the northern reservation lands in a new round of treaties, and Kansas and Nebraska were opened to white settlement.

Indian Removal in the West

A complex set of attitudes drove whites to remove Native Americans forcibly. Most wanted land and had little or no respect for the Indians' rights or culture. Others were aware of the injustice but believed that Indians inevitably had to give way to white settlement. Some, like John Quincy Adams, believed the only way to preserve Indian civilization was to separate Indians and white settlers physically. Others hoped to "civilize" Indians and assimilate them gradually into American culture. Whatever the source of white attitudes, it resulted in the devastation of Native American cultures.

Free People of Color

Free people of color also struggled for recognition and legal rights. Like Native Americans, they were involuntary participants in American society. Unlike Indians, however, they wished to partake fully in American life. During this period, African-Americans fought for equal rights, formed cohesive communities, and maintained their cultural heritage. Most whites, however, treated African-Americans as outsiders in the land of their birth.

On the surface, the Bill of Rights seemed to protect free African-Americans. The Fifth Amendment specified that "no person shall . . . be deprived of life, liberty, or property, without due process of law." But eighteenth-century political theory had defined the republic as being for whites only (see page 181), and early federal legislation reflected this exclusionist thinking: naturalization, for example, was limited to white aliens in 1790. After the admission of Missouri in 1821, every new state admitted until the Civil War banned blacks from voting. When the Oregon

and New Mexico Territories were organized, public land grants were reserved for whites.

African-Americans in the North were second-class citizens. Newly admitted states barred free blacks or required them to post bonds ranging from $500 to $1,000 to guarantee their good conduct, as did Ohio (1804), Illinois (1819), and Oregon (1857). Only in Massachusetts, New Hampshire, Vermont, and Maine could blacks vote on an equal basis with whites throughout the pre–Civil War period. In 1842 African-Americans gained the right to vote in Rhode Island (where all voters faced restrictive property qualifications), but they had lost it earlier in Pennsylvania and Connecticut. Only Massachusetts permitted blacks to serve on juries. Four midwestern states and California did not allow African-Americans to testify against whites. In Oregon, blacks could not own real estate, make contracts, or sue in court. The laws were meant to render African-Americans powerless.

Throughout the North white social custom excluded or segregated free people of color. Hotels and restaurants barred them, as did most theaters and white churches. Abolitionist Frederick Douglass was repeatedly turned away from public facilities during a speaking tour of the North in 1844.

Exclusion and Segregation of African-Americans

African-Americans encountered discrimination in hiring everywhere. Countinghouses, retail stores, and factories refused to hire black men except as janitors and handymen. New England mills hired only whites. Except for a small professional and skilled elite, free black men in the North found steady work elusive; most toiled as unskilled daily laborers. African-American women found jobs more easily because their domestic skills were in great demand in the cities; they worked as servants, cooks, laundresses, and seamstresses. Unlike their white counterparts, these women did not view paid employment as a temporary phase in their lives; around 40 percent of black women worked for wages during their child-rearing years.

Free people of color faced severe legal and social barriers in the southern slave states. Whites viewed their presence as subversive. Fearing free African-Americans, southern states restricted their presence. In 1806, Virginia required newly freed blacks to leave the state. After the Nat Turner Rebellion in 1831,

Southern Free Blacks

This watercolor of Augustus Jones was painted in 1852 when Jones was forty-nine. A leader in the Philadelphia community of free people of color, Jones was the grandson of Absalom Jones, a founder of the African Free Society and the African Episcopal Church in Philadelphia.   Private collection. Photo courtesy of David A. Schorsch.

the position of free blacks deteriorated throughout the South. Within five years nearly every southern state prohibited the freeing of slaves without legislative or court approval, and by the 1850s Texas, Mississippi, and Georgia had banned manumission altogether.

In essence, the legal status of southern free people of color was somewhere between slave and free. Southern states adopted elaborate "black codes" to curtail the activities and opportunities of African-Americans, who provided most of the South's skilled labor. They were barred from a number of occupations. Virginia and Georgia, for instance, denied work to black riverboat captains and pilots. Some states forbade blacks to assemble without a license. Some prohibited them from learning to read and write. In the late 1830s, the codes were tightened, and free people of color moved northward even though northern states discouraged the migration.

In spite of these obstacles, the free African-American population rose from 108,000 in 1800 to almost 500,000 in 1860. Nearly half lived in the North, some in rural settlements but far more in cities like Philadelphia, New York, and Cincinnati. Baltimore had the largest community, but sizable free black populations formed in New Orleans, Charleston, and Mobile. Although differences in occupation, wealth, education, religion, and social status divided free people of color, the common necessity of self-defense promoted solidarity among them.

The ranks of free people of color were constantly increased by ex-slaves. Some, like Frederick Douglass and Harriet Tubman, were fugitives. Douglass, a Baltimore ship caulker, escaped by bluffing his way to Philadelphia and freedom. Tubman, a slave in Maryland, escaped to Philadelphia in 1849 when it was rumored that she would be sold out of the state. Within the next two years she returned twice to free her two children, her sister, her mother, and her brother and his family. Some slaves received freedom in owners' wills when masters sought, at death, to rid themselves of the stain of owning slaves. Some owners freed elderly slaves after a lifetime of service rather than support them in old age.

Free people of color forged cohesive communities and created autonomous institutions within them. Churches became the center of community life, and pastors became political leaders. Church buildings functioned as town halls, and they housed schools, political forums and conventions, protest meetings, and benevolent and self-help associations as well as prayer meetings.

African-American Communities

Like European immigrants, free people of color sought to assist members of their own community. But they had a greater burden. Although their taxes supported white schools, for instance, they had to raise additional funds to establish African-American schools because their children were excluded from the new public schools. A network of voluntary associations—self-help societies, female benevolent societies, and literary and social clubs—became the hallmark of their communities. Most of these organizations were political as well as social.

In the majority of states where free blacks were excluded from the ballot, they formed protest organizations to fight for equal rights. Among the early efforts to organize for self-defense was the Negro Convention movement. From 1830 to 1835, and irregularly thereafter, free blacks held national conventions with delegates drawn from city and state organizations. Under the leadership of the small

How do historians know about African-American political thought and activity in the early nineteenth century? One important source is the published minutes of black conventions, first held in 1830. Free people of color held at least eleven national conventions and about forty state conventions prior to the Civil War. The first national convention, a special meeting in Philadelphia in September 1830, was presided over by Bishop Richard Allen, founder of the African Methodist Episcopal Church. The delegates agreed to explore a settlement in Canada as a haven for free people of color and fugitive slaves. They also called for pursuing "all legal means for the speedy elevation of ourselves and brethren to the scale and standing of men." Less than a year later, delegates to the "First Annual Meeting of the People of Colour" condemned the persecution of African-Americans, appealed for funds to support their work, called for the establish-ment of a college for poor blacks, and stressed the importance of education. They also were consciously building a movement of annual conventions. The report of this convention, and subsequent convention minutes and addresses, demonstrate the involvement of African-Americans in the reforms of the times and the importance they placed on education and equality of opportunity. At conventions held in the 1850s nationalism took hold among African-Americans.

The convention movement was democratic. Most communities elected their delegates to the national conventions at public meetings or at local and state conventions. Although the minutes reveal a wide range of opinion within black communities, there was agreement about the abolition of slavery, immediate emancipation, and equal rights for free people of color. Minutes of the Proceedings of the National Negro Convention, 1831.

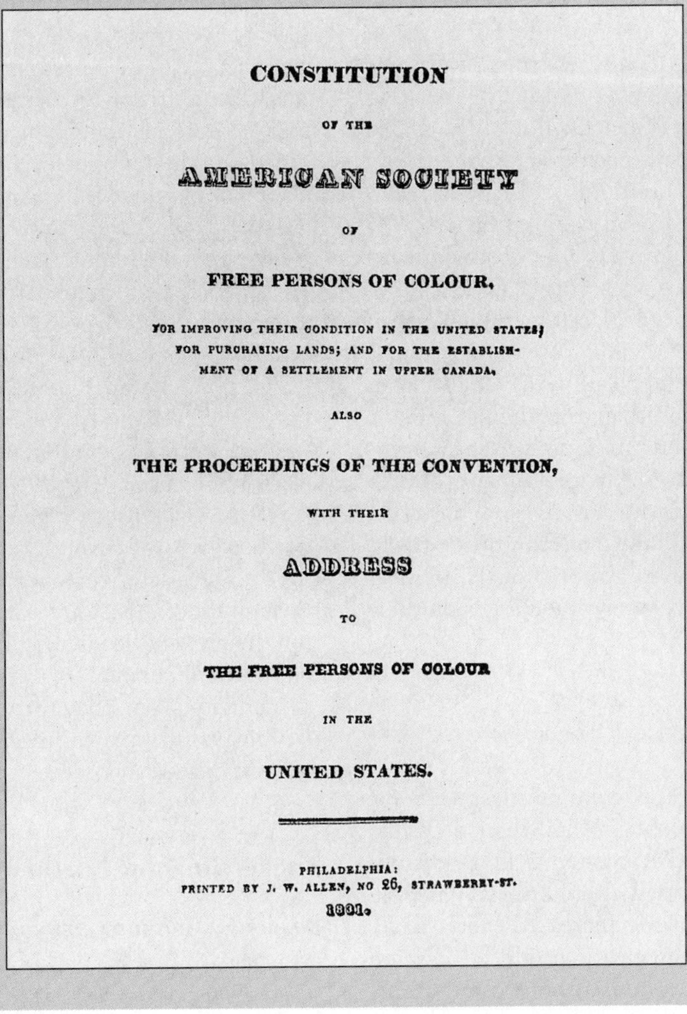

CONSTITUTION

OF THE

AMERICAN SOCIETY

OF

FREE PERSONS OF COLOUR,

FOR IMPROVING THEIR CONDITION IN THE UNITED STATES;
FOR PURCHASING LANDS; AND FOR THE ESTABLISH-
MENT OF A SETTLEMENT IN UPPER CANADA,

ALSO

THE PROCEEDINGS OF THE CONVENTION,

WITH THEIR

ADDRESS

TO

THE FREE PERSONS OF COLOUR

IN THE

UNITED STATES.

PHILADELPHIA:
PRINTED BY J. W. ALLEN, NO 26, STRAWBERRY-ST.
1831.

black middle class, which included the Philadelphia sail manufacturer James Forten and the orator Reverend Henry Highland Garnet, the convention movement served as a forum to attack slavery and agitate for equal rights. Militant new black newspapers joined the struggle. *Freedom's Journal*, the first black weekly, appeared in 1827; in 1837 the *Weekly Advocate* began publication in New York City. Both papers circulated throughout the North, disseminating African-American political analysis and promoting activism.

The mood of free blacks began to shift in the late 1840s and 1850s. Many were frustrated by the failure of the abolitionist movement and angered by the passage of the Fugitive Slave Act of 1850 (see page 383). Some fled to Canada, others became more militant, and a few joined John Brown in his plans for a slave uprising (see page 395). Many more were swept up in a wave of black nationalism that stressed racial solidarity, self-help, and a growing interest in Africa. Before this time, efforts to send African-Americans "back to Africa" had originated with whites seeking to rid the United States of blacks. But in the 1850s blacks held emigrationist conventions of their own under the leadership of abolitionists Henry Bibb and Martin Delany. Delany led an exploration party to the Niger valley as the emissary of a black convention, there signing a treaty with Yoruba rulers allowing him to settle American blacks in their African kingdom.

Black Nationalism

Nothing illustrates the position of free blacks in the United States better than the flight of black Americans to Canada and Africa in search of freedom while millions of European migrants were coming to the United States for liberty and opportunity. With the coming of the Civil War, the status of blacks would move onto the national political agenda, and African-Americans would focus on their position at home.

Conclusion

The American people and communities were far more diverse and turbulent in 1860 than they had been in 1800. The market economy, immigration, and the growth of cities had altered the way people lived and worked. Inequality increased everywhere, and competition and insecurity produced resentment and conflict. Cities housed both ostentatious wealth and abject poverty, and disorder became commonplace. Many Americans felt as if they were strangers to each other.

In the midst of these changes, middle-class families sought to insulate their homes from the competition of the market economy. Many women found fulfillment in the domestic ideal: others found it confining. Middle-class urban women became associated with nurturing roles, first in homes and schools, then in churches and reform societies. Working-class women had more modest goals: escaping poverty and winning respect. Most Americans found some comfort in religion.

Famine and religious and political oppression in Europe propelled millions of people across the Atlantic. They were drawn to the United States by the promise of jobs and tolerance. Although conditions usually were better than in their native lands, most found the going rough. In the process of adapting, immigrants changed the profile of the American people: Americans differed from each other more and shared fewer traditions and experiences. Competition and diversity in turn bred intolerance. Native Americans, free African-Americans, and Hispanics were made to feel like aliens in their own land. Indians, forced off their traditional lands, found themselves uprooted and deprived of much that had given their lives meaning. African-Americans sought acceptance as citizens, but without much success. A small number attempted to return to Africa. Hispanics saw economic and political power shift to English-speaking settlers.

Conflict became increasingly commonplace in the public arena. The manifestations of division in America were many: utopian communities, conflicts over public space, backlash against immigrants, urban riots, black protest, and Indian resistance. Conflict also took the form of reform movements, which came to characterize American life from the 1820s through the 1850s. Through reform and political action, many Americans sought to harness and control the forces of change. Spurred on by religious revival and individualism, they turned to politics as a collective means of restoring harmony and order. In the process, divisions became even sharper.

Suggestions for Further Reading

Rural and Utopian Communities

Leonard J. Arrington and Davis Bitton, *The Mormon Experience: A History of the Latterday Saints* (1979); Priscilla J. Brewer, *Shaker*

Communities, Shaker Lives (1986); David B. Danbom, *Born in the Country: A History of Rural America* (1995); Don H. Doyle, *The Social Order of a Frontier Community: Jacksonville, Illinois, 1825–1870* (1978); John Mack Faragher, *Sugar Creek: Life on the Illinois Prairie* (1986); Laurence Foster, *Religion and Sexuality: Three American Communal Experiments of the Nineteenth Century* (1981); Steven Hahn and Jonathan Prude, eds., *The Countryside in the Age of Capitalist Transformation* (1985); Joan M. Jensen, *Loosening the Bonds: Mid-Atlantic Farm Women, 1750–1850* (1986); Sally McMurry, *Families and Farmhouses in Nineteenth Century America: Vernacular Design and Social Change* (1988); Anthony F. C. Wallace, *Rockdale: The Growth of an American Village in the Early Industrial Revolution* (1978); Kenneth H. Winn, *Exiles in a Land of Liberty: Mormons in America, 1830–1846* (1989).

Urban Communities

Melvin A. Adelman, *A Sporting Time: New York City and the Rise of Modern Athletics, 1820–1870* (1986); Stuart M. Blumin, *The Emergence of the Middle Class: Social Experience in the American City, 1760–1900* (1989); Susan G. Davis, *Parades and Power: Street Theater in Nineteenth-Century Philadelphia* (1986); Timothy J. Gilfoyle, *City of Eros: New York City, Prostitution, and the Commercialization of Sex, 1790–1920* (1992); Karen V. Hansen, *A Very Social Time: Crafting Community in Antebellum New England* (1994); Carl Kaestle, *Pillars of the Republic: Common Schools and American Society, 1780–1860* (1982); Jack Larkin, *The Reshaping of Everyday Life, 1790–1840* (1988); Scott Martin, *Killing Time: Leisure and Culture in Southwestern Pennsylvania, 1800–1850* (1995); Edward Pessen, *Riches, Class and Power Before the Civil War* (1973); Christine Stansell, *City of Women: Sex and Class in New York, 1789–1860* (1986); Richard B. Stott, *Workers in the Metropolis: Class, Ethnicity, and Youth in Antebellum New York City* (1990); Stephan Thernstrom, *Poverty and Progress: Social Mobility in a Nineteenth Century City* (1964); Alexis de Tocqueville, *Democracy in America*, 2 vols. (1835, 1840).

American Families

Virginia K. Bartlett, *Keeping House: Women's Lives in Western Pennsylvania, 1790–1850* (1994); Janet Farrell Brodie, *Contraception and Abortion in Nineteenth-Century America* (1994); Lee Virginia Chambers-Schiller, *Liberty, A Better Husband: Single Women in America: The Generations of 1780–1840* (1984); Clifford Edward Clark, Jr., *The American Family Home, 1800–1960* (1986); Nancy F. Cott, *The Bonds of Womanhood: "Woman's Sphere" in New England, 1780–1835* (1977); Carl N. Degler, *At Odds: Women and the Family in America from the Revolution to the Present* (1980); Linda Gordon, *Woman's Body, Woman's Rights: A Social History of Birth Control in America* (1976); Joan Hoff, *Law, Gender and Injustice: A Legal History of U.S. Women* (1991); Suzanne Lebsock, *The Free Women of Petersburg: Status and Culture in a Southern Town, 1784–1860* (1984); Glenda Riley, *Divorce: An American Tradition* (1991); Mary P. Ryan, *Women in Public: Between Banners and Ballots, 1825–1880* (1990); Mary P. Ryan, *Cradle of the Middle Class: The Family in Oneida County, New York, 1790–1865* (1981); Kathryn Kish Sklar, *Catharine Beecher: A Study in American Domesticity* (1973); Maris A. Vinovskis, *Fertility in Massachusetts from the Revolution to the Civil War* (1981); Robert V. Wells, *Revolutions in Americans' Lives* (1982); Barbara Welter, "The Cult of True Womanhood, 1820–1860," *American Quarterly* 18 (Summer 1966): 151–174.

Immigrants and Hispanics

Gunther Barth, *Bitter Strength: A History of Chinese in the United States, 1850–1870* (1964); Kathleen Neils Conzen, *Immigrant Milwaukee: 1836–1860* (1976); Arnoldo De León, *The Tejano Community, 1836–1900* (1982); Hasia R. Diner, *Erin's Daughters in America: Irish Immigrant Women in the Nineteenth Century* (1983); Jay P. Dolan, *The Immigrant Church: New York's Irish and German Catholics, 1815–1865* (1975); Charlotte Erickson, *Invisible Immigrants* (1972); David A. Gerber, *The Making of an American Pluralism: Buffalo, New York, 1825–60* (1989); Walter D. Kamphoefner, *The Westfalians: From Germany to Missouri* (1987); Walter D. Kamphoefner et al., eds., *News from the Land of Freedom: German Immigrants Write Home* (1991); Dale T. Knobel, *Paddy and the Republic: Ethnicity and Nationality in Antebellum America* (1986); Timothy M. Matovina, *Tejano Religion and Ethnicity: San Antonio, 1821–1860* (1995); Kerby A. Miller, *Emigrants and Exiles: Ireland and the Irish Exodus to North America* (1985); Stanley Nadel, *Little Germany: Ethnicity, Religion, and Class in New York City, 1845–80* (1990); Philip Taylor, *The Distant Magnet: European Emigration to the United States of America* (1971); Mark Wyman, *Immigrants in the Valley: Irish, Germans, and Americans in the Upper Mississippi, 1830–1860* (1984).

Native Americans

Robert F. Berkhofer, Jr., *The White Man's Indian* (1978); James W. Covington, *The Seminoles of Florida* (1993); Grant Foreman, *Indian Removal: The Emigration of the Five Civilized Tribes of Indians*, rev. ed. (1953); Michael D. Green, *The Politics of Indian Removal: Creek Government and Society in Crisis* (1982); William G. McLoughlin, *Cherokee Renascence in the New Republic* (1986); Theda Perdue, *Slavery and the Evolution of Cherokee Society, 1540–1866* (1979); Francis P. Prucha, *American Indian Policy in the Formative Years* (1967); Ronald N. Satz, *American Indian Policy in the Jacksonian Era* (1975); Anthony F. C. Wallace, *The Long, Bitter Trail: Andrew Jackson and the Indians* (1993); Richard White, *The Roots of Dependency: Subsistence, Environment, and Social Change Among the Choctaws, Pawnees, and Navajos* (1983); J. Leitch Wright, Jr., *Creeks and Seminoles: The Destruction and Regeneration of the Muscogulge People* (1986).

Free People of Color

Ira Berlin, *Slaves Without Masters: The Free Negro in the Antebellum South* (1974); Leonard P. Curry, *The Free Black in Urban America, 1800–1850* (1981); James Horton, *Free People of Color: Inside the African American Community* (1993); James O. Horton and Lois E. Horton, *In Hope of Liberty: Culture, Community and Protest Among Northern Free Blacks, 1700–1860* (1996); Luther Porter Jackson, *Free Negro Labor and Property Holding in Virginia, 1830–1860* (1942); David M. Katzman, *Before the Ghetto: Black Detroit in the Nineteenth Century* (1973); Rudolph M. Lapp, *Blacks in Gold Rush California* (1977); Leon Litwack, *North of Slavery: The Negro in the Free States, 1790–1860* (1961); Floyd J. Miller, *The Search for a Black Nationality: Black Colonization and Emigration, 1787–1863* (1975); Gary B. Nash, *Forging Freedom: The Formation of Philadelphia's Black Community, 1720–1840* (1988); Harry Reed, *Platform for Change: The Foundations of the Northern Free Black Community, 1775–1865* (1994); Julie Winch, *Philadelphia's Black Elite: Activism, Accommodation, and the Struggle for Autonomy, 1787–1848* (1988); Arthur Zilversmit, *The First Emancipation: The Abolition of Slavery in the North* (1967).

13

Reform, Politics, and Expansion

1824–1844

"I proceed, Gentlemen, briefly to call your attention to the *present* state of Insane persons confined within this Commonwealth," Dorothea Dix petitioned the Massachusetts legislature in 1843, "in *cages, closets, stalls, pens! Chained, naked, beaten with rods and lashed into obedience*."

Dix described the nether world she had uncovered in her investigations of the treatment of the insane in the previous two years. She reported appalling conditions in Massachusetts towns: men and women in cages, chained to walls, in dark dungeons, brutalized and held in solitary confinement. In a surprise visit to a Newburyport almshouse in the summer of 1842, Dix expressed her surprise at the comfortable conditions for the "one idiotic" and seven insane inhabitants. On the grounds she discovered, however, one man residing in a shed whose door opened to the local "dead room" or morgue; the man's only companions were corpses. Shocked, she heard from an attendant about another insane inmate whom no one spoke of: "a woman in a *cellar*."

She asked to see the woman. The superintendent tried to dissuade her, warning Dix that the *woman "was dangerous to be approached*; that 'she had lately attacked his wife,' *and was often naked*." Dix pressed on: "if you will not go with me," she said, "give me the keys and I will go alone." They unlocked the doors and entered an underground cell. Beneath the staircase was a tiny door. In the shadows Dix saw "a female apparently wasted to a skeleton, partially wrapped in blankets." She was withered, wrote Dix, "not by age, but by suffering." When the inmate saw the visitors, she wailed with despair: "Why am I consigned to hell? dark—dark—I used to pray, I used to read the Bible—I have done no crime in my heart; I had friends, why have all forsaken me!—my God! my God! why hast *those* forsaken me?"

Dix described in the most personal and vivid terms her visits to jails, almshouses, and private homes, and the brutal treatment of the insane. Her petition to the General Court of Massachusetts was so graphic and shocking that the legislature voted to reprint it as a government pamphlet: *Memorial to the Massachustts Legislature* (1843).

The first-person narrative—"*I tell what I have seen*"—gave Dix's message power. She seemed, however, to be an unlikely herald. Reared in Massachusetts, she began teaching in Worcester at age fourteen in 1816. She wrote an elementary science text and published children's devotional verse and poetry. She dressed in a somber manner; she wore dark dresses with starched white collars and pulled her hair back tightly, making her face look more angular and austere. She never married and seemed aloof and remote to other Bostonians.

She became obsessed with exploring the ill treatment of the insane. What drove her was not only a sense of outrage but also a belief in human perfectibility and in the corollary idea that the insane could be treated and cured. Proper humane treatment, Dix argued, could bring them back to the community; they could be healed if they were treated as ill rather than as criminal.

Dix became a one-issue reformer. From teacher and Boston lady, she became a crusader for asylum reform, advocating hospitals for the mentally ill. In the 1840s she traveled more than 40,000 miles, investigating the treatment of the insane and petitioning state legislatures. From 1848 through 1856 she lobbied Congress annually to set aside 5 million acres to fund insane asylums. In 1854 President Franklin Pierce vetoed the bill, which finally had passed Congress. During the Civil War she recruited and supervised nurses for the federal government; afterward she resumed her crusade on behalf of the mentally ill. She died in 1887 in a hospital she had founded.

Dix epitomized so much of early- to mid-nineteenth-century reform. She started with a belief in individual self-improvement that led her to advocate collective responsibility, especially on behalf of those dependent on the kindness of others. She became so personally absorbed in reform that it became her career. She was single-minded, expressing little concern for abolition or women's rights. Unlike Susan B. Anthony, Lucretia Mott, or Elizabeth Cady Stanton, Dix never joined the early feminists in agitating for women's political equality. Nonetheless, her obsession with reform took her into politics. In investigating asylums, in petitioning the Massachusetts General Court in 1843, and in lobbying other state legislatures and Congress, she joined other women in moving from reform to politics, and she helped create a new public role for women.

The reform fervor of the 1820s to the 1850s, which stirred interest in asylum reform, arose in part as a response to the enormous transformation that the United States experienced after the War of 1812. Immigration, internal migration, urbanization, the spread of a market economy, growing inequality, loosening family and community ties, the westward advance of settlement, and territorial expansion all contributed to the remaking of the United States. Many Americans felt they were no longer masters of their own fate. People had difficulty keeping up with the rapid pace of change. And social institutions did not always keep up with change.

Americans had fought the Revolution to make themselves independent, but poverty and wage work made many of them dependent again. Other changes were equally disturbing. Respectable citizens felt threatened by urban mobs and paupers, and the Protestant majority feared the growing Catholic minority. Protestants had waged the Revolution to preserve the rights they claimed as Englishmen, not to protect alien cultures and religions. To many, all these changes seemed to be undermining traditional values.

Religious reformers sought to reimpose order on a society in which economic change and discord had reached a crescendo. Prompted by the evangelical spirit of the Second Great Awakening and convinced of their moral rectitude, they crusaded for individual self-improvement. Many renounced alcohol and gambling. Gradually the personal impulse to reform oneself led to the creation of benevolent and reform societies. Religious ardor drew men and women to reform, in time broadening the political base. Reform soon eclipsed benevolent work and became an instrument for restoring discipline and order in a changing society. "Americans love their country not as it is but as it will be," the English visitor Francis Grund observed in the 1830s. Women became prominent in reform, first to improve life for others, then to secure rights and freedom for themselves.

Members of reform organizations eventually turned to politics, viewing it as an instrument of change; that perception is what led Dorothea Dix to

• *Important Events* •

1790s–1840s	Second Great Awakening spreads religious fervor
1820s	Reformers in New York and Pennsylvania establish model penitentiaries
1824	No presidential candidate wins a majority in the electoral college
1825	House of Representatives elects John Quincy Adams president
1826	American Society for the Promotion of Temperance founded
	Morgan affair is catalyst for Antimasonry movement
1828	Protectionist Tariff stirs nullification
	Andrew Jackson elected president
1830	Webster-Hayne debate explores the nature of the Union
1830s–40s	Democratic-Whig competition gels in second party system
1831	Abolitionist newspaper *The Liberator* begins publication
	First national Antimason convention
1832	Jackson vetoes rechartering of the Second Bank of the United States
	Jackson reelected president
1832–33	South Carolina nullifies the Tariff of 1832, prompting nullification crisis
1836	Republic of Texas established after breaking from Mexico
	Specie Circular ends credit purchase of public lands
	Martin Van Buren elected president
1837	*Caroline* affair sparks Anglo-U.S.-Canadian hostility
	Financial panic ends boom of the 1830s
1838–39	United States and Canada mobilize their militias over Maine–New Brunswick border dispute
1839–43	Hard times spread unemployment and deflation
1840	Whigs win presidency under William Henry Harrison
1841	John Tyler assumes the presidency after Harrison's death
	"Oregon fever" attracts settlers to the Northwest and intensifies expansionism
1843	Dorothea Dix petitions Massachusetts legislative regarding deplorable condition of insane asylums
1844	James K. Polk elected president
1845	Texas admitted to the Union
1848	Woman's Rights Convention at Seneca Falls, New York, calls for women's suffrage
1851	Maine adopts prohibition

political lobbying. The line between social reform and politics was not always clear, however. Temperance, institutional reform, and, most notably, Antimasonry and abolition lured new voters into politics. But opponents of reform were just as concerned with social problems and just as interested in political solutions. What distinguished them from reformers was their skepticism about human perfectibility and their distrust of institutions and the exercise of power, both public and private. To them, government coercion was the greater evil. They sought to reverse, not shape, change.

Two issues in particular served as bridges between reform and politics: the short-lived Antimasonry frenzy and the intense, uncompromising crusade for immediate emancipation. Though Antimasons organized the first third-party movement, abolition eventually overrode all other concerns. No single issue evoked the passion that slavery did. It pitted neighbor against neighbor, settler against settler, section against section. Politicians had long recognized that slavery was a political powder keg, and they had adopted the Missouri Compromise of 1820 to avoid igniting it. Territorial expansion in the 1840s and 1850s, however, made slavery politically explosive. Abolitionism influenced the woman's movement as well.

Opponents of religious reform found a champion in Andrew Jackson and a home in the Democratic Party in the late 1820s. Yet the Jacksonians, too, saw themselves as reformers; they sought to foster individualism and restore restraint in the federal government. They opposed special privileges and the Second Bank of the United States with the same vigor with which reformers opposed sin. President Jackson believed that a strong federal government restricted individual freedom by favoring one group over another. In response, social reformers rallied around the new Whig Party, which became the vehicle of humanitarian reform. Democrats and Whigs constituted a new party system, characterized by strong organizations, intensely loyal followings, and energetic religious and ethnic competition.

Both parties eagerly promoted expansionism during the prosperous 1840s. Democrats saw the agrarian West as an antidote to urbanization and industrialization; Whigs focused on the new commercial opportunities it offered. Expansion from coast to coast seemed to Americans to be the manifest destiny of the United States. Texas, California, and Oregon, unknown to most Americans at the turn of the century, had become familiar places by the 1830s and 1840s, and the United States was on the road to war with Mexico. Then race was added to the brew as the politics of territorial expansion and the antislavery movement boiled over in the 1850s and 1860s.

 ## From Revival to Reform

Religion was probably the prime motivating force behind organized benevolence and reform. Religious revival stimulated by the Second Great Awakening galvanized Protestants, especially women, from the late 1790s to the 1840s. Under its influence, the role of churches and ministers in community life began to change, and Christians in all parts of the country tried to right the wrongs of the world.

Before the Second Great Awakening, churches found themselves diminishing in influence and having to compete with other voluntary societies for members. A new generation of seminary-trained ministers successfully introduced revivals and advocacy of benevolent works—aid to the poor, education of the young, and temperance campaigns—to attract new members, especially women. But while churches grew, their authority continued to erode. They stimulated people emotionally, but less and less they controlled people's behavior.

Revivals—the lifeblood of evangelical Christianity—won converts to a religion of the heart rather than the head. In 1821 New York lawyer Charles G. Finney, the father of modern revivalism, experienced a soul-shaking conversion that he interpreted as "a retainer from the Lord Jesus Christ to plead his cause." Finney abandoned the law to convert souls, taking revival services and three- to four-day camp meetings to towns in western New York. Social reformer Elizabeth Cady Stanton attended a Finney revival and was converted.

Second Great Awakening

Salvation could be achieved, Finney preached, through spontaneous conversion or spiritual rebirth like his own. He evoked emotional responses. Using everyday language, Finney preached that "God has made man a moral free agent." In other words, evil was avoidable: Christians were not doomed by original sin, and anyone could achieve salvation. Finney's brand of revivalism transcended sects, class, and race but had a particularly strong base among Baptists and Methodists. These sects grew the most because their structure maximized democratic participation and they drew their ministers from ordinary folk.

The Second Great Awakening raised people's hopes for the Second Coming of the Christian messiah and establishment of the Kingdom of God on earth. Revivalists resolved to speed the Second Coming by creating a heaven on earth, marshaling the forces of good and light—reform—to combat the forces of evil and darkness. Some revivalists even believed that the United States had a special mission in God's design and therefore a special role in eliminating evil.

Regardless of theology, all revivalists shared a belief in individual self-improvement. Thus the Second Great Awakening bred reform, and evangelical Protestants became missionaries for both religious and secular salvation. Wherever they preached, evangelists generated new religious groups and voluntary reform societies. New sects like the Mormons arose out of this ferment. Evangelical reformers organized associations to address pressing issues: temperance, education, Sabbath observance, dueling, and later antislavery. Collectively these groups constituted a national web of benevolent and moral-reform societies. Finney's doctrine of perfectibility demanded that Christians actively work with other people. By organizing and converting others, and by renouncing their own personal corruptions and dependency, the converted confirmed their status as Christians. They also moved toward reform and ultimately toward public action.

Women's involvement grew remarkably during the Second Great Awakening and invigorated local churches. In Andover, Massachusetts, revivalism gave

Role of Women

rise in 1814 to a men's society dedicated to uplifting morality, banishing swearing, observing the Sabbath, and discouraging drunkenness. The next year local women formed the Female Charitable Society, and a year later youth joined the Juvenile Bible Society. During the 1820s, without any revivals in Andover, the benevolent societies brought in new church members, of whom 70 to 80 percent were women.

Women were the earliest converts to evangelism, and they tended to sustain the Second Great Awakening. Pious middle-class women in Rochester, New York, for instance, responded to Finney's prayer meetings by spreading the word to other women during the day while their husbands were at work. Gradually women brought their families and husbands into church and reform. Although many businessmen recruited their employees to revivalism and benevolent work, women more than men tended to feel personally responsible for counteracting the increasingly secular orientation of the expanding market economy. Many women felt guilty for neglecting their religious duties, and the emotionally charged conversion experience returned them to what they believed was the right path.

Beyond conversion, the great influence of the Second Great Awakening was the spread of women's participation in benevolent societies to ameliorate

Religion and Reform

social ills. The prayer groups and female missionary societies gave rise to organized religious and benevolent activity on an unprecedented scale. In cities women responded both to their inner voices and to the growing inequality, turbulence, and wretched conditions around them. The poverty and vice that accompanied urbanization touched the hearts of women, especially those caught up in the fervor of revival. By 1800 most cities had women's benevolent societies to help needy women and orphans.

Both female and male reformers sometimes opposed traditional political leaders. An exposé of prostitution in New York City illustrates the gulf

between reform-minded men and women and the political establishment. John R. McDowall, a divinity student, published a report in 1830 documenting the prevalence of prostitution in New York City. Philip Hone, a prominent civic leader (see pages 325–326), denounced McDowall's report as "a disgraceful document," and he and other New York businessmen and politicians united to defend the city's good name against "those base slanders." Reform-minded women, however, moved by the plight of "fallen women" and the calls for reform from McDowall and others, organized to fight prostitution. While male reformers made the prostitutes the target of their zeal, the newly organized Female Moral Reform Society focused on the men who victimized young women, publicizing the names of men who entered brothels in New York City.

The New York–based Female Moral Reform Society led the crusade against prostitution. During the 1830s, the organization expanded its activities and geographical scope, calling itself the American Female Moral Reform Society. By 1840 it had 555 affiliated female societies across the nation. They combated prostitution by focusing on men and by assisting poor women whose economic desperation might lead them to turn to prostitution. They also entered the political sphere. In New York State in the 1840s the movement successfully crusaded for criminal sanctions against the men who seduced women into prostitution and against the prostitutes themselves.

As the pace of social change quickened in the 1830s and 1840s, so did religious fervor and reform. In western New York and Ohio, Finney's preaching acted as a catalyst to reform. Western New York experienced such continuous and heated waves of revivalism that it became known as "the burned-over district." The westward migration of New Englanders along the newly opened Erie Canal carried religious ferment to Ohio. There, revivalist institutions—notably Ohio's Lane Seminary and Oberlin College—sent committed graduates out into the world to spread the gospel of reform. The efforts of these early reformers stirred nonevangelical Protestants, Catholics, and Jews, as well as evangelical Christians, and they became involved in new grassroots political movements. In the late 1830s and 1840s they rallied around the Whig Party in hopes of using government as an instrument of reform.

One of the most successful reform efforts was the campaign against alcohol. Drinking was more widespread in the early nineteenth century than it is

Temperance

today. American men gathered in public houses, saloons, and rural inns to gossip, talk politics, play cards, escape work and home, and drink whiskey, rum, and hard cider. Contracts were sealed, celebrations commemorated, and harvests toasted with liquor. Respectable women did not drink in public, but many regularly tippled alcohol-based patent medicines promoted as cure-alls. Why then did temperance become such a vital issue? And why were women especially active in the movement? Like all nineteenth-century reform, temperance had a strong religious foundation.

Evangelicals considered drinking a sin, and forsaking alcohol was part of conversion. The sale of whiskey often involved a Sabbath violation, for workers commonly labored six days a week and spent Sunday at the public house drinking and socializing. Equally important, alcoholism destroyed families. In the early 1840s thousands of ordinary women formed Martha Washington societies to protect families by reforming alcohols, raising children as teetotalers, and spreading temperance. Contemporary imagery was laced with domestic images—abandoned wives, prodigal sons, drunken fathers. Timothy Shay Arthur dramatized all these evils in *Ten Nights in a Barroom* (1853), a classic American melodrama, as did Deacon Robert Peckham in his temperance paintings. Employers complained that drinkers took "St. Monday" as a holiday to recover from Sunday. In the new world of the factory, drinking was unacceptable.

Demon rum became a prime target of reformers. As the temperance movement gained momentum, its goal shifted from moderate use of alcohol to voluntary abstinence and finally to prohibition. The American Society for the Promotion of Temperance, organized in 1826 to sign drinkers to a pledge of abstinence, became a pressure group for state prohibition legislation. By the mid-1830s there were five thousand state and local temperance societies, and more than a million people had taken the pledge. Several hundred thousand children, for instance, enlisted in the Cold Water Army. Thousands of wives and mothers joined the Martha Washingtons in the 1840s.

Temperance Societies

The temperance movement's success was reflected in a sharp decline in alcohol consumption. Per capita consumption fell from five gallons in 1800 to below two gallons in the 1840s. Success bred more victories. Maine prohibited the manufacture and sale of alcohol except for medicinal purposes in 1851, and by 1855 similar laws had been enacted throughout New England, in New York, Pennsylvania, and the Midwest.

Though consumption was declining, opposition to alcohol grew. From the 1820s on, many reformers expressed their prejudices by regarding alcohol as an evil introduced by Catholic immigrants. The Irish and Germans, the *American Protestant Magazine* complained in 1849, "bring the grog shops like the frogs of Egypt upon us." Rum and immigrants defiled the Sabbath; rum and immigrants brought poverty; rum and immigrants supported the feared papacy. Some Catholics took the pledge of abstinence and formed their own organizations, such as the St. Mary's Mutual Benevolent Total Abstinence Society in Boston. Even some nondrinking Catholics tended to oppose state regulation of drinking, however; temperance seemed to them a question of individual choice. They favored self-control, not state coercion.

Another aspect of the temperance movement was opposition to gambling. People gambled in taverns, and reformers believed that both drinking and gambling undermined independence and self-reliance. Of special concern in the nineteenth century was the spread of lotteries.

Lotteries

Lotteries were common in colonial times. The Continental Congress tried to raise $1.5 million from a lottery to wage revolutionary war against England but fell short of that amount. In the early nineteenth century, state and local governments seeking to ease the tax burden used lotteries to raise money for capital improvements. Lotteries, however, became a target of reform, and between 1830 and 1860 every state banned them.

Reformers compared lotteries to slavery and alcohol. Others objected to the abuses inherent in the states' practice of delegating their lottery powers to private sponsors. An 1831 Pennsylvania investigation, for instance, revealed that a state-authorized lottery to raise $27,000 a year for internal improvements, specifically for the Union Canal Company, had generated enormous profits for the lottery company. From annual sales of $5 million, the state received its $27,000, and the sponsors received $800,000. At the urging of Protestant reformers

The evils of drinking and the bliss of temperance were a major theme in popular culture. Deacon Robert Peckham illustrated the contrast in two paintings from the 1840s: The Woes of Liquor (Intemperance) *and* The Happy Abstemious Family (Temperance).   Worcester Historical Museum.

who condemned all forms of gambling, Pennsylvania prohibited lotteries. (When some states revived lotteries in the twentieth century, they learned from the previous century's experiences and chose to run their own contests.)

The age of reform also brought about the construction of asylums and other institutions to house prisoners, the mentally ill, orphans, delinquent children, and the poor. Such institu-

Penitentiaries and Asylums

tions were needed, reformers believed, to shelter victims of society's instability and turbulence and of the lack of discipline in families. In an environment of order, stability, and discipline, inmates would have an opportunity to become self-reliant and responsible.

The penitentiary movement exemplified this outlook. In the 1820s New York and Pennsylvania developed competing models for reforming criminals. Both rejected incarceration simply to punish criminals or remove them from society, believing instead that disciplined regimens would rehabilitate them. New York's Auburn (1819–1823) and Sing-Sing (1825) prisons isolated prisoners in individual cells but brought them together in common workshops. Pennsylvania's Pittsburgh (1826) and Philadelphia (1829) prisons isolated prisoners completely, forcing them to eat, sleep, and work in their individual cells and allowing them contact only with guards and visitors. Both systems sought to separate criminals from evil societal and individual influences and to expose them to a regimen of order and discipline. It was widely believed that criminals came from unstable families whose lack of discipline and restraint led to vice and drink. Idleness was believed to be both a symptom and a cause of individual corruption and crime; thus the clock governed a prisoner's day, and idleness was banished.

Similar approaches were employed in insane asylums, hospitals, and orphanages. By exposing the inhumane treatment of the mentally ill, Dorothea Dix built a national movement. Formerly the prescribed treatment had been to remove disturbed individuals from their families and society and isolate them among strangers; many were incarcerated with criminals. The new asylums removed them from society but attempted to impose discipline and order in a humane fashion. In response to Dix's crusade and reform societies, twenty-eight of the thirty-three states had public institutions for the mentally ill by 1860.

 Antimasonry

More intense than the asylum movement but of shorter duration was the crusade against Freemasonry, a secret middle- and upper-class fraternity that had come to the United States from England in the eighteenth century. Sons of the Enlightenment such as Benjamin Franklin and George Washington were attracted to Masonry, with its emphasis on individual belief in a deity (as opposed to organized religion) and on brotherhood (as opposed to one church). In the early nineteenth century Freemasonry spread, attracting men prominent in commerce and civic affairs. For ambitious young men, the Masons offered access to and fellowship with the leading lights of the community.

Opponents of Masonry charged that the order's secrecy was antidemocratic and antirepublican, as were its elite membership and its use of uniforms. Publications such as the *Anti Masonic Almanac* attacked Masonic initiation rites. Evangelicals labeled the order satanic. Antimasons argued that Masonry threatened the family because it excluded women and encouraged men to neglect their families for alcohol and ribald entertainments at Masonic lodges.

The Antimasonry movement arose overnight in the burned-over district of western New York in 1826 and virtually disappeared in the 1830s. Foreshadowing abolitionism, it quickly became a political movement. Antimasonry created the first third-party movement and drew new white voters into politics at a time when male suffrage was being extended. As the temperance movement sought to liberate individuals from drink, Antimasons sought to liberate society from the grip of what they considered a powerful and antirepublican secret fraternity. Just as asylums would restore individual discipline and harmony, the Antimasons believed, the abolition of Masonry would reestablish communal moral discipline and harmony. The political arena quickly absorbed Antimasonry, and its short life illustrates the close association of politics and reform between the 1820s and the 1840s.

The catalyst for Antimasonry as an organized movement was the Morgan affair. In 1826 William Morgan, a disillusioned Mason, published an exposé,

Morgan Affair

The Illustration of Masonry, By One of the Fraternity Who Has Devoted Thirty Years to the Subject, to which his printer David Miller added a scathing attack on the order. Just prior to the book's appearance, a group of Masons abducted Morgan in Canandaigua, New York. It was widely believed that they murdered him, though his body was never found.

Events seemed to confirm the Antimasonry crusade's depiction of Masonry as a secret conspiracy. Many officeholders in western New York, especially prosecutors, were Masons, and they appeared to obstruct the investigation of Morgan's abduction. The public pressed for justice, and the series of notorious trials that ensued from 1827 through 1831 led many to suspect a conspiracy. The cover-up became as much of an issue as Masonry itself, and the movement spread from the burned-over district to other states.

As a moral crusade, Antimasonry spilled over into the political arena almost immediately. The issue itself was political, because of the perceived obstruction of justice. Furthermore, Antimasonry attracted the lower and middle classes, pitting them against higher-status Masons and exploiting the general public's distrust and envy of local political leaders.

Unwittingly, the Masons stoked the fires of Antimasonry. By their silence they seemed to condone the murder of Morgan, and by their construction of monumental lodges in Boston and elsewhere they called attention to their affluence and prominence. The conflict aroused a high level of public interest in politics. Wherever religious fervor flared and wherever families were entering the market economy for the first time, Antimasonry flourished.

As Antimasonry won a popular following, it introduced the convention system in place of caucuses for choosing political candidates. Invoking public morality and republican principles, the Antimasons held conventions in 1827 to select candidates to oppose Masons. The next year the conventions supported the National Republican candidate, John Quincy Adams, and opposed Andrew Jackson because he was a Mason. The Antimasons held the first national political convention in Baltimore in 1831, and a year later they nominated William Wirt as their presidential candidate. Thus the Antimasons became a rallying point for those opposed to President Andrew Jackson. Their electoral strength lay in New England and New York. In Vermont the Antimasons became the dominant party for a brief time in 1833; in Massachusetts Antimasons replaced the Democrats as the second major party. Antimasonry found little support, however, in the South.

**Convention
System**

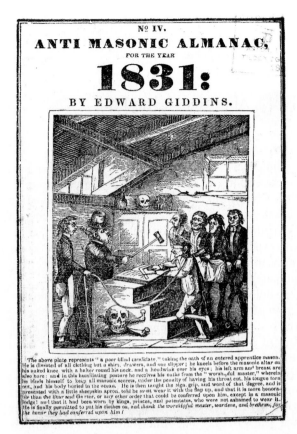

Antimasonic publications, such as this 1831 almanac, made much of the allegedly sinister initiation rites that bound a new member "to keep all Masonic secrets, under the penalty of having his throat cut, his tongue torn out, and his body buried in the ocean." Print collection, Miriam and Ira D. Wallach Division of Art, Prints, and Photographs, New York Public Library.

By the mid-1830s, Antimasonry had lost momentum as a moral and political movement. A single-issue party, the Antimasons declined along with Freemasonry. Yet the movement left its mark on the politics of the era. As a moral crusade focused on public officeholders, it inspired broad participation in the political process. The Antimasons also changed party organization by pioneering the convention system and stimulating grassroots involvement.

Antimasonry also had much in common with abolitionism. Indeed, as Antimasonry waned, the antislavery movement gathered momentum. Abolitionist William Lloyd Garrison at first ignored the frenzy over the Morgan affair but in 1832 he joined the ranks of Antimasons. Echoing his stand on emancipation, Garrison wrote: "I go for the immediate, unconditional and total abolition of Freemasonry." In his eyes, both slavery and Masonry undermined republican values.

 ## Abolitionism and the Women's Movement

The issue of slavery eventually became so compelling that it consumed all other reforms. Passions became so heated that they threatened the nation itself. Those who advocated immediate emancipation saw slavery as, above all, a moral issue—evidence of the sinfulness of the American nation. When territorial expansion forced the issue of slavery to center stage in the 1850s, the abolitionist forces were well prepared (see Chapter 14).

Before the 1830s few whites advocated the abolition of slavery. Quakers had shown the way, freeing their slaves and preaching that bondage was a sin. But in the North, where most states had begun to abolish slavery by 1800, whites took little interest in the issue. Antislavery sentiment appeared strongest in the Upper South, though northern involvement grew with the expansion of benevolent societies after the War of 1812. The American Colonization Society, founded in 1816, advocated gradual, voluntary emancipation and resettlement of former slaves in Africa, and it attracted evangelicals, Quakers, some blacks (briefly), and some slaveholders. The gradualist antislavery movement remained strong, but in the 1830s the immediatists—those who demanded immediate, complete, and uncompensated emancipation—surpassed the gradualists as the dominant strand of abolitionism.

At first only African-Americans demanded an immediate end to slavery. By 1830 there were more than fifty black abolitionist societies. They assisted fugitive slaves, lobbied for emancipation, exposed the evils of slavery, and reminded the nation that its mission as defined in the Declaration of Independence remained unfulfilled. A free black press helped to spread the word. Black abolitionists Frederick Douglass, Sojourner Truth, and Harriet Tubman joined forces in the 1840s with white reformers in the American Anti-Slavery Society. Their militant and unrelenting campaign also won European support. "Brethren, arise, arise, arise!" Henry Highland Garnet commanded the 1843 National Colored

Black Abolitionists

Convention. "Strike for your lives and liberties. Now is the day and hour. Let every slave in the land do this and the days of slavery are numbered. Rather die freemen than live to be slaves."

In the 1830s a small number of white reformers, driven by moral urgency, crusaded for immediate emancipation. The most prominent and uncompromising immediatist, though far from the most representative, was William Lloyd Garrison, who demanded "immediate and complete emancipation." Garrison, a talented journalist, broke with moderate abolitionists in 1831. That year he published the first issue of *The Liberator*, which was to be his major weapon against slavery for thirty-five years. As he declared in the first issue, "I am in earnest—I will not equivocate—I will not excuse—I will not retreat a single inch—*and I will be heard.*"

William Lloyd Garrison

Garrison's staunch refusal to work with anyone who tolerated the delay of emancipation isolated him from other opponents of slavery. He even forswore political action on the grounds that it was government that permitted slavery. (Garrison burned a copy of the Constitution on July 4, 1854, proclaiming, "So perish all compromises with tyranny.") Through sheer rhetorical power, Garrison helped to make antislavery a national issue. His brand of immediatism consisted of a refusal to tolerate delay in ending slavery; he had no specific plan for abolishing it. In essence, what Garrison called for was *conversion* of those who held slaves or cooperated with institutions that supported slavery; they should cast off their sins, repent, and do battle against evil.

It is difficult to differentiate between those who became immediatists and those who did not. But immediatists like Garrison, Elizabeth Chandler, Amos Phelps, and Theodore Weld had much in common. They were young evangelicals active in benevolent societies in the 1820s; many became ordained ministers or flirted with the ministry as a career; and they had personal contact with free blacks and were sympathetic to African-American rights. They were convinced that slaveholding was a sin. Their immediatism made them more concerned about sin in the United States than about converting "heathens across the seas," and their concern in turn made them more political: to abolish sin, they sought to change institutions at home. Finally, they shared

Immediatists

How do historians know how the abolitionists, especially women and African-Americans, built their movement? Abolitionists lived open lives. They used newspapers, pamphlets, speeches, and sermons to expose the evils of slavery, to mount a crusade for emancipation, and to build a network of like-minded people. Much of their correspondence and most of their speeches were printed in abolitionist newspapers, such as The Liberator, *published by William Lloyd Garrison.*

Here, twentieth-century African-American artist Jacob Lawrence depicts abolitionist Frederick Douglass lecturing in eastern Massachusetts, describing his life as a slave and telling of the cruelty of the system. In 1841 Douglass became a supporter of Garrison and a contributor to The Liberator, *which appeared from 1831 to 1866. The newspaper printed passionate attacks on slavery, reported on meetings of antislavery societies, and published letters, especially from women and African-American abolitionists. Under the banners "No Union with Slaveholders" and "The United States Constitution is a 'convenant with death, and an agreement with hell,'" The Liberator circulated to abolitionists advocating immediate emancipation. The subscription lists that have survived indicate that a majority of its subscribers probably were African-Americans.* Hampton University Museum, Hampton, Virginia.

great moral intensity. They were unwilling to compromise their beliefs, and their zeal made them activists. Their main organizational vehicle was the American Anti-Slavery Society, founded in 1833.

Most benevolent workers and reformers kept their distance from the immediatists. Many regarded the intensity of the immediatist approach as unchristian. They shared with immediatists the view that slavery was a sin but believed in gradual emancipation. They feared that if they moved too fast, attacked sinners too harshly, or interfered too aggressively in time-honored customs and beliefs, they would destroy the harmony and order they sought to bring about through benevolent and reform work.

Immediatists' greatest recruitment successes resulted from their defense of their own constitutional and natural rights, not the rights of slaves. Wherever they went, immediatists found their civil rights, especially free speech at risk. Hostile crowds threatened abolitionist speakers and presses. Mobs violently defended what they considered to be American traditions. At Utica, New York, merchants and professionals broke up the state Anti-Slavery Convention in 1835. Abolitionist conventions provoked hostility by welcoming blacks and women. Fear and hatred moved proslavery proponents to take to the streets. In 1837 a mob in Alton, Illinois, murdered abolitionist editor Elijah P. Lovejoy, who had been driven out of slaveholding Missouri. Before killing Lovejoy, rioters sacked his office with the cooperation of local authorities. Public outrage at Lovejoy's murder broadened the base of antislavery support in the North.

Opposition to Abolitionists

In the South, mobs blocked distribution of antislavery pamphlets. Using high-speed printing presses, the American Anti-Slavery Society increased its distribution of antislavery propaganda tenfold in the 1830s by sending out 1.1 million pieces. But southern mobs frequently seized and destroyed the mailings, and South Carolina intercepted and burned abolitionist literature that entered the state. President Andrew Jackson even proposed a law prohibiting the mailing of antislavery tracts.

The opposition saw danger in abolitionism. At a rally in Boston's Faneuil Hall in 1835 former Federalist Harrison Gray Otis portrayed abolitionists as subversives. He attacked Garrison's American Anti-Slavery Society as a "revolutionary society" that not only recruited all men to its "holy crusade" but also asked women to "turn their sewing parties into abolition clubs." If it prevailed, Otis charged, school primers would teach "that A stands for abolition." The abolitionists, he predicted, would soon turn to politics, causing unforeseeable calamity. "What will become of the nation?" Otis asked. "What will become of the union?" Others believed that the immediatists' opposition to sending black people back to Africa undermined the best solution. Keeping blacks in America, they believed, eventually would lead to slave rebellions and racial amalgamation.

Another confrontation focused on the House of Representatives. Abolitionists, exercising their constitutional right to petition Congress, campaigned to abolish slavery and the slave trade in the District of Columbia. (Because the district was under federal rule, states' rights arguments against interfering with slavery did not apply there.) The House responded in 1836 by adopting the "gag rule," which automatically tabled abolitionist petitions, effectively preventing debate on them. Immediatists flooded Congress with nearly seven hundred thousand petitions. In a dramatic defense of the right of petition, former president John Quincy Adams, a Massachusetts representative, took to the floor repeatedly to defy the gag rule and in 1844 succeeded in getting it repealed.

Gag Rule

Frustration with the federal government also fed northern support for antislavery. Generally speaking, politicians and government officials sought to avoid the question of slavery. The Missouri Compromise of 1820 had been an effort to quarantine the issue by adopting a formula—prohibition of slavery north of 36°30', Missouri's southern boundary—that would make debate on the slave or free status of new states unnecessary (see map, page 368). Censorship of the mails and the gag rule also represented attempts to keep the issue out of the political arena. Yet the more intensely national leaders, especially Democrats, worked to avoid the matter, the more they hardened the resolve of the antislavery forces.

The unlawful and violent tactics used by opponents of abolition unified the movement by forcing the various factions to work together for mutual defense. Antislavery was not at the outset a unified movement. It was factionalized, and its adherents fought each other as doggedly and as often as they fought the defenders of slavery. They were divided over Garrison's emphasis on "moral suasion" versus the more practical political approach of James G. Birney, the Liberty Party's candidate for president in 1844 (see page 371). They were split over support for other reforms, especially the rights of women. And they disagreed about the place of free people of color in American society.

Many women joined local female antislavery societies through churches as part of the network of reform societies. Some opposed extending benevolent work into the political arena, and this issue led to the disbanding of the seven-year-old Boston Female Anti-Slavery Society in 1840. Especially in abo-

Women Abolitionists

lition issues and in women's rights, however, women became more politically involved and took an equal role with men. Lydia Maria Child, Maria Chapman, and Lucretia Mott all joined the American Anti-Slavery Society's executive committee; Child edited its official organ, the *National Anti-Slavery Standard*, from 1841 to 1843, and Chapman coedited it from 1844 until 1848. Garrison's *moral* suasion attracted many women because it gave them a platform from which to oppose slavery. Where *political* power was stressed, women were often excluded because they could not vote.

Opposition to women's prominent public roles in reform movements led some women to reexamine their position in society. In the 1830s Angelina and Sarah Grimké challenged slavery and women's right to speak out. Born into a slaveholding family in Charleston, South Carolina, both sisters experienced conversion and independently became Quakers. In 1834 both aspired to be more politically involved in reform, especially in abolitionism. They found in Garrison's immediatism a home. Yet they were soon attacked for speaking before mixed groups of men and women. Some New England Congregationalists and even abolitionists joined in the criticism; as one pastoral letter put it, women should obey, not lecture, men. This reaction turned the Grimkés' attention from slavery to the women's condition. The two attacked the concept of "subordination to man," insisting that men and women had the "same rights and same duties." Sarah Grimké's *Letters on the Condition of Women and the Equality of the Sexes* (1838) and her sister's *Letters to Catharine E. Beecher*, published the same year, were the opening volleys in the long war over the legal and social inequality of women.

Women involved with abolitionism crossed the path from pious and moral opposition against slavery to political engagement. Like the Grimké sisters, other women abolitionists encountered restrictions because they were women. Elizabeth Cady Stanton and Lucretia Mott had traveled to London in 1840 for the World Anti-Slavery Convention and had to sit in a balcony, denied participation, because they were women. But women active in abolitionism had developed the experience to do something about their limited rights: they could organize on their own behalf.

Women's Rights

In July 1848 three hundred women and men reformers gathered at the Woman's Rights Conven-

Women played an activist role in reform, especially in abolitionism. A rare daguerreotype from August 1850 shows women and men, including Frederick Douglass, on the podium at an abolitionist rally in Cazenovia, New York. Collection of J. Paul Getty Museum, Los Angeles, California.

tion at Seneca Falls, New York, to demand political, social, and economic equality for women. Led by Stanton, Mott, and Lucy Stone, they protested women's legal disabilities—inability to vote, limited property rights—and their social restrictions—exclusion from advanced schooling and from most occupations. Their Declaration of Sentiments, modeled after the Declaration of Independence, was an indictment of the injustices suffered by women, and it launched the women's rights movement. "All men and women are created equal," the declaration proclaimed. If women had the vote, participants argued, they could protect themselves and realize their full potential as moral and spiritual leaders.

Advocates of women's rights were slow to garner support, especially from men, who held most of the political and legal power. In the 1840s the question of women's rights split the antislavery movement; the majority declared themselves opposed. Some

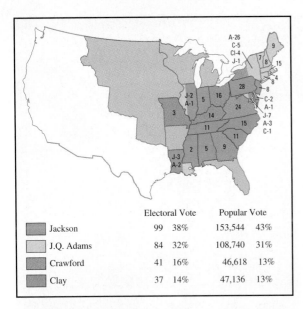

	Electoral Vote		Popular Vote	
Jackson	99	38%	153,544	43%
J.Q. Adams	84	32%	108,740	31%
Crawford	41	16%	46,618	13%
Clay	37	14%	47,136	13%

Presidential Election, 1824 Andrew Jackson *led in both electoral and popular votes but failed to win a majority of electoral college votes. The House elected John Quincy Adams president.*

men joined the ranks, notably Garrison and Frederick Douglass, but most men actively opposed. Not everyone at Seneca Falls signed the resolution on women's suffrage. Of the one hundred who did, only two would live to see the passage of the Nineteenth Amendment to the Constitution seventy-two years later.

Jacksonianism and Party Politics

In the 1820s the distinction between reform and politics began to erode as reform pushed its way into politics. No less than reformers, politicians sought to control the direction of change in the expanding nation. After a brief flirtation with single-party politics after the War of 1812, the United States entered a period of intense political competition. As the age of Virginia presidents came to an end in 1825, the Republican Party was split by hard times, sectional disputes, abolitionism, and reform. The 1824 presidential election ignited a political barn fire that reformers, abolitionists, and expansionists would continuously stoke. By the 1830s, politics had become the great nineteenth-century American pastime.

The election of 1824, in which John Quincy Adams and Andrew Jackson faced off for the first time, heralded a new, more open political system.

End of the Caucus System

From 1800 through 1820 the system in which a congressional caucus chose Jefferson, Madison, and Monroe as the Republican nominees had worked well. Such a system limited voters' involvement in choosing candidates but at first was not an anomaly because in 1800 only five of the sixteen states selected presidential electors by popular vote. (In most cases, state legislatures selected the electors who voted for president.) By 1816, however, ten out of nineteen states chose electors by popular vote, and by 1824 eighteen out of twenty-four did so. With the voters choosing electors, Congress could no longer sustain its control over the nomination system.

The Republican caucus in 1824 chose William H. Crawford, secretary of the treasury, as its presidential candidate. But other Republicans, emboldened by the chance to appeal directly to voters, put themselves forward as sectional candidates. Secretary of State John Quincy Adams drew support from New England, and westerners backed Speaker of the House Henry Clay of Kentucky. Secretary of War John C. Calhoun looked to the South for support and hoped to win Pennsylvania as well. The Tennessee legislature nominated Andrew Jackson, a popular military hero whose political views were unknown. Jackson had the most widespread support, but Crawford led in the party caucus. By boycotting the caucus and by attacking it as undemocratic, the four other candidates and their supporters ended the role of Congress in nominating presidential candidates.

In the four-way presidential election of 1824, Andrew Jackson led in both electoral and popular votes, but no candidate received a majority in the electoral college (see map).

Election of 1824

Adams finished second, and Crawford and Clay trailed far behind. (Calhoun had dropped out of the race before the election.) As required by the Twelfth Amendment to the Constitution, the House of Representatives, voting by state delegation, one vote to a state, selected the next president from among the leaders in electoral votes. Clay, who had received the fewest votes, was dropped. Crawford, a stroke victim, never received serious consideration. The influential Clay—Speaker of the House and leader of the Ohio valley states—

backed Adams, who received the votes of thirteen of the twenty-four state delegations. Clay then became secretary of state in the Adams administration, the traditional steppingstone to the presidency.

Angry Jacksonians denounced the outcome of the election as a "corrupt bargain" that had stolen the office from the front runner. Congressional intrigue had thwarted the will of the people, Jacksonians believed, and Jackson's bitterness reinforced his opposition to elitism and fueled his later emphasis on the people's will. The Republican Party split. The Adams wing emerged as the National Republicans, and the Jacksonians became the Democratic-Republicans (shortened to Democrats). The Jacksonians immediately began planning for 1828.

After taking the oath of office, Adams (the sixth president) proposed a strong nationalist policy incorporating Henry Clay's program of protective tariffs, a national bank, and internal improvements (see page 245). Adams believed the federal government should take an activist role not only in the economy but also in education, science, and the arts. He accordingly proposed the establishment of a national university in Washington, D.C. Brilliant as a diplomat and secretary of state, Adams was an inept president. The political skills he had demonstrated in winning the office eluded him as chief executive. He underestimated the lingering effects of the Panic of 1819 and the resulting bitter opposition to a national bank and protective tariffs. Meanwhile, supporters of Andrew Jackson sabotaged Adams's administration at every opportunity.

The 1828 campaign pitted Adams against Jackson in an intensely personal conflict. Principles gave way to mudslinging by both sides. Jackson's supporters renewed their claim that Adams had stolen the 1824 election. In his diary Adams declared Jackson "incompetent both by his ignorance and by the fury of his passions." The two camps traded charges of adultery and procuring prostitutes. When Rachel Jackson died a month after the election, the president-elect attributed his wife's death to the abuse heaped on him in the campaign. He never forgave her "murderers."

Election of 1828

Adams won the states he had won in 1824, but this time the opposition was unified, and Jackson swamped him (see map). Jackson polled 56 percent of the popular vote and won in the electoral college by 178 to 83 votes. He and his supporters believed

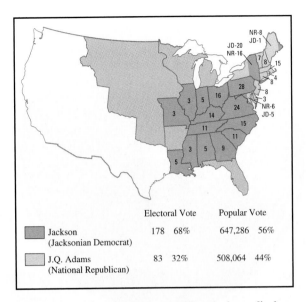

	Electoral Vote		Popular Vote	
Jackson (Jacksonian Democrat)	178	68%	647,286	56%
J.Q. Adams (National Republican)	83	32%	508,064	44%

Presidential Election, 1828 Andrew Jackson *avenged his 1824 loss of the presidency, sweeping the election in 1828.*

that the will of the people had finally been served. Many voters displayed their enthusiasm for Jackson with badges, medals, and other campaign paraphernalia, which were mass-produced for the first time.

Through a lavishly financed coalition of state parties, political leaders, and newspaper editors, a popular movement had elected the president, and an era had ended. The Democratic Party became the first well-organized national political party in the United States. Tightly organized parties would become the hallmark of nineteenth-century American politics.

Andrew Jackson

Nicknamed "Old Hickory" after the toughest of American hardwoods, Andrew Jackson was a rough-and-tumble, ambitious man. Born in South Carolina in 1767, he rose from humble beginnings to become a wealthy Tennessee planter and slaveholder. Jackson was the first American president from the West and the first born in a log cabin; he was a self-made man at ease among both frontiersmen and southern planters. Though vindictive and given to violent displays of temper, he could charm away the suspicions of those opposed to him. A natural leader, Jackson inspired immense loyalty. He had an instinct

President Andrew Jackson is portrayed here on a snuff box, an example of the campaign paraphernalia that were widely sold to partisan Jackson supporters.   Collection of David J. and Janice L. Frent.

for politics and picked both issues and supporters shrewdly.

Few Americans have been as celebrated as Jackson. Having fought in the Revolution as a boy, he bore scars from a redcoat attack. In the Tennessee militia General Jackson led the campaign to remove Creeks from the Alabama and Georgia frontier (see page 243). He burst onto the national scene as the great hero of the War of 1812, and in 1818 enhanced his glory in an expedition against Seminoles in Spanish Florida. Jackson also served as a congressman and senator from Tennessee, and as the first territorial governor of Florida (1821), before running for president in 1824.

Jackson and his Democratic supporters offered a distinct alternative to the strong federal government advocated by John Quincy Adams. The Democrats represented a wide range of views but shared a fundamental commitment to the Jeffersonian concept of an agrarian society. They harkened back to the belief that a strong central government is the enemy of individual liberty, a tyranny to be feared. The 1824 "corrupt bargain" had strengthened their suspicion of Washington

Democrats

politics. Jackson himself, symbol of the backwoodsman and the farmer, affirmed the familiar old values that predated the new party politics and the new market system.

Jacksonians feared the concentration of economic and political power. They believed that government intervention in the economy benefited special-interest groups and created corporate monopolies; they rejected an activist economic program as favoring the rich. They sought to restore the independence of the individual—the artisan and the yeoman farmer—by ending federal support of banks and corporations and restricting the use of paper currency, which they distrusted. Their definition of the proper role of government tended to be negative, and Jackson's political power was largely expressed in negative acts. He exercised the veto more than all previous presidents combined.

Jackson and his supporters also opposed reform as a movement. Reformers eager to turn their programs into legislation were calling for a more activist and interventionist government. But Democrats tended to oppose programs like educational reform and the establishment of public education. They believed, for instance, that public schools restricted individual liberty by interfering with parental responsibility and undermined freedom of religion by replacing church schools. Nor did Jackson share reformers' humanitarian concerns. He showed little sympathy for Native Americans, initiating the removal of the Cherokees along the Trail of Tears (see page 337).

Jackson and the Jacksonians considered themselves reformers in a different way. By restraining government and emphasizing individualism, they sought to restore old republican virtues, such as prudence and economy. No less zealous than reformers, Jackson sought to encourage self-discipline and self-reliance and to restore the harmony and unity that he saw disrupted by economic and social change. In doing so, Jackson looked to Jefferson and the generation of the founders as models of traditional values. "My political creed," Jackson wrote to Tennessee congressman James K. Polk in 1826, "was formed in the old republican school."

Jacksonians as Reformers

Like Jefferson, Jackson strengthened the executive branch of government even as he weakened the federal role. Given his popularity and the strength of his personality, this concentration of power in the presidency was perhaps inevitable, but in combining the roles of party leader and chief of state, he increased the centralization of power in the White House. Jackson relied on political friends, his "Kitchen Cabinet," for advice; he rarely consulted his official cabinet. Enamored of power, Jackson never hesitated to confront his opponents with all the weapons at his disposal. He commanded enormous loyalty, and he rewarded his followers handsomely. Invoking the principle that rotating officeholders would make government more responsive to the public will, Jackson used the spoils system to appoint loyal Democrats to office. He removed fewer than one-quarter of the federal officeholders he inherited, but he used patronage to strengthen party organization and loyalty.

Jackson stressed rejection of elitism and special favors, rotation of officeholders, and belief in popular government. Time and again he declared that sovereignty resided with the people, not with the states or the courts. In this respect Jackson was a reformer; he returned government to majority rule. Yet it is hard to distinguish between Jackson's belief in himself as the instrument of the people and simple egotism and demagogic arrogance. After all, his opponents, too, claimed to represent the people.

Animosity grew year by year among President Jackson's supporters and opponents. Massachusetts senator Daniel Webster feared the men around the president; Henry Clay most feared Jackson himself. Rotation in office, they contended, corrupted government. Opponents mocked Jackson as "King Andrew I," charging him with abusing his presidential powers by ignoring the Supreme Court's ruling on Cherokee rights (see page 336), by his use of the spoils system, and by his dependence on the Kitchen Cabinet. Critics rejected his claim of restoring republican virtue. They charged him with recklessly and impulsively destroying the economy.

Jackson injected new vigor into the philosophy of limited government. In 1830 he vetoed the Maysville Road bill—which would have funded construction of a 60-mile turnpike from Maysville to Lexington, Kentucky. A federally subsidized internal improvement confined to one state was unconstitutional, he charged; such projects were properly a state responsibility. The veto undermined Henry Clay's nationalist program and personally embarrassed Clay because the project was in his home district. Such federal-state issues were to loom even larger in the nullification crisis.

Federalism at Issue: The Nullification and Bank Controversies

Soon Jackson had to face the question of the proper division of sovereignty between state and central government more directly. The slave South feared federal power, no state more so than South Carolina, where the planter class was strongest and slavery most concentrated. Southerners, hard hit by the Panic of 1819, from which they never fully recovered, also resented protectionist tariffs.

To protect their interests, South Carolinian political leaders articulated the doctrine of *nullification*, according to which a state had the right to overrule, or nullify, federal legislation that conflicted with its own. Nullification was based on the idea expressed in the Virginia and Kentucky Resolutions of 1798 (see page 215)—that the states, representing the people, have a right to judge the constitutionality of federal actions. Jackson's vice president, John C. Calhoun of South Carolina, argued in his unsigned *Exposition and Protest* that, in any disagreement between the federal government and a state, a special state convention—like the conventions called to ratify the Constitution—should decide the conflict by either nullifying or affirming the federal law. Only the power of nullification, Calhoun asserted, could protect the minority against the tyranny of the majority.

In public, Calhoun let others take the lead in advancing nullification. As Jackson's running mate in 1828, he had avoided publicly endorsing nullification and thus embarrassing the Democratic ticket; he hoped to win Jackson's support as the Democratic presidential heir-apparent. Thus Calhoun presided silently over the Senate and its packed galleries when Senator Daniel Webster of Massachusetts and Senator Robert Y. Hayne of South Carolina debated nullification in early 1830. The debate explored North-South frictions and the nature of the Union. With Vice President Calhoun nodding in agreement, Hayne charged that the North was threatening to bring disunity, as it had done before at the Hartford Convention (see page 245). Hayne accused reformers in "the spirit of false philanthropy" of wanting to destroy the South.

Webster-Hayne Debate

For two days Webster eloquently defended the New England states and the republic, as he kept nullification on the defense. Though debating Hayne, he really aimed his remarks at Calhoun, depicting the nation as a compact of people, not merely of states. At the climax of the debate, Webster invoked two powerful images. One was the outcome of nullification: "states dissevered, discordant, belligerent; on a land rent with civil feuds, or drenched . . . in fraternal blood!" The other was a patriotic vision of a great nation flourishing under the motto "Liberty *and* Union, now and forever, one and inseparable."

Though sympathetic to states' rights and distrustful of the federal government, Jackson rejected the idea of state sovereignty. He strongly believed that sovereignty rested with the people. Deeply loyal to the Union, he shared Webster's dread of nullification. Soon after the Webster-Hayne debate, the president made his position clear at a Jefferson Day dinner with the toast "Our Federal Union, it *must* and *shall be* preserved." Vice President Calhoun, when his turn came, toasted: "The Federal Union—next to our liberty the most dear." Torn between devotion to the Union and loyalty to his state, Calhoun had revealed his preference for states' rights. Politically and personally, Calhoun and Jackson grew apart, and it soon became apparent that Jackson favored Secretary of State Martin Van Buren, not Calhoun, as his successor.

South Carolina invoked the theory of nullification against the Tariff of 1832, which reduced some duties but retained high taxes on imported iron,

Nullification Crisis

cottons, and woolens. Though a majority of southern representatives supported the new tariff, South Carolinians refused to go along. In their eyes, the constitutional right to control their own destiny had been sacrificed to the demands of northern industrialists. More than the tariff, they feared the consequences of accepting such an act, because it could set a precedent for congressional legislation on slavery. In November 1832 a South Carolina state convention nullified the tariff, making it unlawful for federal officials to collect duties in the state. Recruiters immediately began to organize a volunteer army to ensure nonenforcement of the tariff.

Old Hickory responded with toughness. Privately he threatened to invade South Carolina and hang Vice President Calhoun; publicly he sought to avoid the use of force. In December Jackson issued a presidential proclamation nullifying nullification. He moved troops to federal forts in South Carolina and prepared United States marshals to collect the required duties. At Jackson's request, Congress passed the Force Act, which gave the president renewed authority to call up troops but also offered a way to avoid using force by collecting duties before foreign ships reached Charleston Harbor in South Carolina. At the same time, Jackson extended an olive branch by recommending tariff reductions.

Calhoun, disturbed by South Carolina's drift toward separatism, resigned as vice president and soon won election to represent South Carolina in the United States Senate. There he worked with Henry Clay to draw up the compromise Tariff of 1833. Quickly passed by Congress and signed by the president, the new tariff lengthened the list of duty-free items and reduced duties over nine years. Satisfied, South Carolina's convention repealed its nullification law. In a final salvo, it also nullified Jackson's Force Act. Jackson ignored the gesture.

Nullification offered a genuine debate on the nature and principles of the republic. Each side believed it was upholding the Constitution. Both sides felt they were opposing special privilege and subversion of republican values. South Carolina was fighting the tyranny of the federal government and manufacturers who sought tariff protection. Jackson was fighting the tyranny of South Carolina, whose refusal to bow to federal authority threatened to split the republic. Neither side won a clear victory, though both claimed to have done so. It took another crisis, over a central bank, to define the powers of the federal government more clearly.

At stake was survival of the Second Bank of the United States, whose twenty-year charter was scheduled to expire in 1836. Like its predecessor, the bank

Second Bank of the United States

served as a depository for federal funds and was an important source of credit for business people. Its bank notes circulated as currency throughout the country; they could be readily exchanged for gold, and the federal government accepted them as payment in all transactions. Through its twenty-five branch offices, the Second Bank acted as a clearing-house for state banks, keeping them honest by refusing to accept in transactions state bank notes from any state bank that had insufficient gold in reserve.

Western farmers, urban workers, and many other Americans were suspicious of bank notes, regarding only specie—gold and silver coins—as real money. Coins—hard money—had intrinsic value (the value of the gold or silver contained in the coin).

Bank notes, by contrast, represented only a promise to pay specie on demand; the paper itself had no value. But as long as people had faith in the issuing institutions, bank notes circulated freely. The growing, market-oriented society needed more currency than the nation's supply of gold and silver could accommodate. Manufacturers, wholesalers, and retailers needed capital for investment and cash for transactions and thus were supporters of the Second Bank.

Enemies of the Second Bank made the redemption of bank notes for specie an issue. Most state banks resented the central bank's police role: by presenting a state bank's notes for redemption all at once, the Second Bank could easily ruin a state bank. Moreover, with less money in reserve, state banks found themselves unable to compete on an equal footing with the Second Bank. Many state governments also regarded the national bank, with its headquarters in Philadelphia, as unresponsive to local needs. Westerners and urban workers remembered with bitterness the bank's conservative credit policies during the Panic of 1819 (see page 248). Although the Second Bank served some of the functions of a central bank, it was a private, profit-making institution, and its policies reflected the interest of its owners. Its president, Nicholas Biddle, controlled the bank completely. An eastern patrician, Biddle symbolized all that westerners found wrong with the bank.

Rechartering was a volatile issue in the 1832 presidential campaign. The bank's charter was valid until 1836, but Henry Clay, the National Republican presidential candidate, persuaded Biddle to ask Congress to approve an early rechartering. This strategy was designed to marshal public pressure to force Jackson to sign the rechartering bill or to override his veto of it. The plan backfired, however. The president vetoed the bill, and the Senate failed to override. Jackson's veto message was an emotional attack on the undemocratic nature of the bank. "It is to be regretted," he wrote, "that the rich and powerful too often bend the acts of government to their selfish purposes."

The bank thus became the prime issue in the presidential campaign of 1832. Jackson led the way by denouncing special privilege and economic power. Operating in a system in which every state but South Carolina now chose electors by popular vote, the Jacksonians used their party organization to mobilize voters by advertising the presidential election as the focal point of the political system. When the Antimasons adopted a party platform, the first in the nation's history, the Democrats and the National Republicans quickly followed suit. Jackson and Martin Van Buren, Jackson's first secretary of state and then American minister to Great Britain, were nominated at the Democratic convention; Clay and John Sergeant, at the National Republican convention. South Carolina had its own candidate, John Floyd. Jackson was reelected easily in a Democratic party triumph.

After his sweeping victory and second inauguration, Jackson moved in 1833 to dismantle the Second Bank of the United States and to kill it forever. He deposited federal funds in state-chartered banks (critics called them his "pet banks"). Without federal money, the Second Bank shriveled. When its federal charter expired in 1836, it became just another Pennsylvania-chartered private bank. Five years later it closed its doors.

Jackson's Second Term

In conjunction with this coup de grâce to the Bank of the United States, Congress passed the Deposit Act of 1836 with Jackson's support. The act authorized the secretary of the treasury to designate one bank in each state and territory to provide the services formerly performed by the Bank of the United States. The act provided that the federal surplus in excess of $5 million be distributed to the states as interest-free loans beginning in 1837. These loans were never repaid—a fitting Jacksonian restraint on the federal purse.

Jackson was worried about more than just restraining the government. The surplus had derived from wholesale speculation in public lands: speculators bought public land on credit, used the land as collateral to borrow more money to buy additional acreage, and repeated the cycle. Between 1834 and 1836 federal receipts from land sales rose from $5 million to $25 million. The state banks providing the loans issued bank notes. Jackson, an opponent of paper money, feared that the speculative craze threatened the stability of state banks and undermined the interests of settlers, who could not compete with speculators in bidding for the best land.

Specie Circular

In keeping with his hard-money instincts and opposition to paper currency, the president ordered Treasury Secretary Levi Woodbury to issue the Specie Circular. It provided that after August 1836 only specie or Virginia scrip would be accepted as payment for federal lands. The circular sought to end "the monopoly of the public lands in the hands of speculators and capitalists" and the "ruinous extension" of bank notes and credit. By ending credit sales, it significantly reduced purchases of public land and the federal budget surplus. As a result the government suspended its loan payments to the states soon after they began.

The policy was a disaster. Although federal land sales were sharply reduced, speculation continued as available land for sale became scarce. The ensuing increased demand for specie squeezed banks, and many suspended the redemption of bank notes for specie. Credit contracted further as banks issued fewer notes and gave less credit. Equally damaging was the way Jackson attacked the problem. He instinctively pursued a tight money policy and remained indifferent to its impact. More important, the Specie Circular was similar to a bill defeated in the Senate just three months earlier. Jackson's opponents thus saw King Andrew at work. In the waning days of Jackson's administration, Congress voted to repeal the circular, but the president pocket-vetoed the bill. Finally in mid-1838, a joint resolution of Congress overturned the circular. Restrictions on land sales ended, but the speculative fervor was over. The federal government did not revive loans to states.

From George Washington to John Quincy Adams, presidents had vetoed nine bills; Jackson vetoed twelve. Previous presidents believed that vetoes were justified only on constitutional grounds, but Jackson, as in the veto of the bill rechartering the Second Bank of the United States, considered policy disagreement legitimate grounds as well. He made the veto an effective weapon for controlling Congress, since representatives and senators had to consider the possibility of a presidential veto in their deliberations on any bill. In effect, Jackson made the executive for the first time a rival branch of government, equal in power to Congress.

Use of the Veto

The Whig Challenge and the Second Party System

Historians used to call the 1830s and 1840s the Age of Jackson, and the personalities of leading political figures dominated their accounts of the era. Most historians now view these years as an age of reform and popularly based political parties. Only when the passionate concerns of reformers and abolitionists spilled over into politics did party differences become paramount and party loyalties solidify. For the first time in American history, grassroots political groups, organized from the bottom up, set the tone of political life.

Opponents of the Democrats, including remnants of the National Republican Party, found shelter under a common umbrella, the Whig Party, in the 1830s. Resentful of Jackson's domination of Congress, the Whigs borrowed the name of the British party that had opposed the tyranny of Hanoverian monarchs in the eighteenth century. From 1834 through the 1840s, the Whigs and the Democrats competed on a nearly equal footing. They fought at the city, county, state, and national levels and achieved a stability previously unknown in American politics. The political competition of this period—known as the second party system—was more intense and well organized than that of the first party system of Republicans and Federalists (see page 235).

The two parties were responsive to their supporters, reflecting important changes in the electoral process. Only a handful of states significantly restricted adult white male suffrage by the 1830s. Some even allowed immigrants who had taken out first citizenship papers to vote. Moreover, hotly contested elections stimulated public interest in politics. The net effect of these changes was a sharp increase in the number of votes cast in presidential elections. Between 1824 and 1828 that number increased threefold, from 360,000 to over 1.1 million. In 1840, 2.4 million men cast votes. The proportion of eligible voters who cast ballots also increased, from about 27 percent in 1824 to more than 80 percent in 1840.

Increasingly the parties differed in their approaches. Whigs favored economic expansion through an activist government, Democrats through limited central government. Whigs supported corporate charters, a national bank, and paper currency; Democrats were opposed. Whigs also favored more humanitarian reforms than did Democrats, including public schools, abolition of capital punishment, prison and asylum reform, and temperance.

Whigs

Whigs were more optimistic than Democrats, generally speaking, and more enterprising. They did not object to helping a specific group if doing so would promote the general welfare. The chartering of corporations, they argued, expanded economic opportunity for everyone by providing work for laborers and increasing demand for food from farmers. Democrats, distrustful of concentrated economic power and of moral and economic coercion, held fast to the Jeffersonian principle of limited government.

Neither economics nor class was a key determinant of party affiliation. Instead, religion and ethnicity most influenced party membership. The Whigs' support for energetic government and humanitarian and moral reform won the favor of evangelical Protestants in the North, especially those involved in religious revival. Methodists and Baptists were overwhelmingly Whigs, as were the small number of free black voters. Democrats, by contrast, tended to be foreign-born Catholics and nonevangelical Protestants, both of whom preferred to keep religious and secular affairs separate.

The Whig Party was the vehicle of revivalist Protestantism. In many locales the membership rolls of reform societies overlapped those of the party.

Whigs and Reformers

Indeed, Whigs practiced a kind of political revivalism. Their rallies resembled camp meetings; in their speeches they employed evangelical rhetoric; their programs embodied the perfectionist beliefs of reformers. This potent blend of religion and politics—"intimately united" in America, according to Tocqueville—greatly intensified political loyalties.

In their appeal to evangelicals, Whigs alienated members of other faiths. In the evangelicals' ideal Christian state there was no room for Catholics, Mormons, Unitarians, Universalists, or religious freethinkers. Those groups opposed Sabbath laws and temperance legislation in particular and state interference in moral and religious questions in general. As a result, more than 95 percent of Irish Catholics, 90 percent of Reformed Dutch, and 80 percent of German Catholics voted Democratic.

Vice President Martin Van Buren, handpicked by Jackson, headed the Democratic ticket in the presidential election of 1836. Van Buren was a

Election of 1836

shrewd politician who had built a political machine—the Albany Regency—in New York and had left that state's government to join Jackson's cabinet in 1829. Having helped found the Democratic Party, Van Buren was one member of a new generation of men who made their careers in party politics.

The Whigs in 1836 had not yet coalesced into a national party. They entered three sectional candidates: Daniel Webster of New England, Hugh White of the South, and William Henry Harrison of the West. By splintering the vote, they hoped to throw the election into the House of Representatives. Van Buren, however, comfortably captured the electoral college even though he had only a 25,000-vote edge out of a total of 1.5 million votes cast. No vice-presidential candidate received a majority of electoral votes, and for the only time in American history the Senate decided a vice-presidential race, selecting Democratic candidate Richard M. Johnson of Kentucky.

Van Buren took office just weeks before the American credit system collapsed. In response to the impact of the Specie Circular, New York banks

President Martin Van Buren and Hard Times

stopped redeeming paper currency with gold in mid-1837. Soon all banks suspended payments in hard coin. Thus began a cycle that led to curtailment of bank loans and reduced business confidence. The credit contraction only made things worse; after a brief recovery, hard times persisted from 1839 until 1843.

Ill advisedly, Van Buren followed Jackson's hard-money policies. He cut federal spending, which caused prices to drop further, and he opposed a national bank, which would have expanded credit. Even worse, the president proposed a new regional treasury system for government deposits. The proposed treasury branches would accept and pay out only gold and silver coin; they would not accept paper currency or checks drawn on state banks. Van Buren's independent treasury bill became law in 1840. By creating a constant demand for hard coin, it deprived banks of gold and further accelerated the deflation of prices.

Whigs and Democrats faced off at the state level over these issues. Whigs favored new banks, more paper currency, and more corporations. As the party of hard money, Democrats favored eliminating paper currency altogether. Increasingly the Democrats became distrustful even of state banks, and by the mid-1840s a majority favored eliminating all bank corporations. The Whigs, riding the wave of economic distress into office, made banking and corporate charters more readily available.

Using techniques that look familiar to twentieth-century politicians, General William Henry Harrison in 1840 ran a "log cabin and hard cider" campaign against Jackson's heir, President Martin Van Buren. The campaign handkerchief shows Harrison welcoming two of his comrades to his log cabin, with a barrel of cider outside. The Log Cabin, *a newspaper edited by Horace Greeley, was the voice of the Harrison campaign, and it reached eighty thousand partisans.* Handkerchief: New-York Historical Society. Newspaper: Division of Political History, Smithsonian Institution, Washington, D.C.

With the nation again in the grip of hard times, the Whigs prepared confidently for the election of 1840. Their strategy was simple: hold on to loyal supporters and win over independents distressed by the economic downturn. The Democrats renominated President Van Buren at a somber convention. The Whigs rallied behind a military hero, General William Henry Harrison, conqueror of the Shawnees at Tippecanoe Creek in 1811 (see page 243).

William Henry Harrison Wins Election of 1840

Harrison, or "Old Tippecanoe," and his running mate, John Tyler of Virginia, ran a "log cabin and hard cider" campaign—a people's crusade—against the aristocratic president in "the Palace." Harrison presented himself as an ordinary farmer, though he was descended from a Virginia plantation family. The Whigs wooed supporters and independents alike with huge rallies, parades, songs, posters, campaign mementos, and a campaign newspaper, *The*

Log Cabin. Harrison took a position above the issues, earning himself the nickname "General Mum," but party hacks bluntly blamed the hard times on the Democrats. In a huge turnout, 80 percent of eligible voters cast ballots. Harrison won the popular vote by a narrow margin but swept the electoral college by 234 to 60.

Immediately after taking office in 1841, President Harrison convened a special session of Congress to pass the Whig economic program: repeal of the independent treasury system, a new national bank, and a higher protective tariff. But the sixty-eight-year-old Harrison caught pneumonia and died within a month of his inauguration. His successor, John Tyler, was a former Democrat who had left the party to protest Jackson's nullification proclamation.

In office, Tyler turned out to be more of a Democrat than a Whig. As critical of the Whigs' economic nationalism as he had been of Jackson's use of executive power, Tyler consistently opposed the Whig congressional program. He repeatedly vetoed

Henry Clay's protective tariffs, internal improvements, and bills aimed at reviving the Bank of the United States. The only important measures that became law during his term were repeal of the independent treasury system and passage of a higher tariff. Two days after Tyler's second veto of a bank bill, the entire cabinet except Secretary of State Daniel Webster resigned; Webster, busy negotiating a new treaty with Great Britain, left shortly thereafter. Tyler thus became a president without a party, and the Whigs lost the presidency without losing an election. Whigs referred to Tyler as "His Accidency."

Hard times in the late 1830s and early 1840s deflected attention from a renewal of Anglo-American tensions that had multiple sources: northern commercial rivalry with Britain, the default of state governments and corporations on British-held debts during the Panic of 1837, rebellion in Canada, boundary disputes, southern alarm over West Indian emancipation, and American expansionism.

Anglo-American Tensions

One of the most troublesome disputes arose from the *Caroline* affair. A United States citizen, Amos Durfee, had been killed when Canadian militia set afire the privately owned steamer *Caroline* in the Niagara River. (The *Caroline* had supported an unsuccessful uprising against Great Britain in 1837.) Britain refused to apologize, and American newspapers called for revenge. Fearing that popular support for the Canadian rebels would ignite war, President Van Buren posted troops at the border to discourage border raids. Tensions subsided in late 1840 when Alexander McLeod, a Canadian deputy sheriff, was arrested in New York for the murder of Durfee. McLeod eventually was acquitted. If he had been found guilty and executed, Lord Palmerston, the British foreign minister, might have sought war.

At almost the same time a border dispute disrupted Anglo-American relations. The Treaty of Ghent, ending the War of 1812, had not resolved the boundary dispute between Maine and New Brunswick. Great Britain had accepted an 1831 arbitration decision fixing a new boundary, but the United States Senate rejected it. Thus when Canadian lumbermen cut trees in the disputed region in the winter of 1838–1839, the citizens of Maine attempted to expel them. The lumbermen captured the Maine land agent and posse, both sides mobilized their militias, and Congress authorized a call-up of fifty thousand men. Ultimately, no blood was spilled. General Winfield Scott, who had patrolled the border during the *Caroline* affair, was dispatched to Aroostook, Maine, where he arranged a truce. The two sides compromised on their conflicting claims in the Webster-Ashburton Treaty (1842).

These border disputes with Great Britain prefigured the conflicts that were to erupt in the 1840s over the expansion of the United States. With Tyler's succession to power in 1841 and a Democratic victory in the presidential election of 1844, federal activism in the domestic sphere ended for the rest of the decade, and attention turned to the debate over territorial expansion. Reform, however, was not dead. Its passions would resurface in the 1850s in the debate over slavery in the territories.

Manifest Destiny and Expansionism

The belief that American expansion westward and southward was inevitable, just, and divinely ordained was first labeled *manifest destiny* by John L. O'Sullivan, editor of the *United States Magazine and Domestic Review*. The annexation of Texas, O'Sullivan wrote in 1845, was "the fulfillment of our manifest destiny to overspread the continent allotted by Providence for the free development of our yearly multiplying millions." In the 1840s expansionism reached a new fervor.

Since colonial days Americans had hungered for more land. Acquisition of the Louisiana Territory (1803) and Florida (1819) had set the process in motion (see map, page 368). As the proportion of Americans living west of the Appalachians grew from one-quarter to one-half between 1830 and 1860, both national parties joined the popular clamor for expansion. Agrarian Democrats saw the West as an antidote to urbanization and industrialization. Enterprising Whigs looked to the new commercial opportunities the West offered. Southerners envisioned the extension of slavery and more slave states.

Fierce national pride spurred the quest for land. Subdued during hard times, it reasserted itself in the boom times of the 1840s. Americans were convinced that theirs was the greatest country on earth, with a special role to play in the world. As reform sought to perfect American society, so too expansionism promised to improve foreign lands. The acquisition of new territory, many Americans reasoned, would extend the benefits of America's republican system of government to the less fortunate and the inferior.

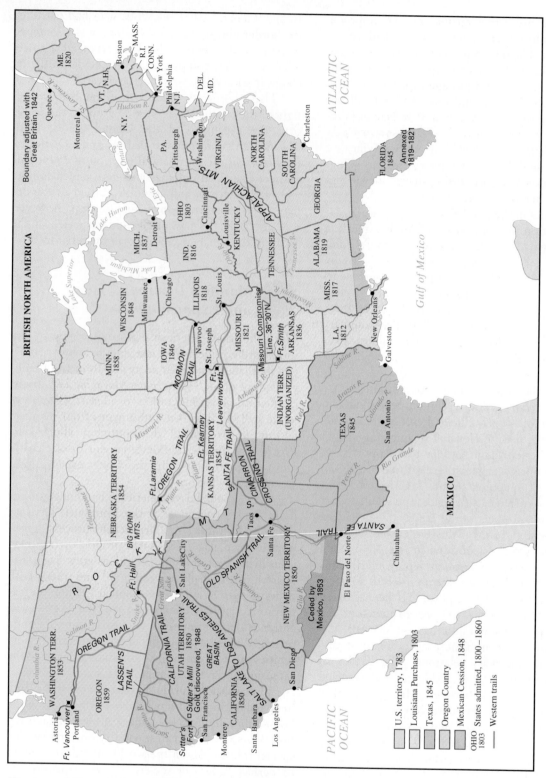

Westward Expansion, 1800–1860 *Through exploration, purchase, war, and treaty, the United States became a continental nation, stretching from the Atlantic to the Pacific.*

In part, racism drove the belief in manifest destiny. Native Americans were perceived as savages best confined to small areas in the West. Hispanics were seen as inferior peoples, best controlled or conquered. Thus the same racism that justified slavery in the South and discrimination in the North supported expansion in the West. For some, expansion also offered a solution to the American race problem: free people of color, unwanted in the North and the South, could find refuge in distant territories. But racism also could limit expansion, for Americans did not look on Mexicans—whether Indian, European, African, or mestizo—with favor.

The desire to secure the nation from perceived external threats also fed expansionist fever. The internal enemies of the 1830s—a monster bank, corporations, paper currency, alcohol, Sabbath violation—seemed pale in comparison to the opportunities Americans saw along their borders in the 1840s. Expansion, some believed, was necessary to preserve American independence.

The establishment of an independent Texas and its annexation by the United States were major events. With the acquisition of Louisiana and California, they were critical steps in the United States's domination of the continent. Among the long-standing objectives of expansionists was the Republic of Texas, which in addition to Texas included parts of present-day Oklahoma, Kansas, Colorado, Wyoming, and New Mexico (see map, page 368). After winning its independence from Spain in 1821, Mexico encouraged the development of its rich but remote northern province, offering large tracts of land virtually free to settlers called *empresarios*. The settlers in turn agreed to become Mexican citizens, adopt the Catholic religion, and bring two hundred or more families into the area. Americans Moses and Stephen Austin, who had helped to formulate the policy, responded eagerly.

Republic of Texas

By 1835, thirty-five thousand Americans, including many slaveholders, lived in Texas. The new settlers' power grew. The dictatorship of General Antonio López de Santa Anna tightened control over the region. In response, Anglos and Tejanos rebelled. At the Alamo mission in San Antonio in 1836, fewer than two hundred Texans made a heroic but unsuccessful stand against three thousand Mexicans under General Santa Anna. "Remember the Alamo" became the Texans' rallying cry. By the end of the year the Texans had won independence, delighting most Americans. Some saw the victory as a triumph of Protestants over Catholic Mexico; others cheered that proslavery Texans had defeated antislavery Mexicans.

Texas established the independent Lone Star Republic but soon sought annexation to the United States. Sam Houston, president of the Texas republic, opened negotiations with Washington, but the issue quickly became politically explosive. Southerners favored annexing proslavery Texas; abolitionists, many northerners, and most Whigs opposed annexation. In recognition of the political dangers, President Jackson reneged on his promise to recognize Texas, and President Van Buren ignored annexation.

Rebuffed by the United States, Texans talked about closer ties with the British and extending their republic all the way to the Pacific coast. With British colonies already entrenched in Canada, the prospect of a rival republic to the south caused some Americans to fear encirclement. If Texas reached the ocean and became an English ally, would not American independence be threatened?

President Tyler, committed to expansion and eager to build political support in the South, pushed for annexation. Tyler was hoping to build a political base in the South to gain the 1844 Democratic nomination. Southerners also pressed for annexation; they lobbied former president Jackson, who responded that the United States must have Texas, "peacefully if we can, forcibly if we must." But the opposition was too strong, and the Senate rejected annexation in 1844. A letter from Secretary of State Calhoun to the British minister, justifying annexation as a step in protecting slavery, so outraged senators that the treaty was defeated 16 to 35.

Like southerners who sought expansion to the Southwest, northerners looked to the Northwest. "Oregon fever" struck thousands in 1841. Lured by the glowing reports of missionaries who seemed as enthusiastic about the Northwest's riches and beauty as about conversion of Indians, migrants in wagon trains took to the Oregon Trail. "Ho for California," Helen Carpenter wrote in her diary, "We are off to the Promised Land." Others' enthusiasm was tempered by apprehension. Lavinia Porter had to face the sober realization that her husband did not have "the training to make a living on the plains of the West or the crossing of the continent in an ox team a successful

Oregon Fever

Texans believed that their war for independence paralleled the Revolutionary War. The lady of liberty on this banner, carried by Texans in 1836, brings to mind similar images that stirred patriots during the American Revolution.   Archives Division, Texas State Library.

venture." The 2,000-mile journey took six months or more, but within a few years five thousand settlers had arrived in the fertile Willamette valley south of the Columbia River.

Britain and the United States had jointly occupied the disputed Oregon Territory since the Anglo-American Convention of 1818 (see pages 246–247). Beginning with the administration of President John Quincy Adams, the United States had tried to fix the boundary at the 49th parallel, but Britain was determined to maintain access to Puget Sound and the Columbia River. Time only increased the American appetite. In 1843 a Cincinnati convention of expansionists demanded the entire Oregon Country for the United States, up to its northernmost border at latitude 54°40'. Soon "Fifty-four Forty or Fight" became the rallying cry of American expansionists.

Expansion into Oregon and rejection of the annexation of Texas, both favored by antislavery forces, worried southern leaders. Anxious about their diminishing ability to control the debate over slavery, they persuaded the 1844 Democratic convention to adopt a rule requiring the presidential nominee to receive two-thirds of the convention votes. In effect, the southern states acquired a veto, and they blocked Van Buren as the nominee; most southerners objected to his antislavery stance and opposition to Texas annexation. Instead, the party chose "Young Hickory," House Speaker James K. Polk, a hard-money Jacksonian, avid expansionist, and slaveholding cotton planter from Tennessee. The Whig leader Henry Clay, who opposed annexation, won his party's nomination unanimously. The Democratic platform called for occupation of the entire Oregon Territory and annexation of Texas. The Whigs, though favoring expansion, argued that

James K. Polk Wins Election of 1844

the Democrats' belligerent nationalism would lead the nation into war with Great Britain or Mexico or both. Clay favored expansion through negotiation.

With a well-organized campaign, Polk and the Democrats won the election by 170 electoral votes to 105. (They won the popular vote by just 38,000 out of 2.7 million votes cast.) Polk won New York's 36 electoral votes by just 6,000 popular votes. Abolitionist James G. Birney, the Liberty Party candidate, had drawn almost 16,000 votes away from Clay, handing New York and the election to Polk. Abolitionist forces thus unwittingly brought about the choice of a slaveholder as president, but they viewed Polk as more moderate than Clay on slavery and the lesser of two evils.

Interpreting Polk's victory as a mandate for annexation, President Tyler proposed in his final days in office that Texas be admitted by joint resolution of Congress. (The usual method of annexation, by treaty negotiation, required a two-thirds vote in the Senate—which expansionists clearly did not have. Joint resolution required only a simple majority in each house.) Congressmen debated the extension of slavery into the territory, and the resolution passed in the House by 120 to 98 and in the Senate by 27 to 25. Three days before leaving office, Tyler signed the measure. Mexico immediately broke relations with the United States; war was inevitable. In October, the citizens of Texas ratified annexation, and Texas joined the Union in December 1845.

An unknown artist depicted, in rich detail, the election campaign of 1844. A team of Polk supporters offers a campaign handbill to the seated voter. Passions were so high and party organization was so extensive that door-to-door politicking became the norm.   Courtesy, Nathan Liverant & Son.

Conclusion

Religion, reform, and expansionism colored politics in the 1830s and 1840s. As the Second Great Awakening spread through villages and towns, the converts, especially women, changed American religion and organized to reform a rapidly changing society. Religion imbued men and women with zeal to right the wrongs of American society and the world. Reformers pursued perfectionism and republican virtue by doing battle with the evils of the growing cities, seeking to ban alcohol and gambling, and expanding education. Two issues elicited particular intensity: Antimasonry flared only briefly; abolitionism smoldered over time. The passions that both aroused were so potent, and success was so elusive, that Antimasons and abolitionists transformed their moral crusades into political movements. But reformers had no monopoly on claims of republican virtue; their opponents laid claim to a heritage of revolutionary values that held individual liberty particularly dear.

Once reform forced itself into politics, it generated a broader-based interest in politics that would remake the political system. The ensuing conflicts, and the highly organized parties that arose during the era, stimulated even greater interest in campaigns and political issues. The Democrats, who rallied around Andrew Jackson, and Jackson's opponents, who found shelter under the Whig tent, competed almost equally for the loyalty of voters. Both parties built strong organizations that faced off in national and local elections. And both parties favored economic expansion. Their world-views, however, were fundamentally different. Whigs were more optimistic and favored greater centralized government initiative. Democrats harbored a deep-seated belief in limited government.

Territorial expansion would provide the kindling for the firestorm that would overtake the United States in 1861. Manifest destiny, the admission of Texas, and debates over territorial expansion awaited a spark. Ultimately, one issue would rivet the attention of nearly all Americans and ignite the fire that would threaten to sever the Union: slavery.

Suggestions for Further Reading

Religion, Revivalism, and Reform

Robert H. Abzug, *Cosmos Crumbling: American Reform and the Religious Imagination* (1994); Michael Barkun, *Crucible of the Millennium: The Burned-over District of New York in the 1840s* (1986); Terry Bilhartz, *Urban Religion and the Second Great Awakening: Church and Society in Early National Baltimore* (1986); Clifford S. Griffen, *Their Brother's Keepers: Moral Stewardship in the United States, 1800–1865* (1960); Keith J. Hardman, *Charles Grandison Finney, 1792–1875: Revivalist and Reformer* (1987); Nathan O. Hatch, *The Democratization of American Christianity* (1989); Curtis D. Johnson, *Islands of Holiness: Rural Religion in Upstate New York, 1790–1860* (1989); Paul E. Johnson, *A Shopkeeper's Millennium: Society and Revivals in Rochester, New York, 1815–1837* (1978); Steven Mintz, *Moralists and Modernizers: America's Pre-Civil War Reformers* (1995); Richard D. Shiels, "The Scope of the Second Great Awakening: Andover, Massachusetts, as a Case Study," *Journal of the Early Republic* 5 (Summer 1985): 223–246; Timothy L. Smith, *Revivalism and Social Reform in Mid–Nineteenth Century America* (1957); Alice Felt Tyler, *Freedom's Ferment* (1944); Ronald G. Walters, *American Reformers, 1815–1860*, 2nd ed. (1997).

Temperance, Asylums, and Antimasonry

David Gollaher, *Voice for the Mad: The Life of Dorothea Dix* (1995); Paul Goodman, *Towards a Christian Republic: Antimasonry and the Great Transition in New England, 1826–1836* (1988); Gerald N. Grob, *Mental Institutions in America: Social Policy to 1875* (1973); Kathleen Smith Kutolowski, "Antimasonry Reexamined: Social Bases of the Grass-Roots Party," *Journal of American History* 71 (September 1984): 269–293; W. J. Rorabaugh, *The Alcoholic Republic: An American Tradition* (1979); David J. Rothman, *The Discovery of the Asylum: Social Order and Disorder in the New Republic* (1971); Ian R. Tyrrell, *Sobering Up: From Temperance to Prohibition in Antebellum America, 1800–1860* (1979); William Preston Vaughn, *The Antimasonic Party in the United States, 1826–1843* (1983).

Women and Reform

Barbara J. Berg, *The Remembered Gate: Origins of American Feminism: The Woman and the City, 1800–1860* (1977); Ellen C. Du Bois, *Feminism and Suffrage: The Emergence of an Independent Woman's Movement in America, 1848–1869* (1978); Barbara Leslie Epstein, *The Politics of Domesticity: Women, Evangelism, and Temperance in Nineteenth-Century America* (1981); Lori D. Ginzberg, *Women and the Work of Benevolence: Morality, Politics, and Class in the Nineteenth-Century United States* (1990); Debra Gold Hansen, *Strained Sisterhood: Gender and Class in the Boston Female Anti-Slavery Society* (1993); Nancy A. Hewitt, *Women's Activism and Social Change: Rochester, New York, 1822–1872* (1984); Sylvia D. Hoffert, *When Hens Crow: The Woman's Rights Movement in Antebellum America* (1995); Gerda Lerner, *The Grimké Sisters of South Carolina* (1967); Mary P. Ryan, *Cradle of the Middle Class: The Family in Oneida County, New York, 1790–1865* (1981); Shirley J. Yee, *Black Women Abolitionists: A Study in Activism, 1828–1860* (1992); Jean Fagan Yellin, *Women & Sisters: The Antislavery Feminists in American Culture* (1989).

Antislavery and Abolitionism

David Brion Davis, *Slavery and Human Progress* (1984); Frederick Douglass, *Life and Times of Frederick Douglass* (1881); George M. Fredrickson, *The Black Image in the White Mind: The Debate on Afro-American Character and Destiny, 1817–1914* (1971); Lawrence J. Friedman, *Gregarious Saints: Self and Community in American Abolitionism, 1830–1870* (1982); Aileen S. Kraditor, *Means and Ends* in *American Abolitionism: Garrison and His Critics on Strategy and Tactics* (1967); William Lee Miller, *Arguing About Slavery: The Great Battle in the United States Congress* (1995); William H. Pease and Jane H. Pease, *They Who Would Be Free: Blacks' Search for Freedom, 1830–1861* (1974); Benjamin Quarles, *Black Abolitionists* (1969); Leonard L. Richards, *"Gentlemen of Property and Standing": Anti-Abolition Mobs in Jacksonian America* (1970); John L. Thomas, *The Liberator: William Lloyd Garrison* (1963); Ronald G. Walters, *The Antislavery Appeal: American Abolitionism After 1830* (1976).

Andrew Jackson and the Jacksonians

Donald B. Cole, *Martin Van Buren and the American Political System* (1984); Daniel Feller, *The Jacksonian Promise: America, 1815–1840* (1995); Mary W. M. Hargreaves, *The Presidency of John Quincy Adams* (1985); Michael F. Holt, *Political Parties and American Political Development from the Age of Jackson to the Age of Lincoln* (1992); Richard B. Latner, *The Presidency of Andrew Jackson* (1979); Marvin Meyers, *The Jacksonian Persuasion* (1960); John Niven, *Martin Van Buren* (1983); Edward Pessen, *Jacksonian America: Society, Personality, and Politics*, rev. ed. (1979); Robert V. Remini, *The Legacy of Andrew Jackson: Essays on Democracy, Indian Removal, and Slavery* (1988); Robert V. Remini, *The Life of Andrew Jackson* (1988); Charles Sellers, *The Market Revolution: Jacksonian America, 1815–1846* (1991); Harry L. Watson, *Liberty and Power: The Politics of Jacksonian America* (1990).

Democrats and Whigs

William J. Cooper, *The South and the Politics of Slavery, 1828–1856* (1978); Ronald P. Formisano, *The Transformation of Political Culture: Massachusetts Parties, 1790s–1840s* (1983); William W. Freehling, *Prelude to Civil War: The Nullification Controversy in South Carolina* (1966); Daniel Walker Howe, *The Political Culture of the American Whigs* (1979); Lawrence Frederick Kohl, *The Politics of Individualism: Parties and the American Character in the Jacksonian Era* (1989); Richard P. McCormick, *The Second American Party System: Party Formation in the Jacksonian Era* (1966); Merrill D. Peterson, *The Great Triumvirate: Webster, Clay, and Calhoun* (1987); Norman Lois Peterson, *The Presidencies of William Henry Harrison and John Tyler* (1989); Robert V. Remini, *Henry Clay: Statesman for the Union* (1991); James Roger Sharp, *The Jacksonians Versus the Banks: Politics in the States After the Panic of 1837* (1970).

Manifest Destiny and Foreign Policy

John M. Belohlavek, *"Let the Eagle Soar!" The Foreign Policy of Andrew Jackson* (1985); T. R. Fehrenbach, *Lone Star: A History of Texas and the Texans* (1968); Norman B. Graebner, ed., *Manifest Destiny* (1968); Thomas R. Hietala, *Manifest Destiny: Anxious Aggrandizement in Late Jacksonian America* (1985); Reginald Horsman, *Race and Manifest Destiny* (1981); Michael Hunt, *Ideology and U.S. Foreign Policy* (1987); Bradford Perkins, *The Creation of a Republican Empire, 1776–1865* (1993); David M. Pletcher, *The Diplomacy of Annexation: Texas, Oregon, and the Mexican War* (1973); Charles G. Sellers, Jr., *James K. Polk: Continentalist, 1843–1846* (1966); Anders Stephanson, *Manifest Destiny: American Expansionism and the Empire of Right* (1995); Paul A. Varg, *United States Foreign Relations, 1820–1860* (1979); Albert K. Weinberg, *Manifest Destiny* (1935).

14

Slavery and America's Future: The Road to War

1845–1861

As the nation expanded, so did slavery, bringing with it a chain of consequences. On the frontier, slavery proved a source of wealth and financial progress for many white slaveowners, but for slaves it brought suffering, pain, and injustice. With slavery also came violence and controversy. Such was the case in Missouri, where Robert Newsom purchased Celia, a female slave, in 1850.

Almost sixty and a widower, Newsom lived with his two adult daughters and four of his grandchildren. Five male slaves worked the family's land. Celia, who was only fourteen, probably assumed that Newsom wanted her to cook and clean for the family. But he had more in mind for Celia. Almost immediately he raped her and made it clear that he would continue to demand her sexual services. He installed her in a small house only fifty yards behind his home. Over the next five years he visited her often, fathering two children. Newsom's adult daughters and his neighbors knew what he was doing to Celia but said nothing. They respected him and knew that slavery spawned such arrangements.

In 1855, Celia began a relationship with George, another of the Newsom slaves, and resolved to end the relationship with her master. She appealed first to Newsom's daughters, but they said they could do nothing to stop their father's behavior. Celia then begged her master to leave her alone, pleading that she was again pregnant and ill. One evening in June 1855, Robert Newsom read until his family was asleep and then walked to Celia's door. When he brushed aside her objections to sex, she grabbed a club and struck him on the skull. As he sank to the floor, she struck him again. He never arose. Panicked at having killed her master, Celia proceeded to burn his body all through the night in her large fireplace.

Physical evidence of Newsom's murder soon came to light, and Celia was arrested. Her trial received only local publicity, but in that district of Missouri it stirred conflicting passions. News of the murder made some slaveowners fear for their safety, but Celia's attorneys sympathized with her plight enough to argue, unsuccessfully, that laws against rape entitled her to defend herself. After a jury of twelve white men convicted her, Celia went to the gallows four days before Christmas.

By the time Celia was hanged, her drama had been overshadowed by a larger drama of violence in the neighboring territory of Kansas. Open warfare had broken out there between advocates and foes of slavery. Proslavery men, intent on spreading the peculiar institution and preserving a balance of free and slave states in the United States Senate, rode across the border from Missouri, stole elections by voting illegally, and physically attacked those who wanted Kansas to be free soil. Antislavery activists organized the New England Emigrant Aid Company to send opponents of slavery to Kansas. Before long the New Englanders were arming their settlers with Sharps rifles, nicknamed "Beecher's Bibles" after the well-known antislavery minister Henry Ward Beecher of New York. On the proslavery side a United States senator, Missouri's David Atchison, publicly advocated violence and pledged his readiness "to shoot, burn and hang." Expansion and slavery proved an incendiary combination, arousing passions in national politics as on the Newsom farm. As the 1850s advanced, slavery pulled Americans deeper and deeper into a maelstrom of conflict and violence.

Between 1845 and 1853 the United States added Texas, the West Coast, and the Southwest to its domain and launched the settlement of the Great Plains. Each time the nation expanded, it confronted a thorny issue: should new territories and states be slave or free? This question stirred disagreements too extreme for compromise. Sensing the danger of conflict, Senator John C. Calhoun of South Carolina called Mexico "the forbidden fruit; the penalty of eating it would be to subject our institutions to political death." A host of political leaders, including Henry Clay, Lewis Cass, Stephen A. Douglas, and Presidents Jackson and Van Buren, tried to postpone or resolve disagreements about slavery in the territories. Repeatedly, though, these disputes injected into national politics the bitterness surrounding slavery. If slavery was the sore spot in the body politic, territorial disputes rubbed salt into the wound.

The United States had always been a diverse, heterogeneous society, not a cohesive unit. Now, however, diverse interests that used to balance each other became linked to a divisive issue. The second party system disintegrated, and a realigned system that emphasized sectional conflict took its place. Sectional parties emphasizing conflict replaced nation-wide organizations that had promoted compromise. The ensuing political storms gave rise to a feeling in both North and South that America's future was at stake. The new Republican Party charged that southerners were taking over the federal government and planning to make slavery legal throughout the Union. Republicans believed that America's future depended on the free labor of free men, whose rights were protected by a government devoted to liberty. Southern leaders defended slavery and charged the North with lawless behavior in violation of the Constitution. To these southerners enslavement of blacks was the foundation of equality and republicanism among whites, and a government that failed to protect slavery was un-American and unworthy of their loyalty.

Not all citizens were obsessed with these conflicts. In fact, the results of the 1860 presidential election indicated that most voters wanted neither disunion nor civil war. Within six months, however, they had both, for slavery aroused passions that could be neither contained nor resolved. What had begun as a dark cloud over the territories became a storm engulfing the nation.

 ## Conflict Begins: The Mexican War

Territorial expansion surged forward under the leadership of President James K. Polk. The annexation of Texas (see page 371) just before his inauguration did not weaken Polk's determination to acquire California and the Southwest, and he desired Oregon as well. Polk achieved his goals but was unaware of the price in domestic harmony that expansion would exact. Territorial conquest divided the Whig Party, drove southern Whigs into a full embrace of slavery, and brought into the open an aggressive new southern theory about slavery's position in the territories. Expansion also sparked protests and proposals from the North that angered southerners.

During the 1844 campaign Polk's supporters had threatened war with Great Britain to gain all of Oregon. As president, however, Polk turned first to diplomacy. Not wanting to fight Mexico and

• *Important Events* •

1846	War with Mexico begins Oregon Treaty negotiated Wilmot Proviso inflames sectional divisions
1847	Lewis Cass proposes idea of popular sovereignty
1848	Treaty of Guadalupe Hidalgo gives United States new territory in the Southwest Free-Soil Party formed Zachary Taylor elected president
1849	California applies for admission to Union as free state
1850	Compromise of 1850 passed in separate bills
1852	Publication of *Uncle Tom's Cabin*, by Harriet Beecher Stowe Franklin Pierce elected president
1854	Publication of "Appeal of the Independent Democrats" Kansas-Nebraska Act wins approval and ignites controversy Republican Party formed Democrats lose ground in congressional elections

1856	"Bleeding Kansas" troubles nation Preston Brooks attacks Charles Sumner in Senate chamber James Buchanan elected president
1857	*Dred Scott* v. *Sandford* endorses southern views on race and territories Lecompton Constitution proposed; President Buchanan supports it
1858	Kansas voters reject Lecompton Constitution Lincoln-Douglas debates attract attention Stephen A. Douglas proposes Freeport Doctrine
1859	John Brown raids Harpers Ferry
1860	Democratic Party splits in two Abraham Lincoln elected president Crittenden Compromise fails South Carolina secedes from Union
1861	Six more Deep South states secede Confederacy established at Montgomery, Alabama Attack on Fort Sumter begins Civil War Four states in the Upper South join the Confederacy

Great Britain at the same time, he tried to avoid bloodshed in the Northwest, where America and Britain had jointly occupied disputed territory since 1818. Dropping the demand for a boundary at latitude 54°40', he pressured the British to accept the 49th parallel. In 1846 Great Britain agreed. The Oregon Treaty gave the United States all of present-day Oregon, Washington, and Idaho and parts of Wyoming and Montana (see map, page 378).

Toward Mexico, Polk was more aggressive. He ordered American troops to defend the border claimed by Texas but contested by Mexico (see map, page 379), and he attempted to buy from the angry Mexicans a huge tract of land in the Southwest. When that effort failed, Polk resolved to ask Congress for a declaration of war. As he was drawing up a list of grievances, word arrived that Mexican forces had engaged American troops on disputed territory and American blood had been shed. Eagerly, Polk declared that "war exists by the act of Mexico itself" and summoned the nation to arms.

Congress recognized a state of war between Mexico and the United States in May 1846, and

soon American forces made significant gains. The troops—as in previous wars, mainly volunteers furnished by the states—proved unruly and undisciplined, and their politically ambitious commanders often quarreled among themselves. Nevertheless, progress was steady. General Zachary Taylor's forces attacked and occupied Monterrey, securing northeastern Mexico (see map, page 379). Polk then ordered Colonel Stephen Kearny and a small detachment to invade the remote and thinly populated provinces of New Mexico and California. Taking Santa Fe without opposition, Kearny pushed into California, where he joined forces with rebellious American settlers led by Captain John C. Frémont and with a couple of United States naval units. A quick victory was followed by reverses, but American soldiers soon reestablished their dominance in distant California.

Because losses on the periphery had not broken Mexican resistance, General Winfield Scott carried the war to the enemy's heartland. From Veracruz on the Gulf of Mexico, he led fourteen thousand men toward Mexico City. This daring invasion was the

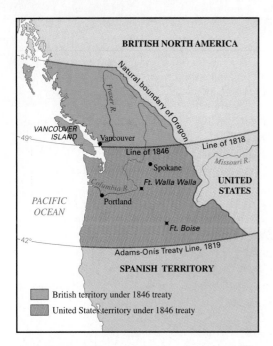

American Expansion in Oregon *The slogan of Polk's supporters had been "Fifty-four forty or fight," but negotiation of a boundary at the 49th parallel avoided the danger of war with Great Britain.*

decisive campaign of the war. Scott's men, outnumbered and threatened by yellow fever, encountered a series of formidable Mexican defenses, but engineers repeatedly discovered flanking routes around the enemy. After a series of hard-fought battles, United States troops captured the Mexican capital and brought the war to an end.

Representatives of both countries signed the Treaty of Guadalupe Hidalgo in February 1848. The United States gained California and New Mexico (including present-day Nevada, Utah, and Arizona) and recognition of the Rio Grande as the southern boundary of Texas. In return, the American government agreed to settle the claims of its citizens against Mexico and to pay Mexico a mere $15 million.

Treaty of Guadalupe Hidalgo

The costs of the war included the deaths of thirteen thousand Americans (mostly from disease) and fifty thousand Mexicans, plus Mexican-American enmity that endured into the twentieth century. The domestic cost to the United States was even higher. Public opinion was sharply divided, despite widespread hostility toward Mexicans. Southwesterners were enthusiastic about the war; New Englanders strenuously opposed it. Whigs in Congress charged that Polk, a Democrat, had "literally provoked" an unnecessary war (which they called "Mr. Polk's war") and "usurped the power of Congress." The aged John Quincy Adams denounced the war; and a tall, young, Illinois Whig named Abraham Lincoln questioned its justification. Abolitionists and a small minority of antislavery Whigs charged that the war was no less than a plot to extend slavery. Congressman Joshua Giddings of Ohio charged that Polk's purpose was "to render slavery secure in Texas" and to extend slavery's domain to vast expanses of new territory.

These charges fed northern fear of the so-called Slave Power. Abolitionists had long warned of a Slave Power—a slaveholding oligarchy that controlled the South and intended to dominate the nation. These dangerous aristocrats had gained power in their region by persecuting critics of slavery and suppressing dissent. The Slave Power's assault on northern liberties, abolitionists argued, had begun in 1836, when Congress passed the gag rule (see page 356). Many white northerners, even those who saw nothing wrong with slavery, had opposed restrictions on free speech and the right of petition. It was the battle over free speech that first made the idea of a Slave Power credible. The Mexican War deepened fears about this sinister power. Why, asked antislavery northerners, had claims to part of Oregon been abandoned and a questionable war begun for slave territory?

Idea of a Slave Power

Northern opinion began to shift, but the impact of events on southern opinion and southern leaders was even more dramatic. At first many southern leaders criticized the war with Mexico. Southern Whigs attacked the Democratic president for causing the war, and few southern congressmen saw defense of slavery as the paramount issue. In 1845 Alexander H. Stephens of Georgia had declared, "I am no defender of slavery in the abstract," and even John C. Calhoun—despite his earlier schemes to annex Texas for slavery—strongly opposed the seizure of large amounts of land from Mexico. A Whig editor in Georgia argued that "we have territory enough, especially if every province, like Texas, is to bring in its train war and debt and death."

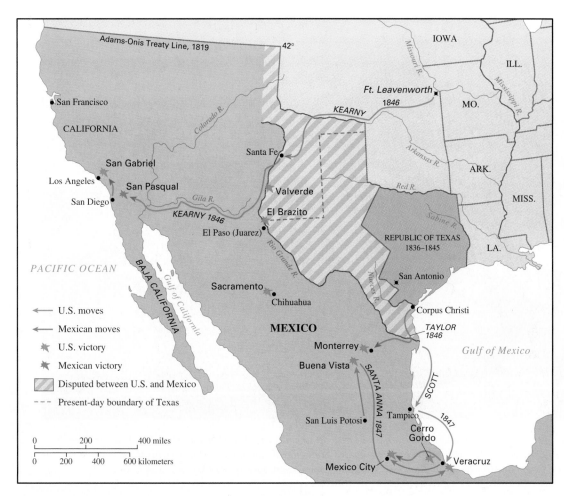

The Mexican War *This map shows the territory disputed between the United States and Mexico. After United States gains in northeastern Mexico and in New Mexico and California, General Winfield Scott captured Mexico City in the decisive campaign of the war.*

But the Mexican War proved generally popular with southern voters, and no southern Whig could oppose it once slavery became the central issue.

Wilmot Proviso That happened in August 1846, when David Wilmot, a Pennsylvania Democrat, proposed an amendment, or proviso, to a military appropriations bill: that "neither slavery nor involuntary servitude shall ever exist" in any territory gained from Mexico. His proviso did not pass both houses of Congress, but it immediately transformed the debate.

Alexander H. Stephens, only recently "no defender of slavery," now declared that slavery was based on the Bible and above moral criticism, and John C. Calhoun asserted a radical new southern position. The territories, Calhoun insisted, belonged to all the states, and the federal government could do nothing to limit the spread of slavery there. Southern slaveholders had a constitutional *right*, Calhoun claimed, to take their slaves anywhere in the territories. This position, which quickly became orthodox for every southern politician, was a radical reversal of history. In 1787 the Confederation Congress had excluded slavery from the Northwest Territory (see pages 187–188); Article IV of the federal Constitution had authorized Congress to make "all needful rules and regulations" for the territories; and the

Enthusiastic publishers vied to furnish the American public with up-to-date news of the Mexican War. This is one of three lithographs issued by Currier and Ives in 1846 to celebrate United States forces' capture of Mexico's General La Vega during the Battle of Resaca, fought near the border of Texas and Mexico.   Amon Carter Museum, Fort Worth, Texas.

Missouri Compromise had barred slavery from most of the Louisiana Purchase. Now, however, southern leaders demanded protection for slavery.

In the North, the Wilmot Proviso became a rallying cry for abolitionists. Eventually the legislatures of fourteen northern states endorsed it—and not because all its supporters were abolitionists. David Wilmot, significantly, was neither an abolitionist nor an antislavery Whig. He denied having any "squeamish sensitiveness upon the subject of slavery" or "morbid sympathy for the slave." Instead, his goal was to defend "the rights of white freemen" and to obtain California "for free white labor." Wilmot sought opportunity for "the sons of toil, of my own race and own color." His involvement in antislavery controversy is a measure of the remarkable ability of the territorial issue to alarm northerners of many viewpoints.

Like Wilmot, most white northerners were racists, not abolitionists. It was possible, however, to be both a racist *and* an opponent of slavery. Fear of the Slave Power was building a potent antislavery movement that united abolitionists *and* antiblack voters. The latter's concern was to protect themselves, not southern blacks, from the Slave Power. Abolition had few followers, but opposition to slavery's extension and fear of the Slave Power was growing. And as northerners became increasingly antislavery, southern slaveholders felt deep alarm.

The slavery question divided northerners and southerners in both parties and could not be kept out of national politics. After Polk renounced a second term as president, the Democrats nominated Senator Lewis Cass of Michigan for president and General William Butler of Kentucky for vice president. Cass, a party loyalist who had served in Jackson's cabinet, in 1847 had devised the idea of "popular sover-

Election of 1848 and Popular Sovereignty

eignty" for the territories—letting residents in the territories decide the question of slavery for themselves. His party's platform declared that Congress lacked the power to interfere with slavery and criticized those who pressed the question. The Whigs nominated General Zachary Taylor, a southern slaveholder and the conqueror of Monterrey; Congressman Millard Fillmore of New York was his running mate. The Whig convention similarly refused to assert that Congress had power over slavery in the territories.

But the issue would not stay in the background. Many southern Democrats distrusted Cass and eventually voted for Taylor because he was a slaveholder. Among northerners, concern over slavery led to the formation of a new party. New York Democrats committed to the Wilmot Proviso rebelled against Cass and nominated former president Van Buren. Antislavery Whigs and former supporters of the Liberty Party then joined them to organize the Free-Soil Party, with Van Buren as its candidate (see table). This party, whose slogan was "Free Soil, Free Speech, Free Labor, and Free Men," won almost 300,000 northern votes. Taylor polled 1.4 million votes to Cass's 1.2 million and won the White House, but the results were more ominous than decisive. In both public opinion and the political parties, a North-South division was deepening.

The conflicts of 1848 would dominate politics throughout the 1850s, as slavery in the territories colored every other national issue. The nation's uncertain attempts to deal with economic and social change gave way to more pressing questions about the nature of the Union itself. Soon the second party system succumbed to the crisis over slavery and the future.

Territorial Problems Are Compromised but Reemerge

The first sectional battle of the decade involved California. More than eighty thousand Americans flooded into California during the gold rush of 1849. With Congress unable to agree on a formula to govern the territories, President Taylor urged these settlers to apply directly for admission to the Union. They promptly did so, proposing a state constitution that did not allow for slavery. Because California's admission as a free state would upset the sectional balance of power in the Senate, southern politicians wanted to postpone admission and make California a slave territory, or at least to extend the Missouri Compromise line west to the Pacific. Representatives from nine southern states, meeting in Nashville, asserted the South's right to part of the territory.

Henry Clay, the venerable Whig leader, sensed that the Union was in peril. Twice before—in 1820 and 1833—Clay, the "Great Pacificator," had taken the lead in shaping sectional compromise; now he struggled one last time to preserve the nation. To hushed Senate galleries Clay presented a series of compromise measures. Over the weeks that followed, he and Senator Stephen A. Douglas of Illinois, the

New Political Parties

Party	Period of Influence	Area of Influence	Outcome
Liberty Party	1839–1848	North	Merged with other antislavery groups to form Free-Soil Party
Free-Soil Party	1848–1854	North	Merged with Republican Party
Know-Nothings (American Party)	1853–1856	Nationwide	Disappeared, freeing some northern voters to join Republican Party
Republican Party	1854–present	North (later nationwide)	Became rival of Democratic Party in third party system

"Little Giant," steered their omnibus bill, or compromise package, through debate and amendment.

The problems to be solved were numerous and difficult. Would California, or part of it, become a free state? How should the territory acquired from Mexico be organized? Texas, which allowed slavery, claimed large portions of the new land as far west as Santa Fe, so that claim, too, had to be settled. Southerners complained that fugitive slaves were not being returned as the Constitution required, and northerners objected to the sale of human beings in the nation's capital. But most troublesome of all was the status of slavery in the territories.

Clay and Douglas hoped to avoid a specific formula, for Lewis Cass's idea of popular sovereignty possessed a vagueness that appealed to practical politicians. Like many others, Cass wanted Congress to stay out of the territorial wrangle. Ultimately Congress would have to approve statehood for a territory, but "in the meantime," he said, it should allow the people living there "to regulate their own concerns in their own way."

Those simple words proved highly ambiguous. When could settlers prohibit slavery? To avoid dissension within their party, northern and southern Democrats explained Cass's statement to their constituents in two incompatible ways. Southerners claimed that neither Congress nor a territorial legislature could bar slavery. Only when settlers assumed sovereignty under a state constitution could they take that step. Northerners insisted that Americans living in a territory were entitled to local self-government and thus could outlaw slavery at any time. Northern and southern Whigs, too, were divided over the issue.

The cause of compromise gained a powerful supporter when Senator Daniel Webster committed his prestige and eloquence to Clay's bill. "I wish to speak today," Webster declaimed, "not as a Massachusetts man, nor as a Northern man, but as an American. I speak today for the preservation of the Union. Hear me for my cause." Abandoning his earlier support for the Wilmot Proviso, Webster urged northerners not to "taunt or reproach" the South with antislavery measures. To southern firebrands he issued a warning that disunion inevitably would cause great convulsion and destruction.

Yet even Webster's influence was not enough. After months of labor, Clay and Douglas finally brought their legislative package to a vote, and lost. But the determined Douglas would not give up. With Clay sick

and absent from Washington, Douglas reintroduced the compromise measures one at a time. Though there was no majority for compromise, Douglas shrewdly realized that different majorities might be created for the separate measures. Because southerners favored some bills and northerners the rest, the small bloc for compromise could vote first with one section and then with the other. The strategy worked, and Douglas's resourcefulness salvaged a positive result from more than eight months of congressional effort. The Compromise of 1850 became law.

Under its various measures, California became a free state, and the Texas boundary was set at its present limits (see map, page 383). The United States

Compromise of 1850

paid Texas $10 million in consideration of the boundary agreement. The territories of New Mexico and Utah were organized with power to legislate on "all rightful subjects . . . consistent with the Constitution." A stronger fugitive slave law and an act to suppress the slave trade in the District of Columbia completed the compromise.

Jubilation greeted passage of the compromise; crowds in Washington celebrated the happy news. "On one glorious night," records a modern historian, "the word went abroad that it was the duty of every patriot to get drunk. Before the next morning many a citizen had proved his patriotism," and several prominent senators "were reported stricken with a variety of implausible maladies—headaches, heat prostration, or overindulgence in fruit."

In reality, there was less cause for celebration than people hoped. Fundamentally, the Compromise of 1850 was not a settlement of sectional disputes; at best, it was an artful evasion. Douglas had found a way to pass his proposals without convincing northerners and southerners to come together and agree. This compromise bought time for the nation, but it did not create guidelines for the settlement of future territorial questions. It merely put them off. Furthermore, the compromise had two basic flaws. The first concerned the ambiguity of territorial legislation: what were "rightful subjects of legislation, consistent with the Constitution"? During debate, southerners said these words meant that there would be no prohibition of slavery during the territorial stage, and northerners declared that settlers could bar slavery whenever they wished. The compromise even acknowledged this disagreement by providing for the appeal of a territorial legislature's action to

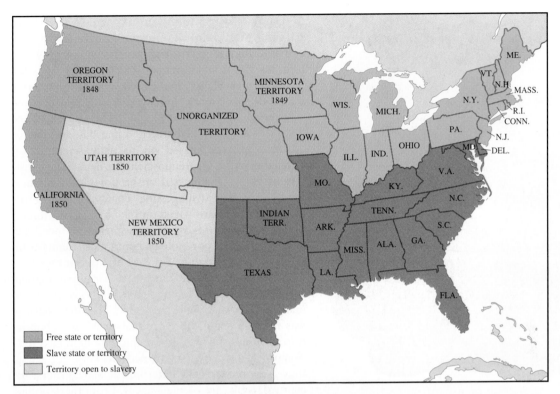

The Compromise of 1850 *The territorial provisions of the Compromise of 1850 made California a free state and set Texas's western boundary. The Utah and New Mexico Territories were opened to slavery, but northerners and southerners disagreed over when settlers could legally decide to prohibit slavery.*

the Supreme Court, but no such case ever arose. One witty politician remarked that the legislators had enacted a lawsuit instead of a law.

The second flaw lay in the Fugitive Slave Act, which gave added—and controversial—protection to slavery. The new law empowered slaveowners to go into court in their own states to present evidence that a slave who owed them service had escaped. The resulting transcript and a description of the fugitive would then serve as legal proof of a person's slave status, even in free states and territories. Court officials would decide only whether the person brought before them was the person described, not whether he or she was indeed a slave. Penalties discouraged citizens from harboring fugitives, and the fees paid to United States marshals seemed to favor slaveholders. (Authorities were paid $10 if the alleged fugitive was turned over to the slaveowner, $5 if not.)

Abolitionist newspapers quickly attacked the Fugitive Slave Act as a violation of fundamental

Fugitive Slave Act

American rights. Why, in a land of freedom, were alleged fugitives denied a trial by jury? Why were they given no chance to present evidence or cross-examine witnesses? Why did the law give authorities a financial incentive to send suspected fugitives into bondage? These arguments convinced some northerners that free blacks could be sent into slavery, mistakenly or otherwise, with no means to defend themselves. Protest meetings were held in Massachusetts, New York, Pennsylvania, northern Ohio, northern Illinois, and elsewhere. In 1851 a mob in Boston grabbed a runaway slave from a federal marshal and sent him to safety in Canada.

At this point a novel portrayed the humanity and suffering of slaves in a way that touched millions of northerners. Harriet Beecher Stowe, whose New England family had produced many prominent ministers, wrote *Uncle Tom's Cabin* out of deep moral conviction. Her story, serialized in 1851 and published as a book in 1852, conveyed the agonies faced by slave families and described a mother's dash to freedom

Uncle Tom's Cabin

The Webb Family toured the North, presenting dramatic readings of Uncle Tom's Cabin. *Performances by the Webbs and others deepened the already powerful impact of Harriet Beecher Stowe's novel.* Harriet Beecher Stowe Center, Hartford, CT.

with her child across the frozen Ohio River. Stowe also portrayed slavery's evil effects on slaveholders, indicting the institution itself more harshly than she indicted the southerners caught in its web. In nine months the book sold over three hundred thousand copies; by mid-1853, over a million. Countless people saw *Uncle Tom's Cabin* performed as a stage play or heard the story in dramatic readings or read similar novels inspired by it. Stowe brought home the evil of slavery to many who had never given it much thought.

The popularity of *Uncle Tom's Cabin* alarmed and appalled anxious southern whites. In the territorial controversies and now in popular literature they saw threats to their way of life. Behind the South's aggressive claims about territorial rights lay fear—fear that if nearby areas became free soil, they would be used as bases from which to spread abolitionism into the slave states. Jefferson Davis of Mississippi, President Franklin Pierce's secretary of war, wrote in 1855 that "abolitionism would gain but little in excluding slavery from the territories, if it were never

to disturb that institution in the States." To defend slavery against political threats, southern leaders relied on Calhoun's territorial theories and the dogmas of states' rights and strict construction.

To protect slavery in the arena of ideas, southerners needed to counter indictments of the institution as a moral wrong. Accordingly, proslavery theorists elaborated numerous arguments based on partially scientific or pseudoscientific data. They discussed anthropological evidence suggesting separate origins of the races and physicians' views on the physical infirmities of blacks. Other proslavery spokesmen expounded the new "science" of phrenology, citing measurements of skulls to "prove" that blacks were an inferior race.

Proslavery Theories

One southern sociologist, a Virginian named George Fitzhugh, focused on relations between management and labor and declared that slavery was morally superior to free labor. Wage labor in northern industry was inhumane, Fitzhugh charged, because factory owners turned workers out when they grew old or sick. Paternalistic slaveowners, he claimed, took care of aged slaves. From these points he drew a startling conclusion: slavery ought to be practiced in all societies, whatever their racial composition. His notions, extreme even for the South, reveal why southern defenses deepened northern fears of the Slave Power.

In private and in their hearts, most southern leaders fell back on two rationales for slavery: their belief that blacks were inferior and biblical accounts of slaveholding. Like many whites, Jefferson Davis believed that whites and blacks could not coexist as equals in freedom and that slavery therefore was unavoidable. Among friends Davis reverted to the eighteenth-century argument that southerners were doing the best they could with a situation they had inherited. "Is it well to denounce an evil for which there is no cure?" he asked.

The 1852 election gave Davis and other southerners hope that slavery would be secure under the administration of a new president. Franklin Pierce, a Democrat from New Hampshire, won an easy victory over the Whig presidential nominee, General Winfield Scott. Pierce believed that the defense of each section's rights was essential to the nation's unity, and southerners hoped that his firm support for the Compromise of 1850 might end sectional divi-

Election of 1852

sions. Because Scott's views on the compromise had been unknown and the Free-Soil candidate, John P. Hale of New Hampshire, had openly rejected it, Pierce's victory suggested strong support for the compromise.

That interpretation of the election, however, was erroneous. Pierce's victory derived less from his strengths than from the Whig Party's weakness. The Whigs were a congressional and state-based party that never had achieved much success in presidential politics. Sectional discord was splitting the party in two, further undermining its national competitiveness, and the deaths of President Taylor, Daniel Webster, and Henry Clay had deprived Whigs of the few dominant personalities they had. In 1852 the Whig Party ran on little but its past reputation, and many observers predicted its demise.

When President Pierce actively supported the compromise, the results appalled many northerners. His vigorous enforcement of the fugitive slave law provoked outrage and fear of the Slave Power. In 1854 Pierce learned that a fugitive slave named Anthony Burns was in custody in Boston. Burns had fled from Virginia by stowing away on a ship. Thinking he was safe in a city known for its abolitionists, Burns wrote to an enslaved relative in Virginia. His letter was intercepted, and federal marshals placed him under guard in Boston's federal courthouse. Abolitionists attacked the courthouse, protesting for Burns's freedom.

Pierce moved decisively to enforce the Fugitive Slave Act. He telegraphed local officials to "incur any expense to insure the execution of the law" and sent marines, cavalry, and artillery to Boston. When Burns's owner seemed willing to sell his property, the United States attorney blocked the sale and won a decision that Anthony Burns must return to slavery. United States troops marched Burns to Boston harbor through streets draped in black and hung with American flags at half mast. At a cost of $100,000, equivalent to roughly $2 million today, a single black man was returned to slavery through the power of federal law.

This demonstration of federal support for slavery radicalized opinion, even among many conservatives. "I put my face in my hands and wept," wrote one man. Textile manufacturer Amos A. Lawrence observed that "we went to bed one night old fashioned, conservative, Compromise Union Whigs & waked up stark mad Abolitionists." Juries refused to convict the abolitionists who had stormed the court-

house, and New England states passed personal-liberty laws designed to impede or block federal enforcement. But where northerners saw evidence that the Slave Power was dominating American government, outraged slaveholders saw northern "faithlessness" to the law.

Pierce seemed unable to avoid sectional conflict in other arenas as well. His proposal for a transcontinental railroad derailed when congressmen fought over its location, North or South. His attempts to acquire foreign territory stirred more trouble. An annexation treaty with Hawai'i failed because southern senators would not vote for another free state, and efforts to acquire slaveholding Cuba angered antislavery northerners. After he tried to purchase Cuba from Spain in 1854, publication of a government document, the Ostend Manifesto, revealed that three administration officials had rashly talked of "wresting" Cuba from Spain. Some northerners concluded that Pierce was determined to acquire more slave territory. Then another territorial bill threw Congress and the nation into a bitter conflict that was to have significant results.

 ## Territorial Problems Shatter the Party System

The new controversy began in a surprising way. Stephen A. Douglas, one of the architects of the Compromise of 1850, introduced a bill to establish the Kansas and Nebraska Territories. A talented and ambitious man, Douglas was known for compromise, not sectional quarreling. But he did not view slavery as a fundamental problem, and he was willing to risk some controversy to win economic benefits for Illinois, his home state. A transcontinental railroad would encourage settlement of the Great Plains and stimulate the economy of Illinois; but no company would build such a railroad before Congress organized the territories it would cross. Thus it was probably for the sake of promoting the construction of a railroad that Douglas introduced a bill that inflamed sectional passions and thwarted his own ambitions for national office. The Kansas-Nebraska bill also finished off the Whig Party, damaged the northern Democrats, and gave birth to a new Republican Party.

The Kansas-Nebraska bill exposed the first flaw of the Compromise of 1850—the conflicting interpretations of popular sovereignty. Douglas's bill

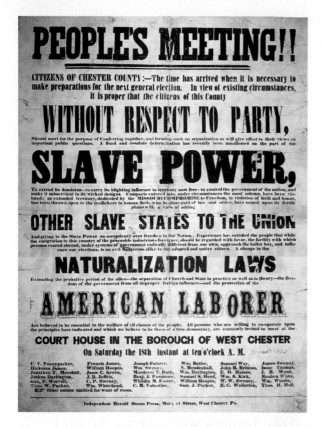

PEOPLE'S MEETING!!

CITIZENS OF CHESTER COUNTY :—The time has arrived when it is necessary to make preparations for the next general election.   In view of existing circumstances, it is proper that the citizens of this County

WITHOUT RESPECT TO PARTY,

Should meet for the purpose of Conferring together, and forming such an organization as will give effect to their views on important public questions.   A fixed and resolute determination has recently been manifested on the part of the

SLAVE POWER,

To extend its dominion—to carry its blighting influence to territory now free—to control the government of the nation, and make it subservient to its wicked designs. Compacts entered into, under circumstances the most solemn, have been violated; an extended territory, dedicated by the MISSOURI COMPROMISE to Freedom, in violation of faith and honor, has been thrown open to the traffickers in human flesh, who in disregard of law and order, have seized upon its fertile plains with a view of adding

OTHER SLAVE STATES TO THE UNION

And giving to the Slave Power an ascendency over freedom in the Nation. Experience has satisfied the people that while the emigration to this country of the peaceable industrious foreigner, should be regarded with favor, the facility with which persons reared abroad, under systems of government radically different from our own, approach the ballot box, and influence our elections, is an evil dangerous alike to the adopted and native citizen. A change in the

NATURALIZATION LAWS

Extending the probative period of the alien—the separation of Church and State in practice as well as in theory—the freedom of the government from all improper foreign influence—and the protection of the

AMERICAN LABORER

Are believed to be essential to the welfare of all classes of the people. All persons who are willing to co-operate upon the principles here indicated and which we believe to be those of a true democracy, are earnestly invited to meet at the

COURT HOUSE IN THE BOROUGH OF WEST CHESTER

On Saturday the 18th instant at ten o'clock A. M.   *August 1855*

U. V. Pennypacker,   Francis Jones,   Joseph Painter,   Wm. Butler,   Samuel Way,   James Sweney,
Hickman Jones,   William Hoopes,   Wm. Sweney,   N. Mendenhall,   John B. Brinton,   Isaac Thomas,
Jonathan T. Marshall,   Jesse C. Green,   Mordecai T. Ruth,   Wm. Darlington,   E. D. Haines,   J. B. Wood,
Joshua Darlington,   J. B. Jeffris,   Benj. J. Passmore,   Samuel S. Heed,   Wm. S. Kirk,   Reuben White,
Geo. J. Worrall,   C. P. Sweney,   Whildin M. Foster,   William Hoopes,   W. W. Sweney,   Wm. Windie,
Thos. W. Parker,   Wm. Whitehead,   C. M. Valentine,   Sam. J. Parker,   Z. C. Wollerton,   Thos. H. Hall.
Other names omitted for want of room.

Independent Herald Steam Press, Mar t Street, West Chester Pa.

Throughout the North the Kansas-Nebraska Act kindled fires of alarm over the Slave Power's "determination to extend its dominion" and "control the government of the nation." Public meetings like the one announced here, held in West Chester, Pennsylvania, aided the new Republican Party.   American Antiquarian Society.

Kansas-Nebraska Bill

left "all questions pertaining to slavery in the Territories . . . to the people residing therein." Northerners and southerners, however, still disagreed violently over what territorial settlers could constitutionally do. Moreover, the Kansas and Nebraska Territories lay within the Louisiana Purchase, and the Missouri Compromise prohibited slavery in all that land from latitude 36°30' north to the Canadian border. If popular sovereignty were to mean anything in Kansas and Nebraska, it had to mean that the Missouri Compromise was no longer in effect and that settlers could establish slavery there.

Southern congressmen, anxious to establish slaveholders' right to take slaves into any territory, pressed Douglas to concede this point. They de-

manded an explicit repeal of the 36°30' limitation as the price of their support. During a carriage ride with Senator Archibald Dixon of Kentucky, Douglas debated the point at length. Finally he made an impulsive decision: "By God, Sir, you are right. I will incorporate it in my bill, though I know it will raise a hell of a storm."

Perhaps Douglas underestimated the storm because he believed that conditions of climate and soil would keep slavery out of Kansas and Nebraska. Nevertheless, his bill threw open to slavery land from which it had been prohibited for thirty-four years. Opposition from Free-Soilers and antislavery forces was immediate and enduring (see broadside). The titanic struggle in Congress lasted three-and-a-half months. Douglas won the support of President Pierce and eventually prevailed: the bill became law in May 1854 (see map, page 387).

Unfortunately, the storm was just beginning. Abolitionists charged sinister aggression by the Slave Power, and northern fears of slavery's influence deepened. Opposition to the Fugitive Slave Act grew dramatically; between 1855 and 1859 Connecticut, Rhode Island, Massachusetts, Michigan, Maine, Ohio, and Wisconsin passed personal-liberty laws. These laws interfered with the Fugitive Slave Act—and enraged southern leaders—by providing counsel for alleged fugitives and requiring trial by jury. More important was the devastating impact of the Kansas-Nebraska Act on political parties. The weakened Whig Party broke apart into northern and southern wings that could no longer cooperate nationally. One of the two foundations of the second party system was now gone. The Democrats survived, but their support in the North fell drastically in the 1854 elections. Northern Democrats lost sixty-six of their ninety-one congressional seats and lost control of all but two free-state legislatures.

The New Republican Party

The beneficiary of northern voters' wrath was a new political party. During debate on the Kansas-Nebraska bill, six congressmen had published an "Appeal of the Independent Democrats." Joshua Giddings, Salmon Chase, and Charles Sumner—the principal authors of this protest—attacked Douglas's legislation as a "gross violation of a sacred pledge" (the Missouri Compromise) and a "criminal betrayal of precious rights" that would make free territory a "dreary region of despotism." Their appeal tapped a reservoir of deep

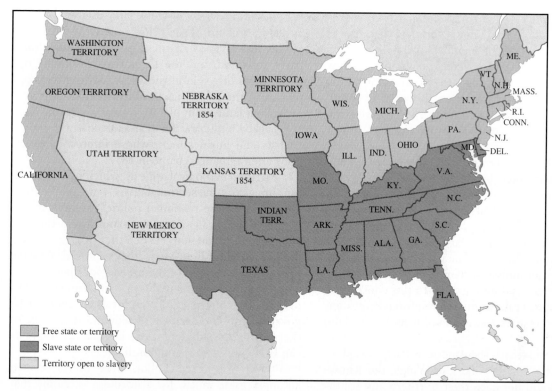

The Kansas-Nebraska Act, 1854 *Stephen Douglas's bill raised a storm of opposition in the North because it repealed the Missouri Compromise's limitation on slavery. In Kansas and Nebraska, land was opened to slavery where it had been prohibited before.*

concerns in the North—concerns that Illinois's Abraham Lincoln cogently expressed.

Although Lincoln did not condemn southerners—"They are just what we would be in their situation"—he exposed the moral bankruptcy and historic significance of the Kansas-Nebraska Act. Denying "that there can be moral right in the enslaving of one man by another," Lincoln argued that the founders, from love of liberty, had banned slavery from the Northwest Territory, kept the word *slavery* out of the Constitution, and treated it overall as a "cancer" that eventually had to be removed. Rather than encouraging liberty, the Kansas-Nebraska Act put slavery "on the high road to extension and perpetuity," and that constituted a "moral wrong and injustice." America's future, Lincoln warned, was being mortgaged to slavery. The nation should "readopt the Declaration of Independence" and commit itself to freedom.

Thousands agreed. During the summer and fall of 1854, antislavery Whigs and Democrats, Free-Soilers, and other reformers throughout the Old Northwest met to form the new Republican Party, dedicated to keeping slavery out of the territories. The influence of the Republicans rapidly spread to the East, and they won a stunning victory in the 1854 elections. In their first appearance on the ballot, Republicans captured a majority of northern House seats. Antislavery sentiment had created a new party and caused roughly a quarter of northern Democrats to desert their party.

For the first time, too, a sectional party had gained significant power in the political system. Previously, every major party was a national organization whose leaders patched up sectional differences to achieve partisan goals. Now the Whigs were gone, and only the Democrats struggled to maintain a national following. The sectional Republican Party, which absorbed the Free-Soil Party, grew rapidly in the North by raising moral issues that angered many southerners.

Nor were Republicans the only new party. For a brief period, an anti-immigrant organization, the American Party, seemed likely to replace the Whigs.

Know-Nothings

This party, popularly known as the Know-Nothings (because its first members kept their purposes secret, answering "I know nothing" to all questions), exploited nativist fear of foreigners. Between 1848 and 1860, nearly 3.5 million immigrants entered the United States—proportionally the heaviest inflow of foreigners ever in American history (see pages 330–334). Democrats courted these new citizens and relied on their votes, but many native-born Americans harbored serious misgivings about them. In 1854 anti-immigrant fears gave the Know-Nothings more supporters in some northern states than either the Republicans or the Free-Soilers. The temperance movement also gained new strength early in the 1850s with its promises to stamp out the evils associated with liquor and immigrants. In this context the Know-Nothings campaigned to reinforce Protestant morality and restrict voting and officeholding to the native-born.

By the mid-1850s the American Party was powerful and growing. But like the Whigs, the Know-Nothings could not keep their northern and southern wings together, and they melted away after 1856. That left the field to the Republicans, who wooed the nativists and in several states passed temperance ordinances and laws postponing suffrage for naturalized citizens (see table, page 381).

Republicans, Know-Nothings, and Democrats were all scrambling to attract former Whig voters. The demise of that party ensured a major realignment of the political system, with nearly half of the old electorate up for grabs. To woo these homeless Whigs, the remaining parties made appeals to various segments of the electorate. Immigration, temperance, homestead bills, the tariff, internal improvements—all played important roles in attracting voters during the 1850s.

Realignment of the Political System

The Republicans appealed strongly to those interested in the economic development of the West. Commercial agriculture was booming in the Ohio–Mississippi–Great Lakes area, but residents of that region desired more canals, roads, and river and harbor improvements to reap the full benefit of their labors. Because credit was scarce, there was also widespread interest in a homestead program: its pro-

Republican Appeals

ponents argued that western land should be made available free to those who would farm it. The Whigs had favored all these measures before their party collapsed, but the Democrats resolutely opposed them throughout the 1850s. Seizing their opportunity, the Republicans added internal improvements and land-grant planks to their platform. They also backed higher tariffs as an enticement to industrialists and businessmen, whose interest in tariffs grew after a financial panic in 1857.

Partisan ideological appeals, which had a significant impact on the sectional crisis, were another major feature of the realigned political system. In the North, Republicans attracted many voters through effective use of ideology. When they preached "Free Soil, Free Labor, Free Men," they captured an image that northerners had of themselves and their future. These phrases resonated with traditional ideals of equality, liberty, and opportunity under self-government—the heritage of republicanism. Use of that heritage also undercut charges that the Republican Party was radical and unreliable.

"Free Soil, Free Labor, Free Men" seemed an appropriate motto for a northern economy that was energetic, expanding, and prosperous. Thousands of farmers had moved west to establish productive farms and growing communities. Midwesterners were using new machines, such as disk harrows and mechanical reapers, which multiplied their yields. Railroads were carrying their crops to urban markets. And industry was beginning to perform wonders of production, making available goods that had been beyond the reach of the average person. As northerners surveyed the general growth and prosperity, they thought they saw a reason for it.

The key to progress appeared, to many people, to be free labor. People believed in the dignity of labor and the incentive of opportunity. Any hard-working and virtuous man, it was thought, could improve his condition and achieve economic independence by seizing opportunities that the country had to offer. Republicans argued that the South, which relied on slave labor and had little industry, was backward and retrograde by comparison, and their arguments captured much of the spirit of the age in the North.

Republican Ideology

Traditional republicanism hailed the virtuous common man as the backbone of the country. In Abraham Lincoln, a man of humble origins who had become a successful lawyer and political leader, Republicans had a symbol of that tradition. They portrayed their party as the guardian of economic opportunity, giving individuals a chance to work, acquire land, and attain success. In the words of an Iowa Republican, the United States was thriving because its "door is thrown open to all, and even the poorest and humblest in the land, may, by industry and application, gain a position which will entitle him to the respect and confidence of his fellow-men."

The Republican Party thus attracted support from a variety of sources. Opposition to the extension of slavery had brought the party into being, but party members carefully broadened their appeal by adopting the causes of other groups. They were wise to do so. As the New York newspaper editor Horace Greeley wrote in 1856, "It is beaten into my bones that the American people are not yet anti-slavery." Four years later, Greeley again observed that "an Anti-Slavery man *per se* cannot be elected." But, he added, "a Tariff, River-and-Harbor, Pacific Railroad, Free Homestead man, *may* succeed *although* he is Anti-Slavery." As these elements joined the Republican Party, they also learned more about the dangers of slavery. Thus the process of party building deepened the sectional conflict.

A similar process was under way in the South. The disintegration of the Whig Party had left many southerners at loose ends politically; they included a good number of wealthy planters, smaller slaveholders, and urban businessmen. Some gravitated to the American Party, but not for long. In the increasingly tense atmosphere of sectional crisis, these people were highly susceptible to strong states' rights positions and defense of slavery. Democratic leaders emphasized such appeals during the 1850s and managed to convert most of the formerly Whig slaveholders, who responded to their class interests.

Southern Democrats

Most Democrats south of the Mason-Dixon line, however, were not slaveholders. Since Andrew Jackson's day, small farmers had been the heart of the Democratic Party. Democratic politicians, though often slaveowners themselves, lauded the common man and argued that their policies advanced his interests. According to the southern version of republicanism, white citizens in a slave society enjoyed liberty and social equality *because* black people were enslaved. Slavery supposedly prevented the evil of aristocracy by making all white men

equal. As Jefferson Davis put it in 1851, in other societies distinctions were drawn "by property, between the rich and the poor." But in the South, slavery elevated every white person's status and allowed the nonslaveholder to "*stand upon the broad level of equality with the rich man.*" To retain the support of ordinary whites, southern Democrats emphasized this appeal to racism. The issue in the sectional crisis, they warned, was "shall negroes govern white men, or white men govern negroes?"

Southern leaders also portrayed sectional controversies as matters of injustice and insult to the South. The rights of all southern whites were in jeopardy, they argued, because antislavery and Free-Soil forces were attacking an institution protected in the Constitution. The stable, well-ordered South was the true defender of constitutional principles; the rapidly changing North did not respect constitutional principles.

Those arguments had their effect. Racial fears and traditional political loyalties helped keep the political alliance between yeoman farmers and planters intact through the 1850s. Potential conflicts of interest between slaveholders and nonslaveholders were not discussed, and no viable party emerged to replace the Whigs. The result was a one-party system that emphasized sectional issues. In the South as in the North, political realignment sharpened sectional divisions.

Political leaders of both sections argued that racial change threatened opportunity, but northerners and southerners saw different futures. The *Montgomery* (Alabama) *Mail* warned southern whites in 1860 that the Republicans intended "to free the negroes and force amalgamation between them and the children of the poor men of the South. The rich will be able to keep out of the way of the contamination." Republicans warned northern workers that if slavery entered the territories, the great reservoir of opportunity for ordinary citizens would be poisoned. Republicans claimed that free labor had to be extended to the territories if coming generations were to prosper.

In the territory of Kansas a succession of events, like hammer blows, deepened the conflict. The Kansas-Nebraska Act spawned hatred and violence as land-hungry claim jumpers and partisans in the sectional struggle clashed repeatedly in Kansas Territory. Abolitionists and religious groups sent in armed Free-Soil settlers; southerners sent in their reinforcements to establish slavery and prevent "northern hordes" from stealing Kansas away. Conflicts led

The Border Ruffians, depicted in this pen-and-ink drawing, were proslavery Missourians who periodically invaded Kansas to vote and help establish slavery there. Conflicts over land claims further complicated the violence in Bleeding Kansas. Yale University Art Gallery, Mabel Brady Garvan Collection.

to bloodshed, and soon the whole nation was talking about "Bleeding Kansas."

Politics in the territory resembled war more than democracy. During elections for a territorial legislature in 1855, thousands of proslavery Missourians—known as Border Ruffians—invaded the polls and ran up a large but fraudulent majority for slavery candidates. The resulting legislature legalized slavery, and in response Free-Soilers held an unauthorized convention at which they created their own government and constitution. A proslavery posse sent to arrest the Free-Soil leaders sacked the town of Lawrence. In revenge John Brown, an antislavery zealot who saw himself as God's instrument to destroy slavery, murdered five proslavery settlers. Soon, armed bands of guerrillas roamed the state, battling over land claims as well as slavery.

Bleeding Kansas

These passions brought violence to the United States Senate in May 1856, when Charles Sumner of Massachusetts denounced "the Crime against Kansas." Radical in his antislavery views, Sumner bitterly assailed the president, the South, and Senator Andrew P. Butler of South Carolina. Soon thereafter Butler's cousin, Representative Preston Brooks, approached Sumner at the latter's Senate desk, raised his cane, and began to beat Sumner on the head. Trapped behind his desk, which was bolted in place, Sumner tried to rise, eventually wrenching the desk free before he collapsed, bleeding, on the floor. Shocked northerners recoiled from what they saw as another southern assault on free speech and the South's readiness to use violence to have its way. William Cullen Bryant, editor of the *New York Evening Post*, asked, "Has it come to this, that we must speak with bated breath in the presence of our southern masters?" As if in reply, the *Richmond En-*

quirer denounced "vulgar Abolitionists in the Senate" who "have been suffered to run too long without collars. They must be lashed into submission." Popular opinion in Massachusetts strongly supported Sumner; South Carolina voters reelected Brooks and sent him dozens of new canes. The country was becoming polarized.

The election of 1856 showed how extreme that polarization had become. When Democrats met to select a nominee, they shied away from prominent leaders whose views on the territories were well known. Instead, they chose James Buchanan of Pennsylvania, whose chief virtue was that for the past four years he had been ambassador to Britain, uninvolved in territorial controversies. This anonymity and superior party organization helped Buchanan win 1.8 million votes and the election, but he owed his victory to southern support. Eleven of sixteen free states voted against him, and Democrats did not regain ascendancy in those states for decades. The Republican candidate, John C. Frémont, won those eleven free states and 1.3 million votes; Republicans had become the dominant party in the North. The Know-Nothing candidate, Millard Fillmore, won almost 1 million votes, but this election was to be his party's last hurrah. The coming battle would be between a sectional Republican Party and an increasingly divided Democratic Party.

The earliest known photograph of John Brown, probably taken in 1846 in Massachusetts, shows him pledging his devotion to an unidentified flag, possibly an abolitionist banner. Already Brown was aiding runaway slaves and pondering ways to strike at slavery. Ohio Historical Society.

Slavery and the Nation's Future

For years the issue of slavery in the territories had convulsed Congress, and for years Congress had tried to settle the issue with vague formulas. In 1857 a different branch of government stepped onto the scene. The Supreme Court took up this emotionally charged subject and attempted to silence controversy with a definitive verdict.

A Missouri slave named Dred Scott had sued his owner for his freedom. Scott based his claim on the fact that his former owner, an army surgeon, had taken him for several years into Illinois, a free state, and into the Wisconsin Territory, from which slavery had been barred by the Missouri Compromise. Scott first won and then lost his case as it moved on appeal through the state courts, into the federal system, and finally after eleven years to the Supreme Court.

Dred Scott **Case**

Normally Supreme Court justices were reluctant to inject themselves into political issues, and it seemed likely that the Court would stay out of this one. An 1851 decision had declared that state courts determined the status of Negroes who lived within their jurisdiction. The Supreme Court had only to follow this precedent to avoid ruling on substantive, and very controversial, issues: Was a black person like Dred Scott a citizen of the United States and thus eligible to sue in federal court? Had residence in a free state or free territory made him free? Did Congress have the power to prohibit slavery in a territory or to delegate that power to a territorial legislature?

Initially the Supreme Court seemed ready to dispose of *Dred Scott* v. *Sandford* by following the 1851 precedent. The chief justice even assigned one justice the task of writing such an opinion. Then, for a number of reasons, the Court decided to rule on the Missouri Compromise after all. Two northern justices indicated that they would dissent from the assigned

Dred Scott, a slave who brought suit in Missouri for his freedom, and Chief Justice Roger Taney, a descendant of Maryland's slave-holding elite, were principal figures in the most controversial Supreme Court decision of the nineteenth century. Dred Scott: Missouri Historical Society; Roger Taney: Maryland Historical Society.

opinion and argue for Scott's freedom and the constitutionality of the Missouri Compromise. Their decision emboldened southerners on the Court, who were growing eager to declare the 1820 compromise unconstitutional. Southern sympathizers in Washington were pressing for a proslavery verdict, and several justices simply felt they should try to resolve an issue whose uncertainties had caused so much strife.

In March 1857, Chief Justice Roger B. Taney of Maryland delivered the majority opinion of a divided Court. Taney declared that Scott was not a citizen of either the United States or Missouri; that residence in free territory did not make Scott free; and that Congress had no power to bar slavery from a territory, as it had done in the Missouri Compromise. The decision not only overturned a sectional compromise that had been honored for years; it also invalidated the basic ideas of the Wilmot Proviso and probably popular sovereignty as well.

The Slave Power seemed to have won a major constitutional victory. African-Americans were espe-

cially dismayed, for Taney's decision asserted that the founders had never intended for black people to be citizens. At the nation's founding, the chief justice wrote, blacks had been regarded "as beings of an inferior order" with "no rights which the white man was bound to respect." Taney was mistaken, however. African-Americans had been citizens in several of the original states. Nevertheless, the *Dred Scott* decision seemed to shut the door permanently on their hopes for justice and equal rights.

Northern whites who rejected the decision's content were suspicious of the circumstances that produced it. Five of the nine justices were southerners; three of the northern justices actively dissented or refused to concur in crucial parts of the decision. The only northerner who supported Taney's opinion, Justice Robert Grier of Pennsylvania, was known to be close to President Buchanan. In fact, Buchanan had secretly brought to bear improper but effective influence.

A storm of angry reaction broke in the North. The decision alarmed a wide variety of northerners

How do historians know what motivated Abraham Lincoln to oppose the extension of slavery? Lincoln, of course, was a public man who made many addresses and public statements. His words as a politician and leader of the Republican Party show his reverence for the Declaration of Independence and America's heritage of freedom. But Lincoln also produced many private writings. The page reproduced below comes from a notebook in which he recorded his reactions to a proslavery book, *Slavery Ordained of God, by Rev. Fred A. Ross.* Criticizing Ross, Lincoln revealed his dislike of privilege and exposed the self-interest of those who would exploit others: "Dr. Ross sits in the shade, with gloves on his hands, and subsists on the bread that Sambo is earning in the burning sun" rather than "delv[ing] for his own bread." Illinois State Historical Society and Library.

and seemed to confirm every charge against the aggressive Slave Power. "There is such a thing as the slave power," warned the *Cincinnati Daily Commercial.* "It has marched over and annihilated the boundaries of the states. We are now one great homogenous slaveholding community." The *Cincinnati Freeman* asked, "What security have the Germans and the Irish that their children will not, within a hundred years, be reduced to slavery in this land of their adoption?" "Where will it end?" asked the *Atlantic Monthly.* "Is the success of this conspiracy to be final and eternal?" The poet James Russell

Lowell expressed the anxieties of poor northern whites when he had his Yankee character Ezekiel Biglow say:

> Wy, it's just ez clear ez figgers,
>   Clear ez one an' one make two,
> Chaps thet make black slaves o' niggers,
>   Want to make wite slaves o' you.

Republican politicians used these fears to strengthen their coalition of abolitionists and other northerners, including racists who feared that slavery jeopardized their interests.

Abraham Lincoln on the Slave Power

Abraham Lincoln stressed that the territorial question affected every citizen. "The whole nation," he declared as early as 1854, "is interested that the best use shall be made of these Territories. We want them for homes of free white people. This they cannot be, to any considerable extent, if slavery shall be planted within them." The territories must be reserved, he insisted, "as an outlet for *free white people everywhere*" so that immigrants could come to America and "find new homes and better their condition in life."

More importantly, Lincoln warned of slavery's increasing control over the nation. The founders had created a government dedicated to freedom, Lincoln insisted. Admittedly they had recognized slavery's existence, but "this Government has endured eighty-two years because," he argued in 1858, "during all that time, until the introduction of the Nebraska Bill, the public mind did rest . . . in the belief that slavery was in course of ultimate extinction." After the *Dred Scott* decision, he charged, it was clear that slavery's advocates, including highly placed government officials, were trying to "push it forward, till it shall become lawful in *all* the states . . . *North* as well as *South*."

The next step in the unfolding Slave Power conspiracy, Lincoln alleged, would be a Supreme Court decision "declaring that the Constitution does not permit a State to exclude slavery from its limits. . . . We shall lie down pleasantly, dreaming that the people of Missouri are on the verge of making their State free; and we shall awake to the reality instead, that the Supreme Court has made Illinois a slave State." This charge was not pure hyperbole, for lawsuits soon challenged state laws that freed slaves brought within their borders.

Lincoln's most eloquent statement against the Slave Power was his famous "House Divided" speech, in which he declared:

> I do not expect the Union to be dissolved—I do not expect the House to fall—but I do expect it to cease to be divided. It will become all one thing or all the other. Either the opponents of slavery will arrest the further spread of it, and place it where the public mind shall rest in the belief that it is in the course of ultimate extinction; or its advocates will push it forward, till it shall become alike lawful in all the States, old as well as new, North as well as South.

Lincoln warned repeatedly that the latter possibility was real, and events convinced countless northerners that slaveholders were nearing their goal of making slavery a national institution.

Politically, these forceful Republican arguments offset the difficulties that the *Dred Scott* decision posed. By endorsing Calhoun's theories, the Court had in effect declared that the central position of the Republican Party—no extension of slavery—was unconstitutional. Republicans could only repudiate the decision, appealing to a "higher law," or hope to change the personnel of the Court. They did both and probably gained politically as fear of the Slave Power grew.

For northern Democrats like Stephen Douglas, the Court's decision posed an awful dilemma. Northern voters were alarmed by the prospect that the territories would be opened to slavery. To retain their support, Douglas had to find some way to reassure them. Yet, given his ambitions to lead the national Democratic Party and become president, Douglas could not afford to alienate southern Democrats. His task was problematic at best; given the emotions of the era, it proved impossible.

Douglas chose to stand by his principle of popular sovereignty, even if the result angered southerners. In 1857 Kansans voted on a proslavery constitution that had been drafted at Lecompton. It was defeated by more than ten thousand votes. The evidence was overwhelming that Kansans did not want slavery, yet President Buchanan tried to force the Lecompton Constitution through Congress.

Never had the Slave Power's influence over the government seemed more blatant; the Buchanan administration and southerners were demanding a proslavery outcome, contrary to the desires of the majority in Kansas. Breaking with the administration, Douglas threw his weight against the Lecompton Constitution. He gauged opinion in Kansas correctly, for in 1858 voters there rejected the constitution again. But his action infuriated southern

Democrats. After the *Dred Scott* decision, southerners like Senator Albert G. Brown of Mississippi believed that slavery was *protected* in the territories: "The Constitution as expounded by the Supreme Court awards it. We demand it; we mean to have it."

Douglas further alienated the southern wing of his party in his well-publicized debates with Abraham Lincoln, who challenged him for the Illinois Senate seat in 1858. Speaking at Freeport, Illinois, Douglas attempted to revive the concept of popular sovereignty with some tortured arguments. Asserting that the Supreme Court had ruled only on the powers of Congress, not on the powers of a *territorial* legislature, Douglas claimed that the latter could bar slavery either by passing a law against it or by doing nothing. Without the patrol laws and police regulations that supported slavery, he reasoned, the institution could not exist. This argument, called the Freeport Doctrine, temporarily shored up Douglas's crumbling position in the North. But it gave southern Democrats further evidence that Douglas was unreliable, and many turned viciously against him. Some, like Representative William L. Yancey of Alabama, studied the trend in northern opinion and concluded that southern rights and slavery would be safe only in a separate nation.

Stephen Douglas Proposes the Freeport Doctrine

Such feelings were not new. As early as 1838, the Louisiana planter Bennet Barrow had written in his diary, "Northern States meddling with slavery . . . openly speaking of the sin of Slavery in the southern states . . . must eventually cause a separation of the Union." In 1856, a calmer, more polished Georgian named Charles Colcock Jones, Jr., rejoiced at James Buchanan's defeat of Republican John C. Frémont for the presidency. The result guaranteed four more years of peace and prosperity, wrote Jones, but "beyond that period . . . we scarce dare expect a continuance of our present relations." Increasingly, slaveowners agreed with Jones and Barrow.

The immediate consequence for politics, however, was the likelihood of a split in the Democratic Party. Northern Democrats could not support the territorial protection for slavery that southern Democrats insisted was theirs as a constitutional right. Thus the issue of slavery in the territories continued to generate wider conflict, even though it had little immediate, practical significance. In territories outside Kansas the number of settlers was small, and in all territories the number of African-Americans was negligible—less than 1 percent of the populations of Kansas and New Mexico. By 1858 even Jefferson Davis had abandoned hopes of agricultural development in the Southwest and admitted that slavery might not succeed in Kansas. Nevertheless, men like Davis and Douglas spent many hours in bitter, alarming debate. The situation had become explosive.

Breakup of the Union

One year before the 1860 presidential election, John Brown, who had slain proslavery settlers in Kansas, led a small band of whites and blacks in an attack on the federal arsenal at Harpers Ferry, Virginia. Hoping to trigger a slave rebellion, Brown failed miserably and was quickly captured, tried, and executed. Yet his attempted insurrection struck fear into the South. Then it became known that Brown had received financial backing from several prominent abolitionists. When northern intellectuals such as Emerson and Thoreau praised Brown as a hero and a martyr, white southerners' fears and anger multiplied many times over.

Many believed that the election of 1860 would decide the fate of the Union. Only the Democratic Party remained as an organization that was truly national in scope. Even religious denominations had split into northern and southern wings during the 1840s and 1850s. "One after another," wrote a Mississippi newspaper editor, "the links which have bound the North and South together, have been severed . . . [but] the Democratic party looms gradually up, its nationality intact, and waves the olive branch over the troubled waters of politics." At its 1860 convention, however, the Democratic Party broke in two.

Stephen A. Douglas wanted his party's presidential nomination, but he could not afford to alienate northern voters by accepting the southern position on the territories. Southern Democrats like William L. Yancey, however, insisted on recognition of their rights—as Chief Justice Roger Taney had defined them—and they moved to block Douglas's nomination.

Splintering of the Democratic Party

When Douglas obtained a majority for his version of the platform, delegates from the five Gulf states plus

THE NATIONAL GAME. THREE "OUTS" AND ONE "RUN".
ABRAHAM WINNING THE BALL.

The 1860 presidential campaign, like great political contests today, rapidly entered popular culture. This cartoon by Currier and Ives was one of the first to apply the terminology of baseball to that other national game: politics. From left to right, the presidential candidates are Breckinridge, Douglas, Bell, and the victorious Lincoln. Museum of American Political Life, University of Hartford.

South Carolina, Georgia, and Arkansas walked out of the party convention in Charleston. After efforts at compromise failed, the Democrats presented two nominees: Douglas for the northern wing, and Vice President John C. Breckinridge of Kentucky for the southern. The Republicans nominated Abraham Lincoln. A Constitutional Union Party, formed to preserve the nation but strong only in the Upper South, nominated John Bell of Tennessee.

Three of the candidates stressed their support for the Union in the ensuing campaign. Bell's only issue was the urgency of preserving the Union, and Douglas desperately wanted to hold his northern and southern supporters together. Even Breckinridge quickly backed away from the appearance of extremism, and his supporters in several states declared that he was not a threat to the Union. Then the *New Orleans Bee* charged that every disunionist in the land applauded Breckinridge, and a Texas paper challenged his association with radicals: "Mr. Breckinridge claims that he isn't a disunionist. An animal not willing to pass for a pig shouldn't stay in the stye." Reacting to such criticism, Breckinridge reversed his decision to give no speeches and delivered one address in which he flatly denied that his aim was secession. Thereafter his supporters stressed his loyalty and even ridiculed the possibility of secession in case of a Republican victory. Although Lincoln and the Republicans denied any intent to interfere with slavery in the states where it existed, they stood firm against the extension of slavery into the territories.

The results of the balloting were sectional in character. Lincoln won, but Douglas, Breckinridge, and Bell together received most of the votes (see cartoon, page 396). Douglas had broad-based support but won few states. Breckinridge, whose strength was concentrated in the Deep South, carried nine southern states. Bell won pluralities in Virginia, Kentucky, and Tennessee. Lincoln prevailed in the North, but in the states that ultimately remained loyal to the Union he gained only a plurality, not a majority (see table). Lincoln's victory was won in the electoral college.

Election of 1860

Given the heterogeneous nature of Republican voters, it is likely that many of them did not view the issue of slavery in the territories as paramount. But opposition to slavery's extension was the core issue of the Republican Party, and Lincoln's alarm over slavery's growing political power was genuine. Moreover, abolitionists and supporters of free soil in the North worked to keep the Republicans from compromising on their territorial stand. Meanwhile in the South, proslavery advocates and secessionists whipped up public opinion and demanded that state conventions assemble to consider secession.

Lincoln made the crucial decision not to soften his party's position on the territories. He wrote of the necessity of maintaining the bond of faith between voter and candidate and of declining to set "the minority over the majority." But Lincoln's party had not won a majority of votes. His refusal to compromise probably derived both from conviction and from concern for the unity of the Republican Party. Although many conservative Republicans—eastern businessmen and former Whigs who did not feel strongly about slavery—hoped for a compromise, the original and most committed Republicans—antislavery voters and "conscience Whigs"—were adamant for free soil. Lincoln chose to preserve party unity by standing firm against slavery's extension.

Southern leaders in the Senate were willing, conditionally, to accept a compromise drawn up by Senator John J. Crittenden of Kentucky. Hoping to don the mantle of Henry Clay and avert disunion, Crittenden proposed that the two sections divide the territories between them at latitude 36°30'. But the southerners would agree to this *only* if the Republicans did, too, for they wanted no less and knew that extremists in the South would demand much more. When Lincoln ruled out concessions on the territorial issue, Crittenden's peacemaking effort

Presidential Vote in 1860

	Lincoln	Other Candidates
Entire United States	1,866,452	2,815,617
North plus border and southern states that rejected secession prior to war[1]	1,866,452	2,421,752
North plus border states that fought for the Union[2]	1,864,523	1,960,842

Source: From David Potter, *Lincoln and His Party in the Secession Crisis.* Copyright 1942, 1967 by Yale University Press. Reprinted by permission.

[1]Kentucky, Missouri, Maryland, Delaware, Virginia, North Carolina, Tennessee, Arkansas

[2]Kentucky, Missouri, Maryland, Delaware

collapsed. Virginians called for a special convention in Washington, to which several states sent representatives. But this gathering, too, failed to find a solution.

Though political leaders in North and South had communicated clearly with each other about the Crittenden proposal, misjudgment also played a role in the coming of war. As the historian David Potter has shown, Lincoln and other prominent Republicans believed that southerners were bluffing when they threatened secession; Republicans expected a pro-Union majority in the South to assert itself. Therefore Lincoln determined not to yield to threats but to call the southerners' bluff. On their side, southern leaders had become convinced, more accurately, that northern leaders were not taking them seriously and that a posture of strength was necessary to win respect for their demands. "To rally the men of the North, who would preserve the government as our fathers found it, we . . . should offer no doubtful or divided front," wrote Jefferson Davis. With such attitudes shaping leaders' actions, confrontation was more likely than compromise.

Meanwhile, the Union was being destroyed. On December 20, 1860, South Carolina passed an ordinance of secession amid jubilation and cheering.

On February 18, 1861, in Montgomery, Alabama, Jefferson Davis took an oath as president of the Confederate States of America. Davis later recalled that he foresaw "troubles innumerable" but was committed to seek independence as his paramount goal.   Boston Athenaeum.

Secession of South Carolina

This step marked the inauguration of a strategy favored by secessionists: separate-state secession. Recognizing the difficulty of persuading all the southern states to challenge the federal government simultaneously, secessionists concentrated their efforts on the most extreme proslavery state. They hoped South Carolina's secession would induce other states to follow, with each decision building momentum for disunion.

The strategy proved effective. By reclaiming its independence, South Carolina raised the stakes in the sectional confrontation. No longer was secession an unthinkable step; the Union was broken. Extremists now argued that other states should secede to support South Carolina and that those who favored

compromise could make a better deal outside the Union than in it. Moderates found it difficult to dismiss such arguments, since most of them—even those who felt deep affection for the Union—were committed to defending southern rights and the southern way of life.

Southern extremists soon got their way in the Deep South. Overwhelming their opposition, they called separate state conventions and passed secession ordinances in Mississippi, Florida, Alabama, Georgia, Louisiana, and Texas. By February 1861 these states had joined South Carolina to form a new government in Montgomery, Alabama: the Confederate States of America. The delegates at Montgomery chose Jefferson Davis as their president, and the Confederacy began to function independently of the United States.

Confederate States of America

This apparent unanimity of action was deceiving. Confused and dissatisfied with the alternatives, many southerners who in 1860 had voted in the United States presidential election stayed home a few months later rather than vote for delegates who would decide on secession. Even so, in some state conventions the vote to secede was close, with secession decided by overrepresentation of plantation districts. Furthermore, the conventions were noticeably unwilling to let voters ratify their acts. Four states in the Upper South—Virginia, North Carolina, Tennessee, and Arkansas—flatly rejected secession and did not join the Confederacy until after fighting had begun. In the border states, popular sentiment was deeply divided; minorities in Kentucky and Missouri tried to secede, but these slave states ultimately came under Union control, along with Maryland and Delaware (see map, page 399).

Such misgivings were not surprising. Secession posed new and troubling issues for southerners, especially the possibility of war and the question of who would die. Analysis of election returns from 1860 and 1861 indicates that slaveholders and nonslaveholders were beginning to part company politically. Heavily slaveholding counties strongly supported secession. But nonslaveholding areas that had favored Breckinridge in the United States presidential election proved far less willing to support secession: most counties with few slaves took an antisecession position or were staunchly Unionist (see figure, page 400). Large numbers of yeomen also sat out the election. With war on the horizon, nonslave-

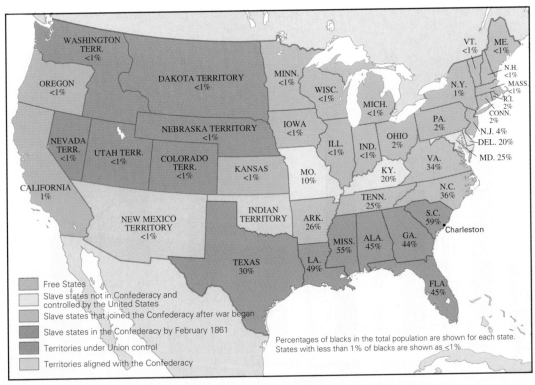

The Divided Nation—Slave and Free Areas, 1861 *After fighting began, the Upper South joined the Deep South in the Confederacy. How does the nation's pattern of division correspond to the distribution of slavery and the percentage of blacks in the population?*

holders were beginning to consider their class interests and to ask how far they would go to support slavery and slaveowners.

Some opponents of secession was fervently pro-Union. After Alabama's convention approved secession, one delegate wrote: "Here I set & from my window see the nasty little thing flaunting in the breeze which has taken the place of that glorious banner which has been the pride of millions of Americans and the boast of freemen the wide world over." Although such sentiments presented problems for the Confederacy, they were not sufficiently developed to prevent secession.

The dilemma facing President Lincoln on inauguration day in March 1861 was how to maintain the authority of the federal government without provoking war. Proceeding cautiously, he sought only to hold on to forts in the states that had left the Union, reasoning that in this way he could assert federal sovereignty while waiting for a restoration of rela-

Attack on Fort Sumter

tions. But Jefferson Davis, who could not claim to lead a sovereign nation if the Confederate ports were under foreign (that is, United States) control, was unwilling to be so patient. A collision was inevitable.

It arrived in the early morning hours of April 12, 1861, at Fort Sumter in Charleston harbor. A federal garrison there ran low on food, and Lincoln notified the South Carolinians that he was sending a ship to resupply the fort. For the Montgomery government, the alternatives were to attack the fort or to acquiesce to Lincoln's authority. After the Confederate cabinet met, the Secretary of War ordered local commanders to obtain a surrender or attack the fort. After two days of heavy bombardment, the federal garrison finally surrendered. No one died in battle, though an accident during postbattle ceremonies killed one Union soldier. Confederates permitted the United States troops to sail away on unarmed vessels while Charlestonians celebrated wildly. The Civil War—the bloodiest war in America's history—had begun.

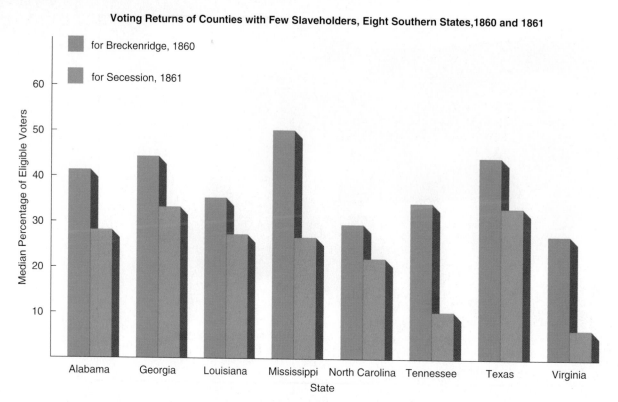

Voting Returns of Counties with Few Slaveholders, Eight Southern States,1860 and 1861

Voting Returns of Counties with Few Slaveholders, Eight Southern States, 1860 and 1861 *This graph depicts voting in counties whose percentage of slaveholders ranked them among the lower half of the counties in their state. How does voters' support for secession in 1861 compare with support for John Breckinridge, the southern Democratic candidate in 1860? Why was their support for secession so weak? At this time counties with many slaveholders were giving increased support to secession.*

Conclusion

Throughout the 1840s and 1850s many able leaders had worked diligently to avert this outcome. Most people, North and South, had hoped to keep the nation together. As late as 1858 even Jefferson Davis had declared, "This great country will continue united," saying that "to the innermost fibers of my heart I love it all, and every part." Secession dismayed northern editors and voters, and it also plunged some planters into depression. Paul Cameron, the largest slave-owner in North Carolina, confessed that he was "very unhappy. I love the Union." Why, then, had war broken out? Why had all efforts to prevent it failed?

Slavery was an issue on which compromise was impossible. The conflict it generated was fundamental and beyond adjustment. The emotions bound up in attacking and defending it were too powerful, and the motives it affected too vital, for compromise. Because it was deeply entwined with major policy questions of the present and the foreseeable future, each

section ultimately regarded slavery as too important to be put aside.

Even if one excludes extreme views, North and South had fundamentally different attitudes toward the institution. The logic of Republican ideology tended in the direction of abolishing slavery, even though Republicans denied any such intention. The logic of southern leaders' arguments led toward establishing slavery everywhere, though southern leaders denied that they sought to do any such thing. Lincoln put these facts succinctly. In a postelection letter to his old friend Alexander Stephens of Georgia, Lincoln offered assurance that Republicans would not attack slavery in the states where it existed. But Lincoln continued, "You think slavery is *right* and ought to be expanded; while we think it is *wrong* and ought to be restricted. That I suppose is the rub."

Fundamental disagreements have not always led to war. A nation may face unresolvable issues yet manage to get past them. New events can capture people's attention; time can alter interests and attitudes, if in the intervening years conflict is contained or restricted. That is precisely what the advocates of compromise sought to achieve. They tried to contain conflict and buy time for the nation, to avoid issues that could not be settled, and to preserve the many areas of consensus among Americans. Their efforts were well intentioned and patriotic but doomed to failure.

The issue of slavery in the territories made conflict impossible to avoid. Territorial expansion generated disputes so frequently that the nation never enjoyed a breathing space. As the conflict recurred, its influence on policy and effect on the government deepened. Every southern victory increased fear of the Slave Power, and each new expression of Free-Soil sentiment made alarmed slaveholders more insistent in their demands. Eventually even those opposed to war could see no way to avoid it.

In the profoundest sense, slavery was tied up with the war. Concern over slavery had driven all the other conflicts. But as the fighting began, this, the war's central issue, was shrouded in confusion. How would the Civil War affect slavery, its place in the law, and African-Americans' place in society? The answers to those questions, and the degree to which answers were sought, would be of fateful import.

Suggestions for Further Reading

Politics: General

Thomas B. Alexander, *Sectional Stress and Party Strength* (1967); Tyler Anbinder, *Nativism and Slavery* (1992); Maurice G. Baxter, *One and Inseparable: Daniel Webster and the Union* (1984); Paul Bergeron, *The Presidency of James K. Polk* (1987); Ray Allen Billington, *The Protestant Crusade, 1800–1860* (1938 and 1964); Frederick J. Blue, *The Free Soilers: Third Party Politics, 1848–1854* (1973); Stanley W. Campbell, *The Slave Catchers* (1968); Don E. Fehrenbacher, *The Dred Scott Case* (1978); George M. Fredrickson, *The Black Image in the White Mind* (1971); Holman Hamilton, *Prologue to Conflict: The Crisis and Compromise of 1850* (1964); Michael F. Holt, *Political Parties and American Political Development* (1992); Michael F. Holt, *The Political Crisis of the 1850s* (1978); Stephen E. Maizlish and John J. Kushma, eds., *Essays on American Antebellum Politics, 1840–1860* (1982); William Lee Miller, *Arguing About Slavery* (1996); Chaplain W. Morrison, *Democratic Politics and Sectionalism: The Wilmot Proviso Controversy* (1967); Paul D. Nagle, *One Nation Indivisible* (1964); Russell B. Nye, *Fettered Freedom* (1949); Merrill D. Peterson, *The Great Triumvirate: Webster, Clay, and Calhoun* (1987); David M. Potter, *The Impending Crisis, 1848–1861* (1976); James A. Rawley, *Race and Politics* (1969); Joel H. Silbey, *The Transformation of American Politics, 1840–1960* (1967); Elbert B. Smith, *The Presidency of James Buchanan* (1975); Kenneth M. Stampp, *America in 1857*
(1991); Kenneth M. Stampp, *And the War Came* (1950); Gerald W. Wolff, *The Kansas-Nebraska Bill* (1977).

The South and Slavery

William L. Barney, *The Secessionist Impulse* (1974); Steven A. Channing, *A Crisis of Fear: Secession in South Carolina* (1970); William J. Cooper, Jr., *The South and the Politics of Slavery, 1828–1856* (1978); Avery O. Craven, *The Growth of Southern Nationalism, 1848–1861* (1953); Daniel W. Crofts, *Reluctant Confederates: Upper South Unionists in the Secession Crisis* (1989); Merton L. Dillon, *Slavery Attacked* (1991); Drew G. Faust, *The Ideology of Slavery* (1981); Drew G. Faust, *A Sacred Circle: The Dilemma of the Intellectual in the Old South* (1978); Lacy K. Ford, Jr., *Origins of Southern Radicalism* (1988); William W. Freehling, *The Road to Disunion* (1990); Eugene D. Genovese, *The World the Slaveholders Made* (1969); Eugene D. Genovese, *The Political Economy of Slavery* (1967); Michael P. Johnson, *Toward a Patriarchal Republic: The Secession of Georgia* (1977); John Niven, *John C. Calhoun and the Price of Union* (1988); David M. Potter, *The South and the Sectional Conflict* (1968); Thomas E. Schott, *Alexander H. Stephens of Georgia* (1988); William R. Stanton, *The Leopard's Spots* (1960); J. Mills Thornton III, *Politics and Power in a Slave Society* (1978); Larry E. Tise, *Proslavery* (1987); Ralph Wooster, *The Secession Conventions of the South* (1962).

The North and Antislavery

Dale Baum, *The Civil War Party System* (1984); Eugene H. Berwanger, *The Frontier Against Slavery* (1967); Frederick J. Blue, *Salmon P. Chase* (1987); David Donald, *Charles Sumner and the Coming of the Civil War* (1960); Louis Filler, *The Crusade Against Slavery, 1830–1860* (1960); Eric Foner, *Free Soil, Free Labor, Free Men* (1970); Louis S. Gerteis, *Morality and Utility in American Antislavery Reform* (1987); William E. Gienapp, *The Origins of the Republican Party, 1852–1856* (1986); Henry V. Jaffa, *Crisis of the House Divided* (1959); Robert W. Johannsen, *Lincoln, the South, and Slavery* (1991); Robert W. Johannsen, *Stephen A. Douglas* (1973); Aileen S. Kraditor, *Means and Ends in American Abolitionism* (1969); Stephen B. Oates, *To Purge This Land with Blood*, 2d ed. (1984); Lewis Perry and Michael Fellman, eds., *Antislavery Reconsidered* (1979); Jeffrey Rossbach, *Ambivalent Conspirators* (1982); Richard Sewell, *Ballots for Freedom: Antislavery Politics in the United States, 1837–1860* (1976); Alice Felt Tyler, *Freedom's Ferment* (1944).

The Mexican War and Foreign Policy

K. Jack Bauer, *Zachary Taylor* (1985); Gene M. Brack, *Mexico Views Manifest Destiny, 1821–1846* (1976); Richard Griswold del Castillo, *The Treaty of Guadalupe Hidalgo* (1990); Neal Harlow, *California Conquered* (1982); Reginald Horsman, *Race and Manifest Destiny* (1981); Robert W. Johannsen, *To the Halls of the Montezumas: The Mexican War and the American Imagination* (1985); Ernest M. Lander, Jr., *Reluctant Imperialists: Calhoun, the South Carolinians, and the Mexican War* (1980); Robert E. May, *The Southern Dream of a Caribbean Empire, 1854–1861* (1973); Frederick Merk, *The Monroe Doctrine and American Expansion, 1843–1849* (1966); Frederick Merk, *Manifest Destiny and Mission in American History* (1963); David M. Pletcher, *The Diplomacy of Annexation: Texas, Oregon, and the Mexican War* (1973); Dirk Raat, *Mexico and the United States* (1992); John H. Schroeder, *Mr. Polk's War: American Opposition and Dissent* (1973); Otis A. Singletary, *The Mexican War* (1960); Anders Stephanson, *Manifest Destiny* (1995); David J. Weber, *The Mexican Frontier, 1821–1846* (1982).

CHAPTER

15

Transforming Fire:
The Civil War
1861–1865

H e was a living legend. A frontiersman who fought with Andrew Jackson at the Battle of Horseshoe Bend, he had a distinguished career as lawyer, congressman, and governor of Tennessee. But in 1829 he abruptly resigned his governorship and spent the next three years living among the Cherokees. In 1836 he reemerged as commander-in-chief of the armies winning Texan independence. Then he became president of the new Republic of Texas, holding that office twice. After Texas joined the Union, he served fourteen years as United States senator. In 1859 voters in Texas elected him governor. No one in Texas rivaled the reputation or prestige of Sam Houston, yet in March 1861 he was deposed. Why? Houston opposed secession, warned of defeat, refused to take an oath of allegiance to the Confederacy, and challenged the authority of the secession convention. Its members ended his career by declaring his office vacant.

A similar reversal of fortune befell Nathaniel Banks in Texas. Banks had built a distinguished public career in Massachusetts. Hard-working and self-educated, he had risen from bobbin boy in a cotton mill to lawyer, state legislator, congressman, Speaker of the United States House of Representatives, and governor of Massachusetts. When the Civil War began, Banks promptly volunteered to fight and was commissioned a major general. His troops met defeat in Virginia, however, and his reputation was slipping when he arrived on Texas's coast to try to capture the Rio Grande valley. After some success in 1863, a failed offensive along the Red River in 1864 led to scathing criticism and his departure from the military.

The Civil War brought astonishing, unexpected changes not only to Sam Houston and Nathaniel Banks but everywhere in both North and South. For some, wealth changed to poverty and hope to despair; for others, the suffering of war spelled opportunity. Contrasts abounded, between noble and crass motives and between individuals seeking different goals. Even the South's slaves, who hoped that they were witnessing God's "Holy War for liberation," encountered unsympathetic liberators. When a Yankee soldier ransacked a slave woman's cabin, stealing her best quilts, she denounced him as a "nasty, stinkin' rascal" who had betrayed his cause of freedom. Angrily the soldier contradicted her, saying, "I'm fightin' for $14 a month and the Union."

Northern troops were not the only ones to feel anger over their sacrifice. Impoverished by the war, one southern farmer had endured inflation, taxes, and shortages to support the Confederacy. Then an impressment agent arrived to take still more from him— grain and meat, horses and mules, and wagons. In return, the agent offered only a certificate promising repayment sometime in the future. Bitter and disgusted, the farmer declared, "The sooner this damned Government falls to pieces, the better it will be for us."

Many northern businessmen, however, viewed the economic effects of the war with optimism and anticipation. The conflict ensured vast government expenditures, a heavy demand for goods, and lucrative federal contracts. *Harper's Monthly* reported that an eminent financier expected a long war—the kind of war that would mean huge purchases, paper money, active speculation, and rising prices. "The battle of Bull Run," predicted the financier, "makes the fortune of every man in Wall Street who is not a natural idiot."

For these people and millions of others, the Civil War was a life-changing event. It obliterated the normal patterns and circumstances of life. Millions of men were swept away into training camps and battle units. Armies numbering in the hundreds of thousands marched over the South, devastating once-peaceful countrysides. Families struggled to survive without their men; businesses tried to cope with the loss of workers. Women in both North and South took on extra responsibilities in the home and moved into new jobs in the work force. No sphere of life was untouched.

Change was most drastic in the South, where the leaders of the secession movement had launched a revolution for the purpose of keeping things unchanged. Never were men more mistaken: their rev-olutionary means were fundamentally incompatible with their conservative purpose. Southern whites had feared that a peacetime government of Republicans would interfere with slavery and upset the routine of plantation life. Instead their own actions led to a war that turned southern life upside down and imperiled the very existence of slavery. Jefferson Davis, president of the Confederate States of America, devised policies more objectionable to the elite than any proposed by President-elect Lincoln. Life in the Confederacy proved to be a shockingly unsouthern experience.

War altered the North as well, but less deeply. Because most of the fighting took place on southern soil, northern farms and factories remained virtually unscathed. The drafting of workers and the changing need for products slowed the pace of industrialization somewhat, but factories and businesses remained busy. Workers lost ground to inflation, but the economy hummed. A new probusiness atmosphere dominated Congress, where the seats of southern representatives were empty. To the alarm of many, the powers of the federal government and of the president increased during the war.

The war created social strains in both North and South. Disaffection was strongest in the Confederacy, where poverty and class resentment fed a lower-class antagonism to the war that threatened the Confederacy from within as federal armies assailed it from without. In the North, dissent also flourished, and antiwar sentiment occasionally erupted into violence.

Ultimately, the Civil War forced on the nation new social and racial arrangements. Its greatest effect was to compel leaders and citizens to deal directly with the issue they had debated and argued over but had been unable to resolve: slavery. This issue, in complex and indirect ways, had given rise to the war. Now the scope and demands of the war forced reluctant Americans to confront it.

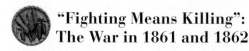

"Fighting Means Killing": The War in 1861 and 1862

Few Americans understood what they were getting into when the war began. The onset of hostilities sparked patriotic sentiments, optimistic speeches, and joyous ceremonies in both North and South. Northern communities, large and small, raised companies of volunteers eager to save the Union and sent them off with fanfare (a scene captured in the

• *Important Events* •

1861	Battle of Bull Run takes place
	General George McClellan organizes Union Army
	Union blockade begins
	United States Congress passes first confiscation act
	Trent affair
1862	Union captures Fort Henry and Fort Donelson
	United States Navy captures New Orleans
	Battle of Shiloh shows the war's destructiveness
	Confederacy enacts conscription
	General Robert E. Lee thwarts McClellan's offensive on Richmond
	United States Congress passes second confiscation act
	Confederacy mounts offensive in Maryland and Kentucky
	Battle of Antietam ends Lee's drive into Maryland
1863	Emancipation Proclamation takes effect
	United States Congress passes National Banking Act
	Union enacts conscription
	African-American soldiers join Union Army
	Food riots occur in southern cities
	Battle of Chancellorsville ends in Confederate victory but General "Stonewall" Jackson's death
	Union wins key victories at Gettysburg and Vicksburg
	Draft riots take place in New York City
	Battle of Chattanooga leaves South vulnerable to General William T. Sherman's march
1864	Battles of the Wilderness and Spotsylvania produce heavy casualties on both sides in the effort to capture and defend Richmond
	Battle of Cold Harbor continues carnage in Virginia
	Abraham Lincoln requests Republican Party plank abolishing slavery
	General Sherman captures Atlanta
	Lincoln wins reelection
	Jefferson Davis proposes emancipation within the Confederacy
	Sherman marches through Georgia
1865	Sherman marches through Carolinas
	United States Congress approves Thirteenth Amendment
	Hampton Roads Conference
	Lee abandons Richmond and Petersburg
	Lee surrenders at Appomattox Courthouse
	Lincoln assassinated

painting *Departure of the Seventh Regiment*). In the South, confident recruits boasted of whipping the Yankees and returning home in time for dinner, and southern women sewed dashing uniforms for men who soon would be lucky to wear drab gray or butternut homespun.

Through the spring of 1861 both sides scrambled to organize and train their inexperienced, undisciplined armies. On July 21, 1861, the first battle took place outside Manassas Junction, Virginia, near a stream called Bull Run. General Irvin McDowell and 30,000 Union troops attacked General

Battle of Bull Run

P. G. T. Beauregard's 22,000 southerners (see map, page 407). As raw recruits struggled amid the confusion of their first battle, federal forces began to gain ground. Then they ran into a line of Virginia troops under General Thomas Jackson. "There is Jackson standing like a stone wall," shouted one Confederate. "Stonewall" Jackson's line held, and the arrival of 9,000 Confederate reinforcements won the day for the South. Union troops fled back to Washington and shocked northern congressmen and spectators, who had watched the battle from a point two miles away, suddenly feared their capital would be taken.

The unexpected rout at Bull Run gave northerners their first hint of the nature of the war to come.

In Departure of the Seventh Regiment *(1861), flags and the spectacle of thousands of young men from New York marching off to battle give a deceptively gay appearance to the beginning of the Civil War.* Museum of Fine Arts, Boston; M. and M. Karolik Collection.

Victory would not be easy, even though the United States enjoyed an enormous advantage in resources. Pro-Union feeling was growing in western Virginia, and loyalties were divided in the four border slave states—Missouri, Kentucky, Maryland, and Delaware. But the rest of the Upper South had joined the Confederacy. Moved by an outpouring of regional loyalty, half a million southerners volunteered to fight; there were so many would-be soldiers that the Confederate government could not arm them all. The United States therefore undertook a massive buildup of troops in northern Virginia.

Lincoln gave command of the army to General George B. McClellan, an officer who proved to be better at organization and training than at fighting. McClellan devoted the fall and winter of 1861 to readying a formidable force of a quarter-million men whose mission would be to destroy southern forces guarding Richmond, the new Confederate capital.

"The vast preparation of the enemy," wrote one southern soldier, produced a "feeling of despondency" in the South for the first time.

While McClellan prepared, the Union began to implement other parts of its overall strategy, which called for a blockade of southern ports and eventual capture of the Mississippi River. Like a constricting snake, this "Anaconda plan" would strangle the Confederacy (see map, page 409). At first the Union Navy had too few ships to patrol 3,550 miles of coastline and block the Confederacy's avenues of commerce and supply. Gradually, however, the navy increased the blockade's effectiveness, though it never bottled up southern commerce completely.

Confederate strategy was essentially defensive. A defensive posture not only was consistent with the South's claim that it merely wanted to be left alone, but also took into account the North's advantage in resources (see figure, page 410). Furthermore, communities all across the South demanded to be defended. Jefferson Davis, however, wisely rejected a static or wholly defensive strategy. The South would pursue an "offensive defensive," taking advantage of opportunities to attack and using its interior lines of transportation to concentrate troops at crucial points.

Strategic thinking on both sides slighted the importance of "the West," that vast expanse of territory between Virginia and the Mississippi River. When the war began, both sides were unprepared for large-scale and sustained operations in the West, but before the end of the war it would prove to be a crucial theater. North and South also shared a fondness for "turning movements," in which an army marched around its opponent to force a withdrawal or unleashed a flank attack in battle. In the Far West, beyond the Mississippi River, the Confederacy hoped to gain an advantage by negotiating treaties with the Creeks, Choctaws, Chickasaws, Cherokees, Seminoles, and smaller tribes of Plains Indians.

The last half of 1861 brought no major land battles, but the North made gains by sea. Late in the summer Union naval forces captured Cape Hatteras and then seized Hilton Head, one of the Sea Islands off Port Royal, South Carolina. A few months later, similar operations secured vital coastal points in North Carolina, as well as Fort Pulaski, which defended Savannah. Federal naval operations were biting into the Confederate coastline (see map, page 409).

Union Naval Campaign

The coastal victories off South Carolina foreshadowed major changes in slave society. At the federal gunboats' approach, frightened planters abandoned their lands and fled. Their slaves greeted what they hoped to be freedom with rejoicing and broke the hated cotton gins. Their jubilation and the constantly growing stream of runaways who poured into the Union lines eliminated any doubt about which side slaves would support, given the opportunity. Unwilling at first to wage a war against slavery, the federal government did not acknowledge the slaves' freedom—though it began to use their labor in the Union cause.

The coastal incursions worried southerners, but the spring of 1862 brought even stronger evidence of the war's seriousness. In March two ironclad ships—the *Monitor* (a Union warship) and the *Merrimack* (a Union ship recycled by the Confederacy)—fought each other for the first time; their battle, though indecisive, ushered in a new era in naval de-

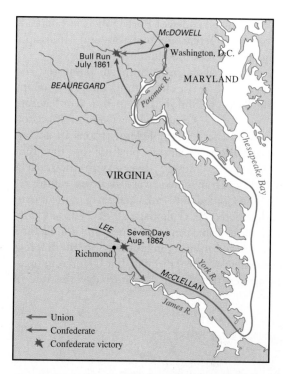

McClellan's Campaign *The water route chosen by McClellan to threaten Richmond during the peninsular campaign.*

sign. In April Union ships commanded by Admiral David Farragut smashed through log booms blocking the Mississippi River and fought their way upstream to capture New Orleans. Farther west a Union victory at Elkhorn Tavern, Arkansas, shattered Confederate control of Indian Territory. (Thereafter, dissension within Native American groups and a Union victory the following year at Honey Springs, Arkansas, reduced Confederate operations in Indian Territory to guerrilla raids.)

In February 1862 land and river forces in northern Tennessee won significant victories for the Union. A hard-drinking, hitherto unsuccessful general named Ulysses S. Grant saw the strategic importance of Fort Henry and Fort Donelson, the Confederate outposts guarding the Tennessee and Cumberland Rivers. If federal troops could capture these forts, Grant realized, two prime routes into the heartland of the Confederacy would lie open. In just ten days he seized the forts, using his forces so well that he was in a position to demand

Grant's Campaign in Tennessee

unconditional surrender of Fort Donelson's defenders. A path into Tennessee, Alabama, and Mississippi now lay open before the Union Army.

Grant moved on into southern Tennessee and the first of the war's shockingly bloody encounters, the Battle of Shiloh. On April 6, Confederate General Albert Sidney Johnston caught federal troops in an undesirable position on the Tennessee River. With their backs to the water, Grant's men were awaiting reinforcements. The Confederates attacked early in the morning and inflicted heavy damage all day. Close to victory, General Johnston was struck and killed by a ball that severed an artery in his thigh. Southern forces almost achieved a breakthrough, but Union reinforcements arrived that night. The next day the tide of

Battle of Shiloh

battle turned, and after ten hours of heavy combat, Grant's men forced the Confederates to withdraw. Neither side won a victory, yet the losses were staggering. Northern troops lost 13,000 men (killed, wounded, or captured) out of 63,000; southerners sacrificed 11,000 out of 40,000. Total casualties in this single battle exceeded those in all three of America's previous wars combined. Now both sides were beginning to sense the true nature of the war. Shiloh utterly changed Grant's thinking about it. He had hoped that southerners soon would be "heartily tired" of the conflict. After Shiloh, he recalled, "I gave up all idea of saving the Union except by complete conquest."

Meanwhile, on the Virginia front, President Lincoln had a different problem. Conquest was impossible without battles, but General McClellan seemed

Both armies experienced religious revivals during the war. This photograph shows members of a largely Irish regiment from New York celebrating Mass at the beginning of the war. Notice the presence of some female visitors in the left foreground.   Library of Congress.

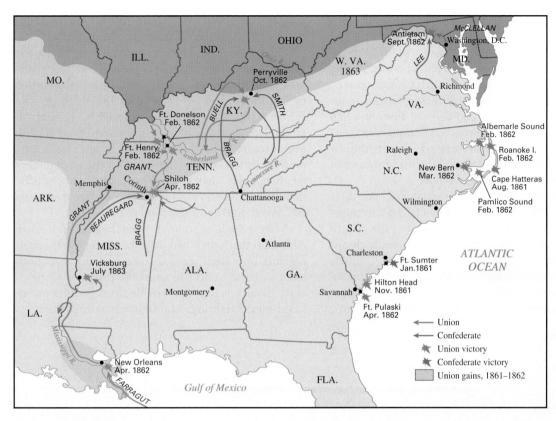

Anaconda Plan   *An overview of the Union's "Anaconda Plan" and key battles on the coast and in the West, 1861–1863.*

unwilling to fight. Only thirty-six, McClellan had already achieved notable success as an army officer and railroad president. Keenly aware of his historic role, he did not want to fail and insisted on having everything in order before he attacked. Habitually overestimating the size of enemy forces, McClellan called repeatedly for reinforcements and ignored Lincoln's directions to advance. Finally McClellan chose to move by a roundabout water route, sailing his troops around the York peninsula and advancing on Richmond from the east (see map, page 407).

By June the sheer size of the federal armies outside the Confederacy's capital was highly threatening. But southern leaders foiled McClellan's legions. First, Stonewall Jackson moved north into the Shenandoah valley behind Union forces and threatened Washington, D.C., drawing some of the federal troops away from Richmond to protect their own capital. Then, in a series of engagements known as the Seven Days Battles, Confederate general Robert E. Lee struck at McClellan's army. Lee never managed to close his pincers around the retreating Union forces, but on August 3 McClellan withdrew to the Potomac. Richmond remained safe for almost two more years.

Buoyed by these results, Jefferson Davis conceived an ambitious plan to turn the tide of the war and gain recognition of the Confederacy by European nations. He ordered a general offensive, sending Lee north into Maryland and Generals Kirby Smith and Braxton Bragg into Kentucky. Calling on residents of Maryland and Kentucky to make a separate peace with his government, Davis also invited northwestern states like Indiana, which sent much of their trade down the Mississippi to New Orleans, to leave the Union.

Confederate Offensive in Maryland and Kentucky

The plan was promising, but every part of the offensive failed. In the bloodiest day of the entire war, September 17, 1862, McClellan turned Lee back from Sharpsburg, Maryland. In the Battle of Anti-etam 5,000 men died (3,500 had died at Shiloh), and another 18,000 were wounded. Lee was lucky to escape destruction, for McClellan had obtained a copy of Lee's marching orders. But McClellan moved slowly, failed to use his larger forces in simultaneous attacks all along the line, and allowed Lee's stricken army to retreat to safety across the Potomac. In Kentucky Generals Smith and Bragg had to withdraw just one day after Bragg attended the inauguration of a provisional Confederate governor.

Confederate leaders had marshaled all their strength for a breakthrough but had failed. Outnumbered and disadvantaged in resources, the South could not continue the offensive. Profoundly disappointed, Davis admitted to a committee of Confederate representatives that southerners were entering "the darkest and most dangerous period we have yet had." Tenacious defense and stoic endurance now

seemed the South's only long-range hope. Perceptive southerners shared their president's despair.

But 1862 also brought painful lessons to the North. Confederate General James E. B. (Jeb) Stuart executed a daring cavalry raid into Pennsylvania in October. Then on December 13 Union general Ambrose Burnside unwisely ordered his soldiers to attack Lee's army, which held fortified positions on high ground at Fredericksburg, Virginia. Lee's men performed so coolly and controlled the engagement so thoroughly that Lee, a restrained and humane man, was moved to say, "It is well that war is so terrible. We should grow too fond of it."

The rebellion was far from being suppressed. Although the North had large reserves, it was learning just how high were the costs of the war. Both sides would have to pay a terrible price. As Confederate cavalry leader Nathan Bedford Forrest put it, "War means fighting. And fighting means killing."

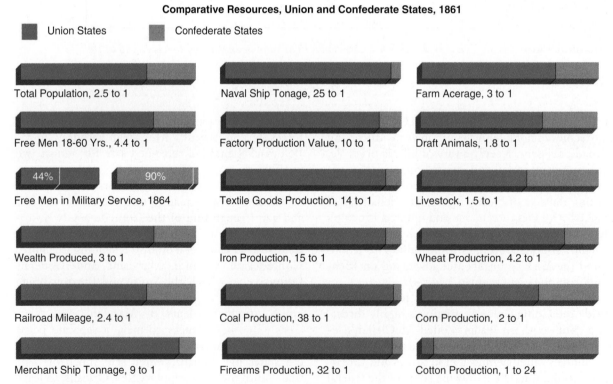

Comparative Resources, Union and Confederate States, 1861

■ Union States   ■ Confederate States

Total Population, 2.5 to 1

Naval Ship Tonage, 25 to 1

Farm Acerage, 3 to 1

Free Men 18-60 Yrs., 4.4 to 1

Factory Production Value, 10 to 1

Draft Animals, 1.8 to 1

44%   90%

Free Men in Military Service, 1864

Textile Goods Production, 14 to 1

Livestock, 1.5 to 1

Wealth Produced, 3 to 1

Iron Production, 15 to 1

Wheat Productrion, 4.2 to 1

Railroad Mileage, 2.4 to 1

Coal Production, 38 to 1

Corn Production, 2 to 1

Merchant Ship Tonnage, 9 to 1

Firearms Production, 32 to 1

Cotton Production, 1 to 24

Comparative Resources, Union and Confederate States, 1861 *The North had vastly superior resources. Although the North's advantages in manpower and industrial capacity proved very important, the South could not really be conquered until it chose to give up the fight.*   Source: From *The Times Atlas of World History.* Time Books, London, 1978. Used with permission.

In October 1862 in New York City, photographer Matthew Brady opened an exhibition of photographs from the Battle of Antietam. The camera, whose modern form had been invented only in 1826, made war's carnage hideously real. Although few knew it, Brady's vision was very poor, and this photograph of Confederate dead was actually made by his assistants, Alexander Gardner and James F. Gibson. Confederate dead: Library of Congress; camera: George Eastman House Collection.

 ## War Transforms the South

Even more than the fighting itself, disruptions in civilian life robbed southerners of their gaiety and nonchalance. The war altered southern society beyond all expectations and with astonishing speed. One of the first traditions to fall was the southern preference for local government. The South had been characterized by limited government. States' rights had been its motto, but by modern standards even the state governments were weak and sketchy affairs. The average citizen, on whom the hand of government had rested lightly, probably knew county authorities best. To withstand the massive power of the North, however, the South needed to centralize;

like the colonial revolutionaries, southerners faced a choice of join or die. No one saw the necessity of centralization more clearly than Jefferson Davis. If the states of the Confederacy insisted on fighting separately, said Davis, "we had better make terms as soon as we can."

Promptly Davis moved to bring all arms, supplies, and troops under his control. But by early 1862 the scope and duration of the conflict required something more. Tens of thousands of Confederate soldiers had volunteered for just one year's service, planning to return home in the spring to plant their crops. To keep southern armies in the

Confederacy Resorts to a Draft

field, the War Department encouraged reenlistments and called for new volunteers. However, as one official admitted, "the spirit of volunteering had died out." Three states threatened or instituted a draft. Finally, faced with a critical shortage of troops, in April 1862 the Confederate government enacted the first national conscription (draft) law in American history. Thus the war forced unprecedented change on states that had seceded out of fear of change.

Though Jefferson Davis was careful to observe the Confederate constitution, he was a strong chief executive. He adopted a firm leadership role toward the Confederate Congress, which raised taxes and later passed a tax-in-kind—a tax paid in farm products. Almost three thousand agents dispersed to collect the tax, assisted by almost fifteen hundred appraisers. Where opposition arose, the government suspended the writ of habeas corpus (which prevented individuals from being held without trial) and imposed martial law. In the face of political opposition that cherished states' rights, Davis proved unyielding.

Centralization of Power

To replace the food that men in uniform would have grown, Davis exhorted farmers to switch from cash crops to food crops; he encouraged the states to require them to do so. But the army remained short of food and labor. In emergencies the War Department resorted to impressing slaves to work on fortifications, and after 1861 the government relied heavily on confiscation of food to feed the troops. Officers swooped down on farms in the line of march and carted away grain, meat, wagons, and draft animals.

Soon the Confederate administration in Richmond was exercising virtually complete control over the southern economy. Because it controlled the supply of labor through conscription, the administration could compel industry to work on government contracts and supply the military's needs. The Confederate Congress also gave the central government almost complete control of the railroads; in 1864 shipping, too, came under extensive regulation. New statutes even limited corporate profits and dividends. A large bureaucracy sprang up to administer these operations: over seventy thousand civilians staffed the Confederate administration. By the war's end, the southern bureaucracy was larger in proportion to population than its northern counterpart.

Clerks and subordinate officials crowded the towns and cities where Confederate departments had their offices. The sudden population booms that resulted overwhelmed the housing supply and stimulated new construction. The pressure was especially great in Richmond, whose population increased 250 percent. Before the war's end, Confederate officials were planning the relocation of entire departments to lessen crowding in Richmond. Mobile's population jumped from 29,000 to 41,000; Atlanta began to grow; and 10,000 people poured into war-related industries in little Selma, Alabama.

Effects of War on Southern Cities and Industry

Another prime cause of urban growth in the South was industrialization. The Union blockade disrupted imports of manufactured products and caused the traditionally agricultural South to become interested in industry. Davis exulted that manufacturing was making the South "more and more independent of the rest of the world." Many planters shared his hope that industrialization would bring "deliverance, full and unrestricted, from all commercial dependence" on the North. Indeed, beginning almost from scratch, the Confederacy achieved tremendous feats of industrial development. Chief of Ordnance Josiah Gorgas increased the capacity of Richmond's Tredegar Iron Works and other factories to the point that by 1865 his Ordnance Bureau was supplying all Confederate small arms and ammunition. Meanwhile, the government constructed new railroad lines to improve the efficiency of the South's transportation system.

Southerners adopted new ways in response to these changes. Women, restricted to narrow roles in antebellum society, gained substantial new responsibilities. The wives and mothers of soldiers now headed households and performed men's work, adding to their traditional chores the tasks of raising crops and tending animals. Women in nonslaveowning families cultivated fields themselves, while wealthier women suddenly had to manage field hands unaccustomed to female overseers. Only the very rich had enough servants to allow a woman's routine to continue undisturbed. In the cities, white women—who had been virtually excluded from the labor force—found a limited number of respectable new paying jobs. Clerks had always been males, but the war changed that, too. "Government girls" staffed the Confederate bureaucracy, and female schoolteachers became commonplace in the South for the first time.

Change in the Role of Southern Women

Some women gained confidence from their new responsibilities. Among these was Janie Smith, a young North Carolinian. Raised in a rural area by prosperous parents, she had faced few challenges or grim realities before the war reached her farm and troops turned her home into a hospital. "It makes me shudder when I think of the awful sights I witnessed that morning," she wrote to a friend. "Ambulance after ambulance drove up with our wounded. . . . Under every shed and tree, the tables were carried for amputating the limbs. . . . The blood lay in puddles in the grove; the groans of the dying and complaints of those undergoing amputation were horrible." But Janie Smith learned to cope with crisis. She ended her account with the proud words, "I can dress amputated limbs now and do most anything in the way of nursing wounded soldiers."

Patriotic sacrifice appealed to some women, but others resented their new burdens. Many among the wealthy found their new tasks difficult and their changed situation distasteful. North Carolina diarist Catherine Devereux Edmondston was enthusiastic for the southern cause but wanted her husband to remain at home. A Texas woman who had struggled to discipline slaves pronounced herself "sick of trying to do a man's business." Others grew angry over shortages and resented cooking and unfamiliar contact with lower-class women.

Yet the Confederate experience produced some new values. Legislative bodies yielded power to the executive branch of government, which could act more decisively in time of war. Achievement and bravery under fire began to take precedence over aristocratic lineage. Men such as Josiah Gorgas, Stonewall Jackson, and Nathan Bedford Forrest gained renown by distinguishing themselves in industry and on the battlefield.

For millions of ordinary southerners, however, change brought privation and suffering. Mass poverty descended for the first time on a large minority of the white population. Many yeoman families had lost their breadwinners to the army. As a South Carolina newspaper put it, "The duties of war have called away from home the sole supports of many, many families. . . . Help must be given, or the poor will suffer." The poor sought help from relatives, neighbors, friends, anyone. Sometimes they pleaded their cases to the Confederate government. "In the name of humanity," begged one woman, "discharge my husband he is not able to do your government much

Human Suffering

This Confederate soldier, like thousands of his comrades, took advantage of an opportunity to pose with his wife and brother. As the death toll mounted and suffering increased, southern women grew less willing to urge their men into battle. Collection of Larry Williford.

good and he might do his children some good . . . my poor children have no home nor no Father."

Other factors aggravated the effect of the labor shortage. The South was in many places so sparsely populated that the conscription of one skilled craftsman could work a hardship on the people of an entire county. Often they begged in unison for the exemption or discharge of the local miller or the neighborhood tanner, wheelwright, or potter. Physicians also were in short supply. Most serious, however, was the loss of a blacksmith. As a petition from Alabama explained, "our Section of County [is] left entirely Destitute of any man that is able to keep in order any kind of Farming Tules."

The blockade of Confederate shipping created shortages of common but important items—salt, sugar, coffee, nails—and speculation and hoarding made the shortages worse. Greedy businessmen cornered the supply of some commodities; prosperous citizens stocked up on food. The *Richmond Enquirer* criticized one man for hoarding

Hoarding and Runaway Inflation

seven hundred barrels of flour; another man, a planter, purchased so many wagonloads of supplies that his "lawn and paths looked like a wharf covered with a ship's loads." "This disposition to speculate upon the yeomanry of the country," lamented the *Richmond Examiner*, "is the most mortifying feature of the war." North Carolina's Governor Zebulon Vance worried about "the cry of distress . . . from the poor wives and children of our soldiers. . . . What will become of them?"

Inflation raged out of control, fueled by the Confederate government's heavy borrowing and inadequate taxes, until prices had increased almost 7,000 percent. Inflation particularly imperiled urban dwellers and the many who could no longer provide for themselves. As early as 1861 and 1862, newspapers reported that "want and starvation are staring thousands in the face," and troubled officials predicted that "women and children are bound to come to suffering if not starvation." Some concerned citizens tried to help. "Free markets," which disbursed goods as charity, sprang up in various cities. Some families came to the aid of their neighbors. But other people would not cooperate: "It is folly for a poor mother to call on the rich people about here," raged one woman. "Their hearts are of steel they would sooner throw what they have to spare to the dogs than give it to a starving child." The need was so vast that it overwhelmed private charity. A rudimentary relief program organized by the Confederacy offered hope but was soon curtailed to supply the armies. Thus southern yeomen sank into poverty and suffering.

As their fortunes declined, people of once-modest means looked around and found abundant evidence that all classes were not sacrificing equally. They saw that the wealthy gave up only their luxuries, while many poor families went without necessities. And they noted that the Confederate government contributed to these inequities through policies that favored the upper class. Until the last year of the war, for example, prosperous southerners could avoid military service by hiring substitutes. Prices for substitutes skyrocketed until it cost a man $5,000 or $6,000 to send someone to the front in his place. Well over 50,000 upper-class southerners purchased such substitutes. South Carolina's Mary Boykin Chesnut knew of one young aristocrat who "spent a fortune in substitutes. Two have been taken from

Inequities of the Confederate Draft

him [when *they* were conscripted], and two he paid to change with him when he was ordered to the front. He is at the end of his row now, for all able-bodied men are ordered to the front. I hear he is going as some general's courier." As Chesnut's last remark indicates, the rich also traded on their social connections to avoid danger. "It is a notorious fact," complained an angry Georgian, that "if a man has influential friends—or a little money to spare he will never be enrolled." A Confederate senator from Mississippi, James Phelan, informed Jefferson Davis that apparently "nine tenths of the youngsters of the land whose relatives are conspicuous in society, wealthy, or influential obtain some safe perch where they can doze with their heads under their wings."

Anger at such discrimination exploded in October 1862 when the Confederate Congress exempted from military duty anyone who was supervising at least twenty slaves. "Never did a law meet with more universal odium," observed one representative. "Its influence upon the poor is most calamitous." Protests poured in from every corner of the Confederacy, and North Carolina's legislators formally condemned the law. Its defenders argued, however, that the exemption preserved order and aided food production, and the statute remained on the books.

Dissension spread as growing numbers of citizens concluded that the struggle was "a rich man's war and a poor man's fight." Alert politicians and newspaper editors warned that class resentment was building to a dangerous level. The bitterness of letters to Confederate officials during this period suggests the depth of the people's anger. "If I and my little children suffer [and] die while there Father is in service," threatened one woman, "I invoke God Almighty that our blood rest upon the South." Another woman swore to the secretary of war that unless help was provided to poverty-stricken wives and mothers "an allwise god . . . will send down his fury and judgment in a very grate manar . . .[on] those that are in power." War was magnifying social tensions in the Confederacy.

 ## The Northern Economy Copes with War

With the onset of war, a tidal wave of change rolled over the North as well. Factories and citizens' associations geared up to support the war, and the federal government and its executive branch gained new powers. The energies of an industrializing, cap-

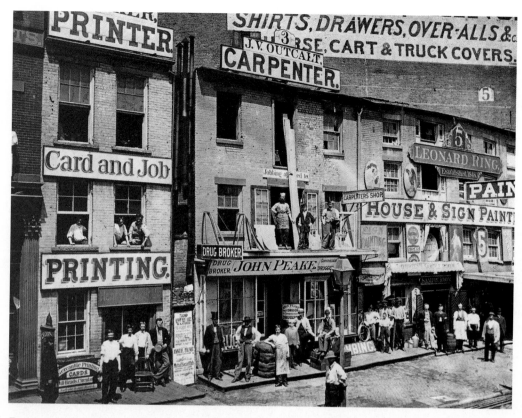

Despite initial problems, the task of supplying a vast war machine kept the northern economy humming. This photograph shows businesses on the west side of Hudson Street in New York City in 1865. New-York Historical Society.

italist society were harnessed to serve the cause of the Union. Idealism and greed flourished together, and the northern economy proved its awesome productivity. Northern factories ran overtime, and unemployment was low. The war did not destroy the North's prosperity. Northern farms and factories came through the war unharmed, whereas most of the South suffered extensive damage. To Union soldiers on the battlefield, sacrifice was a grim reality, but northern civilians experienced only the bustle and energy of wartime production.

At first the war was a shock to business. Northern firms lost their southern markets, and many companies had to change their products and find new customers in order to remain open. Southern debts became uncollectible, jeopardizing not only northern merchants but also many western banks. In farming regions, families struggled with an aggravated shortage of labor. A few enterprises never pulled out of the tailspin caused by the war.

Initial Slump in Northern Business

Cotton mills lacked cotton; construction declined; shoe manufacturers sold few of the cheap shoes that planters had bought for their slaves.

Overall the war slowed the pace of industrialization in the North, but its economic impact was not all negative. Certain entrepreneurs, such as wool producers, benefited from shortages of competing products, and soaring demand for war-related goods swept some businesses to new heights of production. To feed the hungry war machine, the federal government pumped unprecedented sums into the economy. The Treasury issued $3.2 billion in bonds and paper money called greenbacks, and the War Department spent over $360 million in revenues from new taxes (including a broad excise tax and the nation's first income tax). Government contracts soon totaled more than $1 billion.

Secretary of War Edwin M. Stanton's list of the supplies needed by the Ordnance Department indicates the scope of government demand: "7,892 cannon, 11,787 artillery carriages, 4,022,130 smallarms, . . . 1,022,176,474 cartridges for small-arms,

1,220,555,435 percussion caps, . . . 26,440,054 pounds of gunpowder, 6,395,152 pounds of niter, and 90,416,295 pounds of lead." Stanton's list covered only weapons; the government also purchased huge quantities of uniforms, boots, food, camp equipment, saddles, ships, and other necessities. War-related spending revived business in many northern states. In 1863, a merchants' magazine examined the effects of the war in Massachusetts: "Seldom, if ever, has the business of Massachusetts been more active or profitable than during the past year. . . . In every department of labor the government has been, directly or indirectly, the chief employer and paymaster." Government contracts had a particularly beneficial impact on the state's wool, metal, and shipbuilding industries, and also saved Massachusetts shoe manufacturers from ruin.

Nothing illustrated the wartime partnership between business and government better than the work of Jay Cooke, a wealthy New York financier. Cooke threw himself into the marketing of government bonds to finance the war effort. With great imagination and energy, he convinced both large investors and ordinary citizens to invest enormous sums in the war effort, in the process earning hefty commissions for himself. But the financier's profit served the Union cause, as the interests of capitalism and government, finance and patriotism, merged. The booming economy, the Republican alliance with business, and the frantic wartime activity combined to create a new atmosphere in Washington. The notion spread that government should aid businessmen and not interfere with them. Noting the favorable atmosphere, railroad builders and industrialists—men such as Leland Stanford, Collis P. Huntington, John D. Rockefeller, John M. Forbes, and Jay Gould—took advantage of it. Their enterprises grew with the aid of government loans, grants, and tariffs.

War production aided some heavy industries in the North. Coal output rose substantially. Iron makers improved the quality of their product while boosting the production of pig iron from 920,000 tons in 1860 to 1.1 million tons in 1864. Foundries developed new and less expensive ways to make steel. Although new railroad construction slowed, repairs helped the manufacture of rails to increase. Of considerable significance for the future was the railroad industry's adoption of a standard gauge (width) for

Effects of War on Northern Industry and Agriculture

track, which eliminated the unloading and reloading of boxcars and created a unified transportation system.

Another strength of the northern economy was the complementary relationship between agriculture and industry. Mechanization of agriculture had begun before the war. Wartime recruitment and conscription, however, gave western farmers an added incentive to purchase labor-saving machinery. The shift from human labor to machines created new markets for industry and expanded the food supply for the urban industrial work force. The boom in the sale of agricultural tools was tremendous. Cyrus and William McCormick built an industrial empire in Chicago from the sale of their reapers. Between 1862 and 1864 the manufacture of mowers and reapers doubled to 70,000 yearly; even so, manufacturers could not satisfy the demand. By the end of the war, 375,000 reapers were in use, triple the number in 1861. Large-scale commercial agriculture had become a reality. As a result, northern farm families whose breadwinners went to war did not suffer as their counterparts did in the South. "We have seen," one magazine observed, "a stout matron whose sons are in the army, cutting hay with her team . . . and she cut seven acres with ease in a day, riding leisurely upon her cutter."

Northern industrial and urban workers did not fare as well. After the initial slump, jobs became plentiful, but inflation ate up much of a worker's paycheck. By 1863 9-cent-a-pound beef cost 18 cents. The price of coffee had tripled; rice and sugar had doubled; and clothing, fuel, and rent had all climbed. Between 1860 and 1864 consumer prices rose at least 76 percent, while daily wages rose only 42 percent. Workers' families consequently suffered a substantial decline in their standard of living.

As their real wages shrank, industrial workers lost job security. To increase production, some employers were replacing workers with labor-saving machines. Other employers urged the government to promote immigration so they could import cheap labor. Workers responded by forming unions and sometimes by striking. Skilled craftsmen organized to combat the loss of their jobs and status to machines; women and unskilled workers, excluded by the craftsmen, formed their own unions. In recognition of the increasingly national scope of business activity, thirteen occupational groups—including tailors, coal miners, and

New Militancy Among Northern Workers

railway engineers—formed national unions during the Civil War. Because of the tight labor market, unions won many of their demands without striking, but the number of strikes also rose steadily.

Employers reacted with hostility to this new spirit among workers—a spirit that William H. Sylvis, leader of the iron molders, called a "feeling of manly independence." Manufacturers viewed labor activism as a threat to their property rights and freedom of action, and accordingly formed statewide or craft-based associations to cooperate and pool information. These employers shared blacklists of union members and required new workers to sign "yellow dog" contracts (promises not to join a union). To put down strikes, they hired strikebreakers from the ranks of the poor and desperate—blacks, immigrants, and women—and sometimes received additional help from federal troops.

Troublesome as unions were, they did not prevent many employers from making a profit. The highest profits were made from profiteering on government contracts. Unscrupulous businessmen took advantage of the suddenly immense demand for army supplies by selling clothing and blankets made of "shoddy"—wool fibers reclaimed from rags or worn cloth. Shoddy goods often came apart in the rain; most of the shoes purchased in the early months of the war were worthless, too. Contractors sold inferior guns for double the usual price and passed off tainted meat as good. Corruption was so widespread that it led to a year-long investigation by the House of Representatives. A group of contractors that had demanded $50 million for their products dropped their claims to $17 million as a result of the findings of the investigation.

Legitimate enterprises also made healthy profits. The output of woolen mills increased so dramatically that dividends in the industry nearly tripled.

Wartime Benefits to Northern Business

Some cotton mills made record profits on what they sold, even though they reduced their output. Brokerage houses worked until midnight and earned unheard-of commissions. Railroads carried immense quantities of freight and passengers, increasing their business to the point that railroad stocks doubled or even tripled in value. The price of Erie Railroad stock rose from $17 to $126 a share during the war.

Railroads also were a leading beneficiary of government largesse. Congress had failed in the 1850s to resolve the question of a northern versus a southern route for the first transcontinental railroad. With the South absent from Congress, the northern route quickly prevailed. In 1862 and 1864 Congress chartered two corporations, the Union Pacific Railroad and the Central Pacific Railroad, and assisted them financially in connecting Omaha, Nebraska, with Sacramento, California. For each mile of track laid, the railroads received a loan of from $16,000 to $48,000 in government bonds plus 20 square miles of land along a free 400-foot-wide right of way. Overall, the two corporations gained approximately 20 million acres of land and nearly $60 million in loans.

Other businessmen benefited handsomely from the Morrill Land Grant Act (1862). To promote public education in agriculture, engineering, and military science, Congress granted each state 30,000 acres of federal land for each of its congressional districts. The states could sell the land, as long as they used the income for the purposes Congress had intended. The law eventually fostered sixty-nine colleges and universities, but one of its immediate effects was to enrich a few prominent speculators. Hard-pressed to meet wartime expenses, some states sold their land cheaply to wealthy entrepreneurs. For example, Ezra Cornell, a leader in the telegraph industry, invested in 500,000 acres in the Midwest.

Morrill Land Grant Act

Higher tariffs also pleased many businessmen. Northern businesses did not uniformly favor high import duties; some manufacturers desired cheap imported raw materials more than they feared foreign competition. But northeastern congressmen traditionally supported higher tariffs, and after southern lawmakers left Washington, they had their way: the Tariff Act of 1864 raised tariffs generously. According to one scholar, manufacturers had only to mention the rate they considered necessary and that rate was declared. Some healthy industries earned artificially high profits by raising their prices to a level just below that of the foreign competition. By the end of the war, tariff increases averaged 47 percent, and rates were more than double those of 1857.

 ## Wartime Society in the North

The outbreak of war stimulated patriotism in the North just as it initially had done in the South. Northern society, which had suffered the stresses associated with industrialization, immigration, and widespread social change, found a unifying cause in the preservation of the nation and the American form of government. In thousands of self-governing towns and communities, northern citizens felt a personal connection to representative government. Secession threatened to destroy their system, and northerners rallied to its defense. Secular and church leaders supported the cause, and even ministers who preferred to separate politics and pulpit denounced "the iniquity of causeless rebellion."

Such enthusiasm proved useful as northerners encountered a multitude of wartime changes. The powers of the federal government and the president grew steadily during the crisis.

Expanded Powers of the United States President

Abraham Lincoln, like Jefferson Davis, found that war required active presidential leadership. At the beginning of the conflict, Lincoln launched a major shipbuilding program without waiting for Congress to assemble. The lawmakers later approved his decision, and Lincoln continued to act in advance of Congress when he deemed such action necessary. In one striking exercise of executive power, Lincoln suspended the writ of habeas corpus for everyone living between Washington D.C., and Philadelphia. There was scant legal justification for this act, but the president's motive was practical: to ensure the loyalty of Maryland. Later in the war, with congressional approval, Lincoln repeatedly suspended habeas corpus and invoked martial law, mainly in the border states but elsewhere as well. Between fifteen and twenty thousand United States citizens were arrested on suspicion of disloyal acts.

On occasion Lincoln used his wartime authority to bolster his own political fortunes. He and his generals proved adept at furloughing soldiers so they could vote in close elections; those whom Lincoln furloughed, of course, usually voted Republican. He also came to the aid of other officeholders in his party. When the Republican governor of Indiana, who was battling propeace Democrats in his legislature, ran short of funds, Lincoln had the War Department supply $250,000. This procedure lacked constitutional sanction, but it advanced the Union cause.

Among the clearest examples of the wartime expansion of federal authority were the National Banking Acts of 1863, 1864, and 1865. Before the Civil War, the nation lacked a uniform currency, for the federal government had never exercised its authority in this area. Banks operating under state charters issued

no fewer than seven thousand different kinds of notes, which were difficult to distinguish from a variety of forgeries. On the recommendation of Secretary of the Treasury Salmon Chase, Congress established a national banking system empowered to issue national bank notes. At the close of the war in 1865, Congress imposed a prohibitive tax on state bank notes and forced most state institutions to join the national system. This process created a sounder currency and a simpler monetary system—but also inflexibility in the money supply and an eastern-oriented financial structure.

Social attitudes on the home front evolved in directions that would have shocked the soldiers in the field. In the excitement of moneymaking, an eagerness to display one's wealth flourished in the largest cities. A visitor to Chicago commented that "so far as lavish display is concerned, the South Side in some portions has no rival in Chicago, and perhaps not outside New York." *Harper's Monthly* reported that "the suddenly enriched contractors, speculators, and stock-jobbers . . . are spending money with a profusion never before witnessed in our country, at no time remarkable for its frugality. . . . The men button their waistcoats with diamonds . . . and the women powder their hair with gold and silver dust." The *New York Herald* summarized that city's atmosphere: "The richest silks, laces and jewelry are the soonest sold. . . . Not to keep a carriage, not to wear diamonds, . . . is now equivalent to being a nobody. This war has entirely changed the American character. . . . The individual who makes the most money—no matter how—and spends the most—no matter for what—is considered the greatest man."

Extravagance Amid War

Yet idealism coexisted with ostentation. Many churches endorsed the Union cause as God's cause. One Methodist newspaper described the war as a contest between "equalizing, humanizing Christianity" and "disunion, war, selfishness, [and] slavery." Abolitionists, after initial uncertainty over whether to let the South go, campaigned to turn the war into a crusade against slavery. Free black communities and churches both black and white responded to the needs of slaves who flocked to the Union lines, sending clothing, ministers, and teachers to aid the runaways.

Northern women, like their southern counterparts, took on new roles. Those who stayed home organized over ten thousand soldiers' aid societies, rolled innumerable bandages, and raised $3 million to aid injured troops. Thousands served as nurses in front-line hospitals, where they pressed for better care of the wounded. Yet women were only a small minority of all nurses, and they had to fight for a chance to serve at all. The professionalization of medicine since the Revolution had created a medical system dominated by men, and many male physicians did not want women's aid. Female nurses proved their worth, but only the wounded welcomed them. Even Clara Barton, the most famous female nurse, was ousted from her post in 1863.

The poet Walt Whitman left a record of his experiences as a volunteer nurse in Washington, D.C. As he dressed wounds and tried to comfort suffering and lonely men, Whitman found

Walt Whitman

"the marrow of the tragedy concentrated in those Army Hospitals." But despite "indescribably horrid wounds," he also found in the hospitals inspiration and a deepening faith in American democracy. Whitman celebrated the "incredible dauntlessness" and sacrifice of the common soldier who fought for the Union. As he had written in the preface to his great work *Leaves of Grass* (1855), "The genius of the United States is not best or most in its executives or legislatures, but always most in the common people." Whitman worked this idealization of the common man into his poetry, which also explored homoerotic themes and rejected the lofty meter and rhyme of European verse to strive for a "genuineness" that would appeal to the masses.

Thus northern society embraced strangely contradictory tendencies. Materialism and greed flourished alongside idealism, religious conviction, and self-sacrifice. While some soldiers risked their lives willingly out of a desire to preserve the Union or extend freedom, many others openly sought to avoid service. Under the law, a draftee could stay at home by providing a substitute or paying a $300 commutation fee. Many wealthy men chose these options, and in response to popular demand, clubs, cities, and states provided the money for others. In all, 118,000 substitutes were provided and 87,000 commutations paid before Congress ended the commutation system in 1864.

The Strange Advent of Emancipation

At the highest levels of government in the United States and in the Confederacy there was a similar lack of clarity about the purpose of the war. Throughout the first several months of the struggle, both Davis and Lincoln studiously avoided references to slavery. Davis realized that emphasis on the issue could increase class conflict in the South. To avoid identifying the Confederacy only with the interests of slaveholders, he articulated a broader, traditional ideology. Davis told southerners that they were fighting for constitutional liberty: northerners had betrayed the founders legacy, and southerners had seceded to preserve it. As long as Lincoln also avoided making slavery an issue, Davis's line seemed to work.

Lincoln had his own reasons for not mentioning slavery. It was crucial at first not to antagonize the Union's border slave states, whose loyalty was tenuous. Also for many months Lincoln hoped that a pro-Union majority would assert itself in the South. It might be possible, he thought, to coax the South back into the Union and stop the fighting. Raising the slavery issue would severely undermine both goals. Powerful political considerations also dictated that Lincoln remain silent. The Republican Party was a young and unwieldy coalition. Some Republicans burned with moral outrage over slavery; others were frankly racist, dedicated to protecting free whites from the Slave Power and the competition of cheap slave labor; still others saw the tariff or immigration or some other issue as paramount. A forthright stand by Lincoln on the subject of slavery could split the party, gratifying some groups and alienating others. Until a consensus developed or Lincoln found a way to appeal to all the elements of the party, silence was the best approach.

The president's hesitancy ran counter to some of his personal feelings. Lincoln was a sensitive and compassionate man whose humility and moral anguish during the war were evident in his speeches and writings. But as a politician, Lincoln distinguished between his own moral convictions and his official acts. His political positions were studied and complex, calculated for maximum advantage. Frederick Douglass, the astute and courageous black protest leader, sensed that Lincoln was without prejudice toward black people. Yet Douglass judged him "pre-eminently the white man's president."

Lincoln first broached the subject of slavery in a substantive way in March 1862, when he proposed that the states consider emancipation on their own. He

Lincoln's Plan for Gradual Emancipation

asked Congress to promise aid to any state that decided to emancipate, and he appealed to border-state representatives to consider this course seriously. What Lincoln proposed was gradual emancipation, with compensation for slaveholders and colonization of the freed slaves outside the United States. To a delegation of free blacks he explained that "it is better for us both . . . to be separated." Until well into 1864 Lincoln steadfastly promoted an unpromising and wholly impractical scheme to colonize blacks in some region like Central America. Despite Secretary of State William H. Seward's care to insert phrases such as "with their consent," the word *deportation* crept into one of Lincoln's speeches in place of *colonization*. Thus his was as conservative a scheme as could be devised. Moreover, since the states would make the decision voluntarily, no responsibility for it would attach to Lincoln.

Others wanted to go much further. A group of Republicans in Congress, known as the Radicals and led by men such as George Julian, Charles Sumner, and Thaddeus Stevens, dedicated themselves to seeing that the war was prosecuted vigorously. They were instrumental in creating a special House-Senate committee on the conduct of the war, which investigated Union reverses, sought to make the war effort more efficient, and prodded the president to take stronger measures. Early in the war these Radicals, with support from other representatives, turned their attention to slavery.

In August 1861, at the Radicals' instigation, Congress passed its first confiscation act. Designed to punish the Confederate rebels, the law confiscated

Confiscation Acts

all property used for "insurrectionary purposes." Thus if the South used slaves in a hostile action, those slaves were declared seized and liberated. A second confiscation act (July 1862) was much more drastic: it confiscated the property of all those who supported the rebellion, even those who merely resided in the South and paid Confederate taxes. Their slaves were declared "forever free of their servitude, and not again [to be] held as slaves." The logic behind these acts was that the insurrection—as Lincoln always termed it—was a serious revolution requiring strong measures. Let the government use its full powers, free the slaves, and crush the revolution, urged the Radicals.

Lincoln refused to adopt that view. He stood by his proposal of voluntary gradual emancipation by the states and made no effort to enforce the second confiscation act. His stance provoked a public protest from Horace Greeley, editor of the powerful *New York Tribune*. In an open letter to the president entitled "The Prayer of Twenty Millions," Greeley

pleaded with Lincoln to "execute the laws" and declared, "On the face of this wide earth, Mr. President, there is not one disinterested, determined, intelligent champion of the Union cause who does not feel that all attempts to put down the Rebellion and at the same time uphold its inciting cause are preposterous and futile."

Lincoln's reply was an explicit statement of his complex and calculated approach to the question. He disagreed, he said, with all those who would make the maintenance or destruction of slavery the paramount issue of the war. "I would save the Union," announced Lincoln. "If I could save the Union without freeing *any* slave I would do it, and if I could save it by freeing *all* the slaves I would do it; and if I could save it by freeing some and leaving others alone I would also do that. What I do about slavery, and the colored race, I do because I believe it helps to save the Union." Lincoln closed with a personal disclaimer: "I have here stated my purpose according to my view of *official* duty; and I intend no modification of my oft-expressed *personal* wish that all men everywhere could be free."

When he wrote those words, Lincoln had already decided on a new step: issuance of the Emancipation Proclamation. On the advice of the cabinet, however, he was waiting for a Union victory before announcing the proclamation, so that it would not appear to be an act of desperation. Yet the letter to Greeley was not simply an effort to stall; it was an integral part of Lincoln's approach to the future of slavery, as the text of the Emancipation Proclamation would show.

On September 22, 1862, shortly after the Battle of Antietam, Lincoln issued the first part of his two-part proclamation. Invoking his powers as commander-in-chief of the armed forces,

Emancipation Proclamations

he announced that on January 1, 1863, he would emancipate the slaves in states whose people "shall then be in rebellion against the United States." Lincoln made plain that he would judge a state to be in rebellion in January if it lacked bona fide representatives in the United States Congress. Thus his September proclamation was less a declaration of the right of slaves to be free than a threat to southerners: unless they stopped fighting and returned to Congress, they would lose their slaves. "Knowing the value that was set on the slaves by the rebels," said Garrison Frazier, a black Georgian, "the President thought that his proclamation would stimulate them to lay down their arms . . . and their not doing so has now made the freedom of the slaves a part of the war." Lincoln may not actually have expected southerners to give up their effort, but he was careful to offer them the option, thus putting the onus of emancipation on them.

When Lincoln designated the areas in rebellion on January 1, his proclamation excepted every Confederate county or city that had fallen under Union control. Those areas, he declared, "are, for the present, left precisely as if this proclamation were not issued." Nor did Lincoln liberate slaves in the border slave states that remained in the Union. "The President has purposely made the proclamation inoperative in all places where . . . the slaves [are] accessible," charged the anti-administration *New York World*. "He has proclaimed emancipation only where he has notoriously no power to execute it." Partisanship aside, even Secretary of State Seward, a moderate Republican, said sarcastically, "We show our sympathy with slavery by emancipating slaves where we cannot reach them and holding them in bondage where we can set them free." A British official, Lord Russell, commented on the "very strange nature" of the document, noting that it did not declare "a principle adverse to slavery."

By making the liberation of the slaves "a fit and necessary war measure," furthermore, Lincoln raised a variety of legal questions. How long did a war measure remain in force? Did it expire with the suppression of a rebellion? The proclamation did little to clarify the status or citizenship of the freed slaves. And a reference to garrison duty in one of the closing paragraphs suggested that former slaves would have inferior duties and rank in the army. For many months, in fact, their pay and treatment were inferior.

Thus the Emancipation Proclamation was a puzzling and ambiguous document that said less than it seemed to say. It freed no slaves, and serious limitations were embedded in its language. But if as a moral and legal document it was wanting, as a political document it was nearly flawless. Because the proclamation defined the war as a war against slavery, radicals could applaud it, even if the president had not gone as far as Congress. Yet at the same time it protected Lincoln's position with conservatives, leaving him room to retreat if he chose and forcing no immediate changes on the border slave states.

The need for men soon convinced the administration to recruit northern and southern blacks for the Union Army. By the spring of 1863, African-American troops were proving their value. Lincoln came to see them as "the great *available* and yet *un-availed of* force for restoring the Union." African-American leaders hoped that military service would secure equal rights for their people. Once the black soldier had fought for the Union, wrote Frederick Douglass, "there is no power on earth which can deny that he has earned the right of citizenship in the United States." If black soldiers turned the tide, asked another man, "would the nation refuse us our rights?"

In June 1864, Lincoln gave his support to a constitutional ban on slavery. Reformers such as Elizabeth Cady Stanton and Susan B. Anthony were pressing for an amendment that would write emancipation into the Constitution. On the eve of the Republican national convention, Lincoln called the party's chairman to the White House and instructed him to have the party "put into the platform as the keystone, the amendment of the Constitution abolishing and prohibiting slavery forever." The party promptly called for a new amendment, the Thirteenth. Republican delegates probably would have adopted such a plank without his urging, but Lincoln demonstrated his commitment by lobbying Congress for quick approval of the measure. The proposed amendment passed in 1865 and was sent to the states for ratification or rejection. Lincoln's strong support for the Thirteenth Amendment—an unequivocal prohibition of slavery—constitutes his best claim to the title "Great Emancipator."

Yet Lincoln soon clouded that clear stand, for in 1865 the newly reelected president considered allowing the defeated southern states to reenter the Union and delay or defeat the amendment. In February he and Secretary of State Seward met with three Confederate commissioners at Hampton Roads, Virginia. The end of the war was clearly in sight, and southern representatives angled vainly for an armistice that would allow the South to remain a separate nation. But Lincoln was doing some political maneuvering of his own, apparently contemplating the creation of a new national party based on a postwar alliance with southern Whigs and moderate and conservative Republicans. The cement for the coalition would be concessions to planter interests.

Hampton Roads Conference

Pointing out that the Emancipation Proclamation was only a war measure, Lincoln predicted that the courts would decide whether it had granted all, some, or none of the slaves their freedom. Seward observed that the Thirteenth Amendment, which would be definitive, was not yet ratified and that reentry into the Union would allow the southern states to defeat it. Lincoln did not contradict Seward but spoke in favor of "prospective" ratification: approval with the effective date postponed for five years. He also promised to seek $400 million in compensation for slaveholders and to consider their views on related questions such as confiscation. Such financial aid would provide an economic incentive for planters to rejoin the Union and capital to cushion the economic blow of emancipation.

These were startling propositions from a president on the verge of military victory. Most northerners opposed them, and only the opposition of Jefferson Davis, who set himself against anything short of independence, prevented discussion of the proposals in the South. Even at the end of the war, Lincoln was keeping his options open and maintaining the distinction he had drawn between "*official* duty" and "*personal* wish." Lincoln did not attempt to mold public opinion on race, as did advocates of equality in one direction and racist Democrats in the other. Instead, he moved cautiously, constructing complex and ambiguous positions and avoiding the risks inherent in challenging, educating, or inspiring the nation's conscience.

Before the war was over, the Confederacy, too, addressed the issue of emancipation. Jefferson Davis himself offered a strong proposal in favor of liberation. Though emancipation was less popular in the South than in the North, Davis did not flinch or conceal his purpose. He was dedicated to independence, and he was willing to sacrifice slavery to achieve that goal. After considering the alternatives for some time, Davis concluded late in 1864 that the military status of the Confederacy was desperate and that independence with emancipation was preferable to defeat with emancipation. He proposed that the Confederate government purchase forty thousand slaves to work for the army as laborers, with a promise of freedom at the end of their service. Soon Davis upgraded his proposal, calling for the recruitment and arming of slaves as soldiers, who likewise would gain their freedom at the end of the war. The wives and children of these soldiers, he made plain, must also receive freedom from the states. Davis and his advisers did not favor full equality—they envisioned "an intermediate state of serfage or peonage." Thus they shared with Lincoln and their entire generation racial attitudes that blinded them to the massive changes taking place around them.

Davis's Plan for Emancipation

Still, Davis had proposed a radical change for the slaveholding South. Bitter debate resounded through the Confederacy, but Davis stood his ground. When the Confederate Congress approved slave enlistments without the promise of freedom, Davis insisted on more. He issued an executive order to guarantee that owners would emancipate slave soldiers, and his allies in the states started to work for emancipation of the soldiers' families. Some black troops had started to drill as the end of the war approached.

Confederate emancipation began too late to revive southern armies or win diplomatic advantages with antislavery Europeans. By contrast, Lincoln's Emancipation Proclamation stimulated a vital infusion of forces into the Union armies. Beginning in 1863 slaves from the Confederacy and the border states shouldered arms for the North. Before the war was over, 134,000 slaves (and 52,000 free African-Americans) had fought for freedom and the Union. Their participation aided northern victory while it discouraged recognition of the Confederacy by foreign governments. Lincoln's policy, whatever its limitations and lack of clarity, had profound practical effects.

 ## The Soldier's War

The intricacies of policymaking were far from the minds of ordinary soldiers. Military service completely altered their lives. Enlistment took young men from their homes and submerged them in large organizations whose military discipline ignored their individuality. Army life meant tedium, physical hardship, and separation from loved ones even in the best of times. Soldiers in battle confronted fear and danger, and the risk of death from wounds or disease was very high. Yet the military experience had powerful attractions as well. It molded men on both sides so thoroughly that they came to resemble each other far more than they resembled civilians back home. Many soldiers forged amid war a bond with their fellows and a connection to a noble purpose that they cherished for years afterward.

Union soldiers may have sensed most clearly the massive scale of modern war. Most were young; eighteen was the most common age, followed by twenty-one. Many went straight from small towns and farms into large armies supplied by extensive bureaucracies. By late 1861 there were 640,000 volunteers in arms, a stupendous increase over the regular

army of 20,000 men. The increase occurred so rapidly that it is remarkable the troops were supplied and organized as well as they were. Yet many soldiers' first experiences with a large military organization were unfortunate.

Soldiers benefited from certain new products, such as canned condensed milk, but blankets, clothing, and arms were often of poor quality. Vermin abounded. Hospitals were badly managed at first. Rules of hygiene in large camps were badly written or unenforced; latrines were poorly made or carelessly used. One investigation turned up "an area of over three acres, encircling the camp as a broad belt, on which is deposited an almost perfect layer of human excrement." Water supplies were unsafe and typhoid epidemics common. About 57,000 army men died from dysentery and diarrhea. The situation would have been much worse but for the United States Sanitary Commission. A voluntary civilian organization, the commission worked to improve conditions in camps and to aid sick and wounded soldiers. Even so, 224,000 Union troops died from disease or accidents, far more than the 140,000 who died as a result of battle. Confederate troops were less well supplied, especially in the latter part of the war, and they had no sanitary commission. Still, an extensive network of hospitals, aided by many female volunteers, sprang up to aid the sick and wounded.

On both sides troops quickly learned that soldiering was far from glorious. "The dirt of a camp life knocks all its poetry into a cocked hat," wrote

Realities of a Soldier's Life

a North Carolina volunteer in 1862. One year later he marveled at his earlier innocence. Fighting had taught him "the realities of a soldier's life. We had no tents after the 6th of August, but slept on the ground, in the woods or open fields, without regard to the weather. . . . I learned to eat fat bacon raw, and to like it. . . . Without time to wash our clothes or our persons, and sleeping on the ground all huddled together, the whole army became lousy more or less with body lice." Union troops "skirmished" against lice by boiling their clothes or holding them over a hot fire, but, reported one soldier, "I find some on me in spite of all I can do."

Few had seen violent death before, but war soon exposed them to the blasted bodies of their friends and comrades. "Any one who goes over a battlefield after a battle," wrote one Confederate, "never cares to go over another. . . . It is a sad sight to see the dead and if possible more sad to see the wounded—shot in every possible way you can imagine." Many men died gallantly; there were innumerable striking displays of courage. But far more often soldiers gave up their lives in the mass, as part of a commonplace sacrifice. "They mowed us down like grass," recalled one survivor of a Union assault.

Advances in technology made the Civil War particularly deadly. By far the most important were the rifle and the "minie ball." Bullets fired from a smoothbore musket tumbled and wobbled as they flew through the air and thus were not accurate at distances over eighty yards. Cutting spiraled grooves inside the barrel gave the projectile a spin and much greater accuracy, but rifles remained difficult to load and use until the Frenchman Claude Minie and the American James Burton developed a new kind of bullet.

Civil War bullets were sizable lead slugs with a cavity at the bottom that expanded upon firing so that the bullet "took" the rifling and flew accurately. With these bullets, rifles were accurate at four hundred yards and useful up to one thousand yards.

This meant, of course, that soldiers assaulting a position defended by riflemen were in greater peril than ever before. Even though Civil War rifles were

Impact of the Rifle

cumbersome to load (relatively few of the new, untried, breech-loading and repeating rifles were ordered), the defense gained a significant advantage. While artillery now fired from a safe distance, there was no substitute for the infantry assault or the popular turning movements aimed at an enemy's flank. Thus advancing soldiers had to expose themselves repeatedly to accurate rifle fire. Large lead bullets shattered bones and destroyed flesh, and, because medical knowledge was rudimentary, even minor wounds often led to death through infection. Thus the toll from Civil War battles was very high. Never before in Europe or America had such massive forces pummeled each other with weapons of such destructive power. Yet the armies in the Civil War seemed virtually indestructible. Even in the bloodiest engagements, in which thousands of men died, the losing army was never destroyed. As losses mounted, many citizens wondered at what Union soldier (and future Supreme Court justice) Oliver Wendell Holmes called "the butcher's bill."

Still, Civil War soldiers developed deep commitments to each other and to their task. As campaigns dragged on, fighting and dying with their comrades became their reality, and most soldiers who did not desert grew determined to see the struggle through. "We now, like true Soldiers go determined not to yield one inch," wrote a New York corporal. When at last the war was over, "it seemed like breaking up a family to separate," one man observed. Another admitted, "We shook hands all around, and laughed and seemed to make merry, while our hearts were heavy and our eyes ready to shed tears."

The bonding may have been most dramatic among officers and men in the northern black regiments, for there white and black troops took their

Black Soldiers Fight for Acceptance

first steps toward bridging a deep racial divide. Racism in the Union Army was strong. Most white soldiers wanted nothing to do with black people and regarded them as inferior. "I never came out here for to free the black devils," wrote one soldier, and another objected to fighting beside African-Americans because, "We are a too superior race for that." For many, acceptance of black troops grew only because they could do heavy labor and "stop Bullets as well as white people." A popular song celebrated "Sambo's Right to Be Kilt" as the only justification for black enlistments.

But among some a change occurred. White officers who volunteered for black units only to gain promotion found that experience altered their opinions. After just one month with black troops, a white captain informed his wife, "I have a more elevated opinion of their abilities than I ever had before. I *know* that many of them are vastly the *superiors* of those (many of those) who would condemn them all to a life of brutal degradation." One general reported that his "colored regiments" possessed "remarkable apti-

tude for military training," and another observer said, "They fight like fiends."

Black troops created this change through their dedication. They had a mission to destroy slavery and demonstrate their equality. "When Rebellion is crushed," wrote a black volunteer from Connecticut, "who will be more proud than *I* to say, 'I was one of the first of the despised race to leave the free North with a rifle on my shoulder, and give the lie to the old story that the black man will not fight.'" Corporal James Henry Gooding of Massachusetts's black 54th Regiment explained that his unit intended "to live down all prejudice against its color, by a determination to do well in any position it is put." After an engagement he was proud that "a regiment of white men gave us three cheers as we were passing them," because "it shows that we did our duty as men should." Through such experience under fire the blacks and

Black enlistments were vital to the Union Army, and military service made a major impact on those who had been slaves. These photographs, taken by a photographer accompanying the Union troops, show Hubbard Pryor before and after he enlisted in 1864 in Tennessee. Pryor survived the war. He married a former slave, and he and his wife worked as farmers and raised four children.   National Archives.

whites of the 54th Massachusetts forged deep bonds. Just before the regiment launched its costly assault on Fort Wagner, in Charleston harbor, a black soldier called out to abolitionist Colonel Robert Gould Shaw, "Colonel, I will stay by you till I die." "And he kept his word," noted a survivor of the attack. "He has never been seen since."

Such valor emerged despite persistent discrimination. Off-duty black soldiers were sometimes attacked by northern mobs; on duty, they did most of the "fatigue duty," or heavy labor. The Union government, moreover, paid white privates $13 per month plus a clothing allowance of $3.50, whereas black privates earned only $10 per month less $3 deducted for clothing. Outraged by this injustice, the men of the 54th and 55th Massachusetts refused to accept any pay whatever, and Congress eventually remedied the inequity. In this instance, at least, the majority of legislators agreed with a white private that black troops had "proved their title to *manhood* on many a bloody field fighting freedom's battles."

 ## The Tide of Battle Begins to Turn

The fighting in the spring and summer of 1863 did not settle the war, but it began to place clear limits on the outcome. The campaigns began in a deceptively positive way for Confederates, as their Army of Northern Virginia performed brilliantly in the Battle of Chancellorsville. For once a large Civil War army was not slow and cumbersome but executed tactics with speed and precision. On May 2 and 3, some 130,000 members of the Union Army of the Potomac bore down on fewer than 60,000 Confederates (see map, page 427). Boldly, as if they enjoyed being outnumbered, Lee and Stonewall Jackson divided their forces, ordering 30,000 men under Jackson on a day-long march westward to gain position for a flank attack. This classic turning movement was boldly carried out in the face of great numerical disadvantage. Arriving at their position late in the afternoon, Jackson's seasoned "foot cavalry" found unprepared Union troops laughing, smoking, and playing cards. The Union soldiers had no idea they were under attack until frightened deer and rabbits bounded out of the forest, followed by gray-clad troops. The Confederate attack drove the entire right side of the Union Army back in confusion. Eager to press his advantage, Jackson rode forward with

Battle of Chancellorsville

a few officers to study the ground. As they returned, southern troops mistook them for federals in the fading light and fired, fatally wounding their commander. The next day Union forces left in defeat. Chancellorsville was a remarkable southern victory but costly because of the loss of Stonewall Jackson.

July brought crushing defeats for the Confederacy in two critical battles—Vicksburg and Gettysburg—that effectively circumscribed Confederate hopes for independence. Vicksburg was a vital western citadel, the last major fortification on the Mississippi River in southern hands (see map, page 409). After months of searching through swamps and bayous, General Ulysses S. Grant found an advantageous approach to the city. He laid siege to Vicksburg in May, bottling up the defending army of General John Pemberton. If Vicksburg fell, Union forces would control the river, cutting the Confederacy in half and gaining an open path into its interior. To stave off such a result, Jefferson Davis gave command of all other forces in the area to General Joseph E. Johnston and beseeched him to go to Pemberton's aid. Meanwhile, at a council of war in Richmond, General Robert E. Lee proposed a Confederate invasion of the North. Although such an offensive would not relieve Vicksburg directly, it could stun and dismay the North and, if successful, possibly even lead to peace.

Battle of Vicksburg

Lee's troops streamed through western Maryland and into Pennsylvania, threatening both Washington and Baltimore. As his superb army advanced, the possibility of a major victory near the Union capital became more and more likely. Confederate prospects along the Mississippi, however, darkened. Davis repeatedly wired General Johnston, urging him to concentrate his forces and attack Grant's army. Johnston, however, did nothing effective and telegraphed at one point, "I consider saving Vicksburg hopeless." Grant's men, meanwhile, were supplying themselves from the abundant crops of the Mississippi River valley and could continue their siege indefinitely. Their rich meat-and-vegetables diet became so tiresome, in fact, that one day, as Grant rode by, a private looked up and muttered, "Hardtack" (dry biscuits). Soon a line of soldiers was shouting "Hardtack! Hardtack!" demanding respite from turkey and sweet potatoes.

In such circumstances the fall of Vicksburg was inevitable, and on July 4, 1863, its commander surrendered. The same day a battle that had been rag-

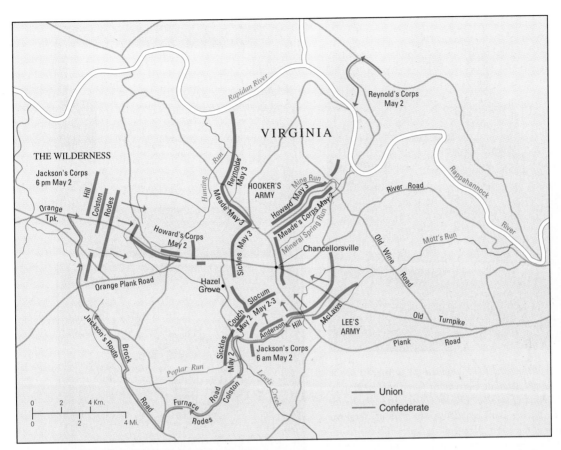

The Battle of Chancellorsville, May 2–3, 1863 *At Chancellorsville on the first day, Jackson and Lee successfully carried out a daring flanking movement to the west, around the Union forces' right. Although federal forces were driven back in confusion, the victory was costly to the Confederacy, for Jackson suffered a fatal wound.*

Battle of Gettysburg

ing for three days concluded at Gettysburg, Pennsylvania. On July 1 Confederate forces hunting for a supply of shoes had collided with part of the Union Army. Heavy fighting on the second day left federal forces in possession of high ground along Cemetery Ridge. There they enjoyed the protection of a stone wall and a clear view of their foe across almost a mile of open field. Undaunted, Lee believed his splendid troops could break the Union line, and on July 3 he ordered a direct assault. Full of foreboding, General James Longstreet warned Lee that "no 15,000 men ever arrayed for battle can take that position." But Lee stuck to his plan. Brave troops under General George E. Pickett methodically marched up the slope in a doomed assault known as Pickett's Charge. For a moment a hundred Confederates breached the enemy's line, but most fell in heavy slaughter. On July 4 Lee had to withdraw, having suffered almost 4,000 dead and about 24,000 missing and wounded. The Confederate general reported to President Davis that "I am alone to blame" and offered to resign. Davis replied that to find a more capable commander was "an impossibility."

Southern troops displayed unforgettable courage and dedication at Gettysburg, but the results there and at Vicksburg were disastrous. The Confederacy was split in two; west of the Mississippi General E. Kirby Smith had to operate on his own, virtually independent of Richmond. Moreover, the heartland of the Confederacy lay exposed to invasion, and Lee's defeat spelled the end of major southern offensive actions. Too weak to prevail in attack, the Confederacy henceforth would have to conserve its limited resources and rely on a prolonged defense. By refusing to be beaten, the South might yet win, but its prospects were darker than ever before.

These "children of the battlefield" aroused great interest in the North after a burial detail at Gettysburg found this ambrotype clutched in the hand of a fallen Union soldier. After thousands of copies of the picture were circulated, the wife of Sergeant Amos Humiston of the 154th New York Infantry (above) recognized her children and knew that she was a widow. The C. Craig Caba Gettysburg Collection, from *Gettysburg*. Larry Sherer © 1991 Time-Life Books, Inc.

 ## The Disintegration of Confederate Unity

Both northern and southern governments waged the final two years of the war in the face of increasing opposition at home. Dissatisfactions that had surfaced earlier grew more intense and sometimes violent. The gigantic costs of a war that neither side seemed able to win fed the unrest. But protest also arose from fundamental stresses in the social structures of North and South.

The Confederacy's problems were both more serious and more deeply rooted than the North's. Vastly disadvantaged in industrial capacity, natural resources, and labor, southerners felt the cost of the war more quickly, more directly, and more painfully than northerners. But even more fundamental were the Confederacy's internal problems; crises that were integrally connected with the southern class system threatened the Confederate cause.

One ominous development was the planters' increasing opposition to their own government, whose actions often had a negative effect on them. Not only did the Richmond government impose new taxes and the tax-in-kind, but Confederate military authorities also impressed slaves to build fortifications. And when Union forces advanced on plantation areas, Confederate commanders burned stores of cotton that lay in the enemy's path. Such interference with plantation routines and financial interests was not what planters had expected of their government, and they complained bitterly.

Nor were the centralizing policies of the Davis administration popular. The increasing size and power of the Richmond administration startled and alarmed planters who had condemned federal usurpations. In fact, the Confederate constitution had granted substantial powers to the central government, especially in time of war. But many planters assumed with R. B. Rhett, editor of the *Charleston Mercury*, that the Confederate constitution "leaves the States untouched in their Sovereignty, and commits to the Confederate Government only a few simple objects, and a few simple powers to enforce them." Governor Joseph E.

Brown of Georgia took a similarly inflated view of the importance of the states. During the brief interval between Georgia's secession from the Union and its admission to the Confederacy, Brown sent an ambassador to Europe to seek recognition for the sovereign republic of Georgia from Queen Victoria, Napoleon III, and the king of Belgium.

Years of opposition to the federal government within the Union had frozen southerners in a defensive posture. Now they erected the barrier of states' rights as a defense against change, hiding behind it while their capacity for creative statesmanship atrophied. Planters sought, above all, a guarantee that their plantations and their lives would remain untouched; they were not deeply committed either to building a southern nation or to winning independence. If the Confederacy had been allowed to depart from the Union in peace and continue as a semideveloped cotton-growing region, they would have been content. When secession revolutionized their world, they could not or would not adjust.

Confused and embittered planters struck out at Jefferson Davis. Conscription, thundered Governor Brown, was "subversive of [Georgia's] sovereignty, and at war with all the principles for the support of which Georgia entered into this revolution." Searching for ways to frustrate the law, Brown bickered over draft exemptions and ordered local enrollment officials not to cooperate with the Confederacy. The *Charleston Mercury* told readers that "conscription . . . is . . . the very embodiment of Lincolnism, which our gallant armies are today fighting." In a gesture of stubborn selfishness, Robert Toombs of Georgia, a former United States senator, refused to switch from cotton to food crops, defying the wishes of the government, the newspapers, and his neighbors' petitions. His action bespoke the inflexibility and frustration of the southern elite at a crucial point in the Confederacy's struggle to survive.

The southern courts ultimately upheld Davis's power to conscript. He continued to provide strong leadership and steered through Congress measures that gave the Confederacy a fighting chance. Despite his cold formality and inability to disarm critics, Davis possessed two important virtues: iron determination and total dedication to independence. These qualities kept the Confederacy afloat, for he implemented his measures and enforced them. But his actions earned him the hatred of most influential and elite citizens.

Meanwhile, for ordinary southerners, the dire predictions of hunger and suffering were becoming a

The impoverishment of nonslaveholding white families was a critical problem for the Confederacy. The sale of this sheet music was intended not only to boost morale but also to raise money that could be used to aid the hungry and needy. This effort and larger government initiatives, however, failed to solve the problem.   Chicago Historical Society.

reality. Food riots occurred in the spring of 1863 in Atlanta, Macon, Columbus, and Augusta, Georgia, and in Salisbury and High Point, North Carolina. On April 2, a crowd assembled in Richmond, the Confederate capital, to demand relief. A passerby, noticing the excitement, asked a young girl, "Is there some celebration?" "We celebrate our right to live," replied the girl. "We are starving. As soon as enough of us get together we are going to the bakeries and each of us will take a loaf of bread." Soon they did just that, sparking a riot that Davis himself had to quell at gunpoint. Later that year, another group of angry rioters looking for food ransacked a street in Mobile, Alabama.

Food Riots in Southern Cities

Throughout the rural South, ordinary people resisted more quietly—by refusing to cooperate with conscription, tax collection, and impressments of food. "In all the States impressments are evaded by every means which ingenuity can suggest, and in some openly resisted," wrote a high-ranking commissary officer. Farmers who did provide food for the army refused to accept payment in certificates of credit or government bonds, as required by law. Conscription officers increasingly found no one to draft—men of draft age were hiding out in the forests. "The disposition to avoid military service is general," observed one of Georgia's senators in 1864. In some areas tax agents were killed in the line of duty.

Jefferson Davis was ill equipped to deal with such discontent. Austere and private by nature, he failed to communicate with the masses. Often he buried himself in military affairs or administrative details, until a crisis forced him to rush off on a speaking tour to revive the spirit of resistance. His class perspective also distanced him from the sufferings of the common people. While his social circle in Richmond dined on duck and oysters, ordinary southerners recovered salt from the drippings on their smokehouse floors and went hungry. State governors who responded to people's needs won the public's loyalty, but Davis failed to reach out to the plain folk and thus lost their support.

Such discontent was certain to affect the Confederate armies. "What man is there that would stay in the army and no that his family is sufring at home?" an angry citizen wrote anonymously to the secretary of war. Worried about their loved ones and resentful of what they saw as a rich man's war, large numbers of men did indeed leave the armies. Their friends and neighbors gave them support. Mary Boykin Chesnut observed a man being dragged back to the army as his wife looked on. "Desert agin, Jake!" she cried openly. "You desert agin, quick as you kin. Come back to your wife and children."

Desertions from the Confederate Army

Desertion did not become a serious problem for the Confederacy until mid-1862, and stiffer policing solved the problem that year. But from 1863 on, the number of men on duty fell rapidly as desertions soared. By mid-1863, John A. Campbell, the South's assistant secretary of war, wondered whether "so general a habit" as desertion could be considered a crime. Campbell estimated that 40,000 to 50,000 troops were absent without leave and that 100,000 were evading duty in some way. Furloughs, amnesty proclamations, and appeals to return had little effect; by November 1863, Secretary of War James Seddon admitted that one-third of the army could not be accounted for. The situation was to worsen.

The defeats at Gettysburg and Vicksburg dealt a body blow to Confederate morale. When the news reached Josiah Gorgas, the genius of Confederate ordnance operations, he confided to his diary, "Today absolute ruin seems our portion. The Confederacy totters to its destruction." In desperation President Davis and several state governors resorted to threats and racial scare tactics to drive southern whites to further sacrifice. Defeat, Davis warned, would mean "extermination of yourselves, your wives, and children." Governor Charles Clark of Mississippi predicted "elevation of the black race to a position of equality—aye, of superiority, that will make them your masters and rulers." Abroad, British officials held back the delivery of badly needed warships, and recognition of the Confederate state became even more unlikely (see page 433).

From this point on, the internal disintegration of the Confederacy quickened. A few newspapers began to call openly for peace. "We are for peace," admitted the *Raleigh* (North Carolina) *Daily Progress*, "because there has been enough of blood and carnage, enough of widows and orphans." A neighboring journal, the *North Carolina Standard*, tacitly admitted that defeat was inevitable and called for negotiations. Similar proposals were made in several state legislatures, though they were presented as plans for independence on honorable terms. Confederate leaders began to realize that they were losing the support of the common people. Governor Zebulon Vance of North Carolina wrote privately that independence would require more "blood and misery . . . and our people will not pay this price I am satisfied for their independence. . . . The great popular heart is not now & never has been in this war."

In North Carolina a peace movement grew under the leadership of William W. Holden, a popular Democratic politician and editor. Over one hundred public meetings took place in the summer of 1863 in support of peace negotiations, and many seasoned political observers believed that Holden had the majority of the people behind him. In Georgia early in 1864, Governor Brown and Alexander H. Stephens, vice president of the Confederacy, led a similar effort. Ultimately, however, these movements came to naught. The lack of a two-party system threw into question the legitimacy of any criticism of the government; even Holden and Brown could not entirely escape the taint of dishonor and disloyalty. That the movement existed at all demonstrates deep disaffection.

Southern Peace Movements

The results of the 1863 congressional elections strengthened dissent in the Confederacy. Everywhere secessionists and supporters of the administration lost seats to men not identified with the government. Many of the new representatives were former Whigs who opposed the Davis administration or publicly favored peace. In the last years of the war, much of Davis's support in the Confederate Congress came from Union-occupied districts, whose people would share no burdens of the war effort until success was achieved.

Having previously secured the legislation he needed, Davis used the government bureaucracy and the army to enforce his unpopular policies. Ironically, as the Confederacy's prospects grew desperate, former critics such as the *Charleston Mercury* became supporters of the administration. They and a core of courageous, determined soldiers kept the Confederacy alive in spite of disintegrating popular support.

By 1864 much of the opposition to the war had moved entirely outside the political sphere. Southerners were simply giving up the struggle and withdrawing their cooperation from the government. Deserters dominated whole towns and counties. Secret societies favoring reunion, such as the Heroes of America and the Red Strings, sprang up. Active dissent spread everywhere and was particularly common in upland and mountain regions. "The condition of things in the mountain districts of North Carolina, South Carolina, Georgia, and Alabama," admitted Assistant Secretary of War John A. Campbell, "menaces the existence of the Confederacy as fatally as either of the armies of the United States." Confederate officials tried using the army to round up deserters and compel obedience, but this approach was only temporarily effective. The government was losing the support of its citizens.

 ## Antiwar Sentiment in the North

In the North opposition to the war was similar but less severe. Alarm intensified over the growing centralization of government, and war-weariness was widespread. Resentment of the draft sparked protest, especially among poor citizens, and the Union Army struggled with a desertion rate as high as the Confederates'. But the Union was so much richer than the South in human resources that none of these problems ever threatened the effectiveness of the government. Fresh recruits were always available, and there were no shortages of food and other necessities.

Also, Lincoln possessed a talent that Davis lacked: he knew how to stay in touch with the ordinary citizen. Through letters to newspapers and to soldiers' families, he reached the common people and demonstrated that he had not forgotten them. The daily carnage, the tortuous political problems, and the ceaseless criticism weighed heavily on him. But this president—a self-educated man of humble origins—was able to communicate his suffering. His moving words helped to contain northern discontent, though they could not remove it.

Much of the wartime protest in the North was political in origin. The Democratic Party fought to regain power by blaming Lincoln for the war's carnage, the expansion of federal powers, inflation and the high tariff, and the emancipation of blacks. Appealing to tradition, its leaders called for an end to the war and reunion on the basis of "the Constitution as it is and the Union as it was." The Democrats denounced conscription and martial law and defended states' rights and the interests of agriculture. They charged repeatedly that Republican policies were designed to flood the North with blacks, depriving white males of their status, their jobs, and their women. These claims appealed to southerners who had settled north of the Ohio River, to conservatives, to many poor people, and to some eastern merchants who had lost profitable southern trade. In the 1862 congressional elections, the Democrats made a strong comeback, and peace Democrats—who would go much farther than others in their party to end the war—had influence in New York State and majorities in the legislatures of Illinois and Indiana.

Peace Democrats

Led by outspoken men like Representative Clement L. Vallandigham of Ohio, the peace Democrats made themselves highly visible. Vallandigham criticized Lincoln as a dictator who had suspended the writ of habeas corpus without congressional authority and had arrested thousands of innocent citizens. Like other Democrats, he condemned both conscription and emancipation and urged voters to use their power at the polling place to depose "King Abraham." Vallandigham stayed carefully within legal bounds, but his attacks seemed so damaging to the war effort that military authorities arrested him for treason after Lincoln suspended habeas corpus. Lincoln wisely decided against punishment—and martyr's status—for the senator and exiled him to the Confederacy, thus ridding himself of a troublesome critic and saddling puzzled Confederates with a man who insisted on talking about "our country." (Eventually Vallandigham returned to the North through Canada.)

Mobs in the New York City draft riots directed much of their anger at African-Americans. Rioters burned an orphanage for black children and killed scores of blacks. This wood engraving, which appeared in the Illustrated London News *on August 8, 1863, depicts a lynching in Clarkson Street.*   Chicago Historical Society.

Lincoln believed that antiwar Democrats were linked to secret organizations that harbored traitorous ideas, such as the Knights of the Golden Circle and the Order of American Knights. These societies, he feared, encouraged draft resistance, discouraged enlistment, sabotaged communications, and plotted to aid the Confederacy. Likening such groups to a poisonous snake, Republicans sometimes branded them—and by extension the peace Democrats—as Copperheads. Though Democrats were connected with these organizations, most engaged in politics rather than treason. And though some saboteurs and Confederate agents were active in the North, they never brought about any major demonstration of support for the Confederacy.

More violent opposition to the government arose from ordinary citizens facing the draft, which became law in 1863. The urban poor and immigrants in strongly Democratic areas were especially hostile to conscription. Federal enrolling officers made up the lists of eligibles, a procedure open to personal favoritism and prejudice. Many men, including some of modest means, managed to avoid the army by hiring a substitute or paying commutation, but the poor viewed the commutation fee as discriminatory, and many immigrants suspected (wrongly, on the whole) that they were called in disproportionate numbers. (Approximately 200,000 men born in Germany and 150,000 born in Ireland served in the Union Army.)

As a result, there were scores of disturbances and melees. Enrolling officers received rough treatment in many parts of the North, and riots occurred in New Jersey, Ohio, Indiana, Pennsylvania, Illinois, and Wisconsin. By far the most serious outbreak of violence occurred in New York City in July 1863. The war was unpopular in that Democratic stronghold, and racial, ethnic, and class tensions ran high. Shippers had recently broken a longshoremen's strike by hiring black strikebreakers to work under police protection. Working-class New Yorkers feared an inflow of black labor from the South and regarded blacks as the cause of the bloody war. Irish workers, many recently arrived and poor, resented being forced to serve in the place of others who could afford to avoid the draft.

New York City Draft Riot

Military police officers came under attack first; then mobs crying "Down with the rich" looted wealthy homes and stores. But blacks became the special target. Those who happened to be in the rioters' path were beaten; soon the mob rampaged through African-American neighborhoods, destroying an orphans' asylum. At least seventy-four people died in the violence, which raged out of control for three days. Only the dispatch of army units fresh from Gettysburg ended the episode.

Discouragement and war-weariness reached a peak in the summer of 1864, when the Democratic Party nominated the popular General George B. McClellan for president and inserted a peace plank into its platform. The plank, written by Vallandigham, condemned "four years of failure to restore the Union by the experiment of war," called clearly for an armistice, and spoke vaguely about preserving the Union. Lincoln, running with Tennessee's Andrew Johnson on a "National Union" ticket, concluded that it was "exceedingly probable that this Administration will not be reelected." During a publicized interchange with Confederate officials sent to Canada, Lincoln insisted that the terms for peace include reunion and "the abandonment of slavery." A wave of protest arose in the North from voters who were weary of war and dedicated only to reunion. Lincoln quickly backtracked, denying that his offer meant "that nothing *else* or *less* would be considered, if offered." He would insist on freedom only for those slaves (about 134,000) who had joined the Union Army under his promise of emancipation. Lincoln's action showed his political weakness, but the fortunes of war soon changed the electoral situation.

Northern Pressure and Southern Will

Northern Diplomatic Strategy

The success of the North's long-term diplomatic strategy was sealed in 1864. From the outset, the North had pursued one paramount goal: to prevent recognition of the Confederacy by European nations. Foreign recognition would belie Lincoln's claim that the United States was fighting an illegal rebellion and would open the way to the financial and military aid that could ensure Confederate independence. The British elite, however, felt considerable sympathy for southern planters, whose aristocratic values were similar to their own. And both England and France stood to benefit from a divided and weakened America. Thus to achieve their goal, Lincoln and Secretary of State Seward needed to avoid both serious military defeats and unnecessary controversies with the European powers.

Aware that the textile industry employed one-fifth of the British population directly or indirectly,

southerners assumed that British leaders would have to recognize the Confederacy. But at the beginning of the war, British mills had a 50 percent surplus of cotton on hand; later on, new sources of supply in India, Egypt, and Brazil helped to meet Britain's needs; and throughout the war, some southern cotton continued to reach Europe, despite the Confederacy's recommendation that southerners plant and ship no cotton. Refusing to be stampeded into recognition of the Confederacy, the British government kept its eye on the battlefield. France, though sympathetic to the South, was unwilling to act independently of Britain. Confederate agents were able to purchase valuable arms and supplies in Europe and obtained loans from European financiers, but they never achieved a diplomatic breakthrough.

More than once the Union strategy nearly broke down. An acute crisis occurred in 1861 when the overzealous commander of an American frigate stopped the British steamer *Trent* and removed two Confederate ambassadors sailing to Britain. They were imprisoned after being brought ashore. This action was cheered in the North, but the British protested this violation of freedom of the seas and demanded the prisoners' release. Lincoln and Seward waited until northern public opinion cooled and then released the two southerners. Then the sale to the Confederacy of warships constructed in England sparked vigorous protest from United States ambassador Charles Francis Adams. A few English-built ships, notably the *Alabama*, reached open water to serve the South. Over a period of twenty-two months, without entering a southern port (because of the Union blockade), the *Alabama* destroyed or captured more than sixty northern ships. But the British government, as a neutral power, soon barred delivery of warships such as the Laird rams, formidable vessels whose pointed prows were designed to end the blockade by battering the Union ships.

On the battlefield, the northern victory was far from won in 1864. General Nathaniel Banks's Red River campaign, designed to capture more of Louisiana and Texas, quickly fell apart, and the capture of Mobile Bay in August did not cause the fall of Mobile. Union general William Tecumseh Sherman commented that the North had to "keep the war South until they are not only ruined, exhausted, but humbled in pride and spirit."

Military authorities throughout history have agreed that deep invasion is very risky: the farther an army penetrates enemy territory, the more vulnerable its own communications and support become.

Both General Grant (left) and General Lee (right) were West Point graduates and had served in the United States Army during the Mexican War. Their bloody battles against each other in 1864 stirred northern revulsion to the war even as they brought its end in sight.   National Archives.

Moreover, observed the Prussian expert Karl von Clausewitz, if the invader encountered a "truly national" resistance, his troops would be "everywhere exposed to attacks by an insurgent population." Thus if southerners were determined enough to mount a "truly national" resistance, their defiance and the South's vast size could make a northern victory virtually impossible.

General Grant, by now in command of all the federal armies, decided to test these conditions—and southern will—with a strategic innovation of his own: raids on a massive scale. Grant proposed to use whole armies, not just cavalry, to destroy Confederate railroads, thus ruining the enemy's transportation and damaging the South's economy. Abandoning their lines of support, Union troops would live off the land while laying to waste all resources useful to the military and to the civilian population of the Confederacy. After General George H. Thomas's troops won the Battle of Chattanooga in November 1863 by ignoring orders and charging up Missionary Ridge, the heartland of the South lay open. Moving to Virginia, Grant entrusted General Sherman with 100,000 men for a raid deep into the South, toward Atlanta.

Jefferson Davis countered by positioning the army of General Joseph E. Johnston in Sherman's path. Davis's entire political strategy for 1864 was based on demonstrating Confederate military strength and successfully defending Atlanta. The United States presidential election of 1864 was approaching, and Davis hoped that southern resolve would lead to the defeat of Lincoln and the election of a president who would sue for peace. When General Johnston slowly but steadily fell back toward Atlanta, Davis grew anxious and sought assurances that Atlanta would be held. From a purely military point of view, Johnston maneuvered skillfully, but the president of the Confederacy could not take a purely military point of view. When Johnston provided no information and continued to drop back, Davis replaced him with the one-legged General John Hood, who knew his job was to fight. "Our all depends on that army at Atlanta," wrote Mary Boykin Chesnut. "If that fails us, the game is up."

For southern morale, the game was up. Hood attacked but was beaten, and Sherman's army occupied Atlanta on September 2, 1864. The victory buoyed northern spirits and ensured Lincoln's reelection. "There is no hope," Mary Chesnut acknowledged, and a government clerk in Richmond wrote, "Our fondly-cherished visions of peace have vanished like a mirage of the desert." Davis exhorted southerners to fight on and win new victories before the federal elections, but he had to admit that "two-thirds of our men are absent . . . most of them absent without leave." Hood's army marched north to cut Sherman's supply lines and force him to retreat, but Sherman began to march sixty thousand of his men straight to the sea, planning to live off the land and destroying Confederate resources as he went (see map).

Sherman's army was an unusually formidable force, composed almost entirely of battle-tested veterans and officers who had risen through the ranks.

The March to the Sea

Before the march began, army doctors weeded out any men who were weak or sick. Tanned, bearded, tough, and unkempt, the remaining veterans were determined, as one put it, "to Conquer this Rebelien or Die." They believed "the South are to blame for this war" and were ready to make the South pay. Although many harbored racist attitudes, most had come to support emancipation because, as one said,

"Slavery stands in the way of putting down the rebellion." Confederate General Johnston later commented, "There has been no such army since the days of Julius Caesar."

As Sherman's men moved across Georgia, they cut a path 50 to 60 miles wide and more than 200 miles long. The totality of the destruction they caused was awesome. A Georgia woman described the "Burnt Country" this way: "The fields were trampled down and the road was lined with carcasses of horses, hogs, and cattle that the invaders, unable either to consume or to carry with them, had wantonly shot down to starve our people and prevent them from making their crops. The stench in some places was unbearable." Such devastation diminished the South's material resources and sapped its will to resist.

After reaching Savannah in December, Sherman marched his armies north into the Carolinas. To his soldiers, South Carolina was "the root of secession." They burned and destroyed as they moved through, encountering little resistance. The opposing army of General Johnston was small, but Sherman's men should have been prime targets for guerrilla raids and harassing attacks by local defense units. The absence

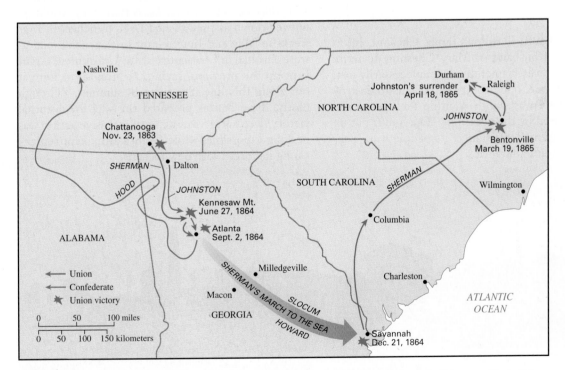

Sherman's March to the Sea *The West proved a decisive theater at the end of the war. From Chattanooga, Union forces drove into Georgia, capturing Atlanta. Then General Sherman embarked on his march of destruction through Georgia to the coast and then northward through the Carolinas.*

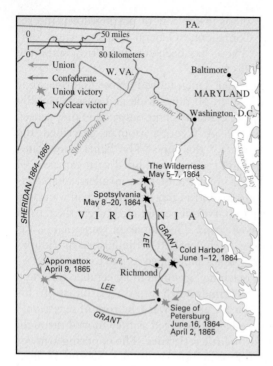

The War in Virginia, 1864–1865 *At great cost, Grant hammered away at Lee's army until the weakened southern forces finally surrendered at Appomattox Courthouse.*

Sherman's march drew additional human resources to the Union cause. In Georgia alone as many as nineteen thousand slaves gladly took the opportunity to escape bondage and join the Union troops as they passed through the countryside. Others remained on the plantations to await the end of the war, either from an ingrained wariness of whites or negative experiences with federal soldiers. The destruction of food harmed slaves as well as white rebels, and many blacks lost blankets, shoes, and other valuables to their liberators. In fact, the brutality of Sherman's troops shocked these veterans of the whip. "I've seen them cut the hams off of a live pig or ox and go off leavin' the animal groanin'," recalled one man. "The master had 'em kilt then, but it was awful."

It was awful, too, in Virginia, where the preliminaries to victory proved protracted and ghastly. Throughout the spring and summer of 1864, intent on capturing Richmond, Grant hurled his troops at Lee's army in Virginia and suffered appalling losses: almost 18,000 casualties in the Battle of the Wilderness, where skeletons poked out of the shallow graves dug one year before; more than 8,000 at Spotsylvania; and 12,000 in the space of a few hours at Cold Harbor (see map). Before the last battle, Union troops pinned scraps of paper bearing their names and addresses to their backs, certain they would be mowed down as they rushed Lee's trenches. In four weeks in May and June, Grant lost as many men as were enrolled in Lee's entire army. Undaunted, Grant kept up the pressure, saying, "I propose to fight it out along this line if it takes all summer." Though costly, these battles prepared the way for eventual victory: Lee's army shrank until offensive action was no longer possible, while Grant's army kept replenishing its forces with new recruits.

of both led South Carolina's James Chesnut, Jr., (a politician and husband of Mary Chesnut) to write that his state "was shamefully and unnecessarily lost. . . . We had time, opportunity and means to destroy him. But there was wholly wanting the energy and ability required by the occasion." The South put up no "truly national" resistance; its people were near the end of their endurance.

At the war's end, the United States flag flew over the state capitol in Richmond, Virginia, which bore many marks of destruction. National Archives.

The death of President Lincoln caused a vast outpouring of grief in the North. As this Currier and Ives print shows, on its way to Illinois, his funeral train stopped at several cities to allow local services to be held. Anne S. K. Brown Military Collection, John Hay Library, Brown University.

The end finally came in the spring of 1865. Grant kept battering Lee, who tried but failed to break through the Union line. With the numerical superiority of Grant's army now greater than two to one, Confederate defeat was inevitable. On April 2 Lee abandoned Richmond and Petersburg. On April 9, hemmed in by Union troops, short of rations, and having fewer than thirty thousand men left, Lee surrendered at Appomattox Courthouse. Grant treated his rival with respect and paroled the defeated troops, allowing cavalrymen to keep their horses and take them home. Within weeks, Davis, who had wanted the war to continue, was captured in Georgia, and the remaining Confederate forces laid down their arms and surrendered. The war was over at last.

Heavy Losses Force Lee's Surrender

With Lee's surrender, Lincoln knew that the Union had been preserved, yet he did not live to see the war's end. On the evening of Good Friday, April 14, he accompanied his wife to Ford's Theatre in Washington to enjoy a popular comedy. There John Wilkes Booth, an embittered southern sympathizer, shot the president in the head at point-blank range. Lincoln died the next day. Twelve days later, troops tracked down and killed Booth. The Union had lost its wartime leader, and millions publicly mourned the martyred chief executive along the route of the funeral train that took his body home to Illinois. Relief at the war's end mingled uncomfortably with a renewed sense of loss and uncertainty about the future.

Costs and Effects

The human costs of the Civil War were enormous (see figure, page 438). The total number of military casualties on both sides exceeded 1 million—a frightful toll for a nation of 31 million people. Approximately 360,000 Union soldiers died, 110,000 of them from wounds suffered in battle. Another 275,175 Union soldiers were wounded but survived. On the Confederate side, an estimated 260,000 lost their lives, and almost as many suffered wounds. More men died in the Civil War than in all other American wars combined until Vietnam. Fundamental disagreements that would continue to trouble the Reconstruction era had caused unprecedented loss of life.

Casualties

Although precise figures on enlistments are impossible to obtain, it appears that 700,000 to 800,000 men served in the Confederate armies. Far more, possibly 2.3 million, served in the Union armies. All

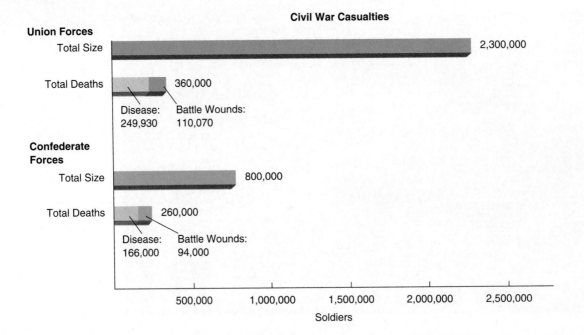

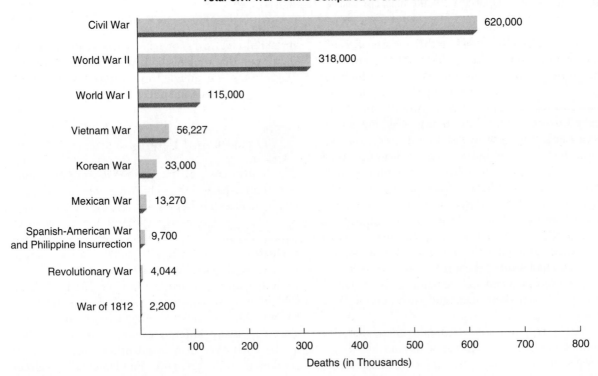

The Unprecedented Human Losses of the Civil War *Month after month newspapers in every community published the names of men who had become casualties. As this graph implies, the newspapers' lists were long.* Source: Shelby Foote, *The Civil War, a Narrative*, 3 vols. (1958–1974); Richard B. Morris, *Encyclopedia of American History* (1982); Archer Jones, *Civil War Command and Strategy* (1992).

these men were taken from home, family, and personal goals and had their lives disrupted in ways that were not easily repaired.

Property damage and financial costs were also enormous, though difficult to tally. United States loans and taxes during the conflict totaled almost $3 billion, and interest on the war debt was $2.8 billion. The Confederacy borrowed over $2 billion but lost far more in the destruction of homes, crops, livestock, and other property. As an example of the wreckage that attended four years of conflict on southern soil, the number of hogs in South Carolina plummeted from 965,000 in 1860 to approximately 150,000 in 1865, leaving many families without their primary source of meat. Scholars have noted that small farmers lost just as much, proportionally, as planters whose slaves were emancipated.

Financial Cost of the War

In southern war zones the landscape was desolated. Soldiers seeking fuel or shelter had cut down many large stands of trees, and artillery shells had blasted many others. Over wide regions fences and crops were destroyed, houses and bridges burned, and fields abandoned and left to erode. Union troops had looted factories and put two-thirds of the South's railroad system out of service. Levees and roads had deteriorated. Visitors to the countryside were struck by how empty and impoverished it looked. Nature would repair much of the damage in time, but large investments of human skill and energy were gone.

Estimates of the total cost of the war exceed $20 billion—five times the total expenditures of the federal government from its creation to 1861. The northern government increased its spending by 700 percent in the first full year of the war; by the last year its spending had soared to twenty times the prewar level. By 1865 the federal government accounted for over 26 percent of the gross national product.

Many of these changes were more or less permanent. In the 1880s, interest on the war debt still accounted for approximately 40 percent of the federal budget and Union soldiers' pensions for as much as 20 percent. The federal government had used its power to support manufacturing and business interests by means of tariffs, loans, and subsidies, and wartime measures left the federal government more deeply involved in the banking and transportation systems. Thus although many southerners had hoped to remove government from the economy, the war made such separation an impossibility. After the war,

federal expenditures shrank but stabilized at twice the prewar level, or at 4 percent of the gross national product.

 ## Conclusion

The Civil War altered American society in many ways. During the war, in both North and South, women had taken on new roles, which could grow or stagnate. Industrialization and large economic enterprises played a larger role than ever before. Ordinary citizens found that their futures were increasingly tied to great organizations. Politically, the defense of national unity brought far-reaching changes in government and policy. Under Republican leadership, the federal government had expanded its power not only to preserve the Union but also to extend freedom. In a sweeping expropriation of what had been considered property, the government emancipated the slaves, and Lincoln had called for "a new birth of freedom" in America. It was unclear, however, whether the nation would use its power to protect the rights of individuals. Would the government guarantee the rights of the former slaves, whose humanity was now recognized? Extreme forms of states' rights dogma clearly were dead, but would Americans continue to favor a state-centered federalism? How would white southerners, embittered and impoverished by the war, respond to efforts to reconstruct the nation?

Closely related to these issues was a question of central importance: what would be the place of black men and women in American life? The Union victory provided a partial answer: slavery as it had existed before the war could not persist. But whether full citizenship and equal rights would take slavery's place remained unclear. Black veterans and former slaves eagerly sought an answer. They would find it during Reconstruction.

Suggestions for Further Reading

The War and the South

Thomas B. Alexander and Richard E. Beringer, *The Anatomy of the Confederate Congress* (1972); Stephen Ash, *When the Yankees Came* (1995); Richard E. Beringer et al., *Why the South Lost the Civil War* (1986); Gabor S. Boritt, *Why the Confederacy Lost* (1992); Richard N. Current, *Lincoln's Loyalists* (1992); William C. Davis, *Jefferson Davis* (1991); Robert F. Durden, *The Gray and the Black: The Confederate Debate on Emancipation* (1972); Paul D. Escott, *Many Excellent People* (1985); Paul D. Escott, *After Secession: Jefferson Davis and the Failure of Confederate Nationalism* (1978); Eli N. Evans, *Judah P. Benjamin* (1987); Mark Grimsley, *The Hard Hand of War* (1995); J. B. Jones, *A Rebel War Clerk's Diary,* 2 vols., ed. Howard Swiggett (1935); Ella Lonn, *Desertion During the Civil War* (1928); Mary Elizabeth Massey, *Refugee Life in the Confederacy* (1964); Larry E. Nelson, *Bullets, Ballots, and Rhetoric: Confederate Policy for the United States Presidential Contest of 1864* (1980); Alan T. Nolan, *Lee Considered* (1991); Harry P. Owens and James J. Cooke, eds., *The Old South in the Crucible of War* (1983); James L. Roark, *Masters Without Slaves* (1977); Daniel Sutherland, *Seasons of War* (1995); Georgia Lee Tatum, *Disloyalty in the Confederacy* (1934); Emory M. Thomas, *The Confederate Nation* (1979); Emory M. Thomas, *The Confederacy as a Revolutionary Experience* (1971); William A. Tidwell, *April '65* (1995); Bell Irvin Wiley, *The Life of Johnny Reb* (1943); Bell Irvin Wiley, *The Plain People of the Confederacy* (1943); W. Buck Yearns, ed., *The Confederate Governors* (1985).

The War and the North

Ralph Andreano, ed., *The Economic Impact of the American Civil War* (1962); Robert Cruden, *The War That Never Ended* (1973); David Donald, ed., *Why the North Won the Civil War* (1960); James W. Geary, *We Need Men* (1991); Wood Gray, *The Hidden Civil War* (1942); Randall C. Jimerson, *The Private Civil War* (1988); Frank L. Klement, *The Copperheads in the Middle West* (1960); Susan Previant Lee and Peter Passell, *A New Economic View of American History* (1979); James M. McPherson, *Battle Cry of Freedom* (1988); James H. Moorhead, *American Apocalypse* (1978); Phillip S. Paludan, *"A People's Contest": The Union and the Civil War, 1861–1865* (1989); Robert Hunt Rhodes, ed., *All for the Union: The Civil War Diary and Letters of Elisha Hunt Rhodes* (1991); George Winston Smith and Charles Burnet Judah, *Life in the North During the Civil War* (1966); George Templeton Strong, *Diary,* 4 vols., ed. Allan Nevins and Milton Hasley Thomas (1952); Paul Studenski, *Financial History of the United States* (1952); Bell Irvin Wiley, *The Life of Billy Yank* (1952).

Women

John R. Brumgardt, ed., *Civil War Nurse: The Diary and Letters of Hannah Ropes* (1980); Beth Gilbert Crabtree and James W. Patton, eds., *"Journal of a Secesh Lady": The Diary of Catherine Ann Devereux Edmondston, 1860–1866* (1979); Jacqueline Jones, *Labor of Love, Labor of Sorrow* (1985); Mary Elizabeth Massey, *Bonnet Brigades* (1966); George C. Rable, *Civil Wars: Women and the Crisis of Southern Nationalism* (1989); Mary D. Robertson, ed., *Lucy Breckinridge of Grove Hill: The Journal of a Virginia Girl, 1862–1864* (1979); C. Vann Woodward and Elisabeth Muhlenfeld, eds., *Mary Chesnut's Civil War* (1981); Agatha Young, *Women and the Crisis* (1959).

African-Americans

Virginia M. Adams, ed., *On the Altar of Freedom: A Black Soldier's Civil War Letters from the Front* (1991); Ira Berlin, ed., *Freedom: A Documentary History of Emancipation, 1861–1867,* Series I, *The Destruction of Slavery* (1979), and Series II, *The Black Military Experience* (1982); David W. Blight, *Frederick Douglass' Civil War* (1989); Dudley Cornish, *The Sable Arm* (1956); Barbara Jeanne Fields, *Slavery and Freedom on the Middle Ground* (1985); Joseph T. Glatthaar, *Forged in Battle* (1990); Leon Litwack, *Been in the Storm So Long* (1979); James M. McPherson, *The Negro's Civil War* (1965); James M. McPherson, *The Struggle for Equality* (1964); Clarence L. Mohr, *On the Threshold of Freedom* (1986); Benjamin Quarles, *The Negro in the Civil War* (1953).

Military History

Nancy Scott Anderson and Dwight Anderson, *The Generals: Ulysses S. Grant and Robert E. Lee* (1987); Albert Castel, *Decision in the West* (1992); Bruce Catton, *Grant Takes Command* (1969); Bruce Catton, *Grant Moves South* (1960); Benjamin Franklin Cooling, *Forts Henry and Donelson* (1988); Peter Cozzens, *This Terrible Sound* (1992); William C. Davis, ed., *The Image of War,* multivolume (1983–1985); Michael Fellman, *Citizen Sherman* (1995); Shelby Foote, *The Civil War, a Narrative,* 3 vols. (1958–1974); Douglas Southall Freeman, *Lee's Lieutenants,* 3 vols. (1942–1944); Douglas Southall Freeman, *R. E. Lee,* 4 vols. (1934–1935); Joseph T. Glatthaar, *The March to the Sea and Beyond* (1985); Herman Hattaway and Archer Jones, *How the North Won* (1983); Laurence M. Hauptman, *Between Two Fires: American Indians in the Civil War* (1995); Archer Jones, *Civil War Command and Strategy* (1992); Alvin M. Josephy, Jr., *The Civil War in the American West* (1991); Gerald F. Linderman, *Embattled Courage* (1989); Thomas L. Livermore, *Numbers and Losses in the Civil War in America* (1957); Grady McWhiney and Perry D. Jamieson, *Attack and Die* (1982); J. B. Mitchell, *Decisive Battles of the Civil War* (1955); Reid Mitchell, *Civil War Soldiers* (1988); Roy Morris, Jr., *Sheridan* (1992); Charles Royster, *The Destructive War* (1991); Stephen W. Sears, *To the Gates of Richmond* (1992); Stephen W. Sears, *George B. McClellan* (1988); Emory M. Thomas, *Robert E. Lee* (1995); Emory M. Thomas, *Bold Dragoon: The Life of J. E. B. Stuart* (1987); Noah Andre Trudeau, *The Last Citadel* (1991); Steven E. Woodworth, *Jefferson Davis and His Generals* (1990).

Foreign Relations

Stuart L. Bernath, *Squall Across the Atlantic: American Civil War Prize Cases and Diplomacy* (1970); Kinley J. Brauer, "The Slavery Problem in the Diplomacy of the American Civil War," *Pacific Historical Review* 46, no. 3 (1977): 439–469; David P. Crook, *The North, the South, and the Powers, 1861–1865* (1974); Charles P. Cullop, *Confederate Propaganda in Europe* (1969); Norman B. Ferris, *The Trent Affair* (1977); Howard Jones, *Union in Peril* (1992); Frank J. Merli, *Great Britain and the Confederate Navy* (1970); Frank L. Owsley and Harriet Owsley, *King Cotton Diplomacy* (1959); Gordon H. Warren, *Fountain of Discontent: The Trent Affair and Freedom of the Seas* (1981).

Abraham Lincoln and the Union Government

Allan G. Bogue, *The Earnest Men: Republicans of the Civil War Senate* (1981); Gabor S. Borit, ed., *The Historian's Lincoln* (1989); Fawn Brodie, *Thaddeus Stevens* (1959); Richard N. Current, *The Lincoln Nobody Knows* (1958); Leonard P. Curry, *Blueprint for Modern America: Non-Military Legislation of the First Civil War Congress* (1968); Christopher Dell, *Lincoln and the War Democrats* (1975); David Donald, *Charles Sumner and the Rights of Man* (1970); Ludwell H. Johnson, "Lincoln's Solution to the Problem of Peace Terms, 1864–1865," *Journal of Southern History* 34 (November 1968): 441–447; Peyton McCrary, *Abraham Lincoln and Reconstruction: The Louisiana Experiment* (1978); James M. McPherson, *Abraham Lincoln and the Second American Revolution* (1990); Mark Neely, *The Fate of Liberty* (1991); Joel Silbey, *A Respectable Minority: The Democratic Party in the Civil War Era* (1977); Benjamin P. Thomas, *Abraham Lincoln* (1952); Hans L. Trefousse, *The Radical Republicans* (1969); Glyndon G. Van Deusen, *William Henry Seward* (1967); T. Harry Williams, *Lincoln and His Generals* (1952); T. Harry Williams, *Lincoln and the Radicals* (1941).

16

Reconstruction:
A Partial Revolution
1865–1877

For both men, war and Reconstruction brought stunning changes and swift reversals of fortune. In 1861 Robert Smalls was a slave in South Carolina, while Wade Hampton was a South Carolina legislator and one of the richest planters in the South. The events of the next fifteen years turned each man's world upside down more than once.

Robert Smalls became a Union hero when he stole a Confederate ship from Charleston harbor and piloted it to the blockading federal fleet. Thereafter, Smalls guided Union gunboats and toured the North recruiting black troops. Though he enjoyed celebrity status, Smalls encountered racial discrimination in the North and found in 1865 that neither his heroism nor his freedom entitled him to vote. But by 1868 that, too, had changed, and he began a career in politics. Robert Smalls helped write his state's constitution, served in the legislature, and won election to Congress. There he denounced white violence and worked for educational and economic opportunity for his people. But Smalls was helpless to prevent the end of Reconstruction or delay the return of white control in South Carolina.

Wade Hampton joined the Confederate Army in 1861 and soon became a lieutenant-general. The South's defeat profoundly shocked him; and as Union forces closed in, he spoke wildly of "forc[ing] my way across the Mississippi" with "a devoted band of Cavalry" and continuing to fight. The postwar years brought further painful and unexpected changes, including forced bankruptcy. In 1867 Hampton surprised other privileged whites by supporting suffrage for a few educated and propertied former slaves. By 1876 Hampton's fortunes were again on the rise: Democrats nominated him for governor, promising that he would "redeem"

On January 6, 1874, Congressman Robert B. Elliott of South Carolina made an eloquent defense of the proposed civil rights bill. After a review of legal issues, he called on Congress to ignore the opposition of southerners, who had tried to destroy the nation, and deal justly with the Negro race, which had faithfully defended the Union. *Chicago Historical Society.*

South Carolina from Republican misrule. While Hampton spoke misleadingly of respect for blacks' rights, each member of the paramilitary Red Shirts who supported him pledged to "control the vote of at least one Negro, by intimidation, purchase," or other means. Hampton won the governor's chair and then a seat in the United States Senate.

As the careers of Smalls and Hampton suggest, Reconstruction's change was extensive but not lasting. Robert Smalls rose from bondage to experience glory, emancipation, political power, and, ultimately, disappointment. Wade Hampton fell from privilege to endure failure, bankruptcy, powerlessness, and, eventually, a return to power. Similarly, American society experienced both extraordinary change and fundamental continuity. Unprecedented social, political, and constitutional changes took place, but the underlying realities of economic power, racial prejudice, and judicial conservatism limited Reconstruction's revolutionary potential.

Nowhere was the turmoil of Reconstruction more evident than in national politics. Lincoln's successor, Andrew Johnson, and Congress fought bitterly over the shaping of a plan for Reconstruction. Though a southerner, Johnson had always been a foe of the South's wealthy planters, and his first acts as president suggested that he would be tough on traitors. Before the end of 1865, however, Johnson's policies changed direction, and southern aristocrats soon came to view Johnson as their friend and protector. Jefferson Davis stayed in prison for two years, but Johnson pardoned other rebel leaders and allowed them to occupy high offices. He also ordered tax officials to return plantations to their original owners, including abandoned coastal lands on which forty thousand freed men and women had settled by order of General William Tecumseh Sherman early in 1865.

This turn of events alarmed northern voters. Republican congressmen began to discuss plans to keep rebels from regaining control of the South or of Congress. Northern legislators produced a new Reconstruction program, embodied in the Fourteenth Amendment. But southern intransigence blocked that plan and forced a more radical step, the Reconstruction Act of 1867. When Congress put the act into effect, Johnson tried to subvert it, and by 1868 the president and Congress were bitterly antagonistic.

Before these struggles were over, Congress had impeached the president, enfranchised the freed men, and given them a role in reconstructing the South. The nation also adopted the Fourteenth and Fifteenth Amendments. Yet some underlying realities never changed. Little was done to open the doors of economic opportunity to black southerners. Judicially, the Supreme Court adopted interpretations of the Thirteenth, Fourteenth, and Fifteenth Amendments that crippled their power for decades. Throughout this period of upheaval, few saw equal rights for African-Americans as the central aim of Reconstruction.

By 1869 the Ku Klux Klan was employing extensive violence to thwart Reconstruction and undermine black freedom. As white Democrats in the South recaptured state governments, undoing the political revolution, they encountered little opposition from the North. Voters had grown weary and suspicious of the use of federal power to prop up failing Republican governments. Moreover, as the 1870s advanced, other issues drew attention away from Reconstruction. Industrial growth accelerated, creating new opportunities and raising new problems. Interest in territorial expansion revived. Political corruption became a nationwide scandal, bribery a way of doing business. "Money has become the God of this country," wrote one disgusted observer, "and men, otherwise good men, are almost compelled to worship at her shrine." Eventually these other forces triumphed. As politics moved on to new concerns, the courts turned their attention away from civil rights, and even northern Republicans abandoned racial reforms in 1877.

Thus only limited change emerged from a period of tremendous upheaval. Congress asserted the principle of equality before the law for African-Americans and gave black men the right to vote. But more far-reaching measures to advance black freedom never had much support in Congress, and when suffrage alone proved insufficient to remake the South, the nation soon lost interest. Reconstruction proclaimed anew the American principle of human equality but failed to secure it in reality.

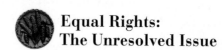 **Equal Rights:
The Unresolved Issue**

For America's former slaves, Reconstruction had one paramount meaning: a chance to explore freedom. A southern white woman admitted in her diary that the black people "showed a natural and exultant joy at being free." Former slaves remembered singing far

• *Important Events* •

into the night after federal troops, who confirmed rumors of their emancipation, reached their plantations. The slaves on a Texas plantation jumped up and down and clapped their hands as one man shouted, "We is free—no more whippings and beatings." A few people gave in to the natural desire to do what had been impossible before. One grandmother who had long resented her treatment dropped her hoe and ran to confront the mistress. "I'm free!" she yelled. "Yes, I'm free! Ain't got to work for you no more! You can't put me in your pocket [sell me] now!" Another man recalled that he and others "started on the move," either to search for family members or just to exercise their newfound freedom of movement.

Most freed men and women reacted more cautiously and shrewdly, taking care to test the boundaries of their new condition. "After the war was over," explained one man, "we was afraid to move. Just like terrapins or turtles after emancipation. Just stick our heads out to see how the land lay." As slaves they had learned to expect hostility from white people, and they did not presume it would instantly disappear. Life in freedom might still be a matter of what was allowed, not what was right. "You got to say master?" asked a freedman in Georgia. "Naw," answered his fellows, but "they said it all the same. They said it for a long time." One sign of this shrewd caution was the way freed people evaluated potential employers. "Most all the Negroes that had good owners stayed with 'em, but the others left. Some of 'em come back and some didn't," explained one man. If a white person had been relatively considerate to blacks in bondage, they reasoned that he might prove a desirable employer in freedom. Others left their plantations all at once, for, as one put it, "that master am sure mean and if we doesn't have to stay we shouldn't, not with that master."

In addition to a fair employer, freed men and women wanted opportunity through education and, especially, through landownership. Land represented their chance to farm for themselves, to enjoy the independence that generations of American farmers valued. It represented compensation for generations of travail in bondage. A northern observer noted that slaves freed in the Sea Islands of South Carolina and Georgia made "plain, straight-forward" inquiries as they settled the land set aside for them by Sherman. They wanted to be sure the land "would be theirs after they had improved it." Everywhere, blacks young and old thirsted for homes of their own.

African-Americans' Desire for Land

But how much of a chance would whites, who were in power in 1865, give to blacks? Northerners' racial attitudes were evolving but remained generally unfavorable. Abolitionists and many Republicans helped African-Americans fight for equal rights, and they won some victories. In 1864 the federal courts accepted black testimony, and the next year the Thirteenth Amendment became law. New York City and the District of Columbia desegregated their streetcars, and Massachusetts enacted a comprehensive public accommodations law. Nevertheless, signs of resistance to racial equality abounded. The Democratic Party fought hard against equality, charging that Republicans favored race-mixing and were undermining the status of white workers. Voters in three states—Connecticut, Minnesota, and Wisconsin—rejected black suffrage in 1865.

Even northern reformers who with Lincoln's encouragement had administered the Sea Islands during the war showed little sympathy for black aspirations. The former Sea Island slaves wanted to establish small, self-sufficient farms. Northern soldiers, officials, and missionaries of both races brought education and aid to the freedmen but also insisted that they grow cotton. They emphasized profit and the values of competitive capitalism. It would be "most unwise and injurious," wrote one worker in the Sea Islands, to give former slaves free land.

"The Yankees preach nothing but cotton, cotton!" complained one Sea Island black. "We wants land," wrote another, but tax officials "make the lots too big, and cut us out." Indeed, the United States government sold thousands of acres in the Sea Islands for nonpayment of taxes, but 90 percent of the land went to wealthy investors from the North. Even after blacks pooled their earnings, they were able to buy fewer than two thousand of nearly seventeen thousand acres sold in March 1863. Thus even from their strongest northern supporters the former slaves received only partial support. How much opportunity would freedom bring? That was a vital question, whose answer depended on the evolution of policy in Washington.

Johnson's Reconstruction Plan

When Reconstruction began under President Andrew Johnson, many expected his policies to be harsh. Throughout his career in Tennessee he had criticized the wealthy planters and championed the small farmers. When an assassin's bullet thrust Johnson into the presidency, many former slaveowners shared the dismay of a North Carolina woman who wrote, "Think of Andy Johnson [as] the president! What will become of us—'the aristocrats of the South' as we are termed?" Northern Radicals also had reason to believe that Johnson would deal sternly with the South. When one of them suggested the exile or execution of ten or twelve leading rebels to set an example, Johnson replied, "How are you going to pick out so small a number? . . . *Treason* is a crime; and *crime* must be punished."

Through 1865 Johnson alone controlled Reconstruction policy, for Congress recessed shortly before he became president and did not reconvene until December. In the following eight months, Johnson devised and put into operation his own plan, forming new state governments in the South by using his power to grant pardons.

Wartime proposals for Reconstruction had produced much controversy but no consensus. In December 1863 Lincoln had proposed a "10 percent" plan for a government being organized in captured parts of Louisiana. Under this plan, a state government could be established as soon as 10 percent of those who had voted in 1860 took an oath of future loyalty to the Union. Only high-ranking Confederate officials would be denied

Lincoln's Reconstruction Plan

a chance to take the oath, and Lincoln urged that at least a few well-qualified blacks be given the ballot. Radicals bristled, however, at such a mild plan, and Congress backed the much stiffer Wade-Davis bill, which required 50 percent of the voters to swear an "iron-clad" oath that they had never voluntarily supported the rebellion. Lincoln pocket-vetoed this measure.

Later, in 1865, Lincoln suggested but then abandoned even more lenient terms. At the Hampton Roads Conference, he raised questions about the extent of emancipation and discussed compensation and restoration to the Union, with full rights, of the very state governments that had tried to leave it. In April he considered allowing the Virginia legislature to convene in order to withdraw its support from the Confederate war effort. Faced with strong opposition in his cabinet, Lincoln reversed himself, denying that he had intended to confer legitimacy on a rebel government. At the time of his death, he had given tentative approval to a plan, drafted by Secretary of War Edwin Stanton, to impose military authority and appoint provisional governors as steps toward the creation of new state governments. Beyond these general outlines, it is impossible to say what Lincoln would have done had he survived.

Johnson began with Stanton's plan. New governments would be created in the South, but which southerners would be allowed to vote? At a cabinet meeting in May 1865, Johnson's advisers split evenly on the question of giving voting rights to black men in the South. Johnson claimed that he favored black suffrage, but *only* if the southern states adopted it voluntarily. A champion of states' rights and no friend of African-Americans, he regarded this decision as too important to be taken out of the hands of the states.

This racial conservatism had an enduring effect on Johnson's policies. Where whites were concerned, however, Johnson seemed to be pursuing radical changes in class relations.

Oaths of Amnesty and New State Governments

He proposed rules that would keep the wealthy planter class out of power. Southerners were required to swear an oath of loyalty as a condition of gaining amnesty or pardon, but Johnson barred several categories of people from taking the oath. Former federal officials who had violated their oaths to support the United States and had aided the Confederacy could not take the oath. Nor

Combative and inflexible, President Andrew Johnson contributed greatly to the failure of his own reconstruction program. Library of Congress.

could high-ranking Confederate officers and political leaders or graduates of West Point or Annapolis who had resigned their commissions to fight for the South. To this list Johnson added another important group: all southerners who aided the rebellion and whose taxable property was worth more than $20,000. All such individuals had to apply personally to the president for pardon and restoration of their political rights; otherwise, they risked legal penalties, which included confiscation of their land.

Thus it appeared that the leadership class of the Old South would be removed from power, for virtually all the rich and powerful whites of prewar days needed Johnson's special pardon. Many observers in both South and North sensed that the president meant to take revenge on the haughty aristocrats whom he had always resented and to raise up a new leadership of deserving yeomen.

Johnson appointed provisional governors who began the Reconstruction process by calling constitutional conventions. The delegates chosen for these conventions had to draft new constitutions that eliminated slavery and invalidated secession. After ratification of these constitutions, new governments could be elected, and the states would be restored to the Union with full congressional representation. But only those southerners who had taken the oath of amnesty and been eligible to vote on the day the state seceded could participate in this process. Thus unpardoned whites and former slaves were not eligible.

If Johnson intended to strip the old elite of its power, his plan did not work as he hoped. The old white leadership proved resilient and influential; prominent Confederates (a few with pardons but many without) won elections and turned up in various appointive offices. Then, surprisingly, Johnson helped to subvert his own plan: he started pardoning aristocrats and leading rebels who should not have been in office. He hired additional clerks to write out the necessary documents and then began to issue pardons to large categories of people. These pardons, plus the return of planters' abandoned lands, restored the old elite to power.

Why did Johnson allow the planters to regain power? Perhaps vanity betrayed his judgment. Wealthy men of the type who previously had scorned him now waited for appointments with him. Too long a lonely outsider, Johnson may have succumbed to the attention and flattery of the pardon seekers. But he also ran out of time. It took months for the constitutional conventions and elections to take place; by the time the process had restored Confederate leaders to powerful positions, the reconvening of Congress was imminent. To scrap his plan and remove the planters would be to admit failure. Since Johnson believed in white supremacy and wanted southern support in the 1866 elections, he decided to endorse the new governments and declare Reconstruction complete. Thus in December 1865 many Confederate congressmen traveled to Washington to claim seats in the United States Congress. Even Alexander Stephens, vice president of the Confederacy, returned to the capital as a senator-elect.

The election of such prominent rebels troubled many northerners. So did other results of Johnson's program. Some of the state conventions were slow to repudiate secession; others admitted only grudgingly that slavery was dead. Two refused to take any action to repudiate the large Confederate debt, which northerners felt should not be paid. Even

Johnson admitted that these acts showed "something like defiance, which is all out of place at this time."

Furthermore, to define the status of freed men and women and control their labor, some legislatures merely revised large sections of the slave codes by substituting the word *freedmen* for *slave*. The new black codes compelled the former slaves, now supposedly free, to carry passes, observe a curfew, live in housing provided by a landowner, and give up hope of entering many desirable occupations. Stiff vagrancy laws and restrictive labor contracts bound supposedly free laborers to plantations, and "anti-enticement" laws punished anyone who tried to lure these workers to other employment. State-supported institutions in the South, such as schools and orphanages, excluded blacks entirely.

Black Codes

It seemed to northerners that the South was intent on returning African-Americans to a position of servility. Thus the Republican majority in Congress decided to take a closer look at the results of Johnson's plan. On reconvening, the House and Senate considered the credentials of the newly elected southern representatives and decided not to admit them. Instead, they established a joint committee to study Reconstruction and consider new policies. Reconstruction thus entered a second phase, one in which Congress would play the decisive role.

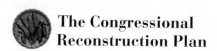 ## The Congressional Reconstruction Plan

Northern congressmen disagreed about what to do, but they did not doubt their right to shape Reconstruction policy. The Constitution mentioned neither secession nor reunion, but it gave Congress an important role in the federal government. Moreover, the Constitution declared that the United States shall guarantee to each state a republican government. This provision, legislators believed, gave them the right to devise policies for Reconstruction.

They soon found that other constitutional questions affected their policies. What, for example, had rebellion done to the relationship between southern states and the Union? Lincoln had always insisted that states could not secede and that the Union remained intact. Not even Andrew Johnson, however, accepted the southern position that state governments of the Confederacy could simply reenter the nation. Johnson argued that the Union had endured, though individuals had erred—thus the use of his power to grant or withhold pardons. Congressmen who favored vigorous Reconstruction measures argued that the war *had* broken the Union. They maintained that the southern states had committed legal suicide and reverted to the status of territories, or that the South was a conquered nation subject to the victor's will. Moderate congressmen held that the states had forfeited their rights through rebellion and thus had come under congressional supervision.

These diverse theories mirrored the diversity of Congress itself. Northern Democrats denounced any idea of racial equality and supported Johnson's policies. Conservative Republicans, despite their party loyalty, favored a limited federal role in Reconstruction. The Radical Republicans, led by Thaddeus Stevens, Charles Sumner, and George Julian, wanted to transform the South. Although they were a minority within their party, they had the advantage of a clearly defined goal. They believed it was essential to democratize the South, establish public education, and ensure the rights of freed people. They favored black suffrage, often supported land confiscation and redistribution, and were willing to exclude the South from the Union for several years if necessary to achieve their goals. A large group of moderate Republicans did not want to go as far as the Radicals but believed some change in Johnson's policies was necessary.

The Radicals

One overwhelming political reality faced all four groups: the 1866 elections were approaching in the fall. Having questioned Johnson's program, Congress needed to develop an alternative plan and avoid going before the voters empty-handed. Thus these politicians had to forge a majority coalition composed either of Democrats and Republicans or of various elements of the Republican Party. The nature of the coalition would determine the kind of plan that Congress developed.

Ironically, Johnson and the Democrats sabotaged the possibility of a conservative coalition. They refused to cooperate with conservative or moderate Republicans and stubbornly insisted that Reconstruction was over, that the new state governments were legitimate, and that southern representatives should be admitted to Congress. These intransigent positions eliminated the Democrats' potential influence and blasted any possibility of bipartisan compromise. To devise a Republican program, conservative and moderate elements in the party had to work with the Radicals. This development and subsequent events enhanced the Radicals' influence. In 1865, however, Republican congressmen were still reluctant to break with the president, who was, for better or for worse, the titular head of their party.

Trying to work with Johnson, Republicans thought a compromise had been reached in the spring of 1866. Under its terms Johnson would agree to two modifications of his program: extension of the life of the Freedmen's Bureau, which Congress had established in 1865 to feed the hungry, negotiate labor contracts, and start schools; and passage of a civil rights bill to counteract the black codes. This bill would force southern courts to practice equality before the law by allowing federal judges to remove from state courts cases in which blacks were treated unfairly. Its provisions applied to discrimination by private individuals as well as by government officials. This was the first major bill to enforce the Thirteenth Amendment's abolition of slavery, and it was to become very important in the twentieth century.

Congress Struggles for a Compromise

Johnson destroyed the compromise, however, by vetoing both bills (they later became law when Congress overrode the president's veto). Denouncing any change in his program, the president condemned Congress's action, questioned its right to make policy, and revealed his own racism. Because the civil rights bill defined United States citizens as native-born persons who were taxed, Johnson claimed it discriminated against "large numbers of intelligent, worthy, and patriotic foreigners . . . in favor of the negro." The bill, he said, operated "in favor of the colored and against the white race."

All hope of working with the president was now dead. But northern Republicans sensed that their constituents remained dissatisfied with Reconstruction. Newspapers reported daily violations of blacks' rights in the South and carried troubling accounts of antiblack violence—notably in Memphis and New Orleans, where police aided brutal mobs in their attacks. Such violence convinced Republicans, and the northern public, that more needed to be done. The various factions of Republican lawmakers therefore continued bargaining among themselves until a plan emerged. It took the form of a proposed amendment to the Constitution, and it represented a compromise between radical and conservative elements of the party. The Fourteenth Amendment was Congress's alternative to Johnson's program of Reconstruction.

In 1866, as Congress reviewed the progress of Reconstruction, news from the South had a considerable impact. Violence against black people, like the riot in Memphis depicted here, helped convince northern legislators that they had to modify President Johnson's policies.   Library of Congress.

Of the four points in the amendment, there was near-universal agreement on one: the Confederate debt was declared null and void, and the war debt of the United States was guaranteed. Northerners rejected the notion of paying taxes to reimburse those who had financed a rebellion, and business groups agreed on the necessity of upholding the credit of the United States government. There was also general support for prohibiting prominent Confederates from holding political office. The amendment therefore barred Confederate leaders from state and federal office. Only Congress, by a two-thirds vote of each house, could remove the penalty.

Fourteenth Amendment

The first section of the Fourteenth Amendment, which would have the greatest legal significance in later years, conferred citizenship on freedmen and prohibited states from abridging their constitutional "privileges and immunities" (see the Appendix). It also barred any state from taking a person's life, liberty, or property "without due process of law" and from denying "equal protection of the laws." These broad phrases became powerful guarantees of African-Americans' civil rights—indeed, of the rights of all citizens—in the twentieth century. They also took on added meaning with court rulings that corporations were legally "persons" (see page 530).

The second section of the amendment dealt with representation and embodied the compromises and political motives that had produced the amendment. Northerners disagreed about whether black citizens should have the right to vote. As a citizen of Indiana wrote to a southern relative, there was strong feeling in favor of "humane and liberal laws for the government and protection of the colored population." But there was prejudice, too. "Although there is a great deal [of] profession among us for the relief of the darkey yet I think much of it is far from being cincere. I guess we want to compel you to do right by them while we are not willing ourselves to do so."

Republican congressmen shied away from confronting this ambivalence, but political reality required them to do something. Representation in Congress depended on population, and each slave had counted as three-fifths of a person. Emancipation made every former slave five-fifths of a person, a fact that would increase southern representation. Thus the postwar South stood to *gain* power in Congress, and if white southerners did not allow blacks to vote, former secessionists would derive all the political benefit from emancipation. What a strange result that would seem to most northerners! They had never planned to reward the South for rebellion, and Republicans in Congress were determined not to hand over power to their political enemies. So they offered the South a choice. According to the second section of the Fourteenth Amendment, states did not have to grant black men the right to vote. But if they did not do so, their representation would be reduced proportionally. If they did enfranchise black men, their representation would be increased proportionally—but, of course, Republicans could seek the support of the new black voters. This compromise protected northern interests and gave Republicans a chance to compete if freedmen gained the ballot.

The Fourteenth Amendment raised the possibility of suffrage for black men but ignored female citizens, black and white. For this reason it provoked a strong reaction from the women's rights movement. Advocates of equal rights for women had worked with abolitionists for decades, often subordinating their cause to that of the slaves. During the drafting of the Fourteenth Amendment, however, female activists demanded to be heard. When legislators defined women as nonvoting citizens, prominent leaders such as Elizabeth Cady Stanton and Susan B. Anthony decided that it was time to end their alliance with abolitionists and fight more determinedly for themselves. Thus the amendment infused new determination into the independent women's rights movement.

In 1866, however, the major question in Reconstruction politics was how the public would respond to the amendment. Johnson did his best to block the Fourteenth Amendment in both North and South. Condemning Congress for its refusal to seat southern representatives, the president urged state legislatures in the South to vote against ratification. Every southern legislature except Tennessee's rejected the amendment by a wide margin. Its best showing was in Alabama,

Southern Rejection of the Fourteenth Amendment

where it failed by a vote of 69 to 8 in the assembly and 27 to 2 in the senate. In three other states the amendment received no support at all.

To present his case to northerners, Johnson organized a National Union Convention and took to the stump himself. In an age when active personal campaigning was rare for a president, Johnson boarded a special train for a "swing around the circle" that carried his message deep into the Midwest and then back to Washington. In cities such as Cleveland and St. Louis, he criticized the Republicans in a ranting, undignified style. Increasingly, audiences rejected his views and hooted and jeered at him.

The elections of 1866 were a resounding victory for Republicans in Congress. Radical and moderate Republicans whom Johnson had denounced won reelection by large margins, and the Republican majority grew as new candidates defeated incumbent Democrats. The North had spoken clearly: Johnson's policies were giving the advantage to rebels and traitors. Although reformers who hoped to eliminate prejudice were only a minority, most northerners feared for "the future peace and safety of the Union." Thus Republican congressional leaders won a mandate to pursue their Reconstruction plan. But, thanks to Johnson and southern intransigence, that plan had reached an impasse. All but one of the southern state governments created by the president had rejected the Fourteenth Amendment and remained adamant. Nothing could be accomplished as long as those governments existed and the southern electorate was constituted as it was. To honor their constituents' wishes, Republicans had little choice but to form new state governments in the South and enfranchise the freedmen. They therefore decided to do both. The unavoidable logic of the situation forced the majority to accept part of the Radical plan.

The Reconstruction Act of 1867 incorporated only a small part of the Radical program. Until new state governments could be set up, Union generals assumed control in five military districts in the South (see map, page 459). Confederate leaders designated in the Fourteenth Amendment were barred from voting until new state constitutions were ratified. The act guaranteed freedmen the right to vote in elections for state constitutional conventions and in subsequent elections under the new constitutions. In addition, each southern state was required to ratify the Fourteenth Amendment and to ratify its new

Reconstruction Act of 1867

Thomas Waterman Wood, who had painted portraits of society figures in Nashville before the war, sensed the importance of Congress's decision in 1867 to enfranchise the freedmen. This oil painting, one of a series on suffrage, emphasizes the significance of the ballot for the black voter.   Cheekwood Museum of Art, Nashville, Tennessee.

of the land affected by his plan was earmarked for freedmen, in forty-acre plots. The rest was to be sold to generate money for veterans' pensions, compensation to loyal citizens for damaged property, and payment of the federal debt. By these means Stevens hoped to win support for a basically unpopular measure. But he failed, and in general the Radicals were not able to generate public support. Northerners were accustomed to a limited role for government, and the business community staunchly opposed any interference with private property rights. Thus black farmers were forced to seek work in a hostile environment in which landowners opposed their acquisition of land, even as renters.

Congress's role as the architect of Reconstruction was not quite over, for its quarrels with Andrew Johnson were growing more bitter. To restrict Johnson's influence and safeguard its plan, Congress passed a number of controversial laws. First, it set the date for its own reconvening—an unprecedented act, for the president traditionally summoned legislators to Washington. Then it limited Johnson's power over the army by requiring the president to issue military orders through the General of the Army, Ulysses S. Grant, who could not be sent from Washington without the Senate's consent. Finally, Congress passed the Tenure of Office Act, which gave the Senate power to interfere with changes in the president's cabinet. Designed to protect Secretary of War Stanton, who sympathized with the Radicals, this law violated the tradition that a president controlled his own cabinet.

Johnson took several belligerent steps of his own. He issued orders to military commanders in the South limiting their powers and increasing the powers of the civil governments he had created in 1865. Then he removed officers who were conscientiously enforcing Congress's new law, preferring commanders who allowed disqualified Confederates to vote. Finally, he tried to remove Secretary of War Stanton. With that attempt the confrontation reached its climax.

constitution and submit it to Congress for approval. Thus African-Americans gained an opportunity to fight for a better life through the political process.

The Radicals had hoped Congress would do much more. Thaddeus Stevens, for example, argued that economic opportunity was essential to the freedmen. "If we do not furnish them with homesteads from forfeited and rebel property," Stevens declared, "and hedge them around with protective laws . . . we had better left them in bondage." Stevens therefore drew up a plan for extensive confiscation and redistribution of land. Only one-tenth

Twice before, the House Judiciary Committee had considered impeachment of Johnson, rejecting the idea once and then recommending it by only a 5-to-4 vote. That recommendation was decisively defeated by the House. After Johnson's last action, however, a third attempt to impeach the president carried easily. In fact, the House was so determined to indict Johnson in 1868 that it voted

Impeachment of President Johnson

Plans for Reconstruction Compared

	Johnson's Plan	Radicals' Plan	Fourteenth Amendment	Reconstruction Act of 1867
Voting	Whites only; Confederate leaders must seek pardons	Give vote to black males	Southern whites may decide but can lose representation	Black men gain vote; whites barred from office by Fourteenth Amendment cannot vote while new state governments are being formed
Officeholding	Many prominent Confederates regain power	Only loyal white and black males eligible	Confederate leaders barred until Congress votes amnesty	Fourteenth Amendment in effect
Time out of Union	Brief	Years; until South is thoroughly democratized	Brief	Brief
Other change in southern society	Little; gain of power by yeomen not realized	Expand public education; confiscate land and provide farms for freedmen	Probably slight	Depends on action of new state governments

before drawing up specific charges. The indictment concentrated on his violation of the Tenure of Office Act, though modern scholars regard his efforts to impede enforcement of the Reconstruction Act of 1867 as a far more serious offense.

Johnson's trial in the Senate began promptly and lasted more than three months. The prosecution, led by Radicals such as Thaddeus Stevens and Benjamin Butler, attempted to prove that Johnson was guilty of "high crimes and misdemeanors." But they also argued that the trial was a means to judge Johnson's performance, not a judicial determination of guilt or innocence. The Senate ultimately rejected such reasoning, which could have made removal from office a political weapon against any chief executive who disagreed with Congress. Although a majority of senators voted to convict Johnson, the prosecution fell one vote short of the necessary two-thirds majority. Johnson remained in office, politically weakened and with only a few months left in his term. His acquittal established a precedent that only serious misdeeds merited removal from office.

In 1869, in an effort to write democratic principles and colorblindness into the Constitution, the Radicals succeeded in presenting the Fifteenth

Fifteenth Amendment

Amendment for ratification. This measure forbade states to deny the right to vote "on account of race, color, or previous condition of servitude." Such wording did not guarantee the right to vote. It deliberately left states free to restrict suffrage on other grounds so that northern states could continue to deny suffrage to women and certain groups of men—Chinese immigrants, illiterates, and those too poor to pay taxes. Ironically, the votes of four uncooperative southern states—compelled by Congress to approve the amendment as an added condition to rejoining the Union—proved necessary to impose even this language on parts of the North. Although several states outside the South refused to ratify, the Fifteenth Amendment became law in 1870.

Reconstruction Politics in the South

From the start, Reconstruction encountered the resistance of white southerners. In the black codes and in private attitudes, many whites stubbornly opposed

Thomas Nast, in this 1868 cartoon, pictured the combination of forces that threatened the success of Reconstruction: southern opposition and the greed, partisanship, and racism of northern interests. Library of Congress.

or "wouldn't let [them] go." Agents of the Freedmen's Bureau reported that "the old system of slavery [is] working with even more rigor than formerly at a few miles distant from any point where U.S. troops are stationed." To hold onto their workers, some landowners claimed control over black children and used guardianship and apprentice laws to bind black families to the plantation.

Whites also blocked blacks from acquiring land. A few planters divided up plots among their slaves, but most condemned the idea of making blacks landowners. One planter in South Carolina refused to sell as little as 1.5 acres to each family. Even a Georgia woman whose family was known for its support of religious education for slaves was outraged that two property owners planned to "rent their lands to the Negroes!" Such action was, she declared, "injurious to the best interest of the community."

Adamant resistance by propertied whites soon manifested itself in other ways, including violence. In one North Carolina town a local magistrate clubbed a black man on a public street, and bands of "Regulators" terrorized blacks in parts of that state and Kentucky. Such incidents were predictable in a society in which many planters believed, as a South Carolinian put it, that blacks "can't be governed except with the whip."

After President Johnson encouraged the South to resist congressional Reconstruction, white conservatives worked hard to capture the new state governments. Many whites also boycotted the polls in an attempt to defeat Congress's plans; by sitting out the elections, whites might block the new constitutions, which had to be approved by a majority of registered voters. This tactic was tried in North Carolina and succeeded in Alabama, forcing Congress to base ratification on a majority of those voting.

Very few black men stayed away from the polls. Enthusiastically and hopefully, they voted Republican. Most agreed with one man who felt he should "stick to the end with the party that freed me." Illiteracy did not prohibit blacks (or uneducated whites) from making intelligent choices. Although Mississippi's William Henry could read only "a little," he testified that he and his friends had no difficulty selecting the Republican ballot. "We stood around and watched," he explained. "We saw D. Sledge vote; he owned half the county. We knowed he voted Democratic so we voted the other ticket so it would be Republican." Women, who could not vote, encouraged their husbands and sons, and preachers exhorted

White Resistance

emancipation, and the former planter class proved especially unbending. In 1866 a Georgia newspaper frankly observed that "most of the white citizens believe that the institution of slavery was right, and . . . they will believe that the condition, which comes nearest to slavery, that can now be established will be the best." Andrew Johnson's encouragement of southern whites to resist Congress only intensified such opposition to change.

Fearing loss of control over their slaves, some planters attempted to postpone freedom by denying or misrepresenting events. Former slaves reported that their owners "didn't tell them it was freedom"

their congregations to use the franchise. Such community spirit helped to counter white pressure tactics, and zeal for voting spread through the entire black community.

Thanks to a large black turnout and the restrictions on prominent Confederates, a new southern Republican Party came to power in the constitutional conventions. Republican delegates consisted of a sizable contingent of blacks (265 out of the total of just over 1,000 delegates throughout the South), some northerners who had moved to the South, and native southern whites who favored change. Together these Republicans brought the South into line with progressive reforms that had been adopted in the rest of the nation. The new constitutions were more democratic. They eliminated property qualifications for voting and holding office, and they turned many appointed offices into elective posts. They provided for public schools and institutions to care for the mentally ill, the blind, the deaf, the destitute, and the orphaned. They also put an end to imprisonment for debt and punishments such as branding.

The conventions broadened women's rights in property holding and divorce. Usually, the goal was not to make women equal with men but to provide relief to thousands of suffering debtors. In families left poverty-stricken by the war and weighed down by debt, it was usually the husband who had contracted the debts. Thus giving women legal control over their own property provided some protection to their families. The goal of some delegates, however, was to elevate women. Blacks in particular called for laws to provide for women's suffrage, but they were ignored by their white colleagues.

Under these new constitutions the southern states elected new governments. Again the Republican Party triumphed, putting new men in positions of power. For the first time, the ranks of state legislators in 1868 included some black southerners. Congress's second plan for Reconstruction was well under way. It remained to be seen what these new governments would do and how much social change they would bring about.

Triumph of Republican Governments

One way to achieve radical change would have been to disfranchise substantial numbers of Confederate leaders. Barring many whites from politics as punishment for rebellion would have given the Republicans a solid electoral majority based on black voters and their white allies. Land reform and the assurance of racial equality would have been possible. None of the Republican governments, however, did this or even gave it serious consideration. Why did the new legislators reject this course of action?

First, they appreciated the realities of power and the depth of racial enmity. In most states, whites were in the majority and former slaveowners controlled the best land and other sources of economic power. James Lynch, a leading black politician from Mississippi, explained why African-Americans shunned the "folly" of disfranchisement. Unlike northerners who "can leave when it becomes too uncomfortable," landless former slaves "must be in friendly relations with the great body of the whites in the state. Otherwise . . . peace can be maintained only by a standing army." Despised and lacking economic or social power, southern Republicans saw mere acceptance and legitimacy as ambitious goals.

Second, blacks believed in the principle of universal suffrage and the Christian goal of reconciliation. Far from being vindictive toward the race that had enslaved them, they treated leading rebels with generosity and appealed to white southerners to adopt a spirit of fairness and cooperation. Henry McNeil Turner, like other black ministers, urged his fellow Georgians to "love whites . . . soon their prejudice would melt away, and with God for our father, we will all be brothers." (Years later Turner criticized his own naiveté, saying that in the constitutional convention his motto had been "Anything to please the white folks.") Therefore southern Republicans quickly (in some cases immediately) restored the voting rights of former Confederates, as Congress steadily released more individuals from the penalties of the Fourteenth Amendment.

The South's Republican Party committed itself to a strategy of winning white support. To put the matter another way, the Republican Party condemned itself to defeat if white voters would not cooperate. Within a few years Republicans were reduced to the embarrassment of making futile appeals to whites while ignoring the claims of their strongest supporters, blacks. But for a time both Republicans and their opponents, who called themselves Conservatives or Democrats, moved to the center and appealed for support from a broad range of groups. Some propertied whites accepted congressional Reconstruction as a reality and declared themselves willing to compete under the new rules. While these Democrats angled for some black votes, Republicans

One notable success in Reconstruction efforts to stimulate industry was Birmingham, Alabama. Here workers cast molten iron into blocks called pigs.   Birmingham Public Library.

sought to attract more white voters. Both parties found an area of agreement in economic policies.

The Reconstruction governments enthusiastically promoted industry. This policy reflected northern ideals, but it also sprang from a growing southern eagerness to build up the region.

Industrialization

Confederates had seen how industry aided the North during the war. Accordingly, Reconstruction legislatures encouraged investment with loans, subsidies, and exemptions from taxation for periods up to ten years. The southern railroad system was rebuilt and expanded, and coal and iron mining made possible Birmingham's steel plants. Between 1860 and 1880, the number of manufacturing establishments in the South nearly doubled. This emphasis on big business, however, produced higher state debts and taxes, drew money away from schools and other programs, and multiplied possibilities for corruption. It also locked Republicans into a conservative strategy. In appealing to elite whites who never joined the Republican Party, they lost the opportunity of building support among poorer whites.

Policies appealing to African-American voters never went beyond equality before the law. In fact, the whites who controlled the southern Republican Party were reluctant to allow blacks a share of offices proportionate to their electoral strength. Aware of their weakness, black leaders did not push for revolutionary economic or social change. In every southern state, they led ef-

Other Republican Policies

forts to establish public schools but usually did not press for integrated facilities. Having a school to attend was the most important thing at the time, for the Johnson governments had excluded blacks from schools and other state-supported institutions. As a result, virtually every public school organized during Reconstruction was racially segregated, and these separate schools established a precedent. By the 1870s segregation was becoming a common though not universal practice in theaters, trains, and other public accommodations in the South.

A few African-American politicians did fight for civil rights and integration. Most were mulattos from cities such as New Orleans or Mobile, where large populations of light-skinned free blacks had existed before the war. Their experience in such communities had made them sensitive to issues of status, and they spoke out for open and equal public accommodations. Laws requiring equal accommodations won passage throughout the Deep South, but they often went unenforced or required an injured party to bring legal action for enforcement.

Economic progress was uppermost in the minds of most freed people and black representatives from rural districts. Black southerners needed land, but only a few promoted confiscation. Some hoped that high taxes would force portions of large estates onto the market (small farmers' lands were protected by homestead exemptions). In fact, much land did fall into state hands for nonpayment of taxes and was offered for sale in small lots. But most freedmen had too little cash to bid against investors or speculators, and few acquired land in this way. South Carolina established a land commission, but it could help only those with money to buy. Any widespread redistribution of land had to arise from Congress, which never supported such action.

Within a few years, as centrists in both parties met with failure, white hostility to congressional Reconstruction began to dominate. Some conservatives had always desired to fight Reconstruction through pressure and racist propaganda. They put economic and social pressure on blacks: one black Republican reported that "my neighbors will not employ me, nor sell me a farthing's worth of anything." Charging that the South had been turned over to ignorant blacks, conservatives deplored "black domination" and "Negro rule."

Such attacks were inflammatory but inaccurate. African-Americans participated in politics but did not dominate or control events. They were a major-ity in only two out of ten state conventions (transplanted northerners were a majority in one). In the state legislatures, only in the lower house in South Carolina did blacks ever constitute a majority; among officeholders, their numbers generally were far inferior to their proportion in the population. Sixteen blacks won seats in Congress before Reconstruction was over, but none was ever elected governor. Only eighteen served in a high state office such as lieutenant governor, treasurer, superintendent of education, or secretary of state.

Conservatives also assailed the allies of black Republicans. Their propaganda denounced whites from the North as "carpetbaggers," greedy crooks planning to pour stolen tax revenues into their sturdy luggage made of carpet material. Immigrants from the North, who held the largest share of Republican offices, were all tarred with this brush.

Carpetbaggers and Scalawags

In fact, most northerners who settled in the South had come seeking business opportunities or a warmer climate and never entered politics. Those who did enter politics generally wanted to democratize the South and to introduce northern ways, such as industry, public education, and the spirit of enterprise. Their ideals were tested by hard times and ostracism by white southerners. Although carpetbaggers supported black suffrage and educational opportunities, most opposed social equality and integration.

Conservatives invented the term *scalawag* to discredit any native white southerner who cooperated with the Republicans. A substantial number of southerners did so, including some wealthy and prominent men. Most scalawags, however, were yeoman farmers, men from mountain areas and nonslaveholding districts who had been restive under the Confederacy. They saw that they could benefit from the education and opportunities promoted by Republicans. Banding together with freedmen, they pursued common class interests and hoped to make headway against the power of long-dominant planters. Cooperation even convinced a few scalawags that "there is but little if any difference in the talents of the two races," as one observed, and that all should have "an equal start."

Yet this black-white coalition was vulnerable to the race issue, and most scalawags shied away from support for racial equality. Republican tax policies also cut into upcountry yeoman support because

Members of the Ku Klux Klan devised ghoulish costumes to heighten the terror inspired by their acts. This photograph shows the costume of a Mississippi Klansman from 1871.   Courtesy, Herbert Peck, Jr.

reliance on the property tax hit many small landholders hard. In addition, poll taxes (whose proceeds often were earmarked for education) endangered the independence of subsistence farmers, pressuring them to participate in the market economy to obtain cash.

Taxation was a major problem for the Reconstruction governments. Republicans wanted to maintain prewar services, repair the war's destruction, stimulate industry, and support important new ventures such as public schools. But the Civil War had destroyed much of the South's tax base. One category of valuable property—slaves—had disappeared entirely. And hundreds of thousands of citizens had lost much of the rest of their property—money, livestock,

fences, and buildings—to the war. Thus an increase in taxes was necessary even to maintain traditional services, and new ventures required still higher taxes. Inevitably, Republican tax policies aroused strong opposition.

Corruption was another serious charge levied against the Republicans. Unfortunately, it often was true. Many carpetbaggers and black politicians engaged in fraudulent schemes, sold their votes, or padded expenses, taking part in what scholars recognize was a nationwide surge of corruption (see page 459). Many white Democrats shared in corruption, and some Republicans fought it, but the Democrats successfully pinned the blame on unqualified blacks and greedy carpetbaggers.

All these problems hurt the Republicans, whose leaders also allowed factionalism along racial and class lines to undermine party unity. But in many southern states the deathblow came through violence. The Ku Klux Klan, a secret veterans' club that began in Tennessee, spread through the South and rapidly evolved into a terrorist organization. Violence against African-Americans occurred from the first days of Reconstruction but became far more organized and purposeful after 1867. Klansmen rode to frustrate Reconstruction and keep the freedmen in subjection. Nighttime harassment, whippings, beatings, and murder became common, and terrorism dominated some areas.

Ku Klux Klan

Although the Klan persecuted blacks who stood up for their rights as laborers or individuals, its main purpose was political. Lawless nightriders made active Republicans the target of their attacks. Leading white and black Republicans were killed in several states. After freedmen who worked for a South Carolina scalawag started voting, terrorists visited the plantation and, in the words of one victim, "whipped every nigger man they could lay their hands on." Klansmen also attacked Union League Clubs— Republican organizations that mobilized the black vote—and schoolteachers who were aiding the freedmen.

Klan violence was not a spontaneous outburst of racism; very specific social forces shaped and directed it. In North Carolina, for example, Alamance and Caswell Counties were the sites of the worst Klan violence. Slim Republican majorities there rested on cooperation between black voters and white yeomen, particularly those whose Unionism or discontent with the Confederacy had turned them against local Democratic officials. Together, these black and white Republicans had ousted officials long entrenched in power. The wealthy and powerful men in Alamance and Caswell who had lost their accustomed political control were the Klan's county officers and local chieftains. They organized a deliberate campaign of terror, recruiting members and planning atrocities. By whipping up racism or intimidating enough Republicans, the Ku Klux Klan weakened the Republican coalition and restored a Democratic majority.

Klan violence injured Republicans across the South. No fewer than one-tenth of the black leaders who had been delegates to the 1867–1868 state constitutional conventions were attacked, seven fatally. In one judicial district of North Carolina the Ku Klux Klan was responsible for twelve murders, over seven hundred beatings, and other acts of violence,

including rape and arson. A single attack on Alabama Republicans in the town of Eutaw left four blacks dead and fifty-four wounded. In South Carolina five hundred masked Klansmen lynched eight black prisoners at the Union County jail, and in nearby York County the Klan committed at least eleven murders and hundreds of whippings. According to historian Eric Foner, the Klan "made it virtually impossible for Republicans to campaign or vote in large parts of Georgia."

Thus a combination of difficult fiscal problems, Republican mistakes, racial hostility, and terror brought down the Republican regimes. In most

Failure of Reconstruction

southern states so-called Radical Reconstruction lasted only a few years (see map). The most enduring failure of Reconstruction, however, was not political; it was social and economic. Reconstruction failed to alter

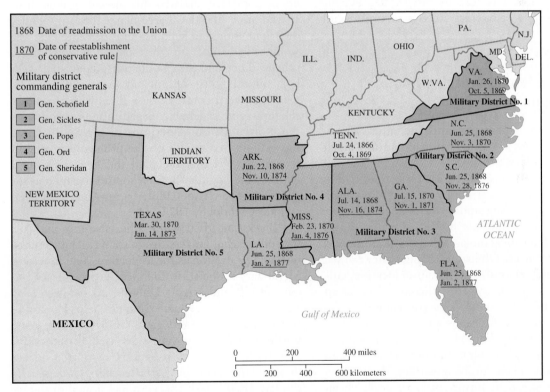

The Reconstruction   *This map shows the five military districts established when Congress passed the Reconstruction Act of 1867. As the dates within each state indicate, conservative Democratic forces quickly regained control of government in four southern states. So-called Radical Reconstruction was curtailed in most of the others as factions within the weakened Republican Party began to cooperate with conservative Democrats.*

the South's social structure or its distribution of wealth and power. Exploited as slaves, freed men and women remained vulnerable to exploitation during Reconstruction. Without land of their own, they were dependent on white landowners who could and did use their economic power to compromise blacks' political freedom. Armed only with the ballot, freed men in the South had little chance to effect major changes.

To reform the southern social order, Congress would have had to redistribute land, but most lawmakers opposed an attack on private property. Radical Republicans like Albion Tourgée condemned Congress's timidity. Turning the freedman out on his own without protection, said Tourgée, constituted "cheap philanthropy." Indeed, African-Americans who had to live with the consequences of Reconstruction considered it a failure, for the North "threw all the Negroes on the world without any way of getting along." Moreover, without careful supervision by Congress, the situation of the freed men and women was sure to deteriorate. Whenever the North lost interest, Reconstruction would collapse.

 ## The Social and Economic Meaning of Freedom

Black southerners entered into life after slavery hopefully but not naively. They had had too much experience with white people to assume that all would be easy. A Texas man recalled his father telling him, even before the war was over, "Our forever was going to be spent living among the Southerners, after they got licked." Expecting hostility, freed men and women tried to gain as much as they could from their new circumstances. Often the changes they valued the most were personal—alterations in location, employer, or living arrangements that could make an enormous difference to individuals or families.

One of the first decisions was whether to leave the old plantation. This choice meant making a judgment about where opportunities for liberty and progress were likely to be greatest. Many cruel slaveholders saw their former property walk off en masse, as former slaves used their experience in bondage to assess the whites with whom they had to deal. Throughout Reconstruction as many as one-third changed employers at the end of a crop year.

After choosing an employer, ex-slaves reached out for valuable things in life that had been denied

them. One of these was education. Blacks of all ages hungered for the knowledge in books that had been permitted only to whites. With freedom, they started schools and filled classrooms both day and night.

Education for African-Americans

On log seats and dirt floors, freed men and women studied their letters in old almanacs, discarded dictionaries, or whatever was available. Young children brought infants to school with them, and adults attended at night or after "the crops were laid by." Many a teacher had "to make herself heard over three other classes reciting in concert" in a small room, but the students kept coming. The desire to escape slavery's ignorance was so great that, despite their poverty, many blacks paid tuition, typically $1 or $1.50 a month. These small amounts constituted one-tenth of many people's agricultural wages and added up to more than $1 million by 1870.

The federal government and northern reformers of both races assisted this pursuit of education. In its brief life the Freedmen's Bureau founded over four thousand schools, and idealistic men and women from the North established and staffed others. The Yankee schoolmarm—dedicated, selfless, and religious—became an agent of progress in many southern communities. Thus with the aid of religious and charitable organizations throughout the North, African-Americans in the South began the nation's first assault on the problems created by slavery. The results included the beginnings of a public school system in each southern state and the enrollment of over 600,000 African-Americans in elementary school by 1877.

Blacks and their white allies also saw the need for colleges and universities to train teachers, ministers, and professionals for leadership. The American Missionary Association founded seven colleges, including Fisk and Atlanta Universities, between 1866 and 1869. The Freedmen's Bureau helped to establish Howard University in Washington, D.C., and northern religious groups such as the Methodists, Baptists, and Congregationalists supported dozens of seminaries, colleges, and teachers' colleges. By the late 1870s black churches had joined in the effort, founding numerous colleges despite limited resources.

Even during Reconstruction, African-American leaders often were highly educated individuals; many of them came from the prewar elite of free people of color. This group had benefited from its association

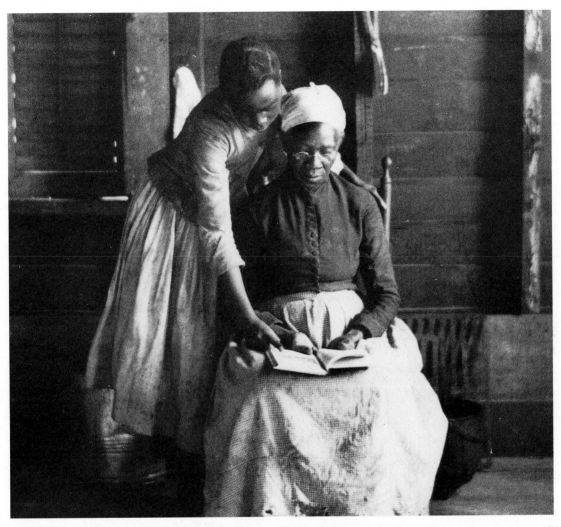

African-Americans of all ages eagerly pursued the opportunity in freedom to gain an education. This young woman in Mt. Meigs, Alabama, is helping her mother learn to read.   Smithsonian Institute, photo by Rudolf Eickmeyer.

with wealthy whites, many of whom were blood relatives; some planters had given their mulatto children outstanding educations. Francis Cardozo, who held various offices in South Carolina, had attended universities in Scotland and England. P. B. S. Pinchback, who became lieutenant governor of Louisiana, was the son of a planter who had sent him to school in Cincinnati. Both of the two black senators from Mississippi, Blanche K. Bruce and Hiram Revels, had had privileged educations. Bruce was the son of a planter who had provided tutoring at home; Revels was the son of free North Carolina mulattos who had sent him to Knox College in Illinois. These men and many self-educated former slaves brought to political office their experience as artisans, businessmen, lawyers, teachers, and preachers.

Meanwhile, millions of former slaves concentrated on improving life on their farms and in their neighborhoods. Surrounded by an unfriendly white population, black men and women sought to insulate themselves from white interference and to strengthen the bonds of their own community. Throughout the South they devoted themselves to reuniting their families, moving away from the slave quarters, and founding black churches. Given the eventual failure of Reconstruction, the gains that African-Americans made in their daily lives often proved the most enduring.

***How do historians know** about the relationships between former slaves and former slaveholders during Reconstruction? The records of the federal Bureau of Refugees, Freedmen, and Abandoned Lands contain a wealth of information on daily conflicts and confrontations. They reveal that one strategy used by planters to retain the labor of their former slaves was to control the slaves' children. The entry shown here, from a Bureau record book in Texas, recounts the complaint of Amanda Hayes. In 1866, her former owner, Captain William Hayes, took her son "to help him drive his cattle." In July 1867, "Mr. Hayes has not returned the boy yet," and Amanda Hayes "wishes the Bureau to compel" his return, with pay.* National Archives.

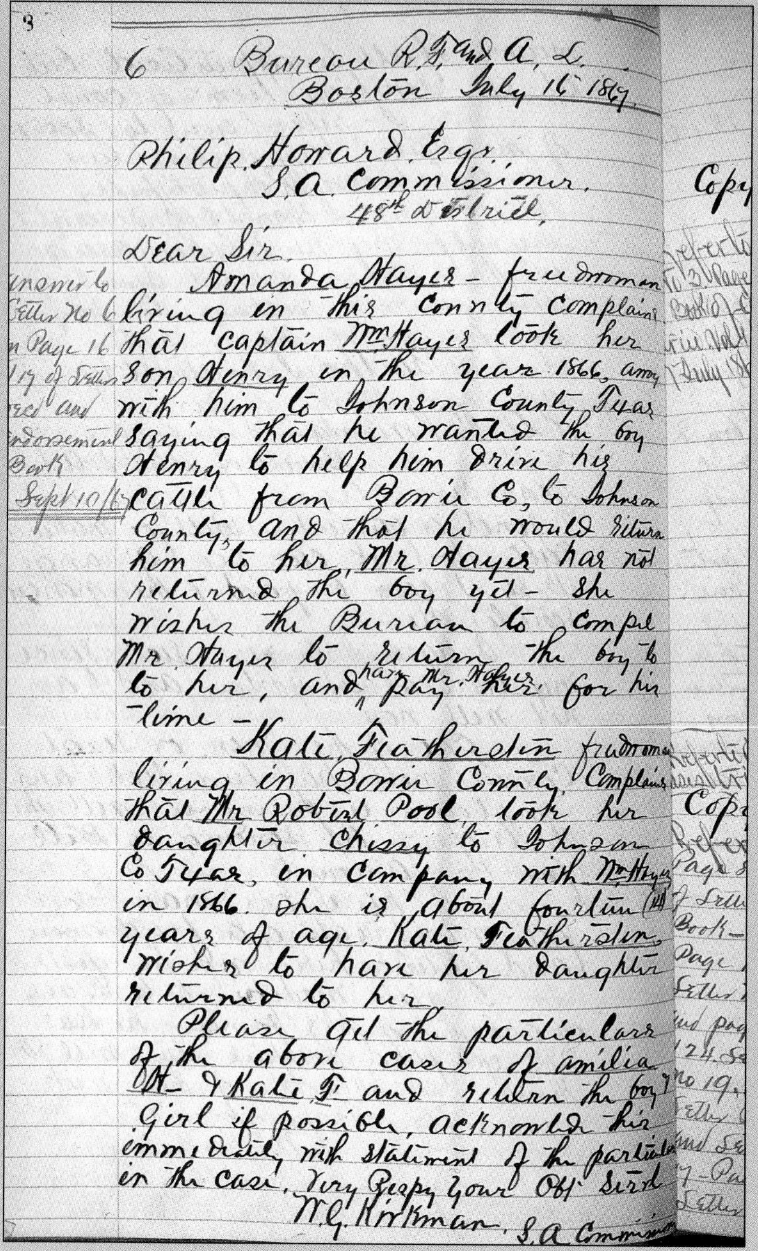
6 Bureau R. F. and A. L.
Boston July 16 1867

Philip Howard Esqr.
S.A. Commissioner
48th District

Dear Sir
Amanda Hayes – freedwoman living in this County complains that captain Wm Hayes took her son Henry in the year 1866, away with him to Johnson County Texas saying that he wanted the boy Henry to help him drive his cattle from Bowie Co, to Johnson County, and that he would return him to her, Mr. Hayes has not returned the boy yet – She wishes the Bureau to compel Mr. Hayes to return the boy to to her, and have Mr. Hayes pay her for his time –

Kate Featherston freedwoman living in Bowie County Complains that Mr Robert Pool, took her daughter Chissy to Johnson Co Texas, in company with Mr Hayes in 1866. she is about fourteen (14) years of age. Kate Featherston wishes to have her daughter returned to her

Please get the particulars of the above cases of Amelia H– & Kate F. and return the boy & Girl if possible, acknowledge this immediately, with statement of the particulars in the case. Very Respy Your Obt Servt
W.G. Kirkman, S.A. Commissioner

Churches became a center of African-American life, for social and political purposes as well as for worship. This engraving, which appeared in Harper's Weekly *in 1874, shows the minister of the First African Baptist Church of Richmond, Virginia, preaching to the congregation from an elevated pulpit.*   The Valentine Museum, Richmond, Virginia.

The search for family members who had been sold away during slavery was awe inspiring. With only shreds of information to guide them, thousands of freed people embarked on odysseys in search of a husband, wife, child, or parent. By relying on the black community for help and information, many succeeded in their quest, sometimes almost miraculously. Others walked through several states and never found loved ones.

Reunification of African-American Families

Husbands and wives who had belonged to different masters established homes together for the first time, and parents asserted the right to raise their own children. A mother bristled when her old master claimed a right to whip her children. She informed him that "he warn't goin' to brush none of her chilluns no more." The freed men and women were too much at risk to act recklessly, but, as one man put it, they were tired of punishment and "sure didn't take no more foolishment off of white folks."

Many black people wanted to minimize contact with whites because, as Reverend Garrison Frazier told General Sherman in January 1865, "There is a prejudice against us . . . that will years to get over." To avoid contact with overbearing whites who were used to supervising and controlling them, blacks abandoned the slave quarters and fanned out to distant corners of the land they worked. "After the war my stepfather come," recalled Annie Young, "and got my mother and we moved out in the piney woods." Others described moving "across the creek to [themselves]" or building a "saplin house . . . back in the woods." Some rural dwellers established small all-black settlements that still exist today along the backroads of the South.

Even once-privileged slaves shared this desire for independence and social separation. One man turned down the master's offer of the overseer's house and moved instead to a shack in "Freetown." He also declined to let the former owner grind his grain for free, because it "make him feel like a free man to pay for things just like anyone else." One couple, a carriage driver and trusted house servant during slavery, passed up the fine cooking of the "big house" to move "in the colored settlement."

The other side of movement away from whites was closer communion within the black community. Freed from the restrictions and regulations of slavery, blacks could build their own institutions as they saw fit. The secret churches of slavery came into the open; in countless communities throughout the South, ex-slaves "started a brush arbor." A brush arbor was

Founding of Black Churches

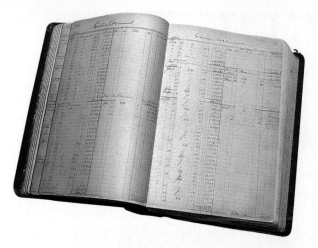

Sharecropping became an oppressive system in the postwar South. At plantation stores like this one, photographed in Mississippi in 1868, merchants recorded in their ledger books debts that few sharecroppers were able to repay.   Recordbook: Smithsonian Institute, Division of Community Life; Plantation store: Amistad Foundation Collection at the Wadsworth Athenaeum, Hartford, Connecticut.

merely "a sort of . . . shelter with leaves for a roof," but the freed men and women worshiped in it enthusiastically. "Preachin' and shouting sometimes lasted all day," they recalled, for the opportunity to worship together freely meant "glorious times." Within a few years independent branches of the Methodist and Baptist denominations had attracted the great majority of black Christians in the South.

The desire to gain as much independence as possible also shaped the former slaves' economic arrangements. Since most of them lacked money to buy land, they preferred the next best thing: renting the land they worked. But few whites would consider renting land to blacks, and most blacks had no means to get cash before the harvest. Thus other alternatives had to be tried.

Northerners and officials of the Freedmen's Bureau favored contracts between owners and laborers. To northerners who believed in "Free Soil, Free Labor, Free Men," contracts and wages seemed the key to progress. For a few years the Freedmen's Bureau helped draw up and enforce such contracts, but they proved unpopular with both races. Owners often filled the contracts with detailed requirements that led to close supervision and reminded blacks of their circumscribed lives under slavery. Besides, cash for wages was not readily available in the early years of Reconstruction. Times were hard, and the failure of Confederate banks had left the South with a shortage of credit facilities.

Black farmers and white landowners therefore turned to sharecropping, a system in which farmers kept part of their crop and gave the rest to the landowner while living on his property. The landlord or a merchant "furnished" food and supplies needed before the harvest, and he received payment from the crop. Republican laws gave laborers the first lien, or legal claim, on the crop, enhancing their sense of ownership. Although

Rise of the Sharecropping System

landowners tried to set the laborers' share at a low level, black farmers had some bargaining power. By holding out and refusing to sign contracts at the end of the year, sharecroppers succeeded in keeping the owners' share at around one-half during Reconstruction.

The sharecropping system originated as a desirable compromise. It eased landowners' problems with cash and credit; blacks accepted it because it gave them more freedom from daily supervision. Instead of working under a white overseer, as in slavery, they farmed a plot of land on their own in family groups. But sharecropping later proved to be a disaster for all concerned. When the Democrats returned to power, they often changed the lien laws to favor landlords; when crop prices were low, landlords received their payment first, even if there was no money left over for the laborer. And in a discriminatory society whites had many opportunities to cheat sharecroppers. Owners and merchants frequently underpaid or overcharged them and manipulated records so that they were always in debt (see page 498).

The fundamental problem, however, was that southern farmers were concentrating on cotton, a crop with a bright past and a dim future. During the Civil War, India, Brazil, and Egypt had begun to supply cotton to Britain, and this loss of markets reduced per capita income, as did a decline in the amount of labor invested by the average southern farmer. In freedom, black women, like their white counterparts, often stayed away from the fields. Black families placed greater value on human dignity than on the reaching the levels of production that they had achieved under the lash. By 1878, the South had recovered its prewar share of British cotton purchases. But even as southerners grew more cotton, eventually surpassing prewar totals, their reward diminished. Cotton prices began a long decline whose causes by chance coincided with the Civil War. From 1820 to 1860, world demand for cotton had grown at a rate of 5 percent per year, but from 1866 to 1895 the rate of growth slowed to only 1.3 percent per year. By 1860 the English textile industry, the world leader in production, had penetrated all the major new markets, and from that point on increases in demand were slight. As a result, when southern farmers planted more cotton, they tended to depress the price.

Over-dependence on Cotton

In these circumstances overspecialization in cotton was a mistake, but for most southern farmers there was no alternative. Landowners required sharecroppers to grow the prime cash crop, whose salability was certain. Because of the shortage of banks and credit in the South, white farmers often had to borrow from a local merchant, who insisted on cotton production to secure his loan. Thus southern agriculture slipped deeper and deeper into depression. Black sharecroppers struggled under a growing burden of debt that reduced their independence and bound them to landowners almost as oppressively as slavery had bound them to their masters. Many white farmers became debtors, too, and gradually lost their land. These were serious problems, but few people in the North were paying attention.

 ## Reconstruction's Decline and Fall

Northerners had always been far more interested in suppressing rebellion than in aiding southern blacks, and by the early 1870s the North's partial commitment to bringing about change in the South was weakening. Criticism of the southern governments grew, new issues captured people's attention, and soon voters began to look favorably on reconciliation with southern whites. In one southern state after another, Democrats regained control, and they threatened to defeat Republicans in the North as well. Before long the situation had returned to "normal" in the eyes of southern whites.

Antagonism between Unionists and rebels was still very strong in 1868. That year Ulysses S. Grant, running as a Republican, defeated Horatio Seymour, a New York Democrat, for president. Grant was not a Radical, but his platform supported congressional Reconstruction and endorsed black suffrage in the South. (Significantly, Republicans stopped short of endorsing it in the North.) The Democrats, meanwhile, vigorously denounced Reconstruction and thus renewed the sectional conflict. By associating themselves with rebellion and with Johnson's repudiated program, the Democrats went down to defeat in all but eight states, though the popular vote was fairly close.

Election of 1868

In office Grant acted as an administrator of Reconstruction but not as its enthusiastic advocate. He vacillated in his dealings with the southern states, sometimes defending Republican regimes and sometimes currying favor with Democrats. On occasion Grant called out federal troops to stop violence or enforce acts of Congress, but only when he had to do so. Neither Andrew Johnson nor he imposed anything approaching a military occupation on the South. Rapid demobilization had reduced a federal army of more than 1 million to 57,000 within a year of the surrender at Appomattox. Thereafter the number of troops in the South continued to fall, until in 1874 there were only 4,000 in the southern states outside Texas. Throughout Reconstruction, the strongest federal units were in Texas and the West, fighting Indians, not white southerners.

In 1870 and 1871 the violent campaigns of the Ku Klux Klan forced Congress to pass two Enforcement Acts and an anti-Klan law. These laws made actions by *individuals* against the civil and political rights of others a federal criminal offense for the first time. They also provided for election supervisors and permitted martial law and suspension of the writ of habeas corpus to combat murders, beatings, and threats by the Klan. Federal prosecutors used the laws rather selectively. In 1872 and 1873 Mississippi and the Carolinas saw many prosecutions; but in other states where violence flourished, the laws were virtually ignored. (Meanwhile, the Republican Party vigorously used the laws in northern cities to combat Democratic election fraud.) Southern juries sometimes refused to convict Klansmen; out of a total of 3,310 cases, only 1,143 ended in convictions. Though many Klansmen (roughly two thousand in South Carolina alone) fled their states to avoid prosecution, and the Klan officially disbanded, the threat of violence did not end. Paramilitary organizations known as Rifle Clubs and Red Shirts often took the Klan's place.

Klan terrorism defied Congress in an especially clear-cut way, yet even on this issue there were ominous signs that the North's commitment to racial justice was fading. Some conservative but influential Republicans opposed the anti-Klan laws. Rejecting other Republicans' arguments that the Thirteenth, Fourteenth, and Fifteenth Amendments had made the federal government the protector of the rights of citizens, these dissenters echoed an old Democratic charge that Congress was infringing on states' rights. Senator Lyman Trumbull of Illinois declared that the states remained "the depositories of the rights of the individual." If Congress could punish

crimes like assault or murder, he asked, "what is the need of the State governments?" For years Democrats had complained of "centralization and consolidation"; now some Republicans seemed to agree with them. This opposition foreshadowed a more general revolt within Republican ranks in 1872.

Disenchanted with Reconstruction, a group calling itself the Liberal Republicans bolted the party in 1872 and nominated Horace Greeley, the well-known editor of the *New York Tribune*, for president. The Liberal Republicans were a varied group, including civil service reformers, foes of corruption, and advocates of a lower tariff. Normally such disparate elements would not cooperate with each other, but two popular and widespread attitudes united them: distaste for federal intervention in the South and a desire to let market forces and the "best men" determine events there.

Liberal Republicans Revolt

The Democrats also gave their nomination to Greeley in 1872. The combination was not enough to defeat Grant, who won reelection, but it reinforced Grant's desire to avoid confrontation with white southerners. He continued to use military force sparingly and in 1875 refused a desperate request for troops from the governor of Mississippi.

Dissatisfaction with Grant's administration grew during his second term. Strong-willed but politically naive, Grant made a series of poor appointments. His secretary of war, his private secretary, and officials in the Treasury and Navy Departments were involved in bribery or tax-cheating scandals. Instead of exposing the corruption, Grant defended some of the culprits. In 1874, as Grant's popularity and his party's prestige declined, the Democrats recaptured the House of Representatives. The Republican Party faced more unfavorable publicity in 1875, when several of Grant's appointees were indicted.

The effect of Democratic gains in Congress was to weaken the legislature's resolve on southern issues. Congress had already lifted the political disabilities of the Fourteenth Amendment from many former Confederates. In 1872 it had adopted a sweeping Amnesty Act, which pardoned most of the remaining rebels and left only five hundred barred from political officeholding. In 1875 Congress passed a Civil Rights Act purporting to guarantee black people equal accommodations in public places, such as inns and theaters, but the bill was

Amnesty Act

watered down and contained no effective provisions for enforcement. (The Supreme Court later struck down this law; see page 501.)

Democrats regained power in the South rather quickly, winning control of state government in four states before 1872 and in a total of eight by January 1876 (see map, page 469). In the North Democrats successfully stressed the failure and scandals of Reconstruction governments. As opinion shifted, historian Brooks Adams, the grandson and great-grandson of presidents, published an article condemning the enfranchisement of blacks as "a wholesale creation of the most ignorant mass of voters to be found in the civilized world." Many Republicans sensed that their constituents were tiring of southern issues.

In fact, new concerns were capturing the public's attention. Both industrialization and immigration were surging, hastening the pace of change in national life. Within only eight years, postwar industrial production increased by an impressive 75 percent. For the first time, nonagricultural workers outnumbered farmers, and only Britain's industrial output was greater than that of the United States. Government financial policies did much to bring about this rapid growth. Soon after the war Congress used a portion of tax revenues to pay off the interest-bearing war debt: the debt fell from $2.33 billion in 1866 to only $587 million in 1893, and every dollar repaid was a dollar injected into the economy for potential reinvestment. Approximately 1 percent of the gross national product was pumped back into the economy from 1866 to 1872, and only slightly less than that during the rest of the 1870s. Low taxes on investment and high tariffs on manufactured goods also aided industrialists. With such help, the northern economy quickly recovered its prewar rate of growth.

Between 1865 and 1873 3 million new immigrants entered the country, most of them joining the labor force of industrial cities in the North and West. As the number of immigrants rose, there was a corresponding revival of ingrained suspicion and hostility among native-born Americans. Also prominent was the question of how Utah's growing Mormon community, which practiced polygamy, could be reconciled to American law.

Then the Panic of 1873 ushered in over five years of economic contraction. Three million people lost their jobs, and the clash between labor and capital became the major issue of the day (see Chapter 18). Class attitudes diverged, especially in the large cities. Debtors and the unemployed sought easy money policies to spur economic expansion. Businessmen, disturbed by the strikes and industrial violence that accompanied the panic, became increasingly concerned about the defense of property.

Class conflict fueled a monetary issue: whether paper money—the Civil War greenbacks—should be kept in circulation. In 1872, Democratic farmers and debtors urged this policy to expand the money supply and raise prices, but businessmen, bankers, and creditors overruled them. Now hard times swelled the ranks of the "greenbackers"—voters who favored greenbacks and easy money. Congress voted in 1874 to increase the number of greenbacks in circulation, but Grant vetoed the bill in deference to the opinions of financial leaders. The next year, "sound money" interests prevailed in Congress, winning passage of a law requiring that greenbacks be convertible into gold after 1878. This law limited the inflationary impact of the greenbacks and aided creditors rather than debtors (such as the hard-pressed and angry farmers).

Greenbacks Versus Sound Money

In international affairs, there was renewed pressure for, and controversy about, expansion (see Chapter 22). In 1867 Secretary of State William H. Seward arranged a vast addition of territory to the national domain through the purchase of Alaska from the Russian government for $7.2 million. Opponents ridiculed Seward's venture, calling Alaska Frigidia, the Polar Bear Garden, and Walrussia. But Seward convinced important congressmen of Alaska's economic potential, and other lawmakers favored the dawning of friendship with Russia. Also in 1867, the United States took control of the Midway Islands, a thousand miles from Hawai'i. And in 1870, President Grant tried to annex the Dominican Republic, but Senator Charles Sumner blocked the attempt. Seward and his successor, Hamilton Fish, also resolved troubling Civil War grievances against Great Britain. Through diplomacy they arranged a financial settlement of claims on Britain for damage done by the *Alabama* and other cruisers built in England and sold to the Confederacy (see page 639).

Meanwhile, the Supreme Court was participating in the northern retreat from Reconstruction. During the Civil War the Court, which in 1857 declared that black people could not be citizens, had been cautious and reluctant to assert itself. Reaction to the *Dred Scott* decision (1857) had been so violent, and the Union's wartime emergency so great, that the Court avoided interference with government actions. The justices breathed a collective sigh of relief, for example, when legal technicalities prevented them from reviewing the case of Clement Vallandigham, a Democratic opponent of Lincoln's war effort, who had been convicted by a military tribunal of aiding the enemy. But in 1866 a similar case, *Ex parte Milligan*, reached the Court through proper channels.

Lambdin P. Milligan of Indiana had plotted to free Confederate prisoners of war and overthrow state governments. For these acts a military court sentenced Milligan, a civilian, to death. Milligan challenged the authority of the military tribunal, claiming that he had a right to a civil trial. The Supreme Court declared that military trials were illegal when civil courts were open and functioning, and its language indicated that the Court intended to reassert itself as a major force in national affairs. This case could have led to a direct clash with Congress, which established military districts and military courts in the 1867 Reconstruction Act. But Congress altered part of the Court's jurisdiction, removing such matters from its purview. (Congress was constitutionally empowered to do so but never had taken such action before and has not done so since.)

In the 1870s the Court successfully renewed its challenge to Congress's actions when it narrowed the meaning and effectiveness of the Fourteenth Amendment. The *Slaughter-House* cases (1873) began in

Supreme Court Decisions on Reconstruction

1869, when the Louisiana legislature granted one company a monopoly on the slaughtering of livestock in New Orleans. Rival butchers in the city promptly sued. Their attorney, former Supreme Court justice John A. Campbell, argued that Louisiana had violated the rights of some of its citizens in favor of others. The Fourteenth Amendment, Campbell contended, had revolutionized the constitutional system by bringing individual rights under federal protection. Campbell thus articulated an original goal of the Republican Party: to nationalize civil rights and guard them from state interference. Over the years his argument would win acceptance, sheltering corporate "persons" from government regulation in the nineteenth century and protecting blacks and other minorities in the twentieth.

But in the *Slaughter-House* decision, the Supreme Court dealt a stunning blow to the scope and vitality of the Fourteenth Amendment. Refusing to accept Campbell's argument, it interpreted the "privileges and immunities" of citizens so narrowly that it reduced them almost to trivialities. State citizenship and national citizenship were separate, the Court declared. National citizenship involved only matters such as the right to travel freely from state to state and to use the navigable waters of the nation, and only these narrow rights were protected by the Fourteenth Amendment. With this interpretation, the words "No state shall make or enforce any law which shall abridge the privileges or immunities of citizens of the United States" disappeared, from that day until now, as a meaningful and effective part of the Constitution.

The Supreme Court also concluded that the butchers who sued had not been deprived of their rights or property in violation of the due-process clause of the amendment. Shrinking from a role as "perpetual censor upon all legislation of the States, on the civil rights of their own citizens," the Court's majority declared that the framers of the recent amendments had not intended to "destroy" the federal system, in which the states exercised "powers for domestic and local government, including the regulation of civil rights." Thus the justices dismissed Campbell's central contention and severely limited the amendment's potential for securing and protecting the rights of black citizens.

The next day the Court decided *Bradwell* v. *Illinois*, a case in which Myra Bradwell, a female attorney, had been denied the right to practice law in Illinois on account of her gender. Pointing to the Fourteenth Amendment, Bradwell's attorneys contended that the state had unconstitutionally abridged her "privileges and immunities" as a citizen. The Supreme Court rejected her claim, alluding to women's traditional role in the home.

In 1876 the Court weakened the Reconstruction-era amendments even further by emasculating the enforcement clause of the Fourteenth Amendment and revealing deficiencies inherent in the Fifteenth Amendment. In *U.S.* v. *Cruikshank* the Court overruled the conviction under the 1870 Enforcement Act of Louisiana whites who had attacked a meeting of blacks and conspired to deprive them of their rights. The justices ruled that the Fourteenth Amendment did not give the federal government power to act against these whites. The duty of protecting citizens' equal rights "was originally assumed by the States; and it still remains there." As for the protection of "unalienable rights," the Court said that "Sovereignty, for this purpose, rests alone with the States." In *U.S.* v. *Reese* the Court noted that the Fifteenth Amendment did not guarantee a citizen's right to vote but merely listed certain impermissible grounds for denying suffrage. Thus a path lay open for southern states to disfranchise blacks for supposedly nonracial reasons—lack of education or property or descent from a grandfather qualified to vote before the Reconstruction Act of 1867. These "grandfather clauses" became a means to give the vote to illiterate whites while excluding blacks (see page 500).

As the 1876 elections approached, most political observers saw that the North was no longer willing to pursue the goals of Reconstruction. The results of a disputed presidential election confirmed this fact. Samuel J. Tilden, the Democratic governor of New York, ran strongly in the South and needed only one more electoral vote to triumph over Rutherford B. Hayes, the Republican nominee. Nineteen votes from Louisiana, South Carolina, and Florida were disputed; both Democrats and Republicans claimed to have won in those states despite fraud committed by their opponents. One vote from Oregon was undecided because of a technicality (see map).

Election of 1876

To resolve this unprecedented situation, on which the Constitution gave no guidance, Congress established a fifteen-member electoral commission. In the interest of impartiality, membership on the commission was to be balanced between Democrats and Republicans. But one independent Republican, Supreme Court Justice David Davis, refused appointment in order to accept his election as a senator. A regular Republican took his place, and the Republican Party prevailed 8 to 7 on every decision, along strict party lines. Hayes would become president if Congress accepted the commission's findings.

Congressional acceptance was not certain. Democrats controlled the House and could filibuster to block action on the vote. Many citizens worried that the nation had entered a major constitutional crisis and would slip once again into civil war. The crisis was resolved when Democrats acquiesced in the election of Hayes. Scholars have found evidence of negotiations between Hayes's supporters and southerners who wanted federal aid to railroads, internal

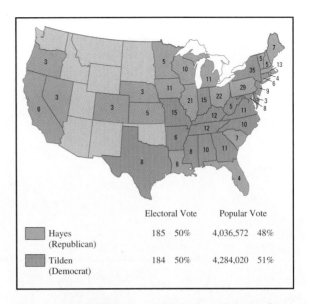

	Electoral Vote		Popular Vote	
Hayes (Republican)	185	50%	4,036,572	48%
Tilden (Democrat)	184	50%	4,284,020	51%

Presidential Election, 1876   *In 1876 a combination of solid southern support and Democratic gains in the North gave Samuel Tilden the majority of popular votes, but Rutherford B. Hayes won the disputed election in the electoral college.*

improvements, federal patronage, and removal of troops from southern states. But studies of Congress conclude that these negotiations did not have a deciding effect on the outcome: neither party was well enough organized to implement and enforce a bargain between the sections. Northern and southern Democrats simply decided they could not win and did not contest the election of a Republican who was not going to continue Reconstruction. Thus Hayes became president, and Reconstruction was unmistakably over.

Southern Democrats rejoiced, but African-Americans grieved over the betrayal of their hopes for equality. Tens of thousands considered leaving the South, where real freedom was no longer a possibility. "[We asked] whether it was possible we could stay under a people who had held us in bondage," said Henry Adams, who led a migration to Kansas. In South Carolina, Louisiana, Mississippi, and other southern states, thousands gathered up their possessions and migrated to Kansas. They were known as Exodusters, disappointed people still searching for

Exodusters Move West

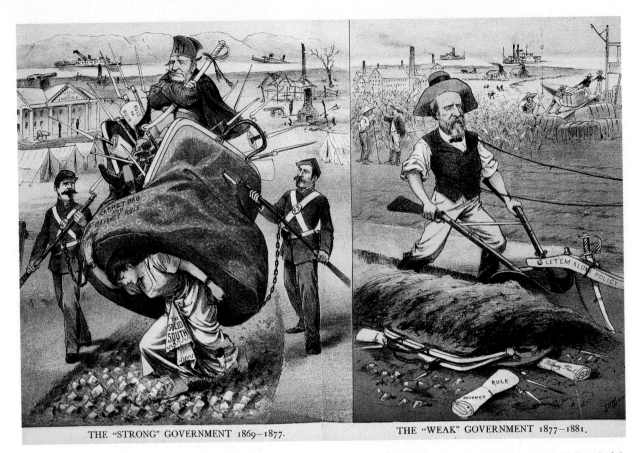

THE "STRONG" GOVERNMENT 1869–1877.   THE "WEAK" GOVERNMENT 1877–1881.

These cartoons reveal the North's readiness to give up on a strong Reconstruction policy. According to the images on the left, only federal bayonets could support the "rule or ruin" carpetbag regimes that oppressed the South. What do the background and foreground of the cartoon on the right suggest will be the results of President Hayes's "Let 'Em Alone Policy"?   Library of Congress.

their share in the American dream. Even in Kansas they met disillusionment, as the welcome extended by the state's governor soon gave way to hostile public reactions.

 Conclusion

The nation ended over fifteen years of bloody Civil War and controversial Reconstruction without establishing full freedom for African-Americans. This contradictory record typified the results of Reconstruction in many other ways. A tumultuous period brought tremendous change, yet many things remained the same. Because extraordinary situations required revolutionary changes, the North acted

strongly for a time. The Union victory brought about an increase in federal power, stronger nationalism, unprecedented federal intervention in the southern states, and landmark amendments to the Constitution. But there was no commitment to make these changes endure, so the revolution remained partial.

The North embraced emancipation, black suffrage, and constitutional amendments strengthening the central government. But it did so to defeat the rebellion, secure the peace, and prevent rebellion from reemerging. As the pressure of these crises declined, strong underlying continuities emerged and placed their mark on Reconstruction. The American people and the courts maintained a preference for state authority and a distrust of federal power. The ideology of free labor dictated that property should be respected and that individuals should take care of themselves without much help from government. Racism endured, and the black minority struggled to gain the attention of the white majority. Concern for the human rights of African-Americans was strongest when their plight threatened to undermine the interests of whites, and reform frequently had less appeal than moneymaking in a diverse, individualistic, and enterprising society. Thus the status of African-Americans would continue to be a major social and political issue.

A host of other issues would arise from industrialization. How would the country develop its immense resources in a growing and increasingly interconnected national economy? How would farmers, industrial workers, immigrants, and capitalists fit into the new social system? Industrialization promised not just a higher standard of living but also a different lifestyle in both urban and rural areas. Moreover, industry increased the nation's power and laid the foundation for an enlarged American role in international affairs. Americans' thoughts again turned to expansion and the conquest of new frontiers. As the United States entered its second hundred years of existence, it confronted these challenging issues. The experiences of the 1860s and 1870s suggested that solutions, if any, might be neither clear nor complete.

Suggestions for Further Reading

National Policy, Politics, and Constitutional Law

Richard H. Abbott, *The Republican Party and the South, 1855–1877* (1986); Herman Belz, *Emancipation and Equal Rights* (1978); Herman Belz, *A New Birth of Freedom* (1976); Michael Les Benedict, *A Compromise of Principle: Congressional Republicans and Reconstruction, 1863–1869* (1974); Michael Les Benedict, *The Impeachment and Trial of Andrew Johnson* (1973); Charles S. Campbell, *The Transformation of American Foreign Relations, 1865–1900* (1976); Adrian Cook, *The Alabama Claims* (1975); Michael Kent Curtis, *No State Shall Abridge* (1987); David Donald, *Charles Sumner and the Rights of Man* (1970); Harold M. Hyman, *A More Perfect Union* (1973); Ronald J. Jensen, *The Alaska Purchase and Russian-American Relations* (1975); William S. McFeely, *Grant* (1981); William S. McFeely, *Yankee Stepfather: General O. O. Howard and the Freedmen* (1968); Eric L. McKitrick, *Andrew Johnson and Reconstruction* (1966); James M. McPherson, *The Abolitionist Legacy* (1975); Brooks D. Simpson, *Let Us Have Peace* (1991); Kenneth M. Stampp, *The Era of Reconstruction* (1965); Hans L. Trefousse, *Andrew Johnson* (1989).

The Freed Slaves

Roberta Sue Alexander, *North Carolina Faces the Freedmen* (1985); Ira Berlin, ed., *Freedom: A Documentary History of Emancipation,* *1861–1867* (1984); Elizabeth R. Bethel, *Promiseland* (1981); Orville Vernon Burton, *In My Father's House Are Many Mansions* (1985); Edmund L. Drago, *Black Politicians and Reconstruction in Georgia* (1982); Paul D. Escott, *Slavery Remembered* (1979); Eric Foner, "Reconstruction and the Crisis of Free Labor," in *Politics and Ideology in the Age of the Civil War,* ed. Eric Foner (1980); Gerald Jaynes, *Branches Without Roots: The Genesis of the Black Working Class in the American South, 1862–1882* (1986); Leon Litwack, *Been in the Storm So Long* (1979); Edward Magdol, *A Right to the Land* (1977); Robert Morris, *Reading, 'Riting and Reconstruction* (1981); Howard Rabinowitz, ed., *Southern Black Leaders in Reconstruction* (1982); Emma Lou Thornbrough, ed., *Black Reconstructionists* (1972); Okon Uya, *From Slavery to Public Service* (1971); Clarence Walker, *A Rock in a Weary Land* (1982).

Politics and Reconstruction in the South

Robert W. Coakley, *The Role of Federal Military Forces in Domestic Disorders, 1789–1878* (1988); Richard N. Current, *Those Terrible Carpetbaggers* (1988); Jonathan Daniels, *Prince of Carpetbaggers* (1958); W. E. B. Du Bois, *Black Reconstruction* (1935); Paul D. Escott, *Many Excellent People: Power and Privilege in North Carolina, 1850–1900* (1985); W. McKee Evans, *Ballots and Fence Rails: Reconstruction on the Lower Cape Fear* (1966); Michael W. Fitzgerald, *The Union League Movement in the Deep South* (1989); Eric Foner, *Reconstruction: America's Unfinished Revolution, 1863–1877* (1988); Eric Foner, *Nothing but Freedom* (1983); William C. Harris, *The Day of the Carpetbagger* (1979); Thomas Holt, *Black over White: Negro Political Leadership in South Carolina During Reconstruction* (1977); J. Morgan Kousser and James M. McPherson, eds., *Region, Race and Reconstruction* (1982); Elizabeth Studley Nathans, *Losing the Peace* (1968); Michael Perman, *The Road to Redemption* (1984); Michael Perman, *Reunion Without Compromise* (1973); Lawrence N. Powell, *New Masters* (1980); George C. Rable, *But There Was No Peace* (1984); James Roark, *Masters Without Slaves* (1977); James Sefton, *The United States Army and Reconstruction, 1865–1877* (1967); Mark W. Summers, *Railroads, Reconstruction, and the Gospel of Prosperity* (1984); Allen Trelease, *White Terror* (1967); Ted Tunnell, *Carpetbagger from Vermont* (1989); Ted Tunnell, *Crucible of Reconstruction* (1984); Michael Wayne, *The Reshaping of Plantation Society* (1983); Sarah Woolfolk Wiggins, *The Scalawag in Alabama Politics, 1865–1881* (1977).

Women, Family, and Social History

Virginia I. Burr, ed., *The Secret Eye* (1990); Ellen Carol Dubois, *Feminism and Suffrage* (1978); Herbert G. Gutman, *The Black Family in Slavery and Freedom, 1750–1925* (1976); Elizabeth Jacoway, *Yankee Missionaries in the South* (1979); Jacqueline Jones, *Labor of Love, Labor of Sorrow* (1985); Jacqueline Jones, *Soldiers of Light and Love* (1980); Robert C. Kenzer, *Kinship and Neighborhood in a Southern Community* (1987); Mary P. Ryan, *Women in Public* (1990); Rebecca Scott, "The Battle over the Child," *Prologue* 10 (Summer 1978): 101–113.

The End of Reconstruction

Michael Les Benedict, "Southern Democrats in the Crisis of 1876–1877," *Journal of Southern History* 66 (November 1980): 489–524; William Gillette, *Retreat from Reconstruction, 1869–1879*

(1980); William Gillette, *The Right to Vote* (1969); Keith Ian Polakoff, *The Politics of Inertia* (1973); John G. Sproat, *"The Best Men": Liberal Reformers in the Gilded Age* (1968); C. Vann Woodward, *Reunion and Reaction* (1951).

Reconstruction's Legacy for the South

Robert G. Athearn, *In Search of Canaan* (1978); Edward L. Ayers, *The Promise of the New South* (1992); Norman L. Crockett, *The Black Towns* (1979); Stephen J. DeCanio, *Agriculture in the Postbellum South* (1974); Steven Hahn, *The Roots of Southern Populism* (1983); Jay R. Mandle, *The Roots of Black Poverty* (1978); Nell Irvin Painter, *Exodusters* (1976); Howard Rabinowitz, *Race Relations in the Urban South, 1865–1890* (1978); Roger L. Ransom and Richard Sutch, *One Kind of Freedom* (1977); Laurence Shore, *Southern Capitalists* (1986); Peter Wallenstein, *From Slave South to New South* (1987); Jonathan M. Wiener, *Social Origins of the New South* (1978); C. Vann Woodward, *Origins of the New South* (1951).

CHAPTER

17

The Development of the West and South

1877–1892

I n August 1867, Roaming Leader, a member of the Skidi band of the Pawnee nation, on orders from his chief, led a scouting party to look for buffalo. The whole band—several dozen men, women, and children—had left its village of mud lodges in northwestern Nebraska two months earlier for the annual buffalo hunt. As the scouts rode along the Platte River, they carefully avoided Cheyenne and Arapaho hunting parties that might attack them and take their horses. Eventually, the Skidi party found three buffalo standing alone by a creek. Quickly and skillfully, they shot the animals and butchered them so they could carry the carcasses back to camp on their five horses. There, outside the tents, which had been carefully arranged according to constellations of stars in the sky, women deftly cut up and dried the meat, then made mats out of the intestines, robes and blankets out of the hides, and implements out of the bones.

In September, Roaming Leader's band returned to its village to harvest the corn the Skidi had planted that spring. When they had left in June to hunt buffalo, the plants stood only a few feet high. Now as autumn approached, the stalks reached ten feet and were ready to be dried along with the beans and pumpkins. The lodges had become infested with fleas while the Skidi were hunting, so they camped near the fields because they could not spare the time to remove the insects. They stayed in the village only long enough to clean out the pits in which they planned to store the dried food. At the harvest, the women again controlled the food preparation, roasting and drying vegetables in a deep pit and grinding grain into flour. Meanwhile, men collected firewood. Finally, after nearly two weeks of strenuous work, the Skidi returned to

This painting (1874) by Thomas Moran shows a solitary American Indian dwarfed but not threatened by nature. The interaction of humans with the environment provided the major themes of western and southern history in the nineteenth century. *Detail of* Cliffs of Green River, *Thomas Moran, oil on canvas, 1874, 1975.28. Copyright Amon Carter Museum, Fort Worth, Texas.*

475

their village to celebrate the harvest with elaborate rituals of song, dance, and food offerings.

Indians had managed land and resources in this way for centuries before covetous white settlers arrived on the scene. The Pawnees planted crops in the spring, then left to hunt buffalo. They sometimes clashed with other Indians, such as the Cheyennes and Arapahos, who wanted hunting grounds and crops for their own purposes. Their technology was simple. Though they sometimes splurged when feasting on buffalo, they tried to survive by developing and using natural resources respectfully; concepts of private property, commercial exchange, and profit had little meaning for them.

For white Americans, however, expanses of land and rivers of water were resources to be utilized for economic gain. As they settled the West and redeveloped the South in the late nineteenth century, they dug into the earth to remove valuable minerals, cut down forests for lumber to build homes, built railroads to link markets, and dammed the rivers and plowed the soil with machines to grow crops. Their goal was not survival; rather, it was buying and selling goods and services and achieving a more comfortable life. As they transformed the landscape, the triumph of their market economies transformed the entire nation.

Throughout American history, the region known as "the South" has had a relatively stable definition, but the meaning of the expression "the West" has changed over time. In the eighteenth century, "the West" was the area beyond the Appalachian Mountains. By the years following the Civil War, "the West" was most of the area between the Mississippi River and the Pacific Ocean, including the flat plains between the Mississippi and the Rocky Mountains, the Rockies themselves, and the mountains and valleys of the Far West. Between 1870 and 1890, migration into the West proceeded at a furious pace; the population living between the Mississippi River and the Pacific Ocean swelled from 7 million to nearly 17 million. Growth characterized the South as well. Shortly after Reconstruction ended, cotton production reached pre–Civil War levels, and southerners found new ways to profit from the region's natural resources.

The abundance of land, food, and raw materials in the West and South filled white Americans with faith that anyone eager and persistent enough could succeed. But their self-confidence rested on an arrogant belief that white people were somehow special, and individualism often asserted itself at the expense of racial minorities and the poor. Americans rarely thought about conserving resources because there always seemed to be more territory to exploit and bring into the market economy.

By 1890, farms, ranches, mines, towns, and cities could be found in almost every corner of the present-day continental United States. The frontier, so long a part of western and southern history, apparently had disappeared. Indeed, in 1890 the superintendent of the United States census declared that the American frontier no longer existed. Though of great symbolic importance, the fading of the frontier had little direct impact on people's behavior, for vast stretches of land remained unsettled. Millions of people continued to stream into the West, and more land in the South came under cultivation. Settlers who failed in one region rarely perished; they moved on and tried again somewhere else. Although life in the West was less comfortable than settlers might have wished, and the South failed to fulfill its potential, expanses of unsettled land in both regions gave Americans the feeling that they would always have a second chance. Belief in an infinity of second chances left a deep imprint on the American character.

The Transformation of Native American Cultures

Historians once defined the American frontier as "the edge of the unused," implying that the frontier faded when white men and women began to use supposedly open land for farming or the building of cities. Scholars now acknowledge that Native Americans had settled the West long before other Americans migrated there. Neither passive nor powerless in the face of nature, Indians had been shaping their environment for centuries. Nevertheless, almost all native economic systems weakened in the late nineteenth century. Why and how did these declines happen?

Western Indian cultures varied. Some Indians lived in permanent settlements, and others moved their camps and villages, but all based their economies to differing degrees on four activities: crop raising; livestock raising; hunting, fishing, and gathering; and raiding. Corn was the most common crop; sheep and horses, acquired from Spanish colonizers, were the livestock; and buffalo were the primary prey of

Subsistence Cultures

• *Important Events* •

1862	Homestead Act grants free land to citizens who live on and cultivate the land for five years	**1889**	Statehood granted to North Dakota, South Dakota, Washington, and Montana
	Morrill Land Grant Act gives states public lands to finance agricultural and industrial colleges	**1890**	Wounded Knee massacre: final suppression of Plains tribes by United States Army
			Census Bureau announces closing of the frontier
1876	Custer's Last Stand (Battle of Little Big Horn): Sioux annihilate federal troops led by Colonel George A. Custer		Statehood granted to Wyoming and Idaho
			Yosemite National Park established
	U.S. v. *Reese* affirms that Congress has no control over states wishing to disfranchise black voters		"Mississippi Plan" disfranchises African-Americans by imposing poll tax and property and literacy requirements
1878	Timber and Stone Act allows citizens to buy timber land cheaply but also enables large companies to acquire huge tracts of forest land	**1896**	*Plessy* v. *Ferguson* upholds doctrine of "separate but equal" among blacks and whites in public facilities
			Rural Free Delivery made available
			Statehood granted to Vermont and Utah
1880–81	George Manypenny's *Our Indian Wards* and Helen Hunt Jackson's *A Century of Dishonor* influence public conscience about poor government treatment of Indians	**1898**	Louisiana enacts first "grandfather clause," using literacy and property qualifications to prevent blacks from voting
1883	Supreme Court, in *Civil Rights* cases, strikes down 1875 Civil Rights Act and reinforces claim that the federal government cannot regulate behavior of private individuals in matters of race relations	**1899**	*Cummins* v. *County Board of Education* applies separate-but-equal doctrine to public schools
		1902	Newlands Reclamation Act passed
	National time zones standardized		
1887	Dawes Severalty Act ends communal ownership of Indian lands and grants land allotments to individual Native American families		
	Hatch Act provides for agricultural experiment stations in every state		

hunts. Indians raided each other for food, hides, and livestock. They also waged war with each other for revenge and to displace each other from hunting grounds. The goal of all these activities was *subsistence*, the maintenance of life at its most basic level. To achieve subsistence, Indians tried to balance their economic systems. When a buffalo hunt failed, they could still subsist on crops. When their crops failed, they could still hunt buffalo and steal food in a raid. Indians also traded with each other and with whites, mainly to obtain necessities such as horses and furs.

For Indians on the Great Plains, whether they were nomads such as the Sioux or village dwellers such as the Pawnees, everyday life focused on the buffalo. They cooked and preserved buffalo meat; fashioned hides into clothing, shoes, and blankets; used sinew for thread and bowstrings; and carved tools from bones and horns. They also depended on horses, which they used for transportation, and hunting and as symbols of wealth. To provide food for their herds, Pawnees and other Plains Indians practiced environmental management by periodically setting fire to tall-grass prairies. The fires burned away dead growth, facilitating the growth of grass in the spring so horses could feed all summer.

In the Southwest, Indians placed great value on sheep, goats, and horses. Old Man Hat (a Navajo) explained, "The herd is money. . . . You know that

Indian Camp at Dawn, painted by Jules Tavernier, a French immigrant who worked as an illustrator for Harper's Weekly, *shows the nomadic life of Plains Indians. Bands would set up a camp near water and stay for several weeks while they hunted, skinned, and processed buffalo.*   Jules Távernier, "Indian Camp at Dawn," oil on canvas, 0136. 1222. From the collection of Gilcrease Museum, Tulsa.

you have some good clothing; the sheep gave you that. And you've just eaten different kinds of food; the sheep gave that food to you. Everything comes from the sheep." He was not speaking of money in a business sense, though. To the Navajos, the herds provided status and security. Like many Indians, they emphasized generosity and distrusted private property and wealth. Within the family, sharing was expected; outside the family, gifts and reciprocity governed personal relations. Thus southwestern Indians, too, controlled the environment, building elaborate irrigation systems to maximize use of scarce water supplies.

This world of subsistence began to dissolve after 1850 when whites entered the West and competed with Indians for access to and control over natural resources. Perceiving the buffalo and the Indians as hindrances to their ambitions on the Great Plains, whites endeavored to eliminate both. As one United States army officer put it, "Kill every buffalo you can. Every buffalo dead is an Indian gone." Railroads sponsored hunts in which eastern sportsmen shot at the bulky targets from slow-moving trains. The army distributed ammunition to hunters and refused

Slaughter of Buffalo

to enforce treaties that reserved hunting grounds for exclusive Indian use. Some hunters collected from $1 to $3 from tanneries for hides that were sent east to be used mainly as belts to drive industrial machinery; others did not even stop to pick up their kill.

By the 1880s only a few hundred remained of the estimated 13 million buffalo that had existed in 1850. As the buffalo herds dwindled, Pawnees and other Plains tribes had to hunt farther from their villages. In so doing, they clashed with rival tribes over scarce buffalo and left their own settlements vulnerable to raids by other Indians seeking food. The scarcity of buffalo disturbed the subsistence system by leaving the Indians with less food to supplement their diets if their crops failed or were stolen.

Government policy reinforced private efforts to remove Indians from the path of white ambitions. North American natives were organized not so much into tribes, as whites believed, but rather into hundreds of bands and confederacies. Some two hundred distinct languages and dialects separated these groups and made it difficult for Indians to unite against white invaders. Although a language group could be defined as a tribe, separate bands and clans within each language group had their own chiefs, and seldom did a "tribal" chief hold significant power. Moreover, bands usually spent more time quarreling with each other than with white settlers.

Nevertheless, the United States government needed some way of categorizing the natives so as to fashion a policy toward them. It did so by imputing more meaning to tribal organization than was warranted.

Territorial Treaties

After the Treaty of Greenville in 1795, American officials considered Indian "tribes" to be separate nations with which they could make treaties that ensured peace and defined boundaries between Indian and white lands. But a chief or chiefs who agreed to a treaty could not guarantee that all bands within the group would abide by it. Moreover, whites seldom accepted treaties as guarantees of the Indians' future land rights; whites assumed that they could settle wherever they wished. As white settlers pressed into Indian territories in the West, treaties made one week were violated the next. Some bands acquiesced; others took revenge by attacking settlements, herds, and troops. The army responded with murders and massacres of entire villages. Often Indians themselves aided the army as scouts and troops against enemy bands. In addition, white settlers openly stole Indian land claims and sold Indians spoiled meat.

By the 1870s, federal officials and reformers, seeking more peaceful means of dealing with western natives, began promoting policies that would treat Indians more like African-Americans and immigrants. Instead of being considered foreign nations, they would be "civilized" and "uplifted" through education. This meant changing their identities, community structures, and relationships to the federal government. With government encouragement, white missionaries and teachers would attempt to force on Native Americans the values of the "new" American work ethic: ambition, thrift, and materialism. To achieve this transformation, however, Indians would have to abandon their traditional cultures.

From the 1860s to the 1880s, the federal government tried to force Indians onto reservations, where, it was thought, they could be "civilized."

Reservation Policy

Reservations usually consisted of those areas of a group's previous territory that were least desirable to whites (see map, page 489). When assigning Indians to restricted territories, the government promised protection from white encroachment and agreed to provide food, clothing, and other necessities.

Intent on removing the huge buffalo herds that impeded their settlement, white Americans engaged in an orgy of killing. Some hunters removed the buffalo hides in order to sell them but left hundreds of thousands of carcasses to rot on the plains. Library of Congress.

Like buffalo kills, reservation policy helped make way for the market economy. In the early years of contact, trade had benefited both Indians and whites and had taken place on a nearly equal footing. Indians had acquired clothing, guns, and horses in return for furs, jewelry, and, sometimes, military service. Gradually, however, the whites' needs and economic power grew disproportionate to the needs and power of Indians. Indians became more dependent, and whites increasingly dictated what was to be traded and on what terms. For example, white traders persuaded Navajo weavers to produce heavy rugs suitable for eastern customers and to adopt new designs and colors to boost sales. Meanwhile, Navajos raised fewer crops and were forced to buy food because the market economy lured them away from subsistence agriculture. Soon they were selling their land and labor to whites as well, which made it easier to force them onto reservations.

Reservation policy had disturbing consequences. First, Indians had no say over their own affairs on reservations. Supreme Court decisions in 1884 and 1886 denied them the ability to become United States citizens, leaving them unprotected by the Fourteenth and Fifteenth Amendments, which had extended to African-Americans the rights and legal protection of citizenship. Second, it was impossible to protect reservations from white farmers, miners, and herders who continually sought Indian lands for their own purposes. Third, the government ignored native history, even combining on the same reservation Indian bands that habitually had waged war with each other. Rather than serving as civilizing communities, reservations made Indians more vulnerable than they had been.

Not all Indians succumbed to market forces and reservation restrictions. Pawnees in the Midwest, for example, resisted extensive trading as well as the liquor that white traders deliberately used to addict Indians and tempt them into disadvantageous deals. And some natives tried to preserve their traditional cultures even as they became dependent on whites. Navajos traded for food in order to restore their subsistence way of life, and Pawnees agreed to leave their Nebraska homelands for a reservation in the hope that they could hunt buffalo and grow corn as they once had done.

Native Resistance

Indians also actively defended their homelands from intrusion by non-Indian would-be settlers and developers in a series of bloody conflicts and revolts. These battles, which had been occurring since colonial times, climaxed in June 1876 when 2,500 Sioux

Reformers established boarding schools to take Indian children off the reservations and teach them a new and allegedly better culture. As one white leader remarked, "They should be educated, not as Indians, but as Americans." Upon their arrival at the Carlisle School in Pennsylvania, one of twenty-four such schools, Sioux youths (on the left) received new attire to make them look (on the right) as their teachers wanted them to look. Smithsonian Institute, Washington, D.C.

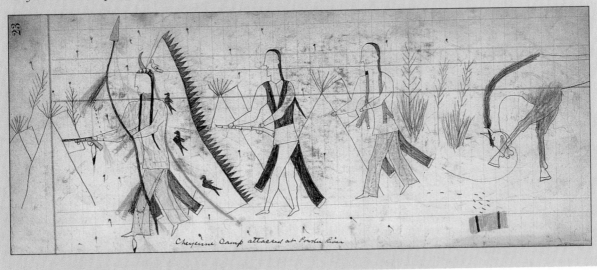

Cheyenne Camp attacked at Powder River

led by Chiefs Rain-in-the-Face, Sitting Bull, and Crazy Horse surrounded and annihilated 256 government troops led by the rash Colonel George A. Custer near the Little Big Horn River in southern Montana. Though Indians consistently demonstrated military skill, shortages of supplies and relentless pursuit by white troops eventually overwhelmed armed Indian resistance. Native Americans were not so much conquered in battle as they were starved into submission.

These conditions kindled new efforts to reform Indian policy in the 1880s. Reform treatises—George Manypenny's *Our Indian Wards* (1880) and Helen Hunt Jackson's *A Century of Dishonor* (1881), for example—and unfavorable comparison with Canada's management of Indian affairs aroused the American conscience. Canada had granted native peoples the rights of British subjects, and the Royal Mounted Police defended them against whites. Canadian officials were more tolerant and proceeded more slowly than Americans in efforts to acculturate Indians. A high rate of intermarriage between Indians and Canadian whites also promoted smoother relations.

In the United States, the two most active Indian reform organizations were the Women's National Indian Association (WNIA) and the Indian Rights Association (IRA). The WNIA, a group composed mainly of white women who sought to use women's domestic skills to help people in need, urged gradual assimilation of Indians. The IRA, which was more important but numbered few Native Americans among its members, supported citizenship and landholding by individual Indians. Most reformers believed Indians were culturally inferior to whites and assumed Indians could succeed economically only if they adopted middle-class values of diligence, monogamy, and education.

Reform of Indian Policy

Reformers particularly deplored Indians' sexual division of labor. Women seemed to do all the work—tending crops, raising children, cooking, curing hides, making tools and clothes—and to be servile to men, who hunted but were otherwise idle. Groups such as the WNIA and IRA wanted Indian men to bear more responsibilities, to treat Indian women more respectfully, and to resemble the male heads of white middle-class households. The effect of their reforms would have been—and sometimes was—to curtail the economic independence of Indian women.

In 1887 Congress reversed its reservation policy and passed the Dawes Severalty Act. The act, which achieved a goal long recommended by reformers,

Dawes Severalty Act

ended communal ownership of Indian lands and granted land allotments to individual Native American families, awarding citizenship (after a twenty-five-year waiting period) to all who accepted allotments. It also authorized the government to sell surplus—unallocated—land, to whites. These provisions applied to western groups except the Pueblo peoples, who retained land rights that were granted to them by the Spanish.

United States Indian policy, as carried out by the Interior Department, now took on three main features. First and foremost, as required by the Dawes Act, the federal government distributed reservation land to individual families in the belief that they would acquire white people's wants and values by learning how to manage their own property. Second, officials believed that Indians would abandon their "barbaric" habits more quickly if their children were educated in boarding schools away from the reservations. In 1879, such schools, which had functioned for decades, were expanded. Third, officials tried to suppress what they believed were dangerous religious ceremonies by funding white church groups to teach Indians to become good Christians.

In 1890 the government made one last show of force—though such a demonstration was hardly necessary. With active resistance having been suppressed, some Sioux and other

Ghost Dance

groups turned to the religion of the Ghost Dance as a spiritual means of preserving native culture. Inspired by a Paiute prophet named Wovoka, the Ghost Dance involved movement in a circle until the dancers reached a trancelike state and envisioned dead ancestors. Some dancers believed these ancestors heralded a day when buffalo would return to the plains and all elements of white civilization, including guns and whiskey, would be buried. The Ghost Dance expressed this messianic vision in a ritual involving several days of dancing and meditation.

Ghost Dancers foreswore violence but looked aggressive when they donned sacred shirts that they believed would repel the white man's bullets. As the religion spread, government agents became alarmed about the possibility of renewed Indian uprisings. Charging that the cult was anti-Christian, they began arresting Ghost Dancers. Late in 1890, the government sent the Seventh Cavalry, Custer's old regiment, to round up some Sioux moving from the north toward Pine Ridge, South Dakota. Though the Indians were starving and seeking protection from the troops, the army believed they were armed for revolt. During an encounter at a creek called Wounded Knee, the troops massacred three hundred men, women, and children in the snow.

The Dawes Act effectively accomplished what whites wanted and Indians feared: it reduced native control over land. Eager speculators induced Indians to sell their newly acquired

The Losing of the West

property, in spite of some federal safeguards against such practices. Between 1887 and the 1930s, Indian landholdings dwindled from 138 million acres to 52 million. Land-grabbing whites were particularly cruel to the Ojibwas of the northern plains. In 1906, Senator Moses E. Clapp of Minnesota attached to an Indian appropriations bill a rider declaring that mixed-blood adults on the White Earth reservation were "competent" enough to sell their land without having to observe the twenty-five-year waiting period stipulated in the Dawes Act. When the bill became law, speculators duped many Ojibwas whom white "experts" had declared "mixed-bloods" on the basis of fraudulent evidence, into signing away their land in return for counterfeit money and worthless merchandise. The Ojibwas lost more than half of their original holdings, and economic ruin overtook them.

The government's policy had other harmful effects on Indians' ways of life. The boarding-school program educated thousands of children, but most returned to their families demoralized and confused rather than ready to assimilate into white society. Polingaysi Qoyawayma, a Hopi woman forced to take the Christian name Elizabeth Q. White, recalled after four years spent at the Sherman Institute in Riverside, California, "As a Hopi, I was misunderstood by the white man; as a convert of the missionaries, I was looked upon with suspicion by the Hopi people."

Ultimately, the western Indians were overcome by political and ecological crises. White military superiority alone did not defeat them. Their economic systems had started to break down before the military campaigns occurred. Buffalo extinction, enemy raids, and disease, in addition to military force, combined to hobble subsistence culture to the point that Native Americans had no alternative but to yield their lands to market-oriented whites. Believing themselves superior, whites determined to transform the Indians into "virtuous" farmers by teaching them the value of private property, educating them in American ideals, and forcefully eradicating their "backward" languages, lifestyles, and religions. Although Indians tried to retain their culture by both adapting and yielding to the various demands they faced, by the end of the century they had lost control of the land and were under increasing pressure to shed their group identity. The West was won at their expense, and to this day they remain casualties of an aggressive age.

By the 1880s, large-scale operations had replaced solitary prospectors in the extraction of minerals from western territories. Here, powerful sprays of water are being used to wash silver from a deposit in Alma, Colorado. Colorado Historical Society.

The Exploitation of Natural Resources

In sharp contrast to the Indians, who used land and water to meet subsistence needs, whites who migrated to the West and the Great Plains, first in the 1850s and increasingly after the Civil War, were driven by the desire to get rich quick. To their eyes, the vast stretches of territory were untapped reservoirs of resources and wealth. Extraction of these resources advanced settlement and created new markets; it also fueled the revolutions in transportation, agriculture, and industry that swept the United States in the late nineteenth century. At the same time, the exploitation of nature's wealth gave rise to careless interaction with the environment and fed habits of racial and sexual oppression.

In the years just before the Civil War, eager prospectors began to comb remote forests and mountains for gold, silver, timber, oil, and copper. The mining frontier advanced rapidly, drawing thousands of people to Nevada, Idaho, Montana, and Colorado. California, already a thriving state with more than 300,000 people in the 1860s, furnished many of the miners, who traveled from west to east in search of riches. Other people followed traditional routes, mov-

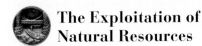

Mining and Lumbering

ing from the East and Midwest to western mining regions.

Prospectors tended to be restless optimists, willing to climb mountains and walk across deserts in search of a telltale glint of precious metal. They shot game for food and financed their explorations by convincing merchants to advance credit for equipment in return for a share of the as-yet-undiscovered lode. Unlucky prospectors whose credit ran out took jobs and saved up for another search for riches.

Prospectors' ultimate goal was to find and sell a large quantity of minerals. Digging for and transporting minerals, however, was extremely expensive, so prospectors who did discover veins of metal seldom mined them. Instead, they sold their claims to mining syndicates. Financed by eastern capital, the mining companies could bring in engineers, heavy machinery, railroad lines, and work crews. Although discoveries of gold and silver first drew attention to the West and its resources, mining companies usually exploited less romantic but equally lucrative bonanzas of lead, zinc, tin, quartz, and copper.

Lumber production, another large-scale extractive industry, required vast amounts of forest land. Lumber companies moving into the Northwest grabbed millions of acres by exploiting the Timber and Stone Act, passed by Congress in 1878 to stimulate settlement in California, Nevada, Oregon, and Washington. It allowed private citizens to buy, at a low price, 160-acre plots "unfit for cultivation" and "valuable chiefly for timber." Lumber companies hired seamen from waterfront boarding houses to register private claims to timberland and then transfer those claims to the companies. By 1900, private citizens had bought over 3.5 million acres, but most of that land belonged to corporations.

While lumber companies were acquiring timberlands in the Northwest, oil companies were beginning to drill for oil in the Southwest. In 1900 most of the nation's petroleum still came from the Appalachians and Midwest, but rich oil reserves had been discovered in southern California and eastern Texas. Although oil and kerosene were still used mostly for lubrication and lighting, oil discovered in the Southwest later became a vital new source of fuel.

The natural-resource frontier was largely a man's world. In 1880, white men outnumbered white women by more than two to one in Colorado, Nevada, and Arizona. Many western communities did have substantial populations of women who had come for the same reason as men: to find a fortune. But on the mining frontier as elsewhere, their independence was limited; they usually accompanied a husband or father and seldom prospected themselves. Even so, many women realized opportunities to earn money by cooking and laundering and in some cases providing sexual services for the miners. Occasionally, a woman became the main breadwinner when her husband failed to strike it rich.

Frontier Society

Women also helped to bolster family and community life as members of the home mission movement. Protestant missions had long carried out benevolent activities overseas, but in the midnineteenth century a number of women broke away from male-dominated missionary organizations. Their efforts focused on aiding women in countries that supported "barbaric" practices such as polygamy and female infanticide. Soon, these women—middle-class and white—were establishing "home" missionary societies in the United States to fulfill their slogan, "Woman's work for woman." In the

West, they exercised moral authority by building homes to rescue women—unmarried mothers, Mormons, Indians, and Chinese immigrants—who they believed had fallen prey to men or who had not yet accepted the conventions of Christian virtue.

The West was a multiracial society, including not only Native Americans and Anglo (native-born white) migrants but also Hispanics, African-Americans, and Asians. Indians could be found throughout the West, and Anglo miners and farmers became an increasing presence after 1850. A crescent of territory, stretching from western Texas through New Mexico and Arizona to northern California, supported Hispanic ranchers and sheepherders, descendants of the Spanish who originally had claimed the land. In New Mexico, Hispanics had mixed with Indians to form a mestizo population of small farmers and ranchers. All along the southwest border, Mexican immigrants streamed into American territory (before 1917, the border was open to all immigrants) to find work; some returned to Mexico seasonally; others stayed. And, before federal law excluded them in 1881 and 1882, some 200,000 Chinese immigrants came to the United States and, because almost all were young males, constituted a sizable proportion of the work force in California and other West Coast states.

A Complex Population

To bring order to this complex population, Anglos and white European immigrants made race the most important distinguishing social characteristic in the West. They usually distinguished among four nonwhite races: Indians, Mexicans (both Mexican-Americans, who had originally inhabited western lands, and Mexican immigrants), "Mongolians" (a term applied to Chinese), and African Americans. In creating these categories, whites imposed racial distinctions on people who, with the possible exception of blacks, had never before considered themselves to be a "race." Whites using these categories ascribed demeaning characteristics to all nonwhites, judging them to be not only inferior but permanently inferior.

Racial minorities in western communities occupied the bottom half of a two-tiered labor system. Whites dominated the top tier of managerial and skilled labor positions. Unskilled laborers, often Chinese and Mexicans, worked in the mines, on railroad construction, and as agricultural laborers. Blacks also worked in railroad and mining camps, doing cooking and cleaning, while Indians barely participated in the

Born in China, Polly Bemis, pictured here, came to America when her parents sold her as a slave. An Idaho saloon-keeper bought her, and she later married a man named Charlie Bemis, who won her in a card game. Her life story was common among the few Chinese women who immigrated to the United States in the 1860s and 1870s (most Chinese immigrants were men). Unlike many Chinese, however, she lived peacefully after her marriage until her death in 1933. Idaho Historical Society Library and Archives.

white-controlled labor system at all. All of these non-white groups encountered prejudice, especially as whites tried to reserve for themselves whatever riches the West might yield. The few Chinese who escaped mining and went into commercial fishing or agriculture found their activities limited by federal laws and local persecution that resulted in loss of their property. Many ended up as low-paid workers in California's laundry, tobacco, and domestic service establishments. Mexicans, many of whom had been the original owners of the land, saw their claims to land ignored or stolen by white miners and farmers. In California, they too became an urban population, working at unskilled, low-paying jobs.

As whites were wresting control of the land from the Indians, new questions arose over control of the nation's oil, mineral, and timber resources.

Use of Western Lands

Much of the undeveloped land west of the Mississippi was in the public domain, and some people believed that the federal government, as its owner, should control its exploitation. Others, however, believed that their own and the nation's wealth depended on unlimited use of the land.

People who supported unrestrained economic growth usually prevailed. Developers of natural resources were seldom interested in landowning. They wanted trees, not forest land that would become useless once they had cut the trees. They wanted oil, not the scrubby plain that would be worthless if—as often happened—they dug wells but found no oil. To avoid purchase costs, oilmen and iron miners often leased property from private owners or from the government and paid royalties on the minerals extracted, then abandoned the land when it was no longer profitable. Some lumbermen simply cut trees on public lands without paying a cent and used trickery to buy land cheaply under the Timber and Stone Act.

Questions about natural resources caught Americans between a desire for progress and a fear of spoiling the land. By the late 1870s, people eager to protect the natural landscape began to organize a conservation movement. Prominent among them was western naturalist John Muir, who helped establish Yosemite National Park in 1890. The next year,

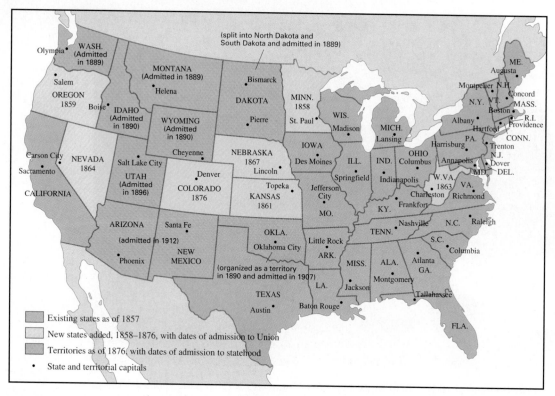

The United States, 1876–1912   *A wave of admissions between 1889 and 1912 brought remaining territories to statehood and marked the final creation of new states until Alaska and Hawai'i were admitted in the 1950s.*

pressured by Muir and others, Congress authorized President Benjamin Harrison to create forest reserves—public land protected from cutting by private interests. Such policies met with strong objections. Lumber companies, lumber dealers, and railroads were joined in their opposition by householders accustomed to cutting timber freely for fuel and building material. Public opinion about conservation also split along sectional lines. Most supporters of regulation came from eastern states, where resources already had become less plentiful. Opposition was loudest in the West, where people still were eager to take advantage of nature's bounty.

Development of the mining and forest frontiers, and of the farms and cities that followed, brought western territories to the threshold of statehood (see map). In 1889, Republicans seeking to solidify their control of Congress passed an omnibus bill granting statehood to North Dakota, South Dakota, Washington, and Montana. Wyoming and Idaho were admitted the following year. Congress denied statehood to Utah until 1896, six years after the Mormons, who

Admission of New States

constituted a majority of the territory's population and controlled its government, agreed to abandon polygamy.

Those states' mining towns and lumber camps spiced American folk culture and fostered a go-getter optimism that distinguished the American spirit. The lawlessness and hedonism of places like Deadwood, in Dakota Territory, and Tombstone, in Arizona Territory, gave the West notoriety and romance. Legends grew up almost immediately about characters whose lives both typified and magnified western experience.

Arizona's mining towns, with their free-flowing cash and loose law enforcement, attracted gamblers, thieves, and opportunists whose names came to stand for the Wild West. Near Tombstone, the infamous Clanton family and their partner John Ringgold (known as Johnny Ringo) engaged in smuggling and cattle rustling. Inside the town, the Earp brothers—Wyatt, Jim, Morgan, Virgil, and Warren—and their friends William ("Bat") Masterson and John Henry ("Doc") Holliday operated on both sides of the law as gunmen, gamblers, and politicians. A feud between the Clanton and Earp clans climaxed on October 26, 1881, in a shootout at the

OK Corral, where three Clantons were killed and Holliday and Morgan Earp were wounded.

Mark Twain, Bret Harte, and other writers captured for posterity the flavor of mining life, and characters like Wild Bill Hickok, Poker Alice, and Bedrock Tom became western folk heroes. But violence and eccentricity were far from common. Most miners and lumbermen worked long hours and had little time, energy, or money for gambling, carousing, or gunfights. Women worked as long or longer as teachers, cooks, laundresses, storekeepers, and housewives. Only a few were sharpshooters or dance-hall queens. For most, western life was a matter of adapting and surviving.

 ## Water and Western Agriculture

Glittering gold, tall trees, and gushing oil shaped the popular image of the West, but water gave it life. If the western territories and states promised wealth from mining, cutting, and drilling, their agricultural potential promised more—but only if settlers could find a way to bring water to the arid land. The economic development of the West is the story of how public and private interests used technology and organization to develop the region's river basins and make the land agriculturally productive. Just as control of the land was central to western development, so too was control of water.

For centuries, Indians had irrigated southwestern lands to sustain their subsistence farming. When the Spanish arrived, they began tapping the Rio Grande to irrigate their farms in southwest Texas and New Mexico; later they channeled water to California mission communities like San Diego and Los Angeles. The first Americans of northern European ancestry to practice extensive irrigation were the Mormons. Arriving in Utah in 1847, they quickly diverted streams and rivers into a network of canals, whose water enabled them to farm the hard-baked soil. By 1890, Utah could boast over 263,000 irrigated acres supporting more than 200,000 people.

Efforts at land reclamation through irrigation in Colorado and California raised controversies over rights to the precious streams that flowed through the West. Americans had inherited the English common-law principle of *riparian rights*, which held that only people who owned land along the banks of a river could appropriate from the water's flow. The

Who Owns the Water?

stream itself, according to riparianism, belonged only to God; those who lived on its banks could take water for normal needs but were not to diminish the river. This principle, intended to protect nature, discouraged economic development because it prohibited each property owner from "artificial" use, such as damming or diverting water at the expense of others who lived along the banks.

Americans, especially those who settled the West, rejected riparianism in favor of the doctrine of *prior appropriation*, which awarded a river's water to the first person who claimed it. Westerners, taking their cues in part from eastern Americans who had appropriated waterways for use in mills and factories, asserted that nature existed to advance human needs and profits. According to this outlook, water, like timber, minerals, and other natural resources, existed for human appropriation. Western farmers wanted to be allowed, as nonriparian property owners, to dam rivers and transport water as far as they wished. Moreover, they believed—a belief eventually supported by the courts—that anyone intending a beneficial or "reasonable" (economically productive) use of river water should have the right to appropriation.

Without appropriated water, agriculture could not have flourished in the West. Most lands were too dry for the rainfall farming that characterized the eastern plains (see page 494). Allowing water-drawing rights only to farmers who lived along riverbanks would give them a monopoly and effectively prevent development of most of the land. The unspoken premise, however, was that *all* land existed for potential human development and that *all* natural resources should be used—even used up—to maximize economic gain. Most white people assumed that the doctrine of appropriation made sense. But, as the Indians knew, there were other ways to view the land.

Riparianism did not permit use of water in a way that would diminish a river's flow. Under appropriation, by contrast, those who dammed and diverted water often reduced the flow of water available to potential users downstream. People disadvantaged by such action could protect their interests either by suing those who deprived them of water or by establishing a public authority to regulate water usage. Thus in 1879 Colorado created a number of water divisions, each with a commissioner to determine and regulate water rights. In 1890 Wyoming enlarged the concept of control with a constitutional provision declaring that the state's rivers were public property subject to state supervision of their use.

Destined to become the most productive agricultural state, California was the scene of the most dramatic water-related developments. In the 1860s a
few individuals controlled huge

California's Solution

tracts of land in the fertile Sacramento and San Joaquin river valleys, which they used for speculation, raising cattle, and growing wheat. But around the edges of the wheat fields lay unoccupied lands that could profitably support vegetable and fruit farming if irrigated properly.

Unlike western states that had opted for appropriation rights over riparian rights, California maintained a mixed legal system that upheld riparianism while allowing for some appropriation. This system put irrigators at a disadvantage and prompted them to seek a change in state law. In 1887 the state legislature passed a law permitting farmers to organize into irrigation districts that would sponsor the construction and operation of irrigation projects. An irrigation district could use its public authority to purchase water rights, seize private property to build irrigation canals, and finance its projects through taxation or by issuing bonds. As a result of this legislation, California became the nation's leader in irrigated acreage, with over 1 million irrigated acres by 1890, and the state boasted the most profitable agriculture in the country.

Though state irrigation provisions stimulated development, the federal government still owned most of the West in the 1890s, ranging from
64 percent of California to

Newlands Reclamation Act

96 percent of Nevada. Prodded by land-hungry developers, the states wanted the federal government to transfer to them all, or at least part, of the public domain lands. States claimed that they could make these lands profitable through *reclamation*—providing them with irrigated water. For the most part, Congress refused such transfers because of the issues they raised. If federal lands were transferred to state control for the purpose of water development, who would regulate waterways that flowed through more than one state or that potentially could provide water to a nearby state? If, for example, California received control of the Truckee River, which flowed westward out of Lake Tahoe, how would Nevadans be assured that California would give them any water? Only the federal government, it seemed, had the power to regulate water development.

In 1902, after many years of proposals and debates, Congress passed the Newlands Reclamation Act. Named for Congressman Francis Newlands of Nevada, the act allowed the federal government to sell western public lands to individuals in parcels not to exceed 160 acres, and to use the proceeds from such sales to finance irrigation projects. The Newlands Act provided for control but not conservation of water, because some three-fourths of the water used in open-ditch irrigation, the most common form, was lost to evaporation. Thus the legislation fell squarely within the tradition of exploitation of nature for human profit. Often identified as an example of sensitivity to natural-resource conservation, the Newlands Reclamation Act represented a direct decision by the federal government to aid the agricultural and general economic development of the West, just as state and federal subsidies to railroads during the 1850s and 1860s had aided the settlement of the West.

 ## The Age of Railroad Expansion

The discovery and development of natural riches provided the base on which the nation's economy expanded. But raw wealth would have been of limited value without the means to carry it to factories and marketplaces. Railroads filled this need, spreading a web of tracks across the country and refashioning the economy in the process.

Railroad construction after the Civil War was extensive and complex. Between 1865 and 1890, total track in the United States grew from 35,000 to
200,000 miles (see map, page

Effects of Railroad Construction

489). By 1910 the nation had one-third of all the railroad track in the world. A diverse mix of workers made up construction crews. The Central Pacific, built eastward from San Francisco, imported seven thousand Chinese to build its tracks; the Union Pacific, extending westward from Omaha, Nebraska, used mainly Irish construction gangs. Workers lived in shacks and tents that could be dismantled, loaded on flatcars, and relocated at intervals of about 60 or 70 miles. After 1880, when durable steel rails began to replace iron rails, railroads helped to boost the nation's steel industry to international leadership. Railroad expansion also spawned a number of related

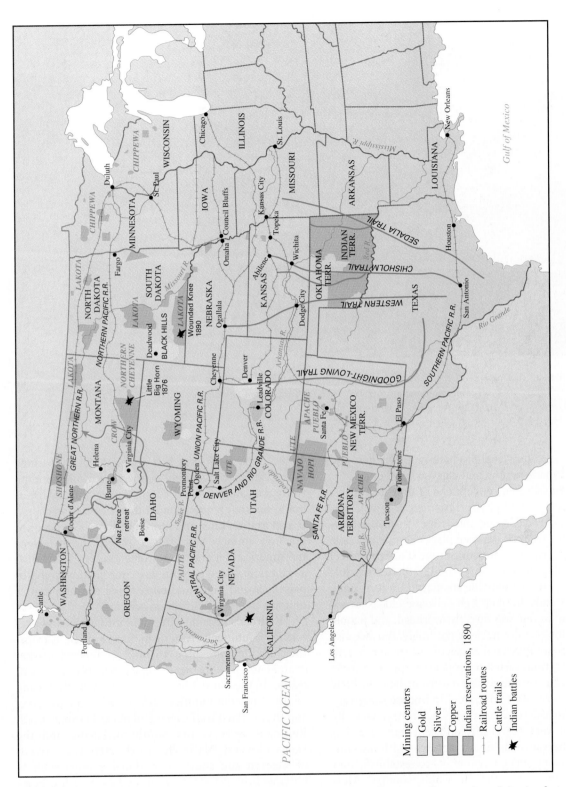

The American West, 1860–1890 *This map shows the dispersed nature of economic activity in the trans-Mississippi West and the importance of railroads in linking those activities.*

Construction crews on western railroads contained people of various ethnicities and races.
This Union Pacific work gang, riding a handcar in 1869, includes Chinese and African-
American laborers as well as a white foreman.   Lightfoot Collection.

industries, including coal production, passenger- and freight-car manufacture, and depot construction.

Railroads altered conceptions of time and space. First, by overcoming physical barriers to travel, railroads transformed space into time. Instead of expressing the distance between places in miles, people began to refer to the amount of time it took to travel from one place to another. Second, railroad scheduling required the nationwide standardization of time. Before railroads, local church bells and clocks struck noon when the sun was directly overhead, and people set their clocks and watches accordingly. But because the sun was not overhead at exactly the same moment everywhere, time varied from place to place. Clocks in Boston, for instance, differed from those in New York by almost twelve minutes. To impose some regularity, railroads created their own time zones. By 1880 there were nearly fifty different standards, but in 1883 the railroads finally agreed—without consulting anyone in government—to establish four standard time zones for the whole country. Most communities adjusted their clocks accordingly, and railroad time became national time.

Railroad construction brought about technological and organizational reforms as well. By the late 1880s, almost all lines had adopted standard-gauge rails so their tracks could connect with one another. Air brakes, automatic car couplers, standardized handholds on freight cars, and other devices made rail transportation safer and more efficient. The need for gradings, tunnels, and bridges spurred the growth of the American engineering profession. Organizational advances included systems for coordinating complex passenger and freight schedules, and the adoption of uniform freight-classification systems.

Railroads became extremely influential and performed a uniquely American function. In Europe, they usually were built to link established market centers and to improve or replace existing routes of traffic. In the United States, they often created many of the very communities they were meant to serve, and they carried traffic that had never before existed. Railroads such as the Southern Pacific and the Louisville and Nashville accelerated the growth of western and southern regional centers such as Omaha, Kansas City, Cheyenne, Los Angeles, Portland, Seattle, Atlanta, and Nashville.

Railroads accomplished these feats with the help of some of the largest government subsidies in American history. Executives argued that because

Government Subsidy of Railroads

railroads benefited the public, the government should aid them by giving them land from the public domain. Congress was sympathetic, as it had been when it aided steamboat navigation on the Great Lakes and the Mississippi River earlier in the nineteenth century. To encourage railroad construction, the federal government granted over 180 million acres, mostly for interstate routes. These grants usually consisted of a right of way, plus alternate sections of land in a strip 20 to 80 miles wide along the right of way. Railroads funded construction by using the land as security for bonds or by selling it for cash. States and localities heaped on further subsidies. State legislators, many of whom had financial interests in a railroad's success, granted some 50 million acres. Counties, cities, and towns also assisted, usually by offering loans or by purchasing railroad bonds or stocks.

Government subsidies had mixed effects. Although capitalists argued against government interference, they nevertheless accepted government aid and pressured governments into meeting their needs. The Southern Pacific, for example, threatened to bypass Los Angeles unless the city came up with a bonus and built a depot. Without public help, few railroads could have prospered sufficiently to attract private investment, yet public aid was not always salutary. During the 1880s, the policy of assistance haunted communities whose zeal had prompted them to commit too much to railroads that were never built or that defaulted on loans. Some laborers and farmers fought subsidies, arguing that companies like the Southern Pacific would become too powerful. Many communities boomed, however, because they had linked their fortunes to the iron horse. Moreover, railroads drew farmers into the market economy.

 Farming the Plains

"You are in a sea of wheat," rhapsodized the author of an 1880 magazine article about Oliver Dalrymple's farm in Dakota Territory's Red River valley. "The railroad train rolls through an ocean of grain. . . . We encounter a squadron of war chariots . . . doing the work of human hands. . . . There are 25 of them in this one brigade of the grand army of 115, under the marksmanship of this Dakota farmer." Dalrymple's farm exemplified two important achievements of the

late nineteenth century: the taming of windswept prairies so that the land would yield crops to benefit humankind, and the transformation of agriculture into big business by means of mechanization, long-distance transportation, and scientific cultivation.

These achievements did not come easily. The climate and landscape of the Great Plains presented formidable challenges, and overcoming them did not guarantee success or security. Agricultural development turned the United States into the world's breadbasket, but it also scarred the lives of hundreds of thousands of men and women who made that development possible.

Settlement of the Farm Frontier

Settlement of the Great Plains and the West involved the greatest migration in American history. During the 1870s and 1880s, hundreds of thousands of people streamed into states like Kansas, Nebraska, Texas, and California. More acres were put under cultivation during these two decades than in the previous 250 years. The number of farms tripled from 2 million to over 6 million between 1860 and 1910.

Most, though not all, migrants came from the eastern states or Europe. Several western states

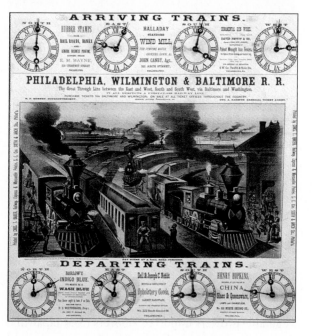

Train schedules not only changed the American economy but also altered how Americans timed their daily lives. As people and businesses ordered their day according to the arrival and departure of trains, distances became less important than hours and minutes. Library of Congress.

HOSPODÁŘ

This cover to a Czech agricultural journal portrays the riches supposedly available in America's fertile farmland. The illustrations show both manual labor, no stranger to immigrant farmers, and mechanized agriculture, a wonder and attraction of the New World. Inside the journal, articles provided advice about farming opportunities to recently arrived and prospective immigrants. Nebraska State Historical Society.

lems of shipping and storage. As a result of population growth, the demand for farm products grew rapidly, and the prospects for commercial agriculture—growing crops for profit—became more favorable than ever.

Life on the farm, however, was much harder than the advertisements and railroad agents suggested. Migrants often encountered scarcities of essentials they had once taken for granted. The open prairies contained little lumber for housing and fuel. Pioneer families were forced to build houses of sod and to burn manure for heat. Water was sometimes as scarce as timber. Few families were lucky or wealthy enough to buy land near a stream that did not dry up in summer and freeze in winter. Machinery for drilling wells was scarce until the 1880s, and even then it was very expensive.

Hardship of Life on the Plains

Even more formidable than the terrain was the climate. The expanse between the Missouri River and the Rocky Mountains divides climatologically along a line running from Minnesota southwest through Oklahoma, then south, bisecting Texas. West of this line, annual rainfall averages less than 28 inches, not enough for most crops (see maps, page 494), and life-giving rain was never certain. Heartened by adequate water one year, farmers gagged on dust and broke their plows on hardened limestone soil the next.

Weather seldom followed predictable cycles. In summer, weeks of torrid heat and parching winds suddenly gave way to violent storms that washed away crops and property. The wind and cold of winter blizzards piled up mountainous snowdrifts that halted all outdoor movement. During the Great Blizzard that struck Nebraska and the Dakota Territory in January 1888, the temperature plunged to 36 degrees below zero, and the wind blew at 56 miles per hour. The storm stranded schoolchildren and killed several parents who ventured out to rescue their children. In the spring, melting snow swelled streams, and floods threatened millions of acres. In the fall, a week without rain could turn dry grasslands into tinder, and the slightest spark could ignite a raging prairie fire.

Nature could be cruel even under good conditions. Weather that was favorable for crops was also good for breeding insects. Worms and flying pests ravaged corn and wheat. In the 1870s and 1880s swarms of grasshoppers virtually ate up entire farms. Heralded only by the din of buzzing wings, a mile-long cloud of insects would smother the land and de-

opened offices in the East and in European ports to lure settlers westward. Land-rich railroads were especially aggressive, advertising cheap land, arranging credit terms, offering reduced fares, and promising instant success. Railroad agents—often former immigrants—traveled to places like Denmark, Sweden, and Germany to recruit settlers and greeted newcomers at eastern ports. In California, fruit and vegetable growers imported laborers from Japan and Mexico to work in the fields and canneries.

Most migrants went west because opportunities there seemed to promise a better life. Railroad expansion made remote farming regions accessible, and the construction of grain elevators eased prob-

Posing in front of their sod house, this proud Nebraska family displays the seriousness that derived from their hard lives on the Great Plains. Though bushes and other growth appear in the background, the absence of trees is notable.   Nebraska State Historical Society, Solomon D. Butcher Collection.

vour everything: plants, tree bark, and clothes. As one farmer lamented, the "hoppers left behind nothing but the mortgage."

Settlers also had to contend with social isolation. Farmers in New England and in Europe lived in villages and traveled each day to their nearby

Social Isolation

fields. This pattern was rare in the American West, where peculiarities of land division compelled American rural dwellers to live apart from each other. The Homestead Act of 1862 and other measures to encourage western settlement offered cheap or free plots to people who would live on and improve their property. Because most plots acquired by small farmers were rectangular—usually encompassing 160 acres—at most four families could live near each other, but only if they congregated around the shared four-corner intersection. In practice, farm families usually lived back from their boundary lines, and at least a half-mile separated farmhouses. Land adjacent to farmhouses often was unoccupied, making neighbors even more distant.

Letters that Ed Donnell, a young Nebraska homesteader, wrote to his family in Missouri reveal how time and circumstances could dull optimism. In the fall of 1885, Donnell wrote to his mother: "I like Nebr first rate. . . . I have saw a pretty tuff time a part

of the time since I have been out here, but I started out to get a home and I was determined to win or die in the attempt. . . . Have got a good crop of corn, a floor in my house and got it ceiled overhead." Already, though, Donnell was lonely. He went on: "There is lots of other bachelors here but I am the only one I know who doesn't have kinfolks living handy. . . . You wanted to know when I was going to get married. Just as quick as I can get money ahead to get a cow."

A year and a half later, Donnell's dreams were dissolving and, still a bachelor, he was beginning to look for a second chance elsewhere. As he explained to his brother, "The rats eat my sod stable down. . . . I may sell out this summer, land is going up so fast. . . . If I sell I am going west and grow up with the country." By fall things had worsened, and Donnell wrote, "We have been having wet weather for 3 weeks. . . . My health has been so poor this summer and the wind and the sun hurts my head so. I think if I can sell I will . . . move to town for I can get $40 a month working in a grist mill and I would not be exposed to the weather." Donnell's doubts and hardships, shared by thousands of other people, fed the cityward migration of farm folk that fueled late-nineteenth-century urban growth (see Chapter 19).

Farm families survived by sheer resolve and by organizing churches and clubs where they could

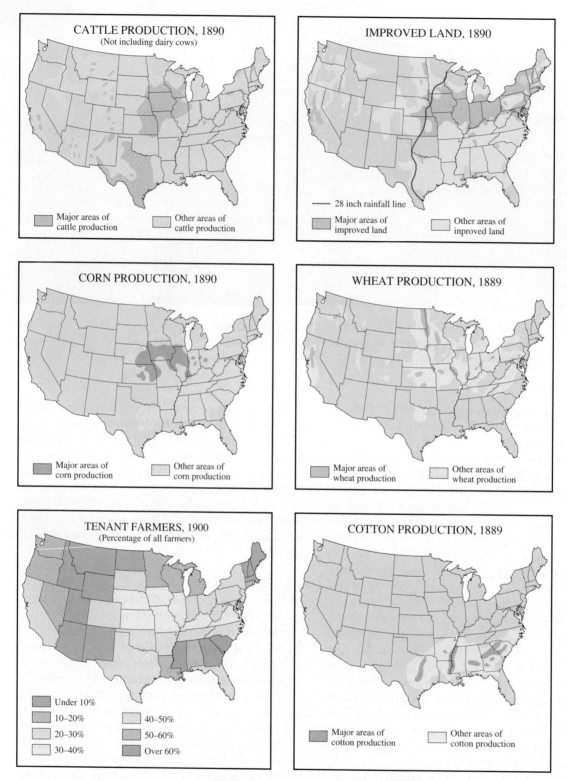

CATTLE PRODUCTION, 1890
(Not including dairy cows)

Major areas of cattle production

Other areas of cattle production

IMPROVED LAND, 1890

—— 28 inch rainfall line

Major areas of improved land

Other areas of inproved land

CORN PRODUCTION, 1890

Major areas of corn production

Other areas of corn production

WHEAT PRODUCTION, 1889

Major areas of wheat production

Other areas of wheat production

TENANT FARMERS, 1900
(Percentage of all farmers)

Under 10%
10–20%
20–30%
30–40%
40–50%
50–60%
Over 60%

COTTON PRODUCTION, 1889

Major areas of cotton production

Other areas of cotton production

Agricultural Regions, 1889–1900 *Commercial agriculture concentrated certain kinds of production in specific regions: cattle and grain in the Midwest, cotton in the South.* Source: From Charles A. Paullin, *Atlas of the Historical Geography of the United States.* Used by permission of Carnegie Institution of Washington.

socialize a few times a month. By 1900, two developments had brought rural settlers into closer contact with modern consumer society (though people in sparsely settled regions west of the 28-inch rainfall line remained isolated for several more decades). First, mail-order companies—Montgomery Ward and Sears, Roebuck—made new consumer products available to almost everyone by the 1870s and 1880s. Emphasizing personal attention to customers, Ward's and Sears were outlets for sociability as well as material goods. Letters from customers to Mr. Ward often reported family news and sought advice on everything from gifts to childcare. A Washington State man wrote, "As you advertise everything for sale that a person wants, I thought I would write you, as I am in need of a wife, and see what you could do for me." Another wrote: "I suppose you wonder why we haven't ordered anything from you since the fall. The cow kicked my arm and broke it and besides my wife was sick, and there was the doctor bill. But now, thank God, that is paid, and we are all well again, and we have a fine new baby boy, and please send plush bonnet number 29d8077."

Second, rural communities petitioned Congress for extension of the postal service during the 1890s, and in 1896 the government made Rural Free Delivery (RFD) widely available. Farmers would no longer lack news and information; they could receive letters, newspapers, and catalogues at home nearly every day. In 1913 the postal service inaugurated parcel post, which enabled people to receive packages, such as orders from Ward's and Sears, more cheaply. By 1920, rural families had regular access to the wider world through the mails.

The agricultural revolution that followed the Civil War would not have been possible without the expanded use of machinery. When the Civil War drew men away from farms in the upper Mississippi River valley, the women and men who remained behind began using reapers and other mechanical implements to satisfy demand for food and take advantage of high grain prices. After the war, continued demand and high prices encouraged farmers to depend more on machines, and inventors developed new implements for farm use. Seeders, combines, binders, mowers, and rotary plows, carried westward by railroads, were introduced on the Great Plains and in California in the 1870s and 1880s.

For centuries, the acreage of grain a farmer could plant had been limited by the amount that could be harvested by hand. Machines—driven first by animals, then by steam—increased productivity beyond farmers' imaginations. Before mechaniza-

Mail-Order Companies and Rural Free Delivery

Mechanization of Agriculture

By the late nineteenth century, the industrial revolution was making a significant impact on farming. This scene from a Colorado wheat farm shows a harvest aided by a steam tractor and belt-driven thresher, equipment that made large-scale commercial crop production possible. Colorado Historical Society.

Time and Cost of Farming an Acre of Land by Hand and by Machine, 1890

Crop	Hours Required		Labor Cost	
	Hand	*Machine*	*Hand*	*Machine*
Wheat	61	3	$3.65	$.66
Corn	39	15	$3.62	$1.51
Oats	66	7	$3.73	$1.07
Loose hay	21	4	$1.75	$.42

Source: Ray Allan Billington, *Westward Expansion: A History of the American Frontier*, 2d ed. (New York: Macmillan, 1960), p. 697.

tion, a farmer working alone could harvest about 7.5 acres of wheat. Using an automatic binder that cut and bundled the grain, the same farmer could harvest 135 acres. Machines dramatically reduced the time and cost of farming other crops as well (see table).

Meanwhile, Congress and scientists worked to improve existing crops and develop new ones. The 1862 Morrill Land Grant Act gave each state federal lands to sell in order to finance the establishment of educational institutions that aided agricultural development. The act prompted establishment of state universities such as those in Wisconsin, Illinois, Minnesota, and California. (A second Morrill Act in 1890 aided more schools, including a number of black colleges.) The Hatch Act of 1887 provided for agricultural experiment stations in every state, further encouraging the advancement of farming technology.

Legislative and Scientific Aid to Farmers

Scientific advances enabled farmers to use the soil more efficiently. Researchers developed the technique of dry farming, a system of plowing and harrowing that minimized the evaporation of precious moisture. Botanists perfected varieties of "hard" wheat whose seeds could withstand northern winters, and millers invented a process for grinding the tougher wheat kernels into flour. Agriculturists also adapted new varieties of alfalfa from Mongolia, corn from North Africa, and rice from Asia. Californian Luther Burbank developed a multitude of new plants by crossbreeding. Chemist George Washington Carver of the Tuskegee Institute cre-

ated hundreds of new products from peanuts, soybeans, sweet potatoes, and cotton wastes, and he taught methods of soil improvement. Other scientists developed means of combating plant and animal diseases. These and other scientific and technological developments helped feed a burgeoning population and make America what one journalist called "the garden of the world."

The Ranching Frontier

While commercial farming was spreading, cattle ranching—one of the West's most romantic industries—was evolving. Early in the nineteenth century herds of cattle, introduced by the Spanish and expanded by Mexican ranchers, roamed southern Texas and bred with cattle brought by Anglo settlers. The resulting longhorn breed multiplied and became valuable by the 1860s, when population growth increased demand for beef and railroads facilitated the transportation of food. By 1870, drovers were herding thousands of Texas cattle northward to Kansas, Missouri, and Wyoming (see map, page 489). On these long drives, mounted cowboys (as many as 25 percent of whom were African-American) supervised the herds, which fed on open grassland along the way. At the northern terminus— usually Abilene, Dodge City, or Cheyenne—the cattle were sold to northern ranches or loaded onto trains bound for Chicago and St. Louis for slaughter and distribution.

The long drive gave rise to romantic lore but was not very efficient. Trekking 1,500 miles made cattle sinewy and tough. Herds traveling through Indian lands and farmers' fields were sometimes shot at and later prohibited from such trespass by state laws. Ranchers adjusted by eliminating long drives and raising herds nearer to railroad routes. When ranchers discovered that crossing Texas longhorns with heavier Hereford and Angus breeds produced animals better able to survive northern winters, cattle raising spread across the Great Plains. Between 1860 and 1880 the cattle population of Kansas, Nebraska, Colorado, Wyoming, Montana, and the Dakotas increased from 130,000 to 4.5 million.

Development of the ranching frontier sparked several kinds of contests over land. In Texas and New Mexico, Anglos had received grants of land previously unoccupied by Mexicans; but driven by hunger for more, they wrested control of additional parcels from Mexican-Americans and Indians through taxation, fraud, and raw economic muscle. Eventually, the Tejanos, as Texas Mexicans were called, became wage laborers as vaqueros (cowboys), railroad workers, and field workers.

Cattle raisers needed vast pastures to graze their herds, and they wanted to incur as little expense as possible from using such land. Thus they often

Open-Range Ranching

bought a few acres bordering a stream and turned their herds loose on adjacent public domain that no one wanted because it lacked water access. By this method, called open-range ranching, a cattle raiser could control thousands of acres by owning only a hundred or so.

Neighboring ranchers often formed associations and allowed their herds to graze together. Owners identified their cattle by burning a brand into each animal's hide. Every ranch had its own brand—an improvised shorthand for labeling movable property. Cowboy crews rounded up the cattle twice each year to brand new calves in the spring and to drive mature animals to market in the fall.

Roundups delighted easterners with colorful images of western life: bellowing cattle, mounted rope-swinging cowboys, and smoky campfires. But roundups and open-range ranching proved short-lived because they lured too many people into the business. Opportunities for profit at first enriched ranchers in Texas and other states. As one publication explained:

> A good sized steer when it is fit for the butcher market will bring from $45.00 to $60.00. The same animal at its birth was worth but $5.00. He has run on the plains and cropped the grass from the public domain for four or five years, and now, with scarcely any expense to its owner, is worth $40.00 more than when he started on his pilgrimage.

But as demand for beef kept rising and ranchers and capital flowed into the Great Plains, cattle began to overrun the range.

The roundup was one of the most important activities of western ranching. In this 1888 photograph, taken at the Cal Snyder ranch in Custer County, Nebraska, a woman and child watch while cowboys rope a steer and singe a brand into its hide. Nebraska State Historical Society.

Meanwhile, sheepherders from California and New Mexico also were using the public domain, starting another conflict over land. Ranchers complained that sheep ruined grassland by eating down to the roots and that cattle refused to graze where sheep had been because the "woolly critters" left a repulsive odor. Armed conflict occasionally erupted when cowboys and sheepherders resorted to violence rather than settle disputes in court, where a judge might discover that both were using public land illegally. More important than these disputes was the fact that the farming frontier was advancing and generating new demands for land.

Fearing loss of control over grazing fields, ranchers began to fence in pastures with barbed wire, even though they had no legal title to such land. In 1886, for example, the Federal Land Office claimed that the Swan Land and Cattle Company of eastern Wyoming had illegally enclosed 130 miles of land. Fences eliminated the open range and often provoked disputes between competing ranchers, between cattle raisers and sheep raisers, and between ranchers and farmers who claimed use of the same territory. In 1885, President Grover Cleveland ordered the removal of illegal fences on public lands and Indian reservations. Enforcement was slow, but the order signaled that free use of public domain was ending.

Open-range ranching made beef a staple of the American diet and created a few fortunes, but its extralegal features could not survive the rush of history. Moreover, a devastating winter in 1886–1887 destroyed countless herds and drove small ranchers out of business. By 1890, big businesses were taking over the cattle industry and applying scientific methods of breeding and feeding. Most ranchers now owned or leased the land they used, though some illegal fencing persisted. The myth of the cowboy's freedom and individualism persisted, but most cowboys became ordinary wage earners.

 ## The South After Reconstruction

While the Great Plains and West were being transformed, the South was developing its own forms of resource exploitation, market economies, and land control. Ravaged by the Civil War, southern agriculture recovered slowly. Rather than diversify, farmers concentrated on growing cotton even more single-

mindedly than before the war. High prices for seed and implements, declining prices for crops, taxes, and, most of all, debt trapped many whites in poverty. Conditions were even worse for blacks, who endured brutal racial prejudice along with economic hardship.

To achieve sectional independence, some southerners tried to promote industrialization. Their efforts partially succeeded, but by the 1900s many southern industries remained mere subsidiaries of northern firms. Moreover, southern planters, shippers, and manufacturers depended heavily on northern banks to finance their operations. Equally important, low wages and stunted opportunities discouraged potential migrants and immigrants who might have brought needed labor and capital. Thus although in some ways the South grew economically, it remained a dependent region locked into a subordinate position in the national economy.

During and after Reconstruction, an important shift in the nature of agriculture swept the South. Between 1860 and 1880, the total number of farms in southern states more than doubled, from 450,000 to 1.1 million. The number of landowners, however, did not increase, because a growing proportion of southern farmers rented, rather than owned, their land. Meanwhile, average farm size actually decreased—from 347 to 156 acres. Southern agriculture, once dominated by laborlords (slave owners), was now dominated by landlords, and the system was characterized by sharecropping and tenant farming (see pages 498–499). One-third of the farmers counted in the 1880 census were sharecroppers and tenants; the proportion increased to two-thirds by 1920.

Sharecropping and tenant farming entangled millions of southerners in a web of debt and humiliation, at whose center stood the crop lien. Most farmers, too poor to have cash on hand, borrowed in order to buy necessities. They could offer as collateral only what they could grow. A farmer in need of supplies dealt with a nearby "furnishing merchant," who would exchange supplies for a *lien*, or legal claim, on the farmer's forthcoming crop. After the crop was harvested and brought to market, the merchant collected his debt by claiming the necessary portion of the crop that would satisfy the loan. All too often, however, the debt exceeded the crop's value. The farmer could pay off only part of the debt to the merchant but still needed food and supplies for the

Crop-Lien System

coming year. The only way he could get these supplies was to sink deeper into debt by reborrowing and giving the merchant a new lien on his next crop.

Merchants frequently took advantage of farmers' powerlessness by inflating prices, charging credit customers 30 to 40 percent more than cash customers paid. Credit customers also had to pay interest ranging from 33 to 200 percent on the advances they received. Suppose, for example, that a cash-poor farmer needed a 20-cent bag of seed or a 20-cent piece of cloth. The furnishing merchant would sell him the goods on credit but would boost the price to 28 cents. At year's end that 28-cent loan would have accumulated interest, raising the farmer's debt to 42 cents—more than double the item's original cost. The farmer, having pledged more than his crop's worth against scores of such debts, fell behind in payments and never recovered. If he fell too far behind, he could be evicted.

The crop-lien system caused hardship in former plantation areas where tenants and sharecroppers—black and white—grew cotton for the same markets that had existed before the Civil War. In the southern backcountry, which in the antebellum era had been characterized by small farms, relatively few slaves, and diversified agriculture, the crop-lien problem was compounded by other economic changes.

New spending habits of backcountry farmers illustrate these changes. In 1884, Jephta Dickson of Jackson County in the northern Georgia hills bought $53.37 worth of flour, peas, meat, corn, and syrup from one merchant and $2.53 worth of potatoes, peas, and sugar from another. Such expenditures would have been rare in the upcountry before the Civil War, when farmers grew almost all the food they needed. But after the war, yeomen like Dickson shifted from semisubsistence agriculture to commercial farming; in the South that meant raising cotton. This change came about for two reasons: debts incurred during the war and Reconstruction forced farmers to grow a crop that would bring in cash, and railroad expansion enabled them to transport cotton to markets more easily than before. As backcountry yeomen devoted more acres to cotton, they raised less of what they needed on a daily basis and found themselves more frequently at the mercy of merchants. In this respect, their economy resembled the economies of western Indians who had been lured into adjusting their economic activities to meet the commercial motives of white merchants.

At the same time, backcountry farmers suffered from laws that essentially closed the southern range (lands owned by the federal government but used freely by southern herders).

Closing the Southern Range

This change, too, resulted from the commercialization of agriculture. Before the 1870s southern farmers, like western open-range ranchers, had let their livestock roam freely in search of food and water. By custom, farmers who wished to protect their crops from foraging animals were supposed to build fences around those crops. But as commercial agriculture reached the backcountry, large landowners and merchants induced county and state governments to require the fencing-in of animals rather than crops. These laws hurt poor farmers who had little land, requiring them to use more of their precious acreage for pasture. Such laws undermined the cooperative customs that yeomen cherished. As one farmer put it, "God makes the grass . . . and corn in the valleys grow, so let's not try to deprive our poor neighbors from receiving his blessing." Yeoman farmers increasingly came to resent merchants, large landowners, and other promoters of commercial agriculture. Their disaffection eventually would find political expression as populism (see Chapter 20).

Poor whites in the rural South, facing economic losses, also feared that newly enfranchised blacks would challenge whatever political and social superiority (real and imagined) they enjoyed. Wealthy white landowners and merchants fanned these fears, using racism to divide whites and blacks and to distract poor whites from protesting their economic subjugation.

The majority of the nation's African-Americans lived in the South and worked in agriculture. Although the abolition of slavery had altered their legal status, it had not improved their opportunities relative to those of whites. In 1880, 90 percent of all southern blacks depended for a living on farming or personal and domestic service—the same occupations they had held as slaves.

Condition of African-Americans

The New South, moreover, proved to be as violent for African-Americans as the Old South had been. Weapons, including a gun commonly known as a "nigger killer," were plentiful, and whites seldom hesitated to use them. One man wrote in his memoirs that all "young blades of the day . . . desired to have

In the years after Reconstruction, lynchings of African-American men occurred with increasing frequency, chiefly in sparsely populated areas where whites looked on strangers, especially black strangers, with fear and suspicion. © R. P. Kingston Collection/ The Picture Cube.

a pistol, a jack knife, and a pair of brass knucks." Whites often added a noose to such weaponry when a black man allegedly broke the racial code.

Between 1889 and 1909 more than seventeen hundred African-Americans were lynched in the South. Most lynchings occurred in sparsely populated rural districts where whites felt threatened by an inflow of blacks and where migrant blacks had no friends, black or white, to vouch for them. Most victims of lynchings were vagrants usually accused of an assault—rarely proved—on a white woman. But behind the accusations, a deep fear that black criminals wanted revenge on whites for slavery drove whites to such extreme measures. As one Kentuckian wrote, "I think there can be no doubt that a considerable amount of crime on the part of colored men against white men and women is due to a spirit of getting even."

Threatened by violence, pushed into sharecropping, and burdened with crop liens, African-Americans also contended with new forms of social and political oppression. With slavery dead, white supremacists fashioned new ways to keep blacks in a position of inferiority. Southern leaders, embittered by northern interference in race relations during Reconstruction and eager to reassert their authority, instituted measures to discourage blacks from voting and to segregate them legally from whites. To humanitarians, discrimination and segregation seemed cruel and demeaning. To whites who supported these measures, the "new order" represented a modern, moderate way to maintain race relations between what they believed to be superior and inferior peoples.

The end of Reconstruction did not stop blacks from voting. Despite threats and intimidation, blacks still formed the backbone of the southern Republican Party and some still won elective offices. In North Carolina, for example, eleven African-American men were elected to the state senate and forty-three to the house between 1877 and 1890. White politicians sought to discourage the "Negro vote" by imposing restrictions that appeared neutral but actually barred blacks from the polls. Beginning with Georgia in 1877, southern states levied taxes of $1 to $2 on all citizens wishing to vote. These *poll taxes* proved prohibitive to most black voters, who were so deeply in debt to merchants and landlords that they never had cash for any purpose. Other schemes disfranchised black voters who could not read. Voters might be required, for instance, to deposit ballots for different candidates in different ballot boxes. To do so correctly, voters had to be able to read the instructions. Such measures also disqualified many poor whites, but their prime objective was to curtail voting by African-Americans.

Disfranchisement was accomplished in other clever and devious ways. The Supreme Court affirmed in *U.S. v. Reese* (1876) that the Fifteenth Amendment prohibited states from denying the vote "on account of race, color, or previous condition of servitude." But, said the Court, Congress had no control over state elections other than the explicit provisions of the Fifteenth Amendment. State legislatures found ways to exclude black voters without mentioning race, color, or servitude. For instance,

Disfranchisement of African-American Voters

an 1890 state constitutional convention established the "Mississippi Plan," which required all voters to pay a poll tax eight months before each election, to present the tax receipt at election time, and to prove that they could read and interpret the state constitution. Registration officials applied stiffer standards to blacks than to whites, even declaring college graduates ineligible on grounds of illiteracy. In 1898 Louisiana enacted the first "grandfather clause," which established literacy and property qualifications for voting but exempted sons and grandsons of those eligible to vote before 1867, the year the Fifteenth Amendment had gone into effect. Other southern states initiated similar measures.

Such restrictions proved highly effective. In South Carolina, for example, 70 percent of eligible blacks voted in the presidential election of 1880; by 1896 the rate had dropped to 11 percent. By the 1900s, African-Americans had effectively lost their political rights in every southern state except Tennessee. Disfranchisement also affected poor whites, few of whom could meet poll tax, property, and literacy requirements. Thus the total number of eligible voters in Mississippi shrank from 257,000 in 1876 to 77,000 in 1892.

Racial discrimination also stiffened in social affairs. Under slavery, a widespread system of separation had governed race relations. After the Civil War, this system was expanded in law. In a series of cases during the 1870s, the Supreme Court opened the door to discrimination by ruling that the Fourteenth Amendment protected citizens' rights only against infringement by state governments (see page 468). The federal government, according to the Court, had no authority over what individuals or organizations might do. If blacks wanted legal protection, the Court said, they must seek it from the states, which under the Tenth Amendment retained all powers not specifically assigned to Congress.

Jim Crow Laws

These rulings climaxed in 1883 when in the *Civil Rights* cases the Court struck down the 1875 Civil Rights Act, which had prohibited segregation in public facilities such as streetcars, hotels, theaters, and parks. Again the Court declared that the federal government could not regulate the behavior of private individuals in matters of race relations. Subsequent lower-court rulings established the principle that blacks could be restricted to "separate-but-equal" facilities. The Supreme Court upheld the separate-but-equal doctrine in *Plessy* v. *Ferguson* (1896) and officially applied it to schools in *Cummins* v. *County Board of Education* (1899).

Thereafter, segregation laws—popularly known as Jim Crow laws—multiplied throughout the South, confronting African-Americans with daily reminders of their inferior status. State and local laws restricted them to the rear of streetcars, to separate drinking fountains and toilets, and to separate sections of hospitals and cemeteries. A Birmingham, Alabama, ordinance required that the races be "distinctly separated . . . by well defined physical barriers" in "any room, hall, theatre, picture house, auditorium, yard, court, ballpark, or other indoor or outdoor place." Local laws defined certain neighborhoods as all-black or all-white. Mobile, Alabama, passed a curfew requiring blacks to be off the streets by 10 P.M, and Atlanta mandated separate Bibles for the swearing-in of black witnesses in court. Thus for thousands of black southerners race relations deteriorated after emancipation. African-Americans adapted to racial bias by creating their own social institutions: churches, schools, and family networks; but their legal rights did not improve markedly until the 1960s.

In industry, new initiatives brought breezes of change, but there too a distinctively southern quality prevailed. Two of the South's leading industries in the late 1800s relied on traditional staple crops—cotton and tobacco. In the 1870s, textile mills began to appear in the Cotton Belt. Powered by the region's abundant rivers, manned cheaply by poor whites eager to escape crop liens, and aided by low taxes, such factories multiplied. By 1900 the South had four hundred mills with a total of 4 million spindles, and twenty years later the region was eclipsing New England in textile-manufacturing supremacy. Proximity to raw materials and cheap labor also aided the tobacco industry, and the invention in 1880 of a cigarette-making machine immensely enhanced the marketability of tobacco.

Industrialization of the South

Cigarette factories, located in cities, employed both black and white workers (though in segregated sections of the factories). Textile mills, concentrated in small towns, developed their own exploitative labor system. Financed mostly by local investors, mills employed women and children from poor white families and paid 50 cents a day for twelve or more hours of work. Such wages barely came to half

Tobacco production was one southern industry that traditionally hired African-American laborers. This scene from a Richmond tobacco factory around 1880 shows women and children preparing leaves for curing by tearing off the stems. Valentine Museum.

of those paid to northern workers. Many companies built villages around their mills, where they controlled the housing, stores, schools, and churches. Inside these towns, companies banned criticism of the company and squelched attempts at union organization. Mill families soon found that factory jobs changed their status very little: the company store replaced the furnishing merchant, and the mill owner replaced the landlord.

Other industries were launched under the sponsorship of northern or European capitalists. Between 1890 and 1900, northern lumber syndicates moved into the pine forests of the Gulf states, boosting production by 500 percent. During the 1880s, northern investors developed southern iron and steel manufacturing, much of it in the boom city of Birmingham. Coal mining and railroad construction also expanded rapidly, but New York and London financiers dominated the boards of directors of most southern companies. To its detriment, the South lacked technological innovators, such as those in the machine-tool industry who had enabled northern industries to compete with those of other industrializing nations. Southern industries had to wait until techniques were developed elsewhere and then adapt them.

Industrialization, regardless of its outside origins, prompted southern boosters to herald the emergence of a New South. Henry Grady, editor of the *Atlanta Constitution* and the most articulate voice of southern progress, proclaimed, "We have sowed towns and cities in the place of theories, and put business in place of politics. We have challenged your spinners in Massachusetts and your iron-makers in Pennsylvania. . . . We have fallen in love with work." Yet in 1900 the South remained as rural as it had been in 1860. Staple-crop agriculture supported its economy, and white supremacy permeated its social and political relations, barring blacks from industrial jobs and the polls. A New South eventually would emerge, but not until after the First World War and a massive black exodus had shaken up old attitudes.

The "New South"

 Conclusion

Americans of all races developed the West with courage and creativity that amazed the rest of the world. The extraction of raw minerals, the use of irrigation and mechanization to bring forth agricultural abundance from the land, and the construction of railroads to tie the nation together transformed half of the continent within a few decades. The optimistic conquerors, however, employed power, violence, and greed that overwhelmed the culture of the land's original inhabitants, left many farmers feeling cheated and betrayed, kindled contests over use of water, and sacrificed environmental balance for market profits. In the South, recovery and growth kindled new optimism, but careless exploitation exhausted the soil and left poor farmers as downtrodden as ever. In an age of expansion, African-Americans saw their rights and opportunities narrowing. Industrialization failed to reduce the dominance of southern staple-crop agriculture, and by 1900 the South was more dependent economically on the North than it had been before the Civil War.

In both the West and the South, the appeal of commercial exchange drew native peoples, freed blacks, and other Americans away from their subsistence ways of life and into the marketplace. The raw materials and agricultural products of both sections improved living standards and contributed to industrial progress, but not without human and environmental costs.

Suggestions for Further Reading

The Western Frontier

Ray A. Billington and Martin Ridge, *Westward Expansion*, 5th ed. (1982); Sara Deutsch, *No Separate Refuge: Culture, Class, and Gender on an Anglo-Hispanic Frontier in the American Southwest* (1987); Robert V. Hine, *The American West*, 2d ed. (1984); Julie Roy Jeffrey, *Frontier Women* (1979); Patricia Limerick, *The Legacy of Conquest: The Unbroken Past of the American West* (1987); Timothy R. Mahoney, *River Towns in the Great West* (1990); Ruth Moynihan, *Rebel for Rights: Abigail Scott Duniway* (1983); Peggy Pascoe, *Relations of Rescue: The Search for Female Moral Authority in the American West* (1990); Rodman W. Paul, *The Far West and the Great Plains in Transition, 1859–1900* (1988); Robert J. Rosenbaum, *Mexican Resistance in the Southwest* (1981); Lillian Schlissel, *Women's Diaries of the Westward Journey* (1982); Kent Ladd Steckmesser, *The Western Hero in History and Legend* (1965); Richard White, *"It's Your Misfortune and None of My Own": A New History of the American West* (1991).

Water and the Environment

Roderick Nash, *American Environmentalism*, 3d ed. (1990); Joseph M. Petulla, *American Environmental History* (1977); Thurman Wilkins, *John Muir: Apostle of Nature* (1995); Donald Worster, *Rivers of Empire: Water, Aridity, and the Growth of the American West* (1985).

Railroads

Alfred D. Chandler, ed., *Railroads* (1965); Robert W. Fogel, *Railroads and Economic Growth* (1964); Edward C. Kirkland, *Men, Cities, and Transportation* (1948); George R. Taylor and Irene Neu, *The American Railroad Network* (1956); Alan Trachtenberg, *The Incorporation of America* (1982); O. O. Winther, *The Transportation Frontier* (1964).

Cliffs of Green River *by Thomas Moran in 1874. A detail of this painting appears at the beginning of the chapter on page 474.* Amon Carter Museum, Fort Worth, Texas.

Native Americans

Ralph K. Andrist, *The Long Death: The Last Days of the Plains Indians* (1964); Leonard A. Carlson, *Indians, Bureaucrats, and Land: The Dawes Act and the Decline of Indian Farming* (1981); Frederick E. Hoxie, *A Final Promise: The Campaign to Assimilate the Indians, 1880–1920* (1984); Janet A. McDonnell, *The Dispossession of the American Indian* (1991); Francis Paul Prucha, *The Great Father: The United States Government and the American Indians* (1984); Robert M. Utley, *The Lance and the Shield: The Life and Times of Sitting Bull* (1993); Robert M. Utley, *The Indian Frontier of the American West, 1846–1890* (1984); Philip Weeks, *Farewell, My Nation: The American Indian and the United States* (1990); Richard White, *The Roots of Dependency* (1983).

Ranching and Settlement of the Plains

Lewis Atherton, *The Cattle Kings* (1961); William Cronon, *Nature's Metropolis: Chicago and the Great West* (1991); Gilbert C. Fite, *The Farmer's Frontier* (1963); Robert V. Hine, *Community on the American Frontier* (1980); Richard W. Slatta, *Cowboys of the Americas* (1990); Walter Prescott Webb, *The Great Plains* (1931).

The New South

Edward L. Ayers, *The Promise of the New South* (1992); Orville Vernon Burton and Robert C. McMath, Jr., eds., *Toward a New South?: Post–Civil War Southern Communities* (1982); Paul Gaston, *The New South Creed* (1970); Steven Hahn, *The Roots of Southern Populism: Yeoman Farmers and the Transformation of the Georgia Upcountry, 1850–1890* (1983); Stanley P. Hirshson, *Farewell to the Bloody Shirt: Northern Republicans and the Southern Negro* (1962); J. Morgan Kousser, *The Shaping of Southern Politics* (1974); Melton A. McLaurin, *Paternalism and Protest: Southern Cotton Mill Workers and Organized Labor* (1971); Howard N. Rabinowitz, *Race Relations in the Urban South, 1865–1890* (1978); Theodore Saloutos, *Farmer Movements in the South, 1865–1933* (1960); C. Vann Woodward, *The Strange Career of Jim Crow*, 3d rev. ed. (1974); C. Vann Woodward, *Origins of the New South*, rev. ed. (1951); Gavin Wright, *Old South, New South* (1986).

18

The Machine Age
1877 – 1920

T he shoemaker known only as "S" was a beaten and bitter man. Interviewed by the Massachusetts Bureau of the Statistics of Labor in 1871, "S" reported that he was fifty years old and had been plying his trade for forty years. He and his three children each worked in a shoe factory ten hours a day, five days a week, and nine hours on Saturdays. His wife worked in another factory, stitching the covering on baseballs from 5:30 A.M. to 10 A.M. every day.

"S" complained to the interviewer that ever since his factory had introduced machinery, he had lost control of his craft. He could no longer teach his sons the skill of shoemaking because they had been moved to another room to carry out just one task instead of having responsibility for assembling the whole product. "S" hoped his sons would not be factory workers all their lives, but he also realized they had little other choice. The cost of living had risen, making it difficult if not impossible for his family to sustain itself in any other way, especially when the shoe factory laid off its work force for four months a year because of slow business.

When asked his opinion about the economic system, "S" responded with frustration and anger. "It is hard to see why it is not better to make the consumer pay two or three cents more a pair for his shoes, than to cut lower down a man who cannot, by hard toil at the wages given, make a comfortable living."

"S" felt embittered by the homage being paid to supply and demand: "We have it constantly dinned in our ears that supply and demand govern prices, but we have found out to a certainty that this is not so. . . . [W]ithout the aid of machinery, six men will make a case of 60 pairs [of shoes] in a day, . . . which would give each man about $1.70 cents [sic] a day; on the other hand, with the machinery, three men will do the same amount of work in the same time, and get about the same pay [$1.70] each, as the men on hand work. . . . Who gets the difference in money saved by machinery? and how far does supply and demand govern in these things?"

The testimony of "S" reflected one worker's reaction to the industrialization that was relentlessly overtaking American society in the late 1800s. The new order was both exciting and ominous. The factory and the machine divided manufacturing into minute, routinized tasks and organized work according to the dictates of the clock. Workers who had long thought of themselves as valued producers found themselves struggling to avoid becoming slaves to machines. Meanwhile, in the quest for productivity, profits, and growth, corporations merged and amassed great power. Defenders of the new system devised theories to justify it, while critics tried to combat what they thought were abuses of power.

Industrialization is a complex process whose chief feature is the production of goods by machine rather than by hand. By using machines, manufacturers lower production costs and significantly raise workers' output. Mechanization relies on the use of standardized parts and specialization in production. In the United States, the results of industrialization have included the concentration of production and laborers in large, organized factories; technological innovation; expanded markets, no longer merely local and regional in scope; a rapid increase in population; and growth of a nationwide transportation network.

In 1860 only about one-fourth of the American labor force worked in manufacturing and transportation; by 1900 over half did so. As the twentieth century dawned, the United States was the world's largest producer of raw materials and food but also the most productive industrial nation (see map, page 508). Between 1879 and 1920 the value of American exports increased twelvefold. Accelerated migration from farms and mass immigration from abroad swelled the industrial work force (see Chapter 19); but machines, more than people, boosted American productivity. Moreover, innovations in business organization and marketing, as well as in technology, fueled the drive for profits.

These developments had momentous effects on standards of living and everyday life. During the years between the end of Reconstruction and the end of the First World War, a new consumer society took shape. Farms and factories produced so much that Americans could afford to satisfy their material

wants. What had once been accessible only to a few was becoming available to many; what had formerly been dreams were becoming necessities. Products such as toilets, canned foods, and ready-made clothing that had hardly existed before the Civil War became common by the turn of the century. Yet the accomplishments of industrial expansion, like expansion into the natural-resources and agricultural frontiers (see Chapter 17), involved waste and greed. The vigor and creativity that marked the era gave rise to both constructive and destructive forces.

Technology and the Triumph of Industrialism

In 1876 Thomas A. Edison and his associates moved into a long wooden shed in Menlo Park, New Jersey, where they intended to turn out "a minor invention every ten days and a big thing every six months or so." Edison envisioned his laboratory as an invention factory, where creative people would pool their ideas and skills to fashion marketable products. Here was the brash American spirit adapting itself to a systematic work ethic. If Americans wanted new products, they had to organize and work purposefully to bring about progress. Such efforts reflected a forward-looking spirit that enlivened American industrialization at the end of the nineteenth century.

In the years between 1865 and 1920, the machine fired American optimism. Like the West, the machine represented opportunity. The patent system, created by the Constitution to "promote the Progress of science and useful Arts," testifies to an outburst of American mechanical inventiveness. Between 1790 and 1860 the United States Patent Office had granted a total of 36,000 patents. In 1897 alone it granted 22,000, and between 1860 and 1930 it registered 1.5 million. As innovative as the inventions themselves was the marriage between technology and business organization. The harnessing of electricity, internal combustion, and industrial chemistry illustrate how this marriage worked.

Many of Edison's more than one thousand inventions used electricity to transmit light, sound, and images. Perhaps the biggest of his "big thing"

Birth of the Electrical Industry

projects began in 1878 when he formed the Edison Electric Light Company and embarked on a search for a cheap, efficient means of indoor lighting. Gas, candles, and oil lamps had proved

• *Important Events* •

1859	Great Atlantic Tea Company (the A&P), the nation's first grocery chain, founded	**1893–97**	Economic depression causes high unemployment and business failures
1860	Knights of Labor founded	**1894**	Workers at Pullman Palace Car Company strike against exploitative policies
1873–78	Economic decline results from overly rapid expansion	**1895**	*U.S.* v. *E. C. Knight Co.* limits Congress's power to regulate manufacturing
1877	Widespread railroad strikes protest wage cuts	**1896**	*Holden* v. *Hardy* upholds law regulating miners' work hours
1878	Edison Electric Light Company founded, leading to development of incandescent bulb	**1898**	Frederick W. Taylor promotes scientific management as efficiency measure in industry
1879	Henry George's *Progress and Poverty* argues against economic inequality	**1901–03**	U.S. Steel Corporation founded E. I. du Pont de Nemours and Company reorganized Ford Motor Company founded
1880s	Chain-pull toilets spread across the United States Doctors accept germ theory of disease Mass production of tin cans begins	**1903**	Women's Trade Union League founded
1881	First federal trademark law begins spread of brand names	**1905**	*Lochner* v. *New York* overturns law limiting bakery workers' work hours and limits labor protection laws Industrial Workers of the World founded
1882	Standard Oil Trust formed	**1908**	*Muller* v. *Oregon* upholds law limiting women to ten-hour workday First Ford Model T built
1884–85	Economic decline results from numerous causes		
1886	Haymarket riot in Chicago protests police brutality against labor demonstrators American Federation of Labor (AFL) founded	**1911**	Triangle Shirtwaist Company fire in New York City leaves 146 workers dead
1888	Edward Bellamy's *Looking Backward* depicts utopian world free of monopoly, politicians, and class divisions	**1913**	First moving assembly line begins operation at Ford Motor Company
1890	Sherman Anti-Trust Act outlaws "combinations in restraint of trade"	**1914**	Ford offers Five-Dollar-a-Day plan to workers
1892	Homestead (Pennsylvania) steelworkers strike against Carnegie Steel Company	**1919**	Telephone operator unions strike in New England

impractical for lighting large buildings, as had electric current flowing between two carbon rods. After tedious trial-and-error experiments, Edison perfected an incandescent bulb that used a filament in a vacuum. At the same time he worked out a *system* of power production and distribution—an improved dynamo and a parallel circuit of wires—to provide convenient power to a large number of customers.

To market his ideas, Edison acted as his own publicist. During the 1880 Christmas season he illuminated Menlo Park with forty incandescent bulbs, and in 1882 he built a power plant that would light eighty-five buildings in New York's Wall Street financial district. When this plant began service, a *New York Times* reporter marveled that working in his office at night "seemed almost like writing in daylight."

Edison's system could send electric power only a mile or two. George Westinghouse, an inventor from Schenectady, New York, who had become famous for

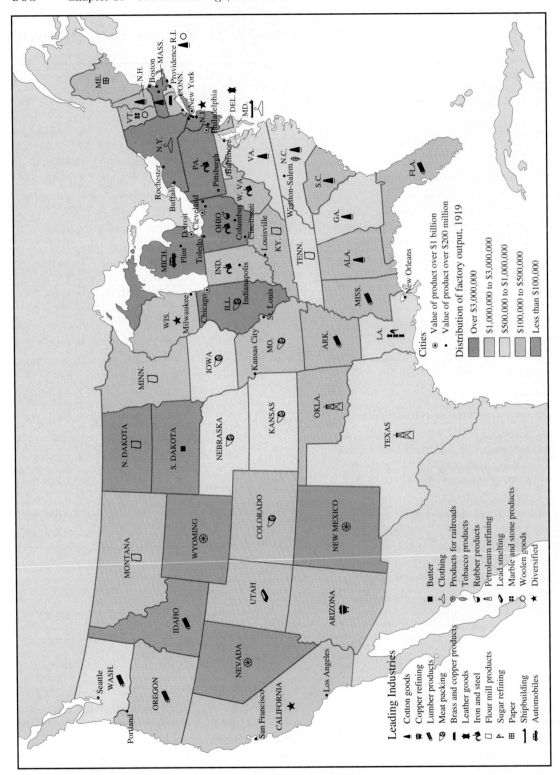

Industrial Production, 1919 *By the early twentieth century, each state could boast of at least one kind of industrial production. Although the value of goods produced was still highest in the Northeast, states like Minnesota and California had impressive dollar values of outputs.*   Source: © American Heritage Publishing Co., Inc., *American Heritage Pictorial Atlas of United States History;* data from U.S. Bureau of the Census, *Fourteenth Census of the United States, 1920,* Vol. IX, *Manufacturing* (Washington, D.C.: U.S. Government Printing Office, 1921).

devising an air brake for railroad cars, solved the problem. Westinghouse purchased patent rights to generators that used alternating current and transformers that reduced high-voltage power to lower voltage levels, thus making transmission over long distances cheaper.

Other entrepreneurs utilized new business practices to market and refine Edison's and Westinghouse's technological breakthroughs. Samuel Insull, Edison's private secretary, who later amassed a huge electric-utility empire, attracted investments and organized Edison power plants across the country, turning energy into big business. In the late 1880s and early 1890s financiers Henry Villard and J. P. Morgan consolidated patents in electric lighting and merged small equipment-manufacturing companies into the General Electric Company. Equally important, General Electric and Westinghouse Electric encouraged the practical application of electricity, formerly an experimental field for scientists, by establishing research laboratories that paid scientists to create new electrical products geared for everyday use.

While corporations in the electricity industry were organizing the process of invention in company labs, individual inventors continued to work independently and tried, sometimes successfully and sometimes not, to sell their handiwork to manufacturing companies. One such inventor was Granville T. Woods, an African-American engineer from Columbus, Ohio. Working in machine shops in Cincinnati and in New York City, Woods patented thirty-five devices vital to electronics and communications. Among his inventions, most of which he sold to companies such as General Electric, were an automatic circuit breaker, an electromagnetic brake, and various instruments to aid communications between railroad trains.

Development of the internal-combustion engine in France and Germany inspired the era's most visionary manufacturer, Henry Ford. In the 1890s Ford, then an electrical engineer in Detroit's Edison Company, experimented in his spare time with a gasoline-burning internal-combustion engine to power a vehicle. George Selden, a lawyer from Rochester, New York, had already been tinkering with internal-combustion engines, but Ford applied his organizational genius to this invention and spawned a massive industry.

Like Edison, Ford had a scheme as well as a product. In 1909 he declared, "I am going to democratize the automobile. When I'm through everybody

Thomas A. Edison was not only an inventor extraordinaire but also a skilled entrepreneur and promoter. This photograph, taken after his rise to fame, conveys the image of a confident technician at home in his laboratory surrounded by gadgets and tools. Library of Congress.

Mass Production of the Automobile

will be able to afford one, and about everyone will have one." Ford proposed to reach this goal through *mass production*—producing thousands of identical cars in exactly the same way. The key to mass production was flow. Adapting methods of the meatpacking and metalworking industries, Ford engineers set up assembly lines that drastically reduced the time and cost of producing cars. Instead of performing numerous tasks,

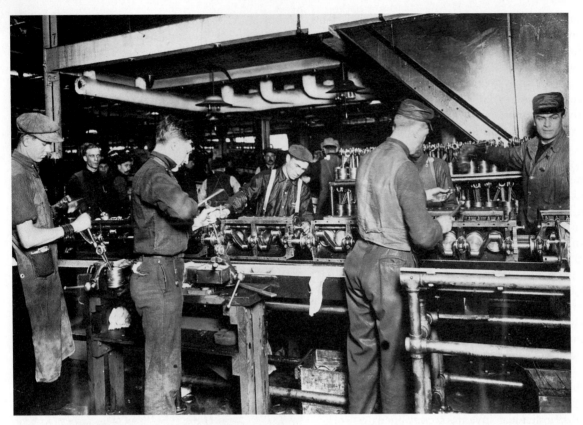

The assembly line broke the production process down into simple tasks that individual workers could efficiently repeat hour after hour. Here, assembly-line workers at the Ford plant in Highland Park, Michigan, outside Detroit, are installing pistons in engines of the Model T around 1914.   Henry Ford Museum and Greenfield Village.

each worker was given responsibility for only one task, performed repeatedly, using the same specialized machine. By means of a continuous flow of these tasks, the work force fashioned each component part and progressively assembled the entire car. The Ford Motor Company began operation in 1903. In 1908, the first year it built the Model T, Ford sold 10,000 cars. In 1913, the company's first full assembly line began producing cars in Highland Park, outside Detroit, and the next year, 248,000 Fords were sold. Rising automobile production created more jobs, higher earnings, and higher profits in related industries such as oil, paint, rubber, and glass. The Model T was indeed replacing the horse.

By 1914, many Ford cars cost $490, only about one-fourth of their cost a decade earlier. Yet even $490 was too much for many workers, who earned at best $2 a day. That year, however, Ford tried to spur productivity, prevent high labor turnover, head off unionization, and better enable his workers to buy the cars they produced by offering them the Five-Dollar-Day plan—combined wages and profit sharing equal to $5 a day.

During the same period, the du Pont family did for the chemical industry what Edison and Ford did for the electrical and automobile industries.

Du Ponts and the Chemical Industry

The du Pont family had been manufacturing gunpowder since the early 1800s. In 1902 three du Pont cousins, Alfred, Coleman, and Pierre, took over E. I. du Pont de Nemours and Company and broadened production. In 1911, du Pont laboratories began to adapt cellulose to the production of materials such as photographic film, rubber, lacquer, and textile fibers. The company also pioneered methods of efficient management, accounting, and reinvestment of earnings, all of which contributed to controlled production, better record-keeping, and higher profits.

The timing of technological innovation varied from one industry to another, but machines altered the economy and everyday life in a pervasive way between 1865 and 1900 by creating new industries. Telephones and typewriters revolutionized communications, making face-to-face conversations less important and facilitating correspondence and record-keeping. Sewing machines made mass-produced clothing available to almost everyone. Refrigeration changed dietary habits by enabling the preservation of meat, fruit, vegetables, and dairy products. Cash registers and adding machines revamped accounting and created new clerical jobs.

Profits from these products resulted from higher production at lower costs. As technological innovations made large-scale production more economical, some owners used their profits to replace small factories with larger ones. Between 1850 and 1900 the average capital investment in a manufacturing firm increased from $700,000 to $1.9 million. Only large companies could afford to buy new machines and operate them at full capacity. And large companies could best take advantage of discounts for shipping products in bulk and for buying raw materials in quantity. Economists call such advantages *economies of scale.*

Profitability depended as much on how production was arranged as on the machines in use. Where once shop-floor workers like the shoemaker "S" had exercised some control over how a product was to be made, by the 1890s engineers and managers with specialized knowledge had assumed this responsibility and planned every task to increase output. Their efforts standardized mass production, which then required less skill and independent judgment from workers.

New Emphasis on Efficiency

The most influential advocate of efficient production was Frederick W. Taylor. As foreman and engineer for the Midvale Steel Company in the 1880s, Taylor concluded that the only way a company could lessen fixed costs and increase profits was to apply scientific studies of "how quickly the various kinds of work . . . ought to be done." The "ought" in Taylor's formulation signified producing more for a lower cost per unit—by eliminating unnecessary workers. Similarly, "how quickly" signified that time and money were equivalent.

In 1898 Taylor took his stopwatch to the Bethlehem Steel Company to illustrate how his principles of scientific management worked. His experiments, he explained, involved studying workers and devising "a series of motions which can be made quickest and best." Applying this technique to the shoveling of ore, Taylor designed fifteen kinds of shovels and prescribed the proper motions for using each one. He succeeded in reducing a crew of 600 men to 140, who received higher wages, though their new jobs were more stressful.

As a result of Taylor's writings and experiments, time, as much as quality, became the measure of acceptable work, and science rather than tradition determined the "best" ways of doing things. As integral features of the assembly line, where work was divided into specific time-determined tasks, employees had become another kind of interchangeable part.

 ## Mechanization and the Changing Status of Labor

By 1880, the status of labor had undergone a dramatic shift in the course of a single generation. Technological innovation and assembly-line production created new jobs, but because most machines were labor-saving devices, fewer workers could produce more in less time, increasing profits for manufacturers. Mechanization destroyed time-honored crafts such as glassmaking and iron molding; it also subordinated men and women workers to rigid schedules and repetitive routines that transformed the nature of work. Most workers could no longer accurately be termed *producers,* as farmers and craftsmen like shoemaker "S" had traditionally thought of themselves. The enlarged working class consisted mainly of *employees*—people who worked only when someone hired them. Producers were paid by consumers in accordance with the quality of what they produced; employees received wages for time they spent on the job.

As mass production subdivided manufacturing into small tasks, workers continually repeated the same specialized operation. One investigator who studied the effects of specialization on a typical laborer found that the worker became "a mere machine. . . . Take the proposition of a man operating a machine to nail on 40 to 60 cases of heels in a day. That is 2,400 pairs, 4,800 shoes in a day. One not accustomed to it would wonder how a man could pick up and lay down 4,800 shoes in a day, to say nothing of putting them . . . into a machine. . . . That is the driving method of the manufacture of shoes under these minute subdivisions."

By reducing the manufacturing process to numerous simplified tasks constantly repeated, and by coordinating production to the running of machinery, assembly-line production also deprived employees of their independence. Workers could no longer decide when to begin and end the workday, when to rest, and what tools and techniques to use. As a Massachusetts factory worker complained in 1879, "During working hours the men are not allowed to speak to each other, though working close together, on pain of instant discharge. Men are hired to watch and patrol the shop." And workers were now surrounded by others who labored at the same rate for the same pay, regardless of the quality of their work.

Those affected by these changes did not accept them passively. Workers struggled to retain inde-

As work became increasingly routinized, workers struggled to hold on to workplace customs like the one shown here: a cigar maker reading the newspaper to his fellow workers. George Eastman House, International Museum of Photography.

pendence and self-respect in the face of employers' ever-increasing power. As new groups encountered the industrial system, they resisted in various ways. Artisans such as cigar makers, glass workers, and coopers (barrel makers), caught in the transition from hand labor to machine production, fought to preserve the pace and quality of their jobs and to retain customs such as appointing a fellow worker to read aloud while they worked. When immigrants went to work in factories, they often persuaded foremen to hire their relatives and friends, thus preserving on-the-job family and village ties. Off the job, workers continued to gather for leisure-time activities like social drinking and holiday celebrations, shunning employers' attempts to control their social lives.

Employers established standards of behavior and work incentives that they thought would enhance efficiency and productivity. To make workers docile (like the machines they operated), employers supported temperance and moral-reform societies, dedicated to combating supposed drinking and debauchery. Managers at Ford Motor Company required workers to meet the company's behavior code before they became eligible for the profit-sharing segment of the Five-Dollar-Day plan. Other employers established piecework rates, paying workers an amount per item produced, rather than an hourly wage, to encourage maximum use of machines.

As machines and assembly-line production reduced the need for skilled workers, employers cut labor costs by hiring women and children.

Employment of Women

Between 1880 and 1900, the numbers of employed women soared from 2.6 million to 8.6 million. At the same time their occupational patterns underwent striking changes (see figure, page 513). The proportion of women in domestic-service jobs (maids, cooks, laundresses)—traditionally the most common and lowest-paid form of female employment—dropped dramatically as jobs opened in other sectors. In manufacturing, jobs for women were usually menial positions in textile mills and food-processing plants that paid as little as $1.56 a week for seventy hours of labor. Though the number of female factory hands tripled between 1880 and 1900, the proportion of women workers in these jobs remained about the same.

Enormous expansion in the industrial and retail sectors, however, caused the numbers and percent-

Distribution of Occupational Categories among Employed Men and Women, 1880–1920

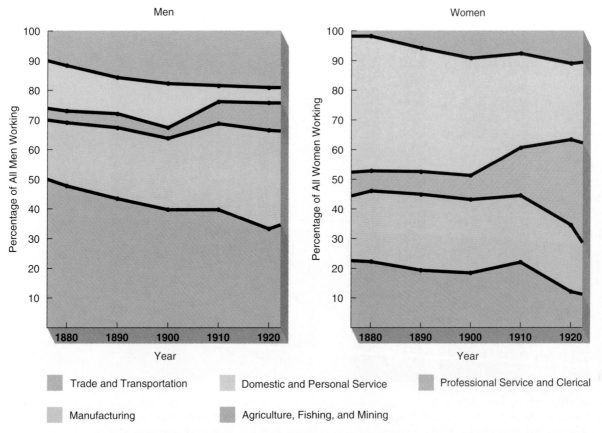

Men

Women

Trade and Transportation

Domestic and Personal Service

Professional Service and Clerical

Manufacturing

Agriculture, Fishing, and Mining

Distribution of Occupational Categories among Employed Men and Women, 1880–1920 The *changing thickness of each part of this graph represents trends in male and female employment. Over the forty years covered by this graph, the agriculture, fishing, and mining segment for men and the domestic service segment for women declined the most, while notable increases occurred in manufacturing for men and services (especially store clerks and teachers) for women.* Source: U.S. Bureau of the Census, *Census of the United States, 1880, 1890, 1900, 1910, 1920* (Washington: U.S. Government Printing Office).

ages of women in clerical jobs—typists, bookkeepers, sales clerks—to skyrocket. By 1920 nearly half of all clerical workers were women; in 1880 only 4 percent had been women. Previously, when sales and office positions had demanded accounting and letter-writing skills, men had dominated such jobs. Then, new inventions such as the typewriter, cash register, and adding machine simplified these tasks. Companies eagerly hired women who had taken courses in typing and shorthand in school and were streaming into the labor market, looking for the better pay and conditions that clerical jobs offered relative to factory and domestic work. An official of a sugar company observed in 1919 that "all the bookkeeping of this company . . . is done by three girls and three

bookkeeping machines . . . one operator takes the place of three men."

Though paid low wages, women also were attracted to sales jobs because of the respectability, pleasant surroundings, and contact with affluent customers that such positions offered. In department stores, male cashiers took in cash and made change; women were given no responsibility for billing or counting money. Sex discrimination pervaded the clerical sector. The new jobs offered women some opportunities for advancement to supervisory positions, but women posed no threat to male managers.

Although most children who worked toiled on their parents' farms, the number in nonagricultural

The rise of new clerical occupations at the beginning of the twentieth century gave women countless employment opportunities. Employers hired women to file company records and type letters and paid them less than they paid male employees. The floor-to-ceiling file cases in the records room of Metropolitan Life Insurance Company in New York was the largest outfit of steel file cases in the world.   Museum of the City of New York, gift of Donald Beggs.

occupations tripled between 1870 and 1900. In 1890, over 18 percent of all children between ages ten and fifteen were gainfully employed (see figure, page 515). In textile factories in particular, many workers were below age sixteen. Shoe factories also employed teenagers, such as "S's" sons. Mechanization created numerous light tasks, such as running errands and helping machine operators, that children could handle at a fraction of adult wages. Conditions were especially hard for child laborers in the South, where burgeoning textile mills needed unskilled hands. Mill owners induced poor white farm families, who otherwise might not have had any jobs or income, to bind their children over to the factories at miserably low wages.

Employment of Children

Several states, especially in the Northeast, passed laws specifying the minimum age and maximum workday hours for child labor. But most large companies could avoid regulations because state statutes did not apply to firms engaged in interstate commerce. Furthermore, it was difficult to enforce age requirements, and to supplement the family income many parents lied about children's ages. One woman who had worked in the Amoskeag Mills of Manchester, New Hampshire, recalled how easy it was to get a job without proof of age. "I was twelve years old when I arrived here and started work," she recalled. "All we had to do was show them that we were fourteen years old. Tall or short, it didn't matter; they'd just ask, 'Are you fourteen years old?' OK. That's all. So that's how I went in to work." By 1900, state laws and automation had reduced the number of children working in manufacturing, but many more worked at street trades—shining shoes and peddling newspapers and other merchandise—and as helpers in stores. Not until the Progressive era did reformers seek federal legislation as the remedy for child labor (see Chapter 21).

Although working conditions were often dangerous and unhealthy, low wages were usually the immediate catalyst of worker unrest. Many employers believed in the "iron law of wages," which dictated that employees be paid according to conditions of supply and demand. Theoretically, because laborers were free to make their own choices and employers competed for their labor, workers would receive the highest wages the employer could pay without being driven out of business. In reality, the "iron law" meant that employers did not have to raise wages—and could even cut them—as long as there were workers who would accept whatever pay was offered. Employers justified the system by invoking individual freedom: a worker who did not like the wages being offered was free to quit and find a job elsewhere.

Courts reinforced this principle, denying workers the right to organize and bargain collectively on the grounds that an employee's wages should be the result of an individual negotiation between employee and employer. Wage earners saw things differently; they believed the system trapped them. As one Massachusetts factory worker testified in 1879, "The market is glutted, and we have seasons of dullness; advantage is taken of men's wants, and the pay is cut down; our tasks are increased, and if we remonstrate, we are told our places can be filled. I work harder now than when my pay was twice as high."

Even steady employment was insecure. Repetitive tasks using high-speed machinery dulled concentration, and the slightest mistake could cause serious injury. Industrial accidents rose steadily before 1920, killing or maiming hundreds of thousands of people each year. As late as 1913, after factory owners had installed safety devices, some 25,000 people died in industrial mishaps, and close to 1 million were injured. Each year sensational disasters, such as explosions, mine cave-ins, and fires, aroused public clamor for better safety regulations. The most notorious tragedy was a fire at New York City's Triangle Shirtwaist Company in 1911, which killed 146 workers, most of them Jewish immigrant women. Equally tragic, however, were the countless accidents that resulted in mangled limbs, infected cuts, chronic illness, and death.

Industrial Accidents

Children in the Labor Force, 1880–1930

— Total Number of Children Aged 10–15
— Total Number of Children Employed

Children in the Labor Force, 1880–1930 The percentage of children in the labor force peaked around the turn of the century. Thereafter, the passage of state laws requiring children to attend school until age fourteen and limiting the ages at which children could be employed caused child labor to decline. Source: Data from *The Statistical History of the United States from Colonial Times to the Present* (Stamford, Conn.: Fairfield Publishers, 1965).

A railroad brakeman described his accident in 1888: "It was four or five months before I 'got it.' I was making a coupling one afternoon. . . . Just before the two cars were come together, the one behind me left the track. . . . Hearing the racket, I sprang to one side, but my toe caught the top of the rail. I was pinned between the corners of the cars as they came together. I heard my ribs cave in like an old box smashed with an ax." Because disability insurance and pensions were almost nonexistent, families stricken by such accidents suffered acutely.

Factories employed children from the early nineteenth century well into the twentieth. In textile mills like the one pictured here, girls operated machines, and boys ran messages and carried materials back and forth. Mill girls had to tie up their hair to keep it from getting caught in the machines. The girl posing here with a shawl over her head would not have worn that garment while she was working. National Archives.

Prevailing free-market views stifled protective legislation for workers, and employers denied responsibility for employees' well-being. As one railroad manager declared, "The regular compensation of employees covers all risk or liability to accident. If an employee is disabled by sickness or any other cause, the right to claim compensation is not recognized." The only recourse for a stricken family was to sue and prove in court that the killed or injured worker had not realized the risks involved and had not caused the accident, an expensive route that very few ever took.

Reformers and union leaders in several states lobbied Congress successfully for laws to improve working conditions, but the Supreme Court limited the scope of such legislation by narrowly defining what jobs were dangerous and which workers needed protection. Initially, in *Holden* v. *Hardy* (1896), the Court upheld a law regulating the working hours of miners because overly long hours would increase the threat of injury. In *Lochner* v. *New York* (1905), however, the Court struck down a law limiting bakery workers to a sixty-hour week and a ten-hour day. In response to the argument that states had the authority to protect workers' health and safety, the Court ruled that baking was not a dangerous enough occupation to justify restricting the right of workers to sell their labor freely. According to the Court, interference with the right of individuals to make contracts for their labor would violate the Fourteenth Amendment's guarantee that no state could "deprive any person of life, liberty, or property without due process of law."

In *Muller* v. *Oregon* (1908), the Court used a different rationale to uphold a law limiting women to a ten-hour workday. In this case, setting aside its *Lochner* argument, the Court asserted that women's health and reproductive functions required protec-

Courts Restrict Labor Reform

tion. According to the Court, a woman's health "becomes an object of public interest and care in order to preserve the strength and vigor of the race." As a result, women were barred from occupations such as printing and transportation, which required long hours or night work, and thus were confined to the menial jobs they always had held.

Throughout the nineteenth century, tensions rose and fell as workers confronted mechanization. Adjustments were made as different groups—rural migrants, foreign immigrants, women, and children—entered the industrial labor force. Some people bent to the demands of the factory, machine, and time clock. Some tried to blend old ways of working into the new system. Some never adjusted and wandered from place to place, job to job. Others, however, turned to organized resistance.

The year 1877 in many ways marked a watershed. In July a series of strikes broke out among unionized railroad workers who were protesting

Strikes of 1877

wage cuts. Violence spread from Pennsylvania to the Midwest, Texas, and California. Venting pent-up anger, rioters attacked railroad property, derailing trains and burning railroad yards. State militia companies, organized and commanded by employers, broke up picket lines and fired into threatening crowds. In several communities, factory workers, wives, and even local merchants aided the strikers, while railroads enlisted strikebreakers to replace union men.

The worst violence occurred in Pittsburgh, where on July 21 militiamen from Philadelphia bayoneted and fired on a crowd of rock-throwing demonstrators, killing ten and wounding many more. Infuriated, the mob drove the soldiers into a railroad roundhouse and set fires that destroyed 39 buildings, 104 engines, and 1,245 freight and passenger cars. The next day, the troops shot their way out of the roundhouse and killed twenty more citizens before fleeing the city. After more than a month of unprecedented carnage, President Rutherford B. Hayes sent federal troops to end the strikes—the first significant use of troops to quell labor unrest.

The immediate cause of these strikes was the squeeze of hard times. In the economic slump that followed the Panic of 1873, railroad managers cut wages, increased workloads, and laid off workers, especially those who had joined unions. Such actions drove workers to strike and riot. Laborers in other industries sympathized with the strikers, as did other residents of their communities. A Pittsburgh militiaman, ordered out to break the 1877 strike, recalled, "I talked to all the strikers I could get my hands on, and I could find but one spirit and one purpose among them—that they were justified in resorting to any means to break down the power of the corporations."

 ## The Union Movement

After 1877, anxiety over the loss of independence and a desire for better wages, hours, and working conditions pushed more workers into unions. The union movement had precedents but few successes. Craft unions dated from the early nineteenth century, but the narrowness of their membership left them without broad power. The National Labor Union, founded in 1866, claimed 640,000 members in 1868 but died when members' loyalty seeped away during the hard times of the 1870s. The only broad-based labor organization to survive that depression was the Knights of Labor.

Founded in 1860 by Philadelphia garment cutters, the Knights opened their doors to other workers in the 1870s. In 1879, Terence V. Powderly, a machinist and former mayor of Scranton, Pennsylvania, was

Knights of Labor

elected grand master. Under his forceful guidance, Knights membership mushroomed, peaking at 730,000 in 1886. At a time when most labor organizations were trade unions—which excluded everyone except skilled workers in particular crafts—the Knights welcomed women, African-Americans, immigrants, and all unskilled and semiskilled workers.

The Knights of Labor tried to avert the bleak future that they believed industrialism portended by building an alliance among all producers that would offer an alternative to profit-oriented industrial capitalism. They believed they could eliminate conflict by establishing a cooperative society in which laborers worked for themselves, not for those who possessed capital. The goal, argued Powderly, was to "eventually make every man his own master—every man his own employer. . . . There is no good reason why labor cannot, through cooperation, own and operate mines, factories, and railroads."

Technological and organizational changes were making it impossible for each worker to be his or her own employer. Like many farmers, the Knights saw

The Haymarket Riot of 1886 was one of the most violent incidents of labor unrest in the late nineteenth century. This drawing, from Frank Leslie's Illustrated Newspaper, *shows workers fleeing while police beat demonstrators with nightsticks. As this clash was occurring, a bomb, allegedly set off by anarchists, exploded, killing both police and workers.*   Library of Congress.

producer and consumer cooperatives as preferable to the forces of greed that surrounded them. They concluded that a society in which all groups lived cooperatively was achievable. This view gave the organization both strength and weakness. The cooperative idea, attractive in the abstract, gave laborers little bargaining power. It was too vague a concept, and employers held most of the economic leverage. Strikes were a means of seeking immediate goals, but Powderly and other Knights leaders opposed strikes for two reasons: they tended to divert attention from the long-term goal of a cooperative society, and workers tended to lose more strikes than they won.

But some Knights leaders and the rank and file did support militant action. In 1886, the Knights demanded higher wages and union recognition from railroads in the Southwest. Railroad magnate Jay Gould refused to negotiate, and a strike began March 1 in Texas and spread to Kansas, Missouri, and Arkansas. As violence increased, Powderly met with Gould and called off the strike, hoping to settle the conflict. But Gould again refused concessions, and the Knights had no choice but to give in. By mid-1886, when Powderly began to denounce radicalism and violence, militant craft unions broke away, upset by Powderly's compromising position and confident that they could attain more on their own. Membership in the Knights dwindled, although the union survived in a few small towns, where it made a brief attempt to unite with Populists in the 1890s. The special interests of craft unions overcame the Knights' broad-based but often vague appeal, and dreams of labor unity faded.

As hard times of the 1870s gave way to better conditions in the early 1880s, labor groups, including the Knights, began to campaign for an eight-hour workday, partly as a means of creating more jobs so as to reduce unemployment. This effort by laborers to regain control of their work gathered momentum

Haymarket Riot

in Chicago, where radical anarchists—who believed that voluntary cooperation should replace all government—as well as various craft unions agitated for the cause. On May 1, 1886, mass strikes and the largest spontaneous labor demonstration in the country's history took place. Some one hundred thousand workers turned out, and Chicago police mobilized to prevent disorder, especially among striking workers at the huge McCormick reaper factory. The day passed calmly, but two days later police stormed an area near the McCormick plant and broke up a battle between striking unionists and nonunion strikebreakers. Police shot and killed two unionists and wounded several others.

The next evening, labor groups rallied at Haymarket Square, near downtown Chicago, to protest police brutality. As a company of police officers approached, a bomb exploded near their front ranks, killing seven and injuring sixty-seven. Mass arrests of anarchists and unionists followed. Eventually eight anarchists were tried and convicted of the bombing, though the evidence of their guilt was questionable. Four were executed and one committed suicide in prison. The remaining three were pardoned in 1893 by Illinois governor John P. Altgeld, who believed they had been victims of the "malicious ferocity" of the courts. Altgeld's act of conscience ruined his political career when law-and-order advocates denounced him as a friend of anarchy.

The Haymarket bombing, like the 1877 railroad strikes, drew attention to the growing discontent of labor and revived middle-class fear of radicalism. The participation of anarchists and socialists, many of them foreign-born, created a sense of crisis, a feeling that forces of law and order had to act swiftly to prevent social turmoil. To protect their city, private Chicago donors helped to establish a military base at Fort Sheridan and the Great Lakes Naval Training Station. Elsewhere, police forces and armories were strengthened. Employer associations—coalitions of manufacturers in the same industry—worked to counter labor militancy by agreeing to resist strikes and by purchasing strike insurance.

The American Federation of Labor (AFL) emerged from the 1886 upheavals as the major workers' organization. An alliance of national craft unions, the AFL had about 140,000 members, most of them skilled native-born workers. Led by Samuel Gompers, a pragmatic and opportunistic immigrant who headed the Cigar Makers' Union, the AFL avoided the idealistic rhetoric of worker solidarity to press for concrete goals—higher wages, shorter hours, and the right to bargain collectively. As Gompers's associate Adolph Strasser explained, "We have no ultimate ends. We are going from day to day. We are fighting only for immediate objects—objects that can be realized in a few years." In contrast to the Knights of Labor, the AFL accepted industrialism and worked to improve conditions within the wage-and-hours system. Member unions retained autonomy in their own areas of interest but tried to develop a general policy that would suit all members. Since these unions were organized by craft (skill) rather than by workplace, they had little interest in recruiting unskilled workers.

American Federation of Labor

Under Gompers the AFL grew to 1 million members by 1901 and 2.5 million by 1917, when it represented 111 national unions and 27,000 local unions. The national organization required constituent unions to hire organizers to expand membership, and it collected dues for a fund to aid members on strike. The AFL avoided party politics, adhering instead to Gompers's dictum to support labor's friends and oppose its enemies, regardless of party.

The AFL and the labor movement suffered a series of setbacks in the early 1890s, when once again labor violence stirred public fears. In July 1892, the AFL-affiliated Amalgamated Association of Iron and Steelworkers refused to accept pay cuts and went on strike in Homestead, Pennsylvania. Henry C. Frick, the president of Carnegie Steel Company, closed the plant. Shortly thereafter, Frick tried to protect the plant by hiring three hundred Pinkerton guards and floating them in by barge under cover of darkness. Lying in wait on the shore of the Monongahela River, angry workers attacked and routed the guards. State militiamen were summoned, and after five months the strikers gave in. By then public opinion had turned against the strike because of an attempt on Frick's life by a young anarchist who was not a striker.

In 1894, workers at the Pullman Palace Car Company walked out in protest over exploitative policies at the company town near Chicago. The paternalistic George Pullman provided everything for the twelve thousand residents of his so-called model town. His company owned and controlled all land and buildings, the school, the bank, and the water and gas systems. It paid wages, fixed rents, and spied on disgruntled employees. As one laborer grumbled, "We are born in a Pullman house, fed from the Pullman shop, taught in the Pullman school, catechized in the Pullman church, and when we die we shall be buried in the Pullman cemetery and go to the Pullman hell."

Pullman Strike

One thing Pullman would not do was negotiate with workers. When the hard times that began in 1893 threatened his business, Pullman maintained profits and stock dividends by cutting wages 25 to 40 percent while holding firm on rents and prices in the town. Hard-pressed workers sent a committee to Pullman to protest his policies. He reacted by firing three members of the committee. Enraged workers, most of whom had joined the American Railway Union, called a strike; Pullman retaliated by closing the plant. The union, led by the charismatic young organizer Eugene V. Debs, voted to aid the strikers by refusing to handle all Pullman cars, but Pullman stood firm and rejected arbitration. The railroad owners' association then enlisted the aid of United States Attorney General Richard Olney, who obtained a court injunction to prevent the union from "obstructing the railways and holding up the mails." President Grover Cleveland sent troops to Chicago, ostensibly to protect the mails but in reality to crush the strike. Within a month strikers gave in, and Debs was jailed for defying the court injunction. The Supreme Court upheld Debs's six-month prison sentence on grounds that the federal government had the power to remove obstacles to interstate commerce.

In the West, radical labor activity arose among Colorado miners, who participated in a series of bitter struggles and violent strikes. In 1905 many of these workers helped form a new labor organization, the Industrial Workers of the World (IWW). Unlike the AFL, the IWW strove like the Knights of Labor to unify all laborers, including the unskilled who were excluded from craft unions. Its motto was "An injury to one is an injury to all," and its goal was "One Big Union." But the "Wobblies," as IWW members were known, went beyond the goals of the Knights and espoused socialism and tactics of violence and sabotage.

Using the rhetoric of class conflict—"The final aim is revolution," according to an IWW organizer—Wobblies believed workers should seize and run the nation's industries. "Mother" Jones, an Illinois coalfield union organizer, Elizabeth Gurley Flynn, a fiery orator known as the "Joan of Arc" of the labor movement, and William D. (Big Bill) Haywood, the brawny, one-eyed founder of the Western Federation of Miners, led a series of IWW-organized, strife-torn strikes. Demonstrations erupted in western lumber and mining camps, in the steel town of McKees Rocks, Pennsylvania (1907), and in the textile mills of Lawrence, Massachusetts (1912). Though the Wobblies' anticapitalist goals and aggressive tactics attracted considerable publicity, IWW membership probably never exceeded 150,000. The organization faded during the First World War when federal prosecution—and persecution—sent many of its leaders to jail.

Many unions, notably those of the AFL, were openly hostile to women. Of the 6.3 million employed women in 1910, fewer than 2 percent belonged to unions. Male unionists often rationalized the exclusion of women by insisting that women should not be employed. According to one labor leader, "Woman is not qualified for the conditions of wage labor. . . . The mental and physical makeup of woman is in revolt against wage service. She is competing with the man who is her

Women and the Labor Movement

father or husband or is to become her husband." Fear of competition was the crucial issue. Because women were paid less than men, males worried that their own wages would be lowered or that they would lose their jobs altogether if women invaded the workplace. Moreover, male workers who were accustomed to sex segregation in employment could not imagine working side by side with women.

Yet female employees could organize and fight employers as strenuously as men could. Since the early years of industrialization, women had formed their own unions. Some, such as the Collar Laundry Union of Troy, New York, organized in the 1860s, had successfully struck for higher wages. The "Uprising of the 20,000" in New York City, a 1909 strike by immigrant members of the International Ladies Garment Workers Union (ILGWU), was one of the largest strikes in the country to that time. Women were also prominent in the 1912 Lawrence (Massachusetts) textile workers' strike. Female trade-union membership swelled during the 1910s, but national trade unions were still led by men, even in industries with large female work forces, such as the garment industry, textiles, and boots and shoes.

Women did dominate, however—as both members and leaders—in one union, the Telephone Operators' Department of the International Brotherhood of Electrical Workers. Organized in Montana and San Francisco early in the twentieth century, the union spread throughout the Bell system, the nation's major telephone company and single largest employer of women. To promote solidarity among their mostly young members, union leaders organized dances, excursions, and bazaars. Influenced by the women's rights movement, they also sponsored educational programs to enhance members' leadership skills. They focused mainly on workplace issues. Intent on developing pride and independence among telephone operators, the union opposed scientific management techniques and tightening of supervision. In 1919 several particularly militant unions paralyzed the phone service of five New England states in the country's largest strike since 1909. The union collapsed after a failed strike, again in New England, in 1923, but not before women had proved that they could advance their own cause.

The first women's labor federation to parallel the AFL was the Women's Trade Union League (WTUL), founded in 1903 and patterned after a similar union in England. The WTUL worked for protective legislation for female workers, sponsored

In 1919, telephone operators, mostly female, went out on strike and shut down phone service throughout New England. These workers, who interrupted their picketing to pose for the photograph, showed that women could take forceful action in support of their labor interests.   Corbis-Bettmann.

educational activities, and campaigned for women's suffrage. It helped telephone operators organize their union, and in 1909 it supported the ILGWU's massive strike against New York City sweatshops. Initially the union's highest offices were held by middle-class women who sympathized with female wage laborers, but control shifted in the 1910s to forceful working-class leaders, notably Agnes Nestor, a glove maker, Rose Schneiderman, a cap maker, and Mary Anderson, a shoe worker. The WTUL advocated changes such as opening apprenticeship programs to women so they could enter skilled trades, and providing leadership training for female workers. It served as a vital link between the labor and women's movements into the 1920s.

Organized labor also excluded most immigrant and African-American workers. Some trade unions welcomed skilled immigrants—in fact, foreign-born

Immigrants, African-Americans, and the Labor Movement

craftsmen were prominent leaders of several unions—but only the Knights of Labor and the IWW had firm policies of accepting immigrants and blacks. Blacks were prominent in the coal miners' union, and they were partially unionized in trades such as construction, barbering, and dock work, which had large numbers of black workers. But they could belong only to segregated local unions in the South, and the majority of northern AFL unions also had exclusion policies. Long-held prejudices were reinforced when blacks and immigrants worked as strikebreakers, hired to take the jobs of striking whites. Probably few strikebreakers understood the full effects of their actions, but even those who did found the lure of employment too great to resist.

The dramatic labor struggles in the half-century following the Civil War make it easy to forget that only a small fraction of American workers belonged to unions. In 1900, about 1 million out of a total of 27.6 million workers were unionized. By 1920, total union membership had grown to 5 million—still only 13 percent of the work force. (See pages 738–739 for a discussion of union participation in the 1930s and 1940s.) Unionization was strong in building trades, transportation, communications, and, to a lesser extent, manufacturing. For many workers, issues of wages and hours were meaningless; getting and holding a job was the first priority. Job instability and the seasonal nature of work seriously hindered union organizing efforts. Few companies employed a full work force all year round; most employers hired workers during peak seasons and laid them off during slack periods. Thus employment rates often fluctuated wildly. The 1880 census showed that in some communities 30 percent of adult males had been unemployed at some time during the previous year. And organizers took no interest in large segments of the industrial labor force and intentionally excluded others.

The millions of men, women, and children who were not unionized tried in their own ways to cope with pressures of the new machine age. Increasing numbers of workers, both native-born and immigrant, turned to fraternal societies such as the Polish Roman Catholic Union and the Jewish B'nai B'rith. For small monthly or yearly contributions these organizations provided their members with life insurance, sickness benefits, and funeral expenses and became widespread by the early twentieth century.

For most American workers, then, the machine age had mixed results. Industrial wages rose between 1877 and 1914, boosting purchasing power and creating a mass market for standardized goods. Yet in 1900 most employees worked sixty hours a week at wages that averaged 20 cents an hour for skilled work and 10 cents an hour for unskilled. Moreover, as wages rose, living costs increased even faster.

 ## Standards of Living

Some Americans distrusted machines, but few could resist the changes that mechanization brought to everyday life. The rapid expansion of railroad, postal, telephone, and electrical service drew even isolated communities into the orbit of a consumer-oriented society. American ingenuity combined with mass production and mass marketing to make available myriad goods that previously had not existed or had been the exclusive property of the wealthy. The new material well-being, heralded by products such as ready-made clothes, canned foods, and home appliances, had a dual effect. It blended Americans of differing status into communities of consumers—communities defined not by place or class but by possessions—and it accentuated differences between those who could afford such goods and services and those who could not.

If a society's affluence can be measured by how it converts luxuries into commonplace articles, the United States was indeed becoming affluent in the years between 1880 and 1920. In 1880, for example, smokers rolled their own cigarettes; only wealthy women could afford silk stockings; only residents of Florida, Texas, and California could enjoy fresh oranges; and people made candy and soap at home. By 1899, manufactured goods and perishable foodstuffs were becoming increasingly widespread. That year Americans bought 2 billion machine-produced cigarettes and 151,000 pairs of silk stockings, consumed oranges at the rate of 100 crates for every 1,000 people, and spent an average of $1.08 per person on store-bought candy and 63 cents per person on soap. By 1921 the transformation had advanced even further. Americans smoked 43 billion cigarettes that year (403 per person), ate 248 crates of oranges per 1,000 people, bought 217 million pairs of silk stockings, and spent $1.66 per person on confectionery goods and $1.40 per person on soap. How did people afford to make these changes in their standard of living?

What people can afford obviously depends on their resources and incomes. Data for the period are incomplete, but there is no doubt that incomes rose. The expanding economy spawned massive fortunes and created a new industrial elite. "The Coming Billionaire," published in *Forum* magazine in 1891, estimated that 120 Americans were worth at least $10 million. By 1920, when income-tax figures made possible accurate tabulations of income distribution, the richest 5 percent of the population received almost one-fourth of all earned income. The same 5 percent received almost half of all interest payments and 85 percent of all stock and bond dividends.

Rising Personal Income

American Living Standards, 1890–1910

	1890	1910
Income and earnings		
Annual income		
Clerical worker	$848	$1,156
Public school teacher	$256	$492
Industrial worker	$486	$630
Farm laborer	$233	$336
Hourly wage		
Soft-coal miner	$0.18[a]	$0.21
Iron worker	$0.17[a]	$0.23
Shoe worker	$0.14[a]	$0.19
Paper worker	$0.12[a]	$0.17
Labor statistics		
Number of people in labor force	28.5 million	41.7 million[b]
Average workweek in manufacturing	60 hours	51 hours

[a]1892.

[b]1920.

Incomes also rose among the middle class. For example, average pay for clerical workers rose 36 percent between 1890 and 1910 (see table). After the turn of the century, employees of the federal executive branch averaged $1,072 a year, and college professors $1,100—not handsome sums, but much more than manual workers received. With such incomes, the middle class, whose numbers were increasing as a result of new job opportunities, could afford relatively comfortable housing. A six- or seven-room house cost around $3,000 to buy or build and from $15 to $20 per month to rent.

Though wages for industrial workers increased, their income figures were deceptive because jobs were not always stable and workers had to expend a disproportionate amount of their income on necessities. On average, annual wages of factory workers rose from $486 in 1890 to $630 in 1910, about 30 percent. In industries with large female work forces, such as shoe and paper manufacturing, hourly rates remained lower than in male-dominated industries such as coal mining and iron production. Regional variations were also wide. Nevertheless, most wages moved upward (see table). Income for farm laborers followed the same trend, though wages remained relatively low because farm workers generally received free room and board.

Wage increases mean little, however, if living costs rise as fast or faster. That is what happened. According to one economic index, the weekly cost of living for a typical wage earner's family of four rose over 47 percent between 1889 and 1913. In other words, a combination of food and other goods that cost $6.78 in 1889 increased, after a slight dip in the mid-1890s, to $10 by 1913. In very few working-class occupations did income rise as fast as the cost of living.

Cost of Living

How then could working-class Americans afford the new goods and services that the machine age offered? Many could not. The daughter of a textile worker, recalling her school days, described how "some of the kids would bring bars of chocolate, others an orange. . . . I suppose they were richer than a family like ours. My father used to buy a bag of candy and a bag of peanuts every payday. . . . And that's all we'd have until the next payday. If we asked for something my mother would say, 'Well, we're too poor. We can't afford to buy that.'" Another woman explained how her family coped with high prices and low wages: "My mother made our clothes. People then wore old clothes. My mother would rip them out and make them over."

Still, a family could raise its income and partake modestly in consumer society by sending children and women into the labor market (see pages 512–515). In a household where the father made $600 a year, the wages of other family members might lift total income to $800 or $900. Many families also rented rooms to boarders and lodgers, a practice that could yield up to $200 a year. These means of increasing family income enabled people to spend more and save more. Between 1889 and 1901, working-class families markedly increased expenditures for items such as life insurance, amusements, alcoholic beverages, and union dues. Workers were able to improve their living standards, but not without sacrifices.

Supplements to Family Income

The work that people did was part of a highly developed wage and money economy. Between 1890 and 1920, the American labor force increased by 50 percent, from 28 million workers to 42 million. These figures, however, are somewhat misleading: in general, they represent a change in the nature of work as much as they indicate an increase in the number of available jobs. In the rural society that predominated in the United States in the nineteenth century, women and children performed jobs that were crucial to the family's daily existence—cooking, cleaning, planting, and harvesting—but often hard to define; they seldom appeared in employment figures because they earned no wages. But as the nation industrialized, and the agricultural sector's share of national income and population declined, paid employment became more common. Jobs in industry and commerce were easier to define and easier to count. The proportion of Americans who worked—whether in fields, households, factories, or offices—probably was not increasing markedly. Most Americans, male and female, had always worked. What was new was the increase in paid employment, making purchases of consumer goods and services more affordable.

Science and technology eased some of life's struggles, and their impact on living standards increased after 1900. Advances in medical care, better diets, and improved housing sharply reduced death rates and extended the life span. Between 1900 and 1920, life expectancy rose by fully six years and the death rate dropped by 24 percent. During this period there were notable declines in death from typhoid, diphtheria, influenza (except for a harsh pandemic in 1918 and 1919), tuberculosis, and intestinal ailments—diseases that had been scourges of earlier generations. There were, however, significantly more deaths from cancer, diabetes, and heart disease, afflictions of an aging population and of new environmental factors. Americans also found more ways to kill one another: although the suicide rate remained stable, homicides and automobile-related deaths—effects of a fast-paced urban society—increased dramatically between 1900 and 1920.

Higher Life Expectancy

Not only were amenities and luxuries more available in the early 1900s than they had been a half-century earlier, but the means to upward mobility seemed more accessible as well. Education increasingly became the key to success. Public education—aided by construction of new schools, particularly high schools, and passage of laws that required children to stay in school to age fourteen—equipped young people to achieve a standard of living higher than their parents'. Between 1890 and 1922 the number of students enrolled in public high schools grew dramatically. The creation of new white-collar jobs in growing service industries helped to stem the downward mobility that resulted when mechanization pushed skilled workers out of their crafts. Yet the inequities that had pervaded earlier eras remained in place. Race, gender, religion, and ethnicity still determined access to opportunity.

 ## The Quest for Convenience

One of the most representative agents of the revolution in American lifestyles at the end of the nineteenth century was the toilet. The chain-pull wash-down water closet, invented in England around 1870, was adopted in the United States in the 1880s. Shortly after 1900 the flush toilet appeared; thanks to the mass production of enamel-coated fixtures, it became standard in American homes and buildings.

Industrialization enhanced the incomes of the middle classes, enabling them to purchase goods previously unavailable and to provide amenities to their families more conveniently. This advertisement for a portable stove shows a father heating up milk for a baby that the mother is coddling. Note the bottle, tube, and nipple that the father is holding as well as the rug, furniture, clothing, vases, clock, and other items of moderate affluence.   Private Collection.

The indoor toilet, cheap and easy to install, brought about a shift in habits and attitudes. Before 1880, only luxury hotels and estates had private bathrooms. By the 1890s, the germ theory of disease had raised fears about carelessly disposed human waste as a source of infection and water contamination. Much more rapidly than Europeans did, Americans combined a desire for cleanliness with an urge for convenience, and water closets became common, especially in middle-class urban houses. (Flush toilets were not common in working-class homes until the 1920s.) Bodily functions took on an unpleasant image, and the home bathroom became a place of utmost privacy. Edward and Clarence Scott, who produced white tissue in perforated rolls, provided Americans a more convenient form of toilet paper than the rough paper they had previously used. At the same time, the toilet and the private bathtub gave Americans new ways to use—and waste—water. These advances in plumbing belonged to a broader democratization of convenience that accompanied mass production and consumerism.

The tin can also altered lifestyles. Before the mid-nineteenth century, Americans typically ate only foods that were in season. Drying, smoking, and salting could preserve meat for a short time, but the availability of fresh meat, like that of fresh milk, was limited; there was no way to prevent spoilage.

Processed and Preserved Foods

A French inventor developed the cooking-and-sealing process of canning around 1810, and in the 1850s an American man named Gail Borden developed a means of condensing and preserving milk. Canned goods and condensed milk became more common during the 1860s, but supplies remained low because cans had to be made by hand. By 1880, however, inventors had fashioned stamping and soldering machines to mass-produce cans from tin plate. Now, even people remote from markets, like sailors and cowboys, could readily consume tomatoes, milk, oysters, and other alternatives to previously monotonous diets. Housewives also did their own preserving of fruits and vegetables, "putting up" foods in glass jars.

Other trends and inventions broadened Americans' diets. Growing urban populations created demands that encouraged fruit and vegetable farmers to raise more produce. Railroad refrigerator cars enabled growers and meatpackers to ship perishables greater distances and to preserve them for longer periods. By the 1890s, northern city dwellers could enjoy southern and western strawberries, grapes, and tomatoes for up to six months of the year. Home iceboxes enabled middle-class families to store perishables. An easy means of producing ice commercially was invented in the 1870s, and by 1900 the nation had over two thousand commercial ice plants, most of which made home deliveries.

The availability of new foods also inspired health reformers to correct the American diet. In the 1870s, John H. Kellogg, a nutritionist and manager of the Western Health Reform Institute in Battle Creek, Michigan, began serving patients new health-providing foods, including peanut butter and wheat flakes. Several years later his brother, William K. Kellogg, invented corn flakes, and Charles W. Post introduced Grape-Nuts, revolutionizing breakfast by replacing eggs, potatoes, meat, and bread with ready-to-eat cereal, which supposedly was healthier. Just before the First World War, scientists discovered the dietetic value of vitamins A and B (C and D were discovered after the war). Growing numbers of published cookbooks and the opening of cooking schools reflected heightened interest in food and its possibilities for health and enjoyment.

Even the working class enjoyed a more diversified diet. As in the past, the poorest people still ate cheap foods, heavy in starches and carbohydrates. Southern textile workers, for example, ate corn mush and fatback (the strip of meat from a hog's back) almost every day. Poor urban families seldom could afford meat. Now, however, many of them could purchase previously unavailable fruits, vegetables, and dairy products. Workers had to spend a high percentage of their income on food—almost half of the breadwinner's wages—but they never suffered the severe malnutrition that plagued other developing nations.

Just as tin cans and iceboxes made many foods widely available, the sewing machine brought about a revolution in clothing. Before 1850, nearly all the clothes Americans wore were made at home or by seamstresses and tailors, and a person's social status was apparent in what he or she wore. Then in the 1850s the sewing machine, invented in Europe but refined by Americans Elias Howe, Jr., and Isaac M. Singer, came into use in clothing and shoe manufacture. Demand for uniforms during the Civil War boosted the ready-made clothing industry, and by 1890 annual retail sales of mass-produced garments reached $1.5 billion. Mass production enabled manufacturers to turn out good-quality apparel at relatively low cost and to standardize sizes to fit different body shapes. By 1900, only the poorest families could not afford "ready-to-wear" clothes. Tailors and seamstresses, once the originators of fashion, had been relegated to repair work. Dress patterns intended for use with a sewing machine simplified the remaining home production of clothing and gave even those who could not afford ready-made clothes access to stylish fashions.

Ready-made Clothing

With mass-produced clothing and dress patterns came a concern for style. Restrictive Victorian fashions still dominated women's clothing, but the most burdensome features were beginning to be abandoned. As women's participation in work and leisure activities became more active, dress styles began to place greater emphasis on comfort. In the 1890s, long sleeves and skirt hemlines receded, and high-boned collars disappeared. Designers used less fabric; by the 1920s a dress required three yards of material instead of ten. Petite was still the ideal, however: the most desirable waist measurement was 18 to 20 inches, and corsets were big sellers. Meanwhile, health reformers complained that women tried to squeeze into dresses, gloves, and shoes that were a size too small. In the early 1900s, long hair tied at the back of the neck was the most popular style. By the First World War, when many women worked in hospitals and factories, shorter and more manageable hairstyles had become fashionable.

Men's clothes, too, became more lightweight and stylish. Before 1900, a man in the middle and affluent working classes would have owned no more than two suits, one for Sundays and special occasions and one for everyday wear. After 1900, however, manufacturers began to produce garments from fabrics of different weights and for different seasons. Men replaced stiff derbies with soft felt hats, and stiff collars and cuffs with soft ones; dark-blue serge gave way to softer shades and more intricate weaves. Workingmen still needed the most durable, least expensive overalls, shirts, and shoes. But even for those of modest means, clothing was becoming something to be bought instead of made and remade at home.

Department stores and chain stores helped to create and serve this new consumerism. Between 1865 and 1900, companies such as Macy's, Wanamaker's, Jordan Marsh, and Marshall Field became fixtures of metropolitan America. Previously, the working classes had bought their goods in stores with

Department and Chain Stores

This photograph of the food counter at R. H. Macy's Department Store in 1902 indicates the large number of processed and preserved foods that became available to Americans at the end of the nineteenth century. The use of tin cans and glass bottles permitted food producers to sell products previously available only at limited times of the year. Museum of the City of New York, the Byron Collection.

limited inventories, and wealthier people had patronized fancy shops; each was discouraged by price, quality of goods, and social custom from shopping at the other's establishments. Now department stores, with their open displays of clothing, housewares, and furniture—all available in large quantities to anyone with the purchase price—caused a merchandising revolution. They offered not only a wide variety but also home deliveries, exchange policies, and charge accounts.

Meanwhile, the Great Atlantic Tea Company, founded in 1859, became the first grocery chain. Renamed the Great Atlantic and Pacific Tea Company in 1869 (familiarly known as the A&P), the firm's stores could buy in volume and sell to the public at low prices. By 1915 there were almost eighteen hundred A&P stores, and twelve thousand more were built in the next ten years. Other chains, such as Woolworth's, grew rapidly during the same period.

The Transformation of Mass Communications

As in the past, most people made up their own minds about what they wanted. But with so much to do and buy, consumers needed fuller information about what was available. Thus new types of communication—modern advertising and popular journalism—arose to influence tastes and opinions.

A society of scarcity does not need advertising: when demand exceeds supply, producers have no trouble selling what they market. But in a society of abundance such as industrial America, supply frequently outstrips demand, necessitating a means to increase or even create demand. Thus advertising took on a new scale and function. In 1865 about $9.5 million was spent on advertising; that sum reached $95 million by 1900 and nearly $500 million by 1919.

Advertising

The salesperson's function has traditionally been to convince a customer that a certain product—whether an insurance policy, article of clothing, or home appliance—is uniquely suited to fill that customer's need. Advertisers, by contrast, aim to *invent* a need by convincing *entire groups* that everyone in that group should buy a specific product—a brand of cigarettes, a particular cosmetic, a company's canned foods. Indeed, growth in the late nineteenth century of large companies that mass-produced consumer goods gave advertisers the task

of creating "consumption communities"—bodies of consumers loyal to a particular brand name.

In 1881, Congress passed a trademark law enabling producers to register and protect brand names. Thousands of companies eventually registered products such as Hires Root Beer, Uneeda Biscuits, and Carter's Little Liver Pills. Advertising agencies—a service industry pioneered by N. W. Ayer & Son of Philadelphia—in turn offered expert advice to companies that wished to cultivate brand loyalty. By the early 1900s, advertising techniques had been so perfected that French composer Jacques Offenbach observed, "Decidedly the American advertising men play upon the human mind as a musician plays on his piano."

The prime vehicle for advertising was the newspaper. In the mid-nineteenth century, publishers began to pursue higher revenues from advertising by selling more ad space, especially to urban department stores. Wanamaker's placed the first full-page ad in 1879, and at about the same time newspapers began to allow advertisers to print pictures of products. Such attention-getting techniques transformed advertising into news. More than ever before, people read newspapers to find out what was for sale as well as what was happening.

Manufacturers used new marketing techniques to advance their technological and organizational innovations. James B. Duke, whose American Tobacco Company made cigarettes a big business, saturated communities with billboards and free samples and offered premium gifts to retailers for selling more cigarettes. Companies like International Harvester and Singer Sewing Machine set up systems for servicing their products and introduced financing schemes to permit customers to buy the machines more easily. In many instances producers sold directly to retailers, squeezing out wholesalers and eliminating excess costs that wholesaling entailed.

The Corporate Consolidation Movement

Neither the industrial wonders nor the new marketing techniques masked unsettling factors in the American economy. The race for higher productivity and new markets had costs as well as benefits. The capital invested in new technology required that factories operate at near capacity to produce goods most economically. But the more manufacturers produced, the more they had to sell. To sell

In their quest for convenience, Americans shopped for mass-produced, standard-size clothing in department stores. Many women, however, continued to make their own clothing, often from standardized patterns. This drawing shows a large millinery shop in New York, where women bought hats that they could trim for themselves and cloth that they could use to make dresses from patterns.   New-York Historical Society.

more, they had to reduce prices. To increase profits and compensate for reduced prices, they further expanded production and often reduced wages. To expand, they had to borrow money. And to repay loans, they had to produce and sell even more. This spiraling process strangled small firms that could not keep pace, and it thrust workers into constant uncertainty. The same cycle affected commerce, banking, and transportation as well as manufacturing.

This environment encouraged rapid growth, but optimism could dissolve at the hint that debtors could not meet their obligations. In the final third of the nineteenth century, financial panics afflicted the economy during every decade, ruining businesses and destroying workers' jobs. Economic declines that began in 1873, 1884, and 1893 each lingered for several years. Business leaders disagreed on what caused them. Some blamed overproduction; others pointed to underconsumption; still others blamed lax credit and investment practices. Whatever the

explanation, businesspeople began seeking ways to combat the uncertainty of boom-and-bust business cycles. Many adopted centralized forms of business organization, notably corporations, pools, trusts, and holding companies.

Unlike laborers, industrialists never questioned the capitalist system. They sought new ways to build on the base that had been supporting economic growth since the early 1800s, when states adopted incorporation laws to encourage commerce and industry. Under such laws, almost anyone could start a company and raise money by selling stock to investors. Stockholders could share in profits without personal risk because laws limited their liability for company debts to the amount of their own investment; the rest of their wealth was protected should the company fail. Nor did investors need to concern themselves with a firm's day-to-day operation;

Role of Corporations

responsibility for company administration rested in the hands of managers.

The corporation proved to be the best instrument to raise capital for industrial expansion, and by 1900 corporations were responsible for two-thirds of all goods manufactured in the United States. Moreover, corporations won judicial protection in the 1880s and 1890s when the Supreme Court ruled that they, like individuals, are protected by the Fourteenth Amendment. In other words, states could not deny corporations equal protection under the law and could not deprive them of rights or property without due process of law. Such rulings insulated corporations against government interference in their operations.

But as economic disorder and the urge for profits mounted, corporation managers sought greater stability in new and larger forms of economic concentration. Between the late 1880s and early 1900s, an epidemic of business consolidation swept the United States, eventually resulting in the massive conglomerates that dominated the economy in the twentieth century. At first such efforts were tentative and informal, consisting mainly of cooperative agreements among firms that manufactured the same product or offered the same service. Through these arrangements, called *pools*, competing companies tried to control the market by agreeing how much each should produce and sharing profits. Employed by railroads (to divide up traffic), steel producers, and whiskey distillers, pools depended on their members' honesty. Such "gentlemen's agreements" worked during good times when there was enough business for all; but during slow periods, the desire for profits often tempted pool members to evade their commitments by secretly reducing prices or by selling more than the agreed quota. The Interstate Commerce Act of 1887 outlawed pools among railroads (see page 578), but by then their usefulness was already fading.

Pools, Trusts, and Holding Companies

John D. Rockefeller disliked pools, calling them "ropes of sand"—weak and undependable. In 1879 one of his lawyers, Samuel Dodd, devised a more stable means of dominating the market. Since state laws prohibited one corporation from holding stock in another corporation, Dodd adapted an old device called a *trust*, which in law existed as an arrangement whereby responsible individuals would manage the financial affairs of a person unwilling or unable to handle them alone. Dodd reasoned that one company could control an industry by luring or forcing the stockholders of smaller companies in that industry to yield control of their stock "in trust" to the larger company's board of trustees. This device allowed Rockefeller to achieve *horizontal integration* of the highly profitable petroleum industry in 1882 by combining his Standard Oil Company of Ohio with other refineries he bought up.

In 1888 New Jersey adopted new laws allowing corporations chartered there to own property in other states and to own stock in other corporations. (Trusts provided for trusteeship, not ownership.) This liberalization facilitated creation of the *holding company*, which owned a partial or complete interest in other companies. Holding companies could in turn merge their companies' assets (buildings, equipment, inventory, and cash) as well as their management. Under this arrangement, Rockefeller's holding company, Standard Oil of New Jersey, merged forty refining companies. By 1898, Standard Oil refined 84 percent of all oil produced in the nation, controlled most pipelines, and had moved into natural-gas production and ownership of oil-producing properties.

Standard Oil's expansion into operations besides refining exemplified a new form of economic integration. To dominate their markets, many holding companies sought control over all aspects of their operations, including raw materials, production, and distribution. The prime example of such *vertical integration*, which fused a broad range of business activities into one entity under unified management, was Gustavus Swift's meat-processing operation. During the 1880s, Swift boldly invested in livestock, slaughterhouses, refrigerator cars, and marketing to ensure the sale of his beef without unexpected inconvenience.

Mergers became the answer to industry's search for order. Between 1889 and 1903, some three hundred combinations were formed, most of them trusts and holding companies. The most spectacular was the U.S. Steel Corporation, financed by J. P. Morgan in 1901. This enterprise, made up of iron-ore properties, freight carriers, wire mills, plate and tubing companies, and other firms, was capitalized at over $1.4 billion. Other mammoth combinations included the Amalgamated Copper Company, American Sugar Refining Company, American Tobacco Company, and U.S. Rubber Company, each worth over $50 million.

The merger movement created a new species of businessman, whose vocation was financial organizing rather than producing a particular good or service. Shrewd operators

Role of Financiers

sought opportunities for combination, formed corporations, and then persuaded producers to sell their firms to the new company. These financiers usually raised money by selling stock and borrowing from banks. Their attention ranged widely. Thus W. H. Moore organized the American Tin Plate Company, Diamond Match Company, and National Biscuit Company, and he acquired control of the mighty Rock Island Railroad. Elbert H. Gary similarly participated in consolidation of the barbed-wire industry and then of U.S. Steel. Investment bankers like J. P. Morgan and Jacob Schiff piloted the merger movement, inspiring awe with their financial power and organizational skills.

The growth of corporations in the late nineteenth century turned financial exchanges into hubs of activity for the sale of stocks and bonds. By 1886 trading on the New York Stock Exchange reached 1 million shares a day. By 1914 the number of industrial stocks traded reached 511, compared with 145 in 1869. Investment could not have occurred without attracting the capital necessary for such purposes. Between 1870 and 1900 foreign investment in American companies rose from $1.5 billion to $3.5 billion. Personal savings and institutional investment also mushroomed: assets of savings banks, concentrated in the Northeast and on the West Coast, rose by 700 percent between 1875 and 1897 to a total of $2.2 billion. States loosened regulations to enable banks to invest in railroads and industrial enterprises. Commercial banks, insurance companies, and corporations also invested heavily. As one journal proclaimed, "Nearly the whole country (including the typical widow and orphan) is interested in the stock market." Though a gross exaggeration, this assertion reflected what optimistic capitalists wanted to believe.

 ## The Gospel of Wealth and Its Critics

Business leaders turned to corporate consolidation not to promote competition but to minimize it. At the same time, defenders of business sought a philosophical theory that would enable them to justify the size and power of the huge companies that resulted from corporate mergers and explain their tactics to a public accustomed to a belief in open competition.

The doctrine of Social Darwinism furnished the needed answers. Developed by English philosopher Herbert Spencer and preached in the United States by Yale professor William Graham Sumner, Social Darwinism

Social Darwinism

loosely grafted Charles Darwin's theory of the evolutionary survival of the fittest onto laissez faire, the doctrine that government should not interfere in private economic affairs. Social Darwinists reasoned that, in an unconstrained economy, power would flow naturally to the most capable people. Acquisition and possession of property were thus sacred rights, and wealth was a mark of well-deserved power and responsibility. Civilization depended on this system, explained Sumner. "If we do not like the survival of the fittest," he wrote, "we have only one possible alternative, and that is survival of the unfittest." Monopolies, therefore, resulted from the natural accumulation of economic power by those best suited for wielding it. Many clergymen and journalists supported this argument.

Social Darwinists reasoned, too, that wealth carried moral responsibilities to provide for those less fortunate or less capable. Steel baron Andrew Carnegie asserted what he called "the Gospel of Wealth"—that he and other industrialists were trustees for society's wealth and that they had a duty to fulfill that trust in humane ways. Over his lifetime, Carnegie donated more than $350 million to libraries, schools, peace initiatives, and the arts. Such philanthropy, however, also implied a right for men like Rockefeller and Carnegie to define what they believed was good and necessary for society as a whole.

Paradoxically, business executives who extolled individual initiative and independence also pressed for government assistance. While denouncing measures to aid unions or regulate factory conditions as interference with natural economic laws,

Government Assistance to Business

they lobbied forcefully and successfully for subsidies, loans, and tax relief to encourage business growth. By far the most extensive form of government assistance to American industry was tariffs, which raised the prices of foreign products by placing an import tax on them. When Congress imposed high tariffs on foreign goods such as kerosene, steel rails, worsted wools, and tin plate, American producers could sell their goods at relatively high prices. Industrialists argued that tariff protection encour-

How do historians know what turn-of-the-century Americans thought about big business? Political cartoons and the symbols that cartoonists often used indicate prevailing attitudes and can serve as a kind of shorthand representation of how the same historical circumstance can arouse differing opinions. These two cartoons illustrate quite different points of view. The top one depicts the Standard Oil Trust as a greedy octopus with sprawling tentacles that are snar-ing Congress, state legislatures, and the taxpayer and are reaching for the White House. The cartoonist obviously believed that the economic giant was exercising dangerous power. The second cartoon portrays a more benevolent view. The cartoonist depicts John D. Rockefeller of Standard Oil and Andrew Carnegie of U.S. Steel at work, using their profits to nurture a garden of colleges and libraries.   Octopus: Library of Congress. Garden: Baker Library, Harvard Business School.

aged the development of new products and the founding of new enterprises. But tariffs also forced consumers to pay artificially high prices for many goods.

Critics of trusts and other new forms of business organization based their arguments on traditional American beliefs in independence and opportunity.

Dissenting Voices

In doing so, they argued within the same framework of values as did the corporate leaders they opposed. While defenders insisted that trusts were a natural and efficient outcome of economic development, critics charged that trusts were unnatural because they were created by greed and stifled opportunity. Such charges gave voice to an ardent fear of *monopoly*, the domination of an economic activity (such as oil refining) by one powerful company (such as Standard Oil). Those who feared monopoly believed that large corporations could manipulate consumers by fixing prices, exploit workers by cutting wages, destroy opportunity by crushing small businesses, and threaten democracy by corrupting politicians—all of which was not only unnatural but immoral. To critics, ethics eclipsed economics.

Many believed in a better path to progress. By the mid-1880s, a number of young professors began to challenge Social Darwinism and laissez-faire economics. Brown University sociologist Lester Ward attacked the application of evolutionary theory to social and economic relations. In *Dynamic Sociology* (1883), Ward argued that human control of nature, not natural law, accounted for the advance of civilization. According to Ward, a system that guaranteed survival only to the fittest was wasteful and brutal; instead, he reasoned, cooperative activity fostered by planning and government intervention was more moral. Economists Richard Ely, John R. Commons, and Edward Bemis agreed that natural forces should be harnessed for the public good. They denounced the laissez-faire system for its "unsound morals" and praised the positive assistance that government could offer.

While academics endorsed intervention in the natural economic order, others more directly questioned why the United States had to have so many poor people while a few became fabulously wealthy. Henry

Utopian Economic Schemes

George was a printer and writer in San Francisco who had fallen into desperate poverty during the depression of the 1870s.

Alarmed at the exploitative power of large enterprises, he came to believe that economic inequality stemmed from the ability of a few to profit from rising land values. George argued that such profits made speculators rich simply because of increased demand for living and working space, especially in cities. To prevent profiteering, George proposed to replace all taxes with a "single tax" on the "unearned increment"—the rise in property values caused by increased market demand rather than by owners' improvements. George's scheme, argued forcefully in *Progress and Poverty* (1879), had great popular appeal and almost won him the mayoralty of New York City in 1886.

Unlike George, who accepted private ownership, novelist Edward Bellamy believed capitalism and competition promoted waste. His solution was establishment of a state in which government owned the means of production. Bellamy outlined his dream in *Looking Backward, 2000–1887* (1888). The novel, which sold over a million copies, depicted Boston in the year 2000 as a peaceful community where everyone had a job and a technological elite managed the economy according to scientific principles. Though in this utopia a council of elders ruled and ordinary people could not vote, Bellamy tried to convince readers that a "principle of fraternal cooperation" could replace vicious competition and wasteful monopoly. His vision, which he called "Nationalism," sparked formation of Nationalist clubs from Boston to Los Angeles and kindled popular appeals for civil service reform, social welfare measures, and government ownership of railroads and utilities.

Before 1900 few people supported the government ownership envisioned by Bellamy, but several states did take steps to prohibit monopolies and regulate business. By the end of the

Antitrust Legislation

nineteenth century, fifteen states had constitutional provisions outlawing trusts, and twenty-seven had laws forbidding pools. Most were agricultural states in the South and West that were responding to antimonopolistic pressure from various farm organizations. But state attorneys general lacked the staff and judicial support for an effective attack on big business, and corporations always found ways to evade restrictions. Only national legislation, it seemed, could work.

Congress moved hesitantly toward such legislation and in 1890 finally passed the Sherman Anti-Trust Act. Introduced by Senator John Sherman of

Ohio and rewritten by probusiness eastern senators, the law made illegal "every contract, combination in the form of trust or otherwise, or conspiracy in the restraint of trade." Those found guilty of violating the law faced fines and jail terms, and those wronged by illegal combinations could sue for triple damages. However, the law was left purposely vague so as to attract broad support. It did not clearly define restraint of trade and consigned interpretation of its provisions to the courts, which at the time were strong allies of business.

Judges used the law's vagueness to blur distinctions between reasonable and unreasonable restraints of trade. When in 1895 the federal government prosecuted the so-called Sugar Trust for owning 98 percent of the nation's sugar-refining capacity, eight of the nine Supreme Court justices ruled that control of manufacturing did not necessarily mean control of trade (*U.S.* v. *E. C. Knight Co.*). According to the Court, the Constitution empowered Congress to regulate interstate *commerce*, but *manufacturing* (which in the *Knight* case took place entirely within the state of Pennsylvania) did not fall under congressional control.

Between 1890 and 1900 the federal government prosecuted only eighteen cases under the Sherman Anti-Trust Act. The most successful cases were those aimed at railroads directly involved in interstate commerce. Ironically, the act equipped the government with a tool for breaking up labor unions: courts that did not consider monopolistic production a restraint on trade willingly applied antitrust provisions to strikes.

 **Conclusion**

Mechanization and new inventions thrust the United States into the vanguard of industrial nations and immeasurably altered daily life between 1877 and 1920. But in industry, as in farming and mining, bigness and consolidation engulfed the individual, changing the nature of work from individual activity undertaken by producers to mass production undertaken by employees. Workers fought to regain control of their efforts but failed to develop well-organized unions that could meet their needs. The outpouring of products created a new mass society based on consumerism, but even the "democratization of consumption" did not benefit all social groups.

The problems of enforcing the Sherman Anti-Trust Act reflected the uneven distribution of power among interest groups. Corporate enterprises had effectively consolidated, and they controlled great resources of economic and political power. Other groups—farmers, laborers, and reformers—had numbers and ideas but lacked influence. Members of these groups desired the material gains that technology and mass production were providing, but they feared that business was acquiring too much influence. In factories and farms, some people were celebrating the industrial transformation while others were struggling with the dilemma of industrialism: whether a system based on ever-greater profits was the best way for Americans to fulfill the nation's democratic destiny.

The march of industrial expansion proved almost impossible to stop, however, because so many people were benefiting from it. Moreover, the waves of people pouring into the nation's cities were increasingly providing both the workers and the consumers for America's expanding productive capacity. The standards of American life now rested in the cities.

Suggestions for Further Reading

General

Daniel J. Boorstin, *The Americans: The Democratic Experience* (1973); Alan Dawley, *Struggle for Justice: Social Responsibility and the Liberal State* (1991); Carl N. Degler, *The Age of the Economic Revolution* (1977); Ray Ginger, *The Age of Excess* (1965); Samuel P. Hays, *The Response to Industrialism* (1975); Thomas J. Schlereth, *Victorian America: Transformations in Everyday Life* (1991).

Technology and Invention

Robert W. Bruce, *Bell: Alexander Graham Bell and the Conquest of Solitude* (1973); David Hounshell, *From the American System to Mass Production* (1984); Thomas Parke Hughes, *American Genesis: A Century of Technological Enthusiasm* (1989); John P. Kasson, *Civilizing the Machine: Technology and Republican Values in America* (1976); Leo Marx, *The Machine in the Garden: Technology and the Pastoral Ideal* (1964); Andre Millard, *Edison and the Business of Innovation* (1990); David E. Nye, *Electrifying America* (1990); Peter Temin, *Steel in Nineteenth-Century America* (1964).

Industrialism, Industrialists, and Corporate Growth

W. Eliot Brownlee, *Dynamics of Ascent: A History of the American Economy*, 2d ed. (1979); Stuart Bruchey, *Growth of the Modern Economy* (1973); Vincent P. Carosso, *The Morgans* (1987); Alfred D. Chandler, *The Visible Hand: The Managerial Revolution in American Business* (1977); Thomas C. Cochran, *Business in American Life*

(1972); Francis L. Eames, *The New York Stock Exchange* (1968); David F. Hawkes, *John D.: The Founding Father of the Rockefellers* (1980); Robert Higgs, *The Transformation of the American Economy, 1865–1914* (1971); Harold C. Livesay, *Andrew Carnegie and the Rise of Big Business* (1975); Glen Porter, *The Rise of Big Business* (1973); Martin J. Sklar, *The Corporate Reconstruction of American Capitalism* (1988); Richard Tedlow, *The Rise of the American Business Corporation* (1991); Joseph Wall, *Alfred I. du Pont: The Man and His Family* (1990).

Work and Labor Organization

Alan Derickson, *Workers' Health, Workers' Democracy: The Western Miners' Struggle, 1891–1925* (1988); Melvin Dubofsky, *We Shall Be All: A History of the Industrial Workers of the World* (1969); Sarah Eisenstein, *Give Us Bread, Give Us Roses: Working Women's Consciousness in the United States* (1983); Leon Fink, *Workingmen's Democracy: The Knights of Labor and American Politics* (1982); Philip S. Foner, *The Great Labor Uprising of 1877* (1977); Herbert G. Gutman, *Work, Culture and Society in Industrializing America* (1976); Tamara K. Hareven, *Family Time and Industrial Time* (1982); Alice Kessler-Harris, *Out to Work: A History of Wage Earning Women in the United States* (1982); Susan Lehrer, *Origins of Protective Labor Legislation for Women* (1987); Harold Livesay, *Samuel Gompers and Organized Labor in America* (1978); Milton Meltzer, *Bread and Roses: The Struggle of American Labor, 1865–1915* (1967); Stephen Meyer III, *The Five Dollar Day: Labor Management and Social Control in the Ford Motor Company, 1908–1921* (1981); Ruth Milkman, ed., *Women, Work, and Protest* (1985); David Montgomery, *The Fall of the House of Labor: The Workplace, the State, and American Labor Activism, 1865–1925* (1987); Stephen H. Norwood, *Labor's Flaming Youth: Telephone Operators and Worker Militancy* (1990); Elizabeth Ann Payne, *Reform, Labor, and Feminism: Margaret Dreier Robins and the Women's Trade Union League* (1988); Daniel J. Walkowitz, *Worker City, Company Town* (1978); Leon J. Wolff, *Lockout: The Story of the Homestead Strike of 1892* (1965).

Living Standards and New Conveniences

Susan Porter Benson, *Counter Cultures: Saleswomen, Managers, and Customers in American Department Stores, 1890–1940* (1986); Stephen Fox, *The Mirror Makers: A History of American Advertising and Its Creators* (1984); T. J. Jackson Lears and Richard W. Fox, eds., *The Culture of Consumption* (1983); Godfrey M. Lebhar, *Chain Stores in America* (1962); Harvey A. Levenstein, *Revolution at the Table: The Transformation of the American Diet* (1988); Daniel Pope, *The Making of Modern Advertising* (1983); Peter R. Shergold, *Working Class Life* (1982); Susan Strasser, *Satisfaction Guaranteed: The Making of the American Mass Market* (1989); Gwendolyn Wright, *Building the Dream: A Social History of Housing in America* (1983).

Attitudes Toward Industrialism

Sidney Fine, *Laissez Faire and the General Welfare State* (1956); Louis Galambos and Barbara Barron Spence, *The Public Image of Big Business in America* (1975); Richard Hofstadter, *Social Darwinism in American Thought*, rev. ed. (1955); T. J. Jackson Lears, *No Place of Grace: Antimodernism and the Transformation of American Culture* (1981); Robert McCloskey, *American Conservatism in the Age of Enterprise* (1951); John L. Thomas, *Alternative America: Henry George, Edward Bellamy, Henry Demarest Lloyd, and the Adversary Tradition* (1983).

NOON HOUR ON
STATE STREET
CHICAGO

CHAPTER

19

The Vitality and Turmoil of Urban Life

1877–1920

In a few short weeks, Antanas Kaztauskis learned just about everything he needed to know about living in Chicago. An immigrant
from Lithuania, Antanas first lived in a boarding house near his job
in the stockyards. One night some friends asked him why he had come to
America. As he later explained to a newspaper reporter,

> I told them . . . "life, liberty, and the pursuit of happiness." They all leaned back and
> laughed. "What you need is money," they said. "It was all right [in Lithuania]. You
> wanted nothing. You ate your own meat and your own things on your farm. You
> made your own clothes and had your own leather. . . . But here you want a hundred
> things . . . and you must have the money to buy everything."

The next morning, Antanas's friends took him to a store and bought him
some American clothes. Then they went for a walk "down town." There,
Antanas discovered the wonders of the city.

> We stood by one theater and watched for half an hour. Then we walked all around a
> store that filled one whole block and had walls of glass. Then we had a drink of
> whiskey, and this is better than vodka. We felt happier and looked into *cafes*. . . . I saw
> men with dress suits, I saw women with such clothes that I could not think at all. . . .
> [My friends said,] "See what money can do?" Then we walked home and I felt poor
> and my shoes got very bad.

Antanas lost his job after a few weeks and out of desperation sought help
from a politician—and learned how the city really worked:

> The Republican boss in our district, Jonidas, was a saloon keeper. A friend took me
> there. Jonidas shook hands and treated me fine. He taught me to sign my name, and
> the next week I went with him to an office and signed some paper, and then I could
> vote. I voted as I was told, and then they got me back into the [stock]yards to work,
> because one big politician owns stock in one of those houses. Then I felt that I was
> getting in beside the game.

*Pulsing with the move-
ment of pedestrians,
horse-drawn buggies,
streetcars, and auto-
mobiles amid bulky
tall buildings, this
postcard of Chicago's
busiest downtown
corner represents the
city's movement and
progress. Another kind
of activity, still vibrant
but even more varied,
could be found in the
neighborhoods in
which all these people
lived.* Lake County (IL)
Museum, Curt Teich
Postcard Archives.

537

As he saved money, Antanas was able to bring his wife from Lithuania and rent an apartment in a respectable part of town. He joined some Lithuanian clubs and on Sundays took trolley rides into the countryside.

The experiences of Antanas Kaztauskis illustrate many themes characterizing urban life in America as the nineteenth century merged into the twentieth. Where to live, where to work, the awesomeness of the consumer economy, the functions of personal and machine politics, the expression of ethnic consciousness, and the rise from rags to respectability—all these things and more made cities places of hope, frustration, satisfaction, and conflict. Their clanging trolleys, smoky air, crowded streets, and jumble of languages contrasted with the slow, quiet pace of village and farm life.

The nation's urban population started to grow much faster than its rural population in the 1830s. But not until the 1880s did the United States begin to become a truly urban nation. By 1920 a symbolic milestone of urbanization was passed: that year's census showed that, for the first time, a majority of Americans (51.4 percent) lived in cities (settlements with more than 2,500 people). This new fact of national life was as symbolically significant as the disappearance of the frontier in 1890. The era of the yeoman farmer was over, and urban growth joined with the development of natural resources and industrialization as an identifiable feature of American expansion in the late nineteenth and early twentieth centuries.

Cities served as marketplaces and forums, bringing together the people, resources, and ideas responsible for many of the changes American society was experiencing. By 1900 a network of small, medium, and large cities spanned every section of the country. Some people relished the opportunities and excitement cities offered. As one newspaper editor wrote, it was "better [to] be the 1/1,000,000,000 of New York than the 1/1 of Aroostook County." Others found the crudeness of American cities disquieting. "Having seen it," British poet Rudyard Kipling wrote of Chicago, "I urgently desire never to see it again." But whatever people's personal impressions, the city had become central to American life. The ways people built their cities and adjusted to the new urban environment have shaped American society.

Transportation and Industrial Growth in the Modern City

By 1900, the compact American city of the early nineteenth century, where residences were mingled among shops, factories, and warehouses, had burst

Electric trolley cars and other forms of mass transit enabled middle-class people like these women and men to reside on the urban outskirts and ride into the city center for work, shopping, and entertainment.   Museum of the City of New York, the Bryon Collection.

• *Important Events* •

1867	First law regulating tenements passes, in New York State	**1895**	William Randolph Hearst buys the *New York Journal*, another major popular yellow-journalism newspaper
1870	One-fourth of Americans live in cities	**1898**	Race riot erupts in Wilmington, North Carolina
1876	National League of Professional Baseball Clubs founded	**1900–10**	Immigration reaches peak Vaudeville rises in popularity
1880s	"New" immigrants from eastern and southern Europe begin to arrive in large numbers	**1903**	Boston plays Pittsburgh in first baseball World Series
1883	Brooklyn Bridge completed Joseph Pulitzer buys *New York World* and creates a major vehicle for yellow journalism	**1905**	Intercollegiate Athletic Association, forerunner of National College Athletic Association (NCAA), is formed and restructures rules of football
1885	Safety bicycle invented	**1906**	Race riot erupts in Atlanta, Georgia
1886	First settlement house opens, in New York City	**1915**	D. W. Griffith directs *Birth of a Nation*, one of the first major technically sophisticated movies
1889	Thomas A. Edison invents the motion picture and viewing device	**1920**	Majority (51.4 percent) of Americans live in cities
1890s	Electric trolleys replace horse-drawn mass transit		
1893	World's Columbian Exposition opens in Chicago		

open. From Boston to Los Angeles, the built environment sprawled several miles beyond the original central core. No longer did walking distance determine a city's size. No longer did different social groups live close together: poor near rich, immigrant near native-born, black near white. Instead, cities subdivided into distinct districts: working-class and ethnic neighborhoods, African-American ghettos, downtown, a ring of suburbs. Two forces were responsible for this new arrangement. One, mass transportation, was centrifugal, propelling people and enterprises outward. The other, economic change, was centripetal, drawing human and economic resources inward.

Mass transportation moved people faster and farther. Before the 1870s, horse- and mule-drawn vehicles had been the main means of transport in cities. But they were inefficient.

Mechanization of Mass Transportation

They could carry relatively few riders, and purchasing, feeding, and cleaning up after the animals was costly. New technology enabled entrepreneurs to adopt better ways to transport people. During the 1850s and 1860s, steam-powered commuter railroads serviced a few cities, such as New York and Boston, but not until the late 1870s did mechanized mass transit appear. The first power-driven devices were cable cars, carriages that moved by clamping onto a moving underground wire. Cheaper than horse cars, cable cars also were more efficient at hauling passengers up and down hills. By the 1880s, cable-car lines operated in Chicago, San Francisco, and many other cities.

In the 1890s, electric-powered streetcars began replacing early forms of mass transit. Designed in Montgomery, Alabama, and Richmond, Virginia, electric trolleys spread to nearly every large American city. Between 1890 and 1902, total extent of electrified track grew from 1,300 to 22,000 miles. In a few cities, trolley companies raised track onto stilts, enabling vehicles to travel without interference above jammed downtown districts. In Boston, New York, and Philadelphia, transit firms dug underground passages for their cars, also to avoid delays. Because elevated railroads and subways were extremely expensive to construct, they appeared

Along with mass-produced consumer goods such as clothing and appliances, Sears, Roebuck and Company marketed architectural plans for middle-class suburban housing. This drawing, taken from the Sears catalogue for 1911, illustrates the kind of housing developed on the urban outskirts in the early twentieth century.   Sears, Roebuck and Company.

only in the few cities where companies could amass enough capital to lay track and buy equipment and where there were enough riders to ensure profits.

Another form of mass transit, the electric interurban railway, not only provided greater convenience for riders but also helped link nearby cities. Usually built over shorter distances than steam railroads, the interurbans operated between cities in areas with growing suburban populations and furthered urban development by making outer regions attractive for settlers and businesses. The extensive network of the Pacific Electric Railway in southern California, for example, facilitated both travel and economic development in that region.

Mass-transit lines launched millions of urban dwellers into outlying neighborhoods and created a commuting public. Those who could afford the fare—usually a nickel a ride—could live beyond the crowded central city and commute there for work, shopping, and entertainment. Working-class fami-

Beginnings of Urban Sprawl

lies, whose incomes rarely topped a dollar a day, found streetcar fares unaffordable. But the growing middle class could escape to quiet neighborhoods on the urban outskirts and live in bungalows with their own yards on tree-lined streets. Real-estate development boomed around the borders of cities. Between 1890 and 1920, for example, developers in the Chicago area opened 800,000 new lots—enough to house at least three times the city's 1890 population. A home several miles from downtown was inconvenient, but the benefits seemed to outweigh the costs. As one suburbanite wrote in 1902, "It may be a little more difficult for us to attend the opera, but the robin in my elm tree struck a higher note and a sweeter one yesterday than any prima donna ever reached."

Urban sprawl was essentially unplanned, but certain patterns did emerge. Eager to capitalize on commuting possibilities, thousands of small investors who bought land in anticipation of settlement paid little attention to the need for parks, traffic control, and public services. Construction of mass transit was guided by the profit motive and thus benefited the urban public unevenly. Streetcar lines serviced mainly those districts that promised the most riders—whose fares, in other words, would increase company profits.

Streetcars, elevateds, and subways altered commercial as well as residential patterns. When consumers moved outward, businesses followed. Secondary commercial centers sprouted at trolley-line intersections and at elevated-railway stations. Branches of department stores and banks joined groceries, theaters, taverns, and specialty shops to create neighborhood shopping centers, the forerunners of today's suburban malls. Meanwhile, the urban core became the work zone, where offices and stores loomed over streets clogged with traffic. Districts like Chicago's Loop and New Orleans's Canal Street employed thousands in commerce and finance.

Cities also became the main arenas for industrial growth. As centers of labor, transportation, and communications, cities provided everything factories needed. Once mass produc-

Urban-Industrial Development

tion became possible, capital accumulated by the cities' mercantile enterprises fed industrial investment. Urban populations also furnished consumers for myriad new products. Thus urban growth and industrialization wound together in a mutually advantageous spiral. The further industrialization advanced, the more opportunities it created for work and investment. Increased opportunity in turn drew more people to cities; as workers and as consumers, they fueled further industrialization.

Most cities housed a variety of industrial enterprises, but product specialization gradually became common. Mass production of clothing concentrated in New York; the shoe industry in Philadelphia, and textiles in several New England cities. Other cities processed products from surrounding agricultural regions: flour in Minneapolis, cottonseed oil in Memphis, beef and pork in Omaha. Still others processed natural resources: gold and copper in Denver, fish and lumber in Seattle, coal and iron in Pittsburgh and Birmingham, oil in Houston and Los Angeles. Such activities increased the magnetic attraction of cities for people in search of steady employment.

Urban and industrial growth transformed the national economy and freed the United States from dependence on European capital and manufactured goods. Imports and foreign investments still flowed into the United States. But by the early 1900s, cities and their factories, stores, and banks were converting America from a debtor agricultural nation into an industrial, financial, and exporting power.

 ## Peopling the Cities: Migrants and Immigrants

Between 1870 and 1920, the number of Americans living in cities exploded almost 550 percent, from 10 million to 54 million. During the same period, the number of cities with more than 100,000 people grew from fifteen to sixty-eight, and the number with more than 500,000 swelled from two to twelve (see maps, page 542). These figures, dramatic in themselves, represent millions of stories of dreams and frustration, adjustment and confusion, success and failure.

A city can increase its population in three ways: by extending its borders to annex land and people; by natural increase (an excess of births over deaths); and by net migration (an

How Cities Grew

excess of in-migrants over out-migrants). Between the 1860s and early 1900s, many cities annexed nearby territory, thereby instantly increasing their populations. The most notable consolidation occurred in 1898 when New York City, which previously consisted only of Manhattan and the Bronx, merged with Brooklyn, Staten Island, and part of Queens and grew overnight from 1.5 million to over 3 million people. Suburbs often desired annexation because they needed the schools, water, fire protection, and sewer systems that cities had developed. Annexation also added vacant land where new city dwellers could live. Cities such as Chicago, Minneapolis, and Los Angeles incorporated hundreds of undeveloped square miles into their borders in the 1880s, only to see them fill up with new residents in succeeding decades. Annexation did increase urban populations, but its major effect was to enlarge the physical size of cities.

Natural increase did not account for much of any city's population growth. In the late nineteenth century, death rates declined in most regions of the country, but birth rates fell as well (see the Appendix). In most cities, the number of people who were born in a given year was roughly equal to the number who died that year. Migration and immigration made by far the greatest contribution to urban population growth. In fact, migration to cities nearly matched the massive migration to the West that was

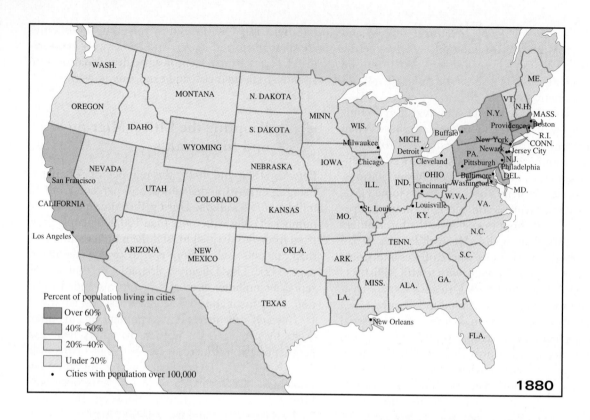

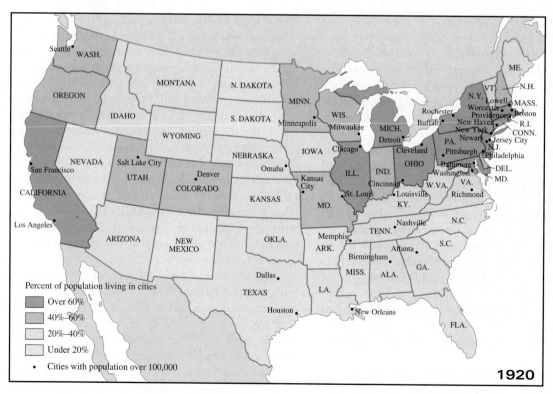

Urbanization, 1880; Urbanization, 1920   *In 1880 the vast majority of states still were heavily rural. By 1920 only a few had less than 20 percent of their population living in cities.*

occurring at the same time. Urban newcomers arrived from two major sources: the American countryside and Europe. Asia, Canada, and Latin America also supplied immigrants, though in smaller numbers.

In general, rural populations declined as urban populations burgeoned. A variety of factors such as low crop prices and high debts dashed farmers' hopes and drove them off the land toward the opportunities that cities seemed to offer.

Major Waves of Migration and Immigration

Such migration affected not only major cities such as Detroit, Chicago, and San Francisco but also secondary cities such as Toledo, Indianapolis, Salt Lake City, Birmingham, and San Diego. The thrill of city life beckoned especially to young people. A character in the play *The City* spoke for many youths when she exclaimed, "Who wants to smell new-mown hay, if he can breathe in gasoline on Fifth Avenue instead! Think of the theaters! The crowds! *Think* of being able to go out on the street and *see some one you didn't know by sight!*"

Many more of the newcomers were immigrants who had fled foreign villages and cities for American shores. The dream of a large number was not to stay but to make enough money to return home and live in greater comfort and security. For every hundred foreigners who entered the country, around thirty left. Still, most of the 26 million immigrants who arrived between 1870 and 1920 and whose numbers peaked between 1900 and 1910 remained, and the great majority settled in cities, where they helped reshape American culture. Antanas Kaztauskis, the Lithuanian stockyards worker, fit this pattern of settlement and adaptation.

Immigrants to the United States participated in a worldwide movement that had two components. One pushed people away from traditional means of support; the other pulled them toward the opportunity for a better life. In many foreign countries, farmers supplemented their incomes by making and selling various products. But as industrialization undercut local crafts like weaving and shoemaking, artisans found it increasingly difficult to sell their wares. In addition, the growth of cities worldwide

Arriving at Ellis Island in New York harbor, perhaps to rejoin her husband, who already had settled in the United States, this woman dressed herself and her children in their best clothes. Relatives and friends often advised immigrants to do everything possible to impress the inspectors who would examine them upon arrival. Brown Brothers.

increased demand for agricultural goods, thereby encouraging large-scale production, which in turn made small farms less profitable. Population pressures and economic changes resulting from land redistribution and industrialization induced millions of small farmers and craftsmen to leave Europe and Asia. They traveled to Canada, Australia, Brazil, Argentina, and other relatively unsettled places, as well as the United States, in search of a better life. Also, religious persecution, particularly the violent pogroms and merciless military conscription that Jews suffered in Russia and Poland, forced people to flee across the Atlantic. Countless others, particularly the poorest peasants, migrated shorter distances in search of better conditions, usually from a rural village to an industrial city. Migration always has been present in human history, but now technology in the form of the telegraph, railroad, and steamship made communications and travel cheaper, quicker, and safer.

Immigrants from northern and western Europe had made the United States their main destination

since the 1840s, but after 1880 economic and demographic changes propelled a second wave of immigrants from other regions. Northern and western Europeans continued to arrive, but the new wave brought more people from eastern and southern Europe, plus smaller contingents from Canada, Mexico, and Japan (see map and figure, page 545). Two-thirds of the newcomers who arrived in the 1880s came from Germany, England, Ireland, and Scandinavia; between 1900 and 1909, two-thirds came from Italy, Austria-Hungary, and Russia.[1] By 1910, arrivals from Mexico were beginning to outnumber arrivals from Ireland, and large numbers of Japanese had moved to the West Coast and Hawai'i. Foreign-born blacks, chiefly from the West Indies, also increased in number. (See the Appendix for the nationalities of immigrants.)

The New Immigration

---

[1]Immigrants from Austria-Hungary and Russia included Poles, Czechs, Slovaks, Serbs, Croats, and Romanians, all of whom could have been Jewish, Catholic, or Greek Orthodox.

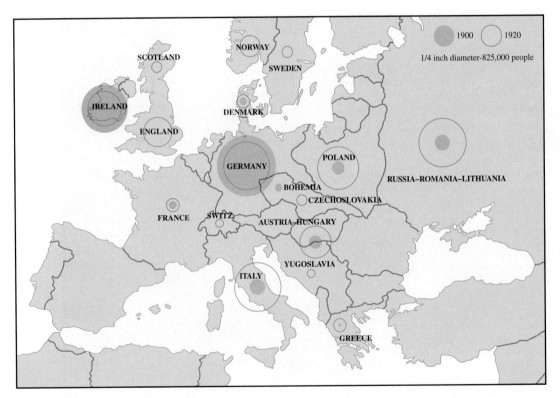

Sources of European-born Population, 1900 and 1920   *In just a few decades, the proportion of European immigrants to the United States who came from northern and western Europe decreased, while the proportion from eastern and southern Europe increased.*

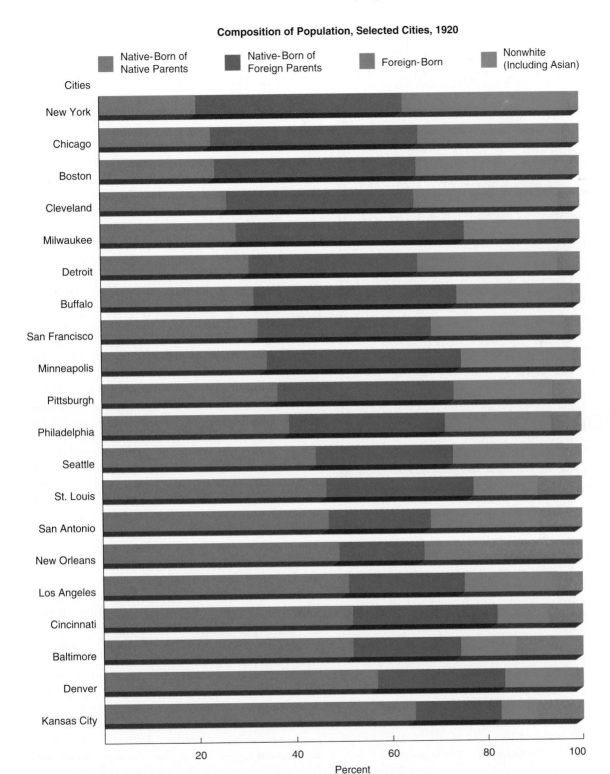

Composition of Population, Selected Cities, 1920

Legend: Native-Born of Native Parents | Native-Born of Foreign Parents | Foreign-Born | Nonwhite (Including Asian)

Cities: New York, Chicago, Boston, Cleveland, Milwaukee, Detroit, Buffalo, San Francisco, Minneapolis, Pittsburgh, Philadelphia, Seattle, St. Louis, San Antonio, New Orleans, Los Angeles, Cincinnati, Baltimore, Denver, Kansas City

Percent: 20, 40, 60, 80, 100

Composition of Population, Selected Cities, 1920 *Immigration and migration made native-born whites of native-born parents minorities in almost every major city by the early twentieth century. Moreover, foreign-born residents and native-born whites of foreign parents (combining the green and purple segments of a line) constituted absolute majorities in numerous places.*

Those who wished to Americanize the immigrants believed the public schools could provide the best setting for assimilation. This 1917 poster from the Cleveland Board of Education and the Cleveland Americanization Committee used the languages most common to the new immigrants—Slovene, Italian, Polish, Hungarian, and Yiddish—as well as English to invite newcomers to free classes where they could learn "the language of America" and "citizenship." National Park Service Collection, Ellis Island Immigration Museum.

The immigrants varied widely in age, marital status, and other characteristics, but certain traits stand out. Approximately two-thirds of the newcomers were males, especially after 1900, and about two-thirds were between the ages of fifteen and thirty-nine. Not all groups were equally educated, but almost three-fourths of the immigrants could read and write, at least in their native languages. Among those reporting occupations at the time of entry, half identified themselves as unskilled laborers or domestic workers (maids, cooks, cleaners). These occupations may have reflected the immigrants' expecta-

tions of how they would be employed in America, but they also suggest that many had lived in cities for at least a short time before emigrating.

In the West, Hispanics, who once had been a predominantly rural population, lived increasingly in cities. They took over ditch-digging and street-grading jobs once held by Chinese laborers who were driven from southern California cities, and in some Texas cities native Mexicans (called Tejanos) held the majority of all unskilled jobs. In places like Los Angeles, males often left for long periods of time to take temporary agricultural jobs, leaving behind many female heads of household.

Many Americans feared the customs, Catholic and Jewish faiths, illiteracy, and poverty of "new" immigrants, considering them less desirable and assimilable than "old" immigrants, whose languages and beliefs seemed less alien. This view received sober support from authorities such as future president Woodrow Wilson, who wrote in his *History of the American People* (1902), "The immigrant newcomers of recent years are men of the lowest class from the South of Italy, and men of the meaner sort out of Hungary and Poland, men out of the ranks where there was neither skill nor energy, nor any initiative or quick intelligence."

In reality, however, old and new immigrants closely resembled each other. The majority of both groups came from societies which made the family the focus of all undertakings. Whether and when to emigrate was decided in light of the family's needs, and family bonds continued to prevail after immigrants reached the New World. New arrivals usually knew where they wanted to go and how to get there because they received aid from relatives who had already immigrated. In many instances, workers helped kin obtain jobs, and family members pooled their resources to maintain, if not improve, their standard of living. The bywords for all immigrants were "cooperate and survive."

All immigrants adjusted to American life guided by the light of memories they brought from their homelands. In their new surroundings—where the language was a struggle, the workday followed the clock rather than the sun, and housing and employment often were uncertain—immigrants anchored their lives to the rock they knew best: their culture. Old World customs persisted in immigrant enclaves of Italians from the same province, Japanese from the same island district, or Russian Jews from the

Immigrant Cultures

same *shtetl* (village). Fraternal societies were re-created along village and provincial lines. For example, Japanese transferred their *ken* societies, which organized social celebrations and relief services, and Chinese from Canton brought *hui* institutions, which raised money to help members acquire businesses. People practiced religion as they always had, held traditional feasts and pageants, married within their group, and pursued old feuds with people from rival villages. Among Jews from eastern Europe, men grew long sidelocks, women wore wigs, and children attended afternoon religious training.

Southern Italians transplanted the system whereby a boss, or *padrone*, found jobs for unskilled workers by negotiating with an employer. Italians also re-created their Old World mutual benefit associations to provide families emergency aid as well as sickness and death benefits. Pasquale Cruci, an immigrant from Salerno, explained that he helped to found such an association in Bridgeport, Connecticut, because "I felt that the Italian people of this city should have some security from death and accidents. The Italian people of this time didn't trust the big insurance companies because they thought they would get cheated. They felt that if some organization was Italian that it was all right."

Yet, as Antanas Katzauskis discovered, the very diversity of American cities forced immigrants to modify their attitudes and habits. Few newcomers could avoid contact with people different from themselves, and few could prevent such contacts from altering their traditional ways of life. Although many foreigners identified themselves by their village or region of birth, native-born Americans categorized them by nationality. People from County Cork and County Limerick were lumped together as Irish; those from Schleswig and Württemberg were Germans; those from Calabria and Campobasso were Italians. Immigrant institutions, such as newspapers and churches, found they had to appeal to the entire nationality in order to survive.

Everywhere, Old World culture mingled with New World realities. Immigrants struggled to maintain their native languages and to pass them down to younger generations. But English was taught in the schools and needed on the job, and it soon penetrated nearly every community. Foreigners cooked ethnic meals using American foods and fashioned European clothes from American fabrics. Italians went to American doctors but still carried traditional amulets to ward off evil spirits. Chinese expanded their traditional gambling games to include poker.

Music especially revealed adaptations. Polka bands entertained at Polish social gatherings, but their repertoires expanded to blend American and Polish folk music; once dominated by violins, the bands added accordions, clarinets, and trumpets so they could play more loudly. Mexican ballads acquired new themes that described the adventures of border crossing and the hardship of labor in the United States.

Eventually most immigrants grew accustomed to trusting American institutions. An Italian woman in Bridgeport, Connecticut, admitted "that time [previously] they had all the societies that give you the money if you die, and that's . . . why all the women they were belonging to these societies. . . . Now they don't do this so much, they get the insurance from the Metropolitan and the other companies. . . . Now us Italian people we are more 'Americanizzata.'"

The inflow of so many immigrants between 1870 and 1920 transformed the United States from a basically Protestant nation into one composed of Protestants, Catholics, and Jews.

Influence on Religion

Newcomers from Italy, Hungary, Poland, and Slovakia joined Irish and Germans to boost the proportion of Catholics in many cities. In Buffalo, Cleveland, Chicago, and Milwaukee, Catholic immigrants and their offspring approached a majority of the population. Catholic Mexicans constituted over half of the population of El Paso. German and Russian immigrants gave New York one of the largest Jewish populations in the world.

Partly in response to Protestant charges that they could not retain Old World religious beliefs and still assimilate into American society, many Catholics and Jews tried to accommodate their faiths to the new environment. Some Catholic and Jewish leaders from more established immigrant groups supported liberalizing trends—the use of English in sermons, the phasing-out of Old World rituals such as saints' feasts, and a preference for public over religious schools. As long as new immigrants continued to arrive, however, these tendencies met stiff opposition.

Newcomers usually sought to retain familiar practices, whether the folk Catholicism of southern Italy or the orthodox Judaism of eastern Europe. Catholic immigrants requested ethnically separate parishes in spite of church attempts to make American Catholicism more uniform. Bishops acceded to pressures from predominantly Polish congregations for Polish- rather than German-born priests. Eastern European Jews, convinced that Reform Judaism sacrificed too much to American ways, established the Conservative branch, which retained traditional ritual, though it abolished the segregation of women in synagogues and allowed English prayers.

In the 1880s, another group of migrants began to enter American cities. Thousands of rural African-Americans moved northward and westward, seeking better employment and fleeing crop liens, the ravages of the boll weevil on cotton crops, racial violence, and political oppression. Though black urban dwellers grew more numerous after 1915, thirty-two cities already had more than ten thousand black residents by 1900, and 79 percent of all blacks outside the South lived in cities. These migrants resembled foreign immigrants in their rural backgrounds and economic motivations, but they differed in several important ways. Because few factories would employ African-Americans, most found jobs in the service sector—cleaning, cooking, and driving—rather than in the industrial trades. Also, because most service openings were traditionally female jobs, black women outnumbered black men in cities such as New York, Baltimore, and New Orleans.

African-American Migration to the Cities

Each of the three major migrant groups that peopled American cities—native-born whites, foreigners of various races, and native-born blacks—helped create modern American culture. The cities nurtured rich cultural variety: American folk music and literature, Italian and Mexican cuisine, Irish comedy, Yiddish theater, African-American jazz and dance, and much more. Like their predecessors, newcomers in the late nineteenth century changed their environment as much as they were changed by it.

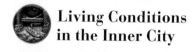

Living Conditions in the Inner City

Urban population growth created intense pressures on the public and private sectors. The masses of people who jammed inner-city districts were recognized more for the problems they bred than for their cultural contributions. American cities seemed to harbor all the afflictions that plague modern society: poverty, disease, crime, and other unpleasant conditions that occur when large numbers of people live close together. City dwellers adjusted as best they could. Although technology, science, private enterprise, and public authority could not solve every problem, city officials and engineers achieved some remarkable successes. In the late nineteenth and early twentieth centuries, construction of buildings, homes, streets, sewers, and schools proceeded at a furious pace. American cities set world standards for fire protection and water purification. But many problems still await solution.

One of the most persistent shortcomings—the failure to provide adequate housing for all who need it—has its roots in nineteenth-century urban development. In spite of massive construction in the 1880s and early 1900s, population growth outpaced housing supplies. The scarcity of inexpensive housing especially afflicted working-class families who, because of low wages, had to rent their living quarters. As cities grew, landlords took advantage of shortages in low-cost rental housing by splitting up existing buildings to house more people, constructing multiple-unit tenements, and hiking rents. Low-income families adapted to high costs and short supply by sharing space and expenses. Thus it became common in many big cities for a "one-family" apartment to be occupied by two or three families or by a single family plus several boarders.

Housing Problems

The result was unprecedented crowding. In 1890, New York City's immigrant-packed Lower East Side averaged 702 people per acre, one of the highest population densities in the world. Low-rent districts had distinctive physical appearances in different cities: six- to eight-story barracks-like buildings in New York; dilapidated row houses in Baltimore and Philadelphia; converted slave quarters in Charleston and New Orleans; and crumbling two- and three-story frame houses in Seattle and San Francisco.

Inside many buildings, living conditions were harsh. The largest rooms were barely ten feet wide, and interior rooms either lacked windows or opened onto narrow shafts that bred vermin and rotten odors. Describing such a shaft, one immigrant housekeeper said, "It's damp down there, and the families, they throw out garbage and dirty papers and the insides of chickens, and other unmentionable filth. . . . I just vomited when I first cleaned up the air shaft." Few buildings had indoor plumbing,

Inner-city dwellers used not only indoor space as efficiently as possible but also what little outdoor space was available to them. Scores of families living in this cramped block of six-story tenements in New York strung clotheslines behind the buildings. Notice that there is virtually no space between buildings, so only rooms at the front and back received daylight and fresh air.   Library of Congress.

and the only source of heat was dangerous, polluting coal-burning stoves.

Housing problems aroused reform campaigns in several places. New York State took the lead by legislating light, ventilation, and safety codes for new tenement buildings in 1867, 1879, and 1901. These and similar laws in other states could not remedy the ills of existing buildings, but they did impose minimal obligations on landlords. A few reformers, such as journalist Jacob Riis and humanitarian Lawrence Veiller, advocated housing low-income families in "model tenements," with more spacious rooms and better facilities. Model tenements, however, required landlords to accept lower profits—a sacrifice few were willing to make. Neither reformers nor public officials would consider government financing of better housing, fearing that such a step would undermine private enterprise. Still, the new housing

Housing Reform

codes and regulatory commissions strengthened the power of local government to oversee construction.

Reformers' earnest concern for the lives of inner-city residents gradually made a difference. As Veiller urged, "We must stop people living in cellars before we concern ourselves with changes in methods of taxation. We must make it impossible for builders to build dark rooms in new houses before we urge the government to subsidize the building of houses. We must abolish privy vaults [latrines] before we build model tenements."

Housing reforms had only limited success, but scientific and technological advances eventually enabled city dwellers and the entire nation to live in greater comfort and safety. By the 1880s, most doctors had accepted the theory that microorganisms (germs) cause disease. In response, cities established more efficient systems of water purification and sewage disposal. Although disease and death rates remained higher in cities than in the countryside,

How do historians know the biases of reformers? *Jacob Riis was a journalist who wrote* How the Other Half Lives *(1890), a landmark investigation of slum life in New York City. He was one of the first to use the camera as a reform tool, supplementing his accounts of poverty and crowding with moving photographs of poor people (mostly immigrants) and their surroundings. For many readers, these photographs provided what one reformer called "added realism" and "an inherent attraction not found in other forms of illustration." But is a photograph always completely "real"? This one taken by Riis shows three "street arabs," homeless boys living and sleeping out-* doors away from adult care. What emotions does it raise? The picture looks unposed, but how can the viewer be sure? The nature of photography in 1890 was such that a photographer had to induce his subjects to remain motionless for thirty seconds or more in order for their image to be fixed on film. Do the boys in this photo seem to be posing? Did Riis exaggerate their plight by perhaps asking them to huddle together and remove their shoes? As is the case with other kinds of evidence, historians must use "realistic" photography carefully and look beyond the image to find out what biases it might represent. Museum of the City of New York, the Jacob Riis Collection.

and tuberculosis and other respiratory ills continued to plague inner-city districts, public health regulations helped to control dread diseases such as cholera, typhoid fever, and diphtheria.

Meanwhile, street paving, modernized firefighting equipment, and electric street lighting spread rapidly across urban America. Steel-frame construc-tion, which supports a building with a metal skeleton rather than with masonry walls, made possible the erection of skyscrapers—and thus more efficient use of scarce and costly urban land. Electric elevators and steam-heating systems serviced these buildings. Steel-cable suspension bridges, developed by John A. Roebling and epitomized by the great Brooklyn

Bridge (completed in 1883), linked metropolitan sections more closely.

None of these improvements, however, lightened the burden of poverty. The urban economy, though generally expanding, advanced erratically.

Urban Poverty

Employment, especially for unskilled workers in manufacturing and construction, rose and fell with business cycles and changing seasons. An ever-increasing number of families lived on the margins of survival.

Since colonial days, Americans have disagreed about how much responsibility the public should assume for poor relief. According to traditional beliefs, still widespread in the late nineteenth and early twentieth centuries, anyone could escape poverty through hard work and clean living; poverty existed only because some people were morally weaker than others. Such reasoning bred fear that aid to poor people would encourage paupers to rely on public relief rather than their own efforts. As poverty increased, this attitude hardened, and city governments discontinued direct grants of food, fuel, and clothing to needy families. Instead, cities provided relief in return for work on public projects and sent special cases to state-run almshouses, orphanages, and homes for the blind, deaf, and mentally ill.

Efforts to professionalize relief fostered some change in attitude. Between 1877 and 1892, philanthropists in ninety-two cities formed Charity Organization Societies, an attempt to put social welfare on a systematic basis by merging disparate charity groups into a coordinated unit. Believing poverty to be caused by personal defects like alcoholism and laziness, members of these organizations spent most of their time visiting poor families and encouraging them to be thriftier and more virtuous.

Close observation of the poor, however, prompted some humanitarians to conclude that people's environments, not their personal shortcomings, caused poverty. In turn, they came to believe that poverty could be prevented and eliminated by improving housing, education, sanitation, and job opportunities rather than admonishing the poor to be more moral. This attitude, which had been gaining ground since the mid-nineteenth century, supported drives for building codes, factory regulations, and public health measures. Still, most middle- and upper-class Americans continued to endorse the creed that in a society of abundance only the unfit were poor and that poverty relief should be tolerated but never encouraged. As one charity worker put it, relief "should be surrounded by circumstances that shall . . . repel every one . . . from accepting it."

More than crowding and pauperism, crime and disorder nurtured fears that urban growth, especially the slums, threatened the nation. The more cities grew, it seemed, the more they shook with violence. While homicide rates declined in industrialized nations such as England and Germany, those in America rose alarmingly: 25 murders per million people in 1881; 107 per million in 1898. Pickpockets, swindlers, and burglars roamed every city. Some acquired as much notoriety as western desperadoes. One infamous urban outlaw was Rufus Minor, alias Rufus Pine. Short, stocky, and bald, Minor resembled a shy clerk, but one police chief labeled him "one of the smartest bank sneaks in America." A sometime associate of Billy "The Kid" Burke, Minor often grew a heavy beard before holding up a bank, then shaved afterward to avoid identification by eyewitnesses to the robbery. Minor was implicated in bank heists in New York City, Cleveland, Detroit, Providence, Philadelphia, Albany, Boston, and Baltimore—all between 1878 and 1882.

Crime and Violence

Despite fears of increasing robberies and violence, urban crime may simply have become more conspicuous and sensational, rather than more prevalent. To be sure, concentrations of wealth and the mingling of different peoples provided new opportunities for larceny, vice, and violence. But urban lawlessness and brutality probably did not exceed that of backwoods mining camps and southern plantations. Anxious natives were quick to blame Irish bank robbers, German pickpockets, and Italian Black Hand murderers for urban disorder, but there is little evidence that more immigrant than native-born Americans populated the rogues' gallery. One investigation of jails in 1900 concluded that "we have ourselves evolved as cruel and cunning criminals as any that Europe may have foisted upon us."

Whatever the extent of criminality, city life in this period supports the thesis that the United States has a tradition of violence. Cities served as arenas for many of the era's worst riots. Violent labor unrest became, in the words of one observer, "a sort of natural and inevitable concomitant" to the uncertainties of industrialization. Ethnic and racial minorities were often victims of violent bigotry that lurked beneath the American myth of equality. The cityward movement of African-Americans roused white fears, and as the twentieth century dawned, a series of race riots spread across the nation: Wilmington, North Carolina, 1898; Atlanta, Georgia, 1906; Springfield, Illinois, 1908. In cities of the Southwest and Pacific coast, Chinese and Mexican immigrants often felt the sting of intolerance. And innumerable disruptions ranging from domestic violence to muggings to gang fights made cities scenes of constant turbulence.

Since the mid-nineteenth century, city dwellers had gradually overcome their resistance to professional law enforcement and increasingly depended on the police to protect life and property. By the early 1900s, however, law enforcement had become complicated and controversial because various groups differed in their views of the law and how it should be enforced. Disadvantaged groups—notably ethnic and racial minorities—could not escape arrest as easily as those with economic or political influence. And police officers applied the law less harshly to members of their own ethnic groups and to people who bought exemptions with bribes.

Role of the Police

As the chief urban law-enforcers, the police were often caught between pressures for swift and severe action on the one hand and leniency on the other. Some people clamored for crackdowns on drinking, gambling, and prostitution at the same time that others privately supported loose law enforcement so they could indulge in these so-called customer crimes. As urban American society diversified, different groups tried to protect their particular interests—such as keeping saloons open late at night, indulging in social gambling, or even applying their own notions of law and order. Achieving a balance between the idealistic intentions of criminal law and people's desire for individual freedom grew increasingly difficult, and it has remained so to this day.

The mounting problems of city life seemed to demand greater government action. Thus city governments passed more ordinances that regulated housing, provided poverty relief, and expanded police power to protect health and safety. Yet public responsibility mostly ended at the boundaries of private property. Eventually advances in housing construction, sanitation, and medical care reached slum dwellers. But for most people, the only hope was that their children would do better or that opportunities would be better somewhere else.

 Family Life

Although the overwhelming majority of Americans continued to live within families, this most basic of social institutions suffered strain during the era of urbanization and industrialization. New institutions—schools, social clubs, political organizations, and others—increasingly competed with the family to provide nurture, education, and security. Observers warned that rising divorce rates, the growing separation between home and work, the entrance of numerous women into the work force, and loss of parental control over children spelled peril for home and family. Yet the family retained its fundamental role as a cushion in a hard, uncertain world.

Throughout modern Western history, most people have lived in two overlapping social units: household and family. A *household* is a group of people, related or unrelated, who share the same residence. A *family* is a group related by kinship, some members of which typically live together. In the late nineteenth and early twentieth centuries, different patterns characterized the two institutions.

Family and Household Structures

The vast majority of households (75 to 80 percent) consisted of *nuclear families*—usually a married couple, with or without children. About 15 to 20 percent of households consisted of *extended families*—usually a married couple, with or without children, plus one or more relatives such as parents, adult siblings, grandchildren, aunts, and uncles. About 5 percent of households consisted of people living alone. Despite slight variations among ethnic, racial, and socioeconomic groups, this pattern held relatively constant.

Several factors explain this pattern. Because immigrants tended to be young, the United States population as a whole was young. In 1880 the median age was under twenty-one, and by 1920 it was still only twenty-five. (Median age at present is over thirty.) Moreover, in 1900 the death rate among people aged forty-five to sixty-four was over twice what it is today. As a result, there were relatively few older people: only 4 percent of the population was sixty-five or older, compared with about 15 percent today. Thus few families could form extended three-generation households. Fewer children than today knew their grandparents, and the experience of be-

Family life provided stability in an age of change, though its activities often were romanticized. Here, parents and children in a middle-class home in Natchez, Mississippi, pose happily amid the comforts of home, including gaslight, an oil lamp, and coal-stove heat.   Collection of Joan W. Gandy and Thomas H. Gandy.

ing a grandparent was rarer. Migration separated many families, and the ideal of a home of one's own encouraged nuclear household organization.

The average size of nuclear families did change over time, though. Most of Europe and North America experienced a fall in birth rates in the nine-

Declining Birth Rates

teenth century. The decline began early in the 1800s in the United States and accelerated toward the end of the century. In 1880 the birth rate was 40 live births per 1,000 people; by 1900 it had dropped to 32; by 1920 to 28. Several factors explain this decline.

First, the United States was becoming an urban nation, and birth rates are generally lower in cities than in rural areas. On farms, where children worked at home or in the fields at an early age, each child born represented a new set of hands for the family work force. In the wage-based urban economy, children could not contribute significantly to the family income for many years, and a new child simply represented another mouth to feed. Second,

infant mortality fell as diet and medical care improved, and families did not have to bear many children just to ensure that some would survive. Third, awareness that smaller families meant an improved quality of life seems to have stimulated decisions to limit family size—either by abstaining from sex during the wife's fertile period or by using contraception and abortion. Although fertility was consistently higher among blacks, immigrants, and rural people than among white native-born city dwellers, birth rates of all groups fell. As a result, families with six or eight children became rare; three or four became more usual. Thus the nuclear family tended to reach its maximum size and then shrink faster than in earlier eras.

The household tended to expand and contract over the lifetime of a given family. Family size grew as children were born. Later, especially in working-

Boarding

class families, it shrank as children of both sexes left home before they were twenty years old, usually to work. The process of leaving home also changed households; huge numbers of young people—and some older people—lived as boarders and lodgers, especially in cities. Middle- and working-class families commonly took in boarders to occupy rooms vacated by grown children and to help pay expenses. Immigrants such as Antanas Katzauskis, often lodged newly arrived relatives and fellow villagers until they could establish themselves. Historians have estimated that at the end of the nineteenth century 50 percent of city residents had lived either as, or with, boarders at some point during their lifetime. Housing reformers charged that boarding caused overcrowding and loss of privacy. Yet for those who boarded or took in boarders, the practice was highly useful. One immigrant woman recalled:

> We had four boarders and I had to cook for them. When I first came here I didn't want to do this because everybody want to have their own house. Well, I change my mind because everybody was doing this thing. That time some of the people that came from the other side didn't have no place to stay and we took some of the people in the house that we knew. . . . This is the way that everybody used to do it that time.

For people on the move, boarding was a transitional stage, providing them with a quasi-family environment until they set up their own households. Also, growing numbers of young people lived independently, away from any family. The "efficiency apartment"—one room with a disappearing or folding bed and collapsible furniture—originated in San Francisco around 1900 to house such people and quickly spread eastward.

Some households took in extended-family members who lived as quasi-boarders. Especially in communities where economic hardship or rapid growth made housing expensive or scarce, newlyweds sometimes lived temporarily with one spouse's parents. Families also took in widowed parents or unmarried siblings who otherwise would have lived alone.

For immigrants and migrants, the family served as a refuge in a strange new place. Having moved from Old World to New, or from one region to another, they sought out relatives who had preceded them. A Russian woman prepared for emigration by writing to relatives in New York: "When I came off the ship, an uncle of mine was supposed to pick me up. . . . But I didn't live with this uncle because I had my mother's sister so I stayed with her."

At a time when welfare agencies were rare, the family was the institution to which people could turn in times of need. Even when relatives did not live together, they often lived nearby and aided each other with childcare, meals, shopping, advice, and consolation. They also obtained jobs for each other. Factory foremen who had responsibility for hiring often recruited new workers recommended by their employees. According to one new arrival, "After two days my brother took me to the shop he was working in and his boss saw me and he gave me the job." A woman who worked in an optical factory recalled, "My uncle was foreman there. . . . That was my first job. I worked there with my mother. . . . My sister worked there a while too."

Importance of Kinship

But obligations of kinship were not always welcome. Immigrant families often put pressure on last-born children to stay at home to care for aging parents, a practice that stifled opportunities for education, marriage, and economic independence. As an aging Italian-American father confessed, "One of our daughters is an old maid [and] causes plenty of troubles. . . . It may be my fault because I always wished her to remain at home and not to marry for she was of great financial help." Tensions also developed when one relative felt that another was not helping out enough. One woman, for example, complained that her brother-in-law "resented the fact that I saved my money in a bank instead of handing it over to him." Nevertheless, for better or worse, kinship provided people a means of coping with the stresses caused by an urban-industrial society. Social and economic change did not burst family ties.

Large numbers of city dwellers lived beyond the haven of traditional family relationships, however. In 1890, almost 42 percent of all American men and 37 percent of women aged fifteen and older were single, the highest these proportions ever have been. About half of them still lived in their parents' household, but many others inhabited boarding houses or rooms in the homes of strangers. Mostly young, these men and women constituted a separate subculture that helped support institutions like dance halls, saloons, cafés, and the YMCA and YWCA.

Some of these unmarried people also numbered among the homosexual population that thrived especially in large cities like New York and Boston. Though their numbers are difficult to estimate, gay men and women had their own subculture complete with clubs, restaurants, coffeehouses, theaters, and support networks. A number of gay couples formed lasting marriage-type relationships (sometimes called "Boston marriages" when they involved middle-class women); others "cruised" in the sexual underground of the streets and bars. People in the gay subculture were categorized more by how they acted—men acting like women, women acting like men—than by who their sexual partners were, and thus the term *homosexual* was not used. For example, men who dressed and acted like women were called "fairies," and men who displayed masculine traits could be termed "normal" even though they might have sexual relations with fairies. The gay world, then, was a complex one that included a variety of relationships and institutions.

Although the family remained resilient and adaptable, subtle but momentous changes began to occur in individual life patterns. Before the twentieth century, stages of life were less distinct than they are today, and generations blended into each other with relatively little differentiation. Childhood, for instance, was regarded as a period during which young people prepared for adulthood by gradually assuming more adult roles and responsibilities. The subdivisions of youth—toddlers, schoolchildren, adolescents, and the like—were not considered or defined. Married couples had more children over a longer time span than is common in the twentieth century, so active parenthood occupied most of their adult lives. Older children, who often cared for younger sisters and brothers, might begin parenting even before reaching adulthood. And because relatively few people lived beyond age sixty-five or seventy or left work voluntarily, and because homes for the elderly were rare, older people were not isolated from other age groups.

Stages of Life

By the turn of the century, demographic and social changes had altered these patterns. Decreasing birth rates shortened the period of parental responsibility, so more middle-age couples experienced an empty-nest stage when all their children grew up and left home. Longer life expectancy and a tendency by employers to force aged workers to retire separated the old from the young. At the same time, work became more specialized and education in graded schools more formalized, especially after states passed compulsory school-attendance laws in the 1870s and 1880s. Childhood and adolescence became more distinct from adulthood. As a result of these and other trends (including the lower birth rate, which gave people fewer sisters and brothers to relate to), Americans became more conscious of age

and peers. People's roles in school, in the family, on the job, and in the community came to be defined by age more than by any other characteristic.

Thus by the early 1900s, family life and functions were both changing and holding firm. New institutions were assuming tasks formerly performed by the family. Schools were making education a community responsibility. Employment agencies, personnel offices, labor unions, and legislatures were taking responsibility for employee recruitment and job security. Age-based peer groups were exerting greater influence over people's values and activities. In addition, migration and a soaring divorce rate seemed to be splitting families apart: 19,633 divorces were granted nationwide in 1880; by 1920, that number had reached 167,105. Popular and scholarly writers predicted the decline of the family, just as they do today. Yet in the face of these pressures, the family adjusted by expanding and contracting to meet temporary needs, and kinship remained a dependable though not always appreciated institution. For the majority of people, family life was vital. "As I grew up, living conditions were a bit crowded," one woman reminisced, "but no one minded because we were a family . . . thankful we all lived together."

The New Leisure and Mass Culture

On December 2, 1889, as hundreds of workers paraded through Worcester, Massachusetts, in support of shorter working hours, a group of carpenters hoisted a banner proclaiming "Eight Hours for Work, Eight Hours for Rest, Eight Hours for What We Will." The phrase "for What We Will" was significant, for it laid claim to a special segment of daily life that belonged to the individual. Increasingly, among all social classes, leisure activities filled this time segment.

American inventors had long tried to create labor-saving devices, but not until the late 1800s did technological development become truly time-saving. Mechanization and assembly-line production not only replaced skilled work but also helped to cut the average workweek in manufacturing from sixty-six hours in 1860 to sixty in 1890 and forty-seven in 1920. These reductions meant shorter workdays and freer weekends. White-collar workers

Increase in Leisure Time

spent from eight to ten hours a day on the job and often worked only half a day or not at all on weekends. To be sure, thousands still spent twelve- or fourteen-hour shifts in steel mills and sweatshops and had no time or energy for leisure. But as the old work ethic eroded and the nation's economy shifted from one of scarcity and production to one of surplus and consumption, more Americans began to partake of a variety of diversions, and a substantial segment of the economy began providing for—and profiting from—leisure. By the early 1900s, many Americans were enmeshed in the business of play.

After the Civil War, amusement became an organized, commercial activity. There was an expansion in the production of games, toys, and musical instruments for indoor, family amusement. Board games such as checkers and backgammon had existed for decades, but improvements in printing and paper production and the rise of new manufacturers such as Milton Bradley and Parker Brothers increased the popularity of board games markedly. Significantly, the content of board games shifted from moral lessons to topics involving transportation, finance, and sports. By the 1890s, mass production of pianos and other instruments plus the widespread circulation of sheet music made the singing of popular songs a favored form of family entertainment.

The vanguard of new leisure pursuits, however, was sports. Formerly a fashionable indulgence of the genteel class, organized sports quickly became the most popular pastime of all classes, attracting huge numbers of participants and spectators. Even those who could not play or watch became involved by reading about sports in the newspapers.

The most popular organized sport was baseball. An outgrowth of older bat, ball, and base-circling games, baseball was formalized in 1845 by a group of wealthy New Yorkers—the Knickerbocker Club—who codified the rules of play. By 1860 at least fifty baseball clubs existed, and informal games were being played on city lots and rural fields across the nation. In 1869 a professional club, the Cincinnati Red Stockings, went on a national tour, and other clubs quickly followed suit. The National League of Professional Baseball Clubs, founded in 1876, gave the sport a stable, businesslike structure. Not all athletes could benefit; as early as 1867, a "color line" excluded black players from professional teams. Nevertheless, by the 1880s, professional baseball was a big business. In 1903, the

Baseball

National League and competing American League (formed in 1901) began a World Series between their championship teams, entrenching baseball as the national pastime. The Boston Red Socks beat the Pittsburgh Pirates in that first series.

Baseball appealed mostly to men. But croquet, which also swept the nation, attracted both sexes. Middle- and upper-class people held croquet parties and even outfitted wickets with candles for night games. In an era when the departure of paid work from the home had separated men's from women's spheres, croquet increased opportunities for social contact between the sexes.

Croquet and Cycling

Meanwhile, bicycling achieved popularity rivaling that of baseball, especially after 1885, when the cumbersome velocipede, with its huge front wheel and tall seat, gave way to the safety bicycle with pneumatic tires and wheels of identical size. By 1900 Americans owned over 10 million bicycles, and clubs like the League of American Wheelmen were pressing state governments to build more paved roads. One journal boasted that cycling cured dyspepsia, headaches, insomnia, and sciatica and gave "a vigorous tone to the whole system." Professional bicycle races brought success to racers such as Major Taylor, an African-American who won fame in Europe and the United States. Like croquet, cycling brought men and women together, combining opportunities for courtship and exercise. Moreover, the bicycle played an influential role in freeing women from the constraints of Victorian fashions. In order to ride the dropped-frame female models, women had to wear divided skirts and simple undergarments. Gradually, freer styles of cycling costumes began to influence everyday fashions. As the 1900 census declared, "Few articles . . . have created so great a revolution in social conditions as the bicycle."

Other sports had their own supporters. Tennis and golf attracted both sexes but remained pastimes of the wealthy. Played mostly at private clubs, these sports lacked baseball's team competition and cycling's informality. American football also began as a sport for people of high social rank. As an intercollegiate sport, football attracted players and spectators wealthy enough to have access to higher education. By the end of the century, however, the game was appealing to a broader audience. The 1893 Princeton-Yale game

Football

drew fifty thousand spectators, and informal games were being played in yards and playgrounds throughout the country.

At the same time, college football became a national scandal because of its violence and use of "tramp athletes," nonstudents whom colleges hired to help their teams win. Critics charged that football mirrored the worst features of American society. An editor of *The Nation* charged in 1890 that "the spirit of the American Youth, as of the American man, is to win, to 'get there,' by fair means or foul; and the lack of moral scruple which pervades the struggles of the business world meets with temptations equally irresistible in the miniature contests of the football field."

The scandals climaxed in 1905, when 18 players died from game-related injuries and over 150 were seriously injured. President Theodore Roosevelt, a strong advocate of athletics, convened a White House conference to discuss ways to eliminate brutality and foul play. The conference founded the Intercollegiate Athletic Association (renamed the National College Athletic Association in 1910) to police college sports. In 1906 the association altered the games to make football less violent and more open. New rules outlawed "flying wedge" rushes, extended from five to ten yards the distance needed to earn a first down, legalized the forward pass, and tightened player eligibility requirements.

As more women enrolled in college, they began to pursue physical activities besides croquet, horseback riding, and cycling. Believing that to succeed intellectually they needed to be active and healthy, college women participated in sports such as rowing, track, and swimming. Eventually basketball became the most popular sport among college women. Invented in 1891 as a winter sport for men, basketball was given women's rules (which limited dribbling and running and encouraged passing) by Senda Berenson of Smith College in the 1890s, and intercollegiate games became common.

Paralleling the rise of sports, American show business also became a mode of leisure created by and for common people. Circuses—traveling shows of acrobats and animals—had existed since the 1820s. But after the Civil War, railroads enabled them to reach more of the country. Circuses offered two main attractions: so-called freaks of nature, both human and animal, and the temptation and conquest of death. At the heart of their appeal was the sheer astonishment that trapeze

Circuses

While baseball, football, boxing, and racing became popular sports for men, basketball became the most appealing sport for women, especially those in college. Special rules established in 1897 lessened the supposed dangers of rough, vigorous play by limiting the number of dribbles, confining players to particular zones on the court, and encouraging passing.   Collection of Sally Fox.

artists, lion tamers, acrobats, and clowns aroused. Writer Hamlin Garland captured the circus's effect on a community:

> From the time the "advance man" flung his highly colored posters over the fence till the coming of the glorious day, we thought of little else. . . . It was our brief season of imaginative life. In one day—in a part of one day—we gained a thousand new conceptions of the world and of human nature. It was the embodiment of all that was skillful and beautiful in human action. . . . It gave us something to talk about.

Three branches of American show business matured with the growth of cities. Popular drama, musical comedy, and vaudeville offered audiences a chance to escape the harshness of urban-industrial life into melodrama, adventure, and comedy. The plots were simple, the heroes and villains recognizable. For urbanized people increasingly distant from the frontier, popular plays brought to life the mythical Wild West and Old South through stories of Davy Crockett, Buffalo Bill, and Civil War romances. Virtue, honor, and justice always triumphed in melodramas like *Uncle Tom's Cabin* and *The Old Homestead*, reinforcing popular faith that even in an uncertain and disillusioning world, goodness would prevail.

Popular Drama and Musical Comedy

Musical comedies raised audiences' spirits with song, humor, and dance. American musical comedy grew out of the lavishly costumed operettas common in Europe. By introducing American themes (often involving ethnic groups), folksy humor, and catchy tunes, these shows launched the nation's most popular songs and entertainers. George M. Cohan, a spirited singer, dancer, and songwriter born into an Irish family of entertainers, became the master of American musical comedy after the turn of the century. Drawing on urbanism, patriotism, and traditional values in songs like "Yankee Doodle Boy" and "You're a Grand Old Flag," Cohan helped bolster national morale during the First World War. Comic opera, too, became popular, and the talented, beautiful Lillian Russell was its most admired performer. The first American comic operas imitated European musicals, but by the early 1900s composers like Victor Herbert were writing for American audiences. Shortly thereafter Jerome Kern began to write more sophisticated musicals, and American musical comedy came into its own.

Because of its variety, vaudeville was probably the most popular entertainment in early-twentieth-century America. Shows included, in rapid succession, acts such as jugglers, dancing bears, pantomimists, storytellers, magicians, puppeteers, acrobats, comedians, and, of course, singers and dancers. Around 1900, the number of vaudeville theaters and troupes skyrocketed. Aided by sharp entrepreneurs who did for entertainment what Edison and Ford did for technology, vaudeville quickly became big business. Its most famous promoter, Florenz Ziegfeld, brilliantly packaged shows in a stylish format—the Ziegfeld Follies—and gave the nation a new model

Vaudeville

of femininity, the Ziegfeld Girl, whose graceful dancing and alluring costumes suggested a haunting sensuality.

Show business provided new economic opportunities for women, African-Americans, and immigrants, but it also encouraged stereotyping and exploitation. Lillian Russell, vaudeville singer and comedienne Fanny Brice, and burlesque queen Eva Tanguay attracted intensely loyal fans, commanded handsome fees, and won respect for their genuine talents. In contrast to the demure Victorian female, they conveyed pluck and creativity. There was something both shocking and refreshingly confident about Eva Tanguay when she sang earthy songs like "I Want Someone to Go Wild with Me," "It's All Been Done Before but Not the Way I Do It," and her theme song, "I Don't Care." But lesser female performers were often exploited by male promoters and theater owners, many of whom wanted only to titillate the public with the sight of scantily clad women.

Before the 1890s, the chief form of commercial entertainment open to African-American performers was the minstrel show. By century's end, however, minstrel shows had given way to more sophisticated musicals, and blacks had begun to break into vaudeville. As stage settings shifted from the plantation to the city, music shifted from folk tunes to ragtime. Pandering to the prejudices of white audiences, composers and performers of both races ridiculed blacks. As songs like "He's Just a Little Nigger, but He's Mine All Mine," and "You May Be a Hawaiian on Old Broadway, but You're Just Another Nigger to Me" confirm, blacks on the stage suffered much as they did in society at large. Even Burt Williams, a talented and highly paid black comedian and dancer who achieved success by playing the stereotypical roles of darky and dandy, was tormented by the humiliation he had to suffer.

African-Americans and Immigrants in Vaudeville

Much of the uniqueness of American mass entertainment arose from its ethnic flavor. Indeed, immigrants occupied the core of American show business. Vaudeville in particular utilized ethnic humor, exaggerating dialects and other national traits. Skits and songs reinforced ethnic stereotypes and made fun of ethnic groups, but such distortions were more self-conscious and sympathetic than those directed at blacks. Ethnic humor often focused on everyday difficulties that immigrants faced. A typical scene

This painting (1912) by Everett Shinn indicates the ornate style of the popular American vaudeville show of the early twentieth century. The entertainment industry provided new employment opportunities for women but also exploited their sex appeal. Notice the performer's coquettish pose and, provocative for the time, exposed leg and ankle. Collecton of Mr. Arthur G. Altschul.

involving Italians, for example, revolved around a character's uncertain grasp of English, which caused him to confuse *mayor* with *mare*, *diploma* with *the plumber*, and *pallbearer* with *polar bear*. Other routines depicted common experiences at a doctor's office or department store:

> Doctor: Do you have insurance?
>
> Patient: I ain't got one nickel insurance.
>
> Doctor: If you die, what will your wife bury you with?
>
> Patient: With pleasure.

or

> Shopper: How much are these scarves?
>
> Clerk: They're on sale; two for five dollars.
>
> Shopper: How much for one?
>
> Clerk: Three dollars.
>
> Shopper: Here's two dollars; I'll take the other one.

Such scenes allowed audiences to laugh at the human condition and reminded them that, deep down, all people—at least all white people—were the same. Blacks, however, were rarely assumed to share the same hopes and frustrations as whites.

Shortly after 1900, live entertainment began to yield to a more accessible form of amusement: moving pictures. Perfected by Thomas Edison in the 1880s, movies began as slot-machine peepshows in penny arcades and billiard parlors. Eventually images were projected onto a screen so that large audiences could view them, and a new medium was born. At first, the subjects of films hardly mattered; it was enough to awe viewers with scenes of speeding trains, acrobats, and writhing belly dancers.

Movies

Producers soon discovered that a film could tell a story in exciting ways. Thanks to creative directors like D. W. Griffith, motion pictures became a distinct art form. Griffith's *Birth of a Nation* (1915), an epic film about the Civil War and Reconstruction, fanned racial prejudice by depicting African-Americans as a threat to white moral values. The infant National Association for the Advancement of Colored People (NAACP) led an organized protest against it. But the film's innovative techniques—close-ups, fade-outs, and battle scenes—gave viewers heightened drama and excitement. From the beginning, movies were popular among all classes (admission usually cost a nickel), and audiences idolized film stars such as Mary Pickford, Lillian Gish, and Charlie Chaplin with a fervor that no stage performer had ever evoked.

The still camera, modernized by inventor George Eastman, enabled ordinary people to make their own photographic images, especially useful

Frank Merriwell, the fictional hero of hundreds of stories written by Burt Standish (the pen name used by Gilbert Patten), was a popular character in the early 1900s. In a series of adventures, most involving sports, Frank used his physical skills, valor, and moral virtue to lead by example, accomplish the impossible, and influence others to behave in an upstanding way. Collection of Picture Research Consultants.

for preserving family memories. The phonograph, another Edison invention, brought musical performances into the home. The spread of movies, photography, and phonograph records meant that access to live performances no longer limited people's exposure to art and entertainment. By making it possible to mass-produce sound and images, technology made entertainment a highly desirable consumer good.

News also became a consumer product. Canny publishers made people crave news just as they craved amusements. City life and increased leisure time seemed to nurture a fascination with the sensational, and from the 1880s onward popular newspapers increasingly whetted that appetite.

Joseph Pulitzer, a Hungarian immigrant who bought the *New York World* in 1883, pioneered journalism as a branch of mass culture. Believing that newspapers should be "dedicated to the cause of the people rather than to that of the purse potentates," Pulitzer filled the *World* with stories of disasters, crimes, and scandals. Sensational headlines, set in large bold type like that used for advertisements, screamed from every page. Pulitzer's journalists not only reported news but sought it out and even created it. *World* reporter Nellie Bly (whose real name was Elizabeth Cochrane) faked her way into an insane asylum and wrote a sensational exposé of the sordid conditions she found. Other reporters staged stunts and sought out heart-rending human-interest stories. Pulitzer also popularized the comics, and the yellow ink they were printed in gave rise to the term *yellow journalism* as a synonym for sensationalism.

Yellow Journalism

Pulitzer's strategy was immensely successful. In one year he increased the *World*'s daily circulation from 20,000 to 100,000, and by the late 1890s it had reached 1 million. Soon other publishers, such as William Randolph Hearst, who bought the *New York Journal* in 1895 and started an empire of mass-circulation newspapers, adopted Pulitzer's techniques. Yellow journalism became a nationwide phenomenon, feeding interest in bizarre aspects of the human condition.

Pulitzer and his rivals boosted circulation even further by emphasizing sports and women's news. Newspapers had always reported on sporting events, but yellow-journalism papers gave such stories far greater prominence by printing separate, expanded sports sections. Such sections did more than anything else to promote sports as a leisure-time attraction. Sports news became a new addiction, re-creating a game's drama through narrative and statistics. While expanding sports news, mostly for male readers, newspapers also added special sections devoted to household tips, fashion, decorum, and club news to capture female readers. Like crime and disaster stories, sports and women's sections helped to make news a mass commodity.

By the early twentieth century, mass-circulation magazines made possible by the steam-driven high-speed printing press—an important technological

Magazines for the Mass Market

innovation—were overshadowing the expensive elitist journals of earlier eras. Publications such as *McClure's*, *Saturday Evening Post*, and *Ladies' Home Journal* offered human-interest stories, muckraking exposés (see page 603), titillating fiction, photographs, colorful covers, and eye-catching ads to a growing mass market. Meanwhile, the total number of books published more than quadrupled between 1880 and 1917. This rising popular consumption of news and books reflected growing literacy. Between 1870 and 1920, the proportion of Americans aged ten or over who could not read or write fell from 20 percent to 6 percent.

Other forms of communication also expanded. In 1891 there was less than one telephone for every 100 people in the United States; by 1901 the number had grown to 2.1, and by 1921 it had swelled to 12.6. In 1900 Americans used 4 billion postage stamps; in 1922 they used 14.3 billion. The term *community* took on new dimensions, as people used the media, mail, and telephone to extend their horizons far beyond their immediate localities. More than ever before, people in different parts of the country knew about and discussed the same news event, whether it was a sensational murder, a sex scandal, or the fortunes of a particular entertainer or athlete. America was becoming a mass society.

To some extent, new amusements and pastimes had a homogenizing influence, bringing together ethnic and social groups to share a common experience. Parks, ball fields, vaudeville shows, movies, and feature sections of newspapers and magazines were nonsectarian and apolitical, designed to appeal to everyone. Yet even though entrepreneurs were responsible for the spread of amusements, different groups of consumers often used them to reinforce their own cultural habits. In some communities, for

example, working-class immigrants occupied parks and amusement areas as sites for family and ethnic gatherings. To the dismay of reformers who hoped that recreation would assimilate newcomers and teach them habits of restraint, immigrants used picnics and Fourth of July celebrations as occasions for boisterous drinking and sometimes violent behavior. Young working-class men and women resisted parents' and reformers' warnings and frequented urban dance halls, where they explored their own forms of courtship and sexual behavior. And children often used the streets and rooftops to create their own entertainment rather than participate in adult-supervised games in parks and playgrounds. Thus as Americans learned to play, their leisure—like their work and politics—was shaped by and expressed pluralistic forces.

 ## Promises of Mobility

Baptist minister Russell Conwell delivered the same sermon more than six thousand times across the United States between the Civil War and the First World War. Titled "Acres of Diamonds," this popular lecture affirmed the faith that any American could achieve success. People did not have to look far for riches, Conwell preached; acres of diamonds lay at their feet. Night after night he would insist to his audience, "the opportunity to get rich, to attain unto great wealth, is here . . . within the reach of almost every man and woman who hears me speak tonight. . . . I say you ought to get rich, and it is your duty to get rich. . . . If you can honestly attain unto riches it is your Christian and Godly duty to do so." Success was not only possible; it was a religious obligation.

Was it really possible for people to improve their lot? The answer is a mixed story of small triumphs but also dashed hopes, discrimination, and failure. Basically, there were three ways a person could get ahead: occupational advancement (and the higher income that accompanied it); acquisition of property (and the wealth it represented); and migration to an area that offered better conditions and greater opportunity. These options were open chiefly to white men.

Many women held paying jobs, owned property, and migrated, but their economic standing was usually defined by the men in their lives—husbands, fathers, or other male kin. Women could improve their status by marrying men with wealth or potential, but other avenues were mostly closed. Laws restricted women's economic rights by limiting what they could inherit; educational institutions blocked their training in professions such as medicine and law; and prevailing assumptions attributed higher aptitude for manual skills and business to men than to women. Men and women who were African-American, American Indian, Mexican-American, or Asian-American had even fewer opportunities. Pinned to the bottom of society by prejudice, they were forced to accept their imposed station.

For large numbers of people, however, occupational mobility was a reality, thanks to urban and industrial expansion. Thousands of new businesses

Occupational Mobility

were needed to supply goods and services to burgeoning urban populations. As corporations grew and centralized their operations, they required new managerial personnel. Capital for a large business was hard to amass, but aspiring merchants could open a saloon or small shop for a few hundred dollars. Knowledge of accounting could qualify one for white-collar jobs that sometimes paid better than manual labor. Thus nonmanual work and the higher social status and income that tended to accompany it were attainable.

Such advancement occurred often. To be sure, only a very few traveled the rags-to-riches path that Andrew Carnegie and Henry Ford discovered. Studies of the era's wealthiest businessmen show that the vast majority began their careers with distinct advantages: American birth, Protestant religion, superior education, and relatively affluent parents. Yet considerable movement occurred along the road from rags to moderate success, as men climbed from manual to nonmanual jobs. Personal successes like that of Meyer Grossman, a Russian immigrant to Omaha, Nebraska, who worked as a teamster before saving enough to open a successful furniture store, were common.

Rates of occupational mobility in American communities were slow but steady between 1870 and 1920. In new, fast-growing cities such as Atlanta, Los Angeles, and Omaha, approximately one in five white manual workers rose to white-collar or owner's positions within ten years—provided they stayed in the city that long. In older cities such as Boston and Newburyport, upward mobility averaged closer to one in six in ten years. Some men slipped from a higher to a lower rung on the occupational ladder, but rates of

upward movement usually doubled those of downward movement. Though patterns were not consistent, immigrants generally experienced less upward and more downward mobility than the native-born did. Still, regardless of birthplace, the chances for a white male to rise occupationally over the course of his career or to have a higher-status job than his father had were relatively good.

It must be remembered, however, that what constitutes a better job depends on one's definition of improvement. Many an immigrant artisan, such as a German carpenter or Italian shoemaker, would have considered an accountant's job demeaning. People with traditions of pride in manual skills neither wanted nonmanual jobs nor encouraged their children to seek them. As one Italian tailor explained, "I learned the tailoring business in the old country. Over here, in America, I never have trouble finding a job because I know my business from the other side [Italy]. . . . I want that my oldest boy learn my trade because I tell him that you could always make at least enough for the family."

Business ownership, moreover, entailed risks. Failure rates were high among shopkeepers, saloon owners, and other small proprietors in working-class neighborhoods because the low incomes of their customers made business uncertain. Many manual workers sought security rather than mobility, preferring a steady wage to the risks of ownership. A Sicilian who lived in Bridgeport, Connecticut, observed that "the people that come here they afraid to get in business because they don't know how that business goes. In Italy these people don't know much about these things because most of them work on farms or in [their] trade."

In addition to, or instead of, advancing occupationally, a person could achieve social mobility by acquiring property. But property was not easy to

Acquisition of Property

acquire. Banks and savings-and-loan institutions had far stricter lending practices than they did after the 1930s, when the federal government began to insure real-estate financing. Before then, mortgage loans carried high interest rates and short repayment periods. Thus renting, even of single-family houses, was common, especially in big cities. A general rise in wage rates nevertheless enabled many families to amass savings, which they could use as down payments on property. Among working-class families who stayed in Newburyport at least ten years, for example, a third to a half managed to accumulate some property; two-thirds did so within twenty years. Owner-ship rates varied regionally—higher in western cities, lower in eastern cities—but 36 percent of all urban American families owned their homes in 1900, the highest homeownership rate of any Western nation except for Denmark, Norway, and Sweden.

Following the maxim that movement means improvement, millions of families each year packed up and moved elsewhere. As early as 1847, a for-

Residential Mobility

eign visitor, amazed by American transiency, wrote, "If God were suddenly to call the world to judgment He would surprise two-thirds of the American pop-ulation on the road like ants." The urge to move af-fected every region, every city. From Boston to San Francisco, from Minneapolis to San Antonio, no more than half of the families residing in a city at any one time were still there ten years later.

Many who migrated, particularly unskilled workers, did not improve their status; they simply floated from one low-paying job to another. Oth-ers did find greener pastures. Studies of Boston, Omaha, Atlanta, and other cities show that most men who rose occupationally or acquired property had migrated from somewhere else. Thus while cities frustrated the hopes of some, they offered op-portunities to others.

In addition to movement between cities, extra-ordinary numbers of people moved within the same city. In American communities today, one in every five families changes residence in a given year. A hundred years ago, the proportion was closer to one in four or one in three. In Omaha between 1880 and 1920, for example, nearly 60 percent of families who remained in the city for as long as fourteen years had lived at three or more addresses during that span of time. Population turnover affected almost every neighborhood, every ethnic and occupational group.

Rapid residential flux undermined the stability of even the most homogeneous neighborhoods. Rarely did a single nationality make up a clear ma-

Ethnic Neighborhoods and Ghettos

jority in any large area, even when that area was known as Little Italy, Jewtown, Polonia, or Greektown. In heavily ethnic Chicago, a survey of one district found a kaleidoscope of immi-grants packed tightly together:

Between Halsted Street and the river live about ten thousand Italians, Neapolitans, Sicilians, and Calabri-

ans. . . . To the South on Twelfth Street are many Germans, and the side streets are given over almost entirely to Polish and Prussian Jews. Further south, three Jewish colonies merge into a huge Bohemian colony. . . . To the north-west are many Canadians . . . and to the north are many Irish.

Moreover, immigrants rapidly dispersed from their original areas of settlement. The families who inhabited a certain neighborhood at one point were not likely to be living there five or ten years later. Ethnically homogeneous districts did exist in New York, Boston, and other eastern ports, and people tended to change residences within those districts rather than leave altogether. Elsewhere, however, most white immigrant families lived in ethnically mixed neighborhoods rather than in ghettos.

In most cities an area's institutions and enter-prises, more than the people who actually lived there, identified a district as an ethnic neighbor-hood. A certain part of town, familiar and accessible to a particular group, served as the location of its churches, clubs, bakeries, markets, and other estab-lishments. Some members of that group might live there; others lived farther away but could travel there on streetcars or on foot. Thus some of the sec-ondary business centers that formed at the intersec-tions of mass-transit routes became locations of eth-nic business and social activity. A Bohemian Town, for example, received its nickname because it was the location of Swoboda's Bakery, Cermak's Drug Store, Cecha's Jewelry, Knezacek's Meats, St. Wenceslaus Church, and the Bohemian Benevolent Association. Such institutions gave the district an ethnic identity even though the surrounding neighborhood was mixed and unstable.

Residential dispersion did not necessarily mean acceptance; immigrants and their children often en-countered hostility in all walks of life. During the depression of the 1890s, the American Protective Association attracted attention by attacking "the di-abolical works of the Catholic Church," spewing anti-Semitic and racist insults, and demanding an end to immigration. Such sentiment influenced na-tional legislation. In 1882, Congress appeased West Coast nativists by prohibiting Chinese immigration for ten years. In 1902 a new federal law excluded the Chinese indefinitely; not until 1943 was the ban lifted. Also, nativists attempted to prevent foreign-born citizens from voting by imposing literacy tests on them.

The West provides an arena for studying con-cepts of race in the late nineteenth century. Anglos

Though Chinese immigrants struggled, like other immigrants, to succeed in American society, they often faced severe discrimination because of their different lifestyles. As this photo of a San Francisco grocery shows, Chinese looked, dressed, and ate differently than did white Americans. Occasionally, they suffered from racist violence that caused them to fear not only for their personal safety but also for the safety of establishments like this one that might suffer damage from resentful mobs.   The Bancroft Library, University of California.

Race and Discrimination

(native-born whites) tended to identify four non-white races but in doing so created racial identities for people who, except for blacks, previously had not thought of themselves as a single race. Hispanics, born in the United States and in Mexico, were mixtures of Spanish, Indian, and African ancestry and had their own racial distinctions. Asians, often called "Mongolians" by whites, also had internal divisions, not only between Chinese and Japanese but within those two nationalities. And whites imposed on Indians a racial unity that never existed.

Whites used racial distinctions to characterize nonwhites with derogatory stereotypes and to make them victims of discrimination, thereby stifling their mobility. Wherever Asians and Mexicans settled, they encountered discrimination in housing, employment, and other facets of public life. Although these groups often preferred to remain separate in Chinatowns and *barrios*, Anglos also made every effort to keep them confined. In the 1880s San Francisco's government, for example, tried to prohibit Chinese laundries from locating in white neighborhoods, and its school board tried to isolate Japanese and Chinese children in Chinatown schools. In *barrios* of Los Angeles and San Antonio, Anglo teachers were insensitive to the needs of Hispanic students.

The same discrimination trapped African-Americans at the bottom of the occupational ladder and limited their housing opportunities. Whites organized protective associations that pledged not to sell homes to blacks and occasionally used violence to scare them away from white neighborhoods. In almost every city, blacks concentrated into homogeneous residential districts. By 1920 in Chicago, Detroit, Cleveland, and other cities outside the South, two-thirds or more of the total African-American population lived in only 10 percent of the residential area. Within these districts, they nurtured cultural institutions that helped them adjust to urban life: storefront churches, business and educational organizations, social clubs, and saloons. But the ghettos also bred frustration, the result of stunted opportunity and racial bigotry.

Virtually all white Americans believed nonwhite "races" were inferior, but their views of the future varied. Some, such as racists in the South and anti-Chinese agitators in the West, believed that people of color were permanently disadvantaged and could never achieve equality with whites. Others, including some urban reformers, believed that the inferiority was temporary and could be overcome if nonwhites learned to imitate whites. In each case, however, racists and reformers both believed people of color should be treated differently from whites, usually in discriminatory ways. Thus race, more than any other factor, made the urban experiences of nonwhites unique from those of whites.

All groups, however, including people of color, could and did move—if not from one neighborhood to another, then from one city to another. Americans were always seeking greener pastures, and hope for better conditions elsewhere acted as a safety valve, relieving some of the tensions and frustrations that simmered inside the city. At times these emotions erupted into violence; more often, people simply left. A railroad ticket to another city cost only a few dollars; there was little to lose by moving.

The possibilities of upward mobility, moreover, seemed to temper people's dissatisfaction. Although the gap between the very rich and the very poor widened, the expanding economies of American cities created room in the middle of the socioeconomic scale. Few could hope to become another Rockefeller, and blocked mobility frustrated others. But many did become respectable shopkeepers, foremen, clerks, and agents. Finally, if migration, occupational mobility, and property acquisition offered little hope of improvement or relief, there was still one sphere to which city dwellers could turn: politics.

 ## The Politics of Bossism and Civic Reform

City governments faced daunting challenges in the late nineteenth century. Burgeoning populations, business expansion, and technological change created urgent needs for sewers, police and fire protection, schools, parks, and other services. Such needs strained municipal resources beyond their capacities. Furthermore, city governments approached these needs in a disorganized fashion. Legislative and administrative functions were typically scattered among a mayor, city council, and independent boards that administered health regulations, public works, poverty relief, and other functions. Philadelphia at one time had thirty different boards, plus a mayor and council. Furthermore, state governments often interfered in local matters, appointing board members and limiting cities' abilities to levy taxes and borrow money.

Power thrives on confusion, and out of this governmental chaos arose political machines, organizations whose main goals were the rewards—money, influence, and prestige—of getting and keeping political power.

Political Machines

Machine politicians routinely used bribery and graft to further their ends. But machines needed popular support, and they could not have succeeded if they had not provided relief, security, and services to large numbers of people, especially to the hordes of newcomers who crowded into cities. By meeting those needs, machine politicians accomplished things that other agencies had been unable or unwilling to attempt.

Machines bred political bosses, leaders who could smooth the way so that special-interest groups could attain their goals and who could simultaneously meet the needs of urban working classes. Bosses and machines established power bases among new immigrant voters and used politics to solve important urban problems. Most bosses had immigrant backgrounds and had grown up in the inner city, so they knew their constituents' needs firsthand. Machines made politics a full-time profession. According to George Washington Plunkitt, a small-time boss in New York City who published his memoirs in 1905, "As a rule [the boss] has no business or occupation other than politics. He plays politics every day and night in the year and his headquarters bears the inscription, 'Never closed.'"

"Big Tim" Sullivan, a New York City ward boss, rewarded "repeat voters" with a new pair of shoes. Sullivan once explained, "When you've voted 'em with their whiskers on, you take 'em to a barber and scrape off the chin fringe. Then you vote 'em again . . . . Then to a barber again, off comes the sides and you vote 'em a third time with the mustache. . . . [Then] clean off the mustache and vote 'em plain face. That makes every one of 'em for four votes." Library of Congress.

Bosses and machines were rarely as dictatorial or corrupt as critics charged. To be sure, fraud, bribery, and thievery tainted the system. Bosses such as Philadelphia's "Duke" Vare, Kansas City's Tom Pendergast, and New York's Richard Croker lived like kings, though their official incomes were slim. A few bosses had no permanent organization; they were freelance opportunists who bargained for power, sometimes winning and sometimes losing. But from the 1880s onward, most machines evolved into highly organized political structures that wedded public accomplishments with personal gain.

The system rested on a popular base and was held together by loyalty and service. Machines were coalitions of smaller organizations that derived power directly from inner-city neighborhoods inhabited by native and immigrant working classes. In return for votes, bosses provided jobs, built parks and bathhouses, distributed food and clothing to the needy, and helped when someone ran afoul of the law. Such personalized service cultivated mass attachment to the boss; never before had public leaders assumed such responsibility for people in need.

Bosses, moreover, were genuinely public people. They attended weddings and wakes, joined clubs, and held open houses in saloons where neighborhood folk could talk to them personally. Each boss had his own style. Pittsburgh's Christopher Magee gave his city a zoo and a hospital. Brooklyn's Hugh McLaughlin provided free burial services. Boston's James Michael Curley would approach a haggard old woman and tell her that "a woman should have three attributes. . . . beauty, intelligence, and money." Then he would press a silver dollar into her hand and say, "Now you have all three."

Techniques of Bossism

To finance their activities and campaigns, bosses exchanged favors for votes or money. Power over local government enabled machines to control the letting of public contracts, the granting of utility or streetcar franchises, and the distribution of city jobs. Recipients of city business and jobs were expected to repay the machine with a portion of their profits or salaries and to cast supporting votes on election day. Critics called this process graft; bosses called it gratitude.

Machines constructed public buildings, sewer systems, and mass-transit lines that otherwise might not have been built; but bribes and kickbacks made such projects costly to taxpayers. In the late nineteenth century, cities financed their expansion with loans from the public in the form of municipal bonds. Critics of bosses charged that these loans were inflated or unnecessary. Whether necessary or not, municipal bonds caused public debts to soar, and taxes had to be raised to repay their interest and principal. In addition, machines dispersed favors to legal and illegal businesses. Payoffs from gambling, prostitution, and illegal liquor traffic became important sources of machine revenue.

Bosses held power because they tended to problems of everyday life. Martin Lomasney, boss of Boston's South End, explained, "There's got to be in every ward somebody that any bloke can come to—no matter what he's done—and get help. Help, you understand, none of your law and justice, but help." The boss system, however, was neither innocent nor fair. Jobs, Christmas turkeys, and funeral money were accompanied by thievery and extortion. Racial minorities and new immigrant groups such as Italians and Poles received only token jobs and favors, if any. But in an age of economic individualism, bosses were no more guilty of self-interest and discrimination than were business leaders who exploited workers, spoiled the landscape, and manipulated government in pursuit of profits. Sometimes humane and sometimes criminal, bosses were brokers between various sectors of urban society and an uncertain world.

While bosses were consolidating their power, others were attempting to destroy them. Many middle- and upper-class Americans feared that immigrant-based political machines menaced the republic and that unsavory alliances between bosses and businesses wastefully depleted municipal finances. Anxious over the poverty, crowding, and disorder that accompanied population expansion, and convinced that urban services were making taxes too high, civic reformers organized to install more responsible leaders at the helm of urban administrations.

Urban reform arose in part from the industrial system's emphasis on eliminating inefficiency. Government could be made more competent, business-minded reformers were convinced, if it were run like a business. The only way to achieve this goal, they believed, was to elect officials who would hold down expenses and prevent corruption. Thus they decided that they must reduce city budgets, make public employees work more efficiently, and cut taxes.

To impose sound business principles on government, civic reformers supported structural changes such as the city-manager and commission forms of government and nonpartisan citywide election of officials. These reforms were meant to put decision making in the hands of experienced experts. Armed with such strategies, reformers believed they could cleanse party politics and undermine bosses' power bases in the neighborhoods. They rarely realized, however, that bosses succeeded because they used government to meet people's needs. Reformers only noticed the waste and corruption that machines bred.

Structural Reforms in Government

A few reform mayors moved beyond structural changes to address social problems. Hazen S. Pingree of Detroit, Samuel "Golden Rule" Jones of Toledo, and Tom Johnson of Cleveland worked to provide jobs for poor people, reduce charges by transit and utility companies, and promote governmental responsibility for the welfare of all citizens. They also supported public ownership of gas, electric, and telephone companies, a quasi-socialist reform that alienated their business allies. But Pingree, Jones, and Johnson were exceptions. Civic reformers achieved temporary successes but could not match the bosses' political savvy; they soon found themselves out of power.

Urban Professionals: Social Workers and Engineers

A different type of reform arose outside politics. Driven by an urge to improve society, social reformers—mostly young and middle class—embarked on campaigns to identify and solve urban problems. Housing reformers pressed local governments for building codes to ensure safety in tenements. Protestant activists

Social Reform

influenced by the Social Gospel reformers, who believed that service to fellow humans was the way to salvation, built churches in slum neighborhoods and urged businesses to be socially responsible. Educational reformers saw public schools as a means of preparing immigrant children for citizenship by teaching them American values as well as the English language.

Perhaps the most ambitious and inspiring feature of urban reform movements was the settlement house. Located in slum neighborhoods and run mostly by women, settlements were buildings where middle-class young people went to live and work in order to bridge the gulf between social classes. The first American settlement house, patterned after London's Toynbee Hall, opened in New York City in 1886, and others quickly appeared in Chicago, Boston, and elsewhere. Early settlement leaders such as Jane Addams, founder of Hull House in Chicago and one of country's most revered women, and Florence Kelley, a brilliant socialist who pioneered laws to protect consumers and working women, wanted to improve the lives of slum dwellers by helping them obtain education, appreciation of the arts, better jobs, and better housing. Although working-class and immigrant neighborhood residents sometimes mistrusted them as outsiders, settlement workers attracted support with activities ranging from vocational classes to childcare and ethnic pageants.

As they broadened their scope to fight for school nurses, building safety codes, public playgrounds, and better working conditions, settlement workers became reform leaders in cities and in the nation. Their efforts to involve national and local governments in the solution of social problems later made them the vanguard of the Progressive era, when a reform spirit swept the nation (see Chapter 21). Moreover, the activities of settlement houses helped create new professional opportunities for women in social work, public health, and child welfare. These professions enabled female reformers to build a dominion of influence over social policy independent of male-dominated professions and to make valuable contributions to national as well as inner-city life.

A contrast developed between white female reformers and black female reformers. Middle-class white women lobbied for government programs to aid needy people and focused on helping mostly white immigrant and native-born working classes.

Black women, barred by their race from white political institutions, raised funds from private institutions and focused on helping members of their own race. African-American women were especially active in financing schools, old-age homes, and hospitals, but they also worked for advancement of the race and protection of black women from sexual exploitation. Their ranks included women such as Jane Hunter, who founded a home for unmarried black working women in Cleveland in 1911 and influenced the establishment of similar homes in other cities, and Modjeska Simkins, who organized a program to address health problems among blacks in South Carolina.

While female reformers tried to revive the neighborhoods, a group of male reformers began the City Beautiful movement to improve cities' attractiveness. Inspired by the World's Columbian Exposition of 1893, a dazzling world's fair held in a specially built "White City" on Chicago's South Side, architects and city planners worked to redesign the urban landscape. Led by architect Daniel Burnham, City Beautiful advocates built civic centers, parks, boulevards, and transportation systems that would make cities more economically efficient as well as beautiful. "Make no little plans," Burnham urged. "Make big plans; aim high in hope and work." This attitude spawned beautifying projects in Chicago, San Francisco, and Washington, D.C., in the early 1900s. Yet most of these big plans turned out to be only big dreams. Neither government nor private businesses could finance large-scale projects, and planners disagreed among themselves and with social reformers over whether beautification really would solve urban problems.

Beautification Campaigns

Whether they focused on government, social services, or city design, urban reformers wanted to save cities, not abandon them. They believed they could improve urban life by restoring cooperation among all citizens. They often failed to realize, however, that cities were places of great diversity and that different people held very different views about what reform actually meant. To civic reformers, distributing city jobs on the basis of civil service exams rather than party loyalty meant progress, but to working-class men civil service signified reduced employment opportunities. Moral reformers believed that prohibiting the sale of alcoholic beverages would prevent working-class breadwinners from wasting their wages and ruining their health, but immigrants saw such crusades as interference in their private drinking customs. Planners saw new streets and civic buildings as modern necessities, but such structures often displaced the poor. Well-meaning humanitarians criticized immigrant mothers for the way they shopped, dressed, did housework, and raised children, without regard for the inability of these mothers to afford the products that the consumer economy created. Thus urban reform merged idealism with naiveté and insensitivity.

At the same time, efforts of still a different sort were making cities more livable. Technical and professional creativity, not political or humanitarian action, was required to address sanitation, street lighting, bridge and street construction, and other such needs. In addressing these issues, American urban dwellers, and the engineering profession in particular, developed new systems and standards of worldwide significance.

Engineering Reforms

Take, for example, the problem of refuse. Experts in 1900 estimated that every New Yorker generated annually some 160 pounds of garbage (food and bones), 1,200 pounds of ashes (from stoves and furnaces), and 100 pounds of rubbish (old shoes, furniture, and other items). Europeans of that era produced only about half as much trash. At the same time, there were as many as 3.5 million horses in American cities, each of which produced about 20 pounds of manure and a gallon of urine daily. City horses worked so hard that they died after only a few years, and each city had to dispose of thousands of carcasses every year. In past eras, trash, excrement, and dead animals could be dismissed as nuisances; by the twentieth century they were public health and safety hazards, and citizens' groups were protesting against inadequate refuse collection and disposal.

The problem raised difficult questions. Who should be responsible for waste removal, city workers or a private contractor hired by the city? Previously, cities had dumped refuse on vacant land and in nearby rivers and lakes. What alternatives were there to these unsafe practices? Should trash be sorted so that some could be salvaged and sold or recycled? How frequently should streets be cleaned, and by whom?

To solve their problems, cities increasingly depended on engineers. By 1900, engineers were applying technical expertise to devise systems for incinerating refuse, and dumping trash while safeguarding water supplies, constructing efficient sewers, and providing for regular street cleaning and snow removal. Engineers also advised officials on budget and contracts. They had similar influence in matters of street lighting, parks, fire protection, and more. City officials, whether bosses or reformers, came to depend on the expertise of engineers, who seemed best qualified to supervise a city's expansion. Insulated within bureaucratic agencies from tumultuous party strife, engineers generally carried out their responsibilities efficiently and without great publicity.

Engineers and their technology also brought about unheralded but momentous changes in home life. As historian Thomas Schlereth has pointed out,

Engineers and the Home

new "systems" of central heating (furnaces), artificial lighting, and modern indoor plumbing created a new kind of consumption first for middle-class households and later for most other households. Whereas formerly families had chopped wood for their cooking and heating, made candles for light, and hauled water for bathing, they now were connected to outside utilities for gas, electricity, and water. Moreover, these utilities helped foment new attitudes about privacy. Bedrooms and bathrooms enabled family members to withdraw into private spaces where they still could have the comfort of light, heat, and water. Instead of doubling or tripling up in one room or even one bed, children could have their own bedroom, complete with its own individualized decoration. Finally, these utilities erased the inconveniences of nature. Central heat and artificial light made it possible to enjoy a steady, comfortable temperature and turn night into day, while indoor plumbing removed the unpleasant experiences of the outhouse.

 ## Conclusion

Much of what American society is today originated in the urbanization of the late nineteenth century. American cities may have been less orderly and beautiful than European cities, but they hummed with energy and excitement. Virtually ungovernable in the 1860s and 1870s, American cities experienced an "unheralded triumph" by the early 1900s. Amid corruption and political conflict, urban engineers modernized local infrastructures with new sewer, water, and lighting services, and urban governments made the environment safer by expanding professional police and fire departments. When old-fashioned native inventiveness met the traditions of European, African, and Asian cultures, a new kind of society emerged. This society seldom functioned smoothly; there really was no coherent urban community, only a collection of subcommunities. Yet the jumble of social classes, ethnic and racial groups, political organizations, and professional experts left important legacies.

American cities exhibited bewildering diversity. Fearful and puzzled, native-born whites tried to Americanize and uplift immigrants, but the newcomers stubbornly strained to protect their cultures. Optimists had envisioned the American nation as a melting pot, where various nationalities would blend to become a unified people. Instead, many ethnic groups proved unmeltable, and racial minorities got burned on the bottom of the pot. As a result of immigration and urbanization, the United States became a culturally pluralistic society—not so much a melting pot as a salad bowl. As one immigrant priest told a social worker, "There is no such thing as an American." He meant the same thing that literary critic Randolph Bourne meant when he dubbed the United States "a cosmopolitan federation of national colonies." This kind of reasoning produced hyphenated identifications: people considered themselves Irish-American, Italian-American, Polish-American, and the like.

Pluralism and interest-group loyalties enhanced the importance of politics. If America was not a melting pot, then different groups were competing for power, wealth, and status. Some people carried polarization to extremes and tried to suppress everything allegedly un-American. Efforts to enforce homogeneity generally failed, however, because the country's cultural diversity prevented domination by a single ethnic majority. By 1920, immigrants and their offspring outnumbered the native-born in many cities, and the national economy depended on these new workers and consumers. Migrants and immigrants transformed the United States into an urban nation. They gave American culture its rich and varied texture, and they laid the foundations for the liberalism that characterized American politics in the twentieth century.

Suggestions for Further Reading

Urban Growth

Howard P. Chudacoff and Judith E. Smith, *The Evolution of American Urban Society*, 4th ed. (1993); David Goldfield and Blaine Brownell, *Urban America*, 2d ed. (1990); Kenneth T. Jackson, *The Crabgrass Frontier: The Suburbanization of the United States* (1985); Raymond A. Mohl, *The New City* (1985); Jon Teaford, *The Unheralded Triumph: City Government in America, 1870–1900* (1984); Sam Bass Warner, Jr., *The Urban Wilderness* (1982).

Immigration, Ethnicity, and Religion

Aaron I. Abell, *American Catholicism and Social Action* (1960); John Bodnar, *The Transplanted* (1985); John Bodnar, Roger Simon, and Michael P. Weber, *Lives of Their Own: Blacks, Italians, and Poles in Pittsburgh, 1900–1960* (1982); Sucheng Chan, ed., *Entry Denied: Exclusion and the Chinese Community in America, 1882–1943* (1990); Elizabeth Ewen, *Immigrant Women in the Land of Dollars* (1985); Mario T. Garcia, *Desert Immigrants: The Mexicans of El Paso, 1880–1920* (1981); Milton Gordon, *Assimilation in American Life* (1964); Victor Greene, *For God and Country: The Rise of Polish and Lithuanian Ethnic Consciousness in America* (1975); Oscar Handlin, *The Uprooted*, 2d ed. (1973); John Higham, *Strangers in the Land: Patterns of American Nativism* (1955); Yusi Ichioka, *The Issei: The World of the First Japanese Immigrants, 1885–1924* (1988); Matt S. Maier and Felciano Rivera, *The Chicanos* (1972); Henry F. May, *Protestant Churches and Industrial America* (1949); Werner Sollors, *Beyond Ethnicity* (1986); Ron Takaki, *Iron Cages: Race and Culture in Nineteenth-Century America* (1979); Stephan Thernstrom, ed., *Harvard Encyclopedia of American Ethnic Groups* (1980).

Urban Services

Charles W. Cheape, *Moving the Masses* (1980); Lawrence A. Cremin, *American Education: The Metropolitan Experience* (1988); David R. Johnson, *American Law Enforcement* (1981); Martin V. Melosi, *Garbage in the Cities* (1981); Eric Monkkonen, *America Becomes Urban* (1988); Barbara Gutmann Rosencrantz, *Public Health and the State* (1972); Stanley K. Schultz, *Constructing Urban Culture: American Cities and City Planning* (1989); Mel Scott, *American City Planning Since 1890* (1969).

Family and Individual Life Cycles

W. Andrew Achenbaum, *Old Age in the New Land* (1979); George Chauncey, *Gay New York* (1995); Howard P. Chudacoff, *How Old Are You? Age in American Culture* (1989); Carl N. Degler, *At Odds: Women and the Family in America* (1980); John D'Emilio and Estelle B. Freedman, *Intimate Matters: A History of Sexuality in America* (1988); Michael Gordon, ed., *The American Family in Social-Historical Perspective*, 3d ed. (1983); Carole Haber, *Beyond Sixty-five: Dilemmas of Old Age in America's Past* (1983); Tamara K. Hareven, *Family Time and Industrial Time* (1981); Joseph Kett, *Rites of Passage: Adolescence in America* (1979); E. Anthony Rotundo, *American Manhood* (1994).

Mass Entertainment and Leisure

Gunther Barth, *City People* (1980); Jessica H. Foy and Thomas J. Schlereth, eds., *American Home Life, 1880–1930* (1992); Allen Guttmann, *A Whole New Ball Game: An Interpretation of American Sports* (1988); George Juergens, *Joseph Pulitzer and the New York World* (1966); John F. Kasson, *Amusing the Million: Coney Island at the Turn of the Century* (1978); Frank L. Mott, *American Journalism*, 3d ed. (1962); David Nasaw, *Going Out: The Rise and Fall of Popular Amusements* (1993); Kathy Peiss, *Cheap Amusements: Working Women and Leisure in Turn-of-the-Century New York* (1986); Benjamin G. Rader, *American Sports* (1983); Steven A. Riess, *City Games* (1989); Roy Rosenzweig, *Eight Hours for What We Will! Workers and Leisure in an Industrial City, 1870–1920* (1983); Robert Sklar, *Movie-Made America* (1976); Ronald A. Smith, *Sports and Freedom: The Rise of Big-Time College Athletics* (1988); Robert V. Snyder, *The Voice of the City: Vaudeville and Popular Culture in New York City, 1880–1920* (1990); Robert C. Toll, *On with the Show: The First Century of Show Business in America* (1976).

Mobility and Race Relations

James Borchert, *Alley Life in Washington* (1980); Howard P. Chudacoff, *Mobile Americans* (1972); Clyde Griffen and Sally Griffen, *Natives and Newcomers* (1977); Jacqueline Jones, *Labor of Love, Labor of Sorrow: Black Women, Work and the Family from Slavery to the Present* (1985); David M. Katzman, *Before the Ghetto* (1973); Kenneth L. Kusmer, *A Ghetto Takes Shape* (1976); Gilbert Osofsky, *Harlem: The Making of a Ghetto* (1966); Elizabeth H. Pleck, *Black Migration and Poverty: Boston, 1865–1900* (1979); Howard N. Rabinowitz, *Race Relations in the Urban South* (1978); Allan H. Spear, *Black Chicago* (1967); Stephan Thernstrom, *The Other Bostonians: Poverty and Progress in the American Metropolis* (1973); Olivier Zunz, *The Changing Face of Inequality* (1982).

Boss Politics

John M. Allswang, *Bosses, Machines and Urban Voters* (1977); Alexander B. Callow, Jr., ed., *The City Boss in America* (1976); Lyle Dorsett, *The Pendergast Machine* (1968); Leo Hershkowitz, *Tweed's New York: Another Look* (1977); Terrence J. McDonald, *The Parameters of Urban Fiscal Policy* (1986); Zane L. Miller, *Boss Cox's Cincinnati* (1968); Bruce M. Stave and Sondra Stave, eds., *Urban Bosses, Machines, and Progressive Reformers* (1984).

Urban Reform

John D. Buenker, *Urban Liberalism and Progressive Reform* (1973); James B. Crooks, *Politics and Progress* (1968); Doris Groshen Daniels, *Always a Sister: The Feminism of Lillian D. Wald* (1989); Allen F. Davis, *Spearheads for Reform* (1967); Lori Ginzberg, *Women and the Work of Benevolence* (1991); Melvin Holli, *Reform in Detroit* (1969); Roy M. Lubove, *The Progressives and the Slums* (1962); Clay McShane, *Technology and Reform* (1974); Robyn Muncy, *Creating a Female Dominion in American Reform* (1991); Martin J. Schiesl, *The Politics of Efficiency* (1977); Kathryn Kish Sklar, *Florence Kelley and the Nation's Work* (1995).

20

Gilded Age Politics
1877 – 1900

E arly one winter evening in 1899, E. L. Godkin, one of the nation's most respected editors, ventured out of his New York townhouse to take the elevated uptown. While waiting on the platform, he happened to look down to the street below, where he spotted two policemen casually conversing. Convinced that the officers were shirking their duty, Godkin filed an indignant complaint with the Police Commissioner. "I [saw] them gossiping with nurse maids and others, and there [was] an air of swagger about them . . . ," Godkin later testified. "From what I [saw], I should judge that the police force had been demoralized a good deal."

What could have made this dignified newspaperman become so irate over an incident so seemingly minor? Godkin believed his society was surrounded by corruption and hypocrisy. The possibilities for quick wealth in business and politics, coupled with the resulting bribery and irresponsibility frightened him. Democracy in the age of industrialism, Godkin believed, had failed. "The first danger [democracy] has encountered," he wrote in his book *Unforeseen Tendencies of Democracy* (1898), "is the enormously increased facility for money-making which the modern world has supplied, and the inevitably resulting corruption. I cannot help doubting whether any regimes would have withstood this. . . . It is breaking down, not simply the old political, but the old social usages and standards."

Godkin was a snob, but he was an influential snob. His indictment of American society in the late nineteenth century impressed not only those of his own time but historians and political analysts ever since. To be sure, there was much in American society to disturb him. So-called robber barons were exercising monumental greed in expanding large corporations across the continent. Public servants, from state legislators to

Politics in the late nineteenth century was a major community activity. In an age before movies, television, shopping malls, and widespread professional sports, forceful orators such as Socialist Party leader Eugene V. Debs, shown speaking in a railroad yard, attracted large audiences for speeches that sometimes lasted for hours. *Brown Brothers.*

congressmen, were swayed and bribed to do the bidding of moneyed men. Officeholders used their positions to amass personal fortunes and dispense patronage appointments to their supporters. And vote fraud poisoned local and national elections. The era's venality seemed so widespread that when, twenty years earlier, novelists Mark Twain and Charles Dudley Warner published their novel, *The Gilded Age*, satirizing America as a land of shallow money grubbers, the name stuck; historians have used the expression "Gilded Age" to characterize the late nineteenth century ever since.

Several of Godkin's contemporaries shared his views about the ineffectiveness of the government and its party system. Henry Adams, son and grandson of presidents, wrote, "one might search the whole list of Congress, Judiciary, and Executive during the twenty-five years from 1870 to 1895, and find little but damaged reputation." Lord James Bryce, the distinguished British author of *The American Commonwealth* (1889), sneered with regard to Democrats and Republicans that "neither party has any principles, any tenets. . . . All has been lost, except office, or the hope of it."

To Godkin, then, those two cops, talking to each other instead of walking their beats as their duty prescribed, were part of the evil undermining American society. But individuals like Godkin, Adams, and Bryce had biases. They thought that everyone should conform to their ideals of duty and nobility, and their personal assessment of their era colored the ways in which Americans have thought about the period. The label "Gilded Age" itself reflects those biases. But like any historical period, the Gilded Age was one of great complexity, accomplishments as well as failings.

Between 1877 and 1900, industrialization, urbanization, and the commercialization of agriculture altered politics and government as much as they shaped everyday life. Congress grappled with railroad regulation, tariffs, currency, civil service, and other important issues and had major accomplishments in spite of powerful partisan and regional rivalries within its ranks. Meanwhile, the judiciary actively supported big business by consistently defending property rights against state and federal regulation. The presidency was occupied by honest, respectable men who, though not as exceptional as Washington, Jefferson, or Lincoln, prepared the office for its more activist character after the turn of the century.

Three phenomena shaped Gilded Age politics: powerful special interests, achievement amid limitations, and exclusion. The influence of powerful private interests—manufacturers, railroad managers, creditors, and wealthy men in general—and the conflict between them and the public interest was the most prominent of the three. Second, despite flaws and corruption and the public's preference for limited government power, governments at the federal and state levels achieved more than historians have credited them for accomplishing. Even so, exclusion—the third phenomenon—prevented the majority of Americans—including women, southern blacks, Indians, uneducated whites, and unnaturalized immigrants—from voting and thus using the tools of democracy to redress their grievances.

Until the 1890s, those phenomena operated within a delicate equilibrium characterized by a stable party system and a balance of power among the country's geographical sections. Then in the 1890s rural discontent erupted in the West and South, and a deep economic depression bared flaws in the industrial system. Amid these crises, a presidential campaign in 1896 stirred Americans as they had not been stirred for a generation. A new party arose, old parties split, sectional unity dissolved, and fundamental disputes about the nation's future climaxed. The nation emerged from the turbulent 1890s with new economic configurations and new political alignments.

 ## The Nature of Party Politics

At no other time in the nation's history was public interest in elections more avid than it was between 1870 and 1896. Consistently, 80 to 90 percent of eligible voters (white and black males in the North, mostly white males in the South) cast ballots in local and national elections. (About 50 percent typically do so today.) Politics was a form of local recreation, more popular than baseball, vaudeville, or circuses. Actual voting was only the final stage in a process that included parades, picnics, and speeches, all of which were as much public amusement as civic responsibility. As one observer remarked, "What the theatre is to the French, or the bull fight . . . to the Spanish . . . [election campaigns] and the ballot box are to *our* people." Politics was indeed the sounding board for local allegiances.

Party loyalties in part reflected the pluralism of American society. As different groups competed for

• *Important Events* •

1873	Congress ends coinage of silver dollars	**1890**	McKinley Tariff raises tariff rates
1873–78	Economic hard times hit		Sherman Silver Purchase Act commits Treasury to buying 4.5 million ounces of silver each month
1876	Rutherford B. Hayes elected president		"Billion-Dollar Congress" passes first federal budget surpassing $1 billion
1877	*Munn* v. *Illinois* upholds state regulation of railroad rates	**1892**	Populist convention in Omaha draws up reform platform
1878	Bland-Allison Act requires Treasury to buy between $2 million and $4 million worth of silver each month		Cleveland elected president
		1893–97	Major economic depression hits United States
	Susan B. Anthony–backed bill for women's suffrage amendment is defeated in Congress	**1893**	Sherman Silver Purchase Act repealed
1880	James Garfield elected president	**1894**	Wilson-Gorman Tariff attempts to reduce tariff rates; Senate Republicans restore cuts made by House
1881	Garfield assassinated; Chester Arthur assumes the presidency		Pullman strike; Eugene V. Debs arrested and turns to socialism
1883	Pendleton Civil Service Act creates Civil Service Commission to oversee competitive examinations for government positions		Coxey's army marches on Washington, D.C.
		1895	President Cleveland deals with bankers to save the gold reserve
1884	Grover Cleveland elected president	**1896**	William McKinley elected president
1886	*Wabash* case declares that only Congress can limit interstate commerce rates	**1897**	Dingley Tariff raises duties
			Maximum Freight Rate decision rules that the Interstate Commerce Commission has no power to set rates
1887	Farm prices collapse		
	Interstate Commerce Act creates commission to regulate rates and practices of interstate shippers	**1900**	Gold Standard Act requires all paper money to be backed by gold
1888	Benjamin Harrison elected president		McKinley reelected president

power, wealth, and status, they formed coalitions to achieve their goals. But such coalitions were fragile, and their membership shifted according to the issue in question. With the exception of some southerners, groups who opposed interference by government in matters of personal liberty identified with the Democratic Party, and those who believed government could be an agent of moral reform identified with the Republican Party. Democrats included immigrant Catholics and Jews, who believed that ritual and sacraments should guide personal behavior and prove one's faith in God. Republicans consisted mostly of native and immigrant Protestants, who believed that religious salvation

Cultural-Political Alignments

could best be achieved by purging the world of evil and that legislation might be necessary to protect people from sin. Democrats took a restricted view of government power. Republicans believed in direct government action.

At the state and local levels, adherents of these two cultural traditions battled over how much control government should exercise over people's lives. The most contentious issues were use of leisure time and celebration of Sunday, the Lord's day. Protestant Republicans tried to prevent desecration of the Sabbath by passing laws to prohibit various commercial and recreational activities; they supported "blue laws," which dictated that no baseball games should be played, or stores be open, on Sunday. Immigrant Democrats, accustomed to feasting and playing after

President Rutherford B. Hayes (1822–1893) entered office amid numerous claims on him by special interests. This cartoon shows Hayes making the precarious journey from the Ohio State House, where he had served as governor, across a field of bayonets to his presidential chair, which is outfitted with a seat of spikes and propped up by the Republican Party.   Library of Congress.

control for any sustained period of time. Between 1877 and 1897, Republicans held the presidency for three terms, Democrats for two. Rarely did the same party control the presidency and both houses of Congress simultaneously: the Republicans did so twice, the Democrats once, each time for only two years. From 1876 through 1892, presidential elections were extremely close. The outcome often hinged on the popular vote in a few populous states—Connecticut, New York, New Jersey, Ohio, Indiana, and Illinois. Both parties tried to gain advantages by nominating presidential and vice-presidential candidates from these states (and also by committing vote fraud there on their candidates' behalf).

Republicans and Democrats competed against each other, but internal quarrels split both parties. Among Republicans, one faction was known as the "Stalwarts," led by New York's pompous Senator Roscoe Conkling. A physical-fitness devotee and former boxer once labeled "the finest torso in public life," Conkling worked the spoils system to win government jobs for his supporters. The Stalwarts' rivals were the "Half Breeds," led by James G. Blaine, who pursued influence as blatantly as Conkling did. On the sidelines were the more idealistic Republicans, or "Mugwumps" (supposedly an Indian term meaning "mug on one side of the fence, wump on the other"). Mugwumps such as Senator Carl Schurz of Missouri disliked the political roguishness that tainted the Republican Party and believed that only righteous, educated men like themselves should govern. Meanwhile, the Democrats tended to subdivide into white-supremacy southerners, immigrant-stock and working-class urban political machines, and business-oriented advocates of low tariffs. Like Republicans, Democrats eagerly pursued the spoils of office.

Party Factions

At the state level, one party usually dominated, and within that party a few men typically held dictatorial power. Often the state "boss" was a senator. Until the Seventeenth Amendment to the Constitution was ratified in 1913, state legislatures elected most United States senators, and a senator could wield enormous influence over the legislature and over federal patronage jobs. Many senators parlayed their state power into national influence. Besides Conkling and Blaine, their ranks included Thomas C. Platt of New York, Nelson W. Aldrich of Rhode Island, Mark A. Hanna of Ohio, Matthew S. Quay of Pennsylvania, and William Mahone of Virginia.

church, fought saloon closings and other restrictions on the only day they had free for fun and relaxation. Similar splits developed over public versus parochial schools and prohibition versus the free availability of liquor.

These issues made politics a personal as well as a community activity. In an era before polls and advertising influenced voters' choices, people formed strong loyalties to individual politicians, loyalties that often overlooked crassness and corruption. James G. Blaine—Maine's flamboyant and powerful congressman, senator, presidential aspirant, and two-time secretary of state—typified this appeal. His followers called him the "Plumed Knight," composed songs and organized parades in his honor, and sat mesmerized by his long speeches, while disregarding his corrupt alliances with businesses and railroads and his animosity toward laborers and farmers.

Allegiances to national parties and candidates were so evenly divided that no faction or party gained

National Issues

In Congress, political and economic issues such as sectional controversies, patronage abuses, railroad regulation, tariffs, and currency provoked heated debates but also important legislation. Well into the 1880s, bitter hostilities left from the Civil War continued to divide Americans. Republicans capitalized on war memories by "waving the bloody shirt" at Democrats. As one Republican orator harangued in 1876, "Every man that tried to destroy this nation was a Democrat. . . . Soldiers, every scar you have on your heroic bodies was given you by a Democrat." In the South, Democratic candidates also waved the bloody shirt, calling Republicans traitors to white supremacy and states' rights.

Sectional Conflict

Other Americans also sought advantages by invoking memories of the war. The Grand Army of the Republic, an organization of more than 400,000 Union army veterans, allied with the Republican Party and cajoled Congress into providing generous pensions for former Union soldiers and their widows. Many pensions were deserved: Union troops had been poorly paid, and thousands of wives had been widowed. But for many veterans, the war's emotional wake provided an opportunity to profit at public expense. Though the Union army spent $2 billion to fight the Civil War, pensions to Union veterans ultimately cost taxpayers $8 billion, one of the largest welfare commitments the federal government has ever made. By 1900, soldiers' pensions accounted for roughly forty percent of the federal budget. Confederate veterans received none of this money, though some southern states funded small pensions and built old-age homes for ex-soldiers.

Few politicians could dare to oppose Civil War pensions, but some attempted to dismantle the spoils system. The practice of awarding government jobs to party workers, regardless of their qualifications, had taken root before the Civil War and flourished after it. As the postal service, diplomatic corps, and other government activities expanded, so did the public payroll. Between 1865 and 1891 the number of federal jobs tripled, from 53,000 to 166,000. Elected officials, often lampooned in cartoons in newspapers and other periodicals, scrambled to control

Civil Service Reform

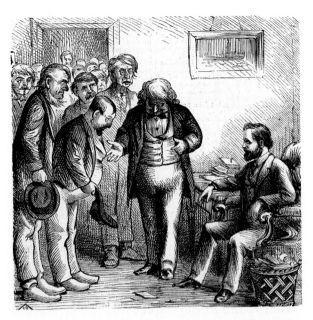

Before the Pendleton Act of 1883, many government positions were filled by patronage; hat in hand, job seekers beseeched political leaders to find a place for them. Here a member of Congress presents office-seeking friends to President Hayes.   Library of Congress.

these jobs as a means of cementing support for themselves and their parties. In return for comparatively short hours and high pay, appointees to federal jobs pledged their votes and a portion of their earnings to their patrons.

Shocked by such corruption, especially when scandals in the Grant administration exposed the defects of the spoils system, some reformers began advocating appointments and promotions based on merit rather than political connections. Civil service became a fervent reform crusade in 1881 with the formation of the National Civil Service Reform League, led by E. L. Godkin and George W. Curtis, editor of *Harper's Weekly*. The same year, the assassination of President James Garfield by a demented job seeker hastened the drive for reform.

The Pendleton Civil Service Act, passed by Congress in 1882 and signed by President Chester Arthur in 1883, outlawed political contributions by officeholders and created the Civil Service Commission to oversee competitive examinations for government positions. The act gave the commission jurisdiction over only about 10 percent of federal jobs, though the president could expand the list. The Constitution barred Congress from interfering in state affairs; thus civil service at the state and local levels developed in a more haphazard manner. Nevertheless, the Pendleton Act marked a beginning and provided the impetus for wider changes.

Civil War pensions and civil service reform were not representative issues of the Gilded Age, however. Rather, economic policymaking occupied congressional business more than ever before in the nation's history. Railroad expansion had become a particularly controversial issue. As the rail network spread, so did competition. In their quest for customers, railroad lines reduced rates to outmaneuver rivals, but rate wars soon cut into profits and wildly fluctuating rates angered shippers and farmers. Ironically, as freight rates generally fell, complaints about high rates rose. On noncompetitive routes, railroads often boosted rates as high as possible to compensate for unprofitably low rates on competitive routes, making pricing disproportionate to distance. Charges on short-distance shipments served by only one line could be far higher than those on long-distance shipments served by competing lines. Railroads also played favorites: they reduced rates to large shippers and offered free passenger passes to preferred customers and politicians.

Such favoritism stirred farmers, small merchants, and reform politicians to demand public regulation of railroad rates. Attempts at regulation occurred first at the state level.

Railroad Regulation

By 1880, fourteen states had established commissions to limit the freight and storage charges of state-chartered lines. Railroads fought these measures, arguing that the Constitution guaranteed them freedom to acquire and use property without government restraint. But in 1877, in *Munn* v. *Illinois*, the Supreme Court upheld the principle of rate regulation by the states, declaring that the grain warehouses owned by the railroads were acting in the public interest and therefore must submit to regulation for "the common good."

State legislatures, however, could not regulate large interstate lines, a limitation affirmed by the Supreme Court in the *Wabash* case of 1886, in which the Court declared that only Congress could limit rates involving interstate commerce. Reformers thereupon demanded federal regulation. Congress responded in 1887 by passing the Interstate Commerce Act. The act prohibited pools, rebates, and long-haul/short-haul rate discrimination, and it created the Interstate Commerce Commission (ICC) to investigate railroad rate-making methods, issue cease-

and-desist orders against illegal practices, and seek court aid to enforce compliance. The legislation, however, proved to be a flimsy roadblock; lack of provisions for enforcement left the railroads ample room for evasion, and federal judges chipped away at ICC powers. In the *Maximum Freight Rate* case (1897), the Supreme Court ruled that the ICC did not have power to set rates; and in the *Alabama Midlands* case (1897), the Court overturned prohibitions against long-haul/short-haul discrimination. Even so, the principle of government regulation, though weakened, remained in force.

The economic issue of tariffs carried strong political implications. Congress initially had created tariffs to protect American manufactured goods and some agricultural products from European competition. But

Tariff Policy

tariffs quickly became a tool by which special interests could protect and enhance their profits. By the 1880s separate tariffs applied to more than four thousand items, and the resulting revenues were producing an embarrassing surplus in the federal Treasury. A few economists and farmers argued for free trade, but most politicians still insisted that tariffs were a necessary form of government assistance to support industry and preserve jobs.

The Republican Party, claiming credit for economic growth, put protective tariffs at the core of its political agenda. Democrats complained that tariffs made prices artificially high by keeping out less expensive foreign goods, thereby benefiting manufacturers while hurting farmers whose crops were not protected and consumers who had to buy manufactured goods. For example, a yard of flannel produced abroad might cost 10 cents, but the imposition of an 8-cent tariff by the United States government raised the price paid by American consumers to 18 cents. An American manufacturer of a similar yard of flannel, also costing 10 cents, could charge consumers 17 cents, underselling the foreign competition by 1 cent yet still pocketing a large profit because he did not have to pay the tariff.

During most of the Gilded Age, taxes, tariffs, and other sources of income created a surplus rather than a deficit in the federal budget. Most Republicans liked the idea that the government was earning more than it spent and hoped to keep the extra money in the Treasury as a reserve or to spend it on projects like harbor improvement and federal buildings that would aid commerce. Democrats, however, pointed out that the national government was not in business to make a profit and insisted that the surplus should be reduced not by spending more but by reducing revenues—by cutting taxes and cutting tariffs. Democrats acknowledged a need for tariff protection of some manufactured goods and raw materials, but they favored lower rates to encourage foreign trade and to reduce the Treasury surplus.

Manufacturers and their congressional allies maintained control over tariff policy. The McKinley Tariff of 1890 boosted already-high rates by another 4 percent. When House Democrats supported by President Grover Cleveland passed a bill to reduce tariff rates in 1894, Senate Republicans, aided by southern Democrats eager to protect their region's infant industries, added six hundred amendments restoring most of the cuts (Wilson-Gorman Tariff). In 1897 the Dingley Tariff raised rates further. Attacks on the tariff, though unsuccessful, made tariffs the symbol of privileged business in the public mind and a target of reformers after 1900.

Monetary policy aroused even stronger emotions than did the tariff. When increased industrial and agricultural production caused prices to fall after the Civil War, debtors and creditors had opposing reactions.

Farmers suffered because the prices they received for their crops were dropping but they had to pay high interest rates on money they borrowed to pay off their mortgages and other debts. They favored schemes like the coinage of silver to increase the amount of currency in circulation. An expanded money supply, they reasoned, would make their debts less burdensome because interest rates would be lower, and thus their costs would be lower relative to the prices they received for their crops.

Monetary Policy

Creditors believed that overproduction had caused prices to decline. They favored a more stable, limited money supply backed only by gold. They opposed an expansion of the money supply. They feared that the value of currency not backed by gold would fluctuate and the resulting uncertainty would undermine investors' confidence in the United States economy.

Arguments over the quantity and quality of money, however, involved more than economics. They grew from a series of conflicts—social, regional, and emotional. Creditor-debtor conflict translated into class divisions between haves and have-nots. The debate also represented sectional cleavages: western silver-mining areas and agricultural regions of the

During the 1880s and 1890s the content of money dominated political debates. These pins of "Gold Bugs" and "Silver Bugs"—the names given to supporters of the gold standard and the silver standard—were common and indicate how dedicated the supporters of each side were to their cause. Collection of David J. and Janice L. Frent.

South and West against the more conservative industrial Northeast. And the issue carried moral, almost religious, overtones. Some Americans believed the beauty, rarity, and durability of gold gave it a magical potency and made it a God-given symbol of value. Others believed the gold standard for currency was too limiting for the machine age; sustained prosperity, they insisted, demanded new attitudes.

By the early 1870s, the currency controversy had boiled down to gold versus silver. Previously, the government had coined both gold and silver dollars. A silver dollar weighed sixteen times more than a gold dollar, meaning that gold was officially worth sixteen times more than silver. Gold discoveries after 1848, however, increased the supply of gold and lowered its market price relative to the price of silver. When silver came to be worth more than one-sixteenth the value of gold, silver producers preferred to sell their metal on the open market rather than to the government. Thus silver dollars disappeared from circulation—because of their inflated value, owners hoarded them—and in 1873 Congress officially stopped coining silver dollars, an act that silver partisans later called the "Crime of '73." Europeans also stopped buying silver, and the United States and many of its trading partners unofficially adopted the gold standard, meaning that their currency was backed chiefly by gold.

Within a few years, new mines in the American West began to flood the market with silver, and its price dropped. Gold then became worth *more* than sixteen times the value of silver, and it became profitable to spend rather than hoard silver dollars. It would have been worthwhile to sell silver to the government in return for gold, but the government was no longer buying silver.

Debtors, hurt by falling prices and the economic hard times of 1873–1878, saw silver as a means of expanding the currency supply. They joined with silver producers to denounce the "Crime of '73" and press for the resumption of silver coinage at the old sixteen-to-one ratio.

Split into silver and gold factions, Congress at first tried to compromise. The Bland-Allison Act of 1878 required the Treasury to buy between $2 million and $4 million worth of silver each month, and the Sherman Silver Purchase Act of 1890 increased the government's monthly purchase of silver by specifying weight (4.5 million ounces) rather than dollars. Neither act satisfied the different interest groups. The minting of silver dollars, which these laws allowed, failed to expand the money supply as substantially as debtors had hoped, and it failed to erase the impression that the government favored creditors' interests. Not until after a depression in the 1890s and an emotional presidential election in 1896 did the money issue subside.

Amid debates over tariffs and money, Congress and the state legislatures heard fervent arguments from supporters of woman suffrage. The Fifteenth

Woman Suffrage

Amendment, adopted in 1869, forbade states to deny the vote "on account of race, color or previous condition" but omitted any reference to sex. For the next twenty years, two organizations—the National Woman Suffrage Association (NWSA) and the American Woman Suffrage Association (AWSA)—battled for female suffrage. The NWSA, led by militants Elizabeth Cady Stanton and Susan B. Anthony, advocated comprehensive women's rights in courts and workplaces as well as at the ballot box. The AWSA, led by former abolitionists Lucy Stone and Thomas Wentworth Higginson, focused more narrowly on suffrage.

In 1878 Susan B. Anthony, who had lost in the courts when she tried to vote in 1872, persuaded Senator A. A. Sargent of California to introduce a constitutional amendment stating that "the right of citizens of the United States to vote shall not be denied or abridged by the United States or by any state on account of sex." A Senate committee killed the bill, but the NWSA had it reintroduced repeatedly over the next eighteen years. On the few occasions when the bill reached the Senate floor, it was voted down by senators who claimed that suffrage would interfere with women's family obligations and ruin female virtue.

While the NWSA fought for suffrage on the national level, the AWSA worked for amendments to state constitutions. (The two groups merged in 1890 to form the National American Woman Suffrage Association.) Though these campaigns had only a few successes, they helped to train a corps of female leaders in political organizing and public speaking. Women did win partial victories. Between 1870 and 1910, eleven states (eight of them in the West) legalized women's suffrage. By 1890 nineteen states allowed women to vote on school issues, and three granted suffrage on tax and bond issues. But the right to vote in national elections awaited a later generation.

National politics was not a glamorous field of endeavor in the Gilded Age. For each constituent who received a patronage job, many more were dis-

Legislative Accomplishments

appointed. Senators and representatives were not highly paid and usually had the financial burden of maintaining two homes: one in their home districts and one in Washington. Life in the nation's capital was bleak, oppressively hot in summer, muddy and icy in winter. Most members of Congress had no private office space, only a desk. They worked long hours responding to constituents' requests, wrote their own speeches, and had to pay for staff out of their own pockets. Yet, cynics to the contrary, most politicians were principled and dedicated.

Some members of Congress undoubtedly were tools of special interests, but most had to satisfy conflicting interests. For example, farmers from a state might have wanted lower tariffs while manufacturers from the same state wanted higher tariffs. The close and intense two-party rivalry often resulted in stalemate, but what is surprising is how much legislation was passed, not how little. Both the tariff and currency issues signaled that Congress believed the federal government should play a large part in determining economic policy and prosperity, and legislation creating the Interstate Commerce Commission and Civil Service Commission represented new directions toward government regulation.

The Presidency Restrengthened

Operating under the cloud of Andrew Johnson's impeachment, Grant's scandals, and doubts about the legitimacy of the election of 1876 (see Chapter 16), American presidents between 1877 and 1900 moved gingerly to restore the authority of their office. Proper and honest, Presidents Rutherford Hayes (1877–1881), James Garfield (1881), Chester Arthur (1881–1885), Grover Cleveland (1885–1889 and 1893–1897), Benjamin Harrison (1889–1893), and William McKinley (1897–1901) tried to act as legislative as well as administrative leaders. Like other politicians, they used symbols. Hayes served lemonade at the White House to emphasize that he, unlike his predecessor Ulysses Grant, was no hard drinker. McKinley put aside his cigar in public so photographers would not catch him setting a bad example for youth. But more importantly, each president initiated legislation and used the veto to combat Congress and guide national policy.

Rutherford B. Hayes had been a Union general and an Ohio congressman and governor before his disputed election to the presidency, an event that prompted opponents to label him "Rutherfraud." Though his party expected him to favor business interests, Hayes played a quiet role as a reformer and conciliator. He emphasized national unity over sectional rivalry and opposed violence of all kinds. When Hayes ordered out troops to disperse railroad strikers in 1877, he acted not to suppress them but because he believed the rioting and looting that the strikes engendered threatened social harmony. He tried to overhaul the spoils system by appointing civil service reformer Carl Schurz to his cabinet and by battling New York's patronage king, Senator Conkling. (He fired Conkling's protégé, Chester Arthur, from the post of New York customs house collector.) Hayes believed society was obligated to help the oppressed, including American Chinese and Indians, and after retiring from the presidency he worked diligently to aid former slaves. But his Victorian sense of propriety caused him to avoid publicity so assiduously that, according to poet-journalist Eugene Field, the only person who would recognize Hayes at a public meeting would be a policeman who would ask him to get off the grass.

When Hayes declined to run for reelection in 1880, Republicans nominated another Ohio Congress member and Civil War hero, James A. Garfield. A solemn and cautious man, Garfield defeated Democrat Winfield Scott Hancock, also a Civil War hero, by just 40,000 votes out of 9 million cast. By carrying the pivotal states of New York and Indiana, however, Garfield carried the electoral college by a comfortable margin of 214 to 155.

Garfield spent most of his brief presidency trying to secure an independent position among party potentates. He hoped to reduce the tariff and develop United States economic interests in Latin America but had to spend most days dealing with hordes of office seekers. "Once or twice I felt like crying out in the agony of my soul," Garfield admitted, "against the greed for office and its consumption of my time." Garfield pleased civil service reformers by rebuffing Conkling's patronage demands, but his chance to make lasting contributions ended in July 1881 when Charles Guiteau, a disappointed patronage seeker, shot him in a Washington railroad station. Garfield lingered for seventy-nine days while doctors tried vainly to remove a bullet lodged in his back, but he succumbed to infection on September 19, 1881.

Garfield's vice president and successor was New York's Chester A. Arthur, the spoilsman whom Hayes had fired in 1878. Republicans had nominated Arthur for vice president only to help Garfield carry New York State. Though his elevation to the presidency made reformers shudder, Arthur became a dignified and temperate executive. He signed the Pendleton Civil Service Act, urged Congress to modify outdated tariff rates, and supported federal regulation of railroads. He wielded the veto aggressively, killing several bills that excessively benefited privileged interests such as railroads and corporations. But congressional partisans frustrated his hopes for reducing the tariff and building up the navy. Arthur wanted to run for reelection in 1884 but lost the nomination to James G. Blaine on the fourth ballot at the Republican national convention.

To oppose Blaine, Democrats named New York governor Grover Cleveland, a bachelor who had tainted his respectable reputation when he fathered an illegitimate son—a fact he admitted during the campaign. Both parties focused on the sordid. (Alluding to Cleveland's bastard son, Republicans chided him with catcalls of "Ma! Ma! Where's my pa?" To which Democrats replied, "Gone to the White House, Ha! Ha! Ha!") Distaste for Blaine was so strong that a number of Mugwump Republicans deserted their party for Cleveland. On election day Cleveland beat Blaine by only 23,000 popular votes; his tiny margin

Hayes, Garfield, and Arthur

Political campaigns contained more than speeches and signs. Some candidates had songs written about them. The "quickstep" dance tune represented here was composed for the campaign of 1880 and sung at rallies for presidential and vice-presidential hopefuls James A. Garfield and Chester A. Arthur.   Collection of David J. and Janice L. Frent.

of 1,149 votes in New York gave him that state's 36 electoral votes, enough for a 219-to-182 victory in the electoral college. Cleveland may have won New York thanks to last-minute efforts of a local Protestant minister, who publicly equated Democrats with "rum, Romanism, and rebellion." The Democrats eagerly publicized the slur among New York's large Irish-Catholic population, urging voters to protest by turning out for Cleveland.

Cleveland, the first Democratic president since James Buchanan (1857–1861), echoed his Republican predecessors' complaints about the "cursed constant grind" of his office and the "want of rest." He tried, however, to exert vigorous leadership. He vetoed excessive pension bills and expanded the merit-based civil service. He acted most forcefully for tariff reform. Worried about the growing Treasury surplus, Cleve-

Cleveland and Harrison

land urged Congress to cut duties on raw materials and manufactured goods. When advisers warned that his stand might weaken his chances for reelection, the president retorted, "What is the use of being elected or reelected, unless you stand for something?" But the Mills tariff bill of 1888, passed by the House in response to Cleveland's wishes, died in the Senate. When Democrats renominated Cleveland for the presidency in 1888, protectionists in the party convinced him to temper his attacks on high tariffs.

Republicans in 1888 nominated Benjamin Harrison, former senator from Indiana and grandson of President William Henry Harrison (1841). The campaign was less savage than that of 1884 but far from clean. Some shrewd Republicans manipulated the British minister in Washington into stating that Cleveland's reelection would be good for England. Irish Democrats, who opposed England because of its colonial rule over Ireland, took offense, as intended, and Cleveland's campaign was weakened. Perhaps more helpful to Harrison were the bribery and multiple voting that helped him to win Indiana by 2,300 votes and New York by 14,000. (Democrats also indulged in bribery and vote fraud, but this time Republicans proved more successful at it.) Those states assured Harrison's victory. Though Cleveland outpolled Harrison by 90,000 popular votes, Harrison carried the electoral vote by 233 to 168.

After the election, Harrison exclaimed to Republican national chairman Matthew Quay, "Providence has given us the victory." Quay later quipped to a friend, "Think of the man. He ought to know that Providence hadn't a damned thing to do with it. . . . [He] would never learn how close a number of men were compelled to approach the gates of the penitentiary to make him president."

Harrison was the first president since 1875 whose party had majorities in both houses of Congress. Using a variety of methods, ranging from threats of vetoes to informal dinners and consultations, Harrison helped guide the course of legislation. The Congress of 1889–1891 passed 517 bills, two hundred more than the average passed by Congresses between 1875 and 1889. Harrison also showed his support for civil service by appointing the energetic reformer Theodore Roosevelt a civil service commissioner. But neither the president nor Congress could resist pressures from special interests, especially those "waving the bloody shirt." Harrison signed the Dependents' Pension Act, which provided disability pensions for Union veterans and granted aid to their

This handkerchief from the presidential campaign of 1892 depicts Democratic candidate Grover Cleveland as a just and patriotic statesman. Cleveland is the only president to have served two nonconsecutive terms, 1885–1889 and 1893–1897.   Collection of David J. and Janice L. Frent.

widows and minor children. The bill doubled the number of welfare recipients from 490,000 to 966,000.

The Pension Act and other grants and appropriations pushed the federal budget past $1 billion in 1890 for the first time in the nation's history. Democrats blamed the "Billion-Dollar Congress" on spendthrift Republicans. Voters reacted by unseating seventy-eight Republicans in the congressional elections of 1890. Seeking to capitalize on voter unrest, Democrats nominated Cleveland to run against Harrison again in 1892. This time Cleveland attracted large contributions from business and beat Harrison by 380,000 popular votes (3 percent of the total) and by 277-to-145 electoral votes.

In office once more, Cleveland moved boldly to address problems of currency, tariffs, and labor unrest. But his actions reflected a narrow orientation toward the interests of business and bespoke political weakness. During his campaign Cleveland had promised sweeping tariff reform, but he made little effort to line up support in the Senate, where protectionists undercut all efforts to reduce rates. And when 120,000 boycotting railroad workers paralyzed commerce in the Pullman strike of 1894, Cleveland bowed to requests from railroad managers and Attorney General Richard Olney to send in troops (see page 519). Though he pursued an expansionist foreign policy (see Chapter 22), throughout Cleveland's second term, events at home—particularly economic downturn and agrarian ferment—seemed too much for the president.

 ## Agrarian Unrest and Populism

While the federal government labored to sustain prosperity, inequities in the new agricultural and industrial order were arousing a mass movement that was to shake American society. The agrarian revolt—a complex mixture of strident rhetoric, nostalgic dreams, desires for economic security, and hard-headed egalitarianism—began in Grange organizations in the early 1870s. The revolt accelerated when Farmers' Alliances formed in Texas in the late 1870s and the Alliance movement spread across the Cotton Belt and Great Plains in the 1880s. The movement caught on chiefly in areas where farm tenancy, crop liens, merchants, railroads, banks, weather, and insects threatened the well-being of hopeful farmers. Once under way, the agrarian rebellion inspired visions of a truly cooperative and democratic society.

Agricultural expansion in the West, Great Plains, and South exposed millions of people to the hardships of rural life (see Chapter 17). Uncertainties might have been more bearable if rewards had been more promising, but such was not the case for farmers of small and middle-size landholdings. As growers cultivated more land, as mechanization boosted productivity, and as foreign competition increased, supplies exceeded national and worldwide demand for agricultural products. Consequently, prices for staple crops dropped steadily. A bushel of wheat that sold for $1.45 in 1866 brought only 80 cents in the

mid-1880s and 49 cents by the mid-1890s. Meanwhile, transportation, storage, and sales fees remained high relative to other prices. Expenses for seed, fertilizer, manufactured goods, taxes, and mortgage interest trapped many farm families in troubling and sometimes desperate circumstances. In order to buy necessities and pay bills, farmers had to produce more. But the spiral wound ever more tightly: the more farmers produced, the lower prices for their crops dropped (see figure).

The West suffered from a variety of special hardships. In Colorado, absentee capitalists seized control of access to transportation and water, and concentration of technology in the hands of large mining companies pushed out small firms. Charges of monopolistic control echoed among farmers, miners, and stockmen in Wyoming and Montana. In California, Washington, and Oregon, wheat farmers and fruit growers found their opportunities reduced by railroads' control of transportation and storage rates.

Even before the full impact of these developments was felt, small farmers began to organize. With

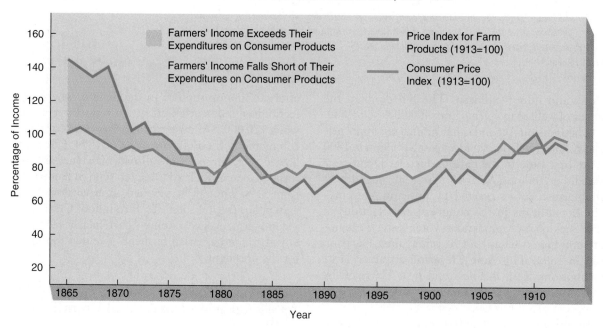

Consumer Prices and Farm Product Prices, 1865–1913

Consumer Prices and Farm Product Prices, 1865–1913 Until the late 1870s, in spite of falling farm prices, farmers were able to receive from their crops more income than they spent on consumer goods. But beginning in the mid-1880s, consumer prices leveled off and then rose while prices for farm products continued to drop. As a result, farmers found it increasingly difficult to afford consumer goods, a problem that plagued them well into the twentieth century.

aid from Oliver H. Kelley, a clerk in the Department

Grange Movement

of Agriculture, farmers in almost every state during the 1860s and 1870s founded a network of local organizations called Granges. By 1875 the Grange had twenty thousand branches and more than a million members. Like other voluntary organizations that were common throughout the country, Granges had constitutions, elected officers, and membership oaths. Strongest in the Midwest and South, Granges at first served a chiefly social function, sponsoring meetings and educational events to help relieve the loneliness of farm life. Family oriented and open to all, local Granges welcomed women's participation.

As membership flourished, Granges turned to economic and political action. Local branches formed cooperative associations to buy equipment and supplies and to market crops and livestock. In a few instances, Grangers operated farm-implement factories and insurance companies. Most of these enterprises failed, however, because farmers lacked capital for cooperative buying and because competition from large manufacturers and dealers undercut them. For example, the mail-order firm Montgomery Ward catered to rural customers and could furnish them with cheaper products more conveniently than could Granges. A requirement that Grange cooperatives run on a cash-only basis excluded large numbers of farmers who rarely had cash.

Despite their efforts, Granges declined in the late 1870s. Their promotion of thrift and hard work hardly helped families already practicing both virtues. Grangers used their numbers to some political advantage, convincing states to establish agricultural colleges, electing sympathetic legislators, and pressing for so-called Granger laws to regulate transportation and storage rates. But these efforts faltered when corporations won court support to overturn Granger laws. Granges disavowed party politics but could not withstand the power of business interests within the two major parties. Thus after a brief assertion of influence, the Granges again became farmers' social clubs.

Rural activism shifted to the Farmers' Alliances, two networks of organizations—one in the Great Plains and one in the South—that by 1890 constituted a genuine mass movement. (The West also had Alliance groups, but in that region they tended to be smaller and more closely linked to other groups

Farmers' Alliances

The Farmers' Alliance movement organized agrarian unrest into a cogent list of reforms. This sarcastic cartoon mocks Alliance members' proposals to protect mortgages and crops and make the currency system more flexible.   Library of Congress.

such as labor radicals, socialist clubs, and antimonopoly organizations.) The first Farmers' Alliances arose in Texas, where hard-pressed small farmers rallied against crop liens, merchants, and railroads in particular, and against "money power" in general. Using traveling lecturers to recruit members, Alliance leaders extended the movement to other southern states. By 1889 the southern Alliance boasted 3 million members, including the powerful Colored Farmers' National Alliance, which claimed over 1 million black members. A similar movement flourished in the Great Plains, where by the late 1880s 2 million members were organized in Kansas, Nebraska, and the Dakotas.

Like Granges, Farmers' Alliances fostered community loyalty by means of secret oaths, rallies, educational meetings, and cooperative buying and selling agreements. Also, women participated in all Alliance activities. But Alliances also opened new paths. Seeing themselves as laborers battling capitalists, some Alliance members advocated unity with the Knights of Labor and other workers' groups in the campaign against unfair privilege.

Beyond urging democratic cooperation, the Alliance movement in 1890 proposed the subtreasury plan to relieve shortages of cash and credit, the most serious rural problems. The plan had two parts. One called for the federal government to construct warehouses where farmers could store nonperishable crops while awaiting higher prices; the government would then loan farmers Treasury notes amounting to 80 percent of the market price that the stored grain or cotton would bring. Farmers could use these notes as legal tender to pay debts and make purchases. Once the stored crops were sold, farmers would repay the loans plus a small amount of interest and storage fees. This provision would enable farmers to avoid the exploitative crop-lien system (see page 498).

Subtreasury Plan

The second part of the subtreasury plan called for the government to provide low-interest loans to farmers who wanted to buy land. These loans, along with the Treasury notes lent to farmers who had temporarily stored their crops in government warehouses, would inject cash into the economy and encourage the kind of inflation that advocates hoped would raise crop prices without raising other prices. If the government subsidized business through tariffs and land grants, reasoned Alliance members, why should it not help farmers earn a decent living, too?

If all the Farmers' Alliances had been able to unite, they would have made a formidable political force; but sectional and racial differences and personality clashes thwarted early attempts at merger. At an 1889 meeting in St. Louis, white southerners, fearing reprisals from landowners and objecting to participation by blacks, rejected proposals that would have ended secret Alliance activities and whites-only membership rules. Northerners, too, evaded amalgamation, fearing domination by more experienced southern leaders. Differences on issues also prevented unity. Northern farmers, who were mostly Republicans, wanted protective tariffs to keep out foreign grain. White southerners, mostly Democrats, wanted low tariffs to hold down the costs of foreign manufactured goods. Northern and southern Alliances did favor government regulation of transportation and

communications, equitable taxation, prohibition of landownership by foreign investors, and currency reform.

Growing membership and rising confidence drew the Alliances more deeply into politics. By 1890, farmers had elected several officeholders sympathetic to their programs, especially in the South, where Alliance members controlled four governorships, eight state legislatures, forty-four seats in the United States House of Representatives, and three seats in the United States Senate. In the Midwest, Alliance candidates often ran on third-party tickets and achieved some success in Kansas, Nebraska, and the Dakotas. Leaders crisscrossed the country organizing camp meetings to solidify community feeling and support for a third party. Rallies and parades resounded with songs and orations; Alliance banners proclaimed "We Are All Mortgaged but Our Votes." During the summer of 1890, the Kansas Alliance held a "convention of the people" and nominated candidates who swept the state's fall elections. Formation of this People's Party, whose members were called Populists (from *populus*, the Latin word for "people"), gave a name to Alliance political activism.

Rise of Populism

Election results in 1890 energized efforts to unite Alliance groups into a single Populist party. A meeting in May 1891 of northern and southern Alliances in Cincinnati failed when southerners chose to remain Democrats rather than risk joining a third party. But by early 1892 southern Alliance members were ready for independent action. Meeting with northern counterparts in St. Louis, they summoned a People's Party convention in Omaha on July 4 to draft a platform and nominate a presidential candidate.

The new party's platform was one of the most comprehensive reform documents in American history. Its preamble charged that the nation had been "brought to the verge of moral, political, and material ruin. Corruption dominates the ballot box, the legislatures, the Congress, and touches . . . even the [judiciary] bench." More important, inequality threatened to split American society. "The fruits of the toil of millions," the platform declared, "are boldly stolen to build up colossal fortunes for a few."

Claiming that "wealth belongs to him that creates it," the Omaha platform addressed the three central sources of rural unrest: transportation, land, and money. Frustrated with weak state and federal regulation, Populists demanded government owner-

How do historians know that President Harrison's support for big ranchers provoked small stock raisers to support the People's Party in the West? In April 1892, large cattle ranchers in Johnson County, Wyoming, hired twenty-five Texas gunmen to suppress a group of small stock raisers with whom they were competing for grazing land. The ranchers claimed that the gunmen were necessary to put an end to cattle rustling, but their real intent was intimidation. After the gunmen had killed two alleged rustlers, an angry band of stockmen besieged the mercenaries and threatened armed revolt in what subsequently was called the Johnson County War. Wyoming's governor and senators then petitioned President Harrison for help, and the president responded with the telegram reproduced below. Federal troops rescued the gunmen and sent them home, but the readiness of the Republican-controlled state and federal government to aid large ranchers and their hired army, as the telegram reveals, caused many small stock raisers to oppose what they believed were monopolistic practices and to join the Populist movement.

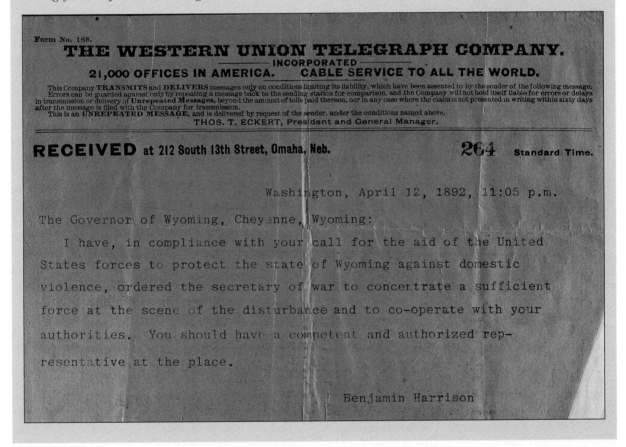

ship of railroad and telegraph lines. They urged the federal government to reclaim all land owned for speculative purposes by railroads and foreigners. The monetary plank called for the government to inflate the currency system by printing money to be made available for farm loans and by basing the money on the free and unlimited coinage of silver. Other planks advocated a graduated income tax, postal savings banks, direct election of United States senators, and a shorter workday. As its presidential candidate, the People's Party nominated James B. Weaver of Iowa, a former Union general and supporter of an increased money supply.

The Populist campaign featured dynamic personalities and vivid rhetoric. The Kansas plains rumbled with speeches by "Sockless Jerry" Simpson, an

Mary E. Lease (1850–1933) was one of the founders of the Populist Party in Kansas. Tall and intense, she had a deep, almost hypnotic voice that made her an effective publicist for the farmers' cause. She gave a seconding speech to the presidential nomination of James B. Weaver in 1892. Library of Congress.

Election Rhetoric

unschooled but canny rural reformer, and by Mary Elizabeth Lease, a fiery orator who urged farmers to "raise less corn and more hell." The South produced equally forceful leaders, such as Charles W. Macune of Texas, Thomas Watson of Georgia, and Leonidas Polk of North Carolina. Colorado's governor Davis "Bloody Bridles" Waite provoked mine owners with his prolabor and antimonopolist stance. Minnesota's Ignatius Donnelly, pseudoscientist and writer of apocalyptic novels, became chief ideologue of the northern plains and was responsible for the thunderous language in the Omaha platform. The campaign also attracted characters such as James Hogg, the 300-pound governor of Texas, and one-eyed Senator "Pitchfork Ben" Tillman of South Carolina, who were

not genuine Populists but used the agrarian fervor for their own political ends.

Weaver garnered 8 percent of the total popular vote in 1892, majorities in four states, and twenty-two electoral votes. Not since 1856 had a third party won so many votes in its first national effort. Nevertheless, disturbing factors had emerged. The party's central dilemma was whether to stand by its principles at all costs or compromise in order to gain power. The election had been successful for Populists only in the West. The vote-rich Northeast had ignored Weaver, and Alabama was the only southern state that gave the Populists as much as one-third of its votes. More ominously, by the end of 1892 most of the Farmers' Alliances had withered. Politics had replaced the social and economic fervor that had inspired the Alliance community spirit, and that spirit had died. Many Alliances either disbanded or converted into People's Party clubs.

Still, Populism gave rural dwellers in the South and West an emotional faith in the future. Although Populists were flawed Democrats—their mistrust of blacks and foreigners gave them a reactionary streak—they sought change in order to fulfill their version of American ideals. Amid hardship and desperation, millions of people began to believe that a cooperative democracy in which government would ensure equal opportunity could overcome corporate power. A banner draped above the stage at the Omaha convention captured the movement's spirit: "We do not ask for sympathy or pity. We ask for justice."

 ## The Depression of the 1890s

In 1893, shortly before Grover Cleveland became president for the second time, an ominous event occurred: the Philadelphia and Reading Railroad, once a thriving and profitable line, went bankrupt. Like other railroads, the Philadelphia and Reading had borrowed heavily to lay track and build stations and bridges. But overexpansion cut into profits, and ultimately the company was unable to pay its debts.

The same problem beset manufacturers. For example, output at McCormick farm machinery factories was nine times greater in 1893 than it had been in 1879, but revenues had only tripled. To compensate, the company bought more machines and squeezed more work out of fewer laborers. This strategy, however, only enlarged debt and increased unemployment. Jobless workers found themselves in the same plight as their employers: they could not pay their creditors. Banks suffered, too, when their customers defaulted. The failure of the National Cordage Company in May 1893 accelerated a chain reaction of business and bank closings. During the first four months of 1893, 28 banks failed. By June the number reached 128. The next year an adviser warned President Cleveland, "We are on the eve of a very dark night." He was right. Between 1893 and 1897, the nation suffered a devastating economic depression.

Personal hardship followed the business failures. Although records are sketchy, it appears that nearly 20 percent of the labor force was jobless for a significant time during the depression. Falling demand caused prices to drop between 1892 and 1895, but layoffs and wage cuts more than offset declining living costs. Many people could not afford basic necessities. The New York police estimated that twenty thousand homeless and jobless people roamed the city's streets. Surveying the depression's impact on Boston, Henry Adams wrote, "Men died like flies under the strain, and Boston grew suddenly old, haggard, and thin."

As the depression deepened, the currency problem reached a crisis. The Sherman Silver Purchase Act of 1890 had committed the government to buy 4.5 million ounces of silver each month. Payment was to be in gold, at the ratio of one ounce of gold for every sixteen ounces of silver. But a western mining boom made silver more plentiful, causing its value relative to gold to fall. Thus every month the government exchanged gold, whose worth remained fairly constant, for cheaper silver. Fearing a decrease in the value of the dollar, which was based on Treasury holdings in silver and gold, merchants at home and abroad began to cash in paper money and securities for gold. The nation's gold reserve soon dwindled, falling below $100 million in early 1893.

Currency Problems

The $100 million level had psychological importance. If investors believed that the country's gold reserve was disappearing, they would lose confidence in its economic stability and refrain from investing. British capitalists, for example, owned some $4 billion in American stocks and bonds. If the dollar were to depreciate too much, they would sell their holdings and stop investing in American economic growth. In fact, the lower the gold reserve dropped, the more people rushed to redeem their money and securities—to get gold before it disappeared. Panic spread, causing more bankruptcies and unemployment.

Vowing to protect the gold reserve, President Cleveland called a special session of Congress to repeal the Sherman Silver Purchase Act. Repeal passed in late 1893, but the run on the Treasury continued through 1894. In early 1895 gold reserves fell to $41 million. In desperation, Cleveland accepted an offer of 3.5 million ounces of gold in return for $62 million worth of federal bonds from a banking syndicate led by financier J. P. Morgan. When the bankers resold the bonds to the public, they profited handsomely at the nation's expense. Cleveland claimed that he had saved the gold reserves, but discontented farmers, workers, silver miners, and even some members of Cleveland's own party saw only humiliation in the president's deal with big businessmen. "When Judas betrayed Christ," charged South Carolina's Senator "Pitchfork Ben" Tillman, "his heart was not blacker than this scoundrel, Cleveland, in betraying the [Democratic Party]."

No one knew what the president was really enduring. At about the time Cleveland called Congress into special session, doctors discovered a malignant tumor on his palate and told the president that it required immediate removal. Fearful that public knowledge of his illness would hasten the run on gold, and intent on preventing Vice President Adlai E. Stevenson, a silver supporter, from gaining influence, Cleveland kept his condition a secret. He announced that he was going sailing, and doctors removed his cancerous upper left jaw while the yacht floated outside New York City. Outfitted with a rubber jaw, Cleveland resumed a full schedule five days later, hiding terrible pain to dispel rumors that he was seriously ill. He eventually recovered, but those who knew of his surgery believed it had sapped his vitality.

Cleveland's Secret

The deal between Cleveland and Morgan did not end the depression. After improving slightly in 1895, the economy plunged again. Farm income, on the decline since 1887, continued to slide; factories closed; banks that remained open restricted withdrawals. The tight money supply depressed housing construction, drying up an important source of jobs and reducing immigration. Cities such as Detroit allowed citizens to cultivate "potato patches" on vacant land to help alleviate food shortages. Each night urban police stations filled up with vagrants who had no place to stay.

Like previous hard times, the depression ultimately ran its course. In the final years of the century, gold discoveries in Alaska, good harvests, and industrial growth brought relief.

Emergence of a New Economic System

But the downturn of the 1890s hastened the crumbling of the old economic system and the emergence of a new one. Since the 1850s, railroads had been the prime mover of American economic development, opening new markets, boosting steel production, and invigorating banking. The central features of the new business system—consolidation and a trend toward bigness—were beginning to solidify just when the depression hit.

The economy of the United States had become national rather than sectional; the fortunes of a large business in one part of the country had repercussions elsewhere. Before the depression of the 1890s many companies had expanded too rapidly. When contraction occurred, their reckless debts dragged them down, and they pulled other industries down with them. In early 1893, for example, thirty-two steel companies, five hundred banks, and sixteen thousand other businesses filed for bankruptcy. European economies also slumped, and more than ever before the fortunes of one country affected the fortunes of other countries.

American farmers had to contend not only with fluctuating transportation rates and falling crop prices at home, but also with Canadian and Russian wheat growers, Argentine cattle ranchers, Indian and Egyptian cotton producers, and Australian wool producers. When farmers fell deeper into debt and lost purchasing power, their depressed condition in turn affected the economic health of railroads, farm-implement manufacturers, banks, and other businesses. As well, the glutted domestic market persuaded businessmen to seek new markets abroad (see Chapter 22). The downward spiral ended late in 1897, but the depression exposed problems that demanded reform and set an agenda for the years to come.

Depression-Era Protests

The depression exposed fundamental tensions in the industrial system. The gap between employees and employers had been widening steadily for half a century in response to technological and organizational changes. By the 1890s workers' protests against exploitation were threatening to spark a full-fledged economic and political explosion. In 1894, the year the economy plunged into depression, there were over thirteen hundred strikes and countless riots. Contrary to the fears of business leaders, only a few protesters were anarchists or communists come from Europe to sabotage American democracy. The disaffected included hundreds of thousands of men and women who believed that in a democracy their voices should be heard.

The era of protest began with the railroad strikes of 1877. The vehemence of those strikes, and the support they drew from working-class people, raised fears that the United States would experience a popular uprising like one in France six years earlier, which had briefly overturned the government and introduced communist principles. The Haymarket riot of 1886 (see page 518), a general strike in New Orleans in 1891, and a prolonged strike at the Carnegie Homestead Steel plant in 1892 (see page 519) heightened anxieties. In the West, too, workers became embittered. In 1892 violence broke out at a silver mine in Coeur d'Alene, Idaho. Angered by wage cuts and a lockout, striking miners seized the mines and battled federal troops sent to subdue them. Such defiance convinced some business owners that only force could counter the radicalism allegedly promoted by socialists and anarchists.

Small numbers of socialists did participate in these and other confrontations. Furthermore, personal experience convinced many workers who never became socialists to agree with Karl Marx (1818–1883), the German philosopher and father of communism, that whoever controls the means of production holds the power to determine how well people live. Marx had written that industrial capitalism generates profits by paying workers less than the value of their labor and that mechanization and mass production alienate workers from their labor. Thus, Marx contended, capitalists and laborers are engaged in an inescapable conflict over how much workers will benefit from their efforts. According to Marx, only by abolishing the return on capital—profits—could labor receive its true value. This outcome would be possible only if workers owned the means of production. Marx predicted that workers throughout the world would become so discontented that they would revolt and seize factories, farms, banks, and transportation lines. The societies resulting from this revolution would establish a socialist order of justice and equality. Marx's vision appealed to some workers because it promised inde-

Socialism

pendence and abundance. It appealed to some intellectuals because it promised an end to class conflict and crude materialism.

American socialism suffered from a lack of strong leadership and disagreement over how to achieve Marx's vision. It splintered into small groups, such as the Socialist Labor Party, led by Daniel DeLeon, a fiery West Indian–born lawyer. DeLeon and other socialist leaders failed to attract the mass of unskilled laborers, even though many immigrant workers had been exposed to socialism in Europe. American socialists often focused on fine points of doctrine while ignoring workers' everyday needs, and they could not rebut the clergy and business leaders who celebrated opportunity, self-improvement, and consumerism. Social mobility and the philosophy of individualism also undermined socialist aims. Workers hoped that they or their children would improve their lives through education and acquisition of property or by becoming their own boss; thus most workers sought individual advancement rather than the betterment of all.

Events in 1894 triggered changes within the socialist movement. That year an inspiring new socialist leader arose in response to the government's quashing of the Pullman strike and of the newly formed American Railway Union. Eugene V. Debs, the intense and animated president of the railway union, had become a socialist while serving a six-month prison term for defying an injunction against the strike (see page 519). Once released, Debs became the leading spokesman for American socialism, combining visionary Marxism with Jeffersonian and Populist antimonopolism. Though never good at organizing, Debs captivated audiences with passionate eloquence and indignant attacks on the free-enterprise system. "Many of you think you are competing," he would lecture. "Against whom? Against Rockefeller? About as I would if I had a wheelbarrow and competed with the Santa Fe [railroad] from here to Kansas City." By 1900 the group soon to be called the Socialist Party of America was uniting around Debs. It would make its presence felt more forcefully in the new century.

Eugene V. Debs

In 1894 Debs shared public attention with Jacob S. Coxey, a quiet businessman from Massillon, Ohio. Like Debs, Coxey had a vision. He was convinced that, to aid debtors, the government should issue $500 million of "legal tender" paper money, make low-interest loans to local

Coxey's Army

governments, and use the loans and money to pay the unemployed to build roads and other public works. He planned to publicize his scheme by leading a march from Massillon to Washington, D.C., gathering a "petition in boots" of unemployed workers along the way. Coxey even christened his newborn son Legal Tender and proposed that his teenage daughter lead the procession on a white horse.

Coxey's army, about two hundred strong, left Massillon in March 1894. Moving across Ohio and into Pennsylvania, they received food and housing in depressed industrial towns and rural villages, and they won new recruits. Elsewhere, a dozen similar armies organized and began the trek eastward. They came from places such as Seattle, Tacoma, San Francisco, and Los Angeles. Sore feet prompted some marchers to commandeer trains, but most of the processions were peaceful and law-abiding. One official called the marchers the "idle, useless dregs of humanity," but the troops kept themselves and their camps clean and well organized.

While other marchers were still on the road, Coxey's troops, including women and children, entered Washington on April 30. The next day (May Day, a date traditionally associated with socialist demonstrations), the citizen army of five hundred, armed with "war clubs of peace," marched to the Capitol. When Coxey and a few others vaulted the wall surrounding the Capitol grounds, mounted police moved in and routed the crowd. Coxey tried to speak from the Capitol steps, but police dragged him away. As arrests and clubbings continued, Coxey's dream of a demonstration of 400,000 jobless workers dissolved. Like the strikes, the first people's march on Washington had yielded to police muscle.

Unlike socialists, who wished to alter the economic system fundamentally, Coxey's troops merely wanted more jobs and better living standards. Today, in an age of union contracts, regulation of business, and government-sponsored unemployment relief, their goals do not appear radical. The brutal reactions of officials, however, reveal how threatening dissenters such as Coxey and Debs seemed to the defenders of the existing social order.

Populists, the Silver Crusade, and the Election of 1896

The Populists did not suffer the kinds of suppression that unions and Coxey's army experienced, but they encountered roadblocks just when their political goals

African-Americans had their own views about the political process. This drawing by African-American cartoonist Henry Jackson Lewis, shows three major parties—Democratic, Temperance, and Republican—courting a black voter in 1888. The size differential emphasized Lewis's view of the importance of black voters.   DuSable Museum of African American History.

seemed attainable. As late as 1894, Populist candidates made good showings in elections in the West and South. Like earlier third parties, though, Populists were underfinanced and underorganized. They had strong and colorful candidates but not enough of them to effectively challenge the major parties. Many voters were reluctant to abandon old loyalties to the Republicans or Democrats.

Issues of race also stymied voters. The possibility of biracial political action posed by the Farmers' Alliances in the early 1890s failed to materialize for two reasons. First, southern white Democrats had succeeded in preventing African-Americans from becoming a political force by establishing various restrictions on voting rights (see pages 500–501). Second, raw racism im-

Stifling of Biracial Political Dissent

peded the acceptance of blacks by white Populists. To be sure, some Populists sought to unite distressed black and white farmers. Tom Watson, Georgia's prominent Populist, noted that "the crushing burdens which now oppress both races in the South will cause each to . . . see a similarity of cause and a similarity of remedy." But poor white farmers could not put aside their racism. Many came from families that had supported the Ku Klux Klan during Reconstruction. Some had owned slaves, considered African-Americans a permanently inferior people, and took comfort in the belief that there always would be people worse off than they were. Thus few Populists addressed the needs of black farmers, and many used white-supremacist rhetoric to evade charges that they encouraged race-mixing.

In the national arena, the Populist crusade against "money power" settled on the issue of silver.

Many people saw silver as a simple solution to the nation's complex ills. To them, free coinage of silver meant the end of special privileges for the rich and the return of government to the people. William H. Harvey, author of the immensely popular *Coin's Financial School* (1894), preached that by coining silver "you increase the value of all property by adding to the number of money units in the land. You make it possible for the debtor to pay his debts [and for] business to start anew, and revivify all the industries of the country."

Adopting this reasoning, Populists made free coinage of silver their political battle cry. But as the election of 1896 approached, they had to decide how to translate their few previous electoral victories into larger success. Should they join with sympathetic factions of the major parties, thus risking a loss of

Free Silver

identity, or should they remain an independent third party and settle for minor successes at best?

Except in the Rocky Mountain states, where free coinage of silver had strong support, Republicans were unlikely allies. Although Republican politicians could be as moralistic as Populists, their conservatism, support for the gold standard, and big-business orientation represented what Populists opposed. In the North and West, alliance with Democrats was more plausible. There, the Democratic Party retained vestiges of antimonopoly ideology and some sympathy for a looser currency system, although "gold Democrats" such as President Cleveland and Senator David Hill of New York retained powerful influence. Populists assumed they also shared common interests with Democratic urban workers, who they believed suffered the same oppression that stifled farmers. In the South, fusion with Democrats seemed less likely,

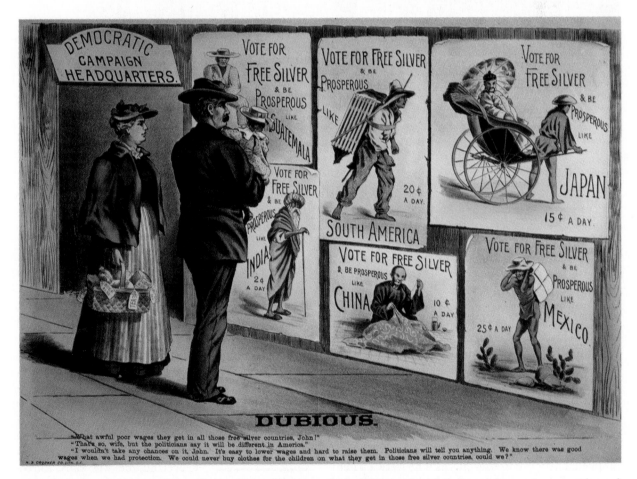

Critics of the free silver policy advocated by Populists and Democrats in the 1896 presidential election tried to convince voters that such a policy would result in poverty and low wages. The message of this broadside is that free silver would make Americans as downtrodden as peasants in the most underdeveloped countries.   Smithsonian Institute, Division of Political History, Washington, D.C.

During the 1896 presidential campaign, Republicans depicted their candidate, William McKinley, as holding the key to prosperity for both the working man and the white-collar laborer, shown here raising their hats to the candidate. Republicans successfully made this economic theme, rather than the silver crusade of McKinley's unsuccessful opponent, William Jennings Bryan, the difference in the election's outcome. Collection of David J. and Janice L. Frent.

since there the party constituted the very power structure against which Populists had revolted in the late 1880s. Whichever option they chose, coalition building or independence, Populists ensured that the political campaign of 1896 was like none before it.

The presidential election of 1896, the most issue-oriented election since 1860, brought the political turbulence to a climax. Each party was divided. Republicans, directed by Marcus A. Hanna, a prosperous Ohio industrialist, had only minor problems. For over a year, Hanna had been maneuvering to win the nomination for Ohio's governor, William McKinley. By the time the party convened in St. Louis, Hanna had corralled enough delegates to succeed. "He had advertised McKinley," quipped Theodore Roosevelt, "as if he were a patent medicine." The Republicans' only distress occurred when the party adopted a moderate platform supporting gold, rejecting a prosilver stance proposed

Republican Nomination of McKinley

by Senator Henry M. Teller of Colorado. Teller, who had been among the party's founders forty years earlier, walked out of the convention in tears, taking a small group of silver Republicans with him.

At the Democratic convention, prosilver delegates wearing silver badges and waving silver banners paraded through the Chicago Amphitheatre. Observing their tumultuous demonstrations, one eastern delegate wrote, "For the first time I can understand the scenes of the French Revolution!" A *New York World* reporter remarked that "All the silverites need is a Moses." They soon found one in William Jennings Bryan.

Bryan arrived at the Democratic convention as a member of a contested Nebraska delegation. A former congressman whose support for coinage of silver had annoyed President Cleveland, he was only thirty-six years old, deeply religious, and highly distressed by the depression's impact on midwest-

William Jennings Bryan

ern farmers. The convention seated Bryan and his colleagues instead of a competing faction that supported the gold standard. Shortly afterward, as a member of the party's resolutions committee, Bryan helped write a platform calling for free coinage of silver. When the committee presented the platform to the full convention, Bryan rose to speak on its behalf. In the heat and humidity of the Chicago summer, Bryan's now-famous closing words ignited the delegates:

> Having behind us the producing masses of this nation and the world, supported by the commercial interests, the laboring interests, and the toilers everywhere, we will answer their [the wealthy classes'] demand for a gold standard by saying to them: You shall not press down upon the brow of labor this crown of thorns, you shall not crucify mankind upon a cross of gold.

The speech could not have been timed better. Friends who had been pushing Bryan for the presidential nomination now had no trouble enlisting support. It took five ballots to win the nomination, but the magnetism of the "Boy Orator" proved irresistible. In accepting the silverite goals of southerners and westerners and repudiating Cleveland's policies in its platform, the Democratic Party became more attractive to discontented farmers. But like the Republicans, it, too, drove away a dissenting minority wing. Some gold Democrats withdrew and nominated their own candidate.

Bryan's nomination presented the Populist Party (as it was now called) with a dilemma. Should Populists join Democrats in support of Bryan, or should they nominate their own candidate? Tom Watson of Georgia, expressing opposition to fusion with Democrats, warned that "the Democratic idea of fusion [is] that we play Jonah while they play whale." Others reasoned that supporting a different candidate would split the anti-McKinley vote and guarantee a Republican victory. In the end the convention compromised, first naming Watson as its vice-presidential nominee to preserve party identity (Democrats had nominated Maine shipping magnate Arthur Sewall for vice president) and then nominating Bryan for president.

The campaign, as journalist William Allen White observed, "took the form of religious frenzy. . . . Far into the night, . . . women's voices, children's voices, the voices of old men, of youths and of maidens, rose on the ebbing prairie breezes, as the crusaders of the revolution rode home, praising the people's will as though it were God's will and cursing wealth for its

William Jennings Bryan (1860–1925) posed for this photograph in 1896, when he first ran for president at the age of thirty-six. Bryan's emotional speeches turned agrarian unrest and the issue of free silver into a moral crusade. Library of Congress.

iniquity." The issues were free silver and moneyed privilege, but campaign rhetoric rang with emotionalism.

Bryan repeatedly preached that "every great economic question is in reality a great moral question." Republicans countered Bryan's moral evangelism and attacks on privilege by predicting chaos if he won. While Bryan raced around the country giving twenty speeches a day, Hanna invited thousands of people to McKinley's home in Canton, Ohio, where the candidate plied them with speeches on moderation and prosperity, promising something for everyone. In an

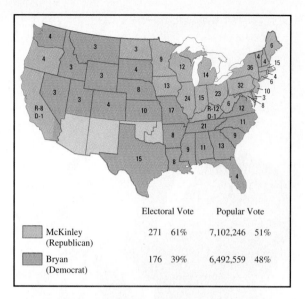

	Electoral Vote		Popular Vote	
McKinley (Republican)	271	61%	7,102,246	51%
Bryan (Democrat)	176	39%	6,492,559	48%

Presidential Election, 1896 William Jennings Bryan had strong voter support in the South and West, but the numerically superior industrial states, plus California, created majorities for William McKinley.

appeal to working-class voters, Republicans particularly stressed the new jobs that a protective tariff would create.

The election results revealed that the political standoff had finally ended. McKinley, symbol of Republican pragmatism and corporate ascendancy, beat Bryan by over 600,000 popular votes and won in the electoral college by 271 to 176 (see map). It was the most lopsided presidential election since 1872.

Election Results

Bryan had worked hard to rally the nation, but obsession with silver undermined his effort and prevented Populists from building the urban-rural coalition that would have broadened their political appeal. The silver issue diverted voters from focusing on the broader reforms deriving from the Alliance movement and the Omaha platform of 1892. Reformer Henry Demarest Lloyd summarized the matter succinctly: "Free silver," he wrote, "is the cowbird of the reform movement. It waited till the nest had been built by the sacrifices and labor of others, and then it laid its eggs in it, pushing out the others which it smashed to the ground." Urban workers, who might have benefited from Populist goals, shied away from the silver issue out of fear that free coinage would inflate prices. Labor leaders such as Samuel Gom-

pers of the AFL, though partly sympathetic, would not commit themselves fully because they viewed farmers as businessmen, not workers. And socialists such as Daniel DeLeon denounced Populists as "retrograde" because they, unlike socialists, believed in free enterprise. Thus the Populist crusade collapsed. Although Populists and fusion candidates won a few state and congressional elections in 1896, the Bryan-Watson ticket of the Populist Party polled only 222,600 votes nationwide.

As president, McKinley signed the Gold Standard Act (1900), which required that all paper money be backed by gold. A seasoned and personable politician, McKinley was best known for his expertise in crafting high protective tariffs; as a congressman from Ohio, he had guided passage of record-high tariff rates in 1890. He accordingly supported the Dingley Tariff of 1897, which raised duties even higher. Domestic tensions subsided during McKinley's presidency; an upward swing of the business cycle and a money supply enlarged by gold discoveries in Alaska, Australia, and South Africa helped restore prosperity. A strong believer in opening new markets abroad to sustain prosperity at home, McKinley encouraged imperialistic ventures in Latin America and the Pacific (see Chapter 22). Good times and victory in the Spanish-American-Cuban-Filipino War enabled him to beat Bryan again in 1900, using the slogan "The Full Dinner Pail."

The McKinley Presidency

 Conclusion

Contrary to the snobbish conclusions of the likes of E. L. Godkin and Henry Adams, government during the Gilded Age was in the hands of many well-meaning people who succeeded in making modest, and some major, accomplishments. Much of what occurred in statehouses, the halls of Congress, and the White House prepared the nation for the twentieth century. Laws encouraging economic growth with some principles of regulation, measures expanding government agencies while reducing crass patronage, federal intervention in trade and currency issues, and the emergence of an energetic presidency all evolved during the 1870s and 1880s. Because the division of power between the major parties was so even, politicians had to avoid extreme stands on issues, and the system could not tolerate radical views such as those expressed by socialists, Coxey, or Populists. But politicians also were concerned with more than patronage and influence; most genuinely wanted to create what they believed was a good society.

The 1896 election realigned national politics. The Republican Party, founded in the 1850s amid a moral crusade against slavery, had become the majority party by emphasizing active government aid to business expansion, broadening its social base to include urban workers, and playing down its moralism. The Democratic Party miscalculated on the silver issue and held its traditional support only in the South; it took three decades to refashion a broader appeal. After 1896, however, party loyalties were not as potent as they once had been. Suspicion of party politics increased, and voter participation rates declined. A new kind of politics was brewing, one in which technical experts and scientific organization would attempt to supplant the back-room deals and favoritism that had characterized the previous age.

In retrospect, it is easy to see that the Populists never had a chance. The political system was not geared for accepting third parties. The structure of Congress was such that the two-party system had enormous power, making it difficult for the few Populist representatives even to speak, let alone serve on important committees and promote reform legislation. Most Populist candidates who did win office held their seats for only one or two terms, and gradually their supporters drifted back into the two major parties. In the West, Republicans captured most former Populists; in the East, Democrats benefited. The Populist vision of democratic capitalism sustained hope for a brief historical moment, but by the late twentieth century the Populist call for a renunciation of "special privilege" would be transformed into a rejection of the welfare state.

By 1920 many Populist goals were achieved, including regulation of railroads, banks, and utilities; shorter workdays; a variant of the subtreasury plan; a graduated income tax; direct election of senators; and the secret ballot. These reforms succeeded because a variety of groups united behind them. Immigration, urbanization, and industrialization had transformed the United States into a pluralistic society in which compromise among interest groups had become a political fact of life. As the Gilded Age ended, business was still in the ascendancy, and large segments of the population were still excluded from political and economic opportunity. But the winds of dissent and reform had begun to blow more strongly.

Suggestions for Further Reading

General

Charles W. Calhoun, ed., *The Gilded Age: Essays on the Origins of Modern America* (1995); Sean Denis Cashman, *America in the Gilded Age* (1984); Ray Ginger, *The Age of Excess*, 2d ed. (1975); H. Wayne Morgan, ed., *The Gilded Age* (1970); Nell Irvin Painter, *Standing at Armageddon* (1987); Alan Trachtenberg, *The Incorporation of America: Culture and Society in the Gilded Age* (1982).

Parties and Political Issues

Paula Baker, *The Moral Framework of Public Life* (1991); Beverly Beeton, *Women Vote in the West: The Suffrage Movement, 1869–1896* (1986); Christine Bolt, *American Indian Policy and American Reform* (1987); Elisabeth Griffith, *In Her Own Right: The Life of Elizabeth Cady Stanton* (1984); J. Rogers Hollingsworth, *The Whirligig of Politics: The Democracy of Cleveland and Bryan* (1963); Ari A. Hoogenboom, *Outlawing the Spoils: The Civil Service Movement* (1961); Richard J. Jensen, *The Winning of the Midwest* (1971); Morton Keller, *Affairs of State* (1977); Paul Kleppner, *The Third Electoral System, 1853–1892* (1979); Paul Kleppner, *The Cross of Culture* (1970); Michael E. McGerr, *The Decline of Popular Politics* (1986); Walter T. K. Nugent, *Money and American Society* (1968); A. M. Paul, *Conservative Crisis and the Rule of Law: Attitudes of Bar and Bench, 1887–1895* (1969); John G. Sproat, *The Best Men: Liberal Reformers in the Gilded Age* (1968); Hal R. Williams, *Years of Decision: American Politics in the 1890s* (1978).

The Presidency

Kenneth E. Davison, *The Presidency of Rutherford B. Hayes* (1972); Justus D. Doenecke, *The Presidencies of James A. Garfield and Chester A. Arthur* (1981); Lewis L. Gould, *The Presidency of William McKinley* (1981); Homer E. Socolotsky and Allen B. Spetter, *The Presidency of Benjamin Harrison* (1987); Richard G. Welch, *The Presidency of Grover Cleveland* (1988).

Protest and Socialism

William M. Dick, *Labor and Socialism in America* (1972); Ray Ginger, *Bending Cross: A Biography of Eugene Victor Debs* (1969); Nick Salvatore, *Eugene V. Debs: Citizen and Socialist* (1982); Carlos A. Schwantes, *Coxey's Army* (1985); David Shannon, *The Socialist Party of America* (1955).

Populism and the Election of 1896

Donna A. Barnes, *Farmers in Rebellion: The Rise and Fall of the Southern Farmers Alliance and People's Party in Texas* (1984); Paolo Coletta, *William Jennings Bryan: Political Evangelist* (1964); Paul W. Glad, *McKinley, Bryan, and the People* (1964); Lawrence Goodwyn, *Democratic Promise: The Populist Movement in America* (1976); Steven Hahn, *The Roots of Southern Populism* (1983); Richard Hofstadter, *The Age of Reform: From Bryan to FDR* (1955); J. Morgan Kousser, *The Shaping of Southern Politics* (1974); Robert C. McMath, Jr., *American Populism* (1993); Walter T. K. Nugent, *The Tolerant Populists* (1963); Jeffrey Ostler, *Prairie Populism* (1993); Norman Pollack, *The Populist Response to Industrial America* (1962); Barton C. Shaw, *The Wool-Hat Boys: Georgia's Populist Party* (1984); Allan Weinstein, *Prelude to Populism: Origins of the Silver Issue* (1970).

CHAPTER

21

The Progressive Era
1895–1920

A coworker once described Florence Kelley as a "guerrilla warrior" in the "wilderness of industrial wrongs." A woman of sharp wit and commanding presence, Kelley accomplished as much as anyone in guiding the United States out of the tangled swamp of unregulated industrial capitalism into the uncharted seas of the twentieth-century welfare state.

Kelley's career traced a remarkable odyssey. Raised in middle-class comfort in Philadelphia, the daughter of a Republican congressman, Kelley graduated from Cornell in 1883. She hoped to prepare for the study of law, but the University of Pennsylvania denied her admission to its graduate school because of her gender. Instead, she went to Europe. In Zurich, Kelley joined a group of socialists who alerted her to the plight of the underprivileged. She married a socialist Russian medical student and returned to New York City in 1886. When debts and physical abuse ended the marriage five years later, Kelley took her three children to Chicago to obtain a divorce under Illinois's more permissive laws. Later that year she moved into Hull House, a residence in the slums where middle-class reformers went to live in order to help and learn from working-class immigrants. There her transforming work truly began.

Until the 1890s, Kelley's life had been male oriented, influenced first by her father, then by her husband. Kelley had tried to enter public life as men did, by attending law school and participating in political organizations. But men had blocked her path at every turn. At Hull House, however, she entered a female-oriented world, where women sought to apply their helping skills to the betterment of society. This environment encouraged Kelley to assert her powerful abilities.

Over the next decade, Kelley became one of the nation's most ardent advocates of improved conditions for working-class women and children. She investigated and publicized abuses of the sweatshop system in Chicago's garment industry, lobbied for laws to prohibit child labor and regulate women's working hours, and served as Illinois's first chief factory inspector. Her work helped create new professions for women in social service, and her strategy of investigating, publicizing, and crusading for action became a model for Progressive reform. Perhaps most significant, she and fellow reformers like Jane Addams and Lillian Wald helped involve government in the solution of pressing social problems.

During the 1890s a severe economic depression, labor violence, political upheaval, and foreign entanglements shook the nation. Technology had fulfilled many promises, but great numbers of Americans continued to suffer from poverty and disease. Many people regarded industrialists as monsters who controlled markets, wages, and prices for the sole purpose of maximizing profits. They believed government was corroded by bosses who used politics to enrich themselves. Tensions created by urbanization and industrialization seemed to be fragmenting society into conflicting interest groups.

By 1900, however, the political tumult of the previous decade had died down, and the economic depression seemed to be over. The nation had just emerged victorious from a war (see Chapter 22), and a new political era of dynamic leaders such as Theodore Roosevelt and Woodrow Wilson was dawning. A sense of renewal served both to intensify anxiety over continuing social and political problems and to raise hopes that somehow such problems could be fixed and democracy could be reconciled with capitalism.

From these circumstances there emerged a broad, complex, and many-sided reform campaign. By the 1910s many reformers were calling them-

This painting (1904) by Everett Shinn depicts the disastrous consequences of poverty and the unkept promise of American life. Unable to pay the rent, thousands of families, along with their meager belongings, were forced into the streets. A painter of the so-called Ashcan School, Shinn captured the distress of poverty-stricken families forced to experience this humiliation.   National Museum of American Art, Washington, D.C./Art Resource, NY.

• *Important Events* •

1893	Anti-Saloon League founded
1895	Booker T. Washington gives Atlanta Compromise speech
	National Association of Colored Women founded
1898	*Holden* v. *Hardy* upholds limits on miners' work hours
1900	William McKinley reelected
1901	McKinley assassinated; Theodore Roosevelt assumes the presidency
1904	Theodore Roosevelt elected president
	Northern Securities case dissolves railroad trust
1905–06	Niagara Falls Convention promotes more militant pursuit of African-American rights
	Lochner v. *New York* removes limits on bakers' work hours
	Hepburn Act tightens control over railroads
1906	Sinclair Lewis's novel *The Jungle* raises public awareness of poor working conditions in meatpacking factories
	Meat Inspection Act passed
	Pure Food and Drug Act passed
1907	Reckless speculation causes economic panic
1908	William H. Taft elected president
	Muller v. *Oregon* upholds limits on women's work hours
1909	NAACP founded
	Payne-Aldrich Tariff passed
1910	Mann-Elkins Act reinforces ICC powers
	White Slave Traffic Act prohibits transportation of women for "immoral purposes"
	Ballinger-Pinchot controversy angers conservationists
1911	Society of American Indians founded
1912	Theodore Roosevelt runs for president on the Progressive (Bull Moose) ticket
	Woodrow Wilson elected president
1913	Sixteenth Amendment ratified, legalizes federal income tax
	Seventeenth Amendment ratified, provides for direct election of United States senators
	Underwood Tariff institutes income tax
	Federal Reserve Act establishes central banking system
1914	Federal Trade Commission created to investigate unfair trade practices
	Clayton Anti-Trust Act outlaws monopolistic business practices
	Margaret Sanger indicted for sending articles on contraception through the mail
1916	Wilson reelected
	Federal Farm Loan Act provides credit to farmers
	Adamson Act mandates an eight-hour workday for railroad workers
1919	Eighteenth Amendment ratified, prohibits manufacture, sale, and transportation of alcoholic beverages
1920	Nineteenth Amendment ratified, gives women the vote in federal elections
1921	Margaret Sanger founds American Birth Control League

selves "Progressives," and in 1912 they formed a new political party by that name to embody their principles. Historians have used the term *Progressivism* to refer to the era's reformist spirit while disagreeing over its meaning and over which groups and individuals actually were Progressive. Nonetheless, the era between 1895 and 1920 experienced a series of movements, each aiming in one way or another to renovate or restore American society, values, and institutions.

The reform impulse had many sources. Industrialization and corporate capitalism had created awesome technology, unprecedented productivity, and a cornucopia of consumer goods. But they also brought overproduction, competition that squashed small companies, labor strife, and the spoiling of

Judge Ben Lindsey (1869–1943) of Denver was a Progressive reformer who worked for children's legal protection. Like many reformers of his era, Lindsey had an earnest faith in the ability of humankind to build a better world.   Library of Congress.

natural resources. Burgeoning cities facilitated the amassing and distribution of goods, services, and cultural amenities; they also bred poverty, disease, and crime. The social order was reconstructed by massive inflows of immigrants and the rise of a new class of managers and professionals. And the depression of the 1890s forced many leading citizens to realize what working people had known for some time: the central promise of American life was not being kept; equality of opportunity was a myth.

In addressing these problems, Progressives organized their ideas and actions around three goals. First, they sought to end abuses of power. Attacks on unfair privilege, monopoly, and corruption were not new in 1900; Jacksonian reformers of the 1830s and 1840s and Populists of the 1890s belonged to the same tradition. In the Progressive era, however, the attacks intensified. Trustbusting, consumers' rights, and good government became compelling political issues.

Second, Progressives aimed to supplant corrupt power with reformed versions of institutions such as schools, charities, medical clinics, and the family. Though eager to protect individual rights, they abandoned the individualistic notions that hard work and

good character automatically ensured success and that the poor had only themselves to blame for their plight. Instead, Progressives acknowledged that society had power to help the individual, and they believed that government, as the agent of society, must intervene in social and economic affairs to protect the common good and elevate public interest above self-interest. Their revolt against fixed categories of thought challenged entrenched views on women's roles, race relations, public education, legal and scientific thought, and morality.

Third, Progressives wanted to apply scientific principles and efficient management to economic, social, and political institutions. Their aim was to establish bureaus of experts that would end wasteful competition and promote social and economic order.

Befitting their name, Progressives had deep faith in the ability of humankind to create a better world. They used phrases such as "humanity's universal growth" and "the upward spiral of human development." Judge Ben Lindsey of Denver, who spearheaded reform in the treatment of juvenile delinquents, expressed the Progressive creed when he wrote, "In the end the people are bound to do the right thing, no matter how much they fail at times."

The Variety of the Progressive Impulse

Progressive reformers addressed vexing issues that had surfaced in the previous half-century, but they did so in a new political climate. As the twentieth century dawned, party loyalty eroded and voter turnout declined. In northern states, voter participation in presidential elections dropped from Gilded Age levels of over 80 percent of the eligible electorate to less than 60 percent. In southern states, where African-Americans were excluded from the polls, it fell below 30 percent. Parties and elections, it seemed, were losing their influence over government policies. At the same time, the political system was opening up to multiple and shifting interest groups, each of which championed its own causes.

Local voluntary associations had existed since the 1790s, but many organizations became nationwide in scope after the 1890s and began trying to shape government policy to meet their own needs and goals. These organizations included professional associations such as the American Bar Association; women's organizations such as the National American Woman Suffrage Association; issue-oriented groups such as the National Consumers League; civic clubs such as the National Municipal League; and associations oriented toward minority groups, such as the National Negro Business League and the Society of American Indians. Because they were not usually tied to either of the established political parties, such groups made politics much more fragmented and issue focused than in earlier eras.

Although goals of the rural-based Populist movement lingered—moral regeneration, political democracy, and antimonopolism—the Progressive quest for social justice, educational and legal reform, and streamlining of government had a largely urban bent. Between 1890 and 1920 the proportion of the nation's population living in cities rose from 35 percent to over 51 percent, and the number of cities with fifty thousand or more people rose from 58 to 144. By utilizing recent communications advances in mail, telephone, and telegraph service, urban reformers shared information and consolidated their efforts to alleviate the consequences of this change.

Urban Middle-Class Reformers and Muckrakers

Organizations and individuals interested in working to achieve the three Progressive goals—ending the abuse of power, reforming social institutions, and promoting bureaucratic and scientific efficiency—existed in almost all levels of society. But the new middle class—men and women in professions of law, medicine, engineering, social work, religion, teaching, and business—formed the vanguard of reform. Offended by inefficiency and immorality in business, government, and human relations, these people set out to apply the scientific techniques they had learned in their professions to problems of the larger society.

Motivated by personal indignation at corruption and injustice, many middle-class Progressive reformers sought to end abuses of power. Their views were voiced by journalists whom Theodore Roosevelt dubbed *muckrakers* (after a character in the Puritan allegory *Pilgrim's Progress* who rejected a crown for a muckrake). Muckrakers fed the public's taste for scandal and sensation by exposing social, economic, and political wrongs. Their investigative articles in *McClure's, Cosmopolitan,* and other popular magazines attacked adulterated foods, fraudulent insurance, prostitution, and other offenses. Lincoln Steffens's articles in *McClure's,* later published as *The Shame of the Cities* (1904), epitomized the muckraking style. Steffens hoped his exposés of bosses' misrule would inspire mass outrage and, ultimately, reform. Other well-known muckraking efforts included Upton Sinclair's *The Jungle* (1906), a novel that disclosed crimes of the meatpacking industry; Ida M. Tarbell's critical history of Standard Oil (1904); Burton J. Hendrick's *Story of Life Insurance* (1907); and David Graham Phillips's *Treason of the Senate* (1906).

Middle-class reformers also deplored the self-serving that they believed infected boss-ridden parties. As journalist William Allen White put it, machines and bosses should be "reduced to mere political scrap iron by the rise of the people." By "the people," however, reformers all too often meant middle-class types like themselves, excluding blacks, immigrants, and the white native-born working class. To improve the political process, Progressives advocated nominating candidates through direct primaries instead of party caucuses and holding nonpartisan elections to prevent the fraud and bribery bred by party loyalties.

To make officeholders more responsible, Progressives advocated three reforms: the *initiative,* which permitted voters to propose new laws; the *referendum,* which enabled voters to accept or reject a law; and the *recall,* which allowed voters to remove offending officials and judges from office before their terms were up. Their goal, like that of the business-consolidation movement, was efficiency: they would reclaim government by replacing the boss system with accountable managers chosen by a responsible electorate.

Middle-class Progressives recoiled from party politics but not from government itself. Rather, they turned to government for aid in achieving their goals, for they were convinced that only government offered the leverage they needed. Members of professions founded on systematic investigation and efficient management agreed with muckrakers that knowledge was the key to progress. Science and scientific method—planning, control, and predictability—were their central values. Just as corporations applied scientific management to achieve economic efficiency, Progressives favored using expertise and planning to achieve social and political efficiency.

The Progressive spirit also stirred some elite business leaders. Successful executives, like Alexander Cassatt of the Pennsylvania Railroad, supported

Upper-Class Reformers

some government regulation and political reforms to protect their interests from more radical political elements. Others, like E. A. Filene, founder of a Boston department store, and Tom Johnson, a Cleveland streetcar magnate, were humanitarians who worked unselfishly for social justice. Business-dominated organizations like the Municipal Voters League and U.S. Chamber of Commerce supported limited political and economic reform. They aimed to stabilize society by running schools, hospitals, and local government like efficient businesses. Elite women often led organizations like the Young Women's Christian Association, which aided growing numbers of unmarried working women, and the Women's Christian Temperance Union, the largest women's organization of its time, which supported numerous causes besides abstinence from drinking.

Not all Progressive reformers were middle- or upper-class. Vital elements of what soon became modern American liberalism derived from working-

Working-Class Reformers

class urban experience. By 1900, many urban workers were pressing for government intervention to ensure safety and security. They wanted "bread-and-butter reforms" like safe factories, a shorter workday, workers' compensation, better housing, and health safeguards. Often these were the same people who supported political bosses, supposedly the enemies of

reform. Workers understood that bosses needed to cultivate allegiance among their constituents and thus would cater to everyday needs. In fact, bossism was not necessarily at odds with humanitarianism. When "Big Tim" Sullivan, an influential boss in New York City's Tammany Hall political machine, was asked why he supported a shorter workday for women, he explained, "I had seen me sister go out to work when she was only fourteen and I know we ought to help these gals by giving 'em a law which will prevent 'em from being broken down while they're still young."

After 1900, voters from urban working-class districts elected several Progressive legislators who had trained in the trenches of machine politics. New York's Alfred E. Smith and Robert F. Wagner, Massachusetts's David I. Walsh, and Illinois's Edward F. Dunne—all from immigrant backgrounds—became spokesmen for reform at the state and national levels. Their goal was to have government take responsibility for alleviating hardships that resulted from urban-industrial growth. They opposed reforms such as prohibition, Sunday closing laws, civil service, and nonpartisan elections, which conflicted with their constituents' interests. They were most successful when they joined forces with other reformers to pass laws aiding labor and promoting social welfare.

Some disillusioned people wanted more than reform; they wanted a different society. These people—a blend of immigrant intellectuals, industrial workers, disaffected Populists, miners, lumbermen, and women's rights activists—turned to the socialist movement. The majority of socialists united behind Eugene V. Debs (see page 591), the American Railway Union organizer who drew nearly 100,000 votes in the 1900 presidential election. Although Debs failed to develop a consistent program beyond opposition to war and bourgeois materialism, he was a spellbinding spokesman for the radical cause. As the Socialist Party's presidential candidate Debs won 400,000 votes in 1904, and in 1912, at the pinnacle of his and his party's career, he polled over 900,000.

Socialists

With stinging rebukes of exploitation and unfair privilege, Debs and socialists like Milwaukee's Victor Berger and New York's Morris Hilquit made compelling overtures to reform-minded people. Some, such as Florence Kelley, joined the Socialist Party. But most Progressives had too much at stake in the capitalist system to want to overthrow it. Municipal ownership of public utilities was as far as they would go toward radical change. In Wisconsin,

Though their objectives sometimes differed from those of middle-class Progressive reformers, socialists also became a more active force in the early twentieth century. Socialist parades on May Day, such as this one in 1910, were meant to express the solidarity of all working people.   Library of Congress.

where Progressivism was most advanced, reformers refused to ally with Berger's more radical group. California Progressives formed a temporary alliance with reactionaries to prevent socialists from gaining power in Los Angeles. And few Progressives objected when Debs was jailed in 1918 for giving an antiwar speech.

It would be a mistake to assume that a Progressive spirit captured all of American society between 1895 and 1920. Large numbers of people, heavily represented in Congress, disliked government interference in economic affairs and found no fault with existing power structures. Defenders of free enterprise opposed many regulatory measures out of self-interest and fear that government programs would undermine the individual initiative and competition that they believed to be basic to the free-market system. Government interference, they contended, contradicted the natural law of survival of the fittest. "Old-guard" Republicans like Senator Nelson W. Aldrich of Rhode Island and House Speaker Joseph Cannon of Illinois championed this ideology. Outside Washington, D.C., this outlook was represented by tycoons like J. P. Morgan, John D. Rockefeller,

Opponents of Progressivism

and other capitalists who insisted that progress would result only from maintaining the profit incentive and an economy unfettered by government regulation.

Progressive reformers operated from the center of the ideological spectrum. Moderate, socially aware, sometimes contradictory, they believed on the one hand that the laissez-faire system was obsolete and on the other that a radical shift away from free enterprise was dangerous. Like Jeffersonians, they believed in the conscience and will of the people; like Hamiltonians, they opted for a strong central government to act in the interests of conscience. Their goals were both idealistic and realistic. As minister-reformer Walter Rauschenbusch wrote, "We shall demand perfection and never expect to get it."

Progressive Contradictions

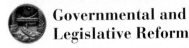 ## Governmental and Legislative Reform

What should be the responsibilities of government? Traditionally, theorists and ordinary citizens had held that because the United States had been born from mistrust of tyranny, democratic government should be small and unobtrusive, should interfere in private affairs only in unique circumstances, and should withdraw when balance had been restored. But in the late 1800s this point of view weakened. Corporations pursued government aid and protection for their enterprises. Discontented farmers sought government regulation of railroads and other monopolistic businesses. City dwellers, accustomed to the favors performed by political machines, came to expect government to act on their behalf.

By the turn of the century, professionals and intellectuals were concluding that government should exert more power to ensure justice and well-being. Increasingly aware that a simple, inflexible government was inadequate in a complex industrial age, they reasoned that public authority needed to counteract inefficiency, corruption, and exploitation. But before reformers could effectively use such power, they would have to capture government from politicians whose greed had soiled the democratic system. Thus eliminating corruption from government was a central thrust of Progressive activity.

Reformers first attacked corruption in cities (see Chapter 19). Between 1870 and 1900, opponents of the boss system tried to restructure government through reforms such as civil service hiring, nonpartisan elections, and tighter scrutiny of public expenditures. A few reformers advocated poverty relief, housing improvement, and prolabor laws, but most worked for efficient—meaning economical—government. After 1900 reform momentum brought into being the city-manager and commission forms of government (in which urban officials were chosen for professional expertise, rather than political connections) and public ownership of utilities (to prevent monopolistic gas, electric, and streetcar companies from profiting at the public's expense).

Reformers found, however, that the city was too small an arena for the changes they sought. Frustrated by limited victories, they came to believe that the state and federal governments offered better opportunities for enacting needed legislation. Their goals tended to vary regionally. In the Great Plains and Far West, they rallied behind railroad regulation and government control of natural resources. In the South reformers continued the Populist crusade against big business and autocratic politicians. In the urban-industrial Northeast and Midwest, they attacked corrupt political machines and unsafe labor conditions.

Faith in a strong, fair-minded executive prompted Progressives to support a number of skillful and charismatic governors who used executive power to achieve change. Their ranks included Braxton Bragg Comer of Alabama and Hoke Smith of Georgia, who introduced business regulation and other reforms in the South; Albert Cummins of Iowa and Hiram Johnson of California, who battled the railroads that dominated their states; and Woodrow Wilson of New Jersey, whose administrative reforms were imitated by other governors. Such men, however, were not saints. Bowing to prevailing racist sentiments, Smith supported disfranchisement of African-Americans, and Johnson promoted discrimination against Japanese-Americans.

Progressive Governors

The most forceful Progressive governor was Wisconsin's Robert M. La Follette. A self-made small-town lawyer whose compact build and thick, bristling hair suited his combative personality, La Follette rose through the state Republican Party and won the governorship in 1900. As governor he initiated a multipronged reform program distinguished by direct primaries, more equitable taxes, and regulation of railroad rates. He also appointed commissions staffed by experts, who supplied him with the facts and figures he used in fiery speeches to arouse public support for his policies. After three terms as governor, La Follette was elected to the United States Senate and carried his ideals into national politics. "Battling Bob" displayed a rare ability to approach reform scientifically while still stirring up the people with moving rhetoric. His goal, he once asserted, "was not to 'smash' corporations, but to drive them out of politics, and then to treat them exactly the same as other people are treated."

Robert M. La Follette

The crusade against corrupt politics brought about some permanent changes. By 1916 all but three states had direct primaries, and many had adopted the initiative, referendum, and recall. Political reformers achieved a major goal in 1913 with adoption of the Seventeenth Amendment, which provided for direct election of United States senators (they had been elected by state legislatures, many of which Progressives thought were corrupt). But political reforms did not

The Seventeenth Amendment

always help. Party bosses, better organized and more experienced than reformers, were still able to control elections. Efforts to use the initiative, referendum, and recall often failed because special-interest groups spent large sums to influence the voting. Political reformers also found that the courts aided rather than reined in entrenched power.

State laws to improve labor conditions had greater impact than did political reforms. Many states broadly interpreted their constitutional

Reform of Labor Conditions

powers to protect public health and safety (police power) and enacted factory inspection laws, and by 1916 nearly two-thirds of the states required compensation for victims of industrial accidents. A coalition of labor and humanitarian groups supported these laws and even induced some legislatures to grant aid to mothers with dependent children. Under pressure from the National Child Labor Committee, nearly every state set a minimum age for employment (varying from twelve to sixteen) and prohibited employers from working children more than eight or ten hours a day. Such laws had limited effect, though, because they seldom provided for the close inspection of factories that full enforcement required. And families that needed extra income evaded the laws by encouraging their children to work and to lie about their ages.

Several groups joined forces to restrict working hours for women. After the Supreme Court, in *Muller* v. *Oregon,* upheld Oregon's ten-hour limit in 1908 (see page 517), more states passed laws protecting female workers. Meanwhile, in 1914 efforts of the American Association for Old Age Security showed signs of success when Arizona established old-age pensions. The courts struck down the law, but demand for pensions continued, and in the 1920s many states enacted laws to provide for needy elderly people.

Reformers themselves were not always certain about what was Progressive, especially in human behavior. The main question was whether it was

Moral Reform

possible to create a desirable moral climate through legislation. Some reformers, notably adherents of the Social Gospel movement, believed that only church-based inspiration and humanitarian work, rather than legislation, could transform society. Others argued that state in-

Robert M. La Follette (1855–1925) was one of the most dynamic of Progressive politicians. As governor of Wisconsin, he sponsored a program of political reform and business regulation known as the Wisconsin Plan. In 1906 he entered the United States Senate and continued to champion Progressive reform. The National Progressive Republican League, which La Follette founded in 1911, became the core of the Progressive Party. State Historical Society of Wisconsin.

tervention was necessary to enforce purity, especially in drinking habits and sexual behavior.

The Anti-Saloon League, formed in 1893, intensified the long-standing campaign against drunkenness and its costs to society. This organization

The War on Alcohol

allied with the Woman's Christian Temperance Union (founded in 1873) to publicize the role of alcoholism in liver disease and other health problems. The League was especially successful in shifting attention from the individual's responsibility for temperance to the alleged link between the drinking that saloons encouraged and the accidents, poverty, and inefficient productivity that were consequences of drinking.

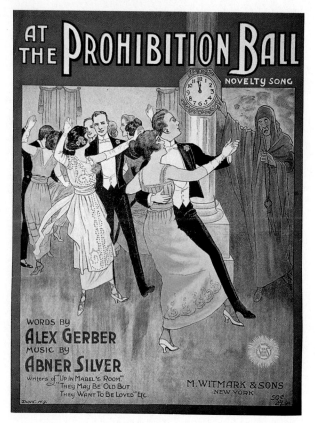

Though not supported by all Progressive reformers, the Eighteenth Amendment to the Constitution passed during this era. The measure, which prohibited the manufacture, sale, and transportation of alcoholic beverages, was intended to uplift morality and protect health. Social satirists exaggerated the belief that no fun could be had after prohibition went into effect. This sheet music cover from 1919 shows partygoers trying to squeeze in one last minute of pleasure before the new law takes effect at midnight. Sheet Music Collection, The John Hay Library, Brown University.

The war on saloons prompted many states, counties, towns, and city wards to restrict consumption of liquor. By 1900 almost one-fourth of the nation's population lived in "dry" communities (which prohibited the sale of liquor). But consumption of alcohol, especially beer, increased after 1900, convincing prohibitionists that a nationwide ban was the only solution. By 1917 they had enlisted support from notables such as Supreme Court Justice Louis D. Brandeis and former president William Howard Taft. In 1918 Congress passed the Eighteenth Amendment (ratified in 1919 and implemented in 1920) outlawing the manufacture, sale,

and transportation of intoxicating liquors. Not all prohibitionists were Progressive reformers, and not all Progressives were prohibitionists. Nevertheless, the Eighteenth Amendment can be seen as an expression of the Progressive urge to protect the family and the workplace through reform legislation.

Public outrage erupted in another area when muckraking journalists charged that international rings were kidnapping young women and forcing them into prostitution, a practice called white slavery. Already alarmed by a perceived link between immigration and prostitution and fearful that prostitutes were producing genetically inferior children, middle-class moralists prodded governments to investigate the problem and pass corrective legislation. The Chicago Vice Commission, for example, undertook a "scientific" survey and published its findings, called *The Social Evil in Chicago*, in 1911. The report underscored the poverty, ignorance, and desperation that drove women into prostitution. Above all, however, it asserted that "it is a man and not a woman problem which we face today—commercialized by men—supported by men—the supply of fresh victims furnished by men. . . . Until the hearts of men are changed we can hope for no absolute annihilation of the Social Evil."

Prostitution and White Slavery

Such investigations found apparently rising numbers of prostitutes but failed to prove that criminal organizations deliberately lured women into prostitution. It appeared instead that women made their own choices to enter "the life"—choices that clearly reflected economic needs but also alarmed moralists about the alleged dangers of young women's sexuality. Reformers nonetheless believed they could attack prostitution by punishing those who promoted it. In 1910 Congress passed the White Slave Traffic Act, known as the Mann Act, prohibiting interstate and international transportation of a woman for immoral purposes. By 1915 nearly every state had outlawed brothels and solicitation of sex.

Like prohibition, the Mann Act reflected growing sentiment that government could improve behavior by restricting it. Reformers believed that the source of evil was not original sin or human nature but the social environment. And if evil was created by human beings, it followed that it could be eradicated by human effort. Intervention in the form of laws could help create a heaven on earth.

New Ideas in Education, Law, and the Social Sciences

While the reform impulse traveled on legislative paths, new vistas opened in education, law, and social service. The preoccupation with efficiency and scientific management challenged teachers, judges, and social scientists to come to grips with modern society. Darwin's theory of evolution had undermined traditional beliefs in a God-created world; immigration had replaced social uniformity with diversity; and technology had made old habits of production and consumption obsolete. Thoughtful people in a number of professions grappled with how to respond to the new era yet preserve what was best from the past.

In education, changing patterns of school attendance called for new ways of thinking. As late as the 1870s, when families needed children at home to do farm work, Americans attended school for an average of only four years. By 1900, however, swelling cities contained multitudes of children who had more time for school. Also, urban taxpayers were providing sufficient revenues to make mass education possible. Boosted by compulsory-attendance laws, enrollments in public schools rose from 7 million in 1870 to 18 million in 1910. Meanwhile, the number of public high schools grew from five hundred to over ten thousand.

In the early 1800s, school curricula had consisted chiefly of moralistic pieties. *McGuffey's Reader,* used throughout the nation, taught homilies such as "By virtue we secure happiness" and "One deed of shame is succeeded by years of penitence."

John Dewey and Progressive Education

But in the late nineteenth century, psychologist G. Stanley Hall and educational philosopher John Dewey asserted that modern education ought to prepare children differently. They insisted that personal development, not subject matter, should be the focus of the curriculum. Education, argued Dewey, must relate directly to experience; children should be encouraged to discover knowledge for themselves. Learning relevant to students' lives should replace rote memorization and outdated subjects.

Progressive education, based on Dewey's *The School and Society* (1899) and *Democracy and Education* (1916), was a uniquely American phenomenon. Dewey believed that learning should focus on real-

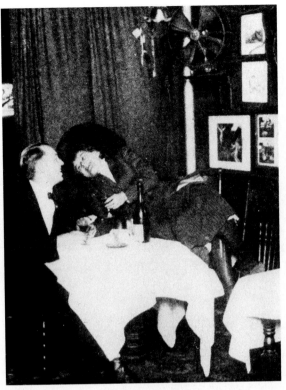

In addition to crusading against drunkenness, moral reformers stirred up emotions over accusations that evil men were seducing innocent young women into prostitution—or white slavery, as it was called. In this posed photograph printed in a 1910 antivice publication, The White Slave Hell: or, With Christ at Midnight in the Slums of Chicago, *the man supposedly has gotten the woman drunk and is about to lure her into a life of sin.* Collection of Perry R. Duis, from The Saloon.

life problems and that children should be taught to use their intelligence and ingenuity as instruments for controlling their environment. From kindergarten through high school, Dewey asserted, children should learn through direct experience. Dewey and his wife Alice put these ideas into practice in the Laboratory School that they directed at the University of Chicago.

Personal growth became the driving principle behind higher education as well. Previously, the purpose of American colleges and universities had been

Growth of Colleges and Universities

that of their European counterparts: to train a select few for the professions of law, medicine, teaching, and religion. But in the late 1800s, institutions of higher education multiplied, aided by

To make children's play more orderly and provide a safer alternative to streets and alleys, progressive playground reformers sponsored a variety of activities, ranging from sports and games to story-telling. In spite of efforts such as this woman telling a story in a New York playground, the reformers never completely succeeded because children wanted to play without adult supervision and continued to use streets and vacant lots for recreation.   Manuscripts and Archives Section, Rare Book and Manuscripts Division, the New York Public Library.

land grants and by an increase in the number of people who could afford tuition. Between 1870 and 1910 the number of colleges and universities in the United States grew from 563 to nearly 1,000. Curricula expanded as educators sought to make learning more appealing and to keep up with technological and social changes. Harvard University, under President Charles W. Eliot, pioneered in substituting electives for required courses and experimenting with new teaching methods. The University of Wisconsin and other public universities achieved distinction in new areas of study such as political science and sociology. Many schools, private and public, considered athletics vital to a student's growth, and intercollegiate sports became a permanent feature of student life as well as a source of school pride and alumni contributions.

Southern states, in keeping with separate-but-equal policies, set up segregated land-grant colleges for blacks. *Separate* was a more accurate description

of these institutions than *equal*. African-Americans continued to suffer from inferior educational opportunities in both state institutions and private all-black colleges.

As colleges and universities expanded, so did female enrollments. Between 1890 and 1910 the number of women in these institutions swelled from 56,000 to 140,000. Of these, 106,000 attended coeducational institutions (mostly state universities); the rest attended women's colleges. By 1920, 283,000 women were attending college, accounting for 47 percent of total enrollment. These numbers disproved contentions that women were unfit for higher learning because they were mentally and physically inferior to men, but discrimination lingered in admissions and curriculum policies. Women were encouraged (indeed, they usually sought) to take home economics and education courses rather than science and mathematics, and most medical schools, including Harvard and Yale, refused to admit women. Shut out from such institutions, women founded their own schools, such as the Women's Medical College of Philadelphia and the many women's colleges, including Smith, Mount Holyoke, and Wellesley.

American educators adopted the prevailing attitude of business: more is better. They justifiably congratulated themselves for increasing enrollments and making instruction more meaningful. By 1920, 78 percent of all children between ages five and seventeen were enrolled in public elementary and high schools; another 8 percent attended private and parochial schools. These figures represented a huge increase over the 1870 attendance rate. And there were 600,000 college and graduate students in 1920, compared with only 52,000 in 1870. Yet few people looked beyond the numbers to assess how well schools were doing their job. Critical analysis seldom tested the faith that schools could promote equality and justice as well as personal growth and responsible citizenship.

The legal profession also embraced the new emphasis on experience and scientific principles. Harvard law professor Roscoe Pound, an influential proponent of the new outlook, urged that social reality should influence legal thinking. Oliver Wendell Holmes, Jr., associate justice of the Supreme Court between 1902 and 1932, led the attack on the traditional view of law as universal and unchanging. "The life of the law," said Holmes, sounding like Dewey, "has not been logic; it has been experience." The opinion that law should reflect society's needs challenged the practice of invoking inflexible legal precedents that often obstructed social legislation. Louis D. Brandeis, a lawyer who later joined Holmes on the Supreme Court, carried legal reform one step further by insisting that judges' opinions be based on factual, scientifically gathered information about social realities. Brandeis collected extensive data on the harmful effects of long hours to convince the Supreme Court, in the landmark case *Muller* v. *Oregon* (1908), to uphold Oregon's law limiting women's working hours.

Progressive Legal Thought

The new legal thinking met with some resistance. Judges raised on laissez-faire economics and strict construction of the Constitution continued to overturn laws Progressives thought necessary for effective reform. Thus despite Holmes's forceful dissent, in 1905 the Supreme Court, in *Lochner* v. *New York*, revoked a New York law limiting bakers' working hours. As in similar cases, the Court's majority argued that the Fourteenth Amendment protected an individual's right to make contracts without government interference and that this protection superseded police power. Judges also weakened federal regulations by invoking the Tenth Amendment, which prohibited the federal government from interfering in matters reserved to the states.

Courts did uphold some regulatory measures, particularly those protecting public safety. A string of decisions beginning with *Holden* v. *Hardy* (1898), in which the Supreme Court upheld Utah's mining regulations, supported the use of state police powers to protect health, safety, and morals. Judges also affirmed federal police powers and Congress's authority over interstate commerce by sustaining federal legislation such as the Pure Food and Drug Act, the Meat Inspection Law (see page 621), and the Mann Act (see page 608). In these instances citizens' welfare took precedence over the Tenth Amendment.

But the concept of general welfare posed thorny legal problems. Even if one agreed that laws should address society's needs, whose needs should prevail? The United States was a mixed nation; gender, race, religion, and ethnicity deeply influenced law. In many localities a native-born white Protestant majority imposed Bible reading in public schools (offending Catholics and Jews), required business establishments to close on Sundays, restricted the religious practices of Mormons and other groups, prohibited interracial marriage, and enforced racial segregation. Justice Holmes asserted that laws should be made for "people of fundamentally differing views," but were such laws possible in a nation of so many different interest groups? The debate continues to this day.

At the same time, social science—the study of society and its institutions—experienced changes similar to those overtaking law and education. In economics a group of young scholars used statistics to argue that laws governing economic relationships were not rock solid. Instead, they claimed, economic theory should reflect prevailing social conditions. Richard T. Ely of Johns Hopkins University and the University of Wisconsin, a spokesman for this point of view, argued that the poverty and impersonality resulting from industrialization required interference by "the united efforts of Church, state, and science." A new breed of sociologists led by Lester Ward, Albion Small, and Edward A. Ross agreed, adding that citizens should

Social Science

The Infant Welfare Society, a typical Progressive organization interested in social reform, had a strong interest in improving the health of children who lived in cramped, unventilated tenements. The organization frequently sponsored regular walks in all kinds of weather—including on cold days such as depicted here—to bring babies into the fresh air. Chicago Historical Society.

actively plan to cure social ills rather than passively waiting for problems to solve themselves. In the field of psychology, female researchers challenged age-old beliefs that women's minds were different from, and inferior to, men's.

Meanwhile, Progressive historians Frederick Jackson Turner, Charles A. Beard, and Vernon L. Parrington were examining the past as a means of explaining present American society and of promoting social change. Beard, like other Progressives, believed that the Constitution was a flexible document amenable to growth and change, not an inviolable code imposed by wise forefathers. His influential *Economic Interpretation of the Constitution* (1913) argued that a group of merchants and business-oriented lawyers had created the Constitution to defend private property. If it had served special interests in one age, it could be changed to serve broader interests in another age. Meanwhile, political scientists like Woodrow Wilson emphasized the

practical over the theoretical, advocating expansion of government power to ensure justice and progress.

In public health, organizations like the National Consumers League (NCL) joined with physicians and social scientists to bring about some of the most far-reaching Progressive reforms. Founded by Josephine Shaw, a socially prominent Massachusetts widow, the NCL initially focused on improving the wages and working conditions of young women. After Florence Kelley became the NCL's general secretary, the organization expanded its activities to encompass women's suffrage, protection of child laborers, and elimination of potential health hazards. Local branches were joined by women's clubs in supporting consumer protection measures such as the licensing of food vendors and inspection of dairies. They also urged city governments to fund neighbor-

National Consumers League and Public Health Reform

hood clinics that provided health education and medical care to the poor. These grassroots reform efforts were basically carried out by women and succeeded where male-based reforms, which either focused on short-term political gains or derived from expert-dominated organizations, did not. Moreover, NCL efforts spurred a consumer and health-awareness movement that has persisted to the present day.

A new breed of men and women pressed for institutional change as well as political reform in the two decades before the First World War. Largely middle class, trained by new professional standards, confident that new ways of thinking could bring about progress, these people helped to broaden government's role to meet the needs of a mature industrial society. But their questioning of prevailing assumptions also unsettled conventional attitudes toward race and gender.

Challenges to Racial and Sexual Discrimination

W. E. B. Du Bois, a forceful black scholar and writer, ended an essay in *The Souls of Black Folk* (1903) with a blunt prediction for American society. "The problem of the Twentieth Century," he wrote, "is the problem of the color line." Du Bois's assertion rang true; people of color continued to endure violent treatment and degradation long after slavery had legally ended. But at the same time, women of all races also suffered from an underprivileged status and were struggling to strive for rights and justice.

Both women and people of color lived in a society dominated by white males. Both suffered disfranchisement, discrimination, and humiliation. And for centuries both groups had been striving for freedom and equality.

The Progressive challenge to entrenched ideas and customs aided African-Americans' and women's struggles for their rights but posed a dilemma. Should women and people of color strive to become just like white men, with white men's values as well as their rights? Or was there something unique about racial and sexual cultures that should be preserved at the risk of sacrificing some gains? Both groups fluctuated between attraction to and rejection of the culture from which they had been excluded.

In 1900 nine out of ten African-Americans lived in the South, where repressive Jim Crow laws had multiplied in the 1880s and 1890s (see page 501). Southern blacks were denied legal and voting rights and were officially segregated in almost all walks of life. They faced constant exclusion; in 1910 only 8,000 out of 970,000 high-school-age blacks in the entire South were enrolled in high schools. And they met with constant violence. Between 1900 and 1914 southern white mobs, usually incensed over rumored sexual assaults by black men on white women, lynched over a thousand blacks.

Blacks began to move northward in the 1880s, accelerating their migration after 1900. The conditions they found represented a relative improvement over their rural sharecropping existence, but job discrimination, inferior schools, and segregated housing existed in northern as well as southern cities. White humanitarians perpetuated segregation by maintaining separate and inferior institutions, such as hospitals and schools, for blacks. A half-century after the abolition of slavery, most whites still agreed with historian James Ford Rhodes, who wrote that blacks were "innately inferior and incapable of citizenship."

African-American leaders differed sharply over how—and whether—to pursue assimilation. In the wake of emancipation, ex-slave Frederick Douglass urged "ultimate assimilation through self-assertion, and on no other terms." Those who favored separation from white society supported migration to Africa or the establishment of all-black communities in Oklahoma Territory and Kansas. Others advocated militancy, believing, as one writer stated, "Our people must die to be saved and in dying must take as many along with them as it is possible to do with the aid of firearms and all other weapons."

Most blacks, however, could neither escape nor conquer white society. They had to find other routes to economic and social improvement. Self-help, a strategy articulated by educator Booker T. Washington, was one popular alternative. Born to slave parents in 1856, Washington worked his way through school and in 1881 founded Tuskegee Institute in Alabama, a vocational school for blacks. There he developed the philosophy that blacks' best hopes for assimilation lay in at least temporarily accommodating to whites. Rather than fighting for political rights, Washington said, blacks should work hard, acquire property, and prove they were worthy of rights.

Booker T. Washington and Self-Help

Washington voiced his views in a widely acclaimed speech at the Atlanta Exposition in 1895. "Dignify and glorify common labor," he urged in what became known as the Atlanta Compromise. "Agitation of questions of racial equality is the extremest folly." Envisioning a society where blacks and whites would remain apart but share the same goals, Washington observed that "in all things that are purely social we can be as separate as the fingers, yet one as the hand in all matters essential to mutual progress."

Whites welcomed Washington's accommodation policy because it urged patience and reminded black people to stay in their place. Because he said what they wanted to hear, white businesspeople, reformers, and politicians chose to regard Washington as representative of all African-Americans. Yet though Washington endorsed a separate-but-equal policy, he projected a subtle racial pride that would find more direct expression in black nationalism later in the twentieth century, when some African-Americans advocated control of their own businesses and schools. Washington never argued that blacks were inferior to whites; he asserted that they could enhance their dignity through self-improvement.

Some blacks thought that Booker T. Washington seemed to favor a degrading second-class citizenship. His southern-based philosophy did not appeal to educated northern African-Americans, such as William Monroe Trotter, the fiery editor of the *Boston Guardian*, or social scientist T. Thomas Fortune. In 1905 a group of "anti-Bookerites" convened near Niagara Falls and pledged a militant pursuit of rights such as unrestricted voting, economic opportunity, integration, and equality before the law. Spokesperson for the Niagara movement was W. E. B. Du Bois, an outspoken critic of the Atlanta Compromise.

A New Englander with a Ph.D. from Harvard, Du Bois was both a Progressive and a member of the black elite. He held an undergraduate degree from all-black Fisk University and had studied in Germany, where he learned about scientific investigation. While a faculty member at all-black Atlanta University, Du Bois compiled fact-filled sociological studies of black ghetto dwellers and wrote poetically in support of civil rights. He treated Washington politely but could not accept white domination. "The way for a people to gain their reasonable rights," Du Bois asserted, "is

W. E. B. Du Bois and the "Talented Tenth"

not by voluntarily throwing them away." Instead, blacks must agitate for what was rightfully theirs.

Du Bois demonstrated that accommodation was an unrealistic strategy, but his solution had its own drawbacks. A blunt elitist, Du Bois believed that an intellectual vanguard of cultured, highly trained blacks, the "Talented Tenth," would save the race by setting an example to whites and uplifting other blacks. Such sentiment had more appeal for middle-class white liberals than for African-American sharecroppers. Thus in 1909 when Du Bois and his allies formed the National Association for the Advancement of Colored People (NAACP), which aimed to end racial discrimination by pursuing legal redress in the courts, the leadership consisted chiefly of white Progressives. By 1914 the NAACP had fifty branch offices and over six thousand members, but only its fight against lynching affected sharecropping and laboring families in the South.

Whatever their views, African-Americans faced continued oppression. Those who managed to acquire property and education encountered bitter resentment, especially when they fought for civil rights. Black editor and reformer Ida B. Wells, whose *On Lynching* (1892) was written in support of antilynching legislation, suffered destruction of her property and threats against her life. The federal government only aggravated biases. During Woodrow Wilson's presidency, discrimination within the federal government expanded: southern cabinet members supported racial separation in restrooms, restaurants, and government office buildings and balked at hiring black workers. Commenting on Wilson's racism in 1913, Booker T. Washington wrote, "I have never seen the colored people so discouraged and so bitter as they are at the present time."

Disfranchisement, instituted by southern states in the late nineteenth century (see page 500), still prevented blacks from becoming full American citizens. Washington seemed to accept disfranchisement, hoping blacks eventually would regain the vote through education and hard work. Du Bois believed suffrage was essential to protect social and economic rights.

African-Americans still sought to fulfill the American dream of success, but many wondered whether their goals should include membership in a corrupt white society. Du Bois voiced these doubts poignantly, observing that "one ever feels his twoness—an American, a Negro, two souls, two thoughts, two unreconciled strivings, two warring ideals in one dark body." Somehow blacks had to reconcile that "twoness" by

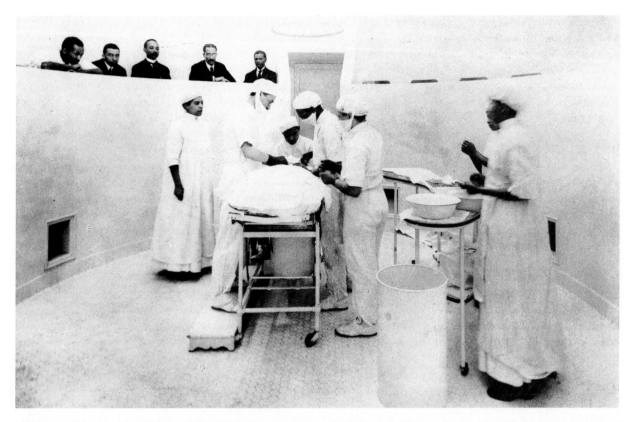

During the Progressive era, African-Americans struggled to share in the various reforms of society. Part of this struggle involved an assertion of their ability in science and economics. This photograph, taken at the surgical amphitheater of the Moorland-Spingarn Research Center at all-black Howard University, shows African-American medical personnel learning and performing medical skills. Moorland-Spingarn Research Center, Howard University, Howard University Archives.

combining racial pride with national identity. As Du Bois wrote in 1903, a black "would not Africanize America, for America has too much to teach the world and Africa. He would not bleach his Negro soul in a flood of white Americanism, for he knows that Negro blood has a message for the world. He simply wishes to make it possible for a man to be both a Negro and an American." That simple wish would haunt the nation for decades to come.

The dilemma of identity haunted Native Americans as well, but it had an added tribal dimension. Since the 1880s, Native American reformers had joined white-led Indian organizations. In 1911 educated, middle-class Indian men and women formed their own association, the Society of American Indians (SAI), which worked for better education, civil rights, and healthcare. It also sponsored "American Indian Days" to cultivate pride and

Society of American Indians

offset Anglo images of tribal peoples promulgated in Wild West shows.

The SAI's emphasis on racial pride, however, was squeezed between pressures for assimilation from one side and tribal allegiance on the other. Its small membership did not genuinely represent the diverse and unconnected Indian nations, and its attempt to establish a governing body faltered. Some tribal governments no longer existed to select representatives, and most SAI members simply promoted their own points of view. At the same time, the goal of achieving acceptance in white society proved elusive. Individual hard work was not enough to overcome white prejudice and condescension, and attempts to redress grievances through legal action bogged down for lack of funds. Ultimately, the SAI had to rely on rhetoric and moral exhortation, which had little effect on poor and powerless Indians who seldom knew the SAI even existed. Torn by internal disputes, the association folded in the early 1920s.

During the same period, the Progressive challenge to established social assumptions also raised among women questions of identity like those faced by blacks: What tactics should women use to achieve equality?

"The Woman Movement"

What should be their role in society? Novelist Henry James expressed the dilemma from a male point of view when he complained that women who wanted to become just like men were disregarding their own uniqueness. Or, as some women put it, could women achieve equality with men and at the same time change male-dominated society?

The answers that women found involved a subtle but important shift in women's politics. Before about 1910, those engaged in the quest for women's rights referred to themselves as "the woman movement." This label was given to middle-class women striving to move beyond the home into social welfare activities, higher education, and paid labor. Like some African-American and Indian leaders, they argued that legal and voting rights were indispensable to such moves. These women's rights advocates based their claims on the theory that women's special, even superior, traits as guardians of family and morality would humanize all of society. Settlement-house founder Jane Addams, for example, supported women's suffrage by asking, "If women have in any sense been responsible for the gentler side of life which softens and blurs some of its harsher conditions, may not they have a duty to perform in our American cities?"

The women's club movement represented a unique dimension of Progressive era reform. Originating as middle-class literary and educational organizations, women's clubs began taking stands on public

Women's Clubs

affairs in the late nineteenth century. Because female activists were excluded from holding office, they were drawn less to government reform than to drives for social betterment, an enterprise called social housekeeping. Rather than pressing for reforms such as trust-busting and direct primaries, women tended to work for factory inspection, regulation of children's and women's labor, housing improvement, upgrading of education, and consumer protection.

Such efforts were not confined to white women. African-American women had their own club movement, which included the Colored Women's Federation, which sought to establish a training school for "colored girls." Founded in 1895, the National Association of Colored Women was the nation's first African-American social service organization; it concentrated on establishing nurseries, kindergartens, and retirement homes. Black women also developed their own reform organizations within the Black Baptist Church.

Around 1910 some of those concerned with women's place in society began using a new term, *feminism*, to refer to their ideas. Whereas members of the woman movement spoke generally of duty and moral purity, feminists—more explicitly

Feminism

conscious of their identity as women—emphasized rights and self-development. Feminism, however, contained an inherent contradiction. On the one hand feminists argued that all women should unite in the struggle for rights because of their shared disadvantages as women. On the other, they insisted that sex-typing—treating women differently than men—must end because it resulted in discrimination. Thus feminists advocated the contradictory position that women should unite as a gender group for the purpose of abolishing all gender-based distinctions.

Feminism focused primarily on economic and sexual independence. Charlotte Perkins Gilman articulated feminist goals in *Women and Economics* (1898), declaring that domesticity and female innocence were obsolete and attacking the male monopoly on economic opportunity. Gilman argued that modern women must take jobs in industry and the professions and that paid employees should handle domestic chores such as cooking, cleaning, and childcare.

Feminists also supported "sex rights"—a single standard of behavior for men and women—and a number of feminists joined the birth-control movement led by Margaret Sanger.

Margaret Sanger's Crusade

As a visiting nurse in New York's immigrant neighborhoods, Sanger distributed information about contraception, in hopes of helping poor women prevent unwanted pregnancies. Her crusade won support from middle-class women who wanted both to limit their own families and to control the growth of the immigrant masses. It also aroused opposition from those who saw birth control as a threat to family and morality.

In 1914, Sanger's opponents caused her to be indicted for defying an 1873 law that prohibited the sending of obscene literature (articles on contracep-

How do historians know that female Progressive organizations combined gender-based notions of service with bureaucratic organization? Visiting nurses, represented in this photograph of a professional nurse entering a tenement, was one of the most effective social welfare programs established during the Progressive era. The photograph was published in The House on Henry Street (1915), a book by Lillian Wald about the early years of the Henry Street Visiting Nurses Service.

Wald, a nurse and one of the movement's leading figures, saw that many people were not sick enough to require hospitalization but needed medical care that could be provided during a house call by a medical professional. Responding to this need, she formed an organization that sent nurses out on home visits. By 1913, home nurses were making 200,000 visits annually in New York, and other cities had copied Wald's model.

She wrote, "[W]e planned to create a service on terms most considerate of the dignity and independence of the patients. . . . The new basis of the visiting nurse service which we thus inaugurated reacted almost immediately upon the relationship of the nurse to the patient, reversing the position the nurse had formerly had. Chagrin at having the neighbors see in her an agent whose presence proclaimed the family's poverty or its failure to give adequate care to its sick member was changed to the gratifying consciousness that her presence . . . proclaimed the family's liberality and anxiety to do everything possible for the sufferer." Those words, with their emphasis on both compassion and organized service, and the sympathetic yet professional appearance of the nurse in the photograph, illustrate one way in which women contributed to Progressive reform. *The House of Henry Street* by Lillian D. Wald, Henry Holt and Company, New York, 1915.

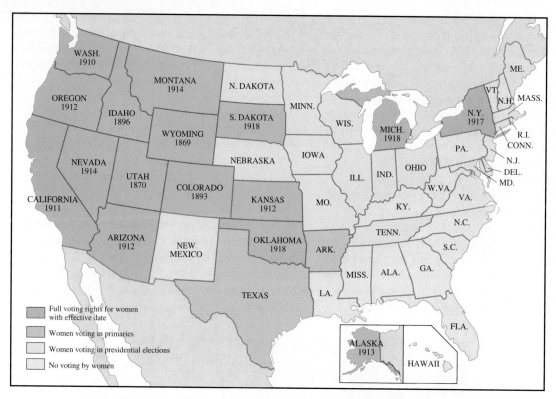

Woman Suffrage Before 1920 *Before Congress passed and the states ratified the Ninetreenth Amendment, woman suffrage already existed, but mainly in the West. Several midwestern states allowed women to vote only in presidential elections, but legislatures in the South and Northeast generally refused such rights until forced to do so by constitutional amendment.*

tion) through the mails, and she fled the country for a year. Sanger persevered and in 1921 formed the American Birth Control League, which enlisted physicians and social workers to convince judges to allow distribution of birth-control information. Most states still prohibited the sale of contraceptives, but Sanger succeeded in introducing the issue into the public debate.

Feminists achieved an important victory in 1920 when enough states ratified the Nineteenth Amendment to give women the vote in federal elections (see map). Until the 1890s, the suffrage crusade was led by elite women who believed that the political system needed more participation by refined and educated people like themselves, and that working-class women would defer to better-educated women on political matters. Elizabeth Cady Stanton, a stalwart of the woman movement who had long fought for equality, voiced this viewpoint when she said that enfranchisement of "educated women"

Woman Suffrage

would best promote "woman's influence in public life."

The younger generation of feminists, represented by Stanton's daughter Harriot Stanton Blatch, ardently opposed this logic. Blatch focused on work, declaring that all women worked, whether they performed paid labor or unpaid housework (like Gilman, she urged that women be paid for whatever work they did), and that all women's efforts contributed to society's betterment. To Blatch, achievement rather than wealth and refinement was the best criterion for public influence. Thus women should exercise the vote not to enhance the power of elites in public life but to promote and protect women's economic roles. This rationale, too, contained ambiguities. It advocated that all women work for pay, especially outside the home. But in doing so, it overlooked the exploitation of working-class women already in the labor force. The tension between the needs of well-to-do women and the needs of poor laboring women haunted the suffrage movement.

Despite internal differences, suffragists achieved some successes. Nine states, all in the West, allowed women to vote in state and local elections by 1912, and women continued to press for national suffrage. Their tactics ranged from the moderate but persistent propaganda campaigns of the National American Woman Suffrage Association, led by Carrie Chapman Catt, to rousing meetings and marches of the National Woman's Party, led by feminist Alice Paul. All these activities heightened public awareness. More decisive, however, were women's performances during the First World War as factory laborers, medical volunteers, and municipal workers (see pages 674–675). By convincing legislators that women could shoulder public responsibilities, women's wartime contributions gave final impetus to passage of the suffrage amendment.

The activities of women's clubs, suffragists, and feminists failed to create an interest group united or powerful enough to dent the political, economic, and social power of men. Like blacks, women knew that voting rights would mean little until society's attitudes changed. The Progressive era helped women to clarify the issues that concerned them, but major reforms were not achieved until a later era. As the feminist Crystal Eastman observed, echoing W. E. B. Du Bois, in the aftermath of the suffrage crusade: "Men are saying perhaps, 'Thank God, this everlasting women's fight is over!' But women, if I know them, are saying, 'Now at last we can begin.'... Now they can say what they are really after, in common with all the rest of the struggling world, is *freedom*."

Theodore Roosevelt and the Revival of the Presidency

The Progressive era's theme of reform—in politics, institutions, and social relations—drew attention to government, especially the federal government, as the foremost agent of change. At first, the federal government seemed incapable of assuming such responsibility. Dominated by political parties that resembled private clubs more than bodies of statesmen, the federal government acted mainly on behalf of special interests when it acted at all. Mostly, its role had been to support rather than control economic expansion, as when it transferred western public lands and resources to private ownership. Then, in September 1901, the political climate suddenly changed. The assassination of President William

McKinley by anarchist Leon Czolgosz vaulted Theodore Roosevelt, the vigorous young vice president, into the White House.

Political manager Mark Hanna had warned fellow Republicans against running Roosevelt for the vice presidency in 1900. "Don't any of you realize," Hanna asked after the nominating convention, "that there's only one life between that madman and the presidency?" As governor of New York, Roosevelt had angered Republican bosses by showing sympathy for regulatory legislation, so they rid themselves of their pariah by pushing him into national politics. Little did they anticipate that they were providing the steppingstone for the nation's most forceful president since Lincoln and a president who infused the office with much of its twentieth-century character.

In contrast to his stout and stolid predecessors, Theodore Roosevelt did not look presidential. Nearsighted, he was helpless without his metal-rimmed glasses. He had prominent teeth and looked shorter than his five-foot-nine height.

Theodore Roosevelt

As a youth he had suffered from asthma. He was driven throughout his later life by an obsession to overcome his physical limitations and exert what he and his contemporaries called "manliness." In his teens he practiced to become an expert marksman and horseman and later competed on Harvard's boxing and wrestling teams. In the 1880s he went to live on a Dakota ranch, where he roped cattle and brawled with cowboys.

Descended from a Dutch aristocratic family, Roosevelt had the wealth to indulge in such pursuits. But he also inherited a sense of civic responsibility that guided him into a career in public service. He served three terms in the New York State Assembly, ran for mayor of New York City in 1886 (finishing third), sat on the federal Civil Service Commission, served as New York City's police commissioner, and was assistant secretary of the navy. In these offices Roosevelt earned a reputation as a combative, politically crafty leader. He also distinguished himself as a historian with *The Naval War of 1812* (1882) and *The Winning of the West* (1889).

In 1898, Roosevelt thrust himself into the Spanish-American-Cuban-Filipino War by organizing a volunteer cavalry brigade, called the Rough Riders, to fight in Cuba (see page 645). Though his dramatic act had little impact on the war's outcome, it excited the public's imagination. A publicity hound who

Theodore Roosevelt (1858–1919) liked to think of himself as a great outdoorsman. He loved the most rugged countryside and believed that he and his country should serve as examples of "manliness." California Museum of Photography, University of California.

craved the center of attention, Roosevelt returned a folk hero.

As president, Roosevelt concurred with Progressives that the small government Jefferson had envisioned would not suffice in the industrial era. Instead, economic development necessitated a Hamiltonian system of government powerful enough to guide national affairs. Like his Progressive supporters, Roosevelt believed in the talents of a select few whose superior backgrounds and education qualified them to coordinate public and private enterprise. "A simple and poor society," he observed, "can exist as a democracy on the basis of sheer individualism. But a rich and complex society cannot so exist." Especially in economic affairs, he wanted the government to act as an umpire, deciding when big business was good and when it was bad. But his brash patriotism and dislike of anything he considered effeminate also recalled the previous era of unbridled expansion when raw power prevailed in social and economic affairs.

The federal regulation of the economy that has characterized twentieth-century American history began with Roosevelt's presidency. Roosevelt turned his attention first to big business, where consolidation had created giant trusts that exerted powerful control. Although Roosevelt was labeled a "trustbuster," he actually considered consolidation the most efficient means to achieve material progress. He believed in distinguishing between good and bad trusts and preventing bad ones from manipulating markets. Thus he instructed the Justice Department to use antitrust laws to prosecute the railroad, meatpacking, and oil trusts, which he believed were unscrupulously exploiting the public. Roosevelt's policy triumphed in 1904 in the *Northern Securities* case. The Supreme Court, convinced by the government's arguments, ordered the breakup of the Northern Securities Company, the huge railroad combination created by J. P. Morgan and his business allies. Roosevelt chose, however, not to attack other gigantic trusts, such as U.S. Steel, another of Morgan's creations.

Regulation of Trusts

When prosecution of Northern Securities began, Morgan reportedly collared Roosevelt and offered, "If we have done anything wrong, send your man to my man and they can fix it up." The president refused but was more sympathetic to cooperation between business and government than his rebuff might suggest. Rather than prosecute, he urged the Bureau of Corporations (part of the newly created Department of Labor and Commerce) to work with companies on mergers and other forms of expansion. Through investigation and cooperation the administration pressured businesses to regulate themselves; corporations often accepted regulation because it helped them make their operations more efficient and reduced overproduction.

Roosevelt also supported regulatory legislation, especially after his resounding electoral victory in 1904, in which he won the votes of Progressives and businesspeople alike. After a year of wrangling, Roosevelt persuaded Congress to pass the Hepburn Act (1906), which gave the Interstate Commerce Commission (ICC) more authority to set the freight and storage rates that railroads charged, though it did allow the courts to overturn rate decisions. Progressives like Robert La Follette complained that Roosevelt had compromised with business allies like Senator Nelson W. Aldrich of Rhode Island to ensure the bill's passage. But Roosevelt's aim was to reaffirm the principle of government regulation rather than risk defeat over unreachable, idealistic objectives.

Roosevelt showed similar willingness to compromise on legislation to ensure the purity of food and drugs. For decades reformers had been urging government regulation of processed meat and patent medicines. Public outrage at fraud and adulteration heightened in 1906 when Upton Sinclair published *The Jungle*, a fictionalized exposé of Chicago meatpacking plants. Sinclair, a young socialist whose prime objective was to improve working conditions, shocked public sensibilities with his vivid descriptions:

Pure Food and Drug Laws

> There was never the least attention paid to what was cut up for sausage; there would come all the way back from Europe old sausage that had been rejected, and that was mouldy and white—it would be dosed with borax and glycerine, and dumped into the hoppers, and made over again for home consumption. . . . There would be meat stored in great piles in rooms; and the water from the leaky roofs would drip over it, and thousands of rats would race about on it. It was too dark in these storage places to see well, but a man could run his hand over these piles of meat and sweep off handfulls of dried dung of rats. These rats were a nuisance, and the packers would put poisoned bread out for them; they would die, and then rats, bread, and meat would go into the hoppers together.

After reading the novel, Roosevelt ordered an investigation. Finding Sinclair's descriptions accurate, the president supported the Meat Inspection Act, which passed in 1906. Like the Hepburn Act, this law reinforced the principle of government regulation. But as part of the compromise to pass the bill, the government, rather than the meatpackers, had to pay for inspections, and meatpackers could appeal adverse decisions in court. Nor were companies required to provide date-of-processing information on their canned goods. Most large companies welcomed the legislation anyway, because it helped them regularize their business, force out smaller competitors, and restore falling confidence in American meat products in foreign markets.

The Pure Food and Drug Act (1906) addressed abuses in the patent medicine industry. Producers of various tonics and pills were not only making undue claims about their products' effects but also liberally using alcohol and narcotics as ingredients. Ads in popular publications, such as one for a "Brain Stimulator and Nerve Tonic" in the Sears, Roebuck catalogue, had wildly exaggerated claims. Although the new law did not ban such products, it did require labels listing the ingredients—a goal consistent with Progressive confidence that if people knew the truth they would make wiser purchases.

Roosevelt's approach to labor resembled his stance toward business. When the United Mine Workers struck against Pennsylvania coal-mine owners in 1902 over an eight-hour workday and higher pay, the president employed the Progressive tactics of investigation and arbitration. Owners stubbornly refused to recognize the union or arbitrate grievances. As winter approached and fuel shortages threatened, Roosevelt roused public opinion. He would use federal troops to reopen the mines, he warned, thus forcing management to accept arbitration of the dispute by a special commission. The commission decided in favor of higher wages and reduced hours and required management to deal with grievance committees elected by the miners, but it did not require recognition of the union. The decision, according to Roosevelt, provided a "square deal" for all. The settlement also embodied Roosevelt's belief that the president or his representatives should have a say in which labor demands were legitimate and which were not. In Roosevelt's mind there were good and bad labor organizations (socialists, for example, were bad), just as there were good and bad business combinations.

In matters of resource conservation, Roosevelt combined the Progressive impulse for efficiency with his love for the great outdoors. He warned Congress in 1907, "We are prone to think of the resources of this country as inexhaustible; this is not so." In this regard, he drastically revised the federal government's stance toward the nation's—particularly the West's—resources. Before Roosevelt, the government's policy had been to transfer ownership and control of natural resources on federal land to the states and to private interests. Roosevelt, however, believed the most efficient way to use and conserve these resources would be for the government to retain public ownership. Ownership did not necessarily mean that no one could have access; rather, it meant that the federal government would manage and control use of those lands that remained in the public domain.

Conservation

Roosevelt took steps to exert federal power in several ways. He tried, though unsuccessfully, to revise an 1873 law under which the government sold coal and oil lands at very cheap prices to private concerns. Roosevelt wanted the government to retain ownership and charge producers lease fees (such a policy was instituted in 1920). He did succeed in withdrawing waterpower sites from sale and instead charged permit fees for users who wanted to produce electricity. He also supported the Newlands Reclamation Act of 1902, which controlled sale of irrigated federal land in the West (see page 488). He tripled the number and acreage of national forests and supported conservationist Gifford Pinchot in creating the United States Forest Service.

As chief forester within the Department of Agriculture, Pinchot advocated scientific management of the nation's forests to protect the land and water from overuse by timber cutters, farmers, and herders. Through bureaucratic manipulation, Pinchot succeeded in getting management of the national forests transferred from the Interior Department to his bureau in the Agriculture Department by arguing that forests were crops grown on "tree farms." Under his guidance, the Forest Service charged fees for grazing within the national forests, supervised bidding for the cutting of timber, and hired university-trained foresters as federal employees.

As historian Richard White has pointed out, Pinchot and Roosevelt did not want to lock up resources permanently; rather they wanted to guarantee their efficient use. Although antifederal, anticonservation attitudes remained in the West, many of those involved in natural-resource exploitation welcomed such a policy because, like the regulation of food and drugs, it enabled them to minimize overproduction and to restrict competition. They simply had to try to influence federal bureaucracies and Congress to act in their behalf while at the same time denouncing federal interference. As a result of new federal policies, the West and its resources had fallen under the Progressive spell of management.

Roosevelt had to compromise his principles in the face of economic crisis. In 1907 a financial panic caused by reckless speculation forced some New York banks to close to prevent frightened depositors from withdrawing money. J. P. Morgan helped to stem the panic by persuading financiers to stop dumping their securities. In return for Morgan's aid, Roosevelt approved a deal allowing U.S. Steel to absorb the Tennessee Iron and Coal Company—a deal at odds with Roosevelt's trustbusting aims.

Panic of 1907

During his last year in office, Roosevelt retreated from the Republican Party's traditional friendliness to big business. He lashed out at the ir-

responsibility of "malefactors of great wealth" and supported stronger regulation of business and heavier taxation of the rich. Having promised that he would not seek reelection, Roosevelt backed his friend Secretary of War William Howard Taft for the Republican nomination in 1908, hoping that Taft would continue his initiatives. Democrats nominated William Jennings Bryan for the third time, but the "Great Commoner" lost again. Aided by Roosevelt, who still enjoyed great popularity, Taft won by 1.25 million popular votes and a 2-to-1 margin in the electoral college.

Early in 1909 Roosevelt went to Africa to shoot game (his passion for the "manly" activity of hunting outweighed his support for conservation), leaving Taft to face political problems that his predecessor had managed to postpone. Foremost among them was the tariff; rates had risen to excessive levels. Honoring Taft's pledge to cut rates, the House passed a bill sponsored by Representative Sereno E. Payne that provided for numerous reductions. Protectionists in the Senate prepared, as in the past, to amend the House bill and revise rates upward. But Senate Progressives, led by La Follette, organized a stinging attack on the tariff for benefiting vested interests. Taft was caught between reformers who claimed to be preserving Roosevelt's antitrust campaign and protectionists who still controlled the Republican Party. In the end, Senator Aldrich and other protectionists restored many of the tariff cuts the Payne bill had made, and Taft—more reluctant than Roosevelt to interfere in the legislative process—signed what became known as the Payne-Aldrich Tariff (1909). In the eyes of Progressives, Taft had failed the test of filling Roosevelt's shoes.

Taft Administration

Progressive and conservative wings of the Republican Party were rapidly drifting apart. Soon after the tariff controversy, a group of insurgents in the House led by Nebraska's George Norris mounted a challenge to Speaker "Uncle Joe" Cannon of Illinois, whose power over committee assignments and the scheduling of debates could make or break a piece of legislation. Taft first supported and then abandoned the insurgents, who nevertheless managed to liberalize procedures by enlarging the influential Rules Committee and removing selection of its members from Cannon's control. In 1910 Taft also angered conservationists by firing Gifford Pinchot when he protested Secretary of the Interior Richard A. Ballinger's plan to reduce federal supervision of western waterpower sites and his questionable sale of coal lands in Alaska.

In reality Taft was as sympathetic to reform as Roosevelt was. He prosecuted more trusts than Roosevelt, expanded national forest reserves, signed the Mann-Elkins Act (1910), which bolstered the regulatory powers of the ICC, and supported labor reforms such as the eight-hour workday and mine safety legislation. The Sixteenth Amendment, which legalized the federal income tax, and the Seventeenth Amendment, which provided for direct election of United States senators, were initiated during Taft's presidency (and ratified in 1913).

Like Roosevelt, Taft compromised with big business, but unlike Roosevelt he lacked the ability to manipulate the public. Roosevelt had worked to expand presidential power and had infused the presidency with vitality. "I believe in a strong executive," he once asserted. "I believe in power." Taft, by contrast, believed in the strict restraint of law. He had been a successful lawyer and judge (and returned to the bench as chief justice of the United States between 1921 and 1930). His caution and unwillingness to offend disappointed those accustomed to Roosevelt's impetuosity.

In 1910, when Roosevelt returned from Africa boasting three thousand animal trophies, he found his party torn and tormented. Reformers, angered by Taft's apparent insensitivity to their cause, formed the National Progressive Republican League and rallied behind Robert La Follette for president in 1912, though many hoped Roosevelt would run. Another wing of the party remained loyal to Taft. Disappointed by Taft's performance (particularly his firing of Pinchot), Roosevelt began to speak out. He filled his speeches with references to "the welfare of the people" and stronger regulation of business. When La Follette became ill early in 1912, Roosevelt, proclaiming himself fit as a "bull moose," threw his hat into the ring for the Republican presidential nomination.

Taft's supporters controlled the convention and nominated Taft for a second term. Protesting parliamentary tactics at the convention, Roosevelt's supporters bolted and reconvened in August to form a third party—the Progressive, or Bull Moose, Party—and nominated the fifty-three-year-old former president. Meanwhile, Democrats took forty-six ballots to select their candidate, New Jersey's Progressive governor Woodrow Wilson. Socialists, by now an organized and growing party, again nominated Eugene V. Debs. The ensuing campaign exposed voters to the most thorough evaluation of the American system since 1896.

Woodrow Wilson and the Extension of Reform

In his acceptance speech before the Progressive Party, Theodore Roosevelt proclaimed, "We stand at Armageddon and we battle for the Lord." But on inauguration day in 1913, it was Woodrow Wilson who assumed command of the forces of good. "The Nation," he exhorted, "has been deeply stirred by a solemn passion. Stirred by the knowledge of wrong, of ideals lost, of government too often debauched and made an instrument of evil. The feelings with which we face this new age of right and opportunity sweep across our heartstrings like some air out of God's own presence, where justice and mercy are reconciled and the judge and the brother are one."

Election results illustrated the extent to which voters had been swept up by the moral fervor of such pronouncements. Wilson won with 42 percent of the popular vote. He was a minority president, though he did capture 435 out of 531 electoral votes (see map, page 624). Roosevelt received 27 percent of the popular vote. Taft finished third, polling 23 percent of the popular vote and only 8 electoral votes. Debs won 902,000 votes, or 6 percent of the total, but no electoral votes. Fully three-quarters of the electorate thus supported some alternative to the view of restrained government that Taft represented.

Sharp debate over the fundamentals of Progressive government had characterized the campaign. Roosevelt offered voters the "New Nationalism," a term coined by reform editor Herbert Croly. Roosevelt foresaw an era of national unity in which government would coordinate and regulate economic activity. He would not destroy big business, which he saw as an efficient organizer of production. Instead, he would establish regulatory commissions of experts who would protect citizens' interests and ensure wise use of concentrated economic power. "The effort at prohibiting all combinations has substantially failed," he claimed. "The way out lies . . . in completely controlling them."

Wilson offered a more idealistic scheme, the "New Freedom," based on the ideas of Progressive

New Nationalism and New Freedom

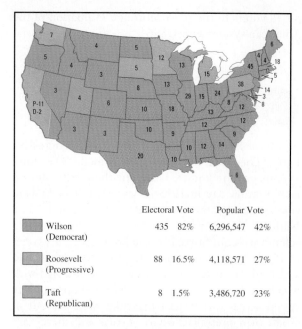

		Electoral Vote		Popular Vote	
	Wilson (Democrat)	435	82%	6,296,547	42%
	Roosevelt (Progressive)	88	16.5%	4,118,571	27%
	Taft (Republican)	8	1.5%	3,486,720	23%

Presidential Election, 1912 *Though he won a minority of the popular votes, Woodrow Wilson captured so many states that he achieved an easy victory in the electoral college.*

lawyer Louis Brandeis. Wilson believed that concentrated economic power threatened individual liberty and that monopolies had to be broken up so the marketplace could become genuinely open. But he did not want to restore laissez faire. Like Roosevelt, Wilson wanted to enhance government authority to protect and regulate. "Freedom today," he declared, "is something more than being let alone. Without the watchful . . . resolute interference of the government, there can be no fair play between individuals and such powerful institutions as the trust." Wilson stopped short of advocating the cooperation between business and government inherent in Roosevelt's New Nationalism. In the campaign at least, he preached economic emancipation, the need to "come out of a stifling cellar into the open . . . breathe again and see the free spaces of the heavens."

Roosevelt and Wilson stood closer together than their rhetoric implied. In spite of his faith in experts as regulators, Roosevelt harbored a belief in individual freedom as strong as Wilson's. And Wilson was not really hostile to concentrated power. Both men strongly supported equality of opportunity (though chiefly for white males), conservation of natural resources, fair wages, and social better-

ment for all classes. Neither would hesitate to expand government activity through strong personal leadership and bureaucratic reform. Thus even though Wilson received a minority of the total vote in 1912, he could interpret the election results as a mandate to subdue trusts and broaden the federal government's role in social reform.

The public fondly called Roosevelt "Teddy" or "TR," but Thomas Woodrow Wilson was too aloof ever to be called "Tommy" or "WW." Born in Virginia in 1856 and raised in the South, Wilson, like

Woodrow Wilson

his mother and his first wife, had a Presbyterian minister for a father. Wilson, however, chose an academic career. He earned a B.A. at Princeton, studied law at Virginia, received a Ph.D. from Johns Hopkins, and became a professor of history, jurisprudence, and political economy. Between 1885 and 1908 he published several respected books on American history and government.

Wilson's manner and bearing reflected his background. Tall, lean, and stiff, he seemed to stare coldly through his pince-nez glasses. Wilson exuded none of Roosevelt's flamboyance, yet he was an effective and charismatic leader. A superb orator, he could inspire intense loyalty with religious imagery and the eloquent expression of American ideals. Wilson's convictions led him early into reform. In 1902 he became president of Princeton, where he upset tradition with curricular reforms and battles against aristocratic elements in the university. In 1910 New Jersey's Democrats, eager for respectability, nominated Wilson for governor. After winning the election, he repudiated the party bosses and promoted Progressive legislation. A poor administrator, he often lost his temper and stubbornly refused to compromise. His accomplishments nevertheless attracted national attention and won him the Democratic nomination for president in 1912.

As president, Wilson found it necessary to blend New Freedom competition with New Nationalism regulation, and in so doing he set the direction of future federal economic policy.

Wilson's Policy on Business Regulation

The corporate merger movement had proceeded so far that restoration of free competition proved impossible. Wilson could only try to prevent corporate abuses by expanding government's regulatory powers. His administration moved toward that end with passage in

1914 of the Clayton Anti-Trust Act and a bill creating the Federal Trade Commission (FTC).

The Clayton Act extended the Sherman Anti-Trust Act of 1890 by outlawing monopolistic practices such as *price discrimination* (efforts to destroy competition by lowering prices in some regions but not in others) and *interlocking directorates* (management of two or more competing companies by the same executives). The FTC was to investigate companies and issue cease-and-desist orders against unfair trade practices. As in ICC rulings, accused companies could appeal FTC orders in court. Nevertheless, the FTC represented another step in consumer protection.

Wilson broadened regulation of finance with the Federal Reserve Act of 1913, which established the nation's first central banking system since Andrew Jackson's destruction of the Second Bank of the United States in 1832. The act created twelve district banks to hold the reserves of member banks throughout the nation. (The act created many banks rather than just one, to allay the fear of a monolithic eastern banking power, which had doomed the central bank in Jackson's time.) The district banks, supervised by the Federal Reserve Board, would lend money to member banks at a low interest rate called the *discount rate*. By adjusting this rate (and thus the amount of money a bank could afford to borrow), district banks could increase or decrease the amount of money in circulation. In other words, in response to the nation's needs, the Federal Reserve Board could loosen or tighten credit. Monetary affairs no longer would depend on the gold supply, and interest rates would be fairer, especially for small borrowers.

The only act of Wilson's first administration that promoted free competition was the Underwood Tariff, passed in 1913. By the 1910s, prices for some

Tariff and Tax Reform

consumer goods were unnaturally high because tariffs had discouraged the importation of cheaper foreign materials and manufactured products. By drastically reducing or eliminating tariff rates, the Underwood Tariff encouraged imports. To replace revenues lost because of tariff reductions, the act levied a graduated income tax on United States residents—an option made possible when the Sixteenth Amendment was ratified earlier that year. The income tax was tame by today's standards. Incomes under $4,000 were exempt; thus almost all factory workers and farmers escaped taxation. Individuals and corpo-

Looking sober and stubborn, Woodrow Wilson (1856–1924) used a preacher's moralism and a professor's reasoning to raise expectations for the fulfillment of his idealistic promises. National Portrait Gallery, Smithsonian Institution. Transfer from the National Museum of American Art, Gift of the City of New York.

rations earning between $4,000 and $20,000 had to pay a 1 percent tax, and rates for higher incomes rose gradually to a maximum of 6 percent on earnings over $500,000. Such rates tore no holes in the pockets of the rich, but the income tax did become an institution of American life.

The outbreak of the First World War (see Chapter 23) and the approaching presidential election campaign prompted Wilson to support stronger reforms in 1916. Concerned that farmers needed a better system of long-term mortgage credit, the president backed the Federal Farm Loan Act. This measure created twelve federally supported banks (not to be confused with the Federal Reserve banks) that would lend money at moderate interest to farmers who belonged to credit institutions—a watered-down version of the subtreasury plan that Populists had promoted a generation earlier (see page 586).

To stave off railroad strikes that might disrupt transportation at a time of national emergency, Wilson pushed passage of the Adamson Act, which mandated an eight-hour workday and time-and-a-half overtime pay for railroad laborers. He also pleased Progressives by appointing Brandeis, the "people's advocate," to the Supreme Court, though an anti-Semitic backlash almost blocked Senate approval of the first Jewish justice on the Court. Finally, Wilson courted support from social reformers by backing laws against child labor and provided workers' compensation for federal employees who suffered work-related injuries or illness.

In selecting a candidate to oppose Wilson in 1916, Republicans snubbed Theodore Roosevelt in favor of Charles Evans Hughes, a Supreme Court justice and former reform governor of New York. Acutely aware of the First World War's impact on national affairs, Wilson ran for reelection on a platform of peace, Progressivism, and preparedness; his supporters used the campaign slogan "He Kept Us Out of War." Hughes and his fractured party could not muzzle Roosevelt, whose bellicose speeches suggested that Republicans would drag Americans into the world war. Wilson received 9.1 million votes to Hughes's 8.5 million, and the president barely won in the electoral college, 277 to 254. The Socialist Party, which had earned 902,000 votes four years earlier, dropped to 600,000, largely because Wilson's reforms had won over some socialists and the ailing Eugene Debs was no longer the party's standard-bearer.

Election of 1916

During Wilson's second term, United States involvement in the First World War brought about a shift away from competition and toward interest-group politics and government regulation. In his first term Wilson had become convinced that regulatory commissions, which could easily fall under the influence of the very interests they were meant to regulate, should not govern social and economic behavior. The war effort, he came to believe, required government coordination of production, and cooperation between the public and private sectors. The War Industries Board (see pages 672–673) exemplified this cooperation: the private businesses regulated by the board submitted to its control on condition that their own profit motives would continue to be satisfied.

After the war the Wilson administration dropped most cooperative and regulatory measures, including farm price supports, guarantees of collective bargaining, and high taxes. This retreat from regulation stimulated a new era of business ascendancy in the 1920s.

 ## Conclusion

By 1920, a quarter-century of reform had wrought momentous changes. Government, economy, and society as they had existed in the nineteenth century were gone forever. The Progressives had established the principle of public intervention to ensure fairness, health, and safety. Concern over poverty and injustice reached new heights. But for every American who suffered some form of deprivation, three or four enjoyed unprecedented material comforts; and amid growing affluence, reformers could not sustain their efforts indefinitely. Although Progressive values lingered after the First World War, a mass consumer society began to refocus people's attention from reform to materialism.

The Progressive era was characterized by multiple and sometimes contradictory goals. By no means was there a single Progressive movement. Reform programs on the national level ranged from Roosevelt's New Nationalism, with its faith in big government as a coordinator of big business, to Wilson's New Freedom, with its promise to dissolve economic concentrations and legislate open competition. At the state and local levels, reformers pursued causes as varied as neighborhood improvement, government reorganization, public ownership of utilities, betterment of working conditions, and moral revival. Local organizations and national associations coordinated their efforts on specific issues, but reformers with different goals often worked at cross-purposes.

The failure of many Progressive initiatives indicates the strength of the opposition, as well as weaknesses within the reform movements themselves. Courts asserted constitutional and liberty-of-contract doctrines in striking down key Progressive legislation, notably the federal law prohibiting child labor. In states and cities, adoption of the initiative, referendum, and recall did not encourage greater participation in government as had been hoped; those mechanisms either were seldom used or became tools of those in power. On the federal level, regulatory agencies rarely had enough resources for thorough investigations; they had to obtain information from the very companies they policed. Progressives thus failed in many respects to redistribute power. In 1920 as in 1900, government remained under the influence of business and industry, a state of affairs that many people considered quite satisfactory.

Yet the reform movements that characterized the Progressive era did shape the nation's future. Trustbusting, however faulty, forced industrialists to become more sensitive to public opinion, and insurgents in Congress partially diluted the power of dictatorial politicians. Progressive legislation equipped government with tools to protect consumers against price fixing and dangerous products. The income tax, created to redistribute wealth, also became a source of government revenue. Social reformers relieved some ills of urban life. And perhaps most important, Progressives challenged old ways of thinking. Although the questions they raised about the quality of American life remained unresolved, Progressives made the nation acutely aware of its principles and promises.

Suggestions for Further Reading

General

Paul M. Boyer, *Urban Masses and Moral Order in America, 1820–1920* (1978); John M. Cooper, Jr., *The Pivotal Decades: The United States, 1900–1920* (1990); Louis Filler, *The Muckrakers*, rev. ed. (1980); Richard Hofstadter, *The Age of Reform* (1955); William R. Hutchinson, *The Modernist Impulse in American Protestantism* (1976); Morton Keller, *Regulating a New Economy* (1990); Gabriel Kolko, *The Triumph of Conservatism* (1963); Arthur Link and Robert L. McCormick, *Progressivism* (1983); David W. Noble, *The Progressive Mind*, rev. ed. (1981); Robert Wiebe, *The Search for Order* (1968).

Regional Studies

Dewey Grantham, *Southern Progressivism* (1983); Richard L. McCormick, *From Realignment to Reform: Political Change in New York State, 1893–1910* (1981); David P. Thelen, *Robert La Follette and the Insurgent Spirit* (1976); Richard White, *"It's Your Misfortune and None of My Own": A History of the American West* (1991); C. Vann Woodward, *Origins of the New South* (1951).

Legislative Issues and Reform Groups

Allen F. Davis, *Spearheads for Reform: The Social Settlements and the Progressive Movement, 1890–1914* (1967); Ruth Rosen, *The Lost Sisterhood: Prostitution in America, 1900–1918* (1982); James H. Timberlake, *Prohibition and the Progressive Crusade* (1963); Walter

I. Trattner, *Crusade for the Children* (1970); Irwin Yellowitz, *Labor and the Progressive Movement in New York State* (1965); James Harvey Young, *Pure Food* (1989). (For works on socialism, see the listings under "Protest and Socialism" at the end of Chapter 20.)

Education, Law, and the Social Sciences

Jerold S. Auerback, *Unequal Justice: Lawyers and Social Change in Modern America* (1976); Lawrence Cremin, *The Transformation of the School: Progressivism in American Education* (1961); Paula S. Fass, *Outside In: Minorities and the Transformation of American Education* (1989); Ellen Fitzpatrick, *Endless Crusade: Women Social Scientists and Progressive Reform* (1990); Lynn D. Gordon, *Gender and Higher Education in the Progressive Era* (1990); Thomas L. Haskell, *The Emergence of Professional Social Science* (1977); Helen Horowitz, *Alma Mater: Design and Experience in Women's Colleges* (1984); David W. Marcell, *Progress and Pragmatism: James, Dewey, Beard, and the American Idea of Progress* (1974); Lawrence Veysey, *The Emergence of the American University* (1970).

Women

Ruth Borden, *Women and Temperance* (1980); Ellen Chesler, *Woman of Valor: The Life of Margaret Sanger* (1992); Nancy F. Cott, *The Grounding of American Feminism* (1987); Carl N. Degler, *At Odds: Women and the Family in America* (1980); Linda Gordon, *Woman's Body, Woman's Right: A Social History of Birth Control in America* (1976); Evelyn Higginbotham, *Righteous Discontent: The Women's Movement in the Black Baptist Church, 1880–1920* (1993); Alice Kessler-Harris, *Out to Work: A History of Wage-Earning Women in the United States* (1982); Robyn Muncy, *Creating a Female Dominion in American Reform* (1991); William L. O'Neill, *Everyone Was Brave: The Rise and Fall of Feminism in America* (1969); Rosalind Rosenberg, *Beyond Separate Spheres: Intellectual Roots of Modern Feminism* (1982); Sheila M. Rothman, *Woman's Proper Place* (1978).

African-Americans

John Dittmer, *Black Georgia in the Progressive Era, 1900–1920* (1977); George Frederickson, *The Black Image in the White Mind* (1971); Louis R. Harlan, *Booker T. Washington* 2 vols. (1972 and 1983); Jacqueline Jones, *Labor of Love, Labor of Sorrow: Black Women, Work and the Family from Slavery to the Present* (1985); August Meier, *Negro Thought in America, 1880–1915* (1963); Elliot M. Rudwick, *W. E. B. Du Bois* (1969).

Roosevelt, Taft, and Wilson

Francis L. Broderick, *Progressivism at Risk: Electing a President in 1912* (1989); Paolo E. Coletta, *The Presidency of William Howard Taft* (1973); John Milton Cooper, Jr., *The Warrior and the Priest: Woodrow Wilson and Theodore Roosevelt* (1983); Lewis Gould, *The Presidency of Theodore Roosevelt* (1991); August Hecksher, *Woodrow Wilson* (1991); Edmund Morris, *The Rise of Theodore Roosevelt* (1979); James Pednick, Jr., *Progressive Politics and Conservation: The Ballinger-Pinchot Affair* (1968).

CHAPTER

22

The Quest for Empire
1865–1914

American lawyers, businessmen, and sugar planters, many of them the sons of Protestant missionaries, decided to become revolutionaries in Hawai'i. These *haole* (foreigners) sought a new order that favored their interests. So, in January 1893, members of this white American elite brought to a climax their treasonous plot to overthrow the native government of Queen Liliuokalani.

Americans had long coveted opportunities in the Hawai'ian Islands, the Pacific Ocean archipelago of eight major islands located 2,000 miles from the west coast of the United States. In the late eighteenth and early nineteenth centuries, American traders cut sandalwood for export to Asia, where it was used for ointments and perfumes. Then came fleets of whaling ships. In the 1830s, Presbyterian and Congregational missionaries from New England founded schools to Christianize—and American-ize—the Hawai'ians. The cultivation of sugar cane and fruit eventually drew other adventurous Americans.

The descendants of the missionaries prospered both economically and politically. As one wag put it, "They came to do good and they did well." By 1890 Americans owned about three-quarters of the islands' wealth, though they represented a mere 2.1 percent of the population. Because diseases brought by foreigners had diminished the native population, causing a labor shortage, the American oligarchy imported Chinese and Japanese workers for the expanding sugar industry. By 1890, 17 percent of Hawai'i's population was Chinese-born, 14 percent was Japanese-born, and native Hawai'ians accounted for only 53.5 percent. Hawai'i became a multiracial society dominated by white Americans who subordinated its economy to that of the United States through sugar exports that entered the American marketplace duty-free.

United States warships in the Strait of Magellan at the southern tip of South America in 1908 during the cruise of the "Great White Fleet," sent around the world by President Theodore Roosevelt to demonstrate American naval power. *Painting by Henry Reuterdahl. Courtesy United States Naval Academy Museum.*

• *Important Events* •

1861–69	Secretary of State Seward sets expansionist course	**1887**	United States gains naval rights to Pearl Harbor, Hawai'i
1866	Transatlantic cable completed France withdraws from Mexico	**1889**	First Pan-American Conference
1867	Alaska and Midway acquired by United States	**1890**	Alfred T. Mahan's *The Influence of Sea Power upon History* is published McKinley Tariff hurts Hawai'ian sugar exports
1868	Burlingame Treaty with China regulates immigration	**1893**	Severe economic depression begins Frederick Jackson Turner sets forth his frontier thesis Americans in Hawai'i overthrow Queen Liliuokalani
1870	Senate rejects annexation of Dominican Republic		
1871	Anglo-American treaty sends *Alabama* claims issue to tribunal	**1894**	Wilson-Gorham Tariff imposes tariff on Cuban sugar
1874	United States foreign trade shifts to favorable balance	**1895**	Venezuelan crisis with Britain Cuban Revolution against Spain begins Japan defeats China to become a major Asian power
1876	Porfirio Díaz, friendly to United States investment, begins long rule in Mexico		
1878	United States gains naval rights to Pago Pago, Samoa	**1896**	McKinley elected president
1880	Treaty with China limits Chinese immigration to the United States	**1898**	De Lôme letter is published Sinking of the *Maine* heightens chances of war Spanish-American-Cuban-Filipino War Hawai'i annexed by the United States
1883	Advent of the New Navy		
1884	Berlin Conference on the Congo		
1885	Josiah Strong's book *Our Country* celebrates Anglo-Saxons		

Many native Hawai'ians heeded King Kalakaua's warning in the 1870s and 1880s that the Americans posed a threat, especially because they were organizing secret clubs and military units to contest the royal government. In 1887 the American conspirators forced the king to accept a constitution that granted foreigners the right to vote and shifted decision-making authority from the monarchy to the legislature. The same year, Hawai'i granted the United States naval rights to Pearl Harbor. Hawai'ians were losing control of their land, their economy, their politics, and their sovereignty.

The McKinley Tariff of 1890 created an economic crisis for Hawai'i that further undermined the native government. The tariff eliminated Hawai'ian sugar's favored status by admitting *all foreign* sugar into the United States duty-free. The measure also provided a bounty of 2 cents a pound to domestic United States growers, making it possible for them to sell their sugar at a price lower than the price charged for foreign sugar. With this new competition from other foreign producers and this advantage for United States producers, planters and their allies in Hawai'i suffered declining sugar prices and profits. Prominent Americans in Hawai'i soon pressed for annexation of the islands by the United States so that their sugar would be classified as domestic rather than foreign.

When Kalakaua's sister Princess Liliuokalani assumed the throne upon his death in 1891, "they were lying in wait," she remembered. The new queen wanted to roll back the political power of the *haole*. She also supported the legalization of opium and a lottery to raise revenues. The next year, the white oligarchy—questioning her moral rectitude, fearing Hawai'ian nationalism, and reeling from the McKinley Tariff—formed the subversive Annexation Club.

In collusion with John L. Stevens, the chief United States diplomat in Hawai'i, the conspirators struck in January 1893—but only after American

• *Important Events* •

1899	Senate approves Treaty of Paris after debate over empire
	United Fruit Company forms and becomes influence in Central America
	First Open Door note calls for equal trade opportunity in China
	Philippine Insurrection against the United States breaks out
1900	Second Open Door note issued during Boxer Rebellion in China
	United States exports total $1.5 billion
	McKinley reelected
1901	Theodore Roosevelt becomes president
	Emilio Aguinaldo captured in Philippines
	Hay-Pauncefote Treaty allows United States development of ship canal
1903	Panama breaks from Colombia and grants canal rights to United States
	Platt Amendment subjugates Cuba
1904	Roosevelt Corollary declares United States a "police power"
1904–05	Russo-Japanese War
1905	Taft-Katsura Agreement gains Japanese pledge to respect Philippines
	Portsmouth Conference ends Russo-Japanese War

	United States financial supervision of Dominican Republic begins
1906	San Francisco school board segregates Asian schoolchildren
	United States invades Cuba to put down rebellion
1907	"Great White Fleet" of the United States Navy makes world tour
	"Gentleman's agreement" with Japan restricts immigration
1908	Root-Takahira Agreement with Japan reaffirms Open Door in China
1910	Mexican Revolution begins against Díaz and United States interests
1911	Treaty bans pelagic sealing in Bering Sea
1912	United States troops invade Cuba again
	United States troops occupy Nicaragua
1914	United States troops invade Mexico
	First World War begins
	Panama Canal opens

troops from the ship U.S.S. *Boston* occupied Honolulu. The queen was forced to surrender to the new regime, headed by Sanford B. Dole, son of missionaries and a prominent attorney. Up went the American flag. "The Hawaiian pear is now fully ripe and this is the golden hour to pluck it," a triumphant Stevens informed the United States Department of State.

Against the queen's protests and those of Japan, President Benjamin Harrison hurriedly sent a treaty of annexation to the Senate. Sensing foul play, incoming President Grover Cleveland withdrew the treaty and ordered an investigation. His investigator's report confirmed a conspiracy by the white economic elite in league with John Stevens and noted that a majority of Hawai'ians opposed annexation. Down came the American flag. But the Dole government arrested the queen and rejected United States attempts to restore the native government. After gaining her freedom, Queen Lilioukalani spoke out; her autobiography, *Hawaii's Story by*

Hawaii's Queen (1898), made the nationalist case against annexation. Nevertheless, annexation came in 1898.

During the late nineteenth and early twentieth centuries, seizing foreign opportunities was common practice for those who governed in Washington, D.C. They were unabashed expansionists and imperialists whose "destiny is always to expand," as the Russian diplomat who negotiated the sale of Alaska to the United States remarked. In the early nineteenth century, Americans had purchased Louisiana; annexed Florida, Oregon, and Texas; pushed Indians out of the path of white migration westward; seized California and other western areas from Mexico; and acquired the Gadsden Purchase (southern parts of present-day Arizona and New Mexico bought from Mexico in 1853). Since the founding of the republic, moreover, they had developed a lucrative foreign trade with most of the world.

From the Civil War to the First World War the United States became one of the world's premier expansionist nations, building, managing, and protecting an overseas empire. In that imperialistic age of "living" and "dying" nations, as British Prime Minister Lord Salisbury observed, the international system was becoming multipolar. Germany challenged an overextended Great Britain, an economic and military giant becoming, said one diplomat, the "weary titan" of the world. Japan expanded in Asia at the expense of both China and Russia. As for the "living" United States, it emerged as a great power with particular clout in Latin America, especially as the "dying" Spain declined. "The old nations of the earth creep on at a snail's pace," declared the industrialist Andrew Carnegie, but the United States "thunders past with the rush of the express [train]."

The United States imperialist surge, however, sparked considerable opposition. Abroad, native nationalists, commercial competitors, and other imperial nations tried to block the spread of United States influence, while anti-imperialists at home stimulated a momentous debate over the fundamental course of American foreign policy. Most Americans applauded *expansionism*—the outward movement of goods, ships, dollars, people, and ideas—as a traditional feature of their nation's history. But many became uneasy whenever expansionism gave way to *imperialism*—the imposition of control over other peoples, undermining their sovereignty so that they lose the freedom to make their own decisions. Imperial control could be imposed either formally (by annexation, colonialism, or military occupation) or informally (by economic domination, political manipulation, or the threat of intervention). As the informal methods indicate, imperialism meant more than the taking of territory.

Critics in the late nineteenth century disparaged territorial imperialism as unbefitting the United States, and they opposed joining other great powers in the scramble for colonies in Asia and Africa. Would not an overseas territorial empire, incorporating people of color living far from the United States, undermine institutions at home, threaten American culture, invite perpetual war, and violate honored principles? Although the United States preferred the "annexation of trade" to the annexation of territory, as Secretary of State James G. Blaine once declared, it became clear that economic expansionism sometimes led to the grabbing of colonies. Most Americans endorsed economic expansion as essential to the nation's prosperity and security, but anti-imperialists drew the line between expansionism and imperialism: profitable and fair trade relationships, yes; exploitation, no. And, some advised, American business activity abroad should not drag the United States into unwanted diplomatic crises and wars. But it did.

In the late nineteenth century the federal government sometimes failed to fund adequately the vehicles of expansion. Washington neglected the navy until the 1880s and continued to tolerate a foreign service weakened by the political spoils system. Most businessmen, moreover, ignored foreign commerce in favor of the domestic marketplace. Still, the direction of United States foreign policy after the Civil War became unmistakable: Americans intended to exert their influence beyond the continental United States, to reach for more space, more land, more markets, and more power. Republican Senator Henry Cabot Lodge, claiming that the "great nations" were seizing "the waste areas of the world," advised that "the United States must not fall out of the line of march," because "civilization and the advancement of the [Anglo-Saxon] race" were at stake.

United States activity abroad heightened in the tumultuous decade of the 1890s, when doubters' voices were drowned out by calls for war and foreign territory, and when American power was sufficient to deliver both. United States entry into the Spanish-American-Cuban-Filipino War in 1898 and the subsequent subjugation of other peoples not only set off a major political debate but also helped carry the United States to great-power status.

Imperial Promoters: The Foreign Policy Elite and Economic Expansion

Foreign policy has always sprung from the domestic setting of a nation—its needs, wants, moods, ideology, and culture. The leaders who guided America's expansionist foreign relations were the same people who guided the economic development of the machine age, forged the transcontinental railroad, built America's bustling cities and giant corporations, espoused ideas of American exceptionalism, and shaped a mass culture. The domestic and foreign spheres, as always, were inseparable.

Unlike domestic policy, foreign policy is seldom shaped by "the people." Most Americans simply do not follow international relations or express themselves on foreign issues. The making of foreign policy, then, is usually dominated by what scholars have labeled the "foreign policy elite"—opinion leaders in politics, business, labor, agriculture, religion, journalism, education, and the military. In the post–Civil War era, this small group, whom Secretary of State Walter Q. Gresham called "the thoughtful men of the country," expressed the opinion that counted. Better read and better traveled than most Americans, more cosmopolitan in outlook, and politically active, they believed that United States prosperity and security depended on the exertion of United States influence abroad. Increasingly in the late nineteenth century, and especially in the 1890s, the foreign policy elite urged not only expansionism but both formal and informal imperialism. These leaders created what the historian Emily Rosenberg has called "the promotional state"—a federal government committed to assisting American entrepreneurs who wished to trade and invest abroad and committed themselves to making the United States a world power.

Ambitious and clannish, the imperialists often met in Washington, D.C., at the homes of Henry Adams or John Hay (who became secretary of state

Network of Imperialists

in 1898) or at the Metropolitan Club. They talked about building a bigger navy and digging a canal across Panama, Central America, or Mexico, establishing colonies, and selling surpluses abroad. Theodore Roosevelt, appointed assistant secretary of the navy in 1897, was among them; so were Senator Henry Cabot Lodge, who became a member of the Foreign Relations Committee in 1895, and the corporate lawyer Elihu Root, who later would serve as both secretary of war and secretary of state. These luminaries kept up the drumbeat for empire.

These American leaders believed that selling, buying, and investing in foreign marketplaces were important to the United States. Why? One reason was profits from foreign sales. "It is my dream," declared the governor of Georgia in 1878, to see "in every valley . . . a cotton factory to convert the raw material of the neighborhood into fabrics which shall warm the limbs of Japanese and Chinese." Fear helped make the case for foreign trade as well, because the nation's farms and factories produced

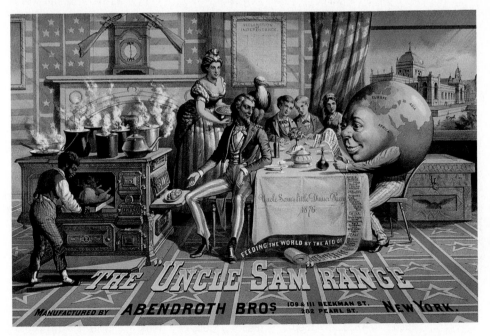

As one expression of the theme of economic expansion, this poster, advertising the Uncle Sam stove manufactured in New York by the Abendroth Bros. company, announces that food links the United States with the rest of the world. Although the foods on the long list are international—potatoes from Ireland and macaroni from Italy, for example—the message here is that the United States itself is "feeding the world." The turkey being removed from the oven seems to be the only unique American offering, but many of the items on the list were also produced in the United States. The poster was issued in 1876, which explains the image of the Centennial building in Philadelphia and the patriotic red, white, and blue colors. The New-York Historical Society.

more than Americans could consume. Foreign commerce might serve as a safety valve to relieve overproduction, unemployment, economic depression, and the social tensions that arise from them. Surpluses had to be exported, the economist David A. Wells warned, or "we are certain to be smothered in our own grease." Economic ties also permitted political influence to be exerted abroad and helped spread the American way of life, creating a world more hospitable to Americans. In an era when the most powerful nations in the world were also the greatest traders, vigorous foreign economic expansion symbolized national stature.

Foreign trade figured prominently in the tremendous economic growth of the United States after the Civil War. Foreign commerce, in turn,

Growth of Foreign Trade

stimulated the building of a larger protective navy, the professionalization of the foreign service, calls for more colonies, and a more interventionist foreign policy. In 1865 United States exports totaled $234 million; by 1900 they had climbed to $1.5 billion (see figure). By 1914, at the outbreak of the First World War, American exports had reached $2.5 billion, prompting some Europeans to protest an American "invasion." In 1874 the United States reversed its historically unfavorable balance of trade (importing more than it exported) and began to enjoy a long-term favorable balance (exporting more than it imported). Most of America's products went to Britain, Europe, and Canada, but increasing

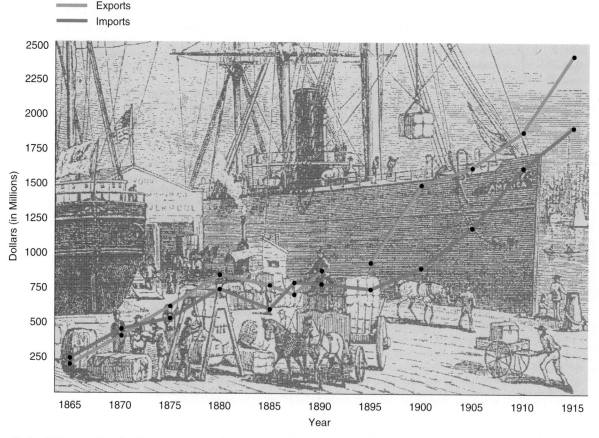

U.S. Trade Expansion, 1865–1914

United States Trade Expansion, 1865–1914 *This figure illustrates two key characteristics of U.S. foreign trade: first, that the United States began in the 1870s to enjoy a favorable balance of trade (exporting more than it imported); second, that U.S. exports expanded tremendously, making the United States one of the world's economic giants.* Source: From Thomas G. Paterson, J. Garry Clifford, and Kenneth J. Hagan, *American Foreign Relations: A History.* 4th edition. © 1995 by D. C. Heath and Company. Used by permission of Houghton Mifflin Company.

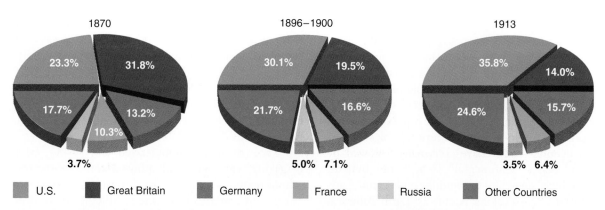

The Rise of U.S. Economic Power in the World

| 1870 | 1896–1900 | 1913 |

U.S. | Great Britain | Germany | France | Russia | Other Countries

The Rise of U.S. Economic Power in the World *These data—percentage shares of world manufacturing production for the major nations of the world—demonstrate that the United States came to surpass Great Britain in this significant measurement of power.* Source: League of Nations data presented in Aaron L. Friedberg, *The Weary Titan: Britain and the Experience of Relative Decline, 1895–1905* (Princeton, NJ: Princeton University Press, 1988), p. 26.

amounts flowed to new markets in Latin America and Asia. Meanwhile, direct American investments abroad reached $3.5 billion by 1914, placing the United States among the top four investor countries.

Agricultural goods accounted for about three-fourths of total exports in 1870 and about two-thirds in 1900, with grain, cotton, meat, and dairy products topping the export list that year. More than half of the annual cotton crop was exported each year. Midwestern farmers transported their crops by railroad to seaboard cities and then on to foreign markets. Farmers' livelihood thus became tied to world-market conditions and the outcomes of foreign wars. Wisconsin cheesemakers shipped to Britain; the Swift and Armour meat companies exported refrigerated beef to Europe. To sell American grain abroad, James J. Hill of the Great Northern Railroad distributed wheat cookbooks translated into several Asian languages.

In 1913, when the United States outranked both Great Britain and Germany in manufacturing production (see figure), manufactured goods led U.S. exports for the first time. Substantial proportions of America's steel, copper, and petroleum were sold abroad, making many workers in those industries dependent on exports. George Westinghouse marketed his air brakes in Europe; almost as many Singer sewing machines were exported as were sold at home; and Cyrus McCormick's "reaper kings" harvested the wheat of Russian fields.

 Ideology, Culture, and Empire

In the American march toward empire, ideology and culture figured prominently. An intertwined set of ideas conditioned United States foreign relations. Nationalism, exceptionalism, capitalism, Social Darwinism, paternalism, and the categorization of foreigners in derogatory race-, age-, and gender-based terms—all influenced American leaders. Fear and prejudice infused many American ideas about the world and "the Other"—fear of the social disorder stirred by revolution, fear of economic depression, fear of racial and ethnic mixing, fear of women's rights, fear of a closed frontier, fear of losing international stature. To calm their fears and promote their values, leaders exported American culture and sought to remake other societies in the image of the United States. "They are children and we are men in these deep matters of government," a future president announced in 1898. Later, as president, Woodrow Wilson declared that "when properly directed there is no people not fitted for self-government." More: "Every nation needs to be drawn into the tutelage of America" and taught "the habit of law and obedience." The intersection of American and foreign cultures, however, bred not only adoption but rejection, not only imitation but clash.

After the Civil War, leaders again put the United States on an expansionist course and championed a nationalism based on notions of American supremacy. The inflated rhetoric of American exceptionalism and manifest destiny revived, giving intensified voice to explanations for expansion based on race. In their idea of a racial hierarchy, Americans ranked "uncivilized" people of black color and Indians at the bottom and "civilized" white Americans of Anglo-Saxon heritage at the top. Near the top but beneath Anglo-Saxons, Americans placed European peoples—"aggressive" Germans followed by "peasant" Slavs, "sentimental" French and Italians, and "Shylock" Jews. In the middle rank came Latinos, the Spanish-speaking people of Latin America. Theodore Roosevelt disparaged Latinos as "dagoes" and "darkeys" who lacked any ability to govern themselves. North Americans debased Latin Americans as half-breeds needing close supervison, distressed damsels begging for manly rescue, or children requiring tutelage. After a visit to Honduras, the writer Richard Harding Davis, author of *Three Gringos in Venezuela and Central America* (1896), called Central Americans "a gang of semi-barbarians." Also midway in the hierarchy were East Asian peoples, the "Orientals" or "Mongolians" whom Americans thought inscrutable, crafty, and immoral, although, as in the case of the Japanese, sometimes capable of success.

Race Thinking

Reverend Josiah Strong's popular and influential *Our Country* (1885) celebrated an Anglo-Saxon race destined to lead others. "As America goes, so goes the world," he declared. A few years later he wrote that "to be a Christian and an Anglo-Saxon and an American . . . is to stand at the very mountaintop of privilege." Social Darwinists saw Americans as a superior people certain to overcome all competition. Secretary of State Thomas F. Bayard (1885–1889) applauded the "overflow of our population and capital" into Mexico to "saturate those regions with Americanism," but, he added, "we do not want them" until "they are fit."

The magazine *National Geographic*, which published its first issue in 1888, chronicled with photographs America's new overseas possessions. The editors chose pictures that reflected prevailing American ethnocentric attitudes toward foreigners. Even when smiling faces predominated, the image portrayed was that of strange, exotic, premodern people who had not become "Western." Emphasizing this point, *National Geographic* regularly pictured women with naked breasts. Fairs,

Images of Foreign Peoples

too, stereotyped other peoples as falling short of civilization. Fair managers not only celebrated the impressive technology of "Western civilization"; they also put people of color on display in the "freaks" or "midway" section. With bearded women and the fattest man in the world were exhibits—as at the 1895 Atlanta and 1897 Nashville fairs—of Cubans and Mexicans in primitive village settings. Dog-eating Filipinos aroused particular comment at the 1904 St. Louis World's Fair.

Race thinking—popularized in world's fairs, magazine cartoons and photographs, postcards, school textbooks, and political orations—reinforced notions of American greatness, influenced the way United States leaders dealt with other peoples, and obviated the need to think about the subtle textures of other societies. Such racism downgraded diplomacy and justified domination and war because self-proclaimed superiors do not negotiate with people ranked as inferiors.

A male ethos also characterized American views of foreigners. The language of American leaders was weighted with words such as *manliness* and *weakling*. The warrior and president Theodore Roosevelt prized the White House as the "bully pulpit" and celebrated the "strenuous life." But, more, he and others often described other nations as effeminate—unable, in contrast to a masculine Uncle Sam, to cope with the demands of world politics. The gendered imagery prevalent in United States foreign relations joined race thinking to place women, people of color, and nations weaker than the United States in the low ranks of the hierarchy of power and, hence, in a necessarily dependent status justifying United States hegemony. During and after the war of 1898, some activists in women's organizations bemoaned the "intoxication with the hashish of conquest" and "martial spirit" prevalent among male imperialists who quite deliberately denied voting rights to both Filipinos and American women.

Male Ethos

Issues of race and gender also marked the experiences of religious missionaries, many of whom were women. Missionaries dispatched to China, Korea, and Africa helped spur the transfer of American culture and power abroad—"the peaceful conquest of the world," as Reverend Frederick Gates put it. One organization, the Student Volunteers for Foreign Missions, began in the 1880s on college campuses and by 1914 had

Missionaries

How do historians know that Americans in the imperial age of the late nineteenth century disparaged people of other societies as "uncivilized" and in need of "civilization" from a superior United States? Historians interpret speeches, diaries, letters, tourist-industry advertisements, cartoons, fair exhibits, and more to identify the derogatory racist, age-based, and gendered language that Americans often used to describe foreigners. Especially revealing are the images on picture postcards of the era, because they capture expressions of supremacy in their depictions of the "civilized" (modern) and the "wild" (premodern). As photographs, postcards provide historians with a detailed documentary record, a testimony of feelings, and a visual representation of the values and attitudes of the time.

Government-made postcards were first issued in Austria in 1869 as a way to reduce the expense of corresponding by mail (they cost just a penny). Privately or commercially printed picture postcards appeared elsewhere in Europe in the 1880s and in the United States in the 1890s. Collecting postcards immediately became popular as a hobby; the collection and study of postcards today is called deltiology. At the turn of the century, card subjects included humor, anniversaries, patriotic events, advertisements, street scenes, historic sites, romantic messages, famous leaders, art, and costumes. The images of foreign peoples on American postcards often communicated a message that denigrated indigenous life through contrast with "Western" ways. The Singer Manufacturing Company handed out the promotional postcard reproduced here as a souvenir from the firm's exhibit at the 1893 Columbian Exposition in Chicago. About three-quarters of all sewing machines sold in the world were Singers. The machine shown in this postcard was marketed in South Africa, where, the company advised, the "Zulus are a fine warlike people" who were moving toward "civilization" with Singer's help.   State Historical Society of Wisconsin.

placed some six thousand missionaries abroad. Like Grace Roberts in China, where by 1900 more than a thousand missionaries labored, missionaries taught the Bible, hoping to convert "natives" and "savages" to Christianity. When American missionary women criticized non-Christian foreign societies as more exploitative of women than the United States was, in essence they perpetuated cultural stereotypes of Anglo-Saxon superiority that undergirded imperialism. The *Mother Goose Missionary Rhymes* betrayed traces of cultural imperialism: "Ten little heathen standing in a line; / One went to mission school, then there were but nine. . . . / Three little heathen didn't know what to do; / One learned our language, then there were two. . . . / One little heathen standing all alone; / He learned to love our flag, then there were

Missionary Grace Roberts taught the Bible to the Chinese in Manchuria in 1903. The promi-nent United States flag indicates that Americanism and religious work intersected overseas. A majority of the American missionaries in China were women.   By permission of Houghton Library, Harvard University.

none." At the same time, missionaries and Singer executives joined hands in promoting the "civilizing medium" of the sewing machine.

With a mixture of self-interest and idealism typical of American thinking on foreign policy, expansionists believed that empire benefited both Americans and those who came under their control. When the United States intervened in other lands or lectured weaker states, Americans claimed that in remaking foreign societies they were extending liberty and prosperity to less fortunate people. William Howard Taft, as civil governor of the Philippines (1901–1904), described the United States's mission in its new colony as lifting up Filipinos "to a point of civilization" that will make them "call the name of the United States blessed." Later, after becoming secretary of war (1904–1908), Taft said about the Chinese that "the more civilized they become . . . the wealthier they become, and the better market they become for us."

Remaking Societies and Gaining Markets

"The world is to be Christianized and civilized," declared Reverend Josiah Strong. "And what is the process of civilizing but the creating of more and higher wants."

To critics at home and abroad, however, American paternalism appeared hypocritical—a violation of cherished principles. To impose on Filipinos an American-style political system, for example, United States officials censored the press, jailed critics, and picked candidates for public office. From this coercive experience, Filipinos may have learned more about how to fix elections than about how to make democracy work.

 Eyes Abroad, 1860s–1880s

The American empire grew gradually, sometimes haltingly. William H. Seward, one of its chief architects, argued relentlessly for extension of the American frontier as senator from New York (1849–1861)

and secretary of state (1861–1869). "There is not in the history of the Roman Empire an ambition for aggrandizement so marked as that which characterizes the American people," he once said. Seward envisioned a large, coordinated United States empire encompassing Canada, the Caribbean, Cuba, Central America, Mexico, Hawai'i, Iceland, Greenland, and Pacific islands. This empire would be built not by war but by a natural process of gravitation toward the United States. Commerce would hurry the process, as would a canal across Central America, a transcontinental American railroad to link up with Asian markets, and a telegraph system to speed communications.

Most of Seward's grandiose plans did not reach fruition in his own day. In 1867, for example, he signed a treaty with Denmark to buy the Danish West Indies (the Virgin Islands),

William H. Seward's Quest for Empire

but his domestic political foes in the Senate and a hurricane that wrecked St. Thomas scuttled his effort. The Virgin Islanders, who had voted for annexation, had to wait until 1917. Also failing was Seward's scheme with unscrupulous Dominican leaders to gain control of a Caribbean naval base at the Dominican Republic's Samaná Bay. The stench of corruption rising over this unsavory deal-making wafted into the Ulysses S. Grant administration to foil Grant's initiative in 1870 to buy the entire island nation. The Senate rejected annexation.

Political foes blocked some territorial schemes, but so did anti-imperialists such as Senator Carl Schurz and E. L. Godkin, editor of the magazine *The Nation*. They argued that the country already had enough unsettled land and that the creation of a showcase of democracy and prosperity at home would best persuade other peoples to adopt American institutions and principles. Some anti-imperialists, sharing the racism of the times, opposed the annexation of territory populated by dark-skinned people.

But Seward did enjoy some successes. In 1866, citing the Monroe Doctrine, he sent troops to the border with Mexico and demanded that France abandon its puppet regime there. Also facing angry Mexican nationalists, Napoleon III abandoned the Maximilian monarchy. In 1867 Seward paid Russia $7.2 million for the 591,000 square miles of Alaska—land twice the size of Texas. Some critics lampooned "Seward's Icebox," but the secretary of state extolled the Russian territory's rich natural resources, and the Senate voted overwhelmingly for the treaty. That same year, Seward laid claim to the Midway Islands in the Pacific Ocean.

Seward realized his dream of a world knit together into a giant communications system. In 1866, through the persevering efforts of the financier

International Communications

Cyrus Field, an underwater transatlantic cable linked European and American telegraph networks. Backed by J. P. Morgan's capital, the communications pioneer James A. Scrymser strung telegraph lines to Latin America, reaching Chile in 1890. In 1903 a submarine cable reached across the Pacific to the Philippines; three years later it reached to Japan and China. Information about markets, crises, and war flowed steadily and quickly. Drawn closer to one another through improved communications and transportation, nations found that faraway events became more important to their prosperity and security. Wire telegraphy—like radio (wireless telegraphy) later—shrank the globe. Because of the communications revolution, "every nation elbows other nations to-day," Amherst College professor Edwin Grosvenor told the American Historical Association in 1898. Indeed, said President Woodrow Wilson many years later, "the world is all now one single whispering gallery."

Seward's successor, Hamilton Fish (1869–1877), inherited the knotty problem of the *Alabama* claims. The *Alabama* and other vessels built in Great Britain for the Confederacy during the Civil War had preyed on Union

Disputes with Britain and Canada

shipping. Senator Charles Sumner demanded that Britain pay $2 billion in damages or cede Canada to the United States, but Fish favored negotiations. In 1871 Britain and America signed the Washington Treaty, whereby the British apologized and agreed to the creation of a tribunal, which later awarded the United States $15.5 million.

Disputing Seward, Canadians did not consider themselves a mere gap in the American empire. They grew alarmed by United States expansion and the repeated, though diminishing, American calls for annexation. In 1867 the Dominion of Canada organized within the British Empire as a confederation of provinces, and three years later the province of Manitoba was created out of fear that the territory would be overrun by Americans. Disputes over fishing rights along the North Atlantic coast dogged Anglo-Canadian-American relations, as did sealing near Alaska.

Beginning in the late 1860s the United States sought to curb "pelagic" sealing—the slaughter of fur seals as they swam in the Bering Sea. Poachers ignored the law. Despite United States seizures of ships, many of them Canadian, the seals faced extermination by the end of the century. Finally, in 1911, Great Britain, Russia, Japan, and the United States banned pelagic sealing altogether and limited land kills. The seal population gradually rejuvenated. A migratory bird treaty signed with Canada in 1916 also restricted hunting and further set standards for environmental protection.

Saving the Fur Seals

In Samoa, a group of South Pacific islands 4,000 miles from San Francisco on the trade route to Australia, the United States once again tussled with Britain. But, as in other cases, an Anglo-American rapprochement developed to protect the interests of both nations. In 1878 the United States gained rights to a naval station at Samoa's strategic port of Pago Pago. The British and Germans also coveted the islands. Year by year tensions grew. To avoid war, Britain, Germany, and the United States met in Berlin in 1889 and, without consulting the Samoans, carved Samoa into three parts. A decade later the United States annexed part of the islands, including Pago Pago.

Pacific Outpost: Samoa

In China the United States experienced both opportunity and trouble. American missionaries became targets of Chinese nationalist anger, while American oil and textile companies sent their wares into a China market they dreamed was boundless. American religious elders and business executives throughout the late nineteenth century appealed for official United States protection (see pages 647–649 on the Open Door policy).

Sino-American Relations

Although the Burlingame Treaty (1868) provided for free immigration between the United States and China and pledged Sino-American friendship, Sinophobia in the American West erupted again and again in riots against Chinese immigrants—in Los Angeles (1871), San Francisco (1877), Denver (1880), and Seattle (1886). A new treaty in 1880 permitted Congress to suspend Chinese immigration to the United States, and it did

so two years later. An especially violent incident occurred in Rock Springs, Wyoming, in 1885, when white coal miners and railway workers rioted and massacred at least twenty-five Chinese. Weakened by internal strife and the imperial powers' encroachments, leaders in Beijing could do little but protest and remember, although a short-lived Chinese boycott of American products in 1905 demonstrated China's anger over racist American practices.

In Latin America, meanwhile, the convening in 1889 of the first Pan-American Conference in Washington, D.C., bore witness to growing United States influence in the Western Hemisphere. Conferees from Latin America toured United States factories and then pledged support for reciprocity treaties to improve hemispheric trade. To encourage inter-American cooperation, they founded the Pan-American Union. In 1891 Latin Americans wondered what Pan Americanism really stood for after the United States flexed its naval muscle and coerced Chile into a humiliating apology and indemnity after drunken sailors from the *Baltimore* battled Chileans outside a Valparaiso bar, costing two American lives. "The American Republic will stand no more nonsense from any power, big or little," boomed Senator George Shoup of Iowa.

Pan-American Conference

In contrast to Latin America, Africa generated little interest in the United States. American tobacco, kerosene, and rum claimed a good share of African markets and the United States Navy patrolled the African coast to protect American lives and property, but through tariff barriers the European colonizers reduced the continent's commerce with the United States. American diplomats sought to preserve the principle of free trade in an increasingly partitioned Africa through participation in the 1884 Berlin Conference, which confirmed Belgium's control of the Congo, but trade doors continued to close. Protestant missionaries in Africa built schools and hospitals, translated the Bible into Zulu, and created seminaries to train an African clergy. The African Methodist Episcopal Church, a major black denomination in the United States, recruited followers in Liberia, Sierra Leone, and South Africa. At a time of rising repression of African-Americans at home, some black missionary leaders urged a back-to-Africa movement. But only several hundred heeded the call.

Modest Interest in Africa

Beginning in the late nineteeth century, Standard Oil (the forerunner of Exxon Corporation) sent agents to China to persuade the Chinese to use American-made kerosene in their lamps and cooking stoves. To promote sales, the American entrepreneurs gave away small lamps, which the Chinese called Mei Foo *(Beautiful Companion). One agent who popularized the lamp was William P. Coltman, shown here with Chinese business associates and an advertisement.*   Agent: EXXON Corporation; Lamp: Private collection.

As the United States acquired new markets and territories and sent its diplomats, missionaries, and naval forces around the world, expansionists argued that a bigger, modernized United States Navy had become imperative and that the navy had to add to its traditional role of "brown water" coastline defense and riverine operations the "blue water" command of the seas. Captain Alfred T. Mahan became a major popularizer for a "New Navy." Because foreign trade was vital to the United States, he argued, the nation required an efficient navy to protect its shipping; in turn, a navy required colonies for bases. "Whether they will or no," Mahan wrote, "Americans must now begin to look outward. The growing production of the country demands it."

Mahan's lectures at the Naval War College in Newport, Rhode Island, where he served as president, were published as *The Influence of Sea Power*

Alfred T. Mahan and the New Navy

upon History (1890). This widely read book sat on every serious expansionist's shelf. German, Japanese, and British leaders turned its pages. Theodore Roosevelt and Henry Cabot Lodge eagerly consulted Mahan, sharing his belief in the links between trade, navy, and colonies.

Moving toward naval modernization, Congress in 1883 authorized construction of the first steel-hulled warships. American factories went to work to produce steam engines, high-velocity shells, powerful guns, and precision instruments. The navy shifted from sail power to steam and from wood construction to steel. Often named for states and cities to kindle patriotism and local support for naval expansion, New Navy ships such as the *Maine*, the *Oregon*, and the *Boston* thrust the United States into naval prominence. When the United States faced crises in the 1890s, the New Navy warships were put to the test.

Crises in the 1890s: Hawai'i, Venezuela, and Cuba

In the depression-plagued 1890s, crises in Hawai'i, Venezuela, and Cuba gave expansionist Americans opportunities to act on their zealous arguments for what Senator Lodge called a "large policy."

Belief that the frontier at home had closed accentuated the expansionist case. In 1893 the historian Frederick Jackson Turner of the University of Wisconsin postulated the thesis that an ever-expanding continental frontier had shaped the American character. That "frontier has gone," Turner wrote, "and with its going has closed the first period of American history." He did not explicitly say that a new frontier had to be found overseas in order to sustain the American way of life, but he did write that "American energy will continually demand a wider field for its exercise."

Turner's Frontier Thesis

Hawai'i emerged as a new frontier for Americans. The Hawai'ian Islands, as described at the beginning of this chapter, had long commanded American attention—commercial, missionary, naval, and diplomatic. Wide-eyed United States expansionists envisioned ships sailing from the eastern seaboard through a Central American canal to Hawai'i and then on to the fabled China market. Secretary of State James Blaine had warned other nations away from the archipelago in 1881, declaring the Hawai'ian Islands "essentially a part of the American system." That is what many Americans living in Hawai'i in the 1890s believed, only to find obstacles placed in their way by Congress (McKinley Tariff) and by native Hawai'ians (Queen Liliuokalani).

Annexation of Hawai'i

Although members of the American elite sought annexation by the United States when they overthrew the queen in 1893, their goal was not achieved until 1898, when Hawai'i gained renewed attention as a strategic and commercial way station to Asia and the Philippines during the Spanish-American-Cuban-Filipino War. On July 7, 1898, President William McKinley maneuvered annexation through Congress by means of a majority vote (the Newlands Resolution) rather than by a treaty, which would have required a two-thirds count. In part because of Hawai'i's mixed racial composition, statehood did not come until 1959.

The Venezuelan crisis of 1895 also saw the United States in an expansive mood. For decades Venezuela and Great Britain had squabbled over the border between Venezuela and British Guiana. The disputed territory contained rich gold deposits and the mouth of the Orinoco River, a commercial gateway to northern South America. Venezuela asked for United States help. President Cleveland decided that the "mean and hoggish" British had to be warned away. In July 1895, Secretary of State Richard Olney brashly lectured the British that the Monroe Doctrine prohibited European intervention in the Western Hemisphere. He aimed his spread-eagle words at an international audience: "To-day the United States is practically sovereign on this continent, and its fiat is law upon the subjects to which it confines its interposition." The British, seeking international friends to counter intensifying competition from Germany, quietly retreated from the crisis. In 1896 an Anglo-American arbitration board divided the disputed territory between Britain and Venezuela. The Venezuelans were barely consulted. Thus the United States displayed a trait common to imperialists: disregard for the rights and sensibilities of small nations.

Venezuelan Crisis

In 1895 came yet another crisis, this one in Cuba. From 1868 to 1878 the Cubans had battled Spain for their independence. Slavery was abolished but independence denied. While the Cuban economy suffered depression, repressive Spanish rule continued. Insurgents committed to "Cuba Libre" waited for another chance. José Martí, one of the heroes of Cuban history, collected money, arms, and men in the United States. This was but one of the many ways the lives of Americans and Cubans were linked. Their cultures, for example, melded. Cubans of all classes settled in Baltimore, New York, Boston, and Philadelphia. Prominent Cubans on the island sent their children to schools in the United States. When Cuban expatriates re-

Cuba in the United States Vortex

turned home, many came in American clothes, spoke English, had American names, played baseball, and jettisoned Catholicism for Protestant denominations. Struggling with competing identities, Cubans admired American culture but resented United States economic hegemony.

The Cuban and United States economies became integrated. American investments of $50 million, most in sugar plantations, dominated the Caribbean island. More than 90 percent of Cuba's sugar was exported to the United States, and most island imports came from the United States. The Florida and Cuban economies also fused. Havana's famed cigar factories relocated to Key West and Tampa to evade protectionist United States tariff laws. Martí feared that this "economic union means political union," for "the nation that buys, commands" and "the nation that sells, serves." Watch out, Marti warned, for the United States's "conquering policy" that reduced Latin American countries to "dependencies." A change in American tariff policy hastened the Cuban Revolution against Spain and the island's further incorporation into "the American system." The Wilson-Gorman Tariff (1894) imposed a duty on Cuban sugar, which had been entering the United States duty-free under the McKinley Tariff. The Cuban economy, highly dependent on exports, plunged into deep crisis.

From American soil, Martí launched a revolution in 1895 that mounted in human and material costs. Rebels burned sugar-cane fields and razed mills, conducting an economic war and using guerrilla tactics to avoid head-on clashes with Spanish soldiers. "It is necessary to burn the hive to disperse the swarm," explained the insurgent leader Máximo Gomez. The Spanish retaliated under the command of General Valeriano Weyler, who instituted a policy of "reconcentration" to separate the insurgents from their supporters among the Cuban people. Some 300,000 Cubans were herded into fortified towns and camps, where hunger, starvation, and disease led to tens of thousands of deaths.

The Cuban Revolution

All across Cuba, United States investments went up in smoke and Cuban-American trade dwindled. As reports of atrocity and destruction became headline news in the American yellow press (see page 560), Americans sympathized increasingly with the insurrectionists. In late 1897, a new government in Madrid modified reconcentration and promised some autonomy for Cuba.

Queen Liliuokalani (1838–1917), ousted from her throne in 1893 by wealthy revolutionaries, vigorously protested in her autobiography and diary, as well as in interviews, the United States's annexation of Hawai'i in 1898. For years she defended Hawai'ian nationalism and emphasized that United States officials in 1893 had conspired with Sanford B. Dole and others to overthrow the native monarchy. Courtesy of the Liliuokalani Trust.

President William McKinley had come to office an imperialist who advocated foreign bases for the New Navy, the export of surplus production, and United States supremacy in the Western Hemisphere. Vexed by the turmoil in Cuba, he came to believe that Spain should give up its colony. At one point he explored the purchase of Cuba by the United States for $300 million. Whatever the outcome of the crisis, McKinley always insisted on "American control."

Events in early 1898 caused McKinley to lose faith in Madrid's ability to bring peace to Cuba. In January, when antireform pro-Spanish loyalists and army personnel rioted in Havana, Washington ordered the battleship *Maine* to Havana harbor to demonstrate United States concern and to protect American citizens. On February 15 an explosion under the enlisted men's quarters ripped the *Maine*,

Sinking of the *Maine*

killing 266 of 354 American officers and crew. Just a week earlier, William Randolph Hearst's inflammatory *New York Journal* had published a stolen private letter written by the Spanish minister in Washington, Enrique Dupuy de Lôme, who belittled McKinley's leadership and suggested that Spain would fight on. Congress soon complied unanimously with McKinley's request for $50 million in defense funds. The naval board created to investigate the sinking of the *Maine* then reported that a mine had caused the explosion. Whether a Spanish mine, Cuban sabotage, or an internal accident caused the disaster did not matter to revengeful Americans bent on blaming Spain.

The impact of these events narrowed McKinley's diplomatic options. He decided to send Spain an ultimatum. In late March the United States insisted that Spain accept an armistice, end reconcentration altogether, and designate McKinley as arbiter. Implicit was the demand that Spain grant Cuba its independence. No Spanish government could have given up Cuba and remained in office, but Madrid nonetheless made concessions. It abolished reconcentration and accepted an armistice on the condition that the insurgents agree first. Wanting more, McKinley drafted a war message. Then he received news that Spain had gone a step further and declared a unilateral armistice. The weary McKinley hesitated, but he would no longer tolerate chronic disorder just 90 miles off the American coast.

On April 11, the president asked Congress for authorization to use United States force against Spain. McKinley listed the reasons: first, the "cause of humanity"; second, the protection of American life and property; third, the "very serious injury to the commerce, trade, and business of our people"; fourth, referring to the destruction of the *Maine*, the "constant menace to our peace." At the very end of his message the president mentioned Spain's recent concessions but made little of them.

McKinley's War Message

On April 19 Congress declared Cuba free and independent and directed the president to use force to remove Spanish authority from the island. The legislators also passed the Teller Amendment, which disclaimed any United States intention to annex Cuba. McKinley beat back a congressional amendment to recognize the rebel government. Believing that the Cubans were not ready for self-government, he argued that they needed a period of American tutoring.

The Spanish-American-Cuban-Filipino War

Diplomacy had failed. By the time the Spanish concessions came forth, events had already pushed the antagonists to the brink. Washington might have been more patient, and Madrid might have faced the fact that its once-grand empire had disintegrated. Still, prospects for compromise appeared dim, because the advancing Cuban insurgents would settle for nothing less than full independence. That Spain could not easily accept. Nor did the United States welcome a wholly independent Cuban government that might attempt to reduce United States interests. In the Cuban crisis, as in the Venezuelan crisis, the United States claimed the right to set the rules for nations in the Western Hemisphere. The British had backed down in 1895, but the Spanish and Cubans stood firm in 1898.

The motives of Americans who favored war were mixed and complex. McKinley's April message expressed a humanitarian impulse to stop the bloodletting, a concern for commerce and property, and the psychological need to end the nightmarish anxiety once and for all. Republican politicians advised McKinley that their party would lose the upcoming congressional elections unless the Cuban question was solved. Many businesspeople, who had been hesitant before the crisis of early 1898, joined many farmers in the belief that ejecting Spain from Cuba would open new markets for surplus production.

Motives for War

Inveterate imperialists saw war as an opportunity to fulfill expansionist dreams. Naval enthusiasts could prove the worth of the New Navy. Some religious leaders also saw merit in war. Social Gospel advocate Washington Gladden remarked that "in saving others we may save ourselves." Conservatives, alarmed by Populism and violent labor strikes, welcomed war as a national unifier. One senator commented that "internal discord" was disappearing in the "fervent heat of patriotism." Sensationalism also figured in the march to war, with the yellow press in particular exaggerating stories of Spanish misdeeds. Assistant Secretary of the Navy Theodore Roosevelt and others too young to remember the bloody Civil War looked on war as adventure and used inflated rhetoric to trumpet the call to arms. Anglo-Saxon supremacists such as the politician Albert Beveridge shouted, "God's hour has struck." Overarching all explanations for the 1898 war were expansionism

On July 1, 1898, United States troops stormed Spanish positions on San Juan Hill near Santiago, Cuba. Both sides suffered heavy casualities. A Harper's *magazine correspondent reported a "ghastly" scene of hundreds killed and thousands wounded. The American painter William Glackens (1870–1938) put to canvas what he saw. Because Santiago surrendered on July 17, propelling the United States to victory in the war, and because Rough Rider Theodore Roosevelt fought at San Juan Hill and later gave a self-congratulatory account of the experience, the human toll has often gone unnoticed.* Wadsworth Atheneum, Hartford, Gift of Henry Schnakenberg.

and imperialism, whose momentum had been moving the nation ever outward in the last half of the nineteenth century.

More than 263,000 regulars and volunteers served in the army and another 25,000 in the navy during the war. The typical volunteer was young (early twenties), white, unmarried, native-born, and working class. Most never left the United States, and 5,462 of them died— but only 379 of them in combat. The rest fell to malaria and yellow fever spread by mosquitoes. About 10,000 African-American troops, assigned to segregated regiments, found no relief from racism and Jim Crow. For all, food was bad and medical care was unsophisticated. Still, Roosevelt could hardly contain himself. He called the Rough Riders—his motley unit of Ivy Leaguers and cowboys—"children of the dragon's blood" eager for a fight. The Rough Riders were undisciplined and not always effective warriors, but largely because of Roosevelt's self-serving publicity efforts they got a good press.

United States Military Forces

To the surprise of most Americans, the first war news actually came from faraway Asia, from the Spanish colony of the Philippines. On May 1, 1898, Commodore George Dewey's New Navy ship the *Olympia*, leading an American squadron, steamed into Manila Bay and wrecked the outgunned Spanish fleet. Dewey's sailors had to be handed volumes of the *Encyclopaedia Britannica* to acquaint them with this strange land, but officials in Washington knew better. Manila ranked with Pearl Harbor and Pago Pago as a choice harbor, and the Philippines sat significantly on the way to China and its potentially huge market.

Dewey in the Philippines

The writer Sherwood Anderson said that fighting Spain was "like robbing an old gypsy woman in a vacant lot at night after a fair." Facing rebels and Americans in both Cuba and the Philippines, Spanish resistance collapsed rapidly. United States ships had blockaded Cuban ports to prevent Spain from reinforcing and resupplying its army on the island. American troops saw their first ground-war action on June 22, the day several thousand of them landed near Santiago de Cuba and laid siege to the city. On July 3, United States warships sank the Spanish Caribbean squadron in Santiago harbor. American forces then assaulted the Spanish colony of Puerto Rico to obtain another Caribbean base for the navy and a strategic site to help protect a Central American canal. Losing on all fronts, Madrid sued for peace.

On August 12, Spain and the United States signed an armistice to end the Spanish-American-Cuban-Filipino War. "Let's see what we get by this," said Secretary of State William R. Day as he twirled the large globe in his office. In Paris in December 1898, American and Spanish negotiators agreed on the peace terms: independence for Cuba; cession of the Philippines, Puerto Rico, and Guam (an island in the Pacific) to the United States; and American payment of $20 million to Spain for the territories. The American empire now stretched deep into Asia; and the annexation of Wake Island (1898), Hawai'i (1898), and Samoa (1899) gave American traders, missionaries, and naval promoters other steppingstones to China.

Treaty of Paris

The Taste of Empire: Imperialists Versus Anti-Imperialists

During the war, the *Washington Post* detected "a new appetite, a yearning to show our strength. . . . The taste of empire is in the mouth of the people." But as the nation debated the Treaty of Paris, it became evident that many Americans found the taste bitter. Anti-imperialists such as Mark Twain, William Jennings Bryan, William Graham Sumner, Jane Addams, Andrew Carnegie, and Senator George Hoar of Massachusetts argued vigorously against annexation of the Philippines. They were disturbed that a war to free Cuba had led to empire.

Some critics appealed to principle, citing the Declaration of Independence and the Constitution: the conquest of people against their will violated the concept of self-determination. The philosopher William James charged that the United States was throwing away its special place among nations; it was, he warned, about to "puke up its

The Anti-Imperialist Case

heritage." Other anti-imperialists argued that the United States could acquire markets without having to subjugate foreign peoples. To those who argued that the Filipinos were not yet fit for self-government, former Senator Carl Schurz retorted that Manila's city council was probably less corrupt than Chicago's. Others claimed that to maintain empire, the president repeatedly would have to dispatch troops overseas. Because he could do so as commander-in-chief, he would not have to seek congressional approval, thus subverting the constitutional checks-and-balances system.

Reform-minded critics of the treaty insisted that domestic issues—including race relations—deserved first priority on the national agenda. Some anti-imperialists predicted that the very character of the American people was being corrupted by the imperialist zeal. Jane Addams, seeing children play war games, pointed out that they were *not freeing Cubans* but were *slaying Spaniards*. An African-American politician from Massachusetts who had just protested a lynching in Georgia cried that the United States was exhibiting quite a spectacle to the world, "offering liberty to the Cubans with one hand, cramming liberty down the throats of the Filipinos with the other, but with both feet planted upon the neck of the negro." Some anti-imperialists, believing in a racial hierarchy, warned that annexing people of color would undermine Anglo-Saxon purity and supremacy.

Samuel Gompers and other labor leaders worried about the possible undercutting of American labor by what Gompers called the "half-breeds and semi-barbaric people" of the new colonies. Might not the new colonials be imported as cheap contract labor to drive down the wages of American workers? Would not exploitation of the weak abroad become contagious and lead to further exploitation of the weak at home? Would not an overseas empire drain interest and resources from pressing domestic problems, delaying reform?

Labor's Fears

The anti-imperialists entered the debate with many handicaps and never launched an effective campaign. Although they organized the Anti-Imperialist League, they differed so profoundly on domestic issues that they found it difficult to speak with one voice on a foreign question. They also appeared inconsistent: Gompers favored the war but not the postwar annexations; Carnegie would accept colonies if they were not acquired by force; Hoar voted for annexation of Hawai'i but not of the

Philippines; Bryan backed the Treaty of Paris but only, he said, to hurry the process toward Philippine independence. Finally, possession of the Philippines was an established fact, very hard to undo.

The imperialists answered their critics with appeals to patriotism, destiny, and commerce. They sketched a scenario of American greatness: merchant ships plying the waters to boundless Asian markets; naval

Advocates of Empire

vessels cruising the Pacific to protect American interests; missionaries uplifting inferior peoples. It was America's duty, they insisted, quoting a then-popular Rudyard Kipling poem, to "take up the white man's burden." Furthermore, insurgents were beginning to resist United States rule, and it was cowardly to pull out under fire. Germany and Japan, two powerful international competitors, were snooping around the Philippine Islands, apparently ready to seize them if the United States did not. National honor dictated that Americans keep what they had shed blood to take. Senator Beveridge asked: "Shall [history] say that, called by events to captain and command the proudest, ablest, purest race of history in history's noblest work, we declined that great commission?"

In February 1899, the Senate passed the Treaty of Paris by a 57-to-27 vote, with most Republicans voting "yes" and most Democrats voting "no." An amendment promising independence as soon as the Filipinos formed a stable government lost only by the tie-breaking ballot of the vice president. The Democratic presidential candidate Bryan carried the anti-imperialist case into the election of 1900, warning that repudiation of self-government in the Philippines would weaken the principle at home. But the victorious McKinley refused to apologize for American imperialism. "It is no longer a question of expansion with us," he asserted. "If there is any question at all it is a question of contraction; and who is going to contract?"

Asian Encounters: Open Door in China, Philippine Insurrection, and Japan

In 1895, the same year as the Venezuelan crisis and the advent of the Cuban Revolution, Japan claimed victory over China in a short war. Outsiders had been pecking away at China since the 1840s, but the Japanese onslaught intensified the international scramble. The Germans carved out a sphere of interest in Shandong; the Russians moved into Manchuria and the Liaodong Peninsula; the French took Guangzhou Bay; the British, already holding Hong Kong, drove in new stakes in Shandong; Japan controlled Formosa and Korea as well as parts of China proper (see map, page 648). Within their spheres, the imperial powers built fortified bases and claimed exclusive economic privileges. American religious and business leaders petitioned Washington to halt the dismemberment before they were closed out.

Secretary Hay knew that the United States could not force the imperial powers out of China, but he was determined to protect American commerce. In

Open Door Policy

September 1899 Hay sent the imperial nations active in China a note asking them to respect the principle of equal trade opportunity—an Open Door. The recipients sent evasive replies, privately complaining that the United States was seeking for free in China the trade rights that they had gained at considerable military and administrative cost. The next year, a Chinese secret society called the Boxers laid siege to the foreign legations in Beijing. The United States joined the imperial powers in sending troops to lift the siege and sent a second Open Door note in July that instructed other nations to preserve China's territorial integrity and to honor "equal and impartial trade." Hay's protests notwithstanding, China continued for years to be fertile soil for foreign exploitation, especially for the Japanese.

Though Hay's foray into Asian politics settled little, the Open Door policy became a cornerstone of United States diplomacy. The "open door" had actually been a long-standing American principle, for as a trading nation the United States opposed barriers to international commerce and demanded equal access to markets. After 1900, however, when the United States began to emerge as the premier world trader, the Open Door policy became an instrument first to pry open markets and then to dominate them, not just in China but throughout the world. The Open Door also developed as an ideology with several tenets: first, that America's domestic well-being required exports; second, that foreign trade would suffer interruption unless the United States intervened abroad to implant American principles and keep foreign markets open; and, third, that the closing of any area to American products, citizens, or ideas threatened the survival of the United States itself.

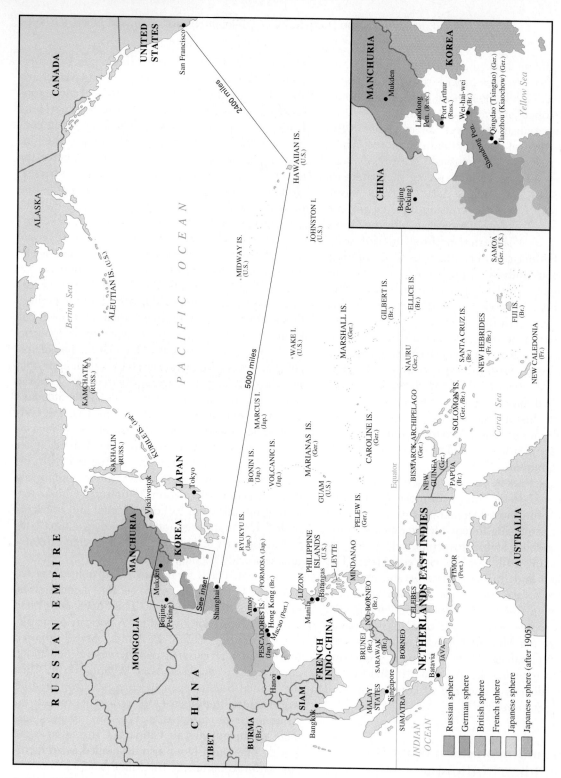

Imperialism in Asia: Turn of the Century *China and the Pacific region had become imperialist hunting grounds by the turn of the century. The European powers and Japan controlled more areas than the United States did, but it participated in the race for influence by annexing the Philippines, Wake, Guam, and Hawai'i, announcing the Open Door policy, and expanding trade in the area. As the "spheres" in China demonstrate, that besieged nation succumbed to imperial outsiders despite the Open Door policy.*

In the Philippines, meanwhile, United States occupation authorities soon antagonized their new "wards," as McKinley labeled them. The president intended to "uplift and civilize" the Filipinos, but they denied that they needed United States paternalism. Emilio Aguinaldo, the Philippine nationalist leader who had been battling the Spanish for years, believed that American officials had promised independence for his country. But after the victory, Aguinaldo was ordered out of Manila and isolated from decisions affecting his nation. Racial slurs—one American teacher wrote home that he had been sent to Leyte "to teach these monkeys to talk"—infuriated nationalistic Filipinos, who also felt betrayed by the Treaty of Paris.

In January 1899, Aguinaldo proclaimed an independent Philippine Republic and took up arms. Before the Philippine Insurrection was suppressed in 1902, more than 200,000 Filipinos and 5,000 Americans lay dead in a war fought viciously by both sides. American soldiers burned villages, tortured captives, and introduced a variant of the reconcentration policy. In the province of Batangas south of Manila, for example, United States troops forced residents to live in designated zones in an effort to separate the insurgents from local supporters. Disaster followed. Poor sanitation, starvation, and malaria and cholera killed several thousand people. Outside the secure areas, Americans destroyed food supplies to starve out the rebels. At least one-quarter of the population of Batangas died or fled. In Batangas and elsewhere, Americans spoke of the "savage" Filipino insurgents who might "injun up" on them. One American soldier declared that the Philippines "won't be pacified until the niggers [Filipinos] are killed off like the Indians." Twenty-six of the thirty United States army generals ordered to the Philippines from 1898 through 1902 had had prior experience battling Native Americans.

After capturing Aquinaldo in 1901, stern United States military rule imposed a policy of "attraction," as the first civil governor of the Philippines William Howard Taft called it. The architect Daniel Burnham, leader of the City Beautiful movement (see page 568), planned modern Manila. American teachers were imported to instruct from the popular American primer *Baldwin Reader* (which included "A" for "apple," a fruit unknown to most Filipinos). English was declared the official language, and the

Philippine Insurrection

The caption of this 1900 photograph reads: "Our young Filipinos in holiday attire at the Fourth of July celebration, Manila, P.I." Converting America's new colonial people in the Philippines to allegiance to the United States, however, proved a great deal more difficult than handing out flags to children. After seizing the Philippines from Spain, the United States blocked Philippine independence, battled and jailed Filipino nationalists who resisted American rule, and imposed a regime on the islands through a combination of the carrot (schools and roads) and the stick (military force and a sedition law to muzzle dissenters). Library of Congress.

University of the Philippines was founded (1908) to train an American-oriented elite. The Philippine economy grew as a United States satellite, and a sedition act silenced critics of United States authority by sending them to prison.

Fiercely independent Muslim Filipinos, the vast majority of the inhabitants of Moro Province, refused to knuckle under. The United States military ordered them to submit or be exterminated. In 1906 the Moros finally met defeat; six hundred of them, including many women and children, were slaughtered at the Battle of Bud Dajo. "Work of this kind," General Leonard Wood wrote Roosevelt, "has its disagreeable side." In 1916 the Jones Act promised independence to the Philippines, but it did not become a reality until thirty years later.

As the United States disciplined the Filipinos, Japan was becoming the dominant power in Asia.

This cloth bandanna celebrated President Theodore Roosevelt's receipt of the Nobel Peace Prize in 1906 for helping to negotiate an end to the Russo-Japanese War. In a bequest, the Swedish inventor-industrialist Alfred Bernhard Nobel created the prize, which was first awarded in 1901. The irony of giving a peace prize to a man who often seemed eager for war is well illustrated at the top of this work, where Roosevelt the Rough Rider is shown charging on horseback into battle in the Spanish-American-Cuban-Filipino War.   Collection of David J. and Janice L. Frent.

Gradually the United States had to make concessions to Japan to protect the vulnerable Philippines and to sustain the Open Door policy. Japan continued to carve out interests in China and then smashed the Russians in the Russo-Japanese War (1904–1905). President Theodore Roosevelt mediated the crisis at the Portsmouth Conference in New Hampshire and won the Nobel Peace Prize for this ultimately vain effort to preserve peace and a balance of power in Asia.

Japan's Expansionism

In 1905, in the Taft-Katsura Agreement, the United States conceded Japanese hegemony over Korea in return for Japan's pledge not to undermine the United States's position in the Philippines. Three years later, in the Root-Takahira Agreement, the United States recognized Japan's interests in Manchuria, whereas Japan again pledged the security of the United States's Pacific possessions and endorsed the Open Door in China. Roosevelt also built up United States naval power to deter the Japanese; in

late 1907 he sent on a world tour the navy's "Great White Fleet" (so named because the ships were painted white for the voyage). Duly impressed, the Japanese began to build a bigger navy of their own.

President William Howard Taft thought he might counter Japanese advances in Asia through *dollar diplomacy*—the use of private funds to serve American diplomatic goals and at the same time to garner profits for American financiers. In this case, Taft induced American bankers to join an international consortium to build a railway in China. Taft's venture seemed only to embolden Japan to solidify and extend its holdings in China, where internal discord continued after the nationalistic revolution of 1911 overthrew the weak Qing (Manchu) dynasty.

Japanese-American relations also became tense over the treatment of Japanese citizens in the United States. In 1906 the San Francisco School Board, reflecting the anti-Asian bias of many West Coast Americans, ordered the segregation of all Chinese, Koreans, and Japanese in a special school. Tokyo protested the discrimination against its citizens. The following year, President Roosevelt quieted the crisis by striking a "gentleman's agreement" with Tokyo restricting the inflow of Japanese immigrants; San Francisco then rescinded its segregation order. Relations with Tokyo were jolted again in 1913 when the California legislature denied Japanese residents the right to own property in the state.

Anti-Japanese Bias in California

In 1914, when the First World War broke out in Europe, Japan seized Shandong and some Pacific islands from the Germans. In 1915 Japan issued its Twenty-One Demands, virtually insisting on hegemony over all of China. The Chinese door was being slammed shut, but the United States lacked adequate countervailing power in Asia to block Japan's imperial thrusts.

Latin America, Europe, and International Rivalry

Intense international rivalry also characterized United States relations with Latin America, where United States economic and strategic interests and usable power towered (see map, page 651), and with Europe, where repeated political and military disputes persuaded Americans to develop friendlier relations with Great Britain while avoiding entrapment in the Continent's troubles.

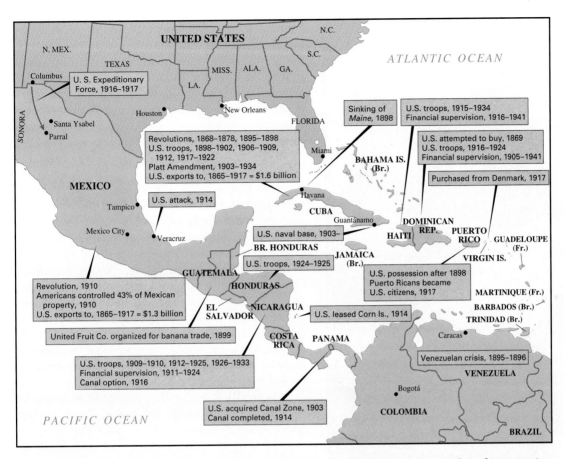

U.S. Hegemony in the Caribbean and Latin America *Through a great number of interventions and persistent economic expansion, the United States became the predominant power in Latin America in the early twentieth century. The United States often backed up the Roosevelt Corollary and its declaration of a "police power" by dispatching troops to Caribbean nations, where they met nationalist opposition.*

As United States economic interests expanded in Latin America, so did United States political influence. United States exports to Latin America, which exceeded $50 million in the 1870s, rose to more than $120 million in 1900 and reached $300 million in 1914. Investments by United States citizens in Latin America climbed to a commanding $1.26 billion in 1914. In 1899 two large banana importers merged to form United Fruit Company. In Central America, United Fruit owned much of the land (more than a million acres in 1913) and the railroad and steamship lines, and the firm became an influential economic and political force in the region. The company also worked to eradicate yellow fever and malaria while it manipulated Central American politics.

With the destructive war in Cuba ended, United States citizens and corporations soon acquired title

Economic Penetration of Latin America

to more than 60 percent of Cuba's rural lands and came to dominate the island's sugar, mining, tobacco, and utilities industries. North American investments in Cuba grew from $50 million before the revolution to $220 million by 1913, and North American exports to the island rose from $26 million in 1900 to $196 million in 1917. Seeing their nation become dependent on the United States, Cuban nationalists developed anti-Yankee views.

The Teller Amendment may have outlawed the annexation of Cuba, but it did not rule out United States control. North American troops remained there until 1902. Under United States rule, the "better classes" were favored. United States authorities, for example, restricted voting rights largely to propertied Cuban males, excluding two-thirds of adult men and all women. North American officials also forced the Cubans to append

Platt Amendment for Cuba

The Panama-Pacific Exposition in San Francisco in 1915 celebrated the opening of the Panama Canal with this official poster by Perham Nahl, "The Thirteenth Labor of Hercules." The artist commemorates the ten-year construction feat using symbols that reflect the imperialism and male hegemony of that time: a gigantic, muscular Hercules (the powerful United States) forcibly opens the land (a yielding Panama) to make space for the canal. When President Theodore Roosevelt asked Secretary of War Elihu Root whether he had adequately defended himself against charges that the United States had acted imperialistically in helping to sever Panama from Colombia in 1903, Root replied: "You have shown that you were accused of seduction and you have conclusively proved that you were guilty of rape." The Oakland Museum, Oakland, California.

to their constitution a frank avowal of United States hegemony known as the Platt Amendment. This statement prohibited Cuba from making a treaty with another nation that might impair its independence; in practice, this meant that all treaties had to have United States approval. Most important,

another Platt Amendment provision granted the United States "the right to intervene" to preserve the island's independence and to maintain domestic order. Cuba was also required to lease to the United States a naval base (at Guantánamo Bay). Formalized in a 1903 treaty, the amendment governed Cuban-American relations until 1934. "There is, of course, little or no independence left Cuba under the Platt Amendment," General Wood privately remarked to President Roosevelt.

The Cubans, like the Filipinos, chafed under their United States masters. A rebellion in 1906 prompted Roosevelt to order another invasion of Cuba. The marines stayed until 1909, returned briefly in 1912, and occupied the island again from 1917 to 1922. All the while, North Americans helped to develop a transportation system, expand the public school system, found a national army, and increase sugar production. When Dr. Walter Reed's experiments, based on the theory of the Cuban physician Carlos Finlay, proved that mosquitoes transmitted yellow fever, sanitary engineers controlled the insect and eradicated the disease.

Puerto Rico, a densely populated Caribbean island that exported sugar and coffee, also developed under United States tutelage. The Puerto Rican elite at first had welcomed the United States as an improvement over Spain. But disillusionment soon set in. The condescending United States military governor, General Guy V. Henry, who regarded Puerto Ricans as naughty, ill-educated children, explained that he was giving them "kindergarten instruction in controlling themselves without allowing them too much liberty." Some residents warned against the "Yankee peril"; others applauded the "Yankee model" and anticipated statehood. Puerto Ricans were granted United States citizenship in 1917, and in 1952 Puerto Rico became a "commonwealth" of the United States.

United States Tutelage of Puerto Rico

Soon after the turn of the century, Panama became the site of a much bolder United States expansionist venture. In 1869 the world had marveled at the completion of the Suez Canal, a waterway that greatly facilitated travel between the Indian Ocean and Mediterranean Sea and enhanced the power of the British Empire. Surely that feat could be duplicated in the Western Hemisphere. One expansionist, United States navy captain Robert W. Shufeldt, predicted that a new canal would convert "the Gulf of Mexico into an American lake." Business interests joined politicians, diplomats, and navy officers in insisting that the United States control such an interoceanic canal.

Before a waterway could be cut across the narrow isthmus of Panama, a province of Colombia, obstacles had to be overcome. The Clayton-Bulwer Treaty with Britain (1850) provided for joint control of a canal.

Panama Canal The British, recognizing their diminishing influence in the region and cultivating friendship with the United States as a counterweight to Germany, stepped aside in the Hay-Pauncefote Treaty (1901) to permit a solely United States canal. But Colombia hesitated to meet the United States's terms. Impatient with Bogotá, Roosevelt encouraged Panamanian rebels to declare independence from Colombia and ordered American warships to the isthmus to back them. In 1903 the new Panama awarded the United States a canal zone and long-term rights to its control. The treaty also guaranteed Panama its independence. (In 1922 the United States paid Colombia $25 million in "conscience money" but did not apologize.)

The completion of the Panama Canal in 1914 marked a major technological achievement. The United States fortified the zone with conspicuous sixteen-inch guns, the nation's largest. During the canal's first year of operation, more than one thousand merchant ships squeezed through its locks. Ten years later the annual rate had risen to five thousand, equal to the Suez Canal traffic.

As for the rest of the Caribbean, Roosevelt did not truck with challenges to United States hegemony. Worried that Latin American nations' defaults on huge debts owed to European banks were provoking European intervention (England, Germany, and Italy sent warships to Venezuela in 1902), the president issued the Roosevelt Corollary to the Monroe Doctrine in 1904. He warned Latin Americans to stabilize their politics and finances. "Chronic wrongdoing," the corollary lectured, might require "intervention by some civilized nation," and "in flagrant cases of such wrongdoing or impotence," the United States would have to assume the role of "an international police power."

Roosevelt Corollary

Roosevelt and his successors were not bluffing. From 1900 to 1917, United States troops intervened in Cuba, Panama, Nicaragua, the Dominican Re-

This chauvinistic Judge *magazine cartoon of 1904 appeared after President Theodore Roosevelt proclaimed the United States a "police power" in the Western Hemisphere (the Roosevelt Corollary to the Monroe Doctrine). "A True American Rough Rider," Roosevelt gallops across Central America and Panama into South America, all the while knocking down or chasing away European nations from the United States's sphere of influence.* Collection of Janice L. and David J Frent.

public, Mexico, and Haiti to quell civil wars, thwart challenges to United States influence, gain ports and bases, and forestall European meddling (see map, page 651). United States authorities ran elections, trained national guards that became politically powerful, and renegotiated foreign debts and shifted them to United States banks. They also took over customs houses to control tariff revenues and government budgets (as in the Dominican Republic, from 1905 to 1941).

In neighboring Mexico, the long-time (1876–1910) dictator Porfirio Díaz recruited foreign investors through tax incentives and land grants.

Economic Links with Mexico

American capitalists came to own Mexico's railroads and mines and invested heavily in petroleum and banking. By the early 1890s, the United States dominated Mexico's foreign trade. By 1910, Americans controlled 43 percent of Mexican property and produced more than half of the country's oil; in the state of Sonora 186 of 208 mining companies were American owned. The Mexican revolutionaries who ousted Díaz in 1910, like nationalists elsewhere in Latin America, set out to reclaim their nation's sovereignty by ending their economic dependency on the United States (see page 665).

As the United States reaffirmed the Monroe Doctrine and demonstrated the power to enforce it, European nations reluctantly honored United States hegemony in Latin America. In

Relations with Europe

turn, the United States held to its tradition of standing outside European embroilments. The balance of power in Europe was precarious, and seldom did an American president involve the United States directly. At Germany's request, Roosevelt helped to settle a Franco-German clash over Morocco by mediating a settlement at Algeciras, Spain (1906). But the president drew American criticism for entangling the United States in a European problem. Americans endorsed the ultimately futile Hague peace conferences (1899 and 1907) and negotiated various arbitration treaties, but on the whole stayed outside the European arena, except to profit from extensive trade with it.

A special feature of European-American relations was growing cooperation with Great Britain. One outcome of the German-British rivalry and the rise of the United States to world power was London's quest for friendship with the United States. Already prepared by ideas of Anglo-Saxon kinship, Americans appreciated British support for the United States in the 1898 war, the Hay-Pauncefote Treaty, and London's virtual endorsement of the Roosevelt Corollary and withdrawal of British warships from the Caribbean. The British overtures paid off in 1917 when the United States threw its weapons and soldiers into the First World War on the British side.

 Conclusion

In the years from the Civil War to the First World War, expansionism and imperialism elevated the United States to world-power status. By 1914 Americans held extensive economic, strategic, and political interests in a world made smaller by modern technology. The victory over Spain in 1898 was but the most dramatic moment in the long process. The outward reach of United States foreign policy from Secretary of State Seward to President Wilson sparked opposition from domestic critics, other imperial nations, and foreign nationalists, but the trend toward empire endured.

From Asia to Latin America, economic and strategic needs and ideology motivated and justified expansion and empire. The belief that the United States needed foreign markets to absorb surplus production to save the domestic economy joined missionary zeal to reform other societies through the promotion of American culture and products. Notions of racial and male supremacy and appeals to national greatness also fed the appetite for foreign adventure and commitments.

The humorist Finley Peter Dunne conveyed the American mood by putting words in the mouths of his fictional Irish-American characters: "'We're a gr-reat people,' said Mr. Hennessy, earnestly. 'We ar-re,' said Mr. Dooley. 'We ar-re that. An' th best iv it is, we know we are.'" In August 1914, having become a *world power* with far-flung interests to protect, the United States had to face a tough test of its self-proclaimed greatness and reconsider its political isolation from Europe, when a *world war* broke out.

Suggestions for Further Reading

General

Robert L. Beisner, *From the Old Diplomacy to the New, 1865–1900*, 2d ed. (1986); Daniel R. Headrick, *The Invisible Weapon* (1991) (on communications); David Healy, *United States Expansionism* (1970); Ronald J. Jensen, *The Alaska Purchase and Russian-American Relations* (1975); Paul Kennedy, *The Rise and Fall of the Great Powers* (1987); Walter LaFeber, *The American Search for Opportunity, 1865–1913* (1993); Walter LaFeber, *The New Empire* (1963); Ernest R. May, *American Imperialism* (1968); Thomas G. Paterson and Stephen G. Rabe, eds., *Imperial Surge* (1992); David M. Pletcher, *The Awkward Years* (1962); Emily Rosenberg, *Spreading the American Dream* (1982); William Appleman Williams, *The Tragedy of American Diplomacy*, new ed. (1988).

Imperial Promoters

Howard K. Beale, *Theodore Roosevelt and the Rise of America to World Power* (1956); John M. Cooper, Jr., *The Warrior and the Priest: Woodrow Wilson and Theodore Roosevelt* (1983); Louis L. Gould, *The Presidency of Theodore Roosevelt* (1991); Lewis L. Gould, *The Presidency of William McKinley* (1981); William H. Harbaugh, *The Life and Times of Theodore Roosevelt* (1975); Frederick Marks III, *Velvet on Iron* (1979) (on Roosevelt); Edmund Morris, *The Rise of Theodore Roosevelt* (1979); Ernest N. Paolino, *The Foundations of the American Empire* (1973) (on Seward); William C. Widenor, *Henry Cabot Lodge and the Search for an American Foreign Policy* (1980).

Economic Expansion

William H. Becker, *The Dynamics of Business-Government Relations* (1982); Robert B. Davies, *Peacefully Working to Conquer the World: Singer Sewing Machines in Foreign Markets, 1854–1920* (1976); Tom Terrill, *The Tariff, Politics, and American Foreign Policy, 1874–1901* (1973); Mira Wilkins, *The Emergence of the Multinational Enterprise* (1970); William Appleman Williams, *The Roots of the Modern American Empire* (1969).

Ideology and Culture

Alexander DeConde, *Ethnicity, Race, and American Foreign Policy* (1992); Thomas G. Dyer, *Theodore Roosevelt and the Idea of Race* (1980); Willard B. Gatewood, Jr., *Black Americans and the White Man's Burden* (1975); Michael H. Hunt, *Ideology and U.S. Foreign Policy* (1987); Robert D. Johnson, ed., *On Cultural Ground* (1994); Amy Kaplan and Donald E. Pease, eds., *Cultures of United States Imperialism* (1993); Catherine A. Lutz and Jane L. Collins, *Reading National Geographic* (1993); Robert Rydell, *All the World's a Fair* (1985); David Spurr, *The Rhetoric of Empire* (1993).

The United States Navy

Benjamin F. Cooling, *Gray Steel and Blue Water Navy* (1979); Frederick C. Drake, *The Empire of the Seas* (1984) (on Shufeldt); Kenneth J. Hagan, *This People's Navy* (1991); Walter R. Herrick, *The American Naval Revolution* (1966); Peter Karsten, *The Naval Aristocracy* (1972); Robert Seager II, *Alfred Thayer Mahan* (1977); Ronald Spector, *Admiral of the New Empire* (1974) (on Dewey).

The Spanish-American-Cuban-Filipino War

Graham A. Cosmas, *An Army for Empire* (1971); Gerald F. Linderman, *The Mirror of War* (1974); Ernest R. May, *Imperial Democracy* (1961); Joyce Milton, *The Yellow Kids* (1989); John Offner, *An Unwanted War* (1992); Julius Pratt, *Expansionists of 1898* (1936); David F. Trask, *The War with Spain in 1898* (1981).

Anti-Imperialism and the Peace Movement

Robert L. Beisner, *Twelve Against Empire* (1968); Kendrick A. Clements, *William Jennings Bryan* (1983); Charles DeBenedetti, *Peace Reform in American History* (1980); C. Roland Marchand, *The American Peace Movement and Social Reform, 1898–1918* (1973); Thomas J. Osborne, *"Empire Can Wait": American Opposition to Hawaiian Annexation, 1893–1898* (1981); David S. Patterson, *Toward a Warless World* (1976); E. Berkeley Tompkins, *Anti-Imperialism in the United States* (1970).

Cuba, Mexico, Panama, and Latin America

Arturo M. Carrión, *Puerto Rico* (1983); Richard H. Collin, *Theodore Roosevelt's Caribbean* (1990); David Healy, *Drive to Hegemony* (1989) (on the Caribbean); Walter LaFeber, *Inevitable Revolutions*, 2d ed. rev. (1993) (on Central America); Walter LaFeber, *The Panama Canal*, rev. ed. (1990); Lester D. Langley, *Struggle for the American Mediterranean* (1980); Lester D. Langley, *The United States and the Caribbean, 1900–1970* (1980); John Major, *Prize Possession* (1993) (on the Panama Canal); David McCullough, *The Path Between the Seas* (1977) (on the Panama Canal); Louis A. Pérez, Jr., *Cuba and the United States* (1990); Louis A. Pérez, Jr., *Cuba Under the Platt Amendment, 1902–1934* (1986); Dexter Perkins, *The Monroe Doctrine, 1867–1907* (1937); Brenda G. Plummer, *Haiti and the Great Powers, 1902–1915* (1988); Stephen J. Randall, *Colombia and the United States* (1992); Ramón E. Ruíz, *The People of Sonora and Yankee Capitalists* (1988); Josefina Vázquez and Lorenzo Meyer, *The United States and Mexico* (1985).

Hawai'i, China, Japan, and the Pacific

Charles S. Campbell, *Special Business Interests and the Open Door Policy* (1951); Warren I. Cohen, *America's Response to China*, 3d ed. (1989); Michael H. Hunt, *The Making of a Special Relationship* (1983) (on China); Jane Hunter, *The Gospel of Gentility* (1984) (on women missionaries in China); Akira Iriye, *Across the Pacific* (1967); Jerry Israel, *Progressivism and the Open Door* (1971); Paul M. Kennedy, *The Samoan Tangle* (1974); Ralph S. Kuykendall, *The Hawaiian Kingdom* (1967); Charles J. McClain, *In Search of Equality* (1994) (on discrimination against the Chinese); Thomas J. McCormick, *China Market* (1967); Charles E. Neu, *The Troubled Encounter* (1975) (on Japan); Craig Storti, *Incident at Bitter Creek* (1991) (on Rock Springs massacre); Merze Tate, *Hawaii: Reciprocity or Annexation* (1968); Merze Tate, *The United States and the Hawaiian Kingdom* (1965); Marilyn Blatt Young, *The Rhetoric of Empire* (1968).

The Philippines

John M. Gates, *Schoolbooks and Krags* (1973) (on the United States Army); Stanley Karnow, *In Our Image* (1989); Brian M. Linn, *The U.S. Army and Counterinsurgency in the Philippine War, 1898–1902* (1989); Glenn A. May, *Battle for Batangas* (1991); Glenn A. May, *Social Engineering in the Philippines* (1980); Stuart C. Miller, *"Benevolent Assimilation"* (1982); Peter Stanley, *A Nation in the Making* (1974); Richard E. Welch, *Response to Imperialism: American Resistance to the Philippine War* (1972); Walter L. Williams, "United States Indian Policy and the Debate over Philippine Annexation," *Journal of American History* 66 (1980): 810–831.

Great Britain and Canada

Robert Bothwell, *Canada and the United States* (1992); Kenneth Bourne, *Britain and the Balance of Power in North America, 1815–1908* (1967); Robert C. Brown, *Canada's National Policy, 1883–1900* (1964); Charles S. Campbell, *From Revolution to Rapprochement: The United States and Great Britain, 1783–1900* (1974); Adrian Cook, *The Alabama Claims* (1975); James T. Gay, *American Fur Seal Diplomacy* (1987); Bradford Perkins, *The Great Rapprochement* (1968).

CHAPTER

23

Americans at War
1914–1920

T he medical case files listed him as "A.P." An eighteen-year-old
Marine Corps private who had volunteered to fight in the First
World War, he thrived on the military life. Like other young
American soldiers, A.P. was ordered to the western front in France. Dur-
ing early 1918 the Germans relentlessly bombarded his position at
Château-Thierry, where screeching shells and deafening explosions
pounded the fresh American troops.

In June, A.P.'s company trudged forward to the battle lines, past the
bodies of French soldiers dismembered by the big guns. His commanding officer detailed A.P. to bury the mangled corpses. For several nights
thereafter the young man could not sleep. Artillery fire frightened him.
During a bombardment on June 14, he began to tremble uncontrollably.
A.P. was evacuated to a hospital, where noise easily startled him and horrifying dreams haunted him.

Doctors who treated military casualties were seeing tens of thousands of such patients, whom they diagnosed as suffering from a mental
illness they called war neurosis or war psychosis—shell shock, for short.
The symptoms became all too familiar: a fixed empty stare, violent
tremors, paralyzed limbs, listlessness, jabbering, screaming, and terrify-
ing dreams. The illness could strike anyone; even those soldiers who appeared most manly and courageous cracked after days of noisy shelling.
"There was a limit to human endurance," one lieutenant explained.

Their nervous systems shattered by explosives, some one hundred
thousand victims went to special military hospitals staffed by psychiatrists. A regimen of rest, military discipline, recreation, exercise, counseling, and reminders about patriotic duty restored many shell-shock
victims to health. Some returned to the front lines, but others remained
riven by anxiety and had to be assigned to noncombat duties. The very ill

**Harvey Dunn's painting
(1918) of weary soldiers
in the First World War
captures the misery
of front-line battle.
Casualties in the war
included 8 million
soldiers and 6.6 million
civilians dead and more
than 21 million people
wounded.** *Smithsonian
Institute, Division of Political
History, Washington, D.C.
(detail)*

went home to the United States. Even cured shell-shocked soldiers had lingering mental problems—flashbacks, nightmares, and a persistent disorientation that made it difficult for them to make decisions or organize their lives. Thousands of the most severely afflicted remained in veterans' hospitals.

Many Progressive era professionals and reformers found rewards and opportunities in the wrenching national emergency of World War I. The psychiatrists who treated the shell-shock victims, for example, wanted to apply their mental health expertise to help win the war. They also hoped to use their wartime medical experience later, at home, to improve care for the mentally ill. For them, the cataclysm of foreign crisis and the opportunity for domestic social betterment went hand in hand. That is what the philosopher and educator John Dewey meant when he said that the war presented "social possibilities."

The outbreak of the Great War in Europe in 1914 at first stunned Americans. For years their nation had participated in the international competition for colonies, markets, and weapons supremacy. But full-scale war seemed unthinkable. "Civilization is all gone, and barbarism come," moaned one social reformer. The French and Germans were using "huge death engines to mow down men and cities," observed *Harper's Weekly*. "We go about in a daze, hoping to awake from the most horrid of nightmares." Articulated by well-organized groups, peace sentiment in the United States strengthened with each grisly report from the European battlefield.

For almost three years President Woodrow Wilson kept America out of the war. During this time, he sought to protect United States trade interests and to improve the nation's military posture should the United States ever decide to join the fight. He lectured the belligerents to rediscover their humanity and to respect international law. But American neutrality, lives, and property fell victim to British and German naval warfare. In early 1917, when the president finally asked Congress for a declaration of war, he did so with his characteristic crusading zeal. America entered the battle not just to win the war but to reform the postwar world—to "make the world safe for democracy," declared Wilson.

Even after more than a decade of Progressive reform, Americans remained a heterogeneous and fractious people at the start of the Great War. Headlines still trumpeted labor-capital confrontations such as the Ludlow Massacre in Colorado, in which two women and eleven children were killed when state militia attempted to break a miners' strike. Racial antagonisms were evident in Wilson's decision to segregate federal buildings in Washington and in continued lynchings of African-Americans (fifty-one in 1914). Nativists protested the pace of immigration; 1.2 million immigrants entered the United States in 1914 alone. Ethnic groups eyed one another suspiciously. Many women argued for equality between the sexes and for the suffrage, but many men wanted to sustain traditional practices.

The war experience accentuated and intensified the nation's social divisiveness. Many whites did not like the northward migration of southern blacks to work in defense plants, and race riots revealed once again the depth of racial prejudice. War hawks harassed pacifists and German-Americans. The federal government itself, eager to stimulate patriotism, trampled on civil liberties to silence critics. And, as communism implanted itself in Russia, a postwar Red Scare in the United States tarnished America's reputation as a democratic society. In the aftermath of war, groups that sought to consolidate gains made during the war vied with those who sought to restore the prewar status quo.

America's participation in the war wrought massive changes and accelerated ongoing trends. Wars are emergencies, and during such times normal ways of doing things surrender to the extraordinary and exaggerated. The United States government, more than ever before, became a manager—of people, prices, production, and minds. A compulsory draft pulled men into the armed services. The presidency assumed greater powers. Unprecedented centralization and integration of the economy, increased standardization of products, and unusual cooperation between government and business also characterized the times. Although reformers did continue to devote themselves to issues such as prohibition and women's suffrage, the war experience helped splinter and thus undermine the Progressive movement. Jane Addams sadly remarked that "the spirit of fighting burns away all those impulses . . . which foster the will to justice."

The United States emerged from the war a major power in an economically hobbled world. Yet Americans who had marched to battle as if on a crusade grew disillusioned. They recoiled from the spectacle of the victors squabbling over the spoils, and they chided Wilson for failing to deliver the "peace without victory" he promised. As in the

• *Important Events* •

1914	United States troops invade Mexico during its revolution
	First World War begins in Europe
1915	Wilson denounces German sinking of the *Lusitania*
	Secretary of State Bryan resigns
1916	Congress votes down the Gore-McLemore resolution limiting travel on belligerent ships
	United States troops invade Mexico again
	After torpedoing *Sussex*, Germany pledges not to attack merchant ships without warning
	National Defense Act provides for larger military
	Wilson reelected on platform of peace, Progressivism, and preparedness
1917	Germany declares unrestricted submarine warfare
	Zimmermann telegram aggravates Mexican–United States troubles
	Russian Revolution ousts the czar
	United States enters First World War
	Selective Service Act sets up compulsory military service (the draft)
	Espionage Act limits First Amendment rights
	Race riot in East St. Louis, Illinois
	War Industries Board created to manage the economy
	War Revenue Act raises taxes to control war profiteering
	Fuel crisis during severe winter

1918	Wilson announces Fourteen Points for new world order
	Sedition Act further limits free speech
	Eugene V. Debs imprisoned for speaking against the war
	American troops at Château-Thierry help turn back German offensive
	American troops intervene in Russian civil war against Bolsheviks
	Flu pandemic
	Republicans hand Wilson a setback by winning congressional elections
	Armistice ends the First World War
1919	Paris Peace Conference punishes Germany and launches League of Nations
	May Day bombings help stimulate Red Scare
	American Legion organizes for veterans' benefits and antiradicalism
	Chicago race riot
	Steelworkers strike
	Communist Party of the United States of America founded
	Wilson suffers stroke after speaking tour
	Senate rejects Treaty of Versailles and United States membership in League of Nations
	Schenck v. *U.S.* upholds Espionage Act
1920	Palmer Raids round up suspected radicals

1790s, the 1840s, and the 1890s, Americans once again engaged in a searching national debate about the fundamentals of their foreign policy. After negotiating the Treaty of Versailles in Paris, the president appealed for United States membership in the League of Nations, which he touted as a vehicle for reforming world politics. But the Senate rejected his call, fearful that the League might further entangle Americans in Europe's problems, impede the growth of the United States's empire, and compromise the country's traditional unilateralism. On many fronts, then, Americans during the era of the First World War were at war with themselves.

 Precarious Neutrality

The war that erupted in August 1914 grew from years of European competition over trade, colonies, allies, and armaments. Two powerful alliance systems had formed: the Triple Alliance of Germany, Austria-Hungary, and Italy, and the Triple Entente of Britain, France, and Russia. All had imperial holdings and ambitions for more, but Germany seemed particularly bold as it rivaled Great Britain for world leadership. Many Americans saw Germany as a threat to United States interests in the Western

Hemisphere and viewed Germans as an excessively militaristic people who embraced autocracy and spurned democracy.

Strategists said that Europe enjoyed a balance of power, but a series of crises in the Balkan countries of southeastern Europe started a chain of events that shattered the "balance." Slavic nationalists in the Balkans sought to enlarge Serbia, an independent Slavic nation, by annexing regions such as Bosnia, then a province of the Austro-Hungarian Empire (see map, page 661). On June 28, 1914, at Sarajevo, a city in Bosnia, a member of the Black Hand, a Slavic terrorist group, assassinated the heir to the Austro-Hungarian throne. Long worried about the prospect of a large Slavic state—an enlarged Serbia—on its southern border, Austria-Hungary consulted its Triple Alliance partner Germany, which urged toughness. When Serbia called on its Slavic friend Russia for help, Russia in turn looked to its ally France. In late July, Austria-Hungary declared war against Serbia, on the grounds that the Serbian government tolerated anti-Austrian terrorists. Russia then began to mobilize its armies.

Outbreak of the First World War

Germany—having goaded Austria-Hungary toward war and then certain that war was next coming Berlin's way—struck first, declaring war against Russia on August 1 and against France two days later. The British hesitated, but when Germany slashed into Belgium to get at France, Britain declared war against Germany on August 4. Eventually Turkey joined Germany and Austria-Hungary (the Central Powers), and Japan and Italy teamed up with Britain, France, and Russia (the Allies). Japan took advantage of the European war to seize Germany's Chinese sphere of influence, Shandong. The world was aflame.

President Wilson at first sought to distance America from the conflagration by issuing a proclamation of neutrality—the traditional United States policy toward European wars. He also asked Americans to refrain from taking sides, to exhibit "the dignity of self-control." In private, the president said that "we definitely have to be neutral, since otherwise our mixed populations would wage war on each other." The United States, he fervently hoped, would stand apart as a sane, civilized nation in a deranged international system.

Wilson's lofty appeal for American neutrality and unity at home collided with several realities between August 1914 and April 1917. First, ethnic groups in the United States took sides. Many German-Americans and anti-British Irish-Americans (Ireland was then trying to break free from British rule) cheered for the Central Powers. Americans of British and French ancestry and others with roots in Allied nations championed the Allied cause. Germany's attack on neutral Belgium at the start of the war confirmed in many people's minds that Germany had become the archetype of unbridled militarism and autocracy.

Taking Sides

The pro-Allied sympathies of Wilson's administration also weakened the United States's proclamation of neutrality. Wilson and his advisers shared the conviction with British leaders that a German victory would destroy free enterprise and government by law. If Germany won the war, Wilson prophesied, "it would change the course of our civilization and make the United States a military nation." Wilson's chief advisers and diplomats—his assistant Edward House, Secretary of State Robert Lansing, and Ambassador to London Walter Hines Page—held similar anti-German views that often translated into pro-Allied policies.

United States economic links with the Allies also rendered neutrality difficult, if not impossible. England had long been one of the nation's best customers. Now the British flooded the United States with new orders for products, including arms. Sales to the Allies helped pull the American economy out of its recession. Between 1914 and 1916, American exports to England and France grew 365 percent, from $753 million to $2.75 billion. In the same period, however, largely because of Britain's naval blockade, exports to Germany dropped by more than 90 percent, from $345 million to only $29 million. Much of United States trade with the Allies was financed through loans from private American banks. These loans totaled $2.3 billion during the period of neutrality; Germany received only $27 million in the same period. The Wilson administration, which at first frowned on these transactions, came to see them as necessary to the economic health of the United States.

Trade and Loans

From Germany's perspective, the linkage between the American economy and the Allies meant that the United States had become the Allied arsenal and bank. Americans, however, faced a dilemma: cut-

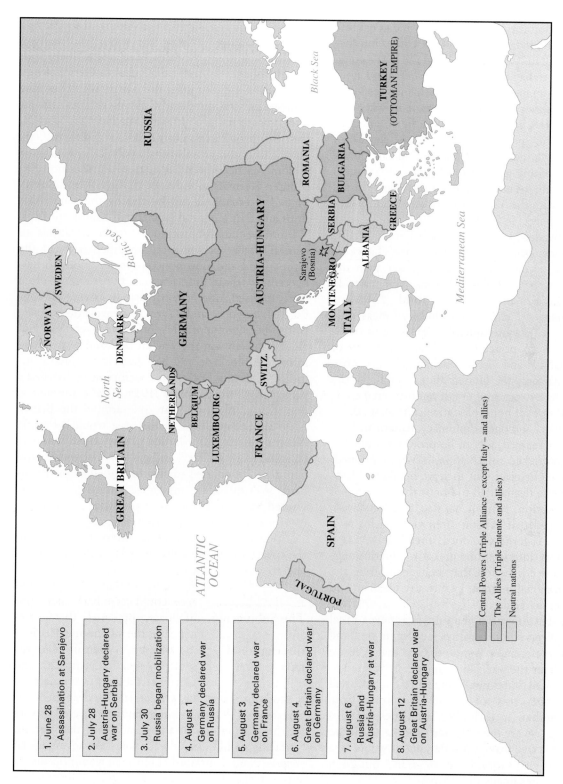

Europe Goes to War, Summer 1914 *Bound by alliances and stirred by turmoil in the Balkans, where Serbians repeatedly upended peace, the nations of Europe descended into war in the summer of 1914. Step by step they escalated a Balkan crisis into the "Great War."*

ting their economic ties with Britain would constitute an unneutral act in favor of Germany. Under international law, Britain—which controlled the seas—could buy both contraband (war-related goods) and noncontraband from neutrals. It was Germany's responsibility, not America's, to stop such trade in ways that international law prescribed—that is, by an effective blockade of the enemy's territory, by the seizure of contraband from neutral (American) ships, or by the confiscation of any goods from belligerent (British) ships. Germans, of course, judged the huge United States trade with the Allies an act of unneutrality that had to be stopped.

The president and his aides believed, finally, that Wilsonian principles stood a better chance of international acceptance if Britain, rather than the Central Powers, sat astride the postwar world. "Wilsonianism," the cluster of ideas Wilson espoused, consisted of traditional American principles and an ideology of internationalism and exceptionalism. The central tenet was that only the United States could lead the world into a new, peaceful era of unobstructed commerce, free-market nonexploitative capitalism, democratic politics, and open diplomacy. American Progressivism, it seemed, was to be projected onto the world. "We created this Nation," Wilson intoned, "not to serve ourselves, but to serve mankind." Empires had to be dismantled to honor the principle of self-determination. Armaments had to be reduced. Critics charged that Wilson often violated his own tenets in his eagerness to force them on others— as his military interventions in Latin America suggested. All agreed, though, that such ideals served the American national interest; in this way idealism and realism were married.

Wilsonianism

To say that American neutrality was never a real possibility given ethnic loyalties, economic ties, and Wilsonian preferences is not to say that Wilson sought to enter the war. He emphatically wanted to keep the United States out. Time and again, he tried to mediate the crisis to prevent one power from crushing another. In early 1917, the president remarked that "we are the only one of the great white nations that is free from war today, and it would be a crime against civilization for us to go in." But go in the United States finally did. Why?

Americans got caught in the Allied–Central Power crossfire. British naval policy aimed to sever neutral trade with Germany in order to cripple the

German economy. The British, "ruling the waves and waiving the rules," declared a blockade of water entrances to Germany and mined the North Sea. They also harassed neutral shipping by seizing cargoes and defined a broad list of contraband (including foodstuffs) that they prohibited neutrals from shipping to Germany; American vessels bearing goods for Germany seldom reached their destination. Furthermore, to counter German submarines (U-boats), the British flouted international law by arming their merchant ships and flying neutral (sometimes American) flags. Wilson frequently protested British violations of neutral rights, pointing out that neutrals had the right to sell and ship noncontraband goods to belligerents without interference. But London often deftly defused American criticism by paying for confiscated cargoes, and German provocations made British behavior appear less offensive by comparison.

British Naval Policy

Unable to win the war on land and determined to lift the blockade and halt American-Allied commerce, Germany looked for victory at sea by using submarines. In February 1915 Berlin announced that it was creating a war zone around the British Isles; all enemy ships in the area would be sunk. Neutral vessels were warned to stay out so as not to be attacked by mistake, and passengers from neutral nations were advised to stay off Allied ships. President Wilson stiffly informed Germany that the United States was holding it to "strict accountability" for any losses of American life and property.

Wilson was interpreting international law in the strictest possible sense. The law that an attacker had to warn a passenger or merchant ship before attacking, so that passengers and crew could disembark safely into lifeboats, predated the emergence of the submarine as a major weapon. When Wilson refused to make adjustments, the Germans thought him unfair. As they saw the issue, the slender, frail, and sluggish *unterseebooten* (U-boats) should not be expected to surface to warn ships of their imminent destruction. Surfacing would deny the U-boats the advantage of surprise, and a surfaced submarine would become a sitting target for a British deck gun. The time required to evacuate passengers, moreover, usually gave the distressed ship the opportunity to radio for help to a British destroyer in nearby waters. Berlin

The Submarine and International Law

frequently complained to Wilson that he was denying the Germans the one weapon they could use to break the British economic stranglehold, disrupt the Allies' substantial connection with American producers and bankers, and win the war. To all concerned—British, Germans, and Americans—this naval warfare became a matter of life and death.

Submarine Warfare and Wilson's Decision for War

"*Here's money for your Americans. I may drown some more,*" *says Kaiser Wilhelm to President Wilson in this anti-German cartoon. It appeared in early 1916 after Germany finally expressed regret for having taken American lives almost a year earlier when a U-boat sank the* Lusitania. *The Germans offered an indemnity, but not until 1925 did a claims commission determine that Germany should pay $2.5 million to American claimants who had suffered losses because of the* Lusitania *tragedy.* Life *magazine, April 13, 1916. The Boston Athenaeum.*

Sinking of the *Lusitania*

Over the next few months the U-boats sank ship after ship. In May 1915 the swift, luxurious British passenger liner *Lusitania* left New York City carrying more than twelve hundred passengers and a cargo of food and contraband, including 4.2 million rounds of ammunition for Remington rifles. Before "Lucy's" departure, the newspapers printed an unusual announcement from the German embassy: travelers on British vessels should know that Allied ships in war-zone waters "are liable to destruction." Few passengers paid attention or shifted to an American vessel for the transatlantic trip. On May 7, off the Irish coast, submarine U-20 unleashed torpedoes at the four-stacked vessel. The *Lusitania* sank quickly, taking to their deaths 1,198 people, 128 of them Americans.

Even if the ship was carrying armaments, argued Wilson, the sinking was a brutal assault on innocent people. But he ruled out a military response. Secretary of State William Jennings Bryan advised that Americans be prohibited from travel on belligerent ships and that passenger vessels be prohibited from carrying war goods. "Germany has a right to prevent contraband going to the Allies," wrote Bryan, "and a ship carrying contraband should not rely on passengers to protect her from attack—it would be like putting women and children in front of an army."

The president rejected Bryan's counsel, insisting on the right of Americans to sail on belligerent ships and demanding that Germany cease its inhumane submarine warfare. When the Germans urged Wilson to rethink the relationship between international law and the submarine, the president fumed. After a stormy White House meeting marked by Bryan's charge that the cabinet was pro-Allied, Wilson reiterated his demand that submarines be kept in port.

When the president refused to ban American travelers from belligerent ships, Bryan resigned in protest—an uncommon act for unhappy secretaries of state, who usually leave quietly. The pro-Allied Robert Lansing, a lawyer with experience in the international field, took Bryan's place. When criticized for pursuing a double standard in favor of the Allies, Wilson responded that the British were taking cargoes and violating property rights but the Germans were taking lives and violating human rights. Wilson's attitude toward Germany had noticeably hardened.

Seeking to avoid war with America, Germany ordered its U-boat commanders to halt attacks on passenger liners. But in mid-August another British vessel, the *Arabic*, was sunk and two American lives were lost. The Germans hastened to pledge that an unarmed passenger ship would never again be attacked without warning. But the sinking of the *Arabic* fueled debate over American passengers on belligerent vessels. Why not require Americans to sail on American craft? asked critics. From August 1914 to March 1917 only three Americans died on an American ship (the tanker *Gulflight* in May 1915), whereas about 190 were killed on belligerent ships.

In early 1916 Congress began to debate the Gore-McLemore resolution to prohibit Americans from traveling on armed merchant vessels or on ships carrying contraband. The resolution, it was hoped, would prevent incidents such as the

Gore-McLemore Resolution

sinking of the *Lusitania* from hurtling the United States into war. But Wilson would tolerate no interference in the presidential making of foreign policy (he had just sent Edward House to Europe to mediate an end to the war) and no restrictions on American travel. The resolution, he argued, would destroy the "whole fine fabric of international law." After heavy politicking, Congress soundly defeated the resolution. Wilson's critics have pointed out that passage of the Gore-McLemore resolution would have avoided or at least delayed a German-American confrontation over the submarine without undercutting United States interests or besmirching national honor.

In March 1916 a U-boat attack on the *Sussex*, a French vessel crossing the English Channel, took the United States a step closer to war. Four Americans were injured on that ship, which the U-boat commander mistook for a minelayer. Stop the marauding submarines, Wilson lectured Berlin, or the United States will sever diplomatic relations. Again the Germans backed off, pledging not to attack merchant vessels without warning. At about the same time, relations with Britain soured. The British crushing of the Easter Rebellion in Ireland and further restriction of United States trade with the Central Powers aroused American anger.

As the United States became more entangled in the Great War, many Americans urged Wilson to keep the nation out. In early 1915, Jane Addams, Carrie Chapman Catt, and other suffragists helped found the Wo-

Peace Movement

men's Peace Party, the United States Section of the Women's International League for Peace and Freedom. "The mother half of humanity," claimed women peace advocates, had a special role as

"the guardians of life." Later that same year, some pacifist Progressives—including Oswald Garrison Villard, Paul Kellogg, and Lillian Wald—organized an antiwar coalition, the American Union Against Militarism. The businessman Andrew Carnegie, who in 1910 had established the Carnegie Endowment for International Peace with $10 million in U.S. Steel bonds, helped finance peace groups. So did Henry Ford, who spent half a million dollars in late 1915 to send a "peace ship" to Europe to propagandize for a negotiated settlement. Socialists such as Eugene Debs added their voices to the peace movement.

The various messages of these antiwar advocates were that war drained a nation of its youth, resources, and impulse for reform; that it fostered a repressive spirit at home; that it violated Christian morality; and that wartime business barons reaped huge profits at the expense of the people. Militarism and conscription, Addams pointed out, were what millions of immigrants had left behind in Europe. Were they now—in the United States—to be forced into the decadent system they had escaped? Although the peace movement was splintered—some of its followers endorsing peace but not pacifism—it carried political and intellectual weight that Wilson could not ignore, and it articulated several ideas that he shared. In fact, he campaigned on a peace platform in the 1916 presidential election. After his triumph, Wilson futilely labored once again to bring the belligerents to the conference table. In early 1917 he advised them to temper their acquisitive war aims, appealing for "peace without victory."

In early February 1917, Germany launched unrestricted submarine warfare. All vessels—belligerent or neutral, warship or merchant—would be attacked if sighted in the declared war zone. This bold decision

Unrestricted Submarine Warfare

represented a calculated risk that submarines could impede American munitions shipments to England and thus defeat the Allies before American troops could be ferried across the Atlantic. Wilson quickly broke diplomatic relations with Berlin. Everybody waited for the inevitable collision.

This German challenge to American neutral rights and economic interests was soon followed by a German threat to American security. In late February, British intelligence intercepted, decoded, and passed to officials in Washington a telegram addressed to the German minister in Mexico from German Foreign Secretary Arthur Zimmermann. If

COs "enemies of the Republic," and the military harassed them. COs who refused noncombat service, such as in the Medical Corps, faced imprisonment.

Before December 1917, when the government prohibited enlistment, hundreds of thousands of citizens volunteered to the sound of the popular song "Johnny Get Your Gun." Asked why he had joined the army, one soldier replied that he was eager "to see a little of the biggest scrap the world has ever known." Other volunteers gave different answers: "Girls like soldiers"; they wanted to become "men"; they were homeless.

The typical American soldier in the First World War was a draftee between twenty-one and twenty-three years old, white, single, and poorly educated (most had not attended high school). Perhaps as many as 18 percent were foreign-born, and 400,000 were African-American. Though women were excluded from military service, some women became navy clerks; others served as telephone operators in the Army Signal Corps or as nurses and physical therapists. On college campuses, 150,000 students joined the Student Army Training Corps or similar navy and marine units. At officer training camps, the army turned out "ninety-day wonders." To overcome the ignorance of the many soldiers who did not know why they were going to war, United States officials put a copy of the president's war message in every knapsack.

American leaders worried that the young soldiers, once away from home, would be tempted by vice—especially by the saloons and houses of prostitution that quickly surrounded training camps. To protect the supposed novices with "invisible armor," the government created the Commission on Training Camp Activities to coordinate the work of the Young Men's Christian Association (YMCA) and other groups that dispensed food, showed movies, held athletic contests, and distributed books. Men in uniform were not permitted to drink. Alarmed by the spread of venereal disease, commission officials declared "sin-free" zones around military bases and exhorted soldiers to abstain from sex. American Federation of Labor President Samuel Gompers thought the moralizing ridiculous and the prohibitions unenforceable because "real men will be men." Navy Secretary Josephus Daniels replied that "men must live straight if they would shoot straight."

Commission on Training Camp Activities

Jim Crow was in the army, too. Although some southern politicians feared arming African-Americans, the army drafted men of color, put them in segregated units, and assigned them to menial labor. Draft boards frequently denied African-Americans' legitimate requests for occupational or dependency deferments. Racist slang became common in the camps. In August 1917 in Houston, Texas, angry African-American soldiers retaliated against whites who had been harassing them, killing sixteen. Nineteen of the black soldiers were ultimately executed; others were court-martialed and given long prison terms.

Seeking to ameliorate conspicuous white racism, W. E. B. Du Bois, in July 1918, endorsed the NAACP's support for the war. He urged blacks to "close ranks" and join the fight for "world liberty," in the hope that a war to make the world safe for democracy might also blur the color line at home. Sparking protest from some other black leaders who thought that wartime accommodationism would not improve race relations, Du Bois also accepted an army captaincy. A year earlier he had backed creation of a segregated, all-black officers' training camp: "We must choose then between the insult of a separate camp and the irreparable injury of strengthening the present custom of putting no black men in positions of authority." Blacks, he insisted, had to "take advantage of the disadvantage." Black colleges such as Hampton Institute and Fisk University encouraged students to join the camp. Eventually fourteen hundred black officers served in the war.

W. E. B. Du Bois Urges Support for the War

In Europe, American soldiers soon learned about the devastation wrought by technological innovations: poison gas, machine guns, artillery. Many suffered shell shock, and by today's standards army medicine and psychiatry were primitive. Away from the front lines, Red Cross canteens staffed by women volunteers served the soldiers as way stations in a strange land, offering haircuts, food, and recreation. Some ten thousand Red Cross nurses also cared for the young warriors. United States troops might even have met some American literary figures. Early in the war Ernest Hemingway, John Dos Passos, and other writers had volunteered for ambulance service in Allied countries.

In Paris, where no fewer than forty large houses of prostitution thrived, it became commonplace to

These black officers in the United States military during the First World War were members of a very small group. Eighty percent of the 400,000 African-Americans in the military were soldiers assigned to noncombat tasks such as assembling coffins, repairing vehicles, cooking meals, and loading supplies. Many of the fourteen hundred African-American commissioned officers were trained at the all-black camp at Des Moines, Iowa. The irony did not go unnoticed that the United States sent abroad a segregated army to make the world "safe for democracy." Collection of William S. Gladstone.

hear that the British were drunkards, the French were whoremongers, and the Americans were both. Venereal disease became a serious problem. French Prime Minister Georges Clemenceau offered licensed, inspected prostitutes in "special houses" to the American army. When the generous Gallic offer reached Washington, Secretary of War Newton Baker gasped, "For god's sake . . . don't show this to the President or he'll stop the war." By war's end, about 15 percent of America's soldiers had contracted venereal disease, costing the army $50 million and 7 million days of active duty. Periodic inspections, chemical prophylactic treat-

Problem of Venereal Disease

ments, and the threat of court-martial for infected soldiers kept the problem from being even more disastrous.

General John J. Pershing, head of the American Expeditionary Forces (AEF), insisted that his troops remain an independent army. He was not about to put his "doughboys"—so called by the French because they looked so clean—under the leadership of Allied commanders, who had become wedded to unimaginative and deadly trench warfare, producing a military stalemate and ghastly casualties on the western front. Zigzag trenches fronted by barbed wire and mines stretched across France. Beyond the

Trench Warfare

muddy and stinking trenches lay "no man's land," denuded by artillery fire. When ordered out, soldiers would charge the German lines, also a maze of trenches. Machine guns mowed them down; chlorine gas, first used by Germany in 1915, poisoned them. Little was gained. At the Battle of the Somme in 1916 the British and French had suffered 600,000 dead or wounded to earn only 125 square miles; the Germans lost 500,000 men.

The influx of American men and materiel decided the outcome of the First World War. With both sides virtually exhausted, the Americans tipped the balance toward the Allies.

AEF Battles in France

American forces did not actually engage in much combat until after the lull in the fighting during the severe winter of 1917–1918. The Germans launched a major offensive in March 1918, after they had knocked Russia out of the war and shifted troops from the eastern front to France. By May, Kaiser Wilhelm's forces had stormed to within 50 miles of Paris. Late that month, troops of the United States First Division helped blunt the German advance at Cantigny (see map, page 670). In June the Third Division helped the French hold positions along the Marne River at Château-Thierry, and the Second Division soon attacked the Germans west of Château-Thierry in the Belleau Wood. American soldiers won the battle after three weeks of fighting, but 5,183 of 8,000 marines died or were wounded after they made almost sacrificial frontal assaults against German machine guns. From this costly victory, the AEF learned to adopt more flexible attack methods.

Allied victory in the Second Battle of the Marne in July 1918 seemed to turn the tide against the Germans. In September French and American forces took St. Mihiel, and the Allies began their massive Meuse-Argonne offensive. More than 1 million Americans joined British and French troops in weeks of fierce combat. More than 26,000 Americans died before the Allies claimed the Argonne Forest on October 10. For Germany—its ground war a shambles, its submarine warfare a dismal failure, its troops and cities mutinous, and its allies Turkey and Austria dropping out—peace became imperative. The Germans accepted an armistice on November 11, 1918.

The belligerents counted 8 million soldiers and 6.6 million civilians dead and 21.3 million people

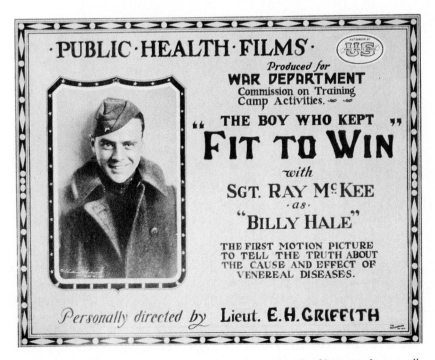

During the First World War, the War Department promoted a film to combat sexually transmitted diseases. After the war, the New York State Board of Censors declared the film obscene. Social Welfare History Archives Center, University of Minnesota.

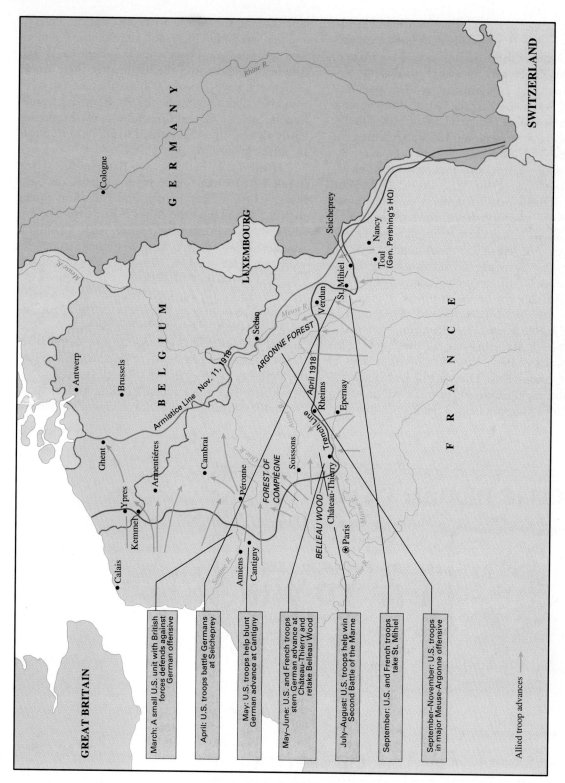

SWITZERLAND

G E R M A N Y

Rhine R.

• Cologne

LUXEMBOURG

Seicheprey

Nancy •

Toul •
(Gen. Pershing's HQ)

Meuse R.

Meuse R.

St. Mihiel •

Verdun •

Sedan •

ARGONNE FOREST

April 1918

F R A N C E

Rheims •
Epernay •

Armistice Line Nov. 11, 1918

B E L G I U M

• Antwerp

• Brussels

Oise R.

Cambrai •

FOREST OF COMPIÈGNE

Soissons •

Trench Line

Aisne R.

• Ghent

• Armentières

Péronne •

Ypres •

Kemmel •

Château-Thierry •

BELLEAU WOOD

Marne R.

Somme R.

• Calais

Amiens •
Cantigny •

✱ Paris

Seine R.

GREAT BRITAIN

March: A small U.S. unit with British forces defends against German offensive

April: U.S. troops battle Germans at Seicheprey

May: U.S. troops help blunt German advance at Cantigny

May–June: U.S. and French troops stem German advance at Château-Thierry and retake Belleau Wood

July–August: U.S. troops help win Second Battle of the Marne

September: U.S. and French troops take St. Mihiel

September–November: U.S. troops in major Meuse-Argonne offensive

Allied troop advances ⟶

American Troops at the Western Front, 1918 *America's two million troops in France met German forces head-on, ensuring the defeat of the Central Powers in 1918.*

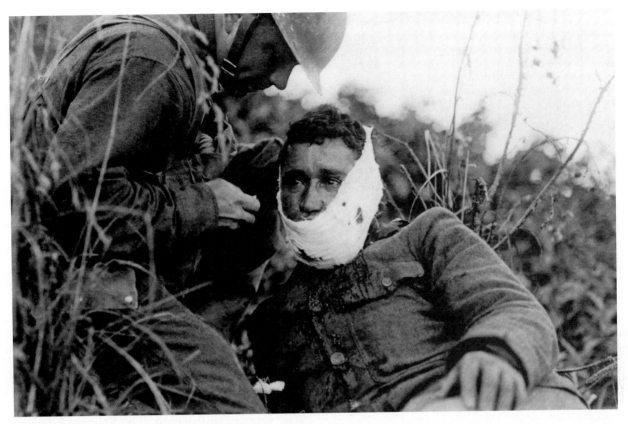

A United States soldier of Company K, 110th Infantry Regiment, receives aid during fighting at Verennes, France.   National Archives.

wounded. Fifty thousand American soldiers died in battle, and another 62,000 died from disease—many from the influenza pandemic (see page 676). More than 200,000 Americans were wounded. Parents and widows pressed the War Department to return the remains of 70 percent of the American dead, but the others were buried in cemeteries in France, Belgium, and England—but not in Germany or Russia.

Casualties

For the surviving doughboys, the army years were memorable, a turning point in their lives. They shed some of their parochialism, as the title of a popular song noted: "How 'Ya Gonna Keep 'Em Down on the Farm, After They've Seen Paree [Paris]?" And they made lasting friendships that would later be cemented by membership in the American Legion. A young soldier from Missouri, Harry S Truman of Battery D, would never lose touch with his wartime buddies, and when he became president in 1945, he would bring some of them into the White House as advisers.

 ## Mobilizing and Managing the Home Front

"It is not an army that we must shape and train for war," declared President Wilson, "it is a nation." The United States was a belligerent for only nineteen months, but the war had a tremendous impact at home. The federal government quickly created a command economy to meet war needs and intervened in American life as never before. The vastly enlarged Washington bureaucracy managed the economy, labor force, military, public opinion, and more. Federal expenditures increased tremendously as the government spent more than $760 million a month from April 1917 to August 1919. War expenses ballooned to $33.5 billion (see figure, page 672). The total cost of the war was probably triple that figure, since future generations would have to pay veterans' benefits and interest on loans. To Progressives of the New Nationalist persuasion, the war-time expansion and centralization of government power were welcome. To others, these changes seemed excessive,

The Federal Budget, 1914–1920

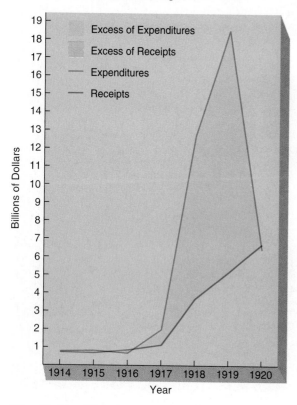

The Federal Budget, 1914–1920 *During the First World War, the federal government spent more money than it received from increased taxes. It borrowed from banks or sold Liberty Loans. To meet the mounting costs of the war, in other words, the federal government had to resort to deficit spending. Expenditures topped receipts by more than $13 billion in 1919. Given this wartime fiscal pattern, moreover, the United States federal debt rose from $1 billion in 1914 to $25 billion in 1919.* Source: U.S. Department of Commerce, *Historical Statistics of the United States: Colonial Times to 1957* (Washington, D.C., Bureau of the Census, 1960), pg. 711.

leading to concentrated, hence dangerous, federal power. "War is the health of the state," the radical intellectual Randolph Bourne had warned.

The federal government and private business became partners during the war. Dollar-a-year executives flocked to the nation's capital from major companies; they retained their corporate salaries while serving in official administrative and consulting capacities. Early in the war, the government relied on several industrial committees

Business-Government Cooperation

for advice on purchases and prices. But evidence of self-interested businesspeople cashing in on the national interest aroused public protest. The head of the aluminum advisory committee, for example, was also president of the largest aluminum company. The committees were disbanded in July 1917 in favor of the War Industries Board (see below). But the government continued to work closely with business through trade associations, which grew significantly, numbering two thousand by 1920. The federal government suspended antitrust laws and signed cost-plus contracts, which guaranteed companies a healthy profit and a means to pay higher wages to head off labor strikes. Competitive bidding was virtually abandoned. Under these wartime practices, big business got bigger.

Hundreds of new government agencies, staffed largely by businesspeople, placed controls on the economy in order to shift the nation's resources to the Allies, AEF, and war-related production. The Food Administration, led by engineer and investor Herbert Hoover, launched voluntary programs to increase production and conserve food—Americans were urged to grow "victory gardens" and to eat meatless and wheatless meals—but it also set prices and regulated distribution. The Railroad Administration took over the snarled railway industry. The Fuel Administration controlled coal supplies and rationed gasoline. When strikes threatened the telephone and telegraph companies, the federal government seized and ran them.

The largest of the superagencies was the War Industries Board (WIB), headed by the financier Bernard Baruch. At one point, this Wall Streeter frankly told Henry Ford that he would dispatch the military to seize his plants if the automaker did not accept WIB limits on car production. Ford relented. Although the WIB seemed all-powerful, in reality it had to conciliate competing interest groups and compromise with the businesspeople whose advice it so valued. Designed as a clearing-house to coordinate the national economy, the WIB made purchases, allocated supplies, and fixed prices at levels that business requested. The WIB ordered the standardization of goods to save materials and streamline production. The varieties of automobile tires, for example, were reduced from 287 to 3.

War Industries Board

The performance of the mobilized economy was mixed, but it delivered enough men and materiel to France to ensure the defeat of the Central Powers.

About a quarter of all American production was diverted to war needs. Farmers enjoyed boom years as they put more acreage into production and received higher prices. Encouraged to produce more at a faster pace, farmers mechanized as never before. From 1915 to 1920 the number of tractors in American fields jumped tenfold. Gross farm income for the period from 1914 to 1919 increased more than 230 percent. Although manufacturing output leveled off in 1918, some industries realized substantial growth because of wartime demand. Steel reached a peak production of 45 million tons in 1917, twice the prewar figure. The cigarette industry profited from a marked wartime increase in smoking: sales rose from 26 billion cigarettes in 1916 to 48 billion in 1918. Overall, the gross national product in 1920 was 237 percent higher than in 1914.

Because massive assignments had to be completed in a hurry, mistakes mounted. Weapons deliveries fell short of demand; the bloated bureaucracy of the War Shipping Board failed to build enough ships. In the severe winter cold of 1917–1918, millions of Americans could not get coal. Coal companies held back on production to raise prices; railroads did not have enough coal cars; and harbors froze, closing out coal barges. In January, blizzards shut down midwestern railroads and factories, impeding the war effort. People died from pneumonia and freezing. A Brooklyn man went out in the morning to forage for coal and returned to find his two-month-old daughter frozen to death in her crib.

Government officials failed to stem inflation. The wholesale price index was 98 percent higher in 1918 than it had been in 1913. Though partly stimulated by demand exceeding supply because of increases in Allied buying, inflation also sprang from the government's liberal credit policies and setting prices at high levels. By fixing prices on raw materials rather than on finished products, moreover, the government lost control of inflation. By bowing to southern politicians who wanted cotton left unregulated, the government permitted runaway cotton prices. Clothing tripled in cost, and food prices more than doubled. A quart of milk that cost 9 cents in 1914 climbed to 17 cents in 1920. Fuel prices also skyrocketed: the price for a 100-pound sack of coal rose 100 percent. Inflation pinched household budgets.

Inflation

Tax policies during the war sought to pull some of the profits reaped from high prices into the treasury. The Wilson administration believed that wealth as well as labor should be conscripted. Still, the gov-

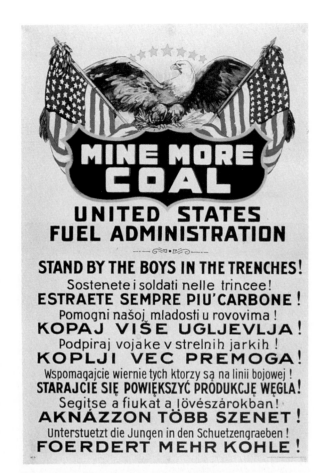

During the First World War, the United States Fuel Administration promoted economic mobilization at home in this poster printed in several languages.   National Park Service Collection, Ellis Island Immigration Museum. Photo Chermayeff and Geismar MetaForm.

ernment financed only one-third of the war through taxes. The other two-thirds came from loans, including Liberty Bonds sold to the American people through aggressive campaigns. The War Revenue Act of 1917 provided for a more steeply graduated personal income tax, a corporate income tax, an excess-profits tax, and increased excise taxes on alcoholic beverages, tobacco, and luxury items. Although these taxes did curb excessive corporate profiteering, they had several loopholes. Sometimes companies inflated costs to conceal profits or paid high salaries and bonuses to their executives. Four officers of Bethlehem Steel, for example, divided bonuses of $2.3 million in 1917 and $2.1 million the next year. Corporate net earnings for 1913 totaled $4 billion; in 1917 they had risen to $7 billion; and in 1918, after the tax bite

FOR EVERY FIGHTER
A WOMAN WORKER

Y·W·C·A·

BACK OUR SECOND LINE OF DEFENSE
UNITED WAR WORK CAMPAIGN

Posters became a familiar tool during the war to mobilize the American people. This one issued by the Young Women's Christian Association demonstrates well the wartime movement of women into the work force and into military uniform. Museum of American Political Life, University of Hartford.

and the war's end, they still stood at $4.5 billion. Profits and patriotism went hand in hand in America's war experience. The abrupt cancellation of billions of dollars' worth of contracts at the end of the war, however, caused a brief economic downturn, a short boom, and then an intense depression (see Chapter 24).

American workers benefited from the full-employment wartime economy, which increased their total earnings and gave many of them time-and-a-half pay for overtime work. Given the high cost of living, however, workers saw minimal improvement in their economic standing. For unions, the war seemed to offer opportunities for recognition and

Workers and the War

better pay through partnership with government. Without consulting rank-and-file members, Samuel Gompers threw the AFL's loyalty to the Wilson administration, promising to deter strikes. Wilson praised Gompers as a man who knew how "to pull in harness," but the president warned that other labor groups would have "to be out in a corral."

Gompers and other moderate labor leaders received appointments to federal agencies, such as the National War Labor Board (NWLB). Created to mediate labor disputes, the NWLB forbade strikes and lockouts and required management to negotiate with existing unions. Union membership climbed from roughly 2.5 million in 1916 to more than 4 million in 1919. The AFL, however, could not curb strikes by the radical Industrial Workers of the World (IWW) or rebellious AFL locals, especially those with a high proportion of antiwar socialists as members. In the nineteen war months, more than six thousand strikes expressed workers' discontent with their wages, working conditions, and inflation. By 1920, in defiance of the national AFL, labor parties sprang up in twenty-three states.

When 16 percent of the male work force trooped off to battle, and when immigration dropped off and some aliens returned to Europe to fight for their homelands, business recruited women to fill the vacancies. Munitions makers in Bridgeport, Connecticut, for example, dropped leaflets from airplanes urging women to work in their factories. Although the total number of women in the work force increased slightly, the real story was that many changed jobs, sometimes moving into formerly male domains. Some white women left domestic service for factories, shifted from clerking in department stores to stenography and typing, or departed textile mills for employment in firearms plants. At least 20 percent of all workers in the wartime electrical-machinery, airplane, and food industries were women. As white women took advantage of these new opportunities, black women took some of their places in domestic service and in textile factories. For the first time, department stores employed black women as elevator operators and cafeteria waitresses. Overall, most working women remained concentrated in sex-segregated occupations ("women's jobs") as typists, nurses, teachers, and domestic servants.

Some male workers, unaccustomed to working beside women, complained that women destabilized

Women in the Work Force

the work environment with their higher productivity. Women answered that they were used to seasonal employment and piecework and hence worked at a faster pace than men. Some men protested that women undermined the wage system by working for lower pay. Women pointed out that male-dominated companies discriminated against them and unions denied them membership. Male employees also resented the spirit of independence evident among women. The women in a Vermont machine-tool company addressed a crude poem to their harping male coworkers:

> We're independent now you see,
> Your bald head don't appeal to me,
> I love my overalls;
> And I would rather polish steel
> Than get you up a tasty meal.
> Or go with you to balls.
> Now, only premiums good and big,
> Will tempt us maids to change our rig.
> And put our aprons on;
> And cook up all the dainty things,
> That so delighted men and kings
> In days now past and gone.[1]

After the war, women lost many of the gains they had made. The attitude that women's proper sphere was the home had changed very little. Married working women found their family relationships growing tense; their husbands and children resented the disruption of home life. Critics charged that working mothers neglected their children and their housework. Day nurseries were scarce and beyond the means of most working-class families, and few employers provided childcare facilities. Whether married or single—the great majority of working women were unmarried—women lost their jobs to the returning veterans. "During the war they called us heroines," observed Mary McDowell of the University of Chicago Settlement, "but they throw us on the scrapheap now."

Women participated in the war effort in other ways. As volunteers, they made clothing for refugees and soldiers, rolled bandages, served at Red Cross facilities, and taught French to nurses assigned to the war zone. Many worked for the Women's Committee of the Council of National Defense, whose leaders included Ida Tarbell and Carrie Chapman Catt. A vast network of state, county, and town volunteer organizations, the Council publicized gov-

Stella Young (1896–1989), a Canadian-born woman from Chelsea, Massachusetts, became widely known as the "Doughnut Girl" because of her service during the First World War with the American branch of the Salvation Army, an international organization devoted to social work. She arrived in France in March 1918 and worked in emergency canteens near the battle front, providing United States troops with coffee, cocoa, sandwiches, doughnuts, pie, and fruit. Stella Young became famous when this picture of her wearing a khaki uniform and a "doughboy" steel helmet was widely circulated as a postcard. She served again in World War II. Chelsea named a city square in her honor in 1968. Collection of Colonel Stuart S. Corning, Jr.

ernment mobilization programs, encouraged home gardens, sponsored drives to sell Liberty Bonds, and continued the push for social welfare reforms. This patriotic work won praise from men and improved the prospects for passage of the Nineteenth Amendment (see page 618).

War mobilization wrought significant change for the African-American community as southern

---

[1]Originally appeared in the *Springfield Reporter*, December 5, 1917. Reprinted by permission of *The Eagle Times*.

A policeman during the Chicago race riot in the summer of 1919 attends a victim, bloodied by stones.   National Archives.

blacks undertook a great migration to northern cities to work in railroad yards, packing houses, steel mills, shipyards, and coal mines. Between 1910 and 1920, Cleveland's black population swelled by more than 300 percent, Detroit's by more than 600 percent, and Chicago's by 150 percent. Much of the increase occurred between 1916 and 1919. All told, about a half-million African-Americans uprooted themselves to move to the North. Families sometimes pooled savings to send one member; others sold their household goods to pay for the journey north. Most of the migrants were males—young (in their early twenties), unmarried, and skilled or semiskilled. Wartime jobs in the North provided an escape from low wages, sharecropping, tenancy, crop liens, debt peonage, lynchings, and political disfranchisement. To a friend back in Mississippi, one African-American wrote: "I just begin to feel like a man. . . . I don't have to humble to no one. I have registered. Will vote the next election."

African-American Migration to the North

But African-Americans continued to experience discrimination in both North and South. When the United States entered the First World War, there was not one black judge in the entire country. Segregation remained social custom. The Ku Klux Klan was reviving, and racist films such as D. W. Griffith's *The Birth of a Nation* (1915) fed prejudice. Lynching statistics exposed the wide gap between wartime declarations of humanity and the American practice of inhumanity at home: between 1914 and 1920, 382 blacks were lynched, some of them in military uniform.

Northern whites who resented "the Negro invasion" vented their anger in riots. In East St. Louis, Illinois, in July 1917, whites opposed to black employment in a defense plant rampaged through the streets; forty blacks and nine whites lost their lives. During the bloody "Red Summer" of 1919, race riots rocked two dozen cities and towns. The worst violence occurred in Chicago, a favorite destination for migrating blacks. In the very hot days of July 1919, a black youth swimming at a segregated white beach was hit by a thrown rock and drowned. Rumors spread, tempers flared, and soon blacks and whites were battling one another. Stabbings, burnings, and shootings went on for days until state police restored some calm. Thirty-eight people died, twenty-three African-Americans and fifteen whites. By the time of this tragedy, a disillusioned W. E. B. Du Bois had already concluded that black support for the war had not diminished whites' adherence to inequality and segregation. That spring he vowed a struggle: "We return. We return from fighting. We return fighting."

Race Riots

Added to the nation's unsettling war experience was another home-front crisis that cut across race, gender, and class lines: the influenza pandemic that engulfed the world in 1918–1919. Before it abated, as many as 40 million people died worldwide. The extremely contagious flu virus first unleashed an epidemic in the United States in the spring of 1918 and then spread to Europe. High fevers, aching muscles, and headaches staggered people. To fend off the virus, people received flu vaccines of questionable value or wore gauze masks. But mostly they had to wait until the virus tailed off. In many cases, severe pneumonia set in, and victims' lungs filled with fluid. Seven hundred thousand people died from the killer disease in the United States.

Influenza Pandemic

Emergence of the Civil Liberties Issue

"Woe be to the man that seeks to stand in our way in this day of high resolution," warned President Wilson. An official and unofficial campaign soon began to silence dissenters who questioned Wilson's decision for war or who protested the draft. In the end, the Wilson administration compiled one of the worst civil liberties records in American history. The targets of governmental and quasi-vigilante repression were the hundreds of thousands of Americans and aliens who refused to support the war: pacifists from all walks of life, conscientious objectors, socialists, the Industrial Workers of the World, the debt-ridden tenant farmers of Oklahoma who staged the Green Corn Rebellion against the draft, the Non-Partisan League, reformers such as Robert La Follette and Jane Addams, and countless others. In the wartime process of debating the question of the right to speak freely in a democracy, the concept of "civil liberties" for the first time in American history emerged as a major public policy issue.

Shortly after the declaration of war in 1917, the president appointed George Creel, a Progressive journalist, to head the Committee on Public Information (CPI). Employing some of the nation's most talented writers and scholars, the CPI used propaganda to shape and mobilize public opinion. Pamphlets and films demonized the Germans, and CPI "four-minute men" spoke at schools and churches to pump up a patriotic mood. The Committee also urged the press to practice "self-censorship" and encouraged people to spy on their neighbors. "Not a pin dropped in the home of any one with a foreign name," Creel claimed with satisfaction, "but that it rang like thunder on the inner ear of some listening sleuth." Exaggeration, fear-mongering, distortion, half-truths—such were the stuff of the CPI's "mind mobilization."

Committee on Public Information

The Wilson administration also guided through an obliging Congress the Espionage Act (1917) and the Sedition Act (1918). The first statute forbade "false statements" designed to impede the draft or promote military insubordination, and it banned from the mails materials considered treasonous. The Sedition Act made it unlawful to obstruct the sale of war bonds and to use "disloyal, profane, scurrilous,

Espionage and Sedition Acts

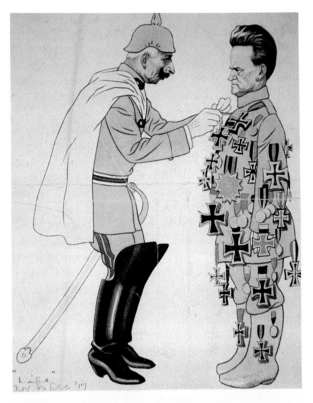

Some critics thought Senator Robert La Follette (1885–1925) was a traitor because he opposed United States entry into the First World War. This harsh cartoon from Life *magazine shows Kaiser Wilhelm of Germany pinning medals on the Wisconsin reformer. La Follette believed that a majority of Americans, if asked in a referendum, would vote his way: "The poor . . . who are the ones called upon to rot in the trenches, have no organized power."* State Historical Society of Wisconsin.

or abusive" language to describe the government, the Constitution, the flag, and the military uniform. These loosely worded laws gave the government wide latitude to crack down on critics. Fair-minded people could disagree over what constituted false or abusive language, but in the feverish home-front atmosphere of the First World War, the Justice Department's definition prevailed. More than two thousand people were prosecuted under the acts, and many others were intimidated into silence.

Stories of repression built up. Tom Watson's *The Jeffersonian* and the Woman's Peace Party's *Four Lights* were denied use of the mails. When federal agents threatened to shut down the large-circulation black newspaper *Chicago Defender,* its editor reluctantly promised to refrain from criticizing the government. Put under surveillance by the Justice

Department, Jane Addams also chose self-censorship, moderating her appeals for peace. The producer of *The Spirit of '76*, a film about the American Revolution complete with redcoats shooting minutemen, was given a ten-year prison sentence for, said the judge, questioning the "good faith of our ally, Great Britain."

The war emergency gave Progressives and conservatives alike an opportunity to throttle the IWW and the Socialist Party. Government agents raided IWW meetings, and the army marched into western mining and lumber regions to put down IWW strikes. By the end of the war most of the union's leaders were in jail. The Socialist Party fared little better. In the summer of 1918, with a government stenographer present, Socialist Party leader Eugene V. Debs delivered a spirited oration extolling socialism and freedom of speech—including the freedom to criticize the Wilson administration for taking America into the war. Federal agents arrested him. Debs told the court what many dissenters—and, later, many jurists and scholars—thought of the Espionage Act: it was "a despotic enactment in flagrant conflict with democratic principles and with the spirit of free institutions." Handed a ten-year sentence, Debs remained in prison until late 1921, when he received a pardon.

Imprisonment of Eugene V. Debs

Intolerance knew few boundaries. Local school boards dismissed teachers who questioned the war. At Wellesley College, economies professor Emily Greene Balch was fired because of her pacifist views (she won the Nobel Peace Prize in 1946). Three Columbia University students were picked up in mid-1917 for circulating an antiwar petition. Columbia also fired Professor J. M. Cattell, a distinguished psychologist, for his antiwar stand. His colleague Charles Beared, a historian with a prowar perspective, resigned in protest: "If we have to suppress everything we don't like to hear, this country is resting on a pretty wobbly basis."

Encouraged by official behavior, groups such as the Sedition Slammers and the American Defense Society sought to cleanse the nation through vigilantism. A German-American miner in Illinois was wrapped in a flag and lynched. In Hilger, Montana, citizens burned history texts that mentioned Germany. By the end of the war, sixteen states had banned the teaching of the German language. Because towns had Liberty Bond quotas to fill, they sometimes bullied "slackers" into making purchases.

Advocates of "100% Americanism" exploited the emotional atmosphere to exhort immigrants to throw off their Old World cultures. Companies offered English-language and naturalization classes in their factories and refused jobs and promotions to those who did not make adequate strides toward learning English.

Prior to World War I, American citizens of good standing could freely express mainstream political views, whereas people more marginal to a community (such as recent immigrants) or local leaders with radical opinions sometimes met with harsh treatment for exercising what today would be termed their freedom of speech. Before the war, few formally questioned these informal restrictions on political dissent. Yet the Wilson administration's vigorous suppression of dissidents led some Americans, most notably a conscientious objector named Roger Baldwin, to reformulate the traditional definition of allowable speech. Baldwin founded the Civil Liberties Bureau (forerunner of the American Civil Liberties Union) to defend the rights of those people accused under the Espionage and Sedition Acts. For the first time, Baldwin advanced the ideas that the content of political speech could be separated from the identity of the speaker and that a patriotic American could—indeed should—defend the right of someone to express political beliefs abhorrent to his or her own.

Roger Baldwin and the Issue of Free Speech

In unanimously upholding the Espionage Act in *Schenck* v. *U.S.* (1919), the Supreme Court adhered to the traditional view rather than the view developed by Baldwin. In time of war, Justice Oliver Wendell Holmes wrote, the First Amendment could be restricted: "Free speech would not protect a man falsely shouting fire in a theater and causing panic." If, according to Holmes, words "are of such a nature as to create a clear and present danger that they will bring about the substantial evils that Congress has a right to prevent," free speech could be limited. A few months later, however, Holmes and Louis Brandeis dissented when the Court similarly upheld the Sedition Act, in *Abrams* v. *U.S.* (1919). In the interim, pressed by friends to adopt Baldwin's approach to freedom of speech and of the press, Holmes had changed his mind and accepted the notion that active political dissent was essential to a democratic government.

Supreme Court Decisions

The Bolshevik Revolution, Labor Strikes, and the Red Scare

The line between wartime suppression of dissent and the postwar Red Scare is not easily drawn. Both put on the mask of patriotism to harass suspected internal enemies and deprive them of their constitutional rights; both had government sanction. Together they stabbed at the Bill of Rights and wounded radicalism in America. In the last few months of the war, guardians of Americanism began to label dissenters not only pro-German but pro-Bolshevik. After the Bolshevik Revolution in the fall of 1917, American hatred for the Kaiser's Germany was readily transferred to communist Russia. When the new Russian government under V. I. Lenin made peace with Germany in early 1918, Americans grew angry because the closing of the eastern front would permit the Germans to move troops west. Many lashed out at American radicals, casually applying the term "Red" (derived from the red flag used by Communists) to discredit them.

Case of Victor Berger

The ordeal of Victor Berger illustrates the blending of the wartime and postwar suppression of civil liberties. A socialist of German descent and a former congressman from Wisconsin, Berger was indicted under the Espionage Act for denouncing United States entry into the European war. The voters of Milwaukee nonetheless elected him once again to Congress in 1918. Early the next year Berger was convicted and sentenced to twenty years in federal prison. The House of Representatives thereupon refused to admit him, calling him a pro-German Bolshevik. While out on bail pending an appeal, Berger won the special election held to replace him. The House again blocked his admission. Berger's nightmare did not end until 1921, when the Supreme Court reversed his conviction. He was elected to Congress again in 1924. This time he took his seat.

Intervention in Russia Against Bolsheviks

The Wilson administration's ardent anti-Bolshevism became clear in mid-1918 when the president ordered five thousand American troops to northern Russia and ten thousand more soldiers to Siberia, where they joined other Allied contingents. Wilson did not consult Congress. He announced that the military expeditions were intended to guard Allied supplies and Russian railroads from German seizure and to rescue a group of Czechs who wished to return home to fight the Germans. Worried that the Japanese were building influence in Siberia and closing the Open Door, Wilson also hoped to deter Japan from further advances in Asia. Mostly he wanted to smash the infant Bolshevik government, a challenge to his new world order. So he waged an undeclared war against the new Russian regime, which entered a civil war with its opponents.

Seemingly unconstrained by his famed embrace of the principle of self-determination, Wilson backed an economic blockade of Russia, sent arms to anti-Bolshevik forces, and refused to recognize the Bolshevik government. The United States also clandestinely passed military information to anti-Bolshevik forces and used food relief to shore up anti-Bolshevik governments in the Baltic region. Later, at the Paris Peace Conference, Russia was

This anti-Bolshevik cartoon, titled "The Bull in the China Shop," represented the view of United States leaders during the Red Scare that Russia's radical Bolshevik revolution was threatening American principles and values. San Francisco Chronicle, February 27, 1919.

denied a seat. United States troops did not leave Siberia until the spring of 1920, after the Bolsheviks had demonstrated their staying power. These interventions in civil war–torn Russia immediately embittered Washington-Moscow relations—a legacy that would persist deep into the twentieth century.

At home, too, the Wilson administration moved against radicals and others imprecisely defined as Bolsheviks or communists. By the war's close, Americans had become edgy. The war had exacerbated racial tensions. It had disrupted the workplace and the family. Americans had suffered an increase in the cost of living, and postwar unemployment loomed. To add to Americans' worries, Russian communists in 1919 established the Comintern to promote world revolution. Already hardened by wartime violations of civil liberties, Americans found it easy to blame their postwar troubles on new scapegoats.

A rash of labor strikes in 1919 sparked the Red Scare. All told, more than thirty-three hundred strikes involving 4 million laborers jolted the nation that year, including the Seattle general strike in January. America, Wilson's press secretary claimed, stood between "organization and anarchy." On May 1, traditionally a day of celebration for workers around the world, bombs were sent through the mails to prominent Americans. Although most of the devices were intercepted and dismantled, police never captured the conspirators. Most people assumed, not unreasonably, that anarchists and others bent on the destruction of the American way of life were responsible. Next came the Boston police strike in September. Some sniffed a Bolshevik conspiracy, but others thought it ridiculous to label Boston's Irish-American Catholic cops "radicals." The conservative governor of Massachusetts, Calvin Coolidge, gained attention by proclaiming that nobody had the right to strike against the public safety. State guardsmen soon replaced the striking policemen.

Labor Strikes in 1919

Unrest in the steel industry in September stirred more ominous fears. Many steelworkers worked twelve hours a day, seven days a week, and lived in squalid housing. They looked to local steel unions, organized by the National Committee for Organizing Iron and Steel Workers, to help them improve their lives. When postwar unemployment in the industry climbed and the U.S. Steel Corporation refused to meet with committee representatives, some 350,000 workers walked off the job demanding the right to collective bargaining, a shorter workday, and a living wage. The steel barons hired strikebreakers and sent agents to club strikers. Worried about both the 1919 strikes and Bolshevism, President Wilson warned against "the poison of disorder" and the "poison of revolt." But in the case of steel, the companies won; the strike collapsed in early 1920.

One of the leaders of the steel strike was William Z. Foster, an IWW member and militant labor organizer who later joined the Communist Party. His presence in a labor movement seeking bread-and-butter goals permitted political and business leaders to dismiss the steel strike as a foreign threat orchestrated by American radicals. There was in fact no conspiracy, and the American left was badly splintered. Two defectors from the Socialist Party, John Reed and Benjamin Gitlow, founded the Communist Labor Party in 1919. The rival Communist Party of the United States of America, composed largely of aliens, was launched the same year. Neither party commanded much of a following—their combined membership probably did not exceed 70,000—and in 1919 the harassed Socialist Party could muster no more than 30,000 members.

Although divisiveness among radicals actually signified weakness, Progressives and conservatives both interpreted the advent of the new parties as a strengthening of the radical menace. That is certainly how the American Legion saw the question. Organized in May 1919 to lobby for veterans' benefits, the Legion soon preached an antiradicalism that fueled the Red Scare. By 1920, 843,000 Legion members, mostly middle and upper class, had become stalwarts of an impassioned Americanism that demanded conformity.

The American Legion

Wilson's attorney general, A. Mitchell Palmer, also insisted that Americans think alike. A Progressive reformer, a Quaker, and an aspirant to the 1920 Democratic presidential nomination, Palmer claimed that "revolution" was "eating its way into the homes of the American workmen, licking the altars of the churches, leaping into the belfry of the school bell." Palmer created a new Bureau of Investigation and appointed J. Edgar Hoover to run it. The young, ambitious official compiled index cards bearing the names of allegedly radical individuals and organizations. During 1919, agents jailed IWW members; Palmer also saw to it that 249 alien radicals, including the anarchist Emma Goldman, were deported to Russia.

Again, state and local governments took their cue from Washington. States passed peacetime sedition acts under which hundreds of people were arrested. Vigilante groups and mobs flourished once again, their numbers swelled by returning veterans. In November 1919, in Centralia, Washington, American Legionnaires broke from a parade to storm the IWW hall. Several were wounded. A number of Wobblies were soon arrested, and one of them, an ex-soldier, was taken from jail by a mob, then beaten, castrated, and shot. The New York State legislature expelled five duly elected socialist members in early 1920.

The Red Scare reached a climax in January 1920 in the Palmer Raids. Using Hoover's file, and having authorization from Attorney General Palmer, government agents in thirty-three cities broke into meeting halls and homes without search warrants. More than four thousand

Palmer Raids

people were jailed and denied counsel. In Boston, some four hundred people were kept in detainment on bitterly cold Deer Island; two died of pneumonia, one leaped to his death, and another went insane. Because of court rulings and the courageous efforts of Assistant Secretary of Labor Louis Post, who deliberately held up paperwork, most of the Palmer Raid arrestees were released, although in 1920–1921 nearly six hundred were deported.

Palmer's disregard for elementary civil liberties drew criticism. Civil libertarians and lawyers charged that his tactics violated the Constitution. Many of the arrested "Communists" had committed no crimes. When Palmer called for a peacetime sedition act, he alarmed both liberal and conservative leaders. His dire prediction that serious violence would mar May Day 1920 proved mistaken. With the steel strike over, the threat of Bolshevism in Europe receding, and the nation returning to postwar "normalcy," Palmer could no longer count on stampeding the public.

The campaigns against free speech from 1917 through 1920 left casualties. Debate, so essential to democracy, was wounded. Reform suffered as reformers either joined in the antiradicalism or became victims of it. Radical groups were badly weakened: the IWW became virtually extinct, and the Socialist Party became paralyzed. Throughout, the president made it appear that his critics were attacking the nation itself when they were actually questioning the policies of his administration. Wilson's intolerance of those who disagreed with him seemed to bespeak a fundamental distrust of democracy. At the very least, it illustrated that some Progressives were willing to use coercion to achieve their goal of a reformed society.

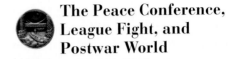

The Peace Conference, League Fight, and Postwar World

While Woodrow Wilson trampled civil liberties at home, he envisioned a brighter future in international relations. In January 1918 he announced his Fourteen Points, and, at the time of the armistice, the combatants reluctantly agreed that Wilson's principles should guide the peace negotiations. For the

The Fourteen Points

first time in its history, the United States offered a framework for world order. The first five points called for diplomacy "in the public view," freedom of the seas, lower tariffs, reductions in armaments, and the decolonization of empires. The next eight points specified the evacuation of foreign troops from Russia, Belgium, and France and appealed for self-determination for nationalities in Europe, such as the Poles. For Wilson, the fourteenth point was the most important—the mechanism for achieving all the others: "a general association of nations" or League of Nations.

When the president departed for the Paris Peace Conference in December 1918, he faced obstacles erected by his political enemies, by the Allies, and by himself. Some observers suggested that a cocky Wilson underestimated his task. During the 1918 congressional elections, Wilson had urged a vote for Democrats as a sign of support for his peace goals. But the American people did just the opposite. The Republicans gained control of both houses, signaling trouble for Wilson in two ways. First, a peace treaty would have to be submitted for approval to a potentially hostile Senate. Second, the election results at home diminished Wilson's stature in the eyes of foreign leaders. Wilson aggravated his political problems by not naming a senator to his advisory American Peace Commission. He also refused to take any prominent Republicans with him to Paris or to consult with the Senate Foreign Relations Committee before the conference.

Another obstacle in Wilson's way was the Allies' determination to impose a harsh, vengeful peace on the Germans. Georges Clemenceau of France, David Lloyd George of Britain, and Vittorio Orlando of Italy—with Wilson, the Big Four—became formidable adversaries. They had signed secret treaties during the war to grab German-controlled territories, and they scoffed at the pious, headstrong, self-impressed president who wanted to deny them the spoils of war while he sought to expand United States power. "How can I talk to a fellow who thinks himself the first man for two thousand years who has known anything about peace on earth," snarled Clemenceau. "Wilson imagines that he is a second Messiah."

At the Paris Peace Conference, held at the ornate palace of Versailles, the Big Four met behind closed doors. Critics quickly pointed out that Wilson had abandoned the first of his Fourteen Points, which urged diplomacy "in the public view." The victors demanded that Germany pay a huge reparations bill. Wilson instead called for a small indemnity, fearing that a resentful and economically hobbled Germany might turn to Bolshevism or disrupt the postwar community in some other way. Unable to moderate the Allied position, the president reluctantly gave way, agreeing to a clause blaming the war on the Germans and to the creation of a commission to determine the amount of reparations (later set at $33 billion).

Paris Peace Conference

As for the breaking up of empires and the principle of self-determination, Wilson could deliver on only some of his goals. Creating a League-administered "mandate" system, the conferees placed former German and Turkish colonies under the control of other imperial nations. France and Britain, for example, obtained parts of the Middle East, and Japan gained authority over Germany's colonies in the Pacific. In other arrangements, Japan replaced Germany as the imperial overlord of China's Shandong Peninsula, and France was permitted occupation rights in Germany's Rhineland. Elsewhere in Europe, Wilson's prescriptions fared better. Out of Austria-Hungary and Russia came the newly independent states of Austria, Hungary, Yugoslavia, Czechoslovakia, and Poland. Wilson and his colleagues also built a *cordon sanitaire* (buffer zone) of new westward-looking nations (Finland, Estonia, Latvia, and Lithuania) around Russia to quarantine the Bolshevik contagion (see map, page 683).

Wilson worked hardest on the charter for the League of Nations. In the long run, he believed, such an organization would moderate the harshness of the Allied peace terms and temper imperial ambitions. The League reflected the power of large nations such as the United States: it consisted of an influential council of five permanent members and elected delegates from smaller states, an assembly of all members, and a World Court. Wilson identified Article 10 as the "backbone" of the League covenant: "The Members of the League undertake to respect and preserve as against external aggression the territorial integrity and existing political independence of all Members of the League. In case of any such aggression or in case of any threat or danger of such aggression the Council shall advise upon the means by which this obligation shall be fulfilled." This collective-security provision, along with the entire League charter, became part of the peace treaty.

League of Nations and Article 10

German representatives at first refused to accept the punitive treaty but ultimately signed it in June 1919. In so doing, they gave up 13 percent of Germany's territory, 10 percent of its population, all of its colonies, and a huge portion of its national wealth. Secretary Lansing and others wondered how the League could function in the poisoned postwar atmosphere of revenge and humiliation. But Wilson waxed euphoric: "The stage is set, the destiny disclosed. It has come about by no plan of our conceiving, but by the hand of God."

In March 1919, thirty-nine senators (enough to deny the treaty the necessary two-thirds vote) had signed a petition stating that the League's structure did not adequately protect United States interests. Wilson denounced his critics as "pygmy" minds, but he persuaded the peace conference to exempt the Monroe Doctrine and domestic matters from League jurisdiction. Having made these concessions to senatorial advice, Wilson would budge no more. Compromises with other nations had been necessary to keep the conference going, he insisted, and the League would rectify wrongs. Could his critics not see that membership in the League would give the United States "leadership in the world"?

The journalist Walter Lippmann asked: "How in our consciences are we to square the results with the promises?" Criticism of the peace process and the treaty mounted: Wilson had bastardized his own principles. He had conceded Shandong to Japan. He personally had killed a provision affirming the racial

Critique of the Treaty

| Boundaries of German, Russian, and Austro-Hungarian Empires in 1914 |
| Areas lost by Austro-Hungarian Empire |
| Areas lost by Russian Empire |
| Areas lost by German Empire |
| Areas lost by Bulgaria |
| Demilatarized Zone |
| Boundaries of 1926 |

Europe Transformed by War and Peace   *After President Wilson and the other conferees at Versailles nego-tiated the Treaty of Paris, empires were broken up. In Eastern Europe, in particular, new nations were established.*

equality of all peoples. The treaty did not mention freedom of the seas, and tariffs were not reduced. Reparations promised to be punishing. Senator La Follette protested that the League would perpetuate empire. Conservative critics feared that the League would limit American freedom of action in world affairs, stymie United States expansion, and intrude on domestic questions. And Article 10 raised serious questions: Would the United States be obligated to use armed force to ensure collective security? And what about colonial rebellions, such as in Ireland or India? Would the League feel compelled to crush them?

Senator Henry Cabot Lodge of Massachusetts boldly disputed Wilson. A Harvard-educated Ph.D. and partisan Republican, Lodge packed the Foreign

How do historians know that President Woodrow Wilson (pictured here on the right) suffered a disabling illness that seriously impaired his ability to conduct government business during the great debate over American membership in the League of Nations and that the severity of his incapacity was deliberately hidden from the public? Historians had long suspected the worst, but not until the diary and medical records kept by Wilson's private physician, Dr. Cary T. Grayson, were published in 1990 and 1991 as part of editor Arthur S. Link's The Papers of Woodrow Wilson *did they have a detailed account of the bedridden president's precarious condition.*

A portion of Dr. Grayson's diary for September 26, 1919, is reproduced on the next page. During the fall of 1919, after a massive stroke had incapacitated the president on October 2, Edith Bolling Wilson insisted that Grayson (pictured here on the left) issue only general statements about her husband's status. No mention was ever made publicly that Wilson had

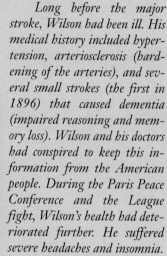

suffered a debilitating stroke; he was said to be down with "nervous exhaustion." When Grayson published a memoir in 1960, he still did not reveal the truth.

Long before the major stroke, Wilson had been ill. His medical history included hypertension, arteriosclerosis (hardening of the arteries), and several small strokes (the first in 1896) that caused dementia (impaired reasoning and memory loss). Wilson and his doctors had conspired to keep this information from the American people. During the Paris Peace Conference and the League fight, Wilson's health had deteriorated further. He suffered severe headaches and insomnia. After a speech in Colorado on September 25, 1919, he collapsed.

The stroke of October 2 left Wilson partially paralyzed and haggard. He could not lead because he seldom could concentrate on any subject for very long and he secluded himself from cabinet members. This irascible, stubborn, very sick man refused to compromise with senators who said that they would vote for United States

Relations Committee with critics and prolonged public hearings. He introduced several reservations to the treaty: one stated that the nation's immigration acts could not be subject to League decision; another held that Congress had to approve any obligation under Article 10.

In September 1919, Wilson embarked on a speaking tour of the United States. Growing more exhausted every day, he dismissed his antagonists as "contemptible quitters." Provoked by Irish-American and German-American hecklers, he lashed out in Red Scare terms: "Any man who carries a hyphen about him carries a dagger which he is ready to plunge into the vitals of the Republic." While doubts about Article 10 multiplied, Wilson tried to highlight neglected features of the League charter—such as provisions for the arbitration of disputes and for an international conference to abolish child labor. In Colorado, a day after delivering another passionate speech, the president awoke to nausea and

uncontrollable facial twitching. "I just feel as if I am going to pieces," he said. A few days later, back in Washington, he suffered a massive stroke that paralyzed his left side. He became peevish and even more stubborn, increasingly unable to conduct the heavy business of the presidency. Advised to placate senatorial critics so the treaty would have a chance of passing, Wilson rejected "dishonorable compromise." From Senate Democrats he demanded utter loyalty—a vote against all reservations.

Twice in November the Senate rejected the Treaty of Versailles. In the first vote, Democrats joined a group of sixteen "Irreconcilables," mostly

Senate Rejection of the Treaty

Republicans who opposed any treaty whatsoever, to defeat the treaty *with* reservations (39 for and 55 against). In the second vote, Republicans and Irreconcilables turned down the treaty *without* reservations (38 for and 53 against). Had

membership in the League of Nations if he would accept changes in, or "reservations" to, the League charter. Given the serious issues raised by the collective security provision of the covenant, some historians wonder whether even a healthy Wilson could have changed the negative Senate vote. But other scholars argue that Wilson's illness so impaired his rationality and the cover-up *so distorted truth that the Senate's defeat of the treaty can be understood only in the context of the stricken president's medical history as documented in Dr. Grayson's records.* Grayson and Wilson: National Archives. Diary entry: From the Grayson papers transcript at Princeton University Library.

Friday, September 26, 1919

This morning at two o'clock I was awakened from my sleep and told that the President was suffering very much. I went at once to the private car and found him unable to sleep and in a highly nervous condition, the muscles of his face were twitching, and he was extremely nauseated. The strain of the trip had at last taken its toll from him and he was very seriously ill. He had a very bad asthmatic attack—the worst that he had had on the trip. For a few minutes it looked as if he could hardly get his breath. I was obliged to give him every possible care and attention. His condition was such that I did not feel that he ought to continue the trip. Although I was reluctant to do so, I felt that it was my duty to suggest to him that he call the trip off and that we return to Washington. He begged me not to make any such suggestion. . . .

As soon as I had secured the President's consent to call the trip off I went out and got Secretary Tumulty and brought him back, telling him definitely that the President had agreed that there should be no further meetings. The President said to Secretary Tumulty: "I don't seem to realize it, but I seem to have gone to pieces. The Doctor is right. I am not in condition to go on. I have never been in a condition like this, and I just feel as if I an going to pieces." The President looked out of the window and he was almost overcome by his emotions. He choked and big tears fell from his eyes as he turned away.

Wilson permitted Democrats to compromise—to accept reservations—he could have achieved his fervent goal of United States membership in the League of Nations.

Who or what was responsible for the defeat of the treaty? The stroke had incapacitated the president, sapping his energy and his ability to lead effectively. The bitter personal feud between Wilson and Lodge accounts for some conflict but does not explain the determination of the Irreconcilables. Certainly Wilson's concessions to a harsh peace at Paris undercut his case in the United States, but, even so, two-thirds of the senators seemed willing to forgive his errors at Versailles if he would only accept some reservations. The uncompromising Wilson had become "a slave to vanity," regretted Secretary Lansing. But Wilsonian "vanity" also lacks adequate explanatory power. Of what was he so proud?

At the core of the debate lay a basic issue in American foreign policy: whether the United States would endorse collective security or continue to travel the path of unilateralism articulated in George Washington's Farewell Address and in the Monroe Doctrine. In a world dominated by imperialist states unwilling to subordinate their selfish ambitions to an international organization, Americans preferred their traditional nonalignment and freedom of choice over binding commitments to collective action. That is why so many of Wilson's critics targeted Article 10 and why the president was so adamant against its revision.

Collective Security versus Unilateralism

In the end, Woodrow Wilson failed to create a new world order through reform. He promised more than he could deliver. Still, the United States emerged from the First World War an even greater world power. By 1920 the United States had become the world's leading economic power, producing 40 percent of its coal, 70 percent of its petroleum, and half of its pig iron. It also rose to first rank in world trade. American companies took advantage of the war to nudge the Germans and British out of foreign markets, especially in Latin America. Goodyear went into the Dutch East Indies for rubber. Meanwhile, the United States shifted from being a debtor to a creditor nation, becoming the world's leading banker.

After the disappointment of Versailles, appeals for arms control accelerated and the peace movement revitalized. At the same time, the military became more professional. The Reserve Officers' Training Corps (ROTC) became permanent; military "colleges" provided upper-echelon training; and the Army Industrial College, founded in 1924, pursued business-military cooperation in the area of logistics and planning. The National Research Council, created in 1916 with government money and Carnegie and Rockefeller funds, continued after the war as an alliance of scientists and businesspeople engaged in research relating to national defense. As before the war, the tendencies toward disarmament on the one hand and preparedness on the other competed.

The international system born in these years was unstable and fragmented. Espousing decolonization and taking to heart the Wilsonian principle

Unstable International System

of self-determination, nationalist leaders active during the First World War, such as Ho Chi Minh of Indochina and Mohandas K. Gandhi of India, vowed to achieve independence for their peoples. Communism became a disruptive force in world politics, and the Russians bore a grudge against those invaders who had tried to thwart their revolution. The new states in central and eastern Europe proved weak, dependent on outsiders for security. Germans bitterly resented the harsh peace settlement, and the war debts and reparations problems dogged international order for years. As it entered the 1920s, the international system that Woodrow Wilson had vowed to reform wobbled.

 ## Conclusion

At the close of the First World War, the historian Albert Bushnell Hart observed that "it is easy to see that the United States is a new country." What had changed? America emerged from the war years an unsettled mix of the old and the new. The war exposed deep divisions among Americans: white versus black, nativist versus immigrant, capital versus labor, "dry" versus "wet," men versus women, radical versus Progressive and conservative, pacifist versus interventionist, nationalist versus internationalist. It is little wonder that Americans—having experienced race riots, labor strikes, disputes over civil liberties, and the League fight—wanted to escape from what John Dewey called the "cult of irrationality" to what President Warren G. Harding called "normalcy."

During the war the federal government intervened in the economy and influenced people's everyday lives as never before. Centralization of control in Washington, D.C., and mobilization of the home front served as a model for the future. The partnership of government and business in managing the wartime economy contributed to the further development of a mass society through the standardization of products and the promotion of efficiency. Wilsonian wartime policies also nourished the continued growth of oligopoly through the suspension of antitrust laws. Business power dominated the next decade. American labor, by contrast, entered lean years.

Although the disillusionment evident after Versailles did not cause the United States to adopt a policy of isolationist withdrawal (see Chapter 26), skepticism about America's ability to right wrongs abroad marked the postwar American mood. The war was grimy and ugly, far less glorious than Wilson's lofty rhetoric suggested. People recoiled from photographs of shell-shocked faces and of bodies dangling from barbed wire. American soldiers, tired of idealism, craved the latest baseball scores and their regular jobs. Those Progressives who had believed that entry into the war would deliver the millennium, later marveled at their naiveté. Many lost their enthusiasm for crusades, and many others turned away in disgust from the bickering of the victors. Some felt betrayed. The journalist William Allen White angrily wrote to a friend that the Allies "have—those damned vultures—taken the heart out of the peace, taken the joy out of the great enterprise of the war, and have made it a sordid malicious miserable thing like all the other wars in the world."

Woodrow Wilson himself had remarked, soon after taking office in 1913 before the Great War, that "there's no chance of progress and reform in an administration in which war plays the principal part." From the perspective of 1920, looking back on distempers at home and abroad, Wilson knew that progress and reform had taken a beating.

Suggestions for Further Reading

General

John W. Chambers, *The Tyranny of Change*, 2d ed. (1992); Stanley Cooperman, *World War I and the American Mind* (1970); Paul Fussell, *The Great War and Modern Memory* (1975); Otis L. Graham, Jr., *The Great Campaigns* (1971); Ellis W. Hawley, *The Great War and the Search for a Modern Order*, 2d ed. (1992); Henry F. May, *The End of American Innocence* (1964); Stuart I. Rochester, *American Liberal Disillusionment in the Wake of World War I* (1977); Ronald Steel, *Walter Lippmann and the American Century* (1980); David P. Thelan, *Robert M. La Follette and the Insurgent Spirit* (1976); John A. Thompson, *Reformers and War* (1987).

Wilson, Wilsonianism, and World War I

Lloyd E. Ambrosius, *Wilsonian Statecraft* (1991); Thomas A. Bailey and Paul B. Ryan, *The Lusitania Disaster* (1975); Frederick S. Calhoun, *Power and Principle* (1986); Kendrick A. Clements, *The Presidency of Woodrow Wilson* (1992); John W. Coogan, *The End of Neutrality* (1981); John M. Cooper, Jr., *The Warrior and the Priest* (1983); Robert H. Ferrell, *Woodrow Wilson and World War I* (1985); Manfred Jonas, *The United States and Germany* (1984); Thomas J. Knock, *To End All Wars* (1992); N. Gordon Levin, Jr., *Woodrow Wilson and World Politics* (1968); Arthur S. Link, ed., *Woodrow Wilson and a Revolutionary World, 1913–1921* (1982); Arthur S. Link, *Woodrow Wilson: Revolution, War and Peace* (1979); Arthur S. Link, *Wilson*, 5 vols. (1947–1965); Bert E. Park, *Ailing, Aging, Addicted* (1993) (on Wilson's health); Hans-Jürgen Schröder, ed., *Confrontation and Cooperation* (1993) (on United States–German relations); J. W. Schulte Nordholt, *Woodrow Wilson* (1991); Tony Smith, *America's Mission* (1994); David Stevenson, *The First World War and International Politics* (1988); Edwin A. Weinstein, *Woodrow Wilson: A Medical and Psychological Biography* (1981).

The Military and the Great War in Europe

Allan M. Brandt, *No Magic Bullet* (1985) (on venereal disease); John W. Chambers, *To Raise an Army* (1987); J. Garry Clifford, *The Citizen Soldiers* (1972); Edward M. Coffman, *The War to End All Wars* (1968); Harvey A. DeWeerd, *President Wilson Fights His War* (1968); Thomas C. Leonard, *Above the Battle* (1978); Dorothy Schneider and Carl J. Schneider, *Into the Breach: American Women Overseas in World War I* (1991); Donald Smythe, *Pershing* (1986); Stephen R. Ward, ed., *The War Generation: Veterans of the First World War* (1975); Russell F. Weigley, *The American Way of War* (1973).

The Home Front

William J. Breen, *Uncle Sam at Home* (1984); Valerie Jean Conner, *The National War Labor Board* (1983); Alfred W. Crosby, *America's Forgotten Pandemic* (1989) (on influenza); Robert D. Cuff, *The War Industries Board* (1973); Maurine W. Greenwald, *Women, War, and Work* (1980); Frank L. Grubbs, Jr., *The Struggle for Labor Loyalty* (1968); David M. Kennedy, *Over Here* (1980); Seward W. Livermore, *Politics Is Adjourned* (1966); Frederick C. Luebke, *Bonds of Loyalty* (1974) (on German-Americans); John F. McClymer, *War and Welfare: Social Engineering in America, 1890–1925* (1980); Ronald Schaffer, *America in the Great War: The Rise of the War Welfare State* (1991); Barbara J. Steinson, *American Women's Activism in World War I* (1982); Stephen L. Vaughn, *Holding Fast the Inner Lines* (1979) (on the CPI); Neil A. Wynn, *From Progressivism to Prosperity* (1986).

Race Relations and the Great Migration

Arthur E. Barbeau and Florette Henri, *The Unknown Soldiers* (1974) (on black troops); Marvin E. Fletcher, *The Black Soldier and Officer in the United States Army, 1891–1917* (1974); James B. Grossman, *Land of Hope: Chicago, Black Southerners, and the Great Migration* (1989); Robert V. Haynes, *A Night of Violence: The Houston Riot of 1917* (1976); Carole Marks, *Farewell—We're Good and Gone* (1989) (on migration); Elliot M. Rudwick, *Race Riot at East St. Louis, July 2, 1917* (1964); Joe William Trotter, Jr., ed., *The Great Migration in Historical Perspective* (1991); William M. Tuttle, Jr., *Race Riot: Chicago in the Red Summer of 1919* (1970).

Dissenters, Wartime Civil Liberties, and the Red Scare

David Brody, *Labor in Crisis* (1965) (on steel strike); Charles Chatfield, *The American Peace Movement* (1992); Stanley Coben, *A. Mitchell Palmer* (1963); Charles DeBenedetti, *Origins of the Modern Peace Movement* (1978); Sondra Herman, *Eleven Against War* (1969); Donald Johnson, *The Challenge to American Freedoms* (1963); C. Roland Marchand, *The American Peace Movement and Social Reform, 1898–1918* (1973); Elizabeth McKillen, *Chicago Labor and the Quest for a Democratic Diplomacy, 1914–1924* (1995); Paul L. Murphy, *World War I and the Origin of Civil Liberties* (1979); Robert K. Murray, *Red Scare* (1955); William Pencak, *For God and Country* (1989) (on the American Legion); H. C. Peterson and Gilbert C. Fite, *Opponents of War, 1917–1918* (1968); Richard Polenberg, *Fighting Faiths* (1987) (on the *Abrams* case); William Preston, *Aliens and Dissenters*, 2d ed. (1995); Francis Russell, *A City in Terror* (1975) (on the Boston police strike); James Weinstein, *The Decline of Socialism in America, 1912–1923* (1967).

The United States and the Bolshevik Revolution

Peter G. Filene, *Americans and the Soviet Experiment, 1917–1933* (1967); David S. Foglesong, *America's Secret War Against Bolshevism* (1995); John L. Gaddis, *Russia, the Soviet Union, and the United States*, 2d ed. (1990); George F. Kennan, *The Decision to Intervene* (1958); George F. Kennan, *Russia Leaves the War* (1956); Christopher Lasch, *The American Liberals and the Russian Revolution* (1962); David McFadden, *Alternative Paths* (1993); Betty M. Unterberger, *The United States, Revolutionary Russia, and the Rise of Czechoslovakia* (1989); Betty M. Unterberger, *America's Siberian Expedition, 1918–1920* (1956).

Paris Peace Conference and League Fight

Lloyd Ambrosius, *Woodrow Wilson and the American Diplomatic Tradition* (1987); Inga Floto, *Colonel House in Paris* (1973); Herbert Hoover, *The Ordeal of Woodrow Wilson* (1958); Warren F. Kuehl, *Seeking World Order* (1969); Arno Mayer, *Politics and Diplomacy of Peacemaking* (1967); Keith Nelson, *Victors Divided* (1973); Ralph A. Stone, *The Irreconcilables* (1970); Arthur Walworth, *Wilson and the Peacemakers* (1986); William C. Widenor, *Henry Cabot Lodge and the Search for an American Foreign Policy* (1980).

CHAPTER

24

The New Era of the 1920s

On the afternoon of June 26, 1926, as an airplane dropped rose petals from above, a crowd of over fifty thousand jammed the Los Angeles railroad station and waited anxiously in the heat for the climax of one of the year's most sensational news stories. When the woman they had come to see stepped gingerly from the train, a band began playing and a parade formed to escort her home. The woman was evangelist preacher Aimee Semple McPherson, and she was returning after disappearing and being presumed dead six weeks earlier. She claimed she had been kidnapped from a California beach and taken to Mexico, where she managed to escape and wander in the desert for hours before finding her way back to civilization. Her story was suspect, but few people cared. Sister, as she liked to be called, was home.

McPherson was a remarkable character in modern American history. She traveled the country, preaching the "old-time religion" of a "Four-Square Gospel" to throngs of people. In 1923 she opened Angelus Temple in Los Angeles, a huge church that presented daily prayer meetings and other religious gatherings with unprecedented pageantry. Sister Aimee's antics, which included riding a motorcycle down the church aisle, dressing in a flowing white dress and blue cape, and carrying a huge corsage of red roses, prompted cynics to label her "the titian-haired whoopee evangelist" and "a frank and simple fraud."

But Sister Aimee was remarkably effective because she gave people what they wanted and needed: a combination of the "tried and true" of Christian spiritual fervor with modern technological apparatus. She provided moral counseling over the telephone, published a monthly magazine promoting God's mercy, and broadcast her theatrical services over her own radio station. Her church regularly sponsored a float in the Rose Bowl Parade and organized Bible conferences for vacationers.

In many ways, Aimee Semple McPherson symbolizes the clash of values that characterized the 1920s. On the one hand was the search to safeguard

This street scene from the Commonwealth Edison Yearbook of 1927 illustrates that the 1920s was the age of electricity and automobiles.
Commonwealth Edison Company.

the "tried and true," whether it was religious certainty, business capitalism, or patriotic commitment. On the other hand, right beside these traditions there existed the increasing appeal of the "modern": new technology, consumer goods, and mass entertainment.

During the 1920s the flower of consumerism reached full bloom. Although poverty beset small farmers, workers in declining industries, and non-whites in inner cities, most other people enjoyed a high standard of living relative to previous generations. Spurred by advertising and new forms of credit, Americans eagerly bought radios, automobiles, real estate, and stocks. As in the Gilded Age, government policies supported the interests of business; Congress, three presidents, and the Supreme Court acted to maintain a favorable climate for profits. And the population at large, unlike people living during the Progressive era, worried little about the abuse of private power. Yet important reforms were undertaken at state and local levels of government, extending the reach of public authority.

Complexity characterized the 1920s. Its fads and frivolities were accompanied by creativity in the arts and by advances in science and technology. Changes in work habits, family responsibilities, and health-care fostered new uses of time and new attitudes about behavior. While material bounty and leisure time enticed Americans into new amusements, winds of change also stirred up waves of reaction. New liberal values repelled various groups and individuals who reacted by trying to create a society in which traditional beliefs prevailed.

Threatening clouds were gathering as well. The consumer culture that dominated everyday life blinded Americans to rising debts and other negative economic signs. Just before the decade closed, a stormy depression swept through the economy, bringing the era to a brutal close.

Private Power Triumphant

The 1920s began with a jolting economic decline. Shortly after the First World War ended, industrial output dropped as wartime orders dried up and consumer spending dwindled. Farm income plunged because of falling exports. Unemployment, around 2 percent in 1919, passed 12 percent in 1921. Railroads and mining industries suffered in the West. Layoffs spread through New England as textile companies abandoned outdated factories for the convenient raw materials and cheap labor of the South.

Aided by electric energy, a recovery began in 1922 and continued unevenly until 1929. By the decade's end, electric motors powered 70 percent of American industry, sending thousands of steam engines to the scrap heap. Electrically driven assembly lines added radios, refrigerators, and other new products to the market. New metal alloys, chemicals, synthetic materials such as rayon, and preserved foods became commonplace. As Americans acquired spending money and leisure time, service industries such as restaurants, beauty and barber shops, and movie theaters boomed. This new consumerism was fueled by the installment or time-payment plan ("A dollar down and a dollar forever," one critic quipped). Of 3.5 million automobiles sold in 1923, some 80 percent were bought on credit.

Beneath the economic expansion, the consolidation movement that had created trusts and holding companies in the late nineteenth century reached a new stage. Although Progressive-era trustbusting had partially harnessed big business, it had not eliminated oligopoly—control of an entire industry by a few large firms. By the 1920s oligopolies dominated not only production but also marketing, distribution, and even finance. In basic industries such as steel production and electrical equipment, a few sprawling companies such as U.S. Steel and General Electric predominated.

Business and professional organizations that had come into being around 1900 also matured in the 1920s. Retailers and manufacturers formed trade associations to swap information and coordinate planning. Farm bureaus promoted scientific agriculture and tried to stabilize markets. Lawyers, engineers, and social scientists expanded their professional organizations. All of these special-interest groups participated in what has been called the "new lobbying." In a complex society in which government was playing an increasingly influential role, hundreds of organizations sought the ear of federal and state legislators in order to convince them to support their interests. Lobbying became so intense that one Washington, D.C., observer remarked that "lobbyists were so thick they were constantly falling over one another."

Business thrived because of government assistance, and legislators often depended on the expertise of lobbyists in making decisions. Congress reduced taxes on corporations and wealthy individuals

• *Important Events* •

1920	Nineteenth Amendment ratified, legalizing the vote for women in federal elections Warren G. Harding elected president KDKA transmits first commercial radio broadcast	**1923–24**	Government scandals (Teapot Dome) exposed
1920–21	Postwar deflation and depression occurs	**1924**	Johnson-Reid Act revises immigration quotas Coolidge elected president
1921	Federal Highway Act funds national highway system Johnson Act establishes immigration quotas Sacco and Vanzetti convicted Sheppard-Towner Act allots funds to states to set up maternity and pediatric clinics Fordney-McCumber Tariff raises rates on imports	**1925**	Scopes trial highlights battle between religious fundamentalists and religious liberals
		1927	Sacco and Vanzetti executed Lindbergh pilots solo transatlantic flight Babe Ruth hits sixty home runs *The Jazz Singer*, the first movie with sound, is released
1922	Economic recovery raises standard of living *Coronado Coal Company* v. *United Mine Workers* rules that strikes may be illegal actions in restraint of trade *Bailey* v. *Drexel Furniture Company* voids restrictions on child labor Federal government ends strikes by railroad shop workers and miners	**1928**	Stock market soars Herbert Hoover elected president
		1929	Stock market crashes; Great Depression begins
1923	Harding dies; Calvin Coolidge assumes the presidency *Adkins* v. *Children's Hospital* overturns a minimum-wage law affecting women Ku Klux Klan activity peaks Aimee Semple McPherson opens Angelus Temple in Los Angeles		

in 1921 and the next year raised tariff rates in the Fordney-McCumber Tariff Act. Presidents Warren G. Harding, Calvin Coolidge, and Herbert Hoover appointed cabinet officers who pursued policies favorable to business. Regulatory agencies such as the Federal Trade Commission and Interstate Commerce Commission, also influenced by lobbyists, cooperated with corporations more than they regulated them.

The Supreme Court, led by Chief Justice William Howard Taft, the former president, protected business and private property as aggressively as it had done in the Gilded Age. Its key decisions sheltered business from government regulation and hindered organized labor's ability to achieve its ends through strikes and legislation. In *Coronado Coal Company* v. *United Mine Workers* (1922), Taft ruled

that a striking union, like a trust, could be prosecuted for illegal restraint of trade. Yet in *Maple Floor Association* v. *U.S.* (1929), the Court ruled that trade associations that distributed antiunion information were not acting in restraint of trade. The Court also voided restrictions on child labor (*Bailey* v. *Drexel Furniture Company*, 1922) and overturned a minimum-wage law affecting women because it infringed on liberty of contract (*Adkins* v. *Children's Hospital*, 1923).

Organized labor suffered other setbacks during the 1920s. Influenced by a fear of communism allegedly brought into the country by radical immigrants, public opinion turned against workers who disrupted everyday life with strikes. Perpetuating tactics used during the Red Scare (see pages 679–680), the Harding administration in 1922 obtained a sweeping court injunction to quash a strike by 400,000 railroad shop workers. The same year, the Justice Department helped put down a nationwide strike by 650,000 miners.

Meanwhile, large corporations countered the appeal of unions by offering pensions, profit sharing (which actually amounted to withholding wages for later distribution), and company-sponsored picnics and sporting events—a policy known as *welfare capitalism*. State legislators aided employers by prohibiting *closed shops* (workplaces where union membership was mandatory). Concerned about job security, workers in turn shied away from unions, and union membership fell from 5.1 million in 1920 to 3.6 million in 1929.

A Business-Minded Presidency

A series of Republican presidents in the 1920s extended Theodore Roosevelt's notion of government-business cooperation, but they made government a compliant coordinator rather than the active director Roosevelt had advocated. A symbol of government's good will toward business was President Warren G. Harding, elected in 1920 when the populace no longer desired national or international crusades. Democrats had nominated Governor James M. Cox of Ohio, who supported Woodrow Wilson's fading hopes for United States membership in the League of Nations. But Cox and his running mate, Franklin D. Roosevelt of New York, failed to excite voters. Harding, who kept his position on the League vague, captured 16 million popular votes to only 9 million for Cox. (The total vote in the 1920 presidential election was 36 percent higher than in 1916, reflecting the participation of women voters for the first time.)

A small-town newspaperman and senator from Ohio, Harding selected some capable assistants, notably Secretary of State Charles Evans Hughes, Secretary of Commerce Herbert Hoover, Secretary of the Treasury Andrew Mellon, and Secretary of Agriculture Henry C. Wallace. Harding also backed some reforms. He helped streamline federal spending with the Budget and Accounting Act of 1921, supported antilynching legislation, approved bills assisting farm cooperatives and liberalizing farm credit, pardoned the jailed socialist Eugene Debs,

Harding Administration

and, unlike his predecessor Wilson, was generally tolerant on civil liberties issues.

Harding's problem was that he had some predatory friends. "Warren, it's a good thing you wasn't born a gal," his father once reputedly remarked. "You'd be in the family way all the time—you can't say no." Harding said "yes" too often, appointing cronies who saw officeholding as an invitation to personal gain. Charles Forbes of the Veterans Bureau went to federal prison after being convicted of fraud and bribery in connection with government contracts. Attorney General Harry Daugherty was implicated in bribery and other fraudulent schemes; he escaped prosecution only by refusing to testify against himself. Most notoriously, a congressional inquiry in 1923 and 1924 revealed that Secretary of the Interior Albert Fall had accepted bribes to lease government property to private oil companies. For his role in the affair—called the Teapot Dome scandal after a Wyoming oil reserve that had been turned over to Mammoth Oil Company—Fall was fined $100,000 and spent a year in jail, the first cabinet officer ever to be so disgraced.

By mid-1923, Harding had become disillusioned. Amid rumors of mismanagement and crime, he told a journalist, "My God, this is a hell of a job. I have no trouble with my enemies. . . . But my friends, my God-damned friends . . . they're the ones that keep me walking the floor nights." On a speaking tour that summer, Harding became ill, and died in San Francisco on August 2. Though his death preceded revelation of the Teapot Dome scandal, some people speculated that Harding had committed suicide rather than face the brewing storm. Most evidence, however, points to death from natural causes, probably a heart attack. At any rate, Harding was truly mourned. A warm, dignified-looking man who relished a good joke and an evening of poker, he seemed suited to a nation recovering from a world war and domestic hard times.

Vice President Calvin Coolidge, Harding's successor, was far more solemn. (Alice Roosevelt Longworth, Teddy's daughter, quipped that Coolidge looked as if he had been weaned on a pickle.) Coolidge had been governor of Massachusetts. He had attracted national attention in 1919 with his active stand against striking Boston policemen, a policy that won him the vice-presidential nomination in 1920. Ordinarily, however, he was content to let events take their course, prompting columnist Walter Lippmann to remark on the "grim, determined, alert inactivity, which keeps Mr. Coolidge occupied constantly."

Coolidge's presidency coincided with unusual business prosperity. Respectful of private enterprise and aided by Andrew Mellon, whom he retained

Coolidge Prosperity

as secretary of the treasury, Coolidge's administration balanced the budget, reduced government debt, lowered income-tax rates (especially for the rich), and began construction of a national highway system. Congress took little initiative during these years, assenting to most measures recommended by the cabinet and by lobbyists from business associations such as the U.S. Chamber of Commerce. The major disputes arose over farm policy. Responding to farmers' complaints of falling prices, Congress twice passed bills to establish government-backed price supports for staple crops (the McNary-Haugen bills of 1927 and 1928). Coolidge, however, vetoed the measure both times.

"Coolidge prosperity" was the decisive issue in the presidential election of 1924. Both major parties ran candidates who favored private initiative. Republicans nominated Coolidge with little dissent. At their national convention, Democrats first debated whether to condemn the newly aroused Ku Klux Klan (see page 706), voting 542 to 541 against condemnation. They then endured 103 ballots deadlocked between southern prohibitionists, who supported former secretary of the treasury William G. McAdoo, and antiprohibition easterners, who backed New York's governor Alfred E. Smith. They finally compromised on John W. Davis, a New York corporation lawyer. Remnants of the Progressive movement, along with various farm, labor, and socialist groups, formed a new Progressive Party and nominated Robert M. La Follette, the aging reformer from Wisconsin. The new party revived issues of the previous decades: public ownership of utilities, aid to farmers, rights for organized labor, and regulation of business.

The election results resembled those of 1912 in reverse: the two probusiness candidates captured most of the votes. Coolidge beat Davis by 15.7 million to 8.4 million popular votes, 382 to 136 electoral votes. Like Taft in 1912, La Follette finished a poor third, receiving a respectable but ineffective 4.8 million popular votes and only 13 electoral votes. The electorate had endorsed the tried and true and voiced its expectation for extended prosperity.

Basically shy and introverted, Calvin Coolidge was content to let business have free rein in the pursuit of profits. This ironic cartoon shows the president accompanying the lively performance of big business with a saxophone and a song of praise. Life, December 10, 1925.

 Extensions of Reform

Struck by the triumph of business influence, political analysts claimed that Progressivism had died. They were partly right. The urgency of political and economic reform that had moved the previous generation faded in the

Extension of Progressive Reforms

1920s. Yet many of the Progressive era's achievements were sustained and extended in these years. Trustbusting declined, but regulatory commissions and other government agencies still monitored company activities and worked to reduce wasteful business practices. A corps of congressional reformers led by George Norris of Nebraska and Robert La Follette of Wisconsin kept Progressive causes alive by supporting labor legislation, aid to farmers, and a government-owned hydroelectric dam at Muscle Shoals, Alabama. (Business-

454

As Native American cultures faded, museums and universities from the 1880s through the 1920s collected Indian art and artifacts. Collectors, however, were concerned more with labeling than with preserving the artwork intact. Thus a museum curator stamped this intricate leather and quill pouch, once used by Great Lakes Indians, as a means of documenting it. Today, there is greater emphasis on appreciating Native American art with the same respect accorded to the aesthetic traditions of other cultures, and an artifact such as this pouch would not be so disfigured.   Peabody Essex Museum, photo by Mark Sexton.

oriented politicians wanted to sell or lease the dam and its nitrate plant to private interests.)

Most reform, however, occurred at state and local levels. Following initiatives begun before the First World War, thirty-four states instituted or expanded workers' compensation laws in the 1920s. Many states established employee-funded old-age pensions and welfare programs for the indigent. In cities, social workers strived for better housing and poverty relief. By 1926 every major city and many smaller ones had planning and zoning commissions that aimed to harness physical growth to the common good. During the 1920s the nation's statehouses, city halls, and universities trained a new generation of reformers who later influenced national affairs.

The federal government's generally apathetic Indian policy disturbed some reformers. Organizations such as the Indian Rights Association, the

Indian Affairs

Indian Defense Association, and the General Federation of Women's Clubs worked to obtain racial justice and social services, including better education and return of tribal lands. But Native Americans, no longer a threat to whites' ambitions, were treated by the general population like other minorities: as objects of discrimination who were expected to assimilate. Severalty, the policy of allotting land to individuals rather than to tribes, had failed to make Indians self-supporting. Indian farmers had to contend with poor soil, lack of irrigation, scarce medical care, and cattle thieves. Deeply attached to their land, they showed little inclination to move to cities. Whites still hoped to convert Native American peoples into "productive" citizens—but in a way that ignored indigenous cultures. Reformers were especially critical of Indian women, who refused to adopt middle-class homemaking methods and balked at sending their children to boarding schools.

Meanwhile, the federal government struggled to clarify Indians' citizenship status. The Dawes Severalty Act (see page 482) had conferred citizenship on all Indians who accepted individual allotments of land but not on those who remained on reservations. Also, over Indian citizens the government retained control that it did not exercise over other citizens. For example, federal law had prevented the sale of liquor to Indians even before ratification of the Eighteenth Amendment. After several court challenges, Congress finally passed a law in 1924 granting full citizenship to all Indians who previously had not received it. Also, the administration of President Herbert Hoover reorganized the Bureau of Indian Affairs and increased expenditures for health, education, and welfare. Much of the money, however, went to enlarge the bureaucracy rather than into Indian hands, and paternalism continued to characterize federal policy.

Even after achieving suffrage in 1920 with final ratification of the Nineteenth Amendment, politically active women still were excluded from party power structures, but they remained active in voluntary organizations whose techniques contributed to modern pressure-group politics. Whether the issue was birth control, peace, education, Indian affairs, or opposition to lynching, women in these associations publicized their cause and lobbied legis-

Women and Politics

lators rather than trying to elect their own candidates. Action by women's groups persuaded Congress to pass the Sheppard-Towner (Maternity and Infancy) Act (1921), which allotted funds to states to set up maternity and pediatric clinics. (The measure ended in 1929 when Congress, under pressure from private physicians, canceled funding.) The Cable Act of 1922 reversed the law under which an American woman who married a foreigner assumed her husband's citizenship; under the new law such a woman could retain United States citizenship. At the state level, women achieved other rights, such as the ability to serve on juries.

As new voters, however, women accomplished relatively little. The National Woman's Party remained the champion of feminism, but categories other than gender affected women's interests. African-American women, for example, fought for the rights of minority women and men without support from either the National Woman's Party or the newly organized League of Women Voters. Some groups, such as the National Woman's Party, pressed for an equal rights amendment, to ensure women's equality with men in all parts of society. But such activity alienated the National Consumers League, the Women's Trade Union League, the League of Women Voters, and other groups that supported sex-based labor legislation to protect employed working-class women. And like men, women of all types seemed preoccupied by the new era's materialism.

 ## Materialism Unbound

Poor Richard's Almanac would have sold poorly in the 1920s, because many Americans found it difficult to

This advertisement indicates two major themes of the 1920s: the need for electricity to power a wonderful variety of home appliances and the use of advertising to promote the purchase of consumer goods. Notice the way in which the ad directs its appeal to women. Private Collection, New York, © 1993.

reconcile the tried and true virtues of thrift and sobriety that Benjamin Franklin had preached with the
modern emphasis on acquisition, amusement, and
salesmanship. Raised on inherited homilies like
"Waste not, want not," they nevertheless succumbed
to the advice of an advertising executive: "Make the
public want what you have to sell. Make 'em pant for
it." Poverty and social injustice still blighted the
country, but the belief prevailed that, as journalist
Joseph Wood Krutch put it, "the future was bright
and the present was good fun at least."

Between 1919 and 1929 the gross national product—the total value of all goods and services produced in the United States—swelled by 40 percent.

Expansion of the Consumer Society

Wages and salaries also grew
(though not as drastically), while
the cost of living remained relatively stable. People had more
purchasing power, and they spent
as Americans had never spent. In
an article in *Survey* magazine, Eunice Fuller Barnard
contrasted one family's expenditures in 1900 with
those of 1928:

1900

2 bicycles	$ 70[1]
wringer and washboard	5
brushes and brooms	5
sewing machine (mechanical)	25
Total	$ 105

1928

automobile	$ 700
radio	75
phonograph	50
washing machine	150
vacuum cleaner	50
sewing machine (electric)	60
other electrical equipment	25
telephone (year)	35
Total	$1,145

Barnard cautioned that education and medical care
had become costlier. Nevertheless, she regarded the
change as worthwhile. "When some of us bewail
the higher cost of living, we may be talking about
the higher cost of *better* living," Barnard concluded.

The benefits of technology were reaching more
people than ever before. By 1929 two-thirds of all
Americans lived in dwellings that had electricity,

[1]From *Another Part of the Twenties* by Paul Carter. Copyright
©1977 by Columbia University Press. Reprinted with permission
of the publisher.

compared with one-sixth in 1912. In 1929 one-
fourth of all families owned vacuum cleaners, and
one-fifth had toasters. Many could afford goods such
as radios, washing machines, and movie tickets only
because more than one family member worked or
because the breadwinner took a second job. Nevertheless, new products and services were available to
more than just the rich.

The automobile stood as vanguard of all the
era's material wonders. During the 1920s automobile registrations soared from 8 million to 23 million. Mass production and com-

Effects of the Automobile

petition brought down prices,
making cars affordable even to
some working-class families. A
Ford Model T cost less than $300
and a Chevrolet sold for $700 by 1926—when work-
ers in manufacturing earned about $1,300 a year and
clerical workers about $2,300. At those prices, people
could consider the car a necessity rather than a luxury.
"There is no such thing as a 'pleasure automobile,'"
proclaimed an ad in a Nashville newspaper in 1925.
"You might as well talk of 'pleasure fresh air,' or of
'pleasure beef steak.' . . . The automobile increases
length of life, increases happiness, represents above
all other achievements the progress and the civilization of our age."

The car altered American life as much as the
railroad had seventy-five years earlier. Women who
learned to drive achieved new-found independence.
By 1927, most autos were enclosed (they had had
open tops in 1919), enabling youths to escape watchful eyes and creating a privacy that bred fears of
"houses of prostitution on wheels." The vast choice
of models (there were 108 automobile manufacturers in 1923) and colors allowed owners to express
their personal tastes. And most important, the car
was the ultimate symbol of social equality. As one
writer observed in 1924, "It is hard to convince
Steve Popovich, or Antonio Branca, or plain John
Smith that he is being ground into the dust by Capital when at will he may drive the same highways,
view the same scenery, and get as much enjoyment
from his trip as the modern Midas."

Americans' new passion for driving necessitated
extensive construction of roads and abundant supplies of fuel. Since the late 1800s farmers and bicy-
clists had been pressing for improved roads. After
the First World War motorists joined the campaign,
and in the 1920s government aid made "automobil-
ity" truly feasible. In 1921 Congress passed the Federal Highway Act, providing money for state roads.

During the 1920s, the desire to own an automobile spread to members of all classes, races, and ethnic groups. Low prices and available credit enabled this family from Beaumont, Texas, to own a "touring car."   Tyrrell Historical Library.

In 1923 the Bureau of Public Roads planned a national highway system. The oil industry, already vast and powerful, shifted its emphasis from illumination and lubrication to propulsion. In 1920 the United States produced about 65 percent of the world's oil. The automobile also forced public officials to pay more serious attention to safety regulations and traffic control. General Electric Company produced the first timed stop-and-go traffic light in 1924.

Demand for automobiles and other goods and services was whetted by advertising. By 1929 more money was spent on advertising than on all types of formal education. Advertising became a new gospel for business-minded Americans. In his best-selling *The Man Nobody Knows* (1925), advertising executive Bruce Barton called Jesus "the founder of modern business" because he "picked up twelve men from the bottom ranks of business and forged them into an organization that conquered the world." About the same time, a pamphlet entitled *Moses, Persuader of Men* declared, "Moses was one of the greatest salesmen and real-estate promoters that ever lived." Blending psy-

Advertising

chological principles with practical cynicism, advertising theorists asserted confidently that any person's tastes could be manipulated.

As newspaper circulation declined in the 1920s, other media assumed vital advertising functions. Radio became one of the era's most influential novelties, as Aimee Semple McPherson proved. By 1929 over 10 million families owned radios, which bombarded them with advertisements. Station KDKA in Pittsburgh pioneered commercial broadcasting in 1920; within two years there were 508 such stations. By 1929 Americans were spending $850 million a year on radio equipment, and the National Broadcasting Company, which had begun to assemble a network of radio stations three years earlier, was charging advertisers $10,000 to sponsor an hour-long show. Highway billboards and commercials projected during intermissions at movie houses also reminded viewers to buy. Packaging and product display became sciences, all intended to entice consumers.

Although low-income people could not afford all modern products and services, some new trends benefited the working classes, especially those living

America Acclaims *the* SUPERETTE
– the smallest *big* radio ever built

Full-size, 8-tube Super-
Heterodyne . . . with new
RCA Super-Control Tubes...
tone color control...exqui-
site small-size
cabinet...only $69.50
COMPLETE

IT'S JUST the radio America wanted. Sales prove
it. Thousands of people are enthusiastically buying it! You'll want it, too, the minute you see how beautiful . . . how compact it is . . . the minute you hear its
marvelous, life-like, "human" tone.

Imagine it. A real big 8-tube radio condensed into a
small cabinet that will fit anywhere . . . living room, dining
room, bedroom, porch, or office! And it costs so little you can
afford it at an extra set . . . even if you already have a radio.

The new SUPERETTE is more than screen-grid . . .
it's a Super-Heterodyne . . . the last word in radios! You
can't be up-to-date without a Super-Heterodyne. You
can't be up-to-date without RCA Super-Control Tubes.
The SUPERETTE has BOTH!

Back of the SUPERETTE are RCA's vast resources and
the world's foremost group of radio engineers. Back of it
are Victor's 30 years of experience in reproducing the
voices of Caruso, Galli-Curci, McCormack and many other
immortals of music.

Only a year ago, an RCA Super-Heterodyne would have
cost you more than *twice as much*. Now it's yours for only
$69.50 *complete with Radiotrons ready to operate* . . . thanks to
the modern methods of the world's largest radio factory.

See the SUPERETTE today. Examine its beautiful cabinet.
Hear its pure, clear, life-like tone. Any Radiola or Victor
dealer will gladly demonstrate it for you.

$11 to $6.000 . . . RCA Victor
instrument range from portable
phonographs and records up to
America's finest radio-phonograph
combination, including automatic
record-changer and remote control.

The Superette . . . An 8-tube Super-Heterodyne employing two Radiotron Super-Control
Screen-Grid Amplifier Tubes, tone color control, improved volume control, push-pull amplifi-
cation; cabinet in either Butt Walnut or Georgian Brown Mahogany. $69.50, COMPLETE.

RCA Victor Radio

*Between 1922 and 1930, the number of families owning
radios swelled from 60,000 to almost 14 million. Manufacturers such as RCA produced a variety of sizes and
shapes and took out full-page advertisements in popular
publications to inform the public about the latest developments in design and technology.* Library of American
Broadcasting, University of Maryland at College Park.

in cities. Indoor plumbing and electricity became
more common in private residences, and canned
foods, ready-made clothes, and mass-produced
shoes became more affordable. A little cash and a lot
of credit enabled many wage earners to purchase an
automobile. And even if a family could not afford a
radio, vacuum cleaner, or vacation right away, there
was always hope. Spending became a national pastime. No wonder many Americans wanted Henry
Ford to run for president in 1924.

Cities, Migrants, and Suburbs

Consumerism signified not merely an economically
mature nation but an urbanized one. The 1920 federal census revealed that for the first time a majority
of Americans lived in urban ar-
eas (defined as places with 2,500
or more people); the city had become the focus of national experience. Indeed, growth in indus-

**Continuing
Urbanization**

try and services was closely tied to urbanization. Industries such as steel, oil, and auto production
energized cities like Birmingham, Houston, and
Detroit; services and retail trades boosted expansion in Seattle, Atlanta, and Minneapolis. Explosive growth also occurred in warm-climate cities—
notably Miami and San Diego—where promises of
comfort and profit attracted thousands of speculators.

During the 1920s, 6 million Americans left their
farms for nearby or distant cities. Midwestern migrants, particularly young single people, moved to
regional centers like Kansas City and Indianapolis or
to the West. Between 1920 and 1930 California's
population increased 67 percent, and California became one of the nation's most urbanized states while
retaining its status as a leading agricultural state.
Meanwhile, a steady stream of rural southerners
moved to that region's burgeoning industrial cities or
rode railroads northward to Chicago and Cleveland.

African-Americans constituted a sizable portion
of the migrants. Pushed from cotton farming by a
boll weevil plague and lured by industrial jobs, 1.5
million blacks moved cityward during the 1920s,
doubling the African-American populations of cities
such as New York, Chicago, Detroit, and Houston.
Forced by low wages and discrimination to seek the
cheapest housing, newcomers squeezed into low-
rent districts from which escape was difficult at best.
Unlike white migrants, who were free to move away
from inner-city ghettos when they could afford to,
blacks found better housing closed to them. The
only way they could expand their housing opportunities was to spill into nearby white neighborhoods,
a process that sparked resistance and violence. Fears
of such expansion prompted white neighborhood associations to adopt restrictive covenants, whereby
homeowners pledged not to sell or rent their property to blacks.

In response to discrimination, threats, and violence, thousands of urban blacks joined movements
that glorified racial independence. The most influential of these nationalist groups
was the Universal Negro Improvement Association (UNIA),
headed by Marcus Garvey, a Ja-
maican immigrant who believed blacks should separate themselves from corrupt white society. Proclaiming "I am the equal of any white man," Garvey
cultivated racial pride with mass meetings and parades. He also promoted black-owned businesses.
Negro World, his newspaper, refused to publish ads

Marcus Garvey

Mexican immigrants, like other immigrants, brought their homeland customs with them to the United States. Every year on May 5, Cinco de Mayo, with events such as this parade, held in 1914 in Mogollon, New Mexico, they commemorated the Mexican victory over French troops in the Battle of Puebla on May 5, 1862.   Library of Congress.

for hair straighteners and skin-lightening cosmetics, and he set up the Black Star shipping line to help blacks emigrate to Africa.

The UNIA declined in the mid-1920s when the Black Star line went bankrupt. Unscrupulous dealers had deceived Black Star managers into buying dilapidated ships and antiradical fears had prompted persecution by the government (ten UNIA leaders were arrested on charges of anarchism, and Garvey was deported for mail fraud). Middle-class black leaders like W. E. B. Du Bois opposed the UNIA, as did black socialists like A. Philip Randolph and Chandler Owen. Nevertheless, in New York, Chicago, Detroit, and other cities, the organization attracted a large following (contemporaries estimated it at 500,000; Garvey claimed 6 million). Garvey's speeches served notice that African-Americans had aspirations that they could and would translate into action.

The newest immigrants to American cities came from Mexico and Puerto Rico. In the 1920s, as in

Mexican and Puerto Rican Immigrants

the nineteenth century, most Mexicans migrated to work as agricultural laborers in the Southwest, but many also were drawn to growing cities like Denver, San Antonio, Los Angeles, and Tucson. Like other immigrant groups, they generally lacked resources and skills, and men outnumbered women. Mexicans crowded into low-rent districts plagued by poor sanitation, poor police protection, and poor schools.

The 1920s also witnessed an inflow of Puerto Ricans to the mainland. Puerto Rico had been a United States possession since 1898, and its natives were granted United States citizenship in 1917. A shift in the island's economy from sugar to coffee production created a surplus of workers. Attracted by contracts from employers seeking cheap labor, most Puerto Rican migrants moved to New York City, where they created *barrios* (communities) in Brooklyn and Manhattan. Puerto Ricans worked in

Wide highways, cheap land, and affordable housing allowed automobile commuters to move to the urban periphery. In this photo, young women wearing 1920s flapper-style outfits celebrate the phenomenal growth of Culver City, outside Los Angeles. Notice the strong presence of the motor car.   Security Pacific National Bank Collection, Los Angeles Public Library.

manufacturing and in hotels, restaurants, and domestic service.

Within their communities, both Puerto Ricans and Mexicans maintained traditional customs and values and developed businesses—*bodegas* (grocery stores), cafés, boarding houses—and social organizations to help themselves adapt to American society. Educated elites—doctors, lawyers, business owners—tended to become community leaders.

As urban growth peaked, suburban growth accelerated. Although towns had clustered around city edges since the nation's earliest years, prosperity

Growth of the Suburbs

and automobile transportation made the urban fringe more accessible to those wishing to flee crowded cities in the 1920s. Between 1920 and 1930, suburbs of Chicago (such as Oak Park and Evanston), Cleveland (Shaker Heights), and Los Angeles (Burbank and Inglewood) grew five to ten times faster than did the central cities. Most suburbs were middle-

and upper-class bedroom communities; some, like Highland Park (near Detroit) and East Chicago, were industrial satellites.

Increasingly, suburbs resisted annexation to core cities. Suburbanites wanted to escape big-city crime, dirt, and taxes, and they fought to preserve control over their own police, fire protection, and water and gas services. Particularly in the Northeast and Midwest, the suburbs' fierce independence choked off expansion by the central city and divided metropolitan areas in ways that would plague future generations. Moreover, with the suburbs' dependence on automobiles and the dispersal of population, the environmental problems of city life—trash, air pollution, water pollution, and noise—spread across the entire metropolitan area.

Cities and suburbs fostered the mass culture that gave the decade its character. Most of the consumers who jammed shops, movie houses, and sporting arenas and embraced fads like crossword puzzles, miniature golf, and marathon dancing were city and suburban dwellers. Cities and suburbs were the places where people defied law and morality by patronizing speakeasies (illegal saloons), wearing outlandish clothes, and listening to jazz. They were also the places where women, ethnic and racial minorities, and devout moralists strained hardest to adjust to the modern era. Yet the tried-and-true ideal of small-town society survived. While millions thronged cityward, Americans reminisced about the innocence and simplicity of a world gone by. This was the dilemma the modern nation faced: how does one anchor oneself in a world of rampant materialism and social change?

 ## New Rhythms of Everyday Life

Amid all the changes to modern society, Americans developed new ways of using time. People increasingly split their daily lives into distinct compartments: work, family, and leisure. Each type of time was altered in the 1920s. For many people, time on the job shrank. The workweek for many industrial laborers shortened from six days to five and a half. Many white-collar employees worked a forty-hour week and enjoyed a full weekend off. Annual vacations were becoming a standard job benefit for white-collar workers.

Family time is harder to measure, but certain trends are clear. Family size decreased between 1920 and 1930 as birth control became more widely practiced. Among American women who had married in the 1870s and 1880s, well over half who survived to age fifty had five or more children; of their counterparts who married in the 1920s, however, just 20 percent had five or more children. Meanwhile, the divorce rate rose. In 1920 there was 1 divorce for every 7.5 marriages; by 1929 the national ratio was 1 in 6, and in many cities it was 2 in 7. In conjunction with longer life expectancy, lower birth rates and more divorce meant that adults were devoting a smaller portion of their lives to raising children.

The availability of ready-to-wear clothes, canned foods, and mass-produced furniture allowed family members to spend less time producing household necessities. Wives still worked long hours cleaning, cooking, and raising children, but machines now lightened some of their tasks. Especially

Household Management

in middle-class households, electric irons and washing machines simplified some chores. Gas- and oil-powered central heating and hot-water heaters eliminated the hauling of wood, coal, and water, the upkeep of a kitchen fire, and the removal of ashes.

Housewives thus used their time differently than their forebears had—though they spent as many, if not more, hours on domestic responsibilities. Although modern technology supposedly made life easier, it also created new demands on a woman's time. By eliminating servants, who had helped with cleaning, cooking, and childcare, machines shifted the entire task of household management to the wife. No longer a producer of food and clothing as her predecessors had been, a wife now became the chief consumer, responsible for making sure the family spent its money wisely.

Prudent expenditure of family money related to a shift in American eating habits. With the discovery of vitamins between 1915 and 1930, nutritionists began advocating the consumption of certain foods to prevent illness. Giant food companies scrambled to advertise their products as filled with vitamins and minerals beneficial to growth and health. Not only did producers of milk and canned fruits and vegetables exploit the vitamin craze, but other companies made lofty claims that were hard to dispute because little was known about these invisible, tasteless ingredients. C. W. Post, for example, claimed that his Grape-Nuts contained "*iron, calcium, phosphorus,* and *other mineral elements* that are taken right up as vital food by the millions of cells in the body." This emphasis on nutrition added a scientific dimension to housewives' responsibilities.

In addition, the availability of washing machines, hot water, and commercial soap put pressure on wives to keep everything clean. Advertisers tried to coax women to buy products by making them feel guilty and inadequate. "Are you unpopular with your own children?" asked the makers of Listerine mouthwash. If so, the ad advised, "more often than you would imagine . . . halitosis is at fault. Children are quick to resent it. . . . Realizing this, [caring mothers] eliminate any risk of offending by the systematic use of Listerine in the mouth. Every morning. Every night." Thus even while technology made the industrial and service sectors more specialized, the same technology gave housewives a wider variety of tasks.

Better diets and shorter workdays made Americans generally healthier. Life expectancy at birth in-

How do historians know about individual and family life in the 1920s? The manuscript census schedules (the pages on which census takers actually recorded information) from the 1920 federal census contain extraordinarily rich information. By sampling, tabulating, and analyzing large numbers of census entries—after trying to decipher often illegible handwriting—historians raise and attempt to answer questions about everyday life and the environments in which ordinary people lived. The excerpt on this page reproduces the records from a few families living on Stamford Street in Boston and yields numerous insights into how these households were organized.

The Bradley household at 16 Stamford consisted of a middle-aged husband, who was born in Massachusetts and worked as a railroad baggage master, his wife, born in New Brunswick (Nova Scotia) and of British descent, and a middle-aged boarder, who worked as a painter. Why was the boarder living there? Did the Bradleys have extra space because their children had grown up and moved away?

The Milkowski household at 10 Stamford was larger and more complex. It contained ten people, including three young children and five lodgers. Mr. and Mrs. Milkowski were from Russia, but their lodgers came from a variety of places. What kinds of social and economic relationships might have existed in this household?

A lone Chinese man lived at 8 Stamford. He worked in a laundry, and the census notes that he was married. Where was his wife?

Census data often must be combined with other sources in order to answer such questions. Nevertheless, manuscript censuses have helped to provide an important place in the historical record for people previously excluded because they did not leave diaries or letters and were not famous enough to be the subject of newspaper stories.   Photo: National Archives Records and Census Bureau.

DEPARTMENT OF COMMERCE-BUREAU OF THE CENSUS
FOURTEENTH CENSUS OF THE UNITED STATES: 1920-POPULATION

STATE *Massachusetts*   ENUMERATOR *Harry Hoffman*
COUNTY *Suffolk*   ENUMERATED BY ME AN THE *7* DAY OF *Jan* 1920

TOWNSHIP OR OTHER DIVISION OF COUNTY *Tract 33 14.13*   NAME OF INCORPORATED PLACE *Boston*

STREET	HOUSE NUMBER	NAME	RELATION	SEX	COLOR OR RACE	AGE	SINGLE, MARRIED WIDOWED OR DIVORCED	YEAR OF IMMIGRATION	CITIZENSHIP	PERSON PLACE OF BIRTH	FATHER PLACE OF BIRTH	MOTHER PLACE OF BIRTH	ENGLISH SPEAKING	OCCUPATION
	22	Garrigan, James	step-son	M	W	20	S			Mass.	New York	Ireland	yes	Chauffeur
		— Ellen	step-dghtr	F	W	16	S			Mass.	New York	Ireland	yes	Laundry
	16	Bradley, George	Head	M	W	53	M			Mass.	Mass.	Mass.	yes	Railroad
		— Carla A.	wife	F	W	52	M	1880		New Brunswick	New Brunswick	New Brunswick	yes	none
		Hart, Dennis	Lodger	M	W	49	wd.			Mass.	Ireland	Ireland	yes	Painter
Stamford Street	12	Sidlinger, Albert	Head	M	W	65	M			Maine	Maine	Maine	yes	none
		— Catherine	wife	F	W	49	M	1886		Nova Scotia	Ireland	Nova Scotia	yes	none
		— Albert K.	son	M	W	29	S			Mass.	Maine	Nova Scotia	yes	Insurance broker
	10	Milkowski, Louis	Head	M	W	34	M	1906		Russia	Russia	Russia	yes	Cook
		— Mary	wife	F	W	27	M	1908		Russia	Russia	Russia	yes	none
		— Helen	dghtr	F	W	6½	S			Mass.	Russia	Russia		none
		— Jennie	dghtr	F	W	5½	S			Mass.	Russia	Russia		none
		— Peter	son	M	W	1¾	S			Mass.	Russia	Russia		none
		McQuaid, Francis	Lodger	M	W	33	M			Mass.	Ireland	Ireland	yes	Reporter
		— Frieda	wife	F	W	22	M	1899		Switzerland	Italy	Germany	yes	none
		White, Irwin	Lodger	M	W	37	M	1897		England	England	England	yes	Hospital Handyman
		Blake, John	Lodger	M	W	38	M	1894		Ireland	Ireland	Ireland	yes	Laborer
		Miller, Harry	Lodger	M	W	44	S	1910		Norway	Norway	Norway	yes	Waiter's ship
	8	Ling, Chin Ting	Head	M	Ch	60	M	1890		China	China	China	no	Laundry
	6	Ross, Frank	Head	M	W	45	M	1899		Italy	Italy	Italy	yes	Marble Polisher
		— Effie	wife	F	W	43	M			New Hampshire	New Hampshire	Maine	yes	none

creased from fifty-four to sixty years between 1920 and 1930, and infant mortality decreased by two-thirds. Sanitation and research in bacteriology and immunology combined with better nutrition to reduce the risks of life-threatening diseases such as tuberculosis and diphtheria. But medical progress did not benefit all groups equally. Rates of infant mortality were 50 to 100 percent higher among non-whites than among whites, and tuberculosis in inner-city slums remained alarmingly common. Moreover, fatalities from car accidents rose 150 percent, and deaths from heart disease and cancer—diseases of old age—increased 15 percent. Nevertheless, Americans in general were living longer: the total population over age sixty-five grew 35 percent between 1920 and 1930, while the rest of the population increased only 15 percent.

Longer life spans and the worsening economic status of the elderly stirred interest in old-age pensions and other forms of assistance. Industrialism

Older Americans and Retirement

put a premium on youth and agility, pushing older people into poverty from forced retirement and reduced income. Recognizing the needs of aging citizens, most European countries had established state-supported pension systems in the early 1900s. Many Americans, however, believed that individuals should prepare for old age by saving in their youth; pensions, they felt, smacked of socialism. As late as 1923 the Pennsylvania Chamber of Commerce labeled old-age assistance "un-American and socialistic . . . an entering wedge of communistic propaganda."

Yet conditions were alarming. Most inmates in state poorhouses were older people, and almost one-third of Americans age sixty-five and older depended financially on someone else. Only a few employers offered pension plans; most, including the federal government, did not provide for retired employees. Noting that the government fed retired horses until they died, one postal worker complained, "For the purpose of drawing a pension, it would have been better had I been a horse than a human being." Resistance to pension plans finally broke at the state level in the 1920s. Led by Isaac Max Rubinow and Abraham Epstein, reformers persuaded voluntary associations, labor unions, and legislators to endorse the principle of old-age assistance through pensions, insurance, and retirement homes. By 1933 almost every state provided at least minimal assistance to

Suburbanization and the demands of white-collar work created new schedules and roles in the middle-class family. Here the housewife, now the chief consumer and household manager, sews a button on the sleeve of the breadwinner husband while he gulps coffee and reads his paper before rushing to catch his commuter train. Library of Congress.

needy elderly people, and a path had been opened for a national program of old-age insurance.

As people were exposed to new influences in their time away from work and family, new habits and values were inevitable. Especially among the middle

Social Values

class but among the working class, too, clothes became a means of self-expression and personal freedom. Both men and women wore more casual and gaily colored styles than their parents would have considered. The line between acceptable and inappropriate behavior blurred as smoking, swearing, and frankness about sex became fashionable. Birth-control advocate Margaret Sanger, who a decade earlier had been accused of promoting race suicide, gained a large following in respectable circles. Newspapers, magazines, motion pictures, and popular songs (such as "Hot Lips" and "Burning Kisses") made certain that Americans did not suffer from "sex starvation." A typical movie ad promised "brilliant men, beautiful jazz babies, champagne baths, midnight revels, petting parties in the purple dawn, all ending in one terrific smashing climax that makes you gasp."

Other modern trends helped to weaken tried-and-true systems. Because child-labor laws and compulsory-attendance laws kept children in school longer than ever before, peer groups played a more influential role in socializing children. In earlier eras, different age groups had shared the same activities: children had worked with older people in fields and kitchens, and young apprentices had toiled in workshops beside older journeymen and craftsmen. Now, graded school classes, sports, and clubs constantly brought together children of the same age, separating them from the company and influence of adults. Meanwhile, parents tended to rely less on family tradition and more on childcare manuals in raising children. Old-age homes, public health clinics, and workers' compensation reduced family responsibilities even further.

After the First World War, women continued to stream into the labor force. By 1930, 10.8 million women held paying jobs, an increase of over 2 million since the war's end (see figure). The sex segregation that had long characterized workplaces persisted; most women took jobs that men seldom held.

Jobs for Women

Over 1 million women were teachers and nurses. Some 2.2 million were typists, bookkeepers, and office clerks, a tenfold increase since 1920. Another 736,000 were store clerks, and growing numbers became waitresses and hairdressers. Though almost 2 million women worked in factories, their numbers grew very little over the decade. Wherever women were employed, their wages seldom exceeded half of the wages paid to men.

For many women, employment outside the home represented an extension of their family roles. Although women worked for a variety of reasons, their families' economic needs were paramount. The consumerism of the 1920s tempted working-class and middle-class families to satisfy their wants by living beyond their means or by sending women and children into the labor force. In previous eras, most of the extra wage earners had been young and single. Even though the vast majority of married women remained outside the work force (only 12 percent were employed in 1930), married women as a proportion of the work force rose by 30 percent, and the number of employed married women swelled from 1.9 million to 3.1 million. These figures omit countless widowed, divorced, and abandoned women who held jobs and who, like married women, often had children to support.

Women of racial minorities were the exception; the proportions of these women who worked for pay

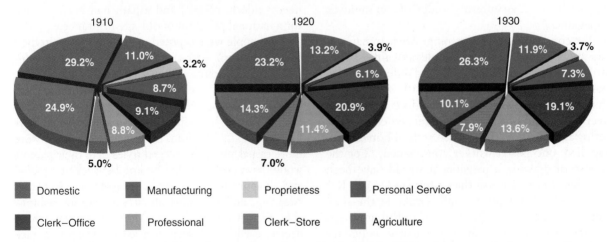

Changing Dimensions of Paid Female Labor, 1910–1930

Changing Dimensions of Paid Female Labor, 1910–1930 These charts reveal the extraordinary growth in clerical and professional occupations among employed women and the accompanying decline in agricultural labor in the early twentieth century. Notice that manufacturing employment peaked in 1920 and that domestic service fluctuated as white immigrant women began to move out of these jobs and were replaced by women of color.

were double that of white women. Often they entered the labor force because their husbands were unemployed or underemployed. The vast majority of African-American women worked in domestic jobs doing cooking, cleaning, and laundry. The few who held factory jobs, such as in cigarette factories and meatpacking plants, had the least desirable, lowest paying tasks. Some opportunities opened for educated black women in social work, teaching, and nursing, but even these women faced harsh discrimination and pressures on their families. Grandmothers and aunts helped with childcare when mothers took outside employment, but such arrangements did not lessen the economic burdens of African-American households beset by poverty and prejudice.

Employment of Minority Women

Economic necessity also drew thousands of Mexican women into wage labor, although their tradition resisted the employment of women. Exact figures are difficult to uncover, but it is certain that many Mexican women worked as pickers in western farm fields and as domestic servants in urban households. Next to black women, Japanese women were the most likely to hold paying jobs. They too worked as field hands and domestics. And, like Mexican and African-American women, Japanese women encountered racial bias, low pay, and little chance for advancement.

Employed or not, women confronted alternative images of femininity. In contrast to the heavy, floor-length dresses and long hair of previous generations, the short skirts and bobbed hair of the 1920s "flapper" signified independent-mindedness and sexual freedom. The flapper look became fashionable among office workers and store clerks as well as college coeds. As models of female behavior, chaste, modest heroines were eclipsed by movie vamps like Clara Bow, known as the "It Girl," and Gloria Swanson, known for her torrid love affairs on and off the screen. Many women, not just flappers, were asserting a new social equality with men. As one observer described "the new woman":

Alternative Images of Femininity

> She takes a man's point of view as her mother never could. . . . She will never make you a hatband or knit you a necktie, but she'll drive you from the station . . . in her own little sports car. She'll don knickers and go skiing with you, . . . she'll dive as well as you, perhaps better, she'll dance as long as you care to, and she'll take everything you say the way you mean it.

The expansion of service-sector jobs and new technology opened new opportunities for women in the 1920s. This telephone operator handled scores of phone calls at the same time and monitored a huge switchboard. Her dress and jewelry contrasted with the simpler styles worn by factory women, who had to be more careful in working with dangerous machines.   George Eastman House.

The era's openness regarding sexuality also enabled the underground homosexual culture to emerge a little more than in previous eras. In nontraditional city neighborhoods, such as New York's Greenwich Village and Harlem, cheap rents and an apparent tolerance of alternate lifestyles attracted gay men and lesbians who patronized dance halls, speakeasies, and other gathering places. Commercial amusement establishments that catered to a gay clientele remained targets for police raids, however, demonstrating that homosexual men and women could not expect respect from the rest of society.

These trends represented a break with the more restrained culture of the nineteenth century. But social change rarely proceeds smoothly. As the decade wore on, various groups prepared to defend tried-and-true older values.

Lines of Defense

Early in 1920 the leader of a newly formed organization hired two public relations experts to recruit members. The experts, Edward Clarke and Elizabeth Tyler, used modern advertising techniques to canvass communities in the South, Southwest, and Midwest, where they found thousands of men eager to pay a $10 membership fee and another $6 for a white uniform. Clarke and Tyler pocketed $2.50 from each membership they sold. No one could argue with their success. By 1923 the organization claimed 5 million members.

This was no ordinary civic club like the Lions or Kiwanis. It was the Ku Klux Klan, a revived version of the hooded order that had terrorized southern communities after the Civil War, and its appeal was based on fear. As one pamphlet distributed by Clarke and Tyler put it, "Every criminal, every gambler, every thug, every libertine, every girl ruiner, every home wrecker, every wife beater, every dope peddler, every moonshiner, every white slaver, every Rome-controlled newspaper, every black spider—is fighting the Klan. Think it over, which side are you on?"

Reconstituted in 1915 by William J. Simmons, an Atlanta evangelist and insurance salesman, the Klan was the most sinister reactionary movement of the 1920s. The new Invisible Empire revived the hoods, intimidating tactics, and mystical terminology of its forerunner (its leader was the Imperial Wizard, its book of rituals the kloran). But the new Klan had broader membership and objectives than the old. It fanned outward from the Deep South and for a time wielded frightening power in every region of the country, its activity peaking in 1923. Unlike the original Klan, which directed its terrorist tactics at emancipated blacks (see page 458–459), the new Klan targeted a variety of racial and religious groups.

Ku Klux Klan

One phrase summed up the Klan's goals: "Native, white, Protestant supremacy." *Native* meant no immigration, no "mongrelization" of American culture. According to Imperial Wizard Hiram Wesley Evans, white supremacy was a matter of survival. "The world," he warned, "has been so made so that each race must fight for its life, must conquer, accept slavery, or die. The Klansman believes the whites will not become slaves, and he does not intend to die before his time." Evans praised Protestantism for fostering "unhampered individual development,"

and he accused the Catholic Church of discouraging assimilation and enslaving people to priests and a foreign pope.

Using threatening assemblies, violence, and political pressure, Klan members menaced many communities in the early 1920s. Assuming the role of moral protector, the Klan meted out vigilante justice to suspected bootleggers, wife beaters, and adulterers; forced schools to adopt Bible reading and to stop teaching the theory of evolution; campaigned against Catholic and Jewish political candidates; and fueled racial tensions against Mexicans in border cities such as El Paso. By 1925, however, the Invisible Empire was on the wane, outnumbered by immigrants and their offspring and rocked by scandal. (In 1925 Indiana Grand Dragon David Stephenson kidnapped and raped a woman who later died either from taking poison or from infection caused by bites on her body; Stephenson was convicted of second-degree murder on grounds that he caused her suicide.) The Klan's negative, exclusive brand of patriotism and purity could not compete in a pluralistic society.

The Ku Klux Klan had no monopoly on bigotry in the 1920s; intolerance pervaded American society. Nativists had been urging an end to free immigration since the 1880s. They charged that Catholic and Jewish immigrants clogged city slums, flouted community norms, and stubbornly held to alien religious and political beliefs. As self-styled expert Madison Grant wrote in *The Passing of the Great Race* (1916): "These immigrants adopt the language of the native American, they wear his clothes, they steal his name and they are beginning to take his women, but they seldom adopt his religion or understand his ideals."

Fear of radicalism, persisting from the Red Scare of 1919, fueled antiforeign flames. The most notorious debate occurred in 1921, when a court convicted Nicola Sacco and Bartolomeo Vanzetti, two immigrant anarchists, of murdering a guard and paymaster during a robbery in South Braintree, Massachusetts. Sacco and Vanzetti's main offenses seem to have been their political beliefs and Italian origins. Though the evidence failed to prove their involvement in the robbery, Judge Webster Thayer openly sided with the prosecution and privately called the defendants "anarchist bastards." Appeals and protests failed to win a new trial, and the defendants, who remained calm and dignified throughout their ordeal, were executed in 1927. Their deaths

Sacco and Vanzetti Case

touched off rallies and riots in Europe, Asia, and South America, chilling those who had looked to the United States as the land that nurtured freedom of belief.

Meanwhile, the movement to restrict immigration gathered support. Labor leaders warned that a flood of aliens would depress wages and raise unemployment. Business executives, who formerly had opposed restrictions because immigrant laborers were easy to exploit, changed their minds, having realized that they could keep labor costs low by mechanizing and by hiring black workers.

Drawing support from such groups, Congress drastically reversed previous policy and set yearly immigration quotas for each nationality. The quotas favored northern and western Europeans, in keeping with nativist prejudices against immigrants from southern and eastern Europe. By stipulating that annual immigration of a given nationality could not exceed 3 percent of the number of immigrants from that nation residing in the United States in 1910, the Quota (Johnson) Act of 1921 mainly limited immigrants from southern and eastern Europe, whose numbers were small in 1910 relative to those from northern Europe. The law also introduced a "nonquota" category that exempted from the quotas individuals with desirable professions, such as artists, nurses, ministers, and professors.

Immigration Quotas

The Johnson Act did not satisfy restrictionists, so Congress replaced it with the Immigration Act (Johnson-Reid Act) of 1924. This law set quotas at 2 percent of each nationality residing in the United States in 1890. It thus further restricted southern and eastern Europeans, since fewer of those groups lived in the United States in 1890 than in 1910. The new law did allow wives and children of United States citizens to enter as nonquota immigrants. The act also established a "national-origins" system, to become effective in 1927. Instead of basing quotas on the 1890 census, national-origins policy set an annual limit of 150,000 immigrants, and each country received a fraction of that number equal to the percentage of people in the United States population in 1920 who derived from that country by *birth or descent*. This system fixed quotas of roughly 66,000 from Great Britain and 26,000 from Germany but allowed only 6,000 from Italy and 2,700 from Russia. It also excluded almost all Asians but set no quotas for peoples from the Western Hemisphere. Soon Canadians, Mexicans, and Puerto Ri-

Anti-immigrationists used songs, as well as speeches and posters, to promote their cause. This 1923 tune urges the government to "O! Close the Gates" lest foreigners betray the hard-won rights of Americans and "drag our Colors down." *National Park Service Collection, Ellis Island Immigration Museum. Photo Chermayeff & Geismar MetaForm.*

cans became the largest groups of newcomers (see figure, page 708).

While various groups lobbied for racial purity, the pursuit of moral purity stirred religious fundamentalists. As they had for many years, millions of Americans sought certainty in a rapidly changing world by following evangelical denominations of Protestantism that accepted a literal interpretation of the Bible. For them, religion provided not only salvation but also a bulwark against the skepticism and irreverence of a materialistic, hedonistic society.

In 1925 Christian fundamentalism clashed with scientific theory in a celebrated case in Dayton, Tennessee. Early that year the state legislature passed a law forbidding public school instructors to teach the theory that humans had evolved from lower forms of life rather than from Adam and Eve. Shortly thereafter, high school

Scopes Trial

Sources of Immigration, 1907 and 1927

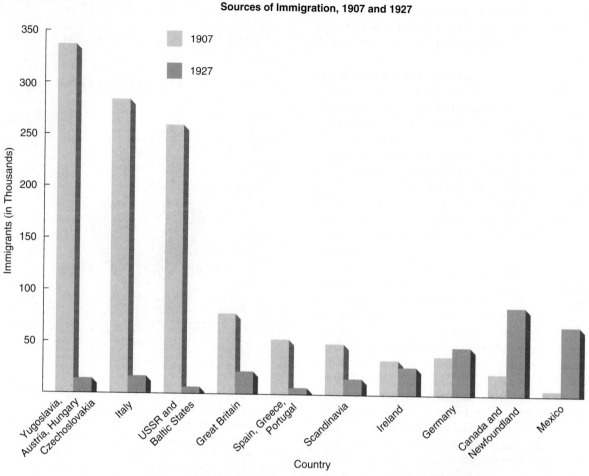

Sources of Immigration, 1907 and 1927 *Immigration peaked in 1907 and 1908, when newcomers from southern and eastern Europe poured into the United States. After immigration restriction laws were passed in the 1920s, the greatest number of immigrants came from the Western Hemisphere (Canada and Mexico), which was exempted from the quotas, and the number coming from eastern and southern Europe shrank.*

teacher John Thomas Scopes was arrested for violating the law; he had volunteered to serve in a test case. Scopes's trial that summer became a headline event. William Jennings Bryan, the former secretary of state and three-time presidential candidate, argued for the prosecution, and a team of civil liberties lawyers headed by Clarence Darrow argued for the defense. News correspondents crowded into town, and radio stations broadcast the trial.

Although Scopes was convicted—clearly he had broken the law—modernists claimed victory. The testimony, they believed, had shown fundamentalism to be illogical. The trial's climax occurred when Bryan took the witness stand as an expert on religion and science. Responding to Darrow's probing, Bryan asserted that Eve really had been created from

Adam's rib, that the Tower of Babel was responsible for the diversity of languages, and that a big fish had swallowed Jonah. The liberal press mocked Bryan's uncritical faith; humorist Will Rogers quipped, "I see you can't say that man descended from the ape. At least that's the law in Tennessee. But do they have a law to keep a man from making a jackass of himself?" Nevertheless, fundamentalists were undeterred and steadfastly denied evolution.

Klan rallies, immigration restriction, and fundamentalist literalism might appear as the last gasps of a rural society yielding to modern urban-industrial values. Yet city dwellers swelled the ranks of all these defensive movements. Nearly half of the Klan's members lived in cities, especially in working-class neighborhoods where fear of invasion by African-

Americans and foreigners was strong. Even urban reformers backed immigration restriction as a means of controlling poverty and quickening the assimilation of foreigners. Cities also housed hundreds of pentecostal churches, which attracted whites struggling with economic insecurity. Such people were swayed by the pageantry and closeness to God that such churches offered. Using modern advertising techniques and elaborately staged services broadcast live on radio, cult leaders such as the magnetic Aimee Semple McPherson of Los Angeles and former baseball player Billy Sunday stirred revivalist fervor. And many urban dwellers supported prohibition, believing that eliminating the temptation of drink would help win the battle against poverty, vice, and corruption.

These defensive and emotional responses represented an attempt to sustain old-fashioned, tried-and-true ways in a fast-moving and materialistic world. Some Americans lashed out at "different" cultures and hedonistic trends in behavior. Millions of otherwise decent Americans firmly believed that nonwhites and immigrants were inferior people who imperiled existing values. And clergy and teachers of all faiths condemned drinking, dancing, new dress styles, and new sexual habits.

Even while worrying about a lost past, most Americans tried to adjust to the modern order in one way or another. Few refrained from listening to the radio and attending movies, activities that proved less corrupting than critics feared. Radio featured music, news, and dramas, most of which did not threaten traditional values. Movie producers, bowing to pressure from legislators, instituted self-censorship in 1927, forbidding nudity, rough language, and plots that did not end with justice and morality triumphant. More than ever, Americans sought fellowship in civic organizations. Membership swelled in Rotary, Elks, and women's clubs, and the number of Community Chests—associations that coordinated civic and welfare projects—grew from 12 in 1919 to 361 in 1930. Perhaps most important, more people were finding release in a world of leisure.

 ## The Age of Play

An insatiable thirst for recreation gripped Americans in the 1920s. In 1919 they spent $2.5 billion on leisure activities; by 1929 such expenditures topped $4.3 billion, a figure not again equaled until after the Second World War. Spectator amusements—

movies, music, and sports—accounted for about 21 percent of the 1929 total; the rest was individual recreation, from participatory sports to hobbies, music, and travel.

Entrepreneurs responded quickly to an appetite for fads, fun, and "ballyhoo"—a blitz of publicity that lent exaggerated importance to some person or event. Games and fancies particularly attracted newly affluent middle-class families. Mahjong, a Chinese tile game, was the rage in the early 1920s. By the mid-1920s people were popularizing crossword puzzles, which mass-circulation newspapers and magazines had begun printing a decade earlier. When Simon and Schuster published a book of crossword puzzles with a pencil attached—people who did a crossword puzzle with a pen were labeled foolish optimists—the volume became an instant bestseller. A few years later fun seekers adopted miniature golf as their new fad. By 1930 the nation boasted thirty thousand miniature golf courses featuring tiny castles, windmills, and waterfalls. Dance crazes like the Charleston riveted public attention throughout the country, aided by live and recorded music on radio and the growing popularity of jazz.

In addition to participating actively in leisure activities, Americans were avid spectators, particularly of movies and sports. In total capital investment, motion pictures became one of the nation's leading industries. Nearly every community had at least one theater, whether it was a hundred-seat Bijou on Main Street or a big-city "picture palace" with ornate lobbies and thousands of cushioned seats. In 1922 movies attracted 40 million viewers a week; by 1930 the number reached 100 million—at a time when the nation's population was 120 million and total weekly church attendance was 60 million. The introduction of sound in *The Jazz Singer* in 1927, and of color a few years later, made movies even more exciting and realistic. The technology for making "talkies" had existed before the 1920s, but producers had continued to make silent movies to attract immigrants who did not speak English. By the late 1920s, after immigration had been restricted and English-speaking offspring had increased, "talkies" could be better understood and had wider appeal.

Movies

Responding to the tastes of mass audiences, the movie industry produced more escapist entertainment than art. The most popular films were spectacles such as Cecil B. DeMille's *The Ten Commandments* (1923) and *The King of Kings* (1927); lurid

This portrait shows Babe Ruth's powerful hands and arms, but more riveting are the penetrating yet sad eyes set in the sensuous, boyish face of the baseball slugger. Museum of Modern Art, Gift of Mrs. Nickolas Murray.

dramas such as *Souls for Sale* (1923) and *A Woman Who Sinned* (1924); and slapstick comedies starring Fatty Arbuckle, Harold Lloyd, and Charlie Chaplin. Ironically, the comedies, with their poignant satire of the human condition, carried the most thought-provoking messages.

Spectator sports also boomed. Each year millions packed stadiums and parks to watch athletic events. Gate receipts from college football alone surpassed $21 million by the late 1920s. In an age when technology and mass production had robbed experiences and objects of their uniqueness, sports provided the unpredictability and drama that people craved. Newspapers and radio magnified this drama, feeding news to an eager public and glorifying events with unrestrained narrative. Thus the otherwise staid *New York Times* resorted to wild hyperbole to summarize a 1920 tennis match between

Bill Tilden, the national champion, and challenger William Johnston:

> The Tilden-Johnston struggle will go down on the records as the most astounding exhibition of tennis, the most nerve-wracking battle that the courts have ever seen. . . . Tilden and Johnston played five acts of incredible melodrama, with a thrill in every scene, with horrible errors leading suddenly to glorious achievements, with skill and courage and good and evil fortune. . . . Tilden's victory was a triumph for supertennis.

With reporting like that, sports promoters did not need to buy advertising.

Baseball's drawn-out suspense, variety of plays, and potential for keeping statistics attracted a huge following. After the "Black Sox scandal" of 1919, when eight members of the Chicago White Sox had been banned from the game for allegedly throwing the World Series to the Cincinnati Reds (even though a jury acquitted them), baseball not only regained its respectability but also transformed itself. Discovering that home runs excited fans, the leagues redesigned the ball to make it livelier. Attendance at games skyrocketed. A record 300,000 people attended the six-game 1921 World Series between the New York Giants and New York Yankees. Millions more gathered regularly to watch local teams.

Sports, movies, and the news created a galaxy of heroes. As technology and mass society made the individual less significant, people clung to heroic personalities as a means of identifying with the unique. Names such as Tilden in tennis, Gertrude Ederle in swimming (in 1926 she became the first woman to swim across the English Channel), and Bobby Jones in golf became household words. But the power and action of boxing, football, and baseball produced the most popular sports heroes. Heavyweight champion Jack Dempsey, a brawler from Manassa, Colorado, attracted the first of many million-dollar gates in his fight with Georges Carpentier in 1921. Harold "Red" Grange, running back for the University of Illinois football team, thrilled thousands and became the idol of sportswriters. During his senior year in 1925, Grange was offered huge contracts by real-estate and motion-picture companies; he collected $42,000 for his first two games as a professional with the Chicago Bears.

Baseball's foremost hero was George Herman "Babe" Ruth, who began his career as a pitcher but

Sports Heroes

Rudolph Valentino became the idol of men and women alike in The Sheik, *his most famous movie. With flashing eyes and wanton smile, Valentino carries a swooning woman to his tent. This immensely popular movie earned $1 million for Paramount Pictures.*   Museum of Modern Art Film Still Archive.

found he could use his prodigious strength to better advantage hitting home runs. Ruth hit 29 in 1919, 54 in 1920 (the year the Boston Red Sox traded him to the New York Yankees), 59 in 1924, and 60 in 1927—each year a record. His exaggerated gestures on the field, defiant lifestyle, and boyish grin endeared him to millions. Known for overindulgence in food, drink, and women, he made fans forgive his excesses by appearing at public events and visiting hospitalized children.

While admiring the physical exploits of sports stars, Americans fulfilled a yearning for romance and adventure through movie stars. The films and personal lives of Douglas Fairbanks, Gloria Swanson, and Charlie Chaplin were discussed in parlors and pool halls across the country. One of the decade's most ballyhooed personalities was Rudolph Valentino, whose smooth seductiveness made women

**Movie Stars
and Public
Heroes**

swoon and men imitate his pomaded hairdo and slick sideburns. Valentino's image exploited the era's sexual liberalism and flirtation with evil. In his most famous film, Valentino played a passionate sheik who carried away beautiful women to his tent, combining the roles of seducer and abductor. When he died at thirty-one of complications from ulcers and appendicitis, the press turned his funeral into a public extravaganza. Mourners lined up for over a mile to file past his coffin.

The news media also created heroes. For two weeks in 1925 newspapers kept readers on edge with reports on Floyd Collins, a young explorer trapped in a Kentucky cave. By the time rescuers found Collins dead, the country had idolized him as a hero battling nature. Flagpole sitters, marathon dancers, and other record seekers regularly occupied the front pages. The most notable news hero was Charles A. Lindbergh, the airplane pilot who made a daring nonstop solo flight across the Atlantic in

1927. A modest, independent midwesterner whom writers dubbed the Lone Eagle, Lindbergh accepted fame but did not try to profit from it. The stark contrast between his personality and the ballyhoo that surrounded him made Americans admire him even more fervently.

Some people may have idolized Lindbergh because they felt guilty at having abandoned virtues of restraint and moderation. In their quest for fun and self-expression, Americans became lawbreakers and supporters of crime. The Eighteenth Amendment (1919) and the federal law (1920) that prohibited the manufacture, sale, and transportation of alcoholic beverages worked well at first. Per capita consumption of liquor dropped, as did arrests for drunkenness, and the price of illegal booze rose higher than average workers could afford. But aside from passing supportive laws, legislators saw little need to enforce prohibition. In 1922 Congress gave the Prohibition Bureau only three thousand employees and less than $7 million for nationwide enforcement.

Prohibition

If the Eighteenth Amendment had applied only to hard liquor and not to beer and wine, it might have succeeded. But after about 1925 the so-called noble experiment broke down in cities, where desire for personal freedom overwhelmed weak enforcement. The law allowed manufacture of beer for dilution into near-beer (with half of the alcoholic content of regular beer) and sale of alcohol for medicinal and sacramental purposes, but criminals cleverly obtained and sold such spirits for other purposes. Smuggling and home manufacture of liquor were rampant. Thousands of people made their own wine and bathtub gin, and bootleg importers along the country's borders and shorelines easily evaded the few patrols that attempted to curb them.

Local officials realized that strict enforcement of prohibition was impossible. Drinking, like gambling and prostitution, was a business with willing customers, and criminal organizations quickly capitalized on public demand. The most notorious of such mobs belonged to Al Capone, a burly tough who seized control of illegal liquor and vice in Chicago and maintained his grip through intimidation, bribery, and violence. Capone and his armed gangsters influenced local politics as well as vice until 1931, when a federal court convicted and imprisoned him for income-tax evasion.

Al Capone

It is important to recognize that prohibition and its weak enforcement did not create organized crime. Gangs like Capone's had provided illegal goods and services long before the 1920s. As Capone put it, "Prohibition is a business. All I do is supply a public demand. I do it in the least harmful way I can." Americans wanted their liquor and their freedom; Capone and others like him took advantage of these desires.

Thus the expansion of leisure activities during the 1920s caught Americans between two value systems. A tradition of hard work, sobriety, and restraint—"Waste not, want not"—still prevailed, especially in rural areas where new diversions were unavailable. Elsewhere, however, modern, liberating opportunities to play beckoned.

Never before had so many types of commercial recreation existed. Not just mass entertainment such as movies, sports, and radio, but individual amusements such as stamp collecting, puzzle working, and listening to the phonograph became commonplace. Few of these activities were illegal or immoral, but Americans were increasingly willing to ignore behavioral restraints and break the law if restrictions interfered with their quest for pleasure. As columnist Walter Lippmann wrote in 1931, "The high level of lawlessness is maintained by the fact that Americans desire to do so many things which they also desire to prohibit."

 ## Cultural Currents

The tension between conflicting value systems pulled artists and intellectuals in new directions. In literature, art, and music, rejection of old beliefs prompted experimentation. Concern over modern materialism and conformity gave the era's artistic output a bitterly critical tinge. Artists seldom voiced a radical message; they wanted not so much to reject modern society as to fend off the era's rampant vulgarity.

The disillusioned writers who found crass materialism at odds with art became known as the Lost Generation. A number of them, including novelist Ernest Hemingway and poets Ezra Pound and T. S. Eliot, moved to Europe. Others, such as novelists William Faulkner and Sinclair Lewis, remained in

Literature of Alienation

America but assailed the racism and irrationality that swirled around them. Along with innovative forms of expression and realistic portrayals of emotion, these writers produced biting social commentary.

Indictments of modern society's materialism and impersonality dominated literature. F. Scott Fitzgerald's *This Side of Paradise* (1920) and *The Great Gatsby* (1925); Lewis's *Babbitt* (1922), *Arrowsmith* (1925), and *Elmer Gantry* (1927); and Eugene O'Neill's plays exposed Americans' preoccupation with money. Edith Wharton explored the clash of old and new moralities in novels such as *The Age of Innocence* (1921). Ellen Glasgow, the South's leading literary figure, lamented the trend toward impersonality in *Barren Ground* (1925). John Dos Passos's *Three Soldiers* (1921) and Hemingway's *A Farewell to Arms* (1929) interwove antiwar sentiment with critiques of the emptiness in modern relationships.

Spiritual discontent quite different from that of white writers inspired a new generation of African-American artists. Middle class, well educated, and proud of their African heritage, these writers rejected white culture and exalted the militantly assertive "New Negro." Most of them lived in Harlem, in upper Manhattan; in this "Negro Mecca" black intellectuals and artists, aided by a few white patrons, celebrated black culture during what became known as the Harlem Renaissance.

Harlem Renaissance

The popular 1921 musical comedy *Shuffle Along* is often credited with initiating the Harlem Renaissance. The musical showcased talented African-American artists such as lyricist Noble Sissle and composer Eubie Blake. It also introduced catchy songs such as "Love Will Find a Way" and "I'm Just Wild About Harry" and boosted the careers of black singers Florence Mills, Josephine Baker, and Mabel Mercer.

Harlem in the 1920s also fostered a number of gifted writers, among them Langston Hughes, whose poems captured the mood and rhythms of blues and jazz; Countee Cullen, a poet of moving lyrical skill; and Claude McKay, whose militant verses urged rebellion against bigotry. Jean Toomer's poems and his novel *Cane* (1923) portrayed black life with passionate realism, and Alain Locke's essays defined the spirit of the artistic renaissance. The movement also included visual artists such as Aaron Douglas, a painter who illustrated many of the books of Harlem Renaissance writers; James A. Porter,

Florence Mills was a talented performer whose singing career received a major boost from her appearance in the musical comedy Shuffle Along, *a show that heralded the beginning of the Harlem Renaissance.* © 1997 Donna VanDer Zee.

whose paintings received wide acclaim; and Augusta Savage, who sculpted busts of famous black personalities and who became an object of controversy in 1923 when the French government rejected her application to an art school because of her race.

Issues of identity troubled the Harlem Renaissance. Although intellectuals and artists cherished their African heritage, they realized that blacks had to come to terms with themselves as Americans. Thus Alain Locke urged that the New Negro should "lay aside the status of beneficiary and ward for that of a collaborator and participant in American civilization." And Langston Hughes wrote, "We younger Negro artists who create now intend to express our individual dark-skinned selves without fear or shame. If white people are pleased we are glad. If they are not, it doesn't matter. We know we are beautiful."

The Jazz Age, as the 1920s is sometimes called, owed its name to music that derived from black culture. Evolving from African and black American folk music, early jazz communicated an exuberance, humor, and authority that African-Americans seldom expressed in their public and political lives. With its emotional rhythms and emphasis on improvisation, jazz blurred the distinction between composer and performer and created intimacy between performer and audience.

Jazz

As African-Americans moved northward, jazz traveled with them. By the 1920s dance halls and bars in major cities featured jazz, sometimes popularized by white musicians such as Paul Whiteman and Bix Beiderbecke. Gifted black performers like trumpeter Louis Armstrong, trombonist Kid Ory, and singer Bessie Smith enjoyed wide fame. Phonograph records and radio, better suited than sheet music to the spontaneity of jazz, helped to popularize it. Jazz greatly boosted the recording industry; music recorded by black artists and aimed at black consumers (sometimes called "race records") gave African-Americans a distinctive place in the consumer culture. More important, jazz endowed America with its most distinctive art form.

In many ways the 1920s were the most creative years the nation had yet experienced. Painters such as Georgia O'Keeffe and John Marin tried to forge a unique American style of painting. European composers and performers still dominated classical music, but Americans such as Henry Cowell, who pioneered electronic music, and Aaron Copland, who built orchestral works around native folk motifs, began careers that later won wide acclaim. George Gershwin blended jazz rhythms, classical forms, and folk melodies in his serious compositions (*Rhapsody in Blue*, 1924, and *Concerto in F*, 1925), musical dramas (*Funny Face*, 1927), and hit tunes such as "Summertime" and "Someone to Watch over Me." In architecture the skyscraper boom drew worldwide attention, and Frank Lloyd Wright's "prairie-style" houses, churches, and schools celebrated the magnificence of the American landscape. At the beginning of the decade, essayist Harold Stearns had complained that "the most . . . pathetic fact in the social life of America today is emotional and aesthetic starvation." By 1929 that contention was hard to support.

The Election of 1928 and the End of the New Era

Intellectuals' uneasiness about 1920s materialism seldom affected the confident rhetoric of politics. Herbert Hoover voiced that confidence in his speech accepting the Republican nomination for president in 1928. "We in America today," Hoover boasted, "are nearer to the final triumph over poverty than ever before in the history of any land. . . . We have not yet reached the goal, but, given a chance to go forward with the policies of the last eight years, we shall soon, with the help of God, be in sight of the day when poverty will be banished from this nation."

Hoover was an apt Republican candidate in 1928 (Coolidge had chosen not to run for reelection), because he fused tried-and-true values of individual hard work with modern emphasis on collective action. A Quaker from Iowa, orphaned at age ten, Hoover worked his way through Stanford University and became a wealthy mining engineer. During and after the First World War, he distinguished himself as United States food administrator and head of food relief for Europe.

Herbert Hoover

As secretary of commerce under Harding and Coolidge, Hoover had what has been called an "associational vision." Recognizing the extent to which large nationwide associations had come to dominate commerce and industry, Hoover tried to stimulate cooperation between business and government. He took every opportunity to make the Department of Commerce a center for the promotion of business, encouraging the formation of trade associations, holding conferences, and issuing reports, all aimed at improving production, marketing, and profits. His active leadership prompted one observer to quip that Hoover was "Secretary of Commerce and assistant secretary of everything else."

As Hoover's opponent, Democrats chose Governor Alfred E. Smith of New York, whose background contrasted sharply with Hoover's. Hoover had rural, native, Protestant, business roots and had never run for public office. Smith was an urbane, gregarious politician of immigrant stock with a career rooted in New York City's Tammany Hall. His relish for the give-and-take of city streets is apparent in his response during the campaign to a heckler who taunted him by shouting,

Al Smith

"Tell them all you know, Al. It won't take long!" Smith unflinchingly retorted, "I'll tell them all we both know, and it won't take any longer!"

Smith was the first Roman Catholic to run for president on a major party ticket. His religion contributed to his considerable appeal among urban ethnics, who were voting in increasing numbers, but intense anti-Catholic sentiments lost him southern and rural votes. Smith had compiled a strong record as a promoter of Progressive reforms and civil rights during his governorship, but his campaign failed to build a coalition of farmers and city dwellers because he stressed issues unlikely to unite these groups, particularly his opposition to prohibition.

Smith waged a spirited campaign, directly confronting anti-Catholic critics, but Hoover, who stressed the nation's prosperity under Republican administrations, won the popular vote by 21 million to 15 million, the electoral vote by 444 to 87. Smith's candidacy nevertheless had beneficial effects on the Democratic Party. He carried the nation's twelve largest cities, which formerly had given majorities to Republican candidates, and he lured millions of foreign-stock voters to the polls for the first time. From 1928 onward, the Democratic Party solidified this urban base, which in conjunction with its traditional strength in the South would make the party a formidable force in national elections.

At his inaugural, Hoover proclaimed a New Day, "bright with hope." His cabinet, composed mostly of businessmen committed to the existing order, included six millionaires. To the lower ranks of government Hoover appointed young professionals who agreed with him that scientific methods could be applied to solve national problems. In time, Hoover and his experts believed, they could establish a stable social order based on cooperation between government and various civic groups.

Hoover's Administration

If Hoover was optimistic, so were most Americans. Reverence for what Hoover called "the American system"—which offered such exciting products as radios and refrigerators—ran high. The belief was widespread that individuals were responsible for their own situations and that unemployment or poverty suggested personal failing. Prevailing opinion also held that the ups and downs of the business cycle were natural and therefore not to be tampered with by government.

This confidence was jolted in the fall of 1929 when stock prices suddenly plunged after soaring in 1928. Analysts explained the drop as a temporary condition caused by a "lunatic fringe." But on October 24, "Black Thursday," panic selling set in. The prices of many stocks hit record lows; some sellers could find no buyers. Stunned crowds gathered outside the frantic New York Stock Exchange. At noon, leading bankers met at the headquarters of J. P. Morgan and Company. To restore faith, they put up $20 million and ceremoniously began buying stocks. The mood changed and some stocks rallied. The bankers, it seemed, had saved the day.

Stock Market Crash

But as news of Black Thursday spread, fearful investors decided to sell their stocks rather than risk further losses. On "Black Tuesday," October 29, stock prices plummeted again. The market settled into a grim pattern of declines and weak rallies. Hoover, who never had approved of what he called "the fever of speculation," assured Americans that the economy was sound. He shared the popular assumptions that the stock market's ills could be quarantined and that the economy was strong enough to endure until the market righted itself.

But instead, the crash ultimately helped to unleash a devastating depression. The economic downturn did not arrive suddenly (see Chapter 25); it was more like a slow leak than a blowout. Had conditions been as sound as businesspeople maintained, the nation might have weathered the Wall Street crash. In fact, however, some historians suggest that the stock market collapse merely moved an ongoing recession into depression.

The economic weakness that underlay the Great Depression had several interrelated causes. The first was declining demand. Coal, railroads, textiles, and some other industries were in distress long before 1929, but the major growth industries—automobiles, construction, and mechanized agriculture—had been able to expand as long as consumers bought their products. Frenzied expansion, however, could not continue unabated. When demand leveled off, owners could not accumulate funds to build new plants and hire new workers. Instead, unsold inventories stacked up in warehouses, and laborers were laid off. The more wages and purchasing power lagged behind industrial production, the greater was the number of workers who produced consumer products but could not afford to buy them in sufficient quantities to sustain the economy's momentum. Farmers, too, had to

Declining Demand

trim their purchases. Thus by 1929 a sizable population of underconsumers was causing serious repercussions.

Underconsumption also resulted from maldistribution of income. As the rich grew richer, middle- and lower-income Americans made only modest gains. Though average per capita disposable income (income after taxes) rose about 9 percent between 1920 and 1929, the income of the wealthiest 1 percent rose 75 percent, accounting for most of the increase. Much of this increase was put into stock market investments instead of being spent on consumer goods.

Furthermore, American businesses were overloaded with debt. In 1929 the top two hundred nonfinancial corporations controlled 49 percent of corporate wealth. Many corpo-

Corporate Debt

rations built pyramid-like empires supported by shady, though legal, manipulation of assets and weakly supported liabilities. The nation's banking system also was on precarious footing. When one part of the edifice collapsed, the entire structure crumbled.

The depression also derived from largely unregulated speculation on the stock market. In the years before the crash, corporations and banks invested huge sums in stocks. Individual

Speculation on the Stock Market

buyers borrowed heavily to purchase stocks, putting up little or no cash, and then used the stocks they had bought but not fully paid for as collateral for more loans. When stock prices collapsed, brokers demanded that buyers repay their loans. Buyers tried to do so by withdrawing their savings from banks or selling their stocks at a loss for whatever they could get. Bankers in turn needed cash and put pressure on brokers to pay back their loans, tightening the vise further. The more obligations went unmet, the more the system tottered; inevitably, banks and investment companies collapsed.

International economic troubles also contributed to the crash and depression. As the world's leading creditor and trader, the United States was

International Economic Troubles

tightly tied to the world economy. Billions of dollars in loans had flowed to Europe during the First World War and during postwar reconstruction. By the late 1920s, however, American

investors were keeping their money at home, to invest it in the more lucrative United States stock market. Europeans, unable to borrow more funds and unable to sell their goods easily in the American market because of high tariffs, began to buy less from the United States and to default on the crippling debts left over from the First World War. Pinched at home, they raised their own tariffs, further disabling international commerce, and withdrew their investments from America. Reacting to the collapse of European economies, Hoover complained that "the European disease had contaminated the United States." He would have been more accurate had he said that the European and American illnesses were mutually infectious.

Government policies also contributed to the crash and depression. The federal government failed to regulate wild speculation, contenting itself with occasionally scolding bankers and

Failure of Federal Policies

businesspeople. The Federal Reserve Board pursued easy credit policies before the crash, charging low discount rates (interest rates on its loans to member banks) even though easy money was financing the speculative mania.

Partly because of optimism and partly because of the relatively undeveloped state of economic analysis, neither the experts nor people on the street realized in 1929 what factors had brought on the depression. Conventional wisdom, based on the experience of previous depressions, held that little could be done to correct economic problems—they simply had to run their course. So in 1929 people waited for the deflation to bottom out, never realizing that the era of expansion and frivolity had come to an end and that society and politics, as well as the economy, would have to be rebuilt.

Conclusion

The onset of the Great Depression revealed with brutal clarity how many of the characteristics of the 1920s had been consequences of prosperity. The decade's consumerism, preoccupation with leisure and entertainment, tendency toward freewheeling behavior, celebration of the automobile, and suburbanization all resulted from higher incomes and shorter workdays. And when the bubble of prosperity broke, these new habits were all the more difficult to modify.

Beneath the "era of excess" lurked two other important phenomena. One was the continued resurfacing of prejudice and intolerance that had long tainted the American dream. As disaffected prohibitionists, Klansmen, and immigration restrictionists made their voices heard, they encouraged discrimination against racial minorities and slurs against supposed "inferior" ethnic groups. Meanwhile, however, the distinguishing forces of twentieth-century life—technological change, bureaucratization, and the growth of the middle class—accelerated, making the decade truly a "new era." Both phenomena would recur as major themes in the nation's history for the rest of the twentieth century.

Suggestions for Further Reading

Overviews of the 1920s

William E. Akin, *Technocracy and the American Dream* (1977); Frederick Lewis Allen, *Only Yesterday* (1931); Paul A. Carter, *Another Part of the Twenties* (1977); Lynn Dumenil, *Modern Temper* (1995); William E. Leuchtenburg, *The Perils of Prosperity* (1958); Robert Lynd and Helen Lynd, *Middletown* (1929); Donald R. McCoy, *Coming of Age* (1973).

Business and the Economy

William W. Barber, *Herbert Hoover, the Economists, and American Economic Policy, 1921–1933* (1986); Irving L. Bernstein, *The Lean Years: A History of the American Worker, 1920–1933* (1960); Morton Keller, *Regulating a New Economy* (1990); David Montgomery, *The Fall of the House of Labor* (1987); Allan Nevins, *Ford*, 2 vols. (1954–1957); Emily Rosenberg, *Spreading the American Dream* (1982).

Politics and Law

Christine Bolt, *American Indian Policy and American Reform* (1987); Paula Eldot, *Governor Alfred E. Smith: The Politician as Reformer* (1983); Allan J. Lichtman, *Prejudice and the Old Politics: The Presidential Election of 1928* (1979); Alpheus Mason, *The Supreme Court from Taft to Warren* (1958); Donald R. McCoy, *Calvin Coolidge* (1967); Robert K. Murray, *The Politics of Normalcy* (1973); George Tindall, *The Emergence of the New South* (1967); James Weinstein, *The Decline of Socialism in America, 1912–1925* (1967); Joan Hoff Wilson, *Herbert Hoover: The Forgotten Progressive* (1975).

African-Americans, Asians, and Hispanics

Rodolfo Acuna, *Occupied America: A History of Chicanos* (1980); Roger Daniels, *Asian America* (1988); James R. Grossman, *Land of Hope* (1989); Jacquelyn Jones, *Labor of Love, Labor of Sorrow* (1985); Kenneth Kusmer, *A Ghetto Takes Shape* (1976); Gilbert Osofsky, *Harlem: The Making of a Ghetto* (1965); Ricardo Romo, *East Los Angeles: History of a Barrio* (1983); Judith Stein, *The World of Marcus Garvey* (1986); Ronald Takaki, *Strangers from a Different Shore* (1989).

Women, Family, and Lifestyles

W. Andrew Achenbaum, *Shades of Gray: Old Age, American Values, and Federal Policies Since 1920* (1983); Dorothy M. Brown, *Setting a Course: American Women in the 1920s* (1987); George Chauncey, *Gay New York* (1995); Howard P. Chudacoff, *How Old Are You? Age in American Culture* (1989); Nancy F. Cott, *The Grounding of Modern Feminism* (1987); John D'Emilio and Estelle B. Freedman, *Intimate Matters: A History of Sexuality in America* (1988); Elizabeth Ewen, *Immigrant Women in the Land of Dollars* (1985); Lillian Faderman, *Odd Girls and Twilight Lovers* (1991); Linda Gordon, *Woman's Body, Woman's Right: A Social History of Birth Control in America* (1976); J. Stanley Lemons, *The Woman Citizen: Social Feminism in the 1920s* (1973); Lois Scharf, *To Work and to Wed* (1980); Susan Strasser, *Never Done: A History of American Housework* (1982); Winifred D. Wandersee, *Women's Work and Family Values, 1920–1940* (1981).

Lines of Defense

Paul Avrich, *Sacco and Vanzetti* (1991); Edith L. Blumhofer, *Aimee Semple McPherson* (1993); Joseph R. Gusfeld, *Symbolic Crusade* (1963); John Higham, *Strangers in the Land: Patterns of American Nativism* (1955); Kenneth T. Jackson, *The Ku Klux Klan and the City* (1967); George M. Marsden, *Fundamentalism and American Culture* (1980); Leonard J. Moore, *Citizen Klansmen* (1991).

Mass Culture

Stanley Coben, *Rebellion Against Victorianism* (1991); Robert Creamer, *Babe* (1974); Kenneth S. Davis, *The Hero, Charles A. Lindbergh* (1959); Susan J. Douglas, *Inventing American Broadcasting* (1987); Paula Fass, *The Damned and the Beautiful: American Youth in the 1920s* (1977); James J. Flink, *The Car Culture* (1975); Richard Wightman Fox and T. Jackson Lears, eds., *The Culture of Consumption* (1983); William R. Leach, *Land of Desire* (1993); Harvey J. Levenstein, *Revolution at the Table: The Transformation of the American Diet* (1988); Roland Marchand, *Advertising the American Dream* (1985); Randy Roberts, *Jack Dempsey, the Manassa Mauler* (1979); Robert Sklar, *Movie-made America* (1976); Ronald A. Smith, *Sports and Freedom: The Rise of Big-Time College Athletics* (1988); Susan Smulyan, *Selling Radio* (1994).

Literature and Thought

Mary Campbell, *Harlem Renaissance: Art of Black America* (1987); Robert Crunden, *From Self to Society: Transition in American Thought, 1919–1941* (1972); George H. Douglas, *H. L. Mencken* (1978); Nathan I. Huggins, *Harlem Renaissance* (1971); Gloria T. Hull, *Color, Sex and Poetry: Three Woman Writers of the Harlem Renaissance* (1987); David L. Lewis, *When Harlem Was in Vogue* (1981); Roderick Nash, *The Nervous Generation: American Thought, 1917–1930* (1969); Kenneth M. Wheller and Virginia L. Lussier, eds., *Women and the Arts and the 1920s in Paris and New York* (1982).

Boom and Bust: The Crash

Peter Fearon, *War, Prosperity, and Depression* (1987); John Kenneth Galbraith, *The Great Crash: 1929* (1989); and Robert T. Patterson, *The Great Boom and Panic, 1921–1929* (1965).

CHAPTER

25

The Great Depression and the New Deal
1929–1941

I n late 1937 on a farm near Stigler, Oklahoma, Marvin Montgomery counted up his assets: $53 and a car—a 1929 Hudson that he had just bought to take himself, his wife, and four children to California. Times in Oklahoma had been tough for Montgomery's family. Like other farm families on the plains, Marvin explained, they had suffered "under the farming conditions, you know, the drought and such as that, it just got so hard, such a hard get-by, I decided it would help me to change countries." Farm families were being dislodged from their homes by the combined disasters of soil exhaustion, drought, and dust storms. In addition, tractors were replacing the labor of men, women, and children in the cotton fields; and farm policies under the New Deal of President Franklin D. Roosevelt often benefited landowners at the expense of tenant farmers and sharecroppers, tens of thousands of whom were "tractored out" and evicted during the 1930s.

Marvin Montgomery believed that he could have held out. "I might have drug by like some of the rest of them," he said, "and sort of lived." But he wanted more than that. Above all, he wanted work. At the same time, circulars and newspaper advertisements held out the promise of jobs aplenty in the fields of California. Dispossessed, as many as 400,000 people decided to make the westward trek. Some of the migrants were from Arkansas, Texas, Missouri, and Kansas, but more came from Oklahoma than from any other state. Among them were Montgomery and his wife and children, who, on December 29, climbed into the rickety Hudson, which was filled with furniture, bedding, and pots and pans. "I had that old car loaded to the full capacity," Marvin acknowledged, "on top, the sides, and everywhere else." Traveling west

Sharecropper, an oil painting by Jerry Bywaters, shows one of the major problems facing farmers on the southern plains in the 1930s: grasshoppers, which along with drought and dust storms ravaged crops in Oklahoma, Kansas, and other states. *Dallas Museum of Art, Allied Arts Civic Prize, Eighth Annual Dallas Arts Exhibition.*

on Route 66, the Montgomerys left Oklahoma for California.

There was never any doubt that the Montgomery family's destination would be California, where their married daughter and oldest son had already moved. "Yes, sir. I knew right where I was coming to," Marvin Montgomery told a congressional committee which in 1940 held hearings in a migratory labor camp in California's San Joaquin valley. But for the Montgomerys the trip was not easy. For one thing, the Hudson proved to be both unreliable and expensive. "On the way, you know my car," Marvin explained, "I got to where I had to blindfold it to get it past a filling station. It was taking on lots of gas and oil." The car also broke down twice. While they were crossing Arizona, their money ran out, and the family had to stop to work in the cotton fields for five weeks before they could afford to resume the trip. And once in California, Marvin said, there was little work: "Well, I hoed beets some; hoed some cotton, and I picked some spuds."

Their dream in coming to California was that one day they would have a home and some land of their own; but they knew that low-paid farm work would never enable them to embrace this dream. In the meantime, though, the Montgomerys were relieved to be able to live in the housing for farm workers provided by the federal government through the Farm Security Administration (FSA). The FSA camp at Shafter in Kern County had 240 tents and forty two-room houses. For nine months the Montgomery family of six lived in a tent 14 by 16 feet, which rented for 10 cents a day plus four hours of volunteer labor a month. Then they proudly moved into an FSA house, "with water, lights, and everything, yes sir; and a little garden spot furnished."

What did the future hold for the Montgomerys? Marvin conceded that he was homesick for Oklahoma and "would rather be back on the farm, if you want to know." But his seventeen-year-old son Harvey saw a future for himself in California. When asked whether he wanted to return to Oklahoma, he said: "I like California. . . . No. I would rather stay out here." And soon there were bountiful employment opportunities in California not only for the Montgomery family but for many other newcomers, in aircraft factories and shipyards mobilizing for the Second World War.

Statistics suggest the magnitude of the Great Depression's human tragedy. Between 1929 and 1933, a hundred thousand businesses failed, corporate profits fell from $10 billion to $1 billion, and

the gross national product was cut in half. Banks failed by the thousands. Americans who believed that saving was a virtue discovered that their deposits had disappeared with the banks. Americans lost jobs as well as savings. Thousands of men and women received severance slips every day. At the beginning of 1930 the number of jobless reached at least 4 million; by November it had jumped to 6 million. When President Herbert Hoover left office in 1933, about one-fourth of the labor force was idle— 13 million workers—and millions more were underemployed, working only part-time. Unemployment strained relations within the family. African-Americans and other minorities sank deeper into destitution. Overall, the economic catastrophe aggravated old tensions: labor versus capital, white versus black, male versus female.

Elected amid prosperity and optimism, Herbert Hoover spent the years from late 1929 to his departure from office in early 1933 presiding over a gloomy and sometimes angry nation. The president appeared cold and indifferent to Americans' suffering. Although he activated more of the federal government's resources than had any of his predecessors in an economic crisis, he opposed direct relief payments for the unemployed. When Hoover refused to take measures strong enough to relieve people's hardships, voters turned him out of office in 1932. His successor in the White House was Franklin D. Roosevelt, the governor of New York, who promised vigorous action and projected hope in a time of despair.

From the first days of his presidency, Roosevelt displayed a buoyancy and willingness to experiment that helped to restore public confidence in the government and the economy. He acted not only to reform the banks and securities exchanges but also to provide central planning for industry and agriculture and direct government relief for the jobless. This sweeping emergency legislation was based on the concept of "pump priming," or deficit financing, to stimulate consumer buying power, business and industrial activity, and employment by pouring billions of federal dollars into the economy. Although Roosevelt's New Deal was opposed from both the left and the right, ultimately he prevailed, vastly expanding the scope of the federal government and the popularity of the Democratic Party, and in the process establishing America's welfare system.

During these years several million workers seized the chance to organize for better wages and working conditions. The new Congress of Industrial

• *Important Events* •

1929	Stock market crash (Oct.); Great Depression begins
	Agricultural Marketing Act establishes Federal Farm Board to support crop prices
1930	Hawley-Smoot Tariff raises rates on imports
1931	Nine African-American men arrested in Scottsboro affair
	President Herbert Hoover declares moratorium on First World War debts and reparations
1932	Reconstruction Finance Corporation established to make loans to banks, insurance companies, and railroads
	Bonus Expeditionary Force marches on Washington
	Franklin D. Roosevelt elected president
	Revenue Act raises corporate, excise, and personal income taxes
1933	13 million Americans unemployed
	National bank holiday suspends banking activities
	Agricultural Adjustment Act encourages decreased farm production
	Civilian Conservation Corps provides jobs to young men
	Tennessee Valley Authority established
	Banking Act creates Federal Deposit Insurance Corporation
	National Industrial Recovery Act attempts to spur industrial growth
	Twentieth (Lame Duck) Amendment sets presidential inaugurations at January 20
	Twenty-first Amendment repeals Eighteenth (Prohibition) Amendment
1934	Francis E. Townsend devises Old Age Revolving Pensions plan
	Huey Long starts Share Our Wealth Society
	Indian Reorganization (Wheeler-Howard) Act restores lands to tribal ownership
	Taylor Grazing Act closes grasslands to further settlement
	Democrats win victories in congressional elections
1935	Emergency Relief Appropriation Act authorizes establishment of public works programs
	Works Progress Administration creates jobs in public works projects

	Schechter v. *U.S.* invalidates NIRA
	National Labor Relations (Wagner) Act grants workers the right to unionize
	Social Security Act establishes insurance for the aged, the unemployed, and needy children
	Committee for Industrial Organization (CIO) established
	Congress passes Public Utility Holding Company Act
	Revenue (Wealth Tax) Act raises taxes on business and the wealthy
1936	9 million Americans unemployed
	U.S. v. *Butler* invalidates AAA
	Roosevelt defeats Alf Landon
	United Auto Workers hold sit-down strike against General Motors
1937	Roosevelt's court-packing plan fails
	NLRB v. *Jones & Laughlin* upholds Wagner Act
	Memorial Day Massacre of striking steelworkers
	Farm Security Administration established to aid farm workers
	National Housing Act establishes United States Housing Authority
1937–39	Business recession
1938	10.4 million Americans unemployed
	AFL expels CIO unions
	Fair Labor Standards Act establishes minimum wage
1939	Marian Anderson performs at Lincoln Memorial
	Social Security amendments add benefits for spouses and widows
1940	Roosevelt defeats Wendell Willkie
1941	African-Americans threaten to march on Washington to protest unequal access to defense jobs
	Fair Employment Practices Committee prohibits discrimination in war industries and government

Organizations (CIO) established unions in the automobile, steel, meatpacking, and other major industries. Blacks registered political and economic gains, too, though they benefited less from the New Deal than did whites. Two-and-a-half million additional women workers joined the labor force during the 1930s. But female workers were segregated in low-income jobs, and New Deal legislation excluded many women from Social Security coverage and minimum-wage protection.

The New Deal was not a revolution, but it transformed the United States. The elderly and disabled still collect Social Security payments. The Federal Deposit Insurance Corporation still insures bank deposits. The Securities and Exchange Commission still monitors the stock exchanges. But the New Deal did not accomplish one of its goals—putting back to work all the people who wanted jobs. That would await the nation's entry into the Second World War in 1941.

Hoover and Hard Times: America's Worsening Depression, 1929–1933

As the Great Depression deepened in the early 1930s, its underlying causes—principally overproduction and underconsumption—grew in severity.

Causes of the Deepening Depression

So too did instability in the banking industry. What happened to America's banks illustrates the cascading nature of the depression. Banks tied into the stock market or foreign investments were badly weakened. When nervous Americans made runs on banks to salvage their threatened savings, a powerful momentum—panic—set in. In 1929, 659 banks folded; in 1930 the number of failures more than doubled to 1,350. The Federal Reserve Board blundered after the crash, drastically raising interest rates and thus tightening the money market when just the opposite was needed: loosening to spur borrowing and spending. In 1931, 2,293 banks shut their doors, and another 1,453 ceased to do business in 1932.

As unemployment soared in the early 1930s, people's fortunes hit bottom. In Detroit, auto workers roamed from plant to plant only to find padlocked gates. Both women and men suffered homelessness. Hundreds of women were sleeping nightly in Chicago's parks. "No fewer than 200 women are sleeping in Grant and Lincoln Parks, on the lake front," reported the city's commissioner of public welfare in 1931. In 1932 a squad of New York City police officers arrested twenty-five men in "Hoover Valley," the shantytown they had constructed in the bed of an old reservoir in Central Park. Twelve shacks made of everything from egg crates to discarded boards and bricks were built in a row called "Depression Street." Shantytowns sprouted up throughout the country.

During these years people's diets deteriorated, malnutrition became common, and the undernourished frequently fell victim to disease. Some people

Deterioration of Health

quietly lined up at Red Cross and Salvation Army soup kitchens or in breadlines. Others ate only potatoes, crackers, or dandelions or scratched through garbage cans for bits of food. Millions of Americans were not only hungry and ill; they were cold. Unable to afford fuel, they huddled in unheated tenements and shacks. Families doubled up in crowded apartments, and those unable to pay the rent were evicted, furniture and all.

In the countryside, hobbled long before the depression struck, economic hardship deepened. Between 1929 and 1933 farm prices dropped 60

Plight of the Farmers

percent. At the same time, production decreased only 6 percent as individual farmers tried to make up for lower prices by producing more, thus adding to the surplus and depressing prices even further. The surplus could not be exported because foreign demand had shrunk. Drought, foreclosure, clouds of hungry grasshoppers, and bank failures also plagued American farmers. Some became transients in search of jobs or food, while others jumped aboard freight trains to seek salvation elsewhere.

Economic woe also affected marriage patterns and family life. People postponed marriage, and married couples postponed having children. Families were beset in other ways as well. Out-of-work fathers felt ashamed of their diminished role. "A child who was playing irritated him," recalled the son of an unemployed tool-and-die maker. "It wasn't just my own father. They all got shook up." Divorces declined, but desertions rose as husbands unable to provide for their families simply took off.

Plagued by dust storms and evictions, thousands of tenant farmers and sharecroppers were forced to leave their land during the Great Depression. Known as "Okies" and "Arkies," they took off for California with their few belongings. These refugees from drought-stricken Oklahoma experienced car trouble and were stalled on a New Mexico highway.   Library of Congress.

Most Americans met the crisis not with protest or violence but with bewilderment and an inability to fix the blame. They scorned businesspeople and bankers, of course, but often blamed themselves as well. Some people were angry, though, and scattered protests raised the specter of popular revolt. Farmers in the Midwest prevented evictions and slowed foreclosures on farm properties by harassing sheriffs, judges, and lawyers. They also tried to stop farm produce from reaching the market. In Nebraska, Iowa, and Minnesota, farmers protesting low prices put up barricades of spiked logs and telegraph poles. They stopped trucks, smashed headlights, and dumped milk and vegetables in roadside ditches. Some of these demonstrations were organized by the Farmers' Holiday Association, whose leader, Milo Reno, encouraged farmers to take a holiday—a farm strike that would

Farmers' Holiday Association

keep their products off the market until they commanded a better price.

Isolated protests also sounded in cities and in mining regions. In Chicago, Los Angeles, and Philadelphia, the unemployed marched on city halls. In Harlan County, Kentucky, when miners struck against wage reductions, mine owners responded with strikebreakers, bombs, the National Guard, the closing of relief kitchens, and evictions from company-owned housing.

The most spectacular confrontation shook Washington, D.C., in the summer of 1932. Congress was considering a bill to authorize immediate issuance of $2.4 billion in bonuses already allotted to First World War veterans but not due for payment until 1945. To lobby for the bill, fifteen thousand unemployed veterans and their families converged on the tense nation's capital, calling

Bonus Expeditionary Force

themselves the Bonus Expeditionary Force (BEF), or "Bonus Army," and camping on vacant lots and in empty government buildings. President Hoover threw his weight against the bonus bill, and after much debate the Senate voted it down. One bonus marcher shouted: "We were heroes in 1917, but we're bums today." Much of the BEF left Washington, but several thousand stayed on during the summer. Hoover carelessly labeled them "insurrectionists" and refused to meet with them. Then in July, General Douglas MacArthur, assisted by Major Dwight D. Eisenhower and Major George S. Patton, confronted the veterans and their families with cavalry, tanks, and bayonet-bearing soldiers. The BEF hurled back stones and bricks. What followed shocked the nation. Men and women were chased down by horsemen; children were tear-gassed; shacks were set afire. When presidential hopeful Franklin D. Roosevelt heard about the attack on the Bonus Army, he turned to his friend Felix Frankfurter and remarked: "Well, Felix, this will elect me."

With capitalism on its knees, American Communists in various parts of the nation organized "unemployment councils" to raise class consciousness and agitate for jobs and food. In 1930 they led urban demonstrations, some of which ended in violent clashes with local police, and in 1931 they led a hunger march on Washington, D.C. The Communists' tangles with authority publicized the human tragedy of the depression. Still, total party membership in 1932 remained small at twelve thousand. The Socialist Party, which took issue with both capitalists and Communists, fared better. More reformist than radical, the Socialists ran well in municipal elections after the stock market crash but scored few victories. Indeed, few Americans looked to left-wing doctrines, protest marches, or violence for relief from their misery. Americans were frightened, and they were angry, but they were not revolutionaries. They turned instead to their local, state, and federal governments.

Communist Party

But when urgent daily appeals for government relief for the jobless reached the White House, Hoover at first became defensive, if not hostile, rejecting direct relief in the belief that it would undermine character and individualism. To a growing number of Americans, Hoover seemed heartless and inflexible. True to his beliefs, the president urged people to help themselves and their neighbors. He applauded private voluntary relief through charitable agencies. Yet when the need was greatest, donations declined. State and urban officials found their treasuries drying up, too. Meanwhile, those calling for federal aid got no sympathy from Secretary of the Treasury Andrew Mellon, who believed that business cycles of boom and bust were not only inevitable but desirable. He advised Hoover to "let the slump liquidate itself. Liquidate labor, liquidate stocks, liquidate the farmers, liquidate real estate. . . . It will purge the rottenness out of the system."

As the depression intensified, Hoover's opposition to federal action gradually diminished. He rejected Mellon's insensitive counsel, hesitantly energizing the White House and federal agencies to take action—more action than the government had taken before. He won pledges from business and labor leaders to maintain wages and production and to avoid strikes. He urged state governors to increase their expenditures on public works. And he created the President's Organization on Unemployment Relief (POUR) to generate private contributions for relief of the destitute.

Hoover's Antidepression Remedies

Though POUR proved ineffective, Hoover's spurring of federal public works projects (including Hoover and Grand Coulee Dams) did provide some jobs. Help also came from the Federal Farm Board, created under the Agricultural Marketing Act of 1929, which supported crop prices by lending money to cooperatives to buy products and keep them off the market. But the board soon found itself short of money, and unsold surplus commodities jammed warehouses. To retard the collapse of the international monetary system, Hoover in 1931 announced a moratorium on the payment of First World War debts and reparations.

The president also asked Congress to charter the Reconstruction Finance Corporation (RFC). Created in 1932 and eventually empowered with $2 billion, the RFC was designed to make loans to banks, insurance companies, and railroads and later to state and local governments. In theory, the RFC would lend money to large entities at the top of the economic system, and benefits would filter down to people at the bottom. It did not work; banks continued to collapse and small companies went into bankruptcy.

Reconstruction Finance Corporation

Despite warnings from prominent economists, Hoover also signed into law the Hawley-Smoot Tariff (1930). A congressional compromise serving special interests, the tariff raised duties by about one-third. Hoover argued that the tariff would help farmers and manufacturers by keeping foreign goods off the market. Actually, the tariff further weakened the economy by making it even more difficult for foreign nations to sell their products and thus to earn dollars to buy American products.

Hawley-Smoot Tariff

Like most of his contemporaries, Hoover believed that a balanced budget was sacred and deficit spending sinful. In 1931 he therefore appealed for a decrease in federal expenditures and an increase in taxes. The following year he supported a sales tax on manufactured goods. The sales tax was defeated, but the Revenue Act of 1932 raised corporate, excise, and personal income taxes. Hoover seemed tangled in a contradiction: he urged people to spend to spur recovery, but his tax policies deprived them of spending money. Nor did he ever balance the budget.

Although Hoover expanded public works projects and approved loans to some institutions, he vetoed a variety of relief bills presented to him by the Congress. In rejecting a public power project for the Tennessee River, he argued that its inexpensive electricity would compete with power from private companies. Hoover's traditionalism also was well demonstrated by his handling of prohibition. Despite the Eighteenth Amendment, Americans were producing and drinking liquor with grand illegality and hypocrisy. Although the law was not and could not be enforced, Hoover resisted mounting public pressure for repeal. Opponents of prohibition argued not only that it encouraged crime but also that its repeal would stimulate economic recovery by reviving the nation's breweries and distilleries. But the president refused to tamper with the Constitution; he declared that the liquor industry, having no socially redemptive value, was best left depressed. After Hoover left office in 1933, prohibition was repealed through ratification of the Twenty-first Amendment.

Hoover's Traditionalism

Still, President Hoover stretched governmental activism as far as he thought he could without violating his cherished principles. Because he mobilized the resources of the federal government as never before, some historians have depicted him as a bridge to the New Deal of the 1930s. If nothing else, he prepared the way for massive federal activity by giving private enterprise the opportunity to solve the depression—and to fail in the attempt.

 ## Franklin D. Roosevelt and the Election of 1932

Herbert Hoover and the Republican Party faced dreary prospects in 1932. The president kept blaming international events for the economic crisis, but Americans were less concerned with abstract explanations than with tomorrow's meal. He grumbled and grew impatient with his critics. But what soured public opinion most was that Hoover did not offer leadership when the times required it. So unpopular had he become by 1932 that Republicans who did not want to be associated with a loser ran independent campaigns.

Franklin D. Roosevelt enjoyed quite a different reputation. Though born into the upper class of old money and privilege, the smiling, ingratiating governor of New York appealed to people of all classes, races, and regions, and he shared the American penchant for optimism. After serving as assistant secretary of the navy under Woodrow Wilson and running as the Democratic Party's vice-presidential candidate in 1920, Roosevelt was stricken with polio and left totally paralyzed in both legs. What should Roosevelt do next? Should he retire from public life, a rich invalid? His answer and his wife Eleanor's was "no." Throughout the 1920s the Roosevelts contended with his handicap. Rejecting self-pity, Franklin Roosevelt worked to rebuild his body. Friends commented that his fight against polio had given him new moral and physical strength. As Roosevelt explained it: "If you had spent two years in bed trying to wiggle your big toe, after that anything would seem easy."

Franklin D. Roosevelt

For her part, Eleanor Roosevelt—who had grown up shy and sheltered—launched her own career in public life. In her memoirs, she described having changed in the 1920s from a depressed, isolated person into an independent woman with significant political commitments and personal relationships in her life. Eleanor Roosevelt worked hard to become an effective public speaker and participated in the activities of the League of Women Voters, the Women's Trade Union League, and the Democratic Party. In a short time, she became the leading figure

Eleanor Roosevelt

In November 1930 Franklin D. Roosevelt (1882–1945) read the good news. Reelected governor of New York by 735,000 votes, he immediately became a leading contender for the Democratic presidential nomination. Notice Roosevelt's leg braces, rarely shown in photographs because of an unwritten agreement by photographers to shoot him from the waist up. Corbis-Bettmann.

in a network of feminist activists. She became deeply committed to equal opportunity for women and for African-Americans and wanted to alleviate the suffering of the poor. On these issues, she served as her husband's conscience.

Roosevelt was elected governor of New York in 1928 and reelected in 1930; his terms coincided with Hoover's presidency. But whereas Hoover appeared hardhearted and unwilling to help the jobless, Roosevelt seemed quite the opposite. He supported direct relief payments for the unemployed, declaring that such aid "must be extended by Government, not as a matter of charity, but as a matter of social duty." As governor of New York, Roosevelt created jobs in publicly funded reforestation, land-reclamation, and hydroelectric-power projects, and he endorsed old-age pensions and protective legislation for labor unions. With his record, Roosevelt became an obvious prospect for the 1932 Democratic presidential nomination.

Roosevelt as Governor of New York

To prepare a national political platform, Roosevelt surrounded himself with a "Brain Trust" of lawyers and university professors. These experts reasoned that bigness was unavoidable in the modern American economy. It thus followed that the cure for the nation's ills was not to go on a rampage of trust-busting but to place large corporations, monopolies, and oligopolies under effective government regulation. "We are no longer afraid of bigness," declared Columbia University professor Rexford G. Tugwell.

Roosevelt's "Brain Trust"

Roosevelt and his Brain Trust also agreed that it was essential to restore purchasing power to farmers, blue-collar workers, and the middle classes, and that the way to do so was to cut production. If demand for a product remained constant and the supply were cut, they reasoned, the price would rise. Producers would make higher profits, and workers would earn more. This method of combating a depression has been called "the economics of scarcity," which the Brain Trust at the time saw as the preferred alternative to deficit spending, or pump priming, in which the government borrowed money to prime the economic pump and thereby revive purchasing power.

Roosevelt and Hoover both campaigned as fiscal conservatives committed to a balanced budget. But Roosevelt, unlike Hoover, also advocated immediate and direct relief to the unemployed. And Roosevelt demanded that the federal government engage in centralized economic planning and experimentation to bring about recovery.

Upon accepting the Democratic nomination, Roosevelt called for a "new deal for the American people." The two party platforms differed little, but

1932 Election Results

the Democrats were willing to abandon prohibition and to launch federal relief. More people went to the polls in 1932 than in any election since the First World War. In a crisis-ridden moment, Americans followed their traditional pattern and exchanged one government for another. The presidential election of 1932 was never much of a contest: Roosevelt's 22.8 million popular votes far outdistanced Hoover's 15.8 million; Roosevelt won forty-two states to Hoover's six (see map). Cities continued the trend, begun in 1928, of voting Democratic. Democrats also won overwhelming control of the Senate and the House.

Once elected, Roosevelt had to wait until his inauguration on March 4, 1933, to act. (To eliminate similar losses of time, the Twentieth Amendment to the Constitution—the Lame Duck Amendment, ratified in 1933—shifted all future inaugurations to January 20.) It was a troubled four months. Millions of jobless Americans walked the streets; prices for agricultural and manufactured goods continued to plummet; industrial production sank to new depths. And throughout the United States, depositors lined up in front of banks to withdraw their savings. Banks with insufficient funds on hand to pay depositors had to close their doors and declare themselves insolvent. In February, Michigan and Maryland suspended banking operations, and by early March thirty-six other states, including New York, had declared bank holidays.

On March 2, 1933, President-elect Roosevelt and his family and friends boarded a train for Washington, D.C., and the inauguration ceremony. Roosevelt was carrying with him rough drafts of two presidential proclamations, one summoning a special session of Congress, the other declaring a national bank holiday, suspending banking transactions throughout the nation.

Launching the New Deal and Restoring Confidence

"First of all," declared the newly inaugurated president, "let me assert my firm belief that the only

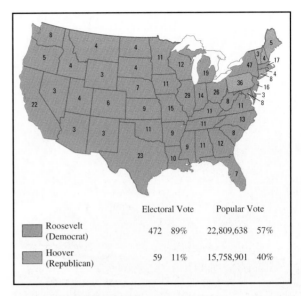

	Electoral Vote		Popular Vote	
Roosevelt (Democrat)	472	89%	22,809,638	57%
Hoover (Republican)	59	11%	15,758,901	40%

Presidential Election, 1932 *One factor above all decided the 1932 presidential election: the Great Depression. Roosevelt won forty-two states, Hoover six.*

thing we have to fear is fear itself—nameless, unreasoning, unjustified terror." In his inaugural address Roosevelt scored his first triumph as president, instilling hope and courage in the rank and file. He invoked "the analogue of war," asserting that, if need be, "I shall ask the Congress for the one remaining instrument to meet the crisis—broad Executive power to wage a war against the emergency, as great as the power that would be given to me if we were in fact invaded by a foreign foe."

The next day, Roosevelt declared a four-day national bank holiday and summoned Congress to an emergency session. Congress convened on March 9

Launching the First New Deal

to launch what observers later called the First Hundred Days. This marked the beginning of the vast legislative output of 1933 and 1934, which historians call the First New Deal. Roosevelt's first measure, the Emergency Banking Relief Bill, was introduced on March 9, passed sight unseen by unanimous House vote, approved 73 to 7 in the Senate, and signed into law by the president that evening. The new law provided for the reopening, under Treasury Department license, of banks that were solvent and for the reorganization and management of those that were not. It also prohibited the hoarding and export of gold. It was, however, a fundamentally conservative law that upheld the status quo and left the same bankers in charge.

A gloomy Hoover and a buoyant Roosevelt ride to the inaugura-tion in 1933. This magazine cover was never published, appar-ently because the editors of The New Yorker *thought it inap-propriate after an assassination attempt on the president-elect just three weeks before.* Franklin D. Roosevelt Library.

On the next day, March 10, the second bill of the New Deal was introduced in Congress. It too was conservative, and ten days later it became law. Called the Economy Act, its purpose was to balance the budget by chopping veterans' benefits and al-lowances and reducing the pay of federal employees. Under Roosevelt, the budget balancers had won a battle that could not have been won under Hoover.

On March 12, a Sunday evening, the president broadcast the first of his "fireside chats," and 60 mil-lion people heard his comforting voice on their

First Fireside Chat

radios. His message: banks were once again safe places for de-positors' savings. On Monday morning the banks opened their doors, but instead of queuing up to withdraw their savings, people were waiting out-side to deposit their money. The bank runs were

over; Roosevelt had reestablished people's confi-dence in their political leadership, their banks, even their economic system.

Roosevelt next pursued a measure, the Beer-Wine Revenue Bill, that was deflationary because it would actually take money out of people's pockets. The bill would generate revenues by legalizing the sale of low-alcohol wines and beers and levying a tax on them. (Congress had proposed repeal of Prohibi-tion in February 1933 in the Twenty-first Amend-ment, and the states ratified it by December 1933.) To many, levying new taxes seemed a strange way to restore purchasing power to people who could not afford to buy what they needed. Roosevelt knew that, but he predicted the situation would change. "It is simply inevitable," he wrote a friend, "that we must inflate." He added that his "banker friends may be horrified" by the large-scale federal spending that was to come.

In mid-March Roosevelt sent to Congress the Agricultural Adjustment Bill to restore farmers' pur-chasing power. If overproduction was the cause

Agricultural Adjustment Act

of farmers' problems—falling prices and mounting surpluses— then the government had to en-courage farmers to grow less food. Under the domestic allot-ment plan, the government would pay farmers to re-duce their acreage or plow under crops already in the fields. Farmers would receive payments based on *parity*, a system of regulated prices for corn, cotton, wheat, rice, hogs, and dairy products that would provide them the same purchasing power they had had during the prosperous period of 1909 to 1914. In effect, the government was making up the differ-ence between the actual market value of farm prod-ucts and the income that farmers needed to make a profit. The subsidies would be funded by taxes levied on the processors of agricultural commodities.

Roosevelt's farm plan immediately encountered vehement opposition. How could there be crop surpluses when some Americans were hungry and even starving? Underconsumption, people argued, was the result of a maldistribution of incomes and wealth. Some politicians wanted to put more money into circulation by coining silver or printing green-backs. Cheap money, they contended, would make it easier for farmers to repay their debts. On May 12, Congress finally overcame opposition to the domes-tic allotment plan and passed the Agricultural Ad-justment Act (AAA). A month later the Farm Credit Act was passed, providing short- and medium-term loans that enabled many farmers to refinance their mortgages and hang onto their homes and land. Another New Deal measure assisted homeowners in the towns and cities; the Home Owners Refinancing Act provided $2 billion in bonds to refinance non-farm home mortgages.

Meanwhile, other relief measures became law. On March 21 the president requested three kinds of massive relief: a job corps called the Civilian Con-

Civilian Conservation Corps

servation Corps (CCC), direct cash grants to the states for relief payments to needy citizens, and public works projects. Ten days later Congress approved the CCC, which ultimately put 2.5 million young men aged eighteen to twenty-five to work planting trees, clearing camping areas and beaches, and building bridges, dams, reservoirs, fish ponds, and fire towers. Then on May 12, Congress passed the Federal Emergency Relief Act, which authorized $500 million in aid to state and local governments.

Roosevelt's proposed plan for public works became Title II of the National Industrial Recovery Act. Passed on June 16, the act established the Public Works Administration (PWA) and appropriated $3.3 billion for hiring the unemployed to build roads, sewage and water systems, public buildings, ships, naval aircraft, and a host of other projects. These were worthwhile projects, but the key purpose of the PWA was to prime the economic pump to spur recovery.

If the AAA was the agricultural cornerstone of the New Deal, the National Industrial Recovery Act was the industrial cornerstone. The act, which es-

National Recovery Administration

tablished the National Recovery Administration (NRA), was a testimony to the New Deal belief in national planning as opposed to an individualistic, intensely competitive, laissez-faire economy. It was essential, planners argued, for businesses to end cutthroat competition and raise prices by limiting production. Under NRA auspices, competing businesses met with representatives of workers and consumers to draft codes of fair competition, which limited production and established prices. With businesses enjoying new concessions, workers wanted a share of the pie, too. Congress responded with Section 7(a) of the National Industrial Recovery Act, which guaranteed their right to unionize and to bargain collectively.

The New Deal also strengthened public confidence in the stock exchanges and banks. Roosevelt signed the Federal Securities Act, which compelled brokers to tell the truth about new securities issues, and the Banking Act of 1933, which set up the Federal Deposit Insurance Corporation (FDIC) for insuring bank deposits. During the First Hundred Days, Roosevelt also took the United States off the gold standard, no longer guaranteeing the gold value of the dollar abroad. Freed from the gold standard, the Federal Reserve Board could expand the supply of currency in circulation, thus enabling monetary policy to become another weapon for economic recovery.

Under the Agricultural Adjustment Act, farmers received government payments for not planting crops or for destroying crops they already had planted. Some farmers, however, needed help of a different kind. The Resettlement Administration, established by executive order in 1935, was authorized to resettle destitute farm families from areas of soil erosion, flooding, and stream pollution to homestead communities. This poster was done by Ben Shahn. Library of Congress.

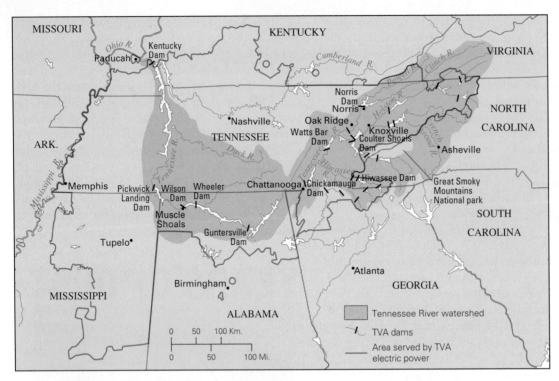

The Tennessee Valley Authority *To control flooding and to generate electricity, the Tennessee Valley Authority constructed dams along the Tennessee River and its tributaries from Paducah, Kentucky, to Knoxville, Tennessee.*

One of the boldest programs enacted by Congress addressed the badly depressed Tennessee River valley, which runs through Tennessee, North Carolina, Kentucky, Virginia, Mississippi, Georgia, and Alabama (see map). For years Progressives had advocated government operation of the Muscle Shoals electric power and nitrogen facilities on the Tennessee River. Roosevelt's Tennessee Valley Authority (TVA), established in May, was a much broader program. Its dams would not only control floods but generate hydroelectric power as well. The TVA also would produce and sell nitrogen fertilizers to private citizens and nitrate explosives to the government; dig a 650-mile navigation channel from Knoxville, Tennessee, to Paducah, Kentucky; and construct public power facilities as a yardstick for determining fair rates for privately produced electric power. The goal of the TVA was nothing less than enhancement of the economic well-being of the entire Tennessee River valley.

The TVA achieved its goals but became—mostly in unforeseen ways—the most notorious polluter in the region. To power its coal-burning generators, the TVA engaged in massive strip mining that caused landslides and soil erosion. The generators also released sulfur oxides, which combined with water vapor to produce acid rain, a poison that not only killed aquatic life and destroyed forests in New England and Canada but also attacked human lungs and promoted heart disease. Above all, the TVA degraded the water by dumping untreated sewage, toxic chemicals, and metal pollutants from strip mining into streams and rivers. The TVA would prove to be a monumental disaster in America's environmental history.

Congress finally adjourned on June 16, 1933. During the First Hundred Days, Roosevelt had delivered fifteen messages to Congress, and fifteen significant laws had been enacted (see table, page 731). Within a few months of Roosevelt's succession to office, the United States had rebounded from hysteria and near collapse. As columnist Walter Lippmann wrote, at the time of the inauguration the

TVA

TVA's Environmental Legacy

End of the First Hundred Days

country was a collection of "disorderly panic-stricken mobs and factions. In the hundred days from March to June we became again an organized nation confident of our power to provide for our own security and to control our own destiny."

Throughout the remainder of 1933 and the spring and summer of 1934, more New Deal bills became law, benefiting farmers, the unemployed, investors, homeowners, workers, and the environment. The Commodity Credit Corporation, organized in 1933, bolstered crop prices by lending farmers money secured by their underpriced crops, thereby al-

Taylor Grazing Act

lowing them to withhold their crops from the market until prices rose. In 1934 additional hundreds of millions of federal dollars were appropriated for unemployment relief and public works. Legislation that year also established the Securities and Exchange Commission, the National Labor Relations Board, and the Federal Housing Administration. In 1934, too, the Taylor Grazing Act was passed. For years, use of the public lands had been largely unregulated, and cattle had caused soil erosion through overgrazing. The Taylor Act, which created the Grazing Service (later to become the Bureau of Land Management), established federal supervision of most of the remaining public domain, and it

New Deal Achievements

Year	Labor	Agriculture	Business and Industrial Recovery	Relief	Reform
1933	Section 7(a) of NIRA	Agricultural Adjustment Act Farm Credit Act	Emergency Banking Relief Act Economy Act Beer–Wine Revenue Act Banking Act of 1933 (guaranteed deposits) National Industrial Recovery Act	Civilian Conservation Corps Federal Emergency Relief Act Home Owners Refinancing Act Public Works Administration Civil Works Administration	TVA Federal Securities Act
1934	National Labor Relations Board				Securities Exchange Act
1935	National Labor Relations (Wagner) Act	Resettlement Administration Rural Electrification Administration		Works Progress Administration National Youth Administration	Social Security Act Public Utility Holding Company Act Revenue Act (wealth tax)
1937		Farm Security Administration		National Housing Act	
1938	Fair Labor Standards Act	Agricultural Adjustment Act of 1938			

Source: Adapted from Charles Sellers, Henry May, and Neil R. McMillen, *A Synopsis of American History*, 6th ed. Copyright © 1985 by Houghton Mifflin Company. Reprinted by permission.

The Economy Before and After the New Deal, 1929–1941

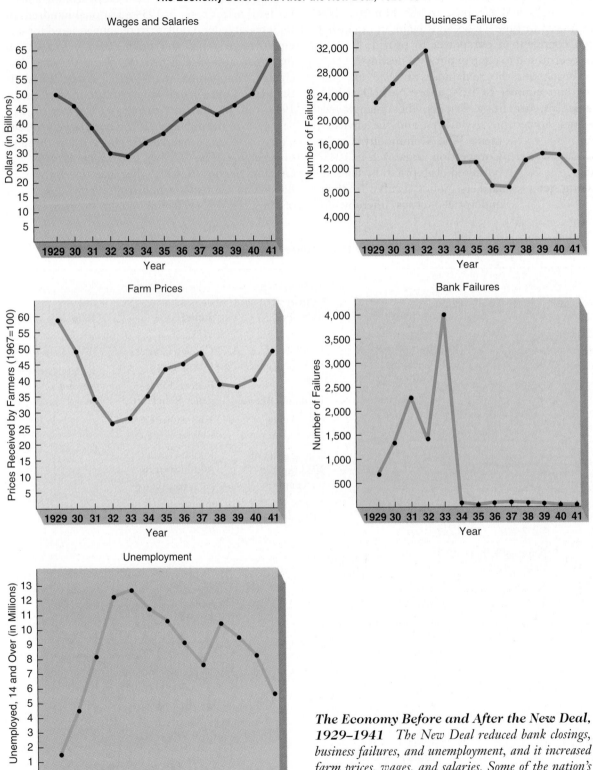

The Economy Before and After the New Deal, 1929–1941 The New Deal reduced bank closings, business failures, and unemployment, and it increased farm prices, wages, and salaries. Some of the nation's most persistent economic problems, however, did not disappear until the advent of the Second World War.

closed 80 million acres of grasslands to further settlement and use.

New Deal legislation seemed to promise something for every group: industrial workers, urban dwellers, landowning farmers, and the jobless, not to mention industrialists, bankers, stockbrokers, educators, and social workers. This was interest-group democracy at work. In the midst of this coalition of special interests was President Roosevelt, the artful broker, who pointed to the economy as proof that this approach was working (see figure, page 732). After the passage of New Deal legislation, unemployment fell steadily from 13 million in 1933 to 9 million in 1936. Net farm income rose from just over $3 billion in 1933 to $5.85 billion in 1935. Manufacturing salaries and wages also increased, from $6.25 billion in 1933 to almost $13 billion in 1937.

Interest-Group Democracy

There was no question about the popularity of either the New Deal or the president during the early years of Roosevelt's presidency. In the 1934 congressional elections, the Democrats gained ten seats in the House and ten in the Senate. The New Deal, according to Arthur Krock of the *New York Times*, had won "the most overwhelming victory in the history of American politics."

Opposition to the First New Deal

There was, however, more than one way to read employment and income statistics and election returns. Although unemployment had dropped from a high of 25 percent in 1933 to 16.9 percent in 1936, it had been only 3.2 percent in 1929. And although manufacturing wages and salaries had reached almost $13 billion in 1937, that figure was less than the total for 1929. Regardless of the New Deal's successes, in other words, it had a long way to go before reaching predepression standards.

With the arrival of partial economic recovery, many businesspeople and conservatives became vocal critics of the New Deal. Some charged that there was too much taxation and government regulation. Others criticized the deficit financing of relief and public works. In 1934, the leaders of several major corporations joined with Al Smith, John W. Davis, and disaffected conservative Demo-

Conservative Critics of the New Deal

crats to establish the American Liberty League. Contending that the New Deal was subverting individual initiative and self-reliance by providing welfare payments, the Liberty League announced that its goal was to abolish welfare and slash taxes.

While businesspeople considered the government their enemy, others thought the government favored business too much. Critics argued that NRA codes favored industry's needs over those of workers and consumers. Farmers, labor unions, and individual entrepreneurs complained that the NRA set prices too high and favored large producers over small businesses. The federal courts also began to scrutinize the constitutionality of the legislation in cases brought by critics.

The AAA also came under attack for its encouragement of cutbacks in production. Farmers had plowed under 10.4 million acres of cotton and slaughtered 6 million pigs in 1933—a time when people were ill clothed and ill fed. Although for landowning farmers the program was successful, the average person found such waste shocking. Tenant farmers and sharecroppers also were supposed to receive government payments for taking crops out of cultivation, but very few received what they were entitled to, especially if they were African-American. Furthermore, the AAA's hopes that landlords would keep their tenants on the land even while cutting production were not fulfilled. In the South the number of sharecropper farms dropped by 30 percent between 1930 and 1940. The result was a homeless population, dispossessed Americans heading to cities and towns in all parts of the country.

Joining the migration to the West Coast were "Okies," such as Oklahoman Marvin Montgomery and his family traveling in their 1929 Hudson, and "Arkies"; many of them had been evicted from their tenant farms during the depression. They also took to the road to escape the drought that plagued the southern plains states of Kansas, Colorado, New Mexico, Oklahoma, Arkansas, and Texas—a region known in the mid-1930s as the Dust Bowl. The Dust Bowl was an ecological disaster. In the 1920s farmers on the southern plains had bought tens of thousands of tractors and plowed millions of acres. Then, in the 1930s, the rain stopped. Soil that had been plowed was particularly vulnerable to the drought that gripped the plains. Strong winds caused enormous dust storms; from 1935 through 1938, 241 dust storms hit the southern plains. Farmers shuttered their homes against the dust as tightly as

The Dust Bowl

The door of this farm shed in Cimarron County, Oklahoma, is blocked by wind-blown sand, which would pile up around the building one day and disappear the next. This photograph was taken by Arthur Rothstein of the Farm Security Administration. Library of Congress.

possible, but, as a woman in western Kansas recounted in 1935, "those tiny particles seemed to seep through the very walls. It got into cupboards and clothes closets; our faces were as dirty as if we had rolled in the dirt; our hair was gray and stiff and we ground dirt between our teeth." Farm animals lacked all protection. The photographer Margaret Bourke-White observed that "cattle quickly become blinded. They run around in circles until they fall and breathe so much dust that they die."

Some farmers blamed the government for their woes; others blamed themselves. As dissatisfaction mounted, so too did the appeal of various demagogues, who presented an analysis of American society that people understood: the wealthy and powerful were ruling people's lives from distant cities, eroding community morale, and ruining family farms and small businesses. One of the best-known demagogues was Father Charles Coughlin, a Roman Catholic priest whose weekly radio sermons offered a curious combination of anticommunism and anticapitalism. In addition to criticizing the

Demagogic Attacks on the New Deal

New Deal, Coughlin became increasingly anti-Semitic, telling his listeners that the cause of their woes was an international conspiracy of Jewish bankers.

Another challenge to the New Deal came from Dr. Francis E. Townsend, a public health officer in Long Beach, California, who was thrown out of work at age sixty-seven with only $100 in savings. Disturbed by the plight of old people, Townsend devised the Old Age Revolving Pensions plan, under which the government would pay monthly pensions of $200 to all citizens older than sixty on condition that they spent the money in the same month they received it. Townsend claimed his plan not only would aid the aged but would cure the depression by pumping enormous purchasing power into the economy. The plan was fiscally impossible but recognized the real needs of elderly Americans.

Then there was Huey Long, perhaps the most successful demagogue in American history. Long was elected governor of Louisiana in 1928 with the slogan "Every Man a King, but No One Wears a Crown." As a United States senator, Long at first supported the New Deal, but he found the NRA too conservative and began to believe that Roosevelt had fallen captive to big business. Long countered in 1934 with the Share Our Wealth Society, which advocated the seizure by taxation of all incomes greater than $1 million and all inheritances of more than $5 million. With the resulting funds, the government would furnish each family a homestead allowance of $5,000 and an annual income of $2,000. By mid-1935 Long's movement claimed 7 million members, and few doubted that Long aspired to the presidency. An assassin's bullet extinguished his ambition in September 1935.

Some politicians, like Governor Floyd Olson of Minnesota, declared themselves socialists in the 1930s. In Wisconsin the left-wing Progressive Party

Left-Wing Critics of the New Deal

reelected Robert La Follette, Jr. (son of "Battling Bob"), to the Senate in 1934, sent seven of the state's ten representatives to Washington, and placed La Follette's brother Philip in the governorship. And the old muckraker and socialist Upton Sinclair won the Democratic gubernatorial

nomination in California in 1934 with the slogan "End Poverty in California."

Perhaps the most controversial alternative to the New Deal was the Communist Party of the United States of America. In 1935 the party leadership changed its strategy. Proclaiming "Communism Is Twentieth Century Americanism," the Communists disclaimed any intention of overthrowing the United States government and began to cooperate with left-wing labor unions, student groups, and writers' organizations in opposition to racism and fascism. Still, in 1938, at its high point for the decade, the party had only fifty-five thousand members.

In addition to challenges from the right and the left, the New Deal was also subject to challenge by the Supreme Court. Many New Deal laws had

Supreme Court Decisions Against the New Deal

been hastily drafted, and the majority of the justices feared that the legislation had vested too much power in the presidency. In 1935, the Court unanimously struck down the NIRA (*Schechter v. U.S.*), asserting that it granted

In the 1930s, Senator Huey Long (center) had a mass following and presidential ambitions. But he was assassinated in 1935, the evening this photograph was taken. When Long was shot, he fell into the arms of James O'Connor (left), a political crony, and Louisiana Governor O. K. Allen (right) seized a pistol and dashed into the corridor in pursuit of the murderer shouting, "If there's shooting, I want to be in on it."   Corbis-Bettmann.

the White House excessive legislative power and that the commerce clause of the Constitution did not give the federal government authority to regulate intrastate businesses. Roosevelt's industrial recovery program was dead. In early 1936, his farm program met a similar fate when the Court invalidated the AAA (*U.S.* v. *Butler*), deciding that agriculture was a local problem and thus, under the Tenth Amendment, subject to state, not federal, action.

As Roosevelt looked ahead to the presidential election of 1936, he foresaw the danger of losing his capacity to lead and to govern. His coalition of all interests was breaking up, radicals and demagogues were offering Americans alternative programs, and the Supreme Court was dismantling the New Deal. In early 1935, Roosevelt took the initiative once more. So impressive was the spate of new legislation that historians call it the Second New Deal.

The Second New Deal and the Election of 1936

The Second New Deal differed in important ways from the First New Deal. When the chief legislative goal had been economic recovery, Roosevelt had cooperated with business. Beginning in 1935, however, he denounced business leaders for placing their own selfish interests above the national welfare. The first triumph of the Second New Deal was an innocuous-sounding but momentous law called the Emergency Relief Appropriation Act, which authorized the president to establish massive public works programs for the jobless. The first such program was the Works Progress Administration (WPA), later renamed the Work Projects Administration. The WPA ultimately employed more than 8.5 million people and built more than 650,000 miles of highways and roads, 125,000 public buildings, and 8,000 parks, as well as numerous bridges, airports, and other structures. But the WPA did more than lay bricks. Its Federal Theater Project brought plays, vaudeville, and circuses to cities and towns across the country, and its Federal Writers' Project hired talent like John Steinbeck and Richard Wright to write local guidebooks and regional and folk histories. The Emergency Relief Appropriation Act also

Emergency Relief Appropriation Act

funded the Resettlement Administration, which resettled destitute families and organized rural homestead communities and suburban greenbelt towns for low-income workers; the Rural Electrification Administration, which brought electricity to isolated rural areas; and the National Youth Administration, which sponsored work-relief programs for young adults and part-time jobs for students.

Roosevelt also wanted new legislation aimed at controlling the activities of big business. The Supreme Court had condemned the government-business cooperation that had been the foundation of the First Hundred Days. In addition, businesspeople had become increasingly critical of Roosevelt and the New Deal, complaining that they were overtaxed and overregulated. If big business would not cooperate with government, Roosevelt decided, government should "cut the giants down to size" through antitrust suits and heavy corporate taxes. In 1935 he asked Congress to enact several major bills, including a labor bill sponsored by Senator Robert Wagner of New York, a Social Security bill, a measure to regulate public-utility holding companies, and a "soak-the-rich" tax bill.

When the summer of 1935, which constituted the Second Hundred Days, was over, the president had everything he had requested. First, the National Labor Relations (Wagner) Act granted workers the right to unionize and bargain collectively with management. The act also empowered the National Labor Relations Board to guarantee democratic union elections and to penalize unfair labor practices by employers, such as firing workers for union membership.

National Labor Relations Act

The Social Security Act was a milestone that established several welfare programs, including a cooperative federal-state system of unemployment compensation and Aid to Dependent Children (later renamed Aid to Families with Dependent Children, AFDC) for needy children in single-parent families. The act also established old-age insurance under which workers who paid Social Security taxes out of their wages, matched by their employers, would receive retirement benefits beginning at sixty-five years of age.

Social Security Act

Social Security was a conservative measure: the government did not pay for old-age benefits; workers and their bosses did. The tax was regressive in that the more workers earned, the less they were taxed proportionally. It was deflationary, because it took out of people's pockets money that it did not repay for years. And the law excluded from coverage farm workers, domestic servants, and many hospital and restaurant workers, among whom were many women and people of color. Nevertheless, the Social Security Act was a highly significant development. With its passage, the federal government acknowledged its responsibility not only for the aged but also for the temporarily jobless, dependent children, and disabled people.

In the next two weeks Roosevelt gained the remainder of what he had asked for, including the Public Utility Holding Company (Wheeler-Rayburn) Act and the Wealth Tax Act, which some critics saw as the president's attempt to "steal Huey Long's thunder." The tax act helped achieve a slight redistribution of income by raising the income taxes of the wealthy. It also imposed a new tax on excess business profits and increased taxes on inheritances, large gifts, and profits from the sale of property.

The Second Hundred Days made it unmistakably clear that the president was once again in charge and preparing to run for reelection. The

Election of 1936

campaign was less heated than might have been expected. The Republican nominee, Governor Alf Landon of Kansas, criticized Roosevelt but did not advocate wholesale repeal of the New Deal. Roosevelt won by a landslide, carrying all but two states and polling 27.8 million votes to Landon's 16.7 million. The Democrats also won huge majorities in the House and Senate. Some observers even worried that the two-party system was about to collapse.

By 1936, Roosevelt and the Democrats had forged what observers have called the "New Deal coalition." The coalition consisted of the urban

New Deal Coalition

masses—especially immigrants from southern and eastern Europe and their sons and daughters—organized labor, the eleven states of the Confederacy (the "Solid South"), and northern blacks (before the 1930s, most African-Americans had voted Republican). With the New Deal coalition, the Democratic Party had become the dominant half of the two-party system and would occupy the White House for most of the next thirty years.

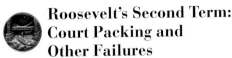

Roosevelt's Second Term: Court Packing and Other Failures

Roosevelt faced a darkening horizon during his second term. The economy faltered again between 1937 and 1939, bringing renewed unemployment and suffering (see figure, page 732). And Europe drew closer to war, threatening to drag the United States into the conflict (see Chapter 26). To gain support for his foreign and military policies, Roosevelt began to court conservative opponents of his domestic reforms. The eventual result was the demise of the New Deal.

In several instances Roosevelt's own actions helped bring about the end of the New Deal. The Supreme Court had invalidated much of the work of

Roosevelt's Court-packing Plan

the First Hundred Days, and Roosevelt feared it would do the same with the fruits of the Second Hundred Days. Four of the justices steadfastly opposed the New Deal; three generally approved of it; two were swing votes. What the federal judiciary needed, the president claimed, was a more enlightened and progressive world-view. His Judiciary Reorganization Bill of 1937 requested the authority to add a federal judge whenever an incumbent failed to retire within six months of reaching age seventy; he also wanted the power to name up to fifty additional federal judges, including six to the Supreme Court. Roosevelt frankly envisioned using the reorganization to create a Supreme Court sympathetic to the New Deal. Liberals joined Republicans and conservative Democrats in resisting the bill, and the president had to concede defeat. The bill he signed into law provided pensions to retiring judges but denied him the power to increase the number of judges.

The episode had a final, ironic twist. During the public debate over court packing, the two swing-vote justices on the Supreme Court began to vote in favor of liberal, pro–New Deal rulings. In short order the Court upheld both the Wagner Act (*NLRB* v. *Jones & Laughlin Steel Corp.*), ruling that Congress's power to regulate interstate commerce also involved the power to regulate the production of goods for interstate commerce, and the Social Security Act. Moreover, the new pensions encouraged judges older than seventy to retire, and the president was able to appoint seven new associate justices in the next four years, including notables such as Hugo Black, Felix Frankfurter, and William O. Douglas.

Another New Deal setback was the renewed economic recession of 1937–1939. Roosevelt had never abandoned his commitment to a balanced budget. In 1937, confident that the depression had largely been cured, he began to order drastic cutbacks in government spending. At the same time the Federal Reserve Board, concerned about a 3.6 percent inflation rate, tightened credit. The two actions sent the economy into a tailspin: unemployment climbed from 7.7 million in 1937 to 10.4 million in 1938. Soon Roosevelt resumed deficit financing.

Recession of 1937–1939

The New Deal was in trouble in 1937 and 1938, and there ensued a wide-ranging ideological struggle to chart the future of the liberal reform movement. Some New Dealers urged vigorous trustbusting; others advocated the resurrection of national economic planning that had existed under the National Recovery Administration. But in the end Roosevelt rejected these alternatives and instead chose deficit financing as a quick fix to stimulate consumer demand and create jobs. And in the spring of 1938, with conflict over events in Europe commanding more and more of the nation's attention, the New Deal came to an end. Roosevelt sacrificed further domestic reforms in return for conservative support for his programs of military rearmament and preparedness. The last significant New Deal laws enacted were the National Housing Act (1937), which established the United States Housing Authority and built housing projects for low-income families; a new Agricultural Adjustment Act (1938); and the Fair Labor Standards Act (1938), which forbade labor by children younger than sixteen and established a minimum wage and forty-hour workweek for many, but by no means all, workers.

Industrial Workers and the Rise of the CIO

Working people gained from the New Deal the right to organize labor unions and bargain collectively with their bosses. Enactment of Section 7(a) of the NIRA (1933) and the Wagner Act (1935) inspired vigorous recruitment of union members. Union membership in 1929 stood at 3.6 million; in mid-1938 it surpassed 7 million. The gains, however, did not always come easily. Management resisted vigor-

ously in the 1930s, relying on the police or hiring armed thugs to intimidate workers and break up strikes. Violence erupted in the steel, automobile, and textile industries and among lumber workers in the Pacific Northwest and teamsters in the Midwest. In 1934 a strike of longshoremen was met with violence by police on the docks of San Francisco; two union members were killed, and workers' anger spread to other industries. Eventually 130,000 workers joined the general strike.

Labor confronted yet another obstacle in the American Federation of Labor (AFL) craft unions' traditional hostility toward industrial unions. Craft unions typically consisted of skilled workers in a particular trade, such as carpentry or plumbing. Industrial unions represented all the workers, skilled and unskilled, in a given industry. The organizational gains of the 1930s were far more impressive in industrial unions than in craft unions, as hundreds of thousands of workers organized in industries such as autos, garments, rubber, and steel.

Rivalry Between Craft and Industrial Unions

Craft and industrial unions competed bitterly for control of the growing labor movement. Personifying this power struggle were John L. Lewis of the United Mine Workers and William Green of the AFL. Lewis, a fighter with a flair for the dramatic, was probably the most colorful and tenacious labor leader in the nation's history. But he presided over only one of the many unions within the AFL, whereas the lackluster Green was president of the entire federation. Attempts to reconcile the craft and industrial union movements failed, and in 1935 Lewis resigned as vice president of the AFL. He and other industrial unionists then formed the Committee for Industrial Organization (CIO). The AFL expelled the CIO unions in 1938, and the CIO reorganized as the Congress of Industrial Organizations. By that time CIO membership had reached 3.7 million, more than the AFL's 3.4 million.

The CIO evolved during the 1930s into a pragmatic, bread-and-butter labor organization that organized millions of workers, including women and African-Americans, who never before had had an opportunity to join a union. One union, the United Auto Workers (UAW), scored a major victory in late 1936. The UAW demanded recognition from General Motors (GM), Chrysler, and Ford. When GM

Sit-down Strikes

refused, workers at the Fisher Body plant in Flint, Michigan, launched a sit-down strike and refused to leave the building. To discourage the strikers, GM turned off the heat. When that tactic failed, GM called in the police, who were met by a barrage of iron bolts, coffee mugs, and bottles. The police then resorted to tear gas, and the strikers turned the plant's water hoses on them.

The strike lasted for weeks. General Motors obtained a court order to evacuate the plant, but the strikers stood firm, risking imprisonment and fines. With the support of their families and neighborhoods, and a women's "emergency brigade" that picketed and delivered food and supplies to the strikers, the UAW prevailed. GM agreed to recognize the union. Chrysler signed a similar agreement, but Ford held out for four more years.

As a tactic, the sit-down strike spread dramatically; it was used by workers in the textile, glass, and rubber industries, as well as by dime-store clerks, janitors, dressmakers, and bakers. Most important, participation in the sit-downs bestowed self-respect on the strikers. One striker in Flint proudly compared his actions to those of Davy Crockett: "Yes sir, Chevy [Plant] No. 4 was my Alamo."

In 1937, the Steel Workers Organizing Committee (SWOC) signed a contract with the nation's largest steelmaker, U.S. Steel, that guaranteed an eight-hour workday and a forty-hour workweek. Other steel companies refused to go along. Confrontations between the so-called little steel companies and the SWOC soon led to violence. On Memorial Day, strikers and their families joined with sympathizers in a picket line in front of the Republic Steel plant in Chicago. Violence erupted, ten strikers were killed, and forty suffered gunshot wounds. The police explained that the marchers had attacked them with clubs and bricks and that they had responded with reasonable force to defend themselves and disperse the mob. Some newspapers agreed, among them the antilabor *Chicago Tribune*, which described the attack as an invasion by "a trained military unit of a revolutionary body." The strikers argued that the police, without provocation, had brutally attacked citizens who were peacefully asserting their constitutional rights.

Memorial Day Massacre

Though senseless, the Memorial Day Massacre was not surprising. During the 1930s industries had hired private police agents and accumulated large stores of arms and ammunition for use in deterring

Among President Roosevelt's earliest supporters were members of the United Mine Workers (UMW). In the 1930s organizers for the union told coal miners, "President Roosevelt wants you to join the union," and many thousands did. To promote Roosevelt's reelection in 1936, a member of a UMW local in Clarksville, Pennsylvania, hand-painted this glass sign. Collection of David J. and Janice L. Frent.

workers from organizing and joining unions. Meanwhile, the CIO continued to enroll new members. By 1938 industrial unions had enlisted 600,000 miners, 375,000 steelworkers, 400,000 auto workers, and 300,000 textile workers. By the end of the decade the CIO had succeeded in organizing most of the nation's mass-production industries. As these industries were converted for war production in the decade ahead, employment would soar and the CIO would register even more impressive membership gains.

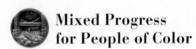

Mixed Progress for People of Color

The Great Depression plunged the vast majority of African-Americans deeper into fear, political disfranchisement, Jim Crow segregation, and privation. In 1930 about three-fourths of all blacks lived in the South. Almost all were prohibited from voting or serving on juries. They were routinely denied access to hospitals, universities, public parks, and swimming pools. And they were hired only for the least desirable, most menial jobs. Blacks living in rural areas in the South were propertyless sharecroppers, tenants, or wage hands. Caught in a cycle of poverty

African-Americans in the Great Depression

tion:sed

How do historians know that police officers were largely responsible for the 1937 Memorial Day Massacre in Chicago? There is both photographic and medical evidence of police culpability. Covering the story at the Republic Steel plant were a cameraman from Paramount News and photographers from Life magazine and Wide World Photos (see photograph). Paramount News suppressed its film footage, claiming that releasing it *"might very well incite local riots,"* but an enterprising reporter alerted a congressional committee to its existence, and a private viewing was arranged. Spectators at this showing, the reporter noted, *"were shocked and amazed by scenes showing scores of uniformed policemen firing their revolvers pointblank into a dense crowd of men, women, and children, and then pursuing the survivors unmercifully as they made frantic efforts to escape."* Medical evidence also substantiated the picketers' version: none of the ten people killed by police were shot from the front. Clearly, the picketers were trying to flee the police when they were shot or clubbed to the ground.   Photo: World Wide Photos.

and disease, their life expectancy was ten years less than that of whites. And the specter of the lynch mob was a continuing threat: in 1929, seven black men were lynched; in 1930, twenty; in 1933, twenty-four.

Racism also plagued African-Americans living in the North. Southern blacks who migrated to northern cities found that employers discriminated against them. Black unemployment rates ran high; in Pittsburgh 48 percent of black workers were jobless in 1933, compared with 31 percent of white laborers.

As African-Americans were aware, President Herbert Hoover shared prevailing white racial attitudes. Hoover sought a lily-white Republican Party and attempted to push blacks out of the party in order to attract white southern Democrats. He appointed few blacks to federal office, rejected appeals for a federal antilynching law, and perpetuated the segregation of the army and of facilities in federal buildings in the nation's capital. In 1930, the president demonstrated his racial insensitivity by nominating Judge John J. Parker of North Carolina to the

Supreme Court. Ten years earlier Parker had endorsed the disfranchisement of blacks. The NAACP remembered and protested his nomination. The AFL joined the protest, and the joint opposition plus liberal votes in the Senate defeated Parker's nomination, 41 to 39.

Shortly thereafter, a celebrated civil rights case revealed the ugliness of race relations in the depression era. In March 1931, nine African-Americans who were riding a freight train near Scottsboro, Alabama, were arrested and charged with roughing up some white hoboes and throwing them off the train. Two white women removed from the same train claimed the nine men had raped them. Medical evidence later showed that the women were lying. But within two weeks, eight of the so-called Scottsboro boys were convicted of rape by all-white juries and sentenced to death.

Scottsboro Trials

After several trials, the first defendant, Haywood Patterson, was condemned to die. A Supreme Court ruling intervened, however, on the ground that African-Americans were systematically excluded from juries in Alabama. Patterson was found guilty again in 1936 and was given a seventy-five-year jail sentence. Four of the other youths were sentenced to life imprisonment. Not until 1950 were all five out of jail—four by parole and Patterson by escaping from a work gang.

African-Americans coped with their white-circumscribed environment and fought racism in a variety of ways. The NAACP, though internally divided, lobbied quietly against a long list of injustices, and the Brotherhood of Sleeping Car Porters, under the astute leadership of A. Philip Randolph, fought for the rights of black workers. In Harlem the militant Harlem Tenants League fought rent increases and evictions, and African-American consumers began to boycott white merchants who refused to hire blacks as clerks. Their slogan was "Don't Buy Where You Can't Work." But America's white leaders made few concessions. Only the Supreme Court provided a measure of protection for African-Americans at this time. It declared unconstitutional the Texas law that barred blacks from voting in the

Numerous African-American families were evicted from their farms during the Great Depression. White planters who received government payments for taking land out of cultivation were supposed to share these payments with their tenants and sharecroppers. Instead, many kicked these families off the land and kept the money for themselves. This family in Putnam County, Georgia, loaded all its possessions into a rickety truck for the trip north.   National Archives.

Mary McLeod Bethune, pictured here with her friend and supporter Eleanor Roosevelt, became the first African-American woman to head a federal agency as director of the Division of Negro Affairs of the National Youth Administration.   Corbis-Bettmann.

Democratic primaries, and it attempted to correct the abuse in the Scottsboro trials.

With the election of Franklin D. Roosevelt, blacks' attitudes toward government changed, as did their political affiliation. For African-Americans— an important component of the New Deal coalition—Franklin D. Roosevelt would become the most appealing president since Abraham Lincoln. For one thing, Roosevelt was a decided improvement over Hoover, and the personal magnetism and buoyancy he exhibited in his fireside chats spoke directly to them. Blacks also were heartened by photographs of African-American visitors at the White House and by news stories about Roosevelt's black advisers. Most important, through the WPA and other relief programs, the New Deal aided black people in their struggle for economic survival.

The "Black Cabinet," or black brain trust, was unique in United States history. Never before had there been so many African-American advisers at the

Black Cabinet

White House. There were black lawyers, journalists, and Ph.D.s and black experts on housing, labor, and social welfare. William H. Hastie and Robert C. Weaver, holders of advanced degrees from Harvard, served in the Department of the Interior. Mary McLeod Bethune, educa-

tor and president of the National Council of Negro Women, was director of the Division of Negro Affairs of the National Youth Administration. Also among the New Dealers were some whites who had committed themselves to first-class citizenship for African-Americans. Foremost among these people was Eleanor Roosevelt. In 1939, when the acclaimed black contralto Marian Anderson was barred from performing in Washington's Constitution Hall by its owners, the Daughters of the American Revolution, Eleanor Roosevelt arranged for Anderson to sing on Easter Sunday at the Lincoln Memorial.

The president himself, however, remained uncommitted to African-American civil rights. Fearful of alienating southern whites, he never endorsed two key goals of the civil rights strug-

The New Deal's Racism

gle: a federal law against lynching and abolition of the poll tax. Furthermore, some New Deal programs functioned in ways that were definitely damaging to African-Americans. Rather than benefiting black tenant farmers and sharecroppers, the AAA had the effect of forcing many of them off the land. The Federal Housing Administration (FHA) refused to guarantee mortgages on houses purchased by blacks in white neighborhoods, the CCC was racially segregated, and the

TVA handed out skilled jobs to whites first. Also, Social Security coverage and the minimum-wage provisions of the Fair Labor Standards Act of 1938 excluded waiters, cooks, hospital orderlies, janitors, farm workers, and domestics, many of whom were African-Americans.

In short, although African-Americans benefited from the New Deal, they did not get their fair share. Even so, the large majorities they gave Roosevelt at election time demonstrated their appreciation of the benefits they did receive. Not all African-Americans, however, trusted the mixed message of the New Deal. Some concluded that they could depend only on themselves and organized self-help and direct-action movements. In 1934, black tenant farmers and sharecroppers joined with poor whites to form the Southern Tenant Farmers' Union. In the North, blacks organized tenants' unions, boycotted stores, and launched "Jobs for Negroes" campaigns. In 1935 when police in Harlem beat to death a black youth, a race riot erupted as mobs of poor and angry people smashed store windows and raided shelves. Working-class blacks criticized the NAACP for ignoring the economics of second-class citizenship and for being too middle class and legalistic in its war on racism. The NAACP was scoring notable victories in opening up graduate and professional schools to black students, but critics charged that these gains benefited only the middle class, not the masses who above all needed jobs.

Black Protest

Nowhere was the trend toward direct action more evident than in the March on Washington movement in 1941. That year, billions of federal dollars flowed into American industry as the nation prepared for the possibility of another world war. Thousands of new jobs were created, but discrimination deprived blacks of their fair share. One executive notified black job applicants that "the Negro will be considered only as janitors and other similar capacities." Randolph, leader of the porters' union, proposed that blacks march on the nation's capital to demand equal access to jobs in defense industries.

March on Washington Movement

By early summer thousands were ready to march. Fearing that the march might provoke riots and that Communists might infiltrate the movement, Roosevelt announced that he would issue an executive order prohibiting discrimination in war industries and in the government if the march was canceled. The result was Executive Order No. 8802, which established the Fair Employment Practices Committee (FEPC). The March on Washington movement anticipated future trends in the civil rights movement: it was all-black; its tactic was direct action—a threat by the masses to take to the streets; and its beneficiaries were the urban working class.

Another group, American Indians, sank further into malnutrition and disease during the early 1930s. In Oklahoma, where the Choctaws, Cherokees, and Seminoles lived with more than twenty other tribes on infertile soil, three-fourths of all Native American children were undernourished. Tuberculosis swept through the reservations. At the heart of the problem was a 1929 ruling by the United States comptroller general that landless tribes were ineligible for federal aid. Not until 1931 did the Bureau of Indian Affairs take steps to relieve the suffering. A federal relief program was launched to provide aid, and Congress substantially increased the bureau's budget that year; yet much of the money went to hire more bureaucrats.

The New Deal approach to Native Americans differed greatly from that of earlier administrations; as a result, Indians benefited more directly than blacks from the New Deal. As commissioner of Indian affairs, Roosevelt appointed John Collier, founder of the American Indian Defense Association. Collier had crusaded for tribal landownership and an end to the allotment policy established by the Dawes Severalty Act of 1887 (see page 482). "The allotment act," Collier wrote, "contemplates total landlessness for the Indians of the third generation of each allotted tribe." First, the Dawes Act sought to dissolve tribes by dividing landholdings among tribal members—160 acres to each head of family and 80 acres to each single adult. Many individuals then sold their allotments to white ranchers, miners, and farmers. Second, reservation land remaining after the distribution of allotments was opened for settlement to non-Indian homesteaders. The result was that, after 1887, Indian landholdings dropped from 138 million acres to 52 million acres, 20 million of which were arid or semi-arid.

A New Deal for Native Americans

The Indian Reorganization (Wheeler-Howard) Act (1934) aimed to reverse the process by restoring lands to tribal ownership and forbidding future division of Indian lands into individual parcels. Other

The New Deal for Native Americans encouraged respect for Indian religions and urged the perpetuation of Indian cultures, including arts and crafts. Indian crafts also had become popular among affluent Americans. This 1937 painting by a Navajo artist, Gerald Nailor, shows eastern shoppers admiring a Navajo rug.   Library of Congress.

provisions of the act enabled tribes to obtain loans for economic development and to establish self-government. Under Collier, the Bureau of Indian Affairs also encouraged the perpetuation of Indian religions and cultures. One order stated: "The cultural history of Indians is in all respects to be considered equal to that of any non-Indian group."

Mexican-Americans also suffered extreme hardship during the Great Depression, but no government programs benefited them. During these years

Depression Hardships of Mexican-Americans

many Mexicans and Mexican-Americans packed up their belongings and moved south of the border, sometimes willingly and sometimes deported by immigration officials or forced out by California officials eager to purge them from the relief rolls. As an inducement, the government offered free one-way train tickets to Mexico. According to the federal census, the Mexican-born population in the United States dropped from 617,000 in 1930 to 377,000 in 1940.

In addition, many employers changed their minds about the desirability of hiring Mexican-American farm workers. Before the 1930s farmers had boasted that Mexican-Americans were an inex-

pensive, docile labor supply and that they would not join unions. But in the 1930s Mexican-Americans overturned the stereotype by engaging in prolonged and sometimes bloody strikes. In the San Joaquin valley, eighteen thousand cotton pickers walked off their jobs in 1933 and set up a "strike city" after being evicted from the growers' camps. Shortly thereafter, their union hall was riddled with bullets, and two strikers died.

The New Deal offered Mexican-Americans little help. The AAA was created to assist property-owning farmers, not migratory farm workers. The Wagner Act did not cover farm workers' unions, nor did the Social Security Act or the Fair Labor Standards Act cover farm laborers. One New Deal agency, the Farm Security Administration (FSA), was established in 1937 to help farm workers, in part by setting up migratory labor camps. But the FSA came too late to help Mexican-Americans, most of whom by then had been replaced in the fields by dispossessed white farmers from the Dust Bowl states.

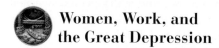

Women, Work, and the Great Depression

During the depression women had to work overtime to maintain themselves and their families. In *It's Up to the Women* (1933), Eleanor Roosevelt wrote that

Mothers and Households Face Hard Times

"women know that life must go on and that the needs of life must be met." Wives and mothers followed the maxim "Use it up, wear it out, make it do, or do without." Women bought day-old bread and cheap cuts of meat; they relined old coats with blankets, and they saved string, rags, and broken crockery for future use. Many families were able to maintain their standard of living only because of astute spending and because women substituted their own labor for goods and services they once purchased. Husbands shared these financial concerns, but it was usually women's responsibility to do the family budgeting; it was estimated that wives and mothers in the 1930s allocated over 80 percent of all family income.

While they were cutting corners to make ends meet, women were also seeking paid work outside the home. In 1930 approximately 10.5 million women were paid workers; ten years later, the female labor force exceeded 13 million. Many women were their families' sole providers and had to do it all, at home and on the job. Despite these social realities, most Americans believed that women should not take jobs outside the home, that they should strive instead to be good wives and mothers, and that women who worked were doing so for "pin money" to buy frivolous things. When a 1936 Gallup poll asked whether wives should work if their husbands had jobs, 82 percent of the respondents (including 75 percent of the women) answered "no."

These attitudes resulted in severe job discrimination. For example, of the fifteen hundred urban school systems surveyed by the National Education

Job Discrimination Against Married Women

Association in 1930 and 1931, 77 percent said that they refused to hire married women as teachers, and 63 percent said that they fired female teachers who married while employed. Most insurance companies, banks, railroads, and public utilities had similar policies against hiring married women. And from 1932 to 1937, federal law prohibited more than one family member from working for the civil service. Because wives usually earned less than their husbands, they were the ones who quit their government jobs.

In part, such thinking stemmed from the widely held belief that a woman who worked caused a man to be unemployed. That view missed the point, for three reasons. First, women were heavily concentrated in "women's jobs," including clerical positions, teaching, and nursing. Men rarely sought these jobs and probably would not have been hired to fill them had they applied. Second, most women workers (71 percent in 1930) were single and thus self-supporting. Third, the wages for "women's jobs" trailed far behind those for "men's jobs." Lagging most were women of color, some of whom lost their low-paying menial jobs to white women during the depression.

More married women went to work during the depression. By 1940, married women constituted 35 percent of the female work force, up from 29 percent in 1930 and 15 percent in 1900. They worked to keep their families from slipping into poverty, but their assistance with family expenses did not improve their status. As the sociologists Robert and Helen Lynd observed at the time: "The men, cut adrift from their usual routine, lost most of their sense of time and dawdled helplessly and dully about the streets; while in the homes the women's world remained largely intact and the round of cooking, housecleaning, and mending became if anything

Many Mexican farm workers (braceros) *were deported in the early 1930s, but by the end of the decade growers eager for the return of this source of cheap labor began to recruit train-loads of Mexicans as farm laborers in southwestern states. This photo, taken by Dorothea Lange in 1938, shows one of these workers.* Dorothea Lange Collection, Oakland Museum of California, City of Oakland. Gift of Paul S. Taylor.

more absorbing." And even though women were making greater contributions to the family, their husbands, including those without jobs, still expected to rule the roost and to remain exempt from childcare and housework.

The New Deal did take women's needs into account, but only when forcefully reminded to do so by the activist women who advised the administration.

Women in the New Deal

These women, mainly government and Democratic Party officials, formed a network united by their commitment to social reform, to protective laws for women's health and safety on the job, and to the participation of women in politics and government. The network's most prominent member was Eleanor Roosevelt, who was her husband's valued adviser. Secretary of Labor Frances Perkins was the nation's first woman cabinet officer. Other historic New Deal appointments included the first woman federal appeals judge and the first women ambassadors. Molly

Social Security has been one of the most enduring of all New Deal programs. Since 1935, tens of millions of Americans have received their Social Security cards. Collection of Faye Kyle/Picture Research Consultants.

Dewson, head of the Democratic Party's Women's Division, noted with pride: "The change from women's status in government before Roosevelt is unbelievable."

Even with increased participation by women, however, New Deal provisions for women were mixed. The maximum-hour and minimum-wage provisions mandated by the NRA won women's support. Women workers in the lowest-paying jobs, many of whom labored under sweatshop conditions, had the most to gain from these standards. Some NRA codes mandated pay differentials based on gender, however, making women's minimum wages lower than men's. Federal relief agencies, such as the Civil Works Administration (1933) and the Federal Emergency Relief Administration, hired only one woman for every eight to ten men placed in relief jobs. A popular New Deal program, the Civilian Conservation Corps, was limited to young men. And women in agriculture and domestic service were not protected by the 1938 Fair Labor Standards Act.

Most important, the 1935 Social Security Act failed to provide coverage for large numbers of women workers, including not only farm women and domestic servants but also many women teachers, nurses, librarians, and social workers. Although Social Security orginally contained no provisions for spouses or widows, in 1939 Congress added such benefits. But the Social Security amendments of 1939 were also far from inclusive. They were based on the government's unstated social policy of preserving the traditional family in which the husband was the breadwinner and the wife was the stay-at-home caregiver. Accordingly, the Social Security amendments of 1939 provided benefits for women who were supported by and lived with their husbands, but not for women who were separated, divorced, or self-supporting.

Nevertheless, significant changes in women's lives were imminent. The reason for the changes, however, was not that the government would suddenly decide to stress women's equality with men, but that beginning in 1941 the country would be at war—a war it could not win without employing womanpower in the nation's aircraft factories, shipyards, and munitions works.

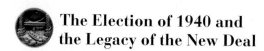

The Election of 1940 and the Legacy of the New Deal

No president had ever served more than two terms, and as the presidential election of 1940 approached, many Americans speculated about whether Roosevelt would run for a third term. Roosevelt seemed undecided until May 1940, when Adolf Hitler's military advances in Europe apparently convinced him to stay on.

The Republican candidate was Wendell Willkie, an Indiana lawyer and utilities executive who was once a Democrat but had become a prominent business opponent of the New Deal. **Wendell Willkie** campaigned against the New Deal, contending that its meddling in business had failed to return the nation to prosperity. He also criticized the government's lack of military preparedness. But Roosevelt preempted the defense issue by beefing up military and naval contracts. As workers streamed into the factories to fill new orders, unemployment figures dropped as well. When Willkie reversed his approach and accused Roosevelt of warmongering, the president promised, "Your boys are not going to be sent into any foreign wars."

Willkie never did come up with an effective campaign issue, and on election day Roosevelt received 27 million popular votes to Willkie's 22 million. In the electoral college Roosevelt buried Willkie 449 to 82 (see map, page 747). Willkie did manage to win the farm and small-town vote in the Midwest, but the New Deal coalition was triumphant. As in 1936, Roosevelt triumphed in the cities, primarily among blue-collar workers, ethnic Americans, and African-Americans. He also won every state in the South. Although the New Deal was over at home, Roosevelt was still riding a wave of public approval.

Any analysis of the New Deal must begin with Franklin Delano Roosevelt himself. Assessments of his career varied widely during his presidency.

Roosevelt and the New Deal Assessed

Most historians consider him a truly great president, citing his courage and buoyant self-confidence, his willingness to experiment, and his capacity to inspire the nation during the most somber days of the depression. Those who criticize him charge that he lacked vision and failed to formulate a bold and coherent strategy of economic recovery and political and economic reform. He was not a socialist but a capitalist: he wanted to alleviate suffering but not at the expense of private property and the profit motive. Essentially he was a pragmatist whose goal was to conserve the system.

Even scholars who criticize Roosevelt's performance agree that he transformed the presidency. "Only Washington, who made the office, and Jackson, who remade it, did more than Roosevelt to raise it to its present condition of strength, dignity, and independence," according to political scientist Clinton Rossiter. Roosevelt personified the presidency, and with his fireside chats he became the first president to use the radio to appeal directly for the people's support. Other scholars, however, have charged that it was Roosevelt who initiated "the imperial presidency." Whether for good or ill, Roosevelt strengthened not only the presidency but the whole federal government. "For the first time for many Americans," the historian William Leuchtenburg has written, "the federal government became an institution that was directly experienced. More than state and local governments, it came to be *the* government."

In the past, the federal government had served primarily as an economic regulator; during the New Deal it became an economic guarantor and stimulator as well. For the first time

Origins of America's Welfare System

the federal government acknowledged a responsibility to offer relief to the jobless and the needy, and for the first time it resorted to deficit spending to stimulate the economy. Millions of Americans benefited from government programs that are still operating today. The New Deal laid the foundation of the welfare system on which subsequent presidential administrations would build.

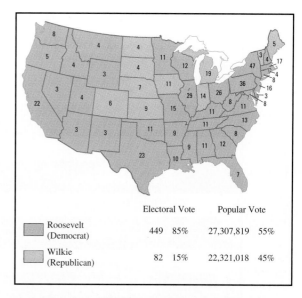

Presidential Election, 1940 *Roosevelt won an unprecedented third term in the 1940 presidential election. He did not repeat his landslide 1936 victory, in which he won all but two states. But he did capture thirty-eight states in 1940 to Republican Wendell Willkie's ten.*

	Electoral Vote		Popular Vote	
Roosevelt (Democrat)	449	85%	27,307,819	55%
Wilkie (Republican)	82	15%	22,321,018	45%

Although the government's role in the economy expanded under the New Deal, the economy itself remained basically capitalistic. The profit motive and private property remained fundamental to the system. Some redistribution of wealth did result from the New Deal, but the wealthy survived as a class. In 1929, for example, the most affluent 5 percent of the population received 30 percent of total family income. By 1941, their share had shrunk but was still a healthy 24 percent. Most of the income lost by the wealthy ended up in the pockets of the middle and upper-middle classes, not those of the poor (see figure, page 748).

 ## Conclusion

The New Deal brought about limited change in the nation's power structure. Beginning in the 1930s, business interests had to share their political clout with others. Labor gained influence in Washington, and farmers got more of what they wanted from Congress and the White House. If people wanted their voices to be heard, they had to organize into labor unions, trade associations, or other special-interest lobbies. Not everybody's voice was heard, however. Because of the persistence of racism, there

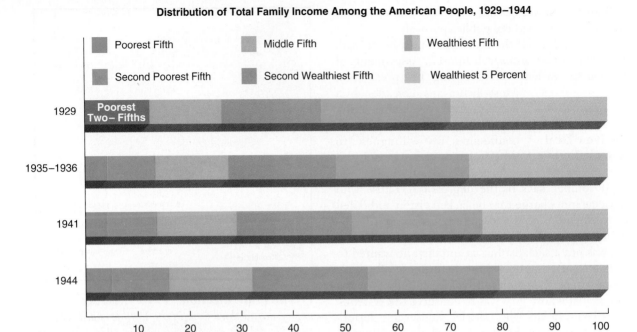

Distribution of Total Family Income Among the American People, 1929–1944

Legend:
- Poorest Fifth
- Middle Fifth
- Wealthiest Fifth
- Second Poorest Fifth
- Second Wealthiest Fifth
- Wealthiest 5 Percent

Years: 1929 (Poorest Two–Fifths), 1935–1936, 1941, 1944

Percent axis: 10, 20, 30, 40, 50, 60, 70, 80, 90, 100

Distribution of Total Family Income Among the American People, 1929–1944 (Percentage) *Although the New Deal provided economic relief to the American people, it did not, as its critics so often charged, significantly redistribute income downward from the rich to the poor.* Source: Adapted from U.S. Bureau of the Census, *Historical Statistics of the United States, Colonial Times to 1970,* 2 parts (Washington, D.C., 1975), Part 1, p. 301.

was no real increase in the power of African-Americans and other minorities.

The New Deal was a liberal, evolutionary reform program, not a revolutionary break with the past. Although the New Deal coalition emerged as a political force in the 1930s, New Deal ideas such as the TVA and Social Security had been around for decades. Moreover, prominent New Dealers had been active in reform movements since the Progressive era. Historians generally view the New Deal as a movement that benefited middle-class Americans. According to William Leuchtenburg, the New Deal "swelled the ranks of the bourgeoisie but left many Americans—sharecroppers, slum dwellers, most Negroes—outside of the new equilibrium."

The New Deal failed in its fundamental purpose: to put people back to work. As late as 1939, more than 10 million men and women were still jobless. That year, unemployment was 19 percent; over the next two years it fell no lower than 14 percent. What plagued the nation throughout the 1930s was underconsumption: people and businesses did not purchase enough goods to sustain high levels of employment. In the end it was not the New Deal but massive government spending during the Second World War that put people back to work. In 1941, as a result of mobilization for war, unemployment declined to 10 percent, and in 1944, at the height of the war, only 1 percent of the labor force was jobless.

The New Deal's most lasting accomplishments were its programs to ameliorate the suffering of unemployed people. The United States has suffered several economic recessions since 1945, but even Republican presidents have primed the pump during the periods of slump. Before the New Deal, the United States had experienced a major depression every fifteen or twenty years. The Great Depression was the last of its kind. Since the New Deal, thanks to unemployment compensation, Social Security, and other measures, the United States has not reexperienced this national nightmare.

Suggestions for Further Reading

Hoover and the Worsening Depression

William J. Barber, *Herbert Hoover, the Economists, and American Economic Policy, 1921–1933* (1986); Michael A. Bernstein, *The*

Great Depression: Delayed Recovery and Economic Change in America, 1929–1939 (1988); David Burner, *Herbert Hoover* (1979); Martin L. Fausold, *The Presidency of Herbert C. Hoover* (1985); John A. Garraty, *The Great Depression* (1986); James S. Olson, *Herbert Hoover and the Reconstruction Finance Corporation, 1931–1933* (1977); Jordan A. Schwarz, *Interregnum of Despair* (1970).

The New Deal

Anthony J. Badger, *The New Deal: The Depression Years, 1933–1940* (1989); William J. Barber, *Designs Within Disorder: Franklin D. Roosevelt, the Economists, and the Shaping of American Economic Policy, 1933–1945* (1996); Roger Biles, *A New Deal for the American People* (1991); Alan Brinkley, *The End of Reform: New Deal Liberalism in Recession and War* (1995); Steve Fraser and Gary Gerstle, eds., *The Rise and Fall of the New Deal Order, 1930–1980* (1989); Colin Gordon, *New Deals: Business, Labor, and Politics in America, 1920–1935* (1994); William E. Leuchtenburg, *The Supreme Court Reborn: The Constitutional Revolution in the Age of Roosevelt* (1995); William E. Leuchtenburg, *Franklin D. Roosevelt and the New Deal* (1963); Albert U. Romasco, *The Politics of Recovery: Roosevelt's New Deal* (1983).

Franklin and Eleanor Roosevelt

James MacGregor Burns, *Roosevelt: The Lion and the Fox* (1956); Blanche Wiesen Cook, *Eleanor Roosevelt: Volume One, 1884–1933* (1992); Kenneth S. Davis, *FDR: Into the Storm, 1937–1940* (1993); Kenneth S. Davis, *FDR: The New Deal Years, 1933–1937* (1986); Frank Freidel, *Franklin D. Roosevelt: A Rendezvous with Destiny* (1990); Joseph P. Lash, *Eleanor and Franklin* (1971); Arthur M. Schlesinger, Jr., *The Age of Roosevelt*, 3 vols. (1957–1960).

Voices from the Depression

James Agee, *Let Us Now Praise Famous Men* (1941); Federal Writers' Project, *These Are Our Lives* (1939); Robert S. McElvaine, ed., *Down and Out in the Great Depression* (1983); Studs Terkel, *Hard Times: An Oral History of the Great Depression* (1970); Tom E. Terrill and Jerrold Hirsch, eds., *Such as Us: Southern Voices of the Thirties* (1978).

Alternatives to the New Deal

Alan Brinkley, *Voices of Protest: Huey Long, Father Coughlin, and the Great Depression* (1982); William Ivy Hair, *The Kingfish and His Realm: The Life and Times of Huey P. Long* (1992); Robin D. G. Kelley, *Hammer and Hoe: Alabama Communists During the Great Depression* (1991); Fraser M. Ottanelli, *The Communist Party of the United States from the Depression to World War II* (1991); Leo Ribuffo, *The Old Christian Right: The Protestant Far Right from the Great Depression to the Cold War* (1983); Donald Warren, *Radio Priest: Charles Coughlin, the Father of Hate Radio* (1996); Frank A. Warren, *An Alternative Vision: The Socialist Party in the 1930s* (1976); Clyde P. Weed, *The Nemesis of Reform: The Republican Party During the New Deal* (1994).

Workers and Organized Labor

Irving Bernstein, *A Caring Society: The New Deal, the Worker, and the Great Depression* (1985); Irving Bernstein, *Turbulent Years: A History of the American Worker, 1933–1941* (1969); Lizabeth Cohen, *Making a New Deal: Industrial Workers in Chicago, 1919–1939* (1991); Melvin Dubofsky and Warren Van Tine, *John L. Lewis* (1977); Sidney Fine, *Sit-Down: The General Motors Strike of 1936–1937* (1969); Gary Gerstle, *Working-Class Americanism: The Politics of Labor in a Textile City, 1914–1960* (1989); Nelson Lichtenstein, *The Most Dangerous Man in Detroit: Walter Reuther and the Fate of American Labor* (1995); Robert H. Zieger, *The CIO, 1935–1955* (1995).

Agriculture and the Environment

William U. Chandler, *The Myth of TVA: Conservation and Development in the Tennessee Valley, 1933–1983* (1984); David E. Conrad, *The Forgotten Farmers: The Story of Sharecroppers in the New Deal* (1965); James N. Gregory, *American Exodus: The Dust Bowl Migration and Okie Culture in California* (1989); David E. Hamilton, *From New Day to New Deal: American Farm Policy from Hoover to Roosevelt, 1928–1933* (1991); Theodore M. Saloutos, *The American Farmer and the New Deal* (1982); John L. Shover, *Cornbelt Rebellion: The Farmers' Holiday Association* (1965); Donald Worster, *Dust Bowl: The Southern Plains in the 1930s* (1979).

People of Color

Dan T. Carter, *Scottsboro*, rev. ed. (1979); James Goodman, *Stories of Scottsboro* (1994); Camille Guerin-Gonzales, *Mexican Workers and American Dreams: Immigration, Repatriation, and California Farm Labor, 1900–1939* (1994); Laurence M. Hauptman, *The Iroquois and the New Deal* (1981); Laurence C. Kelly, *The Assault on Assimilation: John Collier and the Origins of Indian Policy Reform* (1983); John B. Kirby, *Black Americans in the Roosevelt Era* (1980); Donald J. Lisio, *Hoover, Blacks, and Lily-Whites* (1985); Donald L. Parman, *The Navajos and the New Deal* (1975); George J. Sanchez, *Becoming Mexican American: Ethnicity, Culture and Identity in Chicano Los Angeles, 1900–1945* (1993); Harvard Sitkoff, *A New Deal for Blacks* (1978); Patricia Sullivan, *Days of Hope: Race and Democracy in the New Deal Era* (1996); Nancy J. Weiss, *Farewell to the Party of Lincoln: Black Politics in the Age of FDR* (1983).

Women

Glen H. Elder, Jr., *Children of the Great Depression: Social Change in Life Experience* (1974); Linda Gordon, *Pitied but Not Entitled: Single Mothers and the History of Welfare, 1890–1935* (1994); Alice Kessler-Harris, "Designing Women and Old Fools: The Construction of the Social Security Amendments of 1939," in Linda K. Kerber et al., eds., *U.S. History as Women's History* (1995): 87–106; Lois Scharf, *To Work and to Wed: Female Employment, Feminism, and the Great Depression* (1980); Winifred Wandersee, *Women's Work and Family Values, 1920–1940* (1981); Susan Ware, *Holding Their Own: American Women in the 1930s* (1982); Susan Ware, *Beyond Suffrage: Women in the New Deal* (1981).

Cultural and Intellectual History

Daniel Aaron, *Writers on the Left: Episodes in American Literary Communism* (1961); Andrew Bergman, *We're in the Money: Depression America and Its Films* (1971); Jerre Mangione, *The Dream and the Deal: The Federal Writers' Project, 1935–1943* (1972); David P. Peeler, *Hope Among Us Yet: Social Criticism and Social Solace in Depression America* (1987); Richard H. Pells, *Radical Visions and American Dreams: Culture and Social Thought in the Depression Years* (1973); Warren I. Susman, "The Culture of the Thirties," in Warren I. Susman, ed., *Culture as History* (1984): 150–183.

26

Peaceseekers and Warmakers: United States Foreign Relations 1920–1941

In 1921 the Rockefeller Foundation declared war on the mosquito in Latin America. As the carrier of yellow fever, the biting insect *Aedes aegypti* transmitted a deadly virus that threatened public health, political and economic order, and United States hegemony in the region. United States diplomats, military officers, and business executives agreed with foundation officials that the disease that caused severe headaches, vomiting, and jaundice (yellow skin) in its victims, killing many, had to be curbed. With clearance from the United States Department of State, the foundation decided to spend several million dollars on projects to control yellow fever in Latin America, beginning with Mexico. Dedicated scientists, learning from the pioneering work of Carlos Juan Finlay of Cuba, Oswaldo Cruz of Brazil, and United States army surgeon Walter Reed, sought to destroy the mosquito in its larval stage, before it became an egg-laying adult.

Besides killing people, yellow fever disrupted international trade and immigration because ports had to be quarantined. Workers became incapacitated, reducing productivity. The infection struck down American officials, merchants, investors, and soldiers stationed abroad. Throughout Latin America, insufficient official attention to outbreaks of the fever stirred public discontent against regimes the United States supported. The opening of the Panama Canal to ships in 1914, moreover, had raised urgent fears that the death-dealing disease would spread, perhaps infecting Americans in Asia and even reinfecting the southern United States.

Officials of the Brazilian Federal Health Service, in cooperation with the Rockefeller Foundation, spray houses in Bahía to control mosquitoes during a campaign in 1920 to battle yellow fever. *Rockefeller Archive Center.*

751

In Veracruz, a Mexican province of significant United States economic activity where American troops had invaded in 1914, a yellow fever outbreak in 1920 killed 235 people. Gradually overcoming strong anti-Yankee nationalism, Rockefeller Foundation personnel from 1921 to 1923 painstakingly inspected breeding places in houses and deposited larvae-eating fish in public waterworks. In 1924 La Fundación Rockefeller declared yellow fever eradicated in Mexico.

The foundation antimosquito campaign in Latin America proved very successful in maritime and urban areas but less so in rural and jungle regions. Reinfection always lurked as a danger. (Today yellow fever remains endemic in northern South America, although vaccinations have immunized millions of people.) Rockefeller Foundation efforts in the 1920s and 1930s strengthened central governments by providing a national public health infrastructure. Much-welcomed foundation activities also diminished anti–United States sentiment in a region known for virulent anti-Yankeeism.

In the years between the First and Second World Wars, the Rockefeller Foundation became one of many instruments that Americans utilized in their fervent but futile effort to build a stable world order. Despite the tag "isolationist" that is sometimes still applied to United States foreign relations after World War I, Americans did not cut themselves off from international affairs as the misleading term suggests. They wished to avoid entanglements in Europe, but they remained very active in the world in the 1920s and 1930s—from gunboats on Chinese rivers, to negotiations in European financial centers, to marine occupations in Haiti and Nicaragua, to Hollywood films in Germany, to oil wells in the Middle East, to campaigns against diseases in Africa and Latin America.

The most apt description of interwar United States foreign policy is *independent internationalism*. The United States was active on a global scale but retained its independence of action, its traditional unilateralism. Even if Americans had wanted to escape the tumult of international relations, they could not have done so; their interests abroad were too far-flung and too vast—colonies, client states, naval bases, investments, trade, missionaries, humanitarian projects. Nevertheless, many Americans did think of themselves as *isolationists*, by which they meant that they wanted to isolate themselves from Europe's political squabbles, from military alliances and inter-

ventions, and from the League of Nations, which might drag them unwillingly into war. Americans, then, were isolationists in their desire to avoid war but independent internationalists in their behavior.

In the aftermath of the First World War, Americans had grown disenchanted with military methods of achieving order and protecting American prosperity and security. "We can never herd the world into the paths of righteousness with the dogs of war," said Herbert Hoover. American diplomats thus increasingly sought to exercise the power of the United States through conferences, humanitarian programs, moral lectures and calls for peace, nonrecognition of disapproved regimes, arms control, and economic and financial ties in accord with the principle of the Open Door. Downgrading military interventions, for example, United States leaders fashioned a Good Neighbor policy for Latin America.

The United States, however, failed to create a stable world order. Some nations schemed to disrupt it, and severe economic problems undercut it. Public health projects saved countless lives but could not address the low living standards and staggering poverty of dependent peoples across the globe. The debts and reparations bills left over from the First World War bedeviled the 1920s, and the Great Depression of the 1930s shattered world trade and finance. The depression threatened America's prominence in international markets; it also spawned revolutions in Latin America and political extremism, militarism, and war in Europe and Asia. As Nazi Germany marched toward world war, the United States tried to protect itself from the conflict by adopting a policy of neutrality. At the same time, the United States sought to defend its interests in Asia against Japanese aggression by invoking the venerable Open Door policy.

In the late 1930s, and especially after the outbreak of European war in September 1939, many Americans changed their minds. They came to agree with President Franklin D. Roosevelt that Germany and Japan had become menaces to the national interest because those nations were building exclusive, self-sufficient spheres of influence based on military power and economic domination. Roosevelt first pushed for American military preparedness and then for the abandonment of neutrality in favor of aiding Britain and France. A German victory in Europe, he reasoned, would imperil Western political principles, destroy traditional economic ties, threaten United States influence in the Western Hemisphere,

• *Important Events* •

1921	Washington Conference opens and limits naval arms in 1922 Rockefeller Foundation begins battle against yellow fever in Latin America
1922	Mussolini comes to power in Italy Fordney-McCumber Tariff raises duties
1924	Dawes Plan eases German reparations payments United States troops leave the Dominican Republic
1926	United States troops occupy Nicaragua
1927	Jiang Jieshi breaks with Communists to begin civil war in China
1928	Kellogg-Briand Pact outlaws war
1929	Great Depression begins Young Plan reduces German reparations
1930	Hawley-Smoot Tariff raises duties
1931	Japan seizes Manchuria
1932	Stimson Doctrine protests Japanese control of Manchuria Franklin Delano Roosevelt elected president
1933	Hitler establishes Nazi government in Germany United States recognizes Soviet Union Good Neighbor policy announced for Latin America
1934	Fulgencio Batista comes to power in Cuba Reciprocal Trade Agreements Act passed to lower tariffs United States troops withdraw from Haiti Export-Import Bank founded to expand foreign trade
1935	Italy invades Ethiopia Neutrality Act prohibits United States arms shipments
1936	United States votes for nonintervention at Pan-American Conference Germany reoccupies the Rhineland Spanish Civil War breaks out between Loyalists and Franco's fascists Neutrality Act forbids United States loans to belligerents Agreement between Germany and Italy creates the Rome-Berlin Axis

	Germany and Japan unite against Soviet Union in the Anti-Cominterm Pact Roosevelt reelected
1937	Neutrality Act creates cash-and-carry trade with warring nations Sino-Japanese War breaks out ("China incident") Roosevelt's quarantine speech against aggressors Ponce Massacre in Puerto Rico
1938	Mexico nationalizes American-owned oil companies Munich Conference grants part of Czechoslovakia to Germany
1939	Nazi-Soviet Pact carves up eastern Europe Germany invades Poland Second World War begins United States repeals arms embargo to help Allies
1940	Soviet Union invades Finland Germany invades Denmark, Belgium, the Netherlands, and France Committee to Defend America by Aiding the Allies formed Germany, Italy, and Japan join in Tripartite Pact The United States and Great Britain swap destroyers for military bases Roosevelt reelected again Isolationists form America First Committee Selective Training and Service Act starts first peacetime draft
1941	Lend-Lease Act gives aid to Allies Germany attacks Soviet Union United States freezes Japanese assets Atlantic Charter produced at Roosevelt-Churchill meeting Roosevelt exploits *Greer* incident in order to convoy British ships Japanese flotilla attacks Pearl Harbor, Hawai'i United States enters Second World War

and place at the pinnacle of European power a fanatical man—Adolf Hitler—whose ambitions and barbarities seemed limitless.

At the same time, Japan seemed determined to dismember America's Asian friend China, to emasculate the Open Door principle by creating a closed economic sphere in Asia, and to endanger a United States colony—the Philippines. To deter Japanese expansion in the Pacific, the United States ultimately cut off supplies of vital American products such as

oil. But economic warfare had the effect not of containing Japan but rather of intensifying antagonisms. Japan's surprise attack on Pearl Harbor, Hawai'i, in December 1941 finally brought the United States into the Second World War.

Searching for Peace and Order in the 1920s

In the early 1920s Secretary of State Charles Evans Hughes predicted that "there will be no permanent peace unless economic satisfactions are enjoyed." Like the nation's business leaders, Hughes expected American economic expansion to promote international stability—that is, out of economic prosperity would spring a world free from political extremes, revolution, arms races, aggression, and war. Despite valiant efforts, this world never developed.

Europe lay in shambles at the end of the First World War. Between 1914 and 1921, Europe suffered 60 million casualties from world war, civil war, massacre, epidemic, and famine. Germany and France both lost 10 percent of their workers. Crops, livestock, factories, trains, forests, bridges—little was spared. The American Relief Administration and private charities delivered food to needy Europeans, including Russians wracked by famine in 1921 and 1922. Americans hoped not only to feed Europeans but also to create conditions hostile to political radicalism.

The League of Nations, envisioned as a peacemaker, actually proved feeble, its members usually unwilling to use the new organization to settle disputes. Starting in the mid-1920s, American officials participated discreetly in League meetings on public health, prostitution, drug trafficking, and other questions. American jurists served on the Permanent Court of International Justice (World Court) at The Hague, though the United States also refused to join that body.

American peace societies, fully alert to the many obstacles in their path, worked for international stability. During the interwar years, peace groups such

Gassed; Near Dun-sur-Meuse, in the Woods, France

To you who are filled with horror at the sufferings of war-ridden mankind;

To you who remember that **ten million men** were slaughtered in the last war;

To you who have the courage to face the reality of **war, stripped of its sentimental "glory"**;

We make this appeal:—

Eight years since the signing of the Armistice! And peace is still hard beset by preparations for war. In another war men, women and children would be more wantonly, more cruelly massacred, by death rays, gas, disease germs, and machines more fiendish than those used in the last war. Those whom you love must share in its universal destruction.

Can You Afford Not To Give Your Utmost To Cleanse The World Of This Black Plague Of Needless Death and Suffering?

Send your contribution to an uncompromising Peace organization

THE WOMEN'S PEACE UNION
39 Pearl Street, New York

We Believe that Violence and Bloodshed Are Always Wrong in Principle and Disastrous in Practice. We Are working to Make War Illegal and to Ensure World Peace.

The Women's Peace Union (WPU) distributed this flier in the 1920s to remind Americans of the human costs of the First World War. One of many peace societies active in the interwar years, the WPU lobbied for a constitutional amendment requiring a national referendum on a declaration of war. In the 1930s Representative Louis Ludlow (Democrat of Indiana) worked to pass such a measure in Congress, but he failed. Schwimmer-Lloyd Collection, Freida Langer Lazarus Papers. The New York Public Library, Astor, Lenox, and Tilden Foundations.

American Peace Movement

as the Fellowship of Reconciliation and the National Council for Prevention of War drew widespread public support. Women peace advocates gravitated to several of their own organizations because they lacked influence in the male-dominated groups and because of the popular assumption that women—as life givers and nurturing mothers—had a unique aversion to violence and war. Carrie Chapman Catt's moderate National Conference on the Cure and Cause of War, formed in 1924, and the more radical U.S. Section of the Women's International League for Peace and Freedom (WILPF), organized in 1915 under the leadership of Jane Addams and Emily Greene Balch, became the largest women's peace groups.

Most peace groups highlighted the carnage of the First World War and the futility of war as a solution to international problems, but they differed over strategies to ensure world order. Some urged cooperation with the League of Nations and the World Court. Others championed the arbitration of disputes, disarmament and arms reduction, the outlawing of war, and strict neutrality during wars. The WILPF called for an end to United States economic imperialism, which, the organization claimed, compelled the United States to intervene militarily in Latin America to protect United States business interests. The Women's Peace Union (organized in 1921) lobbied for a constitutional amendment to require a national referendum on a declaration of war. The Carnegie Endowment for International Peace (founded in 1910) eschewed political action and promoted peace education through publications. Quakers, YMCA officials, and Social Gospel clergymen in 1917 created the American Friends Service Committee to identify pacifist alternatives to warmaking. All in all, peaceseekers believed that their various reform activities could and must deliver a world without war.

The Washington Conference (November 1921 to February 1922) seemed to mark a substantial step toward peace through arms control. The United

Washington Conference Treaties

States and eight other nations (Britain, Japan, France, Italy, China, Portugal, Belgium, and the Netherlands) met to discuss limits on naval armaments. Britain, the United States, and Japan—the three major powers—were facing a costly naval arms race, and, as Secretary Hughes argued, arms competition had to stop because huge military spending endangered economic rehabilitation.

The conference produced three treaties. The Five-Power Treaty set a ten-year moratorium on the construction of capital ships (battleships and aircraft carriers) and established total tonnage limits of 500,000 for Britain and the United States, 300,000

for Japan, and 175,000 for France and Italy. The first three nations actually agreed to dismantle some existing vessels to satisfy the ratio. They also pledged not to build new fortifications in their Pacific possessions (such as the Philippines). In the Nine-Power Treaty, the conferees reaffirmed the Open Door in China, recognizing Chinese sovereignty. In the Four-Power Treaty, the United States, Britain, Japan, and France agreed to respect each other's Pacific possessions. The three treaties did not limit submarines, destroyers, or cruisers; nor did they provide enforcement powers for the Open Door declaration. By the 1930s, to the great disappointment of peace groups, rearmament was supplanting disarmament.

Peace advocates welcomed the Locarno Pact of 1925, several agreements among European nations that sought to reduce tensions between Germany and France, and the Kellogg-Briand Pact of 1928. In the lat-

Kellogg-Briand Pact

ter document, sixty-two nations agreed to "condemn recourse to war for the solution of international controversies, and renounce it as an instrument of national policy." The accord passed the Senate 85 to 1, but many senators considered it little more than a statement of moral preference because it lacked enforcement provisions. Although weak, the Kellogg-Briand Pact reflected popular opinion that war was barbaric and wasteful and should be outlawed; the accord also stimulated serious public discussion of peace and war. But the peace pact and efforts by peace groups and international institutions failed to muzzle the dogs of war, which fed on the economic troubles that upended world order.

 ## The World Economy and Great Depression

While Europe struggled to recover from the ravages of the First World War, the international economy wobbled and then, in the early 1930s, collapsed. The Great Depression set off a political chain reaction that carried the world to war. Cordell Hull, secretary of state under President Franklin D. Roosevelt from 1933 to 1944, often pointed out that political extremism and militarism sprang from maimed economies. "We cannot have a peaceful world," he warned, "until we rebuild the international economic structure." Hull proved right.

For leaders such as Hughes and Hull, who believed that economic expansion by the United States

John D. Rockefeller, Jr. (1874–1960), second from right, traveled to China in 1921 for the dedication of the Peking Union Medical College, a project of the Rockefeller Foundation, the philanthropic organization founded in 1913 by the oil industrialist John D. Rockefeller, Sr. At the center of this photograph is Hsü Shih-ch'ang (1855–1939), China's president. Rockefeller Archive Center.

United States Economic Expansion

would stabilize world politics, America's prominent position in the international economy seemed opportune. Because of World War I, the United States became a creditor nation and the financial capital of the world (see figure, page 757). From 1914 to 1930, private investments abroad grew fivefold to more than $17 billion. By the late 1920s the United States produced nearly half of the world's industrial goods and ranked first among exporters ($5.2 billion worth of shipments in 1929). For example, General Electric joined international cartels and invested heavily in Germany, American companies began to exploit Venezuela's rich petroleum resources, and American firms began to challenge British control of oil resources in the Middle East. Britain and Germany lost ground to American businesses in Latin America, where Standard Oil operated in eight nations and the United Fruit Company became a huge landowner.

Hollywood movies dominated the global market and stimulated interest in American ways and products. Although some foreigners warned against "Americanization," others aped American mass-production methods and emphasis on efficiency and modernization. Coca-Cola opened a bottling plant in Essen, Germany, and Ford built an automobile assembly plant in Cologne. The German writer Hans Joachim claimed that this cultural adoption might help deliver a peaceful, democratic world because "our interest in elevators, radio towers, and jazz was . . . an attitude that wanted to convert the flame thrower into a vacuum cleaner." Further advertising the American capitalist model were the Phelps-Stokes Fund, exporting to black Africa Booker T. Washington's Tuskegee philosophy of education, and the Rockefeller Foundation, battling diseases in Latin America and Africa, supporting colleges to train doctors in Lebanon and China, and funding medical research and nurses' training in Europe.

Cultural Expansion

The United States government facilitated this cultural expansion by assisting business activities

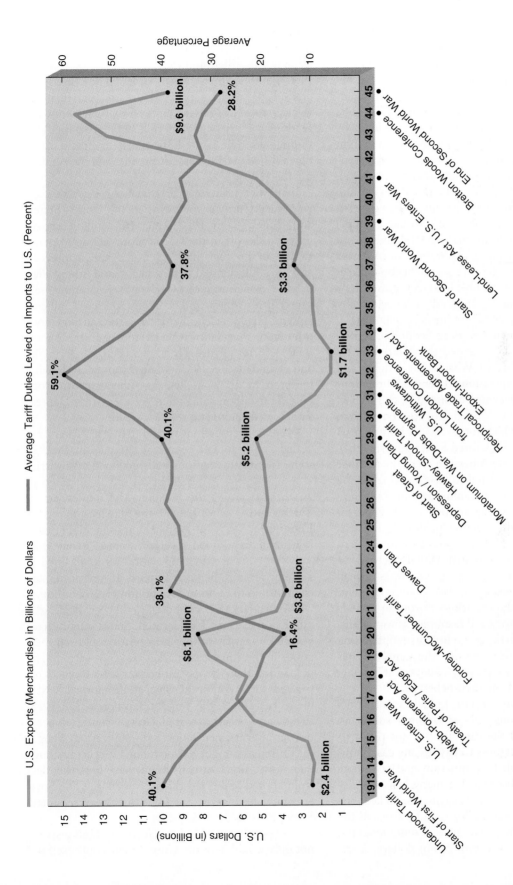

The United States in the World Economy   In the 1920s and 1930s, global depression and war scuttled the United States's hope for a stable economic order. This graph suggests, moreover, that high American tariffs meant lower exports, further impeding world trade. The Reciprocal Trade Agreements program initiated in the early 1930s was designed to ease tariff wars with other nations.   Source: U.S. Bureau of the Census, *Historical Statistics of the United States, Colonial Times to 1970* (Washington, D.C., 1975).

abroad. The Webb-Pomerene Act (1918) excluded from antitrust prosecution those combinations set up for export trade; the Edge Act (1919) permitted American banks to open foreign branch banks; and the overseas offices of the Department of Commerce gathered valuable market information. The federal government also stimulated foreign loans by American investors, discouraging those that might be used for military purposes. "In these days of competition," an American diplomat explained, "capital, trade, agriculture, labor, and statecraft all go hand in hand if a country is to profit." United States government support for the expansion of the telecommunications industry helped International Telephone and Telegraph (ITT), Radio Corporation of America (RCA), and the Associated Press (AP) become international giants by 1930. The United States Navy's cooperation with Juan T. Trippe's Pan American airline company helped its "flying boats" reach Asia.

Europeans watched American economic expansion with wariness and branded the United States stingy for its handling of World War I debts and reparations. Twenty-eight nations became entangled in the web of inter-Allied government debts, which totaled $26.5 billion ($9.6 billion of it owed to the United States government). Europeans owed private American creditors another $3 billion. Europeans urged Americans to erase the government debts as a magnanimous contribution to the war effort. During the war, they angrily charged, Europe had bled while America profited. "There is only one way we could be worse with the Europeans," remarked the humorist Will Rogers, "and that is to have helped them out in two wars instead of one." American leaders insisted on repayment, some claiming that the victorious European nations had gained vast territory and resources as war spoils. Senator George Norris of Nebraska, emphasizing domestic priorities, declared that the United States could build highways in "every county seat" if only the Europeans would pay their debts.

The debts question became linked to Germany's $33 billion reparations bill—an amount some believed Germany had the capacity but not the willingness to pay. In any case, hobbled by inflation and economic disorder, Germany began to default on its payments. To keep the nation afloat and to forestall the radicalism that might thrive on economic troubles, American bankers loaned millions of dollars. A tri-

War Debts

German Reparations

angular relationship developed: American investors' money flowed to Germany, Germany paid reparations to the Allies, and the Allies then paid some of their debts to the United States. The American-crafted Dawes Plan of 1924 greased the financial tracks by reducing Germany's annual payments, extending the repayment period, and providing still more loans. The United States also gradually scaled down Allied obligations, cutting the debt by half during the 1920s.

But the triangular arrangement depended on continued German borrowing in the United States, and in 1928 and 1929 American lending abroad dropped sharply in the face of more lucrative opportunities in the stock market at home (see Chapters 24 and 25). The United States–negotiated Young Plan of 1929, which reduced Germany's reparations, salvaged little as the world economy sputtered and collapsed. That year the British rejected an ingenious offer from President Herbert Hoover to trade their total debt for British Honduras (Belize), Bermuda, and Trinidad. By 1931, when Hoover declared a moratorium on payments, the Allies had paid back only $2.6 billion. Staggered by the Great Depression, they defaulted on the rest.

As the depression accelerated, tariff wars revealed a reinvigorated economic nationalism. By 1932 some twenty-five nations had retaliated against rising American tariffs (created in the Fordney-McCumber Act of 1922 and the Hawley-Smoot Act of 1930) by imposing higher rates on foreign imports. From 1929 to 1933, world trade declined in value by some 40 percent. Exports of American merchandise slumped from $5.2 billion to $1.7 billion.

Tariffs and Economic Nationalism

Many nations contributed to the worldwide economic cataclysm. The United States might have lowered its tariffs so that Europeans could sell their goods in the American market and thus earn dollars to pay off their debts. Americans also might have worked for a comprehensive, multinational settlement. Instead, at the London Conference in 1933, President Roosevelt barred United States cooperation in international monetary stabilization. Vengeful Europeans might have trimmed Germany's huge indemnity. The Germans might have borrowed less from abroad and taxed themselves more. The Soviets might have agreed to pay rather than repudiate Soviet Russia's $4 billion debt.

A revival of world trade, Secretary Hull insisted, not only would help the United States pull itself out of the economic doldrums but also would boost the chances for global peace. Calling the protective tariff the "king of evils," he successfully pressed Congress to pass the Reciprocal Trade Agreements Act in 1934. This important legislation empowered the president to reduce United States tariffs by as much as 50 percent through special agreements with foreign countries. The central feature of the act was the *most-favored-nation principle*, whereby the United States was entitled to the lowest tariff rate set by any nation with which it had an agreement. If, for example, Belgium and the United States granted each other most-favored-nation status, and Belgium then negotiated an agreement with Germany that reduced the Belgian tariff on German typewriters, American typewriters would receive the same low rate.

Reciprocal Trade Agreements Act

In 1934 Hull also helped create the Export-Import Bank, a government agency that provided loans to foreigners for the purchase of American goods. The bank stimulated trade and became a diplomatic weapon, allowing the United States to exact concessions through the approval or denial of loans. But in the short term, Hull's ambitious programs—examples of America's independent internationalism—brought only mixed results.

United States Hegemony in Latin America

Before the First World War the United States had thrown an imperial net over much of Latin America through the Platt Amendment, Roosevelt Corollary, Panama Canal, military intervention, and economic preeminence (see Chapter 22). A North American patronizing attitude could be observed in the comment of a prominent State Department officer who remarked that Latins were incapable of political progress because of their "low racial quality." They were, however, "very easy people to deal with if properly managed."

And managed they were. Schools, roads, telephones, and irrigation systems built by North Americans dotted Caribbean and Central American nations. North American advisers or "money doctors" in Colombia and Peru helped reform tariff and tax laws and invite North American companies to build public works projects. United States soldiers occupied Cuba, the Dominican Republic, Haiti, Panama, and Nicaragua. United States authorities maintained Puerto Rico as a colony (see map, page 760). A distinguished Argentine writer, Manuel Ugarte, asserted that the United States had become a new Rome that annexed wealth rather than territory, but unapologetic North Americans believed that they were bringing not only material improvements to Latin American neighbors but also the blessings of liberty.

Criticism of United States imperialism in the region mounted in the interwar years. Senator William Borah of Idaho urged that Latin Americans be granted the right of self-determination, letting them decide their own future. Others charged that the president was usurping constitutional power by ordering troops abroad without a congressional declaration of war. Businesspeople feared that Latin American nationalists would direct their anti-Yankee feelings against American *gringos* and their property. Some North Americans also became troubled by the double standard that prevailed. Hoover's secretary of state, Henry L. Stimson, acknowledged the problem in 1932 when he was protesting Japanese incursions in China: "If we landed a single soldier among those South Americans now . . . it would put me absolutely in the wrong in China, where Japan has done all this monstrous work under the guise of protecting her nationals with a landing force."

Criticism of United States Interventionism

Renouncing unpopular military intervention, the United States tried other methods to maintain its influence in Latin America: Pan-Americanism, support for strong local leaders, the training of national guards, economic penetration, Export-Import Bank loans, and political subversion. Although this general approach predated his presidency, Franklin D. Roosevelt gave it a name in 1933: the Good Neighbor policy. It meant that the United States would be less blatant in its domination—less willing to defend exploitative business practices, less eager to launch military expeditions, and less reluctant to consult with Latin Americans. "Give them a share," Roosevelt recommended. In 1936, for example, the United States restored some sovereignty to Panama and increased that nation's income from the canal. Such acts greatly enhanced Roosevelt's popularity in Latin America.

Good Neighbor Policy

Meanwhile, United States interests in the Western Hemisphere were growing. From 1914 to 1929,

The United States and Latin America Between the Wars *The United States often intervened in other nations to maintain its hegemonic power in Latin America, where nationalists resented outside meddling in their sovereign affairs. The Good Neighbor policy decreased United States military interventions, but United States economic interests remained strong in the hemisphere.*

direct American investments in Latin America (excluding bonds and securities) jumped from some $1.3 billion to $3.5 billion while United States exports to the area tripled in value. In country after country Latin Americans knew the repercussions of United States economic and political decisions. The price that North Americans set for Chilean copper determined the health of Chile's economy. North American oil executives bribed Venezuelan politicians for tax breaks. Latin American nationalists protested that their resources were being drained away as profits for United States companies, leaving too many nations in a status of dependency.

To secure its interests, the United States trained national guards and supported dictators. For example, before the United States withdrew its troops from the Dominican Republic in 1924, United States personnel created a guard. One of its first officers was Rafael Leonidas Trujillo, who became head of the national army in 1928 and, through fraud and intimidation, became president two years later. Trujillo ruled the Dominican Republic with an iron fist until his assassination in 1961. "He may be an S.O.B.," Roosevelt supposedly remarked, "but he is our S.O.B."

National Guard in the Dominican Republic

Nicaraguans endured a similar experience. United States troops occupied Nicaragua from 1912 to 1925 and returned in late 1926 during a civil war. Washington claimed that it was only trying to stabilize Nicaragua's politics, but critics at home and abroad saw a case of United States imperialism. Nationalistic Nicaraguan opposition, led by César Augusto Sandino, who denounced the Monroe Doctrine as meaning "America for the Yankees," helped persuade Washington to end the occupation. In 1933 the marines departed, but they left behind a powerful national guard headed by General Anastasio Somoza, who "always played the game fairly with us," recalled a top United States officer. With backing from the United States, the Somoza family ruled Nicaragua from 1936 to 1979 through corruption, political suppression, and torture. The revolutionaries who overthrew the Somoza dictatorship in 1979 called themselves Sandinistas in honor of the patriot Sandino, who, more than three decades earlier, had battled the marines before he was assassinated by Somoza henchmen.

Somoza and Sandino in Nicaragua

Nelson A. Rockefeller (1908–1979), at the center of this photograph, enjoys a meal with the dictatorial leader of Nicaragua, General Anastasio Somoza García (1896–1956), who ruled the Central American nation from 1937 to 1956, enriched himself at public expense, and aligned his country with the United States. Born to wealth in an influential family with worldwide economic and philanthropic interests, Nelson was the grandson of John D. Rockefeller, Sr., and the son of John D. Rockefeller, Jr. Nelson worked for the family oil business, especially in Latin America, before becoming coordinator of the office of inter-American affairs in the State Department in 1940. In this position he promoted hemispheric unity against the Axis Powers during World War II. In 1974 he became vice president under President Gerald Ford after President Richard Nixon's resignation during the Watergate scandal. National Archives.

The marine occupation of black, French-speaking Haiti from 1915 to 1934 also left a negative legacy. United States officials censored the Haitian press, manipulated elections, wrote the constitution, jailed or killed protesters, managed government finances, and created a national guard. The National City Bank of New York became the owner of the Haitian Banque Nationale, and the United States became Haiti's largest trading partner. The American high commissioner, General John H. Russell of Georgia, boasted that the Haitian president "has never taken a step without first consulting me." In 1929 Haitians protested violently against United States rule. When a United States commission told President Hoover that the occupation had failed to benefit the Haitian

Occupation of Haiti

This United States government recruiting poster captured the postwar American mood of independent internationalism by offering overseas duty to prospective marines.   Library of Congress.

people, Washington decided to withdraw its soldiers. Haiti continued to suffer Latin America's highest illiteracy rate, lowest per capita income, and poorest health, as well as dictatorship and police-state repression. In 1994, United States troops invaded Haiti again (see page 919).

The Cubans, too, grew restless under North American domination. By 1929 North American investments in the Caribbean nation totaled $1.5 billion, including two-thirds own-

Cuban Revolution of 1933

ership of the sugar industry. The United States military uniform remained conspicuous at the Guantánamo naval base. Especially among elites, North American influences continued to permeate Cuban culture. In 1933, Cubans rebelled against the dictator and United States ally Gerardo Machado. In open defiance of United States warships cruising offshore, Professor Ramón Grau San Martín became presi-

dent and declared the Platt Amendment null and void. His government also seized some North American–owned mills, refused to repay North American bank loans, and debated land reform. Unsettled by this nationalistic "social revolution," United States officials plotted with army sergeant Fulgencio Batista to overthrow Grau in 1934.

During the Batista era, which lasted until Fidel Castro overthrew Batista in 1959 (see page 866), Cuba attracted and protected United States investments while it aligned itself with United States foreign policy goals. The United States provided military aid and Export-Import Bank loans, abrogated the Platt Amendment, and gave Cuban sugar a favored position in the United States market. Cuba became further incorporated into the North American consumer culture, and American tourists flocked to Havana's night life of rum, rhumba, prostitution, and gambling. Nationalistic Cubans grumbled that their nation had become a mere extension—a dependency—of the United States.

In Puerto Rico throughout the 1920s and 1930s, incompetent and often tactless United States officials on the Caribbean island disparaged Puerto Ricans as people of color unfit to govern themselves. The Jones

Puerto Rico

Act of 1917 had granted Puerto Ricans United States citizenship, but the United States rejected calls for the colony's independence or statehood (not until 1947 did the United States permit Puerto Ricans to elect their own governor). A few absentee American landowners and corporate barons made sugar the island's major economic activity. Under United States paternalism, schools and roads were improved, but 80 percent of the island's rural folk were landless, and others crowded into urban slums. New Deal relief programs fell far short of need.

Students, professors, and graduates of the Universidad de Puerto Rico formed the nucleus of islanders critical of United States tutelage. Some founded the Nationalist Party under the leadership of Harvard-trained lawyer Pedro Albizo Campos, who eventually advocated the violent overthrow of United States rule. Police fired on a Nationalist Party march in 1937; nineteen people, including two policemen, died in the Ponce Massacre. Other Puerto Ricans followed the socialist Luis Muñoz Marín, whose Popular Democratic Party ultimately settled for the compromise of commonwealth status (officially conferred in 1952). In the 1950s, under Operation Bootstrap, the island received a huge infusion of capital from the United States and shifted to industrialization. At the same time, increasing numbers of Puerto Ricans journeyed to the United States, creating *barrios* in American cities—especially in New York. To this day, Puerto Ricans remain divided into statehood, commonwealth, and independence factions.

Torn by revolution and civil war, Mexico stood as a unique case in inter-American relations. Woodrow Wilson had sent troops to Mexico in 1914 and

---
United States Clash with Mexican Nationalism

1916 to tame the Mexican Revolution's anti-Americanism. But the opposite occurred. In 1917 the Mexicans openly threatened American-owned landholdings and oil interests by adopting a new constitution specifying that all "land and waters" and all subsoil raw materials (such as petroleum) belonged to the Mexican nation. United States officials worried that if Mexico succeeded in restricting the ownership of private property, other Latin Americans might also defy United States hegemony. For years, with some Americans claiming that Mexico had succumbed to Bolshevism, and Hollywood films disparagingly portraying Mexicans as villainous "greasers" and *bandidos*, Washington and Mexico City wrangled over the rights of United States economic interests.

In 1938, during an oil workers' strike, Mexico boldly expropriated the property of all foreign-owned petroleum companies. The United States countered by reducing purchases of Mexican silver and encouraging a business boycott against the nation. But President Roosevelt decided to compromise because he feared that the Mexicans would sell their oil to Germany and Japan. In a 1942 agreement the United States conceded that Mexico owned its raw materials and could treat them as it saw fit, and Mexico compensated the companies for their lost property. Although American investments in and trade with Mexico remained large, United States power there had been diminished. Nationalists across Latin America drew inspiration from Mexico's defiance of its giant neighbor.

Roosevelt's movement toward nonmilitary methods—the Good Neighbor policy—was also expressed in Pan-Americanism. Throughout the 1920s

---
Pan-Americanism
---

the United States had refused to renounce its self-declared right of intervention in the hemisphere. In 1936, however, at the Pan-American Conference

William E. Borah (1865–1940), chair of the Senate Foreign Relations Committee (left), and Henry L. Stimson (1867–1950), secretary of state (right), often clashed over foreign policy even though both were Republicans. The Idaho senator became a passionate anti-imperialist and isolationist who protested United States interventions abroad. Because of critics such as Borah, Stimson grew eager to find nonmilitary means to maintain United States hegemony in the Western Hemisphere. Corbis-Bettmann.

The German leader Adolf Hitler (1889–1945) is surrounded in this propagandistic painting by images that came to symbolize hate, genocide, and war: Nazi flags with emblems of the swastika, the iron cross on the dictator's pocket, Nazi troops in loyal salute. The anti-Semitic Hitler denounced the United States as a "Jewish rubbish heap" of "inferiority and decadence" that was "incapable of conducting war."   U.S. Army Center of Military History.

in Buenos Aires, United States officials endorsed nonintervention. The new policy marked a distinct change from the Roosevelt Corollary and marine expeditions. One payoff was the Declaration of Panama (1939), in which Latin American governments drew a security line around the hemisphere and warned aggressors away. In exchange for more United States trade and foreign aid, Latin Americans also reduced their sales of raw materials to Germany, Japan, and Italy and increased shipments to the United States. On the eve of the Second World War, then, the United States's sphere of influence in the hemisphere seemed intact, and most Latin American regimes backed United States diplomatic objectives. For a long time, however, memories of strong-arm methods fueled anti-Yankee nationalism throughout the region.

 ## Nazi Germany and Appeasement in Europe

In depression-wracked Germany, Adolf Hitler came to power in 1933. Like Benito Mussolini, who had gained control of Italy in 1922, Hitler was a fascist. Fascism (called Nazism, or National Socialism, in Germany) was a collection of ideas and prejudices that celebrated supremacy of the state over the individual; of dictatorship over democracy; of authoritarianism over freedom of speech; of a regulated, state-oriented economy over a free-market economy; and of militarism and war over peace. The Nazis vowed not only to revive German economic and military strength but also to cripple communism and "purify" the German "race" by destroying Jews and other people, such as homosexuals and Gypsies, whom Hitler disparaged as inferiors.

Resentful of the punitive terms of the 1919 Treaty of Versailles, Hitler immediately withdrew Germany from the League of Nations, ended reparations payments, and began to rearm. While secretly laying plans for the conquest of neighboring states, he watched admiringly as Mussolini's troops invaded the African nation of Ethiopia in 1935. The next year Hitler ordered his own goose-stepping troopers into the Rhineland, an area that the Versailles treaty had demilitarized. When Germany's timid neighbor France did not resist this act, Hitler crowed: "The world belongs to the man with guts!"

Hitler's Aggression

Soon the aggressors joined hands. In 1936 Italy and Germany formed an alliance called the Rome-Berlin Axis. Shortly thereafter Germany and Japan united against the Soviet Union in the Anti-Comintern Pact. To these events Britain and France responded with a policy of appeasement, hoping to curb Hitler's expansionist appetite by permitting him a few nibbles. The policy of appeasing Hitler proved disastrous, for the hate-filled German leader continually raised his demands.

In those hair-trigger times, a civil war in Spain soon turned into an international struggle. From 1936 to 1939, the Loyalists defended Spain's elected republican government against Francisco Franco's fascist movement. About three thousand American volunteers, known as the Abraham Lincoln Battalion of the "International Brigades," joined the fight on the side of the Loyalist republicans, which also had the backing of the Soviet Union. Hitler and Mussolini sent military aid to Franco. France and Britain held to the fiction of a nonintervention pledge that both Italy and Germany had signed. Franco won in 1939, tightening the grip of fascism on the European continent.

Early in 1938 Hitler once again tested the limits of European tolerance when he sent soldiers into Austria to annex the nation of his birth. Then in September he seized the Sudeten region of Czechoslovakia.

Czechoslovakia and Munich

Appeasement reached its apex that month when France and Britain, without consulting the helpless Czechs, agreed at the Munich Conference to allow Hitler another territorial bite. British Prime Minister Neville Chamberlain returned home to proclaim "peace in our time," confident that Hitler was satiated. In March 1939 Hitler swallowed the rest of Czechoslovakia.

Poland was next on the German leader's list. Scuttling appeasement, London and Paris announced that they would stand by their ally Poland. Un-

Poland and the Onset of World War II

daunted, Berlin signed the Nazi-Soviet Pact with Moscow in August. Soviet leader Joseph Stalin believed that the West's appeasement of Hitler had left him no choice but to cut a deal with the Nazi ruler. But Stalin also coveted territory: a top-secret protocol attached to the pact carved eastern Europe into German and Soviet zones and permitted the Soviets to grab half of Poland and the three Baltic states of Lithuania, Estonia, and Latvia. On September 1 Hitler launched *blitzkrieg* attacks—highly mobile land forces and armor combined with tactical aircraft—against Poland. Britain and France declared war on Germany two days later. The Second World War had begun.

As the world hurtled toward war, Soviet-American relations remained embittered. During the 1920s the United States refused to open diplomatic relations with the Soviet government, which had failed to pay $600 million for confiscated American-owned property and had repudiated preexisting Russian debts. To many Americans, the Communists seemed to be godless, radical malcontents bent on destroying the American way of life through world revolution. American businesses such as General Electric and International Harvester nonetheless entered the Soviet marketplace. Henry Ford signed a contract in 1929 to build an automobile plant. By 1930 the Soviet Union had become the largest buyer of American farm and industrial equipment.

In the early 1930s, when trade began to slump, some American business leaders lobbied for diplomatic recognition of the Soviet Union. "We would recognize the Devil with a false face if he would contract for

United States Recognition of the Soviet Union

some pitchforks," quipped Will Rogers. President Roosevelt himself concluded that nonrecognition had failed to alter the Soviet system, and he speculated that closer Soviet-American relations might deter Japanese expansion. In 1933 Roosevelt granted United States diplomatic recognition of the Soviet Union in return for Soviet agreement to discuss the debts question, to forgo subversive activities in the United States, and to grant Americans in the Soviet Union religious freedom and legal rights. The first United States embassy in Moscow opened in 1934, but relations soon deteriorated. Stalin's brutalities against his people and the Nazi-Soviet Pact of August 1939 outraged many Americans—further evidence for them that Europe had gone mad once again.

Isolationism, Neutrality, and Roosevelt's Foreign Policy

As authoritarianism, race hatred, and military expansion descended on Europe in the 1930s, Americans endorsed isolationism to distance themselves from Europe's wars. They had learned powerful negative lessons from the First World War: war wounds reform movements, undermines civil liberties, dangerously expands federal and presidential power, disrupts the economy, and accentuates racial and class tensions (see Chapter 23). A 1937 Gallup poll found that nearly two-thirds of the respondents thought United States participation in the First World War had been a mistake.

Conservative isolationists feared higher taxes and increased executive power if the nation went to war again. Liberal isolationists worried that domestic problems might go unresolved as the nation spent more on the military. Many isolationists predicted that in attempting to spread democracy abroad or to police the world, Americans would lose their freedoms at home. The vast majority of isolationists opposed fascism and condemned aggression, but they did not think the United States should have to do what Europeans themselves refused to do: block Hitler.

It seems odd that a supreme American capitalist such as Henry Ford would be active in communist Russia, a nation that the United States did not even officially recognize in the 1920s. Yet at that very time Ford, seeing economic opportunity, began to market automobiles and tractors in the land of the Bolsheviks. Here some Fordson tractors are readied in Novorossick. The industrializing Russians admired the mass-production techniques Ford used in his American factories. Collections of Henry Ford Museum and Greenfield Village.

Isolationist sentiment was strongest in the Midwest and among anti-British ethnic groups, especially German- and Irish-Americans, but it was a nationwide phenomenon that cut across socio-economic, ethnic, party, and sectional lines and attracted a majority of the American people. Prominent isolationists in the 1930s included Republicans such as Congressman Hamilton Fish of New York, Senator William Borah of Idaho, and former president Herbert Hoover; Democrats such as Congressman Maury Maverick of Texas; Socialists such as Norman Thomas; Communists and Nazi sympathizers; and pacifists such as Congresswoman Jeannette Rankin of Montana. They also included the publisher Robert R. McCormick of the *Chicago Tribune*, the historian Charles Beard, the physicist Albert Einstein, and the anti-Semitic radio priest Charles E. Coughlin. University students in 1936 organized the Veterans of Future Wars and asked for a bonus of $1,000 before going into battle, because, they mockingly proclaimed, few would live through the next war. These dissimilar people united in the opinion that alternatives to American participation in another European war existed.

Some isolationists charged that corporate "merchants of death" had promoted war and were assisting the aggressors. After Dorothy Detzer of the WILPF diligently lobbied Senator Gerald P. Nye to take up the issue, a congressional committee held hearings from 1934 to 1936 on the role of business and financiers in the United States's decision to enter the First World War. The Nye committee did not prove that American munitions makers had dragged the nation into that war, but it did uncover evidence that corporations practicing "rotten commercialism" had bribed foreign politicians to bolster arms sales in the 1920s and 1930s and had lobbied against arms control.

Nye Committee Hearings

The historical record also confirms isolationist suspicions of American business ties with Nazi Germany and fascist Italy that might endanger United States neutrality. Twenty-six of the top one hundred American corporations, including Du Pont, Standard Oil, and General Motors, had contractual agreements in 1937 with German firms. And after Italy attacked Ethiopia in 1935, American petroleum, copper, and scrap iron and steel exports to Italy increased substantially, despite Roosevelt's call for a moral embargo on such commerce. A Dow Chemical official stated: "We do not inquire into the uses of the products. We are interested in selling them." Not all American executives thought this way. The Wall Street law firm of Sullivan and Cromwell, for example, severed lucrative ties with Germany to protest the Nazi persecution of Jews.

Reflecting the popular desire to avoid European squabbles, President Roosevelt signed a series of neutrality acts. Congress sought to protect the nation by outlawing the kinds of contacts that had compromised United States neutrality during World War I. The Neutrality Act of 1935 prohibited arms shipments to either side in a war once the president had declared the existence of belligerency. Roosevelt had wanted the authority to name the aggressor and apply an arms embargo against it alone, but Congress would not grant the president such discretionary power. The Neutrality Act of 1936 forbade loans to belligerents. After a joint resolution in 1937 declared the United States neutral in the Spanish Civil War, Roosevelt embargoed arms shipments to both sides. The Neutrality Act of 1937 introduced the cash-and-carry principle: warring nations wishing to trade with the United States would have to pay cash for their nonmilitary purchases and carry the goods away in their own ships. The act also forbade Americans from traveling on the ships of belligerent nations.

Neutrality Acts

President Roosevelt shared isolationist views in the early 1930s. Although prior to World War I he was an expansionist and interventionist like his older cousin Theodore, during the interwar period Roosevelt talked less about preparedness and more about disarmament and the horrors of war, less about policing the world and more about handling problems at home. In a passionate speech delivered in August 1936 at Chautauqua, New York, Roosevelt expressed prevailing isolationist opinion and made a pitch for the pacifist vote in the upcoming election: "I have seen war. . . . I have seen blood running from the wounded. I have seen men coughing out their gassed lungs. . . . I have seen the agony of mothers and wives. I hate war." The United States, he promised, would remain distant from European conflict. During the Czechoslovakian crisis of 1938 Roosevelt actually endorsed appeasement.

Roosevelt's Changing Views

The Munich accord elicited a "universal sense of relief," he remarked.

All the while, Roosevelt was becoming increasingly troubled by the arrogant behavior of Germany, Italy, and Japan—the aggressors he tagged the "three bandit nations." He condemned the Nazi persecution of the Jews and the Japanese slaughter of Chinese civilians. Privately he chastised the British and French for failing to collar Hitler. Because he worried that the United States was ill prepared to confront the aggressors, his New Deal public works programs included millions for the construction of new warships. In 1935 the president requested the largest peacetime defense budget in American history. Three years later, in the wake of Munich, he asked Congress for funds to build up the air force, which he believed essential to deter aggression. Pressed hard by Roosevelt in early 1938, the House of Representatives defeated a constitutional amendment proposed by Indiana Democrat Louis Ludlow to require a majority vote in a national referendum before a congressional declaration of war could go into effect (unless the United States were attacked). In January 1939 the president secretly decided to sell bombers to France, saying privately that "our frontier is on the Rhine."

In early 1939 the president lashed out at the international lawbreakers and urged Congress to repeal the arms embargo and permit the sale of munitions to belligerents on a cash-and-carry basis. Roosevelt knew that repeal would aid Britain, which dominated the seas. When the Senate Foreign Relations Committee voted down repeal, Roosevelt raged: "I think we ought to introduce a bill for statues of [Senators] Austin, Vandenberg, Lodge and Taft . . . to be erected in Berlin and put the swastika on them."

Europe descended into the abyss of war in September 1939 when Germany attacked Poland. Soviet forces seized eastern Poland at the same time (see map, page 768). Roosevelt declared neutrality. But unlike Woodrow Wilson, he did not ask Americans to be neutral in thought, and he pressed again for repeal of the arms embargo. Senator Arthur Vandenberg, an isolationist from Michigan, roared back that the United States could not be "an arsenal for one belligerent without becoming a target for the other." After much debate, however, Congress in November lifted the embargo on contraband and approved cash-and-carry exports of arms. Using

Repeal of the Arms Embargo

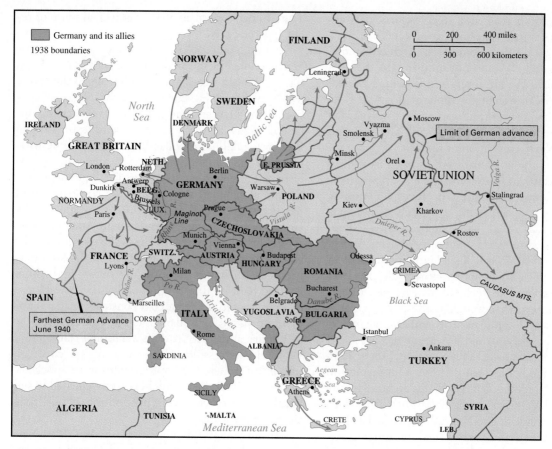

The German Advance, 1939–1942 *Hitler's drive to dominate Europe carried German troops deep into France and the Soviet Union. Great Britain took a beating but held on with the help of American economic and military aid before the United States itself entered the Second World War.*

"methods short of war," Roosevelt was ready to aid the Allies. Hitler dismissed these American stirrings, charging that a "half Judaized, half negrified" United States was "incapable of conducting war."

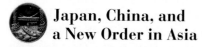

Japan, China, and a New Order in Asia

While Europe succumbed to political turmoil and war, Asia witnessed the aggressive march of Japan. The United States had interests at stake in Asia: the Philippines and Pacific islands, religious missions, trade and investments, and the Open Door in China. In traditional missionary fashion, Americans also believed that they were China's special friend and protector. "With God's help," Senator Kenneth Wherry of Nebraska once proclaimed, "we will lift Shanghai up and up, ever up, until it is just like Kansas City." Pearl Buck's best-selling novel *The Good Earth*

(1931), made into a widely distributed film six years later, confirmed American opinion with its image of the noble, persevering Chinese peasant. By contrast, Japan loomed as a threat to American attitudes and interests. The Tokyo government seemed bent on subjugating China and unhinging the Open Door doctrine of equal trade and investment opportunity.

The Chinese themselves were uneasy about the United States presence in Asia. Like the Japanese, they wished to reduce the influence of Westerners. The Chinese Revolution of 1911 still rumbled in the 1920s as antiforeign riots damaged American property and imperiled American missionaries. Chinese nationalists criticized Americans for the imperialist practice of extraterritoriality (the exemption of foreigners accused of crimes from Chinese legal jurisdiction), and they demanded an end to this affront to Chinese sovereignty.

In the late 1920s, civil war broke out in China when Jiang Jieshi (Chiang Kai-shek) ousted Mao Zedong and his Communist followers from the ruling Guomindang Party. Americans

Rise of Jiang Jieshi in China

applauded this display of anti-Bolshevism and Jiang's conversion to Christianity in 1930. Jiang's new wife, Soong Meiling, also won their hearts. The American-educated daughter of a Chinese businessman, Madame Jiang spoke flawless English, dressed in Western fashion, and cultivated ties with prominent Americans. Warming to Jiang, American officials abandoned one imperial vestige by signing a treaty in 1928 restoring control of tariffs to the Chinese. American gunboats and marines, however, remained in China.

The Japanese grew increasingly suspicious of United States–Chinese ties. In the early twentieth century, Japanese-American relations were seldom cordial, as Japan gained influence in Manchuria, Shandong, and Korea. The Japanese sought not only to oust Western imperialists from Asia but also to dominate Asian territories that produced the raw materials that their import-dependent island nation required. The Japanese also resented the discriminatory immigration law of 1924, which excluded them from entry into the United States. Despite the Washington Conference treaties of 1922, naval competition continued; in fact, American naval officers used Japan as the imaginary enemy in war games at the Naval War College. Also, although the volume of Japanese-American trade was twice that of Chinese-American trade, commercial rivalry strained relations between Japan and the United States. The importation of inexpensive Japanese goods, especially textiles, spawned "Buy America" campaigns and boycotts.

Relations deteriorated further in 1931 after the Japanese military seized Manchuria in China (see map). Manchuria served Japan both as a buffer

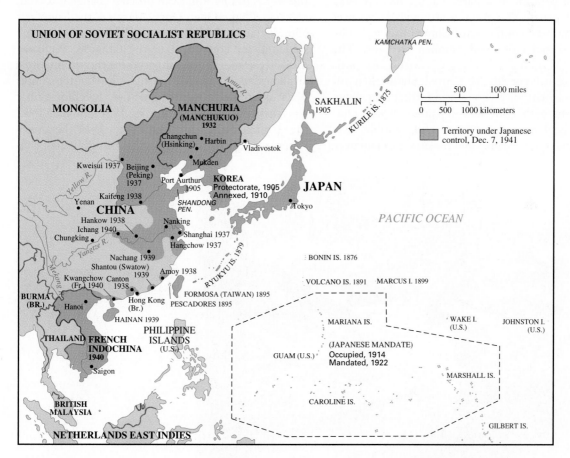

Japanese Expansion Before Pearl Harbor *The Japanese quest for predominance began at the turn of the century and intensified in the 1930s. China suffered the most at the hands of Tokyo's military. Vulnerable United States possessions in Asia and the Pacific proved no obstacle to Japan's ambitions for a Greater East Asia Co-Prosperity Sphere.*

**Japanese
Seizure of
Manchuria**

against the Soviets and as a vital source of coal, iron, timber, and food. More than half of Japan's foreign investments rested in Manchuria. "We are seeking room that will let us breathe," said a Japanese politician, arguing that his tiny, heavily populated nation (65 million people in an area slightly smaller than California) needed to expand in order to survive. Although the seizure of Manchuria violated the Nine-Power Treaty and the Kellogg-Briand Pact, the United States did not have the power to compel Japanese withdrawal. The American response therefore went no further than a moral lecture known as the Stimson Doctrine: the United States would not recognize any impairment of China's sovereignty or of the Open Door policy, Secretary of State Henry L. Stimson declared in 1932.

Hardly cowed by protests from Western capitals, Japan continued to harry China. In mid-1937 the Sino-Japanese War erupted, although Tokyo preferred to call the conflict the "China incident." The Japanese seized cities and bombed civilians. The gruesome bombing of Shanghai intensified anti-Japanese sentiment in the United States. Senator Norris, an isolationist who moved further away from isolationism with each new Japanese thrust, condemned the Japanese as "disgraceful, ignoble, barbarous, and cruel, even beyond the power of language

to describe." In an effort to help China by permitting it to buy American arms, Roosevelt refused to declare the existence of war, thus avoiding activation of the Neutrality Acts.

In a speech denouncing the aggressors on October 5, 1937, the president called for a "quarantine" to curb the "epidemic of world lawlessness."

**Roosevelt's
Quarantine
Speech**

People who thought Washington had been too gentle with Japan cheered. Isolationists warned that the president was edging toward war. On December 12 Japanese aircraft sank the American gunboat *Panay*, an escort for Standard Oil Company tankers on the Yangtze River. Two American sailors died during the attack. Roosevelt was much relieved when Tokyo eventually apologized and offered to pay for damages.

Japan's declaration of a "New Order" in Asia, in the words of one American official, "banged, barred, and bolted" the Open Door. Alarmed, the Roosevelt administration during the late 1930s gave loans and sold military equipment to the Chinese. Secretary Hull declared a moral embargo on the shipment of airplanes to Japan. Meanwhile, the United States Navy continued to grow, aided by a billion-dollar congressional appropriation in 1938. In mid-1939 the United States abrogated the 1911 Japanese-American trade treaty, yet America continued to ship

H. S. Wong's widely circulated photograph of a child after the Japanese bombing of Shanghai, in 1937, helped galvanize world opinion against Tokyo's brutal subjugation of China. National Archives.

oil, cotton, and machinery to Japan. The administration hesitated to initiate economic sanctions because such pressure might spark a Japanese-American war at a time when Germany posed a more serious threat. When war broke out in Europe in the fall of 1939, Japanese-American relations were at a stalemate.

Collision Course, 1939–1941

President Roosevelt remarked in 1939 that the United States could not "draw a line of defense around this country and live completely and solely to ourselves." Thomas Jefferson had tried that with his 1807 embargo—"the damned thing didn't work" and "we got into the War of 1812." America, the president insisted, could not insulate itself from world war. Polls showed that Americans strongly favored the Allies and that most supported aid to Britain and France—but the great majority emphatically wanted the United States to remain at peace. Troubled by this conflicting advice—oppose Hitler, aid the allies, but stay out of the war—the president gradually moved the nation from neutrality to undeclared war against Germany and then, after the Japanese attack on Pearl Harbor, to full-scale war itself.

Because the stakes were so high, Americans vigorously debated the direction of their foreign policy from 1939 through 1941. Unprecedented numbers of Americans spoke out on foreign affairs and joined organizations that addressed the issues. Spine-chilling events and the widespread use of radio, the nation's chief source of news, helped stimulate this high level of public interest. So did ethnic affiliations with the various belligerents and victims of aggression. The American Legion, the League of Women Voters, labor unions, and local chapters of the Committee to Defend America by Aiding the Allies and the isolationist America First Committee (both organized in 1940) provided outlets for citizen participation in the national debate.

National Debate

In April 1940 Germany invaded Denmark and Norway (see map, page 768). In March the Soviet Union had invaded Finland. "The small countries are smashed up, one by one, like matchwood," sighed Winston Churchill, who became Britain's prime minister on May 10, 1940, the day several German divisions attacked Belgium,

Fall of France

This cartoon in a British newspaper on September 22, 1939, suggests how precarious United States neutrality was shortly after the outbreak of war in Europe. The cartoonist obviously feels some pique that the United States is watching rather than joining the war, and his message is clear: bombs inevitably will hit the United States. President Franklin D. Roosevelt turns a quizzical face to Secretary of State Cordell Hull.   "Uncomfortable Grandstand" by David Low, *Evening Standard*, London, September 22, 1939.

the Netherlands, and France, pushing French and British forces back to the English Channel. At Dunkirk, France, between May 26 and June 6, more than 300,000 Allied soldiers frantically escaped to Britain on a flotilla of small boats. The Germans occupied Paris a week later. A new French government located in the town of Vichy decided to collaborate with the conquering Nazis and, on June 22, surrendered France to Berlin. With France knocked out of the war, the German Luftwaffe (air force) launched massive bombing raids against Great Britain in preparation for a full-scale invasion. Stunned Americans asked, could Washington or New York be the Luftwaffe's next target?

Alarmed by the swift defeat of one European nation after another, Americans gradually shed their isolationist sentiment. Some liberals left the isolationist fold; it became more and more the province of conservatives. Emotions ran high. Roosevelt called the isolationists "ostriches" and charged that some were pro-Nazi subversives. The White House began to turn over to the Federal Bureau of Investigation letters that criticized Roosevelt's foreign policy.

The isolationist America First Committee published this bumper sticker in 1941 in a vain attempt to halt the United States's descent into war. America Firsters organized in September 1940 and attracted many prominent members, including the famed aviator Charles Lindbergh.   Herbert Hoover Presidential Library.

After Roosevelt tried futilely to draw the belligerents to the peace table, he told his advisers that he was "not willing to fire the first shot" but was waiting for some incident to bring the United States into the war. In the meantime, assuring Americans that New Deal reforms would not have to be sacrificed to achieve military preparedness, Roosevelt began to aid the beleaguered Allies to prevent the fall of Britain. In May 1940 he ordered the sale of old surplus military equipment to Britain and France. In July he cultivated bipartisan support by naming Republicans Henry L. Stimson and Frank Knox, ardent backers of aid to the Allies, secretaries of war and the navy respectively. In September, by executive agreement, the president traded fifty old American destroyers for leases to eight British military bases, including Newfoundland, Bermuda, and Jamaica.

Two weeks later Roosevelt signed into law the hotly debated and narrowly passed Selective Training and Service Act, the first peacetime military draft in American history. The act called for the registration of all

First Peacetime Military Draft

men between the ages of twenty-one and thirty-five. Soon more than 16 million men had signed up, and draft notices began to be delivered. Meanwhile, Roosevelt won reelection in November with promises of peace: "Your boys are not going to be sent into any foreign wars." Republican candidate Wendell Willkie, who in the emerging spirit of bipartisanship had not made an issue of foreign policy, snapped, "That hypocritical son of a bitch! This is going to beat me!" It did.

Roosevelt claimed that the United States could stay out of the war by enabling the beleaguered British

to win. The United States, he said, must become the "great arsenal of democracy." In January 1941 Congress debated

Lend-Lease Act

the president's lend-lease bill. Because Britain was broke, the president explained, the United States should lend rather than sell weapons, much as a neighbor lends a garden hose to fight a fire. Roosevelt's analogy did not persuade strict isolationist Senator Burton K. Wheeler of Montana, who shouted out another comparison: lend-lease was "the New Deal's triple A foreign policy; it will plow under every fourth American boy." But in March 1941, with pro-British sentiment running high, the House passed the Lend-Lease Act by 317 votes to 71; the Senate followed with a 60-to-31 vote. The initial appropriation was $7 billion, but by the end of the war the amount had reached $50 billion, more than $31 billion of it for England.

To ensure the safe delivery of lend-lease goods, Roosevelt ordered the United States Navy to patrol halfway across the Atlantic, and he sent American troops to Greenland. In June 1941 Hitler attacked the Soviet Union. Two months earlier, in anticipation of just such an attack, the Soviets had signed a neutrality treaty with Japan, thus reducing the chances that they would have to fight a two-front war. In July, arguing that Iceland was essential to the defense of the Western Hemisphere, Roosevelt dispatched four thousand marines there. He also sent lend-lease aid to the Soviet Union. If the Soviets could hold off two hundred German divisions in the east, he calculated, Britain would gain some breathing time. Churchill, who had long thundered against Communists, now applauded aid to the Soviets: "If Hitler invaded Hell, I would make at least a favorable reference to the Devil in the House of Commons."

In August 1941 Churchill and Roosevelt met for four days on a British battleship off the coast of Newfoundland. They got along well, trading naval stories and taking pleasure in the fact that Churchill was half American. The two leaders is-

Atlantic Charter Conference

sued the Atlantic Charter, a set of war aims reminiscent of Wilsonianism (see page 662): collective security, disarmament, self-determination, economic cooperation, and freedom of the seas. On January 1, 1942, twenty-six nations signed the Declaration of the United Nations, pledging allegiance to the Atlantic Charter. Churchill later recalled that the president told him in Newfoundland that he could

President Franklin D. Roosevelt (left) and British Prime Minster Winston Churchill (1874–1965) confer on board a ship near Newfoundland during their summit meeting of August 1941. During the conference, they signed the Atlantic Charter. Upon his return to Great Britain, Churchill told his advisers that Roosevelt had promised to "wage war" against Germany and do "everything" to "force an incident." Franklin D. Roosevelt Library, Hyde Park, New York.

not ask Congress for a declaration of war against Germany but "he would wage war" and "become more and more provocative."

In September 1941 came an incident that Roosevelt could exploit: a German submarine fired on (but did not hit) the American destroyer *Greer*. In a special radio broadcast the presi-

Greer Incident

dent protested German "piracy" and announced a policy he already had promised Churchill in private: American naval vessels would convoy British merchant ships all the way to Iceland and would shoot German submarines, the "rattlesnakes of the Atlantic," on sight. Roosevelt practiced deliberate deception in the *Greer* case, for he did not mention that the *Greer* had been tailing a German U-boat for hours, signaling the submarine's location to British airplanes hunting the ship with depth charges. He and his advisers thought it necessary to manipulate public opinion in order to scare Americans into defending Britain.

Thus the United States entered into an undeclared war with Germany. When in early October a German submarine torpedoed the American destroyer

Kearny off the coast of Iceland, the president announced that "the shooting has started. And history has recorded who fired the first shot." Later that month, when the destroyer *Reuben James* went down with the loss of more than one hundred American lives, Congress scrapped the cash-and-carry policy and further revised the Neutrality Acts to permit transport of munitions to England on armed American merchant ships. The United States was not far from full-scale war in Europe.

 ## Why War Came: Pearl Harbor and the Interwar Era

In retrospect, it seems ironic that the Second World War came to the United States by way of Asia. Roosevelt had wanted to avoid war with Japan in order to concentrate American resources on the defeat of Germany. In September 1940, after Germany, Italy, and Japan had signed the Tripartite Pact, Roosevelt slapped an embargo on shipments of aviation fuel and scrap metal to Japan. Because the president believed the petroleum-thirsty Japanese would consider a cutoff of oil a life-or-death matter, he did not embargo that vital commodity. But after Japanese troops occupied French Indochina in July 1941, Washington froze Japanese assets in the United States, virtually ending trade (including oil) with Japan. "The oil gauge and the clock stood side by side" for Japan, wrote one observer.

Tokyo recommended a summit meeting between President Roosevelt and Prime Minister Prince Konoye, but the United States rejected the idea.

United States Demands on Japan

American officials insisted that the Japanese first agree to respect China's sovereignty and territorial integrity and to honor the Open Door policy—in short, to get out of China. According to polls taken in the fall of 1941, the American people seemed willing to risk war with Japan to thwart further aggression. For Roosevelt, Europe still claimed first priority, but he supported Secretary Hull's hard-line policy against Japan's pursuit of the Greater East Asia Co-Prosperity Sphere—the name Tokyo gave to the vast Asian region it intended to dominate.

Roosevelt told his advisers to string out ongoing Japanese-American talks to gain time—time to fortify the Philippines and check the fascists in Europe. "Let us do nothing to precipitate a crisis," he told the cabinet in November 1941. By breaking the Japanese diplomatic code and deciphering intercepted messages through Operation MAGIC, American officials learned that Tokyo's patience with diplomacy was fast dissipating. In late November the Japanese rejected American demands that they withdraw from Indochina. An intercepted message that American experts decoded on December 3 instructed the Japanese embassy in Washington to burn codes and destroy cipher machines—a sure sign that war was coming. Secretary Stimson explained later that the United States let Japan fire the first shot so as "to have the full support of the American people" and "so that there should remain no doubt in anyone's mind as to who were the aggressors."

The Japanese plotted a daring raid on Pearl Harbor in Hawai'i. An armada of 60 Japanese ships, with a core of 6 carriers bearing 360 airplanes, crossed 3,000 miles of the Pacific Ocean. To avoid detection, every ship maintained radio silence. In the early morning of December 7, some 230 miles northwest of Honolulu, the car-

Surprise Attack on Pearl Harbor

riers unleashed their planes, each stamped with a red sun representing the Japanese flag. They swept down on the unsuspecting American naval base and nearby airfields, dropping torpedoes and bombs and strafing buildings.

The battleship U.S.S. *Arizona* swallowed a Japanese bomb that ignited explosives below deck, killing more than one thousand sailors. The U.S.S. *Nevada* tried to escape the inferno by heading out to sea, but a second wave of aerial attackers struck the ship. Altogether the invaders sank or damaged eight battleships and many smaller vessels and smashed more than 160 aircraft on the ground. Huddled in an air-raid shelter, sixteen-year-old Mary Ann Ramsey watched the injured come in "with filthy black oil covering shredded flesh. With the first sailor, so horribly burned, personal fear left me; he brought me the full tragedy of the day." A total of 2,403 died; 1,178 were wounded. By chance, three aircraft carriers at sea escaped the disaster. The Pearl Harbor tragedy, from the perspective of the war's outcome, was more of a military inconvenience than a disaster.

How could the stunning attack on Pearl Harbor have happened? After all, American cryptanalysts had broken the Japanese diplomatic code. Although the intercepted Japanese messages told policymakers that war lay ahead, the intercepts never revealed naval or military plans and never specifically mentioned Pearl Harbor. Roosevelt did not, as some critics charged, conspire to leave the fleet vulnerable to attack so that the United States could enter the Second World War through the "back door" of Asia. The base at Pearl Harbor was not ready—not on red alert—because a message sent from Washington warning of the imminence of war had been too casually transmitted by a slow method and had arrived too late. Base commanders were too relaxed, believing Hawai'i too far from Japan to be a target for all-out attack. Like Roosevelt's advisers, they expected an assault at British Malaya, Thailand, or the Philippines (see map, page 769). The Pearl Harbor calamity stemmed from mistakes and insufficient information, not from conspiracy.

Explaining Pearl Harbor

On December 8, referring to the previous day as "a date which will live in infamy," Roosevelt asked Congress for a declaration of war against Japan. He noted that the Japanese had also attacked Malaya, Hong Kong, Guam, the Philippines, Wake, and Midway, and he expressed the prevailing sense of revenge when he remarked that Americans would

How do historians know that American leaders knew in December 1941, before the attack on Pearl Harbor, that Japan intended to go to war with the United States? In September 1940, United States cryptanalysts—codebreakers—of the Signal Intelligence Service cracked the most secret diplomatic cipher used by the Japanese government, a machine they called PURPLE. The codebreakers discovered patterns in the incoherent letters of telegraphed messages, produced texts, and even duplicated the complicated PURPLE machine (shown here). Thereafter, under Operation MAGIC, they decoded thousands of intercepted messages sent by Japanese officials around the world. Important intercepts such as the one shown below were delivered to a handful of top American leaders, including the president. These dispatches made increasingly clear through 1941 that Tokyo expected all-out war with the United States. An intercept on December 3, just a few days before the attack on Pearl Harbor, revealed that Tokyo had ordered the Japanese embassy in Washington to destroy all codes and cipher machines, a sure sign that war was imminent.

After the attack against Pearl Harbor, and after it became public knowledge that the United States had broken the Japanese diplomatic code, the cry sounded that President Roosevelt must have known what was coming yet failed to prepare the naval base for the assault. The many messages intercepted in the fall and winter of 1941, however, never revealed Japan's military plans. Not one intercepted message mentioned an attack on Pearl Harbor; indeed, Japanese diplomats in Washington were never told that Pearl Harbor would be hit. National Archives.

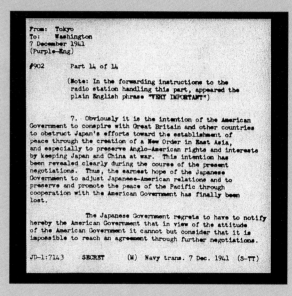

never forget "the character of the onslaught against us." A unanimous vote in the Senate and a 388-to-1 vote in the House thrust America into war. Again, Representative Jeannette Rankin of Montana voted "no," matching her vote against entry into the First World War.

Three days later, Germany and Italy, honoring the Tripartite Pact they had signed with Japan in September 1940, declared war against the United States. "Hitler's fate was sealed," Churchill later wrote. "Mussolini's fate was sealed. As for the Japanese, they would be ground to powder. . . . I went to bed and slept the sleep of the saved and thankful."

Remembering the bitter experience of the First World War, Americans had tried to stay out of the Second. But diplomacy and economic sanctions had not stopped the aggressors, who kept pushing on, threatening United States interests. A fundamental clash of systems explains why diplomacy failed and war came. Germany and Japan preferred a world divided into closed spheres of influence. The United States sought a liberal capitalist world order in which all nations enjoyed freedom of trade and investment. American principles manifested respect for human

Clash of Systems

The stricken U.S.S. California *was one of eight battleships caught in the surprise Japanese attack at Pearl Harbor, Hawai'i, on December 7, 1941. The* California *was sunk, but months later it was refloated and moved to a drydock for modernization. The ship rejoined the United States fleet in 1943 and went on to win seven battle stars during the Second World War.*   National Archives.

rights; fascists in Europe and militarists in Asia defiantly trampled such rights. The United States prided itself on its democratic system; Germany and Japan embraced authoritarian regimes backed by the military.

When the United States protested against German and Japanese expansion, Berlin and Tokyo reminded Washington of the United States's sphere in Latin America. German, Italian, and Japanese leaders also charged that Americans were applying a double standard, conveniently ignoring their own empire built through conquest, military occupation, and economic privilege. Americans rejected such comparisons and claimed that their expansionism had benefited not just themselves but the rest of the world. So many incompatible objectives and outlooks obstructed diplomacy and made war likely.

 Conclusion

By the late 1930s, the earlier American emphasis on independent internationalism and economic and nonmilitary means to peace seemed increasingly archaic. The Great Depression, which had brought on so much international havoc, also faded in memory as the economy geared up for war. The Neutrality Acts, which had been designed to insulate the

United States from European troubles, gradually had been revised and retired in the face of growing danger and receding isolationism. Roosevelt hesitantly moved the nation from neutrality, to aid for the Allies, to outright belligerency.

Looking back with sadness, Americans had to admit that in the 1920s and 1930s they had failed to create a peaceful and prosperous world order. The Washington Conference treaties failed to curb a naval arms race or to protect China; the Dawes Plan collapsed; the Kellogg-Briand Pact proved ineffective; philanthropic activities fell short of need; the process of "Americanization" provided no panacea; Germany and the aggressors ignored repeated United States protests, from the Stimson Doctrine onward; recognition of the Soviet Union barely improved relations; trade policies did not liberate commerce from protectionism; and the Neutrality Acts failed to prevent United States entanglements in Europe. Even where American power and policies seemed to work to satisfy United States goals—in Latin America—nationalist resentments simmered, and Mexico challenged United States hegemony.

The Second World War offered yet another opportunity for Americans to set things right in the world. As the publisher Henry Luce wrote in *American Century* (1941), the United States must "exert upon the world the full impact of our influence, for such purposes as we see fit and by such means as we see fit." As they had so many times before, Americans flocked to the colors. Isolationists joined the president in spirited calls for victory. "We are going to win the war, and we are going to win the peace that follows," Roosevelt predicted.

Suggestions for Further Reading

General

Thomas H. Buckley, *The United States and the Washington Conference, 1921–1922* (1970); Warren I. Cohen, *Empire Without Tears* (1987); Justus D. Doenecke and John E. Wilz, *From Isolation to War, 1931–1941*, 2d ed. (1991); Akira Iriye, *The Globalizing of America, 1914–1945* (1993); Melvyn P. Leffler, *The Elusive Quest* (1979); Elting E. Morison, *Turmoil and Tradition* (1964) (on Stimson); Emily S. Rosenberg, *Spreading the American Dream* (1982); Michael S. Sherry, *The Rise of American Airpower* (1987); Raymond Sontag, *A Broken World, 1919–1939* (1971); Mark A. Stoler, *George Marshall* (1989); Joan Hoff Wilson, *Herbert Hoover* (1975).

Peace Movement

Harriet H. Alonso, *The Women's Peace Union and the Outlawry of War* (1989); Charles Chatfield, *For Peace and Justice: Pacifism in America, 1914–1941* (1971); Charles DeBenedetti, *The Peace Reform in American History* (1980); Charles DeBenedetti, *Origins of the Modern American Peace Movement, 1915–1929* (1978); Carrie A. Foster, *The Women and the Warriors* (1995); Robert D. Johnson, *The Peace Progressives and American Foreign Relations* (1995); Sybil Oldfield, *Women Against the Iron Fist* (1990); Lawrence Wittner, *Rebels Against War* (1984).

The United States in the World Economy

Frederick Adams, *Economic Diplomacy* (1976); Derek H. Aldcroft, *From Versailles to Wall Street, 1919–1929* (1977); Michael J. Hogan, *Informal Entente* (1977) (on Anglo-American relations); Charles Kindleberger, *The World in Depression* (1973); Stephen J. Randall, *United States Foreign Oil Policy, 1919–1948* (1986); Mira Wilkins, *The Maturing of Multinational Enterprise* (1974); Joan Hoff Wilson, *American Business and Foreign Policy, 1920–1933* (1971).

Cultural Expansion and Philanthropy

Frank Costigliola, *Awkward Dominion* (1984); Marcos Cueto, ed., *Missionaries of Science: The Rockefeller Foundation and Latin America* (1994); Mary Nolan, *Visions of Modernity: American Business and the Modernization of Germany* (1994); Thomas J. Saunders, *Hollywood in Berlin* (1994).

Latin America and the Good Neighbor Policy

John A. Britton, *Revolution and Ideology* (1995) (on Mexico); Bruce J. Calder, *The Impact of Intervention* (1984) (on the Dominican Republic); Arturo Morales Carrión, *Puerto Rico* (1983); Paul W. Drake, *The Money Doctors in the Andes* (1989); Alton Frye, *Nazi Germany and the American Hemisphere, 1933–1941* (1967); Irwin F. Gellman, *Good Neighbor Diplomacy* (1979); Walter LaFeber,

Inevitable Revolutions, 2d ed. rev. (1993) (on Central America); Lester D. Langley, *The United States and the Caribbean, 1900–1970* (1980); Abraham F. Lowenthal, ed., *Exporting Democracy* (1991); Thomas F. O'Brien, *The Revolutionary Mission: American Enterprise in Latin America, 1900–1945* (1996); Louis A. Pérez, *Cuba and the United States* (1990); Louis A. Pérez, *Cuba Under the Platt Amendment* (1986); Frederick B. Pike, *FDR's Good Neighbor Policy* (1995); Brenda G. Plummer, *Haiti and the United States* (1992); W. Dirk Raat, *Mexico and the United States* (1992); Stephen G. Rabe, *The Road to OPEC* (1982) (on Venezuela); Bryce Wood, *The Making of the Good Neighbor Policy* (1961).

Isolationists and Isolationism

Wayne S. Cole, *Roosevelt and the Isolationists, 1932–1945* (1983); Wayne S. Cole, *America First* (1953); Manfred Jonas, *Isolationism in America, 1935–1941* (1966); Thomas C. Kennedy, *Charles A. Beard and American Foreign Policy* (1975); Richard C. Lower, *A Bloc of One* (1993) (on Hiram Johnson); Richard Lowitt, *George W. Norris*, 3 vols. (1963–1978); John Wiltz, *In Search of Peace: The Senate Munitions Inquiry, 1934–1936* (1963).

Europe, Roosevelt, and the Coming of World War II

Edward Bennett, *Franklin D. Roosevelt and the Search for Security* (1985) (on the Soviet Union); J. Garry Clifford and Samuel R. Spencer, Jr., *The First Peacetime Draft* (1986); David H. Culbert, *News for Everyman* (1976) (on radio); Robert Dallek, *Franklin D. Roosevelt and American Foreign Policy, 1932–1945*, new ed. (1995); Robert A. Divine, *Roosevelt and World War II* (1969); Frank Freidel, *Franklin D. Roosevelt* (1990); Manfred Jonas, *The United States and Germany* (1984); Warren F. Kimball, *The Juggler* (1991); Warren F. Kimball, *The Most Unsordid Act* (1969) (on lend-lease); Douglas Little, *Malevolent Neutrality* (1985) (on the Spanish Civil War); Thomas R. Maddux, *Years of Estrangement* (1980) (on United States–Soviet relations); Arnold A. Offner, *American Appeasement* (1969); David Reynolds, *The Creation of the Anglo-American Alliance, 1937–1941* (1982); David F. Schmitz, *The United States and Fascist Italy, 1922–1944* (1988); James C. Schneider, *Should America Go to War?* (1989); Richard Steele, *Propaganda in an Open Society* (1985); Donald C. Watt, *How War Came* (1989); Theodore A. Wilson, *The First Summit*, rev. ed. (1991).

China, Japan, and the Coming of War in Asia

Charles A. Beard, *President Roosevelt and the Coming of the War, 1941* (1948); Dorothy Borg and Shumpei Okamoto, eds., *Pearl Harbor as History* (1973); R. J. C. Butow, *Tojo and the Coming of War* (1961); Warren I. Cohen, *America's Response to China*, 3d ed. (1989); Hilary Conroy and Harry Wray, eds., *Pearl Harbor Reexamined* (1990); Herbert Feis, *The Road to Pearl Harbor* (1950); Waldo H. Heinrichs, Jr., *Threshold of War* (1988); Akira Iriye, *The Origins of the Second World War in Asia and the Pacific* (1987); Akira Iriye, *Across the Pacific* (1967); Akira Iriye, *After Imperialism* (1965); Jonathan Utley, *Going to War with Japan* (1985).

Attack on Pearl Harbor

David Kahn, *The Codebreakers* (1967); Robert W. Love, Jr., ed., *Pearl Harbor Revisited* (1995); Martin V. Melosi, *The Shadow of Pearl Harbor* (1977); Gordon W. Prange, *Pearl Harbor* (1986); Gordon W. Prange, *At Dawn We Slept* (1981); John Toland, *Infamy* (1982); Roberta Wohlstetter, *Pearl Harbor* (1962).

CHAPTER

27

The Second World War at Home and Abroad
1941–1945

I n the spring of 1942, when recruiters from the United States Marine Corps came to the Navajo reservation in Shiprock, New Mexico, William Dean Wilson was only sixteen years old and a student at the Shiprock Boarding School. The marines were seeking young men who spoke both English and Navajo, which is an exceedingly complex language; fewer than thirty non-Navajos, none of them Japanese, could understand the language at the outbreak of the war. The Navajo recruits of 1942 would become not only marines but also "code talkers" in the war against the Japanese.

William Dean Wilson volunteered. "I said I was eighteen," he recalled, too young to be drafted but eager to join up. His parents were opposed, but he had removed a note from his file that read "parents will not consent" and was inducted. Wilson was eager to see the world, "kind of like a boy with a new toy . . . everything was new." He was among an initial group of thirty Navajos chosen for a project with an important goal: to prevent the Japanese from deciphering radio messages sent by American troops landing on the shores of Pacific islands. Organized as the 382nd Platoon, Wilson and his fellow recruits went first to marine boot camp, then to Camp Pendleton in California, where they trained as radio operators. At Camp Pendleton, they also helped to devise a code based on the Navajo language; the code had the beauty of being unbreakable. In preparation for battle, the code talkers memorized a special Navajo-coded dictionary of 413 military terms.

By the time William Dean Johnson's seventeenth birthday arrived, he was in the Pacific. From the Battle of Guadalcanal, to Tarawa, Peleliu, and Iwo Jima, he and 420 other Navajo code talkers took part in every

Navajo "code talkers," who were United States Marines, were among the first assault forces to land on Pacific beaches. Dodging enemy fire, they set up radio equipment and transmitted vital information to headquarters, including enemy sightings and targets for American shelling. The Japanese never broke the special Navajo code. The artist is Colonel C. H. Waterhouse, United States Marine Corps (retired). *U.S. Marine Corps Art Collection/Colonel C.H. Waterhouse.*

779

assault the marines conducted in the Pacific from 1942 to 1945. Usually, two code talkers were assigned to a batallion, one going ashore and the other remaining aboard ship. Those who went ashore led the assault forces landing on Pacific beaches. Often under hostile fire, they quickly set up their radio equipment and, using the special code, began transmitting, reporting sightings of enemy forces and directing shelling by American detachments.

While in the marines and even under battle conditions, the code talkers maintained traditional beliefs and practices. To prepare the young men to fight the enemy, Navajo families had special "Blessingway" ceremonies performed for them. Many of the men went to battle carrying bags of sacred corn pollen, and they held traditional beliefs about the evil ghosts of unburied bodies. In late 1943, after battling on the beaches of Tarawa for three straight days, William Dean Wilson still had to face "the real hard test . . . just prior to us leaving the island." They would have to bury the dead. "We had to run around all over the place and find all the bodies that we could of our comrades, that we buried—I think about 500 that one morning."

Since they were responsible for the flow of vital battlefield information back to the ship and between advance units, the code talkers were indispensable. Their work required great courage, and it paid off. "Were it not for the Navajos," declared Major Howard Conner, 5th Marine Division signal officer, "the Marines would never have taken Iwo Jima. The entire operation was directed by Navajo code. . . . During the first forty-eight hours, while we were landing and consolidating our shore positions, I had six Navajo radio sets operating around the clock. In that period alone they sent and received over 800 messages without an error."

As it did for millions of other American fighting men and women, wartime service changed the Navajo code talkers' lives, broadening their horizons and often deepening their ambitions. Many became community leaders. William Dean Wilson, for example, became a tribal judge. From "the service," recalled Raymond Nakai, a navy veteran who became chairman of the Navajo nation, "the Navajo got a glimpse of what the rest of the world is doing." But in 1945 most Navajo war veterans were happy to return to their homes and traditional culture. And in accordance with Navajo ritual, the returning veterans participated in purification ceremonies to dispel the ghosts of the battlefield and invoke blessings for the future.

The Second World War was a turning point in the lives of millions of Americans, as well as in the history of the United States. Most deeply affected were those who fought the war, on the beaches and battlefields, in the skies and at sea. For forty-five months Americans fought abroad to subdue the German, Italian, and Japanese aggressors. After military engagements against fascists in North Africa and Italy, American troops joined the dramatic crossing of the English Channel on D-Day in June 1944. The massive invasion forced the Germans to retreat through France to Germany. Battered by merciless bombing raids, leaderless after Adolf Hitler's suicide, and pressed by a Soviet advance from the east, the Nazis capitulated in May 1945. In the Pacific, Americans drove the Japanese from one island to another before turning to the just-tested atomic bombs, which demolished Hiroshima and Nagasaki in August and helped spur a Japanese surrender.

Throughout the war the Allies—Britain, the Soviet Union, and the United States—were held together by their common goal of defeating Germany. But they squabbled over many issues: when to open a second front; how to structure a new international organization; how eastern Europe, liberated from the Germans, would be reconstructed; how Germany would be governed after defeat. At the end of the war, Allied leaders seemed more intent on retaining and expanding their own nations' spheres of influence than on building a community of mutual interest. The United States and the Soviet Union emerged from the war as direct competitors. The prospects for postwar international cooperation seemed bleak, and the advent of the atomic age frightened everyone.

The war transformed America's soldiers and sailors. Horizons expanded for the more than 16 million men and women who ultimately served in the armed forces, seeing new parts of the world and acquiring new skills. But at war's end they were older than their years, both physically and emotionally; some were psychologically scarred, and many felt they had sacrificed the best years of their lives.

Millions of noncombatant Americans were on the move during the Second World War. Some 12 million Americans, nearly one of every ten, moved permanently to another state during the war (see map, page 782). The farm population declined by one-fifth. Most of the migrants headed for war-production centers; cities on the West Coast registered spectacular population increases. Among the migrants were African-Americans, Mexican-Americans, whites, and women of all races who moved to war-production

• *Important Events* •

1941 Germany invades Russia

Roosevelt issues Executive Order No. 8802, forbidding racial discrimination by defense industry employers

Japan attacks Pearl Harbor

United States enters Second World War

1942 National War Labor Board created to deal with labor-management conflict

War Production Board begins to oversee conversion to military production

West Coast Japanese-Americans interned in prison camps

Congress of Racial Equality established

War Manpower Commission created to manage labor supply

Office of Price Administration created to control inflation

United States defeats Japanese forces at Battles of the Coral Sea and Midway

Office of War Information created to maintain support for the war at home

Manhattan Project set up to produce atomic bomb

Synthetic-rubber program begins

Allies invade North Africa

Republicans gain in Congress

1943 Red Army defeats German troops at Stalingrad

Soft-coal and anthracite miners strike

Congress passes War Labor Disputes (Smith-Connally) Act

Race riots break out in Detroit, Harlem, and forty-five other cities

Allies invade Italy

Hirabayashi v. *U.S.* upholds restrictions on personal liberties of Japanese-Americans because of their ethnicity

Roosevelt, Churchill, and Stalin meet at Teheran Conference

1944 Roosevelt requests Economic Bill of Rights

War Refugee Board established to set up refugee camps in Europe

GI Bill of Rights provides educational benefits for veterans

Allied troops land at Normandy on D-Day

Dumbarton Oaks Conference approves charter for United Nations

Roosevelt reelected

United States retakes the Philippines

Korematsu v. *U.S.* upholds removal of Japanese-Americans from the West Coast

1945 Roosevelt, Stalin, and Churchill meet at Yalta Conference

Battles of Iwo Jima and Okinawa result in heavy American and Japanese losses

Roosevelt dies; Harry S Truman becomes president

United Nations founded

Germany surrenders

First atomic bomb explodes in test at Alamogordo, New Mexico

Potsdam Conference calls for Japan's "unconditional surrender"

Atomic bombs devastate Hiroshima and Nagasaki

Japan surrenders

---

centers in the North and the West. The migration of 112,000 Japanese-Americans on the West Coast was involuntary; in 1942 they were rounded up by the army and placed in internment camps. By contrast, the war offered new economic and political opportunities for numerous African-Americans, encouraging them to demand their full rights as citizens. But the movement of so many people of all colors to these booming areas also created the conditions for

racial violence; in 1943, race riots erupted across the country.

American women made important contributions to the war effort. Though prohibited from engaging in combat, 350,000 women joined the armed forces and worked at a wide range of noncombat jobs, including as transport pilots and as nurses directly behind the front lines. Employers' negative attitudes toward women workers eased during the war, and

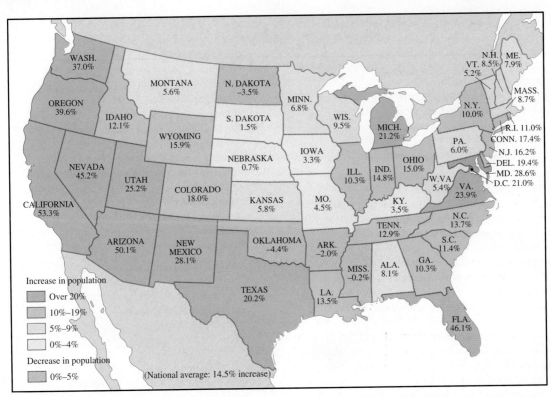

A Nation on the Move, 1940–1950 *American migration during the 1940s was the largest on record to that time. The farm population dropped dramatically as men, women, and children moved to war-production areas and to army and navy bases, particularly on the West Coast. Well over 30 million Americans migrated during the war. Many returned to their rural homes after the war, but 12 million migrants stayed in their new locations. Notice the increases in California, Oregon, and Washington, as well as in the Southwest.*

millions of married middle-class women, many of them over forty-five, took jobs in war industries. For some, work was an economic necessity; for others, it was a patriotic obligation. Whatever the motivation, paying jobs brought women benefits—financial independence and enhanced self-esteem—that many were reluctant to give up at war's end.

The United States underwent profound changes during the course of the war. The American people united behind the war effort, collecting scrap iron, rubber, and newspapers for recycling and planting "victory gardens." But more than national unity and enthusiasm were required to win the war. Essential to victory was the successful mobilization of all sectors of the economy—industry, finance, agriculture, and labor. America's big businesses got even bigger, as did its central government, labor unions, and farms. The federal government had the monumental task of coordinating activity in these spheres, as well as in a couple of new ones: higher education and sci-

ence. For the Second World War was a scientific and technological war, supported by the development of new weapons like radar and the atomic bomb. For all these reasons the Second World War was a watershed in American history.

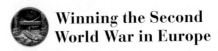 **Winning the Second World War in Europe**

"We are now in the midst of a war, not for conquest, not for vengeance, but for a world in which this Nation, and all that this Nation represents, will be safe for our children." President Franklin D. Roosevelt was speaking just two days after the surprise attack on Pearl Harbor. Americans agreed with Roosevelt that they were defending their homes and families against aggressive, even satanic, Japanese and Nazis. After all, had not Japan provoked the war with its bombing of Hawai'i?

America's men and women responded eagerly to Roosevelt's call to arms. In 1941, only 1.8 million people were serving on active duty, although Selective Service had been functioning for a full year. In 1945 the number of women and men serving in the army, navy, and marines peaked at 12.1 million. Fighting a world war on two fronts required a massive force.

Despite nearly unanimous support for the war effort, government leaders worried that public morale might lag during a long war. To elicit the people's support, in 1942 President Roosevelt established the Office of War Information (OWI), which took charge of domestic propaganda and hired Hollywood filmmakers and New York copywriters to sell the war at home. The army responded by hiring movie director Frank Capra to produce a series of propaganda films called *Why We Fight.* In these widely distributed films, and in the popular mind, the Allies were heroic partners united in a common effort against evil.

Why We Fight

In actuality, wartime relations among the United States, Great Britain, and the Soviet Union ran hot and cold. Although winning the war was the top priority, Allied leaders knew that military decisions had political consequences. If one ally became desperate, for instance, it might destroy the alliance by pursuing a separate peace. Moreover, the positions of troops at the end of the war might determine the politics of the regions they occupied. Thus an undercurrent of mutual suspicion ran just beneath the surface of Allied cooperation.

Roosevelt, British prime minister Winston Churchill, and Soviet premier Joseph Stalin differed vigorously over the opening of a second, or western, front in Europe. After Germany conquered France in 1940 and invaded Russia in 1941, the Russians bore the brunt of the war until mid-1944, suffering millions of casualties. By late 1941, before the fierce Russian winter stalled their onslaught, German troops had nearly reached Moscow and Leningrad and had slashed deeply into the Ukraine, taking Kiev. Stalin pressed for a British-American landing on the northern coast of Europe to draw German troops away from the eastern front, but Churchill would not agree. The Russians therefore did most of the fighting and dying on land, while the British and Americans concentrated on getting lend-lease supplies across the Atlantic and harassing the Germans from the air with attacks on factories and civilians alike.

Second-Front Controversy

BUY WAR BONDS

During the war Americans were urged to make every sacrifice possible for the fighting men at the front. Government posters exhorted people to join the armed forces, conserve gasoline, write daily to the soldiers and sailors, and buy war bonds. Collection of Picture Research Consultants.

Roosevelt was both sensitive to the Soviets' burden and fearful that the Soviet Union might be knocked out of the war, leaving Hitler free to invade England. In 1942 he told the Soviets that they could expect the Allies to cross the English Channel and invade France later that year. This was exactly what Stalin sought to take pressure off his wracked country. But Churchill balked. His preference was a series of small jabs at the enemy's Mediterranean forces. Churchill feared heavy losses in a premature cross-Channel invasion, but some American officials suspected that Churchill's strategy derived from his desire to reassert British imperial power in the Mediterranean.

Churchill won the debate. Instead of attacking France, the British and Americans invaded North Africa in November 1942 (see map, page 784). "We are striking back," Roosevelt declared. The news from the Soviet Union also buoyed Roosevelt. In

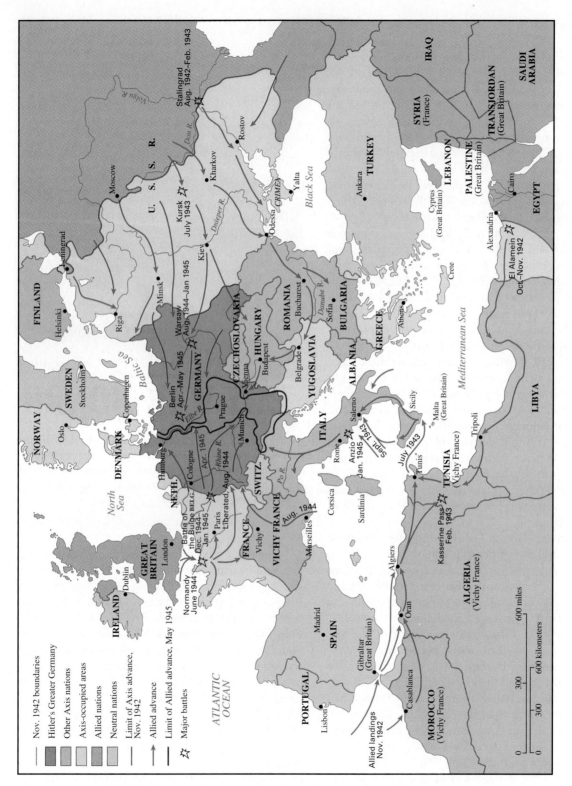

The Allies on the Offensive in Europe, 1942–1945   *The United States pursued a "Europe first" policy: first defeat Germany, then focus on Japan. American military efforts began in North Africa in late 1942 and ended in Germany in 1945 on May 8 (V-E Day).*

On June 6, 1944, an Allied invasion force opened the second front against Germany with an amphibious landing at Normandy Beach, France. Led by the United States, the D-Day invasion was met with ferocious resistance by the enemy.   Corbis-Bettmann.

the battle for Stalingrad (September 1942–January 1943)—probably the turning point of the European war—the Red Army defeated the Germans in bloody block-by-block fighting, forcing Hitler's divisions to retreat. But shortly thereafter, the president once again angered the Soviets by declaring another delay in launching the second front. Stalin was not mollified by the Allied invasion of Italy in the summer of 1943. Italy surrendered in September to American and British officers; Soviet officials were not invited to participate. Stalin grumbled that the arrangement smacked of a separate peace.

With the alliance badly strained, Roosevelt sought reconciliation through personal diplomacy. The three Allied leaders met in Teheran, Iran, in

Teheran Conference

December 1943. Stalin dismissed Churchill's repetitious justifications for further delaying the second front. Roosevelt had had enough, too; he also rejected Churchill's proposal for another peripheral attack, this time through the Balkans to Vienna. The three

finally agreed to launch Operation Overlord—the cross-Channel invasion of France—in early 1944. And the Soviet Union promised to aid the Allies against Japan once Germany was defeated.

The second front opened in the dark morning hours of June 6, 1944—D-Day. In the largest amphibious landing in history, 200,000 Allied troops

D-Day

under the command of American general Dwight D. Eisenhower scrambled ashore at Normandy, France. Thousands of ships ferried the men within a hundred yards of the sandy beaches. Landing craft and soldiers immediately encountered the enemy; they triggered mines and were pinned down by fire from cliffside pillboxes. Meanwhile, Allied airborne troops dropped behind German lines. Although heavy aerial and naval bombardment and the clandestine work of saboteurs had softened the German defenses, the fighting was ferocious.

Allied troops soon spread across the countryside, liberating France and Belgium and entering Germany itself in September. In December, German armored divisions counterattacked in Belgium's Ardennes Forest, hoping to push on to Antwerp to halt the flow of Allied supplies through that Belgian port. After weeks of heavy fighting in what has come to be called the Battle of the Bulge—because of a noticeable bulge in the Allied line—the Allies pushed the enemy back once again. Meanwhile, battle-hardened Soviet troops marched through Poland and cut a path to Berlin. American forces crossed the Rhine River in March 1945 and captured the heavily industrial Ruhr valley. Several units peeled off to enter Austria and Czechoslovakia, where they met up with Soviet soldiers. As the Americans marched east, a new president took office in Washington: Franklin D. Roosevelt died on April 12, and Harry S Truman became president and commander-in-chief. Eighteen days later, in bomb-ravaged Berlin, Adolf Hitler killed himself. On May 8 Germany surrendered.

 ## Winning the Second World War in the Pacific

Allied strategists had devised a "Europe first" formula: knock out Germany and then concentrate on an isolated Japan. Nevertheless, the Pacific theater of operations claimed headlines throughout the war. By mid-1942 Japan had seized the Philippines, Guam, Wake, Hong Kong, Singapore, Malaya, and the Netherlands East Indies. In the Philippines in 1942, Japanese soldiers forced American and Filipino prisoners weakened by insufficient rations to walk 65 miles, clubbing, shooting, or starving to death about ten thousand of them. This so-called Bataan Death March intensified American hatred of the Japanese.

In April 1942, Americans began to hit back, initially by bombing Tokyo. In May, in the momentous Battle of the Coral Sea, carrier-based American planes halted a Japanese advance toward Australia (see map, page 787). The next month American forces defeated the Japanese at Midway, sinking four of the enemy's aircraft carriers. Thanks to the success of Operation MAGIC—the work of American experts who deciphered the secret code used by the Japanese to transmit messages—American naval officers knew ahead of time the approximate date and direction of the Japanese assault. The Battle of Midway was a turning point in the Pacific war, breaking the Japanese momentum and relieving the threat to Hawai'i.

Battle of Midway

Thereafter, Japan was never able to match American fighting power or economic power.

American strategy was to "island-hop" toward Japan, skipping the most strongly fortified islands whenever possible and taking the weaker ones. In an effort to strand the Japanese armies on their island outposts and to cut off the supply of raw materials being shipped from Japan's home islands, Americans also set out to sink the Japanese merchant marine. The first United States offensive—at Guadalcanal in the Solomon Islands in mid-1942—gave American troops their first taste of jungle warfare: tropical heat, thick vegetation, ferocious mosquitoes. In 1943 and 1944 American troops attacked the enemy in the Gilberts, Marshalls, and Marianas. And in October 1944, General Douglas MacArthur landed at Leyte to retake the Philippines for the United States.

Despite those victories, more tough fighting lay ahead in the Pacific. In February 1945 both sides took heavy losses at Iwo Jima, an island less than 5 miles long located 700 miles south of Tokyo. Stationed on the island were 21,000 Japanese troops living in pillboxes and miles of caves, trenches, and connecting tunnels. The American objective was Mount Suribachi, the highest point and most heavily fortified spot on Iwo Jima. From the outset, American casualties were heavy; the mountain had to be taken yard by yard. After twenty days of fighting, victory finally came and marines planted the American flag atop Mount Suribachi. In this bitter battle, 6,821 Americans were killed along with all but 200 of the Japanese troops.

Battles of Iwo Jima and Okinawa

A month later, American troops landed on Okinawa, an island 350 miles from Japan. Fighting raged for two months; death was everywhere. Almost the entire Japanese garrison of 100,000 was killed, and there were 80,000 Okinawan civilian casualties. The American military lost 7,374 men killed. At sea, the supporting fleet reported almost 5,000 seamen killed or missing; most were the victims of *kamikaze* (suicide) attacks, in which Japanese pilots crashed their planes directly into American ships.

Still, Japanese leaders refused to admit defeat. Hoping to avoid a humiliating unconditional surrender (and to preserve the emperor's sovereignty), they hung on even while American bombers leveled their cities. In one staggering attack on Tokyo on May 23, 1945, American planes dropped napalm-filled bombs that engulfed the city in a firestorm, killing 83,000

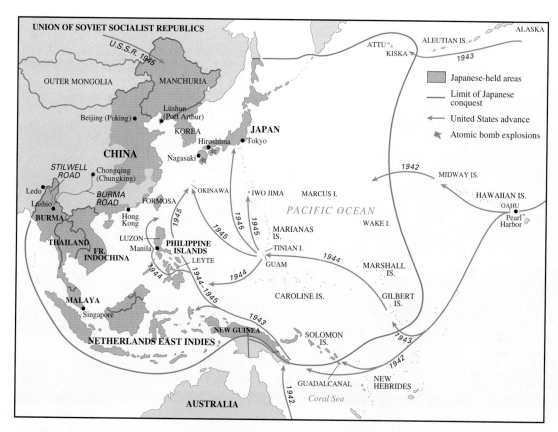

The Pacific War *The strategy of the United States was to "island-hop"—from Hawaii in 1942 to Iwo Jima and Okinawa in 1945. Naval battles were also decisive, notably the Battles of the Coral Sea and Midway in 1942. The war in the Pacific ended with Japan's surrender on August 15, 1945 (V-J Day).* Source: From Paterson et al., *American Foreign Policy: A History*, vol. 2, 3d ed. rev., copyright 1991, page 494. Reprinted by permission of Houghton Mifflin Company.

people. Observers described the ghastly scene as a mass burning.

Impatient for victory, American leaders began to plan a fall invasion of Japan's home islands, an expedition that was sure to incur high casualties. But the successful development of an atomic bomb by American scientists provided another route to victory. The secret atomic program, known as the Manhattan Project, had begun in August 1942, and the first bomb was exploded in the desert near Alamogordo, New Mexico, on July 16, 1945. Only three weeks later, on August 6, the Japanese city of Hiroshima was destroyed by a bomb dropped from an American B-29 plane called the *Enola Gay*. A flash of dazzling light shot across the sky; then a huge purplish mushroom cloud boiled 40,000 feet into the atmosphere. Dense smoke, swirling fires, and suffocating dust soon en-

The Atomic Bomb

gulfed the ground for miles. Much of the city was leveled almost instantly. Approximately 130,000 people were killed; tens of thousands more suffered severe burns and nuclear poisoning.

American planes continued their devastating conventional bombing and also scattered leaflets over other Japanese cities, warning that they, too, would face atomic terror unless the Japanese Empire surrendered. On August 9 another atomic attack flattened Nagasaki, killing at least 60,000 people. Five days later the Japanese, who had been sending out peace feelers since June, surrendered. The victors promised that the Japanese emperor could remain as the nation's titular head. Formal surrender ceremonies were held September 2 aboard the battleship *Missouri*. The Second World War was over.

Use of the bomb to achieve victory had been the primary goal of the Manhattan Project. Most Americans agreed with President Truman that the atomic

This scorched watch, found in the rubble at Hiroshima, stopped at the time of the blast—8:16. The shock waves and fires caused by the atomic bomb leveled great expanses of the city. Radiation released by the bomb caused lingering deaths for thousands who survived the explosion. The photo of Hiroshima shown above was taken eight months after the attack. Watch: John Launois/ Black Star; Hiroshima: National Archives.

Why the Atomic Bomb Was Used

bombing of Hiroshima and Nagasaki was necessary to end the war as quickly as possible and to save American lives. At the highest government levels and among atomic scientists, alternatives had been discussed: detonating the bomb on an unpopulated Pacific island, with international observers as witnesses; blockading and bombing Japan conventionally; following up on Tokyo's peace feelers; encouraging a Soviet declaration of war on Japan. Truman, however, had rejected these options because he believed they would take too long and would not convince the tenacious Japanese that they had been beaten. Then, too, memories of Pearl Harbor played a part. "When you have to deal with a beast, you have to treat him as a beast," Truman said.

Diplomatic considerations also influenced the decision to use the bomb. American leaders wanted to take advantage of the real and psychological power the bomb would bestow on the United States. It might serve as a deterrent against aggression; it might intimidate the Soviet Union into making concessions in eastern Europe; it might end the war in the Pacific before the Soviet Union could claim a role in

How do historians know what motivated President Harry Truman to order the dropping of the atomic bomb? Truman explained that he did it for only one reason: to end the war as soon as possible and thus prevent the loss of a million American lives in an invasion of Japan. An earlier generation of historians, writing in the aftermath of the war, echoed the president's explanation. But more recently historians have revised this interpretation: they argue that Japan might have surrendered even if the atomic bombs had not been dropped, and they dispute Truman's estimate of a million casualties as being many times the actual figure. These revisionists have studied the Potsdam Conference of July 1945 attended by Truman, Joseph Stalin, and Winston Churchill; and they have consulted the diaries kept by certain participants, notably Secretary of War Henry Stimson and Truman himself.

Scholars cite Stimson's diary (excerpted here) as an indication that Truman's chief motivation was the desire to impress the Soviet Union, as well as to minimize Russia's military participation in the final defeat of Japan. On July 21, Stimson reported to Truman that the army had successfully tested an atomic device in New Mexico. Clearly emboldened by the news, Truman said that possession of the bomb "gave him an entirely new feeling of confidence." The next day, Stimson discussed the news with Britain's Prime Minister Winston Churchill. "Now I know what happened to Truman," Churchill responded. "When he got to the meeting after having read this report he was a changed man. He told the Russians just where they got off and generally bossed the whole meeting." A few historians contend that the decision to drop the atomic bomb was at least partly racist. As evidence, they point to Truman's handwritten diary entry in which he

discussed using the bomb against "the Japs," whom he denounced as "savages, ruthless, merciless and fanatic."

The deeply emotional and political question about the necessity for dropping the atomic bomb has stirred debates not only among historians but also within the general public. In 1995, for example, the Smithsonian Institution provoked a public furor with its plans for an exhibit prompted by the fiftieth anniversary of the decision to drop the bomb. Rather than incur the wrath of politicians, veterans' groups, and many other Americans outraged by its interpretation of events, the Smithsonian shelved most of the exhibit.   Diary entry: Henry L. Stinson Papers. Yale University Library

TOP SECRET

I also discussed with him Harrison's two messages. He was intensely pleased by the accelerated timetable. As to the matter of the special target which I had refused to permit, he strongly confirmed my view, and said he felt the same way.

At ten forty Bundy and I again went to the British headquarters and talked to the Prime Minister and Lord Cherwell for over an hour. Churchill read Groves' report in full. He told me that he had noticed at the meeting of the three yesterday, Truman was evidently much fortified by something that had happened, and that he stood up to the Russians in a most emphatic and decisive manner, telling them as to certain demands that they absolutely could not have, and that the United States was entirely against them. Churchill said he now understood how this popping up had taken place and that he felt the same way. His own attitude confirmed this admission. He now not only was not worried about giving the Russians information of the matter, but was rather inclined to use it as an argument in our favor in the negotiations. The sentiment of the four of us was unanimous in thinking that it was advisable to tell the Russians at least that we were working on that subject, and intended to use it if and when it was successfully finished.

At twelve fifteen I called General Arnold over, showed him Harrison's two cables, showed him my answer to them and showed him Groves' report, which he read in its entirety. He told me that he agreed with me about the target which I had struck off the program. He said that it would take considerable hard work to organize the operations now that it was to move forward.

TOP SECRET

the postwar management of Asia. "If it explodes, as I think it will," Truman remarked, "I'll certainly have a hammer on those boys [the Soviets]."

 ## Economic Effects of the War at Home

The Second World War was won at great cost, not only abroad but also on the American home front. While the guns boomed in Europe and Asia, the war was changing American lives and institutions. One month after Pearl Harbor, President Roosevelt established the War Production Board (WPB) and assigned to it the task of converting the economy from civilian to military production. Factories that had manufactured silk ribbons began to turn out silk parachutes; automobile companies switched to the production of tanks and airplanes; adding-machine companies started manufacturing automatic pistols. Factories had to be expanded and new ones built.

War Production Board

The WPB was so successful that the production of durable goods more than tripled. Since this was the world's first massive air war, fighter planes and bombers were crucial, and America's factories responded to the need: the manufacture of military aircraft, which had totaled 6,000 in 1940, jumped to over 47,000 in 1942 and to 85,000 in 1943. Women workers made a major contribution to the rapidly expanding aircraft industry, whose female work force increased from 4,000 in December 1941 to 310,000 two years later.

The wartime emergency also spurred the establishment of totally new industries, most notably synthetic rubber. The Japanese, in their conquest of the South Pacific following Pearl Harbor, had captured 90 percent of the world's supply of crude rubber. The American government resorted to a national speed limit and gasoline rationing to save wear on tires, but the country still could not meet its wartime needs. So in 1942, with an investment of $700 million, the government underwrote the creation of a synthetic-rubber industry. By war's end the nation that had been the world's largest importer of rubber had become the world's largest exporter of rubber—all of it synthetic.

New industries brought with them new and hazardous pollutants. The production of synthetic rubber spewed forth sulfur dioxide, carbon monoxide, and other dangerous gases. War industries fouled the water and the soil with both solid and petrochemical wastes. The dumping of radioactive waste began at Hanford, Washington, where plutonium was produced for the atomic bomb. Air pollution—smog—was first detected in Los Angeles in 1943, the result of that city's rapid wartime industrialization combined with widespread dependence on the automobile. Although these were ominous signs, few people at the time worried about human-made threats to America's seemingly endless supplies of fresh air, water, and soil.

War Production and the Environment

To gain the cooperation of business, the War Production Board and other government agencies met business more than halfway. The government guaranteed profits in the form of cost-plus-fixed-fee contracts, generous tax writeoffs, and exemptions from antitrust prosecution. Such concessions made sense for a nation that wanted vast quantities of war goods manufactured in the shortest possible time.

Government Incentives to Business

From mid-1940 through September 1944 the government awarded contracts totaling $175 billion, no less than two-thirds of which went to the top one hundred corporations. General Motors alone received 8 percent of the total; big awards also went to other automobile companies and to aircraft, steel, electrical, and chemical companies. Although the expression "military-industrial complex" had not yet been coined—President Dwight Eisenhower would do so in 1961 (see pages 820–821)—the web of military-business interdependence had begun to be woven.

In science and higher education, too, the big got bigger as federal contracts mobilized science and technology for the war effort. Massachusetts Institute of Technology was a major recipient for its development of radar. MIT received $117 million, followed by the California Institute of Technology, Harvard, and Columbia. Some wartime contracts accelerated medical progress. Indeed, because of the development of sulfa drugs, which greatly reduced deaths from infected war wounds, the survival rate among injured soldiers was 90 percent, compared with 10 percent in the First World War. Most federal contracts, however, were for weapons.

Universities and War Research

The most spectacular result of government contracts with universities was the atomic bomb. The Manhattan Project, run by the army, financed research at the University of Chicago, which in 1942 was the site of the world's first sustained nuclear chain reaction. The University of California at Berkeley had a contract to operate the Los Alamos Scientific Laboratory in New Mexico, where the atomic bomb was tested. American universities became valued participants in the military-industrial complex.

Organized labor also grew during the war. Membership in unions ballooned from 8.5 million in 1940 to 14.75 million in 1945. Less than a week after Pearl Harbor, a White House labor-management conference agreed to a no-strike/no-lockout pledge to guarantee uninterrupted war production. To minimize labor-management conflict, in 1942 President Roosevelt created the National War Labor Board (NWLB), sometimes referred to as the Supreme Court for labor disputes. Unions were permitted to enroll as many new members as possible, but workers were not required to join a union. Thus the NWLB forged a temporary compromise between the unions' demand for a closed shop, in which only union members could be hired, and management's interest in open shops.

Unions and Wartime Labor Strikes

But when the NWLB attempted in 1943 to limit wage increases to cost-of-living pay increases, workers responded with strikes that tripled the amount of lost production time over that of the previous year. The worst labor disruptions of 1943 occurred in the coal fields, where 450,000 soft-coal miners and 80,000 anthracite miners struck. To discourage further work stoppages, Congress passed the War Labor Disputes (Smith-Connally) Act in June 1943. The act conferred on the president the authority to seize and operate any strike-bound plant deemed necessary to the national security, and it established a mandatory thirty-day cooling-off period before any new strike could be called. The Smith-Connally Act also gave the NWLB the legal authority to settle labor disputes for the duration of the war.

The war demanded sacrifices from Americans, but it also rewarded them with new highs in personal income (see figure, pages 792–793). Savings deposits jumped from $32.4 billion in 1942 to $51.4 billion in 1945. Corporations doubled their net profits between 1939 and 1943, and employees' wages and salaries rose more than 135 percent from 1940 to 1945. The government did not tax this extra income as heavily as

it might have. Instead, it resorted to deficit financing and borrowed much of the cost of waging the war, about half of it in the form of war bonds sold to patriotic citizens. The national debt skyrocketed from $49 billion in 1941 to $259 billion in 1945.

Agriculture also made an impressive contribution to the war effort, through hard work and the introduction of labor-saving machinery to replace men and women who had gone to the front or migrated to war-production centers. Before the war, farming had been in the midst of a transition from the family-owned and -operated farm to the large-scale, mechanized agribusiness dominated by banks, insurance companies, and farm co-ops. The Second World War accelerated the trend, for wealthy financial institutions were better able than family farmers to pay for expensive new machinery. From 1940 to 1945, while the value of farm machinery more than doubled from $3.1 billion to $6.5 billion, the farm population fell from 30.5 million to 24.4 million people.

Wartime Changes in Agriculture

At the apex of the burgeoning national economy stood the federal government, the size and importance of which was mushrooming: from 1940 to 1945 the federal bureaucracy expanded from 1.1 million workers to 3.4 million. The executive branch—which included the Office of the Commander-in-Chief and bore responsibility for directing the war effort—grew most dramatically. Besides raising the armed forces, mobilizing industrial production, and pacifying labor and management, the executive branch also had to manage the labor supply and control inflation. The War Manpower Commission (WMC), established in 1942, recruited new workers for factories and shipyards, while the Office of Price Administration (OPA), also established in 1942, imposed maximum prices on commodities to control inflation and introduced rationing programs. Consumers became skilled at handling ration stamps, each worth ten points—red for meats and cheese, blue for canned goods. Most Americans abided by the rules, but some hoarded sugar and coffee or bought beef on the "black market"—under the counter or from the trunk of a car.

Growth in the Federal Government

Though government-business-labor relations were sometimes bitter, and production was sometimes slowed as a result, Americans were generally ready to make personal sacrifices. They knew the war

The Wartime Economic Boom, 1940–1945

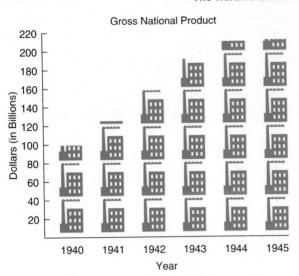

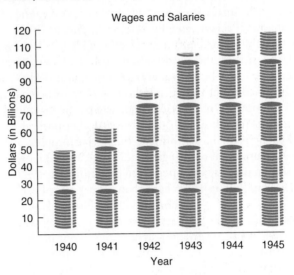

The Wartime Economic Boom, 1940–1945
War production finally ended the Great Depression.
These graphs show the wartime increases in key eco-
nomic indicators: gross national product, wages and
salaries, and value of farm output. They also show the
increase in women's employment and the surge in fed-
eral military and civilian employment, as well as in the
national debt for financing the war.

would be costly and long. In previous conflicts Americans had flocked to the colors with flags, wild rallies, and militaristic songs, but they fought the Second World War with a grim, realistic determination. They were in it "for the duration."

 The Military Life

To American servicepeople in Asia and in Europe, the Second World War was a grimy job. Like cartoonist Bill Mauldin's popular GI characters Willy and Joe, who were more interested in tasty food and dry socks than in abstractions, millions of GIs were simply eager to get it over with. The largest of the services was the army, in which a total of 11.3 million

Americans served; 4.2 million were on active duty in the navy, and 670,000 in the Marine Corps. American troops served overseas for an average of sixteen months. Some never returned: total deaths exceeded 405,000. In terms of lost American lives, the cost of the war was second only to that of the Civil War.

Military service demanded enormous personal adjustments. Soldiers and sailors who never had been more than a few miles from home became homesick; GIs joked, somewhat bitterly, about having found a new home in the army. But loneliness was inconsequential compared with the intense fear that soldiers admitted to feeling in battle. Combat veterans told a group of psychologists that a man who burst out weep-

The Ordeal of Combat

The Wartime Economic Boom, 1940–1945

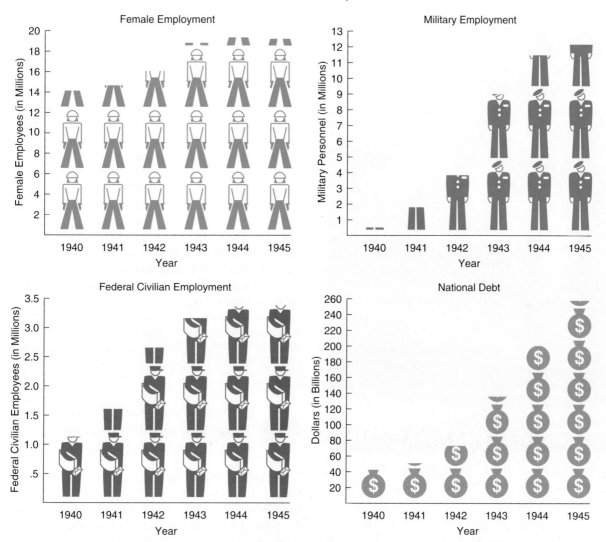

Female Employment

Military Employment

Federal Civilian Employment

National Debt

ing was "not regarded as a coward unless he made no apparent effort to stick to his job." Although the American Psychiatric Association did not identify the illness known as post-traumatic stress disorder until 1980, it is clear in retrospect that American veterans suffered from it after the war. The symptoms included nightmares and flashbacks to the battlefield, depression and anger, and widespread alcoholism.

While combat's cruelties robbed many GIs of their innocence, military service itself broadened the horizons of both men and women, large numbers of whom served in America's armed forces. The WACs (Women's Army Corps) enlisted 140,000 women, while 100,000 served in the navy's WAVES (Women Ac-

Women in the Armed Forces

cepted for Volunteer Emergency Service) and 39,000 in the Marine Corps and Coast Guard. Another 75,000 women served in the army and navy's Nursing Corps, where they saw duty during the invasions of North Africa, Italy, and France. Women also served as pilots in the WASP (Women Air Service Pilots), teaching basic flying, towing aerial targets for gunnery practice, ferrying planes across the country, and serving as test pilots. WASP flying duty was often hazardous; thirty-eight women lost their lives.

Among the millions of Americans who left home to join the armed forces were men and women who had experienced homosexual attraction in peacetime. Freed of their familial environments and serving in sex-segregated units, many acted on their feelings. "When I first got into the navy—in the recreation hall,

For your country's sake today—

For your own sake tomorrow

**GO TO THE NEAREST RECRUITING STATION
OF THE ARMED SERVICE OF YOUR CHOICE**

Women performed valuable service in all branches of the armed forces. This poster urged women to make their wartime contributions by enlisting in the United States Army, Navy, Marine Corps, or Coast Guard. National Archives.

for instance," recalled a chief petty officer, "there'd be eye contact. . . . All of a sudden you had a vast network of friends." The military court-martialed homosexuals, but gay relationships usually went unnoticed by the heterosexual world. For lesbians in the armed forces, the military environment offered friendships and a positive identity. "For many gay Americans," the historian John D'Emilio has written, "World War II created something of a nationwide coming out situation."

Wartime service not only broadened horizons but also fostered soldiers' ambitions. A soldier from the Midwest, who found himself "living among fel-

The GIs' Postwar Ambitions

lows from all over the country," observed that he had "picked up a lot of ideas from them . . . about how to live my own life and to get more out of it. I came out a lot more ambitious than I was before I went in." Many GIs returned to civilian life with new skills they had learned in the military's technical schools. Still others took advantage of the educational benefits provided by the GI Bill of Rights (1944) to study for a college degree.

Still, after two or three years abroad, men and women in the service returned to the United States not knowing what to expect from civilian life. Many GIs returned fearing that life at home had passed them by. They were much older in experience and exposure to brutality; many came back to the United States convinced that they had sacrificed their youth. And they found that home had changed as well. "Our friends are gone," one GI lamented. "The family and the town naturally had to go on even if we weren't there, and somehow it seems things have sort of closed in and filled that space we used to occupy."

 ### Enemy Aliens, Conscientious Objectors, and the Internment of Japanese-Americans

After the United States entered the war, American leaders had to consider whether enemy agents were operating within the nation's borders and threatening the war effort. It was clear that not all Americans were enthusiastic supporters of the nation's participation in the war. After Pearl Harbor, several thousand "enemy aliens" were arrested and taken into custody, including some Nazi agents. And in early 1942, the army prohibited ten thousand German and Italian aliens from living or working in restricted zones along the California coast, including San Francisco and Monterey Bay.

Some Americans had conscientious objections to war, particularly Quakers, Mennonites, and members of the Church of the Brethren. During the Second World War conscientious objectors (COs) had to have a religious (as opposed to a moral or an ethical) reason for refusing military service. About 12,000 COs were sent to civilian public service camps, where they worked on conservation projects or as orderlies in hospitals. Approximately 5,500, three-fourths of whom were Jehovah's Witnesses, refused to participate in any way; they were imprisoned.

Compared with the First World War, the nation's wartime civil liberties record was generally creditable. But there was one enormous exception:

"An Enemy Race"

the internment in "relocation centers" of, ultimately, 120,000 Japanese-Americans. Of these people, 77,000 were Nisei—native-born citizens of the United States. Their imprisonment was based not on suspicion or evidence of treason; their crime was solely their race—the fact that they were of Japanese descent. General John L. DeWitt, chief of the Western Defense Command, warned: "The Japanese race is an enemy race and while many second and third generation Japanese born on United States soil, possessed of United States citizenship, have become 'Americanized,' the racial strains are undiluted. . . . It, therefore, follows that along the vital Pacific Coast over 112,000 potential enemies, of Japanese extraction, are at large today." With strained illogic DeWitt declared: "The very fact that no sabotage [by Japanese-Americans] has taken place to date is a disturbing and confirming indication that such action will be taken."

General DeWitt was not alone in his racist paranoia and hatred. Popular racial stereotypes held that Japanese people abroad and at home were sneaky and evil, and the American people generally regarded Japan as the United States's chief enemy. Moreover, the feeling was widespread that the Japanese—called "monkeys" and "bastards" by angry Americans—had to be repaid for Pearl Harbor. Several factors, however, should have disproved the accusation that Japanese-Americans were members of "an enemy race." In Hawai'i, for example, where 160,000 people—one-third of the population—were of Japanese descent, the paranoia was less than on the West Coast. In Hawai'i, fewer than a thousand people were taken into custody and sent to the mainland for internment.

More to the point, Japanese-American soldiers fought valiantly for the United States. The all-Japanese-American 442nd Regimental Combat Team, drawn heavily from young men in internment camps, was

442nd Regimental Combat Team

the most decorated unit of its size in the armed forces. Suffering heavy casualties in Italy and France, members of the 442nd

were awarded a Congressional Medal of Honor, 47 Distinguished Service Crosses, 350 Silver Stars, and more than 3,600 Purple Hearts.

During the war charges of criminal behavior were never brought against any Japanese-Americans; none was ever indicted or tried for espionage, treason, or sedition. Nevertheless in 1942, all the 112,000 Japanese-Americans living in California, Oregon, and the state of Washington were rounded up and imprisoned. "It was really cruel and harsh," recalled Joseph Y. Kurihara, a citizen and a veteran of the First World War. "To pack and evacuate in forty-eight hours was an impossibility. Seeing mothers completely bewildered with children crying from want and peddlers taking advantage and offering prices next to robbery made me feel like murdering those responsible."

The internees were sent to flood-damaged lands at Relocation, Arkansas; to the intermountain terrain of Wyoming and the desert of western Arizona;

Life in the Internment Camps

and to other arid and desolate spots in the West. Although the names were evocative—Topaz, Utah; Rivers, Arizona; Heart Mountain, Wyoming; Tule Lake and Manzanar, California—the camps were bleak and demoralizing. Behind barbed wire stood tarpapered wooden barracks where entire families lived in a single room furnished only with cots, blankets, and a bare light bulb. Toilets and dining and bathing facilities were communal; privacy was almost nonexistent. Japanese-Americans were forced to sell property valued at $500 million, and they lost their positions in the truck-garden, floral, and fishing industries. Indeed, their economic competitors were among the most vocal proponents of their relocation.

The Supreme Court upheld the government's policy of internment. In wartime, the Court ruled in *Hirabayashi* v. *U.S.* (1943), "residents having ethnic affiliations with an invading enemy may be a greater source of danger than those of different ancestry." In *Korematsu* v. *U.S.* (1944), the Court, with three justices dissenting, approved the removal of the Nisei from the West Coast. One dissenter, Justice Frank Murphy, denounced the decision as the "legalization of racism."

In 1983, forty-one years after he had been sent to a government camp, Fred Korematsu had the satisfaction of hearing a federal judge rule that he—and by implication all detainees—had been the victim of

In February 1942 President Franklin D. Roosevelt ordered that all Japanese-Americans living on the West Coast be rounded up and placed in prison camps. These families were awaiting a train to take them to an assembly center in Merced, California; from there, they would be sent to relocation camps in remote inland areas.   National Archives.

"unsubstantiated facts, distortions and misrepresentations of at least one military commander whose views were affected by racism." A year earlier, the government's special Commission on Wartime Relocation and Internment of Civilians had recommended compensating the victims of this policy. Finally, in 1988, Congress voted to award $20,000 and a public apology to each of the surviving sixty thousand Japanese-American internees.

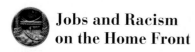 ## Jobs and Racism on the Home Front

At peak enrollment the army had more than 700,000 African-American troops. An additional 187,000

black men and women enlisted in the navy, the Coast Guard, and the once all-white Marine Corps. In response to the March on Washington movement of 1941 (see page 743), the Selective Service System and the War Department agreed to draft black Americans in proportion to their presence in the population: about 10 percent.

Although they served in segregated units, African-Americans made real advances toward racial equality during these years. For the first time the War Department sanctioned the training of blacks as pilots. After instruction at Tuskegee Institute in Alabama, pilots saw heroic service in all-black units such as the Ninety-ninth Pursuit Squadron, winner of eighty Distinguished Flying

African-American Troops

Crosses. In 1940 Colonel Benjamin O. Davis was the first African-American to be promoted to brigadier general. More important, black people distinguished themselves on the battlefield. The performance of black marines in the Pacific theater was such that the corps commandant proclaimed: "Negro Marines are no longer on trial. They are Marines, period."

Serious failures in race relations, however, undercut these accomplishments. Race riots instigated by whites broke out on military bases, and white civilians assaulted black soldiers and sailors throughout the South. In North Carolina a white bus driver who murdered an African-American soldier in full view of the passengers was found not guilty. When the War Department issued an order in mid-1944 forbidding racial segregation in military recreation and transportation, the *Montgomery Advertiser* replied, "Army orders, even armies, even bayonets, cannot force impossible and unnatural social relations upon us."

Experiences such as these caused African-American soldiers and sailors to wonder what, in fact, they were fighting for. They rankled at the remark of the governor of Tennessee when blacks urged him to appoint African-Americans to local draft boards: "This is a white man's country. . . . The Negro had nothing to do with the settling of America." They noted that the Red Cross separated blood according to the race of the donor, as if there were some difference. Many considered black participation in the First World War a mistake, for it had resulted not in social advances but in race riots and lynchings (see page 676). Some even argued that the Second World War was a white man's war and that American racism was little different from German racism.

But there were persuasive reasons for African-Americans to participate in the war effort. Perhaps, as the NAACP believed, this was an opportunity "to persuade, embarrass, compel and shame our government and our nation . . . into a more enlightened at-

A leader of the Tuskegee airmen, Benjamin O. Davis, Jr., was the fourth African-American to graduate from West Point. During the war, Colonel Davis commanded the 332nd Fighter Group, which destroyed over two hundred enemy planes in southern Europe. National Archives.

titude toward a tenth of its people." Proclaiming that in the Second World War they were waging a "Double V" campaign (for victory at home and abroad), blacks were more militant than before and readier than ever to protest. Membership in civil rights organizations soared. The NAACP, 50,000 strong in 1940, had 450,000 members by 1946. And in 1942 civil rights activists founded the Congress of Racial Equality (CORE), which stressed "nonviolent direct action" and staged sit-ins to desegregate restaurants and movie theaters in northern cities.

African-American War Workers

The war also created opportunities in industry. Roosevelt's Executive Order No. 8802, issued in 1941, required employers in defense industries to make jobs available "without discrimination because of race, creed, color or national origin." To secure defense jobs, 1.5 million black Americans migrated from the South to the industrial cities of the North and West in the 1940s. Almost three-fourths settled in the urban-industrial states of California, Illinois, Michigan, New York, Ohio, and Pennsylvania. More than half a million became active members of CIO unions like the United Auto Workers and United Steel Workers. African-American voters in northern cities were beginning to constitute a vital swing vote, not only in local and state elections but also in presidential contests.

But the benefits of urban life came with a high price tag. The migrants had to make enormous emotional and cultural adjustments, and white hostility and ignorance made their task difficult. Southern whites who had migrated north brought with them the racial prejudices of the Deep South. Also hostile were the northern whites. In 1942 more than half of them believed that blacks should be segregated in separate schools and neighborhoods, that black people were receiving all the opportunities they deserved, and that if blacks suffered economically, politically, or socially, it was their own fault. Such attitudes encouraged racial violence in northern cities where whites and blacks competed for housing and jobs.

Race Riots of 1943

Many people, black and white, feared that the summer of 1943 would be like 1919—another "Red Summer" (see page 676). Indeed, in 1943 almost 250 racial conflicts exploded in forty-seven cities. Outright racial warfare bloodied the streets of Detroit in June. At the end of thirty hours of rioting, twenty-five blacks and nine whites lay dead. White mobs, undeterred by police, had roamed the city attacking blacks and overturning cars. Blacks had hurled rocks at police and hauled white passengers off streetcars. A city councilman suggested that the city build a bigger ghetto and pen blacks up in it. Surveying the damage, an elderly black woman said, "There ain't no North any more. Everything now is South."

The federal government did practically nothing to prevent further racial violence. From President Roosevelt on down, most federal officials put the war first, domestic reform second. Unquestionably many government leaders were racists. Secretary of War Henry L. Stimson, for example, blamed the riots on "radical leaders of the colored race" who wanted to use the war to obtain "interracial marriages." But this time government neglect could not discourage African-Americans and the century-old civil rights movement. By war's end they were ready—politically, economically, and emotionally—to wage a struggle for voting rights and for equal access to public accommodations and institutions.

Bracero Program

Racial violence was not directed exclusively against blacks. Some whites judged people of Mexican origin as undesirable as those whose roots were African. In 1942, American farms and war industries needed workers, and the United States and Mexico had agreed to the *bracero* program, whereby Mexicans were admitted to the United States on short-term work contracts. Although the newcomers suffered racial discrimination and segregation, they seized the economic opportunities that had become available. In Los Angeles, seventeen thousand people of Mexican descent found shipyard jobs where before the war none had been available to them.

Ethnic and racial animosities intensified during the war. In 1943 Los Angeles witnessed the "zoot-suit riot," in which whites, most of them sailors and soldiers, wantonly attacked Mexican-Americans. Mexican-American street gangs (*pachucos*) had adopted ducktail haircuts and zoot suits: long coats with wide padded shoulders, pegged pants, wide-brimmed hats, and long watch chains. White racist anger at the presumed arrogance of the zoot-suiters boiled over in June, and for four days mobs invaded Mexican-American neighborhoods. According to one report: "Procedure was standard: grab a zooter. Take off his pants and frock coat and tear them up or burn them." Not only did white police officers look the other way during these assaults, but the city of Los Angeles passed an ordinance that made wearing

The bloodiest race riot of 1943 struck Detroit, where thirty-four people—twenty-five blacks and nine whites—were killed. At the peak of the rioting a white mob overturned an African-American's car, showering trolley passengers with burning gasoline.   UPI/Corbis-Bettmann.

a zoot suit within city limits a crime. Although the Second World War briefly provided economic opportunities for Mexican-Americans, these years were not the transforming experience that they were for African-Americans.

Women and Children in the War Effort

For patriotic as well as economic reasons, more than 6 million women entered the labor force during the war years. During the Great Depression, when millions of men were unemployed, public opinion had been hostile to the hiring of women, but the war brought about a rapid increase in employment. Just when men were going off to war, industry had to recruit millions of new workers to supply the rapidly expanding need for military equipment. Filling these new jobs were African-Americans, southern whites, Mexican-Americans, and, above all, women.

No matter how impressive, statistics tell only part of the story. Changes in people's attitudes were also

important. Until early in the war, employers had insisted that women were not suited for industrial jobs: if women were allowed to work in factories, they would begin to wear overalls instead of dresses, their muscles would bulge, and they might even drink whiskey and swear like men. As labor shortages began to threaten the war effort, employers did an about-face. "Almost overnight," said Mary Anderson, head of the Women's Bureau of the Department of Labor, "women were reclassified by industrialists from a marginal to a basic labor supply for munitions making." Women became riveters, welders, crane operators, tool makers, shell loaders, lumberjacks ("lumberjills"), cowgirls, and police officers.

Women in War Production

During the war years, the number of working women increased by 57 percent. Two million women took clerical jobs; another 2.5 million worked in manufacturing. The significance of these figures lay not just in the numbers themselves but also in the kinds of women who were entering the work force. The economist Claudia Goldin has observed that

Women workers mastered numerous job skills during the war. In 1942 crews of women cared for Long Island commuter trains like this one. UPI/Corbis-Bettmann.

labor-force participation rates increased most for women over age forty-five, and that "married, rather than single women, were the primary means of bolstering the nation's labor force." Of the new women workers, 75 percent were married and 3.7 million were mothers. Before the war the average female wage earner had been young, single, and largely self-supporting; by 1945 more working women were married than single, and more were over age thirty-five than under.

New employment opportunities also increased women's occupational mobility. Especially noteworthy were the gains made by African-American women; over 400,000 quit work as domestic servants to enjoy the better working conditions, higher pay, and union benefits of industrial employment. To take advantage of the new employment opportunities, both black and white women willingly uprooted themselves. Over 7 million women moved to war-production areas, such as Willow Run, Michigan, site of a massive bomber plant, and southern California, home of both shipyards and aircraft factories.

As public opinion shifted to support women's war work, posters and billboards appeared urging women to "Do the Job HE Left Behind." Newspapers and magazines, radio, and movies proclaimed Rosie the Riveter a war hero. But few people asserted that women's war work should bring about a permanent shift in sex roles: it was merely a response to a national emergency. Once the victory was won, women should go back to nurturing their husbands and children, leaving their jobs to returning GIs. Wartime surveys, however, showed that many of the women wanted to remain in their jobs—80 percent of New York's women workers felt that way, as did 75 percent in Detroit. "War jobs have uncovered unsuspected abilities in American women," explained one woman. "Why lose all these abilities because of a belief that 'a woman's place is in the home?' For some it is," she added, "for others not."

Although women's wages rose when they acquired better jobs, they still received lower pay than men. In 1945, women in manufacturing earned only 65 percent of what men were paid.

Discrimination Against Women

An important reason for this inequality was the sex-segregated labor market. Although the wartime emergency caused some traditionally male jobs to be reclassified for women, most jobs were defined as either "women's work" or "men's work." The sociologist Ruth Milkman has written that the absence of a feminist movement in the 1940s was a major reason for the failure "to combat gender inequality in the workplace at that critical historical juncture." Even in factories, most women worked in all-female shops.

Working women, particularly working mothers, suffered in other ways as well. Even as mothers were being encouraged to work in the national defense, there was still opposition to their doing so. One form this campaign took was a series of exaggerated articles in mass-circulation magazines about the suffering of "eight-hour orphans" or "latchkey children," left alone or deposited in all-night movie theaters while their mothers worked eight-hour shifts in war plants. Childcare centers were in short supply in some war-boom areas; communal or neighborhood kitchens were almost nonexistent.

By and large, however, the home-front children of working women were not neglected or abused during the war. Families made their own childcare arrangements, which often involved leaving children in the care of their grandmothers. Some mothers disapproved of public childcare as a form of welfare; others feared their children might contract contagious diseases in childcare centers. Gradually, though, both the demand for and the supply of childcare facilities grew.

Childcare in Wartime

In 1940 Congress passed the Lanham Act to provide federal aid to communities that had to absorb large war-related populations. Benefits included funds for childcare centers, hospitals, sewer systems, and additional police officers and firefighters. In late 1943, fewer than 60,000 children were enrolled in Lanham Act childcare centers; six months later, the number had more than doubled to 130,000. Another government program, Extended School Services, offered care for children before and after school; at the program's peak in 1943, it cared for 320,000 children. Although working mothers and their children re-

ceived less of such help than they needed, the Second World War was a brief time of progress in the provision of childcare. Government support for these programs expired after the war.

Serious social problems affected the nation's youth during the war: there were increases in venereal disease, teenage pregnancy, and juvenile delinquency. The increase in juvenile delinquency was greater for girls than for boys; in San Diego, arrests increased 55 percent for boys and 355 percent for girls. Some teenage girls became prostitutes: in 1943, arrests for that crime climbed 68 percent. Among boys the most common crime was theft, but vandalism and violence were also problems. And teenagers dropped out of school in record numbers.

Juvenile Delinquency

Perhaps because of such statistics, the contributions that children and youth made to the war effort were often overlooked. Children saved their nickels and dimes to buy war bonds, and they pulled wagons from house to house collecting old newspapers, rubber tires, and tin cans. Thousands of young people went to work during the war. In 1940, for example, 900,000 Americans between the ages of fourteen and eighteen were employed. By the spring of 1944 their number had climbed to 3 million—one-third of their age group. Indeed, some observers believed that the most pressing social problem afflicting teenagers was not juvenile delinquency but failure to finish school. High-school enrollments hit new lows during the war, which prompted a back-to-school drive in 1944.

While millions of women were entering the work force, hundreds of thousands of women were also getting married. The number of marriages rose from 73 per 1,000 unmarried women in 1939 to 93 in 1942. Some couples scrambled to get married so they could live together before the man was sent overseas; others doubtless married and had children to qualify for military deferments. But prosperity also fueled the rush to marry. A justice of the peace in Yuma, Arizona, explained that the marriage rate "began going up as soon as those boys were given employment in those plants at San Diego and Los Angeles"; in fact, 90 percent of the marriage licenses issued in Yuma went to aircraft workers.

Increase in Marriage, Divorce, and Birth Rates

Many of these hasty marriages did not survive long military separations, and divorces soared, too—

from 25,000 in 1939 to 359,000 in 1943 and 485,000 in 1945. As might be expected, the birth rate also climbed: total births rose from about 2.4 million in 1939 to 3.1 million in 1943. Many births were "good-bye babies," conceived as a guarantee that the family would be perpetuated if the father died in battle overseas.

Ironically, women's efforts to hold their families together during the war posed problems for returning fathers. Women war workers had brought home the wages; they had taken over the budgeting of expenses and the writing of checks. In countless ways they had proved they could hold the reins in their husbands' absence. Many husbands returned home to find that the lives of their wives and children seemed complete without them.

What of the women who wanted to remain in the labor market? Occupational segregation was pervasive in postwar America, and the better-paying positions were reserved for men. In 1945 many women who wanted to continue working in the factories and shipyards were pushed out to make way for returning veterans. Others chose to leave their jobs for a year or two before returning to work. But those who tried later to return to high-paying industrial work were discouraged, and many were forced into low-paying jobs in restaurants and laundries.

 ## The Decline of Liberalism and the Election of 1944

Even before Pearl Harbor, political liberals had suffered major defeats. Some Democrats hoped to revive the reform movement during the war, but Republicans and conservative Democrats were on guard against such a move. In the 1942 elections, the Republicans, aided by a small voter turnout, scored impressive gains, winning forty-four new seats in the House and nine in the Senate and defeating Democratic governors in New York, California, and Michigan. Part of the Democrats' problem was that the war years, unlike the 1930s, were a time of full employment. Once people had acquired jobs and gained some economic security, they began to be more critical of New Deal policies. The New Deal coalition had always been a fragile alliance: southern white farmers had little in common with northern blacks or white factory workers. In

Republican Gains in 1942

northern cities, blacks and whites who had voted for Roosevelt in 1940 were competing for jobs and housing and soon would collide in race riots.

But though New Deal liberalism was enfeebled, it was far from dead. At its head still stood Franklin D. Roosevelt, and it had a program to present to the American people. The liberal agenda began with a pledge to secure full employment. Roosevelt emphasized the concept in his Economic Bill of Rights, delivered as part of his 1944 State of the Union address. Every American, the president declared, had a right to a decent job, to sufficient food, shelter, and clothing, and to financial security in unemployment, illness, and old age. If to accomplish those goals the government had to operate at a deficit, Roosevelt was willing to do so. But first he had to be reelected.

Wartime Liberalism

In 1944 Franklin D. Roosevelt looked like an exhausted old man. His eyes were tired and puffy, and the loose flesh that hung on his large frame made him appear emaciated. The president's personal physician pronounced "nothing organically wrong with him at all—he's perfectly O.K.," but rumors of his ill health persisted. Whether or not Roosevelt expected to survive his fourth term, he selected a running mate who was inexperienced in international affairs: Senator Harry S Truman of Missouri. Truman, who represented a border state and a big-city machine (the Pendergast machine in Kansas City), was acceptable both to southerners and to the bosses. An ardent and loyal New Dealer, the senator also enjoyed the approval of liberals. There was little evidence, however, that he possessed the capacities for national and world leadership that he would need as president. Nor did Roosevelt take Truman into his confidence, failing even to inform his running mate about the atomic bomb project.

Roosevelt and Truman

Republicans were optimistic about their prospects for regaining the presidency. New York's Governor Thomas E. Dewey, who won the nomination on the first ballot, was moderate in his criticism of Roosevelt's foreign policy and did not advocate repeal of the essentials of the New Deal—Social Security, unemployment relief, collective bargaining, and price supports for farmers. Dewey had one great liability—his public image. He was stiff in manner and bland in personality.

Roosevelt won a fourth term, but with his narrowest-ever margin of victory in the popular vote.

Nevertheless, he won 53.4 percent of the popular vote and 432 electoral votes to Dewey's 99 (see map). It was the urban vote that returned Roosevelt to the White House. Wartime population shifts had enhanced the Democrats' political clout: southern whites who had been lifelong Democrats, along with southern blacks who had never voted before, had migrated to the urban industrial centers and cast Democratic ballots.

Roosevelt's Fourth-Term Victory

Added to the Democrat's urban vote was a less obvious factor. Many voters seemed to be exhibiting what has been called "depression psychosis." Fearful that hard times would return once war contracts were terminated, they remembered New Deal relief programs and voted for Roosevelt. With victory within grasp, many Americans wanted Roosevelt's experienced hand to guide both the nation and the world to a lasting international peace. Roosevelt's death in April 1945, however, rendered that choice moot. The new president who would have to complete the war effort, manage the transition to peace, and deal with the postwar world was Harry Truman.

 ## Wartime Diplomacy

The aftermath of the First World War weighed heavily on the minds of American diplomats throughout the war. Americans vowed to make a peace that would ensure a postwar world free from economic depression, totalitarianism, and war. American goals included the Open Door and lower tariffs; self-determination for liberated peoples; avoidance of the debts-reparations tangle that had plagued Europe after the First World War; expansion of the United States's sphere of influence; and management of world affairs by what Roosevelt once called the Four Policemen: the Soviet Union, China, Great Britain, and the United States.

Although the Allies concentrated on defeating the aggressors, their suspicions of one another undermined cooperation. Questions about eastern Europe proved the most difficult.

Allied Disagreement over Eastern Europe

The Soviet Union sought to fix its boundaries where they had stood before Hitler attacked in 1941. This meant that the part of Poland that the Soviets had invaded and captured in 1939 would become Soviet territory.

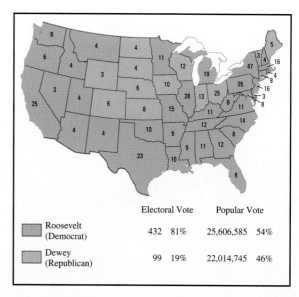

	Electoral Vote		Popular Vote	
Roosevelt (Democrat)	432	81%	25,606,585	54%
Dewey (Republican)	99	19%	22,014,745	46%

Presidential Election, 1944 *Franklin D. Roosevelt's fourth—and last—presidential election was his closest yet, but he still carried thirty-six of the country's forty-eight states.*

The British and Americans hesitated, preferring to deal with eastern Europe at the end of the war. Yet in an October 1944 agreement, Churchill and Stalin struck a bargain: the Soviet Union would gain Romania and Bulgaria as a sphere of influence; Britain would have the upper hand in Greece; and the two countries would share authority in Yugoslavia and Hungary.

Poland was a special case. In 1943, Moscow had broken off diplomatic relations with the conservative Polish government-in-exile in London. The Poles had angered Moscow by asking the International Red Cross to investigate German charges that the Soviets had massacred thousands of Polish army officers in the Katyn Forest in 1940. Then an uprising in Warsaw in 1944 complicated matters still further. Encouraged by approaching Soviet troops to expect assistance, the Warsaw underground rose against the occupying Germans. To the dismay of the world community, Soviet armies stood by as German troops slaughtered 166,000 people and devastated the city. The Soviets then set up a pro-Communist government in Lublin. Thus near the end of the war Poland had two competing governments, one in London, recognized by America and Britain, and another in Lublin.

Early in the war the Allies had begun talking about a new international peacekeeping organization. At Teheran in 1943 Roosevelt called for an

When the British liberated the Bergen-Belsen concentration camp near Hanover, Germany, in April 1945, they found this mass grave. It held the remains of thousands of Holocaust victims who had been starved, gassed, and machine-gunned by their Nazi jailers. This photograph and many others provide irrefutable proof of the Holocaust's savagery. Imperial War Museum.

Creation of the United Nations Organization

institution controlled by the Four Policemen. The next year, at a Washington, D.C., mansion called Dumbarton Oaks, American, British, Russian, and Chinese representatives conferred on the details. The conferees approved a preliminary charter for a United Nations Organization, providing for a supreme Security Council dominated by the great powers and a weak General Assembly. The Security Council would have five permanent members, each with veto power. Britain had insisted that France be one of the permanent members. Meanwhile, the Soviet Union, hoping to counter pro-American and pro-British blocs in the General Assembly, asked for separate membership in the General Assembly for each of the sixteen Soviet republics. This issue was

not resolved at Dumbarton Oaks, but the meeting proved a success nevertheless.

Diplomatic action on behalf of the European Jews, however, proved to be a tragic failure. Even before the war, Nazi officials had targeted Jews throughout Europe for extermination. By war's end, about 6 million Jews had been forced into concentration camps and systematically murdered, most by firing squads and in gas chambers. The Nazis also exterminated as many as 250,000 Gypsies and about 60,000 gay men. During the depression, the United States and other nations had refused to relax their immigration restrictions to save Jews fleeing persecution. The American Federation of Labor argued that new immigrants would

Jewish Refugees from the Holocaust

compete with American workers for scarce jobs, and public opinion polls supported this position. The fear of economic competition was fed by anti-Semitism. Bureaucrats applied the rules so strictly—requiring legal documents that fleeing Jews could not possibly provide—that otherwise-qualified refugees were kept out of the country. From 1933 to 1945, less than 40 percent of the German-Austrian immigration quota was filled.

Even the tragic voyage of the *St. Louis* did not change government policy. The vessel left Hamburg in mid-1939 carrying 930 desperate Jewish refugees who lacked proper immigration documents. Denied entry to Havana, the *St. Louis* headed for Miami, where Coast Guard cutters prevented it from docking. The ship was forced to return to Europe. Some of those refugees took shelter in countries that later were overrun by Hitler's legions. "The cruise of the *St. Louis*," wrote the *New York Times*, "cries to high heaven of man's inhumanity to man."

As evidence mounted that Hitler intended to exterminate the Jews, British and American representatives met in Bermuda in 1943 but came up with no plans. Secretary of State Hull submitted a report to the president that emphasized "the unknown cost of moving an undetermined number of persons from an undisclosed place to an unknown destination." Appalled, Secretary of the Treasury Henry Morgenthau, Jr., charged that the State Department's foot-dragging made the United States an accessory to murder. "It takes months and months to grant the visa and then it usually applies to a corpse," he wrote bitterly. Early in 1944, stirred by Morgenthau's well-documented plea, Roosevelt created the War Refugee Board, which set up refugee camps in Europe and played a crucial role in saving 200,000 Jews from death. But, lamented one American official, "by that time it was too damned late to do too much."

America's Response to the Holocaust

American officials had waited too long to act, and they also missed a chance to destroy the gas chambers and ovens at the extermination camp at Auschwitz in occupied Poland. They possessed aerial photographs and diagrams of the camp, but they argued that bombing it would detract from the war effort or prompt the Germans to step up the anti-Jewish terror. In 1944, American planes bombed factories in the industrial sector of Auschwitz but left untouched the gas chambers and crematoria only 5 miles away.

The Yalta Conference and a Flawed Peace

With the war in Europe nearing an end, and a host of political questions—including what to do with Germany—yet to be settled, President Roosevelt called for another summit meeting. The three Allied leaders met at Yalta, in the Russian Crimea, in early February 1945. Controversy has surrounded the conference ever since. Roosevelt was obviously ill, and critics of the Yalta agreements later charged that he was too weak to resist Stalin's cunning and that he struck a poor bargain. The evidence suggests, however, that Roosevelt was mentally alert and managed to sustain his strength during negotiations.

The Yalta meeting also has been criticized for keeping some of its agreements secret (suggesting that the Allies had something to hide) and for deciding the fates of weakened nations like Poland and China without their consent. Secrecy was necessary because some agreements contained military information that had to be kept from the still-undefeated Japanese and Germans. But the criticism that the Allies paid scant attention to small nations was well deserved. Wartime diplomacy simply assumed that the most powerful of the Allies would dominate international relations after the war.

Each of the Allies arrived at Yalta with definite goals. Britain sought to make France a partner in the postwar occupation of Germany, to curb Soviet influence in Poland, and to ensure protection for the vulnerable British Empire. The Soviet Union wanted reparations from Germany to assist in the massive task of rebuilding at home, possessions in Asia, continued influence in Poland, and a permanently weakened Germany so that Russia would never again suffer a German attack. The United States lobbied for the United Nations Organization, in which it believed it could exercise influence; for a Soviet declaration of war against Japan to aid in ending the war in the Pacific; for recognition of China as a major power; and for compromise between rival factions in Poland.

Allied Goals at Yalta

Military positions at the time of the conference helped to shape the final agreements. Soviet troops had occupied much of eastern Europe, including Poland, and Stalin repeatedly pointed out that twice in the century German armies had marched through Poland into Russian territory, killing millions. He insisted

Compromise on Poland

The three Allied leaders—Winston Churchill, Franklin D. Roosevelt, and Joseph Stalin—met at Yalta in February 1945. Having been president for twelve years, Roosevelt showed signs of age and fatigue. Two months later, he died of a massive cerebral hemorrhage.   Franklin D. Roosevelt Library.

on a government friendly to Moscow—the Lublin regime—in order to prevent another German onslaught. He also demanded boundaries that would give Poland part of Germany in the west and the Soviet Union part of Poland in the east. Churchill boiled over in protest; he wanted the London government-in-exile to return to Poland.

With Roosevelt's help, a compromise was reached: a boundary favorable to the Soviet Union in the east; postponement of the western boundary issue; the creation of a "more broadly based" coalition government that would include members of the London regime; and free elections to be held sometime in the future. The agreement was vague but, given Soviet occupation of Poland, Roosevelt considered it "the best I can do."

As for Germany, the Big Three agreed that it would be divided into four zones, the fourth zone to be administered by France. Berlin, within the Soviet zone, also would be divided among the four victors. On the question of reparations, Stalin wanted a precise figure, but Churchill and Roosevelt insisted on determining Germany's ability to pay. With Britain abstaining, the Americans and Russians agreed that an Allied committee would consider the sum of $20 billion as a basis for discussion in the future, with half of the amount to go to the Soviet Union.

Other issues led to tradeoffs. Stalin promised to declare war on Japan two or three months after Hitler's defeat. Since the Japanese were still resisting the American advance in Asia and since the atomic bomb was still on the drawing boards, American military leaders applauded the commitment. The Soviet premier also agreed to sign a treaty of friendship and alliance with Jiang Jieshi (Chiang Kai-shek), America's ally in China, rather than with the Communist Mao Zedong. In return, the United States agreed to Russia's recovery of holdings it had lost to Japan after the Russo-Japanese War in 1905: the southern part of Sakhalin Island and the Kurile Islands. Regarding the new world organization, Roosevelt and Churchill granted the Soviets three votes in the General Assembly (fifty nations officially launched the United Nations Organization three months later). Finally, the conferees issued the Declaration of Liberated Europe, a pledge to establish order and to rebuild economies by democratic methods.

Yalta marked the high point of the Grand Alliance; in the tradition of diplomatic give-and-take, each of the Allies came away with something it wanted. But as the great powers jockeyed for influence at the close of the war, neither the spirit nor the letter of Yalta held firm. The crumbling of the alliance became evident almost immediately, at the Potsdam Conference, which began in mid-July. Roosevelt had died in April, and Truman—a novice at international diplomacy—was less patient with the Soviets. Truman also was emboldened by learning during the conference that the atomic test in New Mexico had been successful.

Potsdam Conference

Despite major differences at Potsdam, the Big Three did agree on general policies toward Germany: complete disarmament, dismantling of industry used for military production, and dissolution of Nazi institutions and laws. In a compromise over reparations, they decided that each occupying nation should extract reparations from its own zone; but they could not agree on a total figure. The Potsdam Conference also called for the "unconditional surrender" of Japan.

Potsdam left much undone. As the war drew to a close, there was little that bound the Allies together. Roosevelt's cooperative style was gone; the spirit of Yalta was evaporating; the common enemy, Hitler,

was defeated. And the United States, with the awesome atomic bomb in the offing to force defeat on Japan, no longer needed or even wanted Russia in the Pacific war. Moreover, each of the victors was seeking to preserve and enlarge its sphere of influence. Britain claimed authority in Greece and parts of the Middle East; the Soviet Union already dominated much of eastern Europe; and the United States retained its hegemony in Latin America. The United States also seized several Pacific islands as strategic outposts and laid plans to dominate a defeated Japan. Let the Americans have their Pacific bases, responded Churchill, "but 'Hands off the British Empire' is our maxim."

Oil was crucial to victory. Japan and Germany had waged war to secure oil resources in the Dutch East Indies, Russia, and North Africa. Their failure to gain enough oil, while the Allies' supply continued flowing, led directly to their defeat on the battlefield and at sea. American officials, the historian Daniel Yergin has written, recognized that oil was "the critical strategic commodity for the war and was essential for national power and international predominance" both then and in the postwar world. During the war, American interests increased their stake in Middle Eastern oil. By 1944, American petroleum companies controlled 42 percent of the proven oil reserves of the Middle East—a nineteenfold increase since 1936. Both the British and the Russians complained about this new evidence of American expansionism.

Oil's Role in Victory

Hitler once said, "We may be destroyed, but if we are, we shall drag a world with us—a world in flames." Indeed, *rubble* was the word most often invoked to describe the European landscape at the end of the war. Hamburg, Stuttgart, and Dresden had been laid to waste; three-quarters of Berlin was in ruins. In England, Coventry and parts of London were bombed out. Across the continent of Europe transportation systems had been disrupted and water supplies contaminated. In Asia as well as in Europe, ghostlike people wandered about, searching desperately for food and mourning those who would never come home. The Soviet Union had suffered by far the greatest losses: more than 21 million military and civilian war dead—one-ninth of the total Soviet population. The Chinese calculated their war losses at 10 million, the Germans and Austrians at 6 million, and the Japanese at 2.5 million. And 6 million

The War's Death Toll

Jews had been killed during the Holocaust. In all, the Second World War caused the deaths of 55 million people.

Only one major combatant escaped such grisly statistics: the United States. Its cities were not burned and its fields were not trampled. American deaths from the war—405,399—were few compared with the losses of other nations. In fact, the United States emerged from the Second World War more powerful than it had ever been. It alone had the atomic bomb. The United States Air Force and Navy were the largest anywhere. What is more, only the United States had the capital and economic resources to spur international recovery. America, gloated Truman, was "a giant." In the coming struggle to fashion a new world out of the ashes of the old, soon to be called the Cold War (see Chapter 29), the United States held a commanding position.

Postwar Strength of the United States

Conclusion

For many Americans life was fundamentally different in 1945 from what it had been before Pearl Harbor. For one thing, the war finally ended the Great Depression, reducing unemployment practically to zero. But life differed in other ways, too. The Academy Award for 1946 went to *The Best Years of Our Lives*, a painful film about the postwar readjustments of three veterans and their families and friends. Many men returned home suffering flashbacks, nightmares, and deep emotional distress. "Dad came home a different man," recalled one girl; "he didn't laugh as much and he drank a lot."

On another front, the Second World War stimulated the trend toward bigness, not only in business and labor but also in government, agriculture, higher education, and science. Over the next few years, government agencies that had been conceived as temporary became permanent and grew in size and influence, resulting in the Department of Defense (consolidating the War and Navy Departments), the Central Intelligence Agency (succeeding the Office of Strategic Services), and the Atomic Energy Commission. The seeds of the military-industrial complex were sown during these years. Moreover, with the advent of the Cold War, millions of young men would be inducted into the armed forces during the next thirty years. War and the expectation of war would become part of American life.

At the same time, the Second World War was a powerful engine of social change in the United States. The gains made during the war by African-Americans and women were overdue. And by blending New Deal ideology and wartime urgency, the government assumed the responsibility of ensuring prosperity and stepping in when capitalism faltered. Americans emerged from the war fully confident that theirs was the greatest country in the world. The United States, they boasted, had preserved democracy and freedom around the globe. For better or worse—and clearly there were elements of each—the Second World War was a turning point in the nation's history.

Suggestions for Further Reading

Fighting the War

Robert H. Abzug, *Inside the Vicious Heart: Americans and the Liberation of Nazi Concentration Camps* (1985); Stephen E. Ambrose, *D-Day, June 6, 1944* (1994); Stephen E. Ambrose, *Eisenhower: Soldier, General of the Army, President-Elect* (1983); Allan Berube, *Coming Out Under Fire: The History of Gay Men and Women in World War II* (1990); John W. Dower, *War Without Mercy: Race and Power in the Pacific War* (1986); Richard B. Frank, *Guadalcanal* (1991); Paul Fussell, *Wartime* (1989); John Keegan, *The Second World War* (1989); Eric Larabee, *Commander in Chief* (1987); Samuel Eliot Morison, *The Two-Ocean War* (1963); David Reynolds, *Rich Relations: The American Occupation of Britain, 1942–1945* (1995); Ronald Schaffer, *Wings of Judgment: American Bombing in World War II* (1985); Ronald H. Spector, *Eagle Against the Sun: The American War with Japan* (1984); Gerhard L. Weinberg, *A World at Arms: A Global History of World War II* (1994); Daniel Yergin, *The Prize: The Epic Quest for Oil, Money, and Power* (1991).

Wartime Diplomacy

Russell Buhite, *Decisions at Yalta* (1986); Diane Clemens, *Yalta* (1970); Robert Dallek, *Franklin D. Roosevelt and American Foreign Policy, 1932–1945* (1979); Henry L. Feingold, *Bearing Witness: How America and Its Jews Responded to the Holocaust* (1995); George C. Herring, *Aid to Russia, 1941–1946* (1973); Gary R. Hess, *The United States at War, 1941–1945* (1986); Robert C. Hilderbrand, *Dumbarton Oaks* (1990); Akira Iriye, *Power and Culture: The Japanese-American War, 1941–1945* (1981); Warren Kimball, *The Juggler: Franklin Roosevelt as Wartime Statesman* (1991); Verne W. Newton, ed., *FDR and the Holocaust* (1996); Keith Sainsbury, *Churchill and Roosevelt at War* (1994); Michael Stoff, *Oil, War, and American Security* (1980); Mark Stoler, *The Politics of the Second Front* (1977); David S. Wyman, *The Abandonment of the Jews* (1984).

Mobilizing for War

John Chambers, *To Raise an Army* (1980); George Q. Flynn, *The Draft, 1940–1973* (1993); Gregory Hooks, *Forging the Military-Industrial Complex: World War II's Battle of the Potomac* (1991); Nelson Lichtenstein, *Labor's War at Home: The CIO in World War*

II (1983); Bartholomew H. Sparrow, *From the Outside In: World War II and the American State* (1996); Harold G. Vatter, *The U.S. Economy in World War II* (1985); Gerald T. White, *Billions for Defense* (1980); Allen M. Winkler, *The Politics of Propaganda: The Office of War Information, 1942–1945* (1978).

The Home Front

John Morton Blum, *V Was for Victory: Politics and American Culture During World War II* (1976); Alan Brinkley, *The End of Reform: New Deal Liberalism in Recession and War* (1995); John D'Emilio, *Sexual Politics, Sexual Communities: The Making of a Homosexual Minority in the United States, 1940–1970* (1983); Doris Kearns Goodwin, *No Ordinary Time: Franklin and Eleanor Roosevelt: The Home Front in World War II* (1994); Maurice Isserman, *Which Side Were You On? The American Communist Party During the Second World War* (1982); Clayton R. Koppes and Gregory D. Black, *Hollywood Goes to War* (1987); Gerald D. Nash, *The American West Transformed* (1985); William L. O'Neill, *A Democracy at War: America's Fight at Home and Abroad in World War II* (1993); Richard Polenberg, *War and Society: The United States, 1941–1945* (1972); George H. Roeder, Jr., *The Censored War: American Visual Experience During World War II* (1993); Studs Terkel, ed., *"The Good War": An Oral History of World War Two* (1984); William M. Tuttle, Jr., *"Daddy's Gone to War": The Second World War in the Lives of America's Children* (1993).

Japanese-American Internment

Roger Daniels, *Prisoners Without Trial* (1993); Stephen Fox, *The Unknown Internment: An Oral History of the Relocation of Italian Americans During World War II* (1990); Peter Irons, *Justice at War* (1983); Gary Okihiro, *Cane Fires: The Anti-Japanese Movement in Hawaii, 1865–1945* (1991); Page Smith, *Democracy on Trial: The Japanese American Evacuation and Relocation in World War II* (1995); John Tateishi, ed., *And Justice for All: An Oral History of the Japanese-American Detention Camps* (1984).

African-Americans and Wartime Violence

A. Russell Buchanan, *Black Americans in World War II* (1977); Dominic J. Capeci, Jr., *The Harlem Riot of 1943* (1977); Dominic J. Capeci, Jr., and Martha Wilkerson, *Layered Violence: The Detroit Rioters of 1943* (1991); Mauricio Mazon, *The Zoot-Suit Riots* (1984); Patrick S. Washburn, *A Question of Sedition: The Federal Government's Investigation of the Black Press During World War II* (1986); Neil A. Wynn, *The Afro-American and the Second World War*, rev. ed. (1993).

Women at War

Karen T. Anderson, *Wartime Women* (1981); D'Ann Campbell, *Women at War with America* (1984); Sherna Berger Gluck, *Rosie the Riveter Revisited* (1987); Claudia Goldin, *Understanding the Gender Gap: An Economic History of American Women* (1990); Susan M. Hartmann, *The Home Front and Beyond* (1982); Judy Barrett Litoff and David C. Smith, eds., *We're in This War, Too: World War II letters from American Women in Uniform* (1994); Ruth Milkman, *Gender at Work: The Dynamics of Job Discrimination by Sex During World War II* (1987); Leila J. Rupp, *Mobilizing Women for War: German and American Propaganda, 1939–1945* (1978); Peter A. Soderbergh, *Women Marines: The World War II Era* (1992).

The Atomic Bomb and Japan's Surrender

Gar Alperovitz, *The Decision to Use the Atomic Bomb and the Architecture of an American Myth* (1995); Gregg Herken, *The Winning Weapon* (1980); Michael Hogan, ed., *Hiroshima in History and Memory* (1995); Daniel J. Kevles, *The Physicists* (1977); Robert Jay Lifton and Greg Mitchell, *Hiroshima in America: Fifty Years of Denial* (1995); Richard Rhodes, *The Making of the Atomic Bomb* (1987); Martin J. Sherwin, *A World Destroyed: The Atomic Bomb and the Grand Alliance* (1975); Leon V. Sigal, *Fighting to a Finish* (1994); Ronald Takaki, *Hiroshima: Why America Dropped the Atomic Bomb* (1995).

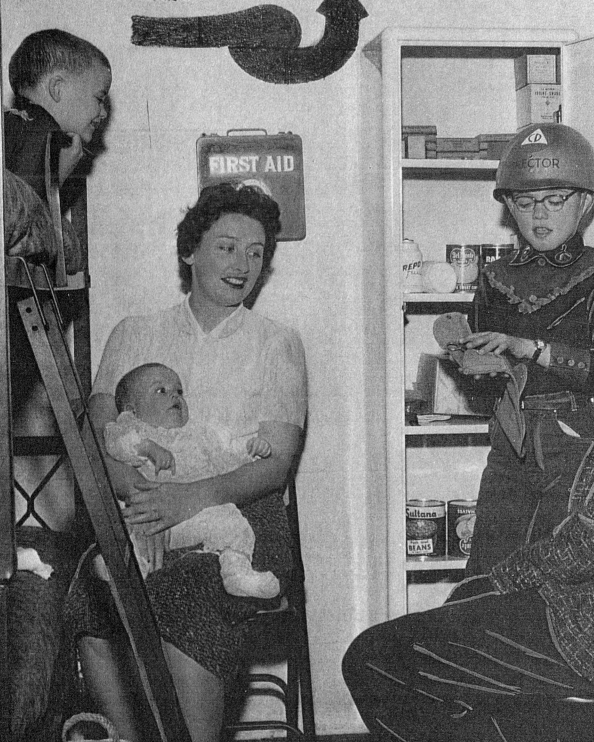

CHAPTER

28

Postwar America:
Cold War Politics,
Civil Rights, and
the Baby Boom
1945–1961

We couldn't wait to be men," recalled Ron Kovic, who as a boy in the 1950s enjoyed nothing more than playing war games with his neighborhood pals in Massapequa, a suburb on Long Island, New York. Ronnie, a baby boomer, was a fervent patriot; most baby boomers were. "For me," Kovic recalled, "it began in 1946 when I was born on the Fourth of July. The whole sky lit up in a tremendous fireworks display. . . . Every birthday after that was something the whole country celebrated. It was a proud day to be born on." Kovic was one of the first of the baby boomers, but millions more followed. From 1946 through 1961 births hit record highs in the United States. During this period 64 million babies were born, compared with only 44 million from 1929 through 1945.

Although Ron Kovic was born after the Second World War, he grew up in its afterglow. Every Saturday afternoon, he and his friends went to a nearby movie theater to see war films. His all-time favorite was *To Hell and Back* (1955) starring Audie Murphy, who at the end of the film "jumps on top of a flaming tank that's about to explode and grabs the machine gun blasting it into the German lines. He was so brave," Kovic remembered, "I had chills running up and down my back, wishing it were me up there." Afterward, Ronnie and his buddies fought war games in woods near their homes, turning the terrain into a battlefield. "We set ambushes, then led gallant attacks, storming over the top, bayonetting and shooting

811

anyone who got in our way. Then we'd walk out of the woods like the heroes we knew we would become when we were men." From films and television shows, as well as from their parents and teachers, the boys also learned who their nation's new enemies were—the Communists. Kovic remembered as a boy fearing that "the Communists were all over the place." He was "certain they were infiltrating our schools, trying to take over our classes and control our minds." Just as their fathers had defeated the Nazis in the Second World War, so they would stop the Communists in the Cold War.

As teenagers in the late 1950s and early 1960s, Ron Kovic and his best friend, Richie Castiglia, read all they could about the Marine Corps. And they "made a solemn promise . . . that the day we turned seventeen we were both going down to the marine recruiter at the shopping center in Levittown and sign up for the United States Marine Corps." Later, the recruiter came to them, speaking at a high-school assembly about "the marines and how they had never lost and [how] America had never been defeated." In the summer of 1964, Ron Kovic kept his promise and enlisted. A year later, he was in Vietnam, where he was severely wounded, losing the use of both legs. For the rest of his life, a wheelchair and catheter bag would be constant companions. Ron Kovic was like millions of other American children growing up in Cold War America. What separated him from other young men and women sacrificed in Vietnam is that he wrote a magnificent autobiography, *Born on the Fourth of July*, about how the fierce anticommunism and super-patriotism of his childhood had led him to the battlefields of Indochina.

Postwar America was proud and boastful. From 1945 to the 1960s, the American people were in the grip of "victory culture"—that is, the belief that unending triumph was the nation's birthright and destiny. From the classroom, the pulpit, and the town hall, as well as from popular culture, came self-congratulatory rhetoric about America's invincibility. Americans believed that their nation was the greatest in the world, not only the most powerful but the most righteous. And, Americans agreed, it was getting better all the time.

As evidence of the nation's perfectibility, Americans pointed to the postwar economic boom. Material comfort was the hallmark of the middle classes, and in both income level and lifestyle more Americans were better off than ever before—and most expected their good fortune to continue. A twenty-five-year economic boom began in 1945, the cornerstones of

which were the automobile, construction, and defense industries. As the gross national product (GNP) grew, income levels rose and property ownership spread. Automobiles rolled off the assembly lines; new houses and schools sprang up throughout the country. More and more people bought homes in the suburbs.

Most important, Americans began to have babies. The postwar baby boom was larger and in other ways different from increases in the birth rate that earlier generations had experienced. Parents who had grown up during the Great Depression were determined that their children's lives would be better than theirs had been. Often both parents worked to pay for a new home and a second car. This meant that women had at least two jobs, for they still were expected to do the housework and cooking. In postwar America, an emphasis on femininity and "family togetherness" concealed the lack of equal opportunities for women. For the baby boomers, family togetherness took on almost religious significance, including evenings watching television in the "family room," family vacations to Disneyland, and regular church attendance.

Although the postwar years comprised an age of consensus, Cold War politics were often volatile. When Harry S Truman became president in 1945, his initial response to the challenge was a deep feeling of inadequacy. As vice president, Truman had been kept ignorant by Franklin D. Roosevelt about crucial foreign and military initiatives; nevertheless, he would have to deal with the closing months of the war (see Chapter 27) and with the onset of the Cold War (Chapter 29). In domestic matters, too, the new president would need a crash course in the intricacies of governing the United States. The nation's reconversion from war to peace was not smooth, and Truman managed to anger liberals, conservatives, farmers, consumers, and union members early in his presidency. In 1946, voters reacted to inflation and a wave of strikes by electing a Republican majority to Congress. Truman's actions also heightened fears that a Communist conspiracy was operating within the federal government. In 1947, he issued an executive order establishing a federal employee loyalty program. Personal beliefs and past associations became criteria for employment, and federal employees accused of disloyalty were presumed to be guilty.

In 1948, Truman was thought to be extremely vulnerable, but he confounded political experts by winning the presidency in his own right. His victory demonstrated the volatility of postwar politics. The key domestic issues of the period—civil rights for

• *Important Events* •

1945 Roosevelt dies; Harry S Truman becomes president
Twelve million GIs demobilized
Truman sends twenty-one-point economic message to Congress

1946 Baby boom begins
Dr. Benjamin Spock's *Baby and Child Care* changes child-rearing practices
Over 1 million GIs enroll in colleges
Coal miners strike
Inflation reaches 18.2 percent
Republicans win both houses of Congress

1947 Truman institutes employee loyalty program
Taft-Hartley Act limits power of unions
To Secure These Rights issued by the President's Committee on Civil Rights
Planned community begun in Levittown, New York

1948 Truman appoints Committee on Equality of Treatment and Opportunity in the Armed Services to oversee racial desegregation of the armed forces
Truman elected president
Dr. Alfred Kinsey's *Sexual Behavior in the Human Male* sparks controversy

1949 Soviet Union explodes an atomic bomb
Communists win revolution in China
National Housing Act promises "a decent home" for every American

1950 Klaus Fuchs arrested as an atomic spy
Alger Hiss convicted of perjury
Senator Joseph McCarthy alleges Communists in government
Korean War begins
Julius and Ethel Rosenberg charged with conspiracy to commit treason
Internal Security (McCarran) Act requires members of "Communist front" organizations to register with the government

1951 *Dennis et al.* v. *U.S.* upholds the Alien Registration (Smith) Act, which outlawed membership in any organization that advocated violent overthrow of the United States government

1952 Ralph Ellison's *Invisible Man* shows African-Americans' exclusion from the American Dream
Dwight D. Eisenhower elected president
Republicans win both houses of Congress

1953 Korean War ends
Rosenbergs executed
Congress adopts termination policy for Native Americans
Kinsey causes a public uproar with *Sexual Behavior in the Human Female*

1954 *Brown* decision rules "separate but equal" is illegal
Communist Control Act makes Communist Party membership illegal
Senate condemns Senator McCarthy

1955 AFL and CIO merge
Rebel Without a Cause idealizes youth subculture
Disneyland opens in Anaheim, California
Montgomery bus boycott begins

1956 Highway Act launches interstate highway project
Eisenhower reelected
Allen Ginsberg's poem *Howl*, the anthem of the Beat generation, is published
Elvis Presley releases his first single recording

1957 Martin Luther King, Jr., is elected first president of the Southern Christian Leadership Conference
Little Rock, Arkansas, has desegregation crisis
Congress passes Civil Rights Act
Soviet Union launches *Sputnik*
Jack Kerouac criticizes white middle-class conformity in *On the Road*

1958 Congress passes National Defense Education Act to improve education in mathematics, foreign languages, and science
Sherman Adams resigns over scandal
St. Lawrence Seaway opens for traffic

1960 Sit-in in Greensboro, North Carolina
Student Nonviolent Coordinating Committee formed
John F. Kennedy elected president

1961 Eisenhower warns against "military-industrial complex"

1962 Michael Harrington's *The Other America* creates awareness of America's poor
Rachel Carson's *Silent Spring* warns of dangers of DDT

African-Americans and the anti-Communist witch-hunt called McCarthyism—were both highly charged. Later, the outbreak of the Korean War in 1950 intensified discontent. The war, inflation, and corruption in the White House caused Truman's popularity to plummet. After twenty years of Democratic presidents, Americans in 1952 elected the Republican nominee, General Dwight D. Eisenhower.

Eisenhower was a war hero, but as president he moved cautiously and hesitantly, particularly in dealing with civil rights and McCarthyism. His major goal was to promote economic growth, and he pursued staunchly Republican goals: a balanced budget, reduced taxes and government spending, low inflation, and a return of power to the states. Still, Eisenhower did not attempt to roll back the New Deal. In fact, however reluctantly, his administration expanded the welfare state.

During Eisenhower's eight-year presidency, the nation was generally quiescent both politically and intellectually. Americans celebrated the American Dream and their economic system for providing a high standard of living, and they liked the president's traditionalism, caution, and moderation. "Ike" reassured them, and they trusted him. These years were comforting to Americans who longed for a respite from social turbulence. "The fifties under Ike," a *New York Times* reporter observed, "represented a sort of national prefrontal lobotomy: tail-finned, we Sunday-drove down the superhighways of life while tensions that later bubbled up in the sixties seethed beneath the placid surface."

It was the infant civil rights movement that challenged the national consensus. Most African-Americans were at the bottom of the economic ladder and were being denied their constitutional rights. How would blacks be incorporated into the consensus? The president, Congress, southern whites, and black civil rights activists all gave different answers as they debated *Brown* v. *Board of Education of Topeka*, the Supreme Court's momentous decision of 1954 invalidating racial segregation in public schools.

Still, however fragile, the age of consensus remained basically intact. President Eisenhower was succeeded in 1961 by a much younger man, Democratic Senator John F. Kennedy of Massachusetts. The 1960s would be a far different decade. For one thing, the exceptions to the American Dream had gone unnoticed by affluent Americans who ignored evidence of poverty. Yet it became clear by the early 1960s that the American poor were much more numerous than many people had imagined. Meanwhile, throughout the country from 1945 to 1961, race relations and urban conditions continued to deteriorate. In the 1960s the nation would have to deal with problems it had postponed for too long.

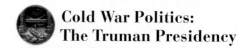

Cold War Politics: The Truman Presidency

After the initial joyous reaction to the Second World War's end, Americans faced a number of important questions. What would be the effect of reconversion—the cancellation of war contracts, termination of wage and price controls, and expiration of wartime labor agreements? Would depression recur as the artificial stimulus of the war was withdrawn, throwing people out of work and sending prices downward? Or would Americans spend the money they had saved during the war years and go on a buying spree?

Even before the war's end, cutbacks in production had caused layoffs. At Ford Motor Company's massive Willow Run plant outside Detroit, where nine thousand Liberator bombers had been produced, most workers were let go in the spring of 1945. Ten days after the victory over Japan, 1.8 million people nationwide received pink slips, and 640,000 filed for unemployment compensation. The employment picture was made more complex by the return of millions of discharged GIs in 1945 and 1946; 12 million GIs were demobilized in 1945 alone. At the peak of postwar unemployment in March 1946, 2.7 million people searched for work.

Postwar Job Layoffs

Fearing that an economic depression might result from the cancellation of war contracts, President Truman declared his determination not only to combat unemployment but also to expand on New Deal programs begun in the 1930s. In September 1945 he delivered to Congress a twenty-one-point message urging extension of unemployment compensation, an increase in the minimum wage, adoption of permanent farm price supports, and new public works projects. Truman also revived Roosevelt's Economic Bill of Rights: the right of every able-bodied American to hold a job. If the economy failed to provide one, the government should create it. Congress responded to Truman's message with the Employment Act of 1946, but the act fell short of Truman's hopes: Congress had deleted a commitment to absolute full employment.

Despite high unemployment immediately after the war, the United States was not teetering on the brink of depression. In fact, after a brief period of readjustment, the economy soon

Beginnings of the Postwar Economic Boom

blasted off into a quarter-century of unprecedented boom. People had plenty of savings to spend in 1945 and 1946, and suddenly there were new houses and cars for them to buy. Easy credit also promoted the buying spree. As a result, despite the winding-down of war production, the gross national product continued to rise in 1945. The nation's most immediate postwar economic problem was not depression; it was inflation, fueled by maddening shortages of consumer goods like meat and housing. Throughout 1945 and 1946 prices skyrocketed; inflation exceeded 18 percent in 1946.

As prices spiraled upward, many people were earning less in real income (actual purchasing power) than they had earned during the war. Industrial work-

Upsurges in Labor Strikes

ers had complained during the war that the National War Labor Board limited them to cost-of-living pay increases. In the immediate postwar period they protested that the end of war production had eliminated much of their overtime work. A primary reason for workers' discontent was that as their wages and salaries declined slightly in 1946, net profits reached all-time highs. Indignant that they were not sharing in the prosperity, workers forced nationwide shutdowns in the coal, automobile, steel, and electric industries and halted railroad and maritime transportation.

By 1946 there was no doubt about the growing unpopularity of labor unions and their leadership. Many Americans blamed the unions for strikes, which restricted the output of consumer goods and inflated prices. In May, when a nationwide railroad strike was threatened, Truman hopped aboard the anti-union bandwagon and made a dramatic appearance before a joint session of Congress. If strikers in an industry deemed vital to the national security refused to honor a presidential order to return to work, he would "request the Congress immediately to authorize the President to draft into the Armed Forces of the United States all workers who are on strike against their government." Truman's speech alienated not just the railroad workers but union members in general. Many vowed to defeat him in the upcoming 1948 presidential election.

Truman fared little better in his direction of the Office of Price Administration (OPA). Now that the war was over, powerful interests wanted price controls lifted. Consumers grew im-

Consumer Discontent

patient with shortages and black-market prices, and manufacturers and farmers wanted to jack up prices legally. Yet when most controls expired in mid-1946 and inflation rose further, consumers grumbled. Truman's approval rating plunged from 87 percent in late 1945 to 32 percent in 1946. Republicans made the most of public discontent. "Got enough meat?" asked Republican Congressman John M. Vorys of Ohio. "Got enough houses? Got enough OPA? . . . Got enough inflation? . . . Got enough debt? . . . Got enough strikes?" In 1946 the Republicans won a majority in both houses of the Eightieth Congress and captured twenty-five of the thirty-two nonsouthern governorships. The White House in 1948 seemed within their grasp.

The politicians who dominated the Eightieth Congress, whether Republicans or southern Democrats, were committed conservatives. They supported Truman's Cold War foreign pol-

The Eightieth Congress

icy but perceived the Republican landslide as a mandate to reverse the New Deal—that is, to curb the power of government and of labor. Truman had had little success with the previous Congress; he would have even less success with this one. Ironically, however, the Eightieth Congress ultimately would help him win the presidency in 1948. For if Truman had alienated labor and consumers, the Eightieth Congress made them livid.

Particularly unpopular with workers was the Taft-Hartley Act, which Congress approved over Truman's veto in 1947. A revision of the Wagner Act of 1935, the bill prohibited the

Taft-Hartley Act

closed shop, a workplace where membership in a particular union was a prerequisite for being hired. It also permitted the states to enact right-to-work laws banning union-shop agreements, which required all workers to join if a majority voted in favor of a union shop. In addition, the law forbade union contributions to political candidates in federal elections, required union leaders to sign non-Communist affidavits, and mandated an eighty-day cooling-off period before carrying out strikes that imperiled the national security. Taft-Hartley became labor's litmus test for political can-

So few pollsters predicted that President Harry S Truman (1884–1972) would win in 1948 that the Chicago Tribune *announced his defeat before all the returns were in. Here a victorious Truman pokes fun at the newspaper for its premature headline.*   Corbis-Bettmann.

didates. Thus Truman's veto vindicated him in the eyes of labor.

Throughout 1947 and 1948, the conservative Eightieth Congress offended a raft of interest groups, which in turn swung back to Truman. The president asked Congress for continued price supports for farmers; the Eightieth Congress responded with weakened price supports. The president requested nationwide health insurance; the Eightieth Congress refused. The pattern was the same with federal funding of public housing and aid to public education; with unemployment compensation and the minimum wage; and with antilynching and fair employment legislation. Truman proposed; Congress rejected or ignored his requests.

Republicans seemed oblivious to public opinion. Not since 1928 had they been so confident of capturing the presidency, and most political experts agreed. "Only a political miracle or extraordinary stupidity on the part of the Republicans," according to *Time*, "can save the Democratic party." At their national convention, Republicans strengthened their position by nominating the governors of

Presidential Campaign of 1948

two of the nation's most populous states: Thomas E. Dewey of New York for president and Earl Warren of California for vice president. Democrats revealed their fragmentation when an alliance of big-city bosses and liberals tried to dump Truman in favor of General Dwight D. Eisenhower. But Eisenhower declined the offer, and Truman ultimately received the nomination.

Democrats were up against more than Republicans in 1948. Two years before, Henry A. Wallace, the only remaining New Dealer in the cabinet, had been fired by Truman for publicly criticizing United States foreign policy. In 1948 Wallace ran for president on the Progressive Party ticket, which advocated friendship with the Soviet Union, racial desegregation, and nationalization of basic industries. A fourth party, the Dixiecrats (States' Rights Democratic Party), was organized by southerners who walked out of the 1948 Democratic convention when it adopted a pro–civil rights plank; they nominated Governor Strom Thurmond of South Carolina. If Wallace's candidacy did not destroy Truman's chances, experts said, the Dixiecrats certainly would.

But Truman had a few ideas of his own. He called the Eightieth Congress into special session and chal-

lenged it to enact all the planks in the Republican platform. If Republicans really wanted

**Truman's
Upset Victory**

to transform their convictions
into law, said Truman, this was
the time to do it. After Congress
had debated for two weeks and
accomplished nothing of significance, Truman took
to the road, delivering scores of speeches denouncing the "do-nothing" Eightieth Congress. Still, no
amount of furious campaigning by Truman seemed
likely to change the predicted outcome.

As the votes were counted, however, it was clear
that Truman had confounded the experts. The final
tally was 24 million popular votes and 303 electoral
votes for Truman; 22 million popular votes and 189
electoral votes for Dewey (see map). How and why
did the upset occur? First, the United States was prosperous, at peace, and essentially united on foreign
policy. Second, Roosevelt's legacy—the New Deal
coalition—had endured: African-Americans, ethnic
Americans, union members, and other voters in
northern cities, along with most southern whites, had
rallied to Truman's support. Many farmers also voted
for Truman, fearful that the Republicans would drastically reduce price supports for agricultural goods.
Finally, the extremist image of the Progressive and
Dixiecrat Parties helped Truman by making the
Democratic Party look moderate. Rather than receiving the predicted 5 million votes each, Wallace
and Thurmond polled just over 1 million each.

Truman began his new term brimming with confidence. It was time, he believed, for government to
fulfill its responsibility to provide economic security
for the poor and the elderly. As he worked on his 1949
State of the Union message, he penciled in an expression of his intentions: "I expect to give every segment of our population a fair deal." Little of Truman's Fair Deal came to fruition, however, and he
would leave office a highly unpopular president. One
reason for the president's unpopularity was the Korean War, which broke out in 1950 (see Chapter 29).

In June 1950, President Truman ordered American troops to fight in Korea. There was much grum-
bling among Americans as the nation again mobilized
for war. People remembered the

**Korean War
Discontent
on the
Home Front**

shortages of the last war and
flocked to their grocery stores for
sugar, coffee, and canned goods.
Fueled by panic buying and large
defense expenditures, inflation
(which had not been a problem
since 1948) began to eat away at the economy again:

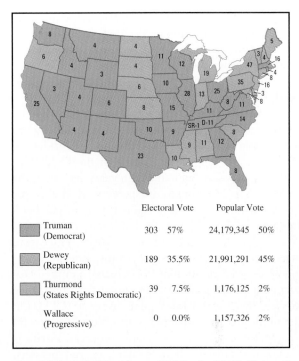

	Electoral Vote		Popular Vote	
Truman (Democrat)	303	57%	24,179,345	50%
Dewey (Republican)	189	35.5%	21,991,291	45%
Thurmond (States Rights Democratic)	39	7.5%	1,176,125	2%
Wallace (Progressive)	0	0.0%	1,157,326	2%

Presidential Election, 1948 *In 1948 Harry S
Truman won perhaps the biggest upset in a presidential
election, defeating not only the Republican candidate
but also challengers from the States' Rights Democratic
and Progressive Parties.*

prices rose 8 percent in the first eight months of the
war.

Draft boards began to call up men between the
ages of nineteen and twenty-six, and national guardsmen and reservists were called to active duty. There
was no rush to join. Husbands and fathers thought single men should go first; parents protested when the
military began to draft eighteen-and-a-half-year-
olds in 1951. "Everybody wants out; no one wants
in," the director of the draft complained. When the
government announced that college students would
be granted deferments, young people enrolled in universities in hopes of the war's ending before their
graduation. But the war did not end quickly, and by
mid-1952 American military personnel numbered
3.6 million, up from 1.5 million two years earlier.

As the 1952 presidential election approached, the
Democrats foundered. Frustration with the Korean
War was exacerbated by the revelation of influence
peddling by some of Truman's cronies. Known as "five
percenters," they had offered government contracts
in return for 5 percent kickbacks. A presidential ap-
pointee admitted under oath, "I have only one thing

to sell and that is influence." In 1951 Truman's public approval rating slumped to an all-time low of 23 percent and hovered at that level for a year. Once again the Democratic Party appeared doomed along with its leader—and this time appearances proved correct.

Although Truman was highly unpopular when he left office in 1953, historians now rate him among the nation's ten best presidents. Truman was president at

Truman's Presidential Legacy

the beginning of the Cold War, and in eight years he strengthened the powers of the presidency. Agencies that had been set up for temporary duty during the Second World War were made permanent, such as the Atomic Energy Commission. And legislation in 1947 created a unified Department of Defense and a permanent intelligence service, the Central Intelligence Agency (CIA). On the domestic front, Truman was a New Dealer who fought for programs to benefit workers, African-Americans, farmers, homeowners, retired persons, and people in need of healthcare. He showed his spunk and courage in 1948 when he pulled off the biggest upset in American political history. Although little of Truman's Fair Deal was enacted during his presidency, much of it became law as part of the Great Society in the 1960s (see Chapter 31).

Consensus and Conflict: The Eisenhower Presidency

In the 1952 presidential election, voters agreed with the Republican campaign slogan "It's Time for a Change." What sealed the fate of the Democratic Party was the Republican candidacy of General Dwight D. Eisenhower. A bona fide war hero who had come from humble origins in Kansas, "Ike" seemed to embody the virtues Americans most admired: integrity, decency, lack of pretense, and native ability. Eisenhower's unlucky Democratic opponent was Adlai Stevenson, the thoughtful and witty governor of Illinois. It was never much of a contest, especially after Eisenhower promised to end the Korean War. The result was a landslide: Eisenhower and his running mate, Senator Richard M. Nixon of California, won almost 34 million popular votes and 442 electoral votes, to the Democrats' 27 million popular and 89 electoral votes, including four states in the once-solid Democratic South. Moreover, Eisenhower's coattails were long enough to carry

other Republicans to victory; the party gained control of both houses of Congress, though with only a one-seat margin in the Senate.

Smiling Ike, with his folksy style, garbled syntax, and frequent escapes to the golf course, provoked Democrats to charge that he failed to lead. But Dwight D. Eisenhower was not that simple. He was no stranger to hard work. His low-key, "hidden-hand" style was a way of playing down his role as politician and highlighting his role as chief of state. Eisenhower relied heavily on staff work, delegating authority to cabinet members. Sometimes he was not well informed on details and gave the impression that he was out of touch with his own government. In fact, he was not, and he remained a very popular president.

During Eisenhower's presidency most Americans clung to the status quo. It was an era of both self-congratulation and constant anxiety. British

The "Consensus Mood"

journalist Godfrey Hodgson has described the "consensus mood," writing that Americans were "confident to the verge of complacency about the perfectibility of American society, anxious to the point of paranoia about the threat of communism." Demand for reform at such a time seemed to most Americans not only unnecessary but downright unpatriotic. Historian Henry Steele Commager saw conformity everywhere in the 1950s, as evidenced by "the uncritical and unquestioning acceptance of America as it is." College students shunned passionate political convictions. A weak minority on the American left advocated checks on the political power of corporations, and a noisy minority on the right accused the government of a wishy-washy campaign against communism. But both liberal Democrats and moderate Republicans avoided extremism, satisfied to be occupying what the historian Arthur M. Schlesinger, Jr., called "the vital center."

In this age of consensus, President Eisenhower approached his duties with a philosophy he called "dynamic conservatism." He meant being "conservative when it comes to money

"Dynamic Conservatism"

and liberal when it comes to human beings." Eisenhower's was unabashedly "an Administration representing business and industry," as Interior Secretary Douglas McKay acknowledged. The president and his appointees gave priority to reducing the federal budget, but they did not always succeed; and they recognized that dismantling New Deal and Fair Deal programs was politically impossible. The administration did try to remove the federal government from agriculture, but the effort failed. Despite several changes in federal farm price support policy, the government found itself spending more money and stockpiling increased amounts of surplus farm commodities.

Eisenhower made headway in other spheres. In 1954 Congress passed legislation to construct a canal, the St. Lawrence Seaway, between Montréal and Lake Erie. This inland waterway, which opened in 1958, was intended to spur the economic development of the Midwest by linking the Great Lakes to the Atlantic Ocean. Also in 1954 Eisenhower signed into law amendments to the Social Security Act that raised benefits and added 7.5 million workers, mostly self-employed farmers, to the program's coverage. Congress also obliged the president with tax reform that raised business depreciation allowances and with the Atomic Energy Act of 1954, which granted private companies the right to own reactors and nuclear materials for the production of electricity.

Eisenhower also presided over a dramatic change in the lives of Native Americans. In 1953, Congress adopted a policy of *termination:* the liquidation of

Termination Policy for Native Americans

Indian reservations and an end to federal services. Another act of the same year made Indians subject to state laws. With little consultation with Native Americans, the government embarked on a radical departure from policies established a century before. Administration officials applauded the changes because they would reduce federal costs and serve states' rights. Critics—including most Indians—denounced termination as one more attempt to grab Indian lands and exploit Native Americans.

Between 1954 and 1960, the federal government withdrew its benefits from sixty-one tribes. About one in eight Indians abandoned the reservations; many joined the ranks of the urban poor in low-paying jobs. The policy of termination and relocation was motivated largely by land greed. The Klamaths of Oregon, for example, lived on a reservation rich in ponderosa pine, which lumber interests coveted. Enticed by cash payments, almost four-fifths of the Klamaths accepted termination and voted to sell their shares of the forest land. With termination, their way of life collapsed. By the time termination was halted in the 1960s, so much human tragedy had struck Native Americans that observers compared the situation to the devastation their forebears had endured in the nineteenth century.

In the 1954 congressional elections, most Americans revealed that, though they still liked Eisenhower, they remained loyal to the Democratic Party.

Interstate Highway System

With a recession just winding down, the voters gave the Democrats control of both houses of Congress. Lyndon B. Johnson of Texas became the Senate's new majority leader. An energetic, pragmatic politician, Johnson worked with the Republican White House to pass legislation. A notable accomplishment was the Highway Act of 1956, which launched the largest public works program in American history. This law authorized the spending of $31 billion over the next thirteen years to build a 41,000-mile interstate highway system, intended to facilitate commerce and enable the military to move around the nation more easily. The interstate highways invigorated the tourist industry, further weakened the railroads, and spurred the growth of suburbs farther and farther from the central cities.

Eisenhower suffered a heart attack in 1955 but regained his strength and declared his intention to run again. The Democrats nominated Adlai E. Stevenson once more. Eisen-

Election of 1956

hower, running again with Nixon, won a landslide victory in 1956: 36 million votes and 457 electoral votes to Stevenson's 26 million and 73. Americans decided to stick with an experienced military man and statesman at a time of world unrest. Still, the Democrats continued to dominate Congress.

Eisenhower faced rising federal expenditures in his second term, in part because of the tremendous expense of America's global activities. In the first three years of his presidency he had managed to trim the budget, largely by controlling defense spending. But the president discovered that he had to tolerate deficit spending to achieve his goals. In 1959 federal expenditures climbed to $92 billion, about half of which went to the military. In fact, Eisenhower balanced only three of his eight budgets. The administration's resort to deficit spending also was fueled by the need to cushion the impact of three recessions—in 1953–1954, 1957–1958, and 1960–1961. A sluggish economy and unemployment also reduced the tax dollars collected by the federal government.

A lingering recession and other setbacks in 1958 made that year the low point for the administration.

During the 1952 presidential campaign, Dwight D. Eisenhower (1890–1969) received a delegation of Republican national committeewomen at his New York City headquarters. As the women chanted "I Like Ike," the Republican candidate opened his arms to welcome them.   Corbis-Bettmann.

Scandal unsettled the White House when the president's chief aide, Sherman Adams, resigned under suspicion of influence peddling. Then came large Republican losses in the 1958 congressional elections. The Democrats took the Senate by 64 votes to 34 and the House by 282 votes to 154. For the last two years of his presidency, Eisenhower had to confront what he called congressional "spenders," who proposed "every sort of foolish proposal" in the name of "national security and the 'poor' fellow."

Assessments of the Eisenhower administration used to emphasize its conservatism, passive style, limited achievements, and reluctance to confront difficult issues. In recent years, interpretations have been changing as scholars have begun examining the now-declassified documents of the consensus era. Many now stress Eisenhower's command of policymaking, sensibly moderate approach to most problems, political savvy, and great popularity. Many historians now argue that Eisenhower was not an aging bystander in the 1950s but a competent, pragmatic leader who gave most Americans what they wanted at the time—a grandfatherly figure in the

Eisenhower Presidency Assessed

White House, economic comfort, and unrelenting anticommunism.

The record of Eisenhower's presidency is nonetheless mixed. At home he failed to deal with poverty, urban decay, and blatant denials of civil rights—problems that would wrack the country in the next decade. But in comparison with his successors in the 1960s, Eisenhower was measured and cautious. He kept military budgets under control and managed crises adroitly so that the United States avoided major military ventures abroad. At home he curbed inflation, strengthened the infrastructure by building an interstate highway system, and expanded Social Security coverage. Eisenhower brought dignity to the presidency, and the American people respected him.

Just before leaving office in early 1961, Eisenhower went on national radio and television to deliver his farewell address to the nation. Because of the Cold War, he observed, the United States had been "compelled to create a permanent industry of vast proportions," as well as a standing army of 3.5 million. "This conjunction of an

The "Military-Industrial Complex"

immense military establishment and a large arms industry is new in the American experience," Eisenhower noted. "The total influence—economic, political, even spiritual—is felt in every city, every statehouse, every office of the federal government." So powerful was this influence that it threatened the nation's "democratic processes." Then Eisenhower issued a direct warning, urging Americans to "guard against . . . the military-industrial complex." They did not.

McCarthyism

The two most volatile political issues in postwar America were the anti-Communist hysteria known as McCarthyism and the growing protest movement for African-American equality. Both Truman and Eisenhower overreacted to the alleged threat of Communist subversion in government. Their alarmist rhetoric heightened public anxiety, and their loyalty programs ruined innocent people's lives and careers.

It is a misconception that McCarthyism began in 1950 with the furious speeches of Senator Joseph R. McCarthy of Wisconsin. Actually, anticommunism had been a prominent strand in the American political fabric ever since the First World War and the Red Scare of 1919 and 1920. The Cold War heightened anti-Communist fears, and McCarthy manipulated the fears to his own advantage; he became the most successful and frightening redbaiter the country had ever seen.

What reason was there to fear Communist influence in the 1940s and 1950s? The Communist Party had never been strong in the United States, even during the hard times of the depression. But anticommunism persisted in the United States, and in 1940 Congress enacted the Alien Registration (Smith) Act, which made it unlawful to advocate the overthrow of the United States government by force or violence or to join any organization that did so. Politicians played on anti-Communist paranoia. Thomas E. Dewey, for example, charged in the 1944 presidential campaign that influential Communists within the Democratic Party were about to take it over.

To a significant extent President Truman shared responsibility for initiating the postwar anti-Communist crusade. He was bothered by the revelation in 1945 that classified government documents had been found in a raid on the offices of *Amerasia*, a little-

known magazine whose editors sympathized with the Communist revolution in China. Who had supplied the documents to the magazine, and why? Similar concerns greeted the release of a Canadian royal commission report in 1946, which claimed that Soviet spies were operating in Canada; among them, the report said, was a scientist who had transmitted atomic secrets to a Soviet agent.

Spurred by these revelations, Truman in 1947 ordered investigations into the loyalty of the more than 3 million employees of the United States government. In 1950 the government began discharging people deemed "security risks," among them alcoholics, homosexuals, and debtors thought to be susceptible to blackmail. In most cases there was no evidence of disloyalty. Others became victims of guilt by association. Their loyalty was considered questionable because they either knew or were related to people thought to be subversive or disloyal.

Truman's Loyalty Probe

The wellspring of this fear of communism was the Cold War: fear of internal subversion was intertwined with fear of external attack. Truman was not alone in peddling fear; conservatives and liberal Democrats joined him. Republicans used the same methods to attack the Democratic candidates for president in 1948 and 1952; liberal Democrats used them to discredit the far-left, pro-Wallace wing of their party. The anti-Communist hysteria of the late 1940s, created by professional politicians, was embraced and promoted by labor union officials, religious leaders, media moguls, and other influential figures.

People began to point accusing fingers at each other. "Reds, phonies, and 'parlor pinks,'" in Truman's words, seemed to lurk everywhere. Hollywood film personalities who had been ardent left-wingers such as Will Geer and Zero Mostel were blacklisted; and ten screenwriters and directors (the "Hollywood Ten") were sentenced to prison for contempt of Congress when they refused to provide names of alleged Communists. Schoolteachers and college professors were fired for expressing dissenting viewpoints. Anti-Communists also exploited the hysteria to drive homosexuals from their jobs. "Sexual perverts have infiltrated our government in recent years," warned the Republican national chairman in 1950, adding that homosexuals were "perhaps as dangerous as the actual Communists."

Victims of Anti-Communist Hysteria

How do historians know that public anxiety about communism was heightened by the media? This comic book, published in 1947 by the Catechetical Guild Educational Society, enjoyed several reprintings; 4 million copies were distributed free to church groups. Claiming that communists already had "wormed their way into . . . government offices, trade unions, and other positions of trust," it warned Americans that, unless they were vigilant, they might be "living in Communist slavery." Films such as Invasion U.S.A. *(1952) and* Red Nightmare *(1962) featured communist-takeover scenarios, as did newspaper and magazine articles. The Hearst media empire, with nine maga-* zines and eighteen daily newspapers, including the Daily Mirror *in New York and the* Los Angeles Examiner, *was vociferous in demanding governmental investigations of alleged left-wing subversives. Right-wing publications also demanded that liberal publications be banned from public libraries. And some libraries responded;* The Nation *was removed from school libraries in New York City and Newark, New Jersey. But some librarians refused. In 1950 Ruth Brown lost her job in Bartlesville, Oklahoma, after a citizens committee objected to her placing copies of* The Nation *and* The New Republic *on the library shelves. Photo: The Michael Barson Collection/Past Perfect.*

IS THIS TOMORROW

AMERICA UNDER COMMUNISM!

In labor union elections and even in local parent-teacher associations, redbaiting became a convenient tactic for discrediting the opposition. The hysteria was particularly damaging to the labor movement, which forsook its class-conscious militancy in favor of anticommunism. In 1949, the CIO expelled eleven unions, with a combined membership of over 900,000, for alleged Communist domination. All this occurred at a time when membership in the Communist Party of the United States of America was rapidly declining, from a high of about 83,000 in 1947 to 55,000 in 1950 and 25,000 in 1954.

Despite the rampant false accusations, there was cause for alarm—especially in 1949. In that year the Soviets detonated their first atomic bomb, and the Chinese Communists, finally victorious in their civil war, proclaimed the People's Republic of China. Furthermore, a former State Department official, Alger Hiss, was on trial for perjury for swearing to a grand jury that he had never passed classified documents to his accuser, for-

Hiss Case

mer American Communist spy Whittaker Chambers, and that he in fact had not seen Chambers since 1936. When Truman and Secretary of State Dean Acheson came to Hiss's defense, some people began to suspect that the Democrats had something to hide. Republican Congressman Richard M. Nixon of California, a member of the House Committee on Un-American Activities (HUAC), which had led the investigation of the Hiss case, harped constantly on that theme.

In early 1950 Hiss was convicted of perjury. At the same time, a British court sentenced Klaus Fuchs, a nuclear scientist and Nazi refugee, to prison for turning over to Soviet agents secrets from the atomic-bomb project at Los Alamos, New Mexico. "Fuchs and Acheson and Hiss and hydrogen bombs threatening outside and New Dealism eating away at the vitals of the nation," exclaimed a Republican senator. "In the name of heaven, is this the best America can do?"

The circumstances were ripe for a demagogue; it was in this atmosphere that Senator Joseph

McCarthy's Attack on the State Department

McCarthy mounted a rostrum in Wheeling, West Virginia, in February 1950 and gave a name to the hysteria: McCarthyism. "The State Department," he asserted, was "thoroughly infested with Communists," and the most dangerous person in the department was Dean Acheson. The senator claimed to have a list of 205 Communists working in the department; McCarthy later lowered the figure to "57 card-carrying members," then raised it to 81. But the number did not matter. What McCarthy needed was a winning campaign issue, and he had found it. Republicans, distraught over losing what had appeared to be a sure victory in the 1948 presidential election, were eager to support his attack.

McCarthy and McCarthyism gained momentum throughout 1950. McCarthy continued to display his unparalleled talent for demagoguery, implying guilt by association, interpreting writings out of context, and telling outright lies. Nothing seemed to slow the senator down, not even attacks by other Republicans. Seven Republican senators broke with their colleagues in 1950 and publicly condemned McCarthy for his "selfish political exploitation of fear, bigotry, ignorance, and intolerance"; a Senate committee reported that his charges against the State Department were "a fraud and a hoax." But McCarthy had much to sustain him, including Julius and Ethel Rosenberg's 1950 arrest for conspiracy to commit espionage. During the war, they allegedly had recruited and supervised a spy who worked at the Los Alamos atomic laboratory. Perhaps even more helpful to McCarthy than the Rosenberg case was the outbreak of the Korean War in June 1950.

Widespread support for anti-Communist measures was also apparent in the adoption, over Truman's veto, of the Internal Security (McCarran) Act of 1950, which required members of "Communist-front" organizations to register with the government and prohibited them from holding defense jobs or traveling abroad. In a telling decision in 1951 (*Dennis et al.* v. *U.S.*), the Supreme Court upheld the Smith Act of 1940, under which eleven Communist Party leaders had been convicted and imprisoned.

During President Eisenhower's first term, the conduct of Senator Joseph R. McCarthy was one of

Congressman Richard M. Nixon (1913–1994) appeared to take little satisfaction in the newspaper headline proclaiming Alger Hiss's perjury conviction in early 1950. As a member of the House Un-American Activities Committee, Nixon had led the investigation into charges that Hiss had been a Communist Party member and a spy in the 1930s. Corbis-Bettmann.

the most vexing problems facing the administration.

Eisenhower's Reluctance to Confront McCarthy

The Wisconsin senator's no-holds-barred search for subversives in government turned up none and was an affront to political fair play, decency, and civil liberties. Eisenhower avoided confronting McCarthy, saying privately that he would not "get into the gutter with that guy"; the president also feared that a showdown would splinter the Republican Party. Instead, he hoped the media and Congress would bring McCarthy down.

While Eisenhower pursued this indirect strategy to undermine the senator, his administration practiced its own brand of anticommunism. A new executive order in 1953 expanded the criteria under which federal workers could be dismissed as "security risks." In its first three years in office, the Eisenhower administration dismissed fifteen hundred people, more than Truman had fired in twice the time. One of Eisenhower's most controversial decisions was his denial of clemency to Julius and Ethel Rosenberg. The two, having been sentenced to death, were executed in 1953.

In 1954 the Communist Control Act demonstrated that both liberals and conservatives shared in the consensus on anticommunism. The measure, which in effect made membership in the Communist Party illegal, passed in the Senate unanimously and in the House by 265 votes to 2. Its chief sponsor, liberal Democratic senator Hubert H. Humphrey of Minnesota, told his colleagues just before he cast his vote: "We have closed all of the doors. These rats will not get out of the trap."

As for Senator McCarthy, he finally transgressed the limits of what the Senate and the public would tolerate. His crucial mistake was taking on the United States Army in front of millions of television viewers. At issue was the senator's wild accusation that the army was shielding and promoting Communists; he cited the case of one army dentist. The so-called Army-McCarthy hearings, held by a Senate subcommittee in 1954, became a showcase for the senator's abusive treatment of witnesses. McCarthy, apparently drunk, alternately ranted and slurred his words. Finally, after he maligned a young lawyer who was not even involved in the hearings, Joseph

Army-McCarthy Hearings

The downfall of Senator Joseph R. McCarthy came in 1954, during the Army-McCarthy hearings, when the army's attorney, Joseph Welch (left), turned to the senator and asked, "Have you no sense of decency, sir?"   Robert Phillips, *Life* magazine © Time Inc.

Welch, counsel for the army, protested, "Have you no sense of decency, sir?" The gallery erupted in applause, and McCarthy's career as a witch-hunter plummeted. The Senate finally condemned McCarthy, in a 67-to-22 vote in December 1954, not for defiling the Bill of Rights, but for sullying the dignity of the Senate. He remained a senator, but exhaustion and alcohol took their toll. McCarthy died in 1957 at the age of forty-eight.

President Eisenhower's reluctance to discredit McCarthy publicly had given the senator, other right-wing members of Congress, and some private and public institutions enough rein to divide the nation and destroy the careers of many innocent people. McCarthyism demoralized and frightened federal workers, some of whom were driven from public service. The anti-Communist campaigns of the 1950s also discouraged people from freely expressing themselves and hence from debating critical issues. Fear and a contempt for the Bill of Rights, in short, helped sustain the Cold War consensus.

The Civil Rights Movement in Postwar America

Ironically, Cold War pressures benefited the civil rights movement. As the Soviet Union was quick to point out, the United States could hardly pose as the leader of the free world or condemn the denial of human rights in Eastern Europe and the Soviet Union if it condoned racism at home. Nor could the United States convince new African and Asian nations of its dedication to human rights if African-Americans were subjected to segregation, disfranchisement, and racial violence. To win the support of nonaligned nations, the United States would have to live up to its own ideals. That the nation was not doing so was evident.

Americans had seen the Second World War as a struggle for democracy and against racism. African-Americans who had helped win the war were determined that their lives in postwar America would be better because of their sacrifices. Moreover, politicians were beginning to pay attention to black aspirations. In the 1940s more than a million African-Americans migrated from the South to the North and West. In some urban-industrial states, black voters began to hold the political "balance of power." Harry Truman and other politicians knew they would have to

African-Americans' Political "Balance of Power"

compete for the growing African-American vote in California, New York, Illinois, Michigan, Pennsylvania, and other large states. Many Republicans cultivated the black vote. Dewey, who as governor of New York had pushed successfully for a fair employment practices commission, was particularly popular with African-Americans.

Clearly, then, President Truman had compelling political reasons for supporting African-American civil rights. But he also felt a moral obligation to do something, for he genuinely believed it was only fair that every American, regardless of race, should enjoy the full rights of citizenship. Truman also was disturbed by the resurgence of racial terrorism. To suppress black aspirations for civil rights unleashed by the war, a revived Ku Klux Klan was again burning crosses and murdering blacks who had had the audacity to vote. But what really horrified Truman was the report that police in Aiken, South Carolina, had gouged out the eyes of a black sergeant just three hours after he had been discharged from the army. Several weeks later, in December 1946, Truman signed an executive order establishing the President's Committee on Civil Rights.

The committee's report, *To Secure These Rights* (1947), would become the agenda for the civil rights movement for the next twenty years. Among its recommendations were the enactment of federal antilynching and antisegregation legislation. *To Secure These Rights* also called for laws guaranteeing voting rights and equal employment opportunity and for the establishment of a permanent commission on civil rights. Although Congress failed to act and some evidence suggests that Truman's real goal was the African-American vote in 1948, his action was significant. For the first time since Reconstruction, a president had acknowledged the federal government's responsibility to protect blacks and strive for racial equality.

President Truman's Committee on Civil Rights

Truman took this responsibility seriously, and in 1948 he issued two executive orders declaring an end to racial discrimination in the federal government. One proclaimed a policy of "fair employment throughout the federal establishment" and created the Employment Board of the Civil Service Commission to hear charges of discrimination. The other ordered the racial desegregation of the armed forces and appointed the Committee on Equality of Treatment and Opportunity in the Armed Services to oversee this change. Despite strong, even fierce, opposition

Jackie Robinson cracked the color line in major league baseball when he joined the Brooklyn Dodgers for the 1947 season. Sliding safely into third base, Robinson displays the aggressive style that won him rookie-of-the-year honors. He was later elected to the Baseball Hall of Fame. Hy Peskin, *Life* magazine © Time Inc.

Smith v. *Allwright* (1944), the Supreme Court also outlawed the whites-only primaries held by the Democratic Party in some southern states, branding them a violation of the Fifteenth Amendment's guarantee of the right to vote. Two years later the Court struck down segregation in interstate bus transportation (*Morgan* v. *Virginia*). And in *Shelley* v. *Kraemer* (1948), the Court held that a racially restrictive covenant (private agreements among white homeowners not to sell to blacks) violated the equal protection clause of the Fourteenth Amendment.

A change in social attitudes accompanied these gains in black political and legal power. Books like Gunnar Myrdal's social science study *An American Dilemma* (1944) and Richard Wright's novels *Native Son* (1940) and *Black Boy* (1945) were increasing white awareness of the social injustice that plagued African-Americans. A new black middle class was emerging, composed of college-educated activists, war veterans, and union workers. Blacks and whites also worked together in CIO unions and service organizations such as the National Council of Churches. In 1947 a black baseball player, Jackie Robinson, broke the major-league color barrier and electrified Brooklyn Dodgers fans with his spectacular hitting and base running.

Segregation was still standard practice in the 1950s, and blacks continued to suffer disfranchisement and severe job discrimination. But in May 1954 the NAACP won a historic victory that stunned the white South and energized African-Americans to challenge segregation on several fronts. *Brown* v. *Board of Education of Topeka* incorporated cases from several states, all involving segregated schools. Written by Earl Warren, whom President Eisenhower had named chief justice in 1953, the Court's unanimous decision concluded that "in the field of public education the doctrine of 'separate but equal' has no place. Separate educational facilities are inherently unequal." Such facilities, Warren wrote, produced in black children "a feeling of inferiority" and deprived them of "the equal protection of the laws guaranteed by the Fourteenth Amendment." But the ruling did not demand immediate compliance. A year later the Court finally ordered school desegregation, but only "with all deliberate speed." This vague timetable encouraged the southern states to resist.

Brown v. Board of Education of Topeka

to desegregation within the military, segregated units were being phased out by the time the Korean War broke out.

African-Americans also benefited from a series of Supreme Court decisions. The trend toward judicial support of civil rights had begun in the late 1930s, when the NAACP established its Legal Defense Fund under Thurgood Marshall (who in 1967 would become the first African-American Supreme Court justice). Marshall and his colleagues set out to destroy the separate-but-equal doctrine established in *Plessy* v. *Ferguson* (1896) by insisting on its literal interpretation. In higher education, the NAACP calculated, the cost of true equality in racially separate schools would be prohibitive. "You can't build a cyclotron for one student," as the president of the University of Oklahoma acknowledged. As a result of NAACP lawsuits in the 1930s and 1940s, African-American students won admission to professional and graduate schools at a number of state universities. In

Supreme Court Decisions on Civil Rights

Some border states quietly implemented the order, and many southern moderates advocated a gradual rollback of segregation. But the forces of white resistance soon came to dominate, urging southern communities to defy the Court. The Klan experienced another resurgence, and business and professional people created White Citizens' Councils for the express purpose of resisting the order. Known familiarly as "uptown Ku Klux Klans," the councils brought their economic power to bear against black civil rights activists. One of the most effective resistance tactics was enactment of state laws that paid the private-school tuition of white children who had left public schools to avoid integration. In some cases, desegregated public schools were ordered closed.

White Resistance to Civil Rights

Unlike Truman, President Eisenhower wanted to avoid dealing with civil rights, preferring instead gradual and voluntary change in race relations. He came to regret his appointment of Earl Warren as "the biggest damn fool mistake I ever made." Although the president disapproved of racial segregation, he objected to "compulsory federal law" in the belief that race relations would improve "only if it starts locally." He also feared that the ugly public confrontations likely to follow rapid desegregation would jeopardize Republican inroads in the South. Thus Eisenhower did not state forthrightly that the federal government would enforce the Court's decision as the nation's law. In short, instead of leading, he spoke ambiguously and thereby tacitly encouraged massive resistance.

Events in Little Rock, Arkansas, forced the president to stop sidestepping the issue. In September 1957 Governor Orval E. Faubus intervened to halt a local plan for the gradual desegregation of Little Rock's Central High School. Faubus mobilized the Arkansas National Guard to block the entry of black students. Eisenhower made no effort to impede Faubus's actions. Later that month, bowing to a federal judge's order, Faubus withdrew the guardsmen. As hundreds of jeering whites threatened to storm the school, eight black children entered Central High. The next day, fearing violence, Eisenhower federalized the Arkansas National Guard and dispatched paratroopers to Little Rock to ensure the children's safety. Troops patrolled the school for the rest of the year; in response, Little Rock officials closed all public high schools in 1958 and 1959 rather than desegregate them.

Crisis in Little Rock, Arkansas

In 1957, paratroopers of the 101st Airborne Division stand at the ready as African-American students enter Central High School in Little Rock, Arkansas, thus desegregating public education in the state. Ed Clarke, *Life* magazine © 1957 Time Inc.

Elsewhere, African-Americans did not wait for Supreme Court or White House decisions to claim equal rights. In 1955 Rosa Parks, a department store seamstress and active member of the NAACP, was arrested for refusing to give up her seat to a white man on a public bus in Montgomery, Alabama. Local black women's organizations and civil rights groups decided to boycott the city's bus system, and they elected Martin Luther King, Jr., a minister, as their leader. King launched the boycott with a moving speech in which he declared: "If we are wrong, the Constitution is wrong. If we are wrong, God Almighty is wrong. If we are wrong, Jesus of Nazareth was merely a utopian dreamer. . . . If we are wrong, justice is a lie."

Montgomery Bus Boycott

Martin Luther King, Jr., was a twenty-six-year-old Baptist minister who recently had earned a

For leading the movement to gain equality for blacks riding city buses in Montgomery, Alabama, Martin Luther King, Jr. (1929–1968) and other African-Americans, including twenty-three other ministers, were indicted by an all-white jury for violating an old law banning boycotts. In late March 1956 King was convicted and fined $500. A crowd of well-wishers cheered a smiling King (here with his wife Coretta) outside the courthouse, where King proudly declared, "The protest goes on!" King's arrest and conviction made the bus boycott front-page news across America. Corbis-Bettmann.

Ph.D. at Boston University. Disciplined and analytical, he was committed to nonviolent, peaceful protest in the spirit of India's leader Mohandas K. Gandhi. Although he was jailed and a bomb blew out the front of his house, King persisted. "Absence of fear," according to civil rights leader Bayard Rustin, was what King gave to black Americans. In 1957, King became the first president of the Southern Christian Leadership Conference, organized to coordinate civil rights activities.

Martin Luther King, Jr.

During the year-long Montgomery bus boycott, blacks young and old walked or carpooled. With the bus company near bankruptcy and downtown merchants hurt by declining sales, city officials adopted harassment tactics to frighten blacks into abandoning the boycott. King urged perseverance, and, bolstered by a Supreme Court decision that declared Alabama's Jim Crow laws unconstitutional, Montgomery blacks triumphed in 1956. They and others

across the nation were further heartened when Congress passed the Civil Rights Act of 1957, which created the United States Commission on Civil Rights to investigate systematic discrimination, such as voting discrimination. But this measure, like a voting-rights act passed three years later, proved ineffective. Critics charged that the Eisenhower administration was interested more in quelling the civil rights question than in addressing it.

African-Americans responded by adopting more aggressive tactics. In February 1960, four black students from North Carolina Agricultural and Technical College in Greensboro ordered coffee at a department-store lunch counter. Told they would not be served, the students refused to budge. "I felt as though I had gained my manhood," recalled one of the young men. Thus began the sit-in movement, which quickly spread northward. Inspired by the sit-ins, southern black college and high-school students met on Easter weekend in

Sit-Ins

1960 and organized the Student Nonviolent Coordinating Committee (SNCC). In the face of angry white mobs, SNCC members challenged the status quo, all the while singing the anthem of the civil rights movement, "We Shall Overcome," which includes the words "We are not afraid."

King personally joined the sit-in movement, and in October 1960 he was arrested in a sit-in to desegregate an Atlanta snack bar. Sent to a cold, cock-

**Civil Rights
and the
1960 Election**

roach-infested state penitentiary where he faced four months at hard labor, he became ill. As an apathetic Eisenhower White House looked on, Senator John F. Kennedy, the Democratic presidential candidate, called King's wife, Coretta Scott King, to express support; and his brother, Robert F. Kennedy, persuaded the sentencing judge to release King on bond. In November, grateful African-Americans cast their ballots for Kennedy in the expectation that, as president, he would provide federal protection of their civil rights movement. Those committed to racial equality looked forward to great gains under Kennedy in the 1960s.

The Postwar Booms: Business and Babies

When the postwar era began in 1945, many Americans wondered whether it would resemble the most recent postwar epoch, the Roaring Twenties. Most Americans, however, expected a replay of the 1930s—not the 1920s. After all, the war had created jobs and prosperity; surely the end of war would bring a slump. Neither prediction was correct: in 1945 the United States entered one of its longest, steadiest periods of growth and prosperity, the keys to which were increasing output and increasing demand. Despite occasional recessions the gross national product more than doubled from $212 billion in 1945 to $520 billion in 1961 (see figure).

When the economy produced more, Americans generally brought home bigger paychecks and had more money to spend. Between the end of the war and 1950, per capita real income

**Increased
Purchasing
Power**

(based on actual purchasing power) rose 6 percent—and that was only the beginning. In the 1950s it jumped another 15 percent; in the 1960s the increase was even greater—32 percent (see figure). The re-

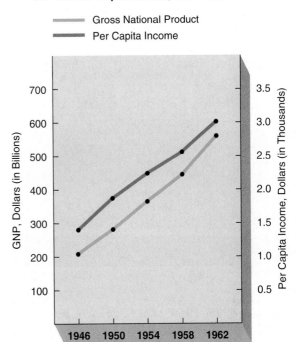

GNP and Per Capita Income, 1946–1962

Gross National Product and Per Capita Income, 1946–1962 Both gross national product and per capita income soared during the economic boom from 1946 to 1970. Source: Adapted from U.S. Bureau of the Census, *Historical Statistics of the United States, Colonial Times to 1970*, Bicentennial Edition (Washington, D.C., U.S. Government Printing Office), p. 224.

sult was a noticeable increase in the standard of living. To the vast majority of Americans, such prosperity was a vindication of the American system of free enterprise.

The baby boom was both a cause and an effect of prosperity. It was natural for the birthrate to soar immediately after a war; what was unusual was that

Baby Boom

the birth rate continued to do so throughout the 1950s (see figure, page 830). During the 1950s, the number of births exceeded 4 million per year, reversing the downward trend in birth rates that had prevailed for 150 years. Births began to decline after 1961 but continued to exceed 4 million per year through 1964. The baby-boom generation was the largest by far in the nation's history. And as this vast age group grew older, it had successive impacts on housing, nursery schools,

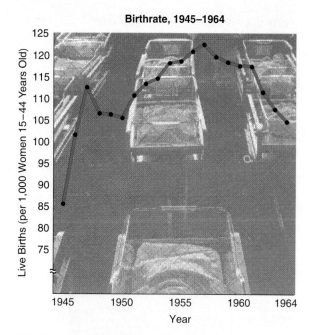

Birthrate, 1945–1964

Birthrate, 1945–1964 *The birthrate began to rise in 1942 and 1943, but it skyrocketed during the postwar years beginning in 1946. Reaching its peak in 1957, the birthrate thereafter subsided throughout the 1960s.* Source: Adapted from U.S. Bureau of the Census, *Historical Statistics of the United States, Colonial Times to 1970*, Bicentennial Edition (Washington, D.C., U.S. Government Printing Office, p. 49).

grade schools, and high schools, fads and popular music, colleges and universities, and the job market.

The baby boom meant business for builders, manufacturers, and school systems. "Take the 3,548,000 babies born in 1950," wrote Sylvia F. Porter in her syndicated newspaper column. "Bundle them into a batch, bounce them all over the bountiful land that is America. What do you get?" Porter's answer: "Boom. The biggest, boomiest boom ever known in history. Just imagine how much these extra people, these new markets, will absorb—in food, clothing, in gadgets, in housing, in services. Our factories must expand just to keep pace."

Of the three cornerstones of the postwar economic boom—construction, automobiles, and defense—two were directly related to the upsurge in

Housing and Auto Sales

births. Demand for housing and schools for all these children generated a building boom, furthered by construction of shopping centers, office buildings, and airports. Much of this construction took place in the suburbs. The postwar suburbanization of America in turn would have been impossible without automobile manufacturing, for in the sprawling new communities a car was a necessity. The number of registered automobiles climbed from 26 million in 1945 to 63 million in 1961.

The third cornerstone of the postwar economic boom was military spending. When the Defense Department was established in 1947, the nation was spending just over $10 billion a year on defense. In 1961, the total was $98 billion. Many defense contracts went to industries and universities to develop weapons, and the government supported space research; funds spent on space research alone zoomed from $76 million in 1957 to almost $6 billion in 1966. Defense spending also helped stimulate rapid advances in the electronics industry. The ENIAC computer, completed at the University of Pennsylvania in 1946, weighed fifty tons and required 18,000 vacuum tubes. The introduction of the transistor in the 1950s accelerated the computer revolution; the silicon microchip in the 1960s inaugurated even more stunning advances in electronics. The microchip facilitated the shift from heavy manufacturing to high-technology industries in fiber optics, lasers, video equipment, robotics, and genetic engineering. Sales of office and business equipment reflected the growth in technology-based production. But in the early 1960s, this was just the beginning. In succeeding decades, the numbers of new computer users in America would continue to skyrocket (see Chapter 33).

The evolution of electronics meant a large-scale tradeoff for the American people. As industries automated, computerized processes replaced slower mechanical ones, generating a rapid rise in productivity. But in doing so, they brought about technological unemployment. Electronic technology also promoted concentration of ownership in industry. Sophisticated technology was expensive. Typically, only large corporations could afford it; small corporations were shut out of the market. Indeed, large corporations with capital and experience in high-tech fields expanded into related industries. General Electric, which during the Second World War had manufactured electrical products, began producing computers, jet engines, and nuclear-powered generators.

Another kind of corporate expansion also marked the early 1950s. The third great wave of mergers swept across American business. The first two such

Military Spending

Conglomerate Mergers

movements, in the 1890s and 1920s, had tended toward vertical and horizontal integration respectively. The postwar era was distinguished by conglomerate mergers. A *conglomerate* brings together companies in unrelated industries as a hedge against instability in a particular market. International Telephone and Telegraph (IT&T), for instance, bought up companies in several fields, including suburban development, insurance, and hotels. In keeping with the thrust of America's postwar boom, the country's ten largest corporations were in automobiles (GM, Ford, Chrysler), oil (Exxon, Mobil, Texaco), and electronics and communications (GE, IBM, IT&T, AT&T).

The labor movement also experienced a postwar merger. In 1955 the American Federation of Labor and the Congress of Industrial Organizations finally put aside their differences and formed the AFL-CIO. Union membership grew slowly during the postwar years, increasing from just around 14.8 million in 1945 to 17.3 million in 1961. Some observers charged that union leaders had become smug and lost the zeal that had won over so many workers in the 1930s and 1940s; revelations of corrupt union practices also tainted the labor movement. But the main reason for the slow growth of union membership was a shift in employment patterns. Most new jobs were being created not in the heavy industries that hired blue-collar workers but in the union-resistant white-collar service trades.

Postwar Labor Movement

The postwar economic boom was good for unionized blue-collar workers, many of whom won real increases in wages sufficient to enjoy a middle-class lifestyle that previously had been the exclusive province of white-collar workers and professionals. Union workers could qualify for mortgages for suburban homes, especially if their spouses also worked. Many enjoyed job security, paid vacations, and retirement plans. They also could aspire to college educations for their children. And they were more protected against inflation: in 1948 General Motors and the United Auto Workers agreed on automatic cost-of-living adjustments (COLAs) in workers' wages, a practice that spread to other industries.

The trend toward economic consolidation also changed agriculture. New machines, such as mechanical cotton-, tobacco-, and grape-pickers and crop-dusting planes revolutionized farming methods, and the increased use of fertilizers and pesticides raised the total value of farm output from $24.6 billion in 1945 to $38.4 billion in 1961. At the same time, farm labor productivity tripled. The resulting improvement in profitability drew large investors into agriculture, and average acreage per farm increased from 195 in 1945 to 306 in 1961. By the 1960s it took money—sometimes big money—to become a farmer. In many regions only banks, insurance companies, and large businesses could afford the necessary land, machinery, and fertilizer.

Decline of the Family Farm

The movement toward consolidation threatened the survival of the family farm. From 1945 to 1961 the nation's farm population declined from 24.4 million to 14.8 million. When the harvesting of cotton in the South was mechanized in the 1940s and 1950s, more than 4 million people were displaced. Southern tobacco growers dismissed their tenant farmers, bought tractors to plow the land, and hired migratory workers to harvest the crop. Many of these displaced farmers traded southern rural poverty for northern urban poverty.

Environmental Costs of Economic Growth

Rapid economic growth also exacted environmental costs, to which most Americans were oblivious. Air, water, soil, and wildlife suffered degradation. Steel mills, coal-powered generators, and internal-combustion car engines burning lead-based gasoline polluted the air and imperiled people's health. America's water supplies suffered as well. Human and industrial waste befouled many rivers and lakes, making them unfit for consumption or recreation. Vast quantities of water were diverted from lakes and rivers to meet the needs of America's burgeoning Sunbelt cities, including the swimming pools that dotted Arizona and southern California. The extraction of natural resources—strip mining of coal, for example—also scarred the landscape, and toxic waste from chemical plants seeped deep into the soil. America was becoming a dumping ground as never before.

DDT

Defense contractors and farmers were among the country's worst polluters. Refuse from nuclear weapons facilities at Hanford, Washington, and at Colorado's Rocky Flats arsenal polluted soil and water resources for years. Agriculture began employing massive amounts of pesticides and other chemicals. A chemical called DDT,

During the Second World War, DDT was used to protect American troops against bug-borne diseases and was hailed as a miracle insecticide. The use of DDT spread in postwar America, but little attention was paid to its often fatal consequences for birds, mammals, and fish. In 1945, even as children ran alongside, this truck sprayed DDT as part of a mosquito-control program at New York's Jones Beach State Park.   Corbis-Bettmann.

for example, which had been used on Pacific islands during the war to kill mosquitoes and lice, was released for public use in 1945. During the next fifteen years, farmers eliminated chronic pests with DDT. In 1962, however, *Silent Spring* by Rachel Carson, a wildlife biologist, specifically indicted DDT for the deaths of mammals, birds, and fish. DDT accumulates in the fatty tissues of eagles, trout, and other animals, causing cancer. Because of Carson's book, many Americans finally realized that there were costs to human conquest of the environment. The federal government banned the sale of DDT in 1972.

Much of America's continued economic growth was based on encouraging habits that would make the country a throwaway society. The auto industry intentionally made cars less durable ("planned obsolescence") and through advertising urged consumers to buy a new car every year or two. Increasing numbers of disposable products such as plastic cups and paper diapers were marketed as conveniences. Moreover, as Amer-

America's Consumption of the World's Resources

icans consumed goods and services, they were using up the world's resources. By the 1960s the United States, with only 5 percent of the world's population, produced and consumed over one-third of the world's goods and services. Consumption of crude petroleum jumped 70 percent from 1945 to 1961, but domestic production increased only 53 percent, and the gap was widening; the extra oil had to be imported. The use of electricity, whether generated by coal, water, or nuclear energy, jumped too, from 275 billion kilowatt-hours in 1945 to 884 billion in 1961.

 ## The Affluent Society, the Sunbelt, and the Suburbs

The Harvard economist John Kenneth Galbraith gave a name to the United States during the postwar economic boom: the "affluent society." As United States productivity increased in the postwar years, so did Americans' appetite for goods and services. During the depression and the Second World War, many Americans had dreamed of buying a home or a car.

In the affluent postwar years they finally could satisfy those deferred desires. Some families bought two cars and equipped their new homes with the latest appliances and amusements. Easy credit was the economic basis of the consumer culture; when people lacked cash to buy what they wanted, they borrowed money. Consumer credit to support the nation's shopping spree grew from $5.7 billion in 1945 to $58 billion in 1961.

Growth of the Sunbelt

Millions of Americans began their search for affluence by migrating to the Sunbelt—roughly, the southern third of the United States, running from southern California across the Southwest and South all the way to the Atlantic coast. Among the Sunbelt's booming cities were Houston, Phoenix, Los Angeles, San Diego, Dallas, and Miami. The population of Houston, which became a center not only of the aerospace industry but also of oil and petrochemical production, jumped from 385,000 in 1940 to 1,243,000 in 1960. California absorbed no less than one-fifth of the nation's entire population increase in the 1950s—enough by 1963 to make it the most populous state in the Union (see map).

The mass migration to the Sunbelt had started during the war, when GIs and their families were ordered to new duty stations and war workers moved to defense plants in the West and South. The economic bases of the Sunbelt's spectacular growth were agribusiness, the aerospace industry, the oil industry, real-estate development, recreation, and defense spending. Government policies—generous tax breaks for oil companies, siting of military bases, and awarding of defense and aerospace contracts—were crucial to the Sunbelt's development. Industry was also drawn to the southern rim by right-to-work laws, which outlawed closed shops, and by low taxes and low heating bills.

Another mass movement in postwar America was from the cities to the suburbs. Almost as many Americans resided in the suburbs as in the cities by

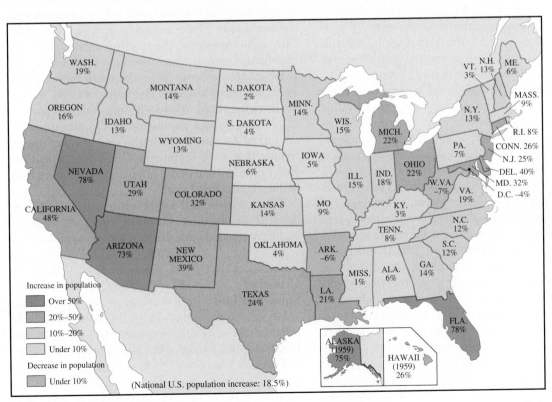

Rise of the Sunbelt, 1950–1960   *The years after the Second World War saw a continuation of the migration of Americans to the Sunbelt states of the Southwest and the West Coast.*

Geographic Distribution of the United States Population, 1930–1970 (in Percentages)

Year	Central Cities	Suburbs	Rural Areas and Small Towns
1930	31.8	18.0	50.2
1940	31.6	19.5	48.9
1950	32.3	23.8	43.9
1960	32.6	30.7	36.7
1970	31.4	37.6	31.0

Source: Adapted from U.S. Bureau of the Census, *Decennial Censuses, 1930–1970* (Washington, D.C., U.S. Government Printing Office).

Growth of the Suburbs

1960 (see table). A combination of motives drew people to the suburbs. Some wanted to leave behind the noise and smells of the city. Some white families moved out of urban neighborhoods because African-American families were moving in. People living in row houses and apartments wanted to move into houses that had yards, family rooms, extra closets, and utility rooms. Many also were looking for a place where they could have a measure of political influence, particularly on the education their children received. Perhaps most important, for this generation of adults—who had suffered economic deprivation during the depression and separation from loved ones during the war—the home became a refuge, and family togetherness fulfilled a psychological need.

Government funding helped new families to settle in the suburbs. Low-interest GI mortgages and Federal Housing Administration (FHA) mortgage insurance made the difference for people who otherwise would have been unable to afford a home. This easy credit, combined with postwar prosperity, produced a construction boom. From 1945 to 1946, housing starts climbed from 326,000 to more than 1 million; they approached 2 million in 1950 and remained above 1.3 million in 1961. Never before had new starts exceeded 1 million.

Housing Boom

To produce so much new housing so fast, contractors had to operate on a massive scale. Arthur Levitt and Sons developed a system, adopted by other companies, of using interchangeable materials and designs to build nearly identical houses on uniform, treeless lots. In 1947 the construction of Levittown, New York, began; Levittowns also arose in New Jersey and Pennsylvania. To supply the new communities, shopping malls soon dotted the countryside.

As suburbia spread, pastures became neighborhoods with astounding rapidity. Highway construction was a central element in the transformation of rural land into suburbia. In 1947 Congress authorized construction of a 37,000-mile chain of highways, and in 1956 President Eisenhower signed the Highway Act (see page 819). Federal expenditures on highways swelled from $79 million in 1946 to $2.6 billion in 1961. State and local spending on highways also mushroomed. Highways both hastened suburbanization and homogenized the landscape. The high-speed trucking that highways made possible also accelerated the integration of the South into the national economy.

Highway Construction

Highway construction in combination with the growth of suburbia produced a new phenomenon, the *megalopolis*, a term coined by urban experts in the early 1960s to refer to the almost uninterrupted metropolitan complex stretching along the northeastern seaboard from Boston 600 miles south through New York, Philadelphia, and Baltimore all the way to Washington, D.C. "Boswash" encompassed parts of eleven states and a population of 49 million people, all linked by interstate highways. Another megalopolis that took shape was "Milipitts," a band of heavy industry and dense population stretching from Milwaukee to Pittsburgh.

Sociologists and other critics denounced the suburbs for breeding conformity and status seeking, and they scolded suburbanites for trying to keep up with the Joneses by buying new cars and appliances. William H. Whyte's *The Organization Man* (1956), a study of Park Forest, Illinois, pronounced these suburbanites mindless conservatives and extreme conformists. And C. Wright Mills castigated white-collar suburbanites who "sell not only their time and energy but their personalities as well." Nonetheless, most residents of suburbia preferred their lifestyle to any other of which they were aware, and the vast majority of college students in the 1950s looked forward to settling in the suburbs.

Critics of Suburban Life

In the 1940s and 1950s prospective homeowners flocked to the suburbs to tour the long rows of new houses being constructed. These clients met in Levittown, New York, with Herbert Richheimer, a building contractor.   Joe Scherschel, *Life magazine* © 1957 Time Warner Inc.

Women's Conflicting Roles and Dilemmas

In 1946, the anthropologist Margaret Mead reflected on society's contradictory expectations of American women: "Choose any set of criteria you like, and the answer is the same: women—and men—are confused, uncertain, and discontented with the present definition of women's place in America." On the one hand, the home was premised on a full-time housewife who, with little regard for her own needs, provided her husband and children with a cozy haven from the outside world. On the other hand, women continued to enter the labor force for a variety of reasons. Many worked because they were their families' sole source of income; they had to work. Others took jobs to supplement the family income. Indeed, the female labor force rose from 19.3 million in 1945 to 23.8 million in 1961 and to 31.6 million in 1970. Despite the cult of motherhood, most new entrants to the job market were married—a trend that had begun during the Second World War—and most were mothers (see figure, page 836).

Women's responsibilities also increased at home after the war. Some of the change was due to the publication in 1946 of Dr. Benjamin Spock's *Baby and Child Care*. Unlike earlier manuals, *Baby and Child Care* urged mothers always to think of their children first (Spock assigned fathers little formal role in child rearing). Dr. Spock based his advice on new findings about the importance of responding to a baby's needs; and the millions of women who embraced his teachings tried to be mother, teacher, psychologist, and playmate to their children. If they "failed" in any of these roles, guilt was the inevitable outcome.

Dr. Spock on Child Rearing

Social critic Philip Wylie denounced such selfless behavior as "Momism." In the guise of sacrificing for her children, Wylie wrote in *Generation of Vipers* (1942, revised 1955), Mom was pursuing "love of herself." She smothered her children with affection to make them emotionally dependent on her and reluctant to leave home. Women, however, were caught in a double bind, for

"Momism"

Marital Distribution of the Female Labor Force, 1944–1970

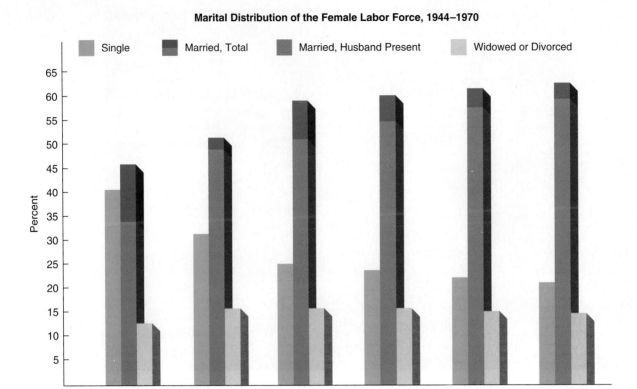

Marital Distribution of the Female Labor Force, 1944–1970 *In 1944, 41 percent of women in the labor force were single; in 1970, only 22 percent were single. During the same years, the percentage of the female labor force that had a husband in the home jumped from 34 to 59. The percentage who were widowed or divorced remained about the same from 1944 to 1970.* Source: Adapted from U.S. Bureau of the Census, *Historical Statistics of the United States, Colonial Times to 1970*, Bicentennial Edition (Washington, D.C., U.S. Government Printing Office, 1975), p. 133.

if they pursued a life outside the home, they were accused of being "imitation men" or "neurotic" feminists. Echoing psychoanalyst Sigmund Freud, critics of working mothers contended that a woman could be happy and fulfilled only through domesticity.

In an era in which wives tended to subordinate their career goals to those of their husbands, the percentage of women earning college degrees declined. College enrollments surged from 1.5 million in 1940, to 2.3 million in 1950, and 3.6 million in 1960, but women in postwar America actually lost ground in higher education. The percentage of women with college degrees dropped from 41 percent in 1940 to 24 percent in 1950. At the postgraduate level, only 10 percent of doctorates earned in the United States went to women, compared with 13 percent in 1940 and 18 percent in 1930. The 1960s would reverse this trend, but it would take another ten years to return to earlier levels.

In postwar America, there was a wide gap between sexual behavior and public discourse on the subject. When Dr. Alfred Kinsey, director of the Institute for Sex Research at Indiana University, published his pioneering study *Sexual Behavior in the Human Male* (1948), the American public was shocked. But five years later Kinsey caused an uproar with *Sexual Behavior in the Human Female*, which revealed that 62 percent of women masturbated and 50 percent had had intercourse before marriage. Some angry Americans condemned the report as a slanderous attack on motherhood and the family, and a congressman charged Kinsey with "hurling the insult of the century against our mothers, wives, daughters and sisters."

Family, church, state, and media alike warned Americans that sex was wrong outside marriage and

Fear of Women's Sexuality

that premarital, extramarital, and homosexual be- havior would bring "familial chaos and weaken the country's moral fiber." Women often were blamed for the impending disaster; despite any evidence of significant increases in women's sexual activity from the 1920s to the 1960s, female lust was perceived to pose the greatest sexual threat to the future of the family. In fact, increased interest in sex was coming from a different direction: in 1953, men began read- ing about the sexual joys of bachelorhood in a new magazine, *Playboy*. Nevertheless, from Momism to promiscuity, American women were the victims of male-inspired stereotypes.

There was confusion for girls, too, in postwar America. Motherhood was venerated in American society, but many daughters sensed that their own mothers were deeply disappointed with their lives. In fact, a 1962 Gallup poll revealed that only 10 per- cent of mothers wanted their daughters to emulate their lives. Some urged their daughters to avoid the trap of early marriage and domesticity and to de- velop personally fulfilling and economically inde- pendent lives. It is clear that the seeds of feminist protest in the later 1960s and 1970s were planted during the postwar years. As the historian Ruth Rosen has observed, the "invisible ghost haunting" young women "wore an apron and lived vicariously through the lives of her husband and children. Against her, the women's liberation movement was forged."

Education, Religion, and the Consumer Culture

Education at all levels, from preschool to graduate school, was a pressing concern for families in post- war America. Immediately after the Second World War, for example, many former GIs enrolled in col- lege and set up housekeeping with their wives and babies in abandoned military barracks on college cam- puses. The legislation that made this possible was the Servicemen's Readjustment Act of 1944, popularly known as the GI Bill of Rights, which provided living allowances and tuition payments to college- bound veterans. Over 1 million veterans enrolled in 1946—accounting for one out of every two students. Despite pessimistic predictions, the veterans, who saw higher education as the key to upward mobility, succeeded as students. The downside of this success story was that colleges made places for male veterans by turning away qualified women.

As the baby boom became a grade-school boom in the 1950s, American families became preoccupied with the education of their children. Convinced that

Education of the Baby-Boom Generation

success in school was a prerequi- site for success in adult life, par- ents joined the parent-teacher association so they would have a voice in the educational process. They worried that schools were overcrowded and that teachers were using obsolete methods. Then in 1957 education became a matter of national security. In that year the Soviet Union launched *Sputnik*, the first earth-orbiting satellite. The Russian triumph threw into question American military and technological superiority, based ulti- mately on the nation's school system. Congress re- sponded in 1958 with the National Defense Edu- cation Act (NDEA), which funded enrichment of elementary and high-school programs in mathemat- ics, foreign languages, and the sciences and offered fellowships and loans to college students.

As education became intertwined with national security, so religion became a matter of patriotism. As President Eisenhower put it, "Recognition of the

Growth of Religion

Supreme Being is the first, the most basic expression of Ameri- canism." And in 1954, Eisen- hower signed a law inserting the words "under God" after "one nation" in the Pledge of Allegiance to the flag. In America's Cold War with an atheistic enemy, relig- ious leaders emphasized traditional values like family togetherness. The Bible topped the bestseller list, and a familiar refrain of the time was "The family that prays together stays together." Most impressive was the growth in membership in religious congre- gations; in the fifteen years after the Second World War, the total jumped 62 percent, from 71.7 million in 1945 to 116 million in 1961.

The postwar religious revival was also spurred by the introduction of a revolutionary influence in American life: television. The evangelist Billy Gra-

TV Enters the American Home

ham, who preached in stadiums throughout the country, could reach mass audiences on televi- sion. The growth of television was phenomenal. In 1946, only 8,000 households had TVs; that number skyrocketed to 3.9 million in 1950 and to more than 47 million in 1961. Most important, the introduction of television transformed family life in America. "And so the monumental change began in

These workers at an RCA plant in Bloomington, Indiana, are making final adjustments to new color television sets in 1954. A year earlier, NBC had broadcast the first commercial television program in color. Color television, however, was somewhat slow to catch on. Seven years passed before RCA made a profit from manufacturing color sets.   Thomson Consumer Electronics, Indianapolis.

our lives and those of millions of other Americans," recalled a man whose parents bought their first television set in 1950. "More than a year passed before we again visited a movie theater. . . . Social evenings with friends became fewer and fewer still because we discovered we did not share the same television program interests." By 1950 television had loosened the grip of both radio and the movies on the American public.

Television was a crucial force in the evolution of the consumer culture. "More appliances make mom's work easier," read a typical 1950s advertisement. TV told people what to buy; and as families strove to acquire the latest luxuries and conveniences, shopping became a form of recreation. TV's number-one product was entertainment, and situation comedies and action series were among the most popular shows. *Father Knows Best* and *Leave It to Beaver* celebrated family life. But as average TV-viewing time reached five hours a day in 1956 and continued to rise, critics worried that TV's distorted presentation of the world would significantly define people's sense of reality.

An obvious casualty of the stay-at-home suburban culture was the motion picture. From 1946 to 1948 Americans had attended movies at the rate of

Rise of the Youth Subculture

nearly 90 million a week. By 1950 that figure had dropped to 60 million a week; by 1960, to 40 million. The postwar years saw the steady closing of movie theaters—with the notable exception of the drive-in, which appealed to car-oriented suburban families and teenagers. In fact, teenagers were the one exception to the downturn in moviegoing. By the late 1950s the first wave of the postwar baby boom had reached adolescence, and teens and young adults were flocking to the theaters. No less than 72 percent of moviegoers during the 1950s were under age thirty. Hollywood catered to this new audience with films portraying young people as sensitive and insightful, adults as boorish and hostile. *Rebel Without a Cause* (1955), starring James Dean, was one such movie. The cult of youth had been born.

Soon the music industry began catering to teens with inexpensive 45-rpm records. Bored with the era's syrupy music, young Americans were electrified by the driving energy and hard beat of Bill Haley and the Comets, Chuck Berry, Little Richard, and Buddy Holly. Although few white musicians acknowledged the debt, the roots of rock 'n' roll lay in African-American rhythm and blues. The release of Elvis Presley's first single, "Heartbreak Hotel," in 1956, and his appearance on Ed Sullivan's Sunday-night TV show, touched off a frenzy of adoration and hero worship. The fact that parents were scandalized by Presley's suggestive gyrations did not lessen his appeal to their children.

Consumerism was strikingly evident in Americans' postwar play and in the era's fads. Slinky, selling for a dollar, began loping down people's stairs in 1947; Silly Putty was introduced in 1950. The era also had 3-D movies and Hula-Hoops. Although most crazes were short-lived, they created multi-million-dollar industries and promoted dozens of movies and TV shows. Another postwar fad was the family vacation. With more money and leisure time and a much-improved highway system, middle-class families took vacations that formerly had been restricted to the rich. The destination of many family vacations was Disneyland, which opened in Anaheim, California, in 1955.

The consumer society was unreceptive to social criticism. The filmgoing public preferred noncontroversial doses of Doris Day and Rock Hudson and Dean Martin and Jerry Lewis.

Beat Generation

Even serious artists tended to ignore the country's social problems. But there were exceptions. Ralph Ellison's *Invisible Man* (1952) gave white Americans a glimpse of the psychic costs to black Americans of exclusion from the American Dream. And one group of writers noisily repudiated the materialistic and self-congratulatory world of the middle class and the suburbs. Beat (for "beatific") writers rejected both social niceties and literary conventions and in the face of middle-class conformity flaunted their freewheeling sexuality and consumption of drugs. The Beats produced some memorable prose and poetry, including Allen Ginsberg's angry incantational poem *Howl* (1956) and Jack Kerouac's novel *On the Road* (1957). Although the Beats were largely ignored during the 1950s, millions of young Americans discovered their writings and imitated their lifestyle in the 1960s.

 ## The Other America

In an age of abundance, most Americans dismissed poverty, if they noticed it at all, as the fault of poor people themselves. But in 1961 about 42.5 million

In this cartoon in which Alfred E. Neuman ("What, me worry?") joins the presidential pantheon on Mount Rushmore, Mad *magazine parodied a venerable icon. Started in 1952,* Mad *was second in popularity only to* Life *magazine among teenagers by the early 1960s.* Mad *mocked suburbia, President Eisenhower, and the smugness of the American middle class.* Mad *magazine Mount Rushmore cover used with permission © 1956, 1984 by E. C. Publications, Inc.*

Americans (nearly one of every four) were poor—too large a group to ignore much longer. Age, race, gender, education, and marital status were all factors in their poverty. One-fourth of the poor were over age sixty-five. One-fifth were people of color, including almost half of the nation's African-American population and more than half of all Native Americans. Two-thirds lived in households headed by a person with an eighth-grade education or less, one-fourth in households headed by a single woman. More than one-third were under age eighteen. Few of these people had much reason for hope.

While millions of Americans (most of them white) were settling in the suburbs, the poor were congregating in the inner cities. Almost 4.5 million

Poverty in the Inner Cities

African-Americans migrated to the cities from the South between the war years and the end of the 1960s. Joining African-Americans in the exodus to the cities were poor whites from the southern Appalachians, many

The Moreira family gathered for an Easter celebration in Los Angeles in 1960. By the end of the 1950s many Mexican-American families had established businesses, bought homes, and entered the middle class. The photograph shows three generations of the Moreira family.   Security Pacific National Bank Collection, Los Angeles Public Library.

of whom moved to Cincinnati, Baltimore, and Detroit. Meanwhile, Latin Americans were arriving in growing numbers from Mexico, the Dominican Republic, Colombia, Ecuador, and Cuba. And New York City's Puerto Rican population exploded from 70,000 to over 600,000 in just twenty years.

Second only to African-Americans in numbers of urban newcomers were Mexican-Americans. Millions came as farm workers during and after the Second

Mexican-Americans

World War, and increasing numbers remained to make their lives in the United States. Despite the initiation in 1953 of Operation Wetback, a federal program to find and deport illegal aliens, Mexicans continued to enter the country in large numbers, many of them illegally. Most settled in cities. According to the 1960 census, over 500,000 Mexican-Americans had migrated to the *barrios* of the Los Angeles–Long Beach area since 1940. Estimates of uncounted illegal aliens suggest that the actual total was far higher. The same was true in the *barrios* in southwestern and northern cities.

Native Americans, whose average annual income was barely half of the poverty level, were the coun-

try's poorest people. Many Native Americans moved to the cities in the 1950s and 1960s, particularly after Congress in 1953 adopted the termination policy (see page 819). Accustomed to semicommunal rural life on the reservation, many had difficulty adjusting to the urban environment. Like other groups who migrated to the cities in hope of finding a place to prosper, they found only a dumping ground for the poor.

Native Americans

Not all of the poor, however, lived in cities. In 1960, 30 percent still lived in small towns, 15 percent on farms. Tenant farmers and sharecroppers, both black and white, continued to suffer severe economic hardship. Migratory farm workers lived in abject poverty. In postwar America, elderly people tended to be poor regardless of where they lived.

Americans living in poverty were poor in part because federal legislation had shortchanged them. Government-sponsored housing and highways were largely intended to improve life for middle-class whites; disadvantaged Americans did not share much in their benefits. For example, the National Housing Act of 1949, passed to make available "a decent home and a suitable living environment for every American family," failed in several respects. A primary feature of the act was "urban redevelopment" (slum clearance); but the slums were replaced not with low-income housing but with luxury high-rise buildings, parking lots, and highways. Many poor people lost what little housing they had.

A disproportionate share of the poor were women. Occupational segregation was pervasive. Men tended to receive the better-paying positions; many women were forced to take low-paying jobs as laundresses, short-order cooks, and janitors. Median annual earnings for full-time women workers stood at 60 percent of men's earnings in 1960. Moreover, many women's jobs were not covered by either the minimum wage or Social Security. And if divorce, desertion, or death did break up a family, the woman was usually left with responsibility for the children. Many divorced fathers did not keep up their regular child-support payments. Single mothers and their children, dependent on welfare or low wages, more often than not slipped into poverty.

Women in Poverty

With the publication of Michael Harrington's *The Other America* in 1962, people became aware of the contradiction of poverty in their midst. America's poor, wrote Harrington, were "the strangest poor in the history of mankind." For they "exist within the most powerful and rich society the world has ever known. Their misery has continued while the majority of the nation talked of itself as being 'affluent.'" Whether living in urban obscurity or rural isolation, the poor had "dropped out of sight and out of mind"—particularly the minds of comfortable suburbanites.

The Election of 1960 and the Dawning of a New Decade

The election of 1960 was one of the closest and most hard fought in the twentieth century. The forty-three-year-old Democratic candidate, Senator John F. Kennedy, was handsome and intelligent; born to wealth, he injected new vigor and glamour into presidential politics. His running mate in 1960 was Senator Lyndon B. Johnson of Texas, added to the ticket to keep white southerners loyal to the Democratic Party as the civil rights issue heated up. The Republican candidate was Richard M. Nixon, the forty-seven-year-old vice president from California. He

and his running mate, Ambassador Henry Cabot Lodge of Massachusetts, expected a rugged campaign.

Kennedy, exploiting the media to great advantage, ran a risky but ultimately brilliant race. Aware that his major liability with voters was his Roman Catholicism, he addressed the issue head-on: he went to the Bible Belt to tell a group of Houston ministers that he respected the separation of church and state and would take his orders from the American people, not the pope. Seeing opportunity in the African-American vote and calculating that Johnson could keep the white South loyal to the Democrats, Kennedy courted black voters. Foreign policy was another major issue. Nixon claimed that he alone knew how to deal with Communists, but Kennedy countered that Eisenhower and Nixon had let American prestige and power erode, and he promised victory instead of stalemate in the Cold War. Kennedy subscribed to the two fundamental tenets of the postwar consensus—economic growth and

How and Why Kennedy Beat Nixon

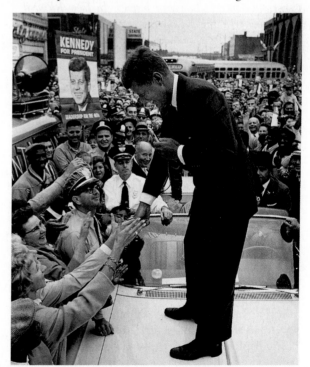

Standing on the hood of a car in Ohio, John F. Kennedy (1917–1963) campaigns for the presidency in 1960. Young, handsome, and articulate, Kennedy introduced new vitality into political campaigning. On television and in person, Kennedy was a popular politician, and when he became president, he became a media star as well. Edward Clark, *Life magazine* © 1959 Time Warner Inc.

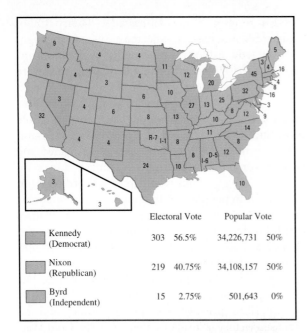

	Electoral Vote		Popular Vote	
Kennedy (Democrat)	303	56.5%	34,226,731	50%
Nixon (Republican)	219	40.75%	34,108,157	50%
Byrd (Independent)	15	2.75%	501,643	0%

Presidential Election, 1960 *In 1960 John F. Kennedy won the closest presidential election in twentieth-century American history. In fact, Richard M. Nixon won the popular votes of twenty-six states to Kennedy's twenty-four. In the electoral college, 15 southerners voted for neither Kennedy nor Nixon but cast protest votes for Harry F. Byrd, a conservative senator from Virginia.*

anticommunism—and asserted that he could expand the benefits of economic progress and win foreign disputes through more vigorous leadership.

As Kennedy gained momentum, Nixon was saddled with the handicaps of incumbency: he had to answer for the recession of 1960 and the Russian downing of a U-2 spy plane (see page 864). Nixon also looked unsavory on TV; in televised debates with Kennedy, he came across as heavy jowled and surly. Perhaps worse, Eisenhower gave him only a tepid endorsement. Asked to list Nixon's significant decisions as vice president, Eisenhower replied: "If you give me a week, I might think of one."

In an election characterized by the highest voter participation (63 percent) in a half-century, Kennedy defeated Nixon by the razor-slim margin of 118,000 votes. Kennedy's electoral college margin, 303 to 219, was much closer than the numbers suggest (see map). Slight shifts in the popular vote in Illinois and Texas—two states where electoral fraud helped produce narrow Democratic majorities—would have made Nixon president. Although Kennedy's Catholicism lost him some votes, religious bigotry

did not decide the election, and Kennedy became the first Roman Catholic president.

Conclusion

Politically and culturally, the 1960s were to prove vastly different from the postwar years that immediately preceded them. During the Cold War presidencies of Truman and Eisenhower, the country was engaged in a moral struggle with communism; and during such a crusade, people believed, one should support, not criticize, the government. Much as they might bicker about how to wage the Cold War or how to manage the economy, they were one when it came to anticommunism and faith in economic progress. Most white Americans believed that the United States was the greatest nation in the world and that its potential was boundless. For middle-class Americans who surrounded themselves with the symbols of economic success—automobiles, televisions, houses in suburbia—the American dream seemed a reality.

Only a few years later, however, comfortable middle-class Americans discovered that millions of poor people were living in their midst and that most of them had been deprived of the civil rights the rest of the nation took for granted. Ironically, it would be the privileged children of suburbia—the generation of the baby boom—who would join the movement to eradicate not only racism and poverty but the whole value system of the postwar American middle class.

Suggestions for Further Reading

An Age of Consensus

Paul A. Carter, *Another Part of the Fifties* (1983); John Patrick Diggins, *The Proud Decades: America in War and Peace, 1941–1960* (1988); David Halberstam, *The Fifties* (1993); Marty Jezer, *The Dark Ages: Life in the United States, 1945–1960* (1982); Douglas T. Miller and Marion Novak, *The Fifties* (1977); William L. O'Neill, *American High: The Years of Confidence, 1945–1960* (1986); James T. Patterson, *Grand Expectations: The United States, 1945–1974* (1996); Richard H. Pells, *The Liberal Mind in a Conservative Age* (1985); Stephen J. Whitfield, *The Culture of the Cold War*, rev. ed. (1996).

The Presidency of Harry S Truman

Robert J. Donovan, *Tumultuous Years: The Presidency of Harry S Truman, 1949–1953* (1982), and *Conflict and Crisis: The Presidency of Harry S Truman, 1945–1948* (1977); Robert H. Ferrell, *Harry S Truman* (1994); Alonzo L. Hamby, *Man of the People: The Life of Harry S Truman* (1995); Donald R. McCoy, *The Presidency of Harry S Truman* (1984); David McCullough, *Truman* (1992).

Eisenhower and the Politics of the 1950s

Charles C. Alexander, *Holding the Line* (1975); Stephen E. Ambrose, *Eisenhower: The President* (1984); Robert F. Burk, *Dwight D. Eisenhower* (1986); Donald L. Fixico, *Termination and Relocation: Federal Indian Policy, 1945–1960* (1986); Fred I. Greenstein, *The Hidden-Hand Presidency* (1982); Chester J. Pach, Jr., and Elmo Richardson, *The Presidency of Dwight D. Eisenhower*, rev. ed. (1991); Mark H. Rose, *Interstate: Express Highway Politics, 1941–1956* (1979).

McCarthyism

Richard M. Fried, *Nightmare in Red* (1990); Robert Griffith, *The Politics of Fear: Joseph R. McCarthy and the Senate*, rev. ed. (1987); Maurice Isserman, *If I Had a Hammer . . . : The Death of the Old Left and the Birth of the New Left* (1987); Harvey Klehr and Ronald Radosh, *The Amerasia Spy Case* (1996); Stanley I. Kutler, *The American Inquisition* (1982); David M. Oshinsky, *A Conspiracy So Immense: The World of Joe McCarthy* (1983); Richard Gid Powers, *Not Without Honor: The History of American Anticommunism* (1995); Thomas C. Reeves, *The Life and Times of Joe McCarthy* (1982); Ellen W. Schrecker, *No Ivory Tower: McCarthyism in the Universities* (1986).

The Civil Rights Movement

Taylor Branch, *Parting the Waters: America in the King Years, 1954–1963* (1988); Robert F. Burk, *The Eisenhower Administration and Black Civil Rights* (1984); William H. Chafe, *Civilities and Civil Rights: Greensboro, North Carolina, and the Black Struggle for Freedom* (1980); Richard M. Dalfiume, *Desegregation of the U.S. Armed Forces* (1969); David J. Garrow, *Bearing the Cross: Martin Luther King, Jr., and the Southern Christian Leadership Conference* (1986); Richard Kluger, *Simple Justice: The History of* Brown v. Board of Education *and Black America's Struggle for Equality* (1975); Stephen B. Oates, *Let the Trumpet Sound: The Life of Martin Luther King, Jr.* (1982); Mark V. Tushnet, *The NAACP's Legal Strategy Against Segregated Education* (1987); Jules Tygiel, *Baseball's Great Experiment: Jackie Robinson and His Legacy* (1983); Stephen J. Whitfield, *A Death in the Delta: The Story of Emmett Till* (1991).

The Baby Boom and Cold War Families

Landon Y. Jones, *Great Expectations: America and the Baby Boom Generation* (1980); Donald Katz, *Home Fires: An Intimate Portrait of One Middle-Class Family in Postwar America* (1992); Paul Leinberger and Bruce Tucker, *The New Individualists: The Generation After the Organization Man* (1991); Elaine Tyler May, *Homeward Bound: American Families in the Cold War Era* (1988); John Modell, *Into One's Own: From Youth to Adulthood in the United States, 1920–1975* (1989); Grace Palladino, *Teenagers* (1996).

Suburbia and the Spread of Education

Robert Fishman, *Bourgeois Utopias* (1987); Herbert J. Gans, *The Levittowners* (1967); Mark I. Gelfand, *A Nation of Cities* (1975); Dolores Hayden, *Redesigning the American Dream* (1984); Kenneth T. Jackson, *Crabgrass Frontier: The Suburbanization of the United States* (1985); Zane L. Miller, *Suburb* (1982); Diane Ravitch, *The Troubled Crusade: American Education, 1945–1980* (1983); Joel Spring, *The Sorting Machine: National Educational Policy Since 1945* (1976).

Women, Work, and Family Togetherness

Wini Breines, *Young, White, and Miserable: Growing Up Female in the Fifties* (1992); Ruth Schwartz Cowan, *More Work for Mother* (1983); Myra Dinnerstein, *Women Between Two Worlds* (1992); Barbara Ehrenreich, *The Hearts of Men: American Dreams and the Flight from Commitment* (1983); Cynthia Harrison, *On Account of Sex: The Politics of Women's Issues, 1945–1968* (1988); Eugenia Kaledin, *Mothers and More: American Women in the 1950s* (1984); Susan Lynn, *Progressive Women in Conservative Times* (1992); Glenna Matthews, *"Just a Housewife"* (1987); Joanne J. Meyerowitz, ed., *Not June Cleaver: Women and Gender in Postwar America, 1945–1960* (1994); Leila J. Rupp and Verta Taylor, *Survival in the Doldrums: The American Women's Rights Movement, 1945 to the 1960s* (1987); Sus.an Strasser, *Never Done: A History of American Housework* (1982).

The Affluent Society

Loren Baritz, *The Good Life: The Meaning of Success for the American Middle Class* (1982); Martin Campbell-Kelly and William Aspray, *Computer: A History of the Information Machine* (1996); John Kenneth Galbraith, *The Affluent Society* (1958); Ann Markusen et al., *Rise of the Gunbelt: The Military Remapping of Industrial America* (1991); Kirkpatrick Sale, *Power Shift: The Rise of the Southern Rim and Its Challenge to the Eastern Establishment* (1975).

Farmers and Laborers

Gilbert C. Fite, *American Farmers* (1981); James R. Green, *The World of the Worker* (1980); Nelson Lichtenstein, *The Most Dangerous Man in Detroit: Walter Reuther and the Fate of American Labor* (1995); George Lipsitz, *Rainbow at Midnight: Labor and Culture in the 1940s* (1994); John L. Shover, *First Majority—Last Minority: The Transforming of Rural Life in America* (1976).

The Other America

Richard B. Craig, *The Bracero Program* (1971); J. Wayne Flint, *Dixie's Forgotten People: The South's Poor Whites* (1979); Mario T. Garcia, *Mexican Americans: Leadership, Ideology, and Identity, 1930–1960* (1990); Michael Harrington, *The Other America*, rev. ed. (1981); Dorothy K. Newman et al., *Politics and Prosperity: Black Americans and White Institutions, 1940–75* (1978); James T. Patterson, *America's Struggle Against Poverty, 1900–1994*, rev. ed. (1994).

Postwar Culture

Peter Biskind, *Seeing Is Believing: How Hollywood Taught Us to Stop Worrying and Love the Fifties* (1983); Paul Boyer, *By the Bomb's Early Light: American Thought and Culture at the Dawn of the Atomic Age* (1985); Thomas Doherty, *Projections of War: Hollywood, American Culture, and World War II* (1993); James Gilbert, *A Cycle of Outrage: America's Reaction to the Juvenile Delinquent* (1986); Charlie Gillett, *The Sound of the City: The Rise of Rock and Roll*, rev. ed. (1983); Todd Gitlin, *Inside Prime Time* (1983); William S. Graebner, *The Age of Doubt: American Thought and Culture in the 1940s* (1991); Karal Ann Marling, *As Seen on TV: The Visual Culture of Everyday Life in the 1950s* (1994); Lary May, ed., *Recasting America: Culture and Politics in the Age of Cold War* (1989); Nora Sayre, *Running Time: Films of the Cold War* (1982); Ella Taylor, *Prime-Time Families: Television Culture in Postwar America* (1989); Allan M. Winkler, *Life Under a Cloud: American Anxiety About the Bomb* (1993).

CHAPTER

29

Foreign Relations Glacier: The Cold War and Its Aftermath
1945–Present

President Harry S Truman's advisers anxiously ranked his March 12, 1947, speech to Congress as important as any presidential address since Pearl Harbor. But they knew that Truman had a selling job to do if he wanted this Congress to endorse his request for $400 million in aid to Greece and Turkey. The Republican 80th Congress wanted less, not more, spending, and many of its members had little respect for the Democratic president whose administration the voters had repudiated in the 1946 elections. Many even wondered if Truman had a coherent foreign policy. Republican Senator Arthur Vandenberg of Michigan, a bipartisan leader who backed Truman's request, bluntly told the president that he would have to "scare hell out of the American people" to gain congressional approval. Already notorious for outspokenness, Truman needed little coaching.

The president delivered a speech laced with alarmist language intended to stake out the United States's role in the postwar world—a statement of "global policy," as Assistant Secretary of State Dean Acheson called it. Truman claimed that communism, feeding on economic dislocations, imperiled the world. "If Greece should fall under the control of an armed minority," he gravely concluded in an early version of the domino theory (see page 898), "the effect upon its neighbor, Turkey, would be immediate and serious. Confusion and disorder might well spread throughout the entire Middle East." At the time, civil war in which communists played a prominent role rocked Greece. Turkey bordered the Soviet Union, considered by American leaders to be masterminding global

Sketch of an intercontinental ballistic missile (ICBM), first launched by the Soviet Union in 1957. The land-based ICBM could travel 3,000 nautical miles to deliver a powerfully destructive nuclear warhead. *The Michael Barson Collection/Past Perfect.*

• *Important Events* •

1945	Yalta Conference charts postwar order Roosevelt dies; Truman becomes president Potsdam Conference sets terms for control of defeated Germany Japan surrenders, and United States occupation begins
1946	Soviets and Americans compete for influence in Iran George Kennan's "long telegram" depicts USSR as uncompromising foe Winston Churchill gives "iron curtain" speech Baruch Plan to control atomic weapons fails Truman fires Wallace for criticizing hard-line Cold War policy
1947	Truman Doctrine launches containment doctrine Walter Lippmann's critique of containment, *The Cold War*, is published Communists take power in Hungary Kennan ("Mr. X") articulates containment doctrine Marshall Plan for European recovery announced National Security Act creates Defense Department and CIA
1948	Organization of American States founded Fulbright Program of academic exchanges begins Communists take power in Czechoslovakia Truman recognizes Israel United States organizes Berlin airlift
1949	North Atlantic Treaty Organization founded USSR explodes atomic bomb Communist victory brings Mao Zedong to power in China
1950	NSC-68 calls for a huge United States military buildup Korean War breaks out in June; China enters in fall
1951	Truman fires General Douglas MacArthur Armistice talks begin in Korea United States occupation of Japan ended; Japanese-American security treaty is signed
1952	United States explodes first H-bomb
1953	Dwight D. Eisenhower becomes president Soviet premier Joseph Stalin dies Eisenhower speaks of "atoms for peace"

	United States Information Agency created as propaganda instrument Korean War ends
1954	Sino-American crisis over Jinmen (Quemoy) and Mazu (Matsu)
1955	Geneva meeting is first United States–USSR summit since 1945 Occupation of Austria ends Soviets organize Warsaw Pact
1956	Soviets crush uprising in Hungary Suez crisis sparks war in Middle East
1957	Soviets fire first intercontinental ballistic missile and launch *Sputnik* Committee for a Sane Nuclear Policy (SANE) founded
1958	United States and USSR sign cultural exchange agreement National Aeronautics and Space Administration created Jinmen-Mazu crisis recurs Berlin crisis erupts
1959	Fidel Castro ousts Fulgencio Batista in Cuba
1960	United States imposes economic embargo on Cuba Soviets shoot down U-2 spy plane
1961	John F. Kennedy becomes president Bay of Pigs invasion fails in Cuba Berlin Wall is built
1962	Cuban missile crisis brings world to brink of nuclear war
1963	Limited Test-Ban Treaty prohibits atmospheric testing of nuclear weapons Kennedy is assassinated; Lyndon B. Johnson becomes president
1967	Summit meeting in Glassboro, New Jersey
1968	Nuclear nonproliferation treaty signed Soviets invade Czechoslovakia
1969	Richard M. Nixon becomes president and, with Henry Kissinger, launches détente
1972	Nixon visits China and ends years of Sino-American isolation SALT-I Treaty limits ABMs and strategic nuclear weapons
1974	Nixon resigns; Gerald Ford becomes president

• *Important Events* •

1975	Helsinki accords pledge support for human rights	**1990**	Communist regimes in Eastern Europe collapse
1977	Jimmy Carter becomes president and presses human-rights policy		Iraq invades Kuwait to spark Persian Gulf War
			Reunification of Germany
1979	SALT-II Treaty acknowledges Soviet-American nuclear parity	**1991**	START-I Treaty reduces nuclear warheads in USSR and the United States
	Soviets invade Afghanistan		USSR dissolves into independent states
			Yeltsin replaces Gorbachev
1980	Carter Doctrine declares United States will defend Persian Gulf area		Agreement bans oil exploration and mining in Antarctica
	United States imposes grain embargo and boycott of Olympic Games against Soviets		Ethnic wars break out in former Yugoslavia
1981	Ronald Reagan becomes president	**1992**	United States in the minority at Rio Earth Summit
	Soviet crackdown in Poland prompts United States trade restrictions on USSR		Canada, Mexico, and United States sign North American Free Trade Agreement
	Nuclear freeze movement grows worldwide		START-II agreement reduces warheads and ICBMs
1982	START negotiations, to reduce strategic nuclear forces, begin	**1993**	Bill Clinton becomes president
			Islamic extremists bomb World Trade Center in New York
1983	United States announces Strategic Defense Initiative ("Star Wars")	**1994**	NAFTA becomes operative, creating the world's largest free-trade bloc
	Soviets shoot down Korean airliner		
	United States deploys Pershing missiles in Western Europe	**1995**	Nuclear nonproliferation treaty renewed
			United States brokers peace agreement for Bosnia
1985	Reagan Doctrine promises United States aid to anti-Soviet "freedom fighters"		American troops join NATO peacekeeping force in Bosnia
	Premier Mikhail Gorbachev initiates *glasnost* and *perestroika* reforms in USSR		World Conference on Women calls for "human rights and fundmental freedoms"
	United States and USSR disagree over "Star Wars" at Geneva summit	**1996**	Clinton criticizes isolationism and calls for a United States "peacemaker" role
1987	Gorbachev and Reagan sign INF Treaty banning land-based intermediate-range nuclear missiles in Europe		Clinton reelected in a campaign largely lacking foreign policy debate
		1997	Madeleine Albright is first woman to become secretary of state
1989	George Bush becomes president		
	United States and other nations agree to phase-out of ozone-destroying chemicals		
	Berlin Wall opens, and East German communist regime collapses		
	Chinese armed forces kill prodemocracy demonstrators in Tiananmen Square		

Note: For events in the nations of the Third World, including Vietnam, Iran, and Iraq, see Chapter 30.

communist expansion. At issue, Truman insisted, was the very security of the United States.

Especially momentous in the dramatic speech were the words, later known as the *Truman Doctrine*, that would guide American policymakers for almost

a half-century: "I believe that it must be the policy of the United States to support free peoples who are resisting attempted subjugation by armed minorities or by outside pressures." Secretary of State George C. Marshall privately questioned the "flamboyant anti-Communism" of the speech, but two new and young members of the House of Representatives, John F. Kennedy and Richard M. Nixon, applauded Truman's message that day. When they assumed the presidency in the 1960s, the Truman Doctrine still guided their policies.

The Truman Doctrine helped launch the *containment doctrine:* the United States had to draw the line against communism everywhere. American presidents from Truman to George Bush believed that a ruthless Soviet Union was directing a worldwide communist conspiracy against peace, free-market capitalism, and political democracy. Soviet leaders from Joseph Stalin to Mikhail Gorbachev protested that a militarized, economically aggressive United States sought nothing less than world domination. This contest between the United States and the Soviet Union soon acquired the name *Cold War.*

The primary feature of world affairs for more than four decades, the Cold War was fundamentally a bipolar contest between the United States and the Soviet Union over spheres of influence, over world power. The two nations never fought one another directly on the battlefield. Instead, they waged the Cold War through competing alliances (the capitalist "West" versus the communist "East"), regional wars between client states, rival ideologies, foreign aid and economic sanctions, covert operations and propaganda, and an arms race that included nuclear weapons. Like a glacier, the Cold War began in the 1940s to cut across the global terrain, changing the topography of international relations. The contest took the lives of millions, emptied the treasuries of the combatants, spawned fears of doomsday, and destabilized politics in one nation after another, dragging localized conflicts into its path. Sometimes the two superpowers negotiated at summit conferences and signed agreements to temper the arms race; at other times they went to the brink of war and armed allies to fight vicious wars in the Third World (see Chapter 30). Decisions made in Moscow and Washington dominated world politics.

Throughout the Cold War era, critics in the United States challenged the architects of the Cold War, questioning their exaggerations of threats from abroad and the expensive militarization of foreign policy. But when leaders such as Truman described the Cold War in extremist terms as a life-and-death struggle against a monstrous enemy, legitimate criticism became suspect and dissenters discredited. The critics' searching questions about the necessity

and consequences of a global, interventionist foreign policy and a nuclear strategy based on the doctrine of "mutual assured destruction" (MAD) were drowned out by redbaiting charges that they were "soft on communism," if not un-American. Decision makers in the United States successfully cultivated a Cold War consensus that dampened debate.

Ultimately the two great powers, weakened by the huge costs of their competition and challenged by other nations and blocs, faced an international system in which power had become diffused. In an effort to stem their relative decline, the two adversaries in the late 1980s began to take steps to end the Cold War. Its end finally came in 1991 with the disintegration of the Soviet Union, the collapse of other communist regimes in Eastern Europe, and the reunification of Germany. Some Americans claimed victory in the Cold War, but others, doubting that there were any winners, thought that the United States, because of its faltering infrastructure, had paid a high price.

Like a retreating glacier, the Cold War left behind a scarred landscape and debris that complicated the shaping of a new world order. For years after the Cold War ended, American leaders found it difficult to define new doctrines and to clarify United States interests, responsibilities, and capabilities in a new era that lacked a Soviet threat. Americans expected a "peace dividend" redirecting Cold War spending to domestic needs, but it failed to materialize. The post–Cold War era became characterized by local conflicts around the world, and the United States, after intense debate at home, often intervened in them (see also Chapter 30).

 ## Sources of the Cold War

After the Second World War, the international system was so unsettled that conflict became virtually inevitable. Economic chaos rocked Europe and Asia.

Unsettled International System

Factories and transportation and communications links had been reduced to rubble. Agricultural production plummeted, and displaced persons wandered around in search of food and family. How would the devastated economic world be pieced back together? The United States and the Soviet Union offered very different answers and models. The collapse of Germany and Japan, moreover, had created power vacuums that drew the two major powers into collision as they sought influence in countries where the Axis once had held sway. And the political turmoil that many nations experienced after the war also spurred Soviet-American competition. For example, in Greece and China, where civil wars raged between leftists and conservative regimes, the two powers supported different sides.

The international system also became unstable because empires were disintegrating. Financial constraints and nationalist rebellions forced the European imperial states to set their colonies free, as Britain did with India (and Pakistan) in 1947 and Burma in 1948. As new nations gained independence in the Middle East and Asia, America and the Soviet Union vied to win these Third World states as allies that might provide military bases, resources, and markets. The shrinkage of the globe also ensured conflict. With the advent of the airplane, the world had become more compact. Faster travel brought nations closer at the same time that it made them more vulnerable to surprise attack from the air. The Americans and the Soviets collided as they strove to establish defensive positions, sometimes far from home.

Driven by different ideologies and different economic and strategic needs in this volatile international climate, the United States and the Soviet Union downgraded diplomacy to build what Secretary of State Dean Acheson (1949–1953) called "situations of strength." Finding the Soviets rude and abusive, this conservative diplomat asserted that "it is a mistake to believe that you can, at any time, sit down with the Russians and solve problems." Both nations marched into the Cold War with convictions of righteousness that gave the contest an almost religious character. Each saw the other as the world's bully. While Americans feared "communist aggression," Soviets feared "capitalist encirclement."

American officials vowed never to repeat the experience of the 1930s; they would accept no more Munichs, no more appeasement, and no more depressions that might spawn political extremism and war. To growing numbers of Americans after the Second World War, it seemed that Soviet Russia had simply replaced Nazi Germany, that communism was simply the flip side of the totalitarian coin. The popular term "Red fascism" captured this sentiment.

American officials also knew that the nation's economic well-being depended on an activist foreign policy. In the postwar years the United States

United States Economic and Strategic Needs

stood as the largest supplier of goods to world markets, but that trade was jeopardized by the postwar economic paralysis of Europe—traditionally America's major customer—and by discriminatory trade practices that violated the Open Door doctrine. If the dollar gap were not closed, the United States might face a severe depression once again. The automobile, steel, and machine-tool industries, as well as wheat, cotton, and tobacco farmers, relied heavily on foreign trade. Indeed, exports constituted about 10 percent of the gross national product. And the United States also needed to import essential minerals such as zinc, tin, and manganese. Thus economic expansionism, so much a part of pre–Cold War history, remained a central feature of postwar foreign relations.

New strategic theory also propelled the United States toward an expansionist, globalist diplomacy. "As top dog, America becomes target No. 1," warned Air Force general Carl Spaatz. To be ready for a military challenge in the postwar "air age," American strategists believed that the nation's defenses had to extend far beyond its own borders. Thus the United States sought overseas bases to guard the approaches to the Western Hemisphere. These bases also would permit the United States to launch offensive attacks with might and speed. When asked where the United States Navy would float, Navy Secretary James Forrestal declared: "Wherever there is a sea."

President Truman, who shared those assumptions, had a personality ill suited for diplomacy. Whereas Franklin D. Roosevelt had been ingratiating, patient, and evasive, Truman was brash, impatient, and direct. The Missouri politician often glossed over nuances, ambiguities, and counterevidence; he preferred the simple answer stated in either-or terms. As Winston Churchill said of him, Truman "takes no notice of delicate ground, he just plants his foot firmly on it." Shortly after Roosevelt's death in early 1945, Truman met the Soviet commissar of foreign affairs, V. M. Molotov, at the White House. When the president sharply demanded that the Soviet Union honor the Yalta agreement on Poland, Molotov stormed out. Truman had self-consciously developed what he called

Truman's Get-Tough Style

Send a warm gift
to a little Russian friend

Merry Christmas, Tanya

RUSSIAN WAR RELIEF, inc.

During the Second World War, when the Soviet Union and the United States were allied, Americans gave generously to Russian War Relief, a private organization that from 1941 to 1946 distributed some $75 million worth of shoes, clothes, and medicine to the hard-hit people of the Soviet republics. After the war, as Soviet-American foreign policy differences widened in the emerging Cold War, such cooperation quickly dissipated and even became suspect as aiding communism, the "Red menace." Poster Collection. Hoover Institution Archives, Stanford, California.

his "tough method," and he bragged after the encounter that "I gave it to him straight 'one-two to the jaw.'" But the Yalta agreements were vague; although the Soviets acted heavy-handedly in Poland, whether they violated the accord remains open to interpretation. Truman's display of toughness nonetheless became a trademark of American Cold War diplomacy.

The Soviets remembered that since the Bolshevik Revolution the hostile West had attempted to defeat and then ostracize them: "We were always outsiders," observed one Soviet diplomat. Fearful of a revived Germany and a resurgent Japan, anticipating that capitalist nations once again would attempt to extinguish the communist flame, facing a monumental task of economic reconstruction, and embracing Marxist-Leninist doctrine, the Soviets made territorial gains in eastern Poland, the Baltic states of Lithuania, Latvia, and Estonia, and parts of Finland and Romania. In Eastern Europe Soviet officials began to suppress noncommunists and install communist clients. The Americans, the steely premier Joseph Stalin protested, were surrounding the USSR with hostile bases and practicing atomic and dollar diplomacy. He nonetheless knew that the Soviets could not realize many of their goals without cooperation from the United States. That is why, historian Melvyn Leffler has written, "Stalin's approach to international affairs at the end of the war [World War II] was relatively cautious" and "expedient," lacking a "distinct strategy."

The Soviet Perspective

Throughout the Cold War era, Americans debated Soviet intentions and capabilities. Many no doubt agreed with Winston Churchill, who said that dealing with the Soviet Union was "like wooing a crocodile. You do not know whether to tickle it under the chin or to beat it over the head. When it opens its mouth you cannot tell whether it is trying to smile or . . . eat you up." Some believed that the Soviet Union—well armed, opportunistic, and aggressive—could never be trusted. Others charged that American officials exaggerated the Soviet/communist threat, imagining a bigger-than-life, monolithic enemy, finding it at work everywhere, blaming it for troubles it never started, attributing to it accomplishments it never achieved.

In the immediate postwar years, in fact, the Soviet Union suffered a hobbled economy and, like the United States, undertook a major postwar demobilization of its armed forces. The Soviet Union was a regional power in Eastern Europe, not a global menace. American leaders feared that the ravaging postwar economic and social unrest abroad would leave American strategic and economic interests vulnerable to political disorders that the Soviets might exploit, perhaps through subversion. In other words, Americans feared Soviet seizure of opportunities to challenge United States interests more than they feared a direct Soviet attack on Western Europe.

The United States took advantage of the postwar power vacuum to expand its overseas interests and shape a peace on American terms. The United States's pursuit of nuclear superiority, outlying bases, raw materials and markets, supremacy in Latin America, and control of the Atlantic and Pacific Oceans aroused many opponents, in particular the Soviet Union. To Americans who thought that vigorous United States globalism must and would save the world, Soviet opposition simply confirmed Moscow's wicked obstructionism. George F. Kennan, one of the chief architects of Cold War policy, later regretted that Americans had created the image of the Soviet Union as "the totally inhuman and malevolent adversary." This distorted view, he believed, had contributed to American abandonment of diplomacy during the rash of crises that shook the global community during the early Cold War.

Europe, Containment, and Global Polarization

One of the first Soviet-American clashes came in Poland in 1945, when the Soviets refused to allow conservative Poles from London to join the communist government in Lublin.

Soviet Sphere in Eastern Europe

Truman officials argued that Stalin at the Yalta Conference had agreed to a democratic government for Poland, but the Soviet Union, fearing Western inroads into its sphere of influence, sustained a pro-communist regime. The Soviets also snuffed out civil liberties in the former Nazi satellite of Romania, justifying their actions by pointing to what they claimed was an equivalent United States manipulation of politics in Italy. They initially allowed free elections in Hungary and Czechoslovakia, but as the Cold War accelerated and United States influence in Europe expanded, the Soviets encouraged communist coups: first Hungary (1947) and then Czechoslovakia (1948) succumbed to Soviet subversion. Yugoslavia was a unique case: its independent communist government, led by Josip Broz Tito, successfully broke with Stalin in 1948.

To justify their actions, the Soviets pointed out that the United States was reviving their traditional enemy, Germany. The Soviets also protested that the United States was meddling in Eastern Europe. They cited clandestine meetings with anti-Soviet groups, repeated calls for elections likely to produce anti-Soviet regimes, and the use of loans to gain political influence (dollar diplomacy). Moscow charged that the United States was pursuing a double standard—intervening in the affairs of Eastern Europe but demanding that the Soviet Union stay out of Latin America and Asia. Americans called for free elections in the Soviet sphere, Moscow noted, but not in the United States sphere in Latin America, where several military dictatorships ruled.

The atomic bomb also divided the two major powers. The Soviets believed that the United States was practicing "atomic diplomacy"—maintaining a nuclear monopoly to scare the Soviets into diplomatic concessions. Secretary of State James F. Byrnes (1945–1947) thought that the atomic bomb gave the United States bargaining power and could serve as a deterrent to Soviet expansion, but Secretary of War Henry L. Stimson thought otherwise in 1945. If Americans continued to have "this weapon rather ostentatiously on our hip," he warned Truman, "their [the Soviets'] suspicions and their distrust of our purposes and motives will increase."

Atomic Diplomacy

In this atmosphere of suspicion and distrust, Truman refused to turn over the "sheriff's" weapon to an international control authority. In 1946 he backed the Baruch Plan, named after its author, financier Bernard Baruch. Largely a propaganda ploy, this proposal provided for the United States's abandonment of its monopoly only after the world's fissionable materials were brought under the authority of an international agency. The Soviets retorted that this plan would require them to shut down their atomic-bomb development project while the United States continued its own. Washington and Moscow soon became locked into an expensive and frightening nuclear arms race.

Soviets and Americans clashed on every front in 1946. When the United States turned down a Soviet request for a reconstruction loan but gave a loan to Britain, Moscow denounced Washington for using its dollars to manipulate foreign governments. The two Cold War powers also backed different groups in Iran, where the United States helped bring the pro-West shah to the throne. Unable to agree on the unification of Germany, they built up their zones independently. The new World Bank and International Monetary Fund, created at the 1944 Bretton Woods Conference to stabilize trade and finance,

On March 5, 1946, former British prime minister Winston S. Churchill (1874–1965) delivered a speech, which he intended for a worldwide audience, at Westminster College in Fulton, Missouri. President Harry S Truman (right) had encouraged Churchill (seated) to speak on two themes: the need to block Soviet expansion and the need to form an Anglo-American partnership. Always eloquent and provocative, Churchill denounced the Soviets for drawing an "iron curtain" across eastern Europe. This speech became one of the landmark statements of the Cold War. Harry S Truman Presidential Library

a Soviet-erected "iron curtain" had cut off Eastern European countries from the West. With an approving Truman sitting on the stage, Churchill called for Anglo-American partnership to resist the new menace.

Secretary of Commerce Henry A. Wallace charged that Truman's get-tough policy was substituting atomic and economic coercion for diplomacy. Wallace told a Madison Square Garden audience in September 1946 that "'getting tough' never brought anything real and lasting—whether for schoolyard bullies or businessmen or world powers. The tougher we get, the tougher the Russians will get." Truman soon fired Wallace from the cabinet, blasting him privately as "a real Commy and a dangerous man" and boasting that he, Truman, had now "run the crackpots out of the Democratic Party." Such extremist words helped kindle the exaggerations so common to the Cold War.

The Cold War escalated further in early 1947, when the British requested American help in Greece to defend their conservative client government against a leftist insurgency. The

Greek Civil War and Truman Doctrine

president asked Congress for aid to Greece and Turkey and enunciated the Truman Doctrine. Critics correctly pointed out that the Soviet Union was hardly involved in the Greek civil war, that the communists in Greece were more pro-Tito than pro-Stalin, and that the resistance movement had noncommunist as well as communist members. Nor was the Soviet Union threatening Turkey at the time. Others suggested that such aid should be channeled through the United Nations. Truman countered that should communists gain control of Greece they might open the door to Soviet power in the Mediterranean. After much debate, the Senate approved Truman's request by 67 votes to 23. Using United States dollars and military advisers, the Greek government defeated the insurgents in 1949, and Turkey became a staunch United States ally on the Soviets' border.

Four months after Truman's speech, State Department official George F. Kennan published an influential statement of the containment doctrine.

George F. Kennan's "X" Article

Writing as "Mr. X" in the magazine *Foreign Affairs*, Kennan advocated a "policy of firm containment, designed to confront the Russians with unalterable counterforce at every point where they show signs of encroaching upon

also became tangled in the Cold War struggle. The Soviets refused to join because the United States so dominated both institutions.

After Stalin gave a speech in February 1946 that depicted the world as threatened by capitalist acquisitiveness, the American chargé d'affaires in Moscow, George F. Kennan, sent

Kennan and Churchill on Soviet Expansion

a pessimistic "long telegram" to Washington. Kennan asserted that Soviet fanaticism made even a temporary understanding impossible. His widely circulated report fed a growing belief among American officials that only toughness would work with the Soviets. The following month, Winston Churchill delivered a stirring speech in Fulton, Missouri. The former British prime minister warned that

the interests of a peaceful and stable world." Such counterforce, Kennan argued, would check Soviet expansion and eventually foster a "mellowing" of Soviet behavior. With the Truman Doctrine, Kennan's "X" article became a key manifesto of Cold War policy.

The veteran journalist Walter Lippmann took issue with the containment doctrine in *The Cold War* (1947), calling it a "strategic monstrosity" that failed to distinguish between areas vital and peripheral to United States security. If American leaders defined every place on earth as strategically important, Lippmann reasoned, the nation's patience and resources soon would be drained. Nor did Lippmann share Truman's conviction that the Soviet Union was plotting to take over the world. The president, he asserted, put too little emphasis on diplomacy.

Debate over Containment

Invoking the containment doctrine, the United States in 1947 and 1948 began to build an international economic and defensive network to protect American prosperity and security and to advance United States hegemony. In Western Europe, the region of primary concern, American diplomats pursued several objectives: economic reconstruction; ouster of communists from governments, as occurred in 1947 in France and Italy; blockage of "third force" or neutralist tendencies; a gradual decolonization of European empires; creation of a military alliance; and unification of the western zones of Germany. At the same time, American culture—Coca-Cola, blue jeans, music, the consumption ethic, and the New Deal corporatist model of business-government-labor cooperation—permeated European societies. Many Europeans resisted Americanization, but transatlantic ties strengthened.

The first instrument designed to achieve United States goals in western Europe was the Marshall Plan. European nations, still reeling economically and unstable politically, lacked the dollars to buy vital American-made goods. Americans, who already had spent billions of dollars on European relief and recovery by 1947, remembered all too well the troubles of the 1930s:

Marshall Plan

Under official postwar relief and recovery programs, including the Marshall Plan, the United States shipped billions of dollars' worth of food and equipment to western European nations struggling to overcome the destruction of the Second World War. Private efforts also succeeded, such as this one in 1950. The people of Jersey City, New Jersey, sent this snowplow to the mountainous village of Capracotta, Italy.   Corbis-Bettmann.

global depression, political extremism, and war born of economic discontent. Such cataclysms could not be allowed to happen again. Western Europe, Dean Acheson declared, was "the keystone in the arch which supports the kind of a world which we have to have in order to conduct our lives."

In June 1947, Secretary of State George C. Marshall (1947–1949) announced that the United States would finance a massive European recovery program. Launched in 1948, the Marshall Plan sent $12.4 billion to Western Europe before the program ended in 1951 (see map, page 855). To stimulate business at home, the legislation provided that the foreign aid dollars must be spent in the United States on American-made products. The Marshall Plan proved a mixed success; some scholars today even argue that Europe could have revived without it. The program caused inflation, failed to solve a balance-of-payments problem, took only tentative steps toward economic integration, and further divided Europe between "East" and "West." But the program spurred impressive Western European industrial production and investment and started the region toward self-sustaining economic growth. From the United States's perspective, moreover, the plan succeeded because it helped contain communism.

To streamline the administration of United States defense, Truman worked with Congress on the National Security Act (July 1947). The act created the Department of Defense (replacing the Department of War), the National Security Council (NSC) to advise the president, and the Central Intelligence Agency (CIA) to conduct spying and information gathering. By the early 1950s the CIA had expanded its functions to include covert (secret) operations aimed at overthrowing unfriendly foreign leaders and, as a high-ranking American official put it, a "Department of Dirty Tricks" to stir up economic trouble in "the camp of the enemy."

In 1948 the United States implemented the Fulbright Program—a "cultural Marshall Plan for the intellectual reconstruction of the West," as historian Richard Pells has written. The brainchild two years earlier of Democratic senator J. William Fulbright of Arkansas, a former Rhodes scholar and university president, this example of "public diplomacy" attempted to overcome cultural barriers to reach foreign peoples with a positive message about the United States.

"Public Diplomacy" and Fulbright Program

The Fulbright Program sponsored educational exchanges; professors and students from the United States went abroad to teach and study, and their counterparts from foreign countries came to the United States. By 1953 influential intellectual elites in twenty-eight nations were participating in the program in Europe, Asia, and the Middle East. In some countries, former Fulbrighters rose to political prominence, keeping their governments allied with the United States. Because considerable anti-Americanism nonetheless persisted, some American and European intellectuals in 1950 created a new organization, the Congress for Cultural Freedom, to blunt it; the CIA secretly subsidized this effort to promote America in Europe.

American officials also made military linkages around the world. The United States granted the Philippines independence in 1946 while retaining military and economic hegemony there. The following year, American diplomats created the Rio Pact in Latin America. To enforce this military alliance, the United States helped found the Organization of American States (OAS) in 1948. Under this and other agreements the Truman administration sent several military missions to Latin America and to Greece, Turkey, Iran, China, and Saudi Arabia to improve the armed forces of those nations.

In May 1948, Truman quickly recognized the newly proclaimed state of Israel, which had been carved out of British-held Palestine after years of Arab-Jewish dispute. Despite State Department objection that recognition would alienate oil-rich Arab nations, Truman made the decision for three reasons: he believed that, after the Holocaust, Jews deserved a homeland; he desired Jewish-American votes in the upcoming election; and he sought another international ally, which Israel became.

Recognition of Israel

One of the most electric moments in the Cold War came in June 1948 after the Americans, French, and British had agreed to fuse their German zones, including their three sectors of Berlin. They sought to integrate West Germany (the Federal Republic of Germany) into the Western European economy, complete with a reformed German currency. Fearing a resurgent Germany tied to the American Cold War camp, the Soviets cut off Western access to the jointly occupied city of Berlin, located well inside the Soviet zone. In response to

Berlin Blockade and Airlift

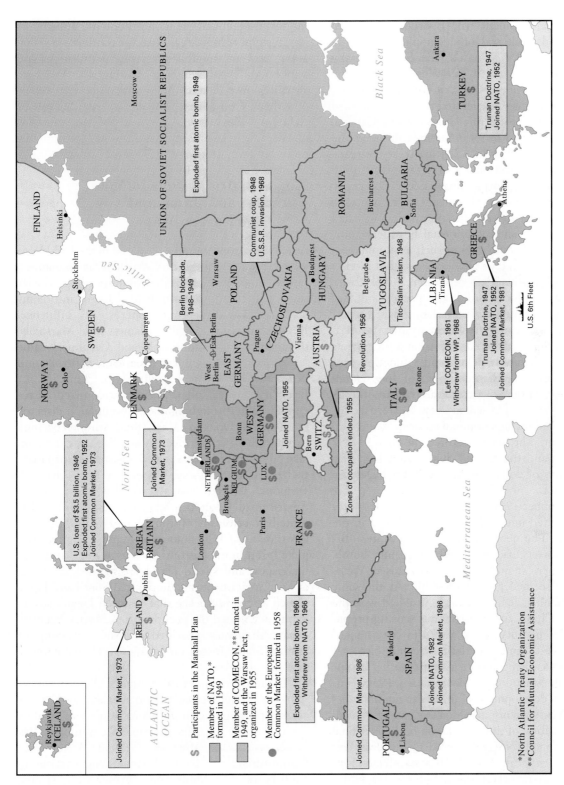

Divided Europe   *After the Second World War, Europe broke into two competing camps. When the United States launched the Marshall Plan in 1948, the Soviet Union countered with its own economic plan the following year. When the United States created NATO in 1949, the Soviet Union answered with the Warsaw Pact in 1955. On the whole, these two camps held firm until the late 1980s.*

this bold move, President Truman ordered a massive airlift of food, fuel, and other supplies to Berlin. Their spoiling effort blunted, the Soviets finally lifted the blockade in May 1949 and founded the German Democratic Republic, or East Germany.

The Berlin crisis accelerated movement toward a Western security pact. The United States, Canada, and many western European nations founded the

Founding of NATO

North Atlantic Treaty Organization (NATO) in April 1949 (see map, page 855). The treaty aroused considerable domestic debate, for not since 1778 had the United States entered a formal European military alliance, and some critics, such as Republican senator Robert A. Taft of Ohio, claimed that NATO would provoke rather than deter war. Other critics argued that the Soviets did not pose a military threat. Administration officials themselves did not anticipate a Soviet military thrust against Western Europe, but they responded that, should the Soviets ever probe westward, NATO would function as a "tripwire," bringing the full force of the United States to bear on the Soviet Union. Truman officials also hoped that NATO would keep Western Europeans from embracing communism or neutralism in the Cold War. The Senate ratified the treaty by 82 votes to 13, and the United States soon began to spend billions of dollars under the Mutual Defense Assistance Act.

In September 1949 an American reconnaissance aircraft detected unusually high radioactivity in the atmosphere. The news stunned United States officials: the Soviets had exploded an atomic bomb. With the American nuclear monopoly erased, Western Europe seemed more vulnerable. At the same time, communists led by Mao Zedong had won the civil war in China, and Moscow was scoring propaganda points by advocating "peaceful coexistence" with the West. American leaders could have responded to this changed state of affairs with a call for high-level negotiations. Instead, in early 1950, Truman ordered development of the hydrogen bomb.

After Mao's victory in China (see page 857) and Soviet acquisition of the atomic bomb, the National Security Council (NSC) delivered to the president

NSC-68

in April 1950 a significant top-secret document tagged NSC-68. Predicting continued tension with expansionistic communists and describing "a shrinking world of polarized power," the report appealed for a much enlarged

military budget and the mobilization of public opinion in support of such an increase. Officials worried about how to sell this prescription to voters and budget-conscious members of Congress. "We were sweating over it, and then—with regard to NSC-68—thank God Korea came along," recalled one of Acheson's aides.

Confrontations in Asia: Japan, China, and the Korean War

Asia, like Europe, became ensnared in the Cold War. The victors in the Second World War dismantled Japan's empire. The United States and the Soviet Union divided Korea into competing spheres of influence.

Reconstruction of Japan

Pacific islands (the Marshalls, Marianas, and Carolines) came under American control, and Formosa (Taiwan) was returned to China. As for Japan itself, the United States monopolized its reconstruction through a military occupation directed by General Douglas MacArthur, who envisioned turning the Pacific Ocean into "an Anglo-Saxon lake." He wrote a democratic constitution for Japan, revitalized its economy, and destroyed the nation's weapons. United States authorities also helped Americanize Japan through censorship; films that hinted at criticism of the United States (for the destruction of Hiroshima, for example) or that depicted traditional customs such as suicide, arranged marriages, and sword play were banned. In 1951, against Soviet protests, the United States and Japan signed a separate peace that restored Japan's sovereignty and ended the occupation. A Mutual Security Treaty that year provided for the stationing of United States forces on Japanese soil, including a base on Okinawa.

Meanwhile, America's Chinese ally was faltering. The United States had long backed the Nationalists of Jiang Jieshi (Chiang Kai-shek) against

Communist Victory in the Chinese Civil War

Mao Zedong's communists. But after the Second World War, Generalissimo Jiang became an unreliable partner who rejected American advice. His government had become corrupt, inefficient, and out of touch with the rebellious peasants, whom the communists enlisted with promises of land reform. Jiang also subverted American efforts to negotiate a cease-fire and a coalition government. "We picked a bad horse," Truman admitted, privately denouncing the Nationalists as "grafters and crooks." Still, seeing Jiang as the only alternative to Mao, Truman backed him to the end.

American officials divided on the question of whether Mao was a puppet of the Soviet Union. Some considered him an Asian Tito—communist but independent—but most believed him to be part of an international communist movement that might give the Soviets a springboard into Asia. Thus when the Chinese communists made secret overtures to the United States to begin diplomatic talks in 1945 and again in 1949, American officials rebuffed them. Mao decided that he had no choice but to "lean" to the Soviet side in the Cold War. But China always maintained a fierce independence that rankled the Soviets and began to foster an ever-widening Sino-Soviet schism. Indeed, Mao deeply resented the Soviets' refusal to aid the communists during the civil war; Stalin offered no help, "not even a fart," Mao once growled.

In the fall of 1949, Jiang fled to the island of Formosa, and Mao proclaimed the People's Republic of China (PRC). Truman hesitated to extend diplomatic recognition to the new government. The British prime minister asked the president: "Are we to cut ourselves off from all contact with one-sixth of the inhabitants of the world?" Washington did precisely that. American officials became alarmed by the 1950 Sino-Soviet treaty of friendship and by the harassment of Americans and their property. Truman also chose nonrecognition because a vocal group of Republican critics, the so-called China lobby, was winning headlines by charging that the United States had "lost" China. Publisher Henry Luce, Senator William Knowland of California, and Representative Walter Judd of Minnesota pinned Jiang's defeat on Truman. The president stoutly answered that the self-defeating Jiang, despite billions of dollars in American aid, had proven a poor instrument of the containment doctrine. The administration nonetheless took the politically safe route and rejected recognition. Not until 1979 did official Sino-American relations resume.

In the early morning hours of June 25, 1950, a large military force of the Democratic People's Republic of Korea (North Korea) moved across

Nonrecognition of the People's Republic of China

CHILDREN'S CRUSADE AGAINST COMMUNISM

2. MacArthur Heads UN Forces

North Korean Reds attacked South Korea in what is believed to be part of a communist plan gradually to conquer the whole world. The United Nations pitched in to help the South Koreans, like your dad would help the folks next door if some bad men were beating them up. The troops sent to Korea for the UN were put under command of General Douglas MacArthur. "Mac" has a long military record. But you know him best as the general who led the Allied forces to victory in the Pacific during the second world war.

Intensely anticommunist groups thrived in the United States during the Cold War. The "Children's Crusade Against Communism" distributed its exaggerated message in the early 1950s through bubble-gum cards such as this one. The Michael Barson Collection/Past Perfect.

Outbreak of the Korean War

the 38th parallel into the Republic of Korea (South Korea). Although the Soviets had armed the North and the Americans had armed the South, the Korean War began as a civil war. Since 1945, when the great powers divided Korea, the two parts had been skirmishing along their supposedly temporary border. Both the North's communist leader Kim Il Sung and the South's president Syngman Rhee sought to reunify their nation. Displaying the Cold War mentality of the time, however, President Truman claimed that the Soviets had masterminded the North Korean attack. "Communism was acting in

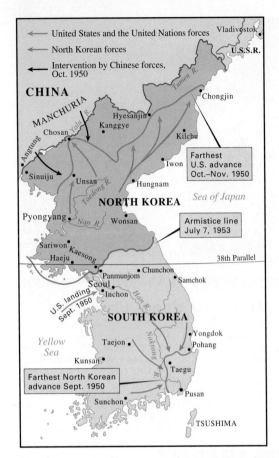

The Korean War, 1950–1953 *Beginning as a civil war between North and South, this war became international when the United States, under the auspices of the United Nations, and the People's Republic of China intervened.* Source: Adapted from Paterson et al., *American Foreign Relations: A History*, vol. 2, 4th ed. rev. Copyright © 1995 by D.C. Heath and Company. Used by permission of Houghton Mifflin Company.

Korea just as Hitler, Mussolini, and the Japanese had acted [in the 1930s]," he said.

Actually, Kim had to press a doubting Joseph Stalin, who only reluctantly approved the attack after Kim predicted an easy, early victory and after Mao Zedong backed Kim. The three communist leaders might have calculated that the United States would not come to South Korea's defense—indeed, that the United States was in the process of abandoning the Korean peninsula. In a public speech in early 1950, Secretary Acheson had drawn the American defense line in Asia through the Aleutians, Japan, and Okinawa to the Philippines. Formosa and Korea clearly lay beyond that line. Acheson did

say, however, that those areas could expect United Nations (and hence United States) assistance if attacked. Kim, Stalin, and Mao must have missed that point. Two other thoughts probably shifted Stalin to support Kim: first, if he did not support North Korea, Mao's China might gain influence over Kim; second, if the United States rearmed Japan, South Korea might once again become a beachhead for Japanese (and American) expansion.

Whatever Stalin's reasoning, his support for Kim's bold venture remained lukewarm. When the United Nations Security Council voted to defend South Korea, the Soviet representative was not even present to veto the resolution because the Soviets were boycotting the United Nations to protest its refusal to grant membership to the People's Republic of China. During the war, Moscow gave limited aid to North Korea and China, which grew angry at Stalin for reneging on promised Soviet airpower. Stalin did not want to be dragged into a costly war.

The president first ordered General Douglas MacArthur to send arms and troops to South Korea. Worried that Mao might attempt to take Formosa,

Truman Commits United States Forces

Truman also directed the Seventh Fleet to patrol the waters between the Chinese mainland and Jiang's sanctuary on Formosa, thus inserting the United States once again into Chinese politics. After the Security Council voted to assist South Korea, MacArthur became commander of United Nations forces in Korea (90 percent of them American). North Korean tanks and superior firepower sent the South Korean army into chaotic retreat. The first American soldiers, taking heavy casualties, could not stop the North Korean advance. Within weeks, the South Koreans and Americans had been pushed into the tiny Pusan perimeter at the base of South Korea (see map).

General MacArthur planned a daring operation: an amphibious landing at heavily fortified Inchon, several hundred miles behind North Korean lines. After United States guns and bombs pounded Inchon, marines sprinted ashore on September 15, 1950; by nightfall, 18,000 American troops had moved inland. They soon liberated the South Korean capital of Seoul and pushed the North Koreans back to the 38th parallel. Even before Inchon, Truman had redefined the United States's war goal from the containment of North Korea to the reunification of Korea by force. Communism not only would be stopped; it would be rolled back.

In September Truman authorized United Nations forces to cross the 38th parallel. These troops drove deep into North Korea, and American aircraft began strikes against bridges on the Yalu River, the border between North Korea and China. The Chinese watched warily, fearing that the Americans would next stab at the People's Republic. Mao publicly warned that China could not permit the bombing of its transportation links with Korea and would not accept the annihilation of North Korea itself. MacArthur shrugged off the warnings, assuring Truman that the Chinese would face the "greatest slaughter" if they entered the war. Officials in Washington agreed with the strong-willed general, drawing further confidence from the fact that the Soviets were not preparing for war.

Chinese Entry into the Korean War

On October 25 Chinese soldiers called "volunteers" entered the war near the Yalu. Perhaps to lure American forces into a trap or to signal willingness to begin negotiations, they pulled back after a brief and successful offensive against South Korean troops. Then, after MacArthur sent the United States Eighth Army northward, tens of thousands of Chinese troops counterattacked on November 26, surprising United States forces and driving them pell-mell southward. An embarrassed MacArthur called for a massive air attack on China. Truman hesitated, reflecting on the costs and consequences of a wider war. He hinted that he might use the atomic bomb. But he seemed chastened, reluctant to pursue a war that might drag on for years.

By early 1951 the front had stabilized around the 38th parallel. Both Washington and Moscow welcomed negotiations, but MacArthur had other ideas. The theatrical general recklessly called for an attack on China and for Jiang's return to the mainland. Now was the time, he insisted, to smash communism by destroying its Asian flank. Denouncing the concept of limited war (war without nuclear weapons, confined to one place), MacArthur hinted that the president was practicing appeasement. In April, fed up with the general's insubordination and backed by the Joint Chiefs of Staff, the heads of the various armed services, Truman fired MacArthur. The general, who had not set foot in the United States for more than a decade, returned home to ticker-tape parades and the lecture circuit but soon faded from the American political scene. Truman's

Truman Fires MacArthur

Often in rugged terrain and in cold weather, United States troops fought in Korea for three years (1950–1953). Here, snow-covered soldiers line up for cold chow during a war that ended in stalemate. National Archives.

popularity sagged because of the MacArthur episode and the stalemated war, but he weathered demands for his impeachment.

Armistice talks began in July 1951, but the fighting and dying went on for two more years. The most contentious point in the negotiations was the fate of prisoners of war (POWs). Defying the Geneva Prisoners of War Convention (1949), United States officials announced that only those North Korean and Chinese POWs who wished to go home would be returned. Responding to the American statement that there would be no forced repatriation, the North Koreans denounced forced retention. Both sides undertook "reeducation" or "brainwashing" programs to persuade POWs to resist repatriation. Tensions built up in prison camps in South Korea. In early 1952, at the Koje camp, United States troops supressed a Chinese/North Korean POW riot, killing more than one hundred. In North Korea's camps, murder and illness took the lives of hundreds of POWs.

The POW Question

As the POW issue stalled negotiations, United States officials made deliberately vague public statements about the possible use of atomic weapons in

War's End and Casualties

Korea. American bombers obliterated dams (whose rushing waters then destroyed rice fields), factories, airfields, and bridges in North Korea. Casualties on all sides mounted. Not until July 1953 was an armistice signed. Stalin's death in March and the coming to power of a more conciliatory Soviet government helped ease the way to a settlement that the Chinese especially welcomed. The combatants agreed to hand over the POW question to a special panel of neutral nations, which later gave prisoners their choice of staying or leaving. (In the end, 70,000 of about 100,000 North Korean and 5,600 of 20,700 Chinese POWs elected to return home; 21 American and 325 South Korean POWs of some 11,000 decided to stay in North Korea.) The North Korean–South Korean borderline was set near the 38th parallel, the prewar boundary, and a demilitarized zone was created between the two Koreas. American casualties totaled 54,246 dead and 103,284 wounded. More than 4 million people died in the war, 2 million of them North Korean civilians.

Thus ended a frustrating war—a limited war that Americans, accustomed to victory, had not won but had wisely kept limited. The Korean War carried major political consequences. The failure to achieve victory and the public's impatience with a limited war undoubtedly helped to elect Eisenhower (see page 819). The powers of the presidency grew as Congress repeatedly deferred to Truman. The president had never asked Congress for a declaration of war, believing that as commander-in-chief he had the authority to send troops wherever he wished. A few dissenters such as Senator Taft disagreed, but Truman saw no need to consult Congress—except when he wanted the $69.5 billion Korean War bill paid.

The implementation of military containment worldwide became entrenched as United States policy. Increased American aid flowed to the French for their die-hard stand in Indochina against nationalist insurgents (see Chapter 30). Because of heightened Sino-American hostility, South Korea and Formosa became major recipients of American foreign aid. The United States's alliance with Japan strengthened as Japan's economy boomed after filling large procurement orders from the United States. Australia and New Zealand joined the United States in a mutual defense agreement, the ANZUS Treaty (1951). The United States Army sent six divisions to Europe, and the administration initiated plans to rearm West Germany. The Korean War, Acheson cheerfully noted, removed "the recommendations of NSC-68 from the realm of theory and made them immediate budget issues." Indeed, the military budget shot up from $14 billion in 1949 to $44 billion in 1953; it remained between $35 billion and $44 billion a year throughout the 1950s. In sum, Truman's legacy was a highly militarized United States foreign policy active on a global scale.

Eisenhower and the Nuclear Arms Race

President Dwight D. Eisenhower largely sustained Truman's Cold War policies. Eisenhower brought considerable experience in foreign affairs to his presidency. He had lived and traveled in Europe, Asia, and Latin America and, as a general during the Second World War, had negotiated with world leaders. After the war, he served as army chief of staff and NATO supreme commander. Eisenhower accepted the Cold War consensus about the threat of communism and the need for global vigilance. Partisan Democrats promoted an image of Eisenhower as a bumbling, passive, aging hero. Although Eisenhower did not always stay abreast of issues because he chose to delegate authority to others, and although he seemed stuck in tired views just when the international system was becoming more fluid, the president commanded the policymaking process and tamed the hawkish proposals of Vice President Richard Nixon and Secretary of State John Foster Dulles.

Eisenhower questioned Dulles's "practice of becoming a sort of international prosecuting attorney," but the president relied heavily on the stern, strong-willed secretary of state.

John Foster Dulles

Few Cold Warriors rivaled Dulles's impassioned anticommunism, often expressed in biblical terms. A graduate of Princeton and George Washington Universities, Dulles had assisted Woodrow Wilson at Versailles. Dulles became a senior partner in a prestigious Wall Street law firm and an officer of the Federal Council of Churches. Though polished and articulate, Dulles impressed people as arrogant, stubborn, and hectoring—too unwilling to compromise, just as he feared that Eisenhower might be too generous. Dulles opposed United States participation in the Geneva summit meeting in 1955, for example, because he feared that the president might accept a Russian "promise or proposition at face value and upset the apple cart."

Like the president, Dulles conceded much to the anticommunist McCarthyites, who claimed that the State Department was infested with communists (see page 823). Dulles appointed one of Senator McCarthy's followers, Scott McLeod, chief security officer of the State Department. Targeting homosexuals and other "incompatibles," and making few distinctions between New Dealers and Communists, McLeod and Dulles forced many talented officers out of the Foreign Service with unsubstantiated charges that they were disloyal. Among them were Asia specialists whose expertise was thus denied to the American leaders who later plunged the United States into war in Vietnam. "The wrong done," journalist Theodore A. White wrote, "was to poke out the eyes and ears of the State Department on Asian affairs, to blind American foreign policy."

**Purge of
the State
Department**

Dulles considered containment too defensive a stance toward communism. He called instead for *liberation*, although he never explained precisely how the countries of Eastern Europe could be freed from Soviet control. *Massive retaliation* was the administration's phrase for the nuclear obliteration of the Soviet state or its assumed client, the People's Republic of China, if either one took aggressive actions. Eisenhower said it "simply means the ability to blow hell out of them in a hurry if they start anything." The ability of the United States to make such a threat was thought to provide *deterrence*, the prevention of hostile Soviet behavior.

In their "New Look" for the American military, Eisenhower and Dulles emphasized airpower and nuclear weaponry. The president's preference for heavy weapons stemmed in part from his desire to trim the federal budget ("More bang for the buck," as the saying went). With its huge military arsenal, the United States in the 1950s practiced *brinkmanship*: not backing down in a crisis, even if it meant taking the nation to the brink of war. Eisenhower also popularized the *domino theory*: small, weak, neighboring nations would fall to communism like a row of dominoes if they were not propped up by the United States.

Eisenhower increasingly utilized the Central Intelligence Agency as an instrument of foreign policy.

Headed by Allen Dulles, brother of the secretary of state, the CIA put foreign leaders on its payroll (such as King Hussein of Jordan), subsidized foreign labor unions and political parties (such as the conservative Liberal Democratic Party of Japan), and planted false stories in newspapers through its "disinformation" projects. The CIA hired American journalists and professors, secretly funded the National Student Association to spur contacts with foreign student leaders, used business executives as "fronts," and conducted experiments on unsuspecting Americans to determine the effects of "mind control" drugs (the MKULTRA program). The CIA also launched covert operations (including assassination schemes) to subvert or destroy governments in the Third World, where new states were emerging from colonialism to nationhood. American leaders declared that revolutionary nationalism in Third World countries threatened United States economic interests and created unstable conditions that communists linked to a Soviet-led international conspiracy could exploit (see Chapter 30).

**CIA
Covert Actions**

The Eisenhower administration also sought to interject American culture into the Soviet Union and its Eastern European allies as a means to popularize democratic principles and to stimulate public discontent with communist regimes. The primary propaganda tool was the United States Information Agency (USIA), founded in 1953. One of the USIA's agencies, Voice of America, broadcast news, editorials, and music worldwide. The CIA secretly funded Radio Free Europe, operated since 1950 by anticommunist Eastern European émigrés headquartered in Munich, West Germany. Radio Liberty, also CIA-subsidized, began in 1951 and beamed incendiary anti-Soviet messages into the "East." The Soviets often jammed such broadcasts, but some got through. Did these broadcasts carry influence? Historians disagree. Some claim that they helped cultivate an anticommunism that eventually undermined pro-Soviet regimes. Others argue that they proved counterproductive because they raised hopes—ultimately false—that the United States would back its propaganda calls for "liberation" with power.

**Propaganda
and Cultural
Infiltration**

The United States and the Soviet Union attempted to regularize cultural relations in January 1958 through an agreement that provided for recip-

On July 22, 1959, in Moscow, the Soviet capital, Vice President Richard M. Nixon (1913–1994) (hands clasped) and Premier Nikita Khrushchev (finger pointing) toured the American National Exhibition, sponsored by the United States Information Agency. When they stopped at this display of a modern American kitchen, Khrushchev doubted Nixon's claim that average American workers owned such appliances. In the "kitchen debate" that followed, the two leaders sparred over comparative national strengths and over whether capitalism or communism best served people's needs. Time-Life Agency © Time Inc..

rocal exchange of radio and television broadcasts, films, students, professors, athletes, and civic groups. One result was Vice President Richard Nixon's trip in July 1959 to Moscow to open an American products fair, where, in the "kitchen debate," he extolled capitalist consumerism in a model six-room ranch-style house, while Soviet premier Nikita Khrushchev touted the merits of communism. Khrushchev followed in September with an eye-opening tour of the United States.

Such expanded cultural relations did not calm the Cold War or tame the nuclear arms race. In November 1952 the United States detonated the first hydrogen bomb. Then, in

Hydrogen Bomb

early 1954, the largest bomb the United States has ever tested destroyed the Pacific island of Bikini. This H-bomb, packing the power of 15 million tons of TNT (750 times as powerful as the atomic bomb that leveled Hiroshima), produced a fallout of radioactive dust that showered a Japanese fishing boat in the area. The crew of the *Lucky Dragon* suffered severe nausea, fever, and blisters. When one of the sailors died, international protest bombarded the United States.

The Soviets tested their first H-bomb in 1953. Four years later they shocked Americans by firing the world's first intercontinental ballistic missile (ICBM) and then propelling *Sputnik* into outer space. Americans felt more vulnerable to air attack and inferior to the Russians in rocket technology. The United States soon tested its own ICBMs. It also enlarged its fleet of long-range bombers (B-52s) and deployed intermediate-range missiles in Europe, targeted against the Soviet Union. By the end of 1960 the United States had added Polaris missile–bearing submarines to its navy. To foster future technological advancement, the National Aeronautics and Space Administration (NASA) was created in 1958.

Missile Development

The CIA's U-2 spy planes collected information demonstrating that the Soviets had deployed very few ICBMs. Yet politically partisan critics charged that Eisenhower had allowed the United States to fall behind in the missile race. The much-publicized "missile gap" was actually not in the Soviets' favor but rather America's. "Everyone knows," air force general Nathan Twining privately told the president, "we already have a [nuclear] stockpile large enough to obliterate the Soviet Union." As the 1950s closed, the United States enjoyed overwhelming strategic dominance because of its air-sea-land "triad" of long-range bombers, submarine-launched ballistic missiles (SLBMs), and ICBMs.

President Eisenhower grew uneasy about the arms race. He feared nuclear war, and the cost of the new weapons made it difficult to balance the budget.

Eisenhower's Critique of Nuclear Arms

In a 1953 speech, the president noted that "every gun that is made, every warship launched, every rocket fired signifies, in the final sense, a theft from those who hunger and are not fed. . . . The cost of one modern heavy bomber is this: a modern brick school in more than 30 cities." He also doubted the need for more and bigger nuclear weapons. How many times, he once asked, "could [you] kill the same man?" Spurred by such thoughts, by citizens' groups such as the Committee for a Sane Nuclear Policy (SANE), founded in 1957, and by neutralist and Soviet appeals, the president cautiously initiated arms control proposals.

Eisenhower's 1953 "atoms for peace" initiative recommended that fissionable materials be contributed to a United Nations agency for use in industrial projects. Two years later, to counter Soviet appeals for disarmament, the Eisenhower administration issued its own propaganda ploy—the "open skies" proposal: aerial surveillance of both Soviet and American military sites to reduce the chances of surprise attacks. In response to worldwide criticism of radioactive fallout, the two powers unilaterally suspended atmospheric testing from 1958 until 1961, when the Soviets resumed it. The United States also began testing again at the same time, but underground. Despite a series of disarmament talks in Geneva, Switzerland, and Eisenhower's meeting there in July 1955 with Stalin's successor Nikita Khrushchev (the first summit meeting in ten years), neither side could agree on bans on nuclear testing or suitable inspection systems to ensure compliance with arms control treaties.

In May 1955, in a rare example of Cold War cooperation, the two great powers ended their ten-year occupation of Austria. But events in Eastern Europe soon revived the customary acrimony of the Cold War. In 1956 Khrushchev called for "peaceful coexistence" between capitalists and communists, denounced

Hungarian Uprising

Precariously balanced on the nuclear warhead of a menacing missile are Soviet premier Nikita Khrushchev (1894–1971) and United States president Dwight D. Eisenhower (1890–1969). In September 1959, Eisenhower hosted Khrushchev in the United States to "melt the ice" of the Cold War. Although the list of outstanding Soviet-American issues was lengthy—including the nuclear arms race and Berlin—their summit meeting did little to ease superpower tensions.

Stalin, and suggested that Moscow would tolerate different brands of communism. Revolts against Soviet power erupted in Poland and Hungary, testing Khrushchev's new permissiveness. After a new Hungarian government in 1956 announced its withdrawal from the Warsaw Pact (the Soviet military alliance formed in 1955 with communist countries of Eastern Europe), Soviet troops and tanks battled students and workers in the streets of Budapest and crushed the rebellion.

Although the Eisenhower administration's propaganda had been encouraging "liberation" efforts and the CIA had been training Eastern European émigrés for paramilitary missions (a program called RED SOX/RED CAP), Eisenhower officials found themselves unable to aid the rebels without igniting a world war. The United States could only welcome Hungarian immigrants in greater numbers than American quota laws allowed. The West could have reaped some propaganda advantage from this display of Soviet brute force had not British, French, and Israeli troops—United States allies—invaded Egypt during the Suez crisis just before the Soviets smashed the Hungarian uprising (see page 894).

Hardly had the turmoil subsided in Eastern Europe when the divided city of Berlin once again became a Cold War flash point. The Soviets railed against the placement in West Germany of American bombers capable of carrying nuclear warheads, and they complained that West Berlin had become an escape route for disaffected East Germans. In 1958, Khrushchev announced that the Soviet Union would recognize East German control of all of Berlin unless the United States and its allies began talks on German reunification and rearmament. The United States refused to give up its hold on West Berlin or to break West German ties with NATO. Khrushchev backed away from his ultimatum but promised to raise the issue at future conferences.

Berlin and Germany were on the agenda of a summit meeting planned for Paris in mid-1960. On May 1, two weeks before the conference, a U-2 spy plane carrying high-powered cameras crashed 1,200 miles inside the Soviet Union. Moscow claimed credit for shooting down the plane, which it put on display along with Francis Gary Powers, the captured CIA pilot, and the pictures he had been snapping of Soviet military sites. Khrushchev demanded an apology for the continued United States violation of Soviet airspace. When Washington refused, the Soviets walked out of the Paris summit.

U-2 Incident

The United States's reconnaisance of the Soviet Union continued, and with far greater sophistication than that provided by the U-2. In August 1960 the CIA's CORONA project saw its first successful mission when a spy satellite circling the globe ejected to earth a film capsule containing photographic coverage of the USSR. CORONA satellites provided data on Soviet missile bases for top-secret intelligence reports to the president.

While sparring over Europe, both sides kept a wary eye on the People's Republic of China, which denounced the Soviet call for peaceful coexistence with the West. Despite evidence of a widening Sino-Soviet split, most American officials still treated communism as a unified world movement. The isolation between Beijing and Washington stymied communication and made continued conflict between China and the United States likely.

Jinmen (Quemoy) and Mazu (Matsu)

In a dispute over Jinmen (Quemoy) and Mazu (Matsu), two tiny islands off the Chinese coast, the United States and the People's Republic of China lurched toward the brink. Jiang used these islands as bases from which to raid the mainland. Communist China's guns bombarded the islands in 1954. Thinking that United States credibility was at stake, Eisenhower decided to defend the outposts; he even hinted that he might use nuclear weapons. Why massive retaliation over such an insignificant issue? "Let's keep the Reds guessing," advised John Foster Dulles. But what if they guessed wrong? critics replied.

Congress passed the Formosa Resolution (1955), authorizing the president to deploy American forces to defend Formosa and adjoining islands, and two years later the United States installed tactical nuclear weapons on Taiwan. Although diplomats from the People's Republic of China and the United States held secret meetings in Geneva and Warsaw, war loomed again in 1958 over Jinmen and Mazu. But this time Washington pressed Jiang to back off, and he promised not to use force against the mainland and withdrew some troops from the islands. China then relaxed its bombardments. One consequence accelerated the arms race: Eisenhower's nuclear threats persuaded the Chinese that they, too, needed nuclear arms. In 1964 China exploded its first nuclear bomb.

As the United States went to the brink with China, it went to the market with Japan, rebuilding Japan with foreign aid as an anticommunist military partner and trader, all the while worrying China, the Soviet Union, and other past victims of Japanese aggression.

"Japanese Miracle"

Huge United States military purchases in Japan during the Korean War and American assistance in developing an export-oriented economy in the 1950s produced what many called the "Japanese miracle"—double-digit economic growth. Japan copied American technology (Motorola, for example, helped start the electronics industry), practiced trade protectionism, and gained a reputation for industrial efficiency and quality control. Before long, Japan became a major economic competitor with the United States.

In eight years of nurturing allies and applying the containment doctrine worldwide, Eisenhower held the line—against the Soviet Union, communist China, neutralism, communism, nationalism, and revolution everywhere. Eisenhower found no way to relax Cold War tensions, and ultimately he accelerated the nuclear arms race he so disliked. Americans feared nuclear holocaust; popular Hollywood films such as *On the Beach* (1959) captured the anxious mood. Even friends of the United States seemed antagonistic; riots against the American military presence in Japan forced Eisenhower to cancel a goodwill trip to that ally in 1960. Also in 1960, during the presidential election, the young Democratic candidate, Senator John F. Kennedy of Massachusetts, went so far as to charge that under Eisenhower's leadership the United States was losing the Cold War.

Kennedy, Johnson, and the Crises of the 1960s

John F. Kennedy's diplomacy owed much to the past. He disparaged the appeasement of the 1930s and praised the containment of the 1940s. An eloquent speaker and fierce competitor, he vowed to rout communism in the 1960s. "Everyone around him thought he had the Midas touch and could not lose," remarked an assistant, historian Arthur M. Schlesinger, Jr. Kennedy appointed a staff of bright, often arrogant "action intellectuals," as journalist Theodore White called them. Adlai Stevenson, an unimpressed United States ambassador to the United Nations, told a friend that "they've got the damnedest bunch of boy commandos running around down there [in Washington] you ever saw." Kennedy's inaugural address suggested no halfway measures: "Let every nation know that we shall pay any price, bear any burden, meet any hardship, support any friend, oppose any foe to assure the survival and the success of liberty."

Kennedy and His Advisers

Khrushchev took up the challenge. Besides endorsing "wars of national liberation" in the Third World, the Soviet Union in the fall of 1961 ended its moratorium on above-ground nuclear testing by exploding a giant 50-megaton bomb. Khrushchev also bragged about Soviet ICBMs, raising American anxiety over Soviet capabilities. Intelligence data soon demonstrated that there was no "missile gap"—except the one in America's favor. Kennedy nonetheless sought to fulfill his campaign commitment to a military buildup based on the principle of *flexible response*: the capability to make any kind of war, from guerrilla combat to nuclear showdown. With this ca-

pability the United States would be able to contain both the Soviet Union and revolutionary movements in the Third World (see Chapter 30).

In 1961 the military budget shot up 15 percent; by mid-1964, United States nuclear weapons had increased by 150 percent. Government advice to citizens to build fallout shelters in their backyards intensified public fear of devastating war. Kennedy inaugurated the Arms Control and Disarmament Agency and signed the Limited Test Ban Treaty with the Soviet Union (1963), which banned nuclear testing in the atmosphere, in outer space, and under water, but his legacy was an accelerated arms race.

Once again, in 1961, the Soviets demanded negotiations to end Western occupation of West Berlin. Calling the city "the great testing place of Western courage and will," Kennedy rejected negotiations and asked Congress for an additional $3.2 billion for defense and the authority to call up reservists. In August 1961 the Soviets, on the urging of the East German regime, erected a concrete and barbed-wire barri-

Berlin Wall

When the East Germans first put up the Berlin Wall in 1961, they hastily constructed it of barbed wire. Later they added concrete blocks to the 28-mile barricade that divided East Berlin (left) and West Berlin (right). The large building with the chariot on top is the Brandenburg Gate. The ugly wall—symbol of the Cold War—came down in 1989, when the long Soviet-American conflict finally waned. Corbis-Bettmann.

cade to halt the exodus of East Germans into the more prosperous and politically free West Berlin. The Berlin Wall inspired protests throughout the noncommunist world, but Kennedy privately sighed that "a wall is a hell of a lot better than a war." The ugly barrier shut off the flow of refugees, and the crisis passed.

United States hostilities with Cuba provoked Kennedy's most serious confrontation with the Soviet Union. Cold War and Third World issues dramatically intersected in Cuba.

The Cuban Revolution

In early 1959 Fidel Castro's rebels, driven by profound anti-American nationalism, had ousted Fulgencio Batista, a long-time United States ally who had welcomed North American investors, United States military advisers, and tourists to the Caribbean island. Batista's corrupt and dictatorial regime had helped turn Havana into a haven for gambling and prostitution run by organized crime.

Cubans had resented United States domination ever since the early twentieth century, when the Platt Amendment was imposed on them (see page 651). Curbing United States influence became a rallying cry of the Cuban Revolution, all the more after the United States conspired secretly but futilely to block Castro's rise to power. From the start Castro sought to roll back the influence of American business, which had invested some $1 billion on the island, and to end United States domination of Cuban trade. His increasing authoritarianism and anti-Yankee declarations alarmed Washington. In early 1960, after Cuba signed a trade treaty with the Soviet Union, Eisenhower ordered the CIA to organize an invasion force of Cuban exiles to overthrow the Castro government. The president also drastically cut United States purchases of Cuban sugar. Castro responded by seizing all North American–owned companies that had not yet been nationalized. Threatened by United States decisions designed to bring him and his revolution down, Castro appealed to the Soviet Union, which offered loans and expanded trade.

Just before leaving office, Eisenhower broke diplomatic relations with Cuba and advised Kennedy to advance plans for the invasion. The scenario sketched by the CIA appealed to Kennedy: Cuban exiles would land and secure a beachhead; the Cuban people would rise up against Castro and welcome a new government brought in from the United States. Because he felt uneasy over such a blatant attempt to topple a sovereign government, Kennedy ordered that the United States's hand be kept hidden. The president never attempted to negotiate Cuban-American troubles with Castro.

Directed by the CIA and escorted by United States warships, some fourteen hundred commandos scrambled ashore at the Bay of Pigs in April 1961. A

Bay of Pigs Invasion

CIA plan to assassinate Castro before the invasion had faltered. The Cuban people did not rise up against Castro. Within two days most of the invaders had been captured by troops loyal to Castro. Although Kennedy refused to order an air strike to aid the invaders when the landing was failing, the operation never had much chance of success. Boats went aground on coral reefs that the CIA had identified as seaweed, and equipment malfunctioned. If the exiles had managed to move inland, they would have faced Castro's large armed militia. Before the operation was over, four Americans had died. As for Castro, the Bay of Pigs invasion helped him remain popular, as did his zealous pursuit of nationalism, land reform, and improvements in healthcare and education. Concluding that the United States would not take defeat well and might launch another invasion, the Cuban leader looked even more toward the Soviet Union for a lifeline.

Kennedy vowed to bring Castro down. His brother, Attorney General Robert Kennedy, promised "to stir things up on the island with espionage, sabotage, [and] general disorder." The CIA soon hatched a project called Operation Mongoose to disrupt the island's trade, support raids on Cuba from Miami, and plot with organized-crime bosses to assassinate Castro. The United States also tightened its economic blockade, engineered Cuba's eviction from the Organization of American States, and undertook military maneuvers that Castro read as threatening. "If I had been in Moscow or Havana at that time," Secretary of Defense Robert McNamara later remarked, "I would have believed the Americans were preparing for an invasion."

Had there been no Bay of Pigs invasion, no Operation Mongoose, no assassination plots, and no program of diplomatic and economic isolation, there probably would have been no Cuban missile crisis because Cuba would have had no urgent need for Soviet military assistance. For Castro, the relentless hostility of the United States represented a real

Cuban Missile Crisis

threat to Cuba's independence. For the Soviets, American actions challenged the only procommunist regime in Latin America. Premier Khrushchev also saw an opportunity to improve the Soviet position in the nuclear arms race. Castro and Khrushchev devised a risky plan to deter any new United States intervention. In mid-1962 they agreed to install in Cuba nuclear-armed missiles capable of hitting the United States. The world soon faced frightening brinkmanship.

In mid-October 1962 a U-2 plane flying over Cuba photographed sites for medium-range missiles. The president immediately organized a special Executive Committee of advisers to find a way to force the missiles and their nuclear warheads out of Cuba. Some members advised a surprise air strike, likely to kill both Soviet technicians and Cubans. The Joint Chiefs of Staff recommended a full-scale military invasion, an option that risked a prolonged war with Cuba, a Soviet attack against West Berlin, or even nuclear holocaust. The Soviet expert Charles Bohlen unsuccessfully urged quiet, direct negotiations with Soviet officials. Secretary of Defense Robert S. McNamara proposed the formula that the president found most acceptable: a naval quarantine of Cuba to prevent further military shipments. Halfway between armed warfare and doing nothing, McNamara's proposal left the administration free to attack or negotiate, depending on the Soviet response.

Kennedy addressed the nation on television on October 22 to demand that the Soviets retreat. United States warships began crisscrossing the Caribbean, while B-52s loaded with nuclear bombs took to the skies. Khrushchev replied that the missiles would be withdrawn if Washington pledged never to attack Cuba. And he added that American Jupiter missiles aimed at the Soviet Union must be removed from Turkey. Edgy advisers predicted war, but on October 28 came a Soviet-American compromise. The United States promised to respect Cuban sovereignty and to withdraw the Jupiters from Turkey in exchange for the withdrawal of Soviet offensive forces from Cuba. Technicians soon dismantled the missiles for shipment back to the Soviet Union. Khrushchev had "shitted in his pants," recalled a Soviet official. "I cut his balls off," Kennedy privately crowed to friends. Forcing the Soviets to back down, many said, was John F. Kennedy's finest hour.

Critics then and now have raised questions about Kennedy's responsibility for and handling of the Cuban missile crisis. Would the crisis have occurred at all if Kennedy had not been hell-bent on overthrowing the Castro regime and expunging the Cuban Revolution from the Western Hemisphere? Should not the president at the start have initiated quiet negotiations rather than practiced dangerous brinkmanship?

Questions About Kennedy's Crisis Management

Hardly an exemplary model of crisis management, Kennedy's handling of the crisis courted disaster. Accidents, near misses, and inadequate information caused events to come close to spinning out of control. On October 27, for example, a Soviet commander shot down a U-2 plane over Cuba. The Americans prepared to retaliate, not knowing that Soviet commanders had tactical nuclear weapons to use against an invasion. Robert Kennedy himself feared "a chain reaction will quickly start that will be very hard to stop." That same day, a United States jet mistakenly crossed into Soviet territory, nearly setting off an air war. Finally, critics have argued that the strategic balance of power was not seriously altered by the missiles in Cuba; the United States still enjoyed a tremendous advantage over the Soviets in the nuclear arms race. Did Kennedy risk doomsday unnecessarily?

The Cuban missile crisis did produce some relaxation in Soviet-American relations. In August 1963, the adversaries signed a treaty banning nuclear tests in the atmosphere, and they installed a Teletype "hot line" staffed around the clock by translators and technicians. They also refrained from further confrontation in Berlin. In June 1963 Kennedy had spoken at American University in conciliatory terms, urging cautious Soviet-American steps toward disarmament. In the aftermath of the missile crisis, some analysts predicted a thaw in the Cold War, but the assassination of President Kennedy in November left unresolved the question of whether he was shedding his strong Cold War views.

Kennedy's successor, Lyndon B. Johnson, held firmly to ideas about United States superiority, the menace of communism, and the necessity of global intervention. He saw the world in simple terms—them against us. Often exaggerating and sometimes lying, he created what became known as a credibility gap. The general problem, said Senator J. William Fulbright of Arkansas, chair of the Foreign

Johnson and the Cold War

How do historians know that, at the outset of the Cuban missile crisis, President John F. Kennedy seemed to downgrade diplomacy in favor of military action to force the Soviet missiles from Cuba? Months before that dangerous October 1962 crisis, Kennedy had ordered the Secret Service to install an audiotape system to record meetings in the Oval Office and the Cabinet Room. The system recorded its first meeting on July 30, 1962. A Dictabelt system for recording telephone conversations was installed later, in early September. Secretary of State Dean Rusk (with the window behind him to Kennedy's right) and Secretary of Defense Robert McNamara (with the flag behind him to Kennedy's left) did not know that their remarks were being taped. Only a few members of the presidential staff knew about the secret system. Whether Kennedy wanted the recordings because he sought an accurate record for the memoirs he intended to write or because he hoped to protect himself against public misrepresen-

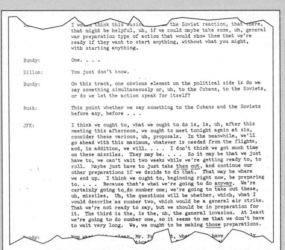

tations of what he said to others in private, he left historians a rich source on high-level decision making in the White House: 127 audiotapes (248 hours) and 73 Dictabelts (12 hours) on wide-ranging foreign and domestic topics.

During the missile crisis of October 1962, President Kennedy regularly convened and taped meetings of an advisory Executive Committee, shown gathered here. Also shown below is an excerpt from the transcript of the very first Executive Committee meeting, 11:50 A.M. to 12:57 P.M., October 16, 1962. The John F. Kennedy presidential library in Boston has declassified many of the recordings and has made them available to researchers. Because of such tapes (some of Kennedy's predecessors and successors also made recordings), historians can study the minute-by-minute, hour-by-hour handling of significant issues, in this case a crisis that brought the Soviet Union and the United States to the nuclear brink. John F. Kennedy Library.

Relations Committee, was that both Johnson and the American people suffered from an "arrogance of power."

Although Johnson improved Soviet-American relations somewhat by meeting with Soviet Premier Alexei Kosygin at Glassboro State College in New Jersey in 1967 and by pushing for the nonproliferation treaty to curb the spread of nuclear weapons in 1968, the Cold War hardly relented. The Soviets—having vowed to catch up with the United States after the Cuban missile crisis—reached nuclear parity with the United States by the end of the decade. Their invasion of Czechoslovakia in 1968 to stymie a nationalist movement caused Johnson to shelve further arms control talks. Meanwhile, Johnson had become preoccupied by the war in Southeast Asia. With the Soviet Union and the United States backing opposing forces in the Vietnam War, opportunities for relaxing the Cold War seemed to diminish (see Chapter 30).

 ## Nixon, Kissinger, and Détente

Richard M. Nixon had been an ardent Cold Warrior as a member of Congress, senator, and vice president, and few observers expected him to produce a thaw in the Cold War during his presidency. Yet he did so dramatically with the assistance of Henry A. Kissinger, a German-born political scientist from Harvard University. Kissinger served as Nixon's national security adviser until 1973, when he became secretary of state. Ambitious, witty, knowledgeable, and egotistical, Kissinger was a formidable negotiator who sought the limelight. He selectively leaked secret information to journalists; he plotted to unseat foreign governments through secret operations, as in Chile (see page 910); he endorsed the sale of massive arms to dictators such as the shah of Iran; and he had his own staff wiretapped.

Nixon and Kissinger pursued a grand strategy designed to promote a global balance of power. The first part of the strategy was *détente:* measured cooperation with the Soviets through negotiations within a general environment of rivalry. Détente's primary purpose, like that of the containment doctrine it resembled, was to check Soviet expansion and limit the Soviet arms buildup. The second part of the strategy sought to curb revolution and radicalism in the

The Pursuit of Détente

Third World so as to quash threats to American interests. The grand design seemed attractive to its architects: the Cold War and limited wars such as in Vietnam were costing too much, and more trade with a friendlier Soviet Union might reduce the huge United States balance-of-payments deficit. Critics faulted the Nixon-Kissinger posture for its assumption that the United States had the right and the ability to manipulate a disorderly world.

Nixon and Kissinger pursued détente with extraordinary energy and fanfare. They expanded trade relations with the Soviet Union; a 1972 deal sent $1 billion worth of American grain to the Soviets at bargain prices. To slow the costly arms race, they initiated the Strategic Arms Limitations Talks (SALT). In 1972 Soviet and American negotiators produced the SALT-I Treaty, which limited antiballistic missile (ABM) systems. (By making offensive missiles less vulnerable to attack, these defensive systems had accelerated the arms race because both sides built more missiles to overcome the ABM protection.) A second agreement imposed a five-year freeze on the number of offensive nuclear missiles each side could possess. At the time of the agreement the Soviets held an advantage in total strategic forces (ICBMs, SLBMs, and long-range bombers)—2,547 to 2,160. But the United States had more warheads per missile because it could outfit each missile with MIRVs (multiple independently targeted reentry vehicles) that could send warheads to several different targets. In short, the United States had a two-to-one advantage in deliverable warheads (5,700 to 2,500). Because SALT did not restrict MIRVs, the nuclear arms buildup actually continued.

SALT

In 1975, at the Conference on Security and Cooperation in Helsinki, Finland, the United States, Canada, and most of the nations of Europe signed several accords that accepted the permanence of existing European boundaries, including adjustments made in Germany and Eastern Europe three decades earlier; they also applauded détente and endorsed human rights for all. Conservatives in the United States excoriated Gerald Ford's administration (which had replaced Nixon's in August 1974) for a sellout to the Soviets, but dozens of "Helsinki groups," including Solidarity in Poland and Charter 77 in Czechoslovakia, sprang up to press communist regimes to honor the human-rights pledge.

Helsinki Accords

During his dramatic trip to the People's Republic of China in February 1972, President Richard M. Nixon (left) and his wife Patricia toured the Great Wall, a 1,500-mile structure first built about 210 B.C.E. as a defensive barrier against invaders. Rebuilt in later centuries, the wall also served as a communications link for the vast country. Nixon's visit to China ended more than two decades of Sino-American hostility and opened an era of détente. Nixon Presidential Materials Project.

While cultivating détente with the Soviet Union, the United States also sought to end almost three decades of Sino-American hostility. The Chinese welcomed the change because they wanted to improve trade and hoped that friendlier Sino-American relations would make their enemy, the Soviet Union, more cautious. Nixon reasoned the same way: "We're using the Chinese thaw to get the Russians shook." In early 1972 Nixon made a historic trip to "Red China," where he and the venerable Chinese leaders Mao Zedong and Zhou Enlai agreed to disagree on a number of issues, except one: the

Opening to China

Soviet Union should not be permitted to make gains in Asia. Official diplomatic recognition and the exchange of ambassadors followed in 1979.

Like disputes in the Middle East, Latin America, and Africa (see Chapter 30), global economic instability bedeviled the Nixon-Kissinger grand design. The worldwide recession early in the 1970s was the worst since the 1930s. Inflation and high oil prices pinched rich and poor nations alike. Protectionist tendencies raised tariffs and impeded world trade. And the debt-ridden developing nations of the Third World—sometimes called the "South"—insisted that the wealthier, industrial "North" share economic resources. The gulf between rich and poor nations threatened world peace. The United States could not escape these problems. It began to suffer a trade deficit—importing more goods than it exported (see figure, page 871). A "dollar glut" abroad threatened to drain the United States's supply of gold. Nixon devalued the dollar and suspended its convertibility into gold and imposed a surtax on imports. But America's slippage in the international economy did not abate.

International Economic Instability

Americans nonetheless remained the richest people in the world. The United States produced about one-third of the world's goods and services. Coca-Cola, Exxon, and many other American companies earned more than half of their profits abroad. One-fourth of agricultural sales came from exports; one out of every nine manufacturing jobs depended on exports. The economy of the United States also depended on imports of strategic raw materials: three-fourths of the tin consumed in the United States and more than 95 percent of the manganese came from abroad. Such ties, as well as American investments abroad totaling more than $133 billion in the mid-1970s, explain in part why the United States welcomed détente as a means to calm international relations and protect the American stake in the world economy.

 Carter and a Reinvigorated Cold War

President Jimmy Carter promised fresh initiatives and diplomatic activism when he took office in 1977. He asked Americans to put their "inordinate fear of

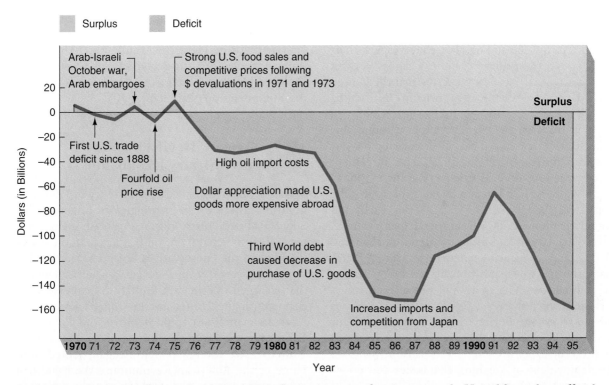

United States Trade Balance, 1970–1995 *Importing more than it exports, the United States has suffered trade deficits for years. Foreign political and economic crises and growing competition from Japanese products in the American marketplace have weakened the United States's position in the world economy. Trade deficits must be financed by borrowing. One result has been a mounting United States external debt.* Source: U.S. Department of State.

Jimmy Carter's Goals

Communism" behind them so that they could attend to North-South issues. With reformist zeal, Carter vowed to reduce the American military presence overseas (by getting NATO countries to increase their defense spending), to cut back arms sales (which had reached unprecedented heights under Nixon), and to slow the nuclear arms race (by spurring a new round of Strategic Arms Limitation Talks). He also promised preventive diplomacy: advancing the peace process in the Middle East, mediating conflict in the Third World, and creating worldwide economic stability through agreements on the law of the sea, energy, and clean air and water. A deeply religious man, Carter said he intended to infuse international relations with moral force. "The soul of our foreign policy," he declared, would be the championing of individual human rights abroad—the freedom to vote, worship, travel, speak out, and get a fair trial.

Carter spoke and acted inconsistently, in part because in the post-Vietnam years no consensus existed in foreign policy and in part because his advisers squabbled among themselves. One source of the problem was the stern-faced Zbigniew Brzezinski, a Polish-born political scientist who became Carter's national security adviser. An old-fashioned Cold Warrior, Brzezinski viewed foreign crises in globalist terms—that is, he blamed them on the Soviet Union. Carter gradually listened more to Brzezinski than to Secretary of State Cyrus Vance, an experienced public servant who advocated quiet diplomacy to find avenues toward Soviet-American cooperation. Vocal neoconservative intellectuals such as Norman Podhoretz, editor of *Commentary* magazine, and the Committee on the Present Danger, founded in 1976 by Cold War hawks such as Paul Nitze, who had composed NSC-68 in 1950, criticized Carter for any relaxation of the Cold War and demanded that he jettison détente.

Under Carter, détente deteriorated and the Cold War deepened. The president at first angered the Soviets by demanding that they respect their citizens' human rights. Soviet leaders protested that the United States was playing its "China card"—building up China in order to threaten the Soviet Union. Despite this rocky start, a new treaty, SALT-II, codified Soviet-American nuclear parity in 1979. The agreement placed a ceiling of 2,250 delivery vehicles (long-range bombers, ICBMs, and SLBMs) on each side, capped MIRVed launchers at 1,200 for each, and limited the number of warheads per delivery vehicle. The Soviet Union had to dismantle more than 250 existing delivery vehicles, whereas the United States was permitted to expand from its existing 2,060 to the new ceiling. The treaty did not affect nuclear warheads, which stood at 9,200 for the United States and 5,000 for the Soviet Union. To win votes for the treaty from skeptical conservatives, Carter announced an expensive military expansion program and deployment of Pershing II missiles and cruise missiles in NATO countries.

SALT-II

As Senate ratification of SALT-II stalled and Moscow fumed over the Pershings, events in Afghanistan led to Soviet-American confrontation. In late 1979 the Red Army bludgeoned its way into Afghanistan to shore up a faltering communist government under siege by Muslim rebels. Carter shelved SALT-II (the two powers nonetheless unilaterally honored its terms later), suspended shipments of grain and high-technology equipment to the Soviet Union, and initiated an international boycott of the 1980 Summer Olympics in Moscow. The Soviets refused to withdraw their forces from Afghanistan.

The president also announced the *Carter Doctrine*: the United States would intervene, unilaterally and militarily if necessary, should Soviet aggression threaten the petroleum-rich Persian Gulf. George F. Kennan called Carter's reaction exaggerated and wrongheaded in assuming that the Soviets would attack elsewhere in the Middle East. Kennan noted that in Afghanistan the Soviet Union was dealing with a local crisis in a strategically important client state on its southern border, not with the entire Gulf region. He faulted Carter for not trying diplomacy first.

Carter Doctrine

Carter lost the 1980 election to Ronald Reagan amid charges that the president had contradicted many of his own goals and had diminished United States power in the world. Carter had earned some diplomatic successes in the Middle East, Africa, and Latin America, but the revived Cold War and the prolonged Iranian hostage crisis had politically hurt the administration (see Chapter 30).

 ## Reagan, Devil Theory, and Military Expansion

Ronald Reagan assumed the presidency in 1981 with no firm grasp of world issues, history, or geography. Superficial and often mistaken about elementary facts, Reagan acted more on instinct than on analysis. He and the conservatives he appointed, including Secretary of State George P. Shultz, believed that enlarged free-market capitalism (expressed, for example, in the United States–Canada Free Trade Agreement of 1988) could help win the Cold War. Expressing the evangelical message so common in United States foreign policy, Reagan quoted Tom Paine of the American Revolution: "We have it in our power to begin the world over again." Reagan also embraced a devil theory: A malevolent Soviet Union, the "evil empire," would "commit any crime," "lie," and "cheat" to achieve a communist world. He attributed Third World disorders to Soviet intrigue as well, rejecting arguments that the civil wars in Central America and elsewhere derived not from Soviet meddling but from deep-seated economic instability, poverty, and class oppression.

Reagan asserted that a substantial military buildup would thwart the Soviet threat and intimidate Moscow, whose defense spending he claimed was greater than that of the United States. Tainted CIA reports overestimating Soviet military strength—tainted because some of the information came from double agents working for the Soviet secret service (the KGB), as the Aldrich Ames spy scandal revealed in the 1990s—reassured the president that he was on the right track. Reagan launched the largest peacetime arms buildup in American history, driving up the federal debt. In 1985, when the military budget hit $294.7 billion (a doubling since 1980), the Pentagon was spending an average of $28 million an hour.

Reagan's Military Expansion

Assigning low priority to arms control talks, in 1983 Reagan announced development of an antimissile defense system in space; he called it the Strategic Defense Initiative (SDI) or "Star Wars." As the veteran diplomat George Ball observed when United States forces overthrew a leftist, pro-Cuban government on the tiny Caribbean island of Grenada in 1983, once again "we shiver in the icy winds of the Cold War."

In 1985 the president declared the *Reagan Doctrine*: the United States will openly support anticommunist movements—"freedom fighters"—wherever they are battling the Soviets or Soviet-backed governments.

Reagan Doctrine Under this doctrine, the CIA funneled aid to insurgents in Afghanistan, Nicaragua, Angola, and Ethiopia. In open defiance of the sovereignty of those nations, Reagan worked to overthrow governments he deemed hostile to the interests of the United States (see Chapter 30).

Reagan's first decision affecting the Soviets was actually friendly. Fulfilling a campaign pledge to help American farmers, in 1981 he lifted the grain embargo that Carter had imposed after the Soviet invasion of Afghanistan, and he sold the Soviet Union grain worth $3 billion. But bitter hostility soon followed when the Soviets cracked down on the Solidarity labor movement in Poland. In response, Washington placed restrictions on Soviet-American trade and hurled angry words at Moscow. In 1983, Reagan restricted commercial flights to the Soviet Union after a Soviet fighter pilot mistakenly shot down a South Korean commercial jet that had strayed some 300 miles off-course into Soviet airspace. The world was shocked by the death of 269 passengers, and Reagan exploited the tragedy to score Cold War points.

Reagan's expansion of the military, his careless utterances about winning a limited nuclear war, and his quest for nuclear supremacy stimulated worldwide debate. In 1981 hundreds of thousands of marchers in London, Rome, Bonn, and other European cities demanded Soviet-American negotiations to prevent a nuclear holocaust. Evangelist Billy Graham joined peace groups and politicians in appeals for a freeze in the nuclear arms race. In the largest peaceful protest in American history, a million people marched through New York City in June 1982 to support a freeze. Towns across the nation and the House of Representatives passed

Debate over Nuclear Weapons

resolutions to freeze the development, production, and deployment of new weapons. Roman Catholic bishops in the United States issued a pastoral letter in 1983 condemning nuclear weapons as "immoral" and urging an end to the arms race, "which robs the poor and the vulnerable." Meanwhile, scientists described the "nuclear winter" that would follow a nuclear war: the earth, cut off from the sun's rays, would turn cold, and food sources would disappear.

In 1982 Reagan substituted the Strategic Arms Reduction Talks (START) for the inactive SALT talks. At the 1985 Geneva summit meeting, Reagan and the new Soviet leader Mikhail S. Gorbachev agreed in principle that strategic weapons should be substantially reduced, and at the 1986 Reykjavik, Iceland, meeting they came very close to a major reduction agreement. SDI, however, continued to block an accord: Gorbachev insisted that the "Star Wars" project be shelved, and Reagan refused to part with it despite widespread scientific opinion that it would cost billions of dollars and never work. But Reagan and "Gorby" warmed toward one another, and the American president toned down his strident anti-Soviet rhetoric in the late 1980s.

Near the end of Reagan's presidency, as the Iran-contra scandal rocked his administration and United States intervention in Central America faltered (see Chapter 30), Soviet-American relations markedly improved. The turnaround stemmed more from changes abroad than from Reagan's decisions. As Reagan said near the end of his presidency, he had been "dropped into a grand historical moment." Under Gorbachev, a younger generation of Soviet leaders came to power in 1985. They began to restructure and modernize the highly bureaucratized, decaying economy (a reform program called *perestroika*) and to liberalize the authoritarian political system (a reform program called *glasnost*). For these reforms to work, Soviet military expenditures had to be reduced and foreign aid decreased.

Mikhail S. Gorbachev's Reforms

In 1987 Gorbachev and Reagan signed a treaty banning all land-based intermediate-range nuclear missiles in Europe (the INF Treaty). Soon began the destruction of 2,800 missiles, including Soviet SS-20s targeted at Western Europe and NATO Pershing and cruise missiles aimed at the Soviet Union. Gorbachev also unilaterally reduced his nation's armed forces and helped settle regional conflicts. In

In one of several summit meetings, top Soviet leader Mikhail Gorbachev (b. 1932) and President Ronald Reagan (b. 1911) met in Moscow in May 1988 in hopes of signing a Strategic Arms Reduction Talks agreement. The "chemistry" of warm friendship that Reagan later claimed characterized his personal relationship with Gorbachev fell short of producing cuts in dangerous strategic weapons. But their cordial interaction encouraged the diplomatic dialogue that helped end the Cold War.   Ronald Reagan Presidential Library.

1989 Soviet troops departed Afghanistan. "Who would have thought that the warmth of that fireplace in Geneva [in 1985] would melt the ice of the Cold War?" Reagan once remarked to Gorbachev. The American president seemed as surprised as anybody.

Bush, Clinton, and the End of the Cold War

George Bush entered the White House in 1989 with solid Cold War experience as director of the CIA, ambassador to China, and vice president. A cautious conservative, Bush seemed to have few long-range foreign policy goals. He and Secretary of State James Baker, finding it difficult to imagine a world without communism, became, in the words of one analyst, "orphans of containment" when the Soviet

Union collapsed and communism lost favor around the world.

Gorbachev had set loose cascading changes in his own country, but he also had encouraged the people of East Germany and Eastern Europe to go their own ways. No longer would Moscow prop up unpopular communist regimes. In 1989 East Germans startled the world by repudiating their communist government, and in November joyful Germans scaled the Berlin Wall to dance atop it and then tore it down. The next year the two Germanys reunited and veteran communist oligarchs fell—in Poland, Hungary, Czechoslovakia, and Romania. Bulgaria and Albania soon held elections.

Meanwhile, the Union of Soviet Socialist Republics itself was unraveling (see map, page 875). In

Communist Regimes Collapse in Eastern Europe

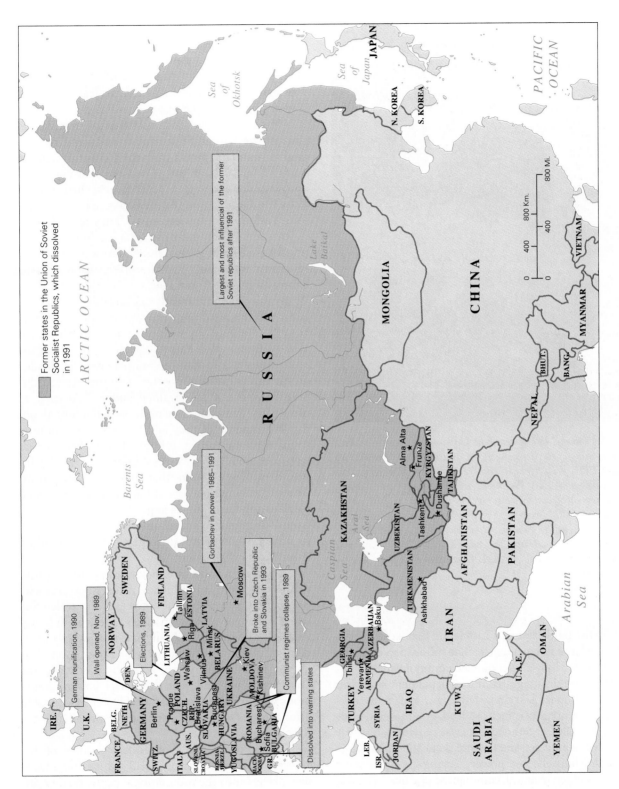

Former states in the Union of Soviet Socialist Republics, which dissolved in 1991

ARCTIC OCEAN

Largest and most influencial of the former Soviet republics after 1991

RUSSIA

Sea of Okhotsk

JAPAN

Sea of Japan

N. KOREA

S. KOREA

PACIFIC OCEAN

MONGOLIA

CHINA

VIETNAM

MYANMAR

Lake Baikal

800 Mi.

800 Km.

400

400

0

0

NEPAL

BHUT.

BANG.

Barents Sea

Gorbachev in power, 1985–1991

Moscow

Alma Alta

Frunze

KYRGYZSTAN

TAJIKISTAN

KAZAKHSTAN

Aral Sea

Dushanbe

Tashkent

UZBEKISTAN

AFGHANISTAN

PAKISTAN

Broke into Czech Republic and Slovakia in 1993

Communist regimes collapse, 1989

Caspian Sea

TURKMENISTAN

Ashkhabad

IRAN

Arabian Sea

SWEDEN

FINLAND

Tallinn

ESTONIA

Riga

LATVIA

Minsk

BELARUS

German reunification, 1990

Wall opened, Nov. 1989

Elections, 1989

NORWAY

DEN.

LITHUANIA

Warsaw

Vilnius

Kiev

UKRAINE

MOLDOVA

Kishinev

GEORGIA

Tbilisi

Yerevan

ARMENIA

AZERBAIJAN

Baku

TURKEY

Dissolved into warring states

IRE.

U.K.

BELG.

NETH.

GERMANY

Berlin

Prague

POLAND

CZECH REP.

Bratislava

SLOVAKIA

Budapest

HUNGARY

ROMANIA

Bucharest

SYRIA

LEB.

ISR.

JORDAN

IRAQ

KUW.

U.A.E.

OMAN

SAUDI ARABIA

YEMEN

FRANCE

SWITZ.

AUS.

ITALY

SLOVENIA

CROATIA

BOSNIA-HERZE.

YUGOSLAVIA

MAC.

ALBANIA

GR.

Sofia

BULGARIA

The End of the Cold War in Europe   *When Mikhail Gorbachev came to power in the Soviet Union in 1985, he initiated reforms that ultimately undermined the communist regimes in Eastern Europe and East Germany and led to the breakup of the Soviet Union itself, ensuring an end to the Cold War.*

In November 1989, a new East German government ordered the opening of the Berlin Wall—a symbol of Cold War division since 1961. West Berliners climbed atop the wall, cheering and dancing, and East Berliners rushed through once heavily guarded checkpoints. Some revelers scratched graffiti on the breached wall: "Freiheit" (freedom). In this photograph, an East Berlin border guard hands a flower back to West Berliners who had come to celebrate the end of an era. The following year the two Berlins and the two Germanys reunited. Corbis-Bettmann.

1990 the Baltic states of Lithuania, Latvia, and Estonia declared independence. The following year, after Gorbachev himself denounced communism, the Soviet Union disintegrated into independent successor states—Russia, Ukraine, Tajikistan, and many others. With no government to lead, and muscled aside by reformers who thought he was moving too slowly toward democracy and free-market economics, Gorbachev himself lost power. Trying to understand these sudden changes, commented one observer, was like trying to paint a speeding train.

One conclusion became clear. The breakup of the Soviet empire, the dismantling of the Warsaw Pact, the repudiation of communism by its own leaders, the shattering of the myth of monolithic communism, the reunification of Germany on October 2, 1990, and the significant reduction in the risk of nuclear war signaled the end of the Cold War. The mammoth glacier had receded, leaving an unsettled world in search of a new order.

The Cold War ended because of the relative decline of the United States and the Soviet Union in the international system from the 1950s through the 1980s. The Cold War ended because the contest had undermined the power of its two major protagonists. They moved gradually toward a cautious cooperation whose urgent goals were the restoration of their economic well-being and the preservation of their diminishing global positions.

Why the Cold War Ended

Four influential trends explain this gradual decline and the resulting attractions of détente. First was the burgeoning economic cost of the Cold War—trillions of dollars spent on weapons and interventions rather than on improvements in the domestic infrastructure. Foreign ventures starved domestic programs and strained budgets. As early as the 1950s President Eisenhower had pointed out that the expense of the Cold War was undermining sound economic policy at home. In the 1960s Americans debated "guns versus butter." In the 1970s, President Nixon, aware that Americans had grown weary of paying the costs of the Cold War, appealed to allies for "burden-sharing." In the 1980s, as the Cold War began to wane, Americans looked eagerly to a "peace dividend" to solve a host of domestic woes. So did the Soviets.

Challenges to the two major powers from within their own spheres of influence also help explain why the United States and the Soviet Union welcomed détente. Cuba's revolution and France's withdrawal from NATO in the 1960s are but two pieces of evidence that the United States was losing power. The uprisings in Hungary and Czechoslovakia and the Sino-Soviet rift undercut the Soviet Union's hegemony within its network of allies. Détente seemed to offer a means to restore great-power management of unruly states.

Third, the Cold War ended because of the emergence of the Third World, which introduced new players into the international game, further diffused power, and eroded bipolarism (see Chapter 30). Soviet-American détente represented a means to deal with the volatile Third World, a fulcrum by which to apply leverage to Third World nations. Fi-

"CONGRATULATIONS....YOU WON THE COLD WAR!"

The veteran cartoonist Jim Borgmann captured the complexity of what many declared a simple matter: American triumph in the Cold War. Borgman reminded his readers that the Cold War had cost the United States itself a great deal—neglect of its domestic problems, including economic malaise, deteriorating infrastructure, unemployment, and millions of people defined by the United States government as poor and homeless. Given the domestic crisis, some analysts argue, it is difficult to claim that either side won the Cold War. Jim Borgmann for the *Cincinnati Enquirer.* Reprinted with special permission of King Features Syndicate.

nally, the worldwide antinuclear movement of the 1980s pressed leaders, especially in western Europe, to seek détente in order to stop the arms race.

These four elements—economic burden, challenges from sphere members, the rise of the Third World, and the antinuclear movement—combined to weaken the standing of the two adversaries and ultimately to persuade them to halt their nations' decline by ending the Cold War. Gorbachev emerged as the primary agent for change, and Reagan and Bush eventually reacted favorably. The Soviet Union fell much harder than the United States, and Americans crowed that they had won the Cold War. But the contest had no winners. Both sides—and all the peoples of the world—paid an enormous price for the waging of the Cold War.

Critics known as declinists spotlighted a fundamental characteristic of the Cold War: large military spending came at the expense of domestic development. According to historian Paul Kennedy's *The Rise and Fall of the Great Powers* (1987), one of the bestselling books in the United States in the late 1980s and early 1990s, the United States suffered from "imperial overstretch." Kennedy argued that the United States, like Spain and Great Britain in earlier centuries, would continue to see American power erode unless it restored the nation's productive vitality and international marketplace competitiveness, reduced its huge federal debt, and improved its educational system. One way to stem economic decline, argued declinists, was to curb America's global interventionism. President Bush dismissed the declinists as "gloomsayers." He and others envisioned the United States as the supreme power in a unipolar world.

Declinists

When the Cold War ended, Bush struggled futilely to explain the dimensions or shape the agenda of a new world order. His administration sustained a large defense budget and continued to use military force abroad (especially in the Persian Gulf War of 1990–1991)—signaling that United States interventionist policies toward the Third World had hardly changed with the end of the Cold War (see Chapter 30). But in mid-1991 the Soviet Union and the United States signed the START-I Treaty to reduce each's nuclear warheads to 6,000 and each's strategic delivery systems to 1,600. In late 1992, Bush signed a START-II agreement with Russia's president Boris Yeltsin, who had ousted Gorbachev. This accord provided for the reduction of warheads to about 3,000 each by the year 2003 and the elimination of land-based intercontinental ballistic missiles (ICBMs) with more than one warhead, leaving each side with about 500 ICBMs.

START Treaties

The Bush administration negotiated the North American Free Trade Agreement (NAFTA) with Canada and Mexico. Signed in late 1992, the pact defined tariff-free trade among the three nations—the world's largest free-trade bloc. Critics claimed that the agreement would cost many United States workers their jobs because corporations would move south to exploit less expensive Mexican labor and minimal environmental controls. The Clinton administration nonetheless lobbied NAFTA through Congress in 1993; the agreement became operative the following year. In 1994, moreover, Congress approved United States membership in the new World Trade Organization, which replaced the General Agreement on Tariffs and Trade as the main body overseeing international trade and settling disputes.

NAFTA and Trade Issues

Trade issues lay at the center of tense United States–Japanese relations in the 1980s and 1990s. Most nettlesome was the huge trade deficit in Japan's favor (about $50 billion in 1989). Japanese products flooded American stores and won customers who appreciated their price and quality. The bestselling car in the United States in 1989 was the Honda Accord (many of which were assembled by American workers in the United States). In 1990 the world's ten largest banks were all in Japan, as were seven of the world's largest

Tense Japanese-American Relations

public companies (ranked by market value). "Some might say the Cold War had indeed ended," observed Chalmers Johnson of the University of California, "and the Japanese won."

American manufacturers complained that Japan's tariffs, cartels, and government subsidies made it difficult for American goods to penetrate Japanese markets. The Japanese countered that obsolete equipment, poor education, and inadequate spending on research and development undercut United States competitiveness. Protectionists championed "Buy American" campaigns. Auto workers in Michigan practiced "Japan-bashing," blaming Americans' woes on the Japanese. Trade talks with Japan proved acrimonious and produced small gains, but both nations knew that their economies were too interdependent for one to punish or isolate the other.

Relations took a negative turn in 1995 after three American servicemen stationed in Okinawa raped a twelve-year-old girl; they were convicted the following year. Okinawans voted by a 10-to-1 margin in a referendum to reduce the United States's military presence on the southern Japanese island, but Toyko chose not to break its military ties with Washington.

Elsewhere in Asia, Sino-American relations became rocky in June 1989, when Chinese armed forces stormed into Beijing's Tiananmen Square. They slaughtered hundreds—perhaps thousands—of unarmed students and other citizens who for weeks had been holding peaceful prodemocracy rallies. China's leader Deng Xiaoping, who had been moving his populous nation toward economic but not political liberalization, crushed the prodemocracy movement. Bush officials initially expressed revulsion, but their response gradually became muted. They believed that America's global security and trade needs required friendly Sino-American ties. In 1994, when granting China most-favored-nation trading status, President Bill Clinton stated that the United States henceforth would decouple trade and human-rights issues.

Tiananmen Square Massacre

Clinton had said little about foreign affairs during his successful 1992 campaign against Bush, and when the former Rhodes scholar and Arkansas governor took office, he said his first priority had to be domestic policy. But he and his secretary of state, the veteran diplomat Warren Christopher (replaced by

Clinton Administration

When President Bill Clinton (b.1946) decided in 1995 to send United States troops into the former Yugoslav republic of Bosnia to enforce a peace accord among warring parties, critics reminded him that he had earlier opposed America's participation in the Vietnam War and that he should be vigilant against another long-term American military commitment. © Tribune Media Services. All rights reserved. Reprinted with permission.

Madeleine Albright in 1997), soon had to deal with the highly volatile, multipolar world of the post–Cold War era. They sustained a large military budget ($256.6 billion for 1996), in part because defense spending served as a federal jobs program. They oversaw a changing CIA, which increasingly practiced economic espionage on the business activities and weapons contracts of other nations and on the destabilizing political effects of rapid population growth, soil erosion, and famine. The promotion of free-market trade and democracy abroad became Clinton goals. The administration patiently moved adversaries toward significant agreements in the Middle East peace process (see Chapter 30).

One consequence of the end of the Cold War in Europe proved savage: ethnic wars in the former Yugoslavia, where, beginning in 1991, Bosnian Muslims, Bosnian Serbs, and Croats killed one another, taking 250,000 lives. Clinton talked tough against Serbian aggression and atrocities in Bosnia-Herzegovina, especially the Serbs' cruel "ethnic cleansing" of Muslims through massacres and rape camps. On occasion he ordered United States airpower to strike Serb positions that threatened vulnerable civilian populations, as in historic Sarajevo. United Nations peacekeeping troops

Bosnia

failed to halt the bloodshed, and Clinton hesitated to commit major United States forces. But in late 1995, after American diplomats brokered an agreement in Dayton, Ohio, among the belligerents for a new multiethnic state in Bosnia, Clinton offered some twenty thousand ground troops to a NATO Implementation Force. American ideals, declared Clinton, had won the Cold War and were being tested in Bosnia. The president denounced an "isolationist backlash" and appealed for United States leadership as the world's "best peacemaker."

Critics challenged the president's case for intervention. With the Cold War over, could and should the United States continue the practice of nation building and policing so common during the previous fifty years? The cost of the Bosnian operation—some $2 billion—seemed expensive just when the administration and Republican Congress were making substantial budgetary cuts in domestic programs (see Chapter 33). "If we've got troops looking for somewhere to help," said a nurse in a high-crime district of St. Louis, "send them in here." One professor of international studies charged that Clinton was dangerously turning American foreign policy into "a branch of social work," seeking to implant American values in areas not vital to the national interest. In contrast, a Missouri trucker saw a moral

To satisfy nuclear arms reduction treaties they had signed, the United States and the Soviet Union had to destroy many existing missiles. Here, in 1995, American secretary of defense William Perry (left) and Russian minister of defense Pavel Grachev initiate the destruction of a Minuteman II missile silo in a Missouri cornfield—one more sign that the Cold War had ended. October 28, 1995, Wide World Photos.

duty for the United States: "You think of the pictures of those poor people, lying in the street, some of them kids, raped, tortured, murdered. That's pretty hard to turn away from."

While Clinton struggled with Bosnia, the global agenda remained crowded with long-term issues. Arms sales, including surface-to-surface missiles, accelerated across the post–Cold War world. In 1993 the United States accounted for 73 percent of the world's total arms-export trade. Nuclear proliferation

Weapons Proliferation

continued to worry leaders. Argentina, Brazil, and South Africa abandoned nuclear weapons programs, but Brazil, Israel, Pakistan, India, and eight other nations refused to sign the nonproliferation treaty, which was renewed in 1995. Terrorists with access to deadly explosives also threatened danger; in early 1993 Islamic extremists bombed the World Trade Center in New York City.

Environmental issues remained high on the international list of troubles, threatening world order because they caused political instability. Acid rain, toxic waste, deterioration of the protective ozone layer (it blocks the sun's ultraviolet rays, which can cause cancer), soil erosion, water pollution, and destruction of tropical forests spoiled the natural environment, killed wildlife, and poisoned land. Warming of the earth's climate due to the greenhouse effect—the buildup of carbon dioxide and other gases in the atmosphere—threatened a rise in ocean levels, flooding farmland and dislocating millions of people. As the world's population swelled to 5.75 billion in 1996 (100 million were added in 1995 alone) and droughts unleashed killer famines and human migrations, ill-equipped governments struggled to provide welfare for the hungry, who sometimes staged food riots (see figure, page 881). A deadly disease also stalked the land: a global AIDS pandemic that by the mid-1990s had taken the lives of millions, including tens of thousands in the United States.

International Environmental Issues

The Bush administration achieved some advances: in 1989 eighty-six nations, including the United States, agreed to phase out use of ozone-destroying chemicals by the year 2000, and Bush signed a tough Clean Air Act in 1990 (see page 990). The following year the United States and twenty-five other nations agreed to protect the fragile environment of Antarctica by banning oil exploration and mining there for fifty years. But at the 1992 Earth Summit held in Rio de Janeiro, Brazil, Bush rejected key international control agreements, charging that they would cost jobs in the United States. The Clinton administration, advised especially by Vice President Al Gore, whose book *Earth in the Balance: Healing the Global Environment* (1992) established his credentials on the topic, worked for more international environmental accords.

In the mid-1990s the State Department and the United Nations studied the treatment of women as a worldwide human-rights issue. The grim findings included not only job and po-

Human Rights and Women

litical discrimination but also forced sterilization and abortion, coerced prostitution, and genital mutilation. Seventy percent of the world's poor people were women. Half of the world's people are women, observed one United States official, "and until you improve their situation, you're not going to improve human rights around the world." The 1995 Fourth World Conference on Women, held in Beijing, called for the "empowerment of women" through "human rights and fundamental freedoms." Gender issues and international relations became intertwined.

 ## Conclusion

The Cold War dominated world affairs for almost a half-century. In the United States in those years, long-neglected domestic needs begged for attention and resources. A large arms industry secured a firm hold on the American economy, and hundreds of thousands of workers owed their jobs to defense contracts. A massive military establishment using an expansive definition of national security tenaciously built a base of power within the American system, which struggled to adjust to new international realities. Americans seemed better equipped to fight wars than to improve their troubled educational system or to make their cities inhabitable and safe.

During the Cold War era, the power of the presidency expanded greatly at the expense of the checks-and-balances system; presidents launched covert operations, dispatched troops, and ordered invasions while barely consulting Congress. Government seemed less accountable because citizens found it difficult to peel away the layers of secrecy that enshrouded decision making. The Cold War also bequeathed a record of political extremism, cover-ups, lies, and scandals that made many Americans feel either cynical about their government and the political process or powerless to influence their leaders.

Throughout the world, the two great powers intervened in civil wars, transforming local class, racial, religious, and economic conflicts into Cold War contests. Given these conflicts, millions probably would have died whether or not there was a Cold War, but millions more surely died because of it.

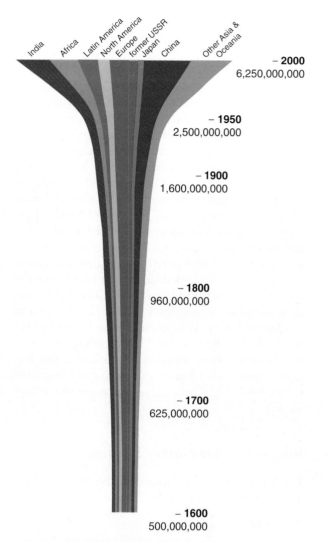

The Population Explosion, 1600–2000   *It is a remarkable story: the world's population has more than doubled since mid-century (1950) and, as this figure indicates, it may reach more than 6 billion by the year 2000. This unprecedented population growth has put heavy pressure on dwindling global natural resources. Food supplies have not kept pace with the population explosion. The United States closely watches this disturbing trend because many nations have been destabilized by eroding soils and food shortages (especially in the developing world), because some nations collide over diminishing resources (such as over oceanic fisheries and river sytems), and because American leaders must decide how foreign aid dollars are spent (on family planning or birth control, for example).*   Source: From *World Military and Social Expenditures* 1993 by Ruth Legar Sivard. Copyright © 1993 by World Priorities, Inc., Washington, D.C. 20007, USA.

While the superpowers waged the Cold War, moreover, they paid scant attention to burgeoning international environmental crises or the injustice of gender inequality.

The central questions of post–Cold War American foreign policy continued in the late 1990s to fuel national debate: Should or could the United States play the expensive role of global policeman and nation builder while at the same time undertaking the expensive task of economic renewal at home? What mix of retrenchment and international activism, of unilateralism and multilateralism, lay ahead? Under what circumstances should the United States apply its predominant military power? Which foreign disturbances threatened vital American interests and which did not? These questions revealed how unsettled Americans were in their foreign policy views in the first years after the Cold War. The 1996 electoral campaign offered few answers. The Republican challenger Robert Dole claimed that "we've lost respect all around the world," but he offered few policy alternatives and emphasized domestic, not foreign, topics. Bill Clinton won reelection primarily on the basis of his domestic policy record (see Chapter 33).

Suggestions for Further Reading

For United States relations with the nations of the Third World since 1945, see Chapter 30.

The Cold War: Overviews

Stephen Ambrose, *Rise to Globalism*, 7th ed. (1993); H. W. Brands, *The Devil We Knew* (1993); Warren Cohen, *America in the Age of Soviet Power, 1945–1991* (1993); Gordon A. Craig and Francis L. Loewenheim, eds., *The Diplomats, 1939–1979* (1994); John L. Gaddis, *Russia, the Soviet Union, and the United States*, 2d ed. (1990); John L. Gaddis, *The Long Peace* (1987); John L. Gaddis, *Strategies of Containment* (1982); Walter Isaacson and Evan Thomas, *The Wise Men* (1986); Robert H. Johnson, *Improbable Dangers: U.S. Perceptions of Threat in the Cold War and After* (1994); Charles W. Kegley, ed., *The Long Post War Peace* (1991); Paul Kennedy, *The Rise and Fall of the Great Powers* (1987); Walter LaFeber, *America, Russia, and the Cold War, 1945–1992*, 8th ed. (1997); Ralph Levering, *The Cold War* (1994); Thomas McCormick, *America's Half-Century*, 2d ed. (1994); Thomas G. Paterson, *On Every Front: The Making and Unmaking of the Cold War* (1992); Thomas G. Paterson, *Meeting the Communist Threat* (1988).

Cold War Origins and the Containment Doctrine

Michael Cohen, *Truman and Israel* (1990); Carolyn W. Eisenberg, *Drawing the Line* (1996) (on the United States and Germany); Frazer Harbutt, *The Iron Curtain* (1986); John L. Harper, *American Visions of Europe* (1994); Walter Hixson, *George F.* *Kennan* (1990); Michael Hogan, *The Marshall Plan* (1987); Lawrence S. Kaplan, *The United States and NATO* (1984); Gabriel Kolko and Joyce Kolko, *The Limits of Power* (1972); Bruce R. Kuniholm, *The Origins of the Cold War in the Near East* (1980); Melvyn Leffler, *The Specter of Communism* (1994); Melvyn Leffler, *A Preponderance of Power* (1992); Alan Milward, *The Reconstruction of Western Europe* (1984); Wilson D. Miscamble, *George F. Kennan and the Making of American Foreign Policy, 1947–1950* (1992); David Reynolds, ed., *The Origins of the Cold War in Europe* (1994); Thomas A. Schwartz, *America's Germany* (1991); Mark A. Stoler, *George C. Marshall* (1989); William Taubman, *Stalin's American Policy* (1982); Graham White and John Maze, *Henry A. Wallace* (1995); Lawrence S. Wittner, *American Intervention in Greece, 1943–1949* (1982); Vladislav Zubok and Constantine Pleshakov, *Inside the Kremlin's Cold War* (1996).

Atomic Diplomacy and Nuclear Arms Race

Howard Ball, *Justice Downwind* (1986) (on testing); Paul Boyer, *By the Bomb's Early Light* (1986); McGeorge Bundy, *Danger and Survival* (1988); Robert A. Divine, *The Sputnik Challenge* (1993); Robert A. Divine, *Blowing in the Wind* (1978) (on the test-ban debate); Gregg Herken, *Counsels of War* (1985); Gregg Herken, *The Winning Weapon* (1981); James G. Hershberg, *James B. Conant* (1993); Richard G. Hewlett and Jack M. Hall, *Atoms for Peace and War, 1953–1961* (1989); David Holloway, *Stalin and the Bomb* (1994); Robert Jervis, *The Meaning of the Nuclear Revolution* (1989); Fred Kaplan, *The Wizards of Armageddon* (1983); Milton Katz, *Ban the Bomb* (1986); Charles Morris, *Iron Destinies, Lost Opportunities* (1988); National Academy of Sciences, *Nuclear Arms Control* (1985); John Newhouse, *War and Peace in the Nuclear Age* (1989); John Newhouse, *Cold Dawn* (1973) (on SALT); Richard Rhodes, *Dark Sun* (1995) (on the H-bomb); David N. Schwartz, *NATO's Nuclear Dilemmas* (1983); Martin Sherwin, *A World Destroyed* (1975); Strobe Talbott, *The Master of the Game* (1988) (on Nitze); Strobe Talbott, *Deadly Gambit* (1984) (on Reagan); Strobe Talbott, *Endgame* (1979) (on SALT-II); Spencer Weart, *Nuclear Fear* (1988); Allan M. Winkler, *Life Under a Cloud* (1993); Lawrence S. Wittner, *One World or None* (1993) (on the disarmament movement).

Occupation and Rebuilding of Japan

Richard B. Finn, *Winners in Peace* (1995); Kyoko Hirano, *Mr. Smith Goes to Tokyo: Japanese Cinema Under the American Occupation, 1945–1952* (1992); Michael Schaller, *Douglas MacArthur* (1989); Michael Schaller, *The American Occupation of Japan* (1985).

China and United States Nonrecognition Policy

Dorothy Borg and Waldo Heinrichs, eds., *Uncertain Years* (1980); Gordon Chang, *Friends and Enemies* (1990); Warren I. Cohen, *America's Response to China*, 3d ed. (1989); Akira Iriye, *The Cold War in Asia* (1974); E. J. Kahn, Jr., *The China Hands* (1975); Paul G. Lauren, ed., *The "China Hands" Legacy* (1987); Robert P. Newman, *Owen Lattimore and the "Loss" of China* (1992); Robert S. Ross, *Negotiating Cooperation* (1995) (on 1969–1989); William W. Stueck, Jr., *The Road to Confrontation* (1981); Nancy B. Tucker, *Patterns in the Dust* (1983).

The Korean War

Roy E. Appleman, *Disaster in Korea* (1992); Roy E. Appleman, *Escaping the Trap* (1990); Roy E. Appleman, *Ridgway Duels for*

Korea (1990); Chen Jian, *China's Road to the Korean War* (1995); Bruce Cumings, *The Origins of the Korean War*, 2 vols. (1980, 1991); Rosemary Foot, *A Substitute for Victory* (1990); Rosemary Foot, *The Wrong War* (1985); Sergei Goncharov et al., *Uncertain Partners: Stalin, Mao, and the Korean War* (1993); John Halliday and Bruce Cumings, *Korea* (1989); Burton I. Kaufman, *The Korean War* (1997); Callum A. MacDonald, *Korea* (1987); Glenn D. Paige, *The Korean Decision* (1968); John W. Spanier, *The Truman-MacArthur Controversy and the Korean War* (1959); William Stueck, *The Korean War* (1995); Richard Whelan, *Drawing the Line* (1990); Allen Whiting, *China Crosses the Yalu* (1960).

Eisenhower-Dulles Foreign Policy

Stephen E. Ambrose, *Eisenhower*, 2 vols. (1982, 1984); Stephen E. Ambrose, *Ike's Spies* (1981); Michael Beschloss, *MAYDAY* (1986) (on the U-2 crisis); Jeff Broadwater, *Eisenhower and the Anti-Communist Crusade* (1992); Robert A. Divine, *Eisenhower and the Cold War* (1981); Fred Greenstein, *The Hidden-Hand Presidency* (1982); Townsend Hoopes, *The Devil and John Foster Dulles* (1973); Richard Immerman, ed., *John Foster Dulles* (1990); Burton I. Kaufman, *Trade and Aid* (1982); Frederick W. Marks, *Power and Peace* (1993) (on Dulles); Richard A. Melanson and David A. Mayers, eds., *Reevaluating Eisenhower* (1986); Jack M. Schick, *The Berlin Crisis* (1971).

Kennedy, Johnson, and Globalism

Michael Beschloss, *The Crisis Years* (1991); H. W. Brands, *The Wages of Globalism* (1995); Warren I. Cohen, *Dean Rusk* (1980); Warren I. Cohen and Nancy B. Tucker, eds., *Lyndon Johnson Confronts the World* (1995); James N. Giglio, *The Presidency of John F. Kennedy* (1991); David Halberstam, *The Best and the Brightest* (1972); Doris Kearns, *Lyndon Johnson and the American Dream* (1976); Montague Kern et al., *The Kennedy Crises* (1984); Diane Kunz, ed., *The Diplomacy of the Crucial Decade* (1994); Herbert S. Parmet, *JFK* (1983); Thomas G. Paterson, ed., *Kennedy's Quest for Victory* (1989); Arthur M. Schlesinger, Jr., *Robert Kennedy and His Times* (1978); Thomas J. Schoenbaum, *Waging Peace and War* (1988); Randall Woods, *Fulbright* (1995). For the Vietnam War, see Chapter 30.

Cuba and the Missile Crisis

Graham Allison, *Essence of Decision* (1971); James G. Blight, *The Shattered Crystal Ball* (1990); James G. Blight et al., *Cuba on the Brink* (1993); James G. Blight and David A. Welch, *On the Brink* (1989); Raymond Garthoff, *Reflections on the Cuban Missile Crisis*, rev. ed. (1989); Trumbull Higgins, *The Perfect Failure* (1987) (on the Bay of Pigs invasion); Richard Ned Lebow and Janice Gross Stein, *We All Lost the Cold War* (1993); Morris Morley, *Imperial State and Revolution* (1987); James Nathan, ed., *The Cuban Missile Crisis Revisited* (1992); Thomas G. Paterson, *Contesting Castro* (1994); Louis A. Pérez, Jr., *Cuba and the United States* (1990); Scott D. Sagan, *The Limits of Safety* (1993); Mark J. White, *The Cuban Missile Crisis* (1996).

Nixon, Kissinger, and Détente

Stephen Ambrose, *Nixon*, 3 vols. (1987–1991); Michael B. Froman, *The Development of the Idea of Détente* (1992); Raymond L. Garthoff, *Détente and Confrontation* (1985); John R. Greene,

The Limits of Power (1992); Seymour Hersh, *The Price of Power* (1983); Joan Hoff, *Nixon Reconsidered* (1994); Walter Isaacson, *Kissinger* (1992); Keith L. Nelson, *The Making of Détente* (1995); Herbert S. Parmet, *Richard Nixon and His America* (1990); Andrew J. Pierre, *The Global Politics of Arms Sales* (1982); Robert D. Schulzinger, *Henry Kissinger* (1989).

The World Economy and Natural Environment

Richard J. Barnet, *The Lean Years* (1980); Richard J. Barnet and John Cavanaugh, *Global Dreams* (1994); Richard J. Barnet and Ronald Müller, *Global Reach* (1974); Richard E. Benedick, *Ozone Diplomacy* (1991); David P. Calleo, *The Imperious Economy* (1982); Alfred E. Eckes, *The United States and the Global Struggle for Minerals* (1979); David E. Fisher, *Fire & Ice* (1990) (on ozone depletion); Edward M. Graham and Paul R. Krugman, *Foreign Direct Investment in the United States* (1989); Stephen D. Krasner, *Defending the National Interest* (1978); John McCormick, *Reclaiming Paradise: The Global Environmental Movement* (1989); Robert A. Pastor, *Congress and the Politics of U.S. Foreign Economic Policy, 1929–1976* (1980); Joan E. Spero, *The Politics of International Economic Relations*, 4th ed. (1990); Herman Van Der Wee, *The Search for Prosperity: The World Economy, 1945–1980* (1986).

Carter Foreign Policy and Human Rights

Erwin C. Hargrove, *Jimmy Carter as President* (1988); Ole R. Holsti and James N. Rosenau, *American Leadership in World Affairs: Vietnam and the Breakdown of Consensus* (1984); Charles O. Jones, *The Trusteeship Presidency* (1988); Burton I. Kaufman, *The Presidency of James Earl Carter, Jr.* (1993); David S. McLellan, *Cyrus Vance* (1985); Richard A. Melanson, *Reconstructing Consensus* (1990); A. Glenn Mower, Jr., *Human Rights and American Foreign Policy* (1987); Kenneth A. Oye et al., *Eagle Entangled* (1979); Herbert D. Rosenbaum and Alezej Ugrinsky, eds., *Jimmy Carter* (1994); Gaddis Smith, *Morality, Reason, and Power* (1986); Sandy Vogelgesang, *American Dream, Global Nightmare* (1980).

Reagan, Bush, Clinton, and the End and Aftermath of the Cold War

Dana H. Allin, *Cold War Illusions* (1995); Michael R. Beschloss and Strobe Talbott, *At the Highest Levels* (1993); Archie Brown, *The Gorbachev Factor* (1996); Lou Cannon, *President Reagan* (1991); Michael Cox, *U.S. Foreign Policy After the Cold War* (1995); Elizabeth Drew, *On the Edge* (on Clinton); John Ehrman, *The Rise of Neoconservatism* (1995); John L. Gaddis, *The United States and the End of the Cold War* (1992); Raymond L. Garthoff, *The Great Transition* (1994); Seymour Hersh, *"The Target Is Destroyed"* (1987) (on the downed Korean airliner); Michael Hogan, ed., *The End of the Cold War* (1992); Haynes Johnson, *Sleepwalking Through History* (1991); Robert G. Kaiser, *Why Gorbachev Happened* (1991); Sean Lynn-Jones, ed., *The Cold War and After* (1991); Michael MccGwire, *Perestroika and Soviet National Security* (1991); Joseph S. Nye, Jr., *Bound to Lead* (1990); Don Oberdorfer, *The Turn* (1991); Kenneth A. Oye et al., eds., *Eagle in a New World* (1992); Kenneth A. Oye et al., eds., *Eagle Resurgent?* (1987); Nicholas X. Rizopoulos, ed., *Sea-Changes* (1990); John G. Ruggie, *Winning the Peace* (1996); Michael Schaller, *Reckoning with Reagan* (1992); Robert W. Tucker and David C. Hendrickson, *The Imperial Temptation* (1992); Daniel Wirls, *Buildup* (1992) (on Reagan military); Susan Woodward, *Balkan Tragedy* (1995).

30

Foreign Relations Storm: Contesting Revolution and Nationalism in the Third World
1945 – Present

The "Deer" Team leader was slammed into a banyan tree on July 16, 1945, when he parachuted into northern Vietnam, near Kimlung, a village nestled in a valley of rice paddies surrounded by mosquito-infested forests. Colonel Allison Thomas could not know that the end of the Second World War was just weeks away, but he and the other five members of his Office of Strategic Services (OSS) unit knew their mission: to work with the Vietminh, a nationalist Vietnamese organization, to sabotage Japanese forces that in March had seized Vietnam from France. Disentangled from parachute and tree, Thomas spoke a "few flowery sentences" to two hundred Vietminh soldiers assembled near a banner proclaiming "Welcome to Our American Friends." Ho Chi Minh, head of the Vietminh, ill but speaking in good English, cordially greeted the OSS team and offered supper. The next day Ho denounced the French but remarked that "we welcome 10 *million* Americans." "Forget the Communist Bogy," Thomas radioed OSS headquarters in China.

A communist who had worked for decades to win his nation's independence, Ho helped supply information on Japanese military forces and rescue downed American pilots during the war. He also met in March 1945 with United States officials in Kunming, China. There he read the *Encyclopaedia Britannica* and *Time* magazine at an Office of War Information facility. Receiving no aid from his ideological allies in the Soviet

• *Important Events* •

1945	OSS "Deer" and "Mercy" Teams cooperate with Vietminh Ho Chi Minh declares independence for Democratic Republic of Vietnam	**1961**	Peace Corps is founded Kennedy initiates Alliance for Progress to spur Latin American economies Kennedy begins to increase aid to Vietnam
1946	United States grants independence to Philippines Anticolonial war against France begins in Vietnam United States backs shah during crisis in Iran	**1962**	Agreement reached on neutralizing Laos Cuban missile crisis
1947	Truman Doctrine launches containment policy National Security Act creates Central Intelligence Agency	**1963**	Strategic Hamlet Program established in South Vietnam United States cooperates in removal of Diem Kennedy assassinated; Lyndon B. Johnson becomes president
1948	State of Israel created amid Arab-Jewish hostilities	**1964**	Tonkin Gulf Resolution authorizes Johnson to handle the Vietnam War his way
1949	Truman announces Point Four technical assistance for developing nations Communists come to power in China	**1965**	United States invades Dominican Republic Operation Rolling Thunder bombs North Vietnam Johnson Americanizes Vietnam War by sending large numbers of troops
1950	United States recognizes Bao Dai government in Vietnam and provides military aid to the French	**1965–66**	Teach-ins at American universities oppose United States intervention in Vietnam
1953	United States helps restore shah to power in Iran	**1967**	Peace rallies held across the United States Six-Day War in the Middle East
1954	Siege of Dienbienphu spells end of French rule in Vietnam CIA overthrows Arbenz government in Guatemala Geneva accords partition Vietnam Southeast Asia Treaty Organization founded	**1968**	Secretary of Defense McNamara resigns Tet offensive in Vietnam sets back United States objectives Dollar/gold crisis threatens United States economy Massacre in My Lai leaves hundreds dead Vietnam peace talks open in Paris
1955	United States backs Diem government in South Vietnam Bandung Conference organizes Non-aligned Movement	**1969**	Under "Vietnamization" President Nixon begins withdrawal of American troops Nixon Doctrine declares United States will help nations that help themselves
1956	Suez crisis pits Nasser's Egypt against Israel, France, and Britain	**1970**	Invasion of Cambodia sets off demonstrations on American college campuses Senate repeals Tonkin Gulf Resolution
1957	Eisenhower Doctrine promises containment of communism in Middle East	**1971**	*Pentagon Papers* indicate that American leaders lied about Vietnam
1958	United States troops land in Lebanon	**1972**	American warplanes pound North Vietnam in "Christmas bombing"
1959	Castro launches Cuban Revolution North Vietnam begins sending aid to communists in the South	**1973**	Vietnam cease-fire agreement reached Salvador Allende ousted in Chile after United States subversive efforts Outbreak of Arab-Israeli war and imposition of Arab oil embargo War Powers Act restricts presidential war-making authority
1960	Eighteen African colonies become independent nations National Liberation Front (Vietcong) organized in South Vietnam		

• *Important Events* •

1974	United Nations proposes "New International Economic Order" for the Third World		**1989**	Third World debt reaches $1.2 trillion United States troops invade Panama to remove General Manuel Noriega
1975	Egyptian-Israeli accord authorizes United Nations peacekeeping force in Sinai Vietnam War ends		**1990**	Sandinistas defeated in Nicaraguan elections After Iraq invades Kuwait, United States forces ordered to Persian Gulf South Africa begins to dismantle apartheid
1977	President Carter announces United States human-rights policy		**1991**	Persian Gulf War Junta ousts Haitian president Jean-Bertrand Aristide Haitian refugees flee to United States Israelis and Arabs negotiate Mideast peace
1978	Congress approves Panama Canal treaties Carter negotiates Egyptian-Israeli peace accord at Camp David		**1992**	United Nations mediation ends Salvadoran civil war United States sends troops to Somalia to ensure delivery of relief supplies
1979	Shah of Iran overthrown; American hostages seized		**1993**	Israel-PLO agreement for Palestinian self-rule
1981	American hostages in Iran released United States steps up role in El Salvador's civil war CIA begins to train contras for attacks against Nicaragua		**1994**	Nelson Mandela elected president in South Africa World's governments react too late to stop genocide in Rwanda United States troops land in Haiti to restore Aristide to presidency
1982	President Reagan sends American troops to Lebanon for peacekeeping		**1995**	AIDS afflicts 4 million people worldwide International Conference on Women held in Beijing
1983	Terrorist bombing kills United States marines in Lebanon Reagan orders invasion of Grenada to remove leftist government		**1996**	Helms-Burton Act tightens United States economic embargo against Cuba United States establishes diplomatic relations with Vietnam Civil war in Guatemala ends through United Nations–brokered peace accord
1984	Reagan administration aids contras, despite congressional ban		**1997**	Israeli troops withdraw from West Bank city of Hebron after United States diplomats manage negotiations
1985	Reagan Doctrine promises United States aid to anti-Soviet "freedom fighters"			
1986	Iran-contra scandal breaks United States imposes economic sanctions against South Africa			
1987	Palestinian uprising occurs in West Bank (*intifada*)			
1988	Terrorist bombing of Pan American flight Negotiated settlement in Namibia			

Note: For events in the history of the Cold War, see Chapter 29.

Union, Ho hoped that the United States, on record in the Atlantic Charter as supporting self-determination for all peoples, would favor his nation's long quest for liberation from colonialism.

A few more OSS personnel parachuted into Kimlung, including a male nurse who diagnosed Ho with malaria and dysentery; quinine and sulfa drugs restored his health, but Ho remained frail. As a sign of friendship, the Americans in Vietnam named Ho OSS Agent 19. Everywhere the Americans went, impoverished villagers thanked them with gifts of food and clothing—interpreting the foreigners' presence as a sign of United States anticolonial and anti-Japanese sentiments. In early August, the "Deer" Team began to give Vietminh soldiers weapons training. During many conversations with the OSS members, Ho said that he hoped young Vietnamese could study in the United States and American technicians could help build an independent Vietnam. Citing history, Ho remarked that "your statesmen make eloquent speeches about . . . self-determination. We are self-determined. Why not help us? Am I any different from . . . your George Washington?"

Another OSS unit, the "Mercy" Team headed by Captain Archimedes Patti, arrived in the city of Hanoi on August 22. When Patti met Ho—"this wisp of a man"—the Vietminh leader applauded America's assistance and called for future "collaboration." But, unbeknownst to these OSS members, who believed that President Franklin D. Roosevelt's general sympathy for eventual Vietnamese independence remained United States policy, the new Truman administration in Washington had decided to let France, America's ally and Vietnam's long-time colonial master, decide the fate of Vietnam. That change in policy explains why Ho never received answers to the several letters and telegrams he sent to Washington—the first dated August 30, 1945.

On September 2, 1945, amid great fanfare in Hanoi, with OSS personnel present, an emaciated but emotional Ho Chi Minh read his declaration of independence for the Democratic Republic of Vietnam: "All men are created equal; they are endowed by their Creator with certain unalienable Rights; among these are Life, Liberty, and the pursuit of Happiness." Having borrowed from the internationally renowned 1776 American document, Ho then itemized Vietnamese grievances against France. At one point in the ceremonies, two American P-38 aircraft swooped down over the crowded square. The Vietnamese cheered, interpreting the flyby as United States endorsement of their independence. Actually, the pilots had no orders to make a political statement; they just wanted to see what was happening.

By late September both OSS teams had departed from Vietnam. In a last meeting with Captain Patti, Ho expressed his sadness that the United States had not opposed France's return to Vietnam and had in fact armed the French to reestablish their colonial rule. Sure, Ho said, United States officials in Washington judged him a "Moscow puppet" because he was a communist. But Ho claimed that he drew inspiration from the American struggle for independence and that he was foremost "a free agent," a nationalist. If necessary, Ho insisted, the Vietnamese would go it alone, with or without American or Soviet help. And

they did—first against the French and eventually against more than half a million United States troops in what became America's longest war. How different world history would have been had President Harry S Truman responded favorably to Ho Chi Minh's last letter to Washington, dated February 16, 1946, which asked the United States "as guardians and champions of World Justice to take a decisive step in support of our independence."

Vietnam was part of the *Third World*, a general term for those nations that during the Cold War era belonged neither to the capitalist "West" (the United States and its allies) nor to the communist "East" (the Soviet Union and its allies). Sometimes called developing countries, Third World nations on the whole were nonwhite, nonindustrialized, and located in the southern half of the globe—in Asia, Africa, the Middle East, and Latin America. Many of them at one point were colonies of European nations or Japan. Often poor and unstable, rife with tribal, ethnic, and class rivalries, their economies often depended on the sale of only one commodity.

After the Second World War, when the United States and the Soviet Union coveted allies, the Third World became entangled in the Cold War. Even though the highly diverse Third World peoples had their own histories, cultures, and aspirations, they often found that they could not escape the pervasive effects of the great-power rivalry, including nuclear confrontations. Vietnam thus became one among many sites where the Cold War and the Third World intersected. American leaders thought of Vietnam as an Asian Berlin, a place to draw the line against communism and to implement the containment doctrine (see Chapter 29).

Americans often interpreted Third World anticolonialism, political instability, and restrictions on foreign-owned property as Soviet or communist inspired—as Cold War matters rather than as expressions of profound nationalism or as consequences of indigenous developments. Although the Soviets supported guerrilla wars and revolution, and some Third World nations worked to forge links with the Soviet Union to fend off counterrevolutionary efforts by the United States, had there been no Soviet Union or Cold War, the Third World still would have challenged the United States and its allies. These anticolonialist developing nations sought to end the economic, military, and cultural hegemony of the "West." As Assistant Secretary of State Thomas Mann told his colleagues in early 1959, when revolutionaries came to power in Cuba: "You fellows better batten down the hatches, because there's going to be some real stormy weather."

Interventions—military and otherwise—in the Third World, United States leaders believed, became necessary. They would impress Moscow with American might and resolve. They would ensure supplies of strategic raw materials. They would build cultural ties with the United States. They would counter nationalism and radical anticapitalist social change that threatened American strategic and economic interests. To thwart nationalist, radical, and communist challenges, the United States directed its massive resources—foreign aid, propaganda, development projects—toward the Third World. Washington also allied with native elites and with undemocratic but anticommunist regimes, meddled in civil wars, and unleashed CIA covert operations. The stormy interaction with the Third World frequently violated American principles. It also diverted billions of dollars from domestic needs. Bitter resentments built up in the Third World, where millions of lives were lost in conflicts aggravated by United States intervention.

The emergence of the Third World in the 1950s began to undermine the bipolar Cold War international system the United States and the Soviet Union had constructed at the end of the Second World War. Secretary of State Henry Kissinger observed in the 1970s that the international order was coming "apart politically, economically, and morally." The world, he feared, was "tilting against us." By the 1980s, power had become more diffused: great-power management of world affairs had diminished, and international relations had become more fluid and less predictable as more and more nations demanded a voice and a vote. Even when the Cold War ended in the early 1990s, the Third World remained to bedevil the United States, which continued its tradition of intervention—in Iraq, Somalia, Haiti, and elsewhere.

Stormy Weather: The Third World Challenge

The process of decolonization began during the First World War but accelerated after the end of the Second World War, when the economically wracked imperial countries proved incapable of resisting their colonies' demands for freedom. A cavalcade of new nations earned independence. The United States granted independence to the Philippines in 1946. India and Pakistan (and

Decolonization

present-day Bangladesh) won their freedom from Britain in 1947, as did Burma (Myanmar) and Ceylon (Sri Lanka) in 1948. The Dutch reluctantly let go of Indonesia in 1949. The French fought on in Indochina (Vietnam, Cambodia, and Laos) but finally gave up in 1954. In 1960 alone, eighteen new African nations became independent. From 1943 to 1989 a total of ninety-six countries cast off their colonial bonds (see map, page 890). At the same time, the long-independent Third World nations of Latin America unsettled the world order by repeatedly challenging the hegemony of the United States.

By the late 1940s, when Cold War lines were drawn fairly tightly in Europe, Soviet-American rivalry shifted increasingly to the Third World. Much was at stake. Third World nations possessed manganese, oil, tin, and other strategic raw materials. Their resources and labor seemed essential to the economic reconstruction of America's allies in Western Europe and Japan. They also attracted foreign investment—more than one-third of America's private foreign investments were in Third World countries in 1959. And Third World nations became markets for American manufactured products and technology. The great powers looked to these new states for votes in the United Nations and sought sites within their borders for military and intelligence bases. In the 1950s, technical assistance, loans, and grants began to flow to developing nations. By 1961 more than 90 percent of United States foreign aid was going to the Third World. Many of these new nations learned to play off the two superpowers against one another to garner more aid and arms.

Many Third World states—notably India, Ghana, Egypt, and Indonesia—did not wish to take sides in the Cold War. To the dismay of both Washington and Moscow, they declared themselves nonaligned, or neutral. Nonalignment became an organized movement in 1955 when twenty-nine Asian and African nations met at the Bandung Conference in Indonesia. Secretary of State John Foster Dulles, alarmed that neutralist tendencies would deprive the United States of potential allies, denounced neutralism as a step on the road to communism. Both he and President Eisenhower insisted that every nation should take a side in the life-and-death Cold War struggle. Neutralism had to be contained.

The Nonaligned Movement

American leaders argued that Third World peoples needed Western-induced capitalist develop-

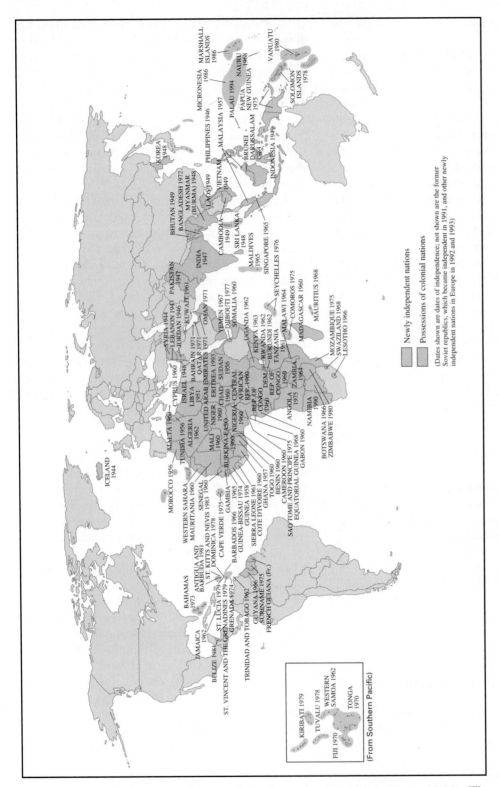

The Rise of the Third World: Newly Independent Nations Since 1943   *The influx of new nations into the international system challenged the United States and Soviet Union. Often voting as a bloc, they pitted one superpower against the other and, suffering economic and political disorder, became targets of great-power intrigue.*

ment and modernization in order to enjoy economic growth, social harmony, and political moderation. Ameri-

American Images of the Third World

can leaders ascribed stereotyped race, age-based, and gendered characteristics to Third World peoples, seeing them as dependent, emotional, and irrational. Cubans, CIA director Allen Dulles told the National Security Council in early 1959, "had to be treated more or less like children. They had to be led rather than rebuffed. If they were rebuffed, like children, they were capable of almost anything." American officials also used gendered language, suggesting that Third World countries were weak women—passive and servile, unable to resist the menacing appeals of communists and neutralists. For example, such thinking conditioned United States relations with India, a neutralist nation that Americans deemed effeminate and submissive—a place where, said President Eisenhower, "emotion rather than reason seems to dictate policy." And American leaders insisted that the peoples of the Third World were technologically "backward." Overall, American policymakers placed these peoples low in the hierarchy of power and claimed that they needed fatherly tutelage by the United States.

Race attitudes and segregation practices in the United States especially influenced relations. In 1955, G. L. Mehta, the Indian ambassador to the

Racism

United States, was refused service in the whites-only section of a restaurant at Houston International Airport. The insult stung deeply, as did many similar rebuffs experienced by other Third World diplomats. Fearing damaged relations with India, a large, neutralist nation whose allegiance the United States sought in the Cold War, Secretary of State John Foster Dulles apologized to Mehta. Dulles knew that racial segregation in the United States was becoming a "major international hazard," spoiling American efforts to win friends in Third World countries. American practices and ideals were conspicuously at odds.

When the United States attorney general appealed to the Supreme Court to strike down segregation in public schools, he underlined that the humiliation of dark-skinned diplomats "furnished grist for the Communist propaganda mills." When the Court announced its *Brown* decision (see page 826), the United States Information Agency's Voice of America quickly broadcast news of the desegregation order around the world in thirty-five different

Indian prime minister Jawaharlal Nehru (1889-1964) in friendly conversation with United States ambassador Chester Bowles (1901-1986), who served in India from 1951-1953 and from 1963 to 1969. Nehru, his nation's first prime minister (1947-1964) after leading the struggle for independence, pursued a policy of neutralism in the Cold War, becoming a leader of the nonaligned movement and thus often at odds with the United States. Still, India became a large recipient of American economic development aid. Bowles championed such aid, believing that India would stand as a noncommunist model in Asia Yale University Library

languages. But the problem did not go away. For example, after the 1957 Little Rock crisis (see page 827), Dulles remarked that racial bigotry was "ruining our foreign policy. The effect of this in Asia and Africa will be worse for us than Hungary was for the Russians."

The hostility of the United States toward revolution also obstructed the American quest for influence in the Third World. In the twentieth cen-

American Intolerance of Revolution

tury, the United States openly opposed revolutions in Mexico, China, Russia, Cuba, Vietnam, Nicaragua, and Iran, among other nations. Americans celebrated the Spirit of '76 but grew intolerant of revolutionary disorder because many Third World revolutions arose against America's Cold War allies and threatened American investments, markets, and military bases. Indeed, by midcentury the United States stood as an established power in world affairs, eager for stability and order to protect American prosperity and security. During revolutionary crises, therefore, the United States usually supported its European allies or the conservative, propertied classes in the Third World. In 1960, for example, when forty-three African and Asian states sponsored a United Nations resolution endorsing decolonization, the United States abstained from the vote, signaling that it stood with the white imperialists.

Believing that Third World peoples craved modernization and that the American economic model of private enterprise and cooperation among business, labor, and government was best for them, American policymakers launched various "development" projects. Such projects held out the promise of sustained economic growth, prosperity, and stability, which the benefactors hoped would undermine radicalism. President Truman—who once labeled Mexico "Greaserdom"—announced in 1949 the Point Four program of sending American know-how to developing nations. In the 1950s the Carnegie, Ford, and Rockefeller Foundations worked with the United States Agency for International Development (AID) to sponsor a "Green Revolution"—a dramatic increase in agricultural production by, for example, the use of hybrid seeds. The Rockefeller Foundation supported foreign universities to train national leaders committed to nonradical development; in Nigeria from 1958 to 1969 the philanthropic agency spent $25 million. Before Dean Rusk became secretary of state in 1961, he served as president of the Rockefeller Foundation (1952–1960).

Development and Modernization

In the 1950s and 1960s the views of Massachusetts Institute of Technology professor Walt W. Rostow influenced United States policy. Rostow wrote in his popular book, *Stages of Economic Growth: A Non-Communist Manifesto* (1959), that if the United States sponsored development projects in the Third World through capital investment, infusions of Western culture and technology, and American government foreign aid, then class conflict, civil war, and revolution would diminish if not disappear. They seldom did, however.

To persuade Third World peoples to abandon radical doctrines and neutralism, American leaders, often in cooperation with the business-sponsored Advertising Council, directed propaganda at the Third World. The United States Information Agency used films, radio broadcasts, the magazine *Free World*, book displays, exhibitions, ex-

USIA Propaganda Campaigns

change programs, and libraries (in 162 cities worldwide by 1961) to trumpet the theme of "People's Capitalism." Citing America's economic success—contrasted with "slave-labor" conditions in the Soviet Union—the message showcased well-paid American workers, political democracy, and religious freedom. To counter ugly pictures of segregation and white attacks on African-Americans and civil rights activists in the South, the USIA applauded success stories of individual African-Americans—such as the boxers Floyd Patterson and Sugar Ray Robinson. The Fulbright Program (see page 854) also brought America's message before the Third World.

Some Third World peoples yearned to be like Americans—to enjoy their consumer goods, their music, their clothes, their economic status, their educational opportunities. American movies offered enticing glimpses of middle-class materialism. In 1969, 70 percent of all films shown in Brazil and Venezuela were American imports, and in 1974, 84 percent of television programs in Guatemala came from the United States. American products drew admiring audiences at trade fairs and native marketplaces. American blue jeans, advertising billboards, and soft drinks dominated some foreign societies.

Third World Views of the United States

If foreigners envied Americans, they also resented them for having so much and wasting so much while poorer peoples went without. The popular American novel *The Ugly American* (1958) spotlighted the "golden ghettoes" where American diplomats lived in compounds separated from their poorer surroundings by high walls. The people of many countries, moreover, resented the ample profits that American corporations extracted from them. Americans often received blame for the persistent poverty of the Third World, even though the leaders of those nations made decisions that hindered their own progress. Underfed India, for example, poured millions of dollars into the production of a nuclear bomb when it might have spent those funds to increase agricultural production. Nonetheless, anti-American resentments could be measured in the late 1950s in attacks on USIA libraries in Calcutta (India), Beirut (Lebanon), and Bogotá (Colombia). The American film and television industries were so active abroad that some foreigners protested "cultural imperialism." Third World peoples also rejected unsavory aspects of American life, including racial segregation, political corruption, and drug abuse.

The Central Intelligence Agency became a major instrument of United States policy in the Third World. Though espionage and the gathering of information had been defined as the CIA's primary functions at its birth in 1947, covert actions soon joined them. The CIA bribed foreign politicians, subsidized foreign newspapers, hired mercenaries, conducted sabotage, sponsored labor unions, dispensed "disinformation" (false information), plotted the assassination of foreign leaders, and staged coups—all in an effort to influence foreign governments toward pro-American positions. The CIA helped overthrow the governments of Iran (1953) and Guatemala (1954) but failed in attempts to topple regimes in Indonesia (1958) and Cuba (for the 1961 Bay of Pigs invasion, see page 866). The CIA trained foreign military leaders, some of whom in Latin America headed death squads that killed government opponents. The agency also subsidized political figures; King Hussein of Jordan received a million dollars a year from the CIA in the 1960s and 1970s.

CIA Covert Activities

The CIA and other components of the American intelligence community followed the principle of *plausible deniability*: covert operations should be conducted in such a way, and the decisions that launched them concealed so well, that the president could

How do historians know that the Central Intelligence Agency tried to assassinate foreign leaders? During the 1970s, Senator Frank Church, Democrat of Idaho, chaired a special investigating committee that looked into the activities of the CIA and other intelligence agencies. Although there had long been speculation that Washington headquarters ordered CIA agents to kill certain foreign leaders, incontrovertible evidence did not come to public light until Church's probe forced the CIA to declassify secret documents. Here, on November 20, 1975, Church holds a copy of his committee's report on assassinaton plots. Among other findings in this report, the committee detailed several bungled attempts on the life of Fidel Castro, the revolutionary leader of Cuba. In this case, the CIA actually hired Mafia crime bosses to help with the unsuccessful schemes. In other cases, the Church committee discovered that the CIA tried to kill Patrice Lumumba of the Congo and either promoted or associated with plots against Rafael Trujillo of the Dominican Republic and Ngo Dinh Diem of South Vietnam. Most of the assassination plots failed. The committee could not confirm whether Presidents Eisenhower, Kennedy, and others personally ordered assassinations, although the report hinted that they gave orders that underlings could only have interpreted as licenses to kill. Because of such revelations, the CIA was later prohibited from conducting assassinations. But until another committee such as Church's opens classified documents, the secrecy that enshrouds CIA operations makes it difficult for historians to know whether the ban has been observed.   Corbis-Bettmann.

deny any knowledge of them. Thus President Eisenhower denied the United States's role in Guatemala, even though he had ordered the operation. He and his successor Kennedy also denied that they had instructed the CIA to assassinate Cuba's Fidel Castro, whose regime after 1959 became stridently anti-American (see page 866).

 ## The Eisenhower Interventions

Anti-Yankee feelings grew in Latin America, long a United States sphere of influence, where poverty, class warfare, overpopulation, illiteracy, economic sluggishness, and foreign exploitation fed discontent (see map, page 913). In 1951 the leftist Jacobo Arbenz Guzmán was elected president of Guatemala, a poor country whose largest landowner was the American-owned United Fruit Company. United Fruit was an economic power throughout Latin America, where it owned 3 million acres of land and operated railroads, ports, ships, and telecommunications facilities. To fulfill his promise of land reform, Arbenz expropriated United Fruit's uncultivated land and offered compensation. United Fruit dismissed the offer and began an aggressive public relations campaign to rally Washington officials against what the company called a communist threat.

Claiming that Arbenz employed too many communists in his government and that they were taking control of Guatemala, the CIA began a secret plot to overthrow him. When Arbenz learned that the CIA was working against him, he turned to Moscow for military aid, thus reinforcing American suspicions. The CIA airlifted arms into Guatemala, dropping them at United Fruit facilities, and in mid-1954 CIA-supported Guatemalans struck from Honduras. American planes bombed the capital city, and the invaders drove Arbenz from power. The new pro-American regime returned United Fruit's land.

CIA in Guatemala

Latin Americans wondered what had happened to the Good Neighbor policy (see page 759). Their accelerating hostility toward the United States surfaced in 1958, when rioters in Venezuela and elsewhere interrupted Vice President Richard M. Nixon's goodwill trip to South America and threatened his life. The following year Panamanians rioted after United States officials denied them permission to raise the Panamanian flag in the Canal Zone. The Cuban Revolution, gathering momentum in 1959 and winning followers in the Western Hemisphere, soon represented the greatest challenge to United States hegemony (see page 652).

In the Middle East the Eisenhower administration confronted challenges to United States influence from Arab nationalists (see map, page 895). American interests were conspicuous: survival of the Jewish state of Israel and extensive oil holdings (American companies produced about half of the region's petroleum in the 1950s). Oil-rich Iran had become a special friend. Its ruling shah had granted American oil companies a 40 percent interest in a new petroleum consortium in return for CIA help in the successful overthrow, in 1953, of his rival, Mohammed Mossadegh, who had attempted to nationalize foreign oil interests.

United States Interests in the Middle East

Egypt's Gamal Abdul Nasser became a towering figure in a pan-Arabic movement to reduce Western interests in the Middle East. Nasser vowed to expel the British from the Suez Canal Zone and the Israelis from Palestine. The United States wished neither to anger the Arabs, for fear of losing valuable oil supplies, nor to alienate its ally Israel, which was supported at home by politically active American Jews. But when Nasser declared neutrality in the Cold War, Dulles lost patience.

In 1956 the United States abruptly reneged on its offer to Egypt to help finance the Aswan Dam, a project to provide inexpensive electricity and water for thirsty farmland. "You fellows are out to kill me," Nasser angrily accused the American ambassador. Secretary Dulles's blunt economic pressure backfired, for Nasser responded by nationalizing the British-owned Suez Canal, intending to use its profits to build the dam. At a mass rally in Alexandria, Nasser expressed the profound nationalism typical of Third World peoples shedding an imperial past: "Tonight our Egyptian canal will be run by Egyptians. *Egyptians!*"

Suez Crisis

Fully 75 percent of Western Europe's oil came from the Middle East, and most of it was transported through the Suez Canal. Fearing an interruption in this vital trade, the British and French conspired with Israel to bring down Nasser. On October 29, 1956, the Israelis invaded Suez, joined two days later by Britain and France. Eisenhower fumed that the United States's allies had not consulted him and that the attack had shifted attention from Soviet intervention in Hungary (see page 863). The president also

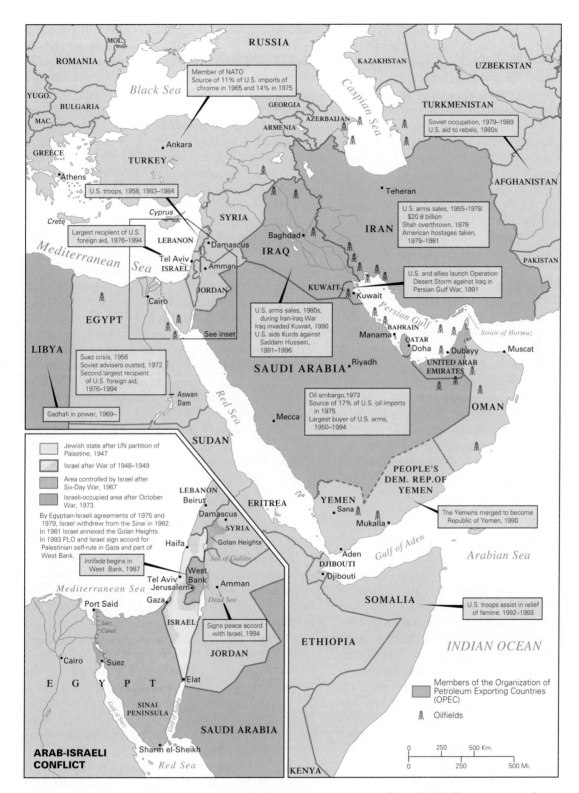

The Middle East *Extremely volatile and often at war, the nations of the Middle East maintained precarious relations with the United States. To protect its interests, the United States extended large amounts of economic and military aid and sold huge quantities of weapons to the area. At times, Washington ordered American troops to the region. The Arab-Israeli dispute particularly upended order.*

speculated that the invasion would cause Nasser to seek help from the Soviets, inviting them into the Middle East. Eisenhower sternly demanded that London, Paris, and Tel Aviv pull their troops out, and they did. Egypt took possession of the canal, and the Soviets built the Aswan Dam. Nasser became a hero to Third World peoples. To counter Nasser's "evil influence," as Eisenhower called it, the United States pursued alignment with the conservative King Saud of Saudi Arabia.

Washington officials worried that a "vacuum" existed in the Middle East—and that the Soviets might fill it. Nasserites insisted that there was no vacuum but rather a growing Arab nationalism that provided the best defense against communism. In an effort to improve the deteriorating Western position in the Middle East and to protect American interests there, the president proclaimed the *Eisenhower Doctrine* in 1957. The United States would intervene in the Middle East, he declared, if any government threatened by a communist takeover asked for help. In 1958 fourteen thousand American troops scrambled ashore in Lebanon to quell an internal political dispute that Washington feared might be exploited by pro-Nasser groups or communists. By 1961, most analysts agreed, the Eisenhower administration had deepened Third World hostility toward the United States.

Eisenhower Doctrine

Kennedy's Quest for Victory

During the 1960 presidential campaign, John F. Kennedy hammered the Eisenhower administration for failing to align the Third World with the United States side in the Cold War. He vowed to win the race for influence in the Third World, as well as the missile race, the arms race, and the space race. After Khrushchev endorsed "wars of national liberation" such as the one in Vietnam, Kennedy called for "peaceful revolution" based on the concept of *nation building*. Drawing on Rostow's ideas, the president set out to help developing nations through the infant stages of nationhood with aid programs aimed at improving agriculture, transportation, and communications. Kennedy thus initiated the multi-billion-dollar Alliance for Progress (1961) to spur economic development in Latin America.

Kennedy also created the Peace Corps in 1961 to serve nation building. This agency sent American teachers, agricultural specialists, and health workers into developing nations. Within three years, ten thousand idealistic young men and women had volunteered for service abroad. The Peace Corps's humanitarian purpose, however, sometimes competed with the administration's political agenda. Conflicts arose between corps members in the field, who identified with Third World peoples' desire for neutrality in the Cold War, and headquarters in Washington, where the goal was aligning those peoples with United States foreign policy.

Peace Corps

Kennedy also relied on *counterinsurgency*—an organized effort to defeat revolutionaries who challenged Third World governments friendly with the United States. American military and technical advisers trained native troops and police forces to quell unrest. And American soldiers—especially the Special Forces units (Green Berets)—were provided a protective shield against insurgents while American civilian personnel worked on economic projects.

The CIA continued its covert operations, including the training of the exile brigade and the launching of Operation Mongoose in Cuba (see page 866). The agency also plotted in the Congo (now Zaire) in 1960 and 1961 to poison Premier Patrice Lumumba with a lethal injection of a virus. A CIA-backed Congolese political faction finally murdered Lumumba, who had turned to the Soviet Union for help during a civil war. In Brazil, the CIA spent $20 million to influence the 1962 elections against President João Goulart, who had expropriated the property of the United States-based firm International Telephone and Telegraph and had refused to vote to oust Cuba from the Organization of American States. When Goulart's supporters won, the CIA helped organize opposition groups. In 1964, with the United States's complicity, the Brazilian military overthrew Goulart.

Nation building and counterinsurgency seldom worked. Americans assumed, as they had for much of the twentieth century in the Caribbean, that the United States model of capitalism and government could be transferred successfully to foreign cultures. But as much as many foreign peoples craved United States economic assistance and praised America's wealth, they resented meddling by outsiders. And because aid was usually funneled through a self-interested elite, it often failed to reach the very poor. To people who preferred the relatively quick solutions of a managed economy, moreover, the American emphasis on private enterprise seemed inappropriate.

Descent into the Longest War: Vietnam

In Southeast Asia the belief that the United States could influence the internal affairs of Third World countries led to outright disaster. How Vietnam became the site of America's longest war, and how the world's most powerful nation failed to subdue a peasant people who suffered enormous losses, is one of the most remarkable and tragic stories of modern history.

For decades after the French takeover of Indochina (Vietnam, Cambodia, and Laos) in the late nineteenth century, France exploited Vietnam for its

French Imperialism in Vietnam

rice, rubber, tin, and tungsten. Although the French beat back recurrent rebellions, Vietnamese nationalists dedicated to independence grew in strength. Their leader Ho Chi Minh, born in 1890, lived in France before the First World War, and at the close of the war he joined the French Communist Party to use it as a vehicle for Vietnamese independence. For the next two decades, living in China, the Soviet Union, and elsewhere, Ho patiently planned and fought to free his nation from French colonialism. During World War II Ho's Vietminh warriors harassed both French and Japanese forces—near the end of the war with OSS help.

The Truman administration rejected Vietnam's independence in favor of the restoration of French rule for several reasons. First, Americans wanted

United States Rejection of Vietnamese Independence

France's cooperation in the Cold War. Second, Southeast Asia was an economic asset; its rice could feed America's soon-to-be ally Japan, and it was the world's largest producer of natural rubber and a rich source of other commodities. Third, the area seemed strategically vital to the defense of Japan and the Philippines. Finally, Ho Chi Minh was a communist, who, it was assumed, would assist Soviet expansionism. Overlooking the native roots of the nationalist rebellion against France, and the tenacious Vietnamese resistance to foreign intruders, American presidents from Truman through Ford took a globalist view of Vietnam, interpreting events through a Cold War lens.

In the 1940s Vietnam was a French problem that few Americans followed with keen interest. More

Ho Chi Minh (1890-1969) had already been working for Vietnamese independence for a quarter-century before this 1945 photograph was snapped. Here Ho (seated third from right with light-colored shirt) and other Vietnamese leaders are pictured with "Deer" Team members of the United States Office of Strategic Services (OSS). Colonel Allison Thomas (second from the right) headed the "Deer" Team's effort to help Ho's Vietminh soldiers battle Japanese forces in Vietnam toward the end of the Second World War. Wartime Vietminh-OSS cooperation did not lead to postwar Vietnamese-American accommodation, however, because the Truman administration opposed Vietnam's independence from America's Cold War ally France. Alan Squires.

dramatic crises in Europe commanded their attention, even after the Vietminh and the French went to war in 1946.

United States Support for the French

But when Jiang Jieshi (Chiang Kai-shek) went down to defeat in China less than three years later (see page 857), the Truman administration made two crucial decisions—both in early 1950, before the Korean War. First, it recognized the French puppet government of Bao Dai, a playboy and former emperor who had collaborated with the French and Japanese. In the eyes of the Vietnamese, the United States thus became in essence a colonial power, an ally of the hated French. Second, the administration agreed to send weapons, and ultimately military advisers, to the French. Eisenhower continued these policies, and by 1954 the United States had provided more than $2 billion in military assistance and was bearing three-fourths of the cost of the war.

Despite American aid, the French lost steadily to the Vietminh. Finally, in early 1954, Ho's forces surrounded the French fortress at Dienbienphu in northwest Vietnam (see map, page 899). Eisenhower huddled

Dienbienphu Crisis

with his advisers. Some suggested a massive American air strike against Vietminh positions, perhaps even using tactical atomic weapons. Eisenhower moved deliberately. Although the United States had been advising and bankrolling the French, it had not committed its own forces to the war. If American airpower did not save the French, would ground troops be required next, and in hostile terrain? As one high-level doubter remarked, "One cannot go over Niagara Falls in a barrel only slightly." Some presidential advisers feared that American units might have to be moved from elsewhere in Asia and Europe, a shift that could leave other regions vulnerable.

Worrying aloud about a communist victory, Eisenhower compared the weak nations of the world to a row of dominoes, all of which would topple if just one fell. He decided to press the British to help form a coalition to address the Indochinese crisis, but they refused. At home, influential members of Congress told the president they wanted "no more Koreas" and warned him to avoid any American military commitment, especially in the absence of cooperation from the United States allies. Some also felt uneasy about supporting colonialism. The issue became moot on May 7, when the weary French defenders at Dienbienphu surrendered.

To compound the administration's problems, the French wanted out of the war. In April they had entered into peace talks at Geneva with the United States, the Soviet Union, Britain, the People's Republic of China, Laos, Cambodia, and the competing Vietnamese regimes of Bao Dai and Ho Chi Minh. Secretary of State John Foster Dulles found the job of negotiating with communists unpleasant; he conducted himself, according to one biographer, like a "puritan in a house of ill repute." Asked at a press conference if he would meet with Chinese delegates, Dulles replied: "Not unless our automobiles collide." The 1954 Geneva accords, signed by France and Ho's Democratic Republic of Vietnam, temporarily divided Vietnam at the 17th parallel; Ho's government was confined to the North, Bao Dai's to the South. The 17th parallel was meant to serve as a military truce line, not a national boundary; the country was scheduled to be unified after national elections in 1956. In the meantime, neither North nor South was to join a military alliance or permit foreign military bases on its soil.

Geneva Accords

Certain that the Geneva agreements ultimately would mean communist victory, the United States and Bao Dai refused to accept the accords and set about to sabotage them. Soon after the conference, a CIA team entered Vietnam and undertook secret operations against the North, including commando raids across the 17th parallel. In the fall of 1954 the United States also joined Britain, France, Australia, New Zealand, the Philippines, Thailand, and Pakistan in the anticommunist Southeast Asia Treaty Organization (SEATO), one purpose of which was to protect the southern part of Vietnam.

In the South, the United States helped Ngo Dinh Diem push Bao Dai aside. A Catholic in a Buddhist nation, Diem had many enemies and no mass support. But he was a nationalist and an anticommunist, and with American aid he staged a fraudulent election that gave him 98 percent of the vote. When Ho called for national elections in keeping with the Geneva agreements, Diem and Eisenhower refused, fearing that the popular Vietminh leader would win. From 1955 to 1961 the Diem government received more than $1 billion in American aid, most of it military. American advisers organized and trained the South Vietnamese army. Police experts from Michigan State University helped build a national guard.

Backing the Diem Regime

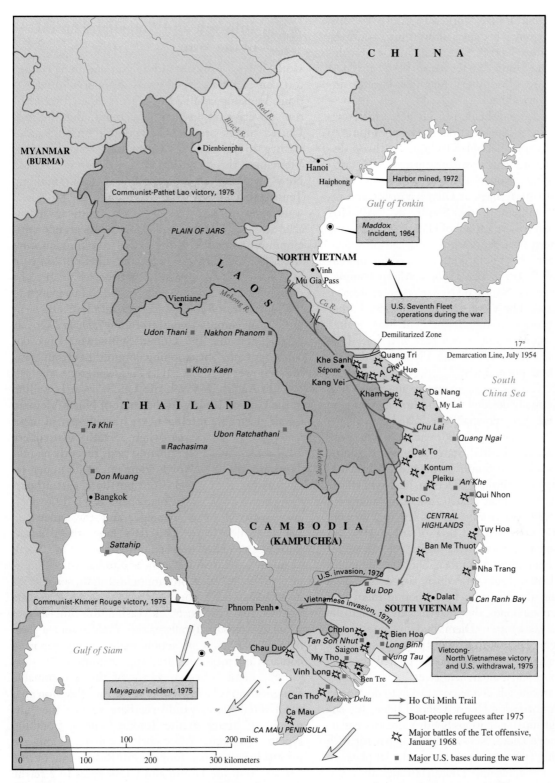

CHINA

Red R.

Black R.

MYANMAR
(BURMA)

• Dienbienphu

Hanoi •

Haiphong

Harbor mined, 1972

Communist-Pathet Lao victory, 1975

Gulf of Tonkin

PLAIN OF JARS

Maddox
incident, 1964

L
A
O
S

NORTH VIETNAM

Vientiane •

Mekong R.

• Vinh
Mu Gia Pass

Udon Thani ■   ■ Nakhon Phanom

Ca R.

U.S. Seventh Fleet
operations during the war

Demilitarized Zone

17°

Quang Tri   Demarcation Line, July 1954

■ Khon Kaen

Khe Sanh •
Sépone •
Kang Vei

A Chau
• Hue

*South
China Sea*

THAILAND

Kham Duc   Da Nang
• My Lai

• Ta Khli

Chu Lai

Ubon Ratchathani ■

■ *Quang Ngai*

• Rachasima

Dak To •
Kontum
Pleiku •   *An Khe*

• Don Muang

Mekong R.

• Duc Co   ☆ *Qui Nhon*

• Bangkok

*CENTRAL
HIGHLANDS*   • Tuy Hoa

CAMBODIA
(KAMPUCHEA)

Ban Me Thuot

☆ ■ Nha Trang

• Sattahip

U.S. invasion, 1970

☆• Dalat   ■ *Can Ranh Bay*

Communist-Khmer Rouge victory, 1975

Bu Dop

Vietnamese invasion, 1978

SOUTH VIETNAM

Phnom Penh •

Cholon ☆
Tan Son Nhut •
Saigon •

☆ Bien Hoa
■ *Long Binh*

Vietcong-
North Vietnamese victory
and U.S. withdrawal, 1975

Gulf of Siam

Chau Duc

My Tho ☆
Vinh Long ☆

☆• *Vung Tau*

☆ ■
• Ben Tre

Mayaguez incident, 1975

Can Tho •
Ca Mau •

Mekong Delta

→ Ho Chi Minh Trail

⇨ Boat-people refugees after 1975

CA MAU PENINSULA

☆ Major battles of the Tet offensive,
January 1968

0		100		200 miles

■ Major U.S. bases during the war

0	100	200	300 kilometers

Southeast Asia and the Vietnam War   *To prevent communists from coming to power in Vietnam,
Cambodia, and Laos in the 1960s, the United States intervened massively in Southeast Asia. The interventions failed, and the remaining American troops made a hasty exit from Vietnam in 1975, when the
victorious Vietcong and North Vietnamese took Saigon and renamed it Ho Chi Minh City.*

American agriculturalists worked to improve crops. American consumer products flowed into southern Vietnamese cities. Diem's Saigon regime became dependent on the United States for its very existence, and the culture of southern Vietnam became increasingly Americanized.

Diem proved a difficult ally. He acted dictatorially, abolishing village elections and appointing to public office people beholden to him. He threw dissenters in jail and shut down newspapers that criticized his regime. Noncommunists and communists alike began to strike back at Diem's corrupt and repressive government in the South. In 1959 Ho's regime in the northern capital of Hanoi began to send aid to southern insurgents who embarked on a program of terror, assassinating hundreds of Diem's village officials. Then, in late 1960, southern communists organized the National Liberation Front, known as the Vietcong. The Vietcong in turn attracted other anti-Diem groups in the South. The war against imperialism had become a two-part civil war: Ho's North versus Diem's South, and Vietcong guerrillas versus the Diem government.

Though fearing entrapment in an Asian war, President Kennedy decided to stand firm in Vietnam. "How do we get moving?" he asked his advisers. In 1961 he ordered more United States military personnel to South Vietnam. By late 1963, Project Beef-up had sent more than 16,000 American "advisers." That year, 489 Americans were killed in Vietnam. Kennedy also increased the flow of aid dollars, but Diem refused to reform. Meanwhile, Diem's opponents in Vietnam grew in number. The United States's Strategic Hamlet Program, which aimed to isolate peasants from the Vietcong by uprooting them into barbed-wire compounds, alienated villagers and actually strengthened resistance to Diem. Buddhist priests protested, charging Diem with religious persecution. In the streets of Saigon, protesting monks poured gasoline over their robes and ignited themselves.

Kennedy's Escalation

American officials divided over what to do. Some, especially Ambassador Henry Cabot Lodge, Jr., encouraged a group of ambitious South Vietnamese generals to remove Diem. Kennedy grew impatient with his squabbling advisers, but in the end he let plans go forward for a coup against Diem. Through the CIA, the United States cooperated with the generals. They struck on November 1, 1963, capturing and murdering Diem just a few weeks before Kennedy himself met death by an assassin's bullet.

Johnson and Americanization of the War

With new governments in Saigon and in Washington, some analysts urged a reassessment. United Nations, Vietcong, and French leaders called for a coalition government in South Vietnam. But the new United States president, Lyndon Johnson, vowed victory to forestall a "Communist take-over" of Vietnam—"this damn little pissant country." An old New Dealer, the president talked about building Tennessee Valley Authorities around the world. "I want them to say, 'This is what Americans left—schools and hospitals and dams.'" An ardent anti-communist wedded to the global containment doctrine, Johnson would draw the line not only in Southeast Asia but also in Latin America. In 1965 he dispatched twenty thousand United States troops to the Dominican Republic to prevent a leftist government from coming to power. In the *Johnson Doctrine*, he declared that the United States would prevent "another Cuba" by stopping communists from coming to power in the Western Hemisphere.

On August 2, 1964, the U.S.S. *Maddox*, sailing in the Gulf of Tonkin off the coast of North Vietnam on an electronic intelligence-gathering patrol in an area where South Vietnamese commando raids recently had hit North Vietnam, came under attack from northern patrol boats (see map, page 899). The small craft suffered heavy damage, and the unharmed *Maddox* sailed away. Two days later, the *Maddox*, joined by another destroyer, moved toward the North Vietnamese shore once again as if to bait the communists. In bad weather on a moonless night, sonar technicians reported torpedo attacks; the two destroyers began firing ferociously. As Washington officials met to decide how to retaliate, the *Maddox* sent a flash message: "Review of action makes many reported contacts and torpedoes fired appear doubtful."

Tonkin Gulf Incident

President Johnson, aware of the questionable evidence, nonetheless announced on television that the United States would retaliate against the "unprovoked" attack in the Tonkin Gulf by bombing North Vietnam. After brief debate, Congress promptly passed the Tonkin Gulf Resolution, by 466 votes to 0 in the House and by 88 votes to 2 in the Senate. Only Wayne Morse of Oregon and Ernest Gruening of Alaska dissented from the resolution's sweeping language, which authorized the president to "take all necessary measures to repel any armed

President Lyndon B. Johnson (1908–1973) (left), here meeting with Secretary of Defense Robert S. McNamara (b. 1919) at the president's Texas ranch in December 1964, agonized over the Vietnam War. That year, recorded telephone conversations reveal, the president remarked that the war was "just the biggest damn mess I ever saw." Johnson also lamented that "I don't think it's worth fighting for, and I don't think we can get out." Later, McNamara wrote in his memoir, In Retrospect: (1995), that United States officials "acted according to what we thought were the principles and traditions of this nation. We made our [Vietnam] decisions in light of those values. Yet we were wrong, terribly wrong." Lyndon B. Johnson Library.

attack against the forces of the United States and to prevent further aggression." By passing the Tonkin Gulf Resolution—which Johnson considered nearly equivalent to a declaration of war—Congress essentially surrendered its powers in the foreign policy process by giving the president wide latitude to conduct the war as he saw fit. The resolution, former secretary of defense Robert McNamara noted, served "to open the floodgates."

In neighboring Laos, meanwhile, American bombers hit the "Ho Chi Minh Trail"—supply routes connecting the Vietcong with the North Vietnamese (see map, page 899).

Laos

The bombings were kept secret from the American Congress and public. The CIA had long manipulated politics in Laos, where in 1962 noncommunists and communists had agreed to a neutralist government. As Ambassador William H. Sullivan admitted, "We ran Laos." After winning the presidency in his own right in the fall of 1964, Johnson directed the military to plan stepped-up bombing of both Laos and North Vietnam. Undersecretary of State George Ball urged caution: "Once on the tiger's back we cannot be sure of picking the place to dismount."

In February 1965 the Vietcong, who controlled nearly half of South Vietnam, attacked the American airfield at Pleiku, killing nine Americans. In response, Johnson ordered carrier-based jets to ravage the North. Soon Operation Rolling Thunder—a sustained bombing program above the 17th parallel—was under way. Before the war was over, more bombs would fall on Vietnam than American aircraft had dropped in the Second World War. The North Vietnamese, however, would not give up. They hid in shelters and rebuilt roads and bridges with a perseverance that frustrated and awed American decision makers. The war was not going well for the United States or its ally, the unstable South Vietnamese government in Saigon.

In late July 1965, Johnson's advisers debated a request from the Joint Chiefs of Staff to add some 100,000 to the 80,000 American troops already in

George Ball's Dissent

Vietnam. Only George Ball dissented, urging that the United States "take our losses, let their government fall apart, negotiate, discuss, knowing full well there will be a probable takeover by the Communists." The president listened but seemed already committed to escalation. Ball warned against possible Chinese intervention, negative world opinion, and domestic political dissent. Because "the enemy cannot be seen in Vietnam," Ball seriously doubted that "an army of Westerners can successfully fight Orientals in an Asian jungle." In the long run, the war "will disclose our weakness, not our strength." Worried about the credibility of the United States, Johnson asked: "But George, wouldn't all these countries say that Uncle Sam was a paper tiger?" "No sir," Ball retorted. "The worse blow would be that the mightiest power on earth is unable to defeat a handful of guerrillas."

President Johnson nonetheless decided in July to give the Joint Chiefs more troops. A turning point in the Vietnam War, this decision meant that the United States for the first time was assuming primary responsibility for fighting the war. Fearing that

he would spark a national debate about deepening United States participation in a Southeast Asian war, Johnson underplayed the importance of the decision when he announced it. By the end of 1965 nearly 200,000 American combat troops were at war in Vietnam. Yet Congress had not passed a declaration of war, and most Americans knew little about the venture.

Month by month the war became Americanized. In 1967 alone United States warplanes flew 108,000 sorties and dropped 226,000 tons of bombs on North Vietnam. In 1968 United

Americanization of the War

States troop strength reached 536,100; in 1969, it peaked at 543,400 before falling by the end of the year to 475,200 (see figure). In 1967 the secret CIA-run Phoenix Program began to kill Vietcong leaders; probably 60,000 were

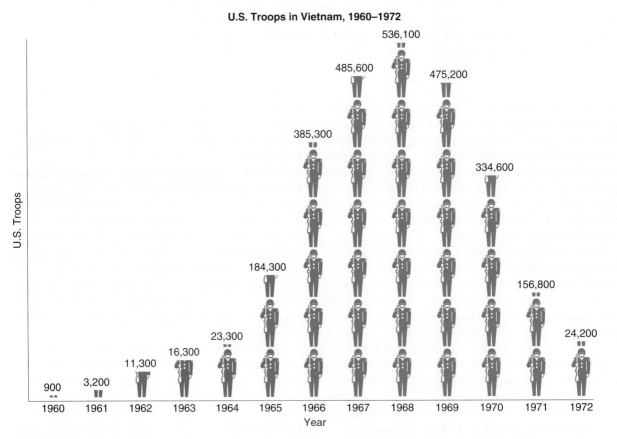

U.S. Troops in Vietnam, 1960–1972

United States Troops in Vietnam 1960–1972   *These numbers show the Americanization of the Vietnam War under President Johnson, who ordered vast increases in troop levels. President Nixon reversed the escalation, so that by the time of the cease-fire in early 1973 fewer than 25,000 American troops remained in Vietnam. Data are for December 31 of each year.*   Source: Data from U.S. Department of Defense.

Aftermath of the My Lai massacre, March 16, 1968, photographed by United States Army photographer Ronald Haeberle of the 11th Infantry Brigade, Americal Division.   Ron Haeberle/*Life* magazine © Time Inc.

assassinated. That year, too, the United States sent $625 million in foreign aid to South Vietnam—25 percent of America's total aid to the entire world. Undeterred, Ho increased the flow of arms and men to the rebels in the South.

In this seemingly endless war of attrition, each American escalation begot a new Vietnamese escalation. "I feel like a hitchhiker caught in a hailstorm on a Texas highway," groaned Johnson. "I can't run, I can't hide, and I can't make it stop." Rejecting the Joint Chiefs' view that United States reserve forces should be mobilized and a national emergency declared, the president kept thinking that the North Vietnamese and Vietcong, taking heavy casualties, had a breaking point. Johnson also worried that if he did not win that "bitch of a war" in Vietnam, members of Congress would cripple his Great Society reform program—"the woman I really loved" (see pages 931–936).

The Americanization of the war under Johnson troubled growing numbers of Americans, especially as television coverage brought the war into their homes every night. The pictures and stories were not pretty. Innocent civilians died; refugees straggled into "pacification" camps; villages went up in flames; crops were destroyed to starve the Vietcong and to make villagers dependent on the central government. To expose and destroy Vietcong hiding places, pilots sprayed chemical defoliants such as Agent Orange

over the landscape to denude it; their swaggering motto was "Only You Can Prevent Forests." This ecological warfare meant that a once-rich agricultural nation became dependent on imports of food.

The Vietcong and North Vietnamese contributed to the carnage and destruction, but American guns, bombs, and chemicals took by far the greatest toll, and the Vietnamese people knew it. Indeed, America's search-and-destroy missions proved counterproductive; rather than winning the war, they were molding an ever-growing population of anti-American peasants who gave secret aid to the Vietcong. Even United States allies among the Vietnamese came to resent their nation's growing dependency. Their politics manipulated and their traditional culture challenged by rock-'n'-roll music, interracial marriages, honky-tonk bars, and prostitution, some anticommunist Vietnamese said that they feared becoming "a little America." One United States official later admitted: "It was as if we were trying to build a house with a bulldozer and wrecking crane."

Stories of atrocities made their way home. Most gruesome was the My Lai massacre of March 16, 1968. Freelance journalist Seymour Hersh broke the story after a military cover-up kept the tragedy out of the news for twenty months. A United States army unit led by Lieutenant William Calley entered

My Lai Massacre

the hamlet of My Lai and for four hours mutilated, raped, sodomized, and killed more than three hundred unarmed Vietnamese civilians, most of them women and children. Herding shrieking, pleading villagers near a ditch, Calley and his troops shot scores of them. When a two-year-old child, its mother dead, began to crawl out of the mass grave, Calley tossed the infant down the slope and shot it. The army awarded Calley's brigade a Special Commendation for 128 "enemy" killed even though there had been no combat and no battle at My Lai.

Much of the massacre at My Lai was recorded in graphic pictures by an army photographer. Why did it occur? Applying a "war is hell" theory, some soldiers explained that they had been trained to kill, and once the bloodletting began they kept killing, especially when their officers urged them on. Calley found the culprit in anticommunism: "I looked at communism as a southerner looks at a Negro. . . . It's evil." Racism certainly played a role: dehumanizing Vietnamese as "gooks" and "slants," GIs murdered in cold blood people they ranked with animals. A culture of male supremacy, accentuated by the military environment, also influenced these infantrymen: girls and young women suffered gang rapes; some victims had their vaginas ripped open with knives and bayonets. Calley and the other rapists and killers had lost their moral bearings. But the aftermath reveals that United States officials had lost theirs too. In 1971 Calley was court-martialed, but President Richard Nixon, exploiting the sentiment of many Americans that Calley should be cheered as a hero serving his nation, ordered him released from jail; three years later the mass murderer was paroled. Army juries acquitted and army officials dismissed murder and cover-up charges against all other personnel connected with the My Lai massacre.

Many incidents of deliberate shooting of civilians, torturing and killing of prisoners, taking of Vietnamese ears as trophies, and burning of villages (by "Zippo squads") have been recorded. Most American soldiers, however, were not committing atrocities. They were trying to save their own young lives (their average age was only nineteen) and to serve the United States's mission of defeating enemy troops. Many of these Americans made up the rear-echelon forces that supported the "grunts" in the field. But wherever they were, the environment was inhospitable, for no place in Vietnam was secure. Well-hidden booby traps blasted away

American Soldiers in Vietnam

Wounded American soldiers after a battle in Vietnam. Larry Burrows/*Life* magazine © Time Warner, Inc.

body parts. And the enemy was everywhere yet no-where, often burrowed into elaborate underground tunnels or melded into the population, where any Vietnamese might be a Vietcong terrorist.

Infantrymen on maneuvers carried heavy ruck-sacks into thick jungle growth, where every step was precarious. Insects swarmed, and leeches sucked at weary bodies. Boots and human skin rotted from the rains, which alternated with withering suns. "It was as if the sun and the land itself were in league with the Vietcong," recalled marine officer Philip Caputo in *A Rumor of War* (1977), "wearing us down, driving us mad, killing us." Wounded GIs shouted for a medic, who in turn might call in a "medevac" (med-ical evacuation helicopter), praying that it would not be shot down. A medevac could carry the wounded within minutes to operating tables in MASH (Mo-bile Army Surgical Hospital) units or hospital ships such as the U.S.S. *Sanctuary.* "What I saw were young men coming in, eighteen or nineteen years old . . . and they would be without a leg," remem-bered Gayle Smith, a nurse at the 3rd Surgical Hos-pital.

As the war ground on to no discernible conclu-sion and became increasingly unpopular at home, growing numbers of GIs became cynical, believing either that United States leaders held them back from clobbering the enemy or that the United States had no business being in Vietnam. Soldiers kept hearing leaders in Washington say that the war was being won. GIs in the field knew better. "This conspiracy of illusion," recalled the then captain Colin Powell, fed on "the secure-hamlet nonsense, the search-and-sweep nonsense, the body-count nonsense, all of which we knew was nonsense, even as we did it." Body counts of killed "enemy" forces became a false measure of success. Powell remembered the litany of each night: "'How many did your platoon get?' 'I don't know. We saw two for sure.' 'Well, if you saw two, there were probably eight. So let's say ten.'" The young captain later regretted the "bull" and "careerism" that dominated the military. "Counting bodies became a macabre statistical competition. Companies measured against companies, battalions against battalions, brigades against brigades. Good commanders scored high body counts. And good commanders got promotions."

Given these corrupting conditions and the unre-lenting war against what Powell called a "phantom enemy," morale in the United States armed forces

"Body-Count Nonsense"

sagged, and discipline sometimes lapsed. Disobedi-ence, desertions, and absent-without-official-leave (AWOL) cases steadily increased. Racial tensions be-tween whites and blacks intensified. Drug abuse be-came serious. Many soldiers smoked plentiful, cheap marijuana; 10 percent of the troops took heroin. "Fragging"—the murder of officers by enlisted men, usually using hand grenades—took at least a thou-sand lives between 1969 and 1972.

At home, some young men were expressing their opposition to the war by fleeing the draft. By the end of 1972 more than thirty thousand draft resisters were living in Canada; thousands more had gone into exile in Sweden or Mexico or were living under false iden-tities in the United States. In the course of the war more than a half-million men committed draft viola-tions, including a quarter-million who never regis-tered and thousands who burned their draft cards.

As American military engagements in Vietnam escalated, so did protest at home. Teach-ins at uni-versities began in 1965, and in April of that year 25,000 people marched on the White House. In October the National Committee to End the War in Vietnam mobilized more than 80,000 in nationwide dem-onstrations. Early the following year, Senator J. William Fulbright held public hearings on whether the national interest was being served by pursuing the war in Asia. What exactly was the threat? sena-tors asked. To the surprise of some, George F. Ken-nan testified before television cameras that his con-tainment doctrine was meant for Europe, not the volatile environment of Southeast Asia. In October 1967, 100,000 people marched on Washington to protest the war. In a direct challenge to Johnson's policies, antiwar senator Eugene McCarthy of Min-nesota announced his candidacy for the Democratic presidential nomination.

Antiwar Protest

Disenchantment also rose in the administration itself. Secretary of Defense Robert McNamara, once a vigorous advocate of prosecuting the war, became aghast over the Joint Chiefs' contemplating the use of nuclear weapons in Vietnam and came to believe that continued bombing would not win the war. "The picture of the world's greatest superpower killing or seriously injuring 1,000 noncombatants a week, while trying to pound a tiny backward nation into submission on an issue whose merits are hotly disputed, is not a

Robert McNamara Questions Bombing

pretty one," the defense secretary told Johnson in mid-1967. But, publicly, McNamara endorsed Johnson's course and remained loyal to the beleaguered president until early 1968, when McNamara left office. Later, in his 1995 autobiography, the former defense secretary lamented that the decisions of the Kennedy and Johnson administrations on Vietnam "were wrong, terribly wrong."

Cheered by opinion polls that showed Americans favored escalation over withdrawal, Johnson dug in, snapping at "those little shits on the campuses." Though on occasion he halted the bombing to encourage Ho Chi Minh to negotiate, such pauses often were accompanied by increases in American troop strength. And the United States sometimes resumed or accelerated the bombing just when a diplomatic breakthrough seemed imminent—as in 1966, when a Polish diplomat's efforts were cut short by a resumption of bombing. The North demanded a complete suspension of bombing raids before sitting down at the conference table. And Ho could not accept American terms: nonrecognition of the Vietcong as a legitimate political organization, withdrawal of Northern soldiers from the South, and an end to North Vietnamese military aid to the Vietcong—in short, abandonment of his lifelong dream of an independent, unified Vietnam.

In January 1968, a shocking event forced Johnson to reappraise his position. During Tet, the Vietnamese holiday of the lunar new year, Vietcong and North Vietnamese forces struck all across South Vietnam, capturing provincial capitals (see map, page 899). Vietcong raiders even penetrated the American embassy compound in Saigon. United States and South Vietnamese units eventually regained much of the ground they lost, including the cities, and inflicted heavy casualties on the enemy. In the process, numerous villages were devastated. As one sober-faced American officer explained about the leveling of Ben Tre to drive the Vietcong out, "It became necessary to destroy the town to save it."

Tet Offensive

The Tet offensive jolted Americans. Although Tet ultimately counted as an American military victory, it proved a psychological defeat for Americans. Had not the Vietcong and North Vietnamese demonstrated that they could strike when and where they wished? Did they not have the advantage of fighting on home territory? Why did "their Vietnamese" fight harder than "our Vietnamese"? If all of America's airpower and dollars and half a million troops could not defeat the Vietcong once and for all, could anything do so? Had the American public been lied to? When the highly respected television anchorman Walter Cronkite somberly raised questions about the war on *CBS Evening News*, President Johnson sensed political trouble: "If I've lost Cronkite, I've lost middle America."

The Tet offensive and its impact on public opinion hit the White House like a thunderclap. The new secretary of defense, Clark Clifford, told Johnson that the war—"a sinkhole"—could not be won, even if the 206,000 more soldiers requested by the army were sent to Vietnam. The ultimate Cold Warrior, Dean Acheson—one of the "wise men" Johnson brought in to advise him—bluntly told the surprised president that the military brass did not know what they were talking about.

Dollar/Gold Crisis

The wise men were aware that the nation was suffering a financial crisis prompted by rampant deficit spending, largely due to heavy United States expenditures abroad to sustain the war and other global commitments. Nervous foreigners were exchanging their United States dollars for gold at an alarming rate. On March 14 alone, foreigners—especially Europeans—redeemed $372 million for gold. A post-Tet effort to take the initiative in Vietnam would surely cost billions more and thus further derail the budget, panic foreign owners of dollars, and wreck the economy. Clifford heard from his associates in the business community: "These men now feel we are in a hopeless bog," he told the president. To "maintain public support for the war without the support of these men" was impossible, Clifford concluded.

Strained by exhausting sessions with skeptical advisers, troubled by the economic implications of escalation, sensing that more soldiers and firepower would not bring victory, meeting protesters wherever he went, and faced with serious opposition within his own party, Johnson changed course. On March 31 he announced on television that he had stopped the bombing of most of North Vietnam, and he asked Hanoi to begin negotiations. Then he stunned the nation by dropping out of the presidential race. American leaders, having come reluctantly to the view that they could not win the war, at least would try not to lose it. Peace talks began in May in Paris, but the war ground on. Johnson demanded North Vietnamese concessions before completely halting the bombing, but Hanoi rejected reciprocity.

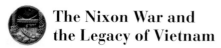

The Nixon War and the Legacy of Vietnam

In July 1969, a few months after his inauguration, the new president, Richard Nixon, announced the *Nixon Doctrine*: the United States will help those

Nixon Doctrine

nations that help themselves. Washington knew that it no longer could afford to sustain its many overseas commitments and that the United States would have to rely more on regional allies to maintain an anticommunist world order. In Southeast Asia this doctrine translated into "Vietnamization"—building up South Vietnamese forces to replace American forces. Nixon began to withdraw United States troops from Vietnam, decreasing their number to 156,800 by the end of 1971. But he also intensified the bombing of the North, hoping to pound Hanoi into concessions: "jugular diplomacy," in the words of Nixon's national security adviser Henry Kissinger. In October 1969, hundreds of thousands of Americans marched peacefully in cities across the nation to call for a moratorium on the war. On November 15, more than a quarter-million marchers protested in Washington, D.C., alone.

On April 1970, South Vietnamese and American forces invaded Cambodia in search of arms depots and enemy forces that used the neutral nation as a

Cambodia and Antiwar Protest

sanctuary. This escalation of the war provoked angry demonstrations on college campuses. At Kent State University in Ohio, national guardsmen ordered to suppress protest killed four people. Across the nation, students went "on strike" to protest the killing in Indochina and America. Nixon dismissed them as "bums." In June the Senate joined the protest against Nixon's broadening of the war by terminating the Tonkin Gulf Resolution of 1964.

Nixon's troubles at home mounted in June 1971 when the *New York Times* began to publish the *Pentagon Papers*, a top-secret official study of United States decisions in the Vietnam War. Secretary McNamara had initiated the study in 1967 to preserve the war's documentary record. Daniel Ellsberg, a former Defense Department official working at the RAND Corporation (a think tank for analyzing defense policy), leaked the report to the *Times*. Nixon secured an injunction to prevent publication, but the Supreme Court overturned the order. The *Pentagon Papers* revealed that American leaders frequently had

lied to the American people. President Johnson, for example, had claimed repeatedly in public that the United States increased its forces in South Vietnam only to respond to escalating North Vietnamese infiltration. The Pentagon study, however, revealed that after mid-1967 the United States itself escalated the war because American officials believed that more troops would deliver victory.

Nixon and Kissinger continued to expand the war, ordering "protective reaction strikes" against the North and the bombing of Cambodia. In December 1972, they launched a massive air strike on the North—the "Christmas bombing." One of Kissinger's aides characterized it as "calculated barbarism." The air terror of 20,000 tons of bombs punished the Vietnamese. At the same time, the United States lost twenty-six planes, including fifteen B-52 bombers. "After B-52s, there doesn't seem to be anything more that they can do," claimed one North Vietnamese. "Apparently they have come to their technological limit."

In Paris, meanwhile, the peace talks begun in 1968 seemed to be going nowhere. The South Vietnamese delegate, who saw defeat coming, purposely stalled the negotiations. But

Cease-Fire Agreement

Kissinger was also meeting privately with Le Duc Tho, the chief delegate from North Vietnam. Nixon instructed Kissinger to make concessions because the president was eager to improve relations with the Soviet Union and China (see page 869), to win back the allegiance of America's allies, and to restore stability at home. When President Nguyen Van Thieu of South Vietnam balked at compromise, Nixon decided to "let Thieu paddle his own canoe." On January 27, 1973, Kissinger and Le Duc Tho signed a cease-fire agreement, and Nixon compelled Thieu to accept it by threatening to cut off United States aid while at the same time promising to defend the South if the North violated the agreement. In the accord, the United States promised to withdraw all of its troops within sixty days. Vietnamese troops would stay in place, and a coalition government that included the Vietcong eventually would be formed in the South.

The United States pulled its troops out of Vietnam, leaving behind some advisers, and reduced but did not end its aid program. Both North and South soon violated the cease-fire, and full-scale war erupted once more. As many had predicted, the feeble South Vietnamese government—for so long an American puppet—could not hold out. Just before its surrender, hundreds of Americans and Vietnamese who had worked for them were hastily evacuated by helicopter from the roof of the American embassy in Saigon. On April 29, 1975, the South Vietnamese government collapsed. Shortly thereafter Saigon was renamed Ho Chi Minh City for the persevering patriot, who had died in 1969.

The overall costs of the war were immense. More than 58,000 Americans and about 1.5 million Vietnamese had died. Civilian deaths in Cambodia and Laos numbered in the millions too. The war cost the United States at least $170 billion, and billions more would be paid out in veterans' benefits. The vast sums spent on the war became unavailable for investment at home to improve the infrastructure and quality of life. Instead, the nation suffered inflation and retreat from reform programs (see Chapters 31 and 32), as well as political schism, violations of civil liberties, and abuses of executive power. The war also delayed détente with the Soviet Union and the People's Republic of China, fueled friction with allies, and alienated Third World nations.

Costs of the Vietnam War

In 1975 communists assumed control and instituted repressive governments in South Vietnam, Cambodia, and Laos, but the domino effect once predicted by prowar United States officials never occurred. Acute hunger afflicted the people of those devastated lands. Soon refugees were crowding aboard unsafe vessels in an attempt to escape their battered homelands. Many of these "boat people" eventually emigrated to the United States, where they were received with mixed feelings by Americans reluctant to be reminded of defeat in Asia. But many Americans faced the fact that the United States, which had relentlessly bombed, burned, and defoliated once-rich agricultural lands, bore considerable responsibility for the plight of the Southeast Asian peoples.

This sad conclusion prompted an American ambassador to pose a central question about the United States's defeat: How was it that "so many with so much could achieve so little for so long against so few"? General Maxwell Taylor, summarizing the reasons why Americans could not win the Vietnam War, answered that "we didn't know our ally. Secondly, we knew even less about the enemy. And, the last, most inexcusable of our mistakes, was not knowing our own people."

Americans seemed both angry and confused about the nation's war experience. For the first time in their history, historian William Appleman Williams observed, Americans were suffering from a serious case of "empire shock"—that is, shock over having had their overseas sphere of influence violently pushed back. Hawkish leaders claimed that America's failure in Vietnam undermined the nation's credibility and tempted enemies to exploit opportunities at the expense of United States interests. They pointed to a "Vietnam syndrome"—a suspicion of foreign entanglements—that they feared would inhibit the United States from exercising its power. Next time, they said, the military should be permitted to do its job, free from the constraints of whimsical public opinion, stab-in-the-back journalists, and meddlesome politicians. America lost in Vietnam, they asserted, because Americans lost their guts and will at home.

Lessons of Vietnam

Dovish leaders drew different lessons, denying that the military had suffered undue restrictions. Some blamed the war on an imperial presidency that had permitted strong-willed men to act without restraint, and on pusillanimous Congresses that had conceded too much power to the executive branch. Make the president adhere to the checks-and-balances system—make him go to Congress for a declaration of war—these critics counseled, and America would become less interventionist. This view found expression in the War Powers Act of 1973, which sought to limit the president's war-making freedom.

Other critics claimed that as long as the United States remained a major power with compelling ideological, strategic, economic, and political needs that could be satisfied only through activism abroad, the nation would continue to be interventionist, especially in the Third World. The United States was destined to intervene abroad, they argued, to sustain its role as the world's policeman, teacher, social worker, banker, and merchant.

Some critics blamed the containment doctrine—that "prison-house" for policymakers, according to historian George C. Herring—for failing to make distinctions between areas vital and peripheral to the national security and for relying too heavily on military means. Containment could not work, they believed, if there were no political stability and no effective popular government in the country where it was being applied.

Public discussion of the lessons of the Vietnam War also was stimulated by veterans' calls for help in dealing with post-traumatic stress disorder, which

Post-traumatic Stress Disorder

afflicted thousands of the 2.8 million Vietnam veterans. Once home, they suffered nightmares and extreme nervousness. Doctors reported that the disorder stemmed primarily from the soldiers' having seen so many children, women, and elderly people killed. Some GIs inadvertently killed these people; some killed them vengefully and later felt guilt. Many vets committed suicide.

Other veterans heightened public awareness of the war by publicizing the effects of Agent Orange and other chemicals they had handled or were accidentally sprayed with in Vietnam. Films such as *Coming Home* (1978), *The Deer Hunter* (1978), and *Apocalypse Now* (1979), personal accounts such as Philip Caputo's *A Rumor of War* (1977), and novels such as James Webb's *Fields of Fire* (1978), all of which depicted the soldier's Vietnam, raised questions about whether defeat had been inevitable, given the inhospitable environment and elusive enemy. The Vietnam Veterans Memorial, erected in Washington, D.C., in 1982, kept such questions alive.

Secretary of State Henry Kissinger (b. 1923) on one leg of his "shuttle diplomacy" between Cairo, Egypt, and Tel Aviv, Israel. In the aftermath of the Arab-Israeli War of 1973 and the oil embargo, Kissinger patiently worked to quiet tempers. Shortly after this 1975 photograph, Egypt and Israel initialed a historic Kissinger-designed agreement that placed a United Nations peacekeeping force in the Sinai region between the two nations.   Gerald Ford Presidential Library.

Wars and Interventions in the 1970s

Besides struggling with Vietnam, the Nixon and Ford administrations repeatedly exerted United States power in the Third World. They calculated that revolutions and radicalism in the Third World still had to be contained and that the Third World challenge to American influence in international organizations such as the United Nations had to be thwarted. Limited wars such as Vietnam cost too much, and they risked drawing the two superpowers into direct conflict. Critics charged that the Nixon administration too often blamed Third World instability on Soviet or communist intrigue, when in fact it derived from indigenous social class, political, religious, and ethnic differences.

Events in the Middle East revealed the fragility of the Nixon-Kissinger grand strategy. Israel, using American weapons, had scored victories against Egypt and Syria in the Six-Day War (1967), seizing the West Bank and the ancient city of Jerusalem from Jordan, the Golan Heights from Syria, and the Sinai Peninsula from Egypt (see map, page 895), creating the enduring problem of the "occupied territories." Israel's Arab adversaries had used Soviet weapons. To

further complicate matters, Palestinians, many of them expelled from their homes in 1948 when the nation of Israel was created, had organized the Palestine Liberation Organization (PLO) and pledged to destroy Israel. PLO sympathizers made hit-and-run raids on Jewish settlements, hijacked jetliners, and murdered Israeli athletes at the 1972 Olympic Games in Munich, West Germany. The Israelis retaliated by assassinating PLO leaders.

In October 1973, Egypt and Syria attacked Israel. In spite of détente, Moscow (backing Egypt) and Washington (backing Israel) put their armed

1973 War in the Middle East

forces—including their nuclear forces—on alert. In an attempt to push Americans into a pro-Arab stance, the Organization of Petroleum Exporting Countries (OPEC) embargoed shipments of oil to the United States. An energy crisis and dramatically higher oil prices rocked the nation. Soon Kissinger arranged a cease-fire and undertook "shuttle diplomacy," flying repeatedly between Middle Eastern capitals in search of a settlement. In March 1974, OPEC lifted the oil embargo. The next year Kissinger persuaded Egypt and Israel to accept a United Nations peacekeeping force in the Sinai. But peace did not come to the region because Palestinian and other Arabs still vowed to destroy Israel, and Israelis insisted on building Jewish settlements in occupied lands.

In 1970, Nixon spotted a communist threat in Chile, when the citizens of that South American nation elected a Marxist president, Salvador Allende.

Intervention in Chile

The CIA began secret operations to disrupt Chile ("make the economy scream") and encouraged military officers to stage a coup. In 1973 a military junta ousted Allende and installed an authoritarian regime in his place. Nixon and Kissinger privately pronounced their policy of "destabilization" successful, while publicly denying any role in the affair that implanted iron-fisted tyranny in Chile for two decades.

In Africa, where United States purchases of oil, chromium, manganese, cobalt, and other strategic minerals were significant, the Nixon administration at first preferred the status quo. Slurring black Africans as

Containing Radicalism in Africa

"jigs" and "niggers," Nixon backed the white-minority regime in Rhodesia (now Zimbabwe); activated the CIA in a failed effort to defeat a Soviet- and Cuban-backed faction in newly independent Angola's civil war; and in South Africa tolerated the white rulers who imposed the racist policy of apartheid on blacks (85 percent of the population), keeping them poor, disfranchised, and segregated in prison-like townships. After the leftist government came to power in Angola, however, Washington took a keener interest in the rest of Africa, building economic ties and sending arms to friendly black nations such as Kenya and Zaire. The administration also began to distance the United States from the white governments of Rhodesia and South Africa. America had to "prevent the radicalization of Africa," said Kissinger, at a time when Soviet-American competition, despite détente, was intensifying.

The United States was interventionist in the Third World in part because the American economy depended on imports of strategic raw materials such as tin, zinc, and manganese. Furthermore, American investments abroad totaled more than $133 billion by the mid-1970s. Ameri-

United States Economic Interests Challenged

can leaders thus read threats to markets, investments, and raw materials as deadly stabs at the

high American standard of living. Particularly alarming was the United Nations's 1974 call for a "New International Economic Order" for the Third World: low-interest loans, lower prices for technology, and higher prices for raw materials. American economic holdings became targets. Venezuela nationalized American oil properties in 1976; India legislated that its nationals own a majority of voting shares in industrial firms; and terrorists around the world destroyed American facilities and kidnapped and sometimes murdered American executives of multinational corporations. In turn, these companies worked to influence foreign politics, as when International Telephone and Telegraph helped undermine President Allende in Chile and Lockheed Aircraft bribed foreign leaders to promote sales. Multinationals also provided "cover" for CIA agents.

 ## Carter's Diplomatic Intervention

When President Jimmy Carter took office in 1977, he promised no more Vietnams. Instead he vowed new departures, including an emphasis on human rights and advancement of the dialogue with Third World nations. Carter promised to be an interventionist, too, but through diplomacy instead of armed force. Like his predecessors, however, he frowned on radicalism and nationalism because they threatened America's prominent global position. At the time, more than 400,000 American military personnel were stationed abroad, the United States had military links with ninety-two nations, United States arms sales overseas had reached $10 billion per year, and the CIA was active on every continent.

Carter worked to overcome the prevalent Third World view that the United States was a selfish imperial power. He appointed Andrew Young, a black civil rights activist and member of Congress, ambassador to the United Nations, earning goodwill among developing nations. Young believed that the United States should stay out of local disputes, even if communists were involved. Carter fired Young in 1979 after the ambassador met privately with representatives of the PLO (at that time, the United States refused to recognize the PLO because the organization did not recognize Israel's right to exist).

In the Middle East, Carter markedly improved the peace process. Through tenacious personal diplomacy at a Camp David meeting in 1978 with

Camp David Agreements

Egyptian and Israeli leaders, the president gained Israel's promise to withdraw from the Sinai (see map, page 895). The agreement was finalized the following year. Other Arab states denounced the agreement for not requiring Israel to relinquish additional occupied territories—namely, the West Bank and Golan Heights—and for not guaranteeing a Palestinian homeland. But the treaty at least ended warfare along one frontier in that troubled area of the world.

In Latin America, Carter sought compromise with nationalists (see map, page 913), even seeking to reduce tensions with Castro's Cuba by establishing limited diplomatic links. But a crisis in 1980, during which the island regime allowed 100,000 Cubans to sail to Florida from the port of Mariel, soured relations once again. When it was discovered that many of the migrants were mentally ill or were prisoners freed from jail, the mayor of Miami charged that "Fidel has flushed his toilet on us."

In Panama, citizens longed for control over the Canal Zone, which they believed had been wrongfully taken from their nation in 1903 (see page 653).

Panama Canal Treaties

Some conservative Americans, such as former California governor Ronald Reagan, running for the presidency, went so far as to claim that the United States had bought and owned the zone, "and we're going to keep it." Carter, however, feared that Panamanians might try to seize the canal by force or might damage the vulnerable waterway. Recognizing also that the canal's value had dwindled because many new, large ships could not squeeze through its locks, he advanced negotiations that had begun after anti-American riots in Panama in 1964. The United States signed two treaties with Panama in 1977. One provided for the return of the Canal Zone to Panama in 2000, and the other guaranteed the United States the right to defend the canal after that time. The Senate narrowly endorsed both agreements in 1978.

Carter met his toughest foreign policy test in Iran. Many Iranians had not forgotten that the United States had meddled in Iranian affairs by backing the shah in the 1946 crisis and restoring him to his throne in 1953. Iranian revolutionaries led by Ayatollah Ruhollah Khomeini, a bitterly anti-American Muslim cleric, also resented the CIA's

Iranian Hostage Crisis

On March 26, 1979, Egypt's president Anwar el-Sadat (1918-1981) on the left, Israel's prime minister Menachem Begin (1913-1992) on the right, and United States president Jimmy Carter (b. 1924) signed a peace treaty known as the Camp David Accords. Studiously negotiated by Carter, the Egyptian-Israeli peace has held to this day—despite conflict in much of the rest of the Middle East. Jimmy Carter Presidential Library.

training of the shah's ruthless secret police and the huge infusion of United States arms into their country—$19 billion worth between 1973 and 1978 alone. When the shah was overthrown in 1979 and then admitted to the United States for medical treatment, mobs stormed the American embassy in Teheran. They took American personnel as hostages, demanding the return of the shah to stand trial. The Iranians eventually released a few American prisoners, but fifty-two others languished more than a year under Iranian guard. They suffered solitary confinement, beatings, and terrifying mock executions.

President Carter would not return the shah to Iran or apologize for past United States aid to his regime. Unable to gain the hostages' freedom through diplomatic intermediaries, Carter felt "the same kind of impotence that a powerful person feels when his child is kidnapped." He took steps to isolate Iran economically, freezing Iranian assets in the United States. The hostage takers continued to grab headlines, often parading their blindfolded and bound captives before television cameras to taunt the United States. Americans seethed in anger.

In April 1980, frustrated and at low ebb in public opinion polls, Carter broke diplomatic relations with Iran and ordered a daring rescue mission. But the rescue effort miscarried after equipment failure in the sandy Iranian desert, and during the hasty withdrawal two aircraft collided, killing eight American soldiers. Critics chided Carter for undertaking a risky operation that surely would have cost the lives of many hostages. Secretary of State Cyrus Vance, already troubled by the growing militancy of Carter's foreign policy and the president's acceptance of the "visceral anti-Sovietism" of National Security Affairs Adviser Zbigniew Brzezinski, resigned in protest. The hostages were not freed until January 1981, after the United States unfroze Iranian assets and promised not to intervene again in Iran's internal affairs.

Carter's diplomatic record failed to meet his aspirations. More American military personnel were stationed overseas in 1980 than in 1976; the defense budget climbed and sales of arms abroad grew to $15.3 billion in 1980. Carter's human-rights policy also proved inconsistent. The president did persuade some nations to release political prisoners, but he left himself vulnerable to the charge of a double standard by applying the human-rights test to some nations (the Soviet Union, Argentina, and Chile) but not to United States allies (South Korea, the shah's Iran, and the Philippines).

Carter's Mixed Record

Carter's performance did not satisfy Americans who wanted a post-Vietnam reinstatement of the economic hegemony and military edge the United States once enjoyed. As one Tennessee woman mused, "Growing up we learned in history that America was the best in everything. . . . But where can you go today and be respected for being American?" An Oklahoma couple urged Carter to take up Teddy Roosevelt's big stick once again. "And club the hell out of them if you need to," urged the blunt husband. During the 1980 presidential election, this nostalgia for old-fashioned American militancy and supremacy found a ringing voice in Ronald Reagan.

Reagan's Confrontations with the Third World

The facts and nuances of international relations often eluded Ronald Reagan. After returning from his first trip to South America, he commented, "Well, I've learned a lot. . . . You'd be surprised. They're all individual countries." Reagan blamed most Third World troubles on the Soviet Union and thought revolutionary movements took their orders from communists. Invoking the Reagan Doctrine (see page 873), the United States intervened both covertly and openly in civil wars in several Third World countries. The Reagan administration also preferred military solutions over negotiations. In 1983, for example, United States forces invaded the tiny Caribbean nation of Grenada to oust a leftist government with ties to Castro's Cuba.

Under the banner of private enterprise, Reagan pressed Third World nations to open their economies to competition and reduce the role of the state in managing economic affairs. The United Nation's Convention on the Law of the Sea, patiently composed during the years 1973 to 1980 through extended negotiations and compromise, became a test case. Developing nations argued that rich sea-bed resources of petroleum and minerals should be shared under international supervision among all nations as a "common heritage of mankind." The industrial states, which alone had the capital and equipment needed to conduct excavating and drilling operations, preferred private exploitation with minimal international management. The treaty, adopted in 1982 but not entered into force until 1994, represented a compromise. The Reagan administration rejected the convention on the grounds that it did not adequately protect private American companies. In 1994 the Clinton administration sent the treaty to the Senate; as of this writing the convention still languishes there.

Law of the Sea Treaty

Reagan officials believed that the Soviets and their Cuban allies were fomenting disorder in Central America (see map, page 913). In small, very poor El Salvador, revolutionaries challenged the government, which was dominated by the military and a small landed elite. The regime used (or could not control) right-wing death squads, which killed thousands of dissidents and other citizens as well as some American missionaries who had been working with landless peasants. Per-

El Salvador

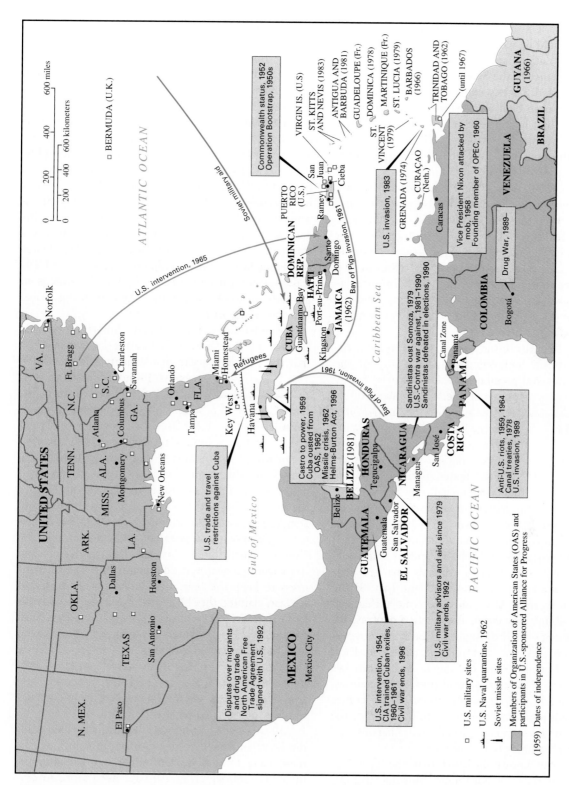

600 miles

600 kilometers

□ BERMUDA (U.K.)

ATLANTIC OCEAN

Commonwealth status, 1952
Operation Bootstrap, 1950s

VIRGIN IS. (U.S)
ST. KITTS
AND NEVIS (1983)
ANTIGUA AND
BARBUDA (1981)
GUADELOUPE (Fr.)
MARTINIQUE (Fr.)
ST. DOMINICA (1978)
ST. LUCIA (1979)
VINCENT   BARBADOS
(1979)   (1966)
TRINIDAD AND
TOBAGO (1962)
(until 1967)
GUYANA
(1966)

BRAZIL

Soviet military aid

U.S. intervention, 1965

San
Juan
Ramey □ □ Cieba
PUERTO
RICO
(U.S.)

DOMINICAN
REP.
HAITI   Santo
Port-au-Prince   Domingo
JAMAICA
(1962) Bay of Pigs invasion, 1961

U.S. invasion, 1983

GRENADA
(1974)   CURAÇAO
(Neth.)

Caracas

VENEZUELA

Vice President Nixon attacked by
mob, 1958
Founding member of OPEC, 1960

Caribbean Sea

COLOMBIA

Drug War, 1989–

Bogotá

Norfolk

VA.
Ft. Bragg
N.C.
Charleston
S.C.
Savannah
Atlanta
Orlando
GA.
Columbus   FLA.
Tampa

Miami
Homestead
Key West   Refugees
Havana

Sandinistas oust Somoza, 1979
U.S.-Contra war against, 1981–1990
Sandinistas defeated in elections, 1990

Canal Zone
Panamá

CUBA
Guantánamo Bay
Kingston

Bay of Pigs invasion, 1961

PANAMA

Anti-U.S. riots, 1959, 1964
Canal treaties, 1978
U.S. invasion, 1989

Castro to power, 1959
Cuba ousted from
OAS, 1962
Missile crisis, 1962
Helms-Burton Act, 1996

BELIZE (1981)

HONDURAS
Tegucigalpa

NICARAGUA
Managua

San José
COSTA
RICA

U.S. trade and travel
restrictions against Cuba

UNITED STATES

TENN.

ALA.
Montgomery
MISS.
New Orleans
LA.

ARK.

GUATEMALA
Guatemala
San Salvador
EL SALVADOR

PACIFIC OCEAN

U.S. military advisors and aid, since 1979
Civil war ends, 1992

OKLA.
Dallas
Houston

TEXAS
San Antonio

MEXICO
Mexico City

U.S. intervention, 1954
CIA trained Cuban exiles,
1960–1961
Civil war ends, 1996

Disputes over migrants
and drug trade
North American Free
Trade Agreement
signed with U.S., 1992

N. MEX.

El Paso

□   U.S. military sites
—†—   U.S. Naval quarantine, 1962
│   Soviet missile sites
▨   Members of Organization of American States (OAS) and
       participants in U.S.-sponsored Alliance for Progress
(1959) Dates of independence

The United States in the Caribbean and Central America   *The United States often has intervened in the Caribbean and Central America. Geographical proximity, economic stakes, political disputes,
security links, trade in illicit drugs, and Cuba's alliance with the Soviet Union and defiance of the United
States have kept North American eyes fixed on events to the south.*

suaded that a United States–funded counterinsurgency war could be won in a short time, Reagan eschewed negotiations and instead in 1981 increased military assistance to the Salvadoran regime.

The United States's controversial intervention in the Salvadoran civil war sparked a debate much like the one that had erupted over Vietnam. Those who urged negotiations thought Reagan wrong to interpret the conflict as a Cold War contest. Oppression and poverty, not communist plots, caused people to pick up guns to fight the regime, they argued. Resurrecting the discredited domino theory, Reagan retorted that the "Communists" would soon be at the Mexican-American border if they were not stopped in El Salvador. Reagan also made a strategic argument: Central America hugs the Caribbean Sea, "our lifeline to the outside world." After intense debate, Congress repeatedly gave Reagan the funds he wanted for El Salvador. The civil war continued, more bloody than before.

In 1979 leftist insurgents in Nicaragua overthrew Anastasio Somoza, a long-time ally of the United States and member of the dictatorial family that had ruled the Central American nation since the mid-1930s.

Contra War Against Nicaragua

The revolutionaries called themselves Sandinistas in honor of the Nicaraguan who had fought United States marines then (see page 761), and they denounced the tradition of United States imperialism in their country. When the Sandinistas aided rebels in El Salvador, bought Soviet weapons, and invited Cubans to work in Nicaragua's hospitals and schools and to help reorganize their army, Reagan officials charged that Nicaragua was becoming a Soviet client. In 1981 the CIA began to train, arm, and direct more than ten thousand counterrevolutionaries, called contras, for the purpose of overthrowing the Nicaraguan government. From CIA bases in Honduras and Costa Rica, the contras crossed into Nicaragua to kill officials and destroy oil refineries, transportation facilities, medical clinics, and daycare centers. As the contra attacks multiplied and the death toll mounted, the Nicaraguan government curbed civil liberties and shifted scarce money to the military.

It became known in 1984 that the CIA had mined the harbors of Nicaragua, blowing up merchant ships. The World Court ruled that Nicaragua had the right to sue the United States for damages. At the same time Congress voted to stop United States military aid to the contras ("humanitarian" aid was soon sent in its place). Secretly, the Reagan administration lined up other countries, including Saudi Arabia, Panama, and Korea, to funnel money and weapons to the contras, and in 1985 Reagan imposed an economic embargo against Nicaragua.

The next year, Congress once again voted military aid for the contras after vigorous White House lobbying and apparent Sandinista intransigence. (The Sandinistas insisted that they would not accept a peace accord until the United States halted support for the contras.) During the undeclared United States war against Nicaragua, Reagan administration officials rejected opportunities for diplomacy, especially the plan proposed by Costa Rica's president Oscar Arias Sanchez in 1987 to obtain a cease-fire in Central America through negotiations and cutbacks in military aid to all rebel forces. Arias won the Nobel Prize for Peace in 1987.

Scandal tainted the North American crusade against the Sandinistas. It became known in 1986 that the president's national security affairs adviser, John M. Poindexter, and an aide, Colonel Oliver North, in collusion with CIA director William J. Casey, had covertly sold weapons to Iran and then diverted the profits to the contras so that they could purchase arms. The diversion occurred after Congress had prohibited military assistance to the contras. During the same period, Washington had been condemning Iran as a terrorist nation and demanding that America's allies not trade with the radical Islamic state. Colonel North later admitted that he illegally had destroyed government documents and lied to Congress to keep the operation under cover. President Reagan claimed that he knew nothing of these activities. In late 1992, outgoing president George Bush pardoned several former government officials who had been convicted of lying to Congress. Critics smelled a cover-up, for Bush himself, as vice president, had participated in high-level meetings on Iran-contra deals. As for Oliver North, his conviction was overturned on a technicality.

Iran-Contra Scandal

In the 1980s, as before, the deeply divided Middle East continued to defy American solutions (see map, page 895). The United States had commitments (Israel, which in 1985 received more American foreign aid—$3 billion—than any other country), political friends (Saudi Arabia, to which the United States sold $8.5 billion worth of military equipment in 1981), and enemies (the Islamic states of Iran and Libya). Mideast oil supplies fueled Western economies. An Iraqi-Iranian war, in which the United States aided Iraq, threatened Persian Gulf shipping. The Middle East was also a major source of the world's terrorism against United States citizens and property. In 1985, Shiite Muslim terrorists from Lebanon hijacked an American jetliner, killed one passenger, and held thirty-nine Americans hostage for seventeen days. Three years later, a Pan American passenger plane was destroyed over Scotland, probably by terrorists who concealed the bomb in a cassette player.

Even Israel gave the United States trouble. In retaliation for PLO shelling of Israel from Lebanon, the Israelis repeatedly bombed suspected PLO

Crisis in Lebanon

camps inside Lebanon, killing hundreds of civilians. And in 1981, without warning, Israel annexed the Syrian territory of the Golan Heights. Many American supporters of Israel, though well aware that the Jewish state faced hostile Arabs, became impatient with Israel's provocative acts toward its neighbors. The following year, Israeli troops invaded civil war–torn Lebanon, reaching the capital Beirut and inflicting massive damage. The beleaguered PLO and various Lebanese factions called on Syria to contain the Israelis. Thousands of civilians died in the multifaceted conflict, and a million people became refugees. Reagan sent United States marines to Lebanon to join a peacekeeping force. American troops soon became embroiled in a war between Lebanese factions. In October 1983, terrorist bombs demolished a barracks, killing 241 American servicemen. Four months later, Reagan recognized failure and pulled the remaining marines out.

Washington, which openly sided with Israel, continued to propose peace plans designed to persuade the Israelis to give back occupied territories and the Arabs to give up attempts to push the Jews out of the Middle East (the "land-for-peace" formula). As the peace process stalled in 1987, Palestinians living in the West Bank began an uprising called *intifada* against Israeli forces. Israel refused to negotiate, but the United States decided to reverse its policy and talk with PLO leaders after PLO chief Yasir Arafat renounced terrorism and accepted Israel's right to live in peace and security.

In South Africa, the Reagan administration at first followed a policy called "constructive engage-

ment"—asking the white government to reform its repressive system. But many

South Africa

Americans demanded economic sanctions: cutting off imports from South Africa and pressing some 350 American companies—led by Texaco, General Motors, Ford, and Goodyear—to cease operations there. By 1985 eleven American cities and five states had passed divestment laws, withdrawing dollars (such as pension funds used to buy stock) from American companies active in South Africa. Public protest and congressional legislation forced the Reagan administration in 1986 to impose economic restrictions against South Africa. Within two years, about half of the American companies in South Africa pulled out.

Elsewhere in Africa, hunger and famine exacerbated by drought and warfare took a ghastly human toll and contributed to political instability as governments failed to satisfy their

Famine in Africa

people's basic needs. In the early 1980s experts estimated that annual hunger-related deaths numbered between 13 million and 18 million people—twenty-four people per minute, many of them in Africa. In Ethiopia and Sudan, both wracked by civil war, hundreds of thousands starved to death. Almost the only good news to come out of Africa was the 1988 agreement, engineered by United States negotiators, among Angola, Cuba, and South Africa: withdrawal of Cuban troops from Angola and black majority rule in Namibia, the former German colony that had come under South Africa's rule after the First World War.

The Third World also continued to suffer economic setbacks that endangered American prosperity. Third World nations had sunk into staggering debt. Having borrowed heavily in the 1970s, they were unable to repay the loans when world prices for sugar, coffee, and other commodities slumped. By 1989 they owed creditors, including American banks, more than $1.2 trillion. Many Third World nations burdened with such debt—Mexico alone owed more than $100 billion—had to cut back on imports of United States goods. Hundreds of thousands of jobs in the United States were lost as a result, while economic instability spawned political unrest throughout the Third World. Reagan had intervened repeatedly in the Third World, but intervention served to aggravate not subdue economic crises, civil wars, and ethnic and class conflicts.

Bush and Clinton in the Storm

When the Cold War ended in the late 1980s and early 1990s, America's stormy relations with the Third World did not improve. In Central America, however, the Bush administration cooled the zeal with which Reagan had intervened, for the interventions had largely failed. The costly, death-dealing United States–financed contra war had not forced the Sandinistas from power in Nicaragua. In 1989 the Central American presidents devised a workable plan for free elections in Nicaragua and the disbanding of the contras. Yet when the Sandinista Front lost the 1990 elections, Washington claimed victory. Bush's efforts to dampen crises in Central America also came to fruition in early 1992 when United Nations mediation led to an agreement between Salvadoran rebels and the government to end their costly civil war. In Guatemala in late 1996 a civil war that had been raging since 1954 and claimed more than 100,000 lives

Ending Civil Wars in Central America

Despite a multi-billion-dollar United States "drug war" to prevent the importation of illegal narcotics such as cocaine from Colombia, Peru, and Bolivia, Americans continued into the 1990s to consume a vast amount of debilitating and death-dealing narcotics. The antidrug campaign ranked high on the agenda of United States–Latin American relations. Schrank/England/Cartoonists and Writers Syndicate.

ended in a peace accord brokered by Norwegian and United Nations diplomats.

The profitable trade in illicit drugs also troubled inter-American relations. By 1990 the United States drug market was probably worth $100 billion. "This is more serious than the Vietnam War," declared Maryland's governor. As the Cold War receded, the "drug war" accelerated, and Washington used the United States military to quash drug producers and traffickers in Colombia, Bolivia, and Peru, sources of cocaine and crack, both processed from coca leaves. North American officials concentrated on interrupting *supply* through interdiction and eradication programs. Others stressed the need to halt *demand* inside the United States itself. Most analysts agree that the "drug war" to this day has not been won.

"Drug War"

The drug issue became conspicuous as relations between Panama and the United States deteriorated. Soon after General Manuel Antonio Noriega took power in Panama in 1983, he cut deals with Colombia's cocaine barons and laundered drug money in Panamanian banks. By the late 1980s his dictatorial rule and drug running had angered North Americans eager to blame the swaggering Panamanian for the United States's drug problems. The American people were unaware—though President Bush knew—that Noriega had long been on the CIA payroll and that he had helped the United States aid the contras. Appreciative, Washington had long turned a blind eye to his drug trafficking. When exposés of Noriega's sordid record provoked protests in Panama, however, the United States decided to dump the dictator. But Noriega would not leave, and he heated up anti-Americanism in Panama.

Operation Just Cause was launched in the early hours of December 20, 1989. The largest American military operation since the Vietnam War, the invasion of Panama by 22,500 troops proved a blood-soaked success. More than 300 Panamanians died; 23 American soldiers perished. Property damage in Panama City amounted to $1 billion. Noriega was captured and taken to Miami, where, in 1992, he was convicted of drug trafficking and imprisoned. Devastated Panama, meanwhile, like war-torn Nicaragua, became all the more dependent on the United States, which offered scant reconstruction aid.

Invasion of Panama

While the United States was managing its sphere of influence in Latin America, it was also helping to end apartheid in South Africa. The United States maintained sanctions against the segregated nation, costing South Africa billions of dollars. Fearing economic disaster and an ultimately successful black revolt, South Africa's president, F. W. de Klerk, in 1990 lifted restrictions on dissent and legalized the militantly anti-apartheid African National Congress (ANC). De Klerk also released from prison his nation's most celebrated critic, ANC leader Nelson Mandela. In mid-1990 Mandela triumphantly toured the United States, even donning a New York Yankees baseball cap. In 1993 Mandela and de Klerk shared the Nobel Peace Prize, and the following year Mandela became his nation's first black president. When apartheid ended, the United States Congress repealed sanctions, and American companies invested once again in South Africa.

End of Apartheid in South Africa

During these tumultuous changes in South Africa, Iraq's dictator Saddam Hussein—resentful that the feudal dynasty of Kuwait would not reduce the huge debt Iraq owed to it and eager to acquire Kuwait's vast petroleum industry—ordered his troops to invade his peaceful neighbor in August 1990. Oil-rich Saudi Arabia, long a United States ally, felt threatened. In Operation Desert Shield, Bush dispatched more than 500,000 United States forces to the region. The Kuwait government-in-exile paid the Hill and Knowlton public relations company more than $10 million to organize a front organization, Citizens for a Free Kuwait; its propaganda helped spruce up undemocratic Kuwait's image in the United States. Likening Saddam to Hitler and declaring the moment the first post–Cold War "test of our mettle," Bush rallied to war a deeply divided Congress (the Senate vote was 52 to 47). The United Nations also endorsed war and helped organize a coalition of forces. Many Americans believed that economic sanctions imposed on Iraq should be given more time to force Saddam's retreat. Bush would not wait. "This will not be another Vietnam," the president said. On the contrary, "Maybe I'll turn out to be a Teddy Roosevelt."

Persian Gulf War

When Operation Desert Storm began on January 16, 1991, the greatest air armada in history began pummeling Iraqi targets. American missiles joined round-the-clock bombing raids on Baghdad, Iraq's capital. In late February, coalition forces launched a ground war that routed the Iraqis from Kuwait in just

Nelson Mandela (b. 1918) founded the African National Congress to end the segregationist policy of apartheid in his white-ruled country of South Africa. Imprisoned from 1962 to 1990, Mandela won election in 1994 as South Africa's first black president. Stout black resistance and United States ecomomic sanctions helped persuade white leaders to yield power to the black majority and to end apartheid. Here Mandela campaigns for the presidency in February 1994 in the Orange Free State. Corbis-Bettmann.

one hundred hours. Hardly a declining power, Bush crowed, the United States was a reborn superpower. The *Wall Street Journal* welcomed the Gulf War because it "lets America, and above all else its elite, recover a sense of self-confidence and self-worth."

The war's toll: at least 35,000 Iraqis dead; 240 coalition soldiers dead, including 148 Americans; and Iraq's infrastructure "relegated to a preindustrial age," as a United Nations inspection team reported. Although defeated, Saddam Hussein held power and even suppressed revolts by Iraqi Shiites and Kurds, whom United States forces only belatedly stepped in to protect. Having achieved the defined mission of driving Iraq from Kuwait, however, American leaders decided not to send ground troops to Baghdad itself in what seemed likely to become a high-casualty operation. Instead, the CIA began to aid Kurds and other anti-Saddam Iraqis who claimed that they could overthrow the dictator. From 1991 through 1996, they received $100 million from the United States, but Saddam remained in power; indeed, he captured or drove away many of his CIA-backed enemies.

After the Persian Gulf War, the chances for peace in the Middle East improved for several reasons: Saudi Arabia, the Gulf states, and the recently collapsed Soviet Union trimmed their financial assistance to the PLO, which had backed Iraq; the war exposed divisions among the Arab nations; and the *intifada* was raising Israel's costs of maintaining control over occupied territories (see map, page 895). "The Palestinian and Israeli leaderships have awakened from illusions," remarked former Israeli foreign minister Abba Eban. Secretary of State James Baker also pressed Israel to reassess its policies: "Lay aside, once and for all, the unrealistic vision of a greater Israel," he implored. "Forswear annexation. Stop settlement activity. . . . Reach out to the Palestinians as neighbors who deserve political

**Gains in
the Mideast
Peace Process**

rights." United States diplomats once again took an arduous, active role in the peace process.

In a major breakthrough in the fall of 1991, Arab and Israeli leaders went to a peace conference in Madrid. In September 1993, the PLO's Yasir Arafat and Israel's Prime Minister Yizhak Rabin signed an agreement for Palestinian self-rule in the Gaza Strip and the West Bank's Jericho (see map, page 895). In 1994, Israel signed a peace accord with Jordan, further reducing the chances of another full-scale Arab-Israeli war. Radical anti-Arafat Palestinians, however, continued to stage bloody terrorist attacks on Israelis, while extremist Israelis killed Palestinians and, in November 1995, even Rabin himself. Nevertheless, the peace process went forward, with Arafat winning Palestine's first national election in early 1996. But the 1996 election of a conservative Israeli government that openly rejected the "land-for-peace" concept sparked new disputes with the Palestinians. Only after intense American-conducted investigations and renewed violence in the West Bank did Israel agree in early 1997 to withdraw its forces from the Palestinian city of Hebron. Secretary of State Warren Christopher said that the agreement "demonstrates that there is a powerful

In the Persian Gulf War of early 1991, Operation Desert Storm forced Iraqi troops out of Kuwait. Much of that nation's oil industry was destroyed by bombs and the retreating Iraqis, who torched oil facilities as they left. Oil wells burned for months, darkening the sky over these American forces and causing considerable environmental damage.   Bruno Barbey/Magnum Photos, Inc.

logic to peace," but difficult issues still lay ahead, especially between Israel and Syria over Israeli occupation of the Golan Heights.

Somalia had long suffered from the effects of soil erosion and famine and was one of the Cold War's orphans. After Somalia jilted its Cold War ally the Soviet Union in the late 1970s, the strategically located Horn of Africa nation became a recipient of United States aid, including large amounts of weapons. That aid stopped with the end of the Cold War, further aggravating the poor country's economic crisis. When Somalia's repressive dictator was driven from power in early 1991, rival clans vied for power and public authority broke down. Gun-toting bandits stole international relief supplies. Hundreds of thousands of Somalis died. President Bush ordered more than 28,000 American troops to Somalia in December 1992 to ensure the delivery of relief aid. A United Nations peacekeeping force, including 9,000 Americans, took over in mid-1993 (see map, page 920).

Operation Restore Hope in Somalia

President Bill Clinton came into office in January 1993 and set a new course: to reform, not just feed, Somalia. The warlords responded by attacking United Nations and United States forces. In early 1994 Clinton pulled all United States troops out; the United Nations peacekeepers left about a year later. The mission had saved perhaps some 250,000 lives, but Somalia returned once again to violent, chaotic politics. Clinton's national security affairs adviser Anthony Lake praised the operation as an example of "pragmatic neo-Wilsonianism."

In 1990 poverty-wracked and environmentally devastated Haiti held its first free elections in decades. But the next year the army overthrew the government of Jean-Bertrand Aristide. The United States imposed economic sanctions against the Caribbean nation, causing further hardship. Tens of thousands of Haitians fled in boats for United States territory, spawning an immigration crisis. The United States demanded that the military dictators restore Aristide to power; at the same time, however, the CIA secretly kept one of the ruling junta's strongmen on its payroll, even though the agency knew him to be an ugly abuser of human rights.

United States Troops to Haiti

After swinging between tough talk and indecision, President Clinton sent Jimmy Carter to Haiti in September 1994. The former president cut a deal with the generals that gave them "honorable retirement" under a general amnesty. Soon, without seeking congressional approval, Clinton ordered United States troops to Haiti in Operation Uphold Democracy. Aristide returned. In early 1996 American forces departed, their mission to revitalize Haiti yet unfulfilled.

Throughout Latin America, the Clinton administration continued to promote liberalized trade, privatized economies, orderly immigration, democratization, and the war against drugs. When politically corrupt Mexico's economy neared collapse in 1995, the United States bailed it out with large loans. As for Cuba, Clinton improved telecommunications linkages and encouraged cultural exchanges while maintaining the punishing economic embargo. In the summer of 1995 Cubans set to sea in all forms of craft for Florida, sparking dispute. Clinton decided to admit thousands of detained Cuban refugees while turning away new arrivals.

In March 1996, after an airplane carrying members of the provocative anti-Castro group Brothers to the Rescue was shot down by Cuban fighter pilots near Cuba, Clinton pandered to the politically influential Cuban-American communities in Florida and New Jersey and signed the Helms-Burton Act. This legislation tightened the economic embargo against the Caribbean island by allowing American nationals and companies to sue in United States courts foreign companies that were using formerly American-owned properties in Cuba. The Castro government had seized these assets in the early days of the Cuban Revolution, and they were valued at $1.8 billion, or $5.5 billion with interest. Canada and the European Union, both of which traded with and invested in Cuba, condemned the measure, promised to retaliate, and took the issue to the World Trade Organization. Alert to international protest, the Clinton administration suspended the act's provision that permitted the suing of foreign companies.

Helms-Burton Act and Cuba

Controversy also surrounded United States ties to Latin American military officers. Evidence became public, for example, that United States military advisers in El Salvador had trained Salvadoran members of death squads. In Guatemala, the CIA had hired and paid Colonel Julio Roberto Alpirez, who killed a Guatemalan revolutionary, husband of Jennifer

United States Links with Latin American Militaries

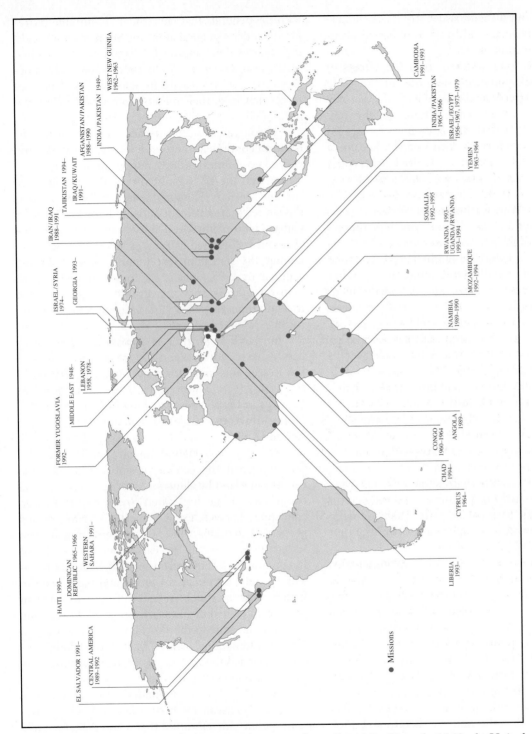

United Nations Peacekeeping Operations as of April 1995   *Since the 1940s the United Nations has conducted significant peacekeeping operations, using the contributed troops of many nations to quiet civil unrest or to monitor compliance with agreements. Often called "blue helmuts" because of the conspicuous light blue hats they wear, United Nations peacekeeping forces have sometimes met violent opposition and suffered casualties.*   Source: Adapted from United Nations, *Yearbook of the United Nations* (New York: Special Edition, 1995).

Harbury, an American lawyer. Clinton's CIA director John M. Deutch admitted that some of the agency's "human assets" were "unsavory people," but he insisted that the information they provided could save American lives, avert conflict, or protect United States interests. Despite revelations that some of their graduates blatantly participated in human-rights violations, the United States Army School of the Americas, the Inter-American Defense College, the United States Navy's Smallcraft Warfare School, and the Inter-American Air Force Academy continued to train Latin American military officers.

In an increasingly fragmented international system, Third World issues filled the international agenda. Clinton administration officials and other internationalists spoke of America's "world responsibilities," humanitarianism, and dedication to spreading democracy abroad. Others argued that the United States had neither the money nor the ability to build or reform other peoples; instead, the United States had to accept its limitations and solve its own domestic problems first. Reasserting traditional notions of United States world leadership, Clinton dismissed such thinking as a dangerous retreat to "isolationism."

Americans Debate the United States's Role in the World

Americans divided over foreign policy issues in a host of ways, and the budget especially sparked debate. People particularly worried about domestic ills such as crime and underfunded education called for cuts in foreign aid; they were joined by budget-slashing conservatives. As a result, in 1996 the United States ranked below Japan, France, and Germany in aid given to developing nations. Americans who followed health questions demanded more funds to combat the global AIDS pandemic. In 1995 17 million people were infected with the H.I.V. virus, and some 4 million suffered the deadly AIDS disease itself.

Congress voted a larger military budget than even the Defense Department wanted ($260 billion in 1995), and the United States by the mid-1990s had built up imposing forces in the Persian Gulf region (see map, page 895). Decline-theorist Paul Kennedy urged reallocating some of these monies "to employ the tens of thousands of scientists and engineers now released from Cold War–related research to seek solutions to environmental problems." Indeed, disappointed environmentalists, predicting a bleak future of ozone-layer depletion, deforestation, polluted water, and global warming, appealed for greater United States activism.

Conservative nationalists demanded less United States cooperation with the United Nations, which they condemned as too expensive, inefficient, and challenging to American sovereignty. Defenders of the world body praised its positive role in the Persian Gulf War and its successful calming of civil wars in El Salvador, Mozambique, Cambodia, and Guatemala. The United Nations also conducted important peacekeeping functions in Africa and the Middle East. Yet the United Nations became strapped for funds for peacekeeping, in part because by 1997 the United States owed the organization $1.5 billion in unpaid contributions.

Dispute over the United Nations

Laborers in declining industries protested NAFTA and other trade agreements that cost them jobs. Women, such as those who attended the International Conference on Women in Beijing in 1995 (see page 881), lobbied for a major American commitment to combat gender discrimination. Seventy percent of the world's poor were women and only 10 percent of national legislative seats were held by women; at the same time, women worldwide earned 30 to 40 percent less than their male counterparts for the same work. Military veterans and families of missing-in-action (MIA) soldiers protested Clinton's 1996 decision to open full diplomatic relations with Vietnam, while American businesses such as Otis, United Airlines, and Pepsico welcomed the new economic opportunities there. Human-rights observers scolded Washington for inadequate focus on abuses. They criticized Clinton's preference for expanding trade rather than pressing for human rights in relations with China. In mid-1994, moreover, the United States and the United Nations responded too late to the Hutus' calculated genocide against the Tutsis in Rwanda, where between 500,000 and 1 million Tutsis were butchered in a ghastly display of ethnic rivalry.

 Conclusion

Since 1945 the United States has been at odds with the Third World. The United States usually stood with its European Cold War allies to resist decolonization, slow the movement toward independence, and preach evolution rather than revolution. The

United States denounced the preference of many Third World nations for nonalignment in the Cold War. And the globalist perspective of the United States prompted Americans to interpret many Third World troubles as Cold War conflicts, inspired if not directed by Soviet-backed communists. The intensity of the Cold War obscured for Americans the indigenous roots of most Third World troubles, as the Vietnam War attested.

Nor could the United States abide Third World nations' drive for economic independence—for gaining control of their own raw materials and economies. Deeply intertwined in the global economy as importer, exporter, and investor, the United States read Third World challenges as threats to the American standard of living and way of life characterized by private enterprise. The Third World, in short, challenged the United States's strategic power by forming a third force in the Cold War, and it challenged American economic power by demanding a new economic order of shared interests. Overall, the rise of the Third World introduced new actors to the world stage, challenging the bipolarity of the international system and diffusing power.

Through foreign aid, trade and investment, CIA covert actions, diplomatic mediation, USIA propaganda, military interventions, arms sales, development projects, cultural exchanges, environmental treaties, and more, the United States has sought for a half-century to help and to discipline Third World peoples. When the Cold War ended, the Third World still remained—higher than ever on the world agenda.

Suggestions for Further Reading

For the Cold War, Soviet-American relations, Sino-American relations, and environmental issues, see Chapter 29. Many works cited in Chapter 29 include discussion of issues related to the Third World.

Third World Relations: Truman to Clinton

Richard J. Barnet, *Intervention and Revolution* (1972); Edward H. Berman, *The Influence of the Carnegie, Ford, and Rockefeller Foundations on American Foreign Policy* (1983); Scott L. Bills, *Empire and Cold War* (1990); H. W. Brands, *The Specter of Neutralism* (1989); Gabriel Kolko, *Confronting the Third World* (1988); James Mayall, ed., *The New Interventionism* (1996); Larry Minear and Thomas G. Weiss, *Humanitarian Politics* (1995); Brenda G. Plummer, *Rising Wind: Black Americans and U.S. Foreign Affairs, 1935–1960* (1996); David M. Reimers, *Still the Golden Door* (1992) (on immigration); Alvin Z. Rubenstein and Donald E. Smith, eds., *Anti-Americanism in the Third World* (1985); Peter J. Schraeder, ed., *Intervention into the 1990s* (1992); Paul B. Stares, *Global Habit*

(1996) (on drugs); Ronald Steel, *Temptations of a Superpower* (1995); Stephen R. Weissman, *A Culture of Deference: Congress's Failure of Leadership in Foreign Policy* (1995). For global economic issues, see works cited in Chapter 29.

The CIA and Counterinsurgency

Douglas S. Blaufarb, *The Counterinsurgency Era* (1977); Peter Grose, *Gentleman Spy* (1994) (on Allen Dulles); Rhodi Jeffreys-Jones, *The CIA and American Democracy* (1989); Loch K. Johnson, *America's Secret Power* (1989); Mark Lowenthal, *U.S. Intelligence* (1984); Thomas Powers, *The Man Who Kept the Secrets* (1979); John Prados, *Presidents' Secret Wars* (1986); John Ranelagh, *The Agency* (1986); Jeffrey T. Richelson, *A Century of Spies* (1995); Jeffrey T. Richelson, *The U.S. Intelligence Community*, 3d ed. (1995); Robin Winks, *Cloak & Gown* (1987).

The Vietnam War and Southeast Asia: General

David L. Anderson, *Shadow on the White House* (1993); Loren Baritz, *Backfire* (1985); Eric M. Bergerud, *The Dynamics of Defeat* (1991); William J. Duiker, *U.S. Containment Policy and the Conflict in Indochina* (1994); Frances FitzGerald, *Fire in the Lake* (1972); William C. Gibbons, *The U.S. Government and the Vietnam War* (1986–1994); Daniel C. Hallin, *The "Uncensored War"* (1986); George C. Herring, *America's Longest War* (1996); Gary R. Hess, *Vietnam and the United States* (1990); Neil L. Jamieson, *Understanding Vietnam* (1993); Stanley Karnow, *Vietnam* (1991); Gabriel Kolko, *Anatomy of a War* (1986); Guenter Lewy, *America in Vietnam* (1978); Joseph G. Morgan, *The Vietnam Lobby: The American Friends of Vietnam, 1955–1975* (1997); William Shawcross, *Sideshow* (1979) (on Cambodia); Anthony Short, *The Origins of the Vietnam War* (1989); Marilyn B. Young, *The Vietnam Wars* (1991). For works on the antiwar movement, see Chapter 31.

Truman, Eisenhower, and Vietnam

David L. Anderson, *Trapped by Success* (1991); James R. Arnold, *The First Domino* (1991); Melanie Billings-Yun, *Decision Against War: Eisenhower and Dien Bien Phu, 1954* (1988); Lloyd C. Gardner, *Approaching Vietnam* (1988); Gary Hess, *The United States' Emergence as a Southeast Asian Power* (1987); Lawrence S. Kaplan et al., eds., *Dien Bien Phu and the Crisis of Franco-American Relations* (1990); David G. Marr, *Vietnam 1945* (1995); Andrew Rotter, *The Path to Vietnam* (1987); Stein Tonnesson, *The Vietnamese Revolution of 1945* (1991).

Kennedy, Johnson, Vietnam, and the Third World

LeRoy Ashby and Rod Gramer, *Fighting the Odds* (1994) (on Senator Frank Church); David M. Barrett, *Uncertain Warriors* (1993); Larry Berman, *Lyndon Johnson's War* (1989); Larry Berman, *Planning a Tragedy* (1982); James A. Bill, *George Ball* (1997); Larry Cable, *Unholy Grail* (1991); Charles DeBenedetti and Charles Chatfield, *An American Ordeal* (1990) (on antiwar movement); David L. DiLeo, *George Ball, Vietnam, and the Rethinking of Containment* (1991); Lloyd C. Gardner, *Pay Any Price* (1995); George C. Herring, *LBJ and Vietnam* (1994); Michael H. Hunt, *Lyndon Johnson's War* (1996); George McT. Kahin, *Intervention* (1986); Yuen Foong Khong, *Analogies at War* (1992); Diane Kunz, ed., *The Diplomacy of the Crucial Decade* (1994); Thomas G. Paterson, ed., *Kennedy's Quest for Victory* (1989); William Prochnau, *Once upon a Distant War* (1995) (on journalists); Gerald T. Rice, *The Bold Experiment: JFK's Peace Corps* (1985); Deborah Shapley, *Promise and Power* (1993) (on Robert McNamara); Kevin Sim and Michael Bilton, *Four Hours in My Lai* (1992); Melvin Small, *Johnson, Nixon and the Doves* (1988); Brian VanDerMark, *Into the Quagmire* (1991); Randall B. Woods, *Fulbright* (1995).

The Vietnam War: Military Aspects

Robert Buzzanco, *Masters of War: Military Dissent and Politics in the Vietnam Era* (1996); Jeffrey J. Clarke, *United States Army in Vietnam* (1988); Mark Clodfelter, *The Limits of Power* (1989) (on bombing); Phillip B. Davidson, *Vietnam at War* (1988); Ronald H. Spector, *After Tet: The Bloodiest Year in Vietnam* (1992); Ronald H. Spector, *United States Army in Vietnam* (1983).

Legacy and Lessons of the Vietnam War

John Hellman, *American Myth and the Legacy of Vietnam* (1986); Herbert Hendin and Ann P. Haas, *Wounds of War: The Psychological Aftermath of Combat in Vietnam* (1984); Ole R. Holsti and James Rosenau, *American Leadership in World Affairs: Vietnam and the Breakdown of Consensus* (1984); David Levy, *The Debate over Vietnam* (1991); Myra MacPherson, *Long Time Passing* (1984); Norman Podhoretz, *Why We Were in Vietnam* (1982); Earl C. Ravenal, *Never Again* (1978); Harrison E. Salisbury, ed., *Vietnam Reconsidered* (1984); Harry G. Summers, Jr., *On Strategy* (1982).

Latin America: General

Cole Blasier, *Hovering Giant* (1974); David W. Dent, ed., *U.S.–Latin American Policymaking* (1995); Guy Gugliotta and Jeff Leen, *Kings of Cocaine* (1989); Lester Langley, *America and the Americas* (1989); Abraham F. Lowenthal, ed., *Exporting Democracy* (1991); Abraham F. Lowenthal, *Partners in Conflict: The United States and Latin America*, rev. ed. (1990); Donald J. Mabry, ed., *The Latin American Narcotics Trade and U.S. National Security* (1989); Brenda G. Plummer, *Haiti and the United States* (1992); W. Dirk Raat, *Mexico and the United States* (1992); Stephen G. Rabe, *Eisenhower and Latin America* (1988); Stephen G. Rabe, *The Road to OPEC: United States Relations with Venezuela* (1982); William F. Sater, *Chile and the United States* (1990); Peter H. Smith, *Talons of the Eagle . . .* (1996). Books on Cuba and the missile crisis are cited in Chapter 29.

Central America and Panama

Cynthia J. Arnson, *Crossroads* (1989) (on Ronald Reagan); Morris J. Blachman et al., eds., *Confronting Revolution* (1986); Kevin Buckley, *Panama* (1991); E. Bradford Burns, *At War in Nicaragua* (1987); John Coatsworth, *Central America and the United States* (1994); Kenneth M. Coleman and George C. Herring, eds., *Understanding the Central American Crisis* (1991); Michael Conniff, *Panama and the United States* (1992); John Dinges, *Our Man in Panama* (1990); Theodore Draper, *A Very Thin Line: The Iran-Contra Affairs* (1991); Piero Gleijeses, *Shattered Hope* (1991) (on Guatemala); J. Michael Hogan, *The Panama Canal in American Politics* (1986); Richard Immerman, *The CIA in Guatemala* (1982); Michael Klare and Peter Kornbluh, eds., *Low Intensity Warfare* (1988); Walter LaFeber, *Inevitable Revolutions* (1993); Walter LaFeber, *The Panama Canal* (1989); Anthony Lake, *Somoza Falling* (1989); Robert A. Pastor, *Whirlpool* (1992); Robert A. Pastor, *Condemned to Repetition* (1987) (on Nicaragua); Peter Dale Scott and Jonathan Marshall, *Cocaine Politics* (1991);

Christian Smith, *Resisting Reagan: The U.S.–Central America Peace Movement* (1996); Thomas W. Walker, ed., *Revolution and Counterrevolution in Nicaragua* (1991).

Middle East

James A. Bill, *The Eagle and the Lion* (1988) (on Iran); William J. Burns, *Economic Aid and American Policy Toward Egypt, 1955–1981* (1985); Michael J. Cohen, *Palestine and the Great Powers, 1945–1948* (1983); Richard W. Cottam, *Iran and the United States* (1988); Mark Gasiorowski, *U.S. Foreign Policy and the Shah* (1991); Peter L. Hahn, *The United States, Great Britain, and Egypt, 1945–1956* (1991); Burton I. Kaufman, *The Arab Middle East and the United States* (1996); Diane Kunz, *The Economic Diplomacy of the Suez Crisis* (1991); George Lenczowski, *The Middle East in World Affairs*, 4th ed. (1980); William Roger Louis and Roger Owen, eds., *Suez 1956* (1989); Aaron D. Miller, *Search for Security* (1980); Donald Neff, *Warriors at Suez* (1981); William B. Quandt, *Peace Process* (1993); Cheryl A. Rubenberg, *Israel and the American National Interest* (1986); David Schoenbaum, *The United States and the State of Israel* (1993); Gary Sick, *October Surprise* (1991) (on Iranian hostage crisis); Steven L. Spiegel, *The Other Arab-Israeli Conflict* (1985); William Stivers, *America's Confrontation with Revolutionary Change in the Middle East* (1986); Robert W. Stookey, *America and the Arab States* (1975); Daniel Yergin, *The Prize* (1991) (on oil).

Persian Gulf War

Deborah Amos, *Lines in the Sand* (1992); Lawrence Freedman and Efraim Karsh, *The Gulf Conflict, 1990–1991* (1993); Stephen Graubard, *Mr. Bush's War* (1992); John MacArthur, *Second Front: Censorship and Propaganda in the Gulf War* (1992); John Mueller, *Policy and Opinion in the Gulf War* (1994); Joseph S. Nye, Jr., and Roger K. Smith, eds., *After the Storm* (1992); Michael Palmer, *Guardians of the Gulf* (1992); Jean Edward Smith, *George Bush's War* (1992); Philip M. Taylor, *War and the Media* (1992).

Africa

Pauline H. Baker, *The United States and South Africa: The Reagan Years* (1989); Thomas Borstelmann, *Apartheid's Reluctant Uncle* (1993); Christopher Coker, *The United States and South Africa, 1968–1985* (1986); David N. Gibbs, *The Political Economy of Third World Intervention* (1991) (on Congo crisis); Jeffrey Lefebvre, *Arms for the Horn* (1992) (on Ethiopia and Somalia); Richard D. Mahoney, *JFK: Ordeal in Africa* (1983); Thomas J. Noer, *Cold War and Black Liberation* (1985); Peter J. Schraeder, *United States Policy Toward Africa* (1994); Jonathan Stevenson, *Losing Mogadishu* (1995) (on Somalia); Penny M. Von Eschen, *Race Against Empire: Black Americans and Anticolonialism, 1937–1957* (1996).

Asia

H. W. Brands, *India and the United States* (1989); Kenton J. Clymer, *Question for Freedom* (1995) (on India's independence); Nick Cullather, *Illusions of Influence* (1994) (on the Philippines); Audrey R. Kahin and George McT. Kahin, *Subversion as Foreign Policy* (1995) (on Indonesia); Stanley Karnow, *In Our Image* (1989) (on the Philippines); Robert J. McMahon, *Colonialism and Cold War* (1981) (on Indonesia); Dennis Merrill, *Bread and the Ballot* (1990) (on India). Works on United States relations with China and Japan are cited in Chapter 29.

31

Reform and Conflict: A Turbulent Era

1961–1974

In 1964 politics and civil rights were in the forefront of the news and were inextricably tied together. It was a presidential election year, and when the Democrats convened in Atlantic City, New Jersey, in August to pick a presidential candidate, they discovered how politically volatile the civil rights issue could be. Two delegations had arrived from Mississippi demanding to be seated. One was all white, composed of the regular Democrats who vehemently opposed President Lyndon B. Johnson's Great Society programs. The other was largely African-American and called itself the Mississippi Freedom Democratic Party (MFDP). Arguing that the state's regular Democratic organization was vehemently segregationist but the MFDP supported civil rights, the MFDP asked the convention to honor its credentials.

In Mississippi, as a result of phony literacy tests, economic intimidation, and (when all else failed) violence, less than 7 percent of the black population could vote. Civil rights activists had decided in 1963 to conduct their own "freedom vote"—a mock election to prove, as one worker put it, "that politics is not 'just white folks' business." And in 1964 the MFDP ran candidates for Congress. The same year, more than a thousand northern students traveled south to Mississippi to work for the Freedom Summer Project, registering voters and organizing protests against Jim Crow segregation. The nation's focus was on Mississippi, and the challenges to white supremacy did not go unanswered. White vigilantes bombed and burned two dozen black churches, and three civil rights workers—one black and two white—were murdered by sheriff's deputies in Philadelphia, Mississippi.

It was in this context that the Democratic Party's credentials committee met on August 22, 1964, to hear the contesting delegations. The hearings were nationally televised. Speaking for the MFDP was Fannie Lou Hamer, a forty-six-year-old African-American field secretary for the Student Nonviolent Coordinating Committee (SNCC). Hamer was an inspiring figure, whose credibility derived from the hard experiences of her own life. Born in 1917, she was the twentieth child of sharecropper parents. At age six, she went to work chopping and picking in the cotton fields, and by the time she was thirteen she was picking from three to four hundred pounds a day on a plantation in Sunflower County. When her boss found out that she could read and write, she was promoted to timekeeper. Still, the pay was pitiful. Hamer married and adopted two daughters, but she and her family were caught in a vicious cycle of political powerlessness and poverty.

In the early 1960s Fannie Lou Hamer began to envision a better future through the direct action of the civil rights movement. Paraphrasing John F. Kennedy's 1961 inaugural address, she explained, "I am determined to give my part not for what the movement can do for me, but what I can do for the movement to bring about a change in the State of Mississippi." In 1962 she lost her job when she attempted to register to vote. Then, fearing violence, she fled to a neighbor's home, but it was riddled with bullets intended for her. The next year, Hamer was arrested with five other SNCC volunteers in Winona, Mississippi, taken to jail, and brutally assaulted by police swinging blackjacks. By 1964, Hamer had become a field worker for SNCC, known for her courage and refusal to surrender as well as for her inspiring speeches and singing. "I'm sick and tired," she told audiences, "of being sick and tired." She began her speeches with a sacred hymn; often it was her favorite, "This Little Light of Mine." Fannie Lou Hamer clearly was not afraid.

Sitting before the credentials committee and the television cameras in Atlantic City, Hamer told the country about her experience in the Winona jail. "I was beaten until I was exhausted," she said. "I began to scream, and one white man got up and began to beat me on the head and tell me to hush. . . . All of this on account we wanted to register, to become first class citizens." She demanded that the MFDP— those who had fought for freedom—be seated, not those who opposed it. If "the Freedom Party is not seated now I question America," she said. Emotion filled her voice as she asked, "Is this America, the land of the free and the home of the brave, where we have to sleep with our telephones off the hooks because our lives be threatened daily, because we want to live as decent human beings, in America?"

The MFDP did not receive justice from President Johnson or the Democratic Party. Offered a consolation prize of two seats, the MFDP refused. "We didn't come all this way for no two seats," Hamer said, "when all of us is tired." In this election year, Johnson was unwilling to alienate powerful southern white politicians by seating the civil rights delegation, but his action threw into question the Democrats' commitment to racial equality. It was already too late for many white southerners, who had begun to switch to the more conservative Republican Party. And, despite Johnson's capitulation to Mississippi's regular Democrats, the state's whites voted for Senator Barry Goldwater, the Republican candidate, in 1964. Civil rights had become the most important political issue in the country, threatening to destroy the New Deal coalition in the South and the North.

The civil rights movement was a dynamic motive force in America society in the 1960s, giving birth in subsequent years to the antiwar movement, the New Left, and a resurgent feminist movement, not to mention the environmental movement and equality movements for other minorities. The civil rights movement also energized the presidential politics of John F. Kennedy and Lyndon B. Johnson. Kennedy's call for a New Frontier had inspired liberal Democrats, idealists, and brave young activists to work to eliminate poverty, segregation, and voting rights abuses. But Americans' dreams were shattered on November 22, 1963, when President Kennedy was assassinated in Dallas. For four days Americans wept, prayed, and gazed at their television sets, numbed by the unbelievable. On the day of the funeral, a million people lined the streets of Washington, and millions more watched on television as the president's body was borne by horse-drawn caisson to Arlington Cemetery. "In retrospect," journalist Godfrey Hodgson has written, "people looked back to Friday, November 22, 1963, as the end of a time of hope, the beginning of a time of troubles."

Lyndon Johnson, who asked for national unity in the wake of the Kennedy assassination, was a strong political leader who knew what he wanted. Johnson presided over what he called the Great Society, an effort to eradicate poverty in the United States and

• *Important Events* •

1960 Sit-ins begin at Greensboro, North Carolina
Birth-control pill approved for use
John F. Kennedy elected president

1961 Freedom Rides protest segregation in transportation
President's Commission on the Status of Women established

1962 John Glenn orbits the globe in space capsule
Students for a Democratic Society issues Port Huron Statement
James Meredith enters University of Mississippi
Baker v. *Carr* establishes "one person, one vote" principle

1963 Betty Friedan's *The Feminine Mystique* published
Civil rights advocates march on Washington
Baptist church in Birmingham, Alabama, bombed
Kennedy assassinated; Lyndon B. Johnson becomes president

1964 Economic Opportunity Act allocates funds to fight poverty
Civil Rights Act outlaws discrimination in jobs and public accommodations
Twenty-fourth Amendment outlaws the poll tax in federal elections
Riots break out in first of the "long hot summers"
Fannie Lou Hamer speaks on behalf of Mississippi Freedom Democratic Party at Democratic convention
Free Speech movement begins at Berkeley
Johnson elected president

1965 Malcolm X assassinated
Voting Rights Act allows federal supervision of voting registration
Medicare program established
Elementary and Secondary Education Act provides federal aid to education
Watts race riot leaves thirty-four dead

1966 National Organization for Women founded
Miranda v. *Arizona* requires police to inform suspects of their rights

1967 Race riots erupt in Newark, Detroit, and other cities
Twenty-fifth Amendment establishes the order of presidential succession

1968 U.S.S. *Pueblo* captured by North Korea
Tet offensive causes fear of losing Vietnam War
Martin Luther King, Jr., assassinated
African-Americans riot in 168 cities and towns
Civil Rights Act bans discrimination in housing
Antiwar protests escalate
Robert F. Kennedy assassinated
Violence erupts at Democratic convention
Richard M. Nixon elected president

1969 Stonewall riot sparked by police harassment of homosexuals
400,000 gather at Woodstock festival
Moratorium Day calls for end to Vietnam War

1970 United States invades Cambodia
Students killed at Kent State and Jackson State Universities
First Earth Day celebrated
Environmental Protection Agency created

1971 *Pentagon Papers* published
Twenty-sixth Amendment extends vote to eighteen-year-olds
Inmates revolt at Attica prison
Swann v. *Charlotte-Mecklenberg* upholds North Carolina desegregation plan

1972 Nixon visits China and Soviet Union
Congress approves Equal Rights Amendment
George Wallace shot and paralyzed
"Plumbers" break into Watergate
Revenue sharing distributes funds to states
Nixon reelected

1973 Watergate burglars tried
Senator Sam Ervin chairs Watergate hearings
White House aides John Ehrlichman and H. R. Haldeman resign
Roe v. *Wade* legalizes abortion
War Powers Act passed
Spiro Agnew resigns; Nixon appoints Gerald R. Ford vice president
"Saturday Night Massacre" provokes public outcry

1974 Supreme Court orders Nixon to release White House tapes
House Judiciary Committee votes to impeach Nixon
Nixon resigns; Ford becomes president
Ford pardons Nixon
Freedom of Information Act passed over Ford's veto

President John F. Kennedy, his wife Jacqueline, and their two young children, John Jr. and Caroline, symbolized youthful energy and idealism. This photograph was taken at their vacation home at Hyannisport on Cape Cod in July 1963.   John F. Kennedy Presidential Library.

guarantee equal rights to all its citizens. Congress responded to Johnson's urgings with a flood of legislation. The 1960s witnessed more economic, political, and social reform than any period since the New Deal, including civil rights legislation, the War on Poverty, and Medicare. But even during these years of liberal triumph, anger and social tension intermittently flared into violence. Beginning with Kennedy's assassination in 1963, ten years of bloodshed—race riots, the murders of other political and civil rights leaders, and the war in Vietnam—shattered the optimism of the Kennedy and Johnson eras.

Urban blacks were angry that poverty and segregation persisted despite the passage of landmark civil rights laws, and their discontent exploded during the "long hot summers" of the 1960s. This social turbulence, in conjunction with the growing antiwar movement, brought down the presidency of Lyndon Johnson, gave rise to the Black Power movement, the radical politics of the New Left, a revived women's movement, and the hippie counterculture.

The perceived excesses of the 1960s, added to snowballing white opposition to the civil rights movement, prompted many Americans to shift to the right politically. In 1968, Richard M. Nixon was elected president, but his presidency polarized the nation still further. The presidencies of Nixon's two immediate predecessors had ended tragically: Dallas and Vietnam were the sites of their undoing. A third location, the Watergate apartment complex in Washington, D.C., became Richard Nixon's downfall. In 1974 he resigned from office, the only American president to do so. Battered by more than a decade of turmoil, many Americans had ceased to believe in any version of the American Dream.

 Civil Rights and the New Frontier

President John F. Kennedy was, as the writer Norman Mailer observed, "our leading man." Young, handsome, and vigorous, the new chief executive was the first president born in the twentieth century. Kennedy had a genuinely inquiring mind, and as a patron of the arts he brought wit and sophistication to the White House. Kennedy was born to wealth and politics: his Irish-American grandfather had been mayor of Boston, and his millionaire father, Joseph P. Kennedy, had served as ambassador to Great Britain. In 1946 the young Kennedy, having returned from the Second World War a naval hero, perpetuated the family tradition by campaigning to represent Boston in the House of Representatives. He won easily, served three terms in the House, and in 1952 was elected to the Senate.

As a Democrat, Kennedy inherited the New Deal commitment to America's social welfare system. He generally cast liberal votes in line with the pro-labor sentiments of his low-income, blue-collar constituents. But he avoided controversial issues such as civil rights and the censure of Joseph McCarthy. Kennedy won a Pulitzer Prize for *Profiles in Courage* (1956), a study of politicians who had acted on principle, but he shaded the truth when he claimed sole authorship of the book, which had been written largely by his staff. As one critic put it, he himself showed "too much profile and not enough courage." Kennedy nevertheless enjoyed an enthusiastic following, especially after his landslide reelection to the Senate in 1958.

Kennedy's vitality and style captured the imagination of many Americans. In a departure from the Eisenhower administration's staid, conservative image, the new president surrounded himself with young men of intellectual verve who proclaimed that they had fresh ideas for invigorating the nation;

"The Best and the Brightest"

the writer David Halberstam called them "the best and the brightest" (Kennedy appointed only one woman to a significant position). Secretary of Defense Robert McNamara (age forty-four) had been an assistant professor at Harvard at twenty-four and later the whiz-kid president of the Ford Motor Company. Kennedy's special assistant for national security affairs, McGeorge Bundy (age forty-one) had become a Harvard dean at thirty-four with only a bachelor's degree. Kennedy himself was only forty-three, and his brother Robert, the attorney general, was thirty-five.

Kennedy's ambitious program, the New Frontier, promised more than the president could deliver: an end to racial discrimination, federal aid to educa-

The New Frontier

tion, medical care for the elderly, and government action to halt the recession the country was suffering. Only eight months into his first year, it was evident that Kennedy lacked the ability to move Congress, which was dominated by a conservative coalition of Republicans and southern Democrats. In 1961 Kennedy saw the defeat of bills providing federal aid to education and a boost in the minimum wage.

Still struggling to appease conservative members of Congress, the new president pursued civil rights with a notable lack of vigor. Kennedy did establish the President's Committee on Equal Employment Opportunity to eliminate racial discrimination in government hiring. But he waited until late 1962 before honoring a 1960 campaign pledge to issue an executive order forbidding segregation in federally subsidized housing. Meanwhile, he appointed five diehard segregationists to the federal bench in the Deep South. The struggle for racial equality was the most important domestic issue of the time, and Kennedy's performance disheartened civil rights advocates.

Despite President Kennedy's lack of support, African-American civil rights activists in the early 1960s continued their struggle through the tactic of nonviolent civil disobedience. Volunteers organized by the Southern Christian Leadership Conference (SCLC), headed by Reverend Martin Luther King, Jr., deliberately violated segregation laws by sitting in at whites-only lunch counters, libraries, and bus stations in the South. The Congress of Racial Equality (CORE) initiated the Freedom Rides in May 1961: an integrated group of thirteen people boarded a bus in Washington, D.C., and traveled into the South, where they braved attacks by white mobs for daring to desegregate interstate transportation. Un-

protected by either federal or state authorities, the Freedom Riders were savagely beaten and their bus was burned outside Anniston, Alabama.

Many black high-school and college students in the South joined the Student Nonviolent Coordinating Committee (SNCC), established in 1960

Student Nonviolent Coordinating Committee

soon after the sit-ins began in Greensboro, North Carolina (see page 828). These young people walked the dusty back roads of Mississippi and Georgia, encouraging African-Americans to resist segregation and register to vote. Some SNCC volunteers were white, and some were from the North; but most were black southerners, and many were from low-income families. These volunteers understood from experience how racism, powerlessness, and poverty intersected in the lives of African-Americans.

As the civil rights movement gained momentum, President Kennedy gradually made a commitment to first-class citizenship for blacks. In 1962 he

"I Have a Dream"

ordered United States marshals to protect James Meredith, the first African-American student to attend the University of Mississippi. The following spring, under court order, federal officials ignored the defiant governor of Alabama, George C. Wallace, and forced the desegregation of the University of Alabama. And in June 1963 Kennedy finally requested legislation to outlaw racial discrimination in employment and racial segregation in public accommodations. When more than 250,000 people, black and white, gathered at the Lincoln Memorial for a March on Washington that August, they did so with the knowledge that President Kennedy was at last on their side. They also heard a most memorable speech: "I have a dream," the civil rights movement's inspirational leader, Martin Luther King, Jr., told the crowd, "that my four little children will one day live in a nation where they will not be judged by the color of their skin but by the content of their character."

The television nightly news programs brought the civil rights struggles into Americans' homes. The story was sometimes grisly. In 1963 Medgar Evers, director of the NAACP in Mississippi, was gunned down in his own driveway. The same year police in Birmingham, Alabama, under the command of Sheriff "Bull" Connor attacked nonviolent civil rights demonstrators, including children, with snarling dogs, fire hoses, and cattle prods. Then two horrifying

A historic moment for the civil rights movement was the March on Washington of August 28, 1963. A quarter of a million people, black and white, stood together for racial equality. Waving to friends, Reverend Martin Luther King, Jr., is about to begin his "I Have a Dream" speech.   Francis Miller, *Life* magazine © Time, Inc.

events helped to convince reluctant politicians that action on civil rights was long overdue. In September white terrorists exploded a bomb during Sunday morning services at Birmingham's Sixteenth Street Baptist Church. Sunday school was in session, and four black girls were killed. A little more than two months later, John Kennedy was assassinated in Dallas. If ever the civil rights movement had the moral support of most of the American people, it was at this time of national tragedy and repugnance over violence.

The first dreadful flash from Dallas clattered over newsroom Teletype machines across the country at 1:34 P.M. Eastern Standard Time, November 22, 1963. Broadcast immediately on radio and television, the news was soon on the streets. Many people still remember precisely where they were and what they were doing when they heard that President John F. Kennedy had been assassinated. Time stopped for Americans, and they experienced what psychologists call flashbulb memory, the freeze-framing of an exceptionally emotional event down to the most incidental detail. For an earlier generation, the indelible memory was of December 7, 1941, when radio reports of the Japanese attack on Pearl Harbor stunned

The Kennedy Assassination

the nation into silence. Now it was November 22, 1963, the day John Kennedy's promise was snuffed out.

In New York City a driver stopped in the middle of a busy intersection and ran over to a sidewalk luncheonette. "Is it true?" he shouted. Without looking up, the counterman replied "Yes, he's dead." The man returned to his car and slumped over the wheel, oblivious to the impatient honking around him. Ken Kesey's play *One Flew over the Cuckoo's Nest* had just opened on Broadway, and Kesey and a couple of friends were driving triumphantly back to the West Coast. They heard the news in Pennsylvania. As "we stopped in at service stations and Howard Johnson's and little fast-food places across the United States," Kesey later recalled, "a really profound thing happened to us. We felt like we were seeing the real soul of America with its shirt torn open in grief."

Kennedy's murder still baffles many Americans. Was the accused assassin, Lee Harvey Oswald, acting alone or as part of a conspiracy? Was he the only gunman? What was his motive? Whatever the answers, Kennedy's death traumatized the entire nation. Then, two days later, in full view of millions of TV viewers, Oswald himself was shot dead by

Who Killed President Kennedy?

a nightclub owner and small-time Mafia figure named Jack Ruby. The same questions were asked again: What was Ruby's motive? Was he silencing Oswald to prevent him from implicating others?

Historians have wondered what John Kennedy would have accomplished had he lived. Although his legislative achievements were meager, he inspired genuine idealism in Americans. When Kennedy exhorted Americans in his inaugural address to "Ask not what your country can do for you; ask what you can do for your country," tens of thousands volunteered to spend two years of their lives in the Peace Corps. "We had such faith in what Kennedy was doing," recalled one volunteer, "and we all wanted to be a part of it."

Kennedy also promoted a sense of national purpose through his vigorous support of the space program. America clearly lagged behind the Soviet Union, which sent a missile carrying cosmonaut Yuri Gagarin into orbit around the earth in April 1961. But Americans celebrated a month later when Alan Shephard, one of the seven original astronauts, rode the Mercury 3 missile into space. After marine lieutenant colonel John Glenn orbited the globe in a space capsule in February 1962, the United States accelerated its Apollo program, which developed more powerful rocket boosters and lunar landing vehicles for the first astronauts to set foot on the moon. And Americans embraced Kennedy's challenge to put a man on the moon before the Soviets did and by the end of the decade.

In recent years, writers have drawn attention to Kennedy's recklessness in world events, such as authorizing the Bay of Pigs invasion of 1961 (see page 866) and CIA attempts to assassinate Cuba's leader Fidel Castro. They also

Kennedy in Retrospect

have criticized his timidity in civil rights and have pointed to his extramarital sex life as evidence of a serious character flaw. It is clear, however, that Kennedy had begun to grow as president during his last few months in office. He made a moving appeal for racial equality and alled for reductions in Cold War tensions. Partly because of the Kennedy aura of glamour and youth and hope, John Kennedy acquired a loftier reputation in death than he had enjoyed in life. And in a peculiar way he accomplished more in death than in life. In the postassassination atmosphere of grief and remorse, Lyndon Johnson pushed through Congress practically the entire New Frontier agenda.

The Great Society and the Triumph of Liberalism

The new president was a big man and a passionate one. As Senate majority leader from 1954 to 1960, Lyndon Johnson had learned how to manipulate people and power to achieve his ends. "This ponderous . . . Texan knows more about the sources of power in the political world of Washington than any president in this century," wrote columnists Rowland Evans and Robert Novak. "He can be gentle and solicitous as a nurse, but as ruthless and deceptive as a riverboat gambler." In the aftermath of the assassination, Johnson resolved to unite the country behind the unfulfilled legislative program of the martyred president. More than that, he wanted to realize Roosevelt's and Truman's unmet goals. He called his new program the Great Society.

Johnson made civil rights his top legislative priority. "No memorial oration or eulogy," he told a joint session of Congress five days after the assassination, "could more eloquently honor President Kennedy's memory than the earliest passage of the civil rights bill." Within months Johnson had signed into law the Civil Rights Act of 1964, which outlawed dis-

Civil Rights Act of 1964

Surrounded by an illustrious group of civil rights leaders and members of Congress, President Lyndon B. Johnson signs the Civil Rights Act of 1964. Standing behind the president is Reverend Martin Luther King, Jr.   Corbis-Bettmann.

crimination on the basis of race, color, religion, sex, or national origin, not only in public accommodations but also in employment. The act also authorized the government to withhold funds from public agencies that discriminated on the basis of race, and it empowered the attorney general to guarantee voting rights and end school segregation. In 1964 African-Americans gained two additional victories. First, President Johnson appointed an Equal Employment Opportunity Commission to investigate and judge complaints of job discrimination. Second, the states ratified the Twenty-fourth Amendment to the Constitution which outlawed the poll tax in federal elections.

Johnson enunciated another priority in his first State of the Union address: "The administration today, here and now, declares unconditional war on poverty." Eight months later, he signed into law the Economic Opportunity Act of 1964, which allocated almost $1 billion to fight poverty. The act became the opening salvo in Johnson's War on Poverty.

In the year following Kennedy's death, Johnson sought to govern by a liberal consensus, appealing

One of several programs established by the 1964 Economic Opportunity Act, VISTA (Volunteers in Service to America) helped poor people to help themselves. In promoting self-help, VISTA workers lived and worked on reservations, in barrios, *and among the homeless. Some worked as advocates for migratory farm families. This VISTA volunteer, JoAnne Eggers, helps two migrant workers in Medford, Oregon.* Paul Conklin.

to the shared values and aspirations of the majority of the nation for continued economic growth and social justice.

Election of 1964

His lopsided victory over his conservative Republican opponent in 1964, Senator Barry Goldwater of Arizona, indicates that he succeeded. Johnson garnered 61 percent of the popular vote and the electoral votes of all but six states. Riding on Johnson's coattails, the Democrats won large majorities in both the House (295 to 140) and the Senate (68 to 32). Johnson recognized that the opportunity to push through further reform had arrived. "Hurry, boys, hurry," he told his staff just after the election. "Get that legislation up to the Hill and out. Eighteen months from now ol' Landslide Lyndon will be Lame-Duck Lyndon." Congress responded in 1965 and 1966 with the most sweeping reform legislation since 1935.

Three bills enacted in 1965 were legislative milestones: the Medicare program insured the elderly against medical and hospital bills; the Elementary and Secondary Education Act provided for general federal aid to education for the first time; and the Voting Rights Act of 1965 empowered the attorney general to supervise voter registration in areas where fewer than half of the minority residents of voting age were registered (see map, page 933). In 1960 only 29 percent of the South's African-American population was registered to vote; when Johnson left office in 1969, the proportion was approaching two-thirds. Even in Mississippi, one of the most resistant states, black registration figures grew from 7 percent in 1964 to 59 percent in 1968.

Voting Rights Act of 1965

The flurry of legislation enacted into law during Johnson's presidency was staggering: establishment of the Department of Housing and Urban Development, the Department of Transportation, and the National Endowments for the Arts and Humanities; water- and air-quality improvement acts; liberalization of immigration laws; and appropriations for the most ambitious federal housing program since 1949, including rent supplements to low-income families. In 1968 Johnson signed another Civil Rights Act—his third—banning racial and religious discrimination in the sale and rental of housing. Another provision of this legislation, known as the Indian Bill of Rights, extended those constitutional protections to Native Americans living under tribal self-government on reservations.

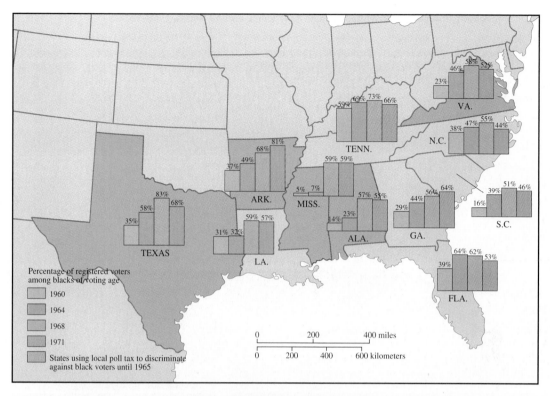

African-American Voting Rights, 1960–1971   *After passage of the 1965 Voting Rights Act, African-American registration skyrocketed in Mississippi and Alabama and rose substantially in other southern states.*   Source: Harold W. Stanley, *Voter Mobilization and the Politics of Race: The South and Universal Suffrage, 1952–1984* (Praeger Publishers, an imprint of Greenwood Publishing Group, Westport, CT, 1987), p. 97. Copyright © 1987 by Harold W. Stanley. Used with permission.

By far the most ambitious of Johnson's initiatives was the War on Poverty. Because the gross national product (GNP) had increased in the mid-1960s, Johnson and his advisers reasoned that the government could expect a "fiscal dividend" of several billion dollars in additional tax revenues. They decided to spend the extra money to wipe out poverty through education and job-training programs. Beginning with a $1 billion appropriation in 1964, the War on Poverty evolved in 1965 and 1966 to include the Job Corps, to provide marketable skills, work experience, and remedial education for young people; Project Head Start, to prepare preschoolers from low-income families for grade school; and Upward Bound, to help high-school students from low-income families to prepare for a college education. Other antipoverty programs were Legal Services for the Poor, Volunteers in Service to America (VISTA), and the Model Cities program, which channeled federal funds to upgrade

War on Poverty

employment, housing, education, and health in targeted neighborhoods.

The War on Poverty was a mixed success. For one thing, it was politically volatile because its "community-action programs" angered powerful mayors: it deliberately bypassed them and encouraged "maximum feasible participation" in decision making by the poor themselves, who served on antipoverty governing boards that allocated large sums of money. Furthermore, confusion abounded in the ambitious program. Not even R. Sargent Shriver, who administered the War on Poverty as head of the Office of Economic Opportunity (OEO), could deny this: "It's like we . . . launched a half-dozen rockets at once," he later conceded. Another failing was that the War on Poverty did little to reduce poverty in rural areas or to discourage the South-to-North migration that was worsening already overwhelming northern urban problems.

Another large group that remained poor despite antipoverty initiatives was women and children living

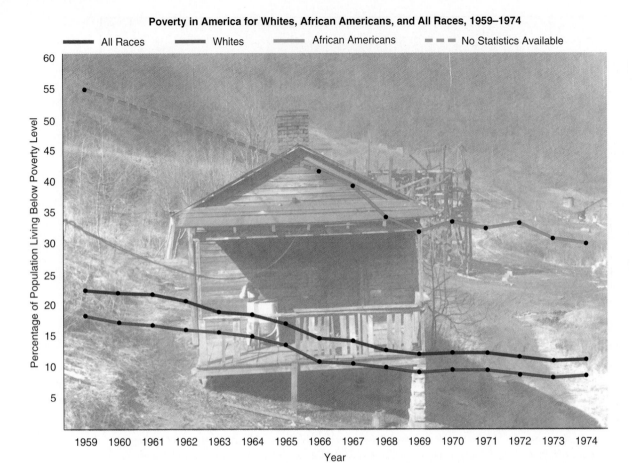

Poverty in America for Whites, African Americans, and All Races, 1959–1974   *Because of rising levels of economic prosperity, combined with the impact of Great Society programs, the percentage of Americans living in poverty in 1974 was half as high as in 1959. African-Americans still were far more likely than white Americans to be poor. In 1959, more than half of all blacks (55.1 percent) were poor; in 1974, the figure remained high (30.3 percent). The government did not record data on African-American poverty for the years 1960 through 1965.*

in female-headed families; they constituted 40 percent of the poor in the United States. The economic boom that lasted from 1963 to 1969 lifted 12 million people in male-headed families out of poverty. Left behind were 11 million in families headed by women (the same number as in 1963) who earned pitiful wages and frequently did not receive child-support payments from ex-husbands.

Even so, in tandem with a rising GNP, the War on Poverty substantially alleviated hunger and suffering in the United States. Its legislation directly addressed the debilitating housing, health, and nutritional deficiencies from which the poor suffered. Between 1965 and 1970, the GNP leaped from $685 billion to $977 billion, and federal

Successes in Reducing Poverty

spending for Social Security, health, welfare, and education more than doubled. Not only did some of this prosperity trickle down to the poor, but also—and more important—millions of new jobs were created. The result was a startling reduction in the number of poor people, from 25 percent of the population in 1962 to 11 percent in 1973 (see figure). Particularly fortunate were the elderly, who benefited from large increases in Social Security benefits; poverty among the elderly dropped from about 40 percent in 1960 to 16 percent in 1974.

The period of liberal ascendancy represented by the War on Poverty was short-lived; most of the Great Society's legislative achievements occurred in 1964, 1965, and 1966 (see table, page 935). Disillusioned with America's deepening involvement in Vietnam (see Chapter 30) and upset by the violence of urban

Great Society Achievements, 1964–1966

	1964	1965	1966
Civil Rights	Civil Rights Act Equal Employment Opportunity Commission 24th Amendment	Voting Rights Act	
War on Poverty	Economic Opportunity Act Office of Economic Opportunity Job Corps VISTA		Model Cities
Education		Elementary and Secondary Education Act Head Start Upward Bound	
Environment		Water Quality Act Air Quality Act	Clean Water Restoration Act
New Government Agencies		Department of Housing and Urban Development National Endowments for the Arts and Humanities	Department of Transportation
Miscellaneous		Medicare Immigration Act	

The Great Society of the mid-1960s saw the biggest burst of reform legislation since the New Deal of the 1930s.

race riots (see pages 937–938), many of Johnson's allies began to reject both him and his liberal consensus.

One branch of government, however, maintained the liberal tradition: the Supreme Court. Under the intellectual and moral leadership of Chief Justice Earl Warren, the Court in the 1960s was disposed by political conviction and a belief in judicial activism to play a central role in the resurgence of liberalism. In 1962 the Court began handing down a series of landmark decisions. *Baker* v. *Carr* (1962) and subsequent rulings established that the principle of "one person, one vote" must prevail at both the state and the national levels. This decision required the reapportionment of state legislatures so that each representative would serve the same number of constituents. The Court also outlawed required prayers

The Warren Court

and Bible reading in public schools, explaining that such practices imposed an "indirect coercive pressure upon religious minorities." Some religious groups denounced these decisions, and a few towns, asserting that they were losing their freedoms, announced their refusal to comply.

The Court also attacked the legal underpinning of McCarthyism, ruling in 1965 that a person need not register with the government as a member of a subversive organization, because doing so would violate constitutional safeguards against self-incrimination. In *Griswold* v. *Connecticut* (1965), the Court ruled that a state law prohibiting the use of contraceptives by married couples violated "a marital right of privacy" and was unconstitutional. The Court upheld the Civil Rights Act of 1964 and the

Civil Rights Rulings

Voting Rights Act of 1965. In other rulings that particularly upset conservatives, the Court decreed that books, magazines, and films could not be banned as obscene unless they were found to be "utterly without redeeming social value."

Perhaps most controversial of all was the Court's transformation of the criminal justice system. Beginning with *Gideon* v. *Wainwright* (1963), the Court ruled that a poor person charged with a felony had the right to a state-appointed lawyer. In *Escobedo* v. *Illinois* (1964), it decreed that the accused had a right to counsel during interrogation and a right to remain silent. *Miranda* v. *Arizona* (1966) established that police had to inform criminal suspects that they had these rights and that any statements they made could be used against them. Critics denounced the decisions as victories for criminals, and the right-wing John Birch Society campaigned to impeach Earl Warren.

Despite conservatives' demands for Warren's removal, constitutional historians consider him one of the two most influential chief justices in the nation's history (the other was John Marshall). Whether or not one approved of the decisions of the Warren Court (which ended with Warren's retirement in 1969), its effect on the American people is undeniable. Bernard Schwartz, a constitutional-law scholar, has made this appraisal: "In expanding civil liberties, broadening political freedom, extending the franchise, reinforcing freedoms of speech, assembly, and religion, limiting the power of the politicians in smoke-filled rooms, [and] defining the limits of police power, the Warren Court had no equal in American history."

 ## Civil Rights Disillusionment, Race Riots, and Black Power

Even while the civil rights movement was winning important victories in the mid-1960s, some activists began to grumble that the federal government was not to be trusted. Fannie Lou Hamer and the Mississippi Freedom Democratic Party felt betrayed by Lyndon Johnson and the Democrats at the 1964 Atlantic City convention, and evidence suggested that the Federal Bureau of Investigation was hostile to the civil rights movement. Indeed, it turned out that at least one FBI informant not only was a member of the Ku Klux Klan but also was a terrorist who instigated violence against the civil rights movement, including the bombing of Birmingham's Sixteenth

Street Baptist Church in 1963. FBI director J. Edgar Hoover was a racist, activists charged, and they were disturbed by rumors (later confirmed) that Hoover had wiretapped and bugged Martin Luther King, Jr.'s hotel rooms and planted allegations in the newspapers about his sexual improprieties.

The year 1964 witnessed the first of the "long hot summers" of race riots in northern cities. In Harlem and Rochester in New York, and in several cities in New Jersey, brutal actions by white police officers, including vicious, unprovoked beatings in police stations, sparked riots in black neighborhoods. African-Americans deeply resented the unnecessary force that police sometimes used. As the black writer James Baldwin put it, the white officers patrolling black neighborhoods represented "the force of the white world."

Explosion of Black Anger

Whites wondered why African-Americans were venting their frustration violently at a time when they were making real progress in the civil rights struggle. The civil rights movement, however, had focused mostly on the South, aiming to abolish Jim Crow and black disfranchisement. In the North, African-Americans could vote, but many were living in deep poverty. The median income of northern blacks was little more than half that of northern whites, and their unemployment rate was twice as high. Among black males from age eighteen to twenty-five the unemployment rate was five times as high. Many African-American families, particularly those headed by women, lived in perpetual poverty. The primary assistance program, Aid to Families with Dependent Children (AFDC), failed to meet the needs of the poor. AFDC payments were inadequate to cover a family's rent, utilities, and household expenses, let alone its food. In 1970 it was estimated that more than 60 percent of African-American children were being raised in poverty.

Northern blacks, surveying the economic and civil rights gains of the 1960s, wondered when they, too, would benefit from the Great Society. Concentrated in the inner cities, they looked around the ghettos in which they lived and knew their circumstances were deteriorating. Their neighborhoods were more segregated than ever; in increasing numbers during the 1960s, whites had responded to the continuing black migration from the South by fleeing to the suburbs. And as inner-city neighborhoods became all black, so did the neighborhood schools. "It doesn't cost anything to move a few feet along a hamburger

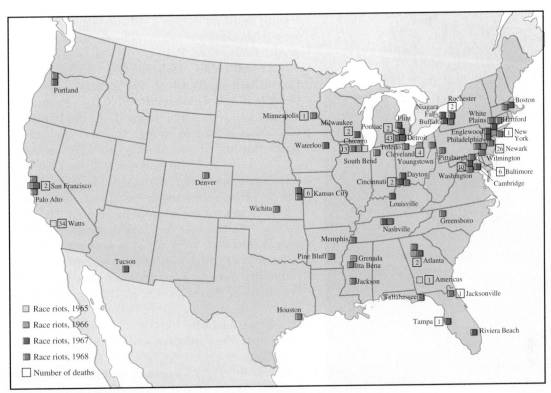

Race Riots, 1965–1968   *The first major race riot of the 1960s exploded in the Los Angeles neighborhood of Watts in 1965. The bloodiest riots of 1967 were in Newark, New Jersey, and Detroit. Scores of riots erupted in the aftermath of Martin Luther King, Jr.'s assassination in 1968.*

counter to make room for a Negro," one writer observed. "But the cost—economic, social, psychological—of abolishing forever a Negro ghetto of half a million souls is only now becoming apparent."

If 1964 was fiery and violent, 1965 was even more so. In August, an altercation between blacks and police sparked rioting in the Watts section of Los Angeles; thirty-four people were killed (see map). White mobs did not initiate the violence (as they had done in 1919 and 1943); instead, blacks exploded in anger over their joblessness and lack of opportunity, as well as police brutality. They looted white-owned stores, set fires, and threw rocks at police and firefighters.

The Watts Race Riot

Other cities exploded in riots between 1966 and 1968. In July 1967 twenty-six people were killed in street battles between blacks and police and army troops in Newark, New Jersey. A week later a race riot in Detroit led to the deaths of forty-three peo-

ple. In 1968 the National Advisory Commission on Civil Disorders, chaired by Governor Otto Kerner of Illinois, released a report blaming white racism for the riots: "The nation is rapidly moving toward two increasingly separate Americas . . . a white society principally located in suburbs . . . and a Negro society largely concentrated within large central cities."

Clearly, many blacks, especially in the North, were beginning to question whether the nonviolent civil rights movement was serving their needs. In 1963 Martin Luther King, Jr., had appealed to whites' humanitarian instincts in his "I Have a Dream" speech. Now another voice was beginning to be heard, one that urged blacks to seize their freedom "by any means necessary." It was the voice of Malcolm X, a one-time pimp and street hustler who had converted while in prison to the Nation of Islam faith, whose followers were commonly known as the Black Muslims.

A small sect that espoused black pride and separatism from white society, the Black Muslims con-

Malcolm X, as chief spokesperson for the Black Muslims, espoused African-American pride and separatism from white society and urged blacks to defend themselves with violence if necessary. Martin Luther King, Jr., preached nonviolence and racial integration. Still, these men agreed on many things. Their common goal was freedom and dignity for all black people in the United States. In 1964 King and Malcolm X met at the United States Capitol and enjoyed a few words together. Wide World Photos.

demned the "white devil" as the chief source of evil in the world. They dissociated themselves from white society,

Malcolm X

exhorted blacks to lead sober lives and practice thrift, and sanctioned violence in self-defense. By the early 1960s Malcolm X had become the Black Muslims' chief spokesperson, and his advice was straightforward: "If someone puts a hand on you, send him to the cemetery."

Malcolm X was murdered in early 1965. His assassins were Black Muslims who believed he had betrayed their cause, because he had modified some of his positions just before his death. He had met whites who were not devils, he said, and he had expressed cautious support for the nonviolent civil rights movement. Still, for both blacks and whites, Malcolm X symbolized black defiance and self-respect. A com-

pelling figure in life, in death he would become a hero to increasing numbers of black nationalists and proponents of Black Power.

A year after Malcolm X's death, Stokely Carmichael, chairman of the Student Nonviolent Coordinating Committee (SNCC), denounced "the betrayal of black dreams by white America" and called

Black Power

on African-Americans to assert "Black Power." To be truly free from white oppression, Carmichael believed, blacks had to elect black candidates, organize their own schools, and control their own institutions. "It's time we stand up and take over," he declared; "move on over [Whitey] or we'll move on over you." Several influential organizations that previously had been committed to racial integration and nonviolence embraced Black Power. SNCC in 1966 and the Congress of Racial Equality (CORE) in 1967 purged their white members and repudiated integration, arguing that black people needed power, not white friendship.

To many white Americans, one of the most fearsome of the new groups was the Black Panther Party. Blending black nationalism and revolutionary communism, the Panthers dedicated themselves to destroying both capitalism and "the military arm of our oppressors," the police in the ghettos. The Panthers defied authority and carried rifles in homage to Mao Zedong's revolutionary slogan "Power flows from the barrel of a gun." But they also instituted free breakfast and healthcare programs for ghetto children, taught courses in African-American history, and demanded jobs and decent housing for the poor. What particularly worried white parents was that some of their own children agreed with the Panthers. Called the New Left, this vocal subset of the baby-boom generation set out to "change the system."

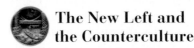

The New Left and the Counterculture

"I'm tired of reading history," Mario Savio, a graduate student at the University of California, complained in a letter to a friend in 1964. "I want to make it." Within a few months Savio realized his ambition as a leader of the campus Free Speech movement, and Berkeley had become synonymous with campus unrest. After teaching in SNCC's Mississippi Freedom Summer Project, Savio and others returned to Berkeley convinced that the power structure that dominated blacks' lives also controlled the bureaucratic machinery of the university.

In fact, the University of California was a model university in 1964, with a worldwide reputation for excellence and public service. Its chancellor, the economist Clark Kerr, had written approvingly that higher education had become "a component part of the 'military-industrial complex,'" and he likened the "multiversity" with its many separate colleges and research institutes to a big business. The largest single campus in the country, with tens of thousands of students, Berkeley had become hopelessly impersonal by the 1960s. Some students complained that they felt like cogs in a machine.

The struggle at Berkeley began when the university administration yielded to pressure from political conservatives and banned recruitment by civil rights and antiwar organizations in Sproul Plaza, the students' traditional gathering place. Savio denounced the ban, saying that the time had come for students to "put [their] bodies against the gears . . . and make the machine stop until we are free." Militant students defied Kerr's ban; the administration suspended them or had them arrested. In December the Free Speech Movement seized and occupied the main administration building. Governor Pat Brown dispatched state police to Berkeley, and more than eight hundred people were arrested. Angry students shut down classes for several days in protest.

Free Speech Movement

The willingness of those in positions of authority to mobilize the police against unruly but not violent students was shocking and radicalizing to many young people. Having grown up comfortable and even indulged, they soon found themselves treated like criminals for questioning what they considered a criminal war in Vietnam and racial injustice in their own country. By the end of the decade, the activism born at Berkeley would spread to hundreds of other campuses.

Two years earlier, another group of students had met in Port Huron, Michigan, to found Students for a Democratic Society (SDS). Like their leaders Tom Hayden and Al Haber, most SDS members were white, middle-class college students. In their platform, the Port Huron Statement, they condemned racism, poverty in the midst of plenty, and the Cold War. SDS sought nothing less than the revitalization of democracy by

Students for a Democratic Society and the New Left

taking power from the corporations, the military, and the politicians and returning it to the people.

Inspired by the Free Speech Movement and SDS, a minority of students allied themselves with the New Left. Though united in their hatred of racism and the Vietnam War, the New Left divided along philosophical and political lines. Some radicals were Marxists, others black nationalists, anarchists, or pacifists. Some believed in pursuing social change through negotiation; others were revolutionaries who regarded compromise as impossible.

By calling into question the basic foundations of American society, the New Left indirectly gave rise to a phenomenon called the counterculture. Exhorted by Timothy Leary—a former Harvard instructor and advocate of expanded consciousness through use of LSD and other mind-altering drugs—to "turn on, tune in, drop out," millions of students experimented with marijuana and hallucinogenic drugs. Their political outrage, drug experiences, and experiments with communal living persuaded them that they lived in a new era unconnected to the past. In fact, in a list of twenty-one academic subjects, students ranked history "the most irrelevant."

Countercultural Revolution

Music more than anything else expressed the countercultural assault on the status quo. Bob Dylan

Beginning in 1964 with the Beatles' sensational television appearance on the Ed Sullivan Show, *Beatlemania swept the nation. In addition to top-selling records, the Beatles made movies that delighted critics and audiences alike. These buttons, each depicting one of the Fab Four, promote the feature-length animated cartoon* The Yellow Submarine *(1968), for which Paul McCartney and John Lennon wrote a number of songs.* Collection of Picture Research Consultants & Archives.

Inspired by Ken Kesey and his Merry Pranksters, who traveled in a 1939 International Harvester school bus, hippies seemed drawn to buses. This bus, named "The Road Hog," carries members of the New Buffalo Commune in the 1968 Fourth of July parade in El Rito, New Mexico.   Lisa Law/Image Works.

Rock 'n' Roll

promised revolutionary answers "blowin' in the wind," and young people cheered Jimi Hendrix, who sang of life in a drug-induced "purple haze," and Janis Joplin, who brought African-American blues to white Americans. Like sex and drugs, the music of the 1960s represented a quest to redefine reality and create a more just and joyful society. Rock festivals became cultural watersheds. In 1969 at Woodstock in upstate New York, more than 400,000 people ignored or reveled in days of rain and mud, without shelter and without violence. A number of them began to dream of a peaceful "Woodstock nation" based on love, drugs, and rock music.

Some young people tried to construct alternative ways of life. In the Haight-Ashbury section of San Francisco, "flower children" created an urban subculture as distinctive as that of any Chinatown or Little Italy. "Hashbury" inspired numerous other communal-living experiments. The counterculture represented only a small proportion of American youth. But to middle-class parents, hippies seemed to be everywhere. Parents were appalled by long hair and patched jeans and feared their children would suffer lifelong damage from drugs.

Sexuality

The "generation gap" was yawning wide, but most disturbing to parents were the casual sexual mores that young people were adopting. In 1960 the government approved the birth-control pill, and use of the pill accelerated among young people. Americans formerly had linked sexuality to romance and marriage and babies. In the 1960s many young people viewed sexuality as a means of self-expression and as a gauge of personal happiness. For them, living together no longer equaled living in sin; and as attitudes toward premarital sex changed, so did notions about homosexuality and sex roles.

Gay Rights Movement

The militancy of the 1960s helped inspire the gay rights movement. Homosexuals had long feared that disclosing their sexual orientation would mean losing not only their jobs but even their friends and families. That attitude began to change in June 1969. In New York City's Greenwich Village, a riot erupted when police raided the Stonewall Inn, a gay bar on Christopher Street, and were greeted with a volley of beer bottles hurled by patrons tired of police harassment. Rioting continued into the night, and graffiti calling for "Gay Power" appeared along Christopher Street. The Stonewall riot, as historian John D'Emilio has written "marked a critical divide in the politics and consciousness of homosexuals and lesbians. A small, thinly spread reform effort suddenly grew into a large, grass-roots movement for liberation . . . as a furtive subculture moved aggressively into the open."

As the slogan "Make Love, Not War" suggests, the New Left and the counterculture discovered a common cause as the war in Vietnam escalated. Students held teach-ins—open forums for discussion of the war by students, professors, and guest speakers—and antiwar marches and demonstrations became a widespread protest tactic (see map). Some young men fled the draft by moving abroad—mostly to Canada and Scandinavia—while others protested, violently and nonviolently, at local draft board offices. The Johnson administration charged that such acts threatened the nation's war-making powers.

Antiwar Protests

By this time, however, growing numbers of Americans, young and old, had quit believing their elected leaders. President Johnson claimed the United States was fighting for honorable reasons, but people wondered what goal could justify the murder of Vietnamese women and children. As troop levels increased, many recalled ruefully that in 1964 they had voted for Johnson as the more cautious of the two presidential candidates. By 1968 almost a half-million American soldiers were stationed in Vietnam, and Johnson's credibility had evaporated.

1968: A Year of Protest, Violence, and Loss

As stormy and violent as the years from 1963 through 1967 had been, many Americans still tried to downplay the nation's distress in the hope that it would go away. But in 1968 a series of shocks hit them harder than ever. The first jolt came in January 1968, when the U.S.S. *Pueblo*, a navy intelligence ship, was captured by North Korea. A week later came the Tet of-

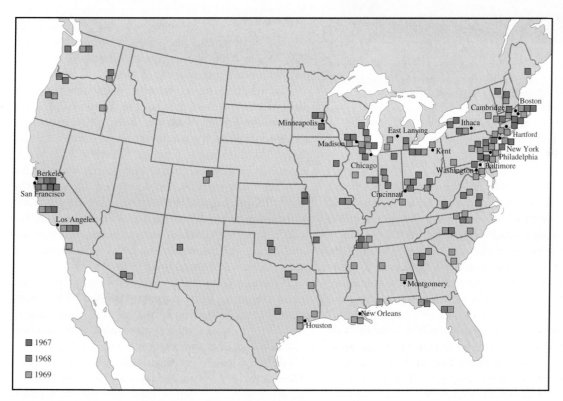

Disturbances on College and University Campuses, 1967–1969 *Students on campuses from coast to coast protested against the Vietnam War. Some protests were peaceful; others erupted into violent confrontations between protesters and police and army troops.*

Cesar Chavez provided charismatic leadership for the United Farm Workers Union and in doing so attracted the support of celebrities and political leaders, most notably Robert F. Kennedy. This poster advertises a 1968 benefit performance for the union to be held at New York City's Carnegie Hall.   Museum of American Political Life, University of Hartford.

fensive (see page 906), and for the first time many Americans believed that they might lose the war. American casualties were climbing. By July 4, 1968, American fatalities had surpassed thirty thousand.

Controversy over the war deepened within the Democratic Party, and two candidates rose to challenge Johnson for the 1968 presidential nomination. Senator Eugene McCarthy of Minnesota entered the New Hampshire primary on March 12 solely to contest Johnson's war policies; he won twenty of New Hampshire's twenty-four convention delegates. Soon another Democrat, Senator Robert F. Kennedy of New York, brother of the dead president, entered the fray. Then, on March 31, President Johnson went on national television to announce a scaling-down of the bombing in North Vietnam and his decision not to run for reelection.

Less than a week later, James Earl Ray, a white man, shot and killed Martin Luther King, Jr., in Memphis. It is still unclear whether Ray was a deranged racist acting alone or a hireling in an organized conspiracy. As an outspoken critic of the Vietnam War and increasingly of American capitalism, King had many enemies. Whatever Ray's motive, the murder touched off massive grief and rage in the nation's ghettos. Riots erupted in 168 cities and towns, including the looting and burning of white businesses (see map, page 937). Thirty-four blacks and five whites died in the violence. The terror provoked a white backlash. Tough talk was the response from Chicago mayor Richard Daley, who ordered police to shoot to kill arsonists.

Assassination of Martin Luther King, Jr.

Gallup polls in April and May reported Robert Kennedy to be the front-running Democratic presidential candidate, and in June he won the California primary. After addressing his joyous supporters in a Los Angeles hotel, Kennedy took a shortcut through the kitchen to a press conference. A young man stepped forward with a .22-caliber revolver and fired. Sirhan Sirhan, the assassin, was an Arab nationalist who despised Kennedy for his unwavering support of Israel.

Assassination of Robert Kennedy

The cumulative effect of so many assassinations drove many Americans to the brink of despair. African-Americans and the poor were especially grief-stricken at the assassination of Martin Luther King. Many antiwar liberals felt they had lost a friend in Robert Kennedy, who in the wake of his brother's assassination had developed deep empathy with the sufferings of the underprivileged and strong opposition to the Vietnam War. Whenever a charismatic, progressive leader with a vision of a more just and peace-loving nation rose to prominence, it seemed, he was mowed down.

Violence erupted again in August at the Democratic national convention in Chicago. The Democrats were divided over the war, and thousands of antiwar protesters and members of the zany and anarchic Youth International Party (Yippies) had traveled to Chicago. The Chicago police force was still in the psychological grip of Mayor Daley's shoot-to-kill directive. Twelve thousand police were assigned to twelve-hour shifts, and another twelve

Violence at the Democratic Convention

Violence erupted in Chicago during the 1968 Democratic convention, as police and national guardsmen used tear gas and clubs to stop twelve thousand protesters from marching to the convention hall. Corbis-Bettmann.

thousand army troops were on call with rifles, bazookas, and flamethrowers. They attacked in front of the Hilton Hotel, wading into the ranks of demonstrators, reporters, and TV camera operators. Throughout the nation, viewers watched as clubswinging police beat protesters to the ground. Inside the convention hall, Senator Abraham Ribicoff of Connecticut put aside his prepared speech to denounce the "Gestapo tactics in the streets of Chicago."

The Democratic convention nominated Vice President Hubert Humphrey for president and Senator Edmund Muskie of Maine for vice president. Like Johnson and Kennedy before him, Humphrey was both an unstinting supporter of the Vietnam War and a political liberal supported throughout his career by big-city bosses, African-Americans, and union members. The Republicans selected Richard M. Nixon as their presidential nominee; his running mate was the tough-talking Governor Spiro Agnew of Maryland. Another tough-talking governor, George C. Wallace of Alabama, ran as the nominee of the American Independent Party. Wallace was a segregationist, a proponent of reducing North Vietnam to rubble with nuclear weapons, and an advocate of "law and order."

Voters' enthusiasm was minimal for both Humphrey and Nixon, but when the votes were tabulated, Nixon emerged the winner. Just four years after Goldwater's debacle, the Republicans captured the White House by the slimmest of margins. Wallace collected nearly 10 million votes, or almost 14 percent of the total, the best performance by a third party since 1924. His strong showing made Nixon a minority president, elected with 43 percent of the popular vote (see map, page 944). Moreover, the Democrats maintained control of the House (243 to 192) and the Senate (58 to 42).

Election of 1968

Still, the 1968 election was a triumph for conservatism, for the combined vote for Nixon and Wallace was 57 percent. The war had hurt the Democrats' appeal, but even more politically damaging was the party's identification with the cause of civil rights and welfare for the poor. In 1968, Humphrey received 97 percent of the black vote but only 35 percent of the white vote. Among the defectors from the New Deal coalition were northern blue-

Unraveling of the New Deal Coalition

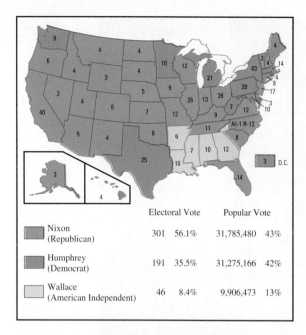

	Electoral Vote	Popular Vote
Nixon (Republican)	301 56.1%	31,785,480 43%
Humphrey (Democrat)	191 35.5%	31,275,166 42%
Wallace (American Independent)	46 8.4%	9,906,473 13%

Presidential Election, 1968 The popular vote was almost evenly split between Richard M. Nixon and Hubert Humphrey, but Nixon won 31 states to Humphrey's 14 and triumphed easily in electoral votes. George Wallace, the American Independent Party candidate, won 5 states in the Deep South.

collar ethnic voters. "In city after city," one observer noted, "racial conflicts had destroyed the old alliance. The New Deal had unraveled block by block."

 ## Rebirth of Feminism

Another liberation movement gained momentum during the turbulence of the 1960s, at first quietly and then on the picket line. The women's rights movement had languished after the adoption of the Nineteenth Amendment in 1920. But in the 1960s feminism was reborn. Many women were dissatisfied with their lives, and in 1963 they found a voice with the publication of Betty Friedan's *The Feminine Mystique*. According to Friedan, women across the country were deeply troubled by "the problem that has no name." Most women had grown up believing that "all they had to do was devote their lives from earliest girlhood to finding a husband and bearing children." The problem was that this "mystique of feminine fulfillment" left many wives and mothers feeling empty and incomplete. Friedan quoted a young mother: "I've tried everything women are supposed to do. . . . I love the kids and Bob and my home. . . . But

I'm desperate. I begin to feel that I have no personality. . . . Who am I?" Although *The Feminine Mystique* failed to address many of the problems faced by working-class women and women of color, it did find a large audience among middle-class white women.

President Kennedy appointed only one woman to a policymaking post in his administration, but she proved to be an effective advocate of women's rights.

National Organization for Women

Esther Peterson served as assistant secretary of labor and director of the Women's Bureau. In 1961, at her urging, Kennedy established the first President's Commission on the Status of Women. Its report, *American Women* (1963), argued that every obstacle to women's full participation in society ought to be removed. By 1967, all fifty states had established commissions to promote women's equality. But little federal action resulted from the release of *American Women*, and the government was failing to enforce the gender-equality provisions of the Civil Rights Act of 1964. The need for action inspired the founding in 1966 of the National Organization for Women (NOW). In the reform tradition, NOW battled for "equal rights in partnership with men" by lobbying for legislation and testing laws in the courts.

Not long after NOW's formation, a new generation of radical feminists emerged. Most radical feminists were white and well educated; many were the daughters of working mothers. Most had been raised in the era of sexual liberation, taking for granted liberation from unwanted pregnancy. The intellectual ferment of their movement produced a new feminist literature. Radical feminists focused not only on legal barriers but also on cultural assumptions and traditions. In the process they introduced the term *sexism* to signify a phenomenon far more pervasive than lack of legal equality, and they challenged everything from women's economic and political inequality to sexual double standards and sex-role stereotypes.

Radical feminists practiced what they called "personal politics." Charlotte Bunch, a feminist, explained, "There is no private domain of a person's life that is not political, and there is no political issue that is not ultimately personal." Unlike NOW, the radical feminists practiced direct action, such as picketing the 1968 Miss America contest in Atlantic City. One woman auctioned off an effigy of Miss America: "Gentlemen, I offer you the 1969 model. . . . She walks. She

"Personal Politics"

talks. She smiles on cue. *And* she does the housework." Into the "freedom trash can" the pickets dumped false eyelashes, curlers, girdles, and *Playboy* magazine to protest the prevailing view of women as domestic servants and sex objects.

Many radical feminists had joined the struggles for black civil rights and against the Vietnam War only to find that they were second-class citizens even in movements dedicated to equality. Instead of making policy, they were expected to make coffee, take minutes, and even provide sexual favors. Many of these feminists organized consciousness-raising groups to discuss wide-ranging and sensitive matters such as homosexuality, abortion, and power relationships in romance and marriage. The issue of homosexuality caused a split in the women's movement. In 1969 and 1970 NOW forced lesbians to resign from membership and offices in the organization. The rift was healed in 1971, largely because lesbians as well as gay men had begun to fight back.

For working women in the 1960s, the most pressing problems were sex discrimination in employment, meager professional opportunities, un-

Working Women's Burdens

equal pay for equal work, lack of adequate daycare for children, and prohibitions against abortion. In 1963 the average woman earned 63 cents for every dollar a man earned. Ten years later the figure had fallen to 57 cents. The main cause of this pay disparity was "occupational segregation": throughout the labor force, work was categorized into men's jobs and women's jobs, and women were concentrated in the low-paying positions. Because many women with college educations earned less than men with eighth-grade educations, it was natural that two of the most important women's goals of the 1960s were equal job opportunity and equal pay for equal work.

Another goal of working women was child daycare. In 1971, a bill passed Congress that would have set up a national system of daycare facilities for the children of working parents, but President Nixon vetoed it. The bill, Nixon asserted, would have committed government to "communal approaches to child-rearing over against the family-centered approach," thus imperiling the American family. In fact, there was a growing need for childcare: 11 million additional women joined the labor force between 1960 and 1972, and many were mothers of young children.

Despite opposition and setbacks, women were making impressive gains. They entered professional

In 1968 protesters from the National Women's Liberation Party marched at the Miss America contest in Atlantic City, New Jersey. Carrying signs that compared the annual pageant to a "cattle auction," or meat market, the picketers condemned the contest as degrading to women.   Wide World Photos.

schools in record numbers: from 1969 to 1973, the

Women's Educational and Professional Gains

number of women law students almost quadrupled, and the number of women medical students more than doubled. Under Title IX of the Educational Amendments of 1972, female college athletes gained the right to the same financial support as male athletes. The same year, Congress approved the Equal Rights Amendment (ERA) and sent it to the states for ratification. (The ERA states: "Equality of rights under the law shall not be denied or abridged by the United States or by any State on account of sex.") Thirty-five states ratified the ERA—three states short of the three-fourths majority needed when the deadline for ratification expired in 1982.

The Supreme Court also ruled on several issues essential to women. In 1973, following the lead of some states, the Court struck down laws that made

Roe v. Wade

abortion a crime. Justice Harry A. Blackmun wrote the majority (7–2) opinion in (*Roe* v. *Wade*): The constitutional "right of privacy . . . is broad enough to encompass a woman's decision whether or not to terminate her pregnancy." Only in the last three months of pregnancy could a state bar abortion. The Court at this time also addressed sex discrimination. In a 1971 ruling (*Reed* v. *Reed*), it held that legislation differentiating between the sexes "must be reasonable, not arbitrary," and in 1973 (*Frontiero* v. *Richardson*) the justices went a step further in declaring that job-related classifications based on sex, like those based on race, were "inherently suspect." These victories gave women new confidence in the 1970s.

 ## Nixon and the Persistence of Chaos

Richard Nixon's presidency was born in chaos. Bloody confrontations occurred at Berkeley, Wisconsin, Cornell, Harvard, and scores of other colleges and universities in 1969. In October three hundred Weathermen—an SDS splinter group—raced through Chicago's downtown district, smashing windows and attacking police officers in a deluded attempt to incite armed class struggle. Violence was absent a month later, however, when a half-million people assembled peacefully at the Washington Monument on Moratorium Day to call for an end to the Vietnam War.

If 1969 was bloody and turbulent, 1970 proved to be even more so. President Nixon appeared on television on April 30 to announce that the United States had launched an "incursion" into Cambodia (see page 907), a neutral country bordering Vietnam. Antiwar protest escalated. On May 4, national guardsmen in Ohio fired into a crowd of fleeing students at Kent State University, killing four young people. Ten days later, police and state highway patrolmen armed with automatic weapons blasted a women's dormitory at Jackson State, an all-black university in Mississippi, killing two students and wounding nine others. The police claimed they had been shot at, but no evidence of sniping could be found; the police fired no tear gas or warning shots.

Kent State and Jackson State

Many Americans, though disturbed by the increasing ferocity of campus confrontations, felt more personally endangered by street crime. Sales of pistols, burglar alarms, and bulletproof vests soared, as did demand for private guards and special police. Crime was on the rise

Fear of Crime

largely because many baby boomers were eighteen to twenty-five years old, the age group that committed far more crime than any other. But conservatives accused liberals and the Supreme Court of causing the crime wave by coddling criminals.

Responding to public calls for crackdowns, government officials sometimes overreacted. Governor Nelson Rockefeller of New York did so in September 1971 when more than a thousand inmates of the state prison at Attica seized thirty-eight guards and took over a cellblock. Rather than agree to come to Attica to negotiate, Rockefeller ordered state troopers, sheriff's deputies, and guards to storm the prison. Under a pall of tear gas Rockefeller's army regained control, but at a horrifying cost: twenty-nine inmates and ten hostages were dead.

This new wave of riots, protests, and violent crime convinced Nixon that the nation was plunging into anarchy. Worried like Lyndon Johnson before him that the antiwar movement was communist inspired, he ordered the FBI, the CIA, the National Security Agency, and the Defense Intelligence Agency in mid-1970 to formulate a coordinated attack on "internal threats." Meanwhile, the administration also worked to put the Democratic Party on the defensive. The theme for the upcoming elections was enunciated in a memorandum by Stuart Magruder, a White House assistant: "The Democrats should be portrayed as being on the fringes: radical liberals who . . . excuse disorder, tolerate crime . . . and undercut the President's foreign policy." But Republican attempts in 1970 to discredit the Democrats failed. The Democrats gained seats in the House, and the Republicans lost eleven state governorships.

Politics of Divisiveness

Nixon's fortunes declined further in 1971. In June the *New York Times* began to publish the *Pentagon Papers*, a top-secret Defense Department study of the Vietnam War (see page 907). Nixon also had to contend with inflation, a problem not entirely of his making. Lyndon Johnson's policy of "guns and butter"—massive deficit financing to support both the Vietnam War and the Great Society—had fueled inflation. By early 1971 the United States was suffering from a 5.3 percent inflation rate and a 6 percent unemployment rate. The word *stagflation* soon would be coined to describe this coexistence of economic recession (stagnation) and inflation.

Stagflation

Nixon shocked both critics and allies by declaring in early 1971 that "I am now a Keynesian." (Accord-

In May 1970, at Kent State University in Ohio, national guardsmen confronted student antiwar protesters with a tear gas barrage. Soon afterward, with no provocation, soldiers opened fire into a group of fleeing students. Four young people were killed, shot in the back; a distraught student hovers over the body of one of the victims. There was outrage throughout the country, campuses closed down, and students by the thousands came to Washington to demonstrate against the war.   John Filo.

ing to the British economist John Maynard Keynes, governments could stimulate economic growth in the private sector by means of "pump priming," or deficit financing.) Nixon's budget for fiscal 1971 would have a built-in deficit of $23 billion, just slightly less than the all-time high of $25 billion (1968 to 1969). Then in August, in an effort to correct the nation's balance-of-payments deficit, Nixon announced that he would devalue the dollar and allow it to "float" in international money markets. Finally, to curb inflation, the president froze prices, wages, and rents for ninety days and set limits on subsequent increases. Nixon's commitment to these controversial wage and price controls buckled the next year under pressure from businesses and unions.

Wage and price controls were just one facet of what surprised observers called Nixon's "great turnabout" from outspoken conservative to pragmatic liberal. Another was his announcement in 1971 that he would travel to the People's Republic of China, a communist enemy Nixon had denounced for years. It was clear that the president was preparing for the 1972 presidential election.

 ## Nixon's Southern Strategy and the Election of 1972

Political observers believed that President Nixon would have a hard time running for reelection on his first-term record. Having urged Americans to "lower our voices," he had ordered Vice President Agnew to denounce the press and student protesters. Having espoused unity, he had practiced the politics of polarization. Having campaigned as a fiscal conservative, he had authorized near-record budget deficits. And having promised peace, he had widened the war in Southeast Asia.

During Nixon's first term, the Democrats dominated both houses of Congress, and they continued to pursue a liberal agenda. Indeed, Congress's accomplishments were more despite Nixon than because of him. Congress increased Social Security payments and food-stamp funding and established the Occupational Safety and Health Administration to reduce hazards in the work place.

Liberal Legislative Victories

Americans concerned about the pollution of the environment celebrated the first Earth Day in 1970. This picture is from the Earth Day celebration in New York City. Covello & Launois/Black Star.

Moreover, in 1971 the states quickly ratified the Twenty-sixth Amendment, which extended the vote to eighteen-year-olds.

The environmental movement, which gained momentum in the 1960s, also bore fruit during Nixon's first term. Alerted to ecological hazards by Rachel Carson's *Silent Spring* (1962), growing numbers of Americans began to heed warnings of impending disaster due to unregulated population and economic growth. Gradually, the Congress responded, establishing the National Wilderness Preservation System (1964) and giving the federal government the power to set water-quality standards (1967).

Environmental Issues

Environmental tragedies such as a 1969 oil spill that fouled the beaches and killed wildlife in Santa Barbara, California, spurred citizen action. The Environmental Defense Fund (founded in 1967) successfully fought the use of DDT, and Greenpeace (founded in 1969) protested radioactive poisoning from nuclear-bomb testing. In 1970 Americans celebrated the first Earth Day, convinced that the earth's fate hung in the balance. Barry Commoner's *The*

Closing Circle (1971) put the issue squarely: "The environment got here first, and it's up to the economic system to adjust to the environment. Any economic system must be compatible with the environment, or it will not survive."

In the 1970s, states took action; Oregon, for example, passed the first bottle-recycling act in 1972. And although President Nixon was personally unsympathetic to the environmental movement, some of his subordinates were not. Nixon acknowledged the movement's political appeal by reluctantly agreeing to the establishment of the Environmental Protection Agency in 1970 and by signing into law the Clean Air Act (1970), Clean Water Act (1972), and Pesticide Control Act (1972).

One of Nixon's chief legislative aims was revenue sharing, a program that distributed federal funds to the states to use as they saw fit. In 1972, the president signed a revenue-sharing bill. Invoking the federalism of the nation's founders, he called this effort to shift responsibility back to state and local governments the New Federalism. The historian Stephen E. Ambrose has written that the program had special appeal to "the surburban, small-town, and rural homeowning Silent Majority," who expressed disgust that they had to pay "high taxes to support giveaway programs for the poor." They wanted to control their own tax dollars.

In his campaign for reelection, Nixon employed a "southern strategy" of political conservatism. A product of the Sunbelt, he was acutely aware of the growing political power of that conservative region. He thus appealed to the "Silent Majority." And as in the 1970 congressional elections, Nixon equated the Republican Party with law and order and the Democrats with permissiveness, crime, drugs, pornography, the hippie lifestyle, student radicalism, black militancy, feminism, homosexuality, and dissolution of the family.

Nixon's "Southern Strategy"

Actually, Nixon had been pursuing a southern strategy all along. A furor had arisen in 1970 when the press published a memorandum by Daniel Moynihan, Nixon's adviser on urban affairs and social welfare, who had recommended that "the issue of race could benefit from a period of benign neglect." Incensed, blacks and white liberals responded that this was another example of how uncaring the Nixon administration was. Moreover, Attorney General John Mitchell had courted southern white voters by trying to delay school desegregation in Mississippi and to prevent extension of the 1965 Voting Rights Act.

The southern strategy also guided Nixon's nomination of Supreme Court justices. After appointing Warren Burger, a conservative federal judge, to succeed Earl Warren as chief justice,

Nixon and the Supreme Court

Nixon had selected two southerners to serve as associate justices, one of whom was a segregationist. When the Senate declined to confirm either nominee, Nixon protested angrily, "I understand the bitter feelings of millions of Americans who live in the South." By 1972, however, the president had managed to appoint three more conservatives to the Supreme Court. Ironically, the new appointees did not always vote as Nixon would have wished: the Court's decisions on abortion, publication of the *Pentagon Papers*, the death sentence, wiretapping, and busing for school desegregation all ran counter to Nixon's views.

The Court was at the center of one of the most emotional issues of the 1972 election: busing of schoolchildren for purposes of integration. In *Swann v. Charlotte-Mecklenberg* (1971), the justices had upheld a desegregation plan that required a school system in North Carolina to work toward racial integration through massive cross-town busing. The decision generated widespread protest. The next year Governor George Wallace of Alabama won the Democratic primary in Florida after taking a strong antibusing stand. Three days later Nixon proposed that Congress pass a busing moratorium, and he appeared on television to denounce busing as a reckless and extreme remedy for segregation. Nixon's opposition to busing was a well-planned aspect of his southern strategy, but it clearly appealed to many northern whites as well.

Besides Governor Wallace, the Democratic candidates for the 1972 presidential nomination were Senators Hubert Humphrey, Edward Kennedy, George McGovern, and Edmund

Election of 1972

Muskie. Wallace fell victim to an assassination attempt: he was shot and paralyzed by a disturbed young man in Maryland and began a long convalescence. After his shooting, the right-wing law-and-order vote had no place to turn but to Nixon. Kennedy had ceased to be a serious contender in 1969; in that year, he left the scene of an accident in which a woman passenger in his car drowned, at Chappaquiddick, an island off the Massachusetts coast near Martha's Vineyard. The other Democratic candidates inspired little enthusiasm. Senator McGovern of South Dakota, who enjoyed the support of many followers of the late Robert F. Kennedy, won several primaries and arrived at the Democratic convention with enough votes to secure the nomination of his party.

Nixon campaigned by assuming the elevated role of world statesman: in early 1972 he traveled to China and to the Soviet Union. Both trips were elaborately staged and televised for maximum political effect. But it was the inept campaign waged by George McGovern that handed victory to the Republicans. When McGovern endorsed a $30 billion cut in the defense budget, people began to fear that he was a neo-isolationist who would reduce the United States to a second-rate power. McGovern's proposals split the Democrats between his supporters—antiwar activists, African-Americans, feminists, young militants—and old-guard urban bosses, labor leaders, white southerners, and growing numbers of blue-collar workers.

Nixon benefited greatly from the rumor planted by his aides that the Vietnam War was near its end. Troops were being pulled out; by September 1972 the American death rate was almost zero. Then in late October, less than two weeks before the election, Henry Kissinger announced a breakthrough in the peace negotiations. "Peace is at hand," he proclaimed. The announcement proved inaccurate but helped persuade some people to vote for Nixon.

Nixon's victory in November was overwhelming: he polled 47 million votes, more than 60 percent of the votes cast. McGovern received only 29

Nixon's Landslide Victory

million and won just one state, Massachusetts, and the District of Columbia. Nixon's southern strategy had been supremely successful. He carried the entire Deep South, which once had been solidly Democratic. He also gained the suburbs and won over a majority of the urban vote, including long-time Democrats such as blue-collar workers, Catholics, and white ethnics. Only blacks, Jews, and low-income voters stuck by the Democratic candidate.

Yet the 1972 election had another significant result, one that would recur in subsequent elections. Despite Nixon's landslide victory, his coattails proved to be short, and the Democrats retained control of both houses of Congress. Democratic voters were becoming independent, resorting to ticket-splitting to reject an unacceptable Democratic presidential candidate but support the party's congressional candidates.

Little noticed during the campaign was a break-in at the Watergate apartment-office complex in Washington, D.C., on June 17, 1972. A watchman

Watergate Break-in

telephoned the police to report an illegal late-night entry into the building through an underground garage. At 2:30 A.M., police arrested five men who were attaching listening devices to telephones in the sixth-floor offices of the Democratic National Committee. The men had cameras and had been rifling through files.

One of those arrested was James W. McCord, a former CIA employee who had become security coordinator of the Committee to Re-Elect the President (CREEP). The other four were anti-Castro Cubans from Miami who had worked with the CIA before. Unknown to the police, two other men had been in the Watergate building at the time of the break-in. One was E. Howard Hunt, a one-time CIA agent who had become a White House consultant. The other was G. Gordon Liddy, a former FBI agent serving on CREEP's staff. What were these men trying to find in the Democrats' offices? What did they hope to overhear on the telephones? And most important, who had ordered the break-in?

Watergate and Nixon's Resignation

The Watergate fiasco actually began in 1971, when the White House established not only CREEP but the Special Investigations Unit, known familiarly as the "Plumbers," to stop the leaking of secret government documents to the press. After publication of the *Pentagon Papers*, the Plumbers burglarized the office of Daniel Ellsberg's psychiatrist in an attempt to discredit Ellsberg, who had leaked the top-secret report to the press. It was the Plumbers who broke into the Democratic National Committee's headquarters to photograph documents and install wiretaps; money raised by CREEP was used to pay the Plumbers' expenses both before and after the break-ins. CREEP's official duty was to solicit campaign contributions, and the committee managed to collect $60 million, much of it donated illegally by corporations, including big oil companies like Gulf Oil and Phillips Petroleum, as well as defense contractors and airlines.

The arrest of the Watergate burglars generated furious activity in the White House. Incriminating documents were shredded; E. Howard Hunt's name

was expunged from the White House telephone directory; and

White House Cover-up

President Nixon ordered his chief of staff, H. R. Haldeman, to discourage the FBI's investigation into the burglary on the pretext that it might compromise national security. Nixon also authorized CREEP "hush-money" payments in excess of $460,000 to keep Hunt and others from implicating the White House in the crime. And he announced to the press that his White House counsel, John W. Dean III, had conducted a "complete investigation" and that no one in the administration "was involved in this very bizarre incident."

Because of successful White House efforts to cover up the scandal, the break-in was almost unnoticed by the electorate. Had it not been for the diligent efforts of reporters, government special prosecutors, federal

Watergate Hearings and Investigations

judges, and members of Congress, President Nixon might have succeeded in disguising his involvement in Watergate. Slowly, however, the tangle of lies and distortions began to unravel. In early 1973, U.S. District Judge John Sirica tried the burglars, one of whom implicated his superiors in CREEP and at the White House. From May until November, the Senate Select Committee on Campaign Practices, chaired by Senator Sam Ervin of North Carolina, heard testimony from White House aides. John W. Dean III acknowledged not only that there had been a cover-up but that the president had directed it. Another aide shocked the committee and the nation by disclosing that Nixon had had a taping system installed in his White House office and that conversations about Watergate had been recorded.

Nixon feigned innocence. In April 1973 he tried to distance himself from the cover-up by announcing the resignations of his two chief White House aides, John Ehrlichman and H. R. Haldeman. The adminstration

Saturday Night Massacre

then appointed Archibald Cox, a Harvard law professor with a reputation for uncompromising integrity, to fill the new position of special Watergate prosecutor. But when Cox sought in October to obtain the White House tapes by means of a court order, Nixon decided to have him fired. Both Attorney General Elliot Richardson and his deputy resigned rather than carry out the dismissal order. It thus fell to the third ranking person in the Department of Justice to fire Cox. The public outcry provoked by the so-called Saturday Night Massacre compelled the president to agree to the appointment of a new special prosecutor, Leon Jaworski. When Nixon still refused to surrender the tapes, Jaworski took him to court.

In the same month as the Saturday Night Massacre, the Nixon administration was stung by another scandal. Vice President Spiro Agnew resigned after pleading no contest to charges of income-tax evasion and acceptance of bribes. Under the provisions of the Twenty-fifth Amendment, ratified in 1967 after President Kennedy's assassination, Nixon nominated Gerald R. Ford, the House minority leader from Michigan, to replace Agnew. Ford's voting record was conservative—he had opposed most of the 1960s reform legislation—but he was popular on Capitol Hill, and his nomination was confirmed promptly by Congress.

Agnew's Resignation

Throughout 1973 and 1974, enterprising reporters uncovered more details of the break-in, the hush money, and the various people from Nixon on down who had taken part in the cover-up. White House aides and CREEP subordinates began to go on trial, and Nixon was cited as an "unindicted co-conspirator." *Washington Post* reporters Carl Bernstein and Bob Woodward found an informant, known as "Deep Throat," who provided damning information about Nixon and his aides. As Nixon's protestations of innocence became less credible, his hold on the tapes became more tenuous. In late April 1974 the president finally released an edited transcript of the tapes.

The edited transcript, however, had a lot of gaps. They swayed neither the public nor the House Judiciary Committee, which had begun to draft articles of impeachment against the president. Nixon still was trying to hang onto the original tapes when the Supreme Court in July, in *U.S. v. Nixon*, unanimously ordered him to surrender the recordings to Judge Sirica. At about the same time, the Judiciary Committee conducted nationally televised hearings. After several days of testimony, the committee voted for impeachment on three of five counts: obstruction of justice through the payment of hush money to witnesses, lying, and withholding evidence; defiance of a congressional subpoena of the tapes; and use of the CIA, the FBI, and the Internal Revenue Service to deprive Americans of their constitutional rights of privacy and free speech.

On August 5 the president finally handed over the complete tapes, which he knew would condemn him. Four days later he resigned the presidency.

How do historians know that President Richard M. Nixon was guilty of obstructing justice in the Watergate affair? That evidence lies in the Watergate tapes. Nixon is pictured here sitting with what he claimed were the full transcripts of the tape recordings made in the White House. But Nixon's version was filled with gaps. What was missing was the tape recording of a specific White House conversation on June 23, 1972, which proved that Nixon had instigated a cover-up and obstructed justice almost from the outset of the scandal. That day, Nixon was recorded ordering his top aide to stop the Federal Bureau of Investigation's inquiry into the Watergate break-in. The Central Intelligence Agency, Nixon thundered, should call the FBI,

claim that the break-in was a secret spy operation, and say, "'Don't go further into this case[,] period'!"

Historians have long wondered what other information the tapes might reveal. Some historians have sued for access to the tapes, but for twenty-one years, Nixon and his family succeeded in keeping them private. In 1996, however, the Nixon estate, the National Archives and Records Administration, and Stanley I. Kutler, a history professor at the University of Wisconsin, reached an agreement that calls for almost three thousand hours of tapes to be made public over the next several years. "All of us," Kutler said, "who believe in open government and full disclosure of history are winners." Photo: Nixon Presidential Materials Project.

Nixon's Resignation

Nixon's successor was Gerald Ford. His congressional colleagues hailed the new president as a decent man, respected by both Republicans and Democrats, who would bind up the wounds of Watergate. Ford's first substantive act, however, was to pardon Nixon, though he had said he would not do so. When the pardon was announced, some people concluded that Ford and Nixon had struck a deal.

The Watergate scandal prompted the reform of abuses that predated the Nixon administration. The executive's usurpation of legislative prerogatives, which historian Arthur M. Schlesinger, Jr., called "the imperial presidency," dated from Franklin D. Roosevelt's administration. Roosevelt had signed executive agreements that were in effect treaties with foreign nations, but he never sent them to the Senate for its advice and consent. Presidents Truman and Johnson had led the nation into the Korean and Vietnam Wars without securing a congressional declaration of war as required by the Constitution. And President Nixon had impounded—that is, refused to spend—federal funds appropriated for health, the environment, space, and other programs.

To end the nation's participation in undeclared wars, Congress in 1973 overrode Nixon's veto and passed the War Powers Act, which mandated that

Post-Watergate Restrictions on Executive Power

"in every possible instance" the president must consult with Congress before sending American troops into foreign wars. Under this law the president could commit American troops abroad for no more than sixty days, after which he had to obtain congressional approval. (The act did not specify what Congress could do if the president refused to comply.) The next year Congress approved the Congressional Budget and Impoundment Control Act, which prohibited the impounding of federal money. In 1972 and 1974, Congress made modest attempts to reduce campaign fundraising abuses, setting ceilings on campaign contributions and expenditures for congressional and presidential elections. Finally, to aid citizens who were victims of dirty-tricks campaigns, in 1974 Congress strengthened the Freedom of Information Act of 1966. The new legislation, which Congress passed over President Ford's veto, permitted access to government documents and provided penalties if the government "arbitrarily or capriciously" withheld such information.

 ## Conclusion

The thirteen years coinciding with the presidencies of John Kennedy, Lyndon Johnson, and Richard Nixon were a period of increasing disillusionment in the United States. As historian James T. Patterson observed, the period began with "grand expectations" about the attainability of "the Good Life." But riots in cities, violence on campus, diminished respect for government leaders, and growing economic uncertainty shattered Americans' illusions and supplanted earlier hopes for peaceful social change. "Americans had gone into the age of Kennedy and Nixon convinced that their government's action . . . could make over the world, at home and abroad," journalist Godfrey Hodgson explained, but "they had been burned." They had learned some hard lessons: how much harder it was to change the world than they thought it would be, and how there often was "little that political action could achieve, however idealistic its intentions, without evoking unforeseen and unwanted reaction."

When John F. Kennedy delivered his inaugural address in 1961, he challenged Americans to "pay any price, bear any burden, meet any hardship" to defend freedom and inspire the world. Twelve years later, Richard M. Nixon echoed that rhetoric: "Let us pledge to make these four years the best four years in America's history, so that on its 200th birthday America will be as young and vital as when it began, and as bright a beacon of hope for all the world." Largely because of his own actions, however, Nixon resigned the presidency before the nation could celebrate its bicentennial in 1976. Rather than young and vital, America seemed bruised and battered.

Suggestions for Further Reading

The 1960s

David Burner, *Making Peace with the 60s* (1996); David Chalmers, *And the Crooked Places Made Straight: The Struggle for Social Change in the 1960s* (1991); David Farber, *The Age of Great Dreams* (1994); David Farber, ed., *The Sixties* (1994); Godfrey Hodgson, *America in Our Time* (1976); Allen J. Matusow, *The Unraveling of America: A History of Liberalism in the 1960s* (1984); James T. Patterson, *Grand Expectations: The United States, 1945–1974* (1996); Tom Shachtman, *Decade of Shocks: Dallas to Watergate, 1963–1974* (1983); Barbara L. Tischler, ed., *Sights on the Sixties* (1992).

The Kennedy Administration

Irving Bernstein, *Promises Kept: John F. Kennedy's New Frontier* (1991); James Giglio, *The Presidency of John F. Kennedy* (1991); David Halberstam, *The Best and the Brightest* (1972); Christopher Matthews, *Kennedy and Nixon: The Rivalry That Shaped Postwar*

America (1996); Herbert S. Parmet, *J.F.K.—The Presidency of John F. Kennedy* (1983); Thomas C. Reeves, *A Question of Character* (1991); Arthur M. Schlesinger, Jr., *Robert Kennedy and His Times* (1978); Arthur M. Schlesinger, Jr., *A Thousand Days: John F. Kennedy in the White House* (1965); Gary Wills, *The Kennedy Imprisonment* (1982).

The Kennedy Assassination

Edward Jay Epstein, *Legend: The Secret World of Lee Harvey Oswald* (1978); Henry Hurt, *Reasonable Doubt* (1985); Gerald Posner, *Case Closed* (1993); Anthony Summers, *Conspiracy* (1980).

The Johnson Administration and the Great Society

Irving Bernstein, *Guns or Butter: The Presidency of Lyndon Johnson* (1996); Paul K. Conkin, *Big Daddy from the Pedernales: Lyndon Baines Johnson* (1986); Doris Kearns, *Lyndon Johnson and the American Dream* (1976); Sar A. Levitan and Robert Taggart, *The Promise of Greatness* (1976); Charles Murray, *Losing Ground: American Social Policy, 1950–1980* (1983); James T. Patterson, *America's Struggle Against Poverty, 1900–1994*, rev. ed. (1994); John E. Schwarz, *America's Hidden Success: A Reassessment of Twenty Years of Public Policy* (1983); Irwin Unger, *The Best of Intentions: The Triumph and Failure of the Great Society Under Kennedy, Johnson, and Nixon* (1996).

Civil Rights, Black Power, and Urban Riots

Taylor Branch, *Parting the Waters: America in the King Years, 1954–1963* (1988); Clayborne Carson, *In Struggle: SNCC and the Black Awakening of the 1960s* (1981); William H. Chafe, *Civilities and Civil Rights: Greensboro, North Carolina, and the Black Struggle for Freedom* (1980); David L. Chappell, *Inside Agitators: White Southerners in the Civil Rights Movement* (1996); John Dittmer, *Local People: The Struggle for Civil Rights in Mississippi* (1994); Sidney Fine, *Violence in the Model City: . . . the Detroit Riot of 1967* (1989); David J. Garrow, *Bearing the Cross: Martin Luther King, Jr., and the Southern Christian Leadership Conference* (1986); Gerald Horne, *Fire This Time: The Watts Uprising and the 1960s* (1996); Malcolm X and Alex Haley, *The Autobiography of Malcolm X* (1965); August Meier and Elliott Rudwick, *CORE* (1973); Kay Mills, *This Little Light of Mine: The Life of Fannie Lou Hamer* (1993); Charles M. Payne, *I've Got the Light of Freedom: The Organizing Tradition and the Mississippi Freedom Struggle* (1995); Mark Stern, *Calculating Visions: Kennedy, Johnson, and Civil Rights* (1992).

The Warren Court

Gerald Dunne, *Hugo Black and the Judicial Revolution* (1977); G. Theodore Mitau, *Decade of Decision: The Supreme Court and the Constitutional Revolution, 1954–1964* (1967); Bernard Schwartz, *Super Chief: Earl Warren and His Supreme Court* (1983); G. Edward White, *Earl Warren* (1982).

The New Left and Protest for Peace and Justice

Terry H. Anderson, *The Movement and the Sixties* (1995); Wini Breines, *Community and Organization in the New Left, 1962–1968*, rev. ed. (1989); Charles DeBenedetti, *An American Ordeal: The Antiwar Movement of the Vietnam Era* (1990); Tom Engelhardt, *The End of Victory Culture: Cold War America and the Disillusioning of a Generation* (1995); Todd Gitlin, *The Sixties* (1987); Maurice

Isserman, *If I Had a Hammer . . . : The Death of the Old Left and the Birth of the New Left* (1987); Peter B. Levy, *The New Left and Labor in the 1960s* (1994); James Miller, *"Democracy Is in the Streets": From Port Huron to the Siege of Chicago* (1987); Kirkpatrick Sale, *The Green Revolution: The American Environmental Movement, 1962–1992* (1993); Tom Wells, *The War Within: America's Battle over Vietnam* (1994).

The Counterculture

Stanley Booth, *Dance with the Devil: The Rolling Stones and Their Times* (1984); Morris Dickstein, *Gates of Eden: American Culture in the Sixties* (1977); Tim Miller, *The Hippies and American Values* (1991); Philip Norman, *Shout! The Beatles in Their Generation* (1981); Charles Perry, *The Haight-Ashbury* (1984); Jay Stevens, *Storming Heaven: LSD and the American Dream* (1987); Jon Weiner, *Come Together: John Lennon in His Time* (1984); Tom Wolfe, *The Electric Kool-Aid Acid Test* (1968).

The Rebirth of Feminism

Alice Echols, *Daring to Be Bad: Radical Feminism in America, 1965–1975* (1989); Sara Evans, *Personal Politics* (1978); Jo Freeman, *The Politics of Women's Liberation* (1975); David J. Garrow, *Liberty and Sexuality: The Right to Privacy and the Making of Roe v. Wade* (1994); Cynthia Harrison, *On Account of Sex: The Politics of Women's Issues, 1945–1968* (1988); Judith Hole and Ellen Levine, *Rebirth of Feminism* (1971); Robin Morgan, ed., *Sisterhood Is Powerful* (1970); Gayle Graham Yates, *What Women Want: The Ideas of the Movement* (1975).

Year of Shocks: 1968

David Caute, *The Year of the Barricades* (1988); Lewis Chester et al., *An American Melodrama: The Presidential Campaign of 1968* (1969); David Farber, *Chicago '68* (1988); Ronald Fraser et al., *1968: A Student Generation in Revolt* (1988); Charles Kaiser, *1968 in America* (1988).

Richard M. Nixon and the Resurgence of Conservatism

Stephen E. Ambrose, *Nixon*, 3 vols. (1987–1991); William C. Berman, *Right Turn: From Nixon to Bush* (1994); Mary C. Brennan, *Turning Right in the Sixties: The Conservative Capture of the GOP* (1995); Dan T. Carter, *The Politics of Rage: George Wallace, the Origins of the New Conservatism, and the Transformation of American Politics* (1995); Robert Alan Goldberg, *Barry Goldwater* (1995); Roger Morris, *Richard Milhous Nixon* (1990); Herbert S. Parmet, *Richard Nixon and His America* (1990); James A. Reichley, *Conservatives in an Era of Change: The Nixon and Ford Administrations* (1981); Tom Wicker, *One of Us* (1991); Garry Wills, *Nixon Agonistes* (1970).

Watergate

Jim Hougan, *Secret Agenda: Watergate, Deep Throat and the CIA* (1984); Stanley I. Kutler, *The Wars of Watergate* (1990); J. Anthony Lukas, *Nightmare: The Underside of the Nixon Years* (1976); Kim McQuaid, *The Anxious Years: America in the Vietnam-Watergate Era* (1989); Arthur M. Schlesinger, Jr., *The Imperial Presidency* (1973); Michael Schudson, *Watergate in American Memory* (1992); Theodore H. White, *Breach of Faith* (1975); Bob Woodward and Carl Bernstein, *The Final Days* (1976); Bob Woodward and Carl Bernstein, *All the President's Men* (1974).

CHAPTER

32

The End of the Postwar Boom: Stagflation, Immigration, and the Resurgence of Conservatism 1974–1989

Nguyet Thu Ha was twenty-two years old when South Vietnam capitulated to North Vietnamese and Vietcong forces in 1975. She had never before spent a night away from her parents; but North Vietnamese soldiers were fighting close to her home, so she fled, taking along her four younger brothers and sisters, all teenagers, and a six-year-old nephew whose distraught parents had entrusted him to Ha for safekeeping. The six were loaded onto a fishing ship dangerously overcrowded with refugees. Their first stop was Guam, a Pacific island controlled by the United States; their second stop was a refugee camp in Arkansas; finally, Nguyet Ha and the children came to Kansas City, Missouri. Ha's immediate challenge was to earn enough money to support six people, but her dream was to reunite her family.

Nguyet Ha got a job working seven days a week as a hotel housekeeper, and at night she taught herself to sew, making shirts and dresses. She next worked as a waitress, saving her tips to buy a house. "I'm very tough about my budget," Ha explained, "even if I know something I really like to buy. I tell myself, 'Hold it, hold it until you can do it. For now, just forget it.'" Within eight months, she had saved enough for a down payment on a $16,000 house; she paid off the mortgage in three years. She married and had two daughters of her own, and in 1989 she bought a Laundromat, five adjoining lots, and a vacant building to house her relatives, should they be allowed to emigrate to the United States.

New immigrants were often eager to become new citizens. In 1996, in a naturalization ceremony held in San Jose, California, a woman from Southeast Asia proudly held an American flag as she took the oath to become a citizen of the United States. *David Butow/Saba.*

955

Ha also began to take college courses; she wanted to become a teacher. After earning two associate of arts degrees, she was hired as a paraprofessional at Northeast High School, a magnet school for law and public service, in Kansas City.

What sustained Nguyet Thu Ha was her dream of bringing her entire family to Kansas City. Soon after she and the children fled Vietnam, Ha's father died, perhaps of sadness, she thought. Her mother and four older siblings and their families remained in Vietnam. Ha often dreamed about her mother, and sometimes her sobbing woke her daughters. "They wake me up and they wipe my tears and they say, 'Mommy, it's OK.'" For ten years, Ha filled out government forms and telephoned and visited the offices of the Immigration and Naturalization Service (INS), but nothing happened. Then she got a call from the INS: Ha's mother, two brothers, a sister-in-law, and a niece would be arriving in a couple of days at Kansas City International Airport. Her mother, the last to leave the airplane, was engulfed by hugs. Ha was overjoyed: "I say, 'Is this real or I still dream?' You wish to have it for long time, and then one moment you have it, and you don't trust it." But it was real. (By 1997, not only Ha's mother but all eight of her siblings, most with their children, were living in the United States.)

Nguyet Thu Ha and her family were part of the "new immigration," which began in the early 1970s, when record numbers of immigrants came to the United States from Asia, Mexico, Central and South America, and the Caribbean. Many of the new immigrants came as families, though some—such as Nguyet Thu Ha's group—arrived a few family members at a time over a period of years. Unlike earlier immigrants, most of the new arrivals were people of color, and race proved to be both a barrier and a spur to success for the new immigrants. Established migration patterns tended to determine where the newcomers, such as Ha's family, went. "People immigrate to where they find connections and a measure of familiarity," explained Alejandro Portes, a sociologist at Johns Hopkins University. Almost 70 percent of the new immigrants settled in six states: California, Florida, Texas, New York, New Jersey, and Illinois. The newcomers redefined urban areas such as Los Angeles, Chicago, and Miami, where nearly three-quarters of city residents spoke a language other than English at home.

Although well-wishers often were on hand to greet the newcomers, the history of the nation's treatment of people of color did not augur well for them. Most found only low-paying jobs, and some suffered hostility and even violence from native-born Americans. Nevertheless, they persevered, pursuing their dreams in a country that was changing racially and ethnically. At Northeast High School, for example, where Nguyet Thu Ha found her first job as a teacher's aide, the student body was richly diverse: white, black, Hispanic, Asian, and American Indian. In their pursuit of both a magnet school and cultural diversity, these teenagers were bused to Northeast from all over Kansas City. Andrea Johnson, a junior and an African-American, explained that it was "beneficial going to a school with different races because you learn about different cultures." Rebecca Hernandez, a senior, agreed, saying she believed it would get monotonous going to school "with the same people your whole life. The world is not separate but equal. I don't want to crawl into my little Hispanic shell."

The American people experienced wrenching economic, political, and social change in the 1970s and 1980s. First, there was the new immigration, which touched millions of people's lives, immigrant and nonimmigrant alike. Second, the postwar economic boom ended. Recessions became more frequent, the rate of economic growth slowed, and the "discomfort index" (the unemployment rate plus the inflation rate) rose. Third, in response to these real changes, there was a resurgence of conservatism, both political and cultural, particularly among Americans who believed that the 1960s had been a period of immoral excesses. President Ronald Reagan became a hero to the conservatives. Fourth, economic inequality and social polarization grew, especially in the 1980s, widening the gap between rich and poor, between whites and people of color, and between the suburbs and the inner cities.

In the 1970s, the twenty-five-year postwar economic boom ended. The rate of economic growth slowed and sometimes stalled, and there were disquieting signs of inflation. The 1973 Arab oil embargo heralded America's misfortunes, leading to the realization that the United States was not a fortress that could stand alone; it was dependent for its survival on imported oil. America's automobile industry suffered from competition from economical imported cars, and other industries found themselves in dire straits.

Filled with uncertainty, Americans in the 1970s reeled under the one-two punch of *stagflation*. First, there was economic *stag*nation. Unemployment was

• *Important Events* •

1974	OPEC oil prices increase Nixon resigns; Gerald Ford becomes president Ford creates WIN program to fight inflation Equal Credit Opportunity Act equalizes loan and credit card terms for men and women	**1981**	AIDS first observed in United States Prime interest rate reaches 21.5 percent Congress approves Reagan's budget and tax cuts Reagan breaks air traffic controllers strike Economic recession; unemployment hits 8 percent
1975	Nuclear accident occurs at Brown's Ferry Antibusing agitation erupts in Louisville and Boston Economic recession hits nation	**1982**	Unemployment reaches 10 percent Voting Rights Act of 1965 renewed
1976	Hyde Amendment cuts off Medicaid funds for abortions Jimmy Carter elected president	**1983**	More than half of adult women work outside the home ERA dies for lack of ratification
1978	*Bakke* v. *University of California* outlaws quotas but upholds affirmative action California voters approve Proposition 13	**1984**	Reagan reelected
		1985	Gramm-Rudman bill calls for balanced budget by 1991
1979	Three Mile Island nuclear accident raises fears of meltdown Moral Majority established Federal Reserve Board tightens money supply American hostages seized in Iran	**1986**	Tax Reform Act lowers personal income taxes Immigration Reform and Control (Simpson-Rodino) Act provides amnesty to undocumented workers Iran-contra scandal breaks Republicans lose control of Senate
1980	Economic recession recurs Race riots break out in Miami and Chattanooga Ronald Reagan elected president Republicans gain control of Senate	**1987**	Stock market prices drop 508 points in one day
		1988	*Understanding AIDS* mailed to 107 million households Reagan travels to the Soviet Union George Bush elected president

on the upswing, particularly in heavy industry. Americans saw once-proud automobile and steel plants close. As a result of such "deindustrialization," many jobs were jeopardized while others disappeared forever. Second, there was in*flation*. As soaring prices eroded the purchasing power of workers' paychecks, people raided their savings, sacrificing future security to current needs. The 1970s was the first decade since the Great Depression in which Americans' purchasing power declined, and the experience shook people's confidence that they could shape their personal destinies.

Although the economy rebounded in the early 1980s, wealth in the United States was being redistributed upward. The rich got richer, as poverty deepened for many others. Women and people of color were particularly hard hit, for they usually were the last hired and the first laid off. Even when they had jobs, they were paid less than white men,

and experts pointed to the growing "feminization" and "blackening" of poverty, which began to climb again in the 1970s and 1980s. In line with the nation's growing conservatism, political opposition to the aspirations of both women and racial minorities also mounted at this time.

The resurgent conservative movement must be understood within the context of America's economic woes and social changes. Conservatives doubted that government had the capacity to serve the people, let alone solve major problems. In the 1970s they worked to repeal the social welfare system. California voters approved a 1978 tax-cutting referendum called Proposition 13, which reduced property taxes and put stringent limits on state spending for social programs. Proposition 13 set off shock waves: nearly a score of other states imposed similar ceilings on taxes and expenditures. On the national level, conservatives lobbied for a constitutional amendment to prohibit federal budget deficits. Perhaps most significant, tax revolts became political vehicles for conservative candidates to win elections.

Moreover, a new conservative political alignment took place in the 1970s and 1980s. Joining the political and economic conservatives were social and cultural conservatives, especially evangelical Christians, who believed they had a moral obligation to enter politics on the side of "a pro-life, pro-traditional family, pro-moral position." President Ronald Reagan appealed mightily to both wings of the movement. A proponent of prayer in the public schools and an opponent of abortion, Reagan argued for a return to the morality that he believed had dominated American culture before the 1960s. He promised a balanced budget, and he blamed government for fettering American economic creativity. Reagan's 1980 presidential victory revealed that conservatism had become the dominant mood of the nation.

Ronald Reagan was a popular president. Although unemployment rose between 1981 and 1983, the economy then rebounded, and by 1984 Reagan's policies had helped lower inflation and interest rates as well as unemployment. Reagan's victory in 1984 was never in doubt, but his forty-nine-state sweep convinced some observers that he had transformed American politics by forging a conservative coalition that could dominate for years. Still, as popular a president as Reagan was in 1984, his programs provoked severe criticism. Liberal opponents lambasted his economic policies ("Reaganomics") as favoring the rich and penalizing the poor. Despite the criticism, Reagan seemed to escape personal blame. Representative Patricia Schroeder, a Colorado Democrat, gave this phenomenon a memorable label: Reagan, she said, was "perfecting a Teflon-coated presidency. . . . He sees to it that nothing sticks to him."

Reagan's favorable image was tarnished by the Iran-contra scandal in late 1986 (see pages 914–915, and 980), and his influence diminished during his final two years in office. Still, when the voters went to the polls in November 1988, the nation was at peace, both unemployment and inflation were at low levels, and Reagan was still a political hero to many Americans. George Bush, his vice president, was the beneficiary of the Reagan legacy and, as the Republican presidential candidate, rode it to victory. The Reagan presidency, however, had bequeathed to the new president and the American people a host of unsolved economic and social problems from the 1970s and 1980s. The challenge of the 1990s would be to find solutions.

The Energy Crisis and End of the Economic Boom

It was evident in the early 1970s that the United States was beginning to suffer economic decline. Recessions—which economists define as at least two consecutive quarters of no growth in the gross national product (GNP)—began to occur more frequently. An eleven-month recession struck the country in 1969 and 1970, the first recession in almost a decade. Between 1973 and 1990, there were four more, and two (1973–1975, 1981–1982) were particularly long and harsh. Americans' economic insecurity, which was pronounced in the 1970s, persisted into the 1980s.

America's economic vulnerability was confirmed by the Arab oil embargo of 1973 (see page 909). The country was importing one-third of its oil supplies. Even before the embargo, the United States had suffered occasional shortages of natural gas, heating oil, and gasoline. But the American people, who had grown up on inexpensive and abundant energy, made few efforts to conserve; they drove big cars and lived in poorly insulated homes.

In 1973, however, the American people had to deal with the oil price increases ordered by the Organization of Petroleum Exporting Countries (OPEC). Oil prices rose 350 percent that year. As Americans grappled with the economic, social, and political costs of the price hikes, multinational oil companies prospered: their profits jumped 70 percent in 1973 and another 40 percent in 1974. Meanwhile, the boost in the price of imported oil reverberated through the entire economy. Inflation jumped from 3 percent in 1972 to a frightening 11 percent in 1974. Many Americans were suffering hard times.

OPEC Price Increases Fuel Inflation

Recession hit the auto industry in 1973 and deepened in 1974. In Detroit, General Motors laid off 38,000 workers indefinitely—6 percent of its domestic work force—and put another 48,000 on leave for up to ten days at a time. Sales of gas-guzzling American autos plummeted as consumers rushed to purchase energy-efficient foreign subcompacts from Japan and Europe. Like Ford and Chrysler, GM was stuck with mostly large-car assembly plants. Moreover, there was an accelerator effect because the ailing American auto companies quit buying steel,

Auto Industry Recession

The Organization of Petroleum Exporting Countries (OPEC) raised oil prices several times in the 1970s. Each increase fueled the rise of inflation in the United States; and Americans, who had expected cheap energy to last forever, saw their expectations dashed. Long lines at the gas pumps were a reminder that an era of easy abundance had passed. Don Wright in the *Miami News*, 1976, Tribune Media Services.

glass, rubber, and tool-and-die products. And as the recession in the auto industry spread, other manufacturers began laying off experienced employees with seniority.

Unlike earlier postwar recessions, this one did not fade away in a year or two. Part of the reason was inflation. In the earlier recessions, Republican as well as Democratic administrations had held to a policy of neo-Keynesianism. To minimize the swings in the business cycle, they had manipulated federal policies—both fiscal policies (taxes and government spending) and monetary policies (interest rates and the money supply). They hoped by so doing to keep employment up and inflation down. Beginning in the 1970s, however, joblessness and prices both began to rise sharply. Policies designed to correct one problem seemed only to worsen the other.

Even in the best of times, the economy would have been hard pressed to produce jobs for the mil-

lions of baby boomers who joined the labor market in the 1970s. As it was, economic activity created 27 million additional jobs during the decade, a remarkable increase of 32 percent. But deindustrialization was causing a shift in the occupational structure. As heavy industries collapsed, laid-off workers took jobs in fast-food restaurants, all-night gas stations, and convenience stores—but at half of their former wages and without healthcare and other benefits. In 1979, 31 percent of households lived on incomes below $25,000; the comparable figure a decade later was 42 percent. Workers who once had held high-paying blue-collar jobs saw their middle-class standard of living slipping away from them.

The Shifting Occupational Structure

A central economic problem was a slowing of growth in productivity—the average output of goods per hour of labor. Between 1947 and 1965 American industrial productivity had increased an average of 3.3 percent a year, raising manufacturers' profits and lowering the cost of products to consumers. From 1966 to 1970 annual productivity growth averaged only 1.5 percent; it fell further between 1971 and 1975 and reached a mere 0.2 percent between 1976 and 1980. Economists blamed lack of business investment in state-of-the-art technology, declining educational standards, the shift from an industrial to a service economy, and an alleged erosion of the work ethic. Whatever the causes, American goods cost more than those of foreign competitors; in the world's increasingly competitive markets, many American products fared poorly. The Joint Economic Committee of Congress warned, "The average American is likely to see his standard of living drastically decline in the 1980s unless the United States accelerates its rate of productivity growth."

Lagging Productivity

The lag in productivity was not matched by a decrease in workers' expectations. Wage increases regularly exceeded production increases, and some economists blamed the raises for inflation. Indeed, wages that went up seldom came down again. Managers of the nation's basic industries—steel, autos, rubber—complained that the automatic cost-of-living adjustments in their labor contracts left them little margin to restrain price hikes.

Another spur to inflation was easy credit. Fearing scarcity, many people went on a buying spree; between 1975 and 1979, household and business borrowing more than tripled (from $94 billion to $328 billion). More people had credit cards; the number of Master-Card cardholders jumped from 32 million in 1974 to 57 million five years later. The credit explosion helped bid up the price of everything, from houses to gold. Farmers bought new farmland and expensive machinery and irrigation equipment. The nation's farm debt, $55 billion in 1971, had reached $166 billion by 1980. Overburdened with debts, many farmers faced bankruptcy in the 1980s.

Easy Credit and Inflation

Every expert had a scapegoat to blame for the nation's economic doldrums. Labor leaders cited foreign competition and called for protective tariffs. Some businesspeople and economists blamed the cost of obeying federal health and safety laws and pollution controls. They urged officials to abolish the Environmental Protection Agency and the Occupational Safety and Health Administration. They also pressed for deregulation of the oil, airline, and trucking industries on the theory that competition would drive prices down. Above all, critics attacked the federal government's massive spending programs; the mounting national debt, they said, was the sad result.

President Ford's Response to the Economic Crisis

By the time Gerald R. Ford became president after Richard M. Nixon's resignation in 1974, OPEC price increases had pushed the inflation rate to 11 percent. Appalled, Ford created Whip Inflation Now (WIN), a voluntary program that encouraged businesses, consumers, and workers to save energy and organize grassroots anti-inflation efforts. In the 1974 congressional elections, voters responded to WIN, Watergate, and Ford's pardon of Nixon by giving the Democrats forty-three additional seats in the House and four in the Senate. Ford showed political courage in 1974 when he offered clemency to Vietnam War draft evaders, but he received blistering criticism from veterans' groups.

Ford's response to inflation was to curb federal spending and encourage the Federal Reserve Board to raise its interest rates to banks, thus tightening credit. Ford was following the tenets of monetary theory, which held that the best way to reduce inflation was to keep the nation's money supply growing at a slow, consistent rate. With less money available to chase the supply of goods, monetarists contended, price increases would gently slow down. But these actions prompted a recession—only this time it was the worst in forty years. Unemployment jumped to 8.5 percent in 1975 and, because the economy had stagnated, the federal deficit for fiscal year 1976–1977 hit a record $60 billion.

Ford devised no lasting solutions to the energy crisis, but the crisis seemed to pass when OPEC ended the embargo—and the incentive to prevent future shortages dissolved as well. The energy crisis, however, did intensify public debate over nuclear power. For the sake of energy independence, advocates asserted, the United States had to rely more on nuclear energy. Environmental activists countered that the risk of nuclear accident was

The Energy Crisis and Nuclear Power

too great and that there was no safe way to store nuclear waste. Accidents in the nuclear power reactors at Brown's Ferry, Alabama (1975), and Three Mile Island, Pennsylvania (1979), gave credence to the activists' argument. By 1979, however, ninety-six reactors were under construction throughout the nation, and thirty more were on order.

In the 1970s, the combined effects of the energy crisis, stagflation, and the flight of industry and the middle class to the suburbs and the Sunbelt were producing fiscal disaster in the nation's cities. Not since 1933, when Detroit defaulted on its debts, had a major American city gone bankrupt. But New York City was near financial collapse by late 1975. President Ford vowed "to veto any bill that has as its purpose a federal bail-out of New York City," but he relented after the Senate and House Banking Committees approved loan guarantees, and the city was saved. New York was not alone in its financial problems; other Frostbelt cities were in trouble, saddled with growing welfare rolls, deindustrialization, and a declining tax base. In 1978 Cleveland became the first major city to default since the Great Depression.

Throughout Ford's two-and-a-half-year presidential administration, relatively little was accomplished. After Vietnam and Watergate, the Ford presidency was a time of healing, not activism. Congress asserted itself and enjoyed new power. Ford almost routinely vetoed its bills, but Congress often overrode his vetoes. For the first time in the nation's history, furthermore, neither the president nor the vice president had been popularly elected. One of Ford's first acts as president had been to select Nelson Rockefeller, former governor of New York, as his vice president. But Republican prospects for retaining the presidency in the 1976 election seemed gloomy.

Gerald Ford's Presidency

 ## The Carter Presidency

While Ford struggled with a Democratic Congress, the Democratic party geared up for the presidential election of 1976. Against the background of Watergate secrecy and corruption, one candidate in particular promised honesty and openness. "I will never lie to you," pledged Jimmy Carter, an obscure former one-term governor

Carter and the Election of 1976

On inauguration day, President Jimmy Carter (b. 1924) and his wife Rosalyn caught the public's fancy by walking from the Capitol to the White House. Despite this symbolic beginning, Carter became increasingly isolated both from the American people and from Congress. Jimmy Carter Presidential Library.

of Georgia. Carter presented himself as both a fiscal conservative who would restrain government spending and a social liberal who would fight for the poor, the aged, people of color, workers, urban dwellers, and farmers. When this born-again Christian promised voters efficiency and decency in government, they believed him. It helped, too, that Carter was a southerner, whose candidacy might block Republican electoral advances in the white South. Carter arrived at the convention with more than enough delegates to win the nomination. His choice of Senator Walter Mondale of Minnesota as his running mate helped cement relations with northern liberals, African-Americans, union members, and political bosses.

Neither Carter nor President Ford, the Republican nominee, inspired much interest, and on election day only 54 percent of the electorate bestirred itself to vote. Nevertheless, an analysis of the turnout was instructive. Carter did carry ten of the eleven states in the Deep South. But as one political commentator observed, the vote nationwide was "fractured to a marked degree along the fault line separating the haves and have-nots." Although Carter won nearly 90 percent of the African- and Mexican-American vote, he squeaked to victory by a slim 1.7 million votes out of 80 million cast. Ford's appeal was strongest among middle- and upper-middle-class white voters.

Carter's most noteworthy domestic accomplishments were in energy, transportation, and conservation policy. To encourage domestic production of oil, he phased in decontrol of oil prices. To moderate the social effects of the energy crisis, he called for a windfall-profits tax on excessive profits resulting from decontrol, and for grants to the poor and elderly for the purchase of heating fuel. Carter also deregulated the airline, trucking, and railroad industries and persuaded Congress to ease federal control of banks. His administration established a $1.6 billion "superfund" to clean up abandoned chemical-waste sites, and created two freestanding departments—the Departments of Energy and Education. Finally, he placed more than 100 million acres of Alaskan land under the federal government's protection as national parks, national forests, and wildlife refuges.

Carter's Accomplishments

Despite these accomplishments, Carter failed to inspire Americans, and he alienated Democratic Party members. Elected as an outsider, he remained one throughout his presidency. Moreover, Carter's conservative economic policies alienated Democrats who had grown up in the party's New Deal liberal tradition. His support of deregulation and his opposition to wage and price controls and gasoline rationing ran counter to liberal Democratic principles. Seeing inflation as a greater threat to the nation's economy than either recession or unemployment, Carter announced that his top priority would be "to discipline the growth of government spending," even though doing so would add to the jobless rolls. But he was unable to gain Congress's cooperation, and both federal expenditures and inflation continued to rise.

Carter's Flagging Popularity

Carter's problems were not entirely of his own making. In 1979 the shah of Iran's government fell to revolutionary forces. When the shah was admitted to the United States for medical treatment, mobs seized the American embassy in Teheran and held fifty-two Americans as hostages for 444 days (see page 911). The new Iranian government also cut off oil supplies to the United States. The same year OPEC raised its prices again, and the cost of crude oil nearly doubled. As Americans waited in long lines at gasoline pumps, and as they bridled at Carter's inability to free the hostages, public approval of the president reached a new low.

Carter also inherited political problems. In the wake of Vietnam and Watergate, power temporarily had shifted from the White House to Capitol Hill. Meanwhile, Congress was filling up with political newcomers, men and women unaccustomed to reflex obedience to established leadership. Despite the large Democratic majorities in Congress following the Watergate scandal, party discipline seemed to be a thing of the past. In addition, Capitol Hill was crawling with lobbyists from special-interest groups: trade associations, corporations, labor unions, and single-issue groups like the National Rifle Association. In 1980, there were 2,765 political-action committees (PACs), more than four times as many as in 1974.

Decline of Presidential Authority

Economic troubles got worse, and by 1980 the economy was in a shambles. Inflation had jumped in 1979 to over 13 percent, and traders around the world had lost confidence in the dollar, causing unprecedented increases in the price of gold. To steady the dollar and curb inflation, the Federal Reserve Board took drastic measures. First, the board cut the money supply—partly by selling Treasury securities to take money out of circulation—thus forcing borrowers to bid up interest rates sufficiently to dampen the economy and reduce inflation. Second, it raised the rate at which the Federal Reserve loaned money to banks. As a result, mortgage-interest rates leaped beyond 15 percent, and the prime lending rate (the rate charged to businesses) hit an all-time high of 20 percent. Inflation fell, but only to 12 percent.

Worse still, by 1980 the nation was in a full-fledged recession. The 1980 unemployment rate of 7.5 percent, combined with the 12 percent inflation rate, had produced a stagger-

Economic Discomfort in 1980

ingly high "discomfort index" of just under 20 percent (see figure). Yet the government was unable to control the causes of the discomfort. In 1976 Carter had gibed at the incumbent president, Gerald Ford, by saying, "Anything you don't like about Washington, I suggest you blame on him." In 1980 Carter was the incumbent, and many Americans blamed him for the problems that beset the country.

Ronald Reagan and the Election of 1980

Political and economic conservatives had long expressed doubt about government's capacity to serve the people. Critics of neo-Keynesian pump priming pointed to stagflation as evi-

Resurgence of Conservatism

dence of the failure of New Deal and Great Society economics. Even some Democrats agreed. Senator Gary Hart, a Colorado Democrat, characterized this mood as "a nonideological skepticism about the old, Rooseveltian solutions to social problems."

In the 1970s, political and economic conservatives joined forces with cultural and religious conservatives and thereby changed the political landscape. In 1979 Reverend Jerry Falwell, a radio-TV minister from Lynchburg, Virginia, helped to found the Moral Majority, which advocated what it called "family values," including opposition to abortion rights and homosexuality. The Moral Majority quickly registered between 2 and 3 million new vot-

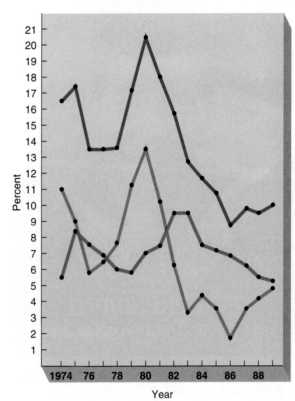

"Discomfort Index" (Unemployment Plus Inflation), 1974–1989 *Americans' economic discomfort directly determined their political behavior. When the "discomfort index" was high in 1976 and 1980, Americans voted for a change in presidents. When economic discomfort declined in 1984 and 1988, Ronald Reagan and George Bush were the political beneficiaries.* Source: Adapted from *Economic Report of the President, 1992* (Washington, D.C., 1992), pp. 340, 365.

ers, started a newspaper, and bought daily time on 140 radio stations. Together with conservative think tanks like the Hoover Institution and conservative magazines like *National Review*, these church groups formed a flourishing network of potential supporters for conservative candidates. By the late 1970s, conservatism was becoming a potent political force.

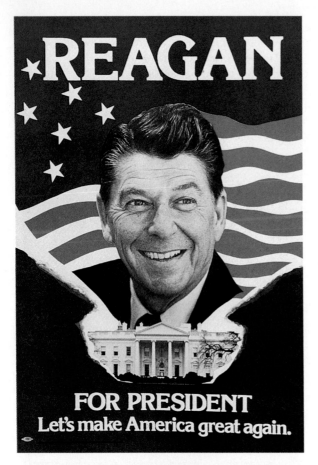

Ronald Reagan, the Republican presidential candidate in 1980, campaigned for "family values," an aggressive anti-Soviet foreign and military policy, and tax cuts. He also exuded optimism and appealed to Americans' patriotism. This poster issued by the Republican National Committee included Reagan's favorite campaign slogan, "Let's make American great again." Collection of David J. and Janice L. Frent.

The 1980 federal census provided additional insights into the reasons for conservatism's resurgence in the United States. First, the 1980 census revealed significant growth in the more politically conservative elderly population—up 24 percent since 1970—and a two-year rise in the median age. In addition, the number of retired people increased by more than 50 percent in the 1970s. Second, the census documented the continuing shift of large numbers of people from the politically liberal Frostbelt states of the Northeast and Midwest to the more conservative

A Shifting Population

Sunbelt states of the South and West (see map, page 965). The census findings also meant that seventeen seats in the House of Representatives would shift from the Frostbelt to the Sunbelt by the 1982 elections. Florida would gain four seats, Texas three, and California two; New York would lose five.

In 1980 several conservative Republican politicians ran for the White House. Foremost among them was Ronald Reagan, former movie star and two-term governor of California. When he was president of the Screen Actors Guild in Hollywood in the 1940s, his politics were those of a New Deal Democrat. But touring the country in the 1950s as host of the television program *General Electric Theatre*, he became increasingly conservative. In 1964 he made a televised appeal for Senator Barry Goldwater, the Republican presidential candidate. Reagan's speech catapulted him to the forefront of conservative politics and became his personal platform for the presidency. America, Reagan said, had come to "a time for choosing" between free enterprise and big government, between individual liberty and "the ant heap of totalitarianism." Two years later he was elected governor of California.

Reagan's Early Career

During his two four-year terms as governor, Reagan maintained his conservate rhetoric but displayed a pragmatic approach to governing. While denouncing welfare, he presided over reform of the state's social welfare bureaucracy. While demanding that student radicals at the University of California either obey the rules or face the prospect of a "bloodbath," he endorsed most of the university's budget requests. And he signed one of the nation's most liberal abortion laws.

In the Republican primaries, Reagan triumphed easily over Representative John Anderson and former CIA director George Bush. His appeal to the voters in the presidential campaign was much broader than experts had predicted. He promised economy in government and a balanced budget, and he committed himself to "supply-side" economics, or tax reductions to businesses to encourage capital investment. Although Reagan planned to slash federal spending, he also pledged to cut income taxes and boost the defense budget—a prescription that George Bush ridiculed as "voodoo economics." Reagan declared that he

Reagan as the Republican Candidate

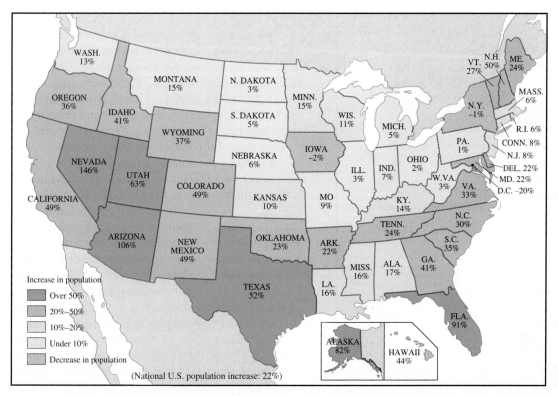

WASH. 13%
OREGON 36%
IDAHO 41%
MONTANA 15%
N. DAKOTA 3%
MINN. 15%
WIS. 11%
MICH. 5%
VT. 27%
N.H. 50%
ME. 24%
MASS. 6%
N.Y. –1%
R.I. 6%
CONN. 8%
N.J. 8%
WYOMING 37%
S. DAKOTA 5%
PA. 1%
NEVADA 146%
UTAH 63%
NEBRASKA 6%
IOWA –2%
OHIO 2%
DEL. 22%
MD. 22%
D.C. –20%
CALIFORNIA 49%
COLORADO 49%
KANSAS 10%
ILL. 3%
IND. 7%
W.VA. 3%
VA. 33%
MO 9%
KY. 14%
ARIZONA 106%
NEW MEXICO 49%
OKLAHOMA 23%
ARK. 22%
TENN. 24%
N.C. 30%
S.C. 35%
TEXAS 52%
MISS. 16%
ALA. 17%
GA. 41%
LA. 16%
FLA. 91%

Increase in population
■ Over 50%
■ 20%–50%
□ 10%–20%
□ Under 10%
■ Decrease in population

(National U.S. population increase: 22%)

ALASKA 82%
HAWAII 44%

The Continued Shift to the Sunbelt in the 1970s and 1980s *Throughout the 1970s and 1980s, Americans continued to leave economically declining areas of the North and East in pursuit of opportunity in the Sunbelt.*

now opposed legalized abortion, and his stand against the Equal Rights Amendment (ERA) recommended him to the "profamily" movement.

Indeed, Reagan's candidacy united the old right wing with the new. The old right had never been very interested in social or cultural issues, explained Richard Viguerie, a conservative fundraiser. "But when political conservative leaders began to . . . strike an alliance with social conservatives—the pro-life people, the anti-ERA people, the evangelical and born-again Christians, the people concerned about gay rights, prayer in the schools, sex in the movies or whatever—that's when this whole movement began to come alive."

In the 1980 election, President Carter faced formidable problems. American hostages were still held captive in Iran, and stagflation beset the economy.

Election of 1980

Carter's major problem was his approval rating of 21 percent, even lower than Richard Nixon's 24 percent during the Watergate crisis. And on election day, vot-

ers gave Reagan and his running mate George Bush 51 percent of the vote to 41 percent for Carter and almost 7 percent for Anderson (see map, page 966). Reagan's sweep was nationwide; Carter carried only six states and the District of Columbia. The vote was not only an affirmation of Reagan's conservatism but also a signal of the nation's deep dissatisfaction with Jimmy Carter's management of both the economy and foreign policy. As startling as Reagan's sweep was the capture of eleven Senate seats by Republican candidates, giving the Republicans a majority in that house. Republicans also gained thirty-three seats in the House and four state governorships.

The preceding fifteen years had been difficult ones for the Democratic Party. Fragmented by the issues of race and war, in the 1970s the party had lost the support of many whites, who viewed the Democrats as the party of welfare, taxes, and African-Americans. With self-proclaimed "Reagan Democrats" supporting Republican candidates, it seemed clear that the Democrats would be running scared in the 1980s.

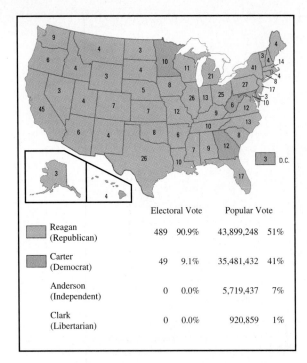

	Electoral Vote		Popular Vote	
Reagan (Republican)	489	90.9%	43,899,248	51%
Carter (Democrat)	49	9.1%	35,481,432	41%
Anderson (Independent)	0	0.0%	5,719,437	7%
Clark (Libertarian)	0	0.0%	920,859	1%

Presidential Election, 1980 Ronald Reagan scored the first of two political landslides in 1980, when he won forty-four states to Jimmy Carter's six.

 "Reaganomics"

Upon taking office, President Reagan wasted little time announcing what he called "a new beginning." He immediately launched a double-barreled attack on problems in the economy. First, he asked Congress to cut billions from domestic programs, including Medicare and Medicaid, food stamps, welfare subsidies for the working poor, and school meals. Congress endorsed most of Reagan's demands; joining the Republicans in support were conservative Democrats, many of them southerners known as "Boll Weevils." Reagan soon initiated a second round of budget cuts, resulting among other things in the trimming of a million food-stamp recipients from government rolls.

Tax cuts were the second facet of Reagan's economic plan. A fervent believer in supply-side economics, he called for reductions in the income taxes of the affluent and of corporations in order to stimulate savings and investments. New capital would be invested, the argument went, and would produce new plants, new jobs, and new products. As prosperity returned, the

Tax Cuts

profits at the top would "trickle down" to the middle classes and even to the poor. Congress responded with a five-year, $750 billion tax cut, the largest ever in American history, featuring a 25 percent reduction in personal income taxes over three years. Other provisions increased business investment tax credits and depreciation allowances and lowered the maximum tax on income from 70 to 50 percent. The wealthy gained the most from these tax cuts.

A third item occupied Reagan's agenda: a vigorous assault on federal environmental, health, and safety regulations that, Reagan believed, excessively reduced business profits and discouraged economic growth. The president appointed opponents of the regulations to enforce them. Some critics likened such appointments to hiring foxes to guard the chicken coop. Reagan officials explained that slackened enforcement was necessary to reduce business costs and make American goods competitive in world markets, but environmentalists countered that such policies invited disaster, such as toxic-waste poisoning or nuclear reactor accidents.

Weakened Environmental Enforcement

Hard times hit labor unions in the 1980s. Faced with recession and unemployment, union negotiators had to settle for less than they were accustomed to receiving. American workers who ratified contracts during the first three months of Reagan's term settled for pay increases averaging only 2.2 percent, the biggest drop in wage settlements since the government began collecting such data in 1954. Unions had suffered large membership losses when unemployment hit heavy industry, and their efforts to unionize the high-growth electronics and service sectors of the economy were failing.

Hard Times for Labor Unions

Reagan made the unions' hard times worse. He presided over the government's busting of the Professional Air Traffic Controllers Organization (PATCO) during the union's 1981 strike. His appointees to the National Labor Relations Board consistently voted against labor and for management. Although Reagan appeared to be an enemy of labor, an estimated 44 percent of union families had voted for him in 1980, and many still responded positively to his genial personality, espousal of old-fashioned values, and vigorous anticommunist rhetoric.

Reagan enjoyed two notable economic successes during his first two years in office. First, the inflation rate plummeted, falling from 12 percent in 1980 to less than 7 percent in 1982. Oil led the way in price declines; after eight years OPEC had at last increased its oil production, thus lowering prices. In 1981 the United States was awash with oil, as world production exceeded demand by 2 million barrels a day. Second, as inflation fell, so too did the cost of borrowing money. Interest rates for bank loans, which had stood at a record high of 21.5 percent in early 1981, dropped to 10.5 percent by 1983.

Falling Inflation

But there was also a second, more sobering, explanation for the decline in inflation. By mid-1981 the nation was mired in a recession that not only persisted but deepened. During the last three months of the year, the GNP fell 5 percent, and sales of cars and houses dropped sharply. With declining economic activity, unemployment soared to 8 percent, the highest level in almost six years.

A year later, in late 1982, unemployment had reached 10 percent, the highest rate since 1940. Most of the jobless were adult men, particularly African-Americans, who suffered an unemployment rate of 20 percent. Many of the unemployed were blue-collar workers in ailing "smokestack industries" such as autos, steel, and rubber. Reagan and his advisers had promised that supply-side economics would produce demand-side results and that consumers would lift the economy out of the recession by spending their tax cuts. But as late as April 1983, unemployment still stood at 10 percent and people were angry. Heavy industry was in a shambles. Jobless steelworkers paraded through McKeesport, Pennsylvania, carrying a coffin that bore the epitaph "American Dream." Agriculture, too, was faltering and near collapse. Farmers suffered from floods and droughts and from burdensome debts they had incurred at high interest rates. Many lost their property through mortgage foreclosures and farm auctions. Others filed for bankruptcy.

Rising Unemployment

As the recession deepened in 1982, poverty rose to its highest level since 1965. The Bureau of the Census reported that the number of Americans living in poverty increased from 26 million in 1979 to 34 million in 1982. The largest single category of poor families consisted of households headed by women (36 percent). With one exception,

Resurgence of Poverty

In the 1980s, this couple in southern Illinois and many other farm families were forced to sell their land, machinery, and personal possessions to pay their debts. Burdened by low prices and, in some areas, by severe drought, few family farmers looked forward to the future.   Roy Roper/Gamma-Liaison.

poverty continued its rise in 1983, returning to the level that had prevailed before the enactment of President Johnson's Great Society. That exception was the elderly; politicians had begun paying attention to this vocal and rapidly growing population whose needs were ably articulated by the American Assocation of Retired Persons (AARP) and other groups.

President Reagan had announced that his administration would halt the expansion of social and health programs but would retain a "safety net" for the "truly needy." But he went back on this promise, and Congress, unwilling to buck the popular president, sustained most of his decisions. Facing a budget deficit in excess of $200 billion in mid-1982, Reagan had three choices. First, he could cut back on his rearmament plans to spend $1.7 trillion over five years. This he refused to do; in fact, the budget he signed raised defense spending another 13 percent. Second, he could suspend or reduce the second installment of his tax cut. This choice, too, he found unacceptable. Third, he could—and did—cut welfare and social programs, pushing through Congress further cuts in Medicare and Medicaid, food stamps,

In 1984 Geraldine Ferraro, Democratic congresswoman from New York, made history by being the first woman nominated to run for the vice presidency on a major party's ticket.   Collection of David J. and Janice L. Frent.

Reagan Triumphant: The Election of 1984

Reagan's key reelection asset in 1984 was the economy, which was showing strong signs of recovery. In 1984 the GNP rose 7 percent, the sharpest increase since 1951, and midyear unemployment fell to a four-year low of 7 percent. The economy was heating up, but without sparking inflation. Indeed, inflation (4 percent in 1984) fell to its lowest level since 1967. A second factor in Reagan's favor was people's perception of him as a strong leader in foreign as well as national affairs. Many Americans were proud that their nation was confronting the Soviets not only with strong words but with military interventions and a large military buildup (see Chapters 29 and 30). Third, Reagan was the enthusiastic choice of political conservatives of all kinds across the country. Patriotism was back in style, and so were traditional values. Reagan won the approval of millions of other Americans who agreed with his television ads that "America is back" after two decades of turmoil and self-doubt.

Reagan's Reelection Assets

Aiding Reagan was the Democrats' failure to field a convincing alternative. The Democratic nominee—former vice president Walter Mondale—did not inspire Americans. Even the policies that Mondale espoused seemed timeworn and out of step with the nation's conservatism. Adding to Mondale's woes was the disarray of the Democratic Party; it had fragmented into separate caucuses of union members, African-Americans, women, Jews, homosexuals, Hispanics, and other groups. Each caucus had its own agenda. The one bright spot for the Democrats was Mondale's historic selection of Representative Geraldine Ferraro of New York as the first woman vice-presidential candidate of a major political party. Ferraro showed herself to be an intelligent, indefatigable campaigner.

Mondale wanted to debate the federal deficit, but Reagan preferred to invoke the theme of leadership and rely on slogans. Mondale chastised Reagan for the mounting deficit, which had reached $175 billion in fiscal year 1984. But when Mondale announced that he would raise taxes to cut the deficit, he lost votes. Voters in 1984 had a clear choice, and in every state but Minnesota—Mondale's home state—they chose the Republican ticket. The election returns

Reagan's 1984 Victory

federal pensions, and government-guaranteed home mortgages. Nevertheless, in the absence of budget cuts in other areas, or higher taxes, the federal debt continued to grow.

Democrats predicted victory for their party in the 1982 congressional elections. Just a week before the elections, however, a *New York Times*/CBS News poll reported that the American public was being tugged sharply in different directions: toward the Democrats by unemployment, toward the Republicans by declining inflation and the president's popularity. Nothing revealed Reagan's winning style better than his courageous response to an attempt on his life by a deranged young man in March 1981. John W. Hinckley, Jr., wounded the president, his press secretary, a Secret Service agent, and a police officer. Reagan's courage and grace caused his popularity ratings to soar.

In the 1982 elections, 26 House seats swung to the Democrats, giving them a lead of 267 to 166. The Senate remained pro-Reagan, with a continued Republican majority of 54 to 46. In another two years, there would be a presidential election. The president had to prove before then that he could restore prosperity to the nation.

1982 Elections

were the most convincing evidence yet that the nation had shifted to the right. The only groups still loyal to the Democratic ticket were African-Americans, Hispanics, Jews, and the poor. Reagan scored solid victories with all other voting groups, including young people, whites in both North and South, high-school and college graduates, and Catholics as well as Protestants.

Fifty years earlier, the Democratic Party had gained the allegiance of millions of Americans, including blue-collar workers, who credited President Franklin Roosevelt's New Deal with having saved them during the Great Depression. The New Deal coalition controlled national politics for the next thirty years. But in the 1970s and 1980s, a deep reaction set in against the liberalized moral standards associated with the Democratic Party. Many Democrats held conservative views on welfare, abortion, homosexuality, and other social issues, and they switched their votes to Ronald Reagan and the Republican Party. Whether Reagan had forged a lasting conservative coalition—one that could repeal the New Deal—remained to be seen. What was not debatable was that, during his first term, he had succeeded in his principal aims.

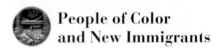 ## People of Color and New Immigrants

Poverty was a growing problem in the 1970s and 1980s, particularly for people of color. Joblessness plagued blacks, Native Americans, and Hispanics, as well as new immigrants. African-Americans made up a disproportionate share of the poor. The overall poverty rate was 13 percent by 1980, but among blacks it was 33 percent and among Hispanics 26 percent, compared with 10 percent for whites. These figures had barely changed by the end of Ronald Reagan's presidency in 1989 (see figure).

The weight of poverty fell most heavily on children, especially African-American children, almost half of whom lived below the poverty line. A 1981 Children's Defense Fund survey reported that black children in the United States were four times more likely than whites to be born into poverty, twice as likely to drop out of school before twelfth grade, three times as likely to be unemployed, and five times as likely to be murdered. "Millions of black children lack self-confidence, feel discouragement, despair, numbness or rage as they try to grow up on islands of poverty, ill health, inadequate education . . . crime

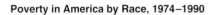

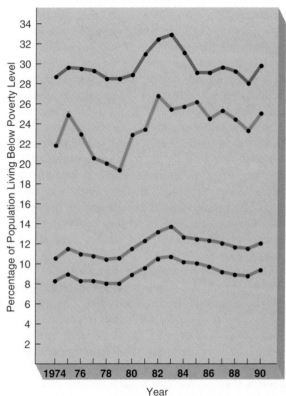

Poverty in America by Race, 1974–1990
Poverty in America rose in the early 1980s but subsided afterward. Many people of color, however, experienced little relief during the decade. Notice that the percentage of African-Americans living below the poverty level was three times higher than that for whites. It also was much higher for Hispanic-Americans. Source: Adapted from U.S. Bureau of the Census, *Statistical Abstract of the United States* (Washington, D.C., 1992), p. 461.

and rampant unemployment in a nation of boastful affluence," the report concluded. Many children lived in poor families headed by single women who earned meager incomes as domestic servants, laundresses, and kitchen helpers, supplemented by welfare assistance.

Some whites and even other blacks grumbled that poor blacks were responsible for their own poverty. But the job market was far different in the 1970s and 1980s from that of twenty-five, fifty, or seventy-five years before. During periods of rapid industrialization, unskilled European immigrants and black migrants from the South had been able to find blue-collar jobs. Beginning in the 1970s, fewer such jobs were available; demand was greatest for skilled workers such as computer operators, bank tellers, secretaries, and bookkeepers. Most jobless people could not qualify. Moreover, blue-collar jobs in the inner cities were disappearing or moving to the suburbs. New York City alone had 234,000 fewer blue-collar workers in 1980 than it had at the beginning of the 1970s. For young African-American men and women who lacked marketable skills, the situation was often tragic. The psychiatrist Alvin Poussaint observed, "A lot of black kids simply feel they don't count. . . . In terms of what makes this society run, they're expendable."

Declining Job Opportunities for African-Americans

But a historical anomaly was at work. For even as the plight of the African-American poor worsened, the black middle class expanded. The number of black college students increased from 282,000 in 1966 to more than 1 million in 1980; by 1980, about one-third of all black high-school graduates were going on to college, the same proportion as among white youths. Some benefited from affirmative-action programs, which sought to compensate for decades of racial discrimination by granting African-American men and women educational opportunities to advance themselves. By 1990, the number of black college students had increased further to 1.3 million. At least at the upper levels of black society, the dream of equality was being realized.

African-American Middle Class

But as middle-class African-Americans made gains, resentful whites complained that they were being victimized by "reverse discrimination." To meet federal affirmative-action requirements, some schools and companies had established quotas for minorities and women; in some cases the standards were lower than those for whites. When Allan Bakke, a white man, was denied admission to medical school, he sued on the grounds that black applicants less qualified than he had been admitted. In a 5-to-4 ruling in 1978, the Supreme

White Backlash

Court outlawed quotas but upheld the principle of affirmative action, explaining that race or ethnicity could be counted as "a 'plus' in a particular applicant's file" (*Bakke* v. *University of California*). Eleven years later, however, the Court ruled that past discrimination did not "justify a rigid racial quota" and that white workers could sue to reopen affirmative-action cases settled in federal courts years earlier (*Richmond* v. *Croson, Martin* v. *Wilks*).

White anger over affirmative action and busing combined with the effects of stagflation to produce an upsurge in racism. In Louisville in 1975, bumper stickers urged people to "honk if you oppose busing," the Ku Klux Klan stepped up its recruiting, and violence soon erupted: one hundred people were injured and two hundred arrested. In Boston, where busing provoked numerous riots, a group of white students attacked a black passerby outside city hall. "Get the nigger; kill him," they shouted as they ran at him with the sharp end of a flagstaff flying an American flag. Racial tension rose in cities across the nation.

African-Americans were tense, and they showed their anger more openly than in the past. Charles Silberman wrote in *Criminal Violence, Criminal Justice* (1978) that "black Americans have discovered that fear runs the other way, that whites are intimidated by their very presence. . . . The taboo against expression of antiwhite anger is breaking down, and 350 years of festering hatred has come spilling out." That hatred erupted several times in 1980, most notably in Miami and Chattanooga, after all-white juries acquitted whites in the killings of blacks. Miami's three days of rioting left eighteen dead and four hundred injured.

Black Anger

African-American civil rights leaders denounced not only the judicial system but also the executive branch headed by President Ronald Reagan. Appointments were one issue: whereas 12 percent of President Jimmy Carter's high-level appointees had been black and 12 percent women, Reagan's were 4 percent black and 8 percent women. (Reagan did appoint four women to his cabinet and made history by appointing Sandra Day O'Connor the first woman associate justice of the Supreme Court.) Moreover, Reagan's civil rights chief in the Justice Department opposed busing and affirmative action, and he was criticized for lax enforcement of fair housing laws and laws banning sexual and racial discrimination in federally funded education programs. He also fought against renewing the Voting Rights Act of

For nearly 115 years, an Arizona land dispute has divided the Hopi and Navajo tribes. A law passed by Congress in 1974 called for the division of 1.8 million acres between the tribes and ordered the relocation of tribal members living on land given to the other tribe. Hopi and Navajo traditionalists claimed that they had no dispute and that powerful economic interests were using the issue as a cover for seizing the area's rich coal and water rights. In 1986 these Hopis and Navajos joined forces to protest federal law directing the secretary of the interior to "expedite" relocation "without regard to any law or regulation." Lawrence Gus/Sygma.

1965, but Congress ignored his efforts and renewed the act in 1982.

"The Kerner report warning is coming true," asserted a group of scholars, politicians, and civil rights leaders who met in 1988 to assess race relations on the twentieth anniversary of the publication of the Kerner Commission report (see page 937). "America is again becoming two separate societies," with whites residing in the suburbs while African-Americans in inner cities lived amid poverty, segregation, and crime. "Even the most pessimistic observers of the social scene in the later 1960s," observed a member of the group, "probably did not foresee or anticipate the sharp increases in the rates of social dislocation and massive breakdown of social institutions in ghetto areas."

Every bit as angry as African-Americans were Native Americans. Their new militancy burst into the headlines in 1969, when a small group of Indians

Native American Militancy

seized Alcatraz Island in San Francisco Bay. Arguing that an 1868 Sioux treaty entitled them to possession of unused federal lands, the group occupied the island until mid-1971. More was at stake than an abandoned federal penitentiary. "Not just on Alcatraz," explained Richard Oakes, a spokesperson for the Indians, "but every place else, the Indian is in his last stand for cultural survival." Two years later, members of the militant American Indian Movement (AIM), demanding the rights guaranteed Indians in treaties with the United States, seized eleven hostages and a trading post on the Pine Ridge Reservation at Wounded Knee, South Dakota, where troops of the Seventh Cavalry had massacred three hundred Sioux in 1890 (see page 482). Their seventy-one-day confrontation with federal marshals ended with a government agreement to examine the treaty rights of the Oglala Sioux.

White society posed more than a cultural threat to Indians. Four in ten Native Americans were unemployed, and nine out of ten lived in substandard housing. Often, being an Indian also meant being unhealthy. Native Americans suffered the highest incidence of tuberculosis, alcoholism, and suicide of any ethnic group in the United States. The American Indian population had risen since the Second World War to 1.7 million in 1990—more than half of whom lived in California, Oklahoma, Arizona, New Mexico, and North Carolina—but that was only a fraction of the population when the first Europeans arrived in North America.

Since 1924, Indians have had dual legal status as United States citizens and as members of tribal nations subject to special treaty agreements with the

Indian Suits for Lost Lands

United States. Their dual status has proved a curse, in large part because the government found it easier to breach its treaty commitments—especially when Indian lands contained valuable minerals. In 1946 Congress established the Indian Claims Commission to compensate Indians for lands stolen from them. Under the legislation, lawyers for the Native American Rights Fund and other groups scored notable victories. In 1980, for example, the Supreme Court ordered the government to pay $106 million plus interest to the Sioux nation for the Black Hills of South Dakota, stolen when gold was found there in the 1870s. Nevertheless, corporations and government agencies continued to covet Indian lands and disregard Indian religious beliefs: a coal company strip-mined a portion of the Hopi Sacred Circle, which according to tribal religion is the source of all life, and the sacred Black Hills of South Dakota are being mined again, this time for uranium.

As Indians fought to regain old rights, Hispanic-Americans struggled to make a place for themselves. An inflow of immigrants unequaled since the turn of

Hispanic-Americans

the century coupled with a high birth rate made Hispanic peoples America's fastest-growing minority by the 1970s. Of the more than 20 million Hispanics living in the United States in the 1970s, 8 million were Mexican-Americans concentrated in California, Texas, Arizona, New Mexico, and Colorado. Several million Puerto Ricans, Cubans, Dominicans, and other immigrants from the Caribbean also lived in the United States, clustered principally on the East Coast in cities in Florida, New York, and other states.

These officially acknowledged Hispanic-Americans were joined by millions of undocumented workers, or illegal aliens. Beginning in the mid-1960s, large numbers of poverty-stricken Mexicans began to cross the poorly guarded 2,000-mile border. The movement north continued in the 1970s and 1980s. By 1990, one out of three Los Angelenos and Miamians was Hispanic, as were 48 percent of the population of San Antonio and 70 percent of El Paso.

Poverty awaited many of these new immigrants, as it had previous groups of newcomers. Like earlier groups, Hispanics faced a language barrier. Most inner-city schools did not provide bilingual education for Spanish-speaking students. And the larger the Hispanic population has become, the more widespread has been the discrimination. "Anglos are afraid," said California assemblyman Richard Alatorre. "They think they will get to be the minorities and we'll be opposing them."

Most of these new Americans preferred their family-centered culture to Anglo culture and, for that reason, resisted assimilation. "We want to be

Hispanic Cultural Pride

here," explained Daniel Villanueva, a TV executive in Los Angeles, "but without losing our language and our culture. They are a richness, a treasure that we don't care to lose."

Like other minorities, Hispanics wanted political power—"brown power." Cesar Chavez's United Farm Workers was the first Hispanic interest group to gain national attention. The militant Brown Berets also attracted notice for their efforts to provide meals to preschoolers and courses in Chicano studies and consciousness raising to older students. And throughout the 1970s the Mexican-American political party La Raza Unida was a potent force in the Southwest and in East Los Angeles.

Still, the group that was becoming the nation's largest minority exercised a disproportionately small share of political power. One reason was that Latin America is tremendously diverse. Although Mexican-Americans, Puerto Ricans, Cubans, and other Hispanic groups shared a language and a religion, they differed in countless ways. And the differences were not only in country of origin: economic immigrants such as Mexican-Americans crowded into West Coast *barrios* side by side with political refugees from Central American wars. Poverty was

How do historians know the extent of the illegal immigration to the United States? In truth, historians do not know precisely how large it has been. The most reliable data come from the United States Census Bureau's reports, but even the Census Bureau concedes that it can only estimate the extent of illegal immigration. In 1992, an estimated 3.4 million immigrants lived illegally in the United States. Academic demographers have contributed to historical understanding through their analyses of government statistics. Philip Martin and Elizabeth Midgley studied recent immigration to the United States and concluded that at least 1 million people move to the United States each year, of whom some 300,000 are undocumented immigrants. The photograph below captures the image that many have of illegal immigrants crossing the border from Mexico; highway crossings such as this one have caused numerous deaths. But as statistics show, this stereotype is misleading. Illegal immigrants come from all over the world, not merely from Mexico, Central America, the Caribbean, or Asia. There also are sizable contigents from Ireland, Poland, Israel, and Iran. Source: Data from Philip Martin and Elizabeth Midgley, "Immigration to the United States: Journey to an Uncertain Destination," *Population Bulletin* 49 (September 1994): 1–46. Photo: Don Bartletti.

most severe where the population was most concentrated. "We need a Spanish Bobby Kennedy or Martin Luther King," observed Daniel Villanueva. "Right now he's just not there."

During the 1970s and 1980s people of color immigrated to the United States in record numbers from Indochina, Mexico, Central and South America, and the Caribbean. Between 1970 and 1980 the United States absorbed more than 4 million immigrants and refugees and uncounted numbers of illegal

New Influx of Immigrants

aliens. High as these figures were, they doubled again during the next decade. With almost 9 million new arrivals, the 1980s surpassed the historic high mark set by the 8.7 million immigrants from Russia, Austria-Hungary, Italy, and other countries who had reached American shores between 1900 and 1909.

Many of the new immigrants came in family units, and women and children accounted for two-thirds of all legal immigrants. Although the new residents faced a long struggle, they were willing to work hard to succeed. Among the newcomers, Asian-Americans seemed to be the most successful.

There had been a burst of Asian immigration; the number of people whose origins were in Asia or the Pacific increased by 385 percent from 1971 to 1990. Asian-Americans were a diverse group, including Korean greengrocers on Manhattan's Upper West Side; Laotian or Vietnamese refugees drawn to Garden City, Kansas, to work in the world's largest meatpacking plant; and Chinese workers assembling integrated circuits in California's Silicon Valley.

The arrival of so many newcomers put pressure on Congress to curtail the flow and perhaps offer amnesty to aliens already living illegally in the United States. In 1978 Congress authorized a comprehensive re-examination of America's immigration policy. The immigration commission completed its study in 1981, but legislative solutions were delayed until 1986, when Congress passed the Immigration Reform and Control (Simpson-Rodino) Act, which provided amnesty to undocumented workers who had arrived before 1982. The act's purpose was to discourage illegal immigration by imposing sanctions on employers who hired undocumented workers, but it failed to stem the flow of people fleeing Mexico's economic woes. In 1988 the number of new immigrants from Mexico approached the record numbers reached before the reform law went into effect.

Immigration Reform

Feminism, Antifeminism, and Women's Lives

Women scored some impressive victories in the 1970s. In 1974, Congress passed the Equal Credit Opportunity Act, which enabled women to get bank loans and obtain credit cards on the same terms as men. In the field of criminal law, many states revised their statutes on rape, prohibiting defense lawyers from discrediting rape victims by revealing their previous sexual experience. Perhaps most significant were women's gains from affirmative action in hiring. As mandated by the Civil Rights Act of 1964 and the establishment of the Equal Employment Opportunity Commission, women and people of color applying for jobs had to receive the same consideration as white males. To take advantage of new opportunities, many women delayed having children until reaching their thirties and establishing themselves in their careers. The number of women enrolled in college rose 45 percent between 1970 and

1975, and numerous women were elected to political offices.

Still, women continued to encounter opposition in their struggle for gender equality. Particularly formidable was the antifeminist or "profamily" movement, which contended that men should lead and women should follow, especially within the family, and that women should stay home and raise children. The conservative backlash against feminism became an increasingly powerful political force in the United States, especially in the Republican Party. In defense of the patriarchal, or father-led, family, antifeminists campaigned against the Equal Rights Amendment, the gay rights movement, and abortion on demand.

Antifeminist Movement

Antifeminists blamed the women's movement for the country's spiraling divorce rate; they charged that feminists would jettison their husbands and even their children in their quest for job fulfillment and gender equality. Although the number of divorces almost tripled from 1960 to 1976, often the decision to divorce was made not by the wives but by the husbands. According to Barbara Ehrenreich, a feminist scholar, men started walking out on their families in large numbers in the 1950s, well before the rebirth of feminism. Tired of fulfilling the role of husband, father, and financial provider, men responded to the image of carefree bachelorhood presented in the pages of men's magazines such as *Playboy*, which attacked wives as parasites who gobbled up their husbands' salaries but were too sexually repressed to give much in return. Many men came to see their wives as the agent of their entrapment; in "flight from commitment," they chose divorce.

Antifeminists successfully stalled ratification of the Equal Rights Amendment, which after quickly passing thirty-five state legislatures fell three states short of success in the late 1970s. Phyllis Schlafly's "Stop ERA" campaign claimed that the ERA would abolish alimony and legalize homosexual marriages. The debate was occasionally vicious. Refusing to acknowledge gender-based discrimination, Schlafly derided ERA advocates as "a bunch of bitter women seeking a constitutional cure for their personal problems." The ERA died in 1983 when the time limit expired for ratification by the states.

Equal Rights Amendment

Many conservative women also participated in the anti-abortion or "prolife" movement, which sprang up almost overnight in the wake of the Supreme Court's 1973 decision in *Roe* v. *Wade* (see page 945). People whose opposition to abortion was heartfelt and uncompromising denounced that ruling and called for an amendment to the Constitution defining human life as beginning at conception. Along with Catholics, Mormons, and other religious opponents of abortion, the anti-abortion movement supported the Hyde Amendment, the successful legislative effort of Representative Henry Hyde of Illinois in 1976 to cut off most Medicaid funds for abortions.

Feminists fought back. Indeed, Ronald Reagan's most vocal critics were women who mobilized in opposition to the conservative agenda of the White House. The *New York Times* reported a "gender gap" between men's and women's opinions of Reagan's performance in 1983: far fewer women (38 percent) than men (53 percent) believed Reagan deserved reelection. What accounted most centrally for the gender gap were Reagan's social welfare, health, and education cuts. Many working mothers expressed shock at the Reagan administration's insensitivity to children's welfare. One feminist critic quipped that for Reagan, "life begins at conception and ends at birth." Children's poverty continued its rise throughout the decade, and, by 1989, children accounted for about 40 percent of America's poor people.

Women Opponents of Reagan's Conservatism

Reagan's critics assailed him for failing to reverse "the feminization of poverty" and for approving cuts in food stamps and school meals. The Reagan administration's opposition to federally subsidized childcare and the feminist goal of "comparable worth" also drew their ire. Because of persistent occupational segregation, 80 percent of all working women in 1985 were concentrated in low-paying "female" occupations such as clerking, selling, teaching, and waitressing. Recognizing this, feminists supplemented their earlier rallying cry of "equal pay for equal work" with a call for "equal pay for jobs of comparable worth." Why, women asked, should a grade-school teacher earn less than an electrician, if the two jobs require comparable training and skills and involve comparable responsibilities? In the 1970s, female workers still took home only 60 cents to every male worker's dollar; by 1990, the figure had risen to 71 cents.

Activists in the women's struggle had to acknowledge certain harsh realities. One was the tight

Women entered the space program as astronauts in the 1970s. Several members of the group shown in this poster from the National Aeronautics and Space Administration (NASA) achieved distinction. The two astronauts on the left side are (above) Shannon W. Lucid and (below) Sally K. Ride. Sally Ride was the first woman in space, spending six days in orbit in 1983. In 1996, Shannon Lucid set a longevity record for American astronauts, female or male: 188 days in orbit. Across from Lucid is Judith Resnik, who died in 1986 in the explosion of the space shuttle Challenger.   Corbis-Bettmann.

job market created by the economic recessions of the 1970s and 1980s. Other problems included a rising divorce rate that left increasing numbers of women and their children with lower standards of living and a high teenage pregnancy rate. The number of single mothers rose to 7.7 million in 1990, up from 5.8 million a decade earlier. The tandem of divorce and teenage pregnancy meant that a progressively smaller proportion of America's

Increased Burdens on Women

children lived with two parents. In 1990, about a quarter of all children—16 million—lived with only one parent—double the percentage of 1970.

Many mothers thus had to find employment. Still others worked to preserve the living standard of two-parent households that otherwise would have experienced substantial declines. Families were paying a higher percentage of their income to buy houses, and often two wage earners were required to pay the bills. In 1983, for the first time in the nation's history, more than half of all adult American women (51 percent) held jobs outside the home. Another milestone was recorded in 1987: the share of women returning to work or actively seeking jobs within a year after the arrival of a baby exceeded 50 percent for the first time. (By contrast, just ten years earlier, the figure had been 31 percent.) The working mother had become the norm in America.

Such women had to contend with what came to be called "the Superwoman Squeeze." According to a report by the Worldwatch Institute, most working wives and mothers, even those with full-time jobs, "retained an unwilling monopoly on unpaid labor at home." Combining housework and outside employ-

ment, wives worked 71 hours a week; husbands worked 55 hours a week. Women traded stories of "couch-potato" husbands who watched television while their wives did chores. Soon only one in four wives would be a full-time housewife and mother. The remainder would be trying to balance the more-than-full-time demands of a family and a career without shortchanging either—or themselves—in the process.

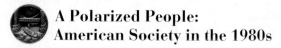

A Polarized People: American Society in the 1980s

The United States became an increasingly polarized society in the 1980s. The rich got richer, while the poor sank deeper into despair (see figure). The incomes of the bottom fifth of American families fell by 13 percent, but the top fifth earned 27 percent more, and the top 1 percent saw their incomes double. Indeed, by 1989 the top 1 percent (834,000 households with $5.7 trillion in net worth) was worth more than the bottom 90 percent (84 million households with $4.8 trillion in net worth). The

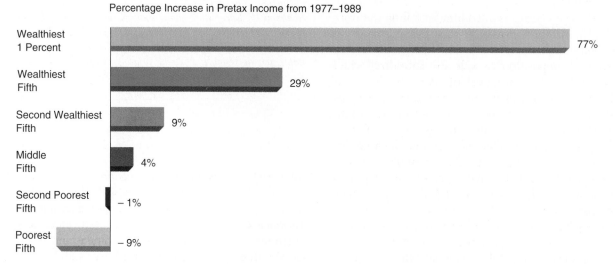

While the Rich Got Richer in the 1980s, the Poor Got Poorer

Percentage Increase in Pretax Income from 1977–1989

Wealthiest 1 Percent	77%
Wealthiest Fifth	29%
Second Wealthiest Fifth	9%
Middle Fifth	4%
Second Poorest Fifth	– 1%
Poorest Fifth	– 9%

While the Rich Got Richer in the 1980s, the Poor Got Poorer *Between 1977 and 1989, the richest 1 percent of American families reaped most of the gains from economic growth. In fact, the average pretax income of families in the top percentage rose 77 percent. At the same time, the typical family saw its income edge up only 4 percent. And the bottom 40 percent of families had actual declines in income.*   Source: Data from the *New York Times*, March 5, 1992.

For this family, which includes a one-week-old baby, homelessness came suddenly. Home had been a squalid motor inn in North Bergen, New Jersey, but the board of health condemned the motel and the police put the family out on the street. In 1988, as many as a million people were homeless.   Eugene Richards/Magnum.

United States was polarizing not only economically but also socially, and societal divisions were exacerbated by new problems: AIDS (acquired immune deficiency syndrome) and the cocaine-derived drug known as crack.

By the end of the 1980s, as many Americans were living in poverty as had been living in poverty in 1964, when 36 million were poor and President Johnson declared war on poverty. But the poor themselves were somewhat different. The poverty of the 1980s, explained the authors of a 1988 report of the Social Science Research Council, "is found less among the elderly and people living in nonurban areas and more among children living with one parent—in households headed principally by young women." In the 1970s, the child poverty rate increased 6 percent; in the 1980s, it jumped 11 percent, and thirty-three states registered increases. As inequality grew, the gap widened between affluent whites and poor blacks, Indians, and Hispanics, and between the suburbs and the inner cities. And as inequality increased, so too did social pathology. Violent crime, particularly homicides and gang warfare, grew alarmingly, as did school dropout rates, crime rates, and child abuse.

Increasing Inequality

Poverty resulted not only from discrimination based on race and gender, but also from economic recessions and from the changing structure of the labor market. As deindustrialization took hold, the job market shifted from high-paying, unionized, blue-collar jobs to low-paying service jobs. Minimum-wage employment burgeoned in fast-food restaurants, but such jobs meant a substantial drop in workers' standard of living. In 1974, blue-collar jobs accounted for half of the employment of African-American males between the ages of twenty and twenty-four. Just ten years later, such jobs accounted for only one-fourth of their employment. North Lawndale, a black neighborhood on Chicago's West Side, exemplified the problem. In prosperous days, the community's economy had depended on the 43,000 jobs at the Hawthorne plant of Western Electric. But the Hawthorne plant closed in 1984. Soon, so did the banks and small stores that depended on the workers' wages.

According to sociologist William Julius Wilson, the issue of "the truly disadvantaged" was "one of the most important social issues of the remainder of the 20th century." Life was becoming precarious not only for the underclass but also for "the working poor," whose numbers increased by more than one-

Changing Job Market

In 1987 the San Francisco–based Names Project started to make quilts in remembrance of those who had died of AIDS. By 1992, when the AIDS quilt was unfolded near the Washington Monument, it contained twenty-one thousand decorated panels and stretched over fifteen acres of land. Jeff Tinsley/Smithsonian Institution.

third during the 1980s. By the end of the decade, 40 percent of the nation's poor were working, but few had full-time, year-round jobs. At the same time, social workers reported that more and more of the nation's homeless were families.

About a third of the homeless were former psychiatric patients who found themselves living on the streets after hospitals emptied their psychiatric wards in a burst of enthusiasm for "deinstitutionalization." By 1985, 80 percent of the total number of beds in state mental hospitals had been eliminated on the premise that small neighborhood programs would be more responsive than large state hospitals to people's needs. The truth was that such programs failed to materialize, and former patients went to live in unsafe boarding houses and cheap hotels. Few provisions were made for medical treatment, and these troubled people increasingly found that they had nowhere to go except the street.

Another cause of homelessness was drug use, which was the scourge of the urban underclass. Mired in hopelessness, poverty-stricken men and

Drugs and Violence

women tried to find forgetfulness in hard drugs, especially cocaine and its derivative crack, which first struck New York City's poorest neighborhoods in 1985. Crack's legacy included destroyed families, abused children, and drug dealers too young for a driver's license but with access to submachine guns and other state-of-the-art firearms. Gang shootouts over drugs were deadly: the toll in Los Angeles in 1987 was 387 deaths; more than half of the victims were innocent bystanders. After a bloody drug murder in New York City's Spanish Harlem, a sixteen-year-old girl moaned, "It's frightening. . . . It's crazy. There's no answer to it. And there's no end to it."

Another lethal byproduct of the 1980s drug epidemic was the spread of AIDS. First observed in the United States in 1981, AIDS is a disease transmittable through the sharing of intravenous needles by drug users or through the exchange of infected body fluids, often during sexual contact. Caused by a virus that attacks cells in the immune system, AIDS makes its victims susceptible to deadly infections and cancers. In the United States, AIDS initially was linked to the sexual practices of male homosexuals, but the disease spread to heterosexuals. Between 1981 and 1988, of the 57,000 AIDS cases reported, nearly 32,000 resulted in death. But because it takes several years for symptoms to appear, the worst had not yet revealed itself. A 1988 study reported that half of the gay men in San Francisco would develop AIDS and another 25 percent would develop the AIDS-related complex within about nine years of infection.

AIDS

AIDS—along with other sexually transmitted diseases such as genital herpes and chlamydia—affected Americans' sexual behavior. Caution replaced the "sexual revolution." "Safe sex" campaigns urged the use of condoms. For years Americans pretended the disease was limited to promiscuous homosexuals and drug addicts. But as writers, artists, athletes, actors, and relatives and friends died, people began to confront the horrifying epidemic.

Nonetheless, AIDS divided communities. Conservative Protestant sects joined the Roman Catholic Church in warning that condom advertising implicitly sanctioned contraception and encouraged promiscuity. Sex education should not be offered in the schools, they contended, citing their deep belief that any sexual activity other than heterosexual matrimonial monogamy was wrong. Gay men expected little assistance from the conservative executive branch, but they were partly wrong. In 1988 the federal government mailed a booklet entitled *Understanding AIDS* to 107 million households. Nevertheless, AIDS continued to be one of several unsolved social problems dividing the nation in the 1980s.

Reagan's Second Term and the Election of 1988

Despite Ronald Reagan's overwhelming reelection victory in 1984, for much of 1985 the president was on the defensive. One reason was the mounting fiscal deficit. Reagan had assailed President Carter's $74 billion deficit during the 1980 campaign, but the deficit exceeded $212 billion in fiscal 1985 and $221 billion in fiscal 1986. Although Republicans blamed the deficit on the Democrats, almost half of the national debt derived from fiscal years 1982 through 1986, when Reagan occupied the White House and the Republicans controlled the Senate.

Mounting Fiscal Deficit

Because of tax reductions and upwardly spiraling defense budgets, the national debt grew by $955 billion during this five-year period (see figure).

A fiscal conservative long committed to balanced budgets, Ronald Reagan nonetheless oversaw the accumulation of more new debt than all previous presidents put together throughout America's history. In response, Reagan and the Congress reluctantly agreed to the 1985 Gramm-Rudman bill, which called for a balanced federal budget by fiscal 1991 through a gradual reduction of the annual deficit. The deficit did drop, but for the three fiscal years from 1987 to 1989, it still totaled $457 billion.

During his second term, Reagan was successful in confronting other challenges. After Warren Burger's decision to retire from the Supreme Court, he nominated William Rehnquist to serve as chief justice and Antonin Scalia to fill Rehnquist's seat; the Senate confirmed both choices. Another victory was the Tax Reform Act of 1986, which lowered personal income taxes while closing some flagrant loopholes and eliminating 6 million poor people from the tax rolls. The law represented a compromise between supply-side conservatives, who argued that lower tax

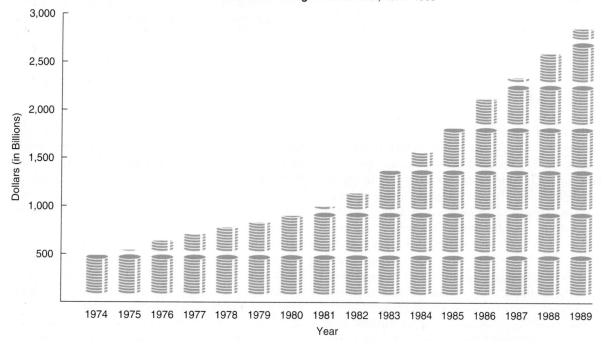

America's Rising National Debt, 1974–1989

America's Rising National Debt, 1974–1989   *America's national debt, which rose sporadically throughout the 1970s, soared to record heights during the 1980s. Under President Reagan, large defense expenditures and tax cuts caused the national debt to grow by $1.5 trillion.*   Source: Adapted from U.S. Bureau of the Census, *Statistical Abstract of the United States* (Washington, D.C., 1992), p. 315.

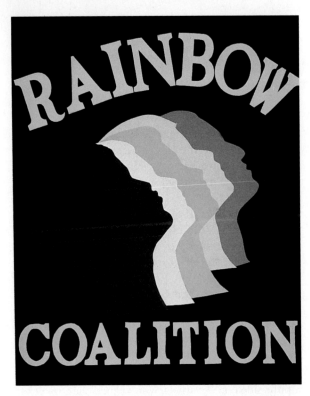

During the 1984 and 1988 campaigns, Reverend Jesse Jackson won a large following as the first African-American to make a serious bid for the presidential nomination of a major party. His multiethnic political organization, the Rainbow Coalition, included people of all colors. Smithsonian Institution, Division of Political History, Washington, D.C.

rates would act as an incentive to savings, investment, and growth, and liberals whose focus was the unfairness of the tax codes.

Until late 1986, Reagan's place in history was secure. But the Iran-contra disclosures caused his aura to fade, not only sullying his last two years in office but also endangering his historical reputation and raising the Democrats' hopes for a presidential victory in 1988. Reagan's political troubles began on election day 1986. First, the Republicans lost control of the Senate, stripping the president of a crucial power base. Second, from Lebanon came a bizarre story that the president's national security adviser had traveled to Iran with a Bible, a cake, and a planeload of weapons seeking the release of Americans held hostage in the Middle East. "No comment," Reagan told reporters, but details of the Iran-contra scandal soon began to surface (see page 914).

Iran-Contra Scandal

"An irony of the Reagan era," wrote Senator Daniel Patrick Moynihan, Democrat of New York, "is that having at midpoint reached a crescendo of triumphalism—morning in America—it is closing amid talk of decline." On a personal level, President Reagan had lost his mastery; the "great communicator" had taken on the appearance of a tired, bumbling old man. "Who's in Charge Here?" asked a *Time* magazine headline. The Iran-contra hearings focused attention on President Reagan's "hands-off" management style. Some observers, both outsiders and insiders, argued that Reagan was unengaged and uninformed. Donald T. Regan described his experience: "In the four years that I served as Secretary of the Treasury I never saw President Reagan alone and never discussed economic philosophy or fiscal and monetary policy with him one-on-one."

Reagan's Decline

Half of the people in the country believed that Reagan was lying about his lack of involvement in the Iran-contra scandal. Doubtless any lame-duck president would have suffered a loss of power in his second term, but the scandal encouraged Reagan's opponents. "No one is afraid of him anymore," said one political observer. And the political satirists were in hot pursuit. The real question, went one gibe, was not "what did the President know and when did he know it?" but "what didn't the President know, and why didn't he know it?"

Reagan's problems continued in 1987 and 1988. Congress overrode his veto of a massive highway-construction bill, and twice his choices for the Supreme Court failed to win confirmation by the Senate. His first nominee, federal judge Robert Bork, failed to convince the Senate that he was not a right-wing ideologue; his second choice, another federal judge, withdrew his name from consideration after revelations that he had smoked marijuana while a professor at Harvard Law School. Then, on October 19, 1987, the stock market went into a nosedive and fell 508 points.

Reagan's Ongoing Political Woes

Still, as the 1988 elections approached, there was also some excellent political and economic news for Republicans. First, Reagan had moderated his anti-Soviet rhetoric and in 1988, to the applause of most Americans, had traveled to the Soviet Union—the first American president to visit Moscow

Continuing Economic Recovery

since Richard Nixon in 1972. Second—and of greater importance to voters—after the economic recession of 1981 and 1982, the United States had embarked on a six-year business recovery. The discomfort index, which had risen alarmingly in the 1970s and early 1980s, dropped to more comfortable levels in the later 1980s. And although unemployment dropped to a decade-low 5.4 percent in April 1988, it did so without refueling inflation (see figure, page 963).

The Reagan administration pointed to the economy as proof of the success of supply-side economics. Critics retorted that Reagan's policy of pursuing massive tax cuts while greatly increasing the defense budget was just another form of Keynesianism—in this case, massive deficit financing to stimulate the economy. But the average American, caring little about this kind of debate, was content to enjoy the economic recovery. It was true that the poor had little to rejoice over and that Americans viewed the economic future with uncertainty. But it was also true that in the 1980s most Americans had jobs and were living very comfortably.

Had Reagan been allowed by the Constitution to run for a third term, he probably would have ridden the economic boom to victory. But the 1988 election was for his successor, and the competition in both parties was intense. On the Republican side the candidates included Vice President George Bush, Senate minority leader Bob Dole, and Pat Robertson, a television evangelist. Bush emerged with the nomination after bitter Republican infighting in state primaries. A native of Connecticut and a Yale graduate, Bush had served heroically as a navy pilot during the Second World War. He had moved to Texas to enter the oil business and had become involved in politics. Bush possessed broad government experience, including service as a congressman, ambassador to China, and director of the Central Intelligence Agency. He had contested Reagan for the Republican nomination in 1980 and then served as Reagan's vice president.

George Bush

On the Democratic side there was also a scramble for the presidential nomination. Beginning with a half-dozen campaigners, the race narrowed to a two-person contest between Michael Dukakis, under whose governorship Massachusetts had seemed a model of economic recovery and welfare reform, and Jesse Jackson, a former colleague of Reverend Martin Luther King, Jr., who had moved to Chicago to organize economic and educational programs for the poor. An eloquent preacher, Jackson campaigned on his dream of forming a "Rainbow Coalition" of the "rejected"—African-Americans, women, Hispanics, the disabled. Jackson was the first African-American to win mass support in seeking the presidential nomination of a major political party.

Both Bush and Dukakis avoided serious debate of the issues: drugs, environmental collapse, poverty, rising medical and educational costs, childcare, and the fiscal and trade deficits. Despite the gravity of the problems, the candidates relied on clichés and negative campaigning. Television dominated the presidential election as never before. Bush aimed his appeals at the "Reagan Democrats" by pushing emotional "hot buttons" such as "patriotism" and the death penalty. A Republican advertisement for television appealed to racism and fear by accusing Dukakis of being soft on crime for furloughing Willie Horton, a black convict who while on weekend leave had stabbed a white man and raped a white woman. Voters expressed their disgust at the 1988 race. Former president Richard Nixon, no stranger to political combat, called the presidential campaign "trivial, superficial and inane."

Presidential Campaign of 1988

But with America at peace and inflation and unemployment both low, Bush's victory was seldom in doubt. His margin over Dukakis was substantial: 53 percent of the popular vote to 46 percent (see map, page 982). Bush retained 85 percent of Reagan's supporters by promising to keep the nation on the course set by his predecessor. Significantly, "Reagan Democrats" again crossed over, this time voting for Bush in sufficient numbers for him to carry Michigan, Pennsylvania, and other key industrial states.

Bush's Victory in 1988

The 1988 election also confirmed that the "Solid South," once a Democratic stronghold, had become solidly Republican. Bush won every state in the region. In both South and North, race was a key factor, as it had been in every presidential election since 1964: for twenty-five years, the Republican vote had been almost exclusively white, and almost all blacks had voted Democratic. Another political constant was low voter turnout. Only 50 percent of Americans who were eligible to vote in 1988 voted, compared with 63 percent in 1960. Voter turnout had declined markedly after the 1968 election, but after turning slightly upward in 1984 (53 percent), it fell again in 1988.

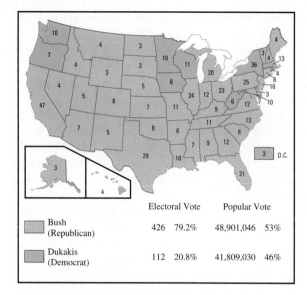

	Electoral Vote		Popular Vote	
Bush (Republican)	426	79.2%	48,901,046	53%
Dukakis (Democrat)	112	20.8%	41,809,030	46%

Presidential Election, 1988 *George Bush easily defeated Michael Dukakis in both popular and electoral votes. The key to Bush's victory was his ability to retain the political support that Ronald Reagan had enjoyed in 1980 and 1984.*

Many Americans seemed unconcerned as they confronted the new decade. College students in the 1990s, unlike many of their predecessors in the 1960s, aspired to join the system. They yearned not to save the world but to scramble up the corporate ladder, and many educated young people worked long hours in pursuit of that goal. "If the 1970s were the Me Decade," *Newsweek* declared, "the 1980s have been the Work Decade." Baby boomers and their younger sisters and brothers reported frustration in their efforts to replicate their parents' standard of living, particularly because of high housing costs.

But polls in 1989 reported that Americans were generally happy with their lives. Many expressed pleasure with the new toys and comforts in their lives. Sales of videocassette recorders (VCRs), microwave ovens, camcorders, and compact disc players soared in the 1980s. At-home comfort was an important reason for buying a VCR. In just four years, from 1980 to 1984, the number of videotapes rented by Americans for viewing movies at home jumped from 26 million to 304 million.

Even more impressive was the phenomenal spread of computers, which revolutionized not only communications but also people's workplaces and lifestyles. In 1981, the number of personal computers in use in America numbered 2 million; in 1988, the figure was 45 million. Companies raced to market with ever-speedier technology. In 1985, a new computer was introduced to the public at the Lawrence Livermore Laboratory in California. "What took a year in 1952," explained a scientist, "we can now do in a second."

 Conclusion

The United States changed in fundamental ways between 1974 and 1989. The spread of technological developments was part of that change. So too was the new immigration, which in the 1970s and 1980s not only swelled tremendously but shifted in origin. People came from Mexico, Central and South America, and the Caribbean, as well as from the Philippines, Korea, Taiwan, and India. Refugees of the Vietnam War also arrived, and Cubans and Haitians risked their lives in flimsy boats to come to America. The totals of the new immigration eclipsed those of the turn-of-the century immigration of millions of people from southern and eastern Europe.

Another change was the country's shift to the right politically. The champion of this change was President Ronald Reagan, whose supporters included both economic and social conservatives and both Republicans and disillusioned Democrats. Moreover, after two presidents, Gerald Ford and Jimmy Carter, who were perceived to be weak or ineffective leaders, Reagan restored the presidency to its central role in politics and the government.

Despite Reagan's successes, when he left office in 1989, the country faced unsolved economic, social, and political issues of great importance. "Ronald Reagan leaves no Vietnam War, no Watergate, no hostage crisis," reported the *New York Times*. "But he leaves huge question marks—and much to do." First, inequality had escalated in the 1980s, as the poor got poorer and the rich got richer. The poorest Americans of all were children, and economics and racism had conspired to widen racial divisions. Second, the rise of the federal debt continued unabated. In 1981, the debt stood at $994 billion; by the time Reagan left office, it had jumped to almost 2.9 trillion. Third, the effects of mismanagement and outright fraud were beginning to show in certain industries, forcing the federal government to consider massive bailouts and threatening greater fiscal deficits. In 1989 Congress debated legislation to rescue insolvent savings-and-loan associations by paying the government's insurance obligations to depositors; the eventual cost was $153 billion.

When George Bush was inaugurated as the forty-first president of the United States on January 20, 1989, the American people prepared to greet not only a new presidency but also a new decade. It was clear that Americans and their leaders would have to make difficult economic, social, and political choices in the 1990s.

Suggestions for Further Reading

Deficits, Deindustrialization, and Other Economic Woes

Barry Bluestone and Bennett Harrison, *The Deindustrialization of America* (1982); Richard Feldman and Michael Betzold, *End of the Line: Autoworkers and the American Dream* (1988); Robert Heilbroner and Peter Bernstein, *The Debt and the Deficit* (1989); John P. Hoerr, *And the Wolf Finally Came: The Decline of the American Steel Industry* (1988); Gregory Pappas, *The Magic City: Unemployment in a Working-Class Community* (1989).

The Ford and Carter Administrations

John Dumbrell, *The Carter Presidency* (1993); John Robert Greene, *The Presidency of Gerald R. Ford* (1995); Erwin C. Hargrove, *Jimmy Carter as President* (1989); Charles O. Jones, *The Trusteeship Presidency: Jimmy Carter and the United States Congress* (1988); Burton I. Kaufman, *The Presidency of James Earl Carter, Jr.* (1993); A. James Reichley, *Conservatives in an Age of Change: The Nixon and Ford Administrations* (1981).

Women and Children's Struggles

Marian Wright Edelman, *Families in Peril* (1987); Barbara Ehrenreich, *The Hearts of Men: American Dreams and the Flight from Commitment* (1983); David T. Ellwood, *Poor Support: Poverty in the American Family* (1988); Susan Faludi, *Backlash: The Undeclared War Against American Women* (1991); Sylvia Ann Hewlett, *When the Bough Breaks: The Cost of Neglecting Our Children* (1991); Arlie Russell Hochschild, *The Second Shift: Working Parents and the Revolution at Home* (1989); Rebecca E. Klatch, *Women of the New Right* (1987); Kristin Luker, *Abortion and the Politics of Motherhood* (1984); Maggie Scarf, *Unfinished Business: Pressure Points in the Lives of Women* (1980); Winifred D. Wandersee, *On the Move: American Women in the 1970s* (1988).

People of Color and New Immigrants

John Crewdson, *The Tarnished Door: The New Immigrants and the Transformation of America* (1983); Leslie W. Dunbar, ed., *Minority Report: What Has Happened to Blacks, Hispanics, American Indians, and Other Minorities in the Eighties* (1984); Reynolds Farley and Walter R. Allen, *The Color Line and the Quality of Life in America* (1987); Nancy Foner, ed., *New Immigrants in New York* (1987); Ronald P. Formisano, *Boston Against Busing* (1991); Troy R. Johnson, *The Occupation of Alcatraz Island: Indian Self-Determination and the Rise of Indian Activism* (1996); Joane Nagel, *American Indian Ethnic Revival: Red Power and the Resurgence of Identity and Culture* (1996); David M. Reimers, *Still the Golden Door: The Third World Comes to America* (1985); Sanford J. Ungar, *Fresh Blood: The New Immigrants* (1995); William Julius Wilson,

The Truly Disadvantaged: The Inner City, the Underclass, and Public Policy (1987).

The New Conservatism and the Election of 1980

William C. Berman, *America's Right Turn* (1994); Alan Crawford, *Thunder on the Right* (1980); Thomas Byrne Edsall, *The New Politics of Inequality* (1984); Jack W. Germond and Jules Witcover, *Blue Smoke and Mirrors: How Reagan Won and Why Carter Lost the Election of 1980* (1981); Godfrey Hodgson, *The World Turned Right Side Up: A History of the Conservative Ascendancy in America* (1996); Gillian Peele, *Revival and Reaction* (1984).

Ronald Reagan and His Presidency

Lou Cannon, *President Reagan* (1991); Paul D. Erickson, *Reagan Speaks: The Making of an American Myth* (1985); Mark Hertsgaard, *On Bended Knee: The Press and the Reagan Presidency* (1988); Haynes Johnson, *Sleepwalking Through History: America in the Reagan Years* (1991); Jane Mayer and Doyle McManus, *Landslide: The Unmaking of the President, 1984–1988* (1988); Michael Schaller, *Reckoning with Reagan* (1992); Larry M. Schwab, *The Illusion of a Conservative Reagan Revolution* (1991); David Thelen, *Becoming Citizens in an Age of Television: How Americans Challenged the Media and Seized Political Initiative During the Iran-Contra Debate* (1996); John Kenneth White, *The New Politics of Old Values* (1988); Garry Wills, *Reagan's America* (1987).

"Reaganomics"

Joan Claybrook, *Retreat from Safety: Reagan's Attack on America's Health* (1984); Benjamin Friedman, *Day of Reckoning: The Consequences of American Economic Policy Under Reagan and After* (1988); Jonathan Lash, *A Season of Spoils: The Story of the Reagan Administration's Attack on the Environment* (1984); Robert Lekachman, *Greed Is Not Enough: Reaganomics* (1982); William A. Niskanen, *Reaganomics* (1988); Charles Noble, *Liberalism at Work: The Rise and Fall of OSHA* (1986); Kevin Phillips, *The Politics of Rich and Poor* (1990); Lawrence J. White, *The S & L Debacle* (1991).

A Polarized Society in the 1980s

Chandler Davidson, *Race and Class in Texas Politics* (1990); Michael Harrington, *The New American Poverty* (1984); Katherine S. Newman, *Declining Fortunes: The Withering of the American Dream* (1993); Randy Shilts, *And the Band Played On: Politics, People and the AIDS Epidemic* (1987); Studs Terkel, *The Great Divide* (1988); Edward N. Wolff, *Top Heavy: A Study of Increasing Inequality in America* (1995).

Presidential Politics: The Elections of 1984 and 1988

Sidney Blumenthal, *Pledging Allegiance: The Last Campaign of the Cold War* (1990); Richard Ben Cramer, *What It Takes* (1992); Thomas Byrne Edsall and Mary D. Edsall, *Chain Reaction: The Impact of Race, Rights, and Taxes on American Politics* (1991); Thomas Ferguson and Joel Rogers, *Right Turn: The Decline of the Democrats and the Future of American Politics* (1986); Marshall Frady, *Jesse: The Life and Pilgrimage of Jesse Jackson* (1996); Jack W. Germond and Jules Witcover, *Wake Us When It's Over: Presidential Politics of 1984* (1985); Peter Goldman and Tom Mathews, *The Quest for the Presidency: The 1988 Campaign* (1989).

CHAPTER

33

Anxiety and Anger: America in the 1990s

Chase Smith, age three, and his two-year-old brother, Colton, were eating powdered doughnuts as their mother Edye Smith drove them to the American Kids daycare center in downtown Oklahoma City. The boys, their mouths jammed full, were in a playful mood; and when they kissed Edye goodbye at the daycare center on the second floor of the Alfred P. Murrah Federal Building, they left powdered sugar on her cheeks. As Edye turned to walk back to her car, Colton called out and ran to give her a big hug. "I love you, Mommy." Not to be outdone, Chase did likewise, hugging his mother and saying he loved her. It was Wednesday morning, April 19, 1995.

Jumping into her car, Edye Smith hurried to her job as a secretary at the Internal Revenue Service five blocks away. What awaited Edye was a birthday party—her own. Knowing that she would be twenty-three in two days, her coworkers had bought a cake to celebrate. Edye had just stood up to slice the cake when she heard a blast and felt the building shake. From the window, she could see smoke rising. Thinking it was a nearby bank, she turned to a coworker and said, "That's so sad. That's some little child's mother that's been killed."

Office workers from neighboring buildings soon flooded into the streets below, including Edye Smith and her mother, who also worked for the Internal Revenue Service. As they got closer to the area of the blast, they sensed the worst. They walked past dead bodies and saw bloodied children huddled with rescue workers. When they could not find the boys, Edye's brother, Daniel Coss, a police officer, took up the search. Several hours later, he identified Colton at a temporary morgue set up near the rubble; then he located Chase's body at the medical examiner's office. Chase and Colton Smith were buried together, holding hands in a small white coffin, along with their stuffed animals and a favorite book, *Animal Sounds*.

This was the worst act of terrorism in United States history. One hundred sixty-eight children, women, and men were killed in the blast. They were in or near the Murrah Building at 9:02 that morning, when a yellow rental truck containing a homemade two-ton bomb of fuel oil and ammonium nitrate fertilizer exploded. A reddish-orange fireball illuminated the sky as the blast tore upward through the nine-story building, ripping a huge crater from street to roof. The roof collapsed, and what had been the daycare center lay at the bottom of the rubble.

Americans were dazed, saddened, and angry. In the aftermath of the tragedy, they called in to radio talk shows to denounce the bombers and express their sorrow for the victims and their families. People also phoned in to spin conspiracy theories about who really was behind the bombing and to express outrage at both the media and the United States government, even suggesting that the Oklahoma City bombing was a government plot to discredit the "Patriot movement" in America. Callers compared it to the tragedy in Waco, Texas, in 1993, when the FBI led an assault on the compound of a religious sect known as the Branch Davidians, a fire broke out, and some eighty people died. "If anyone is responsible for the bombing," explained a woman caller in Richmond, Virginia, "it's the mainstream press for covering up the real story about Waco and the horrible things the Government, [President] Bill Clinton and [Attorney General] Janet Reno did to those women and children." In the 1990s, as evidenced by those calls, a climate of fear and hatred was growing, and some critics blamed the radio talk shows for fueling people's dark suspicions and anger.

At first, most Americans wanted to think that the bomb had come from abroad, perhaps set off by Middle Eastern terrorists. But a charred piece of truck axle located two blocks from the explosion, with the vehicle identification number still legible, proved otherwise. Arrested and convicted of the crime in 1997 was Timothy McVeigh, a native-born white American and a veteran of the Persian Gulf War. He hated the federal government, which he condemned for betraying the American people and the Constitution. The conflagration at Waco had agitated McVeigh; he saw it as deliberate slaughter by the Federal Bureau of Investigation.

In the months that followed, reporters and government investigators discovered networks of Mili-

tiamen, Patriots, tax resisters, and various Aryan-supremacist groups. The Southern Poverty Law Center identified well over four hundred paramilitary groups operating across the country. Computer-literate "patriots" used the Internet to rally support for their view that the federal government had to be resisted or even overthrown because it was controlled not by the people but by Zionists, corrupt politicians, cultural elitists, the Russians, the United Nations, and other "sinister" forces.

It was not just the far right, however, that was politically disaffected in the 1990s. People of far more moderate beliefs also abjured political participation, denouncing the government for being corrupt, arrogant, and downright stupid. In *Why Americans Hate Politics* (1991), E. J. Dionne, Jr., a columnist, ventured that voters were disgusted with the divisive debate that dominated politics in an era of negative attack advertisements. In the 1990s, moreover, many Americans did not know where to turn to make real political choices in their lives. They rejected the Democratic Party for having lost touch with their cultural and moral values, and they rejected the Republicans for failing to represent their economic and social needs. Some Americans spoke of the need for new political parties.

In 1989, as the political scientist James MacGregor Burns concluded his multivolume history of the United States, he took a final look at the American experiment. He was discouraged by what he saw. The American people seemed caught in a state of "political immobility," and few troubled to vote. What the nation needed, he wrote, was "creative and transforming leadership" that would mobilize the country and "carry through great projects." Surely in the 1990s the challenges were there, but would the presidential leadership be there to meet them?

From 1989 to 1993, America's presidential leader was George H. W. Bush. Bush had a rough ride as president. With victory in the Persian Gulf War in 1991, his popularity rating in the polls soared to 89 percent, tied with the high set by Harry S Truman in June 1945 after the surrender of Germany. Bush's re-election in 1992 seemed guaranteed. The president, however, had already sown the seeds of his own defeat. Bush had proclaimed in 1988, "Read my lips: no new taxes," but he betrayed that pledge in 1990 when he agreed to a tax hike as part of a tradeoff to reduce the spiraling fiscal deficit.

The early 1990s was a time of economic stagnation and deepening poverty. Probably no president

• *Important Events* •

1989 George Bush becomes president
Bush vetoes increase in minimum wage

1990 Clean Air Act reauthorization requires reduction in emission of pollutants
Bush-Congress budget agreement raises taxes; Bush reneges on "no new taxes" pledge
Americans with Disabilities Act prohibits discrimination
Recession begins; personal incomes fall

1991 Persian Gulf War
Anita Hill testifies at Senate hearings to confirm Clarence Thomas's Supreme Court nomination
Thomas is confirmed

1992 Federal deficit hits $4 trillion
Los Angeles riots erupt
Bill Clinton and George Bush win nominations
Planned Parenthood v. *Casey* upholds the right to an abortion
California pays employees with IOUs
Clinton elected president
H. Ross Perot's third-party candidacy wins one-fifth of the vote
Bush pardons former government officials indicted in Iran-contra scandal
Twenty-seventh Amendment prohibits future midterm congressional pay raises

1993 Clinton becomes president
Hillary Rodham Clinton heads task force on healthcare reform
Clinton lifts restrictions on abortion counseling
Clinton's proposal to lift ban on homosexuals in the military stirs controversy
Congress approves the North American Free Trade Agreement
Branch Davidian compound burns in Waco, Texas, killing at least 80 people
Clinton appoints Ruth Bader Ginsburg to the Supreme Court
Motor-voter and family-leave acts become law
Gun control laws require a waiting period for handguns and ban the sale of assault weapons

1994 Clinton appoints Stephen Breyer to the Supreme Court
Clinton signs crime bill into law
Republican candidates for Congress offer voters the "Contract with America"
Republicans win the House and Senate

1995 Bombing of federal building in Oklahoma City kills 168 people

1996 Telecommunications Act allows telephone and cable companies to compete
Freedom to Farm Act mandates phaseout of federal subsidies to farmers
Convictions in the first of several Whitewater trials
Clinton signs welfare act eliminating Aid to Families with Dependent Children
Clinton reelected

1997 Madeleine Albright becomes first woman confirmed as Secretary of State

---

could have prevented these problems, but during Bush's presidency the discouraging economic news was unstinting. By 1992, several million Americans had joined the unemployment rolls, and factory employment was skidding to its lowest level since the recession of 1982. Because of the mounting annual fiscal deficits, however, as well as the existing $4 trillion federal debt, the federal government could afford to do little to stimulate the economy and create jobs. And in 1992, the number of poor people in America reached the highest level since 1964.

Bush's greatest handicap as president was his inability to give American voters a sure sense of who he was and what remedies he would prescribe for the economy, which had slipped into a recession in 1990 and 1991. He also seemed perplexed and without a plan when Los Angeles erupted in race rioting in 1992. Opposition to Bush grew not only from Democrats but from independents as well.

Americans sensed that 1992 was an important election year. The Cold War was over. The economy was in trouble. Anti-incumbent sentiment was on the rise, along with calls for term limits. In fact, in 1992 the American people saw the most successful third-party campaign in eighty years. H. Ross Perot, a multibillionaire who spoke plain language and said he could fix the deficit, garnered 19 percent of the popular vote. But the winner and president-elect was the Democratic candidate, Governor Bill Clinton of Arkansas.

Born in 1946—the first baby boomer to be a major party nominee—Bill Clinton had wanted to be president most of his life. Calling himself a "New Democrat," he sought to move his party to the right to make it more attractive to white suburbanites, Reagan Democrats, and members of the business community. Clinton hoped, said an ally, "to modernize liberalism so it could sell again." As president, however, Clinton alienated both liberals and conservatives. He failed to deliver on healthcare reform, and his "Don't ask, don't tell" policy for gays in the military angered homosexuals as well as the military. And throughout his administration, Clinton battled charges of unethical behavior.

As Clinton's public approval rating plummeted, Republican conservatives under the leadership of Representative Newt Gingrich of Georgia launched an assault to win control of government, beginning with Congress. In 1994, "the Republican revolution" was triumphant; the Republicans won control of both houses of Congress for the first time since 1954. But the Republicans failed to enact most of their agenda, and their behavior angered the American public. Twice, the government shut down when Congress and the president failed to agree on routine appropriations bills. Most voters, perceiving Gingrich as ideologically rigid and Clinton as flexible, blamed the shutdowns on the Republicans.

Just two years after the Republicans' historic 1994 triumph, it seemed possible that Bill Clinton could make a political comeback. The Republican candidate in 1996 was Bob Dole, the Senator majority leader from Kansas. Dole was a veteran legislator, but his political vision was vague, and he did not inspire the voters. For his part, Clinton stole some of the conservative thunder by moving to the right himself, declaring that the "era of big government" was over and running as a budget-balancing cultural conservative. The voters seemed to be listening, and on the eve of the voting, Clinton's approval rating stood at 56 percent.

The 1996 election was a triumph for Bill Clinton, who carried thirty-one states. President Clinton had promised that, if reelected, his administration would build "a bridge to the twenty-first century, wide enough and strong enough to take us to America's best days." A new millennium was on the horizon, and Clinton's historical legacy would rest on his success in fulfilling his promise.

Economic and Social Anxieties: The Presidency of George H. W. Bush

In the 1990s, public apathy, even disgust, grew as Americans witnessed gridlock in the federal government. Instead of compromise and negotiated solutions, there was partisanship and stalemate; Republican president George H. W. Bush and the Democratic Congress seemed unable to work together or agree on anything. Beginning in 1989 with his veto of an increase in the minimum wage, Bush vetoed thirty-seven bills during his presidency, only one of which was overridden by a two-thirds vote of both houses of Congress. Rarely in American history had the relationship between Congress and the president been as sour and the legislative results so meager. Among the major issues left unresolved were healthcare, the budget deficit, taxes, crime, and family leave.

Decisive presidential leadership might have broken the gridlock, but Bush was a political chameleon. Once a supporter of family planning and a woman's right to an abortion, he had switched his position and denounced abortion as murder. In the 1980 Republican primaries, he had dismissed Ronald Reagan's "supply-side" economic ideas as "voodoo economics," but he quickly endorsed these policies when he became Reagan's running mate in 1980. In loyally supporting all Reagan's policies, even those that he formerly had opposed, Bush seemed to lack firm convictions of his own. Still, when President Bush was inaugurated in 1989, the future appeared bright. There had been six straight years of economic growth, and both unemployment and inflation were low. Bush hoped the good news would continue; and on inauguration day, when he called for a "kinder, gentler nation," it seemed that a compassionate president would be occupying the White House.

Bush's Political Shifts

Soon, however, the economy took a nosedive, and Bush's inactivity on the home front revealed the shallowness of his inaugural promise. The Bush administration, one columnist wrote, was "leading a retreat from social responsibility." Referring to the Republican who had served as president at the outset of the Great Depression, punsters began to call him George Herbert Hoover Bush. In 1989 Bush vetoed an increase in the minimum wage. And he did seem uncaring when he defended tax breaks for the rich but opposed extending relief payments to the long-term

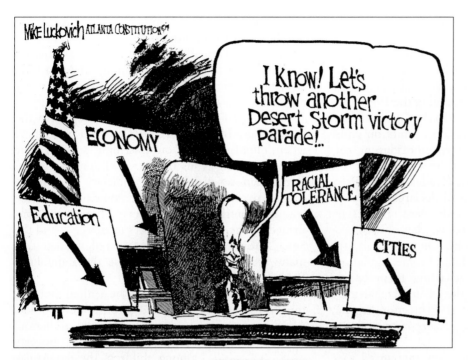

Cartoonist Mike Luckovich seemed to know what President Bush and his advisers were thinking inside the White House when signs of trouble were cropping up in 1991. Bush officials had hoped to turn victory in the Persian Gulf War into votes for the president's re-election, but Americans wearied of Desert Storm celebrations when Bush seemed unwilling to take the lead in solving domestic problems.   © 1991 Mike Luckovich—*Atlanta Constitution*/Creators Syndicate.

unemployed. In October 1990 alone, the president's popularity plummeted 25 points. Kevin Phillips, a political analyst, wrote that Bush's "dithering" over domestic issues was responsible for the decline and that "for now, Washington's vultures are beginning to think about what could be another political death watch."

In the fall of 1990, Bush earned high praise for assembling the multinational force stationed in Saudi Arabia. And the Persian Gulf War (1991) temporarily saved his floundering presidency (see pages 917–918). The war "brought us a year of complacency," acknowledged a Republican close to the White House. But Bush's inaction on healthcare, unemployment, and other pressing domestic concerns drew mounting criticism. Bush's slogan, "First, do no harm," reflected his aversion to government action to solve economic and social problems. Moreover, Bush's advisers believed that he would win re-election easily in 1992 without having to undertake

"First, Do No Harm"

any major new domestic initiatives. "The idea," recalled a senior administration official, "was that he'd ride the wave from the war for the twenty-one months to reelection."

Bush's domestic problems began in 1990, when he betrayed the pledge he had made at the 1988 Republican convention: "Read my lips: no new taxes." During the 1990 budget summit with Congress, the White House agreed to a tax increase in exchange for the acquiescence of congressional Democrats in budget cuts. Without this agreement, the deficit would have risen even higher than it did. Many applauded Bush's action as responsible leadership, but his press secretary was shocked: "That means we've broken the pledge." And soon the television news began running the videotape of Bush's "Read my lips" statement, and questioning whether the president could be trusted in the future.

"Read My Lips: No New Taxes"

Some of Bush's political problems resulted from his failure to fulfill campaign pledges. As a candidate in 1988, he had promised that he would be the "environmental president"

Bush's Assault on the Environment

as well as the "education president"; but he failed in both areas. While Bush accepted high praise for signing the 1990 reauthorization of the Clean Air Act, which required limits on emissions of sulfur dioxide and nitrogen oxides, he gutted enforcement of the act by establishing the Council on Competitiveness. Headed by Vice President Dan Quayle, the council declared that environmental regulations not only were unnecessary but should be eliminated because they slowed economic growth and cost jobs. On this basis, the council halted the enforcement of some regulations and weakened others by rewriting them behind closed doors. In addition, the Justice Department overruled the Environmental Protection Agency when it sought to have large corporate polluters prosecuted.

In education, President Bush announced that, by the year 2000, American students would be second to none in science and mathematics. But he was unable, and perhaps unwilling, to tackle the difficult problem of a nation with thousands of local school systems and much disagreement about education. Other than argue for government vouchers that parents could use to pay tuition at public or private schools of their choice, his administration did little to support educational reform.

The president's credibility also suffered during the confirmation hearings of Clarence Thomas, nominated in the fall of 1991 to serve on the Supreme

Nomination of Clarence Thomas to the Supreme Court

Court. Few people believed that this inexperienced federal judge was, as Bush put it, the "best man for the job." But Thomas, an African-American, was highly conservative; and although he insisted that he had formulated no legal opinions on controversial issues predicted to come before the Court, his writings and speeches made it clear that he opposed affirmative action in hiring, believed in returning prayer to the schools, and opposed abortion because of his belief that a fetus had an inalienable right to life.

Bush's nomination of a black conservative was a clever but cynical political move. One opponent, Eleanor Holmes Norton, the African-American congressional delegate from Washington, D.C., denounced the choice as "calculated . . . to mute the ex-

pected reaction to yet another conservative nominee." Despite the opposition, it seemed that Thomas would be confirmed. In October, however, the nation was electrified by the testimony of Anita Hill, an African-American law professor at the University of Oklahoma, who charged that Thomas had sexually harassed her when she worked for him in the early 1980s. She told the senators of her discomfort when Thomas insisted on describing pornographic movies, as well as his own sexual interests, to her. Republican senators on the Judiciary Committee sought to discredit Hill, but women around the country identified with her story. Thomas was confirmed by the Senate, but Hill's testimony—and the Senate's disregard of it—so angered women that many thousands vowed to oppose the Republican Party in 1992.

Social ills that had plagued the United States in the 1980s persisted unabated into the new decade: AIDS, homelessness, drug and alcohol addiction,

Persistent Social Problems

racism and inequality, poverty among children, the day-to-day struggles of single-parent families. In the 1990s, however, economic and social problems that once had afflicted only the poor now touched the lives of the middle classes, who saw their standard of living decline. Scholars who tracked the "social health" of the nation reported that it was at its lowest level since 1970, when the data were first analyzed. Problems that reached their worst recorded levels in 1990 were child abuse, teen suicide, the gap between rich and poor, and health insurance coverage. "If you look at it as a report card," observed the director of Fordham University's Institute for Innovation in Social Policy, "the country gets an F."

One group, however, made real progress in 1990. That year, President Bush signed the Americans with Disabilities Act, which banned job dis-

Americans with Disabilities Act

crimination, in companies with twenty-five or more employees, against the blind, deaf, mentally retarded, and physically impaired as well as against those who are H.I.V. positive or have cancer. The act, which covered 87 percent of all wage earners, also required that "reasonable accommodations," such as wheelchair ramps, be made available to people with disabilities. Many businesses opposed the bill, but the U.S. Chamber of Commerce supported it. As a Chamber official explained, the bill "opens up a huge untapped resource of workers."

As numerous Americans saw their economic fortunes and social welfare decline in the early 1990s, the criticism of President Bush's performance grew. In November 1991 panic struck the White House. In Pennsylvania, Democrat Harris Wofford defeated Bush's former attorney general, Richard Thornburgh, in a Senate race that focused on people's anxieties over economic issues, particularly healthcare. In advocating national health insurance, Wofford ignited a time bomb.

Healthcare Problems

In the United States, there were few incentives to control healthcare costs, and with the spread of expensive technologies, medical expenses were rising rapidly. In 1992, healthcare costs absorbed 12 percent of the national income, appreciably more than in other industrialized nations. Health insurance also had become a leading labor issue in the country, as steeply rising insurance premiums ate into both profits and wages. In 1990, for example, disputes over health insurance caused 55 percent of the strikes in the United States.

Still worse, some 33 million Americans, about 13 percent of the population, had no health insurance at all. Three-fourths of these people were employed but worked at minimum-wage jobs that did not provide health benefits. Additional tens of millions had such limited coverage that they constantly were at risk of financial devastation. The Price family of Mebane, North Carolina, already $1,000 in debt for medical expenses, was typical of many Americans. The family's major worry was how they could afford treatment for an emergency to William or Paula or their two sons. Self-employed, William could not afford the family policy available at $350 per month; and at Paula's job, there was no group health insurance. As William said, "We just have to hope the family stays healthy."

"Downsizing" and "Outsourcing"

Also fueling American's anxieties were the growing numbers of job layoffs, some of them temporary but many of them permanent. Sensing that economic recovery would be slow and would proceed in fits and starts, businesses were hesitant to take back workers even if the economy did pick up. In a practice called "outsourcing," companies stopped making their components and began ordering them from factories in other states, as well as in other countries, where wages were far lower and benefit packages nonexistent. Other busi-

The Americans with Disabilities Act of 1990 was the result of many people's efforts, including activists with disabilities. Daniel Wilkins became a paraplegic in an automobile accident at age twenty-three. An outdoorsman, he was determined not to be isolated from nature, even though he was confined to a wheelchair. Wilkins led efforts to devise trail-accessibility programs in Ohio and, with his mother, founded a chapter of the National Spinal Cord Injury Association. "Physical barriers are easily overcome," said Dan Wilkins, "once attitudinal barriers vanish." © Junebug Clark.

nesses replaced workers with computers and other machines, in efforts not only to cut costs but also to increase productivity. Employment in the chemical industry, for example, had been declining for several years. "Companies in our industry," said the chief economist of the Chemical Manufacturers Association, "don't want to hire more people because people cost money." In the 1990s, numerous industries were deciding whether to reduce labor costs by opting for technology, outsourcing, or moving their plants to Mexico, South Korea, and other low-wage countries.

Republicans denied that the country was in a recession, but signs to the contrary were everywhere. In late 1989 *Newsweek* called it a "Peek-a-Boo Recession," pointing to slumping car and housing sales and declining orders for manufacturing products. By mid-1990 there was no doubt the United States was mired in a recession. American businesses were eliminating tens of thousands of jobs. "The recession that won't go away," *Newsweek* reported in November 1991, "has average Americans spooked and politicians running scared." And a poll that month showed that for the first time in Bush's presidency, less than a majority of the voters (47 pecent) were inclined to reelect him in 1992. What had seemed unlikely just a few months before was now shaping up: a real battle for the presidency.

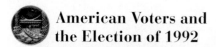

American Voters and the Election of 1992

Prior to the 1992 presidential election, the Republican Party had been on a roll. Beginning with Richard M. Nixon's electoral victory in 1968, the Republicans had captured the White House five of the last six times by building a coalition of ideologically diverse constituencies. First, there were economic conservatives who had always voted Republican. Second, there were cultural conservatives, particularly fundamentalist and evangelical Christians who advocated "family values," stressing their opposition to abortion and homosexualty. Third, there were the "Reagan Democrats," blue-collar workers and one-time Democrats who had supported Bush in 1988 as Reagan's heir. Fourth, there were white voters in the South, where Republican growth had been impressive since the 1960s. Fifth, there were young Americans between eighteen and thirty who had come of age politically during the Reagan years.

Last, and in some ways most significant, there were voters in America's ever-growing suburbs, which in 1990 were home to almost half (46.2 percent) of the country's population. There was no denying the sheer size of the suburban vote, which tended to be antitax and antigovernment. In the 1980s what had held the Republican coalition together were economic growth, anticommunism, and Ronald Reagan. In 1992, these three factors were absent.

As the 1992 presidential election neared, Republicans from all parts of the country pleaded with

the White House to take action on the economy. Between 1989 and 1992, the economy had grown slowly or not at all; the gross national product averaged an increase of only 0.7 percent a year, the worst showing since the Great Depression of the 1930s. Even for Americans with jobs, personal income was stagnant. In fact, in 1991 median household incomes fell by 3.5 percent, the most severe decline since the 1973 recession.

A Stagnant Economy

Even worse off were some city and state governments that faced bankruptcy. The state of California, out of money in mid-1992, paid its workers and bills in IOUs. A series of "tax revolts," beginning with Proposition 13 in 1978, had cut property taxes at just the time California's population was booming. But California was not alone; some thirty states were in serious financial difficulty in the 1990s. Businesses too were deeply burdened with debt; real-estate, home-building, and insurance companies were all overextended. And as companies tottered, the American people were anxious about their jobs.

Some presidential advisers urged Bush to call a special session of Congress to deal with the economy. But he waited, and by January 1992 his approval rating had dropped to half of what it had been ten months before. The president seemed to be out of touch with the American people. He "lacks any fingertip feel," noted one political analyst, "for what it is to be a member of the wage-earning middle class in America." In January 1992 eight of ten Americans polled rated the economy as "fairly bad" or "very bad"; most blamed Bush.

Since this was an election year, Democratic hopefuls took to the road in search of their party's presidential nomination. But the Democrats had problems of their own, particularly in the 102nd Congress, which they controlled. The most blatant scandal involved the House bank, where representatives wrote thousands of bad checks, all of which the bank covered at no fee. The Senate angered the public not only with the Clarence Thomas hearings but also with ethical violations by several of its members who did favors for Charles Keating, who had plundered a large California savings and loan association, causing many unsuspecting small investors to lose their savings. Many Americans also blamed Congress for the gridlock in Washington. The members of Congress had little to boast of to their con-

Scandals in Congress

stituents, but to add insult, they voted themselves a pay raise. (In 1992, the necessary number of states ratified the new Twenty-seventh Amendment to the Constitution to prohibit midterm congressional pay raises.) Said Representative Leon Panetta, a Democrat from California, "When people look back on the 102nd Congress, they will say, 'Let's never repeat this experience again.'"

Among the Democratic presidential hopefuls in 1992 was Bill Clinton, governor of Arkansas. As a college student in the 1960s, Clinton had opposed the Vietnam War and pulled strings to avoid being drafted (as

Bill Clinton

had Vice President Dan Quayle, also of the Vietnam generation). After studying in England as a Rhodes scholar and graduating from the Yale law school, Clinton returned to Arkansas and dived into politics, becoming governor in 1979 at the age of thirty-two. He slugged it out in the 1992 presidential primaries with Paul Tsongas, former senator from Massachusetts, and Jerry Brown, former governor of California. But by July, when the Democrats met for their convention, Clinton emerged the clear victor.

Bill Clinton's message to the voters was mixed. He emphasized the need to move people off welfare, and he called for more police officers on the streets and for capital punishment. But he also advocated greater public investment in building roads, bridges, and communications infrastructure; universal access to apprenticeship programs and college educations; basic healthcare for all Americans; and a shift of funds from defense to civilian programs. Clinton's running mate, Tennessee senator Albert Gore, came from the same mold. He too was a baby boomer, a white southerner, a Baptist, and a moderate Democrat. Gore also appealed to environmentalists as the author of a bestselling book, *Earth in the Balance: Ecology and the Human Spirit* (1992).

Clinton was not Bush's only opponent in 1992. The case against the president was also being made by Patrick J. Buchanan, a conservative television talk-show regular and former Nixon speechwriter, who entered

Ross Perot

the New Hampshire primary to contest Bush for the Republican nomination. And in April 1992, Ross Perot, who had amassed a fortune in the computer industry, announced on a television call-in show that he would run for president if voters in all fifty states put his name on the ballot. Many people responded to Perot's candidacy, convinced that he had the answers

The televised presidential debates took on an informal air in 1992. At this debate at the University of Richmond, George Bush (left) and Ross Perot (right) listen while Bill Clinton speaks. In the debates, Clinton used the talk-show format to his advantage, demonstrating his ability to connect with people.   Corbis-Bettmann.

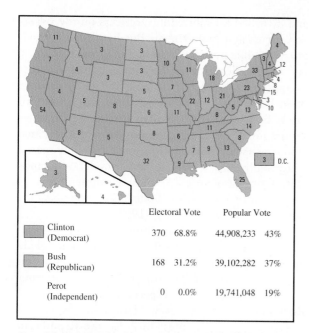

	Electoral Vote		Popular Vote	
Clinton (Democrat)	370	68.8%	44,908,233	43%
Bush (Republican)	168	31.2%	39,102,282	37%
Perot (Independent)	0	0.0%	19,741,048	19%

Presidential Election, 1992 Although a minority of voters cast ballots for Bill Clinton, he won handily in the electoral college. Clinton's share of the popular vote was the lowest for anyone elected president since Woodrow Wilson won with 42 percent of the popular vote in 1912. Exit polls revealed that the votes cast for Perot would have divided about evenly between Clinton and Bush had Perot not been in the race.

and intrigued by the possibility of electing the first president since George Washington who belonged to no party. "He stands for a fresh start," explained one backer. "He doesn't have to answer to anybody but the people."

Still the chameleon, in 1992 Bush changed his colors again. Battling during the New Hampshire primary campaign, he reverted to an earlier identity: "I care," Bush told the voters.

Los Angeles Riots

Bush won the New Hampshire presidential primary, but just weeks later, during race riots in Los Angeles, he revealed his inability to respond to a domestic crisis. As unemployment and poverty rose in the early 1990s, so too did racial tensions. In April 1992, violence erupted in Los Angeles after a California jury had discounted videotaped evidence and acquitted four police officers charged with beating Rodney King, an African-American motorist pulled over after a high-speed chase. In the bloodiest urban riot since the 1960s,

forty-four people died and two thousand were injured. Entire blocks of houses and stores went up in flames, leaving $1 billion in charred ruins. According to a California legislative committee, the 1965 Watts riot (see page 937) had sprung from "poverty, segregation, lack of education and employment opportunities, [and] widespread perceptions of police abuse.... Little has changed in 1992 Los Angeles."

President Bush paid a two-day trip to Los Angeles and advocated emergency aid, but he missed an opportunity to take a bold step in addressing the nation's urban and racial problems. He gave no civil rights talks, and he avoided meeting with the nation's mayors. "So much for the Los Angeles riots," said a dispirited Jack Kemp, Bush's secretary of housing and urban development. It seemed to increasing numbers of voters that President Bush did not really care after all.

In August, when the Republicans held their national convention, Bush assumed the identity of guardian of "family values." In joining the Reagan team in 1980, Bush had learned to practice the politics of cultural conservatism. And cultural conservatism dominated the 1992 Republican national convention, where speaker after speaker called for a return to "family values." Buchanan called for a "religious war" and a "cultural war" against the nation's internal enemies, including homosexuals. In his acceptance speech Bush had little new to offer. The "vision thing," Bush once conceded, had eluded him, and he was unable to chart a bold course in domestic policy. For a presidential candidate in changing times, this was a fatal flaw.

The 1992 Republican Convention

The Republicans renominated George Bush and Dan Quayle. The Bush-Quayle election strategy featured negative campaigning, particularly attacks on Bill Clinton's character. Beginning in the New Hampshire primary, the press had questioned Bill Clinton about his Vietnam draft status as well as about alleged extramarital affairs. His public image suffered, and he was caricatured as "Slick Willie," a draft-dodger, and a ladies' man. During the campaign, Bush said the issue was "trust," and he asked whether the American people could trust Clinton's international leadership. Bush's strategy seemed to be working, and in the closing days of the campaign, he narrowed the gap with Clinton. With three can-

Bush's Campaign

didates in the race, it had become much closer than the pundits had predicted.

On November 3, with the highest voter turnout (55 percent) since 1976, the American people voted to make a change. The Clinton-Gore ticket swept all of New England and the West Coast and much of the industrial heartland of the Middle West (see map, page 994). It also made the deepest Democratic inroads

Clinton's Victory

into the South since Jimmy Carter's 1976 near-sweep (see figure). The Democrats won 43 percent of the vote and 370 electoral votes, while the ticket of Bush and Quayle gained 37 percent and 168 electoral votes. The Republican coalition had not held. Clinton captured Democrats who earlier had fled to Ronald Reagan, and he ran well in the suburbs and among voters who labeled themselves independent and moderates. Although Perot won no electoral votes, he captured almost one-fifth of the popular

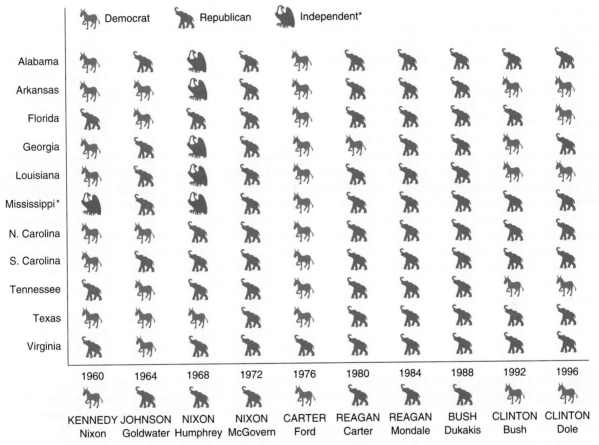

Southern States in Presidential Elections, 1960–1996

Democrat   Republican   Independent*

	1960	1964	1968	1972	1976	1980	1984	1988	1992	1996

KENNEDY JOHNSON NIXON NIXON CARTER REAGAN REAGAN BUSH CLINTON CLINTON
Nixon Goldwater Humphrey McGovern Ford Carter Mondale Dukakis Bush Dole

*Mississippi Voters elected Harry Byrd in 1960. In 1968, George Wallace carried Alabama, Arkansas, Georgia, Louisiana, and Mississippi.

Southern States in Presidential Elections, 1960–1996 *A major shift in modern American political history occurred in the 1960s and 1970s. In those years, the once-solid Democratic South became Republican in presidential elections; in 1972 Richard M. Nixon won every state in the region. In the aftermath of the Watergate scandal, a southern Democrat, Jimmy Carter of Georgia, won all but one state in the South. But the Republicans' ascendancy returned in 1980, when Ronald Reagan won every southern state but Georgia. And in 1984 and 1988, the Republican ticket handily won all of the South. Even though a southerner, Bill Clinton of Arkansas, won the presidential elections of 1992 and 1996, the Republican tickets led by George Bush and Bob Dole still managed to carry a majority of states in the region.*

vote, demonstrating the public's dissatisfaction with both major parties.

Voters also changed the Congress. The party distribution remained about the same, with the Democrats in control of both houses, but four more women were sent to the Senate and nineteen more to the House. Voters also elected more African-American and Hispanic-American representatives. When the 103rd Congress met in January 1993, it had 110 new representatives and eleven new senators. Many of the first-term members of Congress were—like Clinton—in their forties with advanced degrees, no military service, and considerable experience in politics at the state level. "The baby boomers' generation—or at least some of its most upwardly mobile members—is taking over," observed *Washington Post* columnist David Broder. "It will be different."

One of Bush's last decisions as president smacked of the discredited past. Just before leaving office, the president pardoned Reagan's secretary of defense Caspar Weinberger and other Iran-contra figures who had been indicted on felony counts for lying to Congress and obstructing a congressional inquiry (see page 914). Had nothing been learned from the Watergate scandal, asked David Broder, especially "their duty to obey the law"? The veteran journalist added: "We have failed as a society to express our contempt and disgust for those who violate their oaths of office with such impunity."

Bush's Pardon of Iran-Contra Officials

Bill Clinton, Newt Gingrich, and Political Stalemate

President Bill Clinton was every bit the political chameleon his immediate predecessor had been. In fact, Clinton was one of the most paradoxical presidents in American history. In a 1996 story for the *New York Times*, journalist Todd S. Purdum observed of Clinton: "One of the biggest, most talented, articulate, intelligent, open, colorful characters ever to inhabit the White House [Clinton] can also be an undisciplined, fumbling, obtuse, defensive, self-justifying rogue. . . . He is essentially sunny, yet capable of black cloudbursts of thundering rage. He is a splendid salesman and tireless storyteller but confesses that he has failed to tell his Administration's

story. . . . He is breathtakingly bright while capable of doing really dumb things."

Clinton's immediate goal as president was to mobilize the nation to pull itself out of its economic, social, and political doldrums. He named to his cabinet a mix of seasoned politicos, young politicians, intellectuals, women, and minorities. In his inaugural address, he called on Americans to "take more responsibility, not only for ourselves and our families, but for our communities and our country." One of Clinton's first acts was to overturn Bush's "gag rule," which had prohibited abortion counseling in clinics that received federal funds. And he appointed his wife, Hillary Rodham Clinton, to draft a plan for healthcare reform. He seemed to be off to a fast start.

Clinton soon ran into trouble, however, largely because of excessive optimism and sloppy staff work. In the 1992 campaign, he had pledged to lift the ban on homosexuals in the military. But when he acted to do so, the military brass joined Republicans in harshly criticizing the move. Critics charged that Clinton was still a 1960s activist out of step with mainstream American values. Seeing that the American people were evenly divided on the issue, and fearful of losing support for his economic proposals, Clinton delayed a decision for months. Finally, he accepted a "Don't ask, don't tell" compromise that prohibited discrimination against gays in the military as long as they did not reveal their homosexuality; if their sexual orientation became known, however, they would be discharged "for the good of the service." In trying to split the difference, Clinton alienated both liberals and conservatives and both the gay community and the military.

The Issue of Gays in the Military

In 1993, the economy drew the president's close scrutiny. When Clinton took office, the unemployment rate stood at 7.2 percent, and IBM, General Motors, Sears, AT&T, and other major corporations were laying off thousands of workers. The troubled economies of Europe and Japan portended lower United States exports and a bigger trade deficit; the trade deficit already had reached $84.3 billion in 1992, a 29 percent jump from 1991. Still reeling from losses on real-estate loans, banks were hesitant to lend to small businesses, although interest rates had begun to drop. Mounting healthcare costs threatened to drive up the federal deficit.

The economic plan that the president sent to Congress in February 1993 called for higher taxes for the middle class, a 10 percent surtax on individuals with taxable incomes over $250,000, an energy tax, and a higher corporate tax. Clinton promised to end business deductions for expense accounts, such as memberships in country clubs. He also proposed to cut government spending through a smaller defense budget and a downsized bureaucracy, and he offered an immediate stimulus to the economy through public works projects.

Clinton's Economic Proposals

Interest-group lobbyists wasted no time in attacking Clinton's economic plan. Republicans protested that Clinton was not cutting back enough on spending, and other critics hammered him for going back on his campaign pledge to provide tax relief for middle-class Americans. The president fought back, arguing that federal indebtedness was graver than anticipated and that all Americans must pay to clean up the mess the deficit-spending Republicans had left them. Intent on avoiding the "trappings of Washington," he crisscrossed the nation to speak directly to people.

Congress killed Clinton's economic stimulus proposal but passed other requests, including the "motor-voter" act, which enabled people to register to vote when they applied for drivers' licenses, and the Family and Medical Leave Act, which required employers to grant workers unpaid family or medical leave of up to twelve weeks. Clinton also signed into law measures dealing with the sale of firearms. The Brady bill (1993) required a short waiting period before the sale of a handgun; a second law banned the sale of assault weapons. And in 1994, Clinton, with the help of three Republican senators who broke with their party, secured the enactment of $30.2 billion crime bill. The new law provided funds for building more prisons and increasing the size of urban police forces. Finally, with considerable opposition from his own party and from organized labor, Clinton secured congressional approval of the North American Free Trade Agreement.

Clinton's Legislative Successes

Clinton altered the outlook of the Supreme Court in 1993 when Byron R. White, a conservative, retired. Clinton appointed as justice Ruth Bader Ginsburg, an experienced women's rights advocate and federal appeals court judge. The next year he made another appointment to the Supreme Court, naming Stephen Breyer, a fed-

Clinton's Supreme Court Appointments

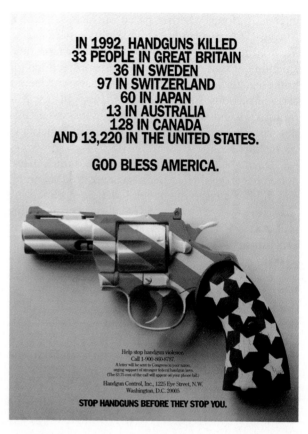

IN 1992, HANDGUNS KILLED 33 PEOPLE IN GREAT BRITAIN 36 IN SWEDEN 97 IN SWITZERLAND 60 IN JAPAN 13 IN AUSTRALIA 128 IN CANADA AND 13,220 IN THE UNITED STATES.

GOD BLESS AMERICA.

Help stop handgun violence.
Call 1-900-860-8787.
A letter will be sent to Congress in your name, urging support of stronger federal handgun laws. (The $3.75 cost of the call will appear on your phone bill.)
Handgun Control, Inc., 1225 Eye Street, N.W. Washington, D.C. 20005

STOP HANDGUNS BEFORE THEY STOP YOU.

In 1993 Congress took action on gun control, passing the Brady Bill into law. Named for James Brady, paralyzed by a gunshot wound during an assassination attempt on President Ronald Reagan in 1981, the new law mandated a short waiting period before the purchase of a handgun. Brady and his wife Sarah founded Handgun Control, Inc., which sponsored this magazine advertisement. Handgun Control, Inc

eral judge from Massachusetts, to succeed Justice Harry Blackmun. The Court would be less conservative, but it was deeply divided over cases involving gay rights, free speech, and voting rights. The right to an abortion had survived a Court challenge in 1992 by a 5-to-4 vote (*Planned Parenthood* v. *Casey*), but the issue had not been laid to rest.

Clinton's appointments bolstered the moderate wing of the Supreme Court. The 1994–1995 term produced conservative rulings that placed limits on affirmative action and school desegregation. But a year later, the new justices began to speak up. In *U.S.* v. *Virginia*, the Court held that the Virginia Military Institute could not exclude women, because to do so would violate the constitutional guarantee of "equal protection of the laws"; thus separate-but-equal was unconstitutional whether based on race or gender. Also in 1996, in a landmark gay rights case (*Romer* v. *Evans*), the Court ruled unconstitutional a Colorado amendment that nullified civil rights protections for homosexuals. Declaring that a state may not "deem a class of persons a stranger to its laws," Justice Anthony M. Kennedy wrote for a 6-to-3 majority: "It is not within our constitutional tradition to enact laws of this sort."

During Clinton's presidency, the annual fiscal deficit began to shrink. Because of reduced spending and higher taxes, the federal deficit declined by some $83 billion during Clinton's first fiscal year in office.

Declining Fiscal Deficit

The president touted the accomplishment but could not take credit alone. The economy rebounded in 1993, outperforming estimates, increasing tax revenues, and cutting interest on the federal debt. Spending for healthcare and for Social Security fell below estimates. The decline in the fiscal deficit begun in 1993 continued throughout the Clinton administration.

Despite the president's legislative accomplishments, it became apparent that Clinton's healthcare plan and welfare proposals would determine his success or failure on the domestic front. Almost everyone—liberal and conservative, Democrat and Republican—agreed that the nation's healthcare system was in crisis and that its welfare system was a failure. Different constituencies, however, had vastly different "solutions" to offer. The result was gridlock between Democrats and Republicans and between the White House and Congress.

The failure to deliver on healthcare was Clinton's major defeat, and it was one he shared with his wife, who cochaired the president's task force on healthcare reform. In trying to transform healthcare "in one bite," Clinton himself later conceded, he had "overestimated how much the system could change." Opposed to substantive reform were powerful interests, including corporations, the insurance industry, and small business. Most important of all, Clinton had been elected a minority president in 1992, with a fragile plurality of 43 percent. And as Haynes Johnson and David Broder, two respected journalists, noted, "conventional wisdom holds that you do not

Clinton's Defeat on Healthcare Reform

In 1994 Hillary Rodham Clinton spoke at a healthcare rally sponsored by Families U.S.A., a watchdog group that monitored the number of Americans without health insurance. The large clock in the background tabulated the number of families recently losing their health coverage.   Jeffrey Markowitz, SYGMA.

build bold agendas on small majorities, and Bill Clinton had no majority at all."

President Clinton's honeymoon in office was brief, and his public approval ratings were mixed in 1993 and 1994. People protested higher taxes and showed impatience with the slowness of his plan to revive the economy. Critics charged that Clinton backed down when pressed and was unwilling to take risks. Liberals complained that Clinton was too conservative, conservatives that he was too liberal. Public relations gaffes and late-hour White House abandonment of controversial appointees raised doubts about the president's management ability.

On the stump in 1992, Bill Clinton had praised his wife, Hillary Rodham Clinton, as a major asset, promising the voters, "Buy one, get one free." A

A Controversial Couple

Yale law school graduate, Hillary Clinton had shaped her own career as a partner in a law firm in Little Rock and as a feminist and social activist. Both she and her husband were controversial. Bill Clinton conceded that he had smoked marijuana in the 1960s but insisted that he had not inhaled. Few people, conservative or liberal, believed him. As president, Clinton was the defendant in a civil lawsuit alleging sexual harassment, and he was the most frequent butt of jokes on the Jay Leno and David Letterman late-night television shows. Letterman cracked, for example, that Clinton had agreed to play a cameo role in an upcoming film, but "was disappointed that he didn't have to sleep with anybody to get the part."

Hillary Clinton was also a magnet for criticism, having been in the middle of several of the defining controversies of the Clinton administration, including the firing of the White House travel office staff in 1993; the suicide later that year of her friend and former law partner, deputy White House counsel Vincent Foster; and the Whitewater land deal. In fact, Hillary Clinton became more controversial than her husband.

In 1993, a scandal dating back to the mid-1980s began to dog the Clintons. The scandal involved the failed Madison Guaranty Savings and Loan and the

Whitewater Indictments and Investigations

Whitewater Development Company. Then-Governor Bill Clinton and Hillary Clinton had been partners in the Whitewater company with James McDougal, who was indicted for conspiracy and mail fraud, along with his wife Susan and Governor Jim Guy Tucker, Clinton's

successor in Arkansas. In 1994, Webb Hubbell, former managing partner of the law firm in which Hillary Clinton had worked and a close friend whom President Clinton had appointed deputy attorney general, entered a plea agreement with the special prosecutor investigating Whitewater. In return for his cooperation in the ongoing investigation, Hubbell was allowed to plead guilty to one count of tax evasion and one count of mail fraud. A Senate committee also launched an investigation into Whitewater, including the role of the Clintons.

In 1992, American voters had thrown the incumbent out of the White House. Taken together, the challengers, Clinton and Perot, had received 62

Newt Gingrich

percent of the vote. Two years later, disgusted and angry voters vowed again to "throw the rascals out." This time the target was the Democratic-controlled Congress, and conservative Republicans stood ready to lead the assault. Meeting in 1989 and 1990, a group led by Newt Gingrich, a Republican representative from Georgia and former history professor, had pondered ways to break America's habit of electing Democrats to the House even as it gave landslide victories to Republican presidents. Gingrich's goal, he said in 1989, was "to figure out a vision large enough (a) to seal off the left, and (b) to have everybody who's left, which is about 65 percent, cheerfully stay together in between fights." Gingrich and his allies drafted a ten-point legislative agenda, which, if events went as Gingrich hoped, would be tested in focus groups, endorsed by all Republican candidates, and enacted in the first one hundred days of the new Congress. Bush rejected the plan in 1992, and he went down to defeat. Gingrich resurrected the plan for the 1994 congressional elections and this time found many takers.

Standing on the steps of the United States Capitol in September 1994, more than three hundred Republican candidates for the House of Representatives proclaimed their

"Contract with America"

endorsement of the "Contract with America." An ambitious document, the ten-point contract called for a balanced-budget amendment to the Constitution; a presidential line-item veto; the prohibition of welfare payments to unmarried mothers under eighteen and a two-years-and-out limit on welfare benefits; more prisons and longer prison sentences; a $500-per-child tax credit; increased defense spending; a

At an outdoor press conference in April 1995, Speaker of the House Newt Gingrich reported on the state of the "Contract with America." The 104th Congress after its first hundred days, enacted few of the items in the contract. Even so, as Gingrich said, Republican victories "changed the whole debate in American politics," forcing liberals to confront conservatism's appeal.   John Harrington/Black Star.

and of the House by 230 seats to 204, with one independent. Not a single Republican incumbent lost, and many newcomers were elected, 73 in the House alone. Gingrich became Speaker of the House, and Bob Dole of Kansas became majority leader of the Senate.

The "Contract with America" was the blueprint for substantial change. "I will cooperate, but I won't compromise," Gingrich asserted. Postelection surveys showed that most Americans had never heard of the contract, but no matter. Ideological passions ran high among Republicans. With their electoral rout of the Democrats, Republicans launched a "counter-revolution" to reverse more than sixty years of federal dominance and to dismantle the welfare state. "It's the Russian Revolution in reverse," gloated Bill Kristol, a Republican strategist.

The 104th Congress convened in January 1995. Confronted with the "Contract with America," Democrats appeared helpless, and President Clinton even took time at a press conference to insist that he was still "relevant." A year later, however, "the Republican Revolution" had stalled on Capitol Hill. Political stalemate gripped the government. Twice, in 1995 and 1996, failure to enact routine appropriations bills caused the government to close most of its offices. The American people were disgruntled; some were angry. And as the 1996 election approached, hostility to the government was both widespread and intense.

 ### Disgruntled Americans: Anger and Apathy

In mid-1996 federal agents in Arizona arrested twelve members of a paramilitary group called the Viper Militia for plotting to blow up government buildings in Phoenix, including the offices of the Federal Bureau of Investigation, Internal Revenue Service, Bureau of Alcohol, Tobacco, and Firearms, and Secret Service. Later that year, five Viper Militia members pleaded guilty to illegally conspiring to make explosive devices. The home of one militia member had yielded several hundred pounds of ingredients for ammonium nitrate bombs, like the one used in Oklahoma City in 1995. Office workers in Phoenix were terrified. "We're scared to go to work," said one. "Now we know these people are here—you don't know who your neighbor is."

Terrorism, which to Americans had seemed remote and foreign, now seemed nearby and home-

reduced capital gains tax; and congressional term limits. Lobbyists from conservative organizations, including the National Rifle Association, the Christian Coalition, and the National Federation of Independent Business, applauded the contract and gave money to Republican candidates.

In 1994, the Republican Party scored one of the most smashing victories in American political history, winning both houses of Congress for the first time since 1954. Republicans also made huge gains in state-houses and legislatures; thirty of fifty governorships would be held by Republicans. In the 104th Congress, the Republicans gained control of the Senate by 53 seats to 47

The 1994 Congressional Elections

How do historians know that militia and similar far-right groups have grown and spread in the United States in the 1990s? Investigators from civil rights and human rights organizations, as well as from governmental agencies, have identified networks of Klansmen, skinheads, tax resisters, Militiamen, Patriots, and Freemen, and members of Aryan supremacist groups such as Christian Identity and the Order. One of the most reliable investigative sources is the Southern Poverty Law Center, which, in its Klanwatch Intelligence Report (winter 1997) year-end edition for 1996 (see below), identified 241 white supremacist hate groups in the United States. Another

inportant source is the Anti-Defamation League of the B'Nai B'rith; its chief investigator, Kenneth S. Stern, is the author of a definitive study, A Force upon the Plain: The American Militia Movement and the Politics of Hate (1996).

Historians can also turn to the daily media for information about hate groups. In 1996, for example, mewspapers ran frequent stories about an epidemic of suspicious fires at black churches across the South. In the first half of the year, there were more than thirty such fires; in a case in South Carolina, Klansmen pleaded guilty to arson.   Photo: Klanwatch.

grown. But while terrorism was relatively new to the American experience, hostility to the government was not. In fact, the American Revolution was an antigovernment movement directed against George III and his rule in the colonies. The Civil War began as a revolt against the federal Union. In the twentieth century, antigovern-

Americans' History of Hostility to Government

ment ideas and movements have taken various forms, ranging from McCarthyism in the 1950s, to the New Left a decade later, to the militias in the 1990s. As historian Michael Kazin has noted, "Throughout American history groups on the right and the left have seen the Federal Government as an alien force, inimical to their interests." Some antigovernment movements have been bitter and resentful, lashing out at people of color, Jews, and Roman Catholics.

Yet, whatever form these movements have taken, they have shared certain articles of faith: the government has betrayed the people, its leaders are corrupt, and the Constitution has been subverted. In the 1990s increasing numbers of Americans seemed to share this outlook.

For many Americans, the roots of their hostility to the federal government were planted in the 1960s during the Vietnam War. "What happened in the 1960s," stated Gerald Marwell, a sociologist at the University of Wisconsin, "was that the Government was successfully 'delegitimated.' We had a period from World War II through the 1950s," Marwell explained, "where the Government was seen as having rescued the nation from the Depression and successfully prosecuted the war, and then we were told in the 1960s that the emperor has no clothes and people shouldn't accept what they're told. And rather than going away, that sensibility has grown over the past 30 years."

The 1960s bequeathed two antigovernment legacies to American politics. One was a leftist critique of government as an instrument of the ruling classes. The other was a libertarian critique calling for freedom from government restraints. Student radicals in the 1960s opposed the draft and demanded

Legacies of the 1960s

the right to smoke marijuana. Conservatives in the 1990s railed against taxes and proclaimed the unfettered right to own handguns and assault weapons. Michael Kazin observed that conservatives today have a "don't-tread-on-me, get-off-my-back" attitude that "fits in perfectly with the anti-draft attitudes of the 60's."

Building on the disillusionment of the 1960s, subsequent decades have deepened Americans' distrust of the federal government. In the 1970s, the Watergate scandal and Richard Nixon's resignation from the presidency convinced many that politics was inherently corrupt. In the 1980s, the administration of Ronald Reagan added the Iran-contra scandal to the public's concerns about government corruption and cover-ups. And in the 1990s, Bill Clinton's White House was tainted by a variety of special investigations and trials, as well as by allegations about his character.

In quite a different way, President Ronald Reagan also had been effective in fueling hostility to the government, in the process shifting American politics to the right. In his inaugural address in 1981, Reagan asserted that "government is not the solu-

tion to our problem; government *is* the problem." Reagan's contribution to antigovernment sentiment in America was twofold. First, even though he was the head of the government, his rhetoric continued to be staunchly antigovernment; and he had many devoted listeners. Second, the Reagan administration—aided by a fiscally irresponsible Congress—bequeathed an enormous federal debt to future generations. As a result, there were significant financial constraints on what the government could afford to do in the future.

When Reagan became president in 1981, the total debt stood at just under $1 trillion; when he left office eight years later, it was almost $3 trillion. Under his successor, the federal

Growing Federal Debt

debt climbed even faster; when George Bush left office in 1993, it was $4.4 trillion. Massive federal funds were needed to pay the interest on the debt, not to mention to fund entitlement programs such as Social Security, Medicare, and veterans' benefits. Thus when Bill Clinton took office in 1993, not much money was available to finance his program objectives: healthcare; investments in roads, technologies, and training; increased spending for children and the poor.

Although Ronald Reagan left office in 1989, his legacy—some scholars have called it "Reagan's revenge"—profoundly influenced American politics in the 1990s. "By the time Bill Clinton got ready to run for the Presidency," sociologist Theda Skocpol has written, "Americans' distrust of the Federal Government was at an all-time high." Americans were ill tempered and quick to vote for change, as they did both in 1992 and in 1994. With the approach of the 1996 elections, unemployment was at its lowest level in six years; wages were up as well, and inflation remained low. Nevertheless, pollsters reported that Americans had not felt so disconsolate since 1980, when American hostages were held in Iran and both unemployment and inflation were very high. Americans' political alienation had deep roots. People confessed to a growing pessimism over the future of the country. When a man in Michigan was asked why Americans were complaining, his simple response was, "The Unknown. What could be."

Americans in the 1990s faced ecomomic uncertainties, such as wage stagnation and job insecurity caused by downsizing. Some Americans blamed their plight on job competition from immigrants, and they condemned affirmative action for giving what they perceived to be an unfair advantage to

African-Americans and to women. Anti-immigration sentiment found political expression in the 1990s. Politicians decried what they called the "flood" or the "invasion" of new immigrants. A *Newsweek* poll in 1993 reported that 60 percent of Americans believed that immigration was "bad for the country." And in 1994, voters in California approved Proposition 187, a ballot initiative to cut off social services to illegal aliens.

It was clear that American voters were deeply alienated from politics. They had had their fill of negative attack advertisements and political "dirty tricks." They expressed disgust not only with the presidency and Congress but also with political parties, special-interest groups, and the press. They found few politicians to admire or even trust. "They're all a bunch of leeches," stated a steelworker in Michigan. "Politics is like life insurance," chimed in a fellow worker. "It's something I got to have but I don't want to know nothing about it." Americans, at bottom, were deeply cynical in the 1990s.

Americans' Political Alienation

Clearly, the media had changed American politics. Television dominated family life, "privatizing" leisure time, as one critic noted, because "it comes at the expense of nearly every social activity outside the home, especially social gatherings and informal conversations." Most Americans got their news from television, and for some, this meant not ABC News or CNN but rather *A Current Affair* or *Hard Copy*. People seemed inattentive to political issues. "Given the increasing domination of television as the key medium of public discourse," the political scientist James Fishkin observed, "the primary process has become a duel of attack ads and sound bites fighting for the attention of an inattentive public."

Television's Influence

Many in the public were not only inattentive but pitifully uninformed. A survey in 1996 asked for the name of the vice president of the United States; four in ten did not know or got it wrong. Two out of three could not name the person who represented them in the House of Representatives; half did not know whether their representative was a Republican or Democrat. And, the survey found, less knowledgeable Americans were much more likely to be cynical about government and to

Americans' Political Ignorance

A White House aide bemoaning a spate of administration setbacks

American voters were both angry and alienated in the 1990s. This cartoon, which appeared in 1994, pictured the "voters'" delight in being able to turn the tables on Congress, which many Americans considered corrupt and unresponsive. Bill Day © *Detroit Free Press*, Tribune Media Services.

believe that actions by the federal government invariably make every problem worse. "Lack of knowledge has a practical short-term political effect," explained Robert J. Blendon of Harvard's Kennedy School of Politics. "It makes it more difficult for the president or Congress to get credit for efforts they have made; thus it supports the sense that neither group ever gets anything done."

In the 1990s American voters were angry, particularly white men. Journalists described the electorate as "cross" and "cranky" and pointed to "the raw tomato-hurling fury that has characterized and transformed modern American politics." The Republican 104th Congress elected in 1994 under Gingrich's leadership failed with much of its legislative program, but it did recast the American political debate. Many Democrats conceded that the government could not solve all problems and needed to be shrunk. Federalism was back in fashion, and both Congress and the president urged returning power to the states. Sacred cows from the New Deal and the Great Society, such as Social Security and Medicare, were under scrutiny as never before. Civil rights issues seemingly became of secondary political importance to both major parties.

As the 1996 election neared, some political observers predicted that angry voters would send Bill Clinton back to Arkansas and put a conservative Republican in the White House.

Women Voters But these pundits overlooked an essential segment of the electorate: women. Women tended to view the 104th Congress as hostile to measures essential to family welfare. Marge Roukema, a Republican representative from New Jersey, recognized the magnitude of her party's shortcomings with women when she got a phone call from her daughter. "She said, 'Mother, there are these TV ads . . . and they make you Republicans look like you're taking food out of the mouths of little babies. Are you?'" For years, political scholars had identified a "gender gap" in voting behavior: women were more likely than men to vote Democratic. In the mid-1990s, that gap threatened to become a chasm.

"Women are still bigger believers in government," explained Andrew Kohut, a veteran pollster, in 1996. "Women are stronger environmentalists, more critical of business and less critical of government. This drives their party preferences. . . ." Issues like health insurance, daycare for children, and edu-

cation were also of keen importance to women, who were more likely than men to want to see an activist government. They also were more suspicious of attempts to downsize government, fearing for the future of safety-net programs and believing that the government should do more to help families. Looking to the 1996 elections, Democrats hoped that women could do for them what "angry white men" had done for the Republicans in 1994.

 Clinton Fights Back: The Election of 1996

As the 1996 elections neared, some political observers predicted that angry voters would send Bill Clinton back to Arkansas and put a conservative Republican in the White House. But the Republicans in the 104th Congress, led by Newt Gingrich, proceeded to make the voters even angrier than Clinton had made them in his first two years. For one thing, they underestimated Clinton, believing that he would fold under pressure. But Clinton fought back. He frustrated the Republicans by positioning himself as the protector of the federal programs and policies under assault, thereby gaining support from grateful citizens who benefited from the programs.

While Americans applauded economy in government, they were resistant to personal sacrifice. And under the "Contract with America," most of those whose benefits would be cut were members of the middle class. People worried especially about Medicare and Medicaid, aid to education and college loans, highway construction and farm subsidies, Social Security and veterans' benefits. When the Republicans attempted to turn over to the states responsibility for child nutrition programs, including school lunches, the Democrats resisted and the public was on their side. Republicans later repeated the mistake in pushing to cut spending for education and to repeal decades of environmental and occupational safety legislation.

The Republicans also made a mistake when they used the threat of a federal government shutdown as a bargaining chip in their quest for a balanced budget by the year 2002. When the government closed its doors in 1995 and 1996, the public was inconvenienced and angry. Most Americans perceived the

Government Shutdowns

Congress as ideologically inflexible but tended to see

Clinton as moderate and "reasonable." Speaker of the House Gingrich conceded that "our strategy failed" because Clinton and his allies, instead of surrendering and making a budget deal, "were tougher than I thought they would be be."

Republicans in the 104th Congress were frustrated. Their proposed constitutional amendments were defeated, and Clinton vetoed their tax cuts. Congress did make some cuts in domestic spending, but these were more than offset by increases in defense spending. Congress did pass several significant acts, including the line-item veto, which allowed the president to cut specific spending items from the federal budget. It also passed a measure to curb the federal government's practice of imposing duties—known as "unfunded mandates"—on the states without paying for them. Of far-reaching influence, the Telecommunications Act of 1996 made sweeping changes in federal law, allowing telephone companies and cable companies to compete, deregulating cable rates, and permitting media companies to own more television and radio stations. With the Freedom to Farm Act of 1996, Congress also made historic changes in farm policy, throwing out the 1938 law that established the existent system of agricultural subsidies and mandating the seven-year phase-out of payments to farmers.

As campaigns for the 1996 elections took shape, Republicans focused on Bill Clinton and the "character" issue. The special prosecutor investigating

Hint of Scandal in the White House

Whitewater began to produce indictments and even convictions. The president gave videotaped testimony, but in 1996 the McDougals and Governor Tucker were found guilty. Hillary Clinton testified before a Senate committee investigating Whitewater. She could not explain how long-lost law-firm billing records from Little Rock, which had been subpoenaed by the committee, disappeared for two years before surfacing in the family quarters of the White House. Republican anger erupted in mid-1996 when the Clinton administration acknowledged that in 1993 and 1994, on orders from the White House, the Federal Bureau of Investigation had sent over the confidential records of some nine hundred Republicans. The White House said it was a mistake; others thought it smelled of an earlier scandal, Watergate.

Misconduct and scandals had tainted the Clinton White House from the beginning. Republicans charged that the Clintons and their aides were left-

President Bill Clinton suffered political repudiation in the Republican sweep of Congress in 1994. But two years later his popularity was on an upswing. One highlight of his political recovery was the 1996 Democratic convention in Chicago. Here he enjoys the closing ceremonies with wife Hillary Rodham Clinton (left) and daughter Chelsea (center) Robert Kusel © Tony Stone Images.

overs from the 1960s counterculture; they called them "leftwing elitists" and "McGovernicks" after the young activists who supported George McGovern in 1972. During his administration, Bill Clinton was the object of frequent criticism, and often his character was the issue as he wavered on issues and as allegations of infidelity abounded. But, as one reporter noted, "If Ronald Reagan was the Teflon President, then Bill Clinton is the Timex President. He takes his lickings, keeps on ticking." The 1996 presidential election with Bill Clinton as the incumbent would test how durable he really was.

A number of Republicans entered the 1996 presidential primaries, confident that President Clinton was vulnerable to defeat. Among the hopefuls was Senator Bob Dole of Kansas.

The Campaigns Unfold

Dole, the Senate majority leader, was an army veteran of the Second World War who had been badly wounded while fighting in Italy. He had served in Congress for thirty-five

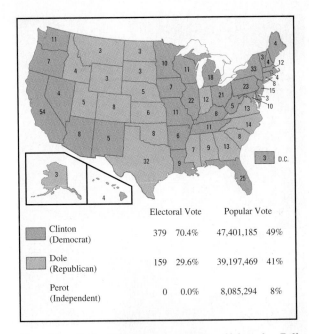

Electoral Vote   Popular Vote

	Electoral Vote		Popular Vote	
Clinton (Democrat)	379	70.4%	47,401,185	49%
Dole (Republican)	159	29.6%	39,197,469	41%
Perot (Independent)	0	0.0%	8,085,294	8%

Presidential Election, 1996 *Although Bill Clinton did not win a majority of the vote, he came close at 49 percent, winning thirty-one states to nineteen for Bob Dole. Ross Perot, with 8 percent of the vote, was less of a factor than in 1992, when he had earned 19 percent of the vote. Despite Clinton's victory, the Republicans retained control of both houses of Congress.*

years, and many Republicans, believing that he had earned his party's presidential nomination, cast their votes for him. Dole chose Jack Kemp, a former congressman, cabinet officer, and professional football player, to be his running mate.

Both the Clinton-Gore and the Dole-Kemp tickets were amply funded by campaign contributors. Businesses and labor unions alike used loopholes in the campaign-financing laws to donate tens of millions of dollars, much of it used for costly attack advertisements on television. Candidates running for federal offices in 1996 spent a total of $2 billion. Negative advertisements offended many voters, who eschewed both parties. In fact, when Americans went to the polls in 1996, turnout was a mere 49 percent, the lowest rate since before the Second World War.

Bill Clinton was reelected with 49 percent of the popular vote. Although he did not achieve his goal of winning a majority of the vote, he easily defeated Dole (41 percent) and Ross Perot (8 percent), who

again had run as an independent. Clinton won the entire Northeast and Northwest and most of the Midwest, as well as crucial battleground states, including Pennsylvania, Illinois, Florida, Arizona, and California. Dole carried most of the South, the western states of Idaho, Wyoming, and Utah, and several plains states (see map). Although the Republicans lost the contest for the White House, they retained control of both houses of Congress.

In 1996 Clinton ran as a conservative, calling for a balanced budget and family values such as "fighting for the family-leave law or the assault-weapons ban or the Brady Bill or the V-chip for parents or trying to keep tobacco out of the hands of kids." Clinton also called for an end to federal welfare "as we know it." And in 1996, he signed two laws that repealed New Deal benefits that had been in existence for sixty years. One act eliminated the section of the Social Security Act of 1935 that provided Aid to Families with Dependent Children (AFDC). The other, the Freedom to Farm Act, authorized the phasing out of agricultural subsidy payments to farmers.

Bill Clinton, the first Democratic president to be reelected since Franklin D. Roosevelt in 1936, accomplished that feat partly by running against Roosevelt's New Deal. It was evident that the conservative revolution that had germinated in the 1970s, and that had come to fruition during the Reagan years of the 1980s, was very much alive in the late 1990s as the United States prepared to enter the twenty-first century.

 Conclusion

Throughout American history, the closing decade of a century has been a time of turbulence and transformation. In the 1690s, as the colonists struggled to adjust to the Navigation Acts that governed their membership in the far-flung British mercantile empire, King William's War pitted the French and their Indian allies against British-Americans, and accusations of witchcraft in Massachusetts revealed political disorder and a society in stress. In the 1790s, a new republic with a new constitution confronted the Whiskey Rebellion, the Alien and Sedition Acts, the rise of partisan political parties, and entanglement in Europe's wars. The 1890s witnessed devastating depression, agrarian revolt, burgeoning cities, bloody labor strikes, the emergence of corporate giants, the

From the beginning of the American republic, all secretaries of state had been men. This changed in 1997, when Madeleine Albright, the ambassador to the United Nations, was nominated by President Clinton to be the secretary of state. Immediately after being sworn in, Secretary Albright traveled to trouble spots around the world. Here she is speaking at her first press conference.   Corbis-Bettmann.

onset of a major reform movement, and a new empire abroad that anti-imperialists considered a violation of United States principles.

As the twenty-first century beckoned, the later 1990s, too, promised to be a period of adjustment for Americans. As in prior centuries, Americans had lost faith in their government; confidence in government, which was expressed by 76 percent of Americans in 1964, had plummeted to 19 percent by 1996. Events in 1997 reinforced the public's disdain for government. Whitewater and charges of sexual harassment dogged Bill Clinton. And in January, the day after Clinton's second presidential inauguration, the House of Representatives voted (395 to 28) to reprimand Speaker Newt Gingrich and fine him $300,000 for using tax-exempt donations for political purposes and submitting false statements about this money to the House.

In his second inaugural address, President Bill Clinton spoke of the past, and of the enduring challenges facing the United States as it stood "at the edge of a new century, in a new millennium. . . ." Three times, he pointed out, the United States had

entered a new century. And still, "the challenge of our past remains the challenge of our future—will we be one nation, one people, with one common destiny, or not?" In the poem he read at the inauguration, Miller Williams also evoked America's history. Titled "Of History and Hope," his poem called upon Americans to remember their heritage of justice and compassion, of freedom and equality, and to convey that heritage to the children, who are the future:

> All this in the hands of children, eyes already set
> on a land we can never visit—it isn't there yet—
> but looking through their eyes, we can see
> what our long gift to them may come to be.
> If we can truly remember, they will not forget.

Suggestions for Further Reading

The Bush Administration

Donald L. Bartlett and James B. Steele, *America: What Went Wrong?* (1992); Colin Campbell and Bert A. Rockman, eds., *The Bush Presidency* (1991); Michael Duffy and Don Goodgame,

Marching in Place: The Status Quo Presidency of George Bush (1992); Dilys M. Hill and Phil Williams, eds., *The Bush Presidency* (1994).

Politics and the Election of 1992

Alan Ehrenhalt, *The United States of Ambition: Politicians, Power, and the Pursuit of Office* (1991); William Greider, *Who Will Tell the People: The Betrayal of American Democracy* (1992); Kathleen Hall Jamieson, *Dirty Politics* (1992); Kevin Phillips, *The Politics of Rich and Poor* (1990); Gerald Posner, *Citizen Perot* (1996); Ruy A. Teixeira, *The Disappearing American Voter* (1992); George F. Will, *Restoration: Congress, Term Limits and the Recovery of Deliberative Democracy* (1992).

The Clinton Administration

Haynes Johnson and David S. Broder, *The System: The American Way of Politics at the Breaking Point* (1996); David Maraniss, *First in His Class: A Biography of Bill Clinton* (1995); Roger Morris, *Partners in Power: The Clintons and Their America* (1996); Richard Reeves, *Running in Place: How Bill Clinton Disappointed America* (1996); James B. Stewart, *Blood Sport: The President and His Adversaries* (1996); Martin Walker, *The President We Deserve* (1996); Bob Woodward, *The Agenda: Inside the Clinton White House* (1994).

American Society in the 1990s

Sheldon Danziger and Peter Gottschalk, *American Unequal* (1996); Robert H. Frank and Philip J. Cook, *The Winner-Take-All Society* (1995); Herbert J. Gans, *The War Against the Poor* (1995); David M. Gordon, *Fat and Mean: The Corporate Squeeze of Working Americans and the Myth of Managerial "Downsizing"* (1996); Jennifer L. Hochschild, *Facing Up to the American Dream: Race, Class, and the Soul of the Nation* (1995); Jonathan Kozol, *Amazing Grace: The Lives of Children and the Conscience of a Nation* (1995); Katherine S. Newman, *Declining Fortunes: The Withering of the American Dream* (1993); New York Times, *The Downsizing of America* (1996); Michael D. Yates, *Longer Hours, Fewer Jobs* (1994).

Disgruntled Americans: Political Apathy and Antigovernment Movements

Stephen Ansolabehere and Shanto Iyengar, *Going Negative: How Attack Ads Shrink and Polarize the Electorate* (1995); Sara Diamond, *Roads to Dominion: Right-Wing Movements and Political Power in America* (1995); E. J. Dionne, Jr., *Why Americans Hate Politics* (1991); James Fallows, *Breaking the News: How the Media Undermine American Democracy* (1996); Thomas Ferguson, *Golden Rule: The Investment Theory of Party Competition and the Logic of Money-Driven Political Systems* (1995); William Martin, *With God on Our Side: The Rise of the Religious Right in America* (1996); Larry J. Sabato and Glenn R. Simpson, *Dirty Little Secrets: The Persistence of Corruption in American Politics* (1996); Robert J. Samuelson, *The Good Life and Its Discontents: The American Dream in an Age of Entitlements* (1995); Kenneth S. Stern, *A Force upon the Plain: The American Militia Movement and the Politics of Hate* (1996).

The Election of 1994: "The Republican Revolution"

Dan Balz and Ronald Brownstein, *Storming the Gates: Protest Politics and the Republican Revival* (1996); Elizabeth Drew, *Showdown: The Struggle Between the Gingrich Congress and the Clinton White House* (1996); David Frum, *Dead Right* (1994); David Maraniss and Michael Weisskopf, *"Tell Newt to Shut Up!"* (1996).

The 1996 Election and the Future of American Politics

E. J. Dionne, Jr., *They Only Look Dead: Why Progressives Will Dominate the Next Political Era* (1996); James S. Fishskin, *The Voice of the People: Public Opinion and Democracy* (1995); Jake H. Thompson, *Bob Dole* (1994); Michael Tomasky, *Left for Dead: The Life, Death, and Possible Resurrection of Progressive Politics in America* (1996); Ben J. Wattenberg, *Values Matter Most: How Republicans or Democrats or a Third Party Can Win and Renew the American Way of Life* (1995); Jacob Weisberg, *In Defense of Government: The Fall and Rise of Public Trust* (1996); Bob Woodward, *The Choice* (1996).

Historical Reference Books by Subject:
Encyclopedias, Dictionaries, Atlases, Chronologies, and Statistics

American History: General

Gorton Carruth, ed., *The Encyclopedia of American Facts and Dates* (1993); *Dictionary of American History* (1976) and Joan Hoff and Robert H. Ferrell, eds., *Supplement* (1996); Eric Foner and John A. Garraty, eds., *The Reader's Companion to American History* (1991); Bernard Grun, *The Timetables of History* (1991); *International Encyclopedia of the Social Sciences* (1968–); Richard B. Morris and Jeffrey B. Morris, eds., *Encyclopedia of American History* (1996); Harry Ritter, *Dictionary of Concepts in History* (1986); Arthur M. Schlesinger, Jr., ed., *The Almanac of American History* (1983); Lawrence Urdang, ed., *The Timetables of American History* (1996); U.S. Bureau of the Census, *Historical Statistics of the United States* (1975).

American History: General, Twentieth Century

John D. Buenker and Edward R. Kantowicz, eds., *Historical Dictionary of the Progressive Era, 1890–1920* (1988); Robert H. Ferrell and John S. Bowman, eds., *The Twentieth Century: An Almanac* (1984); George H. Gallup, *The Gallup Poll: Public Opinion, 1935–1971* (1972), *1972–1977* (1978), and annual reports (1979–); Stanley Hochman and Eleanor Hochman, *A Dictionary of Contemporary American History* (1993); Stanley I. Kutler, ed., *Encyclopedia of the United States in the Twentieth Century* (1995); Peter B. Levy, *Encyclopedia of the Reagan-Bush Years* (1996); James S. Olson, *Historical Dictionary of the 1920s* (1988); Thomas Parker and Douglas Nelson, *Day by Day: The Sixties* (1983).

American History: General Atlases and Gazetteers

Geoffrey Barraclough, ed., *The Times Atlas of World History* (1994); Rodger Doyle, *Atlas of Contemporary America* (1994); Robert H. Ferrell and Richard Natkiel, *Atlas of American History* (1987); Edward W. Fox, *Atlas of American History* (1964); Archie Hobson, *The Cambridge Gazetteer of the United States and Canada* (1996); Eric Homberger, *The Penguin Historical Atlas of North America* (1995); Kenneth T. Jackson and James T. Adams, *Atlas of American History*

(1978); Catherine M. Mattson and Mark T. Mattson, *Contemporary Atlas of the United States* (1990); National Geographic Society, *Historical Atlas of the United States* (1994); U.S. Department of the Interior, *National Atlas of the United States* (1970). Other atlases are listed under specific categories.

American History: General Biographies

Lucian Boia, ed., *Great Historians of the Modern Age* (1991); John S. Bowman, *The Cambridge Dictionary of American Biography* (1995); *Current Biography* (1940–); *Dictionary of American Biography* (1928–); John Garraty and Jerome L. Sternstein, eds., *The Encyclopedia of American Biography* (1996); *National Cyclopedia of American Biography* (1898–). Other biographical works appear under specific categories.

African Americans

Molefi Asante and Mark T. Mattson, *Historical and Cultural Atlas of African-Americans* (1991); John N. Ingham, *African-American Business Leaders* (1993); Bruce Kellner, *The Harlem Renaissance* (1984); Rayford W. Logan and Michael R. Winston, eds., *The Dictionary of American Negro Biography* (1983); W. A. Low and Virgil A. Clift, eds., *Encyclopedia of Black America* (1981); Sharon Harley, *The Timetables of African-American History* (1995); Darlene C. Hine et al., eds., *Black Women in White America* (1994); Charles D. Lowery and John F. Marszalek, eds., *Encyclopedia of African-American Civil Rights* (1992); Randall M. Miller and John D. Smith, eds., *Dictionary of Afro-American Slavery* (1997); Larry G. Murphy et al., eds., *Encyclopedia of African American Religions* (1993); Harry A. Ploski and James Williams, eds., *The Negro Almanac* (1989); Dorothy C. Salem, ed., *African American Women* (1993).

American Revolution and Colonies

Richard Blanco and Paul Sanborn, eds., *The American Revolution* (1993); Lester J. Cappon, ed., *Atlas of Early*

American History: The Revolutionary Era, 1760–1790 (1976); Jacob E. Cooke, ed., *Encyclopedia of the American Colonies* (1993); John M. Faragher, ed., *The Encyclopedia of Colonial and Revolutionary America* (1990); Jack P. Greene and J. R. Pole, eds., *The Blackwell Encyclopedia of the American Revolution* (1991); Douglas W. Marshall and Howard H. Peckham, *Campaigns of the American Revolution* (1976); Gregory Palmer, ed., *Biographical Sketches of Loyalists of the American Revolution* (1984); John W. Raimo, ed., *Biographical Directory of American Colonial and Revolutionary Governors, 1607–1789* (1980); *Rand-McNally Atlas of the American Revolution* (1974); Seymour I. Schwartz, *The French and Indian War, 1754–1763* (1995).

Architecture

William D. Hunt, Jr., ed., *Encyclopedia of American Architecture* (1980).

Business and the Economy

Christine Ammer and Dean S. Ammer, *Dictionary of Business and Economics* (1983); Douglas Auld and Graham Bannock, *The American Dictionary of Economics* (1983); Michael J. Freeman, *Atlas of World Economy* (1991); Douglas Greenwald, *Encyclopedia of Economics* (1982); John N. Ingham, *Biographical Dictionary of American Business Leaders* (1983); John N. Ingham and Lynne B. Feldman, *Contemporary American Business Leaders* (1990); William H. Mulligan, Jr., ed., *A Historical Dictionary of American Industrial Language* (1988); Glenn G. Munn, *Encyclopedia of Banking and Finance* (1973); Glenn Porter, *Encyclopedia of American Economic History* (1980); Richard Robinson, *United States Business History, 1602–1988* (1990). See also "African Americans" and "Transportation."

Cities and Towns

Charles Abrams, *The Language of Cities: A Glossary of Terms* (1971); John L. Androit, ed., *Township Atlas of the United States* (1979); Melvin G. Holli and Peter d'A. Jones, eds., *Biographical Dictionary of American Mayors, 1820–1980: Big City Mayors* (1981); Kenneth T. Jackson, ed., *Encyclopedia of New York City* (1995); Ory M. Nergal, ed., *The Encyclopedia of American Cities* (1980); David D. Van Tassel and John J. Grabowski, eds., *The Dictionary of Cleveland Biography* (1996); David D. Van Tassel and John J. Grabowski, eds., *The Encyclopedia of Cleveland History* (1987). See also "Politics and Government."

Civil War and Reconstruction

Mark M. Boatner III, *The Civil War Dictionary* (1988); Richard N. Current, ed., *Encyclopedia of the Confederacy* (1993); John T. Hubbell and James W. Geary, eds., *Biographical Dictionary of the Union* (1995); Kenneth C. Martis, *The Historical Atlas of the Congresses of the Confederate States of America: 1861–1865* (1994); James M. McPherson, ed., *The Atlas of the Civil War* (1994); Mark E. Neely, Jr., *The Abraham Lincoln Encyclopedia* (1982); Craig L. Symonds, *A Battlefield Atlas of the Civil War* (1983); Hans L. Trefousse, *Historical Dictionary of Reconstruction* (1991); U.S. War Department, *The Official Atlas of the Civil War* (1958); Jon L. Wakelyn, ed., *Biographical Dictionary of the Confederacy* (1977); Ezra J. Warner and W. Buck Yearns, *Biographical Register of the Confederate Congress* (1975); Steven E. Woodworth, ed., *The American Civil War* (1996). See also "South" and "Politics and Government."

Constitution, Supreme Court, and Judiciary

Congressional Quarterly, *The Supreme Court A to Z* (1994); Kermit L. Hall, ed., *The Oxford Companion to the Supreme Court of the United States* (1992); Richard F. Hixson, *Mass Media and the Constitution* (1989); Robert J. Janosik, ed., *Encyclopedia of the American Judicial System* (1987); John W. Johnson, ed., *Historic U.S. Court Cases, 1690–1990* (1992); Arthur S. Leonard, ed., *Sexuality and the Law* (1993); Leonard W. Levy et al., eds., *Encyclopedia of the American Constitution* (1986); Fred R. Shapiro, *The Oxford Dictionary of American Legal Quotations* (1993); Melvin I. Urofsky, ed., *The Supreme Court Justices* (1994). See also "Politics and Government."

Crime, Violence, Police, and Prisons

William G. Bailey, *Encyclopedia of Police Science* (1994); Sanford H. Kadish, ed., *Encyclopedia of Crime and Justice* (1983); Marilyn D. McShane and Frank P. Williams III, eds., *Encyclopedia of American Prisons* (1995); Michael Newton and Judy Ann Newton, *The FBI Most Wanted* (1989); Michael Newton and Judy Ann Newton, *Racial and Religious Violence in America* (1991); Michael Newton and Judy Newton, *The Ku Klux Klan* (1990); Carl Sifakis, *Encyclopedia of Assassinations* (1990); Carl Sifakis, *The Encyclopedia of American Crime* (1982).

Culture and Folklore

Hennig Cohen and Tristam Potter Coffin, eds., *The Folklore of American Holidays* (1987); Richard M. Dorson, ed., *Handbook of American Folklore* (1983); Robert L. Gale, *A Cultural Encyclopedia of the 1850s in America* (1993); Robert L. Gale, *The Gay Nineties in America* (1992); M. Thomas Inge, ed., *Handbook of American Popular Culture* (1979–1981); Wolfgang Mieder et al., eds., *A Dictionary of American Proverbs* (1992); J. F. Rooney, Jr., et al., eds., *This Remarkable Continent: An Atlas of United States and Canadian Society and Cultures* (1982); Jane Stern and Michael Stern, *Encyclopedia of Pop Culture* (1992); Justin Wintle, ed., *Makers of Nineteenth Century Culture, 1800–1914* (1982). See also "Entertainment," "Mass Media and Journalism," "Music," and "Sports."

Education and Libraries

Lee C. Deighton, ed., *The Encyclopedia of Education* (1971); Joseph C. Kiger, ed., *Research Institutions and Learned*

Societies (1982); John F. Ohles, ed., *Biographical Dictionary of American Educators* (1978); Wayne A. Wiegard and Donald E. Davis, Jr., eds., *Encyclopedia of Library History* (1994).

Entertainment

Tim Brooks and Earle Marsh, *The Complete Directory to Prime Time Network and Cable TV Shows, 1946–Present* (1995); Barbara N. Cohen-Stratyner, *Biographical Dictionary of Dance* (1982); John Dunning, *Tune in Yesterday* (radio) (1967); Larry Langman and Edgar Borg, *Encyclopedia of American War Films* (1989); Larry Langman and David Ebner, *Encyclopedia of American Spy Films* (1990); *Notable Names in the American Theater* (1976); *New York Times Encyclopedia of Television* (1977); Andrew Sarris, *The American Cinema: Directors and Directions, 1929–1968* (1968); Anthony Slide, *The American Film Industry* (1986); Anthony Slide, *The Encyclopedia of Vaudeville* (1994); Evelyn M. Truitt, *Who Was Who on Screen* (1977); Don B. Wilmeth and Tice L. Miller, eds., *The Cambridge Guide to American Theatre* (1993). See also "Culture and Folklore," "Mass Media and Journalism," "Music," and "Sports."

Environment and Conservation

André R. Cooper, ed., *Cooper's Comprehensive Environmental Desk Reference* (1996); Forest History Society, *Encyclopedia of American Forest and Conservation History* (1983); Irene Franck and David Brownstone, *The Green Encyclopedia* (1992); Robert J. Mason and Mark T. Mattson, *Atlas of United States Environmental Issues* (1990); Robert Paehlke, ed., *Conservation and Environmentalism* (1995); World Resources Institute, *Environmental Almanac* (1992).

Exploration: From Columbus to Space

Silvio A. Bedini, ed., *The Christopher Columbus Encyclopedia* (1992); Michael Cassutt, *Who's Who in Space* (1987); W. P. Cumming et al., *The Discovery of North America* (1972); William Goetzmann and Glyndwr Williams, *The Atlas of North American Exploration* (1992); Clive Holland, *Arctic Exploration and Development* (1993); Adrian Johnson, *America Explored* (1974); Kenneth Nebenzahl, *Atlas of Columbus and the Great Discoveries* (1990). See also "Science and Technology."

Foreign Relations

Thomas S. Arms, *Encyclopedia of the Cold War* (1994); Gerard Chaliand and Jean-Pierre Rageau, *Strategic Atlas* (1990); Alexander DeConde, ed., *Encyclopedia of American Foreign Policy* (1978); Margaret B. Denning and J. K. Sweeney, *Handbook of American Diplomacy* (1992); Graham Evans and Jeffrey Newnham, eds., *The Dictionary of World Politics* (1990); John E. Findling, *Dictionary of American Diplomatic History* (1989); Chas. W. Freeman, Jr., *The Diplomat's Dictionary* (1997); Michael Kidron and Ronald Segal, *The State of the World Atlas* (1995); Bruce W.

Jentleson and Thomas G. Paterson, eds., *Encyclopedia of U.S. Foreign Relations* (1997); Warren F. Kuehl, ed., *Biographical Dictionary of Internationalists* (1983); Edward Lawson, *Encyclopedia of Human Rights* (1991); Jack C. Plano and Roy Olton, eds., *The International Relations Dictionary* (1988); Bruce W. Watson et al., eds., *United States Intelligence: An Encyclopedia* (1990). See also "Peace Movements and Pacifism," "Politics and Government," "Military and Wars," and specific wars.

Immigration and Ethnic Groups

James P. Allen and Eugene J. Turner, *We the People: An Atlas of America's Ethnic Diversity* (1988); Gerald Chaliand and Jean-Pierre Rageau, *The Penguin Atlas of Diasporas* (1995); Francesco Cordasco, ed., *Dictionary of American Immigration History* (1990); Nicolás Kanellos, ed., *The Hispanic-American Almanac* (1993); Hyung-Chan Kim, ed., *Dictionary of Asian American History* (1986); Judy B. Litoff and Judith McDonnell, eds., *European Immigrant Women in the United States* (1994); Matt S. Meier, *Mexican American Biographies* (1988); Matt S. Meier and Feliciano Rivera, *Dictionary of Mexican American History* (1981); Sally M. Miller, ed., *The Ethnic Press in the United States* (1987); Stephan Thernstrom, ed., *Harvard Encyclopedia of American Ethnic Groups* (1980). See also "Jewish-Americans."

Jewish-Americans

American Jewish Yearbook (1899–); Jack Fischel and Sanford Pinsker, eds., *Jewish-American History and Culture* (1992); Geoffrey Wigoder, *Dictionary of Jewish Biography* (1991). See also "Immigration and Ethnic Groups."

Labor

Ronald L. Filippelli, *Labor Conflict in the United States* (1990); Gary M. Fink, ed., *Biographical Dictionary of American Labor* (1984); Gary M. Fink, ed., *Labor Unions* (1977); Philip S. Foner, *First Facts of American Labor* (1984).

Literature

James T. Callow and Robert J. Reilly, *Guide to American Literature* (1976–1977); *Dictionary of Literary Biography* (1978–); Eugene Ehrlich and Gorton Carruth, *The Oxford Illustrated Literary Guide to the United States* (1982); Jon Tuska and Vicki Piekarski, *Encyclopedia of Frontier and Western Fiction* (1983). See also "Culture and Folklore," "The South," and "Women."

Mass Media and Journalism

Robert V. Hudson, *Mass Media* (1987); Joseph P. McKerns, ed., *Biographical Dictionary of American Journalism* (1989); William H. Taft, ed., *Encyclopedia of Twentieth-Century Journalists* (1986). See also "Constitution, Supreme Court, and Judiciary," "Entertainment," and "Immigration and Ethnic Groups."

Medicine and Nursing

Rima D. Apple, ed., *Women, Health, and Medicine in America* (1990); Vern L. Bullough et al., eds., *American Nursing: A Biographical Dictionary* (1988); Martin Kaufman et al., eds., *Dictionary of American Nursing Biography* (1988); Martin Kaufman et al., eds., *Dictionary of American Medical Biography* (1984); George L. Maddox, ed., *The Encyclopedia of Aging* (1987).

Military and Wars

William M. Arkin et al., *Encyclopedia of the U.S. Military* (1990); Charles D. Bright, ed., *Historical Dictionary of the U.S. Air Force* (1992); Andre Corvisier, ed., *A Dictionary of Military History* (1994); R. Ernest Dupuy and Trevor N. Dupuy, *The Harper Encyclopedia of Military History* (1993); John E. Jessup, ed., *Encyclopedia of the American Military* (1994); Stanley I. Kutler, ed., *Encyclopedia of the Vietnam War* (1996); Kenneth Macksey and William Woodhouse, *The Penguin Encyclopedia of Modern Warfare* (1992); Franklin D. Margiotta, ed., *Brassey's Encyclopedia of Naval Forces and Warfare* (1996); James I. Matray, ed., *Historical Dictionary of the Korean War* (1991); Trevor Royle, *A Dictionary of Military Quotations* (1990); Stanley Sandler, ed., *The Korean War* (1995); Roger J. Spiller and Joseph G. Dawson III, eds., *Dictionary of American Military Biography* (1984); Jerry K. Sweeney, ed., *A Handbook of American Military History* (1996); Peter G. Tsouras et al., *The United States Army* (1991); U.S. Military Academy, *The West Point Atlas of American Wars, 1689–1953* (1959); Bruce W. Watson et al., eds., *United States Intelligence* (1990); *Webster's American Military Biographies* (1978); Bruce W. Watson and Susan M. Watson, *The United States Air Force* (1992); Bruce W. Watson and Susan M. Watson, *The United States Navy* (1991). See also "American Revolution and Colonies," "Civil War and Reconstruction," "Vietnam War," and "World War II."

Music

John Chilton, *Who's Who of Jazz* (1972); Donald Clarke, ed., *The Penguin Encyclopedia of Popular Music* (1989); Edward Jablonski, *The Encyclopedia of American Music* (1981); Roger Lax and Frederick Smith, *The Great Song Thesaurus* (1984); Philip D. Morehead, *The New International Dictionary of Music* (1993); Austin Sonnier, Jr., *A Guide to the Blues* (1994). See also "Culture and Folklore" and "Entertainment."

Native Americans and Indian Affairs

Gretchen M. Bataille, ed., *Native American Women* (1992); Michael Coe et al., *Atlas of Ancient America* (1986); Mary B. Davis, ed., *Native America in the Twentieth Century* (1994); Frederick J. Dockstader, *Great North American Indians* (1977); *Handbook of North American Indians* (1978–); Sam D. Gill and Irene F. Sullivan, *Dictionary of Native American Mythology* (1992); J. Norman Heard et al., *Handbook of the American Frontier: Four Centuries of Indian-White Relationships* (1987–); Barry Klein, ed., *Reference Encyclopedia of the American Indian* (1993); Francis P. Prucha, *Atlas of American Indian Affairs* (1990); Paul Stuart, *Nation Within a Nation: Historical Statistics of American Indians* (1987); Helen H. Tanner, ed., *Atlas of Great Lakes Indian History* (1987); Carl Waldman, *Encyclopedia of Native American Tribes* (1988); Carl Waldman, *Atlas of the North American Indian* (1985).

The New Deal and Franklin D. Roosevelt

Otis L. Graham, Jr., and Meghan R. Wander, eds., *Franklin D. Roosevelt: His Life and Times* (1985); James S. Olson, ed., *Historical Dictionary of the New Deal* (1985). See also "Politics and Government."

Peace Movements and Pacifism

Harold Josephson et al., eds., *Biographical Dictionary of Modern Peace Leaders* (1985); Ervin Laszlo and Jong Y. Yoo, eds., *World Encyclopedia of Peace* (1986); Robert S. Meyer, *Peace Organizations Past and Present* (1988); Nancy L. Roberts, *American Peace Writers, Editors, and Periodicals* (1991). See also "Military and Wars" and specific wars.

Politics and Government: General

Erik W. Austin and Jerome M. Clubb, *Political Facts of the United States Since 1789* (1986); *The Columbia Dictionary of Political Biography* (1991); Jack P. Greene, ed., *Encyclopedia of American Political History* (1984); Leon Hurwitz, *Historical Dictionary of Censorship in the United States* (1985); Earl R. Kruschke, *Encyclopedia of Third Parties in the United States* (1991); Edwin V. Mitchell, *An Encyclopedia of American Politics* (1968); Philip Rees, *Biographical Dictionary of the Extreme Right Since 1890* (1991); Charles R. Ritter et al., *American Legislative Leaders, 1850–1910* (1989); William Safire, *Safire's Political Dictionary* (1978); Edward L. Schapsmeier and Frederick H. Schapsmeier, eds., *Political Parties and Civic Action Groups* (1981); Robert Scruton, *A Dictionary of Political Thought* (1982); Jay M. Shafritz, *The HarperCollins Dictionary of American Government and Politics* (1992). See also "Cities and Towns," "Constitution, Supreme Court, and Judiciary," "States," and the following sections.

Politics and Government: Congress

Donald C. Brown et al., eds., *The Encyclopedia of the United States Congress* (1995); Stephen G. Christianson, *Facts About the Congress* (1996); Congressional Quarterly, *Biographical Directory of the American Congress, 1774–1996* (1997); Congressional Quarterly, *Congress and the Nation, 1945–1984* (1965–1985); Kenneth C. Martis, *Historical Atlas of Political Parties in the United States Congress, 1789–1989* (1989); Kenneth C. Martis, *Historical Atlas of United States Congressional Districts, 1789–1983* (1982); Joel H. Silbey, ed., *Encyclopedia of the American Legislative System* (1994).

Politics and Government: Election Statistics

Congressional Quarterly, *Guide to U.S. Elections* (1975); L. Sandy Maisel, ed., *Political Parties and Elections in the United States* (1991); Richard M. Scammon et al., eds., *America Votes* (1956–); Harold W. Stanley and Richard G. Niemi, *Vital Statistics on American Politics* (1990); G. Scott Thomas, *The Pursuit of the White House: A Handbook of Presidential Election Statistics and History* (1987).

Politics and Government: Presidency and Executive Branch

Henry F. Graff, *The Presidents* (1996); Bernard S. Katz and C. Daniel Vencill, eds., *Biographical Dictionary of the United States Secretaries of the Treasury, 1789–1995* (1996); Richard S. Kirkendall, ed., *The Harry S Truman Encyclopedia* (1989); Leonard W. Levy and Louis Fisher, eds., *Encyclopedia of the American Presidency* (1993); Merrill D. Peterson, ed., *Thomas Jefferson: A Reference Biography* (1986); Robert A. Rutland, ed., *James Madison and the American Nation* (1994); Robert Sobel, ed., *Biographical Directory of the United States Executive Branch, 1774–1977* (1977). See other categories for various presidents.

Politics and Government: Radicalism and the Left

Mari Jo Buhle et al., eds., *The American Radical* (1994); Mari Jo Buhle et al., eds., *Encyclopedia of the American Left* (1990); David DeLeon, ed., *Leaders of the 1960s* (1994); Bernard K. Johnpoll and Harvey Klehr, eds., *Biographical Dictionary of the American Left* (1986).

Religion and Cults

Henry Bowden, *Dictionary of American Religious Biography* (1993); S. Kent Brown et al., eds., *Historical Atlas of Mormonism* (1995); John T. Ellis and Robert Trisco, *A Guide to American Catholic History* (1982); Edwin S. Gaustad, *Historical Atlas of Religion in America* (1976); Samuel S. Hill, Jr., ed., *Encyclopedia of Religion in the South* (1984); Bill J. Leonard, *Dictionary of Baptists in America* (1994); Donald Lewis, ed., *A Dictionary of Evangelical Biography* (1995); Charles H. Lippy and Peter W. Williams, eds., *Encyclopedia of the American Religious Experience* (1988); J. Gordon Melton, *The Encyclopedia of American Religions* (1987); J. Gordon Melton, *Biographical Dictionary of American Cult and Sect Leaders* (1986); J. Gordon Melton, *The Encyclopedic Handbook of Cults in America* (1992); Mark A. Noll and Nathan O. Hatch, eds., *Eerdmans Handbook to Christianity in America* (1983); Arthur C. Piepkorn, *Profiles in Belief: The Religious Bodies of the United States and Canada* (1977–1979); Paul J. Weber and W. Landis Jones, *U.S. Religious Interest Groups* (1994). See also "African Americans."

Science and Technology

James W. Cortada, *Historical Dictionary of Data Processing* (1987); Clark A. Elliott, *Biographical Index to American Science: The Seventeenth Century to 1920* (1990); Charles C. Gillispie, ed., *Dictionary of Scientific Biography* (1970–); National Academy of Sciences, *Biographical Memoirs* (1877–); Roy Porter, ed., *The Biographical Dictionary of Scientists* (1994). See also "Exploration."

Social History and Reform

Mary K. Cayton et al., eds., *Encyclopedia of American Social History* (1993); Wayne R. Dynes, ed., *Encyclopedia of Homosexuality* (1990); Louis Filler, *Dictionary of American Social Change* (1982); Louis Filler, *A Dictionary of American Social Reform* (1963); Robert S. Fogarty, *Dictionary of American Communal and Utopian History* (1980); Joseph M. Hawes and Elizabeth I. Nybakken, eds., *American Families* (1991); David Hey, ed., *The Oxford Companion to Local and Family History* (1996); Harold M. Keele and Joseph C. Kiger, eds., *Foundations* (1984); Mark E. Lender, *Dictionary of American Temperance Biography* (1984); Patricia M. Melvin, ed., *American Community Organizations* (1986); Randall M. Miller and Paul A. Cimbala, eds., *American Reform and Reformers* (1996); Roger S. Powers and William B. Vogele, eds., *Protest, Power, and Change* (1996); Alvin J. Schmidt, *Fraternal Organizations* (1980); Peter N. Stearns, ed., *Encyclopedia of Social History* (1993); Walter I. Trattner, *Biographical Dictionary of Social Welfare in America* (1986); Alden Whitman, ed., *American Reformers* (1985). See also "Crime, Violence, Police, and Prisons."

South

Edward L. Ayers and Brad Mittendorf, eds., *The Oxford Book of the American South* (1997); Robert Bain et al., eds., *Southern Writers* (1979); Kenneth Coleman and Charles S. Gurr, eds., *Dictionary of Georgia Biography* (1983); William S. Powell, ed., *Dictionary of North Carolina Biography* (1979–1996); David C. Roller and Robert W. Twyman, eds., *The Encyclopedia of Southern History* (1979); Walter P. Webb et al., eds., *The Handbook of Texas* (1952, 1976); Charles R. Wilson and William Ferris, eds., *Encyclopedia of Southern Culture* (1986). See also "Civil War and Reconstruction," "Politics and Government," and "States."

Sports

Peter C. Bjarkman, ed., *Encyclopedia of Major League Baseball Team Histories* (1991); Ralph Hickok, *The Encyclopedia of North American Sports History* (1991); Zander Hollander, *The NBA's Official Encyclopedia of Pro Basketball* (1981); Frank G. Menke and Suzanne Treat, *The Encyclopedia of Sports* (1977); *The NFL's Official Encyclopedic History of Professional Football* (1977); David L. Porter, *Biographical Dictionary of American Sports: Baseball* (1987), *Basketball and Other Indoor Sports* (1989), *Football* (1987), and *Outdoor Sports* (1988); David L. Porter, ed., *Biographical Dictionary of American Sports: 1989–1992 Supplement* (1992) and *1992–1995 Supplement* (1995); Paul

Soderberg et al., *The Big Book of Halls of Fame in the United States and Canada* (1977); David Wallechinsky, *The Complete Book of the Summer Olympics* (1996); David Wallechinsky, *The Complete Book of the Winter Olympics* (1993). See also "Culture and Folklore."

States

Roy R. Glashan, comp., *American Governors and Gubernatorial Elections, 1775–1978* (1979); John Hoffmann, ed., *A Guide to the History of Illinois* (1991); Joseph E. Kallenback and Jessamine S. Kallenback, *American State Governors, 1776–1976* (1977); Joseph N. Kane et al., eds., *Facts About the States* (1994); John E. Kleber et al., eds., *The Kentucky Encyclopedia* (1992); Thomas A. McMullin and Marie Mullaney, *Biographical Directory of the Governors of the United States, 1983–1987* (1988) and *1988–1993* (1994); Marie Mullaney, *Biographical Directory of the Governors of the United States 1988–1994* (1994); Thomas J. Noel, *Historical Atlas of Colorado* (1994); John W. Raimo, ed., *Biographical Directory of the Governors of the United States, 1978–1983* (1985); James W. Scott and Ronald L. De Lorme, *Historical Atlas of Washington* (1988); Benjamin F. Shearer and Barbara S. Shearer, *State Names, Seals, Flags, and Symbols* (1994); Robert Sobel and John W. Raimo, eds., *Biographical Directory of the Governors of the United States, 1789–1978* (1978); Richard W. Wilkie and Jack Tager, eds., *Historical Atlas of Massachusetts* (1991). See also "Politics and Government," "South," and "West and Frontier."

Transportation

Keith L. Bryant, ed., *Railroads in the Age of Regulation, 1900–1980* (1988); Rene De La Pedraja, *A Historical Dictionary of the U.S. Merchant Marine and Shipping Industry* (1994); Robert L. Frey, ed., *Railroads in the Nineteenth Century* (1988). See also "Business and the Economy."

Vietnam War

John S. Bowman, ed., *The Vietnam War: An Almanac* (1986); James S. Olson, ed., *Dictionary of the Vietnam War* (1988); Harry G. Summers, Jr., *Vietnam War Almanac* (1985). Also see "Peace Movements and Pacifism" and "Military and Wars."

West and Frontier

William A. Beck and Ynez D. Haase, *Historical Atlas of the American West* (1989); Doris O. Dawdy, *Artists of the American West* (1974–1984); J. Norman Heard, *Handbook of the American Frontier* (1987); Howard R. Lamar, ed., *The Reader's Encyclopedia of the American West* (1977); Clyde A. Milner III et al., eds., *The Oxford History of the American West* (1994); Jay Robert Nash, *Encyclopedia of Western Lawmen and Outlaws* (1992); Doyce B. Nunis, Jr., and Gloria R. Lothrop, eds., *A Guide to the History of California* (1989); Charles Phillips and Alan Axelrod, eds., *Encyclopedia of the American West* (1996); Dan L. Thrapp, *The Encyclopedia of Frontier Biography* (1988–1994); David Walker, *Biographical Directory of American Territorial Governors* (1984). See also "Literature" and "Native Americans and Indian Affairs."

Women

Anne Gibson and Timothy Fast, *The Women's Atlas of the United States* (1986); Karen Greenspan, *The Timetables of Women's History* (1996); Maggie Humm, *The Dictionary of Feminist Theory* (1990); Edward T. James et al., *Notable American Women, 1607–1950* (1971); Lina Mainiero, ed., *American Women Writers* (1979–1982); Kirstin Olsen, *Chronology of Women's History* (1994); Barbara G. Shortridge, *Atlas of American Women* (1987); Barbara Sicherman and Carol H. Green, eds., *Notable American Women, The Modern Period* (1980); Helen Tierney, ed., *Women's Studies Encyclopedia* (1991); Angela H. Zophy and Frances M. Kavenik, eds., *Handbook of American Women's History* (1990). See also "African Americans," "Immigration and Ethnic Groups," "Medicine and Nursing," and "Native Americans and Indian Affairs."

World War I

Arthur Banks, *A Military History Atlas of the First World War* (1975); Martin Gilbert, *Atlas of World War I* (1994); Holger H. Herwig and Neil M. Heyman, *Biographical Dictionary of World War I* (1982); George T. Kurian, *Encyclopedia of the First World War* (1990); Stephen Pope and Elizabeth-Anne Wheal, *The Dictionary of the First World War* (1995); Anne C. Venzon, *The United States in the First World War* (1995). See also "Military and Wars."

World War II

Marcel Baudot et al., eds., *The Historical Encyclopedia of World War II* (1980); David G. Chandler and James Lawton Collins, Jr., eds., *The D-Day Encyclopedia* (1993); I. C. B. Dear and M. R. D. Foot, eds., *The Oxford Companion to World War II* (1995); Simon Goodenough, *War Maps: Great Land Battles of World War II* (1988); Robert Goralski, *World War II Almanac, 1931–1945* (1981); John Keegan, ed., *The Times Atlas of the Second World War* (1989); George T. Kurian, *Encyclopedia of the Second World War* (1991); Norman Polmer and Thomas B. Allen, *World War II: America at War* (1991); Louis L. Snyder, *Louis L. Snyder's Historical Guide to World War II* (1982); U.S. Military Academy, *Campaign Atlas to the Second World War: Europe and the Mediterranean* (1980); Peter Young, ed., *The World Almanac Book of World War II* (1981). See also "Military and Wars."

Documents

DECLARATION OF INDEPENDENCE IN CONGRESS, JULY 4, 1776

When, in the course of human events, it becomes necessary for one people to dissolve the political bonds which have connected them with another, and to assume, among the powers of the earth, the separate and equal station to which the laws of nature and of nature's God entitle them, a decent respect to the opinions of mankind requires that they should declare the causes which impel them to the separation.

We hold these truths to be self-evident: That all men are created equal; that they are endowed by their Creator with certain unalienable rights; that among these are life, liberty, and the pursuit of happiness; that, to secure these rights, governments are instituted among men, deriving their just powers from the consent of the governed; that whenever any form of government becomes destructive of these ends, it is the right of the people to alter or to abolish it, and to institute new government, laying its foundation on such principles, and organizing its powers in such form, as to them shall seem most likely to effect their safety and happiness. Prudence, indeed, will dictate that governments long established should not be changed for light and transient causes; and accordingly all experience hath shown that mankind are more disposed to suffer, while evils are sufferable, than to right themselves by abolishing the forms to which they are accustomed. But when a long train of abuses and usurpations, pursuing invariably the same object, evinces a design to reduce them under absolute despotism, it is their right, it is their duty, to throw off such government, and to provide new guards for their future security. Such has been the patient sufferance of these colonies; and such is now the necessity which constrains them to alter their former systems of government. The history of the present King of Great Britain is a history of repeated injuries and usurpations, all having in direct object the establishment of an absolute tyranny over these states. To prove this, let facts be submitted to a candid world.

He has refused his assent to laws, the most wholesome and necessary for the public good.

He has forbidden his governors to pass laws of immediate and pressing importance, unless suspended in their operation till his assent should be obtained; and, when so suspended, he has utterly neglected to attend to them.

He has refused to pass other laws for the accommodation of large districts of people, unless those people would relinquish the right of representation in the legislature, a right inestimable to them, and formidable to tyrants only.

He has called together legislative bodies at places unusual, uncomfortable, and distant from the depository of their public records, for the sole purpose of fatiguing them into compliance with his measures.

He has dissolved representative houses repeatedly, for opposing, with manly firmness, his invasions on the rights of the people.

He has refused for a long time, after such dissolutions, to cause others to be elected; whereby the legislative powers, incapable of annihilation, have returned to the people at large for their exercise; the state remaining, in the mean time, exposed to all the dangers of invasions from without and convulsions within.

He has endeavored to prevent the population of these states; for that purpose obstructing the laws for naturalization of foreigners; refusing to pass others to encourage their migration hither, and raising the conditions of new appropriations of lands.

He has obstructed the administration of justice, by refusing his assent to laws for establishing judiciary powers.

He has made judges dependent on his will alone, for the tenure of their offices, and the amount and payment of their salaries.

He has erected a multitude of new offices, and sent hither swarms of officers to harass our people and eat out their substance.

He has kept among us, in times of peace, standing armies, without the consent of our legislatures.

He has affected to render the military independent of, and superior to, the civil power.

He has combined with others to subject us to a jurisdiction foreign to our constitution, and unacknowledged by our laws, giving his assent to their acts of pretended legislation:

For quartering large bodies of armed troops among us;

For protecting them, by a mock trial, from punishment for any murders which they should commit on the inhabitants of these states;

For cutting off our trade with all parts of the world;

For imposing taxes on us without our consent;

For depriving us, in many cases, of the benefits of trial by jury;

For transporting us beyond seas, to be tried for pretended offenses;

For abolishing the free system of English laws in a neighboring province, establishing therein an arbitrary government, and enlarging its boundaries, so as to render it at once an example and fit instrument for introducing the same absolute rule into these colonies;

For taking away our charters, abolishing our most valuable laws, and altering fundamentally the forms of our governments;

For suspending our own legislatures, and declaring themselves invested with power to legislate for us in all cases whatsoever.

He has abdicated government here, by declaring us out of his protection and waging war against us.

He has plundered our seas, ravaged our coasts, burned our towns, and destroyed the lives of our people.

He is at this time transporting large armies of foreign mercenaries to complete the works of death, desolation, and tyranny already begun with circumstances of cruelty and perfidy scarcely paralleled in the most barbarous ages, and totally unworthy the head of a civilized nation.

He has constrained our fellow-citizens, taken captive on the high seas, to bear arms against their country, to become the executioners of their friends and brethren, or to fall themselves by their hands.

He has excited domestic insurrection among us, and has endeavored to bring on the inhabitants of our frontiers the merciless Indian savages, whose known rule of warfare is an undistinguished destruction of all ages, sexes, and conditions.

In every stage of these oppressions we have petitioned for redress in the most humble terms; our repeated petitions have been answered only by repeated injury. A prince, whose character is thus marked by every act which may define a tyrant, is unfit to be the ruler of a free people.

Nor have we been wanting in our attentions to our British brethren. We have warned them, from time to time, of attempts by their legislature to extend an unwarrantable jurisdiction over us. We have reminded them of the circumstances of our emigration and settlement here. We have appealed to their native justice and magnanimity; and we have conjured them, by the ties of our common kindred, to disavow these usurpations, which would inevitably interrupt our connections and correspondence. They, too, have been deaf to the voice of justice and of consanguinity. We must, therefore, acquiesce in the necessity which denounces our separation, and hold them, as we hold the rest of mankind, enemies in war, in peace friends.

We, therefore, the representatives of the United States of America, in General Congress assembled, appealing to the Supreme Judge of the world for the rectitude of our intentions, do, in the name and by the authority of the good people of these colonies, solemnly publish and declare, that these United Colonies are, and of right ought to be, FREE AND INDEPENDENT STATES; that they are absolved from all allegiance to the British crown, and that all political connection between them and the state of Great Britain is, and ought to be, totally dissolved; and that, as free and independent states, they have full power to levy war, conclude peace, contract alliances, establish commerce, and do all other acts and things which independent states may of right do. And for the support of this declaration, with a firm reliance on the protection of Divine Providence, we mutually pledge to each other our lives, our fortunes, and our sacred honor.

JOHN HANCOCK
and fifty-five others

CONSTITUTION OF THE UNITED STATES OF AMERICA AND AMENDMENTS*

Preamble

We the people of the United States, in order to form a more perfect union, establish justice, insure domestic tranquillity, provide for the common defense, promote the general welfare, and secure the blessings of liberty to ourselves and our posterity, do ordain and establish this Constitution for the United States of America.

Article 1

Section 1 All legislative powers herein granted shall be vested in a Congress of the United States, which shall consist of a Senate and a House of Representatives.

Section 2 The House of Representatives shall be composed of members chosen every second year by the people of the several States, and the electors in each State shall have the qualifications requisite for electors of the most numerous branch of the State Legislature.

No person shall be a Representative who shall not have attained to the age of twenty-five years, and been seven years a citizen of the United States, and who shall not, when elected, be an inhabitant of that State in which he shall be chosen.

---

*Passages no longer in effect are printed in italic type.

Representatives and direct taxes shall be apportioned among the several States which may be included within this Union, according to their respective numbers, *which shall be determined by adding to the whole number of free persons, including those bound to service for a term of years and excluding Indians not taxed, three-fifths of all other persons.* The actual enumeration shall be made within three years after the first meeting of the Congress of the United States, and within every subsequent term of ten years, in such manner as they shall by law direct. The number of Representatives shall not exceed one for every thirty thousand, but each State shall have at least one Representative; *and until such enumeration shall be made, the State of New Hampshire shall be entitled to choose three, Massachusetts eight, Rhode Island and Providence Plantations one, Connecticut five, New York six, New Jersey four, Pennsylvania eight, Delaware one, Maryland six, Virginia ten, North Carolina five, South Carolina five, and Georgia three.*

When vacancies happen in the representation from any State, the Executive authority thereof shall issue writs of election to fill such vacancies.

The House of Representatives shall choose their Speaker and other officers; and shall have the sole power of impeachment.

Section 3   The Senate of the United States shall be composed of two Senators from each State, *chosen by the legislature thereof,* for six years; and each Senator shall have one vote.

Immediately after they shall be assembled in consequence of the first election, they shall be divided as equally as may be into three classes. The seats of the Senators of the first class shall be vacated at the expiration of the second year, of the second class at the expiration of the fourth year, and of the third class at the expiration of the sixth year, so that one-third may be chosen every second year; and if vacancies happen by resignation or otherwise, during the recess of the legislature of any State, the Executive thereof may make temporary appointments until the next meeting of the legislature, which shall then fill such vacancies.

No person shall be a Senator who shall not have attained to the age of thirty years, and been nine years a citizen of the United States, and who shall not, when elected, be an inhabitant of that State for which he shall be chosen.

The Vice-President of the United States shall be President of the Senate, but shall have no vote, unless they be equally divided.

The Senate shall choose their other officers, and also a President *pro tempore*, in the absence of the Vice-President, or when he shall exercise the office of President of the United States.

The Senate shall have the sole power to try all impeachments. When sitting for that purpose, they shall be on oath or affirmation. When the President of the United States is tried, the Chief Justice shall preside: and no person shall be convicted without the concurrence of two-thirds of the members present.

Judgment in cases of impeachment shall not extend further than to removal from the office, and disqualification to hold and enjoy any office of honor, trust or profit under the United States: but the party convicted shall nevertheless be liable and subject to indictment, trial, judgment and punishment, according to law.

Section 4   The times, places and manner of holding elections for Senators and Representatives shall be prescribed in each State by the legislature thereof; but the Congress may at any time by law make or alter such regulations, except as to the places of choosing Senators.

The Congress shall assemble at least once in every year, and such meeting *shall be on the first Monday in December, unless they shall by law appoint a different day.*

Section 5   Each house shall be the judge of the elections, returns and qualifications of its own members, and a majority of each shall constitute a quorum to do business; but a smaller number may adjourn from day to day, and may be authorized to compel the attendance of absent members, in such manner, and under such penalties, as each house may provide.

Each house may determine the rules of its proceedings, punish its members for disorderly behavior, and with the concurrence of two-thirds, expel a member.

Each house shall keep a journal of its proceedings, and from time to time publish the same, excepting such parts as may in their judgment require secrecy; and the yeas and nays of the members of either house on any question shall, at the desire of one-fifth of those present, be entered on the journal.

Neither house, during the session of Congress, shall, without the consent of the other, adjourn for more than three days, nor to any other place than that in which the two houses shall be sitting.

Section 6   The Senators and Representatives shall receive a compensation for their services, to be ascertained by law and paid out of the treasury of the United States. They shall in all cases except treason, felony and breach of the peace, be privileged from arrest during their attendance at the session of their respective houses, and in going to and returning from the same; and for any speech or debate in either house, they shall not be questioned in any other place.

No Senator or Representative shall, during the time for which he was elected, be appointed to any civil office under the authority of the United States, which shall have been created, or the emoluments whereof shall have been increased, during such time; and no person holding any office under the United States shall be a member of either house during his continuance in office.

Section 7   All bills for raising revenue shall originate in the House of Representatives; but the Senate may propose or concur with amendments as on other bills.

Every bill which shall have passed the House of Representatives and the Senate, shall, before it become a law, be presented to the President of the United States; if he approve he shall sign it, but if not he shall return it with objections to that house in which it originated, who shall enter the objections at large on their journal, and proceed to reconsider it. If after such reconsideration two-thirds of that house shall agree to pass the bill, it shall be sent, together with the objections, to the other house, by which it shall likewise be reconsidered, and, if approved by two-thirds of that house, it shall become a law. But in all such cases the votes of both houses shall be determined by yeas and nays, and the names of the persons voting for and against the bill shall be entered on the journal of each house respectively. If any bill shall not be returned by the President within ten days (Sundays excepted) after it shall have been presented to him, the same shall be a law, in like manner as if he had signed it, unless the Congress by their adjournment prevent its return, in which case it shall not be a law.

Every order, resolution, or vote to which the concurrence of the Senate and House of Representatives may be necessary (except on a question of adjournment) shall be presented to the President of the United States; and before the same shall take effect, shall be approved by him, or being disapproved by him, shall be repassed by two-thirds of the Senate and House of Representatives, according to the rules and limitations prescribed in the case of a bill.

Section 8   The Congress shall have power

To lay and collect taxes, duties, imposts, and excises, to pay the debts and provide for the common defense and general welfare of the United States; but all duties, imposts and excises shall be uniform throughout the United States;

To borrow money on the credit of the United States;

To regulate commerce with foreign nations, and among the several States, and with the Indian tribes;

To establish an uniform rule of naturalization, and uniform laws on the subject of bankruptcies throughout the United States;

To coin money, regulate the value thereof, and of foreign coin, and fix the standard of weights and measures;

To provide for the punishment of counterfeiting the securities and current coin of the United States;

To establish post offices and post roads;

To promote the progress of science and useful arts by securing for limited times to authors and inventors the exclusive right to their respective writings and discoveries;

To constitute tribunals inferior to the Supreme Court;

To define and punish piracies and felonies committed on the high seas and offenses against the law of nations;

To declare war, grant letters of marque and reprisal, and make rules concerning captures on land and water;

To raise and support armies, but no appropriation of money to that use shall be for a longer term than two years;

To provide and maintain a navy;

To make rules for the government and regulation of the land and naval forces;

To provide for calling forth the militia to execute the laws of the Union, suppress insurrections, and repel invasions;

To provide for organizing, arming, and disciplining the militia, and for governing such part of them as may be employed in the service of the United States, reserving to the States respectively the appointment of the officers, and the authority of training the militia according to the discipline prescribed by Congress;

To exercise exclusive legislation in all cases whatsoever, over such district (not exceeding ten miles square) as may, by cession of particular States, and the acceptance of Congress, become the seat of government of the United States, and to exercise like authority over all places purchased by the consent of the legislature of the State, in which the same shall be, for erection of forts, magazines, arsenals, dockyards, and other needful buildings; — and

To make all laws which shall be necessary and proper for carrying into execution the foregoing powers, and all other powers vested by this Constitution in the government of the United States, or in any department or officer thereof.

Section 9   *The migration or importation of such persons as any of the States now existing shall think proper to admit shall not be prohibited by the Congress prior to the year 1808; but a tax or duty may be imposed on such importation, not exceeding \$10 for each person.*

The privilege of the writ of habeas corpus shall not be suspended, unless when in cases of rebellion or invasion the public safety may require it.

No bill of attainder or ex post facto law shall be passed.

No capitation, or other direct, tax shall be laid, unless in proportion to the census or enumeration herein before directed to be taken.

No tax or duty shall be laid on articles exported from any State.

No preference shall be given by any regulation of commerce or revenue to the ports of one State over those of another; nor shall vessels bound to, or from, one State, be obliged to enter, clear, or pay duties in another.

No money shall be drawn from the treasury, but in consequence of appropriations made by law; and a regular statement and account of the receipts and expenditures of all public money shall be published from time to time.

No title of nobility shall be granted by the United States: and no person holding any office of profit or trust under them, shall, without the consent of the Congress, accept of any present, emolument, office, or title, of any kind whatever, from any king, prince, or foreign state.

Section 10   No State shall enter into any treaty, alliance, or confederation; grant letters of marque and reprisal; coin money; emit bills of credit; make anything but gold and silver coin a tender in payment of debts; pass any bill of attainder, ex post facto law, or law impairing the obligation of contracts, or grant any title of nobility.

No State shall, without the consent of Congress, lay any imposts or duties on imports or exports, except what may be absolutely necessary for executing its inspection laws: and the net produce of all duties and imposts, laid by any State on imports or exports, shall be for the use of the treasury of the United States; and all such laws shall be subject to the revision and control of the Congress.

No State shall, without the consent of Congress, lay any duty of tonnage, keep troops or ships of war in time of peace, enter into any agreement or compact with another State, or with a foreign power, or engage in war, unless actually invaded, or in such imminent danger as will not admit of delay.

Article II

Section 1 The executive power shall be vested in a President of the United States of America. He shall hold his office during the term of four years, and, together with the Vice-President, chosen for the same term, be elected as follows:

Each State shall appoint, in such manner as the legislature thereof may direct, a number of electors, equal to the whole number of Senators and Representatives to which the State may be entitled in the Congress; but no Senator or Representative, or person holding an office of trust or profit under the United States, shall be appointed an elector.

The electors shall meet in their respective States, and vote by ballot for two persons, of whom one at least shall not be an inhabitant of the same State with themselves. And they shall make a list of all the persons voted for, and of the number of votes for each; which list they shall sign and certify, and transmit sealed to the seat of government of the United States, directed to the President of the Senate. The President of the Senate shall, in the presence of the Senate and House of Representatives, open all the certificates, and the votes shall then be counted. The person having the greatest number of votes shall be the President, if such number be a majority of the whole number of electors appointed; and if there be more than one who have such majority, and have an equal number of votes, then the House of Representatives shall immediately choose by ballot one of them for President; and if no person have a majority, then from the five highest on the list said house shall in like manner choose the President. But in choosing the President the votes shall be taken by States, the representation from each State having one vote; a quorum for this purpose shall consist of a member or members from two-thirds of the States, and a majority of all the States shall be necessary to a choice. In every case, after the choice of the President, the person having the greatest number of votes of the electors shall be the Vice-President. But if there should remain two or more who have equal votes, the Senate shall choose from them by ballot the Vice-President.

The Congress may determine the time of choosing the electors and the day on which they shall give their votes; which day shall be the same throughout the United States.

No person except a natural-born citizen, *or a citizen of the United States at the time of the adoption of this Constitution,* shall be eligible to the office of President; neither shall any person be eligible to that office who shall not have attained to the age of thirty-five years, and been fourteen years a resident within the United States.

In cases of the removal of the President from office or of his death, resignation, or inability to discharge the powers and duties of the said office, the same shall devolve on the Vice-President, and the Congress may by law provide for the case of removal, death, resignation, or inability, both of the President and Vice-President, declaring what officer shall then act as President, and such officer shall act accordingly, until the disability be removed, or a President shall be elected.

The President shall, at stated times, receive for his services a compensation, which shall neither be increased nor diminished during the period for which he shall have been elected, and he shall not receive within that period any other emolument from the United States, or any of them.

Before he enter on the execution of his office, he shall take the following oath or affirmation:—"I do solemnly swear (or affirm) that I will faithfully execute the office of the President of the United States, and will to the best of my ability preserve, protect and defend the Constitution of the United States."

Section 2 The President shall be commander in chief of the army and navy of the United States, and of the militia of the several States, when called into the actual service of the United States; he may require the opinion, in writing, of the principal officer in each of the executive departments, upon any subject relating to the duties of their respective offices, and he shall have power to grant reprieves and pardons for offenses against the United States, except in cases of impeachment.

He shall have power, by and with the advice and consent of the Senate, to make treaties, provided two-thirds of the Senators present concur; and he shall nominate, and by and with the advice and consent of the Senate, shall appoint ambassadors, other public ministers and consuls, judges of the Supreme Court, and all other officers of the United States, whose appointments are not herein otherwise provided for, and which shall be established by law: but Congress may by law vest the appointment of such inferior officers, as they think proper, in the President alone, in the courts of law, or in the heads of departments.

The President shall have power to fill up all vacancies that may happen during the recess of the Senate, by granting commissions which shall expire at the end of their next session.

Section 3 He shall from time to time give to the Congress information of the state of the Union, and recommend to their consideration such measures as he shall judge necessary and expedient; he may, on extraordinary occasions, convene both houses, or either of them, and in case of disagreement between them, with respect to the time of adjournment, he may adjourn them to such time as he shall think proper; he shall receive ambassadors and other public ministers; he shall take care that the laws be faithfully executed, and shall commission all the officers of the United States.

Section 4   The President, Vice-President and all civil officers of the United States shall be removed from office on impeachment for, and on conviction of, treason, bribery, or other high crimes and misdemeanors.

Article III

Section 1   The judicial power of the United States shall be vested in one Supreme Court, and in such inferior courts as the Congress may from time to time ordain and establish. The judges, both of the Supreme and inferior courts, shall hold their offices during good behavior, and shall, at stated times, receive for their services a compensation which shall not be diminished during their continuance in office.

Section 2   The judicial power shall extend to all cases, in law and equity, arising under this Constitution, the laws of the United States, and treaties made, or which shall be made, under their authority;—to all cases affecting ambassadors, other public ministers and consuls;—to all cases of admiralty and maritime jurisdiction;—to controversies to which the United States shall be a party;—to controversies between two or more States;—*between a State and citizens of another State;*—between citizens of different States;—between citizens of the same State claiming lands under grants of different States, and between a State, or the citizens thereof, and foreign states, citizens or subjects.

In all cases affecting ambassadors, other public ministers and consuls, and those in which a State shall be party, the Supreme Court shall have original jurisdiction. In all the other cases before mentioned, the Supreme Court shall have appellate jurisdiction, both as to law and fact, with such exceptions, and under such regulations, as the Congress shall make.

The trial of all crimes, except in cases of impeachment, shall be by jury; and such trial shall be held in the State where said crimes shall have been committed; but when not committed within any State, the trial shall be at such place or places as the Congress may by law have directed.

Section 3   Treason against the United States shall consist only in levying war against them, or in adhering to their enemies, giving them aid and comfort. No person shall be convicted of treason unless on the testimony of two witnesses to the same overt act, or on confession in open court.

The Congress shall have power to declare the punishment of treason, but no attainder of treason shall work corruption of blood, or forfeiture except during the life of the person attainted.

Article IV

Section 1   Full faith and credit shall be given in each State to the public acts, records, and judicial proceedings of every other State. And the Congress may by general laws

prescribe the manner in which such acts, records, and proceedings shall be proved, and the effect thereof.

Section 2   The citizens of each State shall be entitled to all privileges and immunities of citizens in the several States.

A person charged in any State with treason, felony, or other crime, who shall flee from justice, and be found in another State, shall on demand of the executive authority of the State from which he fled, be delivered up, to be removed to the State having jurisdiction of the crime.

No person held to service or labor in one State, under the laws thereof, escaping into another, shall, in consequence of any law or regulation therein, be discharged from such service or labor, but shall be delivered up on claim of the party to whom such service or labor may be due.

Section 3   New States may be admitted by the Congress into this Union; but no new State shall be formed or erected within the jurisdiction of any other State; nor any State be formed by the junction of two or more States, or parts of States, without the consent of the legislatures of the States concerned as well as of the Congress.

The Congress shall have power to dispose of and make all needful rules and regulations respecting the territory or other property belonging to the United States; and nothing in this Constitution shall be so construed as to prejudice any claims of the United States, or of any particular State.

Section 4   The United States shall guarantee to every State in this Union a republican form of government, and shall protect each of them against invasion; and on application of the legislature, or of the executive (when the legislature cannot be convened), against domestic violence.

Article V

The Congress, whenever two-thirds of both houses shall deem it necessary, shall propose amendments to this Constitution, or, on the application of the legislatures of two-thirds of the several States, shall call a convention for proposing amendments, which, in either case, shall be valid to all intents and purposes, as part of this Constitution, when ratified by the legislatures of three-fourths of the several States, or by conventions in three-fourths thereof, as the one or the other mode of ratification may be proposed by the Congress; provided *that no amendments which may be made prior to the year one thousand eight hundred and eight shall in any manner affect the first and fourth clauses in the ninth section of the first article;* and that no State, without its consent, shall be deprived of its equal suffrage in the Senate.

Article VI

All debts contracted and engagements entered into, before the adoption of this Constitution, shall be as valid against the United States under this Constitution, as under the Confederation.

This Constitution, and the laws of the United States which shall be made in pursuance thereof; and all treaties made, or which shall be made, under the authority of the United States, shall be the supreme law of the land; and the judges in every State shall be bound thereby, anything in the Constitution or laws of any State to the contrary notwithstanding.

The Senators and Representatives before mentioned, and the members of the several State legislatures, and all executive and judicial officers, both of the United States and of the several States, shall be bound by oath or affirmation to support this Constitution; but no religious test shall ever be required as a qualification to any office or public trust under the United States.

Article VII

The ratification of the conventions of nine States shall be sufficient for the establishment of this Constitution between the States so ratifying the same.

Done in Convention by the unanimous consent of the States present, the seventeenth day of September in the year of our Lord one thousand seven hundred and eighty-seven and of the Independence of the United States of America the twelfth. In witness whereof we have hereunto subscribed our names.

GEORGE WASHINGTON
and thirty-seven others

Amendments to the Constitution*

Amendment I

Congress shall make no law respecting an establishment of religion, or prohibiting the free exercise thereof; or abridging the freedom of speech, or of the press; or the right of the people peaceably to assemble, and to petition the government for a redress of grievances.

Amendment II

A well-regulated militia being necessary to the security of a free State, the right of the people to keep and bear arms shall not be infringed.

Amendment III

No soldier shall, in time of peace, be quartered in any house without the consent of the owner, nor in time of war, but in a manner to be prescribed by law.

Amendment IV

The right of the people to be secure in their persons, houses, papers, and effects, against unreasonable searches and seizures, shall not be violated, and no warrants shall issue but upon probable cause, supported by oath or affirmation, and particularly describing the place to be searched, and the persons or things to be seized.

---

*The first ten Amendments (the Bill of Rights) were adopted in 1791.

Amendment V

No person shall be held to answer for a capital, or otherwise infamous crime, unless on a presentment or indictment of a grand jury, except in cases arising in the land or naval forces, or in the militia, when in actual service in time of war or public danger; nor shall any person be subject for the same offense to be twice put in jeopardy of life or limb; nor shall be compelled in any criminal case to be a witness against himself, nor be deprived of life, liberty, or property, without due process of law; nor shall private property be taken for public use without just compensation.

Amendment VI

In all criminal prosecutions, the accused shall enjoy the right to a speedy and public trial, by an impartial jury of the State and district wherein the crime shall have been committed, which district shall have been previously ascertained by law, and to be informed of the nature and cause of the accusation; to be confronted with the witnesses against him; to have compulsory process for obtaining witnesses in his favor, and to have the assistance of counsel for his defense.

Amendment VII

In suits at common law, where the value in controversy shall exceed twenty dollars, the right of trial by jury shall be preserved, and no fact tried by a jury shall be otherwise reexamined in any court of the United States, than according to the rules of the common law.

Amendment VIII

Excessive bail shall not be required, nor excessive fines imposed, nor cruel and unusual punishments inflicted.

Amendment IX

The enumeration in the Constitution, of certain rights, shall not be construed to deny or disparage others retained by the people.

Amendment X

The powers not delegated to the United States by the Constitution, nor prohibited by it to the States, are reserved to the States respectively, or to the people.

Amendment XI

[Adopted 1798]

The judicial power of the United States shall not be construed to extend to any suit in law or equity, commenced or prosecuted against one of the United States by citizens of another State, or by citizens or subjects of any foreign state.

Amendment XII

[Adopted 1804]

The electors shall meet in their respective States, and vote by ballot for President and Vice-President, one of whom, at least, shall not be an inhabitant of the same State with themselves; they shall name in their ballots the person voted for as President, and in distinct ballots the person voted for as Vice-President, and they shall make distinct lists of all persons voted for as President, and of all persons voted for as Vice-President, and of the number of votes for each, which lists they shall sign and certify, and transmit sealed to the seat of government of the United States, directed to the President of the Senate;—the President of the Senate shall, in the presence of the Senate and House of Representatives, open all the certificates and the votes shall then be counted;—the person having the greatest number of votes for President shall be the President, if such number be a majority of the whole number of electors appointed; and if no person have such majority, then from the persons having the highest numbers not exceeding three on the list of those voted for as President, the House of Representatives shall choose immediately, by ballot, the President. But in choosing the President, the votes shall be taken by States, the representation from each State having one vote; a quorum for this purpose shall consist of a member or members from two-thirds of the States, and a majority of all the States shall be necessary to a choice. And if the House of Representatives shall not choose a President whenever the right of choice shall devolve upon them, before *the fourth day of March* next following, then the Vice-President shall act as President, as in the case of the death or other constitutional disability of the President.

The person having the greatest number of votes as Vice-President shall be the Vice-President, if such number be a majority of the whole number of electors appointed; and if no person have a majority, then from the two highest numbers on the list the Senate shall choose the Vice-President; a quorum for the purpose shall consist of two-thirds of the whole number of Senators, and a majority of the whole number shall be necessary to a choice. But no person constitutionally ineligible to the office of President shall be eligible to that of Vice-President of the United States.

Amendment XIII

[Adopted 1865]

Section 1   Neither slavery nor involuntary servitude, except as a punishment for crime whereof the party shall have been duly convicted, shall exist within the United States, or any place subject to their jurisdiction.

Section 2   Congress shall have power to enforce this article by appropriate legislation.

Amendment XIV

[Adopted 1868]

Section 1   All persons born or naturalized in the United States, and subject to the jurisdiction thereof, are citizens of the United States and of the State wherein they reside. No State shall make or enforce any law which shall abridge the privileges or immunities of citizens of the United States;

nor shall any State deprive any person of life, liberty, or property, without due process of law; nor deny to any person within its jurisdiction the equal protection of the laws.

Section 2   Representatives shall be apportioned among the several States according to their respective numbers, counting the whole number of persons in each State, excluding Indians not taxed. But when the right to vote at any election for the choice of Electors for President and Vice-President of the United States, Representatives in Congress, the executive and judicial officers of a State, or the members of the legislature thereof, is denied to any of the male inhabitants of such State, being twenty-one years of age and citizens of the United States, or in any way abridged, except for participation in rebellion, or other crime, the basis of representation therein shall be reduced in the proportion which the number of such male citizens shall bear to the whole number of male citizens twenty-one years of age in such State.

Section 3   No person shall be a Senator or Representative in Congress, or Elector of President and Vice-President, or hold any office, civil or military, under the United States, or under any State, who, having previously taken an oath, as a member of Congress, or as an officer of the United States, or as a member of any State legislature, or as an executive or judicial officer of any State, to support the Constitution of the United States, shall have engaged in insurrection or rebellion against the same, or given aid or comfort to the enemies thereof. Congress may, by a vote of two-thirds of each house, remove such disability.

Section 4   The validity of the public debt of the United States, authorized by law, including debts incurred for payment of pensions and bounties for services in suppressing insurrection or rebellion, shall not be questioned. But neither the United States nor any State shall assume or pay any debt or obligation incurred in aid of insurrection or rebellion against the United States, or any claim for the loss of emancipation of any slave; but all such debts, obligations, and claims shall be held illegal and void.

Section 5   The Congress shall have power to enforce, by appropriate legislation, the provisions of this article.

Amendment XV

[Adopted 1870]

Section 1   The right of citizens of the United States to vote shall not be denied or abridged by the United States or by any State on account of race, color, or previous condition of servitude.

Section 2   The Congress shall have power to enforce this article by appropriate legislation.

Amendment XVI

[Adopted 1913]

The Congress shall have power to lay and collect taxes on incomes, from whatever source derived, without apportionment among the several States, and without regard to any census or enumeration.

Amendment XVII

[Adopted 1913]

Section 1   The Senate of the United States shall be composed of two Senators from each State, elected by the people thereof, for six years; and each Senator shall have one vote. The electors in each State shall have the qualifications requisite for electors of [voters for]the most numerous branch of the State legislatures.

Section 2   When vacancies happen in the representation of any State in the Senate, the executive authority of such State shall issue writs of election to fill such vacancies: Provided, that the Legislature of any State may empower the executive thereof to make temporary appointments until the people fill the vacancies by election as the Legislature may direct.

Section 3   This amendment shall not be so construed as to affect the election or term of any Senator chosen before it becomes valid as part of the Constitution.

Amendment XVIII

[Adopted 1919; Repealed 1933]

Section 1   After one year from the ratification of this article the manufacture, sale, or transportation of intoxicating liquors within, the importation thereof into, or the exportation thereof from the United States and all territory subject to the jurisdiction thereof, for beverage purposes, is hereby prohibited.

Section 2   The Congress and the several States shall have concurrent power to enforce this article by appropriate legislation.

Section 3   This article shall be inoperative unless it shall have been ratified as an amendment to the Constitution by the legislatures of the several States, as provided by the Constitution, within seven years from the date of the submission thereof to the States by the Congress.

Amendment XIX

[Adopted 1920]

Section 1   The right of citizens of the United States to vote shall not be denied or abridged by the United States or by any State on account of sex.

Section 2   The Congress shall have power to enforce this article by appropriate legislation.

Amendment XX

[Adopted 1933]

Section 1   The terms of the President and Vice-President shall end at noon on the 20th day of January, and the terms of Senators and Representatives at noon on the 3rd day of January, of the years in which such terms would have ended if this article had not been ratified; and the terms of their successors shall then begin.

Section 2   The Congress shall assemble at least once in every year, and such meeting shall begin at noon on the 3d day of January, unless they shall by law appoint a different day.

Section 3   If, at the time fixed for the beginning of the term of the President, the President-elect shall have died, the Vice-President-elect shall become President. If a President shall not have been chosen before the time fixed for the beginning of his term, or if the President-elect shall have failed to qualify, then the Vice-President-elect shall act as President until a President shall have qualified; and the Congress may by law provide for the case wherein neither a President-elect nor a Vice-President-elect shall have qualified, declaring who shall then act as President, or the manner in which one who is to act shall be selected, and such persons shall act accordingly until a President or Vice-President shall have qualified.

Section 4   The Congress may by law provide for the case of the death of any of the persons from whom the House of Representatives may choose a President whenever the right of choice shall have devolved upon them, and for the case of the death of any of the persons from whom the Senate may choose a Vice-President whenever the right of choice shall have devolved upon them.

Section 5   Sections 1 and 2 shall take effect on the 15th day of October following the ratification of this article.

Section 6   This article shall be inoperative unless it shall have been ratified as an amendment to the Constitution by the Legislatures of three-fourths of the several States within seven years from the date of its submission.

Amendment XXI

[Adopted 1933]

Section 1   The eighteenth article of amendment to the Constitution of the United States is hereby repealed.

Section 2   The transportation or importation into any State, Territory, or Possession of the United States for delivery or use therein of intoxicating liquors, in violation of the laws thereof, is hereby prohibited.

Section 3   This article shall be inoperative unless it shall have been ratified as an amendment to the Constitution by conventions in the several States, as provided in the Constitution, within seven years from the date of submission thereof to the States by the Congress.

Amendment XXII

[Adopted 1951]

Section 1   No person shall be elected to the office of President more than twice, and no person who has held the office of President, or acted as President, for more than two years of a term to which some other person was elected

President shall be elected to the office of President more than once. But this article shall not apply to any person holding the office of President when this article was proposed by the Congress, and shall not prevent any person who may be holding the office of President, or acting as President, during the term within which this article becomes operative from holding the office of President or acting as President during the remainder of such term.

Section 2   This article shall be inoperative unless it shall have been ratified as an amendment to the Constitution by the legislatures of three-fourths of the several States within seven years from the date of its submission to the States by the Congress.

Amendment XXIII

[Adopted 1961]

Section 1   The District constituting the seat of Government of the United States shall appoint in such manner as the Congress may direct:

A number of electors of President and Vice-President equal to the whole number of Senators and Representatives in Congress to which the District would be entitled if it were a State, but in no event more than the least populous State; they shall be in addition to those appointed by the States, but they shall be considered for the purposes of the election of President and Vice-President, to be electors appointed by a State; and they shall meet in the District and perform such duties as provided by the twelfth article of amendment.

Section 2   The Congress shall have the power to enforce this article by appropriate legislation.

Amendment XXIV

[Adopted 1964]

Section 1   The right of citizens of the United States to vote in any primary or other election for President or Vice-President, for electors for President or Vice-President, or for Senator or Representative in Congress, shall not be denied or abridged by the United States or any State by reason of failure to pay any poll tax or other tax.

Section 2   The Congress shall have the power to enforce this article by appropriate legislation.

Amendment XXV

[Adopted 1967]

Section 1   In case of the removal of the President from office or of his death or resignation, the Vice-President shall become President.

Section 2   Whenever there is a vacancy in the office of the Vice-President, the President shall nominate a Vice-President who shall take office upon confirmation by a majority vote of both Houses of Congress.

Section 3   Whenever the President transmits to the President pro tempore of the Senate and the Speaker of the House of Representatives his written declaration that he is unable to discharge the powers and duties of his office, and until he transmits to them a written declaration to the contrary, such powers and duties shall be discharged by the Vice-President as Acting President.

Section 4   Whenever the Vice-President and a majority of either the principal officers of the executive departments or of such other body as Congress may by law provide, transmit to the President pro tempore of the Senate and the Speaker of the House of Representatives their written declaration that the President is unable to discharge the powers and duties of his office, the Vice-President shall immediately assume the powers and duties of the office as Acting President.

Thereafter, when the President transmits to the President pro tempore of the Senate and the Speaker of the House of Representatives his written declaration that no inability exists, he shall resume the powers and duties of his office unless the Vice-President and a majority of either the principal officers of the executive department[s] or of such other body as Congress may by law provide, transmit within four days to the President pro tempore of the Senate and the Speaker of the House of Representatives their written declaration that the President is unable to discharge the powers and duties of his office. Thereupon Congress shall decide the issue, assembling within forty-eight hours for that purpose if not in session. If the Congress, within twenty-one days after receipt of the latter written declaration, or, if Congress is not in session, within twenty-one days after Congress is required to assemble, determines by two-thirds vote of both Houses that the President is unable to discharge the powers and duties of his office, the Vice-President shall continue to discharge the same as Acting President; otherwise, the President shall resume the powers and duties of his office.

Amendment XXVI

[Adopted 1971]

Section 1   The right of citizens of the United States, who are eighteen years of age or older, to vote shall not be denied or abridged by the United States or by any State on account of age.

Section 2   The Congress shall have power to enforce this article by appropriate legislation.

Amendment XXVII

[Adopted 1992]

No law, varying the compensation for the services of the Senators and Representatives, shall take effect, until an election of Representatives shall have intervened.

The American People and Nation: A Statistical Profile

Population of the United States

Year	Number of States	Population	Percent Increase	Population Per Square Mile	Percent Urban/ Rural	Percent Male/ Female	Percent White/ Non-white	Persons Per House-hold	Median Age
1790	13	3,929,214		4.5	5.1/94.9	NA/NA	80.7/19.3	5.79	NA
1800	16	5,308,483	35.1	6.1	6.1/93.9	NA/NA	81.1/18.9	NA	NA
1810	17	7,239,881	36.4	4.3	7.3/92.7	NA/NA	81.0/19.0	NA	NA
1820	23	9,638,453	33.1	5.5	7.2/92.8	50.8/49.2	81.6/18.4	NA	16.7
1830	24	12,866,020	33.5	7.4	8.8/91.2	50.8/49.2	81.9/18.1	NA	17.2
1840	26	17,069,453	32.7	9.8	10.8/89.2	50.9/49.1	83.2/16.8	NA	17.8
1850	31	23,191,876	35.9	7.9	15.3/84.7	51.0/49.0	84.3/15.7	5.55	18.9
1860	33	31,443,321	35.6	10.6	19.8/80.2	51.2/48.8	85.6/14.4	5.28	19.4
1870	37	39,818,449	26.6	13.4	25.7/74.3	50.6/49.4	86.2/13.8	5.09	20.2
1880	38	50,155,783	26.0	16.9	28.2/71.8	50.9/49.1	86.5/13.5	5.04	20.9
1890	44	62,947,714	25.5	21.2	35.1/64.9	51.2/48.8	87.5/12.5	4.93	22.0
1900	45	75,994,575	20.7	25.6	39.6/60.4	51.1/48.9	87.9/12.1	4.76	22.9
1910	46	91,972,266	21.0	31.0	45.6/54.4	51.5/48.5	88.9/11.1	4.54	24.1
1920	48	105,710,620	14.9	35.6	51.2/48.8	51.0/49.0	89.7/10.3	4.34	25.3
1930	48	122,775,046	16.1	41.2	56.1/43.9	50.6/49.4	89.8/10.2	4.11	26.4
1940	48	131,669,275	7.2	44.2	56.5/43.5	50.2/49.8	89.8/10.2	3.67	29.0
1950	48	150,697,361	14.5	50.7	64.0/36.0	49.7/50.3	89.5/10.5	3.37	30.2
1960	50	179,323,175	18.5	50.6	69.9/30.1	49.3/50.7	88.6/11.4	3.33	29.5
1970	50	203,302,031	13.4	57.4	73.6/26.4	48.7/51.3	87.6/12.4	3.14	28.0
1980	50	226,542,199	11.4	64.0	73.7/26.3	48.6/51.4	85.9/14.1	2.75	30.0
1990	50	248,718,301	9.8	70.3	75.2/24.8	48.7/51.3	83.9/16.1	2.63	32.8
1995	50	263,034,000	5.1	70.7	NA	48.8/51.2	83.0/17.0	2.65	34.3

NA = Not available.

Vital Statistics

| Year | Birth Rate* | Death Rate* | Life Expectancy in Years | | | | | Marriage Rate | Divorce Rate |
			Total Population	White Females	Nonwhite Females	White Males	Nonwhite Males		
1790	NA	NA	NA	NA	NA	NA	NA	NA	NA
1800	55.0	NA	NA	NA	NA	NA	NA	NA	NA
1810	54.3	NA	NA	NA	NA	NA	NA	NA	NA
1820	55.2	NA	NA	NA	NA	NA	NA	NA	NA
1830	51.4	NA	NA	NA	NA	NA	NA	NA	NA
1840	51.8	NA	NA	NA	NA	NA	NA	NA	NA
1850	43.3	NA	NA	NA	NA	NA	NA	NA	NA
1860	44.3	NA	NA	NA	NA	NA	NA	NA	NA
1870	38.3	NA	NA	NA	NA	NA	NA	NA	NA
1880	39.8	NA	NA	NA	NA	NA	NA	NA	NA
1890	31.5	NA	NA	NA	NA	NA	NA	NA	NA
1900	32.3	17.2	47.3	48.7	33.5	46.6	32.5	NA	NA
1910	30.1	14.7	50.0	52.0	37.5	48.6	33.8	NA	NA
1920	27.7	13.0	54.1	55.6	45.2	54.4	45.5	12.0	1.6
1930	21.3	11.3	59.7	63.5	49.2	59.7	47.3	9.2	1.6
1940	19.4	10.8	62.9	66.6	54.9	62.1	51.5	12.1	2.0
1950	24.1	9.6	68.2	72.2	62.9	66.5	59.1	11.1	2.6
1960	23.7	9.5	69.7	74.1	66.3	67.4	61.1	8.5	2.2
1970	18.4	9.5	70.8	75.6	69.4	68.0	61.3	10.6	3.5
1980	15.9	8.8	73.7	78.1	73.6	70.7	65.3	10.6	5.2
1990	16.6	8.6	75.4	79.4	75.2	72.7	67.0	9.8	4.7
1994	15.3	8.8	75.7	79.6	75.8	73.2	67.5	9.1	4.6

Data per one thousand for Birth, Death, Marriage, and Divorce rates.

NA = Not available. *Data for 1800, 1810, 1830, 1850, 1870, and 1890 for whites only.

Immigrants to the United States

| Immigration Totals by Decade | | | |
Years	Number	Years	Number
1820–1830	151,824	1911–1920	5,735,811
1831–1840	599,125	1921–1930	4,107,209
1841–1850	1,713,251	1931–1940	528,431
1851–1860	2,598,214	1941–1950	1,035,039
1861–1870	2,314,824	1951–1960	2,515,479
1871–1880	2,812,191	1961–1970	3,321,677
1881–1890	5,246,613	1971–1980	4,493,314
1891–1900	3,687,546	1981–1990	7,338,062
1901–1910	8,795,386	1991–1994	4,509,852
		Total	61,503,866

Major Sources of Immigrants by Country or Region (in thousands)

Period	Asia[a]	Germany	Mexico	Italy	Great Britain (UK)[b]	Ireland	Canada	Austria and Hungary	Soviet Union (Russia)	Caribbean	Central America and South America	Norway and Sweden
1820–1830	—	8	5	—	27	54	2	—	—	4	—	—
1831–1840	—	152	7	2	76	207	14	—	—	12	—	1
1841–1850	—	435	3	2	267	781	42	—	—	14	4	14
1851–1860	42	952	3	9	424	914	59	—	—	11	2	21
1861–1870	65	787	2	12	607	436	154	8	3	9	1	109
1871–1880	124	718	5	56	548	437	384	73	39	14	1	211
1881–1890	70	1,453	2[c]	307	807	655	393	354	213	29	3	568
1891–1900	75	505	1[c]	652	272	388	3	593	505	33	2	321
1901–1910	324	341	50	2,046	526	339	179	2,145	1,597	108	25	440
1911–1920	247	144	219	1,110	341	146	742	896	921	123	59	161
1921–1930	112	412	459	455	340	211	925	64	62	75	58	166
1931–1940	17	114	22	68	32	11	109	11	1	16	14	9
1941–1950	37	227	61	58	139	20	172	28	—	50	43	21
1951–1960	153	478	300	185	203	48	378	104	—	123	136	45
1961–1970	428	191	454	214	214	33	413	26	2	470	359	33
1971–1980	1,588	74	640	129	137	11	170	16	39	741	430	10
1981–1990	2,738	92	2,336	67	160	32	182	25	58	872	930	15
1991–1994	1,315	43	1,400	49	77	47	88	13	193	333	505	8
Total	7,334	7,126	5,970	5,422	5,196	4,772	4,408	4,356	3,637	3,036	2,575	2,154

Notes: Numbers for periods are rounded. Dash indicates less than one thousand; [a]Includes Middle East;[b]Since 1925, includes England, Scotland, Wales, and Northern Ireland data; [c]No data available for 1886–1894.

The American Worker

Year	Total Number of Workers	Males as Percent of Total Workers	Females as Percent of Total Workers	Married Women as Percent of Female Workers	Female Workers as Percent of Female Population	Percent of Labor Force Unemployed	Percent of Workers in Labor Unions
1870	12,506,000	85	15	NA	NA	NA	NA
1880	17,392,000	85	15	NA	NA	NA	NA
1890	23,318,000	83	17	14	19	4 (1894 = 18)	NA
1900	29,073,000	82	18	15	21	5	3
1910	38,167,000	79	21	25	25	6	6
1920	41,614,000	79	21	23	24	5 (1921 = 12)	12
1930	48,830,000	78	22	29	25	9 (1933 = 25)	11.6
1940	53,011,000	76	24	36	27	15 (1944 = 1)	26.9
1950	62,208,000	72	28	52	31	5.3	31.5
1960	69,628,000	67	33	55	38	5.5	31.4
1970	82,771,000	62	38	59	43	4.9	27.3
1980	106,940,000	58	42	55	52	7.1	21.9
1990	125,840,000	55	45	54	58	5.6	16.1
1995	132,304,000	54	46	55	59	5.6	15.5

NA = Not available.

The American Economy

Year	Gross National Product (GNP) (in $ billions)	Steel Production (in tons)	Automobiles Registered	New Housing Starts	Foreign Trade (in millions of dollars)	
					Exports	Imports
1790	NA	NA	NA	NA	20	23
1800	NA	NA	NA	NA	71	91
1810	NA	NA	NA	NA	67	85
1820	NA	NA	NA	NA	70	74
1830	NA	NA	NA	NA	74	71
1840	NA	NA	NA	NA	132	107
1850	NA	NA	NA	NA	152	178
1860	NA	13,000	NA	NA	400	362
1870	7.4[a]	77,000	NA	NA	451	462
1880	11.2[b]	1,397,000	NA	NA	853	761
1890	13.1	4,779,000	NA	328,000	910	823
1900	18.7	11,227,000	8,000	189,000	1,499	930
1910	35.3	28,330,000	458,300	387,000 (1918 = 118,000)	1,919	1,646
1920	91.5	46,183,000	8,131,500	247,000 (1925 = 937,000)	8,664	5,784
1930	90.7	44,591,000	23,034,700	330,000 (1933 = 93,000)	4,013	3,500
1940	100.0	66,983,000	27,465,800	603,000 (1944 = 142,000)	4,030	7,433
1950	286.5	96,836,000	40,339,000	1,952,000	9,997	8,954
1960	506.5	99,282,000	61,682,300	1,365,000	19,659	15,093
1970	1,016.0	131,514,000	89,279,800	1,434,000	42,681	40,356
1980	2,819.5	111,835,000	121,601,000	1,292,000	220,626	244,871
1990	5,764.9	98,906,000	143,550,000	1,193,000	394,030	485,453
1995	7,237.5	104,930,000	133,930,000[c]	1,354,000	584,742	743,445

[a]Figure is average for 1869–1878.

[b]Figure is average for 1879–1888.

[c]Figure for 1994.

NA = Not available.

Federal Budget Outlays and Debt

Year	Defense[a]	Veterans Benefits[a]	Income Security[a]	Social Security[a]	Health and Medicare[a]	Education[ad]	Net Interest Payments[a]	Federal Debt (dollars)
1790	14.9	4.1[b]	NA	NA	NA	NA	55.0	75,463,000[c]
1800	55.7	.6	NA	NA	NA	NA	31.3	82,976,000
1810	48.4 (1814: 79.7)	1.0	NA	NA	NA	NA	34.9	53,173,000
1820	38.4	17.6	NA	NA	NA	NA	28.1	91,016,000
1830	52.9	9.0	NA	NA	NA	NA	12.6	48,565,000
1840	54.3 (1847: 80.7)	10.7	NA	NA	NA	NA	.7	3,573,000
1850	43.8	4.7	NA	NA	NA	NA	1.0	63,453,000
1860	44.2 (1865: 88.9)	1.7	NA	NA	NA	NA	5.0	64,844,000
1870	25.7	9.2	NA	NA	NA	NA	41.7	2,436,453,000
1880	19.3	21.2	NA	NA	NA	NA	35.8	2,090,909,000
1890	20.9 (1899: 48.6)	33.6	NA	NA	NA	NA	11.4	1,222,397,000
1900	36.6	27.0	NA	NA	NA	NA	7.7	1,263,417,000
1910	45.1 (1919: 59.5)	23.2	NA	NA	NA	NA	3.1	1,146,940,000
1920	37.1	3.4	NA	NA	NA	NA	16.0	24,299,321,000
1930	25.3	6.6	NA	NA	NA	NA	19.9	16,185,310,000
1940	17.5 (1945: 89.4)	6.0	16.0	.3	.5	20.8	9.4	42,967,531,000
1950	32.2	20.3	9.6	1.8	.6	.6	11.3	256,853,000,000
1960	52.2	5.9	8.0	12.6	.9	1.0	7.5	290,525,000,000
1970	41.8	4.4	8.0	15.5	6.2	4.4	7.3	308,921,000,000
1980	22.7	3.6	14.6	20.1	9.4	5.4	8.9	909,050,000,000
1990	23.9	2.3	11.7	19.8	12.4	3.1	14.7	3,206,564,000,000
1995	17.9	2.5	14.5	22.1	18.1	3.6	15.3	5,207,298,000,000[e]

[a]Figures represent percentage of total federal spending for each category. Not included are categories of transportation, commerce, and housing.

[b]1789–1791 figure.

[c]1791 figure.

[d]Includes training, employment, and social services.

[e]1996 figure.

NA = Not available.

The Fifty States, District of Columbia, and Puerto Rico

State	Date of Admission (with Rank)	Capital City	Population (1995) (with Rank)	Racial/Ethnic Distribution (1995)	Per Capita Personal Income (1995) (with Rank)	Total Area in Square Miles (with Rank)
Alabama (AL)	Dec. 14, 1819 (22)	Montgomery	4,253,000 (22)	White: 3,140,000; Black: 1,083,000; Hispanic: 29,000; Asian: 33,000	$18,781 (41)	52,423 (30)
Alaska (AK)	Jan. 3, 1959 (49)	Juneau	604,000 (48)	White: 477,000; Black: 26,000; Hispanic: 22,000; Asian: 29,000; Native American: 102,000	$24,182 (10)	656,424 (1)
Arizona (AZ)	Feb. 14, 1912 (48)	Phoenix	4,218,000 (23)	White: 3,606,000; Black: 123,000; Hispanic: 853,000; Asian: 91,000; Native American: 251,000	$20,421 (35)	114,006 (6)
Arkansas (AR)	June 15, 1836 (25)	Little Rock	2,484,000 (33)	White: 2,047,000; Black: 386,000; Hispanic: 27,000; Asian: 26,000	$17,429 (49)	53,182 (29)
California (CA)	Sept. 9, 1850 (31)	Sacramento	31,589,000 (1)	White: 25,701,000; Black: 2,512,000; Hispanic: 9,143,000; Asian: 3,908,000; Native American: 277,000	$23,699 (12)	163,707 (3)
Colorado (CO)	Aug. 1, 1876 (38)	Denver	3,747,000 (25)	White: 3,431,000; Black: 156,000; Hispanic: 511,000; Asian: 89,000; Native American: 34,000	$23,449 (16)	104,100 (8)
Connecticut (CT)	Jan. 9, 1788 (5)	Hartford	3,275,000 (28)	White: 2,915,000; Black: 293,000; Hispanic: 258,000; Asian: 60,000	$30,303 (1)	5,544 (48)
Delaware (DE)	Dec. 7, 1787 (1)	Dover	717,000 (46)	White: 570,000; Black: 132,000; Hispanic: 22,000; Asian: 14,000	$24,124 (11)	2,489 (49)
District of Columbia (DC)	U.S. Capital, Dec. 1, 1800*	Washington (coextensive with DC)	554,000 (not ranked)	White: 185,000; Black: 384,000; Hispanic: 35,000; Asian: 16,000	$32,274*	68*
Florida (FL)	Mar. 3, 1845 (27)	Tallahassee	14,166,000 (4)	White: 11,867,000; Black: 2,073,000; Hispanic: 1,948,000; Asian: 231,000	$22,916 (20)	65,756 (22)
Georgia (GA)	Jan. 2, 1788 (4)	Atlanta	7,201,000 (10)	White: 5,025,000; Black: 1,955,000; Hispanic: 144,000; Asian: 109,000	$21,278 (28)	59,441 (24)
Hawai'i (HI)	Aug. 21, 1959 (50)	Honolulu	1,187,000 (40)	White: 499,000; Black: 36,000; Hispanic: 106,000; Asian: 679,000	$24,738 (9)	10,932 (43)
Idaho (ID)	July 3, 1890 (43)	Boise	1,163,000 (41)	White: 1,118,000; Black: 5,000; Hispanic: 74,000; Asian: 15,000; Native American: 18,000	$19,264 (38)	83,574 (14)
Illinois (IL)	Dec. 3, 1818 (21)	Springfield	11,830,000 (6)	White: 9,603,000; Black: 1,843,000; Hispanic: 1,086,000; Asian: 383,000	$24,763 (8)	57,918 (25)
Indiana (IN)	Dec. 11, 1816 (19)	Indianapolis	5,803,000 (14)	White: 5,275,000; Black: 476,000; Hispanic: 122,000; Asian: 55,000	$21,273 (29)	36,420 (38)
Iowa (IA)	Dec. 28, 1846 (29)	Des Moines	2,842,000 (30)	White: 2,763,000; Black: 57,000; Hispanic: 45,000; Asian: 33,000	$21,012 (30)	56,276 (26)
Kansas (KS)	Jan. 29, 1861 (34)	Topeka	2,565,000 (32)	White: 2,365,000; Black: 159,000; Hispanic: 116,000; Asian: 50,000	$21,825 (23)	82,282 (15)
Kentucky (KY)	June 1, 1792 (15)	Frankfort	3,860,000 (24)	White: 3,535,000; Black: 286,000; Hispanic: 23,000; Asian: 24,000	$18,612 (43)	40,411 (37)

The Fifty States, District of Columbia,
and Puerto Rico, Continued

State	Date of Admission (with Rank)	Capital City	Population (1995) (with Rank)	Racial/Ethnic Distribution (1995)	Per Capita Personal Income (1995) (with Rank)	Total Area in Square Miles (with Rank)
Louisiana (LA)	Apr. 30, 1812 (18)	Baton Rouge	4,342,000 (21)	White: 2,909,000; Black: 1,371,000; Hispanic: 109,000; Asian: 60,000	$18,827 (39)	51,843 (31)
Maine (ME)	Mar. 15, 1820 (23)	Augusta	1,241,000 (39)	White: 1,217,000; Black: 5,000; Hispanic: 9,000; Asian: 8,000; Native American: 6,000	$20,527 (34)	35,387 (39)
Maryland (MD)	Apr. 28, 1788 (7)	Annapolis	5,042,000 (19)	White: 3,500,000; Black: 1,368,000; Hispanic: 158,000; Asian: 196,000	$25,927 (5)	12,407 (42)
Massachusetts (MA)	Feb. 6, 1788 (6)	Boston	6,074,000 (13)	White: 5,445,000; Black: 340,000; Hispanic: 342,000; Asian: 180,000	$26,994 (3)	10,555 (44)
Michigan (MI)	Jan. 26, 1837 (26)	Lansing	9,549,000 (8)	White: 7,958,000; Black: 1,417,000; Hispanic: 242,000; Asian: 140,000; Native American: 61,000	$23,551 (15)	96,705 (11)
Minnesota (MN)	May 11, 1858 (32)	Saint Paul	4,610,000 (20)	White: 4,344,000; Black: 104,000; Hispanic: 68,000; Asian: 113,000; Native American: 58,000	$23,118 (19)	86,943 (12)
Mississippi (MS)	Dec. 10, 1817 (20)	Jackson	2,697,000 (31)	White: 1,688,000; Black: 952,000; Hispanic: 18,000; Asian: 17,000	$16,531 (50)	48,434 (32)
Missouri (MO)	Aug. 10, 1821 (24)	Jefferson City	5,324,000 (16)	White: 4,629,000; Black: 581,000; Hispanic: 71,000; Asian: 56,000	$21,627 (26)	69,709 (21)
Montana (MT)	Nov. 8, 1889 (41)	Helena	870,000 (44)	White: 798,000; Black: 2,000; Hispanic: 15,000; Asian: 6,000; Native American: 55,000	$18,482 (44)	147,046 (4)
Nebraska (NE)	Mar. 1, 1867 (37)	Lincoln	1,637,000 (37)	White: 1,550,000; Black: 64,000; Hispanic: 53,000; Asian: 17,000; Native American: 14,000	$21,703 (25)	77,358 (16)
Nevada (NV)	Oct. 3, 1864 (36)	Carson City	1,530,000 (38)	White: 1,281,000; Black: 100,000; Hispanic: 195,000; Asian: 70,000; Native American: 27,000	$25,013 (7)	110,567 (7)
New Hampshire (NH)	June 21, 1788 (9)	Concord	1,148,000 (42)	White: 1,109,000; Black: 7,000; Hispanic: 13,000; Asian: 14,000	$25,151 (6)	9,351 (46)
New Jersey (NJ)	Dec. 18, 1787 (3)	Trenton	7,945,000 (9)	White: 6,405,000; Black: 1,156,000; Hispanic: 898,000; Asian: 356,000	$28,858 (2)	8,722 (47)
New Mexico (NM)	Jan. 6, 1912 (47)	Santa Fe	1,685,000 (36)	White: 1,460,000; Black: 32,000; Hispanic: 686,000; Asian: 25,000; Native American: 159,000	$18,055 (47)	121,598 (5)
New York (NY)	July 26, 1788 (11)	Albany	18,136,000 (3)	White: 14,025,000; Black: 3,249,000; Hispanic: 2,372,000; Asian: 846,000; Native American: 57,000	$26,782 (4)	54,471 (27)
North Carolina (NC)	Nov. 21, 1789 (12)	Raleigh	7,195,000 (11)	White: 5,378,000; Black: 1,594,000 Hispanic: 100,000; Asian: 88,000 Native American: 90,000	$20,604 (33)	53,821 (28)
North Dakota (ND)	Nov. 2, 1889 (39)	Bismarck	641,000 (47)	White: 600,000; Black: 4,000; Hispanic: 5,000; Asian: 5,000; Native American: 28,000	$18,663 (42)	70,704 (19)
Ohio (OH)	Mar. 1, 1803 (17)	Columbus	11,151,000 (7)	White: 9,806,000; Black: 1,253,000; Hispanic: 170,000; Asian: 122,000	$22,021 (21)	44,828 (34)
Oklahoma (OK)	Nov. 16, 1907 (46)	Oklahoma City	3,278,000 (27)	White: 2,699,000; Black: 244,000; Hispanic: 106,000; Asian: 52,000; Native American: 276,000	$18,152 (46)	69,903 (20)

The Fifty States, District of Columbia, and Puerto Rico, Continued

State	Date of Admission (with Rank)	Capital City	Population (1995) (with Rank)	Racial/Ethnic Distribution (1995)	Per Capita Personal Income (1995) (with Rank)	Total Area in Square Miles (with Rank)
Oregon (OR)	Feb. 14, 1859 (33)	Salem	3,141,000 (29)	White: 2,929,000; Black: 54,000; Hispanic: 151,000; Asian: 111,000; Native American: 47,000	$21,736 (24)	98,386 (9)
Pennsylvania (PA)	Dec. 12, 1787 (2)	Harrisburg	12,072,000 (5)	White: 10,768,000; Black: 1,167,000; Hispanic: 297,000; Asian: 185,000	$23,279 (18)	46,058 (33)
Puerto Rico (PR)	Ascession 1898; Commonwealth Status 1952	San Juan	3,720,000*	White: >1,000; Black: >1,000; Hispanic: 3,621,000; Asian: >1,000	$6,360*	3,427*
Rhode Island (RI)	May 29, 1790 (13)	Providence	990,000 (43)	White: 927,000; Black: 44,000; Hispanic: 58,000; Asian: 25,000	$23,310 (17)	1,545 (50)
South Carolina (SC)	May 23, 1788 (8)	Columbia	3,673,000 (26)	White: 2,561,000; Black: 1,131,000; Hispanic: 40,000; Asian: 31,000	$18,788 (40)	32,008 (40)
South Dakota (SD)	Nov. 2, 1889 (40)	Pierre	729,000 (45)	White: 663,000; Black: 3,000; Hispanic: 7,000; Asian: 5,000; Native American: 62,000	$19,506 (37)	77,121 (17)
Tennessee (TN)	June 1, 1796 (16)	Nashville	5,256,000 (17)	White: 4,327,000; Black: 845,000; Hispanic: 42,000; Asian: 46,000	$20,376 (36)	42,146 (36)
Texas (TX)	Dec. 29, 1845 (28)	Austin	18,724,000 (2)	White: 15,814,000; Black: 2,251,000; Hispanic: 5,260,000; Asian: 461,000	$20,654 (32)	268,601 (2)
Utah (UT)	Jan. 4, 1896 (45)	Salt Lake City	1,951,000 (34)	White: 1,843,000; Black: 14,000; Hispanic: 106,000; Asian: 54,000; Native American: 33,000	$18,223 (45)	84,904 (13)
Vermont (VT)	Mar. 4, 1791 (14)	Montpelier	585,000 (49)	White: 570,000; Black: 2,000; Hispanic: 4,000; Asian: 4,000; Native American: 2,000	$20,927 (31)	9,615 (45)
Virginia (VA)	June 25, 1788 (10)	Richmond	6,618,000 (12)	White: 5,127,000; Black: 1,284,000; Hispanic: 193,000; Asian: 220,000	$25,597 (14)	42,777 (35)
Washington (WA)	Nov. 11, 1889 (42)	Olympia	5,431,000 (15)	White: 4,915,000; Black: 164,000; Hispanic: 291,000; Asian: 318,000; Native American: 101,000	$23,639 (13)	71,302 (18)
West Virginia (WV)	June 20, 1863 (35)	Charleston	1,828,000; (35)	White: 1,756,000; Black: 54,000; Hispanic: 10,000; Asian: 11,000	$17,915 (48)	24,231 (41)
Wisconsin (WI)	May 29, 1848 (30)	Madison	5,123,000 (18)	White: 4,750,000; Black: 288,000; Hispanic: 118,000; Asian: 76,000; Native American: 45,000	$21,839 (22)	65,499 (23)
Wyoming (WY)	July 10, 1890 (44)	Cheyenne	480,000 (50)	White: 467,000; Black: 4,000; Hispanic: 31,000; Asian: 4,000; Native American: 12,000	$21,321 (27)	97,818 (10)

*Not ranked.

Presidential Elections

Year	Number of States	Candidates	Parties	Popular Vote	% of Popular Vote	Electoral Vote	% Voter Participation[b]
1789	11	**George Washington**	No party			69	
		John Adams	designations			34	
		Other candidates				35	
1792	15	**George Washington**	No party			132	
		John Adams	designations			77	
		George Clinton				50	
		Other candidates				5	
1796	16	**John Adams**	Federalist			71	
		Thomas Jefferson	Democratic-Republican			68	
		Thomas Pinckney	Federalist			59	
		Aaron Burr	Democratic-Republican			30	
		Other candidates				48	
1800	16	**Thomas Jefferson**	Democratic-Republican			73	
		Aaron Burr	Democratic-Republican			73	
		John Adams	Federalist			65	
		Charles C. Pinckney	Federalist			64	
		John Jay	Federalist			1	
1804	17	**Thomas Jefferson**	Democratic-Republican			162	
		Charles C. Pinckney	Federalist			14	
1808	17	**James Madison**	Democratic-Republican			122	
		Charles C. Pinckney	Federalist			47	
		George Clinton	Democratic-Republican			6	
1812	18	**James Madison**	Democratic-Republican			128	
		DeWitt Clinton	Federalist			89	
1816	19	**James Monroe**	Democratic-Republican			183	
		Rufus King	Federalist			34	
1820	24	**James Monroe**	Democratic-Republican			231	
		John Quincy Adams	Independent Republican			1	

Presidential Elections, Continued

Year	Number of States	Candidates	Parties	Popular Vote	% of Popular Vote	Electoral Vote	% Voter Participation[b]
1824	24	**John Quincy Adams**	Democratic-Republican	108,740	30.5	84	26.9
		Andrew Jackson	Democratic-Republican	153,544	43.1	99	
		Henry Clay	Democratic-Republican	47,136	13.2	37	
		William H. Crawford	Democratic-Republican	46,618	13.1	41	
1828	24	**Andrew Jackson**	Democratic	647,286	56.0	178	57.6
		John Quincy Adams	National Republican	508,064	44.0	83	
1832	24	**Andrew Jackson**	Democratic	688,242	54.5	219	55.4
		Henry Clay	National Republican	473,462	37.5	49	
		William Wirt	Anti-Masonic	101,051	8.0	7	
		John Floyd	Democratic			11	
1836	26	**Martin Van Buren**	Democratic	765,483	50.9	170	57.8
		William H. Harrison	Whig			73	
		Hugh L. White	Whig	739,795	49.1	26	
		Daniel Webster	Whig			14	
		W. P. Mangum	Whig			11	
1840	26	**William H. Harrison**	Whig	1,274,624	53.1	234	80.2
		Martin Van Buren	Democratic	1,127,781	46.9	60	
1844	26	**James K. Polk**	Democratic	1,338,464	49.6	170	78.9
		Henry Clay	Whig	1,300,097	48.1	105	
		James G. Birney	Liberty	62,300	2.3		
1848	30	**Zachary Taylor**	Whig	1,360,967	47.4	163	72.7
		Lewis Cass	Democratic	1,222,342	42.5	127	
		Martin Van Buren	Free Soil	291,263	10.1		
1852	31	**Franklin Pierce**	Democratic	1,601,117	50.9	254	69.6
		Winfield Scott	Whig	1,385,453	44.1	42	
		John P. Hale	Free Soil	155,825	5.0		
1856	31	**James Buchanan**	Democratic	1,832,955	45.3	174	78.9
		John C. Frémont	Republican	1,339,932	33.1	114	
		Millard Fillmore	American	871,731	21.6	8	
1860	33	**Abraham Lincoln**	Republican	1,865,593	39.8	180	81.2
		Stephen A. Douglas	Democratic	1,382,713	29.5	12	
		John C. Breckinridge	Democratic	848,356	18.1	72	
		John Bell	Constitutional Union	592,906	12.6	39	
1864	36	**Abraham Lincoln**	Republican	2,206,938	55.0	212	73.8
		George B. McClellan	Democratic	1,803,787	45.0	21	
1868	37	**Ulysses S. Grant**	Republican	3,013,421	52.7	214	78.1
		Horatio Seymour	Democratic	2,706,829	47.3	80	
1872	37	**Ulysses S. Grant**	Republican	3,596,745	55.6	286	71.3
		Horace Greeley	Democratic	2,843,446	43.9	[a]	

Presidential Elections, Continued

Year	Number of States	Candidates	Parties	Popular Vote	% of Popular Vote	Electoral Vote	% Voter Participation[b]
1876	38	**Rutherford B. Hayes**	Republican	4,036,572	48.0	185	81.8
		Samuel J. Tilden	Democratic	4,284,020	51.0	184	
1880	38	**James A. Garfield**	Republican	4,453,295	48.5	214	79.4
		Winfield S. Hancock	Democratic	4,414,082	48.1	155	
		James B. Weaver	Greenback-Labor	308,578	3.4		
1884	38	**Grover Cleveland**	Democratic	4,879,507	48.5	219	77.5
		James G. Blaine	Republican	4,850,293	48.2	182	
		Benjamin F. Butler	Greenback-Labor	175,370	1.8		
		John P. St. John	Prohibition	150,369	1.5		
1888	38	**Benjamin Harrison**	Republican	5,477,129	47.9	233	79.3
		Grover Cleveland	Democratic	5,537,857	48.6	168	
		Clinton B. Fisk	Prohibition	249,506	2.2		
		Anson J. Streeter	Union Labor	146,935	1.3		
1892	44	**Grover Cleveland**	Democratic	5,555,426	46.1	277	74.7
		Benjamin Harrison	Republican	5,182,690	43.0	145	
		James B. Weaver	People's	1,029,846	8.5	22	
		John Bidwell	Prohibition	264,133	2.2		
1896	45	**William McKinley**	Republican	7,102,246	51.1	271	79.3
		William J. Bryan	Democratic	6,492,559	47.7	176	
1900	45	**William McKinley**	Republican	7,218,491	51.7	292	73.2
		William J. Bryan	Democratic; Populist	6,356,734	45.5	155	
		John C. Wooley	Prohibition	208,914	1.5		
1904	45	**Theodore Roosevelt**	Republican	7,628,461	57.4	336	65.2
		Alton B. Parker	Democratic	5,084,223	37.6	140	
		Eugene V. Debs	Socialist	402,283	3.0		
		Silas C. Swallow	Prohibition	258,536	1.9		
1908	46	**William H. Taft**	Republican	7,675,320	51.6	321	65.4
		William J. Bryan	Democratic	6,412,294	43.1	162	
		Eugene V. Debs	Socialist	420,793	2.8		
		Eugene W. Chafin	Prohibition	253,840	1.7		
1912	48	**Woodrow Wilson**	Democratic	6,296,547	41.9	435	58.8
		Theodore Roosevelt	Progressive	4,118,571	27.4	88	
		William H. Taft	Republican	3,486,720	23.2	8	
		Eugene V. Debs	Socialist	900,672	6.0		
		Eugene W. Chafin	Prohibition	206,275	1.4		
1916	48	**Woodrow Wilson**	Democratic	9,127,695	49.4	277	61.6
		Charles E. Hughes	Republican	8,533,507	46.2	254	
		A. L. Benson	Socialist	585,113	3.2		
		J. Frank Hanly	Prohibition	220,506	1.2		
1920	48	**Warren G. Harding**	Republican	16,143,407	60.4	404	49.2
		James M. Cox	Democratic	9,130,328	34.2	127	

Presidential Elections, Continued

Year	Number of States	Candidates	Parties	Popular Vote	% of Popular Vote	Electoral Vote	% Voter Participation[b]
		Eugene V. Debs	Socialist	919,799	3.4		
		P. P. Christensen	Farmer-Labor	265,411	1.0		
1924	48	**Calvin Coolidge**	Republican	15,718,211	54.0	382	48.9
		John W. Davis	Democratic	8,385,283	28.8	136	
		Robert M. La Follette	Progressive	4,831,289	16.6	13	
1928	48	**Herbert C. Hoover**	Republican	21,391,993	58.2	444	56.9
		Alfred E. Smith	Democratic	15,016,169	40.9	87	
1932	48	**Franklin D. Roosevelt**	Democratic	22,809,638	57.4	472	56.9
		Herbert C. Hoover	Republican	15,758,901	39.7	59	
		Norman Thomas	Socialist	881,951	2.2		
1936	48	**Franklin D. Roosevelt**	Democratic	27,752,869	60.8	523	61.0
		Alfred M. Landon	Republican	16,674,665	36.5	8	
		William Lemke	Union	882,479	1.9		
1940	48	**Franklin D. Roosevelt**	Democratic	27,307,819	54.8	449	62.5
		Wendell L. Wilkie	Republican	22,321,018	44.8	82	
1944	48	**Franklin D. Roosevelt**	Democratic	25,606,585	53.5	432	55.9
		Thomas E. Dewey	Republican	22,014,745	46.0	99	
1948	48	**Harry S Truman**	Democratic	24,179,345	49.6	303	53.0
		Thomas E. Dewey	Republican	21,991,291	45.1	189	
		J. Strom Thurmond	States' Rights	1,176,125	2.4	39	
		Henry A. Wallace	Progressive	1,157,326	2.4		
1952	48	**Dwight D. Eisenhower**	Republican	33,936,234	55.1	442	63.3
		Adlai E. Stevenson	Democratic	27,314,992	44.4	89	
1956	48	**Dwight D. Eisenhower**	Republican	35,590,472	57.6	457	60.6
		Adlai E. Stevenson	Democratic	26,022,752	42.1	73	
1960	50	**John F. Kennedy**	Democratic	34,226,731	49.7	303	62.8
		Richard M. Nixon	Republican	34,108,157	49.5	219	
1964	50	**Lyndon B. Johnson**	Democratic	43,129,566	61.1	486	61.7
		Barry M. Goldwater	Republican	27,178,188	38.5	52	
1968	50	**Richard M. Nixon**	Republican	31,785,480	43.4	301	60.6
		Hubert H. Humphrey	Democratic	31,275,166	42.7	191	
		George C. Wallace	American Independent	9,906,473	13.5	46	
1972	50	**Richard M. Nixon**	Republican	47,169,911	60.7	520	55.2
		George S. McGovern	Democratic	29,170,383	37.5	17	
		John G. Schmitz	American	1,099,482	1.4		
1976	50	**James E. Carter**	Democratic	40,830,763	50.1	297	53.5
		Gerald R. Ford	Republican	39,147,793	48.0	240	
1980	50	**Ronald W. Reagan**	Republican	43,899,248	50.8	489	52.6
		James E. Carter	Democratic	35,481,432	41.0	49	
		John B. Anderson	Independent	5,719,437	6.6	0	
		Ed Clark	Libertarian	920,859	1.1	0	
1984	50	**Ronald W. Reagan**	Republican	54,455,075	58.8	525	53.1
		Walter F. Mondale	Democratic	37,577,185	40.6	13	

Presidential Elections, Continued

Year	Number of States	Candidates	Parties	Popular Vote	% of Popular Vote	Electoral Vote	% Voter Participation[b]
1988	50	**George H. W. Bush**	Republican	48,901,046	53.4	426	50.2
		Michael S. Dukakis	Democratic	41,809,030	45.6	111[c]	
1992	50	**William J. Clinton**	Democratic	44,908,233	43.0	370	55.0
		George H. W. Bush	Republican	39,102,282	37.4	168	
		H. Ross Perot	Independent	19,741,048	18.9	0	
1996	50	**William J. Clinton**	Democratic	47,401,054	49.2	379	49.0
		Robert J. Dole	Republican	39,197,350	40.7	159	
		H. Ross Perot	Reform	8,085,285	8.4	0	
		Ralph Nader	Green	684,871	0.7	0	

Candidates receiving less than 1 percent of the popular vote have been omitted. Thus the percentage of popular vote given for any election year may not total 100 percent.

Before the passage of the Twelfth Amendment in 1804, the Electoral College voted for two presidential candidates; the runner-up became vice president.

Before 1824, most presidential electors were chosen by state legislatures, not by popular vote.

[a]Greeley died shortly after the election; the electors supporting him then divided their votes among minor candidates.

[b]Percent of voting-age population casting ballots.

[c]One elector from West Virginia cast her Electoral College presidential ballot for Lloyd Bentsen, the Democratic party's vice-presidential candidate.

Presidents, Vice Presidents, and Cabinet Members

Washington Administration, 1789–1797

President	George Washington	1789–1797
Vice President	John Adams	1789–1797
Secretary of State	Thomas Jefferson	1789–1793
	Edmund Randolph	1794–1795
	Timothy Pickering	1795–1797
Secretary of the Treasury	Alexander Hamilton	1789–1795
	Oliver Wolcott, Jr.	1795–1797
Secretary of War	Henry Knox	1789–1795
	Timothy Pickering	1795–1796
	James McHenry	1796–1797
Attorney General	Edmund Randolph	1789–1793
	William Bradford	1794–1795
	Charles Lee	1795–1797
Postmaster General	Samuel Osgood	1789–1791
	Timothy Pickering	1791–1795
	Joseph Habersham	1795–1797

John Adams Administration, 1797–1801

President	John Adams	1797–1801
Vice President	Thomas Jefferson	1797–1801
Secretary of State	Timothy Pickering	1797–1800
	John Marshall	1800–1801
Secretary of the Treasury	Oliver Wolcott, Jr.	1797–1800
Secretary of War	James McHenry	1797–1800
	Samuel Dexter	1800–1801
Attorney General	Charles Lee	1797–1801
Postmaster General	Joseph Habersham	1797–1801
Secretary of Navy	Benjamin Stoddert	1798–1801

Jefferson Administration, 1801–1809

President	Thomas Jefferson	1801–1809
Vice President	Aaron Burr	1801–1805
	George Clinton	1805–1809
Secretary of State	James Madison	1801–1809
Secretary of the Treasury	Samuel Dexter	1801
	Albert Gallatin	1801–1809
Secretary of War	Henry Dearborn	1801–1809
Attorney General	Levi Lincoln	1801–1804
	Robert Smith	1805
	John Breckinridge	1805–1806
	Caesar Rodney	1807–1809
Postmaster General	Joseph Habersham	1801
	Gideon Granger	1801–1809
Secretary of Navy	Benjamin Stoddert	1801
	Robert Smith	1801–1809

Madison Administration, 1809–1817

President	James Madison	1809–1817
Vice President	George Clinton	1809–1813
	Elbridge Gerry	1813–1814
Secretary of State	Robert Smith	1809–1811
	James Monroe	1811–1817
Secretary of the Treasury	Albert Gellatin	1809–1814
	George Campbell	1814
	Alexander Dallas	1814–1816
	William Crawford	1816–1817
Secretary of War	William Eustis	1809–1812
	John Armstrong	1813
	James Monroe	1814–1815
	William Crawford	1815–1816
	George Graham	1816–1817
Attorney General	Caesar Rodney	1809–1811
	William Pinkney	1811–1814
	Richard Rush	1814–1817
Postmaster General	Gideon Granger	1809–1814
	Return Meigs	1814–1817
Secretary of Navy	Paul Hamilton	1809–1813
	William Jones	1813–1814
	Benjamin Crowninshield	1815–1817

Monroe Administration, 1817–1825

President	James Monroe	1817–1825
Vice President	Daniel Tompkins	1817–1825
Secretary of State	John Quincy Adams	1817–1825

Presidents, Vice Presidents, and Cabinet Members, Continued

Secretary of the Treasury	William Crawford	1817–1825
Secretary of War	George Graham	1817
	John C. Calhoun	1817–1825
Attorney General	Richard Rush	1817
	William Wirt	1817–1825
Postmaster General	Return Meigs	1817–1823
	John McLean	1823–1825
Secretary of Navy	Benjamin Crowninshield	1817–1818
	John C. Calhoun	1818–1819
	Smith Thompson	1819–1823
	Samuel L. Southard	1823–1825

John Quincy Adams Administration, 1825–1829

President	John Quincy Adams	1825–1829
Vice President	John C. Calhoun	1825–1829
Secretary of State	Henry Clay	1825–1829
Secretary of the Treasury	Richard Rush	1825–1829
Secretary of War	James Barbour	1825–1828
	Peter Porter	1828–1829
Attorney General	William Wirt	1825–1829
Postmaster General	John McLean	1825–1829
Secretary of Navy	Samuel Southard	1825–1829

Jackson Administration, 1829–1837

President	Andrew Jackson	1829–1837
Vice President	John C. Calhoun	1829–1833
	Martin Van Buren	1833–1837
Secretary of State	Martin Van Buren	1829–1831
	Edward Livingston	1831–1833
	Louis McLane	1833–1834
	John Forsyth	1834–1837
Secretary of the Treasury	Samuel Ingham	1829–1831
	Louis McLane	1831–1833
	William Duane	1833
	Roger B. Taney	1833–1834
	Levi Woodbury	1834–1837
Secretary of War	John H. Eaton	1829–1831
	Lewis Cass	1831–1836
	Benjamin F. Butler	1836–1837
Attorney General	John M. Berrien	1829–1831
	Roger B. Taney	1831–1833
	Benjamin Butler	1833–1837
Postmaster General	William Barry	1829–1835
	Amos Kendall	1835–1837
Secretary of Navy	John Branch	1829–1831
	Levi Woodbury	1831–1834
	Mahlon Dickerson	1834–1837

Van Buren Administration, 1837–1841

President	Martin Van Buren	1837–1841
Vice President	Richard M. Johnson	1837–1841
Secretary of State	John Forsyth	1837–1841
Secretary of the Treasury	Levi Woodbury	1837–1841
Secretary of War	Joel Poinsett	1837–1841
Attorney General	Benjamin Butler	1837–1838
	Felix Grundy	1838–1840
	Henry D. Gilpin	1840–1841
Postmaster General	Amos Kendall	1837–1840
	John M. Niles	1840–1841
Secretary of Navy	Mahlon Dickerson	1837–1838
	James Paulding	1838–1841

William Harrison Administration, 1841

President	William H. Harrison	1841
Vice President	John Tyler	1841
Secretary of State	Daniel Webster	1841
Secretary of the Treasury	Thomas Ewing	1841
Secretary of War	John Bell	1841
Attorney General	John J. Crittenden	1841
Postmaster General	Francis Granger	1841
Secretary of Navy	George E. Badger	1841

Tyler Administration, 1841–1845

President	John Tyler	1841–1845
Vice President	None	
Secretary of State	Daniel Webster	1841–1843
	Abel P. Upshur	1843–1844
	John C. Calhoun	1844–1845
Secretary of the Treasury	Thomas Ewing	1841
	Walter Forward	1841–1843
	John C. Spencer	1843–1844
	George Bibb	1844–1845
Secretary of War	John Bell	1841
	John C. Spencer	1841–1843
	James M. Porter	1843–1844
	William Wilkins	1844–1845
Attorney General	John J. Crittendon	1841
	Hugh S. Legaré	1841–1843
	John Nelson	1843–1845
Postmaster General	Francis Granger	1841
	Charles Wickliffe	1841–1845
Secretary of Navy	George E. Badger	1841
	Abel P. Upshur	1841–1843
	David Henshaw	1843–1844
	Thomas Gilmer	1844
	John Y. Mason	1844–1845

Polk Administration, 1845–1849

President	James K. Polk	1845–1849
Vice President	George M. Dallas	1845–1849

Presidents, Vice Presidents, and Cabinet Members, Continued

Secretary of State	James Buchanan	1845–1849
Secretary of the Treasury	Robert J. Walker	1845–1849
Secretary of War	William L. Marcy	1845–1849
Attorney General	John Y. Mason	1845–1846
	Nathan Clifford	1846–1848
	Isaac Toucey	1848–1849
Postmaster General	Cave Johnson	1845–1849
Secretary of Navy	George Bancroft	1845–1846
	John Y. Mason	1846–1849

Taylor Administration, 1849–1850

President	Zachary Taylor	1849–1850
Vice President	Millard Fillmore	1849–1850
Secretary of State	John M. Clayton	1849–1850
Secretary of the Treasury	William Meredith	1849–1850
Secretary of War	George Crawford	1849–1850
Attorney General	Reverdy Johnson	1849–1850
Postmaster General	Jacob Collamer	1849–1850
Secretary of Navy	William Preston	1849–1850
Secretary of Interior	Thomas Ewing	1849–1850

Fillmore Administration, 1850–1853

President	Millard Fillmore	1850–1853
Vice President	None	
Secretary of State	Daniel Webster	1850–1852
	Edward Everett	1852–1853
Secretary of the Treasury	Thomas Corwin	1850–1853
Secretary of War	Charles Conrad	1850–1853
Attorney General	John J. Crittenden	1850–1853
Postmaster General	Nathan K. Hall	1850–1852
	Samuel D. Hubbard	1852–1853
Secretary of Navy	William A. Graham	1850–1852
	John P. Kennedy	1852–1853
Secretary of Interior	Thomas McKennan	1850
	Alexander Stuart	1850–1853

Pierce Administration, 1853–1857

President	Franklin Pierce	1853–1857
Vice President	William R. King	1853–1857
Secretary of State	William L. Marcy	1853–1857
Secretary of the Treasury	James Guthrie	1853–1857
Secretary of War	Jefferson Davis	1853–1857
Attorney General	Caleb Cushing	1853–1857
Postmaster General	James Campbell	1853–1857
Secretary of Navy	James C. Dobbin	1853–1857
Secretary of Interior	Robert McClelland	1853–1857

Buchanan Administration, 1857–1861

President	James Buchanan	1857–1861
Vice President	John C. Breckinridge	1857–1861
Secretary of State	Lewis Cass	1857–1860
	Jeremiah S. Black	1860–1861
Secretary of the Treasury	Howell Cobb	1857–1860
	Philip Thomas	1860–1861
	John A. Dix	1861
Secretary of War	John B. Floyd	1857–1861
	Joseph Holt	1861
Attorney General	Jeremiah S. Black	1857–1860
	Edwin M. Stanton	1860–1861
Postmaster General	Aaron V. Brown	1857–1859
	Joseph Holt	1859–1861
	Horatio King	1861
Secretary of Navy	Isaac Toucey	1857–1861
Secretary of Interior	Jacob Thompson	1857–1861

Lincoln Administration, 1861–1865

President	Abraham Lincoln	1861–1865
Vice President	Hannibal Hamlin	1861–1865
	Andrew Johnson	1865
Secretary of State	William H. Seward	1861–1865
Secretary of the Treasury	Samuel P. Chase	1861–1864
	William P. Fessenden	1864–1865
	Hugh McCulloch	1865
Secretary of War	Simon Cameron	1861–1862
	Edwin M. Stanton	1862–1865
Attorney General	Edward Bates	1861–1864
	James Speed	1864–1865
Postmaster General	Horatio King	1861
	Montgomery Blair	1861–1864
	William Dennison	1864–1865
Secretary of Navy	Gideon Welles	1861–1865
Secretary of Interior	Caleb B. Smith	1861–1863
	John P. Usher	1863–1865

Andrew Johnson Administration, 1865–1869

President	Andrew Johnson	1865–1869
Vice President	None	
Secretary of State	William H. Seward	1865–1869
Secretary of the Treasury	Hugh McCulloch	1865–1869
Secretary of War	Edwin M. Stanton	1865–1867
	Ulysses S. Grant	1867–1868
	Lorenzo Thomas	1868
	John M. Schofield	1868–1869
Attorney General	James Speed	1865–1866
	Henry Stanbery	1866–1868
	William M. Evarts	1868–1869

Presidents, Vice Presidents, and Cabinet Members, Continued

Postmaster General	William Dennison	1865–1866
	Alexander Randall	1866–1869
Secretary of Navy	Gideon Welles	1865–1869
Secretary of Interior	John P. Usher	1865
	James Harlan	1865–1866
	Orville H. Browning	1866–1869

Grant Administration, 1869–1877

President	Ulysses S. Grant	1869–1877
Vice President	Schuyler Colfax	1869–1873
	Henry Wilson	1873–1877
Secretary of State	Elihu B. Washburne	1869
	Hamilton Fish	1869–1877
Secretary of the Treasury	George S. Boutwell	1869–1873
	William Richardson	1873–1874
	Benjamin Bristow	1874–1876
	Lot M. Morrill	1876–1877
Secretary of War	John A. Rawlins	1869
	William T. Sherman	1869
	William W. Belknap	1869–1876
	Alphonso Taft	1876
	James D. Cameron	1876–1877
Attorney General	Ebenezer R. Hoar	1869–1870
	Amos T. Ackerman	1870–1871
	G. H. Williams	1871–1875
	Edwards Pierrepont	1875–1876
	Alphonso Taft	1876–1877
Postmaster General	John A. J. Creswell	1869–1874
	James W. Marshall	1874
	Marshall Jewell	1874–1876
	James N. Tyner	1876–1877
Secretary of Navy	Adolph E. Borie	1869
	George M. Robeson	1869–1877
Secretary of Interior	Jacob D. Cox	1869–1870
	Columbus Delano	1870–1875
	Zachariah Chandler	1875–1877

Hayes Administration, 1877–1881

President	Rutherford B. Hayes	1877–1881
Vice President	William A. Wheeler	1877–1881
Secretary of State	William B. Evarts	1877–1881
Secretary of the Treasury	John Sherman	1877–1881
Secretary of War	George W. McCrary	1877–1879
	Alex Ramsey	1879–1881
Attorney General	Charles Devens	1877–1881
Postmaster General	David M. Key	1877–1880
	Horace Maynard	1880–1881
Secretary of Navy	Richard W. Thompson	1877–1880
	Nathan Goff, Jr.	1881
Secretary of Interior	Carl Schurz	1877–1881

Garfield Administration, 1881

President	James A. Garfield	1881
Vice President	Chester A. Arthur	1881
Secretary of State	James G. Blaine	1881
Secretary of the Treasury	William Windom	1881
Secretary of War	Robert T. Lincoln	1881
Attorney General	Wayne MacVeagh	1881
Postmaster General	Thomas L. James	1881
Secretary of Navy	William H. Hunt	1881
Secretary of Interior	Samuel J. Kirkwood	1881

Arthur Administration, 1881–1885

President	Chester A. Arthur	1881–1885
Vice President	None	
Secretary of State	F. T. Frelinghuysen	1881–1885
Secretary of the Treasury	Charles J. Folger	1881–1884
	Walter Q. Gresham	1884
	Hugh McCulloch	1884–1885
Secretary of War	Robert T. Lincoln	1881–1885
Attorney General	Benjamin H. Brewster	1881–1885
Postmaster General	Timothy O. Howe	1881–1883
	Walter Q. Gresham	1883–1884
	Frank Hatton	1884–1885
Secretary of Navy	William H. Hunt	1881–1882
	William E. Chandler	1882–1885
Secretary of Interior	Samuel J. Kirkwood	1881–1882
	Henry M. Teller	1882–1885

Cleveland Administration, 1885–1889

President	Grover Cleveland	1885–1889
Vice President	Thomas A. Hendricks	1885–1889
Secretary of State	Thomas F. Bayard	1885–1889
Secretary of the Treasury	Daniel Manning	1885–1887
	Charles S. Fairchild	1887–1889
Secretary of War	William C. Endicott	1885–1889
Attorney General	Augustus H. Garland	1885–1889
Postmaster General	William F. Vilas	1885–1888
	Don M. Dickinson	1888–1889
Secretary of Navy	William C. Whitney	1885–1889
Secretary of Interior	Lucius Q. C. Lamar	1885–1888
	William F. Vilas	1888–1889
Secretary of Agriculture	Norman J. Colman	1889

Benjamin Harrison Administration, 1889–1893

President	Benjamin Harrison	1889–1893
Vice President	Levi P. Morton	1889–1893

Presidents, Vice Presidents, and Cabinet Members, Continued

Secretary of State	James G. Blaine	1889–1892
	John W. Foster	1892–1893
Secretary of the Treasury	William Windom	1889–1891
	Charles Foster	1891–1893
Secretary of War	Redfield Proctor	1889–1891
	Stephen B. Elkins	1891–1893
Attorney General	William H. H. Miller	1889–1891
Postmaster General	John Wanamaker	1889–1893
Secretary of Navy	Benjamin F. Tracy	1889–1893
Secretary of Interior	John W. Noble	1889–1893
Secretary of Agriculture	Jeremiah M. Rusk	1889–1893

Cleveland Administration, 1893–1897

President	Grover Cleveland	1893–1897
Vice President	Adlai E. Stevenson	1893–1897
Secretary of State	Walter Q. Gresham	1893–1895
	Richard Olney	1895–1897
Secretary of the Treasury	John G. Carlisle	1893–1897
Secretary of War	Daniel S. Lamont	1893–1897
Attorney General	Richard Olney	1893–1895
	Judson Harmon	1895–1897
Postmaster General	Wilson S. Bissell	1893–1895
	William L. Wilson	1895–1897
Secretary of Navy	Hilary A. Herbert	1893–1897
Secretary of Interior	Hoke Smith	1893–1896
	David R. Francis	1896–1897
Secretary of Agriculture	Julius S. Morton	1893–1897

McKinley Administration, 1897–1901

President	William McKinley	1897–1901
Vice President	Garret A. Hobart	1897–1901
	Theodore Roosevelt	1901
Secretary of State	John Sherman	1897–1898
	William R. Day	1898
	John Hay	1898–1901
Secretary of the Treasury	Lyman J. Gage	1897–1901
Secretary of War	Russell A. Alger	1897–1899
	Elihu Root	1899–1901
Attorney General	Joseph McKenna	1897–1898
	John W. Griggs	1898–1901
	Philander C. Knox	1901
Postmaster General	James A. Gary	1897–1898
	Charles E. Smith	1898–1901
Secretary of Navy	John D. Long	1897–1901
Secretary of Interior	Cornelius N. Bliss	1897–1899
	Ethan A. Hitchcock	1899–1901
Secretary of Agriculture	James Wilson	1897–1901

Theodore Roosevelt Administration, 1901–1909

President	Theodore Roosevelt	1901–1909
Vice President	Charles Fairbanks	1905–1909
Secretary of State	John Hay	1901–1905
	Elihu Root	1905–1909
	Robert Bacon	1909
Secretary of the Treasury	Lyman J. Gage	1901–1902
	Leslie M. Shaw	1902–1907
	George B. Cortelyou	1907–1909
Secretary of War	Elihu Root	1901–1904
	Willim H. Taft	1904–1908
	Luke E. Wright	1908–1909
Attorney General	Philander C. Knox	1901–1904
	William H. Moody	1904–1906
	Charles J. Bonaparte	1906–1909
Postmaster General	Charles E. Smith	1901–1902
	Henry C. Payne	1902–1904
	Robert J. Wynne	1904–1905
	George B. Cortelyou	1905–1907
	George von L. Meyer	1907–1909
Secretary of Navy	John D. Long	1901–1902
	William H. Moody	1902–1904
	Paul Morton	1904–1905
	Charles J. Bonaparte	1905–1906
	Victor H. Metcalf	1906–1908
	Truman H. Newberry	1908–1909
Secretary of Interior	Ethan A. Hitchcock	1901–1907
	James R. Garfield	1907–1909
Secretary of Agriculture	James Wilson	1901–1909
Secretary of Labor and Commerce	George B. Cortelyou	1903–1904
	Victor H. Metcalf	1904–1906
	Oscar S. Straus	1906–1909

Taft Administration, 1909–1913

President	William H. Taft	1909–1913
Vice President	James S. Sherman	1909–1913
Secretary of State	Philander C. Knox	1909–1913
Secretary of the Treasury	Franklin MacVeagh	1909–1913
Secretary of War	Jacob M. Dickinson	1909–1911
	Henry L. Stimson	1911–1913
Attorney General	George W. Wickersham	1909–1913
Postmaster General	Frank H. Hitchcock	1909–1913
Secretary of Navy	George von L. Meyer	1909–1913
Secretary of Interior	Richard A. Ballinger	1909–1911
	Walter L. Fisher	1911–1913
Secretary of Agriculture	James Wilson	1909–1913
Secretary of Labor and Commerce	Charles Nagel	1909–1913

Presidents, Vice Presidents, and Cabinet Members, Continued

Wilson Administration, 1913–1921

President	Woodrow Wilson	1913–1921
Vice President	Thomas R. Marshall	1913–1921
Secretary of State.	William J. Bryan	1913–1915
	Robert Lansing	1915–1920
	Bainbridge Colby	1920–1921
Secretary of the Treasury	William G. McAdoo	1913–1918
	Carter Glass	1918–1920
	David F. Houston	1920–1921
Secretary of War	Lindley M. Garrison	1913–1916
	Newton D. Baker	1916–1921
Attorney General	James C. McReynolds	1913–1914
	Thomas W. Gregory	1914–1919
	A. Mitchell Palmer	1919–1921
Postmaster General	Albert S. Burleson	1913–1921
Secretary of Navy	Josephus Daniels	1913–1921
Secretary of Interior	Franklin K. Lane	1913–1920
	John B. Payne	1920–1921
Secretary of Agriculture	David F. Houston	1913–1920
	Edwin T. Meredith	1920–1921
Secretary of Commerce	William C. Redfield	1913–1919
	Joshua W. Alexander	1919–1921
Secretary of Labor	William B. Wilson	1913–1921

Harding Administration, 1921–1923

President	Warren G. Harding	1921–1923
Vice President	Calvin Coolidge	1921–1923
Secretary of State	Charles E. Hughes	1921–1923
Secretary of the Treasury	Andrew Mellon	1921–1923
Secretary of War	John W. Weeks	1921–1923
Attorney General	Harry M. Daugherty	1921–1923
Postmaster General	Will H. Hays	1921–1922
	Hubert Work	1922–1923
	Harry S. New	1923
Secretary of Navy	Edwin Denby	1921–1923
Secretary of Interior	Albert B. Fall	1921–1923
	Hubert Work	1923
Secretary of Agriculture	Henry C. Wallace	1921–1923
Secretary of Commerce	Herbert C. Hoover	1921–1923
Secretary of Labor	James J. Davis	1921–1923

Coolidge Administration, 1923–1929

President	Calvin Coolidge	1923–1929
Vice President	Charles G. Dawes	1925–1929
Secretary of State	Charles E. Hughes	1923–1925
	Frank B. Kellogg	1925–1929
Secretary of the Treasury	Andrew Mellon	1923–1929

Secretary of War	John W. Weeks	1923–1925
	Dwight F. Davis	1925–1929
Attorney General	Henry M. Daugherty	1923–1924
	Harlan F. Stone	1924–1925
	John G. Sargent	1925–1929
Postmaster General	Harry S. New	1923–1929
Secretary of Navy	Edwin Derby	1923–1924
	Curtis D. Wilbur	1924–1929
Secretary of Interior	Hubert Work	1923–1928
	Roy O. West	1928–1929
Secretary of Agriculture	Henry C. Wallace	1923–1924
	Howard M. Gore	1924–1925
	William M. Jardine	1925–1929
Secretary of Commerce	Herbert C. Hoover	1923–1928
	William F. Whiting	1928–1929
Secretary of Labor	James J. Davis	1923–1929

Hoover Administration, 1929–1933

President	Herbert C. Hoover	1929–1933
Vice President	Charles Curtis	1929–1933
Secretary of State	Henry L. Stimson	1929–1933
Secretary of the Treasury	Andrew Mellon	1929–1932
	Ogden L. Mills	1932–1933
Secretary of War	James W. Good	1929
	Patrick J. Hurley	1929–1933
Attorney General	William D. Mitchell	1929–1933
Postmaster General	Walter F. Brown	1929–1933
Secretary of Navy	Charles F. Adams	1929–1933
Secretary of Interior	Ray L. Wilbur	1929–1933
Secretary of Agriculture	Arthur M. Hyde	1929–1933
Secretary of Commerce	Robert P. Lamont	1929–1932
	Roy D. Chapin	1932–1933
Secretary of Labor	James J. Davis	1929–1930
	William N. Doak	1930–1933

Franklin D. Roosevelt Administration, 1933–1945

President	Franklin D. Roosevelt	1933–1945
Vice President	John Nance Garner	1933–1941
	Henry A. Wallace	1941–1945
	Harry S Truman	1945
Secretary of State	Cordell Hull	1933–1944
	Edward R. Stettinius, Jr.	1944–1945
Secretary of the Treasury	William H. Woodin	1933–1934
	Henry Morgenthau, Jr.	1934–1945
Secretary of War	George H. Dern	1933–1936
	Henry A. Woodring	1936–1940
	Henry L. Stimson	1940–1945
Attorney General	Homer S. Cummings	1933–1939
	Frank Murphy	1939–1940
	Robert H. Jackson	1940–1941
	Francis Biddle	1941–1945

Presidents, Vice Presidents, and Cabinet Members, Continued

Postmaster General	James A. Farley	1933–1940
	Frank C. Walker	1940–1945
Secretary of Navy	Claude A. Swanson	1933–1939
	Charles Edison	1939–1940
	Frank Knox	1940–1944
	James V. Forrestal	1944–1945
Secretary of Interior	Harold L. Ickes	1933–1945
Secretary of Agriculture	Henry A. Wallace	1933–1940
	Claude R. Wickard	1940–1945
Secretary of Commerce	Daniel C. Roper	1933–1938
	Harry L. Hopkins	1938–1940
	Jesse H. Jones	1940–1945
	Henry A. Wallace	1945
Secretary of Labor	Frances Perkins	1933–1945

Truman Administration, 1945–1953

President	Harry S Truman	1945–1953
Vice President	Alben W. Barkley	1949–1953
Secretary of State	Edward R. Stettinius, Jr.	1945
	James F. Byrnes	1945–1947
	George C. Marshall	1947–1949
	Dean G. Acheson	1949–1953
Secretary of the Treasury	Henry Morgenthau, Jr.	1945
	Fred M. Vinson	1945–1946
	John W. Snyder	1946–1953
Secretary of War	Henry L. Stimson	1945
	Robert P. Patterson	1945–1947
	Kenneth C. Royall	1947
Attorney General	Francis Biddle	1945
	Tom C. Clark	1945–1949
	J. Howard McGrath	1949–1952
	James P. McGranery	1952–1953
Postmaster General	Frank C. Walker	1945
	Robert E. Hannegan	1945–1947
	Jesse M. Donaldson	1947–1953
Secretary of Navy	James V. Forrestal	1945–1947
Secretary of Interior	Harold L. Ickes	1945–1946
	Julius A. Krug	1946–1949
	Oscar L. Chapman	1949–1953
Secretary of Agriculture	Claude R. Wickard	1945
	Clinton P. Anderson	1945–1948
	Charles F. Brannan	1948–1953
Secretary of Commerce	Henry A. Wallace	1945–1946
	W. Averell Harriman	1946–1948
	Charles W. Sawyer	1948–1953
Secretary of Labor	Frances Perkins	1945
	Lewis B. Schwellenbach	1945–1948
	Maurice J. Tobin	1948–1953
Secretary of Defense	James V. Forrestal	1947–1949
	Louis A. Johnson	1949–1950
	George C. Marshall	1950–1951
	Robert A. Lovett	1951–1953

Eisenhower Administration, 1953–1961

President	Dwight D. Eisenhower	1953–1961
Vice President	Richard M. Nixon	1953–1961
Secretary of State	John Foster Dulles	1953–1959
	Christian A. Herter	1959–1961
Secretary of the Treasury	George M. Humphrey	1953–1957
	Robert B. Anderson	1957–1961
Attorney General	Herbert Brownell, Jr.	1953–1957
	William P. Rogers	1957–1961
Postmaster General	Arthur E. Summerfield	1953–1961
Secretary of Interior	Douglas McKay	1953–1956
	Fred A. Seaton	1956–1961
Secretary of Agriculture	Ezra T. Benson	1953–1961
Secretary of Commerce	Sinclair Weeks	1953–1958
	Lewis L. Strauss	1958–1959
	Frederick H. Mueller	1959–1961
Secretary of Labor	Martin P. Durkin	1953
	James P. Mitchell	1953–1961
Secretary of Defense	Charles E. Wilson	1953–1957
	Neil H. McElroy	1957–1959
	Thomas S. Gates, Jr.	1959–1961
Secretary of Health, Education, and Welfare	Oveta Culp Hobby	1953–1955
	Marion B. Folsom	1955–1958
	Arthur S. Flemming	1958–1961

Kennedy Administration, 1961–1963

President	John F. Kennedy	1961–1963
Vice President	Lyndon B. Johnson	1961–1963
Secretary of State	Dean Rusk	1961–1963
Secretary of the Treasury	C. Douglas Dillon	1961–1963
Attorney General	Robert F. Kennedy	1961–1963
Postmaster General	J. Edward Day	1961–1963
	John A. Gronouski	1963
Secretary of Interior	Stewart L. Udall	1961–1963
Secretary of Agriculture	Orville L. Freeman	1961–1963
Secretary of Commerce	Luther H. Hodges	1961–1963
Secretary of Labor	Arthur J. Goldberg	1961–1962
	W. Willard Wirtz	1962–1963
Secretary of Defense	Robert S. McNamara	1961–1963
Secretary of Health, Education, and Welfare	Abraham A. Ribicoff	1961–1962
	Anthony J. Celebrezze	1962–1963

Lyndon B. Johnson Administration, 1963–1969

President	Lyndon B. Johnson	1963–1969
Vice President	Hubert H. Humphrey	1965–1969

Presidents, Vice Presidents, and Cabinet Members, Continued

Secretary of State	Dean Rusk	1963–1969
Secretary of the Treasury	C. Douglas Dillon	1963–1965
	Henry H. Fowler	1965–1969
Attorney General	Robert F. Kennedy	1963–1964
	Nicholas Katzenbach	1965–1966
	Ramsey Clark	1967–1969
Postmaster General	John A. Gronouski	1963–1965
	Lawrence F. O'Brien	1965–1968
	Marvin Watson	1968–1969
Secretary of Interior	Stewart L. Udall	1963–1969
Secretary of Agriculture	Orville L. Freeman	1963–1969
Secretary of Commerce	Luther H. Hodges	1963–1964
	John T. Connor	1964–1967
	Alexander B. Trowbridge	1967–1968
	Cyrus R. Smith	1968–1969
Secretary of Labor	W. Willard Wirtz	1963–1969
Secretary of Defense	Robert F. McNamara	1963–1968
	Clark Clifford	1968–1969
Secretary of Health, Education, and Welfare	Anthony J. Celebrezze	1963–1965
	John W. Gardner	1965–1968
	Wilbur J. Cohen	1968–1969
Secretary of Housing and Urban Development	Robert C. Weaver	1966–1969
	Robert C. Wood	1969
Secretary of Transportation	Alan S. Boyd	1967–1969

Nixon Administration, 1969–1974

President	Richard M. Nixon	1969–1974
Vice President	Spiro T. Agnew	1969–1973
	Gerald R. Ford	1973–1974
Secretary of State	William P. Rogers	1969–1973
	Henry A. Kissinger	1973–1974
Secretary of the Treasury	David M. Kennedy	1969–1970
	John B. Connally	1971–1972
	George P. Shultz	1972–1974
	William E. Simon	1974
Attorney General	John N. Mitchell	1969–1972
	Richard G. Kleindienst	1972–1973
	Elliot L. Richardson	1973
	William B. Saxbe	1973–1974
Postmaster General	Winton M. Blount	1969–1971
Secretary of Interior	Walter J. Hickel	1969–1970
	Rogers Morton	1971–1974
Secretary of Agriculture	Clifford M. Hardin	1969–1971
	Earl L. Butz	1971–1974
Secretary of Commerce	Maurice H. Stans	1969–1972
	Peter G. Peterson	1972–1973
	Frederick B. Dent	1973–1974
Secretary of Labor	George P. Shultz	1969–1970
	James D. Hodgson	1970–1973
	Peter J. Brennan	1973–1974

Secretary of Defense	Melvin R. Laird	1969–1973
	Elliot L. Richardson	1973
	James R. Schlesinger	1973–1974
Secretary of Health, Education, and Welfare	Robert H. Finch	1969–1970
	Elliot L. Richardson	1970–1973
	Casper W. Weinberger	1973–1974
Secretary of Housing and Urban Development	George Romney	1969–1973
	James T. Lynn	1973–1974
Secretary of Transportation	John A. Volpe	1969–1973
	Claude S. Brinegar	1973–1974

Ford Administration, 1974–1977

President	Gerald R. Ford	1974–1977
Vice President	Nelson A. Rockefeller	1974–1977
Secretary of State	Henry A. Kissinger	1974–1977
Secretary of the Treasury	William E. Simon	1974–1977
Attorney General	William Saxbe	1974–1975
	Edward Levi	1975–1977
Secretary of Interior	Rogers Morton	1974–1975
	Stanley K. Hathaway	1975
	Thomas Kleppe	1975–1977
Secretary of Agriculture	Earl L. Butz	1974–1976
	John A. Knebel	1976–1977
Secretary of Commerce	Frederick B. Dent	1974–1975
	Rogers Morton	1975–1976
	Elliot L. Richardson	1976–1977
Secretary of Labor	Peter J. Brennan	1974–1975
	John T. Dunlop	1975–1976
	W. J. Usery	1976–1977
Secretary of Defense	James R. Schlesinger	1974–1975
	Donald Rumsfeld	1975–1977
Secretary of Health, Education, and Welfare	Casper Weinberger	1974–1975
	Forrest D. Mathews	1975–1977
Secretary of Housing and Urban Development	James T. Lynn	1974–1975
	Carla A. Hills	1975–1977
Secretary of Transportation	Claude Brinegar	1974–1975
	William T. Coleman	1975–1977

Carter Administration, 1977–1981

President	James E. Carter	1977–1981
Vice President	Walter F. Mondale	1977–1981
Secretary of State	Cyrus R. Vance	1977–1980
	Edmund Muskie	1980–1981
Secretary of the Treasury	W. Michael Blumenthal	1977–1979
	G. William Miller	1979–1981
Attorney General	Griffin Bell	1977–1979
	Benjamin R. Civiletti	1979–1981
Secretary of Interior	Cecil D. Andrus	1977–1981

Presidents, Vice Presidents, and Cabinet Members, Continued

Secretary of Agriculture	Robert Bergland	1977–1981
Secretary of Commerce	Juanita M. Kreps	1977–1979
	Philip M. Klutznick	1979–1981
Secretary of Labor	F. Ray Marshall	1977–1981
Secretary of Defense	Harold Brown	1977–1981
Secretary of Health, Education, and Welfare	Joseph A. Califano	1977–1979
	Patricia R. Harris	1979
Secretary of Health and Human Services	Patricia R. Harris	1979–1981
Secretary of Education	Shirley M. Hufstedler	1979–1981
Secretary of Housing and Urban Development	Patricia R. Harris	1977–1979
	Moon Landrieu	1979–1981
Secretary of Transportation	Brock Adams	1977–1979
	Neil E. Goldschmidt	1979–1981
Secretary of Energy	James R. Schlesinger	1977–1979
	Charles W. Duncan	1979–1981

Reagan Administration, 1981–1989

President	Ronald W. Reagan	1981–1989
Vice President	George H. W. Bush	1981–1989
Secretary of State	Alexander M. Haig	1981–1982
	George P. Shultz	1982–1989
Secretary of the Treasury	Donald Regan	1981–1985
	James A. Baker III	1985–1988
	Nicholas F. Brady	1988–1989
Attorney General	William F. Smith	1981–1985
	Edwin A. Meese III	1985–1988
	Richard L. Thornburgh	1988–1989
Secretary of Interior	James G. Watt	1981–1983
	William P. Clark, Jr.	1983–1985
	Donald P. Hodel	1985–1989
Secretary of Agriculture	John Block	1981–1986
	Richard E. Lyng	1986–1989
Secretary of Commerce	Malcolm Baldrige	1981–1987
	C. William Verity, Jr.	1987–1989
Secretary of Labor	Raymond J. Donovan	1981–1985
	William E. Brock	1985–1987
	Ann Dore McLaughlin	1987–1989
Secretary of Defense	Casper Weinberger	1981–1987
	Frank C. Carlucci	1987–1989
Secretary of Health and Human Services	Richard S. Schweiker	1981–1983
	Margaret Heckler	1983–1985
	Otis R. Bowen	1985–1989
Secretary of Education	Terrel H. Bell	1981–1984
	William J. Bennett	1985–1988
	Lauro F. Cavazos	1988–1989

Secretary of Housing and Urban Development	Samuel R. Pierce, Jr.	1981–1989
Secretary of Transportation	Drew Lewis	1981–1982
	Elizabeth Hanford Dole	1983–1987
	James H. Burnley IV	1987–1989
Secretary of Energy	James B. Edwards	1981–1982
	Donald P. Hodel	1982–1985
	John S. Herrington	1985–1989

Bush Administration, 1989–1993

President	George H. W. Bush	1989–1993
Vice President	J. Danforth Quayle	1989–1993
Secretary of State	James A. Baker III	1989–1992
	Lawrence Eagleburger	1992–1993
Secretary of the Treasury	Nicholas F. Brady	1989–1993
Attorney General	Richard L. Thornburgh	1989–1991
	William P. Barr	1991–1993
Secretary of Interior	Manuel Lujan, Jr.	1989–1993
Secretary of Agriculture	Clayton K. Yeutter	1989–1991
	Edward Madigan	1991–1993
Secretary of Commerce	Robert A. Mosbacher	1989–1992
	Barbara Hackman Franklin	1992–1993
Secretary of Labor	Elizabeth Hanford Dole	1989–1991
	Lynn Martin	1991–1993
Secretary of Defense	Richard B. Cheney	1989–1993
Secretary of Health and Human Services	Louis W. Sullivan	1989–1993
Secretary of Education	Lauro F. Cavazos	1989–1990
	Lamar Alexander	1991–1993
Secretary of Housing and Urban Development	Jack F. Kemp	1989–1993
Secretary of Transportation	Samuel K. Skinner	1989–1992
	Andrew H. Card	1992–1993
Secretary of Energy	James D. Watkins	1989–1993
Secretary of Veterans Affairs	Edward J. Derwinski	1989–1993

Clinton Administration, 1993–

President	William J. Clinton	1993–
Vice President	Albert Gore	1993–
Secretary of State	Warren M. Christopher	1993–1997
	Madeleine K. Albright	1997–
Secretary of the Treasury	Lloyd Bentsen	1993–1995
	Robert E. Rubin	1995–
Attorney General	Janet Reno	1993–
Secretary of Interior	Bruce Babbitt	1993–

Presidents, Vice Presidents, and Cabinet Members, Continued

Secretary of Agriculture	Mike Espy Daniel R. Glickman	1993–1995 1995–	Secretary of Education	Richard W. Riley	1993–
Secretary of Commerce	Ronald H. Brown Mickey Kantor William Daley	1993–1996 1996–1997 1997–	Secretary of Housing and Urban Development	Henry G. Cisneros Andrew Cuomo	1993–1996 1997–
Secretary of Labor	Robert B. Reich Alexis M. Herman	1993–1997 1997–	Secretary of Transportation	Federico F. Peña Rodney E. Slater	1993–1997 1997–
Secretary of Defense	Les Aspin William J. Perry William S. Cohen	1993–1994 1994–1997 1997–	Secretary of Energy	Hazel O'Leary Federico F. Peña	1993–1997 1997–
Secretary of Health and Human Services	Donna E. Shalala	1993–	Secretary of Veterans Affairs	Jesse Brown	1993–

Party Strength in Congress

Period	Congress	House Majority Party		House Minority Party		Others	Senate Majority Party		Senate Minority Party		Others	Party of President	
1789–91	1st	Ad	38	Op	26		Ad	17	Op	9		F	Washington
1791–93	2nd	F	37	DR	33		F	16	DR	13		F	Washington
1793–95	3rd	DR	57	F	48		F	17	DR	13		F	Washington
1795–97	4th	F	54	DR	52		F	19	DR	13		F	Washington
1797–99	5th	F	58	DR	48		F	20	DR	12		F	J. Adams
1799–1801	6th	F	64	DR	42		F	19	DR	13		F	J. Adams
1801–03	7th	DR	69	F	36		DR	18	F	13		DR	Jefferson
1803–05	8th	DR	102	F	39		DR	25	F	9		DR	Jefferson
1805–07	9th	DR	116	F	25		DR	27	F	7		DR	Jefferson
1807–09	10th	DR	118	F	24		DR	28	F	6		DR	Jefferson
1809–11	11th	DR	94	F	48		DR	28	F	6		DR	Madison
1811–13	12th	DR	108	F	36		DR	30	F	6		DR	Madison
1813–15	13th	DR	112	F	68		DR	27	F	9		DR	Madison
1815–17	14th	DR	117	F	65		DR	25	F	11		DR	Madison
1817–19	15th	DR	141	F	42		DR	34	F	10		DR	Monroe
1819–21	16th	DR	156	F	27		DR	35	F	7		DR	Monroe
1821–23	17th	DR	158	F	25		DR	44	F	4		DR	Monroe
1823–25	18th	DR	187	F	26		DR	44	F	4		DR	Monroe
1825–27	19th	Ad	105	J	97		Ad	26	J	20		C	J. Q. Adams
1827–29	20th	J	119	Ad	94		J	28	Ad	20		C	J. Q. Adams
1829–31	21st	D	139	NR	74		D	26	NR	22		D	Jackson
1831–33	22nd	D	141	NR	58	14	D	25	NR	21	2	D	Jackson
1833–35	23rd	D	147	AM	53	60	D	20	NR	20	8	D	Jackson
1835–37	24th	D	145	W	98		D	27	W	25		D	Jackson
1837–39	25th	D	108	W	107	24	D	30	W	18	4	D	Van Buren
1839–41	26th	D	124	W	118		D	28	W	22		D	Van Buren
1841–43	27th	W	133	D	102	6	W	28	D	22	2	W	W. Harrison
												W	Tyler
1843–45	28th	D	142	W	79	1	W	28	D	25	1	W	Tyler
1845–47	29th	D	143	W	77	6	D	31	W	25		D	Polk
1847–49	30th	W	115	D	108	4	D	36	W	21	1	D	Polk
1849–51	31st	D	112	W	109	9	D	35	W	25	2	W	Taylor
												W	Fillmore
1851–53	32nd	D	140	W	88	5	D	35	W	24	3	W	Fillmore
1853–55	33rd	D	159	W	71	4	D	38	W	22	2	D	Pierce
1855–57	34th	R	108	D	83	43	D	40	R	15	5	D	Pierce
1857–59	35th	D	118	R	92	26	D	36	R	20	8	D	Buchanan

Party Strength in Congress, Continued

Period	Congress	House Majority Party		House Minority Party		Others	Senate Majority Party		Senate Minority Party		Others	Party of President	
1859–61	36th	R	114	D	92	31	D	36	R	26	4	D	Buchanan
1861–63	37th	R	105	D	43	30	R	31	D	10	8	R	Lincoln
1863–65	38th	R	102	D	75	9	R	36	D	9	5	R	Lincoln
1865–67	39th	U	149	D	42		U	42	D	10		R	Lincoln
												R	A. Johnson
1867–69	40th	R	143	D	49		R	42	D	11		R	A. Johnson
1869–71	41st	R	149	D	63		R	56	D	11		R	Grant
1871–73	42nd	R	134	D	104	5	R	52	D	17	5	R	Grant
1873–75	43rd	R	194	D	92	14	R	49	D	19	5	R	Grant
1875–77	44th	D	169	R	109	14	R	45	D	29	2	R	Grant
1877–79	45th	D	153	R	140		R	39	D	36	1	R	Hayes
1879–81	46th	D	149	R	130	14	D	42	R	33	1	R	Hayes
1881–83	47th	D	147	R	135	11	R	37	D	37	1	R	Garfield
												R	Arthur
1883–85	48th	D	197	R	118	10	R	38	D	36	2	R	Arthur
1885–87	49th	D	183	R	140	2	R	43	D	34		D	Cleveland
1887–89	50th	D	169	R	152	4	R	39	D	37		D	Cleveland
1889–91	51st	R	166	D	159		R	39	D	37		R	B. Harrison
1891–93	52nd	D	235	R	88	9	R	47	D	39	2	R	B. Harrison
1893–95	53rd	D	218	R	127	11	D	44	R	38	3	D	Cleveland
1895–97	54th	R	244	D	105	7	R	43	D	39	6	D	Cleveland
1897–99	55th	R	204	D	113	40	R	47	D	34	7	R	McKinley
1899–1901	56th	R	185	D	163	9	R	53	D	26	8	R	McKinley
1901–03	57th	R	197	D	151	9	R	55	D	31	4	R	McKinley
												R	T. Roosevelt
1903–05	58th	R	208	D	178		R	57	D	33		R	T. Roosevelt
1905–07	59th	R	250	D	136		R	57	D	33		R	T. Roosevelt
1907–09	60th	R	222	D	164		R	61	D	31		R	T. Roosevelt
1909–11	61st	R	219	D	172		R	61	D	32		R	Taft
1911–13	62nd	D	228	R	161	1	R	51	D	41		R	Taft
1913–15	63rd	D	291	R	127	17	D	51	R	44	1	D	Wilson
1915–17	64th	D	230	R	196	9	D	56	R	40		D	Wilson
1917–19	65th	D	216	R	210	6	D	53	R	42		D	Wilson
1919–21	66th	R	240	D	190	3	R	49	D	47		D	Wilson
1921–23	67th	R	301	D	131	1	R	59	D	37		R	Harding
1923–25	68th	R	225	D	205	5	R	51	D	43	2	R	Coolidge
1925–27	69th	R	247	D	183	4	R	56	D	39	1	R	Coolidge
1927–29	70th	R	237	D	195	3	R	49	D	46	1	R	Coolidge
1929–31	71st	R	267	D	167	1	R	56	D	39	1	R	Hoover
1931–33	72nd	D	220	R	214	1	R	48	D	47	1	R	Hoover
1933–35	73rd	D	310	R	117	5	D	60	R	35	1	D	F. Roosevelt
1935–37	74th	D	319	R	103	10	D	69	R	25	2	D	F. Roosevelt
1937–39	75th	D	331	R	89	13	D	76	R	16	4	D	F. Roosevelt
1939–41	76th	D	261	R	164	4	D	69	R	23	4	D	F. Roosevelt
1941–43	77th	D	268	R	162	5	D	66	R	28	2	D	F. Roosevelt
1943–45	78th	D	218	R	208	4	D	58	R	37	1	D	F. Roosevelt
1945–47	79th	D	242	R	190	2	D	56	R	38	1	D	Truman

Party Strength in Congress, Continued

Period	Congress	House Majority Party		House Minority Party		Others	Senate Majority Party		Senate Minority Party		Others	Party of President	
1947–49	80th	R	245	D	188	1	R	51	D	45		D	Truman
1949–51	81st	D	263	R	171	1	D	54	R	42		D	Truman
1951–53	82nd	D	234	R	199	1	D	49	R	47		D	Truman
1953–55	83rd	R	221	D	211	1	R	48	D	47	1	R	Eisenhower
1955–57	84th	D	232	R	203		D	48	R	47	1	R	Eisenhower
1957–59	85th	D	233	R	200		D	49	R	47		R	Eisenhower
1959–61	86th	D	284	R	153		D	65	R	35		R	Eisenhower
1961–63	87th	D	263	R	174		D	65	R	35		D	Kennedy
1963–65	88th	D	258	R	117		D	67	R	33		D	Kennedy
												D	L. Johnson
1965–67	89th	D	295	R	140		D	68	R	32		D	L. Johnson
1967–69	90th	D	246	R	187		D	64	R	36		D	L. Johnson
1969–71	91st	D	245	R	189		D	57	R	43		R	Nixon
1971–73	92nd	D	254	R	180		D	54	R	44	2	R	Nixon
1973–75	93rd	D	239	R	192	1	D	56	R	42	2	R	Nixon
1975–77	94th	D	291	R	144		D	60	R	37	3	R	Ford
1977–79	95th	D	292	R	143		D	61	R	38	1	D	Carter
1979–81	96th	D	276	R	157		D	58	R	41	1	D	Carter
1981–83	97th	D	243	R	192		R	53	D	46	1	R	Reagan
1983–85	98th	D	267	R	168		R	55	D	45		R	Reagan
1985–87	99th	D	253	R	182		R	53	D	47		R	Reagan
1987–89	100th	D	258	R	177		D	55	R	45		R	Reagan
1989–91	101st	D	259	R	174		D	54	R	46		R	Bush
1991–93	102nd	D	267	R	167	1	D	56	R	44		R	Bush
1993–95	103rd	D	258	R	176	1	D	56	R	44		D	Clinton
1995–97	104th	R	230	D	204	1	R	52	D	48		D	Clinton
1997–99	105th	R	227	D	207	1	R	55	D	45		D	Clinton

AD = Administration; AM = Anti-Masonic; C = Coalition; D = Democratic; DR = Democratic-Republican; F = Federalist; J = Jacksonian; NR = National Republican; Op = Opposition; R = Republican; U = Unionist; W = Whig. Figures are for the beginning of first session of each Congress, except the 93rd, which are for the beginning of the second session.

Justices of the Supreme Court

	Term of Service	Years of Service	Life Span		Term of Service	Years of Service	Life Span
John Jay	1789–1795	5	1745–1829	*Salmon P. Chase*	1864–1873	8	1808–1873
John Rutledge	1789–1791	1	1739–1800	William Strong	1870–1880	10	1808–1895
William Cushing	1789–1810	20	1732–1810	Joseph P. Bradley	1870–1892	22	1813–1892
James Wilson	1789–1798	8	1742–1798	Ward Hunt	1873–1882	9	1810–1886
John Blair	1789–1796	6	1732–1800	*Morrison R. Waite*	1874–1888	14	1816–1888
Robert H. Harrison	1789–1790	—	1745–1790	John M. Harlan	1877–1911	34	1833–1911
James Iredell	1790–1799	9	1951–1799	William B. Woods	1880–1887	7	1824–1887
Thomas Johnson	1791–1793	1	1732–1819	Stanley Mathews	1881–1889	7	1824–1889
William Paterson	1793–1806	13	1745–1806	Horace Gray	1882–1902	20	1828–1902
*John Rutledge**	1795	—	1739–1800	Samuel Blatchford	1882–1893	11	1820–1893
Samuel Chase	1796–1811	15	1741–1811	Lucius Q. C. Lamar	1888–1893	5	1825–1893
Oliver Ellsworth	1796–1800	4	1745–1807	*Melville W. Fuller*	1888–1910	21	1833–1910
Bushrod Washington	1798–1829	31	1762–1829	David J. Brewer	1890–1910	20	1837–1910
Alfred Moore	1799–1804	4	1755–1810	Henry B. Brown	1890–1906	16	1836–1913
John Marshall	1801–1835	34	1755–1835	George Shiras, Jr.	1892–1903	10	1832–1924
William Johnson	1804–1834	30	1771–1834	Howell E. Jackson	1893–1895	2	1832–1895
H. Brockholst Livingston	1806–1823	16	1757–1823	Edward D. White	1894–1910	16	1845–1921
Thomas Todd	1807–1826	18	1765–1826	Rufus W. Peckham	1895–1909	14	1838–1909
Joseph Story	1811–1845	33	1779–1845	Joseph McKenna	1898–1925	26	1843–1926
Gabriel Duval	1811–1835	24	1752–1844	Oliver W. Holmes	1902–1932	30	1841–1935
Smith Thompson	1823–1843	20	1768–1843	William D. Day	1903–1922	19	1849–1923
Robert Trimble	1826–1828	2	1777–1828	William H. Moody	1906–1910	3	1853–1917
John McLean	1829–1861	32	1785–1861	Horace H. Lurton	1910–1914	4	1844–1914
Henry Baldwin	1830–1844	14	1780–1844	Charles E. Hughes	1910–1916	5	1862–1948
James M. Wayne	1835–1867	32	1790–1867	Willis Van Devanter	1911–1937	26	1859–1941
Roger B. Taney	1836–1864	28	1777–1864	Joseph R. Lamar	1911–1916	5	1857–1916
Philip P. Barbour	1836–1841	4	1783–1841	*Edward D. White*	1910–1921	11	1845–1921
John Catron	1837–1865	28	1786–1865	Mahlon Pitney	1912–1922	10	1858–1924
John McKinley	1837–1852	15	1780–1852	James C. McReynolds	1914–1941	26	1862–1946
Peter V. Daniel	1841–1860	19	1784–1860	Louis D. Brandeis	1916–1939	22	1856–1941
Samuel Nelson	1845–1872	27	1792–1873	John H. Clarke	1916–1922	6	1857–1945
Levi Woodbury	1845–1851	5	1789–1851	*William H. Taft*	1921–1930	8	1857–1930
Robert C. Grier	1846–1870	23	1794–1870	George Sutherland	1922–1938	15	1862–1942
Benjamin R. Curtis	1851–1857	6	1809–1874	Pierce Butler	1922–1939	16	1866–1939
John A. Campbell	1853–1861	8	1811–1889	Edward T. Sanford	1923–1930	7	1865–1930
Nathan Clifford	1858–1881	23	1803–1881	Harlan F. Stone	1925–1941	16	1872–1946
Noah H. Swayne	1862–1881	18	1804–1884	*Charles E. Hughes*	1930–1941	11	1862–1948
Samuel F. Miller	1862–1890	28	1816–1890	Owen J. Roberts	1930–1945	15	1875–1955
David Davis	1862–1877	14	1815–1886	Benjamin N. Cardozo	1932–1938	6	1870–1938
Stephen J. Field	1863–1897	34	1816–1899	Hugo L. Black	1937–1971	34	1886–1971

Justices of the Supreme Court, Continued

	Term of Service	Years of Service	Life Span		Term of Service	Years of Service	Life Span
Stanley F. Reed	1938–1957	19	1884–1980	Byron R. White	1962–1993	31	1917–
Felix Frankfurter	1939–1962	23	1882–1965	Arthur J. Goldberg	1962–1965	3	1908–1990
William O. Douglas	1939–1975	36	1898–1980	Abe Fortas	1965–1969	4	1910–1982
Frank Murphy	1940–1949	9	1890–1949	Thurgood Marshall	1967–1991	24	1908–1993
Harlan F. Stone	1941–1946	5	1872–1946	*Warren C. Burger*	1969–1986	17	1907–1995
James F. Byrnes	1941–1942	1	1879–1972	Harry A. Blackmun	1970–1994	24	1908–
Robert H. Jackson	1941–1954	13	1892–1954	Lewis F. Powell, Jr.	1972–1987	15	1907–
Wiley B. Rutledge	1943–1949	6	1894–1949	*William H. Rehnquist*	1972–	—	1924–
Harold H. Burton	1945–1958	13	1888–1964	John P. Stevens III	1975–	—	1920–
Fred M. Vinson	1946–1953	7	1890–1953	Sandra Day O'Connor	1981–	—	1930–
Tom C. Clark	1949–1967	18	1899–1977	Antonin Scalia	1986–	—	1936–
Sherman Minton	1949–1956	7	1890–1965	Anthony M. Kennedy	1988–	—	1936–
Earl Warren	1953–1969	16	1891–1974	David H. Souter	1990–	—	1939–
John Marshall Harlan	1955–1971	16	1899–1971	Clarence Thomas	1991–	—	1948–
William J. Brennan, Jr.	1956–1990	34	1906–	Ruth Bader Ginsburg	1993–	—	1933–
Charles E. Whittaker	1957–1962	5	1901–1973	Stephen Breyer	1994–	—	1938–
Potter Stewart	1958–1981	23	1915–1985				

*Appointed and served one term, but not confirmed by the Senate.

Note: Chief justices are in italics.

Index

struction plan of, 453 (illus.); carpet-baggers, scalawags, and, 457. *See also* Reconstruction; Republican Party

Radicals and radicalism: labor strikes and, 518; fear of, 519; among workers, 520; Red Scare and, 679; after First World War, 680; counterculture and, 939; among feminists, 944–945. *See also* Labor strikes; Socialism

Radio, 639; National Broadcasting Company (NBC) and, 697; ownership of, 698 (illus.); jazz and, 714; fireside chats and, 728, 747. *See also* Mass media

Radio Corporation of America (RCA), 758, 838 (illus.)

Radio Free Europe, 861

Radio Liberty, 861

Railroad Administration, 672

Railroads, 257–258, 257 (map), 258 (illus.), 489 (map); land sales by, 282; in South, 291, 412; growth during Civil War, 417; transcontinental, 417; buffalo and, 478; expansion of, 488–491; government subsidy of, 490–491; construction crews on, 490 (illus.); train schedules and, 491 (illus.); accessibility of farm-land and, 492; in South, 502; pools among, 530; antitrust prosecution of, 534; commuter, 539; electric interur-ban, 540; expansion of, 578; regulation of, 578, 606; after First World War, 690. *See also* Labor strikes

Rainbow Coalition, 980 (illus.), 981

Rainfall, in Great Plains, 492

Rain-in-the-Face, 481

Raleigh, Walter, 28, 39

Ramsey, Mary Ann, 774

Ranching, 496–498, 497 (illus.)

Randolph, A. Philip, 741

Randolph, Edmund, 192, 206

Randolph, John, 228

Range: open-range ranching and, 497–498; closing southern, 499

Rankin, Jeannette, 665–666, 665 (illus.), 766, 775

Rape: of female slaves, 304, 375–376; in Vietnam, 904

Rate discrimination, prohibition of, 578

Ratford, Jenkin, 236

Ratification: of Articles of Confederation, 183; of Constitution, 195–196, 200, 201 (illus.)

Rationalism, 104

Ration stamps, 791

Rats, 26

Rauschenbusch, Walter, 605

Rawick, George P., 299n

Raw materials: strategic, 870; in Third World, 889; in Southeast Asia, 897; from Africa, 910; international access to, 912. *See also* Natural resources

Ray, James Earl, 942

RCA, *see* Radio Corporation of America (RCA)

Reactors (nuclear), *see* Nuclear power

Ready-made clothing, 526–527

Reagan, Ronald: election of 1980 and, 872; military expansion by, 872–873; foreign policy of, 872–874; Gorbachev and, 873–874 and *illus.*; Third World and, 912–915; Iran-Contra scandal and, 914; Nicaragua intervention by, 914; Lebanon crisis and, 915; South African policy of, 915; conservative movement and, 956, 958; presidency of, 958; early career of, 958; election of 1980 and, 964–965, 964 (illus.), 966 (map); social and health programs and, 967–968; wounding of, 968; election of 1984 and, 968–969, 979; minority appointments by, 970; women's opposi-tion to, 975; Iran-Contra scandal and, 980; development of antigovernment attitudes and, 1002

Reagan Doctrine, 873, 912

Reaganomics, 958, 966–968

Real estate, urban sprawl and, 540–541

Real income, 815

Real Whigs, 128–129, 138, 195. *See also* Whig Party

Rearmament, 738, 755

Rebates, 578

Rebellion: by slaves, 110; Stono Rebellion, 113; Shays's, 171–172, 190; Whiskey Rebellion as, 207; by Tous-saint L'Ouverture, 221; Gabriel's Rebel-lion, 221–222 and *illus.*; by Sancho, 222; by female mill workers, 272; by Nat Turner, 305–306; against slavery, 305–306; by blacks, 342; John Brown and, 395; in Cuba, 652. *See also* Protest(s); Revolution(s); Wars and warfare

Rebels, *see* Confederate States of Amer-ica; South (U.S. region)

Rebel Without a Cause (movie), 838

Recall, 603, 606

Recessions, 956; of 1937–1939, 738; under Eisenhower, 819–820; in 1970s, 870, 958–960; in automobile industry, 958–959; in 1980s, 967, 981; women and, 975; under Bush, 992

Reciprocal Trade Agreements Act (1934), 757 (illus.), 759

Reck, Philip Georg Friedrich von, 77 (illus.), 96 (illus.)

Reclamation, 488

Reconstruction, 442 (illus.), 443–471; end of, 170 (illus.); Lincoln's plan for, 446–447; Johnson's plan for, 446–448; Con-gressional plan for, 448–453; politics in South during, 453–460, 453 (illus.), 456 (illus.), 459 (map); social and economic meaning of, 460–465; Grant and, 465; election of 1868 and, 465–466; fall of, 465–470; South after, 498–502. *See also* South (U.S. region)

Reconstruction Act (1867), 451–452, 453 (illus.); military districts established by, 459 (map)

Reconstruction Finance Corporation (RFC), 724

Recording industry, 714

Recordings, *see* Tapings

Recovery program, *see* New Deal

Recreation: of slaves, 302; in 1920s, 709–712; postwar fads and, 839

"Red": use of term, 679; anticommunism and, 821

Red Army, 785

Redbaiting, 821–822

Redcoats, 125. *See also* Armed forces; Revolutionary War

Red Cross, 667, 675, 722, 797

"Red fascism," 849

Red Nightmare (movie), 822

Red River campaign, 433

Red River valley, 491

Red Scare, 658, 679–681, 691, 821. *See also* McCarthyism

Red Shirts, 444, 466

RED SOX/RED CAP program, 863

Red Sticks, 243 and *illus. See also* Creek peoples

Red Strings, 431

"Red Summer" (1919), 676, 798

Reed, John, 680

Reed, Walter, 652

Reed v. Reed, 946

Referendum, 603, 606

Reform and reformers: in education, 176–177; among Iroquois, 187; in banking, 270; electoral, 308; religion and, 346, 348–352; of treatment of insane, 346; asylums and, 352; penitentiaries and, 352; abolitionism and, 357 (illus.); pol-itics and, 358; Jackson's opposition to, 360; Whigs and, 365; Republican Party and, 387; emancipation and, 421; Native Americans and, 480 (illus.), 481–482; child labor and, 514–515; labor and, 516–517; housing and, 549–551; city government and, 567; social, 567–568; moral, 568–569; civil service and, 577–578; agrarian, 583–586; free silver and, 596; in Progressive Era, 599–627; paci-fism and, 677; in 1920s, 693–695; old-age assistance and, 703; in Soviet Union under Gorbachev, 873–874; Great So-ciety program and, 928, 935 (illus.); New Frontier and, 929–931; of immigration laws, 974. *See also* Great Society programs; Mental illness; Progressives and progressivism; specific reform movements

Reformation, 41

Reformed Church of the Netherlands, 331

Reform politics, 273

Reform societies, 346

Refrigeration, 511, 526

Refugees, 804–805

Refuse disposal, 569

Regan, Donald T., 980

Regionalization, transportation and, 254–259

Regions: differences in, 74, 99; labor and farming in, 109; monetary policy and, 579; Progressive reforms in, 606; inten-sity of isolationism in, 766. *See also* spe-cific regions